ABSTRACTS

OF

OLD NINETY-SIX

AND

ABBEVILLE DISTRICT WILLS AND BONDS

AS ON FILE IN THE
ABBEVILLE, SOUTH CAROLINA, COURTHOUSE

Compiled by
WILLIE PAULINE YOUNG
LIBERTY, SOUTH CAROLINA

Please Direct All Correspondence and Book Orders to:

Southern Historical Press, Inc.
PO Box 1267
375 West Broad Street
Greenville, S.C. 29602

ISBN # 0-89308-036-5

Printed in the United States of America

PREFACE

"Let us have done with vain regrets and long-ings for the days that will never be ours again. Our work lies in front, not behind us, and forward is our motto."

—JEROME K. JEROME

Genealogical research has its griefs as well as its triumphs. So it is with life and every thing worth while. It has given me great pleasure to preserve these records of the families who came to this district so early to enrich history, and who now have descendants in every state in the union, who may find their progenitors in this book. I hope that this book will prove useful to the many who may search its contents.

James Savage once made this statement. "By an instinct of our nature, we all learn to love the places of our birth, and the chief circumstances in the lives of our progenitors." Abbeville, South Carolina, is known the world over for every day there are people coming here to seek out their ancestry, as Abbeville was settled by the Scotch-Irish, the English, the French Hugenots, etc.

In copying abstracts of these old records, I made copies from the original papers that were found in the Probate Judge's office. I also wish to give thanks to Judge Wilbur J. Blake and Mrs. Elizabeth F. Robison who have made it possible for me to copy these records.

PAULINE YOUNG

"Without genealogy, the study of history is comparatively lifeless."

---John Fiske

*The Abbeville Courthouse where I labored so long and so faithfully,
in copying these records for the future generations.*

*The Stark Home, where the last Cabinet Meeting
of the Confederacy was held.*

ABBREVIATIONS

Est.	Estate	Cit.	Citation
Admnr.	Administrator	Pub.	Published
Byrs.	Buyers	Lbs.	Pounds
Dist.	District	Decd.	Deceased
Wid.	Widow	Rec.	Recorded
Exr.	Executor	Sett.	Settlement
Wit.	Witness	b. l.	Brother-in-law
Ment.	Mentioned	Gdn.	Guardian
s. l.	Son-in-law	Gr. f.	Grandfather
d. l.	Daughter-in-law	Co. and Ct.	County
Sis.	Sister	Ch.	Church
f. l.	Father-in-law	Prov.	Proved
Gr. chn.	Grandchildren		
Chn.	Children		
Inv.	Inventory		

Words that are printed in italics indicate information about which the author is doubtful.

ABSTRACTS OF OLD NINETY-SIX
And
ABBEVILLE DISTRICT WILLS AND BONDS
As On File In The
Abbeville, South Carolina, Courthouse

ARNOLD, JAMES—BOX 1, PACK 1:
Will dated Aug. 3, 1827 in Abbeville Dist. Rec. Mar. 16, 1836. Exrs: Son, Archibald Arnold, s. l. John Cochran, Alexr. B. Arnold. Wit: Jno. V. Reynolds, David Lewis Wardlaw, Jesse S. Adams. Lived one mile from the Dead-fall. Chn: Alexr. B., Archibald Arnold, Nancy Lumsden, wife of Jno. Cochran. Sett: Jan. 22, 1840. Jno. Cochran gdn. his sons, Jas., Alexr. B., John W. Cochran. Wm. McNairy husband of Mary Ann L. dtr. of Nancy Lumsden Cochran decd. who died Sept. 24, 1835. Testator died Mar. 5, 1836.

ADAMS, BENJAMIN, SR.—BOX 1, PACK 2:
Will dated Jan. 10, 1826 in Abbeville Dist. Exrs: Patrick Noble, Alex. Hamilton Esq. Wit: Amos Edwards, G. or E? Lomax. Wife, Mary. Chn: Lusy Wilson, Benjamin Adams. "Have given to all my chn. by my first wife and to my last 5 chn. by my last wife Mary," viz: James, Hezekiah, Gideon, Nathaniel, Irmsey Adams.

ALLEN, JOHN—Box 1, Pack 3:
Est. admr. Nov. 8, 1838, by Jane L. Allen, Jno. Livingston, David Lesley to Moses Taggart Ord. Sum $20,000.00. Inv. made Dec. 4, 1838, by Jas. L Bowie, Jno. White, Thos. Jackson.

ANDREWS, ARCHIBALD—Box 1, Pack 4:
Bond not rec. Jno. Evans admnr. appeared before Moses Taggart Ord. before Mar. 23, 1832. Alexr. Wilson gdn. Margaret, Jane, Alexr., Benjamin Andrews.

ARNOLD, BENJAMIN—Box 1, Pack 5:
On Nov. 7, 1784, Rebecca Arnold the widow, John Arnold his eldest son appointed Saml. Garrett, Nathaniel Robertson, Daniel McClary the appraisers.

ARMSTRONG, HUGH—Box 1, Pack 6:
Inv. made Feb. 19, 1833, by David Armstrong, admnr. (No other papers)

ANDERSON, MARY—Box 1, Pack 7:
Will dated Oct. 31, 1835, in Abbeville Dist. Proved Dec. 2, 1836.

Exrs: sons, John, Robert Anderson. Wit: Wm. Campbell, Edward Vann. Chn: Wm. (decd.), Jno., Robt. Anderson, Rebecca Reynolds, Nancy Gibson, Mary Foster, Elizabeth Motes. Gr. chn., Jefferson, Benjamin, Mary, Robt., Wm., Larkin Reynolds, Margaret, Robt., Edmund, Mary, Wm., Jno., Nathaniel Anderson chn. of Wm. Anderson decd., Nancy Gibson, Louisa Motes. "Bequeath to Margaret Jordon, Margaret Bearden, Elizabeth Scott. Land on which I now reside bounded by lands of David Whitman, Geo. Marshall, Robt. Anderson."

ANSLEY, MARGARET—BOX 1, PACK 8:
Admnr. not rec. Wm. Ansley was admnr. Cit: pub. at Cedar Springs Church. Sale, Dec. 15, 1835. Byrs. Wm., Jesse Ansley etc. (Written Ansley & Ainsley.)

AGNEW, ANDREW S.—BOX 1, PACK 9:
Samuel Agnew Sr. the admnr. in Nov. 2, 1837. Sett: Feb. 10, 1846 by Enoch, S. W. Agnew, sons of Saml. Agnew Sr. admnr. of Andrew S. Agnew decd.

ATKINS, THOMAS—BOX 1, PACK 10:
Hamilton Hill admnr. Cit. pub. at Bulah Church. Inv. made Jan. 7, 1835 by Jas. Devlin, Barton Jordon. Sale made Jan. 8, 1835. Byrs: Widow Atkins, David, Daniel, Henry, Saml. Atkins.

ATKINS, JAMES—BOX 1, PACK 11:
Est. admnr. Aug. 26, 1833 by Rosamond, Francis, Thomas Atkins to Moses Taggart Ord. Abbeville Dist. sum $10,000.00. Sett: Sept. 30, 1844 ment. Rosanna widow, chn: Robt., Joseph, Jas., Mary J., Nancy Atkins.

ASTON, JAMES—BOX 1, PACK 12:
Will dated Aug. 24, 1788 in Abbeville Dist. Proved Oct. 5, 1789. Exrs: Wife, no name given, Robt. Anderson Esq., Alexr. Aston. Wit: Alexr. Young, Jno. McMahan, Wm. Walker. Chn. Jno., Saml., Wm., Mary, Sarah Aston. Sis. Elizabeth Aston. Inv. made Oct. 25, 1789 by Jno. Dealwood, Thos., Jno. Harris.

ANDERSON, AMOS, SR.—BOX 1, PACK 13:
Est. admnr. June 10, 1808 by Jean, Amos Anderson Jr., Wm. Hutchison to Andrew Hamilton Ord. Abbeville Dist. sum $5,000,00. Cit. pub. at Rocky Springs Church. Sale, July 26, 1808. Byrs: Amos, Jane Anderson, Jas. Forest, Elizabeth Dornes, Joseph Thornton, John Youngblood, etc.

ALEXANDER, AARON—BOX 1, PACK 14:
Will dated Feb. 19, 1796 in Abbeville Dist. Filed Mar. 25, 1796. Exrs: Joseph Black, Thomas Alston Harris. Wit: Saml. McClelin, Andw. Pickens, Saml. McClelin. Wife and chn. ment. no names given. Sale made April 28, 1796. Byrs: Jane Alexander, Mathew Parker, Thos. Harris, Joseph, Robt. Black, Isaac Bain, Elizabeth Riley, etc.

AGNEW, SAMUEL—BOX 1, PACK 15:
Will dated Dec. 10, 1790, in Abbeville Dist. Exrs: Wife, Elizabeth, Adam Crain Jones Esq., Saml. Wall Esq. Wit: Jas. Wardlaw, Mary Seawright,

Jno. Sharp. Chn: Jas., Andw., Saml., Mary, Jane Agnew. Inv. made April 5, 1791, by Capt. Saml. Reid, Jno. Wardlaw, Edward Sharp, Richard Hodges.

ARNETT, EDWARD—BOX 1, PACK 16:
Est. admr. Sept. 20, 1783, by Ann Arnett, Wm. Bouland, Ralph Smith to Jno. Thomas Jr. Ord. 96 Dist. sum 2,000 lbs. Sale, Oct. 13, 1783. Byrs: Ann, Mary Arnett, Wm. Bowland, Benjamin Wofford, Larnard Smith, Gowen Clayton, Wm. Cleylon.

ARMSTRONG, SAMUEL—BOX 1, PACK 17:
Will dated Aug. 26, 1809, in Abbeville Dist. Proved Sept. 11, 1809. Exrs: sons, David, Saml. Armstrong, Abraham Livingston. Wit: Robt. Russell, Wm. Black, Jr., Abraham Livingston. Wife, no name given. Chn: Jno., David, Mathew, Hugh, James, Saml., Martha Armstrong, Mary Emerson. Expend: Oct. 27, 1826 Paid Matilda V. Armstrongs board $9.00. Feb. 6, 1826 Paid Watt Bowie for Eliza Armstrong $14.56¼. Feb. 24, 1827 Paid gdn. for Matilda V., Amanda Armstrong $3.00. Jan. 1, 1824 Paid Mary Ann Armstrong legacy $105.88. Saml. Armstrong had notes on Mathew, Martin, Henry and Wm. Emerson.

ALLEN, CHARLES—BOX 1, PACK 18:
Admnr. Lucy Allen. Lived in 96 Dist. Inv. made Dec. 30, 1777 by Nehemiah Franks, Robt. Ross, Marshall Franks.

ADKINS, JOSEPH—BOX 1, PACK 19:
Est. admr. Dec. 16, 1785, by George Morgan, Joshua Saxon, Lewis Banton to Jno. Thomas, Jr. Ord. 96 Dist. sum 100 lbs. Inv. made Dec. 16, 1786, by Nimrod William, Wm. Anderson, Zachariah Simms, Jno. Richey.

ALLEN, JOSIAH—BOX 1, PACK 20:
Admnr. Jas. Allen of Richland Creek in 96 Dist. was next of kin. Inv. made Sept. 13, 1782 by Wm. Lisson, Enoch Grissbe, Jno. Davis, Russell Wilson.

ALEXANDER, JEAN— BOX 1, PACK 21:
Inv. made Mar. 3, 1801, by Thos. Lackey, Anthony M. Eiton, David Pressly, Jno. Austin, Jno. Calewood of Abbeville Dist.

ARMENT, MAGNUS—BOX 1, PACK 22:
George Harland admr. of est. of Magnus and Sarah Arment decd. of 96 Dist. Inv. made Dec. 1784, by Nehemiah Howard, Archer Smith, Geo. Harland. Byrs: Thos. Blassingham, Moses Collyer, Wm. Plummer.

ADAMS, WILLIAM—BOX 2, PACK 23:
Will dated Sept. 29, 1794, in Abbeville Dist. Rec. Mar. 25, 1795. Exrs: Wife, Mary; Son, Jno. Wit: Jas. Lomax, Andrew Bradley, Jas. Cain. Chn: Jno., Andrew, Wm., Nancy Adams, Rosey Moor. Inv. made Mar. 26, 1795 by Wm. Hairston, Simeon Williams, Peter Hairston, Capt. Jno. Irwin, Reuben Shotwell.

ALLISON, WILLIAM—BOX 2, PACK 24:
Will dated Dec. 15, 1780, in 96 Dist. Exrs: Wm. Pugh, Thos. Richardson.

Wit: Richard Pugh, Thos. Richardson, Charles Brody. Wife, Margaret. Chn: Thos., David, Ellenor, Nancy, Margaret Allison. s. 1. Charles Brody. Inv. made Jan. 9, 1783, by Wm. Baugh, Saml. Scott, Richard Owings, Sr. (Thos. Allison's records in same package.) Benjamin Kilgore Esq. of Duncans Creek, 96 Dist. admr. of est. of Thomas Allison late of Reaburns Creek. Inv. made April 26, 1783 by Basil Holland, Thos. Murphey, Robt. Hanna.

ANDERSON, CHARITY—BOX 2, PACK 25:
    Est. admr. Nov. 6, 1782, by Jno. Watson Sr. of Clouds Creek, Edward Couch, Jas. Harrison to Jno. Ewing Calhoun Ord. 96 Dist. sum 2,000 lbs. Inv. made by Arthur Watson, Jacob Adams, Saml. Lotcher.

ALEXANDER, WILLIAM—BOX 2, PACK 26:
    Will dated April 16, 1793. Rec. Nov. 10, 1793. Exrs: Wife, Margaret. Jas. Cochran, Benjamin Clarke. Wit: Jas. Foster Sr. Jno., Wm. Norris. Chn: Mary, Agness, James Alexander. Stepson, Wm. Thompson. "Order that Mary's mothers clothes be divided by her stepmother and Christian Robertson."

ATCHISON, SAMUEL—BOX 2, PACK 27:
    Admnr. Joseph Eakins. Sale made July 24, 1809. Byrs: Jno. Baird, Hughey McCormick, Prudence Atchison, etc. Expend: April 26, 1815 Paid Wm. Runnels gdn. for Wm. Atchison $2.10. May 10, 1815 Paid Geo. Marshall gdn. for Saml., Rachel Atchison $442.49.

ALEXANDER, JOHN—BOX 2, PACK 28:
    Est. admnr. Feb. 25, 1784 by Alexander Alexander, Jno. McCrory, Wm. Earnest of Jemmies Creek to Jno. Thomas Jr. Ord. 96 Dist. sum 2,000 lbs. Inv. made Feb. 28, 1784 by Tobias Wright, Wm. Earnest, Jno. McCrory.

ALLISON, JAMES—BOX 2, PACK 29:
    Will dated Aug. 10, 1778 in 96 Dist. Proved Aug. 23, 1784. Exrs: Capt. Wm. Berry, W. Robt. Templeton. Wit: Wm. Berry, Peter, Brookes, Hugh Smith. Chn: Joseph, Robt., Margaret, Jean, Isabel, Elizabeth Allison. Gr. Chn: Jas. Sr., Jas. Jr., Joseph Linch, Jean dtr. of Edward Linch, Jean dtr. of Aaron Linch, Jas. Joseph Casey, Jean dtr. of Wm. Casey. "Bequeath a four gallon pot to Elizabeth Stone."

ADAIR, JOHN—BOX 2, PACK 30:
    Est. admr. May 5, 1784 by Sarah, James, Joseph Adair, James Montgomery to Jno. Thomas Jr. Ord. 96 Dist. sum 1,000 lbs. Inv. made June 9, 1784 by Thos. Ewing, Jas. Cragg, Benjamin Adair.

APPLETON, THOMAS—BOX 2, PACK 31:
    Est. admr. Sept. 13, 1782 by Joachim Bulow of Beach Island, Wm. Shinholser, David Zubly to Jno. Ewing Calhoun Ord. 96 Dist. sum 2,000 lbs. Inv. made Sept. 13, 1782 by Jno. Murray, Wm. Dunbar Esq.

ADAIR, WILLIAM—BOX 2, PACK 32:
    Est. admr. May 5, 1784 by Robt. Scott, Jas. Montgomery, Jas. Adair to Jno. Thomas Jr. Ord. 96 Dist. sum 1,000 lbs. Inv. made May 5, 1784 by Thos.

Ewing, Jas., Joseph Adair. Byrs at sale. Sarah, Benjamin, Jas. Adair, Thos. McCreery, Robt. Scott, Saml. Ewing, Wm. Price, Jas. Cragg, Jas. Dilerd.

ANDERSON, ROBERT—Box 2, Pack 33:
Est. admr. Feb. 17, 1816 by Wm. Anderson, Joseph Eakin, Wm. Reynolds, Bartholomew Jordon to Taliaferro Livingston Ord. Abbeville Dist. sum 10,000 lbs. Expend: 1812 Paid Jno. Anderson $1.75. Robt. Anderson $1.75. Meary Anderson $6.00. Edgefield Dist. the Inv. of Colbert Anderson made Mar. 10, 1786 by Richard Lanier, Obediah Fields, Thos. Ross. Admr: were Mary, Jas. Anderson. (This last in same package.)

ADAMS, WILLIAM—Box 2, Pack 34:
Est. admr. Aug. 27, 1819 by Saml. Adams, Arthur Gray, Wm. Gray, Wm. McColloch to Moses Taggart Ord. Abbeville Dist. sum $1,000.00. Cit. pub. at Willington Church. Inv. made Sept. 9, 1819 by Jno., Wm. Gray, Saml. Young. Sale made Sept. 10, 1819. Byrs: Mary, Saml. Adams, Jno. Gray, Capt. Wm. Gray, Jno. Norris, Andrew McClane, etc.

ATKINS, ROBERT—Box 2, Pack 35:
Est. admr. June 7, 1816 by Jas., Thos. Atkins, Wm. Paul, Anthony Yeldell to Taliaferro Livingston Ord. Abbeville Dist. sum $20,000.00. Expend: May 23, 1818. Paid Jane Atkins share $3,067.00. Jno. Adams share $560.00. Abraham Lites share $562.00. Thomas Atkins gdn. of Francis Atkins part share $370.00. Thos., Jane Atkins gdns. of Joseph, Thos., David, Teresa, Ravenna, Phebe Atkins part share $2,230.00. June 5, 1824 Paid Jno. Donald share $29.30. Robt. Atkins was f.l. of Elias Teague.

ADAMS, JOHN—Box 2, Pack 36 :
Admnrs. Mrs. Lucy Adams, Col. Jas. Lomax. Sale, Jan. 22, 23, 1827. Byrs: Mrs. Rosey Moore, Mrs. Nancy Norris, Gabriel Treatland, Joseph Travis, Archibald Arnold, H. P. Arnold, Wiley Watson, Robt. Well, Wm. L. Jones, Thos. Gary, Jno. Phillips, etc.

ARNOLD, JOHN, Sr.—Box 2, Pack 37:
Saml. O. Arnold Exr. of Wm. P. Arnold of Madison Co., Georgia appointed Paschal D. Klugh of Abbeville Dist. to collect his part of Jno. Arnold's est. late of Abbeville Dist. which is and of right ought to belong to est. of Wm. P. Arnold decd. as one of the legatees of said Jno. Arnold decd. Dated Feb. 20, 1833. Signed in presence of Elisha Ware, J. P. Richardson Hancock. Jno. Arnold died Sept. 1827. (Will gone).

ARNOLD, SAMUEL O.—Box 2, Pack 38:
Est. admr. July 19, 1824, by Hart P., Jno. Arnold, Geo. Lomax Esq. to Moses Taggart Ord. Abbeville Dist. sum $3,000.00.

ANDERSON, WILLIAM—Box 2, Pack 39:
Est. admr. Nov. 17, 1827, by Nancy, Jno. Anderson, Edmund Cobb to Moses Taggard Ord. Abbeville Dist. sum $3,000.00. Nancy Anderson gdn. minor chn. of Wm. Anderson decd. viz. Margaret, Robt., Edmund, Mary, Wm.,

Jno., Nathaniel Anderson. Inv. made Dec. 24, 1827 by Nathaniel Cobb. Robt. Anderson, Owen Selby.

ANDERSON, WILLIAM—Box 2, Pack 40:
Est. admr. Oct. 12, 1816, by William Anderson Sr., Wm. Anderson Jr., Thos. Heron, David Taggartto, to Taliaferro Livingston Ord. Abbeville Dist. sum $10,000.00. Expend: Feb. 21, 1823. Paid admr. of est. of Jas. Anderson decd. $268.00. Feb. 2, 1823, Wm. Anderson Sr. $200.00. Oct. 4, 1825, Thos. Anderson in full $244.66. Oct. 10, 1825, Paid S. and Mary Austin in full $125.34. Jno. Anderson on acct. $11.81¼. (Same pack a paper of Robt. Anderson decd.) Admnrs. Wm. Anderson, Joseph Eakins. Expend: May 23, 1816, Paid Wm. Runnold part share $42.04. Wm. Anderson part share $83.00. Jno. Anderson share $300.00. Nancy Y. Anderson share $348.94. C. Anderson, wid. of Wm. Anderson.

ALLEN, LEWIS—Box 3, Pack 41:
Will dated June 26, 1816, in Abbeville Dist. Proved July 13, 1816. Exr: b.l. Jno. Gray. Wit: B. H. Saxon, Robt. Wadell, Jno. McGaw. Niece, Anna Craig Gray. Sis. Hannah Gray. "Give to Mary Gray Weed dtr. of Major Andrew Weed $100.00. Inv. made July 15, 1816 by Andrew Weed, Jno. Weed, Jas. Gray.

ALLEN, GEORGE B.—Box 3, Pack 42:
Est. admr. Oct. 15, 1817, by Deborah Allen, Saml. McQueen, Jno. Morrow, Jas. McQueen to Taliaferro Livingston Ord. Abbeville Dist. sum $5,000.00. Expend: Jan. 2, 1821, Paid A. Norris wife's share $53. 40½. Saml. Anderson wife's share $11.58. April 23, 1819, Paid Wm. Robison for tutition of his dtr. $12.00. Mar. 12, 1824, the est. of Geo. B. Allen decd. to Alexr. McQueans in right of his wife, to boarding 2 chn. of said decd. at $35.00 each.

ANDERSON, JACOB—BOX 3, PACK 43:
Sept. 28, 1839, Stephen Ross, Geo. Holloway, Jno. R. Tarrant bound to Moses Taggart Ord. Abbeville Dist. sum $1,000.00. Stephen Ross gdn. of Jacob Newton Anderson minor under 21 yrs. Est. admnr. Dec. 16, 1823, by Elizabeth, Perry F. Anderson, Wm. A. Huggins to Moses Taggart Ord. Abbeville Dist. sum $4,500.00. Expend: 1828 Board of Franklin, Nathan, Newton, Elizabeth Anderson each $25.00. Sett. of Jacob Anderson, Jr., for his share of his father Jacob Anderson decd. Present, Elizabeth Ross, wid. and admr. her husband Stephen Ross by second marriage being dead made June 1, 1846, Martha Anderson a dtr. died soon after her father leaving a mother, 4 brothers, 1 sis. Benjamin H. Anderson died Oct. 1831 leaving a mother, 3 brothers, 1 sis. Elizabeth Anderson died Sept. 1832.

ALLEN, ROBERT, SR.—BOX 3, PACK 44:
Will dated Sept. 7, 1815. Proved April 13, 1816. Exrs: son, Jas. Allen, s. l. Jno. Gray. Wit: Andrew Norris, Wm., Anna C. Gray. Chn. Jas., Lewis, George B., Robt. Allen, Hannah Gray. Gr. chn. Robt. H. Allen, Arthur A. Gray, Inv. made April 15, 1816, by Andrew, Jno. Weed, Wm. Gray.

ANSLEY, DAVID—BOX 3, PACK 45:
Est. admr. Dec. 20, 1824, by Margaret Ansley, Abraham Lites, Wm.
Mantz to Moses Taggart Ord. sum $3,000.00. Sale, Jan. 13, 1825. Byrs: Peggy
Ansley, Mary Norris, Jas. Devlin, Saml., Jonathan jordan, Benjamin, Jno.
Adams, Miriam Moor, Jas., Joseph Conn, etc.

ANDERSON, JAMES—BOX 3, PACK 46:
Est. admr. Oct. 21, 1820, by Wm., Jno. Mattison, Jno. Anderson, Wm.
Cullins to Moses Taggart Ord. Abbeville Dist. sum $3,000.00. Sale, Nov. 24,
1820. Byrs: David Anderson, Robt. V. Posey, Andrew Agnew, Jno. Calvert,
Christian Rasor, Jabish Vines, Jno. Richey, Wm. Dunn, etc.

ATKINSON, TIMOTHY—BOX 3, PACK 47:
Est. admr. Jan. 7, 1786, by Nathaniel Howell, Casper Nail, Sr,. Jno.
Meyer bound to Jno. Thomas, Jr., Ord. 96 Dist. sum 500 lbs. Inv. made Feb. 14,
1786, by Jonathan, Jno. Meyer, Casper Nail. Byrs: at sale. Jean, Jane Atkinson,
Saml. Burris, Nathaniel Howell, Joe Hix, Benjamin Harris, Jno. Savage, Jno.
Clark.

ADAMSON, LYDIA—BOX 3, PACK 48:
Will dated June 6, 1819, in Abbeville Dist. Proved Feb. 5, 1827. Exr.
son, Jonathan. Wit: Saml. Perrin, Jas. Thompson. Chn. Peggy wife of Jno.
Argo, Sally, Harriet Adamson. Inv. made Feb. 26, 1827, by Wm. Chiles, Jas.
Wiley, Thos. W. Chiles.

ANDERSON, WILLIAM—BOX 3, PACK 49:
Will dated Sept. 20, 1827, in Abbeville Dist. Proved Nov. 24, 1827.
Exr. Jno. Brown. Wit: Jno., Jas. Lindsay. Mother, Christian Anderson. Sis.
Mary Austin. Brothers, Thos., Jas., Jno., David Anderson. "To the chn. of Jas.
Anderson decd. viz. Thos. A., Wm., Daly C., Betsy Anderson. To Mary
Austin's son, Wm. H. Austin.

ADAMS, JAMES—BOX 3, PACK 50:
Aug. 20, 1782, Elizabeth Adams of Cuffe Town, 96 Dist. applied for
Letters of Admnr. on est. of Jas. Adams, Jr. Cit. pub. at Little Mountain Church
April 1, 1821, stated that Elizabeth Adams was next of kin on the est. of
Joseph Adams late a soldier in the United States Army. Sale, May 16, 1804.
Byrs: Jas., Peter Barmore, Robt. Posey, Alexr. Elgin, Jas., Nipper, Nancy Adams,
Wm. Lord, etc.

ANDERSON, DANIEL—BOX 3, PACK 51:
Est. admr. Nov. 21, 1833, by Wm. Speer, Wm. L. Buford, Elijah Hunt
to Moses Taggart Ord. Abbeville Dist. sum $4,000.00. Left wid. Martha Ander-
son and 2 chn. one died in minority and Wm. Anderson. On May 3, 1847, The-
opholius White was gdn. of Wm. Anderson both of Russell Co. Alabama.

AGNER, JOHN—BOX 3, PACK 52:
Est. admr. Sept. 29, 1828, by Saml. Morris, Wm. McDonald, Wm.
Patton to Moses Taggart Ord. Abbeville Dist. sum of $700.00. Saml. Morris gdn.

of Saml., Mary, Lucy, John Agner. The minor Jno. Agner was taken as an orphan child at 9 mos. old and raised and schooled by Saml. Morris to his death. Expend: April 1, 1845 Paid Mary's schooling in Alabama $15.00 Oct. 1, 1835 Recd. of Richard Morris a legacy left by Saml. Morris of Chestershire County, Great Britain $317.25.

ADAMS, WILLIAM (MINORS)—BOX 3, PACK 53:
On Jan. 13, 1833, Jno. D. Adams, Joseph, Henry Norrell bound to Moses Taggart Ord. Abbeville Dist. sum $500.00. Jno. D. Adams made gdn. of Elizabeth Adams minor under 14 yrs. Feb. 6, 1843 Jno. Adams, Saml. Hill, N. J. Davis bound to David Lesly Ord. Abbeville Dist. sum $900.00. Jno. Adams made gdn. of Martha Jane dtr. Wm. Adams a minor about 18 yrs. Jno. N. and Martha Jane Lowry of Winston County, Miss. appointed Quincy B. Adams of said county to receive their part of est. from Jno. Adams of Abbeville Dist. S. C. On Oct. 23, 1847 appeared Martha J. Lowry stated that she was separated from her husband. (Letter)

Louisville, Miss.
Febry 3, Mr. Jno. Adams,
Abbeville Co. House,
South Carolina   January 30, 1848
Dear Cousin John Adams,
I take this opportunity of writing you a few lines for explanation of Quincey B. Adams. He left this state Nov. 4, 1847. I gave him the power of Attorney to Corlict the money that was coming to my wife from you and Aaron Lindsay. I have not herd a word from him since he left this State I want you writ me wether he has corlicted that money or not I am very oneasy about him I want you to write to me soon and gave me all the information you can and write me the amount you paid him and how much was a coming to me we are all well at present and the Condition is generally well I have nothing of importance to write or communicate at present by Reman yours forever untill death. Amanda N. F. Allen sends her best respects to Ann Adams and Family Jan. 30, 1848.

                                                John N. Lowery
                                                Martha J. Lowery

ATKINS, RAVENNA—BOX 3, PACK 54:
On Dec. 13, 1828 Dewy E. Lipford, Geo. W. Hodges, Donald Douglass bound to Moses Taggart Ord. Abbeville Dist. sum $3,000.00. Dewy Lipford made gdn. Ravenna Atkins minor over 14 yrs. Feb. 6, 1830 Paid David Atkins $30.00.

ANDERSON, MINORS—BOX 3, PACK 55:
Mar. 8, 1825 Thos. Anderson, Jno. Douglass, L. I. C. Deyampert bound to Moses Taggart Ord. Abbeville Dist. sum $4,000.00. Thos. Anderson made gdn. of Thos., Amelia, Mary, Elenor, Daniel Anderson, minors.

ALLEN, JAMES—BOX 3, PACK 56:
Will dated June 28, 1837, in Hall County, Ga. Proved Mar. 4, 1839.

Exr: Wm. E. Wilson. Wit: Saml. H., Robt., A. L. Wilson. Wife, Sarah. Chn. Anna G., Jas. J., Theresa, Robt. H. Allen. "Desire that my son Robt. H. Allen have a lot of land in Cobb Co. Ga. and Abbeville Dist. and in State of Indiana."

ALEXANDER, WILLIAM—BOX 3, PACK 57:
Est. admr. Sept. 1, 1832, by Paul Rogers, Robt., James McCraven bound to Moses Taggart Ord. Abbeville Dist. sum $500.00. Cit. pub. at Hopewell Church.

ASHLEY, JOHN—BOX 3, PACK 58:
Will dated May 13, 1838, in Abbeville Dist. Proved Mar. 5, 1840. Exrs. son, Richard Ashley, Jno. B. Black. Wit: Ann Smith, Elizabeth J. H., Margaret Burnett. Wife, Amey. Chn. Jno., Aaron, Richard Ashley. Sett. ment. Amey Ashley died 1851. Present, Aaron Ashley agent for Richard Ashley who named Frances a dtr. of said decd. Ment. 11 legatees, no names given. Sale, June 24, 1852. Byrs: R. W. Shaw, Jno. Smith, Richard Ashley, Jas. W. Black, Aaron, Moses Ashley, Capt. Jno. Swilling, Pinckney Ashley, Thos. Davis, etc.

ANDERSON, DAVID—BOX 3, PACK 59:
Est. admr. Mar. 25, 1839, by Labon, Landy G. Shoemaker, Hamilton Hill bound to Moses Taggart Ord. Abbeville Dist. in sum $1,000.00. Inv. made April 10, 1839, by Jno. Ruff, Jno. H. Armstrong, Landy G. Shoemaker. Byrs: Lina Anderson, Col. Jno. Hearst, Saml. Jordon, Mathew Foster, Jesse Jester, G. W. Pressly, Wm. Nelson.

ANDERSON, WILLIAM (Minors)—BOX 3, PACK 60:
On Sept. 19, 1837 Henry Thos. Riley, Ephraim Davis bound to Moses Taggart Ord. Abbeville Dist. sum $10,000.00. Henry Riley made gdn. of Margaret, Mary, Robt., Edmond, Wm., Jno., Nathaniel Anderson, minors. Aug. 23, 1842 Edmund Cobb, Nancy Beazley made the gdns. Nathaniel Anderson the last minor to become of age on May 16, 1848.

ANDERSON, THOMAS—BOX 4, PACK 61:
Will dated June 12, 1839, in Abbeville Dist. Proved Aug 11, 1840. Exrs: sons, Jas., Thomas Anderson. Wit: Littleton Yarbrough, Wm. Arnet, A. Pearson. Wife, Didama. Chn. Jas., Thos., Amelia, Mary, Eliza, Daniel Anderson. Gr. son, Wm. L. Anderson. "Gave lands to Daniel in Ga." Eliza marired Jno. G. Paschall. Mary married a Harris.

ASHLEY, JOSHUA—BOX 4, PACK 62:
Will dated Sept. 29, 1840 in Abbeville Dist. Proved Feb. 26, 1842. Exr: Son, Joshua Ashley. Wit: Jno. Pratt, Jr., Wm. Pratt, Sr., Robeson Ashley. Chn: Charlotte, Nancy, Moses, Joshua Ashley. "Bequeath land to Moses Ashley's 2 sons, Geo. W., Joshua Ashley. Expend: May 8, 1843 Left 2 legacies to his 2 dtrs. Nancy Shaw, Charlotte Fraser. Paid C. Frances and Charlotte his wife $200.00.

ANSLEY, JOHN A.—BOX 4, PACK 63:
Est. admr. Feb. 27, 1843, by Saml. Jordon, Wm. Ansley, Hanly Lipford

bound to David Lesly Ord. Abbeville Dist. sum $5,000.00. Wid. Sarah A. Ansley. Wm. Ansley gdn. Margaret, Wm., Jno. Ansley.

AIKEN, NANCY—BOX 4, PACK 64:
Will dated Nov. 25, 1842, in Abbeville Dist. Proved Feb. 7, 1843. Exr. Son, Joseph. Wit: Saml. Marshall, Mary A. Jordon, Susan C. Barnett. Chn: Joseph, George Aiken.

ARNOLD, JONATHAN—BOX 4, PACK 65:
Will dated July 17, 1837. Proved Aug. 19, 1841. Exr: Wife, Nancy. Wit: Henry Rush, S. B. Cook, Jno. Hearst. Chn: Susannah, Sarah Arnold. Sale: Sept. 29, 1841. Byrs: Wm. P. Sullivan, Pleasant Morris, Charles Varner, Jno. Spikes, Wm. Butler, Col. Hearst.

AGNEW, SAMUEL—BOX 4, PACK 66:
Est. admr. Oct. 7, 1844, by Dr. Enoch, Jas., Saml. W., Wm. Agnew bound to David Lesly Ord. Abbeville Dist. sum $30,000.00. Wid: Malinda. Expend: Feb. 11, 1847 Paid E. E. Pressly $186.79 in right of his wife Elizabeth a dtr. of Saml. Agnew who was also gdn. of Malinda Jane. Legatees: S. W., Wm., Joseph, Alfred, Washington Agnew.

ARMSTRONG, JOHN H.—BOX 4, PACK 67:
Will dated Jan. 7, 1843. Proved Sept. 26, 1843. Exr: Saml. L. Hill. Wit: Andrew Kennedy, Hugh Armstrong, Robt. Devlin. Wife: Sarah. Dtr: Nancy K. Armstrong. S. L. Nancy Kennedy.

ATKINS, SAMUEL—BOX 4, PACK 68:
Est. admr. Sept. 17, 1844, by Barton Jordon, Francis Atkins, Abraham Lites bound to David Lesly Ord. Abbeville Dist. sum $500.00. Sale, Oct. 5, 1844. Byrs: Wid. Ann R. Atkins, David, Jas., Daniel Atkins, Jas. Watson, Benjamin Nealey, Wm. Sanders, Silas Anderson, etc.

BELL, JOHN—BOX 4, PACK 69:
Will dated July 31, 1813. Rec. Sept. 4, 1813. Exrs: brother, Lewis Bell, Thos. Chiles Esq. Jno. Meriwether. Wit: Austin Pollard, Thos. Cheatham, Peter Ball. Chn: Fanny, Sally Bell. Sale, Nov. 27, 1813. Byrs: Lewis Bell, Capt. Jno. Moore, Wm. Young, Richard Garland, Wm. Swift, Peter Ball, etc.

BELL, JOHN—BOX 4, PACK 70:
Est. admr. Dec. 7, 1802, by Sarah, Jno. Bell, Isham Harris bound to Andrew Hamilton Ord. Abbeville Dist. sum $10,000.00. Inv. made Dec. 15, 1802, by Robt. Cheatham, Elisha Weatherford, Robt. Pollard.

BOYD, WILLIAM—BOX 4, PACK 71:
Est. admr. Feb. 22, 1803, by Elenor Boyd, Jas. Bradley, Andrew Bowie, Adam Sanders bound to Andrew Hamilton Ord. Abbeville Dist. sum $5,000.00. Expend: Dec. 27, 1805 Wm. Wilson recd. his part of est. $286.63¼. Saml. Armstrong recd. his part $300.27. Sale, April 13, 1803. Byrs: Elenor, Thos. Boyd, Amos Spiller, Joseph Downey, etc.

BROWNLEE, WILLIAM—BOX 4, PACK 72:
Will dated May 23, 1833. Proved Dec. 29, 1834. Exrs: Son, John.
Jno. B. Black, Jas. Cowan. Wit: Jno. W. Smith, Wm. B. Porter, Wm. E.
Daniel. Wife, Mary. Chn: Andrew, Sarah, Jas. Brownlee. Gr. chn: Cinthia, Jno.,
Wm., Susanna, Porter, Mary, Andrew, Robt. Brownlee. Gr. chn. of Sarah by her
first husband, Susanna, Wm., Sarah, Alfred. Legatees: Susannah N., L. P.
Brownlee, Jas. Morrah, Jas. Cowan, Robt. C. Harkness, W. B. Porter, Jno.
Brownlee, Marion Davis, Jno. Wimbish, T. L. Harris. Mary Harkness had 5 chn.
Sallie Harris, Anna Morrow, Mrs. Laney Davis. Elizabeth Black had 7 chn.

BIGBY, JOHN, SR.—BOX 4, PACK 73:
Est. admr. Oct. 1, 1832, by Jno. W., Archibald Bigby, Jno. Seawright
bound to Moses Taggart Ord. Abbeville Dist. sum $2,000.00. Expend: Dec.
12, 1832. Paid Geo. Bigby leg. $118.20. Nov. 15, 1933 Paid Widow Bigby
$140.00. Mrs. Elizabeth Dunlap share of Jno. Bigby's est. to be divided between
her children $200.67. Was wid. of Bryce Dunlap.

BUCHANAN, ROBERT—BOX 4, PACK 74:
Will dated Oct. 8, 1838. Proved Nov. 5, 1838. Exrs: son, Wm., Robt. E.,
Francis A. Buchanan. Wit: Jno. Mathews, Jno. Irwin, W. B. Arnold. Chn: Wm.,
Robt., Francis A., Jas. Buchanan, Mary Logan. Gr. chn: Robt. B., Jas. W., Mary
C. Buchanan heirs of my son Jas. Buchanan decd., Jane Logan. Mary C.
Buchanan died in infancy.

BROUGH, THOMAS—BOX 4, PACK 75:
Will dated Aug. 5, 1834. Proved Sept. 17, 1834. Exrs: Joseph Mathews,
Peter Bevill. Wit: Joseph Callahan, Emanuel Wiss, Henry H. Townes. Wife,
Nancy. Chn: Margaret Mathews, Jas. L. Brough, Nelly Scott. s. l. Peter Bevill.
Gr. chn: Jno. L., John Lewis Brough. Expend: Mar. 1836 Paid Nancy Brough,
Sr. $200.00. Eliiah Legard $132.67. Jno. Scott Esq. $169.23.

BLAIR, SAMUEL—BOX 4, PACK 76:
Will dated Feb. 10, 1813. Proved Feb. 6, 1815. Exr· son, Jno. Wit·
Sarah Milligan, A. Milligan, S. Steadman. Chn: Jno., Thos., Wm., Abigail
Blair.

BIRDSHAW, JOHN—BOX 4, PACK 77:
Est. admr. Aug. 2, 1819, by Peter Birdshaw, Wm. Truitt, Joshua Hill
bound to Moses Taggart Ord. sum $1,000.00. Inv. made by Joshua Hill, Jas.
Dillishaw, Wm. Truett, Drewer Breazeale.

BEAL, DUKE—BOX 4, PACK 78:
Est. admr. Jan. 29, 1814, by Martha Beal, Benjamin H. Saxon, Jno. H.
Miller, W. Shackelford bound to Taliaferro Livingston Ord. Abbeville Dist.
sum $10,000.00. Sale, Dec. 27, 1814. Byrs: Martha, Joshua, Jeremiah, Leonard
Beal, Andrew Lee, Thos. Casey, Thos. Brock, etc.

BLACKSTOCK, JOHN—BOX 4, PACK 79:
Will date left out. Proved Sept. 17, 1785. Exr: Brother, Jas. Blackstock

Wit: Thos. Murphey, Solomon Langston. Was of Laurens County. Wife, Neomy. Son, Wm. Inv. made by Solomon Langston, Thos. Murphey, Jesse Holder.

BARKSDALE, HIGGERSON—BOX 4, PACK 80:
Will dated July 8, 1800. Rec. Jan. 3, 1805. Exrs: Sons, Wm., Steth Barksdale, Col. Thomas Murry of Lincoln Co. Ga. Wit: Alexr., Wm. Noble, Hugh Milligan. Chn: Wm., Steth, Sarah Lou Barksdale, Pheoby Stinson, Jane Murry. Gr. dtr. Nancy Stinson. Sale, Jan. 14, 1805. Byrs: Phebe, Hickerson, Mary, Henry, Sally Lou, Joseph Barksdale, Thos. Murry, etc.

BARKSDALE, HIGGERSON, SR.—BOX 5, PACK 81:
Est. admr. Jan. 31, 1800, by Fanny Barksdale, Geo. Bowie, Esq. bound to Andrew Hamilton Ord. Abbeville Dist. sum $5,000.00. Inv. made Jan. 14, 1805, by Wm. Noble, Jas. Calhoun, Jr.

BURDINE, REGINALD—BOX 5, PACK 82:
Est. admr. Oct. 25, 1787, by Jno. Grisham, Sr., Jno. Burdine, Jno. Hallum bound to the Judges of Abbeville Dist. sum 1,000 lbs. Inv. made Nov. 5, 1787, by Wm. Poor, Peter Acker, Reuben Johnson.

BATES, STEPHEN—BOX 5, PACK 83:
Will dated Aug. 25, 1788. Proved Oct. 8, 1788. Exrs: Alexr. Clark, Ann, Fleming Bates. Wit: Wm. Hall, Arthur Patton, Jas. Hutcheson. Wife, Anne. Son, Jas. Alexander Bates. Inv. made Oct. 8, 1788, by Wm. Clark, Wm. Scott, Saml. Blair.

BAKER, ELIJAH—BOX 5, PACK 84:
Est. admr. Jan. 10, 1803, by Wm. Cain, Joseph Barksdale, Charles Latham bound to Andrew Hamilton Ord. Abbeville Dist. sum $10,000.00. Sale, Feb. 26, 1803. Byrs: Allen, Joseph Barksdale, Wm. Cain, Richard Stanfield, Abram Campbell, Elijah Breazeal, Charles Latham.

BOND, ROBERT—BOX 5, PACK 85:
Will dated Feb. 5, 1791. Proved April 5, 1791. Exrs: Wife, no name given, Jas. Carlile. Wit: Wm. Pickens, Jas. Carlile. Chn: Robt., Mary Bond. "Bequeath to Jas. Campbell 50 lbs. sterling. Bequeath to Robert's oldest son Robt. Bond."

BOYD, WILLIAM, SR.—BOX 5, PACK 86:
Will dated May 20, 1801. Rec. Sept. 2, 1803. Exrs: Son, Jas. Boyd, Jno. Glasgo, Jr. Wit: P. McCarter, Fleming Bates, Josiah Patterson. Chn: Joseph, Saml., Mary Boyd. Bequeath 200 acres of land in Georgia to sons, Wm., Jas., Robt., Jno. Boyd.

BROWNLEE, JOHN—BOX 5, PACK 87:
Will dated Feb. 25, 1802. Rec. June 12, 1802. Exrs: Wife, Alley, Sons, Joseph, George Brownlee. Wit: Saml. Anderson, Joseph Brownlee. Chn: Geo., Sr., Joseph Brownlee, Nancy Richey. Gr. son, Joseph Richey. Inv. made by Col. Jno. Weatherall, Capt. Jno. Hodges, Robt. Swain.

BRIGGS, JOHN—BOX 5, PACK 88:
Inv. made July 5, 1783, by Jas. Montgomery, Joseph Green, Jno. Owens of 96 Dist. Admr. Elizabeth Briggs. No other papers.

BISHOP, ROBERT—BOX 5, PACK 89:
Est. admr. Oct. 17, 1783, by Elizabeth Bishop, Alexr. Kilpatrick bound to Jno. Thomas, Jr. Ord. 96 Dist. sum 2,000 lbs. Inv. made Jan. 14, 1784, by Wm. Benson, Alexr. Kilpatrick, Alexr. Vernon, Alexr. Rea.

BELL, JOHN—BOX 5, PACK 90:
Est. admr. April 12, 1813, by Wm., Saml. Bell, Robt. Wallace bound to Taliaferro Livingston Ord. Abbeville Dist. sum $2,000.00. Sale, April 30, 1813. Byrs: Elizabeth, Wm., Saml. Bell, etc.

BOYD, JOHN—BOX 5, PACK 91:
Est. admr. Nov. 22, 1833, by Jas., Jno. L. Boyd, Wm., Henry Brooks, Archibale McMullan bound to Moses Taggart Ord. Abbeville Dist. sum $30,000.00. Expend: Jan. 15, 1835 Paid Jas. Murray for Frances Boyd $23.43. Jno. L. Boyd $11.50. Jan. 13, 1835 Paid Jno. L. Boyd for his trouble of a trip to Alabama $38.87½.

BUSBY, STEPHEN—BOX 5, PACK 92:
Est. admr. Nov. 21, 1836, by Joel, Wm. Smith, Jno. White bound to Moses Taggart Ord. Abbeville Dist. sum $300.00 Inv. made Dec. 10, 1836, by Jas. M. Calvert, Nicholas Long, Jas. Wood. Byrs: Micajah Busby, Andrew Cobb, etc.

BOYD, JOHN—BOX 5, PACK 93:
Est. admr. Sept. 12, 1836, by Wm. Campbell, Joseph Hughey, Thos. J. Foster bound to Moses Taggart Ord. Abbeville Dist. sum $2,000.00. Cit. pub. at Mt. Moriah Church. Sett. ment. Hugh, Wm., Jno. Boyd out of the state. Elener Boyd wid. Ebenezer, A. P., Hannah, Jane, Robt., Adam Boyd.

BEASLEY, EDWARD—BOX 5, PACK 94:
Est. admr. May 1, 1837, by Ephraim R. Calhoun, Richard Griffin, Ephraim Davis, Robt. Anderson bound to Moses Taggart Ord. Abbeville Dist. sum $15,000.00. Cit. pub. at Mt. Moriah Church. Expend: Jan. 1, 1839 Paid gdn. of Benjamin C. Beasley $400.00. Williamson Beasley $400.00. Washington Beasley $400.00. Heardon Beasley $200.00. Nancy Beasley for Jesse Beasley $100.00.

BUCHANAN, JOHN—BOX 5, PACK 95:
Est. admr. Dec. 26, 1837, by Wm., Elizabeth, William Buchanan bound to Moses Taggart Ord. Abbeville Dist. sum $20,000.00. Sett. made Feb. 21, 1842. Present, Wm. Buchanan admr. Elizabeth Buchanan wid. Jno., William Buchanan gdn. of infant distributees, Elizabeth, Geo., Saml., Andrew Buchanan. Abner P. Jones and wife Lacinda.

BONNER, DR. ANDREW—BOX 5, PACK 96:
Est. admr. Oct. 6, 1828, by Patrick Calhoun, Samuel Young bound to

Moses Taggart Ord. Abbeville Dist. sum $20,000.00. Wm. Bonner, Joseph Jones of Wilcox Co. Alabama appointed Saml. Bonner of same county their Atty. for their part of est. of Dr. Andrew Bonner of Abbeville Dist. S. C. Joseph Jr., Jas. N., Mary, Robt., Elizabeth Jones chn. of Margaret Jones decd. of Wilcox Co. Alabama appointed Saml. Bonner their Atty. Robt. Jones gdn. of Andrew, Sarah, Wm., Cynthia, Jane Jones minor chn. of Robt. Jones and Margaret Jones decd. formerly Bonner.

BUCHANAN, WILLIAM, SR.—BOX 6, PACK 97:
Will dated April 20, 1836, in Abbeville Dist. Exrs: Sons, Jno., Wm. Buchanan. Wit: Thos. Wier, Jno. Irwin, Saml. Turner. Chn: Jno., Wm., Margaret, Isabella, Martha Buchanan, Mary Bruce (or Brice) Sett: Jan. 31, 1842. Legs: Wife, Polly, Wm., Thos., Peggy Buchanan, Kennedy Blake and Isabella his wife. Jno. Buchanan died after intestate leaving no will. Elizabeth his wid. Wm., Jno., Geo., Saml., Andrew Buchanan, Abner Jones and wife Lacinda. Chn: of Romans (first name not plain) Wm., Jno. Romans. Smith Romans died under age. Wm. of age. Paschall D. Klugh gdn. of Jno., Robt., Stephen, Daniel Romans. Wm. Buchanan gdn. of Elizabeth, Geo., Saml., Andrew Buchanan.

BLACK, ROBERT—BOX 6, PACK 98:
Est. admr. Nov. 6, 1837, by Jno. B., Wm. C. Black, Hudson Prince bound to Moses Taggart Ord. Abbeville Dist. sum $20,000.00. H. M. Prince gdn. of the minor chn. wid. Susan C. Black.

BEAZLEY, ELIZABETH—BOX 6, PACK 99:
Est. admr. Dec. 5, 1836, by Franklin Beazley, Jas. Calvert, Jno. Irwin bound to Moses Taggart Ord. Abbeville Dist. sum $4,000.00. Expend: Feb. 25, 1837 Recd. of Jesse C. Beazley admr. of Wm. Beazley decd. $350.00.

BLACK, JAMES A.—BOX 6, PACK 100:
Will dated Nov. 7, 1836. Proved Dec. 1836. Exrs. Jno. B. Black, Hugh M. Prince, Francis B. Clinkscales. Wit: Joseph Black, Jno. Young, Ester M. Burnett. Ment. wife and chn. no names given. Sett. made Feb. 1851 ment. Hugh M. Prince, Elizabeth, Jas. A. Black Jr. James Young and wife, Wesley A. Black, J. M. and Matilda E. Shirley.

BROWNLEE, SANDERS—BOX 6, PACK 101:
Est. admr. Sept. 4, 1837 by Wm. B. Beazley, Downs Calhoun, Wm. Turner bound to Moses Taggart Ord. Abbeville Dist. sum $1,000.00. Sale, Sept. 13, 1837. Byrs. Bevley Brownlee, Jno. H. Sample, Downs Calhoun, Franky Long, S. G. Cook, Aaron Pinson, Wm. Rogers, Jas. Caldwell, etc.

BROWNLEE, GEORGE—BOX 6, PACK 102:
Will dated Dec. 30, 1833 in Abbeville Dist. Proved Feb. 25, 1836. Exrs. Geo., Harrey Brownlee, Francis B. Clinkscales, Hugh Morrah, Aaron Lomax. Wit: Wm. Hill, Saml. Donald, Jas. Webb. Chn. Jno., Geo., Brownlee, Elizabeth Lomax, Jane Morrah, Elsey Clinkscales, Sarah Miller, Martha Richey, Isabella Kay. Gr. chn. Sally Rasor dtr. my son Jno. Brownlee, Eliza-

beth dtr. Jno. Brownlee. d. l. Maria widow Jno. Brownlee. "Bequeath $150.00 to the Greenville Presbyterian Church." Expend: Mar. 3, 1836. Leg. Jas. Miller, Jas. Seawright, Jno. Rasor, Aaron Lomax, Jno. Cowan, Hugh Morrah, Jas. Richey, Robt. H. Kay.

BEAZLEY, WILLIAM—BOX 6, PACK 103:
    Est. admr. Sept. 7, 1835 by Jesse C. Beazley, Downs Calhoun, Walter Anderson bound to Moses Taggart Ord. Abbeville Dist. sum $12,000.00. Sale, Nov. 18, 1835. Byrs. Franklin, Elizabeth, Jno., Willison B. Beazley, Walter Anderson, Silas Bailey, Wm. H. Green, Jesse Caldwell.

BLACK, HENRY S.—BOX 6, PACK 104:
    Est. admr. June 6, 1836 by Stephen Whitley, Larkin G. Carter, Richard C. Griffin bound to Moses Taggart Ord. Abbeville Dist. sum $2,000.00. Sett. made Sept. 10, 1846 between Meady Mays admr. of Stephen Whitley who was admnr. of H. S. Black and David Lesly Ord. Sale, June 23, 1836. Byrs. Richard White, Stephen Whitley, Wm. Carter, Jno. Cheathem, Jno. Pressly, Thos. Cheatham, Larkin Griffin, Jno. McCain, A. P. Pool, etc.

BOWMAN, WILLIAM W.—BOX 6, PACK 105:
    Est. admr. Sept. 7, 1835 by Sarah C. Bowman, Jas., Jno. G. Caldwell bound to Moses Taggart Ord. Abbeville Dist. sum $1,000.00. Sale, Oct. 30, 1835. Byrs. S. C. Bowman, Isaac Carlile, J. H. Crainshaw, Jno. Martin, Jas. Kelly, Michael Kennedy, etc.

BURTON, MOLLY—BOX 6, PACK 106:
    Will dated Aug. 6, 1829 in Abbeville Dist. Proved Nov. 27, 1829. Exr. Son, Peter Burton. Wit: Wm. Pratt, Saml. C. Jones, Jas. Wilson, Chn. Robt., Sarah, Caleb, Wm., Jno., Peter, Josiah, Elizabeth, Mary Burton. Expend: 1831 Heirs. Sarah Burton alias Hall, Saml. Black and wife Elizabeth, Joshua Ashley and wife Mary.

BARMORE, PETER—BOX 6, PACK 107:
    Est. admr. Nov. 27, 1829 by Wm., Larkin Barmore, Ezekiel Rasor bound to Moses Taggart Ord. Abbeville Dist. sum $4,000.00. Chn. Larkin. Nancy, Elizabeth, Makaly Barmore. Nov. 20, 1830 Recd. of Saml. Agnew $12.43¾. Recd. of Lucy Barmore widow $475.00.

BURTON, JOHN—BOX 6, PACK 108:
    Will dated July 9, 1836 in Abbeville Dist. Proved July 25, 1836. Exrs. Wife, Caroline C. Sons, Jas., Jno. A. Burton. Wit: Wesley C. Norwood, Donald Douglass, L. A. Bowie, Sarah Downey. Chn. Wm., Jas., Jno. A. Butron, Margaret Foreman, Mary Thacker, Mariah Chandler, Gr. dtr. Mary Hodges. Inv. made Aug. 24, 1836 by Jno. Gray, Jas. Moore, Donald Douglass.

BARMORE, JAMES—BOX 6, PACK 109:
    Will dated June 8, 1829 in Abbeville Dist. Proved June 7, 1830. Exr. Son. Wm. Wit: N. W., Wm., Malinda S., Louisa A. Ware. Wife, Molly. Ment. heirs of Geo., Peter Barmore, heirs of Asa Franklin namely

Wm., Jas., Franklin. Sett. April 7, 1831 Leg. Jas., Lewis, Wm. Jr., Nancy Barmore.

BARMORE, MARGARET—BOX 6, PACK 110:
On Dec. 4, 1838 Enoch, Wm. Barmore, Abner H. McGee, Burrel McGee the last of Anderson Dist. bound to Moses Taggart Ord. Abbeville Dist. sum $20,000.00. Enoch Barmore made gdn. of Margaret Barmore minor under 21 yrs. Expend: Feb. 14, 1840 Paid Wm. Donnald who married Margaret Barmore $582.68¾.

BOND, WRIGHT—BOX 6, PACK 111:
Est. admr. June 3, 1833 by Wm. P. Bond, Edward Carter, Wm. Hanvey bound to Moses Taggart Ord. Abbeville Dist. in sum $300.00. Inv. made Aug. 1, 1833 by Jas. Gray, Alexr. Laughlin, Thos. Calhoun.

BEAZLEY, JESS—BOX 6, PACK 112:
Est. admr. Dec. 9, 1834 by Willison B. Beazley, Downs Calhoun, Joel Smith bound to Moses Taggart Ord. Abbeville Dist. sum $10,000.00. Sale, Dec. 25, 1834. Byrs. Jesse Caldwell, Downs Calhoun, Isaac Sample, Aaron Pinson, Jesse C. Beazley, etc.

BRADLEY, PATRICK—BOX 7, PACK 113:
Will dated Oct. 13, 1828 in Abbeville Dist. Proved Jan. 29, 1835. Exrs. Jno., Archibald Bradley. Wit. Jno., Robt. McComb, Alexr. Laughlin. Chn. Isabella, Mary Bradley.

BOSTICK, WILLIS—BOX 7, PACK 114:
Est. admr. Aug. 7, 1826 by Jas. A. Ward, Charles Neely, Jno. D. Adams bound to Moses Taggart Ord. Abbeville Dist. sum $5,000.00. Est. admr. again Mar. 5, 1827 by Henry Pritchard, Jas. Patterson, Geo. Pressly bound to Moses Taggart Ord. sum $3,000.00. Inv. made Aug. 26, 1826 by Jno. McLennan, A. B. Crook, E. R. Calhoun.

BEAL, BENJAMIN—BOX 7, PACK 115:
Will dated Aug. 15, 1827 in Abbeville Dist. Exr. Jas. Calhoun. Wit. Moses W. Houston, Jas. L. Brough, Rebeckah Calhoun. "Bequeath to Lucinday Gray and Mourning Roberts." Inv. made Dec. 4, 1827 by Peter Bevill, Joshua Dubose, Jas. Mathews, Nathaniel Banks. Byrs. at sale. Mourning Roberts, Duke Beall, Robt. Green, Jas. Mathews, Thos. Brough, Jas. Calhoun, Peter Bevill.

BELL, BENJAMIN—BOX 7, PACK 116:
Est. admr. Feb. 10, 1824 by Littleton Myrick, Eli S. Davis, C. Daniel bound to Moses Taggart Ord. Abbeville Dist. sum $3,000.00. Inv. made Feb. 16, 1824 by Thos. Goodman, Wm. Collins, Jno. D. Williams.

BROOKS, SARAH R.—BOX 7, PACK 117:
Will dated Feb. 20, 1826 in Abbeville Dist. Proved Feb. 28, 1826. Exr. Thos. Livingston Esq. Wit: A. Hunter, Wm. McCaw, Mary A. Fraser.

Chn. Sarah Amanda Brooks, Thomas A. Sanders. Sale, April 1, 1826. Byrs. Thos. Livingston, Henry Brooks, Polly Stewart, Thos. A. Sanders.

BROUGH, GEORGE—BOX 7, PACK 118:
Est. admr. Jan. 23, 1835 by Jno., Alexr. Scott, Benjamin McKittrick, Henry Furr bound to Moses Taggart Ord. Abbeville Dist. sum $10,000.00. Expend: Mar. 14, 1836 Paid Jno. W. Brough $20.00. Jno. Livingston $36.13. Philip Leroy for board of Nancy $27.50. For board of Elizabeth $16.50. Board of Geo. Brough $45.00. Had 1 note signed by Jas. L. Brough.

BROUGH, GEORGE AND NANCY (Minors)—BOX 7, PACK 119:
On Jan. 4, 1836 Benjamin McKittrick, Jno. Scott, Isaac W. Waddel bound to Moses Taggart Ord. Abbeville Dist. sum $10,000.00. Benjamin McKittrick made gdn. of Nancy and George Brough minors.

BULLOCK, WILLIAM—BOX 7, PACK 120:
Est. admr. Dec. 5, 1830 by Jno. White, Jno. McLeman, Joel Smith bound to Moses Taggart Ord. Abbeville Dist. sum $3,000.00. Expend: Dec. 5, 1830 Paid Jas. W. Chiles tuition of Wm. Bullock minor $2.12½. Jno. W. Bullocks acct. $1.00. Wm. Bullock decd. was gdn. of Jno., Mary A., Len, Richard White minor chn. of Geo. White decd. $3.00. Jan. 15, 1833 Paid Vincent, Agness Griffin's share est. $335.43: Wm., Martin L. Bullock were minors.

BLAIN, WILLIAM—BOX 7, PACK 121:
Will dated Jan. 16, 1829 in Abbeville Dist. Proved Mar. 31, 1829. Exrs. Wife, Mary, Jas. W. Blain, Wm. Barmore. Wit: Isaac, Jas. Cowan, Jno. Weatherall. Chn: Jno., Jas., Daniel, Yancey Blain. Sett. ment. 9 leggs. Jas., Jno., Daniel, Wm. Y. Blain, Richard D. Shirley & wife Mary, Wm. P. Martin & wife Mahala, Saml. Smith & wife Jane, W. Norris & wife Martha. Richard, Mary Shirley were of Green Co. Alabama. Jno. Blain was of Attalla Co. Miss.

BLACK, MARY—BOX 7, PACK 122:
Will dated Jan. 6, 1826 in Abbeville Dist. Proved Mar. 19, 1828. Exrs. Jas. A., Jno. B. Black. Wit: Ebenezer Ashley, Jas. A., Elizabeth Black. Chn: Molly, Ann Pickens, Abby wife of Jesse Campbell of Georgia, Alexr. Black. Gr. dtr. Mary Ann Black. Inv. made Aug. 26, 1828 by Alexr. L. McClint, Majoy Lewis, Wm. N. Buchanan.

BUSBY, ELIZABETH—BOX 7, PACK 123:
Est. admr. Oct. 10, 1828 by Downs, Wm. Calhoun, Saml. Crawford bound to Moses Taggart Ord. Abbeville Dist. sum $2,000.00. Inv. made Nov. 28, 1828 by Alexr. Stewart, Wm. Beazley, Edmund Caldwell. Byrs: Benjamin, Jno., Stephen, Jane Micajah Busby, Smith Romans, etc.

BELL, ABRAM—BOX 7, PACK 124:
Est. admr. Jan. 24, 1834 by Wm., Jas. Lomax, Wm. Tennent bound to Moses Taggart Ord. Abbeville Dist. sum $8,000.00. Est. admr. again

24   ABSTRACTS OF OLD NINETY-SIX AND

Sept. 18, 1837 by Armistead Burt, Wm. Calhoun, Wm. Tennent to Moses Taggart Ord. sum $10,000.00. Sett: made Oct. 6, 1837 of est. made by Armistead Burt, Geo. Graves admnrs. of Wm. Lomax who was the first admnr. of Abraham Bell. Abraham Bell died Oct. 1833. Wm. Lomax died 1834. Jas. Lomax died Sept. 1835. Present: Jas. E. G. Bell who represents also the interest of his mother, Jane, the wid. of Abraham Bell as admr. she being dead. Jno. English married Sarah a dtr. Legs: Wm., Jno. L., Allen L., Napoleon, Robt. T., Constantine Bell minors not present. Had 9 chn.

BLACK, ROBERT—BOX 7, PACK 125:
    Est. admr. Jan. 8, 1831 by Charles Dendy, Leanden Bryan, Thos. D. Gray bound to Moses Taggart Ord. Abbeville District sum $600.00. Inv. made Jan. 21, 1831 by Jno. Boyd, Robt. Monroe, Robt. Hunter. Byrs: Nancy Black.

BOZEMAN, EDWARD—BOX 7, PACK 126:
    Est. admr. July 14, 1818 by Susanna Bozman, Joseph, Robt. F. Black to Taliaferro Livingston Ord. Abbeville Dist. sum $10,000.00. Expend: Jan. 25, 1818 the heirs of Edward Bozman. Wid. Susanna. Paid Robt. F. Black for boarding Thos. Bozeman $28.00, who was 24 yrs. old last Aug. Boarding Elizabeth Taylor $75.00 who was 26 yrs. old the 5th of Nov. last. Jas. Bozeman will be 21 yrs. the 16th of Feb. next. Katharine Smith will be 18 yrs. old the 16th July next.

BURTON, JOHN—BOX 7, PACK 127:
    Est. admr. Feb. 12, 1823 by Beverly Burton, Jno. Hearst Jr. Jas. Carson bound to Moses Taggart Ord. Abbeville Dist. sum $4,000.00. Sale, March 27, 1823. Byrs: Mary, Beverly, Allen, Mrs. Mary Burton, Thos. Harris, Jno. Briskey, Jno. Hearst.

BICKLEY, JOSEPH—BOX 7, PACK 128:
    Will dated 1816 in Abbeville Dist. Rec. Dec. 21, 1816. Exrs: wife, Frances, Brothers, Jno., Waller O. Bickley. Wit: Geo. Whitefield, Jas. W. Speed, Wm. Bradshaw. Chn: Mary Ann. Wm. Bickley, Caroline Covington. "Advanced property in lifetime to Caroline, Richard Covington." Inv. made Jan. 13, 1817 by Jeremiah S. Terry, Michael Speed, Wm. Norwood.

BRANYON, HENRY—BOX 7, PACK 129:
    Est. admr. Mar. 6, 1820 by Agness, Jno. W. Branyon, Robt., Wm. Ellis bound to Moses Taggart Ord. Abbeville Dist. sum $1,000.00. Sale, Mar. 28, 1820. Byrs: Jno., Thos., Elizabeth, Mary Ann, Nancy Branyon, Robt. H. Kay, Jno. Armstrong, David Taggart, Robt. Rutherford, etc.

BOUCHELON, JEAN—BOX 7, PACK 130:
    Will dated Nov. 8, 1818 in Abbeville Dist. Proved May 4, 1819. Exr: Wife, Jeanne. Wit: Jacob, Jno. Bellot, Philip LeRoy Jr. Chn: Isaac, Elizabeth, Josephine, Joseph Louis Bouchillon. Inv. made July 16, 1819 by J. Gibert, R. Watkins, Pierre Guillval, Jacob Bellot.

BRIGHTMAN, THOMAS, SR.—BOX 7, PACK 131:
Will dated Mar. 15, 1823. Proved Nov. 28, 1823 in Abbeville Dist.
Exrs: Nathaniel Marion, Jas. Shackelford, Joseph N. Whitner. Wit: Elihu
Creswell, Lewis Gwyn, Jno. C. McGehee. Wife, Maria. Chn: Wm., Thos.
Brightman Jr. decd. Gr. chn: Ann wife of Jas. Butler, Violet, Thos., Rebecca
Brightman chn. of Wm. Brightman. "Give to Jno. Porter $500.00. Give my
little friend Masselon Glenn $1,000.00. to be paid over by her father the Rev.
Jas. E. Glenn. Owned land in the Village of Cambridge." Inv. made Jan.
10, 1824 by Richard Griffin, Jno. Logan, Zachary Meriwether.

BULLOCK, ELIHU—BOX 8, PACK 132:
Est. admr. Dec. 14, 1819 by Mary Ann Bullock, Jas. Vaughn, Frederick
Slappy Sr., Vincent Griffin bound to Moses Taggart Ord. Abbeville Dist.
sum $7,000.00. Sale, Jan. 20, 1820. Byrs: Jas., B. S. Bullock, Jesse Jay Jr.,
Saml. Cochran, Jacob Slappy, Thos., Nathan Lipscomb, Jno. Anderson, Hugh
Robinson, Willis Glover, Ira Griffin, Frederick Slappy.

BLACKBURN, WILLIAM—BOX 8, PACK 133:
Est. admr. Oct. 6, 1817 by Lidia Blackburn, Malon Morgan, Jno. H.
Spruce bound to Taliaferro Livingston Ord. Abbeville Dist. sum $5,000.00.
Expend: April 3, 1823 Paid Robt. Powell for schooling $4.25. Sarah Black-
burn $40.50. April 27, 1820 Jno. Blackburn $153.00. Jan. 15, 1823 Thos.
Blackburn $118.00. Jan. 24, 1824 Nancy Blackburn $55.00. Aug 4, 1826
Isabel Blackburn $80.00.

BEATTY, JOHN—BOX 8, PACK 134:
Est. admr. April 17, 1824 by Jas. Beatty, Geo. Palmer, Wm. Bond
bound to Moses Taggart Ord. Abbeville Dist. sum $2,000.00. Sale, May 3,
1824. Byrs: Thos., Jas. Beatty, Edward Carter, Hiram, Geo. Palmer, Singleton Hughes, Thos. Creswell Sr. Peter LeRoy.

BURTON, JOSIAH—BOX 8, PACK 135:
Est. admr. Sept. 5, 1829 by Peter, Robt., Wm., Caleb Burton bound
to Moses Taggart Ord. Abbeville Dist. sum $3,000.00. Expend: Nov. 4, 1830
Saml. Black recd. $450.00 for his claim against est. of Josiah, Molly Burton
both decd. Inv. made Oct. 2, 1829 by Jas. Hill, Wm. Young, Wm. Breazeal.

BURNS, LUKE—BOX 8, PACK 136:
Est. admr. Nov. 12, 1819 by Jno. Cain, Andrew Milligan, Wm. Cal-
houn bound to Moses Taggart Ord. Abbeville Dist. sum $1,000.00. Expend:
Oct. 27, 1820 Recd. of Jno. Cain in full my demands against est. Jno. Clay.
Jas. Herring recd. $6.00 for Wm. B. Herring, Sale, Dec. 18, 1819. Byrs:
Matty Burns, W. Burns, Jno. Cain, David Richardson, Drury Breazeal.

BRADLEY, THOMAS—BOX 8, PACK 137:
Est. admr. Sept. 1, 1823 by Patrick, Jno. Bradley, Geo. McFarlin
bound to Moses Taggart Ord. Abbeville Dist. sum $1,000.00. Sale, Nov. 18,
1823. Byrs: Archibald, Isabell Bradley, Adam Cole, Alexr. Patterson Sr.,
Jas. Cason, David Blackwell, Edward Carter, Saml. Ross, Thos. Parker, etc.

BIBB, RICHARD—BOX 8, PACK 138:
Est. admr. July 28, 1819 by wid. Susannah B. Bibb, Wm. McMarten, Jeremiah Beall bound to Moses Taggart Ord. Abbeville Dist. sum $2,000.00. Inv. made Aug. 12, 1819 by Jeremiah Beall, Jno. H. Cofer, Peter Bevill.

BROOKS, CHRISTOPHER—BOX 8, PACK 139:
Will dated Sept. 15, 1819 in Abbeville Dist. Proved April 1, 1820. Exrs: Wife, Sarah, Wm., Henry Brooks. Wit: Wm. H. Caldwell, Wm. Lesley Jr., Jane Caldwell. Lived in Abbeville District. Wife, Sarah Brooks. Chn: Henry, Wm. Brooks, Sally Wilson, Polly Prince, Betey, Nancy Brooks. Inv. made May 19, 1820 by Wm. H. Caldwell, John Boyd, Andrew Gillespie, Dudley Jones. Byrs: Henry Brooks, Silvanus, Edward Prince, Elizabeth Brooks, John Boyd, Wm., Sarah Brooks.

BEATY, WM. W.—BOX 8, PACK 140:
Will dated May 21, 1826, in Abbeville Dist., Proved July 3, 1826. Exrs.: Lewis Pyles. Wit: Jno. Stevenson, Lewis Pyles, Catharine Pyles. Brother, Thos. Beaty Jr.

BLACK, ARCHIBALD—BOX 8, PACK 141:
Est. admnr. Dec. 13, 1820 by Jno. McPhail, Jonathan Swift, Douglass McKellar bound to Moses Taggart Ord. Abbeville Dist. sum $500.00 Inv. made Dec. 20, 1820 by Jonathan Swift, Isaac Logan.

BEALL, JEREMIAH—BOX 8, PACK 142:
Est. admnr. Oct. 27, 1826 by Jas. W. Prather, Jas. Allen, Alexr. Scott bound to Moses Taggart Ord. Abbeville Dist. Sum $10,000.00 Expend: Paid Benjamin Beall $1200.00, property to James W. Prather before his death. Sale, Nov. 30, 1826. Buyers: Benjamin Beall, Joseph B. Gibert, Orville Tatom, Benjamin McKittrick, Joseph H. Stanton, Catherine Tanehill, Richard Luzter, Robt. McKinley, Mathew Young, Lewis Howland.

BEATTY, ANN—BOX 8, PACK 143:
Est. admnr. Nov. 8, 1825 by Edward Carter, Andrew Bonner, Singleton Hughes bound to Moses Taggart Ord. Abbeville Dist. sum of $3,000.00 Inv. made Nov. 15, 1825, by Adam Wideman, Jno. Lindsay, Mathew Goodwin, Robt. McCaslan. Sale Nov. 29, 1825. Byrs: James Beatty, Jas. Hughes, Jas. Spence, Jas. Cain, Joshua Wallace, Jas. Adams, Peter LeRoy, Saml. Wideman, Mary McCanery, Owen Findley, Joseph Tilman.

BRIDGES, JOHN—BOX 8, PACK 144:
Est. admnr. Dec. 12, 1825, by Bennett McAdams, Saml. W. Tribble, Archibald Mattison bound to Moses Taggart Ord. Abbeville Dist. sum $500.00 Inv. made Dec. 30, 1825 by Jno. Clinkscales, Lewis Pyles, Jacob Loaner. Sale made at the home of Charlotte McAdam, wid. Cit. pub. at Little Mountain Church. House Rent paid Mrs. Charlotte McAdams $10.00.

BEVINS, IRA—BOX 8, PACK 145:
Est. admnr. June 17, 1831 by Jno. Hanley, Thos. P. Spiencen, Jno. Brown

Pressly bound to Moses Taggart Ord. Abbeville Dist. sum $1,000.00 Inv. made July 16, 1831 by Jas. Alston, Jno. Allen, Wm. H. Kyle. Byrs.: Charles Dansby, Isaac Hobart, Giles W. Glasgow, Francis Pitman, Wm. Moore, Wm. Marsh.

BOWEN, STERLING—BOX 8, PACK 146:
Will dated Jan. 23, 1822 in Abbeville Dist. Proven Dec. 2, 1822. Exrs: Sons, Woody Bowen, Lacey Bowen. Wit: Jno. Bowen, Andrew Brownlee, A. Hunter. Wife, Susannah, ch. Susannah, Drury, Clarey, Woody, Meridith, Nancy, Lacey, Polly, Sterling, Patsy, Jincey Bowen. Inv. made Dec. 17, 1822 by Jno. Powell Sr. Wm. Brownlee, Wm. Anderson, David Christopher. Aug 28, 1846. Elizabeth, Alfred B., Nancy Gailey, Harriet Lomax, chn. of Polly Gailey decd. Wife of Andrew Gailey, of Habersham County, Georgia, put in for their part of est. of Sterling Bowen decd. Sett. stated that Meridith Bowen was in Arkansas, Nancy in Georgia, Jas. Gailey, Polly Gailey dead, Chn. in Georgia all of age, Andrew Gailey her husband living, Patsey dead, Jincey in Abbeville, S. C. a wid. Susannah had 2 sets of chn. present husband Saml. McIlwain in Abbeville. Nov. 27, 1845. Jane McCurry recd. of her father's estate $33.21. One place written Jincy McCurry.

BREAZEALE, MARY ANN—BOX 8, PACK 147:
Est. admnr. Oct. 12, 1828 by Michael R. Breazeal, Jacob Bellot,. Saml. McCarter bound to Moses Taggart Ord. Abbeville Dist. sum of $1,000.00. Inv. made Oct. 31, 1828 by Jacob Bellott, Isaac Bouchillon, Isaac W. Waddell. Paid C. W. Breazeale $8.77½. Sale Nov. 1, 1828. Byrs.: Henry Breazeale, Robt. T. Jennings, Andrew Guillebeau, Isaac Bouchillon, Elizabeth Todd, Jno. Hodges, Benjamin McKittrick, Charles Vaughn, Singleton Hughes, Lazarus Guillebeau, Jacob Bellott, Hague Lawton.

BARKSDALE, HENRY—BOX 8, PACK 148:
Est. Admnr. Jan. 17, 1818 by Vincent Griffin, Jas. Hutchison, Joseph C. Matthews bound to Taliaferro Livingston Ord. Abbeville Dist. sum of $20,000.00 Inv. made Jan. 31, 1818 by Ezekiel, Wm. Noble, Geo. Patterson. Expend: Jan. 1, 1818 For boarding Steth Barksdale $100.00. Delia Ann Barksdale $100.00. Jno. Barksdale $335.00. B. Barksdale $281.00. G. Barksdale $95.00.

BROUGH, JOHN—BOX 8, PACK 149:
Est. admr. May 19, 1820 by Thos. Brough, Dr. Eli S. Davis, Jas. Tatom bound to Moses Taggart Ord. sum $500.00. Cit. pub. at Willington Church. Expend: Jan. 25, 1823 Paid Elizabeth Brough $268.22. Geo. Brough bought at sale.

BELL, LEWIS—BOX 8, PACK 150:
Will dated Feb. 23, 1816 in Abbeville Dist. Proved Mar. 18, 1816. Exrs: Joseph Meriwether, Jno. Meriwether Jr. Peter Coleman. Wit: Zachary Meriwether, David Cunningham, Willis Bartee. Wife, Frances. Brother, Benjamin. Nephew, Jno. Bostick. Inv. made Mar. 22, 1816 by Jno. Hatter, Robt., Austin Pollard, Jno. H. Meriwether.

BALL, PETER—BOX 8, PACK 151:
    Will dated Feb. 25, 1816 in Abbeville Dist. Rec. Mar. 12, 1816. Exrs.
Brother, Lewis, Henry Hitt, Geo. Ball. Wit: Zachary Meriwether, Jno. Hatter,
Polly Whitlow. Wife, Elizabeth. Chn: Jeremier, Polly, Lucay, Nancy, Jinsay,
Elizabeth Ball. Inv. made Mar. 13, 1816 by Peter H. Coleman, Jno. Hatter,
Dudley Richardson.

BROWN, WILLIAM—BOX 8, PACK 152:
    Est. admr. Mar 2, 1801 by Elizabeth Brown, Jno. Connon Esq. Dr.
Zachary Meriwether, Carr McGehee bound to Andrew Hamilton Ord. Abbeville
Dist. sum $8,000.00. (Will of Wm. Brown Sr. in same pack:) Will dated Jan.
8, 1791 in Abbeville Dist. Proved June 12, 1792. Exrs: Wife, Isbel, Son, Wm.
Brown, Jas. Black. Chn: Isbel, Sarah, Martha, Wm. Brown, Margaret Ruford.
Gr. chn: Jno. son to Wm. Brown, David son to Jas. Black, Margaret, Elizabeth,
Frances Brown dtrs. to my son Jno. Brown decd., William Ruford.

BROWN, CORNELIUS—BOX 9, PACK 153:
    Will dated Oct. 31, 1792 in Abbeville Dist. Exrs: Nephew, Peter Brown,
Robt. Allen, Wm. McKinley, Wm. Hutton. Wit: Jas. Bynum, Peter Thompson,
Joseph Hutton. Gr. chn: Cornelius Brown Williams, Sarah, Jas. chn. of Peter
Brown. Delilah, Elizabeth stepdtrs. of Peter Brown. Nephew, Robt. Brown.
Expend: One paper for 1793 ment. that Peter Brown was of Elbert Co., Georgia.
July 1795 Recd. from Duke, Sarah Bell 4 lbs. 4 shillings sterling. April 18, 1796
Recd. of Wm. Hutton 4 shillings for certifying a Power of Atty. given to Peter
Brown for conveying a tract of land in Virginia & for the receiving the balance of
money due from the sale, which land was sold by Cornelius Brown decd. in his
life time & conveyed by said Hutton & Brown. Mar. 22, 1796 To Peter Brown
for going to Virginia in Montgomery Co. about 300 miles to make titles for land
sold by Cornelius Brown decd. to Cornelius Brown Jr.

BROWN, ELIZABETH—BOX 9, PACK 154:
    Will dated Dec. 24, 1804. Rec. Sept. 2, 1805. No Exrs: Wit: Jno.
Lummus, Wm. Steal, Geo. Connor. Chn: Shadrick, Nancy Brown, Elizabeth
Nighting. Sale, Sept. 21, 1805. Byrs: Wm., Nancy Brown, Jno. Hagood, Thos.
Moore, Abraham Smith, Cornelius Austin, Wm. Georgee, Robt. Lummus.

BOWMAN, JAMES—BOX 9, PACK 155:
    Est. admr. July 20, 1790 by Hugh, Jno. Wardlaw Jr, Joseph Reid bound
to Judges of Abbeville Co. sum 500 lbs. Inv. made Aug. 2. 1790 by Joseph, Saml.
Reid, Edward Sharp.

BALL, NANCY—BOX 9, PACK 156:
    Will dated May 2, 1814 in Abbeville Dist. Rec. Aug. 16, 1814. Exrs:
Sons, Wm., Lewis Ball, Brother, Zachary Pulliam. Wit: Charles Fooshe, Wm.
Hill, Chn: Lewis, Wm., Juda, Anney, Burwell, Parkes Ball, Betsey Davis, Sally
Glover. Expend: Feb. 11, 1816 Paid Wm. H. Glover leg. $241.43. & gdn. for
Juda Ball. Paid Wm. Davis leg. & gdn. for Burwell Ball.

BROWN, ANDREW—BOX 9, PACK 157:
Est. admr. Jan. 21, 1808 by Mary Brown, Wm. Hutchison, Wm. Gaston, Robt. McCord bound to Andrew Hamilton Ord. Abbeville Dist. sum $2500.00. Inv. made Feb. 5, 1808 by Jno. Jay, Jesse Reagin.

BEARD, DAVID—BOX 9, PACK 158:
Est. admnr. May 2, 1786 by Elizabeth Beard, Jno. Miller bound to Jno. Thomas Jr. Ord. 96 Dist. sum 500 lbs. Inv. made July 1786 by Capt. Jno. Norwood, Jno. Miller Sr., Jno. Miller Jr.

BARKSDALE, WILLIAM—BOX 9, PACK 159:
Est. admr. 4, 1805 by Henry Hickerson Barksdale, Thos. Tillery, Wm. Goodman bound to Andrew Hamilton Ord. Abbeville Dist. sum $10,000.00. Mary Barksdale the widow & mother of Henry, Hickerson Barksdale. Sale, Feb. 27, 1807. Byrs: Wm., Nancy, Hickerson, Henry Barksdale, Harrison Posey, Col. Thos. Murray, Andrew Goodger, etc.

BRYAN, PHILIP—BOX 9, PACK 160:
Est. admr. Oct. 16, 1784 by Hannah, Richard Bryan, Wm. Littlefield bound to Jno. Thomas Jr. Ord. 96 Dist. sum 2,000 lbs. Sale, Oct. 6, 1784. Byrs: Elizabeth, Hannah, Wm. Bryan, Thos. Bearding, Lewis Bobo, Mark Jackson, etc. (Written Bryan & Bryant.)

BRUMMETT, PETERSON—BOX 9, PACK 161:
Est. admr. Mar. 26, 1787 by Lettice, Thos.,. Saml. Brummett, Henry Wolf bound to Jno. Thomas Jr. Ord. 96 Dist. sum 500 lbs. Inv. made April 21, 1787 by Henry Wolf, Elias, Saml. Earl.

BYRD, SAMUEL—BOX 9, PACK 162:
Inv. made April 10, 1783 by Hugh Means, Andrew Mays, Joseph Buffington. Sale, May 12, 1783. Byrs: Isaac Cruse, Mark Jackson, Jno. Harris, Thos. Bearding, Wm. Simpson, Jno. Foster, David Brown, Jas. Wofford. Lived in 96 Dist. (No other papers.)

BROWN, JOHN—BOX 9, PACK 163:
Est. admr. June 18, 1784 by Andrew, Jas. Compton Edwards, Jno. Lockridge bound to Jno. Thomas Jr. Ord. 96 Dist. sum 2,000 lbs. Inv. made July 2, 1784 by Jno. Cochran, Thos. Weems, Jno. Lockridge. Sale, Aug. 6, 1784. Byrs: Robt. Pulliam, Jas. Edwards, Mary Norris.

BERRY, USLEY—BOX 9, PACK 164:
Est. admnr. Jan. 2, 1784 by Geo. Berry bound to Jno. Thomas Jr. Ord. 96 Dist. sum 2,000 lbs. Inv. made Jan. 1784 by Andrew Cunningham, Jas. McLaughlin, Thos. Deane.

BOZEMAN, JOHN—BOX 9, PACK 165:
Est. admr. Dec. 1785 by Philip Fagan, Gibson Jones, Thos. Eastland bound to Jno. Thomas Jr. Ord. 96 Dist. sum 1,000 lbs. Keziah Bozeman bought at sale, etc.

BAGLEY, JAMES—BOX 9, PACK 166:
Lived in 96 Dist. Inv. made July 12, 1783 by Nehemiah Howard, Jeremiah Stokes, Joseph Little. Wid. Lucy Bagley. (No other papers.)

BAKER, BARNABAS—BOX 9, PACK 167:
Est. admr. Nov. 29, 1785 by Margaret Baker, Jas. Gray, Wm. Shinholser bound to Jno. Thomas Jr. Ord. 96 Dist. sum 1,000 lbs. Inv. made Dec. 24, 1785 by Jacob Tim, Jno. Williams, Jonathan, Jno. Meyer.

BULLION, THOMAS—BOX 9, PACK 168:
Est. admr. Aug. 5, 1786 by Thos. Manson, Andrew Thomsom, Andrew Barry bound to Jno. Thomas Jr. Ord. 96 Dist. sum 200 lbs. Admnr. also granted to Thos. Manson & Mary Bullion his wife. Inv. made Oct. 2, 1786 by Alexr. Vernon, Robt. Foster, Andrew Thomson. Byrs: Thos. Manson, Jno. Collings, Thos. Moore, Jas. Jordan.

BRYAN, JOHN—BOX 9, PACK 169:
Est. admr. Aug. 1, 1783 by Rebecca Bryan, Jno. Brown bound to Jno. Thomas Jr. Ord. 96 Dist. sum 2,000 lbs. Inv. made by Wm. Hanna, David Dunlap, Besdell Holland.

BRADLEY, JAMES—BOX 9, PACK 170:
Est. admr. Jan. 13, 1807 by Hugh Morrah, Jno. Bowie, Jas. Wardlaw Esq. bound to Andrew Hamilton Ord. Abbeville Dist. sum $10,000.00. Expend: Feb. 3, 1812 Paid Wm. McGaw for schooling $5.81. June 2, 1810 Paid Jas. McCord for boarding, schooling Betey, Jno. Bradley minors $9.50.

BELL, MATHEW—BOX 9, PACK 171:
Will dated Dec. 25, 1803 in Abbeville Dist. Rec. Jan. 16, 1804. Exrs: Alexr. Clark, Jas. Hutcheson, Wm. McGaw. Wit: Saml. Hutcheson, Alexr. Houston, Wm. L. Wills. Wife, Elenor. Chn: Ely, Jas. Bell. Sale, June 4, 1824. Byrs: Thos., Peter, David, Wm. Bell Jr. etc. Cash recd. from Arthur Bell $1.00. From Ellender Bell $51.33.

BURDEN, JOHN—BOX 9, PACK 172:
Est. admnr. May 14, 1823 by Sarah Burden, Hugh Saml. Porter bound to Moses Taggart Ord. Abbeville Dist. sum $3,000.00. Expend: Sarah Burden makes oath that Nancy Gibson recd. a bed at or before her marriage. May 24, 1826 Paid Canady Gibson leg. $15.00. May 25, 1823 Paid Saml. Hill gdn. Wm. Burden $32.00. July 4, 1823 Paid Abraham Burden leg. $20.00. Feb. 5, 1820 Paid Valentine Young gdn. Abraham Burden $100.00.

BALL, ELIZABETH—BOX 9, PACK 173:
Will dated 1816. Proved May 20, 1816. in Abbeville Dist. Exrs: Elihu Creswell. Wit: left out. Chn: Charlotte, Catharine Davenport, Wm., Jonathan Swift.

BOLE, ANN—BOX 9, PACK 174:
Est. admr. Oct. 5, 1801 by Wm. Bole, Thos. Ramsay, Saml. McMullen

bound to Andrew Hamilton Ord. Abbeville Dist. sum $10,000.00. Sale, Nov. 1801. Byrs: Henry, Isaac, Wm. Bole, Jno. Hamilton, Jas. Keown, Dudley Cook, Henry Steel. April 7, 1804 Paid Harvey Bole $19.75.

BOYD, ROBERT—BOX 9, PACK 175:
Will dated June 21, 1779 in Granville Co. 96 Dist. Proved April 20, 1782. Exrs: Patrick McMaster, Wm. Hays. Wit: Robt. Boyd, Patrick McMaster. Wife, Mary. Chn: Agnes, Robt., Wm. Boyd. Inv. made July 27, 1782 by Moses Davis, Hugh Calhoun, Wm. McKeen.

BOWMAN, JACOB—BOX 10, PACK 176:
Est. admnr. Oct. 2, 1782 by Sarah Bowman, Saml. Rosemond, Saml. Wharton yeoman bound to Jno. Ewing Calhoun Ord. 96 Dist. sum 2,000 lbs. Sarah Bowman was of Reedy River in 96 Dist.

BURDETTE, GILES—BOX 10, PACK 177:
Est. admnr. Feb. 1, 1783 by Henry King, Wright Nicholson, Michael DeLoach bound to Jno. Ewing Calhoun Ord. 96 Dist. sum 14,000 lbs. Cit. ment. that Henry King was of Little Saluda. Inv. made Feb. 25, 1783 by Jesse Jernigin, Wright Nicholson, Michael DeLoach.

BRYAN, ROBERT—BOX 10, PACK 178:
Est. admr. April 2, 1782 by Sarah Bryan, Benjamin Tutt, David Maxwell bound to Jno. Ewing Calhoun Ord. 96 Dist. sum 14,000 lbs. Lived in Cuffetown, 96 Dist. Sale, May 30, 1782. Inv. made by Saml. Anderson, Jas. Harrison, Benjamin Glanton.

BRACKENRIDGE, JAMES—BOX 10, PACK 179:
Est. admnr. Jan. 16, 1804 by David Brackenridge, Thos. Ross, Jas. Cowan bound to Andrew Hamilton Ord. Abbeville Dist. sum $5,000.00. Sale, Feb. 13, 1804. Byrs: David, Jas., Elizabeth, Mary, Margaret, Janet, Widow Brackenridge, Austin Smith, Wm. Ross, etc.

BRACKENRIDGE, JOHN—BOX 10, PACK 180:
Est. admnr. Mar. 27, 1797 by Elizabeth Brackenridge widow, Jno. Miller blacksmith, Wm. Mayn bound to the County Court sum $1,000.00. Sale, July 4, 1797. Byrs: Elizabeth, David, Jas. Brackenridge, Wm. Mayn.

BOYES, ARTHUR—BOX 10, PACK 181:
Est. admnr. May 29, 1782 by Alexr. Boyes, Col. Geo. Reid, Jas. Seawright bound to Jno. Ewing Calhoun Ord. 96 Dist. sum 14,000 lbs.

BUCHANAN, JAMES—BOX 10, PACK 182:
Will dated Oct. 18, 1802 in Abbeville Dist. Proved Mar. 29, 1805. Exr: Son, Robt. Wit: Benjamin Hatter, Margaret Rice, Z. Rice. Wife, Frances. Chn: Mary, Rebekah, Frances, Robt. Bonds, Robertson, Jas. Buchanan. Inv. made April 30, 1805 by Wm. P. Arnold Humphrey Klugh, Stephen Watson.

BENTON, JAMES—BOX 10, PACK 183:
Est. admnr. Jan. 7, 1785 by Jas. Adair, Jno. Owens, Jno. Jones bound

to Jno. Thomas Jr. Ord. 96 Dist. sum 2,000 lbs. Inv. made Feb. 4, 1785 by Benjamin Adair, Jno. Jones, Jno. Owens.

BUTLER, JAMES—BOX 10, PACK 184:
Est. admnr. Oct. 11, 1782 by Russell Wilson, Jas. Allen, Wm. Sisson bound to Jno. Ewing Calhoun Ord. 96 Dist. sum 14,000 lbs. Cit. pub. at Clouds Creek Meeting House. Widow, Mary.

BENNETT, JOHN—BOX 10, PACK 185:
Est. admnr. Jan. 4, 1783 by Jas. Brewer, Mathew Devore, Sr., Brayn Green bound to Jno. Ewing Calhoun Ord. 96 Dist. sum 2,000 lbs. Cit. ment. was of Stephens Creek. Sale, April 4, 1800. Byrs: Mary Bennett, Jacob Free, Wm. Pitman, Mark Wideman, Robt. Clinton, etc.

BOGGS, JOHN—BOX 10, PACK 186:
Est. admnr. Jan. 17, 1803 by Francis Rene LeRoy Duverqueil, Dillary Carrel, Jas. Dillyshaw bound to Andrew Hamilton Ord. Abbeville Dist. sum $5,000.00. Sale, Feb. 4, 1803. Byrs: Jas., Ann Boggs, Polly Campbell, etc.

BOUCHILLON, JOSEPH—BOX 10, PACK 187:
Will dated Nov. 30, 1802 in Abbeville Dist. Rec. Jan. 3, 1803. Exrs: Brother, Jno. Jas. Guillebaut. Wit: P. Gilbert, Pierre Guillebaut, Lazare Causain. Wife, Susannah. Chn: Jno., Jenny, Joseph Leonard Bouchillon. Inv. made Jan. 10, 1803 by Drury Breazeale, Jno. Prince, Peter B. Rogers.

BURTON, JOSEPH—BOX 10, PACK 188:
Will dated Sept. 5, 1809 in Abbeville Dist. Rec. Mar. 14, 1811. Exrs: Sons, Jno., Wm. Burton. Wit: Ann, Revd. Benjamin R. Montgomery, Mary Dunlap, Saml. Geddis. Chn: Jno., Wm., Mary & her dtr. Edy, Elizabeth, Sarah, Catharine, Mahatabel, Josiah, Douglass Burton. Expend: Mar. 8, 1811 Paid Ord. in Camden for proving said will $1.50. To 12 days going twice to Camden & Abbeville to have will rec. $18.60. Dec. 12, 1811 Paid Wm. Howard for paling in graves at Cambridge $4.00. May 2, 1814 Paid Catharine Wray $1.06.

BOIN, JOHN—BOX 10, PACK 189:
Will dated Oct. 22, 1780 in 96 Dist. Proved Oct. 3, 1783. Exrs: Wife, Hannah, Son, Wm. Wit: Edward Pugh, Salley Pryan, Holloway Power. Chn: Jno., Wm., Jacob, Isaac, Jas. Boin. Inv. made Feb. 22, 1785 by Jno. Brockman, Jas. Walker More, Holloway Power.

BUSBY, STEPHEN—BOX 10, PACK 190:
Est. admnr. Mar. 7, 1812 by Wm. Smith, Alexr. Sample bound to Taliaferro Livingston Ord. Abbeville Dist. sum $1,000.00. Sale, Mar. 24, 1812. Byrs: Elizabeth Busby, Jno. Sample Sr., Obediah Wilson, etc.

BIGBY, ARCHIBALD—BOX 10, PACK 191:
Est. admnr. Sept. 16, 1815 by Daniel F. Lucius, Wm. Bigby, Abner Nash, Andrew Richey bound to Taliaferro Livingston Ord. Abbeville Dist. sum $10,000.00. Cit. stated that Daniel F. Lucius & Wm. Bigbea made suit for Letters of Admnr. of Archibald Bigby (late 2nd Lieutenant in the 43rd Regiment

of the United States Infantry.) as next of kin. Pub. at the store of Lt. Col. Reuben Nash.

BANKS, RIVERS—BOX 10, PACK 192:
Will dated April 11, 1800 in Abbeville Dist. Proved Nov. 19, 1800. Exrs: Wife, Mary. Son, Jas. Wit: Richard Tuh Jr. Stephen Smith. Chn: Geo., Jas. Banks. Inv. made Jan. 1, 1801 by Jas. Newby, Jno. Standard, Jas. Tucker.

BOYD, JAMES—BOX 10, PACK 193:
Will dated Aug. 10, 1784 in Craven Co. 96 Dist. Proved Oct. 26, 1784 before Andrew Foster & Jas. Barnes of Camden Dist. Exrs: Wife, Martha. Son, Saml. Boyd. Wit: Barnett Sr., Wm. Barnett Jr., Jas. Barnett. Chn: Mary, Jno., Saml., Abraham Boyd. s. l. Robt. Barnes. "Bequeath to Saml. Horse Creek Mill & plantation on Reburns Creek."

BURGESS, WILLIAM—BOX 10, PACK 194:
Est. admnr. May 1, 1784 by Wm. Rucks, Jas. Puckett, Jas. Finney bound to Jno. Thomas Jr. Ord. 96 Dist. sum 1,000 lbs. Inv. made Nov. 15, 1784 by Geo. Neely, Jas. Puckett, Robt. Swansey.

BARKSDALE, CLEVIUS—BOX 10, PACK 195:
Est. admnr. April 28, 1784 by Jno., Wm. Barksdale, Jno. Martin bound to Jno. Thomas Jr. Ord. 96 Dist. sum 2,000 lbs. Inv. made Aug. 4, 1784 by Daniel Ramsay, Jno. Harris, Geo. Whitefield.

BERAUD, JOHN—BOX 10, PACK 196:
Will dated Jan. 1796 in New Bordeaux, Abbeville Co. 96 Dist. Rec. Mar. 27, 1799. (This was a translation from the French will & the wit. names omitted. Signed in Columbia.) Exrs: Jno. Gervais Esq. residing in Charleston, Peter Gibert Sr. of New Bordeaux. Nephews at Ste Foi sons of my late brother Jas. Beraud surnamed Rousseau and of Elizabeth Battide Beraud the mother, residing at the Canton Bourg D'Tnessee Jurisdiction of Ste Foi in Aginez province of Guiennee in France.

BRASSWELL, DAVID—BOX 10, PACK 197:
Est. admnr. Nov. 8, 1782 by Russel Wilson, Lewis Clark, Jno. Douglass bound to Jno. Ewing Calhoun Ord. 96 Dist. sum 14,000 lbs. Dated at White Hall. Russell Wilson was of Little Saluda. Inv. made Nov. 22, 1782 by Andrew Lee, Levi Manning, Thos. Gibson.

BROOKS, ELISHA—BOX 10, PACK 198:
Est. admnr. Mar. 4, 1782 by Frances Brooks, Jno. Wyld, Jno. Wallace bound to Jno. Ewing Calhoun Ord. 96 Dist. sum 14,000 lbs. Made in presence of Ann Boyman. Inv. made June 26, 1782 by Bartlett Satterwhite, Morris Guinn, Jno. Caldwell.

BROWN, ANDREW—BOX 10, PACK 199:
Inv. made Feb. 10, 1808 by Wm. Hutcheson. Byrs: Mary, Margaret, Mary Ann Brown, Jesse Ragan, Thos. Livly, etc. (No other papers.)

BRANSON, CAPT. ELI—BOX 10, PACK 200:
Will dated May 30, 1796. Rec. Mar. 27, 1797. Exrs: Wife, Keziah. Nathaniel Henderson. Wit: Julius Nichols Jr., Jeffery Lively, Jno. Stevens. "Was one of his Majestys Subjects of the King of Great Britian, but now resident of Abbeville Dist." Chn: Jemima, Jno., Daniel, Thos., Levi, Eli Branson, Rebekah, Mary Jones, Naomi Ward. "Left 636 acres of land lying in Newberry Co. on Indian Creek to Jno., Daniel, Thos. Branson." His part of est. that was willed to him by his Grandfather Benjamin Burden est. in Virginia left to his chn.

BENNISON, GEORGE—BOX 10, PACK 201:
Est. admnr. Dec. 27, 1785 by Sarah Benison, Abel Pearson, Jeremiah Files bound to Jno. Thomas Jr. Ord. 96 Dist. sum 500 lbs. Sale, Jan. 27, 1786. Byrs: Sarah Benison, Mary, Jeremiah Files, Wm. McCalleb.

BYRD, WILLIAM—BOX 10, PACK 202:
Est. admnr. Mar. 12, 1785 by Jordon, Thos,. Saml. Jackson bound to Jno. Thomas Jr. Ord. 96 Dist. sum 1,000 lbs. Sale, April 6, 1785. Byrs: Esther, Elizabeth Byrd, Arthur Crawford, Ezekiel Farmer, Robt. White.

BRATCHEY, ARTHUR—BOX 10, PACK 203:
Est. admnr. 1783 by Margaret Bratchey, Jno. Hall bound to Jno. Thomas Ord. 96 Dist. sum 2,000 lbs. Expend: July 25, 1784 Recd. of Margaret Cracken 1 lb. 17 and 6 pense. Feb. 21, 1784 Recd. of Margaret Bradshaw $1.00.

BETTIS, JOHN—BOX 10, PACK 204:
Est. admnr. April 28, 1784 by Stephen Bettis, Lacon Ryan, Joel McClendon bound to Jno. Thomas Jr. Ord. 96 Dist. sum 2,000 lbs. Inv. made June 26, 1784 by Stephen Bettis, Van Swearingen Sr.

BARRY, JOHN—BOX 11, PACK 205:
Will dated Oct. 1, 1786 in Spartanburg Co. 96 Dist. Exrs: Wife, Rebeccah. Brother, Andrew. Wit: Richard Barry, Thos. Peden, Charles Moore. Chn: Jno., Jas., Elizabeth Barry. s. l. Esebella McCord. Owned land lying in the forks of Tyger River. Inv. made Oct. 29, 1786 by Charles Moore, Richard Barry, Michael Miller.

BEAZLEY, EDMOND—BOX 11, PACK 206:
Est. admnr. April 24, 1794 by Jno. Hairston, Isaac Logan bound to County Court of Abbeville Dist. sum $2,000.00. Est. admnr. again Mar. 28, 1794 by Oliver & Elizabeth Louden his wife, (alias Beazley.) Jas., Saml. Houston, Capt. Jno., Wm. Calhoun to the Judges of Abbeville County sum 2,000 lbs.

BEAZLEY, JAMES—BOX 11, PACK 207:
Est. admnr. Dec. 15, 1802 by Edmond Beazley, Robt. Thompson, Henry Fleming bound to Andrew Hamilton Ord. Abbeville Dist. sum $5,000.00. Next of kin, Edmond Beazley. Sale, Jan. 7, 1803. Byrs: Edmond, Wm. Beazley, Wm. Neely, Stephen Busby, Oliver Louden, Jno. Shotwell, etc.

BLAND, ROBERT—BOX 11, PACK 208:
Will dated Dec. 21, 1786 in Edgefield County. Exrs: Wife, Ann., Joseph

Nun, Solomon Pope. Wit: Edward, Saml. Bland, Joel Swaney. Chn: Jno., Jas., Pressly, *Wormley?'* Elisha, Payton, Liddey Bland. Gr. son, Micapa son of Jno. Bland. Inv. made May 15, 1787 by Wm. Humphrey, Henry King, Jacob Brown.

BAYLAND, JACOB—BOX 11, PACK 209:
Will dated Sept. 23, 1784 in Hillsborough Township. Proved Oct. 15, 1785. Exrs: Nicholas Vinzel, Peter Gibert. Wit: Henry Wilson, Jno. Poncheere, Nicholas Bascon. Wife, Mary Susan Bouchomeau. Chn. ment. no names given. "I give full power to my wife to sign to Dr. Jno. Delahow, the titles of a plantation of 150 acres joining lands of said doctor, the mill of Jeremiah Rogers, lands of Peter Bayle, Peter Boutition." Inv. made at Hillsborough, Amelia Township Oct. 20, 1785 by Geo. Crawford, Peter Engerven, Peter Belott, Henry Wilson, Thos. Matthews.

BEARD, SIMEON—BOX 11, PACK 210:
Est. admnr. Jan. 3, 1803 by Margaret Baird, Jno., Archibald Douglass bound to Andrew Hamilton Ord. Abbeville Dist. sum $5,000.00. Inv. made Jan. 7, 1803 by Jno. Gray, Jno. Jack, Robt. Gibson.

BICKETT, JOHN—BOX 11, PACK 211:
Est. admnr. Feb. 20, 1803 by Nancy Bicket, Joseph Creswell, Jno. Stewart bound to Andrew Hamilton Ord. Abbeville Dist. sum $5,000.00. Sale, Mar. 14, 1803. In 1806 Nancy Bicket was dead.

BARKSDALE, RICHARD—BOX 11, PACK 212:
Est. admnr. July 16, 1801 by Mary Ann Barksdale, Benjamin Cant bound to Andrew Hamilton Ord. Abbeville Dist. sum $10,000.00. Sale made Aug. 24, 1801 in Edgefield Dist. Mary Ann Barksdale alias Martin late of Abbeville Dist. Higgerson & Allen Barksdale names were ment.

BECKWITH, ISAAC—BOX 11, PACK 213:
Est. admnr. Sept. 26, 1814 by Else Beckwith, Abner Nash, Jno. H. Miller, Jno. Calvert bound to Taliaferro Livingston Ord. Abbeville Dist. sum $10,000.00. Sale, Oct. 13, 1814. Byrs: Else Beckwith, Wm. Anderson, Wm. Adams, Alexr. Bowie, Joseph Cooper, etc.

BUTLER, THOMAS—BOX 11, PACK 214:
Admnrs. next of kin, Wm. Butler, Jas. Cain. Sale, April 23, 1799. Byrs: Wm. Lumbus, Wm. Brown, Jas., Richard Perry, Mary Steel, etc.

BELL, SARAH—BOX 11, PACK 215:
Will dated Aug. 6, 1803 in Abbeville Dist. Rec. Aug 21, 1809. Exr: Husband, Duke. Wit: Jno. Clark, Jas. Tannehill, Jane Levesten. Sis: Janey Leviston, Easther Clark, Mary Boyd. "Give Peter Brown, Cornelius Brown Williams each 1 shilling." Est. also admnr. Nov. 8, 1813 by Lewis Bell next of kin, Jno. Meriwether bound to Taliaferro Livingston Ord. Abbeville Dist. sum $1,000.00.

BEVIL, JOHN—BOX 11, PACK 216:
Est. admnr. Oct. 23, 1813 by Hudson Prince, Elijah Horn, Jas. Fleming

bound to Taliaferro Livingston Ord. Abbeville Dist. sum $1,000.00. Sale, Dec. 3, 1813. Byrs: Sarah Bevil, Edward Prince Jr., Saml. Savage Esq. Hudson Prince.

BUCHANAN, JAMES—BOX 11, PACK 217:
Est. admnr. Dec. 27, 1837 by Wm., Robt., Francis A. Buchanan bound to Moses Taggart Ord. sum $7,000.00. Cit: pub. at Cokesbury. Chn: Jas. Willis, Robt. P., Buchanan. Mary Catharine died about 1844. Wid: Nancy.

BURNEY, ANDREW—BOX 11, PACK 218:
Will shows no date. Wit. David Zubly Sr. and Britton Dawson were sworn on May 9, 1782, they were present signature. Lived in 96 District. Stepson, George Bender. "Bequeath unto Andrew Thomas, Wm. Bassett Smith." Sister, Elizabeth Milling, give her 2 lotts in Augusta, Georgia, situated on Broad and Reynolds St. (This will was badly torn.)

BALL, JOHN—BOX 11, PACK 219:
Est. admnr. April 17, 1807 by Charles Fooshe, Joseph Hill, Daniel Mitchel bound to Andrew Hamilton Ord. Abbeville Dist. sum $10,000.00 Cit: ment. Charles Fooshe next of kin. Pub. at Fellowship Church. Expend: May 21, 1810 Paid Sally Ball leg. $30.00. July 9 Lewis Ball lef. $196.40. July 13 Paid Jas. Foster for schooling Wm. Ball $4.00. Oct. 19 Paid Wm. Davis leg. $114.75. Nov. 2 Paid Nancy Ball wid. dowery $861.37. May 3, 1813 Paid Wm. Davis gdn. Burwell Ball leg. $246.10. June 20, 1807 Wm. Davis to est. Jno. Ball decd. for personal property given after marriage to the said decd. dtr. Betey Davis. Aug 7, 1815 Paid Wm. H. Glover gdn. Judith Ball leg. $267.21. Wm. Ball gdn. Ann Ball $264.09½. Wm. Glover leg. $16.00.

BERRY, WILLIAM—BOX 11, PACK 220:
Admnrs. Elizabeth, George Berry. Inv. made Aug. 3, 1783 by Andrew Cunningham, Jno. Lindsay, Benjamin Kilgore. Lived in 96 Dist.

BUFORD, LUNSFORD—BOX 11, PACK 221:
Est. admnr. Aug. 5, 1816 by Philemon, Wm. Buford, Alexr. Speer bound to Taliaferro Livingston Ord. Abbeville Dist. sum $20,000.00. Cit: pub. at Rocky River Church. Byrs: Margaret, Morgan A., Wm., Philemon, Jane Buford, etc.

BAIRD, JOHN—BOX 11, PACK 222:
Will dated Nov. 28, 1798 in Abbeville Dist. Exrs: Thos. McBride, David Pressly. Wit: Simeon Baird, Alexr., Jno. White. Wife ment. no name given. Chn: Adam, Jno., Andrew, Simeon Baird. Sale, Apirl 24, 1798. Byrs: Martha, Mary, Hugh, Adam Baird, Wm. Quay, Saml. Morris, etc.

BUFORD, WARREN—BOX 11, PACK 223:
Est. admnr. June 15, 1809 by Philemon, Lunsford, Wm. Buford bound to Andrew Hamilton Ord. Abbeville Dist. sum $10,000.00. Expend: ment. that property was given to Charles Johnson. Inv. made Sept. 18, 1809 by Jas. R. Baird, Alexr. Wimbus, Wm. P. Rayford.

BENISON, WILLIAM—BOX 11, PACK 224:
Will dated April 30, 1817 in Abbeville Dist. Proved Feb. 2, 1818. Exrs:
Jno. McAdam Sr., Jas. Richey Sr. Wit: Jno. Shirley, Jno. McAdam Jr., Wm.
Bennison. Wife, Margaret. Chn: Jno., Wm., Jas. Benison, Fanny Wallace,
Margaret Bell, Mary Ann McWhorter, Betsey, Jean Step. Sale. Feb, 17, 1818.
Byrs: Wm. Wallace, Wm. Bell, Saml., Alexr. McKinney, etc.

BUCHANAN, PATRICK—BOX 11, PACK 225:
Will dated Mar. 11, 1812 in Abbeville Dist. Rec. Aug. 31, 1812. Exrs:
Wm. Wedgeworth, Alexr. Simpson. Wit: Edward Forbes, Jno. Simpson, Jno.
Buchanan. Wife, Martha. Chn: Jno., Margaret Buchanan. Cit: pub. at Johns
Creek Meeting House.

BARMORE, GEORGE—BOX 11, PACK 226:
Will dated July 15, 1816 in Abbeville Dist. Rec. Sept. 19, 1816. Exrs:
Wm. Barmore, Wm. Pyles. Wit: Abner Nash, Jas. W. Kay. Wife, Nancy. Chn:
ment. no names given. Inv. made Oct. 5, 1816 by Abner, Reuben Nash, Charles
Kay.

BIGBEE, ARCHIBALD—BOX 11, PACK 227:
Est. admnr. July 27, 1836 by Chester Kingsley, Jno. W. Bigbee, Thos.
E. Owen bound to Moses Taggart Ord. Abbeville Dist. sum $1,000.00. Cit: pub.
at Moseleys Meeting House.

BASKIN, WILLIAM ESQ.—BOX 11, PACK 228:
Est. admnr. May 25, 1804 by Anne, Wm. C. Baskin, Wm. Harkness,
Thos. Shanklin, Vachal Clary bound to Moses Taggart Ord. Abbeville Dist.
sum $10,000.00. Inv. made July 21, 1804 by Thos. Shanklin, Wm. Nichols,
Saml. Porter. Sale, Sept. 20, 1804: Byrs: Anne Baskin, Wm., Jas. Harkness,
Capt. Stuart Baskin, Wm. C., Jno. A., Jno. Baskin, etc.

BLACK, JOHN—BOX 11, PACK 229:
Est. admnr. April 16, 1814 by Wm. Black, Jas. Cochran Esq. bound
to Taliaferro Livingston Ord. Abbeville Dist. sum $1,000.00. Inv. made April
3, 1814 by Jas. Foster, Wm. Hill, Jno. M. Cochran.

BOWMAN, JOHN—BOX 11, PACK 230:
Will dated Nov. 2, 1789 in Abbeville Dist. Proved April 6, 1790. Exrs:
Saml. Reid, Hugh Wardlaw. Wit: Wm., Jno. Wardlaw Jr., Wm. Herd. Wife,
Jean. Chn: Margaret, Wm. Bowman.

BOWMAN, WILLIAM—BOX 12, PACK 231:
Est. admnr. Aug 10, 1814 by Rosannah Bowman, Jno., Wm. Ravlin
bound to Taliaferro Livingston Ord. Abbeville Dist. sum $2,000.00. Sale. Aug.
3, 1790. Byrs: Jean Bowman, Jas. Buchanan, Wm. Ross, etc. (There could have
been 2 bonds, if so one is missing for 1790.)

BOYD, MARY—BOX 12, PACK 232:
Will dated Mar. 19, 1820 in Abbeville Dist. Proved Jan. 21, 1824. Exrs:

Jno. Rogers, Robt. McKinley. Wit: Thos. Finley, Jno. Clark. Son, Jno. Gr. Son, Wm. Boyd Scott.

BLACK, WILLIAM—BOX 12, PACK 233:
Est. admnr. Aug. 16, 1803 by Mathew Robinson, Robt. Black, Wm. Russell bound to Andrew Hamilton Ord. Abbeville Dist. sum $10,000.00. Sale. Sept. 8, 1803. Byrs: Capt. Robt., Wm., Jas., Joseph Black, Widow Black, Mathew Fox, Isabel Pickens, Jas. Able, Jno. Cameron, Jno. Miller, etc.

BAIRD, ADAM—BOX 12, PACK 234:
Will dated Feb. 9, 1807 in Abbeville Dist. Rec. April 8, 1807. Exrs: Wm. Dale, Joseph McCrery. Wit: Elizabeth Weed, Mary Dale, Joseph McCrery. Chn: Jean Vickery, Mary Baird. Gr. chn: Lily, Jno., Agness Baird, Elizabeth Hathorn otherwise Baird. Sale, May 7, 1807 Byrs: Jas. Hathorne Jr. Jno. Baird, Thos., David Hathorn, Jno. Baird Jr., etc.

BANKS, JAMES—BOX 12, PACK 235:
Est. admnr. Mar. 6, 1811 by Benjamin Glover, Saml. B. Shields bound to Taliaferro Livingston Ord. Abbeville Dist. sum $1,000.00. Cit: pub. at Hopewell Church. Sale, April 22, 1811. Byrs: Edward, Peter Smith, Vicey, Wm. Banks, Edward Collier, Wm. Cain, Isaac Haws etc. Inv. of James Banks made July 24, 1794 by Thom. Banks admnr. Hickerson Barksdale, Wm. Goodman, Pyrum Olds. (No other record)

BREDDEN, MARGERY—BOX 12, PACK 236:
Will dated July 21, 1798 in Abbeville Dist. Rec. Sept. 13, 1798. Exrs: Dtr. Jean. & Jas. Wadsworth. Wit: Capt. Saml. Rosamond, Wm. Robertson. Chn: David, Jane, Rachel, Susannah Bredden, Ann Wadsworth, Mary McGee, Betty Clark. Est. of Jas. Bredden in same pack. admnr. Oct. 15, 1789 by Margery Bredden wid., David Bredden, David Hunter bound to the Judges Abbeville County sum 1,000 lbs. Cit: pub. at Long Cane Church.

BASKIN, JAMES—BOX 12, PACK 237:
Est. admnr. Oct. 5, 1790 by Prudence Baskin, Jno. Green, Wm. Boles bound to Judges Abbeville County sum 1,000 lbs. Sale, Oct. 29, 1790. Byrs: Prudence, Wm. Baskin, Jno. McNeal, Saml. Young, Adam Foyls, etc.

BALL, MARK—BOX 12, PACK 238:
Est. admnr. Nov. 10, 1795 by Catey Ball wid. Jas. Ball, Capt. Reuben Nash, Jeremiah McWhorter bound to the Judges Abbeville Co. in sum 1,000 lbs. Inv. made Dec. 16, 1795 by Herod Freeman, Wm. Davis, Reuben Nash.

BROWN, SHADRICK—BOX 12, PACK 239:
Will dated Feb. 18, 1815 in Abbeville Dist. Rec. Mar. 2, 1815. Exrs: Wm. Ware, Robt. Jones. Wit: Ephraim Hampton, Sarah H. Brown, Wm. Forgason. Wife, Hannah. Chn: Daniel Brown, Elizabeth N. Meloy wife of Jno. Meloy.

BROWN, JOSEPH—BOX 12, PACK 240:
Will dated Aug. 27, 1802 in Abbeville Dist. Rec. Oct. 9, 1802. Exrs:

Wife, Sarah, Abraham Livingston, Wit: Jno. Cameron, Joseph Carmechel, Wm. Brown. Chn: Jno., Joseph Brown. "Owned land on Ponch Creek." Expend: April 8, 1812 Paid Mr. Yarbrough for Miss Jane Brown boarding & schooling at the dancing school $7.00. April 8, 1809 Paid Mr. Webster for 2 bonnets for Miss Polly & Miss Jane Brown $12.00. Paid for 4 negro chn. property of the est. from Baldwin Co. Georgia carried away by James Gamble $6.00. Jan. 1. 1812 Paid Josiah Mathews of Baldwin Co. Georgia for the benefit of the heirs $78.00. Inv. made Oct. 30, 1802 by Charles Holland, Henry Purdy, Wm. Brown.

BREAZEALE, WILLIS SR.—BOX 12, PACK 241:
Will dated Nov. 6, 1794 in Abbeville Dist. Rec. Mar. 25, 1795. Exrs: Wife, Sarah, Son, Elisha, Brother, Drury Breazeale Sr. Wit: Alexr., Robt. Clark, Thos. McKedy. Chn: Elisha, Benjamin Frankling, Kinsman, Archibald, Drury, Willis, Elijah, George Washington, Mary, Sarah, Patty Breazeal. Inv. made May 5, 1795 by Richard Barksdale, Wm. Scott, Wm. McGaw.

BASKIN, HUGH—BOX 12, PACK 242:
Will dated Mar. 30, 1796 in Abbeville Dist. Rec. June 13. 1797. Exrs: Wife, Sarah, Wm. Baskin. Wit: Bartley Tucker, Thos. Wilson Harris, Jas. Pettigrew. Chn: Elizabeth Stuart, Wm., Robt. Baskin, Esther Wilson, Susannah McKinley. Inv. made Aug. 23. 1797 by Capt. Thos. Shanklin, Jas. Pettigrew, Jno. McMaham.

BROOKS, CHRISTOPHER SR.—BOX 12, PACK 243:
Will dated Jan. 8, 1796 in Abbeville Dist. Rec. June 13, 1796. Exr: Wife, no name given. Wit. Richard Ford, Wm. White. Son, Christopher Brooks. Inv. made Nov. 14, 1796 by Richard Ford, Wm. White, Alexr. Davis. One paper ment. that Sarah, Henry, Wm. Brooks were Exrs.

BLACK, MARTHA—BOX 12, PACK 244:
Est. admnr. Jan. 15, 1839 by Jno. Cunningham, Robt. McNaire, Jno. W. Miller bound to Moses Taggart Ord. Abbeville Dist. sum $20,000.00. Cit: pub at Little Mountain Church. Sett. made Mar. 13, 1847. Present, Jno. Cunningham admnr. Robt. Black the husband of Martha died first in Alabama & Robt. Black admnr. his est. then. David Russell was employed agent by Mrs. Martha Black to receive her portion of personal est. in Alabama & did receive $500.00. Martha died before the return of David Russell. The heirs of said decd. are scattered over the U. S. & not particularly known.

BOND, BAZALL—BOX 12, PACK 245:
Est. admnr. Sept. 26, 1782 by Wm. Moore, Peter Stubles, Robt. McAlpin bound to Jno. Ewing Calhoun Ord. 96 Dist. sum 14,000 lbs. Inv. made May 15, 1783 by Solomon Pope, Joseph Nun, Dudley Prewitt, Jno. Logan, Jno. Wardlaw, Wm. Brown.

BEAZLEY, MINORS—BOX 12, PACK 246:
On Oct. 27, 1835 Downs Calhoun, Walter Anderson, Wm. A. Moore bound to Moses Taggart Ord. Abbeville Dist. sum $4,000.00. Downs Calhoun

40

made gdn. Franklin. Amanda, Robt. Beazley minors. Expend: Mar. 20, 1837 Recd. of Franklin Beazley admnr. est. of Elizabeth Beazley $30.00. Nov. 1837 Recd. of Jesse Beazley admnr. est. of Wm. Beazley decd. $201.00. (Name written Beazley & Beasley.)

BOYD, ADAM—BOX 12, PACK 247:
On Dec. 7, 1838 Hugh Boyd, Wm. Campbell, Jefferson Hughey bound to Moses Taggart Ord. Abbeville Dist. sum $5,000.00. Hugh Boyd made gdn. Adam Boyd a minor. Sett. of Adam Boyd a decd. minor made Nov. 11, 1845. Present, Hugh Boyd. Left as his distributes, mother Elenor Boyd. Brother, Hugh Boyd his gdn. Robt. Boyd, Hannah who married Wm. Malone. Martha H. who married Major Wm. Campbell. Jane not in the state, Jno. B., Wm. H., Alexr. Ebenezer Boyd. Jno. Boyd decd. was the father. Had land in Georgia.

BOYD, ROBERT—BOX 12, PACK 248:
On Dec. 7, 1838 Wm. Campbell, Thos. J. Foster, Hugh Boyd bound to Moses Taggart Ord. Abbeville Dist. sum $5,000.00. Wm. Campbell made gdn. Robert Boyd a minor.

BULLOCK, MINORS—BOX 12, PACK 249:
On Oct. 10, 1832 Jno. White, Vincent Griffin, Jas. F. Watson bound to Moses Taggart Ord. Abbeville Dist. sum $2,000.00. Jno. White made gdn. Wm. W., Luther M. Bullock minors under 14 yrs. Expend: Jan. 15, 1833. Their share of their father Wm. Bullocks est. $671.16.

BEAZLEY, JESSE—BOX 12, PACK 250:
On Sept. 19, 1837. Nancy Beazley, Ephrain Davis, Thos. Riley bound to Moses Taggart Ord. Abbeville Dist. sum $2,000.00. Nancy Beazley made gdn. Jesse Beazley a minor leg. of Edmund Beazley decd.

BEAZLEY, MARIA L.—BOX 12, PACK 251:
On Sept. 7, 1835 Willison B. Beazley, Downs Calhoun, Walter Anderson bound to Moses Taggart Ord. Abbeville Dist. sum $6,000.00. Willison B. Beazley made gdn. Maria L. Beazley, a minor over 14 yrs.

BRADY, JOHN—BOX 12, PACK 252:
Est. admnr. Oct. 19, 1832 by Robt. Brady, Jas. Taggart, Thos. Parker bound to Moses Taggart Ord. Abbeville Dist. sum $1,000.00. Cit: pub. at Lebanan Church. Inv. made Nov. 9, 1832 by Jas. Gray, Ninen Thompson, Dr. Jno. S. Reid. Byrs: Robt. Brady, Wm. Wilson, Thos. Rowan, Harris Tiner, Jno. S. Weed, Jas. Gray.

BARTEE, JAMES—BOX 12, PACK 253:
Est. admnr. Oct. 3, 1814 by Jno. Bartee, Peter Coleman, Dudley Richardson bound to Taliaferro Livingston Ord. Abbeville Dist. sum $2,000.00.

BURTON, ELIZABETH—BOX 12, PACK 254:
On Jan. 5, 1818 Caleb, Jno., Jno. Burton Jr. bound to Moses Taggart Ord. Abbeville Dist. sum $1,000.00. Caleb Burton made gdn. Elizabeth Burton, minor.

BANKS, PETER—BOX 12, PACK 255:
On Feb. 12, 1821 Abner Banks, Jas. Olds, Geo. Patterson bound to Moses Taggart Ord. Abbeville Dist. sum $300.00. Abner Banks made gdn. Peter Banks a minor over 14 yrs.

BOYD, MINORS—BOX 12, PACK 256:
On Sept. 30, 1820 Jno. Jr., Jas. McCord Sr., Wm. Stuart McCord bound to Moses Taggart Ord. Abbeville Dist. sum $500.00. Jno. McCord Jr. made gdn. Mary, Martha Boyd, minors.

BOYD, MARTHA—BOX 12, PACK 257:
Est. admnr. Oct. 6, 1832 by Robt. Boyd, Jas. Robinson, Jas. Stewart bound to Moses Taggart Ord. Abbeville Dist. sum $800.00. Cit: pub. at New Harmony Church.

BROOKS, SIMEON—BOX 12, PACK 258:
Est. admnr. Mar. 4, 1839 by Jas. Brooks, Wm. Ansley, Alexr. Scott bound to Moses Taggart Ord. Abbeville Dist. sum $20,000.00 Expend: Recd. of Jas. Brooks admnr. sum $440.15 due the minor chn. of Simon Brooks decd. viz. J. N., Isabella Brooks with interest from the 1st April 1845. Jno. Trapp gdn.

BOYD, JAMES—BOX 12, PACK 259:
Will dated Jan. 5, 1840 in Abbeville Dist. Exr: Brother, Jno. L. Boyd. Wit: Jas. Murray, F. B. Clinkscales, Andrew Gillespie Sr. Wife, Sarah. Chn: Frances Eliza, Sarah Amanda, Thos., Wm. Benjamin Boyd. Inv. made Feb. 17, 1840 by Jas. Murray, Jas. Calhoun, Jno. Gray, Edward Tilman, Andrew Gillespie. Frances Eliza maried Thos. J. Mabry.

BIGBY, SARAH—BOX 12, PACK 260:
Will dated Nov. 3, 1832 in Abbeville Dist. Proved Oct. 10, 1838. Exr: Son, Jno. Wesley Bigby. Wit: Robt. H. Kay, Archibald Bigby, Hezekiah Day. Chn: Jno. Wesley, Nancy Bigby, Sarah Gaines, Step chn: Arah Lucius, Wm. Bigby. "U to my dtrs. Betseys children $1.00." Sale, Aug. 11, 1838. Byrs: Geo. Mattison, Archibald Bigby, Jas. E. Robinson, Wm. Davis Jr., Mason Kay, etc.

BEALL, SARAH—BOX 12, PACK 261:
Will dated July 12, 1839 in Abbeville Dist. Exr: b. l. Pleasant T. Tullis. Wit: Alexr. Hughey, Meridith McGehee, Jno. Clark. Halfsisters, Eliza B., Charlotte P. Shoemaker. Nieces, Martha S. Tullis, Sarah E. Prather. Sis. Mary Ann Tullis, Martha C. Cowls. Inv. made Oct. 5, 1839 by Jno. Clark, Meridith McGehee, Joshua Dubose.

BELL, JANE—BOX 13, PACK 262:
Est. admnr. Dec. 2, 1839 by Jas. E. G. Bell, Thos. Graves, Jno. English bound to Moses Taggart Ord. Abbeville Dist. sum $20,000.00. Minor chn: A. Bell, M. Bell, R. T. Bell, C. Bell. Jno. L. Bell recd. $460.00 his share est. Abraham Bell recd. also $460.00.

BROWNLEE, MARY—BOX 13, PACK 263:
Will dated June 10, 1836 in Abbeville Dist. Proved Oct. 19, 1839. Exr:

Son, John. Wit: Wm. E. Daniel, Mary L. Campbell, A. Hunter. Chn: Jno. Brownlee, Jas. Brownlee decd. Gr. chn: Arrabella, Sarah Jane chn. Jas. Brownlee decd. Wm. son of Jno. Brownlee. Inv. made Nov. 9, 1839 by Jno. Swilling, A Morrow, Hugh Prince. Sarah Jane maried Tillman Lomax.

BROWNLEE, JAMES—BOX 13, PACK 264:
   Est. admnr. Aug. 9, 1830 by Wm., Alexr., Langdon Bowie bound to Moses Taggart Ord. Abbeville Dist. sum $1,000.00. Was late of the State of Tenn Cit. pub. at Little Mountain Church.

BOWIE, MAJOR JOHN, SR.—BOX 13, PACK 265:
   Will dated Feb. 1, 1820 in Abbeville Dist. Proved Nov. 19, 1827. Exrs: Son, Alexr. Bowie, Jas. Wardlaw Esq. Wit: Saml. L. Watt, Francis H. Wardlaw, Thos. Spierin. Chn: Geo., Jno., Wm., Alexr., Saml. Bowie. Andrew decd. d. l. Rosey Ann Bowie. Gr. dtr. Eliza Bowie. "Left nephew Dr. Jas. Bowie late from Scotland 50 lbs."

BRADLEY, ISABELLA—BOX 13, PACK 266:
   Will dated May 28, 1840 in Abbeville Dist. Proved June 7, 1840. Exrs: Joseph C. Lindsay Jr. Adam Wideman Jr. Wit: Archibald S. McFarlin. Braxton Cason, Mary Harris. Sis. Mary Bradley, Jane Lindsay. Ment. Isabella dtr. of Jane Lindsay. Inv. made June 12, 1841 by Jno. Wideman, Jas. Spence, Matthew Goodwin. Sett. ment. Wilson Watkins a leg.

BARTRAM, MARY—BOX 13, PACK 267:
   Will dated Sept. 10, 1836 in Abbeville Dist. Proved Oct. 4, 1836. Exrs: David Stuart, Downs Calhoun. Wit: Saml. S. Smith, Lewis Busbee, Willison B. Beazley. Chn: Elizabeth, Margaret Brown, Katharine Spence, Edna Waugh. s. l. Jas. W. Waugh. Gr. dtr. Mary Brown. Mary Louisa Spence, Tabitha Waugh each recd. bed and furniture.

BROWNLEE, MINORS—BOX 13, PACK 268:
   On June 2, 1845 Jas. Seawright, Robt. Brownlee, Jas. Cowan bound to David Lesly Ord. Abbeville Dist. sum $2,000.00. Jas. Seawright made gdn. Sarah, Jas. H. Brownlee minors. Sarah A. of age in 1847. Jas. H. of age in 1853. Gr. chn. of George Brownlee decd.

BURRELLE, JOHN—BOX 13, PACK 269:
   Est. admnr. Dec. 4, 1844 by Dr. Jno. Davis, McKinney Thomas, J. F. Marshall bound to David Lesly Ord. Abbeville Dist. sum $400.00. Left a wid. Vasti Burrelle and 2 chn.

BULL, DICY—BOX 13, PACK 270:
   Est. admnr. Sept. 17, 1844 by Jno. Bull, Jno. Huskison, Jas. Moore bound to David Lesly Ord. Abbeville Dist. sum $200.00. Jno. a son of decd. Expend: Paid Thos. Bull share $8.51. Mary, Martin Bull each $8.51. Jno. Smith and wife $8.51.

BLACK, ROBERT—BOX 13, PACK 271:
   Est. admnr. Mar. 2, 1840 by David, Jno. Russell, Jno. B. Black bound

to Moses Taggart Ord. Abbeville Dist. sum $2,000.00. Left no chn. but 3 brothers and 1 sis. to wit: Jas. Black living, Saml. Black died before Robt. having chn. Wm. Black no record of his death, he left chn. Mary Black married Robt. Davis and died before Robt. Black. She had 2 chn. Eleanor wife of Joseph Carter living, Jane wife Jno. C. Black, no record of her death. Saml. Black left 9 chn. viz. Robt. J., W. R., Saml. F., Catharine S., Rebecca Black, Jane wife of Charles Connor, Martha wife Jno. H. Martin, Isabella wife of Jno. C. Black, Mary wife of W. H. Norris.

BASKIN, F. Y.—BOX 13, PACK 272:
Est. admnr. May 12, 1845 by Jas., Jane, Jno. Baskin, Wm. S. McBride bound to David Lesly Ord. Abbeville Dist. sum $8,000.00. Died April 12, 1845. Francis Y. Baskin left a wid. Jane and 7 chn. Jas. Baskin f. l. of Jane Baskin purchased a small place for the family to live on near Willington.

BOWIE, WILLIAM—BOX 13, PACK 273:
Est. admnr. April 16, 1845 by Saml. Reid, Robt. H. Wardlaw, Allen T. Miller, Jno. R. Wilson, Wm. A. Wardlaw bound to David Lesly Ord. Abbeville Dist. sum $50,000.00. He died about Mar. 12, 1845 leaving wid. Nancy Jane and chn: Louisa A., Robt. E., Andrew Bowie.

BUTLER, LARKIN—BOX 13, PACK 274:
Est. admnr. April 16, 1845 by Jno. Burnett, Nathaniel Cobb, Thos. Strawhorn bound to David Lesly Ord. Abbeville Dist. sum $1300.00. Died about Mar. 3, 1845. Left a wid. Elizabeth and 6 infant chn. Inv. made May 16, 1845 by Aaron, Jno. W. Lomax, Nathaniel Cobb, Thos. Strawhorn.

BROOKS, JOHN—BOX 13, PACK 275:
Est. admnr. Jan. 13, 1845 by Sterling Williams, Wm. Brooks, Bartlett Cheatham, Jno. McIlwain bound to David Lesly Ord. Abbeville Dist. sum $4,000.00. Left wid. Mary A. but no chn. Died in the fall 1844. Mary A. was dtr. of Sterling Williams the admnr. Wm. Brooks was father of Jno. Brooks. The wid. is without the state and her father is her agent.

BEARD, MARY—BOX 13, PACK 276:
Est. admnr. Nov. 1, 1813 by Jane Vickry, Jno. Boyd, Wm. Ward bound to Taliaferro Livingston Ord. Abbeville Dist. sum $1,000.00. Jane Vickry next of kin. Sale, Nov. 26, 1813. Byrs: Mary, Nancy Buck. Thos. Osborn, Jean Vickry, Wm. Ward, Jno. Boyd, Jno., Margaret Baird, Jas., Ebenezer Foster.

BRANCH, SAMUEL—BOX 13, PACK 277:
Will dated July 17, 1840. Proved July 21, 1840. Exrs: Dr. Isaac Branch, Jno. Wilson. Wit: Armstead Burt, David J. Red, F. A. Sale. Wife, Betsey. Chn. ment. no names given. Sale, Feb. 22, 1842. Byrs: Jno. Branch, etc.

BREWER, JASPER—BOX 13, PACK 278:
Est. admnr. Feb. 17, 1841 by Geo. J. Cannon, Geo. W. Pressly, Richard Hill bound to Moses Taggart Ord. Abbeville Dist. sum $500.00. Wid. Elizabeth Brewer.

BEAL, EMSLEY—BOX 13, PACK 279:
Est. admnr. April 28, 1841 by McKinney Thomas, Jas. H. Cobb, Johnson Ramey bound to Moses Taggart Ord. Abbeville Dist. sum $2,000.00.

BLACK, WILLIAM B. (Minors)—BOX 13, PACK 280:
Died in 1841. Left 4 minors viz. Isabella E., Wm. S., Anna R. Nancy B., Jas. B. Black. On Jan. 8, 1856 B. Z. Blackman recd. from Saml. B. Major gdn. in right of his wife, Isabella E. Black, Mary Jane, wife of W. H. Blackman. Nancy B. married Rd. Burns. 1854 Paid tuition to G. H. Round $12.50 for Wm. S. Black.

BROUGH, JOHN L.—BOX 13, PACK 281:
On Oct. 31, 1835 Peter E. Legard, Jacob Bellott, Jas. P. Waddell bound to Moses Taggart Ord. Abbeville Dist. sum $10,000.00. Peter E. Legard gdn. Jno. L. Brough a minor. Sett. made Mar. 3, 1836 of Jno. L. Brough decd. the ward of Peter E. Legard with Rebecca R. Brough the wid. Jno. L. Brough entitled to a small legacy by the will of Thos. Brough decd. Left no chn. but a wid. and a mother Elizabeth Legard as his heirs.

BAIRD, THOMAS—BOX 13, PACK 282:
On Feb. 26, 1847 by Jno. S. Moragne of Benton Co. Alabama, Dionius M. Rogers, Isaac Morgane of Abbeville Co. bound to David Lesly Ord. sum $480.00. Jno. S. Moragne made gdn. Mary Ann, Robt., Martha Thomas Beard (alias Bairds.) State of Ala. Benton Co. Orphans Court. Feb. 11, 1847 came Jno. S. Moragne and asked to be made gdn. of Mary Ann Baird an infant under age & produced the certificate of Mary E. Baird the mother. Were the chn. of Thos. Baird decd. The petition of Jno. S. Moragne sheweth that some years ago Thos. Beard (alias Baird) of said state and dist. died leaving a wid and 2 chn. and another child born after his death (perhaps Illegimate) & some time afterward the wid. and chn. removed to Benton Co. Ala. Dec. 23, 1843 Jas. Beard recd. $28.86 his share of est.

BUTLER, WILLIAM—BOX 13, PACK 283:
Will dated Jan. 19, 1844 in Abbeville Dist. Proved June 29, 1844. Exrs: Son, Wm. Aaron Lomax. Wit: Jno. W., Jesse, J. N. Lomax. Chn: Larkin, Wm., Washington Butler, Elizabeth MCoole, Nancy Hix, Susannah Norrell.

BUSBEE, MICAJAH—BOX 13, PACK 284:
Est. admnr. May 18, 1844 by Lewis, Benjamin Busbee, Jas. T. Day bound to David Lesly Ord. Abbeville Dist. sum $500.00. Left no wid. or chn. but a brother Lewis Busbee. Sale, June 4, 1844. Byrs: Lewis Busbee, Jas. F. Puckett, Jas. Fuller, Thos. Stewart, Jones Tullis, Saml. Trobridge, Thos. Ramsey.

BLACK, WILLIAM B.—BOX 13, PACK 285:
Inv. made Dec. 15, 1841 by Stephen Herndon, Thos. B. Gary, Gabriel Hodges. Jan. 20, 1845 Nancy Black requested that her brother Saml. B. Major be made gdn. of her chn.

BURTON, JOSIAH—BOX 13, PACK 286:
Josiah Burton, a minor over 14 yrs. sheweth that he is entitled to a small est. of Sally Osborn dtr. of Jno. Osborn decd. who maried Josiah Burton decd. Parents dead, but brother, sister survive. viz. Polly and Jas. Burton their gdn. Benjamin Johnson. Also entitled to one third of est. of his parents from the est. of his gr. father Jno. Osborn decd. Dated this 5th Jan. 1842. Of age Nov. 13, 1845.

BUCHANAN, MARTHA—BOX 13, PACK 287:
Will date not given. Proved Jan. 3, 1842. Exr: Wm. Buchanan Jr. Wit: Paschal D. Klugh, Jno. Irwin, Wm. Buchanan Jr. Lived in Abbeville Dist. Dtr. Margaret Roman. Gr. dtr. Martha Roman. Sale, April 1842. Byrs. Robt. Woods, Wm., F. J. Buchanan, H. B. Campbell, Andrew Cobb, Jno. Irwin, A. Turner.

BARRETT, THOMAS—BOX 13, PACK 288:
Est. admnr. Nov. 3, 1842 by Thos. Fergerson, Isaac Hawes, Saml. C. Edmonds bound to David Lesly Ord. Abbeville Dist. sum $8,000.00. Sett. made Jan. 7, 1845. Present, Thos. Fergerson admnr. Martha Barrett wid., Richard Barrett. Heirs: Henry, Wm. Barrett of Georgia, Permelia Barrett, Mary White wife of Jno. White, Catharine Martin wife of Tandy Martin, Elizabeth Tomkins wid. S. Tomkins, Eliza wife Jno. Briggs, Thos., Jas., Saml., Susan Barrett, Martha wife Alexr. Edmunds.

BURTON, JAMES—BOX 13, PACK 289:
Est. admnr. Jan. 13, 1843 by Jno. E., Jas. C. Ellis, Zachariah Haddon bound to David Lesly Ord. Abbeville Dist. sum $6,000.00. b. l. of Jno. E. Ellis. Inv. made Feb. 17, 1843 by Wm. Morrison, Jno. Richardson, Thos. Eakins.

BRADSHAW, WILLIAM—BOX 13, PACK 290:
Will dated Dec. 12, 1842 in Abbeville Dist. Proved Feb. 6, 1843. Exrs: son, Henry, Dr. L. Yarbrough. Wit: Jacob, Saml., Jas. Hill. Wife, Elizabeth. Gr. chn: Wm., Elizabeth Pearson, Caroline Bradshaw the only child of Jas. and Lucinda. Jno. Pearson the supposed elligitamate dtr. of Jno. Bradshaw decd. and Sarah Pearson. (Letter)
South Carolina, Abbeville Dist.
Mr. Lesly Dear Sir,
I want you git old Mr. Bradshawa will and to read it to my brother if you please as I am not able to come my self now I come to the courthouse last Friday to see you my self and you was gone from house I have not had one cts. worth of the old mans estate me nor my husband nor children and the rest of the legatees is made away will all the rest of the property but the land the old man died while I was in Alabama and they never let even me know what was in the will my husband is also dead he died in Alabama and I want to see if I cant get something for my children this the 10 of August 1848.
Mary Ann Bradshaw   John Bradshaw's widow.

BARR, DR. WILLIAM H.—BOX 14, PACK 291:
Will dated Aug. 9, 1843 in Abbeville Dist. Proved Oct. 16, 1843. Exrs:

Wife, Rebecca, Son, Wm. Wit: Jno. Wier, Jas. F. Gibert, Jno. Barnett. Chn: Wm., Margaret, Elizabeth, Jas., Alexr. Barr. "Minister of the Gospel." "Left a tract of land in *Henry* Co. Tenn. to Jas., Alexr. Barr." Inv. made Mar. 17, 1843 by Jno. Wier, Robt. H., Wm. Lesly, Robt. Richey.

BIGBY, ARCHIBALD—BOX 14, PACK 292:
    Will dated Aug. 9, 1843 in Abbeville Dist. Proved Oct. 16, 1843. Exrs: Sons, Geo., Benjamin Bigbee. Wit: Saml., Edward Robinson, Geo. Mattison. Chn: Catharine, Margaret Spruill, Geo., Thos., Jno., Milly Ann, Archibald Bigbee, Susannah Robinson. "Owned real est. in Georgia." Susannah wife of Jas. E. Robinson, Margaret wife of Thos. Spruill. Jan. 1846 Jno. S. Spruill recd. $289.05.

BARKSDALE, ALLEN—BOX 14, PACK 293:
    Est. admnr. Dec. 5, 1843 by Wm., Benjamin Barksdale, Merideth McGehee bound to David Lesly Ord. Abbeville Dist. sum $10,000.00. On Jan. 1, 1844 the petition of Wm. Barksdale sheweth that his father Allen Barksdale died some two yrs. ago leaving a wid. Margaret who is since dead and several chn. Sale, Feb. 15, 1844. Byrs: Esq. Collier, Davis, Allen Barksdale, Jno. Price, Jas. McCaslan, Hiram Palmer.

BROWNLEE, GEORGE—BOX 14, PACK 294:
    Admnrs. Jas., Robt. Brownlee. Wid. Ann Brownlee. Dated Mar. 12, 1844. Geo. Brownlee died Feb. 28, 1844. Sett: made May 20, 1845. Present, Robt., Jas., Jno. Brownlee, R. C. Sharp who married Mary Ann. Absent: Anny, Geo. H., Wm. A., Sarah Jane, Elizabeth, Martha, Saml. R. Brownlee (the last 4 minors.) Est. admnr. Mar. 25, 1844 by Robt., Jas. Brownlee, Liddell Williams, Saml. Donald, Jas. B. Richey bound to David Lesly Ord. Abbeville Dist. sum $50,000.00.

BLACK, JOHN—BOX 14, PACK 295:
    Est. admnr. May 6, 1844 by Jas. W. Black, Geo. B. Clinkscales, Jno. Brownlee, Robt. C. Harkness, Francis L. Kay bound to David Lesly Ord. Abbeville Dist. sum $30,000.00. Sett: made Feb. 9, 1848. Present, Jas. W. Black, Geo. B. Clinkscales admnrs. and distributees, Washington B. Black for himself and Sarah L. Black his ward, Francis L. Kay, husband of Mary E. and Joseph R. Black. Absent, Jno. Brownlee admr. and Elizabeth Black wid. W. P., Jno. C. Black the last 3 having sent consent in writing. April 5, 1848 Geo. B. Clinkscales recd. $623.00 the share of his wife.

CONNER, DR. FRANCIS—BOX 14, PACK 296:
    Will dated Aug. 2, 1836 in Abbeville Dist. Proved Sept. 5, 1836. Exrs: Son, Francis A., Gabriel E. Trentlen, Geo. Conner. Wit: Stephen Herndon, Thos. R. Gary, Jno. W. Conner. Wife, Mary. Chn: Caroline S. DuBose, Mary A. D. Hodges, Belinda W., Sarah T., Francis A., Geo. D., Wesley F., Julia Ann E., Glenn B., Dosytheus L. O., Wm. Conner. s. l.s. Dr. Edwin E. Dubose, Saml. A. Hodges. Owned house & lot at Cokesbury. (Letter)

ABBEVILLE DISTRICT WILLS AND BONDS 47

Anderson April 8 H 1845
Dear Husband
   I was some what surprised when I received your letter as it was the first you have ever written to me. I am very sorry to hear that you had to take a cow that you did not buy for I always thought that many cows were expensive particularly to those who have corn to buy. Brother John is much better than he was when you left he rode out in his carriage last saturday four or five miles he was quite cherrful I am fearful that it will be some time before he can walk much his family have all had the measles and are doing well. Ma has two or three cases in her family Margaret is broke out with out with them today but they do not appear to make her very sick. I feel something better than I did when you left all though I am not able to do much at present I have had a bad cold for the last five or six days is better today I bought a piece of factory to have negro clothe Ma will have it wove for me I want you to bring with you the yarn that dinah has spun since I left home I wish you would have the hopper fixed and see that dine makes some soap I do not wish you to buy more I hope that you will not neglect the garden for we cant furnish a table with out vegetables the gardens up this way look very promising not with standing the dry weather. Another day has dawned and it will long be remembered by the people of Anderson this morning about three or four oclock a fire broke out in the village between Mr. Grigins store and the postoffice. Mr. Browns house next took fire he lost his house and nearly all his furniture but he saved most of his goods Rices store house was consumed the house next Cratons store was in burnt down every house on Bensons lot was consumed by the fire. The merchants save most of their goods with the exception of Mr. Griffin he lost every thing he had but his account book and his bed. It required great exertion to save Mr. McCully's and Orrs houses The village presents a strange appearance I tell you I hope you will soon come up and see for your self You must excuse my writing as my pen and ink is very bad. Take care of your self and the house I am ever your
                    Caroline, To Mr. James Brownlee
                              Duewest Corner
                              Abbeville District, S. C.

CUNNINGHAM, ROBERT A.—BOX 14, PACK 297:
   Will dated Aug. 26, 1836 in Abbeville Dist. Proved Aug. 23, 1838. Exrs: Nephew, Robt. Pulliam, Jabez W. H. Johnson. Wit: Robt. Cunningham, B. C. Yancey, Jno. Calhoun. Wife, Sarah. Nieces, Harriot Ware, Caroline Steward, Jane Johnson, Elizabeth Wood, Fanny Campbell. Nephews: Zachary, Robt. Pulliam. "I desire that my Exrs: purchase tombstones and have them put over the graves of my mother, sister, first wife & child, b. l. Zachary Pulliam and my grave." Expend: Dec. 1, 1838 Paid Capt. Cunningham for Margaret C. his ward $3752.98. Harriot married Jas. A. Ware. Caroline married Mark A. Steward.

CHASTAIN, JOHN—BOX 14, PACK 298:
   Will dated May 28, 1834 in Abbeville Dist. Proved July 17, 1837.

Exrs: Son, Allen. s. l. Henry Hoes. Wit: Thos. Fergason, Saml. C. Edmunds, Frederick Smith. Chn: Jas., Wm., Allen, Jno. Chastain, Bersheba Hoes. Inv. made Oct. 2, 1837 by Thos. Harmon, Robt. Jennings, Geo. Crawford.

CHEVES, MARGARET—BOX 14, PACK 299:
    Will dated Dec. 16, 1837 in Abbeville Dist. Proved Jan. 1, 1838. Exrs: Jno. Reid, Thos. Parker. Wit: Andrew McClane, Peter Roberts, Robt. Brady. Dtr. Polly. Gr. dtr. Margaret Polly Ann Shirley. Expend: Recd. of Jno. Reid Exr: of Margaret Cheves the legacy bequeathed to me by the said Margaret Cheves in her will. Dated this Feb. 26, 1856. Mary Strickland.

CALDWELL, SAMUEL—BOX 14, PACK 300:
    Est. admnr. Mar. 1, 1837 by Jno. Cochran, J. L. Pearson, Anthony G. Caldwell, Wade L. Cochran, Lewis Perrin bound to Moses Taggart Ord. Abbeville Dist. sum $20,000.00. Inv. made Mar. 9, 1837 by Wade L. Cochran, Wm. Harris, Vincent Griffin, Thos. Ross.

COLLINS, CHARLES—BOX 14, PACK 301:
    Will dated July 12, 1836 in Abbeville Dist. Proved Aug. 19, 1836. Exrs: Manasa, Charles Collins. Wit: Adam Crain Jones Jr. Isaac, Andrew Agnew. Wife, Jane. Chn: Nancy, Mahala, Elizabeth, Franky, Charles, Ephraim, Noah, Manasa Collins. (Name also written Cullins.)

COLLINS, CHARLES SR.—BOX 14, PACK 302:
    Will dated May 31, 1836 in Abbeville Dist. Proved July 16, 1836. Exr. Son, Charles Collins Jr. Wit: Stephen Jones Sr. Zeckariah Graham, Benjamin Rosemond. Wife, Sarah. Chn: Charles Jr., Jas., Cealea Graham, Ester, Mary Pope. Gr. chn: of Ester Pope viz. Jas. Maderson, Elizer, Elizabeth Pope. Sale, Oct. 20, 1836. Byrs: Geo. Pope, Wm. Graham Sr. Wm. Graham Jr., etc.

CALDWELL, GEORGE F.—BOX 14, PACK 303:
    Est. admnr. Dec. 1, 1834 by Stanmore, Wm. B. Brooks, Saml. Perryman, bound to Moses Taggart Ord. Abbeville Dist. sum $20,000.00. He died Mar. 12, 1834 having 5 chn. Expend: April 13, 1836 Paid Edna Caldwell $100.81. Ann Caldwell $2.88. Rebecca Caldwell $2.75. Geo. Caldwell $3.25. Jas. Caldwell $1.00.

CHILD, JOHN—BOX 14, PACK 304:
    Est. admnr. Jan. 17, 1837 by Robt. Child, Jno. McLeman, Abraham P. Pool bound to Moses Taggart Ord. Abbeville Dist. sum $20,000.00. Inv. made Feb. 1, 1837 by S. C. Sullivan, Abraham P. Pool, Martin Hackett, Wm. B. Smith.

CALHOUN, JOHN E.—BOX 14, PACK 305:
    Est. admnr. May 17, 1839 by Sarah A. Calhoun, Merideth McGehee, H. H. Townes bound to Moses Taggart Ord. Abbeville Dist. sum $20,000.00. Cit. pub. at Hopewell Church. Inv. made June 18, 1836 by Joseph Mathews, Jacob Bellot, Philip LeRoy, Jno. Dickson.

ABBEVILLE DISTRICT WILLS AND BONDS   49

CALHOUN, MARTHA—BOX 15, PACK 306:
Will dated Sept. 2, 1835 in Abbeville Dist. Proved Oct. 7, 1835. Exrs:
Son, Wm., Jno. E. Calhoun. Wit: A. Houston, Jno. Dickson, Nancy Ann
Mathews. Chn: Wm. M., Martha. Jane, Jno. Ewin Calhoun. Gr. chn: Elizabeth,
Martha Holt. Inv. made Nov. 4, 1835 by Joseph C. Mathews, Jno. Dickson,
Jas. Calhoun.

CRAWFORD, SAMUEL—BOX 15, PACK 307:
Est. admnr. Nov. 8, 1834 by Robt. Crawford, Saml. Reid, Hugh Kirk-
wood, Allen Miller bound to Moses Taggart Ord. Abbeville Dist. sum $12,000.00.
On Oct. 20, 1834 Robt., Rosanna Crawford made Suit for Letters of Admnr.
Cit. pub. at Rocky Creek Church. Expend: Nov. 7, 1846 Jno. T. Haddon recd.
his share in right of his wife Jane. Sale, Nov. 26, 1834. Byrs: Robt., Wm.
Crawford, etc.

CRAWFORD, GEORGE—BOX 15, PACK 308:
Est. admnr. Sept. 6, 1825 by Esther, Greenberry, Mathews Crawford,
Jas. Connor, Wm. Struit bound to Moses Taggart Ord. Abbeville Dist. sum
$4,000.00. Chn: Isbel, Jas. Crawford. Sale, Sept. 25, 1825. Byrs: Geo., Hester,
Greenberry Crawford, etc.

CRENSHAW, PLEASANT—BOX 15, PACK 309:
Est. admnr. Jan. 1, 1838 by Mathew Young, Jas. Huey, Michael Kennedy
bound to Moses Taggart Ord. Abbeville Dist. sum $1,000.00. Cit: pub. at New
Harmony Church. Sale, Jan. 16, 1838. Byrs: Major Crenshaw, Jno. Crenshaw,
Robt. McCants, etc.

CARTER, WILLIAM, SR.—BOX 15, PACK 310:
Est. admnr. Dec. 9, 1836 by Daniel, Larkin G., Wm. Carter Jr. bound
to Moses Taggart Ord. Abbeville Dist. sum $20,000.00. Sett: ment. wid. Eliza
Carter, Wm., L. G., Benny A., Jno. T., Elizabeth Carter.

CHEVIS, JOHN—BOX 15, PACK 311:
Est. admnr. June 7, 1830 by Martha Chevis, Jas., Patrick Calhoun bound
to Moses Taggart Ord. Abbeville Dist. sum $2,000.00. Cit. pub. at Lebanon
Church. Sale, Dec. 28, 1837. Byrs: Martha Chevis, Miss Martha A. Chevis, etc.

COVINGTON, RICHARD—BOX 15, PACK 312:
Will dated Jan. 11, 1836 in Abbeville Dist. Proved Feb. 2, 1836. Exrs:
Brother, Wm. Covington, Alexr. Bowie, Dr. Wm. Tennent. Wit: Dr. J. Lockhart,
Eleazer Shockley, Jno. G. Adair. Son, Josephus. Nephews: Edmund, Benjamin
R., Charles, Jas., Samuel Watt Covington, Wm. sons of Wm. Covington.
Niece, Emily wife of Morgan McMorris. "To my little friend Andrew Wm.
son of Alexr. Bowie I leave one colt. To Tacitus Johnson son of Gideon H
Johnson decd."

CUNNINGHAM, DAVID—BOX 15, PACK 313:
Est. admnr. Jan. 15, 1826 by Robt., Robt. A. Cunningham, Jno. C. Mc-

Gehee, Nathan Lipscomb bound to Moses Taggart Ord. Abbeville Dist. sum $20,000.00.

COLE, ISAAC—BOX 15, PACK 314:
Will dated Mar. 21, 1835 in Abbeville Dist. Exr: Jas. Conner. Wit: Jas., M. O. McCaslan, Elizabeth Foster. Wife & chn. ment. no names given. Sett: ment. wid. & 5 chn. No names given. Richard Cole recd. a legacy. Sale, April 24, 1835. Byrs: Sarah, Adam, Wm. Cole, etc.

CASEY, JOHN—BOX 15, PACK 315:
Est. admnr. Dec. 21, 1832 by Thos., Elias, Jno. Lake of Edgefield Dist. bound to Moses Taggart Ord. Abbeville Dist. sum $8,000.00. Sett. made Jan. 2, 1851. Present, Thos. Lake admnr. Thos. Henderson gdn. of Lucian, Wm. Casey chn. of said decd. Esine Jones married the wid. No name given.

CROSSAN, ROBERT—BOX 15, PACK 316:
Est. admnr. Sept. 30, 1831 by Jacob Richard, Jeremiah Hinton, Daniel Keller bound to Moses Taggart Ord. Abbeville Dist. sum $500.00. (Letter)
Mr. Jacob Rikards
Sir after my best respects to you and all enquiring friends I shall take this opportunity to address a few lines to let you know that I received your letter dated the 6th of this instant. I was truly glad to hear that you went to west Tennessee and as sincerely sorry to hear that the business would not be settled with out the trouble and expense of law I wish for all the just debts to be paid if it does take every cent and I wish you to see that Dr. Cooper gets his money if payable you wrote for me to come and see you settle, or send you my consent I have already given given you my consent and authority too when I gave you the power of attorney legally executed but I will add it is out of my power to come and I wish you to settle your business in Abbeville and then if there is anything coming to the legatees from *Ramy* in Tennessee if he will not settle without sued I wish you to see or authorize your agent to do so upon the authority I have given you. I wish you after you make your settlements to write to me and give me a statement of all the demands against the estate and what both the sale bills amounted to no word but revises your affectionate friends   Thomas Crossan
Newberry District, So. Ca.   William Bruce
April 14, 1835

CALDWELL, CHARLES—BOX 15, PACK 317:
Est. admnr. Mar. 4, 1816 by Abigail Caldwell wid. Hugh Morrah, Hugh Dickson bound to Taliaferro Livingston Ord. Abbeville Dist. sum $10,000.00. Louisa W. Cochran was a child of Charles Caldwell & wid. of Jno. C. Cochran decd. Feb. 12, 1817 Paid Wm. Morrow part of his wife's legacy from her Uncle Jno. Caldwell decd. $20.00.

CALDWELL, ABIGAIL—BOX 15, PACK 318:
Est. admnr. Mar. 10, 1828 by Jno., Robt. W. Wilson, Geo. W. Hodges bound to Moses Taggart Ord. Abbeville Dist. sum $400.00. Cit. pub. at Upper

Long Cane Church. Est. admnr. again May 12, 1830 by Saml. L. Watt, Jas., L. Bowie bound to Moses Taggart Ord. sum $3,000.00. Had a dtr. Elizabeth.

COOK, PETER—BOX 15, PACK 319:
Est. admnr. Oct. 29, 1829 by Jno., Dr. Saml. Pressly, Patrick Giblson bound to Moses Taggatr Ord. Abbeville Dist. sum $400.00. Inv. made Nov. 16, 1829 by Jas. Patterson, Jno. Lipscomb, Wm. Cook. Byrs: Robt., Wm. Cook, Robt. Gibson, Jno. Falkner, Saml. Goff.

COX, ELIJAH—BOX 15, PACK 320:
Est. admnr. Dec. 21, 1829 by Alice Cox, Jas. Findly, Stephen B. Elmore bound to Moses Taggart Ord. Abbeville Dist. sum $500.00. Sale, Jan. 26, 1830. Byrs: Allis, Wm. Cox, Daniel Evans, etc.

COOPER, AGRIPPA—BOX 15, PACK 321:
Est. admnr. Nov. 12, 1830 by Grigsby Appleton, Stanley Crews, Joel Smith bound to Moses Taggart Ord. Abbeville Dist. sum $6,000.00. Expend: April 6, 1834 Paid W. D. Cooper on his share $15.00. Jan. 4, 1832 Joshua Moody for Jas. Cooper $175.00. Jan. 18, 1832 Elizabeth Cooper $110.00. Anny Cooper $1053.00.

COCHRAN, JAMES—BOX 15, PACK 322:
Will dated July 2, 1828 in Hall Co., Georgia. Proved Oct. 2, 1828. Exrs: Joseph Davis Esq, Dr. Geo. W. Pressly of S. C. Wit: Thos. Sanford, Norman L. Chester, Wiley Harben. "Give unto Pleasant Lowe of Augusta two thirds of the property which I declare to be his of justice and right. I constitute Dr. Jno. L. Cooper of S. C. or who ever may apply for my effects at Gainesville, Ga. where I am now at & expect not to be removed to receive all my effects in the hands of Wiley Harben with whom I am staying. Rest to be divided between my brothers & sisters."

CALHOUN, REBECCA—BOX 15, PACK 323:
Will dated Nov. 27, 1828 in Abbeville Dist. Proved Dec. 24, 1828. Exr: Jas. Calhoun. Wit: Thos. Parker, Jas. Taggart, Catharine Tannehill. Chn: Rachel, Jas. Montgomery, Joseph, my helpless son, Leroy Calhoun. "My son Joseph I leave in the care of his cousin Joseph Calhoun Sr. but entreat him not to keep my son at Calhouns Mills during the sickly season. Inv. made Dec. 31, 1828 by Jas. Taggart, Patrick, Joseph Calhoun.

CRAWFORD, JAMES—BOX 16, PACK 324:
Est. admnr. Nov. 11, 1829 by Mary Crawford, wid., Andrew Giles, Jno. McCalla, A. Hunter bound to Moses Taggart Ord. Abbeville Dist. sum $40,000.00. Mar. 15, 1833 Paid A. Hunter admnr. of Wm. Crawford in part amount due by Jas. Crawford to the est. of Wm. Crawford $2334.69¼. Sale, Dec. 30, 31, 1829. Byrs: Jas. Arabella C., Wm. Crawford Sr. Jas. Moore, etc.

CRISWELL, JOSEPH—BOX 16, PACK 325:
Est. admnr. Dec. 3, 1832 by Dr. Samuel, George W. Pressly, Patrick Gibson bound to Moses Taggart Ord. Abbeville Dist. sum $5,000.00. Cit. pub.

at Long Cane Church. Inv. made Dec. 13, 1832 by John C. Covey, Samuel Young, Robert McCaslan. Sale, Dec. 14, 1832. Buyers: John, Thomas Criswell, Mathew Shanks, Jane Criswell, Caleb Cain, etc.

CAMERON, JOHN—BOX 16, PACK 326:
    Est. admnr. Jan. 13, 1832 by Jane Cameron, Jas. Sr., Jas. Lomax Jr. bound to Moses Taggart Ord. Abbeville Dist. sum $20,000.00. Cit. pub. at Rocky River Church. On Mar. 9, 1789 another cit. was pub. at public worship on Little Generstee when Alexr. Cameron applied for Letters of Admnr. of Jno. Cameron decd.

CALHOUN, WILLIAM—BOX 16, PACK 327:
    Est. admnr. Oct. 16, 1833 by Nathan Calhoun, Jabez W. H. Johnson, Jas. A. Ware bound to Moses Taggart Ord. Abbeville Dist. sum $40,000.00. Will dated July 12, 1833 in Abbeville Dist. Proved Oct. 16, 1833. Wit: J. W. H. Johnson, Robt. A. Cunningham, Sarah White. Chn: Nathan, Wm., Agness, Jno., Downs Calhoun, Sarah Fooshe, Milley McCrady.

CRAWFORD, JOHN—BOX 16, PACK 328:
    Est. admnr. Oct. 12, 1832 by Joel, Charles, Wm. Smith bound to Moses Taggart Ord. Abbeville Dist. sum $3,000.00. Cit. pub. at Providence Church. Heirs: Saml., Elizabeth, Martha, Robt. Crawford.

CALHOUN, SAMUEL—BOX 16, PACK 329:
    Est. admnr. Jan. 31, 1834 by Wm., Jno. E. Calhoun, Joseph C. Matthews bound to Moses Taggart Ord. Abbeville Dist. sum $10,000.00. Cit. pub. at Hopewell Church. Byrs: Miss Martha, Wm., J. E. Calhoun.

COBB, THOMAS—BOX 16, PACK 330:
    Est. admnr. Dec. 3, 1828 by Charles, Lewis B. Cobb, Stephen Watson bound to Moses Taggart Ord. Abbeville Dist. sum $20,000.00. Sale, Dec. 18, 1828. Byrs: Sarah, Charles, Thos. A. Cobb, etc.

COBB, THOMAS SR.—BOX 16, PACK 331:
    Est. admnr. Jan. 11, 1828 by Jas., Thos. Cobb Jr. Donald Douglass, Thos. Osburn bound to Moses Taggart Ord. Abbeville Dist. sum $1,000.00. Mar. 10, 1828 Paid to Thos. Cobbs Sr. est. in Virginia. Byrs at sale. Edmund, Elijah, Jas. Cobb, etc.

COFER, THOMAS LAWSON—BOX 16, PACK 332:
    Est. admnr. June 10, 1815 by Elizabeth, Jno. H. Cofer, Jno. Clark bound to Taliaferro Livingston Ord. Abbeville Dist. sum $2,000.00.

CROZIER, SUSANNAH—BOX 16, PACK 333:
    Est. admnr. Sept. 4, 1826 by Jno. S., Dr. Saml. Pressly, Jno. Hearst Jr. bound to Moses Taggart Ord. Abbeville Dist. sum $6,000.00. Expend: Paid Mary Crozier heir $10.00. Margaret Crozier heir $10.00. Michael Crozier for acct. $20.77½.

COFER, THOMAS—BOX 16, PACK 334:
Est. admnr. Oct. 10, 1822 by Thos. T. Hamilton, Elijah E. Turnbull, Francis Young bound to Moses Taggart Ord. Abbeville iDst. sum $2,000.00. Cit. pub. at Rocky River Church.

CALDWELL, JOHN—BOX 16, PACK 335:
Will dated April 15, 1812 in Abbeville Dist. Proved May 27, 1816. Exrs: Sons, Jas., Mathew Caldwell. Wit: Isaac Beckwith, Peter Robertson, Geo. W. Liddle. Wife, Elizabeth. Chn: Jno., Wm. H., Sally C. Caldwell, Ann Speer, Jean Jones. Expend: Mar. 6, 1840 Paid Jno. Speer for surveying land $5.00. Aug. 21, 1841 Paid Stephen Jones leg. $250.00. April 3, 1827 Paid Wm. W. and Sarah C. Bowman his wife $374.50.

CALDWELL, JOHN—BOX 16, PACK 336:
Est. admnr. July 8, 1818 by Peggy Caldwell, Thos. Brightman, Jesse Beazley, Jno. Sample bound to Taliaferro Livingston Ord. Abbeville Dist. sum $20,000.00. Cit. pub. at Siloam Church. Byrs. at sale. Alexr. Wm., Peggy Caldwell, etc.

CALDWELL, JOHN—BOX 16, PACK 337:
Expend: Jan. 1, 1819 Paid Elizabeth Caldwell $37.62½. Margaret Caldwell $24.00. Edmund Caldwell $50.00. Jas. Caldwell $50.00. Jno. Caldwell $54.50. Polly Caldwell $54.50. Jesse Caldwell for 1 hat $1.25. Jan. 1, Paid to the leg.'s of Andrew Wardlaw decd. $341.25. Nov. 13, To Jesse Beasley in full of his portion due from the est. of Andrew Wardlaw decd. $153.34. Feb. 23, 1829 Paid Alexr. Caldwell $380.12½. Feb. 19, 1820 Paid Wm. Caldwell $380.12½. Jan. 1, 1820 Paid Drury Wilson $461.793/4. Paid to Edmund Beasley gdn. $350.00.

CHILES, BEAUFORD—BOX 16, PACK 338:
Est. admnr. Jan. 26, 1826 by Robt. Turner, Jas. Pulliam, Thos. B. Byrd bound to Moses Taggart Ord. Abbeville Dist. sum $4,000.00. Sale, Feb. 13, 1826. Byrs: Lucinda, Mrs. Judith Chiles, etc.

CARITHERS, WILLIAM—BOX 16, PACK 339:
Est. admnr. Nov. 5, 1826 by Mary, Robt. Carithers, Jas. Hunt, Jonathan Johnston bound to Moses Taggart Ord. Abbeville Dist. sum $6,000.00. Cit. pub. at Rocky River Church.

CALVERT, JACKSON W.—BOX 16, PACK 340:
Est. admnr. April 26, 1825 by Charles Neely, Jesse Beazley, G. W. Hodges bound to Moses Taggart Ord. Abbeville Dist. sum $12,000.00. Sale, Dec. 8, 1825. Byrs: Permelia, H. H. Calvert, etc.

COLEMAN, PETER H.—BOX 16, PACK 341:
Will dated Jan. 4, 1817 in Abbeville Dist. Proved May 27, 1817. Exrs: Wife, Jas., Zachariah Pulliam. Wit: Thos. J. Anderson, Jno. Logan Jr. Thos. Gaines. Wife and chn. ment. no names given. Inv. made May 26, 1817 by Jno. R. Long, Joseph Meriwether, Dudley Richardson.

CHILES, BENJAMIN—BOX 16, PACK 342:
Will dated Aug. 2, 1822 in Abbeville Dist. Proved Aug. 16, 1822. Exr:
Wm. P. Sullivan. Wit: Lewis Chiles, Wm. Carnal, Jno. McGehee. s. ls. Jas.
Dozier, Wm. P. Sullivan. Est. admnr. also July 7, 1823 by Jas. Dozier, Jno.
Partlow, Richard Culpepper bound to Moses Taggart Ord. sum $10,000.00. Cit.
pub. at Mount Moriah Church.

COBB, LITTLEBURY—BOX 17, PACK 343:
Est. admnr. Nov. 5, 1827 by Thos. Cobb, Thos. J. Spraggin, Agrippa
Cooper bound to Moses Taggart Ord. Abbeville Dist. sum $2,000.00. Inv. made
Nov. 23, 1827 by Stephen Watson, Robt., Jas. Buchanan. Byrs: Thos. Cobb, etc.

CALHOUN, WILLIAM SR.—BOX 17, PACK 344:
Will dated Dec. 5, 1821 in Abbeville Dist. Proved Aug. 6, 1827. Exrs:
Wife, Rebecca. Son, Ezekiel Noble Calhoun. Wit: Joseph Hutton, Joseph
Houston, Alexr. Calhoun. Chn: Rachel, Rebecca Catharine, Mary Elizabeth,
Leroy, Joseph, Ezekiel Noble, Wm., Jas. Calhoun.

COCHRAN, JAMES—BOX 17, PACK 345:
Will dated Oct. 1, 1822 in Abbeville Dist. Proved Oct. 21, 1822. Exrs:
Son, Reuben, Thos. M. Downey. Wit: Jas. Devlin Jr., Wm. Hamilton. Andrew
Crawford. Wife ment. no name given. Chn: Martha, Nancy, Sarah, Jas., Reuben
Cochran. Expend: Mar. 7, 1825 Recd. of Margaret Cochran $26.02½. Paid
Elizabeth Cooper $56.34. Jan. 2, 1826 Paid Jas. H. Cooper his share of P. M.
Cooper's legacy $8.50. Paid Silas Cooper $8.50. Paid Jas. Wilson his legacy $8.04.

CUMMINS, ROBERT—BOX 17, PACK 346:
Will dated Dec. 7, 1818 in Abbeville Dist. Proved Feb. 10, 1824. Exrs:
Hugh Morrah Esq., Saml. Watt. Wit: Andrew Hamilton, Jno. Finley. Wife, Mary
M. Gr chn: Alexr. Martin Cummins, Salley Williams Cummins, Jenny Robison
Cummins, Polly Ann Eliza Cummins. Sett. made Jan. 9, 1838. Isaac Holsonback
married Polly Cummins. Jenny Sally Cummins decd.

CHAMBERS, BENJAMIN—BOX 17, PACK 347:
Will dated Nov. 28, 1826 in Abbeville Dist. Proved June 18, 1827. Exr:
Thos. Ruffin of Hillsborough, N. C. Wit: Dr. A. B. Arnold, Geo. A., Jno. H.
Miller. Dtr. Arabella Crawford. Gr. dtr. Mary Crawford. Est. admnr. July 2,
1827 by Alexr. B. Arnold, Jno. Cochran, Geo. Miller to Moses Taggart Ord.
Abbeville Dist. sum $5,000.00.

CLARY, VACHEL—BOX 17, PACK 348:
Est. admnr. Dec. 1, 1821 by Thos. Wooldridge, Edward Tilman, Alexr.
B. Arnold bound to Moses Taggart Ord. Abbeville Dist. sum $10,000.00. Est.
admnr. again Jan. 9, 1815 by Mrs. Sarah Clary, Thos., Robt Wooldridge, Benjamin Murray, to Taliaferro Livingston Ord. Abbeville Dist. sum $10,000.00.

CLARKE, DR. BENJAMIN & REV. THOS.—BOX 17, PACK 349:
Will of Benjamin Clark dated May 24, 1796 in 96 Dist. Rec. Nov. 8,
1796. Exrs: Jas., Mary Cochran. Wit: David, Jane, Agness Cochran Jr. Chn:

Elizabeth, Jean N. Brother, Ebenezer. m. l. Agness Cochran. "Bequeath my wearing apparel to Jno., Jas., David Cochran." Est. of Rev. Thos. Clark admnr. Mar. 26, 1792 by Benjamin Clark, Fleming Bates, Jno. Hearst bound to Judges of Abbeville Co. sum 1,000 lbs.

CUNNINGHAM, JOHN R.—BOX 17, PACK 350:
Est. admnr. Feb. 13, 1818 by Thos. Cunningham, Francis Young Jr. Joseph B. Gibert bound to Taliaferro Livingston Ord. Abbeville Dist. sum $2,000.00. Cit. pub. at Rocky River Church.

CHEATHAM, WILLIAM—BOX 17, PACK 351:
Est. admnr. April 12, 1816 by Richard Cheatham, Wm. White bound to Taliaferro Livingston Ord. Abbeville Dist. sum $10,000.00. Inv. made May 4, 1816 by J. McCracken, Jno., Robt. Cheatham. Sale made in Cambridge. Byrs: Richard Cheatham, Wm. Swift, Jno. Marsh, Jno. McKellar, Jno. McBryde, Jesse Paine.

CUMMINS, JESSE—BOX 17, PACK 352:
Est. admnr. Jan. 12, 1807 by Nancy Cummins, David Henderson, Timothy Chandler bound to Andrew Hamilton Ord. Abbeville Dist. sum $2,000.00. One paper written, the est. of Jesse Cummins to Nancy Cummins alias Youngblood and Jacob Youngblood admnrs. Sale, Feb. 16, 1807. Byrs: Nancy, Peggy Cummins, Jno. Youngblood, Jno. Woods, etc.

COVEY, SAMUEL—BOX 17, PACK 353:
Will dated Nov. 23, 1789 in 96 Dist. Rec. Mar. 28, 1797. Exrs: Mary Covey, Wm. McBride, Moses Thompson. Wit: Jas. Young, Rowley McMullan, Jas. Cox. Wife ment. name not given. Dtr. Sarah Covey. Inv. made May 9, 1797 by Jno. Miller, Andrew McCormick, Abraham Russell.

COWAN, COL. ISAAC—BOX 17, PACK 354:
Will dated Dec. 22, 1831 in Abbeville Dist. Proved Jan. 2, 1832. Exrs: Sons, Jas., Jno. Cowan. Wit: Jno., Jas. Lindsay, Jas. Martin. Wife, Jane. Chn: Jno., Jas. Cowan, Elizabeth Lions, Polly Evans, Jane Ellis, Anny Hawthorn. Gr. chn: Isaac C., Elizabeth D. Richey, Jane F. Hawthorn. Sale, Jan. 24, 1832. Byrs: S. R. Evans, Robt. Richey, Capt. Cowan, Robt. Ellis, Abram Haddon, Andrew C. Hawthorn, Jas. C. Ellis, etc.

CRISSWELL, GEORGE—BOX 17, PACK 355:
Will dated May 7, 1823 in Abbeville Dist. Proved June 7, 1830. Exrs: Dr. Saml. Marshall, Leroy Watson. Wit: Geo. Marshall, Joseph, Wm. Eakins. Wife. Sarah. Chn: Jas., Wm., Jno. Creswell, Rebecca wife of Drury Glover, Mary Ann wife of Jno. Grey, Jenny Grey.

COWAN, WILLIAM—BOX 17, PACK 356:
Est. admnr. Aug. 17, 1810 by Margaret, wid. Isaac Cowan, Jno. Seawright, Dist. sum $5,000.00. Paid Anne Cowan for lent money $120.00. Wm. Blain, Andrew Seawright bound to Jno. Hamilton Esq. Ord. Abbeville

CHEATHAM, JOHN L.—BOX 17, PACK 357:
    Will dated Feb. 29, 1828 in Abbeville Dist. Proved Jan. 14, 1830. Exrs: Isaac Bunting, Robt. Cunningham. Wit: Jas. T. Livingston, Jas. Sills, Jno. Hefferman. Wife, Patsey. Sons, Jno., Robt. Cheatham. Other chn. ment. names not given. s. l. Richard Cheatham. Est. also admnr. Jan. 29, 1830 by Jno., Charles B. Fooshe, Isaac Bunting bound to Moses Taggart Ord. Abbeville Dist. sum $20,000.00. Cit. pub. at Rocky Creek Church. Martha Cheatham relinquished her right of admnr. to Jno. Fooshe Jan. 28, 1830.

CALHOUN, COL. JOSEPH—BOX 17, PACK 358:
    Will dated Mar. 17, 1817 in Abbeville Dist. Proved May 12, 1817. Exrs. Wife, Patsey, Son, Joseph Calhoun, Dr. Moses Waddel. Wit: Wm., E. Noble, Stephen Lee. Chn: Joseph, Wm., Saml., Jno. Ewing, Ann Eliza, Martha, Mary Jane Calhoun. "Give to my son Joseph whatever part of tract of land conveyed to Nancy Perrin."

COLEMAN, JAMES—BOX 17, PACK 359:
    Est. admnr. Dec. 21, 1829 by Albert Waller, Larkin, Ira Griffin, Westly Brooks bound to Moses Taggart Ord. Abbeville Dust. sum $20,000.00. Expend: July 5, 1830 Paid P. Noble for making sett. with Jno. Waller a ward of Jas. Coleman. Aug. 10, Paid Abraham P. Pool in right of himself and wife in right of minor chn. of Jas. Coleman. Mar. 2, 1832 Madison J. Coleman leg. $283.70. Jan. 3, 1833 Nancy Coleman wid. $457.36. Jan. 17 Jno. White gdn. for 2 minors $415.83.

CRAWFORD, ANDREW—BOX 17, PACK 360:
    Est. admnr. Dec. 22, 1826 by Alexr., Jno. B., Wm. Foster, Enos Crawford, Nathaniel Weed to Moses Tagart Ord. Abbeville Dist. sum $10,000.00. (On back of bond some one had written that he was the son of Robt. Crawford pioneer from Londonderry, Ireland 1771 and married Elizabeth Dole). Cit. pub. at Hopewell Church. Ibby, Andrew Crawford minor chn. May 28, 1829 Paid A. R. Foster leg. $17.00.

CHEATHAM, FRANCES—BOX 17, PACK 361:
    Est. admnr. April 22, 1815 by Peter Cheatham, Jno. Fooshe, Thos. Hill bound to Taliaferro Livingston Ord. Abbeville Dist. sum $2,000.00. Expend: Jan. 6, 1816 Paid Abraham Chaney leg. $35.00. Mar. 18, Nathan Chaney leg. $27.50. May 3, 1815 Recd. of Charles Fooshe Exr. of est. of Robt. Cheatham decd. $232.27.

CLEM, JOHN—BOX 17, PACK 362:
    Est. admnr. Nov. 6, 1824 by Anas Clem, Rhoda Eves, Jas. Yeldell bound to Andrew Hamilton Ord. Abbeville Dist. sum $3,000.00. Jan. 7, 1806 Paid Mary Clem on acct. $8.50.

CLAY, JOHN—BOX 17, PACK 363:
    Will dated Sept. 16, 1828 in Abbeville Dist. Proved Sept. 29, 1828. Exrs: Jas. Morrow, O. Houston. Wit: Jno. Crawford, Mary Dale, O. Houston. Wife, Judy. Recpts. 1829 Note to Simeon Clay $67.95. To Nancy Clay $9.32. Edmund Clay $100.00.

COTHRAN, SAMUEL—BOX 17, PACK 364:
Will dated Sept. 25, 1826 in Abbeville Dist. Proved Dec. 13, 1826. Exrs: Sons, Jno., Wade S. Cothran, Wm. Harris. Wit: Jno. P. Barnett, Lewis L. Simmons, Wm. Hammond. Wife, Polley. Chn: Jno., Wade S., Dolly Ann Cothran, Charlotte Stephens. Gr. son, Franklin Stephens. "All the chn. recd. a part of a tract of land in Alabama." "Land to Dempsey Cothran during his life the Lively tract."

CORBY, ADKIN—BOX 17, PACK 365:
Est. admnr. Dec. 14, 1819 by Charlotte Corby, Geo. Palmer, Jas. Findley bound to Moses Taggart Ord. Abbeville Dist. sum $3,000.00. Chn: Woody, Nancy Corby. (Name written Adkin and Adran Corby.) Sale, Jan. 21, 1820. Byrs: Charlotte, Nancy, Catlett Corby, etc.

CHILES, JOHN—BOX 18, PACK 366:
Will dated Nov. 16, 1813. Rec. Dec. 20, 1813. Exrs: Jas., Zachary Pulliam. Wit: Wm., Jonathan Swift, Thos. Hill Sr. Wife, Juda. Chn: Levinda, Blooford Chiles.

COFER, JOHN H.—BOX 18, PACK 367:
Est. admnr. Aug. 13, 1824 by Joshua Dubose, Andrew Defoor, Orville Tatom bound to Moses Taggart Ord. Abbeville Dist. sum $3,000.00. Sale, Sept. 7, 1824. Byrs: Mrs. Elizabeth Cofer, Isabella, Jane, Miss Elizabeth Cofer, etc.

CAMERON, ARCHIBALD W.—BOX 18, PACK 368:
Est. admnr. Nov. 2, 1824 by Jno. McLennan, Jno. C. McGehee, Thos. Livingston bound to Moses Taggart Ord. Abbeville Dist. sum $3,000.00. Inv. took place at the home of Nathan Lipscomb.

CARMICHAL, WILLIAM—BOX 18, PACK 369:
Will dated April 18, 1818. Filed May 23, 1820. Exrs: Joseph Young, Francis Hatton. Wit: Jno. A. Burn, Saml. Hollinghead. Wife, Mary. "Bal. of est. to be divided between Arthur, Abraham, Robt. Carmichal, Abraham Young."

CAMPBELL, JOHN—BOX 18, PACK 370:
Expend: Feb. 17, 1823. Paid Wm. Crawford for his wife's legacy $4,000. Feb. 22, 1823 Recd. from Edwards of N. C. on note $1729.69. July 5, 1824 Recd. of Jane McKee in payment for certain lands bequeathed to in the will of said decd. Mar. 13, 1823 Paid Thos. Cobb's legacy $50.00. May 4, 1824 Geo. Miller legacy $1,292.34. May 8, 1824 Thos. Simmon's legacy $3,960.88. Sept. 17, 1824 Isham Edward's legacy $6338.87. Patrick Johnson and Jno. Morow surviving Exrs. and Isham Edwards and Thos. Simmons in right of their wives. Jno. Campbell Martin in his own right and as sole heir of his mother Abrabella and his Father Thos. P. Martin. (Will not in pack.)

CONNER, JOHN ESQ.—BOX 18, PACK 371:
Est. admnr. Oct. 21, 1822 by Jno. Swilling, Francis Clinkscales, Henry Johnson bound to Moses Taggart Ord. Abbeville Dist. sum $10,000.00. One paper thought to be his will was: Ment. dtr. Molley Johnson. "Bequeath to

Nancy, Jno. Johnson, Dolley Conner." Bal. of est. to be divided between his 4 chn: Fanny Swilling, Lewis Conner, Molley Johnson, Betsy Nash.

COCHRAN, JOHN C.—BOX 18, PACK 372:
Est. admnr. Aug 7, 1826 by Jas. Cochran, Andrew Stewart, Thos. M. Downey, Jno. L. Cooper to Moses Taggart Ord. Abbeville Dist. sum $3,000.00. Inv. made Aug. 23, 1826 by Jas. Devlin, Thos. Downey, Jno. Gallavgher.

CHILES, JOHN—BOX 18, PACK 373:
Will dated Jan. 30, 1814 in Abbeville Dist. Proved Mar. 21, 1816. Exrs Wife, Sarah, Thompson Chiles, Archey Mayson. Wit: Jas. C. Dozier, Thos. Miller, Charles C. Mayson. Chn. ment. but names not given. Expend: Mar. 1820 Paid traveling expenses to and from Yorkville Academy for F. E. Chiles $8.00. Frances Emily, Jas. M., Jno. R. Chiles were minors.

CRYMES, JOHN—BOX 18, PACK 374:
Will dated Nov. 6, 1821 in Abbeville iDst. Proved Dec. 19, 1821. Exr: Saml. Marshall. Wit: Jno. Galldugher. (In another place written Galaher,) Thos. Cobb, Jno. Gibson. Sis. Nancy Hubbard and her dtr. Sarah S. C. Johnstone of Kentucky. Left $2,000.00 in hands of Wm. Berry of Lexington, Ky. for education of nephew Jno. Crymes Farmer. Niece, Nancy N. Farmer. Nephew, Leopard D. Farmer of Ky. Brother, Leonard Crymes of Lunenburg Co., Va.

CROMER, GEORGE—BOX 18, PACK 375:
Est. admnr. Oct. 14, 1822 by Henry, Jno. F. Gray, Jno. Marshall to Moses Taggart Ord. Abbeville Dist. sum $12,000.00. Byrs: Elizabeth, Elias Cromer, Jas., Jno. McCord, etc.

CAMPBELL, JAMES SR.—BOX 18, PACK 376:
Est. admnr. July 19, 1803 by Jas. Campbell, Lewis Mitchell, Alexr. Adams bound to Moses Taggart Ord. Abbeville Dist. sum $5,000.00. Inv. made Feb. 18, 1785 by Jas. Seawright, Saml. Reid, Adam Crain Jones as shewn to them by Margaret Campbell. Admnr. Expend: Aug. 28, 1804 Paid Elizabeth Campbell her legacy $1000.00. Paid Wm. Philip's legacy $25.00.

CHILES, JONATHAN—BOX 18, PACK 377:
Will dated Mar. 5, 1798 in 96 Dist. Rec. Feb. 26, 1800. Exrs: Wife, Judah, Jas. Chiles, Ellexander Deale, Nimrod Chiles. Wit: Wm. Pollard, Jno. Purvis, Jno. Richardson. Chn: Wm., Elihew, Jemema, Peremele, Jonathan, Ezekiel Chiles. Expend: Jan. 1, 1801 Paid David Gains for schooling $10.12. Feb. 28, 1807 Paid to a surveyor to run around a tract of land that is in dispute in Georgia to see if platt covered it $3.75.

COCHRAN, DAVID—BOX 18, PACK 378:
Will dated Aug. 31, 1825 in Abbeville iDst. Proved Oct. 5, 1825. Exr: Thos. M. Downey. Wit: Jas. Devlin, Jas. Cochran, Jno. Henderson. Chn: Alexr. Porter, Sarah Shaw, Hannah F. Cochran. "Desire that Thos. M. & Martha Downey should take care my youngest child Hannah as if she was their own until 18 yrs."

CALDWELL, HENRY—BOX 18, PACK 379:
Bond. missing. On petition of Julius Nichols Esq. and Lattice his wife for a cit. to issue against Charles Martin Esq. admnr. to shew cause why he should not settle up the est. Inv. made May 8, 1806 in Edgefield Dist. by Saml., Robt. Perrin, Richard Quarles. Sale, June 7, 1806. Byrs: Jane, Charles, Letty Caldwell, etc.

CHEATHAM, THOMAS—BOX 18, PACK 380:
Est. admnr. Mar. 4, 1816 ny Jency Cheatham, Moses Drummond, Ezekiel Nash bound to Taliaferro Livingston Ord. Abbeville Dist. sum $10,000.00. Expend: 1816 To Boarding Eliza, Benjamin Cheatham, chn. of Thos. Cheatham, $40.00 each. Byrs. at sale: Jeney, Robt., Jno. Cheatham, etc.

CONNOR, CHRISTOPHER—BOX 18, PACK 381:
Est. admnr. Sept. 12, 1799 by Jno. Connor, Jno. Pettigrew, Andrew McBride bound to Andrew Hamilton Ord. Abbeville Dist. sum $5,000.00. Cit. ment. Jno. Connor next of kin. Inv. made Sept. 20, 1799 by Wm. Boyd, Jas. Bonner, Thos. Morrow.

CALLAHAN, DELPHIA—BOX 18, PACK 382:
Est. admnr. Nov. 17, 1809 by Jehu Foster, Joseph Sanders, Saml. H. Owen bound to Andrew Hamilton Ord. Abbeville Dist. sum $10,000.00. Est. admnr. again Oct. 17, 1810 by Robt., Saml. Perrin to Jno. Hamilton Ord. Abbeville Dist. sum $5,000.00. Expend: Jan. 10, 1813 To boarding Thos. Callahan 3 yrs. $45.00. Boarding Wm. Callahan 2 yrs. $90.00. Sundries for Elizabeth Callahan $24.37½. Paid Jas. Noble leg. $90.00.

CHILES, NIMROD—BOX 18, PACK 383:
Will dated May 7, 1805 in Abbeville Dist. Rec. Oct. 22, 1807. Exrs: Wife, Elizabeth, Walter Chiles, Archey Mayson. Wit: Jno. C. Mayson, Robt. Cox, Jno. Chiles. Chn: Lewraney, Leucindy, Elizabeth, Ferreby Chiles. Expend: Oct. 20, 1815 Paid Jno. son of Jas. Chiles $4.37½. Thompson Chile's note $26.24

CHANEY, NATHAN—BOX 18, PACK 384:
Will dated Dec. 21, 1827 in Abbeville Dist. Proved Nov. 22, 1831. Exrs: Son, Robt., Jas. Gillam, Peter Cheatham. Wit: Wm. Eddins, Wm. Ward, Jas. T. Livingston. Wife ment. no name given. Chn: Simeon, Robt., Thos. Chaney. s. l. Daniel Hitt. Expend: Sept. 12, 1836 Acct. of the funeral expenses of Elizabeth Chaney $6.50.

CALDWELL, EZEKIEL—BOX 18, PACK 385:
Est. admnr. Dec. 29, 1820 by Alexr. Hunter, Thos. Shanklin Sr., Jno. Power Sr. bound to Moses Taggart Ord. Abbeville Dist. sum $2,000.00. Cit. pub. at Rocky River Church. Expend: Jan. 9, 1821 Paid Thos. Shanklin on acct. of Thos. Caldwell for boarding $49.31 ¾. Joseph Caldwell $50.06¼. Elizabeth Caldwell $35.90. Paid Gideon Johnson proven accts. vs. Ezekiel, Sarah Caldwell $2.50. Wid. Sarah Caldwell.

CHEVES, THOMAS—BOX 18, PACK 386:
Est. admnr. April 6, 1790 by Margaret, Alexr. Cheves, Philip Mathews bound to the Justices of Abbeville Co. Court sum 200 lbs. Inv. made June 10, 1790 by Reuben Weed, Andrew Jones, Josiah Crawmer.

CALHOUN, HUGH, SR.—BOX 18, PACK 387:
Will dated Aug 25, 1794 in Abbeville Dist. Rec. Mar. 25, 1799. Exrs: Son, Hugh, Jas. Noble, Fleming Bates. Wit: Wm. Dunlap, Alexr. Noble, Archibald McClene. Wife, Jennet. Chn: Hugh, Ezekiel Calhoun, Mary Morrow. Inv. made May 3, 1799 by Peter Brown, Ezekiel Calhoun Jr., Wm. White.

COWAN, ANDREW—BOX 18, PACK 388:
Will dated Nov. 6, 1786 in 96 Dist. Exrs: Ann, Jno. Cowan, Wm. Ross, Wm. Mayn to be gdns. over Ann Cowan. Wit: Rowley McMillan, Wm. Ross. Wife, Ann. Chn: Jno., Isaac, Wm., Mary, Elizabeth, Ann, Leaney Cowan. Inv. made May 1, 1789 by Wm. Ross, Wm. Mayne, Jas. Stevenson.

CAMPBELL, JESSE—BOX 18, PACK 389:
Est. admnr. Oct. 9, 1789 by Jas. Campbell, Joseph Trimble, Saml. Morr is bound to Justices of Abbeville Co. sum 1,000 lbs. Est. admnr. again April 30, 1816 by Jas. Campbell, Wm., Philemon Buford to Taliaferro Livingston Ord. Abbeville Dist. sum $1,000.00. Inv. made Dec. 19, 1789 by Saml. Scott, Richard Ross, Aaron Steel who met at the house of Jno. Harris and appraised the goods of Jesse Campbell.

CHAMBERLAIN, JOHN—BOX 19, PACK 390:
Est. admnr. Dec. 15, 1813 by Rebecca Chamberlain, Ezekiel Calhoun, Dr. Joseph B. Gibert bound to Taliaferro Livingston Ord. Abbeville Dist. sum $2,000.00. Sale, Jan. 4, 1814. Byrs: Rebecca, Thos. Chamberlain, Thos. Cobb, etc.

CALHOUN, ALICE—BOX 19, PACK 391:
Est. admnr. Feb. 10, 1826 by Wm., Geo. Sims, Jno. McGaw, Richard H. Kester bound to Moses Taggart Ord. Abbeville Dist. sum $2,000.00. Cit. pub. at Hopewell Church. Inv. made Feb. 24, 1826 by Jas. Calhoun, Richard H. Lester, Christopher Connor.

CAIN, RICHARD—BOX 19, PACK 392:
Will dated Dec. 14, 1793 in Abbeville Dist. Rec. Mar. 25, 1794. Exr: Wife, Mary. Wit: Thomas Ramsay, Daniel McKenzie. Chn: Sara, Jas. Cain, Elizabeth Bradley. Inv. made June 12, 1794 by Wm. Patterson, Wm. Bell, Jno. Fletcher.

CALHOUN, PATRICK—BOX 19, PACK 393:
Will dated May 19, 1784 in 96 Dist. Rec. Nov. 7, 1796. Exrs: Wife, Martha, Jno. Ewing Calhoun. Wit: Jno. Herndon, Jas. Cunningham, Sarah Cross. Chn: Catharine. (Other chn. ment. but names not given.) Inv. made Jan. 25, 1797 by Jas. Esq., Col. Joseph Calhoun, Major Alexr. Noble.

CALDWELL, JOHN—BOX 19, PACK 394:
Will dated Oct. 25, 1797 in Abbeville Dist. Rec. Mar. 28, 1798. Exrs: Charles, Jas. Caldwell, Jno. Ravling. Wit: Betsey Ravlin, Jenny Ravling, Jas. Wardlaw. Wife, Nancy. Brothers: Charles, Jas., Joseph, Henry Caldwell. "Bequeath silver watch to Jno. Wm. Caldwell, son of my brother Jas. Caldwell. Leave 500 lbs. to Jenny, Jas. Caldwell Reid chn. of Capt. Saml. Reid." Inv. made July 1798 by Capt. Charles, Jas. Caldwell, Jno. Ravlin.

CRAWFORD, JOSEPH—BOX 19, PACK 395:
Est. admnr. June 11, 1798 by Agness Crawford wid. Archibald Scott, Alexr. White, Jr., Jno. Caldwell of Savannah River bound to the Judges Abbeville Co. sum $10,000.00. Inv. made by Jno. Caldwell, Robt. Davis, Jas. Steel.

CHILES, JAMES—BOX 19, PACK 396:
Will dated Dec. 5, 1803 in Abbeville Dist. Rec. Jan. 9, 1804. Exrs: Wife, Polly, Jno. Ball, Jas. Gowdy. Wit: Jno. Pulliam, Richard Pollard, Salley Bell. Chn: Patsey, Jno., Jas., Larkin, Lewis, Fanney Chiles.

CAMPBELL, MARGERY—BOX 19, PACK 397:
Will dated Nov. 23, 1801 in Abbeville Dist. Proved Dec. 17, 1801. Exrs: Josiah Patterson Sr., Abraham Little. Wit: Jno., Saml. Tullock. Brother, Dinnes Foy. "Bequeath to Margery Conn dtr. of Geo. Conn $18.00. Unto Josiah Patterson Sr. $75.00. Unto Abraham Little husband of my niece Hannah $100.00. Left property to Margery, Jno., Abraham chn. of Abraham Little." Expend: May 6, 1815 Paid Archibald McFerron his wife's legacy $764.25. Jan. 12, 1803 Margaret Carson recd. $29.00 in full demands against said est. (Name Tullock appeared as Tulloch in one place.)

CHAPMAN, JOHN—BOX 19, PACK 398:
Est. admnr. Jan. 9, 1804 by Nathan, Benjamin Chapman, Charles Fooshe, Joseph Hill, Jno. Ball bound to Andrew Hamilton Ord. Abbeville Dist. sum $10,000..00 Expend: May 30, 1812 Paid Randall Chapman's legacy $644.86. Dec. 8, 1809 Thos. Chapman $15.00. Nov. 16, 1808 L. B. Bostick $644.86. Cit. ment. that Nathan, Benjamin Chapman next of kin.

CHANDLER, JESSE—BOX 19, PACK 399:
Will dated June 11, 1804 in Abbeville Dist. Rec. Nov. 3, 1804. Exrs: Son, Timothy, David Henderson. Wit: Wm., Jas. Henderson. Wife, Joyse Allen Chandler. Chn. and gr. chn. ment. but no names given. Inv. made by Gabriel Long, Michael Henderson, Jas. Green.

CALDWELL, JOHN ESQ.—BOX 19, PACK 400:
Est. admnr. Jan. 21, 1783 at Pages Creek by Wm., Jas. Caldwell, Richard Griffin, Bartlett Saterwhite bound to Jno. Ewing Calhoun Ord. Abbeville Dist. sum 14,000 lbs. Inv. made May 24, 1783 by Sims Brown, Wm. Houseal, David Glyn.

CALHOUN, EZEKIEL—BOX 19, PACK 401:
Est. admnr. Feb. 14, 1817 by Frances Calhoun, Andrew, Alexr. Hamilton

bound to Taliaferro Livingston Ord. Abbeville Dist. sum 10,000 lbs. Inv. made Feb. 27, 1817 by Patrick, Wm. Calhoun, Joseph Houston.

COLEMAN, PHILIP—BOX 19, PACK 402:
Est. admnr. Aug. 2, 1785 by Jno. Haile, Adam Potter, Wm. Coleman bound to Jno. Thomas Jr. Ord. 96 Dist. sum 2,000 lbs. On Aug. 4, 1785 1 negro boy Sam was appraised in Union Court, S. C. by Adam Potter, Samuel Littlejohn, Lawrence Esterwood.

CALHOUN, JAMES—BOX 19, PACK 403:
Inv. made Aug. 1, 1794 by Jno. Calhoun, Geo. Heard, Michael Blain. Inv. made again Nov. 13, 1804 by Saml. Foster, Andrew English Jr., Benjamin Hill. Sale, Nov. 23, 1804. Byrs: Wm., Peggy, Jno. Calhoun, Wm. Cameron.

CALDWELL, JOHN SR.—BOX 19, PACK 404:
Will dated June 21, 1795 in Abbeville Dist. Rec. Nov. 10, 1795. Exrs: Jno. Caldwell Jr. Joseph Black. Wit: Saml. Linton, Mathew Wilson, Wm. Caldwell. Wife, Elizabeth. Chn: Jane, Andrew, Wm., David, Jas. Caldwell, Mary Black, Ann Kolb, Isabella Pickens.

CAIN, JONATHAN—BOX 19, PACK 405:
Byrs: Jno., Barbary, Abner, Harold Cain, Jno. Townsend, Josiah Duckett, Mahlon Pearson. (No date. No other papers.)

COZBY, JOHN—BOX 19, PACK 406:
Est. admnr. Aug. 10, 1793 by Saml. Sr., Jas. Jr., Saml. Foster Jr., Adam Hill bound to Judges of Abbeville Co. sum 500 lbs. Inv. made Aug. 26, 1793 by Jas. Devlin, Enos Crawford, Thos. Jordon. Byrs: Elizabeth Cozby. Cit. pub. at Cedar Springs Church ment. Saml. Foster Sr. as next of kin.

CRAFTON, BENNETT—BOX 19, PACK 407:
Will dated June 13, 1774. Proved Mar. 16, 1786. Exr: Jno. Pomfrett. Wit: Robt. King, Martha Humphrey. Was of the County of King William. (No state given.) Brother, Saml. Crafton. Inv. made July 22, 1786 in Edgefield Dist. by Joseph, Jno. Covington, Isaac Evans. (Richard Crafton was a heir.)

CRAWFORD, GEO. AND PATRICK—BOX 19, PACK 408:
Est. of Patrick Crawford admnr. Aug. 20, 1785 by Mary Crawford, Jno. Caldwell, Andrew Cowan bound to Jno. Thomas Jr. Ord. 96 Dist. sum 2,000 lbs. Est. Geo. Crawford admnr. June 11, 1785 by Sarah Crawford, Richard Nalley, Abenego Green bound to Jno. Thomas Jr. Ord. 96 Dist. sum 2,000 lbs. Inv. of Patrick made by Jno. Caldwell, Thos. Pedin. Inv. of George made June 25, 1785 by Joseph Wofford, Jno. Butler, David Grims, Thos. Young.

COLLINS, JOHN—BOX 19, PACK 409:
Est. admnr. Mar. 21, 1801 by Andrew Collins, Capt. Jno. Hamilton, Campbell Kennedy bound to Andrew Hamilton Ord. Abbeville Dist. sum $1,000.00. Cit. ment. Andrew Collins next of kin. Inv. made May 18, 1801 by Jno. Hamilton, Jeremiah S. Terry, Patrick Cain. Inv. of Peter Collins Jr. made May 13, 1786 by Francis Carlile, Jas. Baskin, Wm. McKinley.

COOK, DUDLEY—BOX 19, PACK 410:
Est. admnr. Aug. 4, 1803 by Thos., Joshua Cook, Robt. Vernon bound
to Andrew Hamilton Ord. Abbeville Dist. sum $5,000.00. Sale, Sept. 2, 1803.
Byrs: Joshua, Thos., Nancy Cook, etc.

CRAWFORD, ELIZABETH—BOX 19, PACK 411:
Will dated May 11, 1807 in Abbeville Dist. Rec. Nov. 2, 1807. Exrs:
Josiah Patterson, Thos. Morrow. Wit: Jno. Moore, Geo. W. Breazeal, Richard
Terry. Gr. chn: James C., Jno., Ebenezer, Rhoda C. Crawford. Niece, Catharine
Miller. Nephew, Robt. Miller. "Bequeath to Elizabeth C., child of Catharine
Miller." Sis. Agness. Inv. made Nov. 6, 1807 by Jno. Moore, Wm. Clark, Jas.
McCarter.

COOK, NATHANIEL—BOX 19, PACK 412:
Est. admnr. 1785 by Philip Anderson, in 96 Dist. Inv. made Jan. 7, 1785
by David Watson, Wm. Rodgers, David Truit. (No more papers.)

CALLIS, JAMES—BOX 19, PACK 413:
Will dated Sept. 3, 1814 in Abbeville Dist. Rec. Oct. 19, 1814. Exr:
Thos. Chiles. Wit: Elizabeth Jackson, Susannah Roe, Thos. Chiles. Wife ment.
no name given. Chn: Dudly, Jno., Wm., Polly Lucindy Callis. "Wife now
pregnant with child." Inv. made Oct. 20, 1814 by Moody Burt, Wm. Jackson,
Adino Griffin.

CARLILE, FRANCIS ESQ.—BOX 19, PACK 414:
Will dated Nov. 13, 1785 in 96 Dist. Proved Nov. 29, 1785. No Exr:
Wit: Nathaniel Howell, Casper Nail Jr., Goodrich Howell. "Bequeath to
Susannah Shinholser and Jno. Stare's son 100 lbs. Elizabeth Stare sis. of Jno., John
Sturzenegger Jr., Wm. Shinholser, Geo. Bender." Inv. made Feb. 1, 1815 by
Jeremiah S. Terry, Ezekiel Calhoun, Thos. Cunningham.

CALDWELL, JAMES SR.—BOX 19, PACK 415:
Will dated April 15, 1804 in Abbeville Dist. Rec. May 15, 1805. Exrs:
Wm., Jas. Caldwell. Wit: Jno. Cameron, Jno. Harris, Martha Boles. "Bequeath
to Jno., David, Jas., Thos. Caldwell, Rebecca Pickens, Elizabeth Wilson, Mary
Davis. Rest of property to be divided among Jas. Lesley, Jas. son of Jno. Cald-
well, Jas. son of David Caldwell, Jas. Caldwell Pickens, Jas. Wilson, Jas. Davis,
Elizabeth Harris Caldwell, Eliza Harris Caldwell, Elizabeth Harris Kerr."

CAMPBELL, ELIZABETH—BOX 20, PACK 416:
Will dated Jan. 23, 1807 in Abbeville Dist. Rec. Feb. 7, 1807. Exrs:
Jas. Campbell, Wm. Phillips. Wit: Sam Moseley, Reuben Butler. Chn: Jno.
Edmiston, Jno., Jas., Lydda Campbell. "Give 1 calico habit to Lucy Edmiston."
Inv. made Feb. 12, 1807 by Jas. Loveless, Christopher Watson, Jas. Smith.

CUNNINGHAM, DAVID—BOX 20, PACK 417:
Will dated Oct. 30, 1793. Rec. Mar. 25, 1794. Exrs: Wife, Jane. Brother,
Patrick and his son Jno. Cunningham. Wit: Jno., Walter Chiles, D. Lilly. Chn:
David, Robt., Polly, Jno., Betsey, Pamale, Margaret Cunningham.

CRANE, CHARLES—BOX 20, PACK 418:
Est. admnr. Nov. 28, 1786 by Judah Crane, Thos. Brandon bound to Jno. Thomas Jr. Ord. 96 Dist. sum 200 lbs. Inv. made by Stephen Phillips, Wm. Simmons, Jas. Reynolds. Byrs: Judith, Wm., Saml. Crane.

CROSSAN, THOMAS—BOX 20, PACK 419:
Est. admnr. Jan. 1, 1786 by Alexr. Crossan, Jeremiah Williams, Jno. Riley bound to Jno. Thomas Jr. Ord. 96 Dist. sum 200 lbs. Inv. made Jan. 13, 1787 by Joseph Caldwell, Wm. Dawkins, Jno. Riley.

CARGILE, CORNELIUS—BOX 20, PACK 420:
Est. admnr. April 26, 1784 by Sarah Cargill, Wm. Harris, Saml. Goode bound to Jno. Thomas Jr. Ord. 96 Dist. sum 2,000 lbs. Inv. made June 23, 1784 by Andrew Rogers, Thos. Dendy, Tandy Walker.

COWDRY, JOHN—BOX 20, PACK 421:
Est. admnr. Jan. 24, 1805 by Nancy Cowdry, Jas., Jonathan Moore, Jas. Goody, Richard Eskridge, Thos. Livingston bound to Andrew Hamilton Ord. Abbeville Dist. sum $15,000. Cit. pub. at Fellowship Church. Inv. of Jno. Cowdry late merchant of Cambridge made Feb. 1805 by Jas. McCracken, Thompson Chiles, Jno. Wilson.

COX, WILLIAM—BOX 20, PACK 422:
Admnr. Beverly Cox. Lived in 96 Dist. Inv. made Aug 2, 1783 by Wm. Mitchuson, Zadock Tard, Andrew Cunningham. Inv. made again Aug. 21, 1809 by Joel Eddins, Jno. Shotwell, Wm. Smith.

CAUDEL, RICHARD—BOX 20, PACK 423:
Est. admnr. Jan. 6, 1789 by Elijah and his wife Barsheba Baker, Uel Hill, Lazarus Benton bound to the Judges Abbeville Co. sum 1,000 lbs. Inv. made at Cambridge Jan. 16, 1789 by Gabriel Smithers, Jas. Wilson, Wm. Huggins.

COOK, HENRY—BOX 20, PACK 424:
Est. admnr. Sept. 15, 1801 by Susannah Cooke, Frederick Knob, Philip Stiefel bound to Andrew Hamilton Ord. Abbeville Dist. sum $5,000.00. Inv. made Oct. 13, 1801 by Wm. Wade, Geo. Hearst, Frederick Knob. Sale, Nov. 9, 1801. Byrs: Susannah Cook, Polly Clark, etc.

CALDWELL, JOSEPH—BOX 20, PACK 425:
Est. admnr. Jan. 8, 1803 by Charles, Henry Caldwell, Wm. Hamilton, Jas. Kyle bound to Andrew Hamilton Ord. Abbeville Dist. sum $5,000.00. Inv. made Jan. 15, 1803 by Jehy Foster, Jno. Ravlin, Joseph Sanders.

CRAWFORD, GEORGE—BOX 20, PACK 426:
Est. admnr. Jan. 15, 1837 by Thos. Fergerson, Wm. Chastain, Peter Smith bound to Moses Taggart Ord. Abbeville Dist. sum $6,000.00. Expend: Nov. 30, 1845 Paid Vicey Banks for clothing $9.87. May 1, 1840 Paid F. Mitchell for schooling Wade Crawford. On Dec. 25, 1839 Vicey Crawford stated that it wasn't convenient for her to attend the sett. Martha a minor married Geo. Martin. Mary married Jas. Covang.

CROW, JOHN—BOX 20, PACK 427:
Est. admnr. Jan. 15, 1784 by Elizabeth, Wm., Isaac Crow, Joseph Barnett
bound to Jno. Thomas Jr. Ord. 96 Dist. sum 2,000 lbs. Inv. made Feb. 3, 1784
by Henry Hamilton, Jno. Stone, Ebenezer Morse.

CLARKE, MARY—BOX 20, PACK 428:
Will dated Nov. 8, 1802 in Abbeville Dist. Rec. 29, 1802. Exrs: Alexr.
Houston, Alexr. Clark Jr. Wit: Saml. Blair, Jno. Hemphill. Brother, Alexr. Sis.
Susannah Houston. "Will negro to Margaret Hemphill and my sadel to her dtr.
Nancy. Will negro to Jas. Bates. My colt to Jas. C. Hemphill."

CHILES, WILLIAM—BOX 20, PACK 429:
Will dated May 4, 1804 in Abbeville Dist. Rec. Oct. 8, 1804. Exrs: Sons,
Reuben, Thos., Jno., Wm. Chiles. Wit: Jas. Adamson, Robt. Jones, Jno. White.
Chn: Jno., Reuben, Wm., Elizabeth, Salley, Eunice, Thos. Chiles. Expend:
April 8, 1804 Paid Jas. Coleman's legacy $314.00. Paid Joel Lipscomb's legacy
$96.12½.

CARGO, SAMUEL—BOX 20, PACK 430:
Est. admnr. Sept. 12, 1791 by Jno. McConnel, Wm. Huggins, Jas. Wilson
bound to Judges Abbeville Co. sum 500 lbs. Inv. of Saml. Cargo late merchant
at Cambridge made Oct. 19, 1791 by Jas. Gouedy, Thos. Livingston, Elijah
Moore.

COODIE, ARTHUR—BOX 20, PACK 431:
Est. admnr. Mar. 24, 1783 by Edeth Coodie, Edward Vann, Drury Murfey.
Cit. ment. Edeth Coodie of Horns Creek, 96 Dist. next of kin. Inv. made April
21, 1783 by Littlejohn Pardue, Drury Murfey, Edward Vann. (Name also
written Coodey.)

CRAWFORD, ANDREW—BOX 20, PACK 432:
Est. admnr. June 1, 1818 by Mary B., Robt. F. Crawford, Edmund Cobb,
Elijah Foster bound to Taliaferro Livingston Ord. Abbeville Dist. sum $10,000.00.
Expend: Jan. 2, 1820 Paid Andrew Crawford $20.00. Jan. 22, 1820 Robt. Craw-
ford $45.00.

COOPER, DR. JAMES—BOX 20, PACK 433:
Will dated Mar. 9, 1807 in Abbeville Dist. Rec. April 6, 1807. Exrs:
Wife, Margaret, Jas. Cochran Sr. Wit: Jno. Weems, Jno. Frazer, Sarah Morrow.
Chn: Jno. Linn Cooper, Ebenezer, Arthur M., Martha, Mary, Elizabeth, Jas.
H., Silas Cooper.

COWAN, JOHN—BOX 20, PACK 434:
Will dated Feb. 9, 1789 in Abbeville Dist. Proved Sept. 12, 1792. Exrs:
Wife, Margaret. Sons, Jno. Archibald Cowan. Wit: Isaac, Mary Herbert, Isabel
Walton. Chn: Jno., Archy, Jas., Saml., Susan, Eleanor, Mary Cowan, Newel,
Elizabeth P. Walton. Inv. made Oct. 27, 1792 by Willis, Drury Breazeale, Uel
Hill.

COLLYER, BARNETT—BOX 20, PACK 435:
Est. admnr. Jan. 4, 1784 by Sarah, Moses Collyer, Wm. Plumer, Aaron Fincher bound to Jno. Thomas Jr. Ord. 96 Dist. sum 2,000 lbs. (Name written Collier and Collyer.) Sale, Feb. 5, 1784. Byrs: Sarah, Moses, Jno. Collyer, Saml. Jackson, Henry Long, Jno. Birdsong.

CARMICHAEL, JOSEPH—BOX 20, PACK 436:
Est. admnr. Nov. 30, 1785 by Eleanor, Joseph Carmichael, Timothy McKinney bound to Jno. Thomas Jr. Ord. 96 Dist. sum 1,000 lbs. Inv. made Dec. 24, 1785 by Thos. Hamilton, Jno. Beard, Joseph Limaster.

CONWAY, EDWARD BOX 20, PACK 437:
Est. admnr. Mar. 14, 1785 by Robt. Cunningham, Jno. Rodgers, Peter Hamilton bound to Jno. Thomas Jr. Ord. 96 Dist. sum 1,000 lbs. Inv. made June 1, 1785 by Andrew, Wm. Cunningham, Thos. Murphey. Byrs: Jas. Parks, Margaret Cunningham.

CRAWFORD, JAMES JR.—BOX 20, PACK 438:
Est. admnr. April 27, 1784 by Barbara Crawford, Benjamin Tutt, Michael Duvall bound to Jno. Thomas Jr. Ord. 96 Dist. sum 2,000 lbs. Heirs, Jas., Catharine Crawford. Inv. made June 25, 1784 by Saml. Foster, Thos. Weems, Wm. Alexander.

COLEMAN, CHRISTOPHER—BOX 20, PACK 439:
Admnr: Wm. White. Lived in 96 Dist. (Bond missing.) Inv. made Dec. 8, 1784 by Adam Potter, Thos. Draper, Charles Hames. Sale, Dec. 28, 1784. Byrs: Wm., Jno. White, Wm. Coleman Jr. Isaac Samson, Thos. Palmer, etc.

CONE, JAMES—BOX 20, PACK 440:
Est. admnr. Nov. 26, 1782 by Simeon Cushman, Daniel Shaw, Jesse Roundtree of New Windsor bound to Jno. Ewing Calhoun Ord. 96 Dist. sum of 14,000 lbs. Cit. ment. Simeon Cushman of Beech Island next of kin. Inv. made Jan. 6, 1783 by Jesse Roundtree, Capt. Nathaniel Bacon, Vachal Davis.

COBB, JOHN—BOX 20, PACK 441:
Est. admnr. Nov. 8, 1782 at White Hall by Judy Cobb, Wm., Jno. Calhoun both of Cornacre bound to Jno. Ewing Calhoun Ord. 96 Dist. sum 14,000 lbs. Judy Cobb of Saludy River next of kin. Cit. pub. at the Blockhouse. Inv. made Jan. 1, 1783 by Isaac Benjamin Mitchell, Geo. Heard.

COLLIER, CORNELIUS—BOX 20, PACK 442:
Est. admnr. July 7, 1790 by Elizabeth, wid., Edward Collier, Wm. Pettigrew bound to Judges Abbeville Co. sum 5,000 lbs. Cit. pub. at Long Cane Church. Inv. made Sept. 1790 by Wm. Stanfield, Uel Hill, Adam Wideman.

COCHRAN, ANDREW—BOX 20, PACK 443:
Will dated Dec. 9, 1795 in Abbeville Dist. Rec. Mar. 26, 1796. Exrs: Robt. Smith, Thos. McBride. Wit: Jno. Covey, Saml. Patterson, Andrew Taylor. Chn: Andrew, Jno., Wm. Hugh Cochran, Rachel Paterson, Jean Beatty, Jean

McCreary. "Leave unto Ellenor McCreary 6 lbs. Unto Mary Little 1 guinea. Allow my 3 sons to live with my 2 dtrs. two to go to Saml. Patterson, the other to Jno. Beaty." Gr. son, Saml. Glasgow. (Name written Cochran and Coughran.)

CHALMERS, MAJOR JAMES—BOX 20, PACK 444:
Est. admnr. Mar. 28, 1799 by Saml. Morris, Elizabeth Chalmers, Wm. Callahan, Thos. Weems Jr. bound to Andrew Hamilton Ord. Abbeville Dist. sum $5,000.00. Cit. ment. Stephen Chalmers next of kin. Inv. made April 8, 1799 by Jehu, Jas. Foster, Robt. Henderson.

CAIN, JONATHAN—BOX 20, PACK 445:
Est. admnr. Nov. 30, 1784 by Jno. Cain, Jno. Pearson Robt. Burns bound to Jno. Thomas Jr. Ord. 96 Dist. sum 2,000 lbs. Jno. Cain next of kin. Inv. made Dec. 6, 1784 by Abel Pearson, Jno. Clarke, David Smith.

CHANEY, JAMES—BOX 20, PACK 446:
Est. admnr. May 3, 1782 by Jno., Priscilla Chaney, Jas. Thomas, Jno. Gray bound to Jno. Ewing Calhoun Ord. 96 Dist. sum 2,000 lbs. Cit. ment. Jno. Chaney of Horns Creek next of kin. Inv. made July 2, 1782 by Jno. Gray, Jas. Thomas, Jno. Turner.

CARTER, ROBERT—BOX 20, PACK 447:
Est. admnr. Oct. 21, 1786 by Jno., Patty Sharp, Joseph Calhoun, Geo. Carswell bound to Jno. Thomas Jr. Ord. 96 Dist. sum 2,000 lbs. Jno. and his wife Patty Sharp next of kin. Inv. made Nov. 2, 1786 by Wm. Clark, Joseph Calhoun, Geo. Carswell, Robt. Patterson.

COLLINS, JOSEPH—BOX 20, PACK 448:
Inv. made July 2, 1783 by Adam Goudylock, Jno. Montgomery, Moses Meek. Joseph Collins lived on Thickety Creek, 96 Dist. (Bond or will missing.)

CLARK, WILLIAM—BOX 20, PACK 449:
Will dated Nov. 18, 1803 in Abbeville Dist. Rec. Sept. 2, 1809. Exrs: Brothers, Alexr., Robt. Clark. Wit: Thos. Finley, Robt. McClinton, Jno. Prince. Sis: Jane, Susanna Clark. "Leave my brother Alexr. Clark and Saml. Mackey my wearing apparel." Inv. made Oct. 17, 1809 by Wm. Scott, Jno. Guthrie, Peter Hemmenger.

CHEATHAM, ROBERT—BOX 20, PACK 450:
Will dated Oct. 12, 1812 in Abbeville Dist. Rec. Oct. 31, 1812. Exrs: Wife, Francy, Charles Fooshe, Joseph Hill. Wit: Robt., Catharine Pollard, Robt. Pollard Jr. Chn: Peter, Jno., Nancy Cheatham, Lurany Evans, Betsey, Mary Chaney. Expend: Jan. 1, 1816 Paid Abraham Chaney leg. $700.00, Mar. 31, 1815 Nathan Chaney leg. $550.00. Jan. 9, 1830 Dawson B. Sullivan and wife Nancy their share $321.62½.

CLARK, ALEXANDER—BOX 20, PACK 451:
Est. admnr. Mar. 13, 1804 by Jean, Wm., Robt. Clark, Abel Jackson bound to Andrew Hamilton Ord. Abbeville Dist. sum $10,000.00. Expend:

Nov. 13, 1810 To boarding Wm., Patrick Clark $18.00. Sally Clark $9.00. Byrs: David, Wm., Robt. Clark, etc.

CHASTAIN, RANE—BOX 20, PACK 452:
Will dated Jan. 27, 1786 in Edgefield Dist. Proved Dec. 6, 1786. Exrs: Leroy Hammond, Peter Chastain. Wit: Joseph Collier, Christian Burckhalter. Chn: Peter, Rane, Makinne, Sarah Chastain, Jude Winfree, Fanne Winfree. Gr. son, Jno. Chastain. "The slaves to return to son & dtrs. in Virginia." Inv. made April 24, 1787 by Charles, Bartley Martin, Jas. Lesure. (Name also written Raney.)

CALHOUN, CAPT. JOHN—BOX 20, PACK 453:
On May 29, 1782 Capt. Jno. Calhoun Jr. of Wilsons Creek, 96 Dist. applied for Letters of Admnr. Inv. made Oct. 25, 1782 by Jno. Wilson, Wm. Calhoun, Jno. Irwin, Victor Mathews. (No other papers.)

CHILES, GARLAND—BOX 20, PACK 454:
Est. admnr. Mar. 5, 1827 by Littleton Myrick, Isaac Bunting, Jno. Mc-Lennan bound to Moses Taggart Ord. Abbeville Dist. sum $2,000.00. Inv. made Mar. 6, 1827 by E. H. Calhoun, Jno. Williams, Jas. Coleman. Mrs. Chiles bought at sale.

CALDWELL, CURTIS—BOX 20, PACK 455:
Est. admnr. June 5, 1784 by Sarah Caldwell, Jno. Fondren, Jas. Wilkison bound to Jno. Thomas Jr. Ord. 96 Dist. sum 2,000 lbs. Inv. made by Daniel McClanen, Geo. Taylor, Jas. Wilkinson. Certifield by us in Virginia money.

CAIN, MICHAEL—BOX 21, PACK 456:
Est. admnr. Feb. 7, 1803 by Mary Cain, Jesse Kennedy, Robt. Black, Jas. Pringle bound to Andrew Hamilton Ord. Abbeville Dist. sum $5,000.00. Inv. made Feb. 21, 1803 by Capt. Robt., Wm. Black, Wm. Brownlee.

CARTER, JAMES—BOX 21, PACK 457:
Will dated Nov. 9, 1779 in 96 Dist. Exrs: Wife, no name given. Brothers, Thos., Robt. Carter. Wit: Thos., Sarah Carter, Benjamin Jonston. Wife and chn. ment. no names given. Will probated Aug. 2, 1782 by Thos. & Sarah Carter in N. C. Wid. Lettice McFarland. Inv. made Dec. 22, 1786 by Jno. Cowan, Wm., Alexr. Clark.

COLLIER, WILLIAM—BOX 21, PACK 458:
Est. admnr. Jan. 16, by Jas. Collier, Joshua Hill, Andrew Weed bound to Taliaferro Livingston Ord. Abbeville Dist. sum $10,000.00.00. Expend: Sept. 1, 1814 Paid Elizabeth C. Collier $95.62½. Wm. Herring a leg. in right of his wife. Beatrice Collier a minor. In same pack. was the admnr. bond of Willie Collier who died Nov. 24, 1920 intestate. Left as heirs his mother Sarah Miller, sisters and brothers.

COLEMAN, ROBERT—BOX 21, PACK 459:
Est. admnr. Aug. 15, 1783 by Thos. Draper, Jno. Haile bound to Jno.

Thomas Jr. Ord. 96 Dist. sum 2,000 lbs. Admnr. granted also to his wife, Lucy Draper. Inv. made Dec. 20, 1783 by Major Zachariah Bullock, Jno. Tollison, Adam Potter.

CAIN, WILLIAM—BOX 21, PACK 460:
Est. admnr. Mar. 20, 1817 by Mary Cain, Isaac Moragne, Jno. Chastain bound to Taliaferro Livingston Ord. Abbeville Dist. sum 5,000 lbs. Inv. made April 12, 1817 by Drury Breazeale, Jno. Moragne, Peter Smith, Joshua Hill.

COCHRAN, JOHN M.—BOX 21, PACK 461:
Est. admnr. Nov. 27, 1817 by Martha, Jas. Cochran, Jno. L., Jas. H. Cooper bound to Taliaferro Livingston Ord. Abbeville Dist. sum $3,000.00. Sale, Dec. 16, 1817. Byrs: Martha, Reuben, Jas. Cochran Esq. etc.

CALVERT, MAYSON—BOX 21, PACK 462:
Est. admnr. Mar. 16, 1807 by Jas. Lomax, Rev. Saml Watson, Merideth Bryan bound to Andrew Hamilton Ord. Abbeville Dist. sum $5,000.00. Sale, April 6, 1807. Byrs: Jno., Frances, Jesse Calvert, etc.

CAULEY, STUTELEY—BOX 21, PACK 463:
Est. admnr. July 29, 1808 by Elizabeth Cauley, wid., David McClaskey, Alexr. Hunter bound to Andrew Hamilton Ord. Abbeville Dist. sum $2,000.00. Sale, Aug. 13, 1808. Byrs: Charles Holland, Saml. Linton Esq., etc.

COWDRESS, GEORGE—BOX 21, PACK 464:
Est. admnr. Jan. 6, 1808 by Elizabeth Cowdress, Jno. Thomson, Saml. Saxon, Thos. Lee Jr. bound to Andrew Hamilton Ord. Abbeville Dist. sum $1500.00. (One part of bond name written Sarah Cowdress.) Cit. ment. that Elizabeth Cowdress and Jno. Thompson next of kin.

CHAMBERS, STEPHEN—BOX 21, PACK 465:
Est. admnr. April 15, 1809 by Jno., Joseph Sanders, Jno. Brannon bound to Andrew Hamilton Ord. Abbeville Dist. sum $5,000.00. Inv. made May 4, 1809 by Joseph Sanders, Jno. Brannon, Robt. Henderson.

CALHOUN, JOHN—BOX 21, PACK 466:
Admnr. Jno. L. Calhoun. Inv. made Feb. 24, 1826 by Jas. Calhoun, Richard H. Lester, Christopher Conner, Jno. Reid. (No other papers.)

COX, MARGARET—BOX 21, PACK 467:
Est. admnr. Feb. 11, 1822 by Jas., Robt. Young, Alexr. Adams bound to Moses Taggart Ord. Abbeville Dist. sum $3,000.00. Inv. made Mar. 11, 1822 by Thos. Edwards, Alexr. Sample, Robt. Young. Wid. of Wm. Cox.

CHILES, REUBEN—BOX 21, PACK 468:
Will dated Mar. 3, 1808 in Abbeville Dist. Rec. Sept. 2, 1808. Exrs: Wife, Fanney. Son, Thos. Brothers: Jno., Wm. Chiles. Wit: Joseph Hearst, Jno. Wallace, Tabitha Chiles. Chn: Reuben, Thos., Moriah Chiles. "Wife now pregnant with child." Inv. made Sept. 20, 1808 by Jno. Pressly, Philip Stiefle, Saml. Perrin.

CLARK, JOHN HUSTON—BOX 21, PACK 469:
Will dated Jan. 8, 1803 in Abbeville Dist. Rec. Jan. 17, 1803. Exrs:
Brothers, Robt., Wm. Clark. Wit: Thos. Crawford. Sisters, Jean, Susanna Clark.
Brothers, Wm. Robt., Alexr. Clark.

COIL, MARTHA—BOX 21, PACK 470:
Est. admnr. June 13, 1796 by Saml. Watt Esq., Ezekiel Evans Sr., Saml.
Houston bound to Judges Abbeville Co. sum $4,000.00. Cit. pub. at Upper Long
Cane Church. Sale, July 1, 1796. Byrs: Gedeon Coil, Robt. Boggs, Elizabeth
Beard, Margaret Miller, Sarah Hufman, Jean Alexander, Elizabeth McCollough,
etc.

CANE, MARY—BOX 21, PACK 471:
Will dated Oct. 1795 in Abbeville Dist. Rec. Mar. 27, 1798. Exrs: Son,
Jas. Cane, Jas. Lomax. Wit: Hugh Porter, Jenny Watters, Jane Lomax. Chn:
Jas., Sarah Cane, Elizabeth Bradley. Inv. made May 11, 1798 by Geo. Conner,
Wm. Hairston, Wm. Bell.

CALAHAN, WILLIAM—BOX 21, PACK 472:
Est. admnr. Feb. 4, 1804 by Jehu Foster, Wm. Hamilton, David Wardlaw
Esq. bound to Andrew Hamilton Ord. Abbeville Dist. sum $5,000.00. Sale,
Mar. 2, 1804. Byrs: Delphy Callahan, Robt. Henderson, Josiah Chambers,
Frederick Hart. etc.

CRAWFORD. THOMAS—BOX 21, PACK 473:
Est. admnr. April 6, 1807 by Rhoda Crawford, Jas. Craig, Jas. M. Petti-
grew bound to Andrew Hamilton Ord. Abbeville Dist. sum $5,000.00. Sale,
April 27, 1807. Byrs: Rhoda Crawford, Jas. Craig, Margaret Bates, Joseph
Hutton, Anne Pettigrew, Robt. Boyd.

CARSON, WILLIAM, SR.—BOX 21, PACK 474:
Will dated Oct. 16, 1801 in Abbeville Dist. Proved April 3, 1802. Exrs:
Sons, Robt., Wm. Carson. Wit: Thos. Lindsay, Jas. Paterson, Sarah Howard.
Wife, Margaret. Chn: Wm. Robt., Jean Carson, Martha Hearst, Margaret Patter-
son, Elizabeth McGouch, Mary Patterson. Gr. son, Wm. son to Robt. Carson.
"Bequeath to Sarah Rafferty." Inv. made Aug. 24, 1802 by Jno. Robinson, Wm.
McBride, Andrew Caughran.

COOK, ANNE—BOX 21, PACK 475:
Est. admnr. Feb. 22, 1803 by Jno., Robt. Pettigrew, Jno. Clark bound
to Andrew Hamilton Ord. Abbeville Dist. sum $2,000.00. Cit. pub. at Upper
Long Cane Church ment. Jno. Pettigrew next of kin. Inv. made Mar. 23, 1803
by Andrew Weed, Jno. Gray, Joseph Crammer.

CLARK, JACOB—BOX 21, PACK 476:
Est. admnr. Nov. 1, 1824 by Jno. Hearst, Luke Matthews, Alexr. Mc-
Queans bound to Moses Taggart Ord. Abbeville Dist. sum $500.00. Cit. pub.

at Upper Long Cane Church. Inv. made Nov. 20, 1824 by Ira Griffin, Jno. Gibson, Jno. Lipscomb.

CHEW, CAPT. JOHN DRURY—BOX 21, PACK 477:
Will dated Feb. 7, 1780 in 96 Dist. Proved May 20, 1783. Exrs: Margaret Cohune, Edward Mitcherson. Wit: Jno., Sarah, Lucrettia Cohune, Martha Parsons. Chn: Cassander, Saml. Chew. "Leave to Margaret Cohune while a single woman to care for the 2 chn. if marrys to Edward Mitcherson. Leave to Anne Johnsons eldest son Jno. to be learned at my expense." One paper stated that Mrs. Margaret McElheney was an Exr. and that will was in hands of Jas. McElheney.

CRAWFORD, WILLIAM—BOX 21, PACK 478:
Admnr. Geo. Reid. Lived in 96 Dist. Inv. made Mar. 1, 1785 by Jas. Caldwell, Jno. Luckie, Joseph Reid. (No other papers.)

CLARK, SAMUEL—BOX 21, PACK 479:
Will dated Oct. 19, 1803 in Abbeville Dist. Rec. 5, 1803. Exrs: Wife, Rosanna. Son, Saml. Clark. Wit: Geo. Tillman, Jno. Oakley, Jno. Salor. Chn: Jno., Leviey, Moses, Geo., Permeley, Aaron, Elizabeth Cassia, Peggy, Saml., Mary, Thos. Clark. Inv. made Jan. 5, 1804 by Jno. Saylor, Elijha Trible, Jno. Oakley.

COCHRAN, WILLIAM—BOX 21, PACK 480:
Est. admnr. Mar. 4, 1800 by Jno. Calhoun, David Pressly, Arthur Morrow Sr., Jno. Gaston bound to Andrew Hamilton Ord. Abbeville Dist. sum $1,000.00. Sale, Mar. 21, 1800. Byrs: Elizabeth Chalmers, Jno. Brady, Mary Cochran, etc.

COVINGTON, WILLIAM, SR.—BOX 21, PACK 481:
Will dated April 20, 1785 in 96 Dist. Proved Feb. 7, 1786 in Edgefield Co. Exrs: Sons, Joseph, Wm., Jno. Covington. Wit: Daniel Mathews, Joseph Day, Geo. Piper. Chn: Joseph, Wm., Jno. Covington, Mary Blackwell, Rosamond Hinton, Amey Savage. Gr. dtrs. Betsey Christopher, Amey Blackwell.
(In same pack. also.) Will of William Covington dated July 23, 1799 in Abbeville Dist. Proved Mar. 3, 1800. Exrs: Wife, Phebe, Wm. Fuguay, Barkley Martin (later 2 of Edgefield Co.) Wit: Rev. Francis, Sarah Cummins, Jno. B. Covington. Chn: Charles, Richard, Wm. Covington, Nancy Fuguay. Gr. dtr. Marriet dtr. of Geo. B. and Patsy Moor his wife.

CUNNINGHAM, AGNESS—BOX 21, PACK 482:
Will dated Nov. 28, 1807 in Abbeville Dist. Rec. Sept. 22, 1810. Exrs: Jno. Jones Jr., Jeremiah S. Terry. Wit: Benjamin Terry, Saml. Young, Margaret Calhoun. Chn: Thos., Jno. R. Cunningham. Gr. son, Jno. Cunningham Boles.

CONN, JOHN, JR.—BOX 21, PACK 483:
Est. admnr. Oct. 11, 1814 by Jas. Cobb, Jno. Campbell, Jacob Martin bound to Taliaferro Livingston Ord. sum $2,000.00. Inv. made Nov. 2, 1814 by Jno. White, Wm., Thos. Weems. Expend: Feb. 5, 1816 Recd. of Jno. Conn Sr. $85.25.

CROOKS, ANDREW—BOX 21, PACK 484:
Will dated Mar. 6, 1782 in Abbeville Dist. Proved Aug. 29, 1783. Exrs: Alexr., Jno. Dickey. Wit: Ann, Alexr. Wife, Jenne. Chn: Jno., Elizabeth, Andrew, Nancy, Saml. Crooks. Inv. made Nov. 26, 1783 by Geo. Montgomery, Jno. Riley, Joseph Caldwell. (His wife's name may have been Jonne)

COOK, JOHN—BOX 21, PACK 485:
Inv. made Sept. 6, 1783 by Nehemiah Howard, Thos. Greer, Wm. Wool-banks. (No other papers.)

CANE, JAMES, SR.—BOX 21, PACK 486:
Will dated Aug. 21, 1777 in Granville Co. Proved Oct. 27, 1783. Exrs: Jno. Cowan, Geo. Walton. Wit: Jno. Cowan, Geo. Walton. Wife, Frances. Chn: Wm., Jas., Peggy, Randal Cain, Frances Norrell, Hannah Caudle. Inv. made Nov. 25, 1783 by Robt. Patterson, Rivers Banks, Daniel Walker.

COATES, HENRY—BOX 21, PACK 487:
Est. admnr. June 11, 1784 by Jno. Coate, Benjamin Pearson, Geo. Powell bound to Jno. Thomas Jr. Ord. 96 Dist. sum 2,000 lbs. Henry Coate was of Bush River. Inv. made Aug. 10, 1784 by Saml. Kelly, Hugh Creighton, Benjamin Pearson. Byrs: Henry, Jno. Coate, etc.

CASTELTON, THOMAS—BOX 21, PACK 488:
Est. admnr. Sept. 22, 1783 by Elizabeth Inman, Joseph Miller, Thos. Rennolds bound to Jno. Thomas Jr. Ord. 96 Dist. sum $2,000.00. Inv. made at the house of Mrs. Mary Castelton Nov. 22, 1783 by Jas. Booth, Drury Napper.

CALDWELL, MARGARET R.—BOX 22, PACK 489:
On Feb. 14, 1837 Stanmore B., Wm. B. Brooks, Dr. Saml. Perryman bound to Moses Taggart Ord. Abbeville Dist. sum $2,000.00. Stanmore B. Brooks made gdn. of Margaret Rebecca Caldwell a minor.

CALDWELL, MINORS—BOX 22, PACK 490:
On Feb. 14, 1837 Wm. B., Stanmore B. Brooks, Saml. Perryman bound to Moses Taggart Ord. Abbeville Dist. sum $3,000.00. Wm. B. Brooks made gdn. Jas. B., Geo. R. Caldwell minors. Recd. $880.17 from est. of Geo. Caldwell decd. Jas. B. of age Oct. 27, 1845, Geo. of age Jan. 1851.

COLEMAN, MILTON W. AND THOS. L.—BOX 22, PACK 491:
On Mar. 6, 1832 Nancy Coleman, Jno. White, Jno. McLennan bound to Moses Taggart Ord. Abbeville Dist. sum $4,000.00. Jno. White made gdn. Milton W. and Thos. L. Coleman minors. Jan. 2, 1834 Paid trustees of Wood Academy 2 yrs. tuition $900.00.

CHANEY, MINORS—BOX 22, PACK 492:
Simeon Chaney was father of Jno. F., Elizabeth, Emily Chaney. Elmore Chaney their gdn. Mar. 4, 1850 Alfred Cheatham recd. $37.00 in right of his wife Emily Chaney. Robt. Elmore Chaney recd. $47.73. Sett. of Emily Chaney made Mar. 4, 1850, Recd. Jan. 1, 1837 of J. Sample admnr. of est. of Luke Day decd. Her portion of said est. $43.66.

CHILES, MINORS—BOX 22, PACK 493:
On July 4, 1830 Joseph, Hugh Dickson, Wm. Means bound to Moses Taggart Ord. Abbeville Dist. sum $2,000.00. Joseph Dickson made gdn. Willie C., Elizabeth Ann R. Chiles by their father April 26, 1836 who was then living in another state. July 10, 1837 Recd. Commissioner of Newberry Dist. selling lands belonging to Jas. Chiles decd. $132.75. Elizabeth A. R. Chiles married Jno. Williams.

CALDWELL, MINORS—BOX 22, PACK 494:
On Jan. 11, 1830 Jas., Jno. B. Huey, Wm. H. Caldwell bound to Moses Taggart Ord. Abbeville Dist. sum $4,000.00. Jno. B. Huey made gdn. Thos. L. and Wm. Ezekiel Caldwell minors. Expend: Jan. 12, 1833 Paid Wm. B. Scott for boarding W. C. Caldwell 10 months $34.00. Jan. 9, 1831 Recd. of Mathew McNeil on acct. of E. W. Caldwell $22.50.

CALDWELL, SARAH—BOX 22, PACK 495:
On July 16, 1835 Peggy Stuart, Jno. Logan, Jesse Beazley bound to Moses Taggart Ord. Abbeville Dist. sum $4,000.00. Peggy Stuart made gdn. Sarah Caldwell dtr. of Jno. Caldwell decd. June 10, 1831 Recd. from David Stewart Exr. of Alexr. Stewart in part $155.00. (One place written Mrs. Margaret Stuart gdn. Name written Stuart and Stewart.)

CHILES, EMILY—BOX 22, PACK 496:
On Feb. 19, 1830 Benjamin, Speers, Robt. Y. Jones bound to Moses Taggart Ord. Abbeville Dist. sum $3,000.00. Robt. Y. Jones made gdn. Emily Chiles minor. She died July 1841 having no chn, brothers or sisters of the whole blood but a mother Lucinda who married her gdn. R. Y. Jones.

CALHOUN, COL. JAMES (Minors)—BOX 22, PACK 497:
On Mar. 19, 1827 Martha, Joseph Jno. E. Calhoun bound to Moses Taggart Ord. Abbeville Dist. sum $5,000.00. Martha Calhoun made gdn. Martha S. minor over 14 yrs. and Mary Jane Calhoun a minor under 14 yrs.

CASEY, MINORS—BOX 22, PACK 498:
On Nov. 23, 1838 Thos. Henderson, Wright N. Moore, Gaines Rushton bound to Moses Taggart Ord. Abbeville Dist. sum $12,000.00. Thos. Henderson made gdn. Jno. Lucian and Wm. Casey minors. Jan. 7, 1851 Paid Thos. Lake amt. over paid by him to the gdn. when sett. of est. of Jno. Casey decd. was made $118.93. Esma Jones married the mother of said minors.

CALHOUN, MARIA L.—BOX 22, PACK 499:
On Mar. 20, 1838 Nathan Calhoun, Jno. N. Sample, Jas. Gillam bound to Moses Taggart Ord. Abbeville Dist. sum $20,000.00. Nathan Calhoun was the f. l. and gdn. of Maria L. Calhoun formerly a Beazley. May 22, 1838 Recd. of Wm. B. Beazley $3280.36.

CUNNINGHAM, MARGARET—BOX 22, PACK 500:
On Aug. 22, 1838 Robt. Cunningham, J. W. H. Johnson, Nathan Calhoun bound to Moses Taggart Ord. Abbeville Dist. sum $20,000.00. April 28,

1843 Recd. of Robt. Cunningham gdn. of Margaret Cunningham now wife of Saml. Trowbridge. $4141.72. Saml. Trowbridge.

COWAY, ELENOR—BOX 22, PACK 501:

On Jan. 16, 1833 Martha Coway, Jno. B., Jas. M. Foster bound to Moses Taggart Ord. Abbeville Dist. sum $1,000.00. On July 25, 1832 Joseph Coway made gdn. Nancy Ann Elenor Coway minor uner 14 yrs. Mar. 11, 1834 Recd. of Andrew Covey admnr. $66.93¾. Recd. of Martha Covey $355.37½. (Name written Coway and Covey.)

CRAWFORD, ISABELLA—BOX 22, PACK 502:

On Dec. 6, 1830 Jno. B., Alexr. P., Jas. Foster bound to Moses Taggart Ord. Abbeville Dist. sum $2,000.00 Alexr. P. Foster made gdn. of Ibby Crawford minor over 14 yrs. Jan. 3, 1832 Recd. from A. P. Foster $651.20.

CRAWFORD, MINORS—BOX 22, PACK 503:

On Oct. 20, 1832 Saml. Crawford, Joel Smith, Downs Calhoun bound to Moses Taggart Ord. Abbeville Dist. sum $5,000.00. Saml. Crawford made gdn. Elizabeth, Patsy, Saml. Crawford. Mr. Saml. Crawford was an Uncle to said minors who were the chn. of Jno. Crawford decd. Dec. 24, 1833 Cash sent to Elizabeth while in Alabama $30.00.

CALDWELL, MINORS—BOX 22, PACK 504:

On Feb. 14, 1837 Dr. Saml. Perryman, Stanmore B., Wm. B. Brooks bound to Moses Taggart Ord. Abbeville Dist. sum $3,000.00. Dr. Saml. Perryman made gdn. Charlotte S., Anne Elizabeth Caldwell minors. Feb. 14, 1837 Recd. from Stanmore B. Brooks admr. of Geo. Caldwell decd. $880.17 May 23, 1837 Recd. of Commission of Newberry Dist. the 1st and 2nd instalment of share of land of est. of Jas. Caldwell $55.45.

COLEMAN, MINORS—BOX 22, PACK 505:

On July 5, 1830 Abraham P. Pool, Jno. Logan, Jno. Coleman bound to Moses Taggart Ord. Abbeville Dist. sum $2,000.00. Abraham P. Pool made gdn. Mary, Ann Coleman minors under 14 yrs. Aug. 1830 Recd. of the admnr. of Jas. Coleman decd. $510.72. Mar. 20, 1845 Mary S. Coleman recd. in full $523.11 of est. of Jas. Coleman decd. and of the legacy of Col. Jas. Williams decd. Abraham Pool married her mother Sarah Coleman. Ann Coleman died in infancy.

CHILES, MINORS—BOX 22, PACK 506:

On Mar. 20, 1811 Benjamin Chiles, Jno. Meriwether Sr., Nathan Lipscomb Jr. bound to Taliaferro Livingston Ord. Abbeville Dist. sum $2,000.00. Benjamin Chiles made gdn. Lewis, Larkin Chiles minors under 14 yrs. Austin Pollard gdn. Fanny Chiles. Wm. Chiles gdn. of Maria L. Chiles. Jno. Swilling gdn. of Thos. Chiles. Dec. 25, 1810 By the hire of a negro boy Edmund belonging to est. of Reuben Chiles decd. $18.00. (One paper ment. est. of Jno. Chiles decd. for sons Jas., Jno. Chiles Jr.)

COCHRAN, SAMUEL W.—BOX 22, PACK 507:

On Oct. 6, 1828 Saml., Bartholomew, Jonathan Jordon bound to Moses

Taggard Ord. Abbeville Dist. sum $5,000.00. Saml. Jordon made gdn. Saml. Cochran minor under 14 yrs.

CALDWELL, SAMUEL—BOX 22, PACK 508:

On Mar. 2, 1835 Thos. P. Spierin, Charles Dendy, Franklin Branch, Andrew Giles bound to Moses Taggart Ord. Abbeville Dist. sum $3,000.00. On Nov. 10, 1834 Saml. Caldwell was a minor over 14 yrs. Wm. Caldwell was the former gdn. Sett. made Mar. 11, 1843. Evidence of T. P. Spierin taken by consent. Saml. Caldwell the minor came to his house April 1832 and continued to live with witness until April 8, 1836. At first the witness did not intend to charge the ward with board, but on justice to his own chn. he afterwards did make the charge. The ward had his hand shot off while living with witness. The ward was brought to his house by Mr. *Henry* on a visit. He was anxious to live with Mr. Spierin and on this acct. Mr. Spierin kept him. Expend: To boarding Saml. Caldwell from April 5 to Jan. 1, 1836 at $6.00 per month deducting therefrom 3 months absence at school on Rocky River with Col. Wm. H. Caldwell $251.00. April 8, 1836 Paid expenses to Miss. $38.00.

COLLIER, BEATRICE—BOX 22, PACK 509:

On May 3, 1813 Jas. Collier, Josiah Patterson bound to Moses Taggart Ord. Abbeville Dist. sum $10,000.00. Jas. Collier Esq. made gdn. Beatrice Collier a minor under 14 yrs.

CALHOUN, CAPT. JOSEPH—BOX 22, PACK 510:

Est. admnr. Nov. 12, 1838 by Frances, Wm. Calhoun, Patrick Noble bound to Moses Taggart Ord. Abbeville Dist. sum $40,000.00. Inv. of Joseph Calhoun late of Calhoun Mills made Nov. 16, 1838 by Patrick Noble, Jas. Taggart, Meredith McGehee. Cit. pub. at Hopewill Church. Frances Calhoun married Moses O. Talman.

CARWILE, JOSIAH—BOX 23, PACK 511:

Will dated Aug. 9, 1840 in Abbeville Dist. Proved April 13, 1841. Exrs: Sons, Jno., Jas. Carwile. Wit: Jno. L. Wright, Wm. Bowan, Saml. Carlile. Wife, Elizabeth. Chn: Jas., Wm., Jno., Polly, Nancy Carwile. Sett. made May 13, 1845. Present, Jno. Carwile, Charles Collins who married Mary Carwile, Wm. McClain married Elizabeth, Wm. L. Bryant married Clarissa Nancy Carwile, Jas. M. Carwile. Absent: Wm. M., Candis C., Sarah, Addison F., Maddison M., Milton S., Margaret J., Josiah Carwile his half brother.

CALHOUN, WILLIAM—BOX 23, PACK 512:

Will dated Aug. 6, 1840 in Abbeville Dist. Proved Dec. 18, 1840. Exrs: Wm. Tennent, Armstead Burt, Henry H. Townes, Geo. McDuffie. Wit: Edward, Frances A. Calhoun, Hayden Lawton. Chn: Thos. J., Jas. L. Calhoun, Lucretia A. Towns, Martha C. Burt.

CHEATHAM, PETER—BOX 23, PACK 513:

Will dated April 24, 1839 in Abbeville Dist. Proved Nov. 23, 1840. Exrs: Son, Richard Cheatham, Jas. Gillam. Wit: Wm. Carter, Henry C. Culbreath, J. R. Boulware. Wife ment. no name given. Chn: Jas., Lucy, Frances,

Jackson, Richard Cheatham. Following were the legatees: Dison Henderson, Jackson, Elizabeth, Lucy, Susan, Agness, Calvin, Sopronia Cheatham, Frances Henderson, Elizabeth Dodson.

CARLILE, ROBERT E.—BOX 23, PACK 514:
    Est. admnr. Oct. 14, 1840 by Isaac Carlile, Wm. C. Cozby Esq., Jno. G. Caldwell bound to Moses Taggart Ord. Abbeville Dist. sum $1200.00. Wid. Margaret B. Carlile. Chn: Jas. M., Robt. H., Isabella F. Carlile. Inv. made Nov. 24, 1840 by Robt., Wm. C. Cozby, Jno. Carlile.

CURTIS, BROOKS—BOX 23, PACK 515:
    The petition of Wm. N. Blake sheweth that Brooks Curtis died intestate not having any relations known to be in this dist. to whom admnr. could be granted. Prays that he may be appointed the admnr. Dated this Nov. 17, 1841. Inv. made by Jno. Logan, David Gullam, P. D. Klugh, Henry Riley.

CRAYTON, MARY—BOX 23, PACK 516:
    Will dated Mar. 29, 1834 in Abbeville Dist. Proved Aug. 31, 1841. Exrs: Henry Weed, Hezekiah Wakefield. Wit: Benjamin Griffin, Jas. A. Gantt, Jno. L. Wright. Chn: Saml., Thos., Wm. Crayton, Easter Reed. Gr. chn: Mary Jane, Balis Franklin chn. of Saml. Crayton. Mary dtr. of Easter Reed. Expend: Thos. Crayton a minor recd. $100.00 from his grandmother's est. Dec. 10, 1842 Recd. of Thos. L. Reed $26.00. Henry Reed recd. $32.62½. Oct. 15, 1841 Alfred E. Reed recd. $50.00.

CRAWFORD, GREENBERRY—BOX 23, PACK 517:
    Will dated May 27, 1841 in Abbeville Dist. Proved July 10, 1841 Exrs Wm. Harris, Jno. Kennedy. Wit: Jno. Patterson, Washington Freeman, J. C. Williard. Chn: George B., Jas. Bunion, Mary Louisa Crawford. Inv. made Nov. 31, 1841 by Joshua Wideman, Jas. McCaslan, M. O. McCaslan.

CLELLAND, DAVID—BOX 23, PACK 518:
    On Jan. 14, 1842 David Cleland sheweth that he is a minor about 17 yrs., that his grandfather Wm. Plunket decd. died in Newberry Dist. leaving a small est. The mother of your petr. Hannah Plunket married Wm. Cleland and both are dead leaving 6 living chn. Your petr. desires that his b. l. Thos. C. Milford be appointed his gdn. Thos. Milford married Jane Cleland dtr. of Wm. and Hannah Cleland. (In another place name written Sarah.)

CLARK, WILLIAM—BOX 23, PACK 519:
    Will dated Nov. 1, 1841 in Abbeville Dist. Proved Feb 7, 1842. Exrs: Jas., Wm. Caldwell. Wit: Jas. Calhoun, Jas. Harris, Bartley Tucker. Son, Jno. Clark. Nephew, Wm. Clark. "To eldest dtr. of my decd. brother Patrick C. Clark one negro girl." Ment. several nephews and nieces but could not recollect their names. Niece, Margaret Ann and husband Wm. Kelley of Gonzales Co., Tex. appointed Jno. A. Clark of same county their attorney to receive their part of Wm. Clarks est. in Abbeville Dist. S. C. Dated this Oct. 29, 1856. Wm. Clark died Jan. 18, 1842. Sett. made Dec. 26, 1843 to ascertain the share of Sarah Clark now Sarah McCallister. Jane Amanda Clark married Stephen C. Neal.

"I, Jno. Oldham, gdn. of Wm. Clark child of Patrick C. Clark decd. do appoint Alexr. McCallister of said county our attorney to receive Wm. Clark's part of est. of Wm. Clark decd. of Abbeville Dist. S. C."

CRAWFORD, AGNESS—BOX 23, PACK 520:
Will dated Mar. 18, 1838 in Abbeville Dist. Proved Mar. 22, 1842. Exrs: Dtr. Nancy Crawford, Stephen Jones. Wit: Jno. Speer, Jane M. Pressly, Elizabeth Hutchison. Chn: Nancy, Mary, Elizabeth, Wm. Crawford, Margaret Harris, Isabella Allen. On Mar. 22, 1842 Jno. Speer ment. that Stephen Jones had removed from the limits of this state.

CAIN, THOMAS—BOX 23, PACK 521:
On Mar. 8, 1842 the petition of Michael Hackett sheweth that Thos. Cain died intestate leaving a wid. in Alabama and a small est. in this state and Alabama. Thos. Cain was late of Abbeville and Georgia. Inv. made June 28, 1842 by D. Douglass, Wm. R. Swain, Jno. A. Burton.

CORNETT, DRAYTON—BOX 23, PACK 522:
Est. admnr. Oct. 3, 1842 by Thos. Nichols, Jno. Holland, Saml. Baird, Richard White bound to David Lesly Ord. Abbeville Dist. sum $2,000.00. He left no parents, wife or chn. but a brother as next of kin. Had one note on Joseph Cornett dated Dec. 26, 1832 for $32.50. Recd. from Albert Cornet $4.87.

CALDWELL, JAMES—BOX 23, PACK 523:
Est. admnr. Nov. 28, 1842 by Wm. H. Harris, Jno. G. Caldwell, Wm. H. Caldwell bound to David Lesly Ord. Abbeville Dist. sum $24,000.00. Left a wid and 9 chn. some minors. s. l. Wm. H. Harris. J. J. Caldwell recd. $615.00. Saml. Caldwell $1125.00. D. O. Mecklin and wife $750.00.

COBB, CHARLES—BOX 23, PACK 524:
Est. admnr. Dec. 5, 1842 by Jno. W., Charles A. Cobb, Jno. Cochran, Hart P. Arnold, Jas. Jay bound to David Lesly Ord. Abbeville Dist. sum $9,000.00. The petition of J. W. and Charles A. Cobb sheweth that their father Charles C. Cobb died in intestate, leaving no wid. but 4 chn. Nancy married R. A. Kirkpatrick. Mary A. married Jno. Cheatham.

CLARK, MINORS—BOX 23, PACK 525:
On Dec. 13, 1842 Charles H. Allen, Jno. F. Livingston, Jno. White bound to David Lesly Ord. Abbeville Dist. sum $1,000.00. Charles Allen made gdn. of Laura A., Louisa, Sarah B. Clark. The petition of Charles Allen sheweth that Joseph Clark of Orange Co. Virginia died leaving a will in which Reuben T. Clark was Exr. did bequeath property to the chn. of his son Jas. Clark decd. That your Petr. married Catharine L. Clark dtr. of said Jas. Clark and gr. dtr. of said Joseph Clark decd.

CALHOUN, JAMES—BOX 23, PACK 526:
Will dated July 21, 1842 in Abbeville Dist. Proved Feb. 21, 1843. Exrs. Sons, Jas. M., Jno. A., Wm. H. Calhoun. Wit: Jas. Taggart, Charles T. Haskell, T. W. Thomas. Wife, Sarah. Chn: Sarah, Jas. M., Jno. A,. Wm. H. Calhoun.

Ment. friends, Thos. Parker, Joseph Dixson. (Will of Jas. Calhoun Sr. in same pack.) Will dated May 9, 1786 in 96 Dist. Proved Oct. 2, 1787. Exrs: Wm., Jno. Calhoun. Wit: Wm. Heard, Jno. Gaw. Wife, Jannet. "Bequeath to wife Jannet and Alexr. Calhoun Moody 1 note upon Jno. Gaw. Unto Jas. son of Wm. Calhoun. Bequeath to Andrew Chalmers. Unto Jas. son of Jno. Calhoun. Chn: Wm., Maria Calhoun. s. l. Wm. Anderson.

CHEATHAM, JOHN—BOX 23, PACK 527:
Will dated Aug. 23, 1843 in Abbeville Dist. Proved Nov. 27, 1843. Wit: Peter M. Keller, Stanmore Brooks, Jas. C. Ray. Wife, no name given. "My will that my wife and her 2 chn. have no part of my property." Chn: J. W., W. H., M. E., J. H., A. H., J. R. Chatham. Edmund Cobb married the wid. Elizabeth Chatham. Augustus A. Chatham by his last wife died soon after his death. (Name written Cheatham and Chatham.)

CARLILE, MINORS—BOX 23, PACK 528:
On Jan. 26, 1844 Margaret B., Isaac Carlile, Wm. C. Cozby bound to David Lesly Ord. Abbeville Dist. sum $1292.00. Margaret B. Carlile made gdn. of Jam. M., Robt. H., Isabella E. Carlile minors. Margaret B. was the wid. of R. Carlile and mother of said minors.

CHEATHAM, HENRY—BOX 23, PACK 529:
Est. admnr. May 6, 1844 by Daniel Carter, Meedy Mays, Robt. Cheatham bound to David Lesly Ord. Abbeville Dist. sum $500.00. Left a wid. Charlotte T. Cheatham but no chn. Martha Cheatham was mother of said decd. Daniel Carter was father of Charlotte T. Cheatham.

CALDWELL, ANN—BOX 23, PACK 530:
On Feb. 8, 1842 Mrs. Edna Caldwell was gdn. of Ann Caldwell a minor. Amt. of Ann's portion paid into my hands by Jno. P. Baratt Exr. of est. of Saml. Perryman former gdn. of Ann Caldwell.

CALHOUN, KITTY—BOX 23, PACK 531:
On July 3, 1815 Joseph Hutton, Andrew Weed, Jas. Craig bound to Taliaferro Livingston Ord. Abbeville Dist. sum $10,000.00. Joseph Hutton made gdn. Kitty Calhoun minor over 14 yrs. Expend: Aug. 30, 1817 Paid Archibald McClain for hauling her trunk from Pendleton $2.92. July 3, 1815 Paid for a copy of the sale of est. of Jas. Johnson decd. in which she was interested $2.23. Jan. 17, 1816 To my expense going to Edgefield to prove the will of Jas. Johnson decd. $7.82½. Oct. 31 Paid Joseph Owen for riding with a commission to Orangeburg Dist. $5.00. Feb. 21, 1814 Recd. in trust for Kitty J. Calhoun of Jas. Johnson Sr. decd. negroes and also about 500 acres of land in Barnwell and Orangeburg Dist.

CHATHAM, RICHARD—BOX 23, PACK 532:
Will dated Jan. 22, 1836 in Abbeville Dist. Exrs: Wm. Harris, Leroy Watson. Wit: Jemima Lipscomb, Matilda Vaughan, Jno. Harris. Wife, Margaret Ann Chatham. Inv. made Aug. 31, 1836 by Robt. Turner, Thos. Ross, Richmond Still, Maximilan Hutcheson.

ABBEVILLE DISTRICT WILLS AND BONDS 79

COTTRELL, REVD. THOMAS—BOX 23, PACK 533:
Will dated Mar. 17, 1830 at Mount Ariel. Exr. Wife, Susan L. Cotterell. Wit. F. Connor, J. E. Glenn. (Will rejected having but 2 wit.) Names written Cottrell and Cotterell. Est. admnr. Nov. 14, 1834 by Saml. A., Gabriel Hodges, Jas. Shackelford bound to Moses Taggart Ord. Abbeville Dist. sum $3,000.00.

CHILES, JOHN SR.—BOX 23, PACK 534:
Will dated Feb. 28, 1803 in Abbeville Dist. Rec. June 28, 1803. Exrs: Wife, Mary Ann. Sons, Walter, Jno., Thompson Chiles. Wit: Benjamin, Thos. B. Waller, Geo., Wm. White. Chn: Walter, Jno., Thompson Chiles, Agness Waller, Anne Dawson, Mary Livingston, Betey Goudey, Raney Livingston, Phebe Mayson. Inv. made April 12, 1816 by Jno. C. Mayson, W. O. Bickley. Inv. made again July 28, 1803 by Nathan Lipscomb, Geo. White, Thos. B. Waller.

CHEATHAM, ROBERT—BOX 24, PACK 535:
Est. admnr. Mar. 9, 1827 by Nancy Cheatham, Jno. H., Albert Waller bound to Moses Taggart Ord. Abbeville Dist. sum $20,000.00. Inv. made May 9, 1827 by Albert, Jno. H. Waller, Martin Hackett, Jno. Cheatham.

CARITHERS, JAMES—BOX 24, PACK 536:
Will dated Dec. 11, 1823 in Abbeville Dist. Proved April 9, 1824. Exrs: Benjamin Terry, Francis Young. Wit: Geo. Whitefield, Benjamin Terry. Sis. Margarette Carithers. Brother, Saml. Carithers. Ment. Jas. son of Saml. Carithers. Inv. made April 12, 1824 by Geo. Whitefield, W. H. Bickley.

CROMER, ELIZABETH—BOX 24, PACK 537:
Est. admnr. June 27, 1839 by Jno. Ruff, Philip Cromer, Saml. Morris, Jno. Keller bound to Moses Taggart Ord. Abbeville Dist. sum $20,000.00. Cit. pub. at Asbury Church. Inv. made July 16, 1839 by David, J. Kellar, W. Connor.

COCHRAN, ROBERT ESQ.—BOX 24, PACK 538:
Est. admnr. Feb. 3, 1840 by Jno. Cochran, Thos. J. Douglass, Jas. C. Ellis bound to Moses Taggart Ord. Abbeville Dist. sum $12,000.00. Cit. pub. at Cokesbury. Sett. made Jan. 13, 1843. Present, Jno. Cochran admnr. and distributee, Jas., Daniel, Wm. Cochran, Elizabeth decd. wife of Douglas. Chn: viz. D. Douglass, Jno., Thos. J. Douglass, Rebecca, Phebe Hodges, Deborah decd. wife of Wm. Norris, Phebe Drennan, Milly Mathis. Robt. Cochran died Jan. 1840. Elizabeth Douglass was a sis. Elias Mathis recd. $391.00 as a legg. Gabriel Hodges legatee recd. $122.22. D. Douglass $156.76.

CRAWFORD, MINORS—BOX 24, PACK 539:
Josiah Crawford in 1808 was gdn. Jas., Elenera, Rhoda C., Jno. Crawford. (No other papers.)

CALHOUN, JAMES SR.—BOX 24, PACK 540:
Will dated Jan. 25, 1814 in Abbeville Dist. Rec. June 22, 1815. Exr. Capt. Jas. Calhoun. Wit: Jas. Noble, Sarah C. Calhoun, Thos. S. Baskin. Nephews, Saml, Patrick, Jno. L. Calhoun. "Bequeath to Caroline Calhoun my

sorel mare." Inv. made Sept 21, 1815 by Joseph Hutton, Patrick Calhoun, Joseph Houston.

CRAWFORD, WILLIAM M.—BOX 24, PACK 541:
Est. admnr. Feb. 1, 1830 by Alexr. Hunter, Josiah Patterson, Joseph Black bound to Moses Taggart Ord. Abbeville Dist. sum $20,000.00. Cit. pub. at Upper Long Cane Church. Cit. pub. Dec. 27, 1829 at Rocky River Church ment. Alexr. Hunter. Arabella Crawford made suit for Letters of Admnr. Jas. Crawford former admnr. and father of Wm. Crawford died about 1830.

CROWTHER, NANCY—BOX 24, PACK 543:
Will dated Oct. 15, 1834 in Abbeville Dist. Proved June 10, 1839. Exr: Saml. Tribble. Wit: Wm., Milley Covington, C. Stark. "Bequeath to Robt. Stuckey $40.00. To chn. of Jno. Fowler $150.00. To Elizabeth Fowler a bed. To Nancy dtr. of Thos. Fisher a dress. To Jno. Osborne Jr. $20.00. Sis. Catharine McAdams.

CLIZBE, SAMUEL—BOX 24, PACK 544:
Est. admnr. Mar. 8, 1821 by Timothy Chiles, Jacob Martin, Thos. Botts bound to Moses Taggart Ord. Abbeville Dist. sum $1,000.00. Saml. Cilzbe was late of Georgia. (No other papers.)

CALVERT, JESSE—BOX 24, PACK 545:
Est. admnr. Jan. 7, 1839 by Wm., Joel Smith, Jno. White bound to Moses Taggart Ord. Abbeville Dist. sum $20,000.00. He died Dec. 1838. Left a wid. Caroline and 7 chn. all of age but one. 3 are in Abbeville, one the wife of Wm. Smith, 3 are in Alabama (one the minor) and one in Texas. Legs. Lucy E., Robt. J., Mary E., H. H. Calvert, Wm. Leake, Caroline Dunn now Caroline Anderson, Mary E. Calvert now Mary E. Anderson.

CAROTHERS, MARGARET—BOX 24, PACK 546:
Will dated Sept. 19, 1828 in Abbeville Dist. Proved April 22, 1829. Exrs: Benjamin Terry, Jane Gibert. Wit: Joseph, Harriet Hillhouse, A. Hunter. "Beloved grandniece, Mrs. Jane Gibert with whom I now reside at this time." Cit. pub. at Rocky River Church. Inv. made June 5, 1829 by Jas. Gillam, Major Thos. T. Hamilton, Mathew Young.

COLLINS, SARAH—BOX 24, PACK 547:
Est. admnr. Aug. 29, 1837 by Charles Collins Jr., Stephen Jones Jr. Zachariah Graham bound to Moses Taggart Ord. Abbeville Dist. sum $1,000.00. Cit. pub. at Walnut Grove Church.

CROZIER, MICHAEL C.—BOX 24, PACK 548:
Will dated Jan. 11, 1831 in Abbeville Dist. Proved Feb. 16, 1831. Exrs: Wife, Mary, Dr. Saml. Pressly. Wit: Jeremiah, Saml. Cook, Jno. W. Foster. Chn: Andrew, Emuline, Elizabeth Crozier. Inv. made Mar. 3, 1831 by Archibald Campbell, Saml. Cook, Mathew Goodwin. (Name written Crozier & Crosier.)

COOK, HENRY P.—BOX 549:
On June 17, 1845 Frederick Cook, Jno. W. Hearst, Thos. C. Perrin bound

to David Lesly Ord. Abbeville Dist. sum $196. 00. Frederick Cook made gdn. Henry P. Cook a minor. Dec. 19, 1846 Jno. W. Thornton recd. $191.91 for Sophronia Cook now his wife given to her by the will of Elizabeth Irwin decd. On Mar. 14; 1845 Henry P. Cook of Jasper County, Miss. chose his brother Frederick Cook his gdn.

CHATHAM, ROBERT NEWTON—BOX 24, PACK 550:
Will dated Mar. 14, 1864 at Dalton, Georgia. Filed Dec. 4, 1865. Exrs: Armstead Burt, Jas. A. Norwood. Wit: J. L. White, J. M. Latimer, A. Clinkscales. Lived also in Abbeville Dist. Brothers: Jas. Medley Cobb, J. Richard Chatham.

CALHOUN, ANDREW—BOX 24, PACK 551:
Est. admnr. April 14, 1845 by Geo. W. Blackburn, Henry Boozer, Andrew Riley bound to David Lesly Ord. Abbeville Dist. sum $1,000.00. Petition of Geo. W. Blackburn sheweth that Andrew Calhoun left no wid. but several infant chn. that the decd. was sick in his last days at my house. Dated this Mar. 14, 1845.

CARWILE, JOSIAH—BOX 24, PACK 552:
Statement for sett: of Josiah N. Carwile a minor ward of Jno. S. Carlile. The gdn. expects to leave this state and this sett. is in order to transfer the funds. Addison F. Carwile a minor on Nov. 28, 1850 recd. $125.85. Margaret Jane Carwile now of age Nov. 24, 1855 appointed her brother Jas. Carwile her gdn. Her father Josiah Carwile decd. She lived in Lebanan, Dekalb Co. Alabama. On May 31, 1845 Elizabeth Carwile appointed Jno. S. Carwile gdn. for her son Josiah N. Carwile. Dec. 8, 1851 Madison M. Carwile recd. $129.44. Milton S. Carwile of age Jan. 2, 1854. In 1845 the 7 minors were: Candice C., Sarah J., Addison F., Madison M., Milton S., Margaret J., Josiah N. Carwile. On Mar. 21, 1848 Candice C. was the wife of Wm. C. Graham.

CALDWELL, JAMES H.—BOX 24, PACK 553:
Est. admnr. Dec. 2, 1844 by Jefferson Davis, Jno. C. Red, McKinney Thomas bound to David Lesly Ord. Abbeville Dist. sum $2,000.00. Left a wid. Jude and 1 child. On Feb. 6, 1846 Judass Hughey recd. $273.17 her share of husband's est. Her son Jas. Caldwell recd. $530.53.

CHEATHAM, MILTON—BOX 24, PACK 554:
Est. admnr. Jan. 13, 1845 by Zebidee, Robt. Cheatham, Meedy Mays Sr. bound to David Lesly Ord. Abbeville Dist. sum $300.00. Left a wid. Amanda and 2 infant chn. Zebidee was a brother to Milton Cheatham.

COOK, SOPHRONIA—BOX 24, PACK 555:
Petition of Sophronia Cook sheweth that she is a minor of age and entitled to a small legacy from the will of Elizabeth Irwin decd. to her mother Mary Cook now decd. Prays that her brother be appointed her gdn. Jan. 14, 1845.

CHALMERS, MARTHA—BOX 24, PACK 556:
Will dated April 21, 1824 in Abbeville Dist. Proved Mar. 16, 1832. Exrs:

Sis. Sarah Wilson. Nieces, Martha, Anna Maria Wilson. Wit: Richard B. Cater, Stephen Lee, Washington Langford. "Leave est. to Thos. Parker in trust that during the life of my sis. Sarah Wilson, wid. to have use, possession of my est."

CROZIER, JAMES—BOX 24, PACK 557:
Will dated May 27, 1778. Proved April 7, 1789. Exrs: Wm. *Pressly,* Thos. Crozier. Wit: Wm. Doris, Andrew Crozier. Wife, no name given. Chn: Saml., Agness Crozier.

CHAMBERLAIN, THOMAS—BOX 24, PACK 558:
Inv. made May 17, 1845 by Obadiah Campbell, Alexr. Oliver, Michael Kennedy, Alexr. McAlister. Wid. Margaret. Chn: Wm., Alexr., Alfred, Jas. Chamberlain, Caroline Bowen.

DAWKINS, GEORGE—BOX 25, PACK 559:
Will dated Jan. 20, 1781. Proved May 9, 1783. Exrs: Thos. Dawkins, Geo. Harris, Thos. Harbert. Wit: Daniel Gartman, Jno. Buchanan, Thos. Allison. Lived in Craven Co., S. C. Wife, Chole. Chn: Joseph, Polly, Geo., Thos., Hannah Dawkins. "Give unto Nancy Norman 1 negro girl." Joseph recd. 50 acres lying in the forks between Broad and Sandy Rivers. Inv. made May 9, 1783 by Jno. Buchanan, Daniel Gartman, Wm. Hutcheson.

DAVIS, GERAH—BOX 25, PACK 560:
Est. admnr. Oct. 22, 1822 by Dr. Eli S., Joseph Davis, Benjamin Adams bound to Moses Taggart Ord. Abbeville Dist. sum $20,000.00. Cit. pub. at Upper Long Cane Church. Expend: Jan. 7, 1823 Paid Mr. Pressly tuition for P. H. Davis $4.00. Sept. 14 Cash sent to P. H. Davis in Tenn. $90.00. Oct. 25, By cash of Col. Carr's est. in Georgia $700.00. Nov. 8, 1882 Cash advanced Richard D. Davis $4.00. Advanced Patrick Davis $1.00. Mar. 15, 1823 By cash of Ben Martin's est. in Georgia $36.37.

DAVIS, WILLIAM—BOX 25, PACK 561:
Will dated April 26, 1819 in Abbeville Dist. Proved Aug. 6, 1819. Exrs: Wife, Elizabeth. Jas. Pulliam, Wm. Spraggins. Wit: Jas. Franklin, Charles Neely, Turner A. Davis. Chn. ment. no names given. Inv. made Aug. 28, 1819 by Robt. Young, Jas. Franklin, Wm. Neely. (One place ment. Elizabeth Wardlaw as Exr.)

DEVLIN, JAMES—BOX 25, PACK 562:
Est. admnr. Jan. 7, 1826 by Jno., Jas. Devlin bound to Moses Taggart Ord. Abbeville Dist. sum $1,000.00. Cit. pub. at Tranquil Church. "We the heirs and legatees of said est. have agreed to relinquish our shares unto Jannet Devlin." Signed, Jas. Devlin, Isaac Kennedy.

DEVALL, SAMUEL—BOX 25, PACK 563:
Will dated Dec. 30, 1800 in Abbeville Dist. Filed Mar. 7, 1818. Exr. Wife, Sarah Devauld. Wit: Moses Tullis, Jesse Dobbs, Margaret Cochran. Chn: Joseph, Eliza, Jas. Otes, Matilday Ann Devauld, Siscela Bevly. Inv. made Mar.

23, 1818 by Adam Wideman, Robt. M. Steger, Uel Hill, Jno. Harris, Jesse Dobbs. (Name written Devall & Devauld.)

DODSON, ENOCH—BOX 25, PACK 564:
Will dated April 23, 1811 Proved May 6, 1816. Exrs: Wife, Elizabeth. Son, Wm. Dodson, Saml. Agnew. Wit: Ezekiel Nash, Jno. Cheatham, Michael Magee. Chn: Wm., Jas., Polly, Mahaley Dodson, Nancy, Lucy Barmore, Malinda Agnew. Enoch Dodson died April 12, 1816.

DAVIS, DEMPSEY—BOX 25, PACK 565:
Will dated Aug. 30, 1822 in Abbeville Dist. Proved Oct. 7, 1822. Exr: Patrick Calhoun. Wit: Wm. Carson, H. Reid, Eli Giddings. Wife, Elizabeth. Dtr. Caroline Davis. Nephews, Vincent Woods, Dempsey Dutton. Inv. made Nov. 6, 1822 by Wm. Carson, Jas. Taggart, Jas. Calhoun. (One paper stated Elizabeth Johnson formerly Davis.)

DAY, JOHN R.—BOX 25, PACK 566:
Est. admnr. Jan. 3, 1827 by Jas. Sills, Charles B. Fooshe, Wm. C. Owen bound to Moses Taggart Ord. Abbeville Dist. sum $1,000.00. Cit. pub. at Silome Meeting House. Inv. made Jan. 9, 1827 by Jas. Mitchel, Wm. Ward, Peter Chatham. 1828 Paid Ransom Day $2.25. Leroy Day $27.37½.

DOAN, WILLIAM H.—BOX 25, PACK 567:
Est. admnr. Mar. 25, 1831 by Isaac, Franklin Branch, Jas. S. Wilson bound to Moses Taggart Ord. Abbeville Dist. sum $1,000.00. On May 21, 1831 appeared before me Wm. Patton, a Justice in Charleston Dist. S. C., Kerr Boyce, Jas. S. Wilson, Geo. Henry appraisers appointed to appraise the est. of Wm. H. Doan decd. late of Abbeville Dist.

DELPH, COL. HENRY—BOX 25, PACK 568:
Will dated June 15, 1823 in Abbeville Dist. Proved Aug. 4, 1823. Wit: Wm. Barmore, Reuben Powell, Wm. Braden. Brothers, Robt., Muymons Delph. "Rest of est. to be divided between Austin Arnold and family, Nathaniel Jeffries family." Inv. made Nov. 29, 1823 by Edmond Ware, Charles Pitts, Wm. Braden N. J. Rosamond.

DUNLAP, BRYCE—BOX 25, PACK 569:
Est. admnr. Dec. 4, 1826 by Jno. W., Wm., Jno. Bigby bound to Moses Taggart Ord. Abbeville Dist. sum $4,000.00. Mar. 11, 1834 To clothing for Wm., Emily D. Dunlap $7.00. Paid Jno. Case for boarding Sarah Dunlap at school 6 months $13.00. Nov. 7 To dressing for Caroline $17.00.

DUNN, MICHAEL—BOX 25, PACK 570:
Est. admnr. June 17, 1836 by Abner W. McGee, Saml. Agnew, Benjamin Smith bound to Moses Taggart Ord. Abbeville Dist. sum $10,000.00. Cit. pub. at Turkey Creek Church. Inv. made Aug. 8, 1836 by Wm. Barmore, Benjamin Smith, Ezekiel Rasor.

DUNLAP, ELIZABETH—BOX 25, PACK 571:
Est. admnr. Nov. 26, 1830 by Jno. W. Bigby, Wm. Gaines, Waller Sims

bound to Moses Taggart Ord. Abbeville Dist. sum $1500.00. Inv. made Dec. 2, 1830 by Geo. Bigby, Waller Sims, Robt. Benson Kay, Wm. Gaines. Dec. 29, 1832 To cloth for Wm. Dunlap $2.00. Shoes for Wm. and Emily Dunlap $2.00. Paid Wm. Gaines for boarding Emily, Jno., Sarah Dunlap $49.00.

DOUGLASS, AGNESS—BOX 25, PACK 572:
Will dated July 17, 1835 in Abbeville Dist. Proved Aug. 26, 1836. Exr: Wm. Douglass. Wit: Nathaniel Moore, Isaiah Johnson, Jno. W. Cranner. "Left est. to Wm. H. Douglass and his heirs."

DAVIS, CHESLEY—BOX 25, PACK 573:
Will dated Aug. 4, 1827 in Abbeville Dist. Exrs: Sons, Saml., Daniel, Gabriel Davis. Wit: Charles Smith, Wm., Robt. E. Buchanan. Chn: Saml., Gabriel, Susanna, Jesse, Little Berry, Nancy, Heszecah, Bulah Davis. "Bequeath to Francis Harris $3.00. To Wm. Gains $3.00." Inv. made Nov. 22, 1836 by Wm. Taggart, Jesse Calvert, Robt. Turner.

DUNN, JAMES—BOX 25, PACK 574:
Est. admnr. Dec. 7, 1835 by Wm. Dunn, Robt., Jno. Richey bound to Moses Taggart Ord. Abbeville Dist. sum $10,000.00. Sale, Dec. 26, 1835. Byrs: R. L. Anderson, Jno. Richey Sr. Wm. Dunn Jr. etc.

DOUGLASS, MATHEW—BOX 25, PACK 575:
Est. admnr. Dec 11, 1837 by Jas. Foster, Archibald Kennedy, Hamilton Hill bound to Moses Taggart Ord. Abbeville Dist. sum $1,000.00. Cit. pub. at Cedar Springs Church. Sale, Dec. 25, 1837. Byrs: Catharine, Jno. Douglass, etc.

DAWKINS, JOHN—BOX 25, PACK 576:
Will dated May 14, 1837 in Abbeville Dist. Proved July 21, 1828. Exr. Jno. R. Wilson. Wit: Jno. C. Griffin, Jas. Dixon, Benjamin Low. Wife, Margaret. Chn: Thos., Elijah Dawkins, the heirs of my dtrs. Sally and Elizabeth, Jno. Dawkins, my wifes dtr. Elizabeth Dawkins. Gr. son, Lewis Dawkins.

DRENNAN, JOSEPH—BOX 25, PACK 577:
Est. admnr. April 3, 1836 by Jno. Isaac Kennedy, Jas. Foster bound to Moses Taggart Ord. Abbeville Dist. sum $10,000.00. Cit. pub. at Long Cane Church. Inv. made April 8, 1836 by Josiah McGaw, Jno. Bradley, Reuben Weed. Byrs: Feby, Wm. Drennan, etc.

DRENNAN, CHARLES—BOX 25, PACK 578:
Est. admnr. Nov. 27, 1835 by Wm. T. Drennan, Thos. Dickson, Wm. McCaslan bound to Moses Taggart Ord. Abbeville Dist. sum $5,000.00. Cit. pub. at Hopewell Church. Inv. made Jan. 27, 1836 by Wm. McCaslan, Jno. Bradley, Josiah McGaw. Byrs: Wm. T., Joseph Drennan, etc.

DOBBS, JESSE—BOX 25, PACK 579:
Will dated Nov. 2, 1819 in Abbeville Dist. Proved Nov. 6, 1819. Exr. Wife, Elizabeth. Son, Elipah Dobbs. Other chn. ment. but no names given. Sale, Feb. 6, 1834. Byrs: E. H., Polly, E., Mary, Susan Dobbs.

DAVIS, NANCY—BOX 25, PACK 580:
Est. admnr. Sept. 18, 1823 by Robt., Moses Davis, Wm. H. Caldwell,
Jno. Baskin bound to Moses Taggart Ord. Abbeville Dist. sum $8,000.00. Cit. pub.
at Rocky River Church. Sale, Oct. 15, 1823. Byrs: Robt., Moses, Jane, Eliza,
Sarah, Jas. Davis.

DIXON, STARLING—BOX 26, PACK 581:
Est. admnr. Jan. 12, 1827 by Wm. Pettigrew, Jas. Dixon, Oswell Houston
bound to Moses Taggart Ord. Abbeville Dist. sum $3,000.00. Sale, Feb. 1, 1827.
Byrs: Hannah, Ellis, Mary Ann, Jas. Dixon, etc.

DOWNEY, JOHN—BOX 26, PACK 582:
Will dated May 15, 1826 in Abbeville Dist. Proved Oct. 1, 1827. Exrs:
Jno. Burton, Alexr. C. Hamilton. Wit: Eli S. Davis, Jno. Douglass, Thos.
Spierin. Wife, Sarah.

DAY, MANSFIELD—BOX 26, PACK 583:
Est. admnr. Jan. 5, 1824 by Willis Holms, Thos. Goodman, Joseph
Talbert bound to Moses Taggart Ord. Abbeville Dist. sum $5,000.00. Cit. pub.
at Mount Garrison Meeting House in Cambridge. Byrs. at sale. Jno. R., Leroy
Day, etc.

DOWNEY, RICHARD—BOX 26, PACK 584:
Est. admnr. June 10, 1794 by Martha Downey wid. Jas. Foster Sr. Adam
Hill bound to Judges Abbeville County sum 500 lbs. Cit. read at a public meeting
at David Cannedays on Mountain Creek. Inv. made by Saml. Foster Sr., Capt.
Jas. Chalmers, Enos Crawford, Jno. Devlin.

DOUGLASS, JOHN—BOX 26, PACK 585:
Est. admnr. April 6, 1790 by Sarah Douglass, Jno. Wardlaw, Andrew
McAllister bound to Judges Abbeville County sum 1,000 lbs. Sale, July 5, 1790.
Byrs: Sarah Douglass, Joseph Bowen, Nancy Duncan, etc.

DAVIS, ROBERT—BOX 26, PACK 586:
Est. admnr. Oct. 7, 1801 by Martha, Israel, Robt. Davis, Ezekiel Calhoun
bound to Andrew Hamilton Ord. Abbeville Dist. sum $10,000.00. Byrs. at sale.
Martha, Israel, Rebecca, Milley, Andrew, Wm. Davis, etc.

DAVENPORT, JOHN—BOX 26, PACK 587:
Will dated May 27, 1798 in Abbeville Dist. Rec. Sept. 13, 1798. Exrs:
Brother, Charles Davenport, Jno. Arnold, Geo., Jno. Connor. Wit: Jas. Pettus,
Wm. P., Jno. P. Arnold. Wife, Susannah. Chn: Carles, Richard, Peggy, Patsy
Davenport. "Leave part of a legacy coming from my father's est. in Virginia to
Charles Davenport."

DUGAN, ROBERT—BOX 26, PACK 588:
Books accts. for 1768. Names, Joseph Greer, Saml. Cunningham, Joseph
Kelly, Geo. Ray, Wm. Adair, Jno. Edward, Jacob Anderson, Arthur McCracken,
Wm. Neighbors, Joseph Davis, Patrick Riley, Jno. Gent, Anthony Park, etc.
(No other papers.)

DAVIS, ROBERT—BOX 26, PACK 589:
Est. admnr. Aug. 12, 1811 by Nancy, Wm. Davis, Wm. H. Caldwell, Jno. H. Lesley, Jno. Brannon bound to Taliaferro Livingston Ord. Abbeville Dist. sum $10,000.00. Inv. made Sept. 11, 1811 by Wm. Buford, Saml. Scott, Robt. Harris. Byrs: Nancy, Jane H., Rachel W., Wm. Davis, etc.

DAVIS, ALEXANDER—BOX 26, PACK 590:
Est. admnr. June 5, 1809 by Jas. Foster, Wm. H., Jno. Caldwell Esq. Nathaniel Alston bound to Andrew Hamilton Ord. Abbeville Dist. sum $5,000.00. Est. admnr. again Aug. 5, 1803 by Mary, Wm. Davis, Wm. H., Jas. Caldwell bound to Andrew Hamilton Ord. Abbeville Dist. spm $5,000.00. Expend: Nov. 23, 1805 Paid Davis for schooling Moses, Jas. Davis $7.00. April 9, 1808 Paid Polly Davis $39.88. Paid Wm. Davis $4.00.

DEALL, MARY—BOX 26, PACK 591:
Will dated June 2, 1828 in Abbeville Dist. Proved July 7, 1828. Exrs: Jas., Geo. McLin Morrow. Wit: O., A. L. Houston, Mary Morrow. Chn: David, Elizabeth Deall, Martha Taylor, Jane Shanks, Molly McGaw, Jonathan, Jno. Anderson. Expend: July 22, 1829 Paid Elizabeth Anderson $225.00.

DEAN, JULIUS—BOX 26, PACK 592:
Est. admnr. April 10, 1826 by Jno., Nathan Lipscomb bound to Moses Taggart Ord. Abbeville Dist. sum $2,000.00. Cit. pub. at Smyrna Church. Sale, Mar. 28, 1826. Byrs: Edward Dean, etc.

DICKENSON, JOSEPH B.—BOX 26, PACK 593:
Est. admnr. Mar 1, 1816 by Elizabeth C. Dickenson, Billups Gayle, Jas. Spann bound to Taliaferro Livingston Ord. Abbeville Dist. sum $10,000.00. Elizabeth C. married Jno. Madison White. (One place ment. Elizabeth Heard the admnr.)

DRAKE, BENJAMIN—BOX 26, PACK 594:
Est. admnr. Mar. 28, 1817 by Sarah Drake, Charles Pitts, Joseph Hill, Wm. Young, Edmund Ware bound to Taliaferro Livingston Ord. Abbeville Dist. sum $10,000.00. Byrs: Sarah, Jno. Drake, etc.

DILBONE, HENRY—BOX 26, PACK 595:
Est. admnr. Oct. 1, 1817 by Jno., Joseph, Wm. Hearst bound to Taliaferro Livingston Ord. Abbeville Dist. sum $2,000.00. Byrs: Mary Hanie, Margaret P. Sullivan, Jno. Dilbone, etc.

DAVIS, ZACHARIAH—BOX 26, PACK 596:
Est. admnr. Dec. 31, 1814 by Robt. Davis, Jno., Abraham Hadden, Isaac Cowan bound to Taliaferro Livingston Ord. Abbeville Dist. sum $10,000.00. Cit. pub. at Crib Branch Meeting House. Legs: Jno. Haddan, Jas. McKee, Luke Wright, Wm. Craton, Catharine Davis bought at sale.

DONALD, WEST—BOX 26, PACK 597:
Est. admnr. Dec. 19, 1834 by Jno. A. Donald, Hiram Moore, Robt. D.

Gray bound to Moses Taggart Ord. Abbevile Dist. sum $2,000.00. Cit. pub. at Asbury Chapel. Jno. A. Donald next of kin.

DAVIS, ISRAEL—BOX 26, PACK 598:
Will dated Jan. 26, 1817 in Abbeville Dist. Rec. May 5, 1817. Exrs: Wife, Martha, Alexr Hunter Esq., Wm. H. Caldwell. Wit: Jno. B. Huey, D. H. McClaskey, Wm. Kirkwood. Chn: *Flowing* Warren, Marion Jasper, Israel Pickens Davis. Inv. made May 21, 1817 by Wm. Davis, Robt. Kirkwood, Bruce Livingston. (Martha was also written Marthew Davis.)

DELPH, ROBERT P.—BOX 26, PACK 599:
Est. admnr. Feb. 19, 1838 by Jno. F. Gray, David L. Wardlaw, Thos. C. Perrin bound to Moses Taggart Ord. Abbeville Dist. sum $10,000.00. Cit. pub. at Cokesbury. Est. admnr. again Nov. 6, 1827 by Edmund Ware, Alexr. Hunter, Jas. A. Black bound to Moses Taggart Ord. Abbeville Dist. sum $1,000.00. Sale, Nov. 23, 1827. Byrs: Mary Delph, etc.

DAVIS, WILLIAM, ESQ.—BOX 26, PACK 600:
Est. admnr. Nov. 20, 1824 by Wm. H. Caldwell, Jno. Gray, Saml. L. Watt bound to Moses Taggart Ord. Abbeville Dist. sum $3,000.00. Cit. pub. at Rocky River Church. Inv. made Dec. 6, 1824 by Jno. Cameron, Thos. Jones, Saml. Buchanan. Byrs: Margaret, Martha, Jane, Robt., Moses Davis, Wm. Baker, Christian Barns.

DOZIER, ABRAHAM GILES—BOX 26, PACK 601:
Est. admnr. April 2, 1817 by Lyttleton Myrick, Benjamin F. Whitner, Waller O. Bickley bound to Taliaferro Livingston Ord. Abbeville Dist. sum $20,000.00. Est. admnr. again Mar. 10, 1816 by Rebecca F. Dozier, Jas. Spann, Benjamin F. Whitner bound to Taliaferro Livingston Ord. Abbeville Dist. sum $20,000.00.

DONALD, JOHN—BOX 26, PACK 603:
Est. admnr. June 17, 1831 by Jno. A. Donald, Joel J., Duey Lipford bound to Moses Taggart Ord. Abbeville Dist. sum $6,000.00. Expend: Feb. 4, 1833 Paid Jane Donald $25.00. Byrs: Jno. A., West, Alexr. Donald, etc.

DORRIS, WILLIAM—BOX 26, PACK 604:
Will dated Mar. 24, 1818 in Abbeville Dist. Proved Oct. 6, 1818. Exrs: Wife, no name given. Sons, Wm., Jno. Dorris. Wit: Saml. Perrin, Saml. Caldwell, Hugh Moseley. Chn: Catharine, Margaret, Wm., Jno. Dorris. Stepson, Henry Mark. Gr. chn: Wm. Gable, Mary Ethridge. "Will Catharine a tract of land lying in Edgefield Dist."

DUNCAN, JAMES—BOX 26, PACK 605:
Will dated Oct. 19, 1814. Rec. Nov. 5, 1814. Exrs: David Wardlaw, Alexr. Bowie. Wit: Jas. Kyle, Wm. Hutcheson, Lawrance Brock. Mother, Hannah. Brother, Robt. Berry Duncan. Sis. Pamelia Carr Duncan. Inv. made Dec. 10, 1814 by Jas. Wardlaw, Wm. Anderson, Thos. Jones.

DONALDSON, THOMAS, SR. AND JANET—BOX 27, PACK 606:
Est. admnr. Nov. 3, 1811 by Mary, Wm. Donaldson, Edward, Wm.
McCraw bound to Taliaferro Livingston Ord. Abbeville Dist. sum $2,000.00.
Legatees: Jas., Wm., Thos., Reuben Donaldson, Geo. Spruell, Benjamin Maddox,
Robt. Webb, Thornton Davis, Benjamin Milten.

DOUGLASS, ARCHIBALD—BOX 27, PACK 607:
Est. admnr. April 25, 1815 by Nancy Douglass, Jno. Cochran, Jno.
Donald, Andrew Gray, Jas. Pettus, Wm. Cochran bound to Moses Taggart Ord.
Abbeville Dist. sum $20,000.00. Cit. to acct. on petition of Wm. Cochran a
distributee of est. of Phebe Hearst alias Phebe Cochran. July 8, 1816 Paid Nancy
Douglass $510.00. Jan. 16, 1817 Paid Jno. McGee for schooling and boarding
Jno., David Douglass 1 yr. $96.00. Paid Wm. Butler on Amt. probated due the
est. of Polly Cain decd. $24.44. April 12, 1817 Paid Joseph Foster for boarding
Phebe Douglass to school $27.50.

DALE, ALEXANDER—BOX 27, PACK 608:
Est. admnr. Mar. 21, 1826 by Enos, Andrew Crawford, Andrew Stuart
bound to Moses Taggart Ord. Abbeville Dist. sum $700.00. Paid Elizabeth Dale
$42.18. Sale, April 12, 1826. Byrs: Betsy, Wm. Jr., Wm. Sr., Dale, etc.

DAVISON, JOHN—BOX 27, PACK 609:
Est. admnr. Oct. 22, 1823 by Aaron Lomax, Hugh Morrah, Nathaniel
Cobb bound to Moses Taggart Ord. Abbeville Dist. sum $2,000.00. Byrs: Martha,
Margaret Davison, etc.

DURRET, PLEASANT—BOX 27, PACK 610:
Est. admnr. Dec. 11, 1817 by Mary Durrett, Lewis Mathews, Lecretia
Goode bound to Taliaferro Livingston Ord. Abbeville Dist. sum $10,000.00.
Mar. 15, 1820 Paid Henry Duret on note $88.00. Nov. 16, 1819 Paid the
Cambridge Library Society $13.00. On Feb. 9, 1828 the petition of Swilling
Goode sheweth that Mary Durett married Isaac Bunting and that said Mary is
now dead.

DRINKWATER, CO. SAMUEL—BOX 27, PACK 611:
Est. admnr. April 6, 1824 by Martha B. Drinkwater, Jno. Gray, Wm. H.
Caldwell, Joseph Baker bound to Moses Taggart Ord. Abbeville Dist. sum
$3,000.00.

DAVIS, JOHN—BOX 27, PACK 612:
Est. admnr. Mar. 1, 1826 by Wm. Davis Sr., Edmond Ware bound to
Moses Taggart Ord. Abbeville Dist. sum $700.00. Cit. pub. at Pleasant Grove
Church. Sale, Mar. 18, 1826. Byrs: Wm., Malinda, Jno., Thornton Davis, etc.

DAVIS, ABSALOM—BOX 27, PACK 613:
Est. admnr. Nov. 4, 1811 by Robt., Gibson Wooldridge bound to
Taliaferro Livingston Ord. Abbeville Dist. sum $1,000.00. Inv. made Dec. 26,
1811 by Abraham Livingston, Wm. Yarbrough, Titus Murry.

DAVENPORT, CHARLES ESQ.—BOX 27, PACK 614:

Will dated Jan. 21, 1806. Rec. Feb. 3, 1806. Exrs: Wife, name not given, s. l. Jas. Pollard, Jas. McCracken, Sons, Burket, Jno. Marshal Davenport. Wit: Charles Maxwell, Thos. J. Anderson, Julius Nichols. Chn: Charlotte, Kitty, Burket, Nancy, Jno. Marshall, Polly Thompson Davenport. Father, Richard Davenport. Stepmother, Elizabeth Davenport.

DOWNEY, JOHN—BOX 27, PACK 615:

Inv. made Aug. 4, 1784 by Thos. Weems, Jno. Cochran, Jno. Lockridge. Byrs: Frances Downey. (No other papers.)

DICK, JOHN—BOX 27, PACK 616:

Will dated April 20, 1776 in Granvill County. Probated April 8, 1782. Exrs: Wife, Mary, Son, Joseph Dick. Wit: Ann, Jno,. Alexr. Newman. Chn: Joseph, Wm., Jno., Thos. Dick. Ment. girls but names not given. Inv. made Dec. 10, 1782 by Michael Meyer, Jno. Sturzenegger, Nathaniel Howell.

DURBOROUGH, BENJAMIN—BOX 27, PACK 617:

Est. admnr. July 4, 1782 by Mary Duborow, Frederick Glover, Isaac Crowther bound to Jno. Ewing Calhoun Ord. 96 Dist. sum 2,000 lbs. Inv. made July 17, 1782 by Thos. Wilson, Wm. Robison, Isaac Crowther. (Name written Douborough and Duborow.)

DUNCAN, WILLIAM—BOX 27, PACK 618:

Est. admnr. Aug. 19, 1785 by Keturah, Wm. Duncan, Jacob Pennington bound to Jno. Thomas Jr. Ord. 96 Dist. sum 2.000 lbs. Inv. made by Jno. Williams, Wm. Moore, Wm. Linvill.

DOROUGH, MARMADUKE—BOX 27, PACK 619:

Est. admnr. May 20, 1785 by Simon Pack, Joseph Wofford bound to Jno. Thomas Jr. Ord. Abbeville Dist. sum 2,000 lbs. Inv. made by Wm. Watson, Daniel Megin, Jno. Johnson.

DIXON, JOHN—BOX 27, PACK 620:

Est. admnr. Dec. 1, 1785 by Wm. Dixon, Jas. Seawright, Adam McKee bound to Jno. Thomas Jr. Ord. 96 Dist. sum 1,000 lbs. Inv. made Dec. 16, 1785 by Adam McKee, Jas. Seawright, Patrick Lancy.

DENDY, CHARLES—BOX 27, PACK 621:

Est. admnr. Oct. 5, 1785 by Nancy, Thos. Dendy, Silvanus Walker of Laurens County bound to Jno. Thomas Jr. Ord. 96 Dist. sum 1,000 lbs. Inv. made Oct. 18, 1785 by Jas. Saxon, Thos. Cargill, Jno. Milam.

DUVALL, MICHAEL—BOX 27, PACK 622:

Est. admnr. Jan. 15, 1803 by Elizabeth Devaul, Uel Hill, Edward W. Collier bound to Andrew Hamilton Ord. Abbeville Dist. sum $10,000.00. Sale, Mar. 1, 1803. Byrs: Elizabeth, Saml., Macklin Devaul, etc. (Name written Devall & Devaul.)

DUNLAP, JOHN—BOX 27, PACK 623:
Inv. made July 31, 1783 by Capt. Jas. Mulwee, Robt. McNier, Anthony Griffin. Lived in 96 Dist. Admnr. Margaret Dunlap. (No other papers.)

DAVIS, MARTHA—BOX 27, PACK 624:
Will dated Dec. 26, 1803 in Abbeville Dist. Rec. Feb. 4, 1804. Exr: Son, Robt. Davis. Wit: Prudence Baskin, Anna Harris, Joseph Irving. Chn: Jas., Robt., Saml., Martha, Mildridge, Israel, Margaret, Jean, Rebecca Davis. Ment. wid. of Robt. Davis decd. Sale, Feb. 29, 1804. Byrs: Robt., Martha, Wm., Israel Davis, etc.

DAVIS, JOHN—BOX 27, PACK 625:
Will dated Dec. 30, 1830 in Abbeville Dist. Proved Oct. 6, 1831. Exr: Stephen Jones. Wit: Jno. White, Jno. A., Jas. H. Baskin. Wife, Elizabeth Davis. Chn: Jno. Timothy, Nancy, Polly Davis. Gr. son, Jno. Davis Christopher "give him land in Dooley County, Georgia." "Bequeath to Margaret McCalister."

DENNIS, ROBERT—BOX 27, PACK 626:
Will dated May 8, 1785 in Rediriver Sett. 96 Dist. Proved July 15, 1785. Exrs: David Dunlap, Wm. Norris. Wit: Joseph Dorsett, Jonathan Waller, Jno. Put. Ment. wife and mother but no names given. Inv. made July 2, 1785 by Joseph Dorsett, Thos. Cunningham, Jno. Rogers. Made in Laurens Dist.

DUGAN, ROBERT, SR.—BOX 27, PACK 627:
Est. admnr. Jan. 6, 1787 by Margaret, Thos. Dugan, Jas. McElwayn, Geo. Storey bound to Jno. Thomas Jr. Ord. 96 Dist. sum 2,000 lbs. Inv. made May 2, 1787 by Wm. Murry, Robt. Johnston, Wm. Wilson. Sale, June 25, 1787. Byrs: Margaret, Thos. Dugan, Joseph Green, Anthony Parks, Thos. McCracken.

DODDS, THOMAS—BOX 27, PACK 628:
Will dated Sept. 25, 1771 in Craven County. Proved Aug. 16, 1785. Exr: Wife, Sarah Dodd. Wit: Jno. Nudarman, Jesse Dodd, Jno. Pearson. Ment. chn. but names not given. Inv. made Sept. 8, 1785 by Richard Burgiss, Jno. Martindell, Jno. Wideman.

DINWOODY, WILLIAM—BOX 27, PACK 629:
Est. admnr. 1800 by Jas. McCollough, Jas. Frazer bound to Andrew Hamilton Ord. Abbeville Dist. sum $1,000.00. Cit. pub. at Upper Long Cane Church. Inv. made by Wm. Gray, Jno. McCarter, Abel Jackson, Jas. Bonner.

DALE, JAMES—BOX 27, PACK 630:
Est. admnr. Mar. 3, 1817 by Elizabeth Dale, Peter Tutton, Andrew Crawford bound to Taliaferro Livingston Ord. Abbeville Dist. sum $5,000.00. Inv. made Mar. 13, 1817 by Andrew, Enos, Robt. Crawford, Sr.

DENHAM, ROBERT—BOX 27, PACK 631:
Est. admnr. Oct. 5, 1802 by Mary Denham, Jas. S. Baskin, Jas. Caldwell, David Gillespie bound to Andrew Hamilton Ord. Abbeville Dist. sum $3,000.00. Inv. made Nov. 10, 1802 by Anthony Elton, Wm. Bole, Dudley Cook.

DICKSON, MARY ANN—BOX 27, PACK 632:
Est. admnr. Nov. 26, 1827 by Jas. N. Dixon, Jno. Dale, Jno. McFarland,
Wm. Pettigrew bound to Moses Taggart Ord. Abbeville Dist. sum $2,000.00.
Cit. pub. at Lebanon Church. Paid Hannah Dixon $133.81½. Paid Jno. Mc-
Farland, gdn. for 2 minors, $267.63½. Inv. made Dec. 4, 1827 by Jno. Cheves,
Geo. Roberts, Robt. Pettigrew.

DRENNAN, ROBT—BOX 27, PACK 633:
Est. admnr. Jan. 12, 1822 by Charles, Wm. T. Drennan, Jas. Thompson,
Thos. Gray bound to Moses Taggart Ord. Abbeville Dist. sum $10,000.00. Cit.
pub. at Smyrna Church. Inv. made Mar. 8, 1822 by Jas. Devlin, Jno. Hearst,
Sr., Hugh McCormick, Wm. Drennan.

DONALDSON, MATTHEW—BOX 27, PACK 634:
Will dated Nov. 13, 1802 in Abbeville Dist. Rec. 11, 1802. Exrs: Jno.
Sr., Geor., Andrew Bowie, Jas. Wardlaw. Wit: Jno. Logan, Jno., Nancy Bracken-
ridge. Wife, Jennet. Niece, Jean wife of Robt. Campbell. Nephews: Andrew,
Matthew Cowan all now living in the Kingdom of Ireland. Inv. made Dec. 23,
1802 by Ezekiel Evans, Robt. C. Gordon, Jas. Gilmer.

DRENNAN, NATHAN—BOX 28, PACK 635:
Est. admnr. Aug. 20, 1830 by Robt., Wm. Drennan, Jno. Devlin bound
to Moses Taggart Ord. Abbeville Dist. sum $500.00. Inv. made Sept. 7, 1830
by Jas. Devlin, Archibald Little, Jonathan Jordon. May 15, 1832 Paid Wm.
Drennan $39.15. June 9 Paid Mary Hunter $59.00.

DALE, JOHN, JR.—BOX 28, PACK 636:
Est. admnr. Feb. 13, 1826 by Polly Dale, Enos, Andrew Crawford Sr.,
Jno. B. Foster bound to Moses Taggart Ord. Abbeville Dist. sum $1,000.00.
Cit. pub. at Hopewell Church. Sale, Mar. 3, 1826. Byrs: Elizabeth, Jno. N.
Polly Deal, Joseph Williams, etc.

DAVIS, JOSEPH ESQ.—BOX 28, PACK 637:
Est. admnr. May 23, 1840 by Ephraim, Nathaniel J. Davis, Jas. S. Wilson,
Charles Dendy, Jas. A. Davis bound to Moses Taggart Ord. Abbeville Dist. sum
$50,000.00. (Letter.)
Missippi, Monroe County Nov. 5th, 1842
Mr. John C. Red
Sir it is with pleasure that I take my pen in hand to submit ad lines
for your permissal in the first place to let you know that we are all in good
health at this present time hoping these few lines may find you & your family
enjoying the same blessing I have nothing of importance to write now as I just
started you a letter last week but one thing I expect to send the power of attorney
to you by Mr. Spence empowering you to collect all my dews there & pay
my debts conserning my fathers effects & give brother Jefferson a receipt for
what you receive & no more provided the legatees allow me wages for my
labor in the year 1840 if they do you can give brother Jefferson a cleare receipt
& not without I expect to come out there next fall if I can to see you all once

more Mr. Red I want you to buy me a little two horse waggon for Mr. Spence to bring my negroes to this Contry sister Elizabeth ows me $80.00 which she will give Robert Brady to pay to you and you can pay cash for the waggon if you have nought bought it yet brother Jefferson wrote to me that he had swaped my mare off for a mule if he still has it I want it put in the waggon if it is an owld mule I would be glad that you or Jefferson would swap it off for a young mule I would rather have a mule as a horse here in this Contry doctor I dont wat you not to be backward in tranacting my business for I assure you whatever you do will satisfy me but to proceeds I want you to pay yourself for the trouble you have for me & that will satisfy me write me a letter back as soon as you can all about the settlement of my fathers estate and all other matters who is married and who they are married to has been a good my marriage here this year but that is no new to you for you know that I was agoing to get married and that would be news I have seen a great many puerty girls in this contry I have become acquained with a good many and like them first site and dont know now but what I shall do some tall courting this winter I have become almost tired of a single life and have forgotten the Abbeville girls most entirely I have thought that I would start every week for the last six weeks past but have not had time yet you need not be surprised if I should bring Mrs. Davis to see you next fall if I should be fortunate I shall be *subserving* my self

Yours truly

John C. Red   Jas A. Davis

Mississippi, Nov. 1842, Monroe County

Dear Brother and Sister I will write you a few lines to let you no that we are in good health at this time hoping these few lines may find you all enjoying the same Blessing though I myself have lately recovered out of a hard spell I had a severe (word not plain) of Conjestive fever I was ill few days it was hardly expected that I would recover but it has pleased God through his kind mercy to restore me back to my little family again and what a great blessing that is there has been a right smart sickness in our family this year though all and very light except budy and myself Jerry had the third day chills for about four weeks so on as we give him medicine they quit him I received your letter the 13 of July which I was glad to see and its contents was a great satisfaction to me although I have neglected writing until the present I have intended all year to write you what I now intend to write and I thought it best we wait until I knew what to write Dear Brother I shall hace to trouble you to do some business for me I will send you the power of attorney by Cousin William Gray to appear for me at the settlement of my fathers estate to draw the money that is due me there I want you to draw it as my own money not as belonging to our estate here atall I expect to apply it to the use of the estate as soon as I can get it but I cant pay the unnessary expense for administering on it if any thing is charged I have too many poor little children who is depending on me for to pay any thing for that which was not necessary and if there is any expense for administering brother (word worn) as regards the demand that is out there I want you to settle all the just debts is I heard something about a horse that was not right but you are there and you no haw things are and you can act the way you think best and that will satisfy me I thought it first I would pay anything that would come against me as long as the money would hold but I have been well tried in that matter there has come the most against us that was unjust to my certain knowledge Dear Brother I want you to send me about 30 dollars of silver or gold to pay our taxes as that is all the sort of money they will take our taxes ever so high and I ant you to pay Doctor John C Red *30 to 80* dollars for Brother James for money we got from him here you wrote to me conscrning my poor husband's grave that you thought a tomb stone could be got for about 15 dollars and if you will put your self to the trouble to get it and place it there I will be a thousand times thankful to you I am very glad you thought of it so if any of his children should go there they could no where he was buried you can reserve as much as will get and when you are done with all the trouble of my business I want you to satisfy yourself for all your trouble for it will be right smart and what ever you do I assure you that I will be satisfied Mr. Robert Spence is agoing out to your contry and he has promised to bring the money you can pay it over to him when you settle all I always intended for you to settle with mother out there when ever I had the chance of drawing the money and I wrote to you to that effect but Alfred Roberts received a letter a few days from that he must recieved it here (word) we can pay it here as well as there only I was afraid she thought I would not pay her there but I never intended for her to lose one thing for she has been a kind mother to me and every just debt shall be paid if it takes every cent but I no we were unjust to pay as regards our affairs here I will state to you as near as I can our crop is burning all very well have gathered 35 thousand pounds of cotton and brothei thinks there is fully 15 thousand pounds to gather and they will make right smart by the gin we have gathered six hundred bushels of corn and there is between three and four hundred to gather as respect other matter the Judge of probate court appointed commissioners to value the third part our land they allowed us the north west quater and included all the buildings but we believe the ginhouse and screw is not on that quarter and the east half and south west quater will be sold on the day of sale which will come on the 27 of December they will be a great sacrifice I expect it is uncertain what I can get it will be altogether owing to the way the property sells whether I can save much or not I should like to have some more of the land as the quater that is left to is one half it cleared and the balance lies so that we cant get more than three little fields to clear on it and I would be glad to save as mush of the personal property it was wish of my poor husband but I want enough to go so what little is left there will be no danger of my being distressed about it far I have enough to distress me with out that I want to be on a sure footing so if cant add nothing to it I am in hopes they will be nothing taken from it Caroline had a fine boy on the 16 of last month dear sister as respect my little children there are tolerable hearty at this time except one of my babys that was weaned when I sick it was only nine and a half old it is better at this time but has been a great deal of trouble it was a very (word) hearty before that little George is the fleshed child now Joseph send howdy to his little Cousins and tell his uncle Robert he is mighty plased with his present give my best respects to mother and I will write her belong Jack is here wished me to give his respect to his mistress and tell her he was well and was a doing first rate he wished her to no would make 20 bags of cotton this year and he wishes to no haw she come on there give my best respect to all of children and except the same your selves may that all wise and great being guide and direct us all through lifes end ways is the sincere desires of yours

To Robert and Sarah Brady   Elizabeth Roberts

Christiana Davis refused to act as admnr. on her husband's est. On Nov. 23, 1842 John C. Red recd. $802.48 from estate in right of his wife Frances C. Davis a Dtr. of Joseph Davis decd. Settlement made Nov. 22, 1842. Present, N. J. Davis, Dr. John C. Red, husband of Frances Davis, Adam Wideman, husband of Caroline A. Davis, Christiana Davis, widow, Damuel L. Hill, guardian of Lewis Davis, Addison Davis, Benjamin Davis, minors. Absent, James Davis, Elizabeth Roberts, widow of George Roberts. Antoinette Davis is dead. N. J. Davis, James Davis, Elizabeth Roberts, Frances Red, Caroline Wideman were children of the first marriage. Antoinette, Addison, Lewis and Benjamin Davis were children of the second marriage and of the widow Christiana Davis. Joseph Davis died April 8, 1840.

DANIEL, CHESLEY, ESQ.—BOX 28, PACK 638:
Est. admnr. Nov. 20, 1828 by Thos. W. Williams, Wm. Tennent, Geo. McDuffie bound to Moses Taggart Ord. Abbeville Dist. sum $20,000.00. Cit. pub. at Glovers Chapel. Heirs were: Robt. Giles and wife Martha, Daniel, Thos. D. Turpin and wife Ann, Thos. Evans and wife Jane B. Evans. Dec. 10, 1831 Paid John G. Daniel $144.50.

DELPH, POLLY—BOX 28, PACK 639:
Est. admnr. April 16, 1829 by Gen. Edmund Ware, Donald Douglass, Wm. Graham bound to Moses Taggart Ord. Abbeville Dist. sum $2,000.00.

DELLISHAW, JAMES—BOX 28, PACK 640:
Will dated Sept. 6, 1820 in Abbeville Dist. Proved Oct. 21, 1820. Exr: Son, Jacob Dellishaw. Wit: Dale Palmer, Daniel Chambers, Charles Britt. Wife, Nancy. Chn: Peter, Jacob Dellishaw, Sarah Breazeal, Elizabeth Mann. Gr. Son, Joseph. Inv. made Oct. 28, 1820 by Charles Britt, Peter Dellishaw, Daniel Chambers. Byrs: Elizabeth Graham, etc.

DEAL, JOHN—BOX 28, PACK 641:
Inv. made July 22, 1791 by Isaac Matthews, Patrick Norris, Robt. Messer. Admnrs. Rebecca, Wm. Deal, Jr. (No other papers.)

DALE, MINORS—BOX 28, PACK 642:
On Aug. 27, 1830 Wm. Dale, Saml. Jordon, Robt. A. Crawford bound to Moses Taggart Ord. Abbeville Dist. sum $1,000.00. Wm. Dale made gdn. of Jno. A. Donald from the est. of Jno. Donald decd. $68.00. Paid Mary Dale $1.75.

DONALD, MINORS—BOX 28, PACK 643:
On Nov. 17, 1831 Thos. Lyon, Abraham Thompson, Saml. Jordon

bound to Moses Taggart Ord. Abbeville Dist. sum $1,000.00. Thos. Lyon made gdn. Laura Ann, Mary Lyon minors under 14 yrs. Expend: Feb. 4, 1833 Recd. of Jno. A. Donald from the est. of Jno. Donald decd. 68.00. Paid Mary Stiefel $6.00. Paid board for Mandy $13.00. Polly's board $12.00. Patsy recd. $279.67. Martha Donald $10.00.

DRINKARD, MARION F.—BOX 28, PACK 644:
Est. admnr. May 22, 1843 by Thos. C. Botts, W. B., J. B. Martin bound to David Lesly Ord. Abbeville Dist. sum $400.00. He died having no parents, brothers or sisters. Thos. C. Botts sheweth that his wife is an aunt of said decd. and that he died at his house.

DEALE, JAMES—BOX 28, PACK 645:
Will dated June 13, 1836 in Abbeville Dist. Proved Aug. 1, 1836. Exr: b. l. Jas. Cason. Wit: Geo. Roberts, Thos. P. Dowton, Jas. C. Willard. Sis. Mary Cason. Nephew, Jas. son of Mary and Jas. Cason. Inv. made Sept. 2, 1836 by Geo. Roberts, Saml. Zimmerman, Oliver McCaslan.

DODSON, WESLEY—BOX 28, PACK 646:
Est. admnr. Jan. 4, 1836 by Peter Cheatham, Jas. Gillam, Simeon Chaney bound to Moses Taggart Ord. Abbeville Dist. sum $300.00. Cit. pub. at Siloam Church. Mar. 6, 1837 Paid Elizabeth Dodson $10.00. Recd. of Jas. Dodson note $13.90. Inv. made Jan. 19, 1836 by Isaac Bunting, Jas. Gillam, Simeon Chaney.

DAY, LUKE—BOX 28, PACK 647:
Est. admnr. Mar. 14, 1836 by Isaac Sample, Wm. Eddins, Jno. Weatherall bound to Moses Taggart Ord. Abbeville Dist. sum $2,000.00. Cit. pub. at Rocky Creek Church. Dec. 28, 1836 Paid Fedrick Ward legatee $70.00. Jan. 1, 1837 Paid Jno. Day leg. $80.33. Philip Day leg. $9.37½. Inv. made April 9, 1836 by Jno. N. Sample, Nathan, Jno. Calhoun.

DAVIS, WILLIAM—BOX 28, PACK 648:
Est. admnr. Sept. 13, 1782 by Jas. Christopher, Michael Harvey, Allen Hinton bound to Jno. Ewing Calhoun Ord. 96 Dist. sum 14,000 lbs. Cit. ment. Jas. Christopher was of Cherokee Ponds. Inv. made Mar. 20, 1783 by Wm. Covington, Allen Hinton, Jno. Currie.

DYSON, JAMES—BOX 28, PACK 649:
Will dated Mar. 7, 1784 in 96 Dist. Proved June 5, 1784. Exrs: Wife, Margaret, Son, Daniel Dyson, Wm. Anderson. Wit: Jas., Hannah Hollingsworth, Amey Wallace. Chn: Jas., Jno., Abraham, Isaac, Daniel Dyson. "Owned land on Saludy River and Goose Pond Creek." Inv. made June 12, 1784 by Thos. Anderson, Jno. Wallace, Jas. Long.

DONAHOE, THOMAS—BOX 28, PACK 650:
Est. admnr. Feb. 7, 1784 by Jno. Leath, Nathaniel Bacon, Simeon Cushman bound to Jno. Thomas, Jr. Ord. 96 Dist. sum $2,000.00. Inv. made by Jno. Savage, Jas. Richards, Jno. de Yampert. (Name also written Donohugh.)

DAVIS, GEORGE—BOX 28, PACK 651:
Est. admnr. Feb. 21, 1784 by Jno. Houston, Joseph, Benjamin Adair bound to Jno. Thomas, Jr. Ord. 96 Dist. sum 2,000 lbs. Elizabeth Houston was wife of admnr. Inv. made Mar. 10, 1784 by Thos. Ewing, Joseph, Benjamin Adair.

DRUMMOND, BENJAMIN—BOX 28, PACK 652:
Will dated Oct. 18, 1803 in Abbeville Dist. Rec. Nov. 11, 1803. Exrs: Leonard, Wm. Waller. Wit: Nathan Lipscomb, Benjamin Waller, Robt. Marsh. Wife, Anna. Chn: Nathaniel, Norman, Jenny, Moses Drummond, Betsy Godfrey, Carlile Ball. Gr. dtr. Anna dtr. of decd. son Benjamin Drummond. Sarah, relect of Ben Drummond. "Give Betsy Godfrey 100 acres in Laurens Dist." Inv. made Nov. 30, 1803 by Wm. Ansley, T. Keelen Smith, Jno. Scogin.

DAWKINS, THOMAS, SR.—BOX 28, PACK 653:
Inv. made July 16, 1783 by Wm. Hutcheson, Thos. Harbert. Byrs: Jno., Elizabeth, Wm. Jr., Thos. Dawkins, Jr. One paper stated that Elizabeth Dawkins was admnr. and there were 8 chn. (No other papers.)

DARRACOTT, GARLAND M.—BOX 28, PACK 654:
Will dated Nov. 1, 1821 in Wilkes County, Georgia. Proved June 16, 1829. Exrs: Thos. Jones of Elbert Co. Georgia, Jas. Wingfield, Thos. Terrell of Wilkes Co. Georgia, Herbert Darracott of S. C. Wit: Jas. Wingfield, Thos. Terrell, Edward Ballard. Wife, Mary Ann. Chn: Francis, Rebecca Darracott. Expend: June 30, 1836 Recd. of Jno. D. Thompson for a lot of land in Washington, Georgia.

DRINKARD, JOHN—BOX 28, PACK 655:
Est. admnr. May 4, 1818 by Lucy Drinkard, Robt. Russell, Christopher Brooks bound to Taliaferro Livingston Ord. Abbeville Dist. sum $1,000.00. Sale, June 4, 1818. Byrs: Francis, Lucy, Jno. Drinkard, Elizabeth Campbell.

DELLECHAUX, JACOB—BOX 28, PACK 656:
Will dated Mar. 17, 1790 in Hillsborough Township, Abbeville Dist. Proved July 6, 1790. Exr: Wife, Elizabeth. Wit: Peter Engevin, Jacob Langel, Peter Gibert. Was a Blacksmith. Chn: Jas., Peter, Susanna, Sara, Elizabeth, Jacob Dellechaux. Stepson, Charles Britt. Inv. made Aug. 2, 1790 by Uel Hill, Daniel Ramsey, Adam Wideman.

DAVIS, MOSES—BOX 28, PACK 657:
Will dated Sept. 6, 1804 in Abbeville Dist. Rec. Dec. 5, 1804. Exrs: Wife, no name given, Wm., Robt. Davis, Wm. Caldwell. Wit: Wm. Lesly, Israel Davis, Sarah Noble. Chn: Wm., Alexr. decd., Robt., Jane Davis. Ment. 3 sons of Alexr. decd. no names given. s. ls. Wm. Caldwell, Thos. Harris. Gr. son, Moses Davis Harris. Inv. made Dec. 20, 1804 by Charles Johnson, Jacob Irving, Saml. Harris.

DUNN, JAMES—BOX 28, PACK 658:
Will dated Feb. 8, 1799 in Abbeville Dist. Rec. Jan. 12, 1805. Exrs:

Wife, Agness, Son, Saml. Dunn. Wit: Robt., Hannah McCann, Jno., Wm. Robertson. Chn: Margaret, Thos., Saml., Wm., Robt. Dunn, Mary Drake, Jinny Lyon, Elizabeth Richey, Sarah Martin. Inv. made Jan. 22, 1805 by Jno. Robertson, Michael Magee, Jno. Richey.

DUNN, JAMES, MINORS—BOX 30, PACK 660:
Jas. Dunn died 1835. Chn: Ally Ann, Jane, Margaret, Elizabeth Dunn were minors in 1842. His wid. Caroline later married Jas. L. Anderson. Jane married Wm. A. Richey. Margaret married B. F. Smith. Elizabeth Jane married J. R. Swansey. Alley Ann married Jno. Nickles. Wm. Dunn, Sr. was the gdn.

DOWTON, KETURAH—BOX 30, PACK 661:
Est. admnr. Jan. 1, 1845 by Thos. P. Dowton, Oliver. Alexi. McCaslan bound to David Lesly Ord. Abbeville Dist. sum $2,000.00. Father, Thos. P. Dowton. Caturah left a father, brothers and sisters of the whole as well of the half blood. Thos. Dowton was gdn. Jno., Drusilla Dowton and Elihu Spruill who maried Mary Ann. Keturah was an infant. (Name written Keturah and Caturah.)

DUNN, ROBERT—BOX 30, PACK 662:
Will dated Oct. 28, 1844 in Abbeville Dist. Proved Nov. 16, 1844. Exrs: Sons, Andrew, Wm. Dunn. Wit: Jno. Miller, Jas. Webb, E. W. Seawright. Wife, Jane Dunn. Chn: Andrew, Wm., Jno., Elizabeth Dunn, Phebey Hodges, Polley Richey. Expend: Nov. 2, 1846 Polley and H. T. Richey recd. $326.27. Dec. 21, 1846 B. F. Moseley recd. his legacy of $163.13.

DRENNAN, WILLIAM—BOX 30, PACK 663:
Est. admnr. Jan. 13, 1845 by Robt. Drennan, Jas. J., Robt. Devlin bound to David Lesly Ord. Abbeville Dist. sum $6,000.00. Wm. Drennan left no wid. but 4 living chn. and a decd. sister's 2 chn. Power of Atty. "Know that I Mary Robinson of Wilcox County, Alabama on the 1st May 1845 appointed Wm. H. Drennan of Holmes Co. Miss. my Atty. to receive my share of my father Wm. Drennan's est." Mary Robison was wid. of B. Robinson. Sett. made May 26, 1845. Present, Robt. Drennan admnr. Wm. H. Drennan from Holmes Co., Miss. for self and holds Power of Atty. from his sister Mary Robinson du. of Wm. Drennan decd., Jas. Drennan. Eliza Jane married Marcus Upson who died before intestate having 2 chn., Jno. D. and Rachel E. J. Upson. Wm. Drennan died Dec. 1844.

DONALD, JNO. A.—BOX 30, PACK 664:
Est. admnr. Dec. 20, 1844 by A. R. Ramey, Jno. W. Ramey bound to David Lesly Ord. Abbeville Dist. sum $1,000.00. Left a wid. Mary and 2 chn. Inv. made Jan. 8, 1845 by Thos. McDill, David M. Wardlaw, Wm. Riley.

DUNCAN, MINORS—BOX 30, PACK 665:
On Sept. 25, 1844, Elizabeth, Wm. Duncan, Wm. Loaner bound to David Lesly Ord. Abbeville Dist. sum $600.00. Elizabeth Duncan made gdn. of Jno. R., Polly C., Wm. P., Margaret E. Duncan, minors. Elizabeth Duncan was the mother, and wid. of Geo. A. Duncan decd. Jno. W., Mary E. Brough, Polly and Jno. R. Duncan agreed to the sett.

DUNN, JOHN—BOX 30, PACK 666:
Will dated Sept. 1, 1841 in Abbeville Dist. Proved Sept. 11, 1841. Exr:
Jno. Wier. Wit: Wm. Dunn, Joseph Lyon, Thos. Thomson. Wife, Jane C.
Dunn. Nieces, Ally Ann, Jane, Margaret, Elizabeth J. Dunn chn. of my brother
Jas. Dunn. Inv. made Sept. 29, 1841 by Joseph Eakin, Robt. Richey, Sr., Joseph
Lyon.

DOUGLASS, WILLIAM—BOX 30, PACK 667:
Admnr. Leonard J. White. Expend: Feb. 1, 1843 Paid Jas. Anderson
distributee share $378.66. Jas. Peart his share $411.00. Jas. Douglass his share
$397.36. Jno. Douglass share $231.71. Wm. A. Douglass share $413.68. Jas. L.
Mayson his share $400.00. Jas. Waites his share $400.00. Mrs. Mary Douglass
her share $659.59. Mrs. Nancy Douglass her share $400.00.

DALE, JOHN—BOX 30, PACK 668:
Will dated Jan. 13, 1840 in Abbeville Dist. Proved Nov. 18, 1840. Exr:
Nathaniel Moore. Wit: Jas. Gray, Jno. S. Reid, Robt. Brady. Chn: Jno. S.,
Sarah, Nancy Dale, Betsy Ann Pettigrew. Sett. made Feb. 15, 1842. Present,
Jno. Dale, Jr., Robt. Pettigrew in right of wife Betsy Ann, Robt. Wilson in right
of wife Nancy Dale. H. Wilson married Sarah Dale.

DUNLAP, MINORS—BOX 30, PACK 669:
On Jan. 3, 1839 Jas. S., Daniel F. Lucius, Berry Clinkscales of Anderson
Dist. bound to Moses Taggart Ord. Abbeville Dist. sum $10,000.00. Jas. S.
Lucius made gdn. Jno., Sarah, Emily, Wm. Dunlap, minors under 21 yrs, chn.
of Bryce, Elizabeth Dunlap decd. Wm. F. Dunlap recd. $792.59 from said est.
and of Jno. Bigbee decd.

DAVIDSON, ANDREW—BOX 30, PACK 670:
Est. admnr. Feb. 5, 1844 by J. F. Marshall, Benjamin Y. Martin, Joseph
W. Marshall bound to David Lesly Ord. Abbeville Dist. sum $400.00. He had
no wid. or chn. Inv. made May 3, 1844 by Aaron, Jno. W., Jas. Lomax, Wm.
Butler.

DOBBS, ELIZABETH—BOX 30, PACK 671:
Est. admnr. Feb. 10, 1844 by Jas. C. Willard, Wm. Harris bound to
David Lesly Ord. Abbeville Dist. sum $800.00. Died leaving no husband but
chn. Inv. made Feb. 27, 1844 by Saml. Cowan, Saml. Wideman, Sherod
Barksdale.

DUNCAN, GEORGE A.—BOX 30, PACK 672:
Est. admnr. Feb. 2, 1843 by Wm. Duncan, Lemuel W. Tribble, Wm.
Clinkscales bound to David Lesly Ord. Abbeville Dist. sum $200.00. Sale, Feb.
17, 1843. Byrs: Elizabeth, Wm. Duncan, Jacob, Wm. Loner, etc. Elizabeth
Duncan was the wid. Wm. was a brother to Geo. Duncan.

DAVIS, MARTHA—BOX 30, PACK 673:
Est. admnr. Feb. 14, 1843 by Nathaniel McCants, Jno. Fooshe, Robt.
E. Buchanan bound to David Lesly Ord. Abbeville Dist. sum $4,000.00. She

died in 1842. Sett. made Feb. 19, 1845 by Nathaniel McCants, admnr. and distributee in right of his wife Eliza Davis, Robt. E. Buchanan in right of wife Elizabeth.

EVANS, WILLIAM, SR.—BOX 30, PACK 674:
Will dated June 17, 1836 in Abbeville Dist. Proved Feb. 11, 1839. Exr: s. l. Blumer White. Wit: Joseph C. Lindsay, Sarah Wideman, A. Perrin. Chn: Wm., Peter, Henry Evans, Polly, Elizabeth, Martha White. Est. also admnr. Feb. 11, 1839 by Jno. Lyon, Leonard Wideman, Frederick Cook bound to Moses Taggart Ord. Abbeville Dist. sum $20,000.00. Cit. pub. at Tranquil Church. 1841 Paid Stephen White legatee $292.54.

ELDER, JAMES—BOX 31, PACK 675:
Est. admnr. Oct. 8, 1785 by Robt., Sarah Sterling, Jas. McElwain, David Brown bound to Jno. Thomas Jr. Ord. 96 Dist. sum 500 lbs. Inv. made by Isaac Patton, Wm. Smith, Wm. Elder.

ELLIS, JAMES G.—BOX 31, PACK 676:
Est. admnr. Oct. 6, 1817 by Jas. Brownlee, Robt. Ellis, Jno. Lindsay, Jno. McKee bound to Taliaferro Livingston Ord. Abbeville Dist. sum $5,000.00. Expend: April 6, 1831 Recd. interest from Robt. N. Ellis. From J. E. Ellis $4.76. July 1 From Robt. Ellis, Jr. $13.00. Jan. 7, 1823 From Jno. L. Ellis $13.50.

EDWARDS, JAMES CUMTON—BOX 31, PACK 677:
Will dated July 31, 1772. Proved Nov. 12, 1792. Exr: Brother, Thos. Edwards. Wit: Matthew Edwards, Jno. Brannan. Ment. wife and chn. but no names given. The est. of Jas. Edwards decd. in acct. with Jno. Oliver, Exr., by virtue of his intermarriage with Betsy Edwards, Extrx. of said decd. Paid Benjamin Glover for tuition of Augustine, Jas. Edwards, chn. of said decd.

EVANS, DUNWIDDIE—BOX 31, PACK 678:
Est. admnr. Dec. 1831 by Washington Belcher, Jas. C. Willard bound to Moses Taggart Ord. Abbeville Dist. sum $2,000.00. Power of Atty. Jas. E. Cook and wife Matilda of Monroe County, Miss. appointed Allen S. Evans of Abbeville Dist. S. C. their Atty. to receive their part of said est. who was the father of Matilda Cook. Dated this Jan. 30, 1847. Expend: May 4, 1833 Recd. of Col. Key admnr. of C. Evans decd. $744.46. Recd. of the Ord. of Edgefield Dist. $14.31½. Oct. 21, 1845 Recd. of W. W. Belcher, Exr. of his father W. Belcher decd., who was the admnr. of Dunwiddie Evans decd. and as gdn. of 4 minor chn. of said decd. $42.09 in full of the share of Laura Ann Evans supposed to be dead from her long absence of 15 yrs. and not heard from in that time. Simpson Evans. Was also a sis. to Matilda Cook. Wid. was Eliza Evans.

ENGLISH, ANDREW—BOX 31, PACK 679:
Will dated April 3, 1805. Rec. May 4, 1805. Exrs: Wife, Jean, Sons, Jno., Jas. B. English. Wit: Abraham Livingston, Charles, Jno. Spence. Chn: Jno., Jas. B., Jean, Mary D., Hannah English. s. ls. Daniel Gillespie, Francis Kennedy. Inv. made June 29, 1805 by Hugh Calhoun, Gilbert Mann, Charles Spence.

EVANS, EZEKIEL, SR.—BOX 31, PACK 680:
Will dated Jan. 29, 1803. Rec. Dec. 31, 1806. Exr: Son, Jas. Evans. Wit: Andrew Bowie. s. ls. Abraham Howard, Nathaniel Thacker. Nephew, Ezekiel, son of Jas. Evans. Inv. made Jan. 8, 1807 by Ezekiel Evans, Isaac Thacker, Robt. C. Gordon.

ELLIS, JAMES—BOX 31, PACK 681:
Est. admnr. Sept. 12, 1791 by Elizabeth Ellis wid., Robt. Ellis, Wm. Ross, Jno. Lindsay bound to Judges of Abbeville County sum 500 lbs. Cit. pub. at Long Cane Church. Inv. made Oct. 25, 1791 by Wm. Ross, Saml. Lindsay, Jno. Murphey.

EDDIS, THEOPHILAS—BOX 31, PACK 682:
Will dated Mar. 12, 1784 in 96 Dist. Proved April 27, 1784. Exrs: Wife, no name given, Brother, Benjamin Eddins. Wit: Wm. Eddins, Jno. McGehee, Charles Cooper. Chn: Jas., Wm., Patsy, Becky, Benjamin, Joel, Parky, Polly, Betsey Eddins. "Wife now pregnant with child." Inv. made June 12, 1784 by Thos., Jas. Wilson, Wm. Beal.

EAGAN, LAURENCE—BOX 31, PACK 683:
Est. admnr. Mar. 7, 1803 by Archibald Douglass, Jno. Gray, Jas. Arnold bound to Andrew Hamilton Ord. Abbeville Dist. sum $2,000.00. Inv. made May 31, 1803 by Jas. Lomax, Jas. Perry, Abraham Overbey. Sale made at the home of Archibald Douglass. Byrs: Archibald Douglass, Jno. Gray, Abraham Overbey, Alexr. Gray.

EWART, ANDREW—BOX 31, PACK 684:
Will dated April 2, 1795. Rec. Sept. 13, 1799. No Exrs. No. Wit: b. l. Adam Stewart. Nephew, Jas. Stewart. Uncle, Jas. Milligan. Aunt, Mary McBride. Cousins: Andrew McBride, Andrew, Hugh, Rachel, Mary Milligan. Nieces: Ann, Mary Stewart. Sis. Mary Stewart. (He was a school master.) Inv. made Oct. 30, 1799 by Andrew, Reuben Wood, Jas. Foster, Sr. (Poem found in pack:)

> Tis (word) of a sluggard I heard him complain
> You have waked me to soon, I must slumber again,
> As the door on its hinges, so he on his bed,
> Turns his sides and his shoulders and his hearry head.
> A little more sleep and a little more slumber,
> Thus he wastes half his days and his hours without number,
> And when he gets up he sits folding his hands,
> Or walks about sauntering or trifling he stands,
> I passed by his garden and saw the wild brier,
> The thorn and the thistle grow broader and higher,
> The cloathes that hang on him are turning to rags,
> And his money still wastes till he starves or he beggs
> I made him a visit still hoping to find,
> He had took better care for improving his mind,
> He told me his dreams, talked of eating and drinking,

But he scarce reads his bible and never loves thinking,
Said I then to my heart heres a lesson for me,
That many but a picture of what I might be,
But thanks to my friends for their care in my breeding,
Who taught me betimes to love working and reading.
(Note. On the front of pack. some one had written that the Stewarts had moved
to Tenn.)

EYMERIE, JOHN—BOX 31, PACK 685:
Will dated Feb. 10, 1781 in Hillsborough Township, 96 Dist. Rec.
Sept. 13, 1798. Exrs: Peter Moragne, Francis Gros of Charleston, formerly
Tavern Keeper. Wit: Pierre Guearineau, Jno. Bert, Jas. Cowan. Wife, Angelicica
Elizabeth Boar, dtr. of Adam Boar of Hardlabor. Sis. Henrie Eymerie, wife of
Peter der Chany. Brother, Jno. Eymerie.

ELGIN, ANN—BOX 31, PACK 686:
Will dated July 25, 1791 in Abbeville Dist. Rec. Nov. 11, 1794. No
Exr. Wit: Mary, Adam Crain, Sr. Adam Crain Jones, Jr. Chn: Ann, Catharina,
Elizabeth Elgin. Inv. made April 14, 1795 by Capt. Reuben, Abner Nash,
Benjamin Mattison. The chn. appointed Robt. Elgin to admnr. on est.

EALES, JOHN—BOX 31, PACK 687:
Est. admnr. Sept. 16, 1825 by Joseph, Jas. Conn, Jas. Weems bound to
Moses Taggart Ord. Abbeville Dist. sum $2,000.00. Cit. pub. at Smyrna Church.
Joseph Conn acct. against said est. To boarding for Jno. Eales from fall 1819
until his death which took place in April 1825 $266.66. Inv. made Oct. 6, 1825
by Jas. Conn, Robt. C. Wilson.

EDWARDS, ANDREW—BOX 31, PACK 688:
Will dated April 3, 1791 in Abbeville Dist. Proved June 13, 1791. Exrs:
Thos., Matthew Edwards, Jas. Lockridge. Wit: Jno. Lockridge, Robt. Messer,
Jas. C. Edwards. Wife, Jean Edwards. Chn: Ibale, Elizabeth Edwards. "After
my dtrs. decease their part to be given to Thos. Edwards second and third dtrs.
Rebecca, Jenney Edwards." Inv. made July 7, 1791 by Capt. Thos. Weems,
Jno. Norris, Jas. C. Edwards.

EDDINGS, ISAAC—BOX 31, PACK 689:
Est. admnr. June 11, 1798 by Betsey Eddings wid., Charles Davenport
Esq., Capt. Richard Pollard, Benjamin Eddins bound to Andrew Hamilton Ord.
Abbeville Dist. sum $5,000.00. Aug. 14, 1798 Paid Jas. Eddins $4.16. Inv.
made July 2, 1798 by Richard Pollard, Benjamin Chiles, Thos. Poole. (Name
written Eddings and Eddins.)

ELLIS, JOSEPH—BOX 31, PACK 690:
Est. admnr. Sept. 24, 1806 by Jno. Burton, Adam Crain Jones, Jr., Jno.
Colbert bound to Andrew Hamilton Ord. Abbeville Dist. sum $10,000.00. Wid.
Rachel Ellis. Inv. made Oct. 10, 1806 by Jno., Robt. Lindsay, Robt. Ellis.

ENGEVINE, PETER—BOX 31, PACK 691:
Est. admnr. Aug. 7, 1805 by Joseph, Peter Gibert Esq., Thos. Finley

bound to Andrew Hamilton Ord. Abbeville Dist. sum $10,000.00. Inv. made Aug. 27, 1805 by Joshua Hill, Charles Britt, Jas. Dilleshaw.

ELLINGTON, DEWI—BOX 31, PACK 692:
    Will dated Sept. 29, 1810 in Abbeville Dist. Rec. Mar. 22, 1814. Exrs: Jno. Wooldridge, Jno. Ellington. Wit: Wm., Mary Yarbrough, Jno. Cain. Brothers: David, Jno. Ellington. Sis: Lucy Waldon, Patsey Wooldridge, Obedience Lipford. "Bequeath to Dewi Lipford, Wm. son of Jno. Wooldridge, Fanney dtr. of Patsey Wooldridge, Dewi Ellington Lipford son of Obedience Lipford." Expend: Jan. 1, 1822 Rented Flat Woods tract for 2 yrs. $65.00. Amt. due heirs of Obedience Lipford say $2151.22 to be divided between 9 chn. Amt. due heirs Patsey Wooldridge, Fanny Harris $2151.22. divided between 9 chn. Paid Daniel Weed his part $227.91. Thos. Ellington his part $227.91. Thompson Allen his part $227.91. Asa Lipfords part $221.91. To 5 days traveling to Georgia on business $7.52. Paid W. B. Wimbish, one of the heirs of Lucy Waldon, $100.00.

ELLIS, ROBERT, SR.—BOX 31, PACK 693:
    Will dated July 18, 1831 in Abbeville Dist. Rec. Nov. 5, 1831. Exrs: Jno. L., Robt. Ellis Jr. Wit: Robt. Lindsay, Jno. Haddon, Isaac Murdock. Wife, Margaret Ellis. Chn: Wm., Margaret, Joseph, Robt. Jr., Jno. L. Ellis, Jane Branyon, Elizabeth Tribble, Nancy Latimer. Gr. son, Robt. B. Ellis. Dec. 27, 1843 Paid Stephen Lattimer, Richardson Tribble, Benet McAdams, Jno. Branyon each $673.82.

ELLINGTON, JOHN—BOX 31, PACK 694:
    Est. admnr. July 5, 1820 by Bedy H. Ellington, Jas., Jno. G. Caldwell. Jas. Murray, David Lesly bound to Moses Taggart Ord. Abbeville Dist. sum $20,000.00. Cit. pub. at Upper Long Cane Church. April 1830 Paid Joel Lipford part of what was coming to him from Dewi Lipford $100.00. Nov. 12 Paid Jno. Speer for Mary Ellington $16.37½. Jan. 7, 1831 Paid A. Maldenhis wife's legacy $233.00.

ENGLISH, JANE—BOX 31, PACK 695:
    Will dated Mar. 13, 1825 in Abbeville Dist. Proved Oct. 5, 1826. Exrs: Jas. B. English, Jno. H. Armstrong. Wit: Jas. B., Hugh P. English, Jno. H. Armstrong. Chn: Mary, Jas. B., Andrew English. "Left property to Nancy Kennedy, also said Nancy to take care my dtr. Mary." The following recd shares: Jas. Alexander, Daniel Gillespie, Ann Kennedy, Nancy Kennedy, Wm. McGaw's share or Hannah's.

EDGAR, JOHN, JR.—BOX 31, PACK 696:
    Will dated July 17, 1823 in Abbeville Dist. Proved June 17, 1825. Exr: Wife, Judeth Edgar. Wit: Wm. Robinson, Jno. Golden. "Bequeath to my wife tract granted to John Edgar, Sr. conveyed to me." Inv. of Jno. Edgar, Sr. in same pack. made Mar. 15, 1819 by Jno. Guthrie, Peter Hemmenger, W. McElhenney.

EVANS, JAMES, SR.—BOX 31, PACK 697:
    Will dated Jan. 22, 1822. Proved Mar. 30, 1822. Wit: Jno., Robt. Gilmer,

Joseph Gouge. Wife, Jane Evans. Chn: Robt., Joseph, Jas. Evans. Inv. made June 1, 1822 by Joseph Gouge, Jno., Col. Henry Fulton.

EDWARDS, THOMAS—BOX 31, PACK 698:
Est. admnr. Nov. 4, 1826 by Elizabeth Edwards, Joel, Wm. Smith, Wm. Campbell bound to Moses Taggart Ord. Abbeville Dist. sum $20,000.00. Cit. pub. at Providence Church. "Know that we this 20th Dec. 1826, Isaac Edwards and Christopher Clarke both of Georgia do agree to acct. for the property ment. in settling of our parts of est. of said decd." Expend: Ambrose Edwards book acct. $2.00. David Hudson, Jas. J. Banks, Shelton White appraised the property in Elbert Co. Georgia.

EDMISTON, JOHN—BOX 31, PACK 699:
Will dated Mar. 7, 1789. Proved Oct. 8, 1789. Exrs: Wife, Elizabeth Edmiston, Jno. Wardlaw. Wit: Victor, Isabel, Joseph Matthews. Chn: Jno., Andrew, Jas. Edmiston. "One yet unborn child."

EDWARDS, JAMES—BOX 31, PACK 700:
Will dated May 23, 1783. Proved July 16, 1784. Exrs: Wife, Betsy Edwards, Davis Terry. Wit: Dabney Gholson, Philip Day, Charles Powell. Was of Halifax Co. Virginia. Chn: Augustine, Jas. Judith Crawford Edwards, Jno., Betsy Terry Edwards.

ESKRIDGE, BURDITT—BOX 31, PACK 701:
Will dated Mar. 23, 1779 in Collenton Co. 96 Dist. Proved Aug. 20, 1782. Exrs: Wife, Nancy Eskridge, Enoch Grigsbee, Jacob Smith. Wit: Jno. Davis, Jacob, Sarah Smith. Chn: Saml., Griggsbey, Richard, Eskridge. "Wife ·no pregnant with child." Burditt Eskridge was of Richland Creek, 96 Dist.

EDWARDS, RANDOLPH—BOX 32, PACK 702:
Est. admnr. Sept. 15, 1838 by Thos. Strawhorn, Aaron Lomax, Jno. Burnett bound to Moses Taggart Ord. Abbeville Dist. sum $800.00. Cit. pub. at Beulah Church. Had 6 minors. Jno. was of age in 1842. Mar. 1853 Paid Saml. M. Edwards $56.59.

EVANS, RICHARD—BOX 32, PACK 703:
Est. admnr. Sept. 20, 1782 by Jamima Evans wid. of Beach Island, Wm. Jones, Daniel Evans bound to Jno. Ewing Calhoun Ord. 96 Dist. sum 2,000 lbs. Inv. made Oct. 8, 1782 by Henry Jones, David Bowen, Adam Kiles.

ELLINGTON, JEREMIAH—BOX 32, PACK 704:
Est. admnr. Nov. 7, 1796 by Fanny, Leonard Ellington, Wm. Harris, Jno. Norwood bound to Judges of Abbeville Co. sum $8,000.00. Cit. pub. at Upper Long Cane Church. Expend: Dec. 20, 1800 Cash paid in Virginia for redemption of the land it being returned insolvent $1.21. Legatees, Lucy Waldon, Francis Drinkard, Jno. Wooldridge, Royall N. Lipford, Dewi Ellington, Jno. Ellington. Paid expenses going 3 trips to Virginia, Pittsylvania Co. Paid Sarah Terry her claim of dowry $70.00.

EDWARDS, THOMAS—BOX 32, PACK 705:
Inv. made Mar. 29, 1796 by Jehu Foster, Mathew Edwards, Andrew

Paul. Mar. 29, 1811 Jane Edwards recd. her third of est. Paid the Exrs. of Andrew Edwards, not included in a former return, $22.53. July 27, 1805 Paid for a saddle for Peggy $18.00. April 1808 Paid Margaret Edwards $7.12. Paid Amos Edwards $58.75. Paid Thos. Edwards $11.00. Est. admnr. Mar. 6, 1796 by Jane Edwards wid., Jno. Brannan, Robt. Smith. Josiah Chambers bound to the Judges Abbeville Co. sum 1,500 lbs.

ELLIS, MINORS—BOX 32, PACK 706:
On Mar. 24, 1817 Jno. E. Ellis, Jno. Lindsay, Wm. Martin bound to Taliaferro Livingston Ord. Abbeville Dist. sum $10,000.00. Jno. E. Ellis made gdn. Robt. Nicholson, Mary Ellis, minors over 14 yrs.

EDWARDS, DAVID—BOX 32, PACK 707:
Est. admnr. Feb. 12, 1840 by Jas. M. Edwards, Owen Selby, Andrew Riley bound to Moses Taggart Ord. Abbeville Dist. sum $1,000.00. Cit. pub. at Beulah Church. Sett. made Sept. 16, 1844. Present, Matthew Campbell who married Rebecca, Thos. Edwards. Absent, Mary Edwards, Henry Boozer gdn. David, Jno. Edwards.

EMERSON, MINORS—BOX 32, PACK 708:
On Nov. 22, 1858 Martha E. Emmerson formerly of Abbeville Dist. but now of Hinds Co. Miss. appointed Joel J. Cunningham of Abbeville Dist. her Atty. to receive her claim of her father Jno. Emmerson decd. Martha was also entitled to a small sum of her grandfather's est. in S. C. Jno. Osborne decd. in right of her mother who was a dtr. of said decd. That there are chn. of Jno. Emmerson who married Eveline Osborn, the mother Eveline being dead. Minor chn: Jno. Wm., Frances A., Martha E. Emmerson. Frances A. married A. E. McClelland. Mother, Hannah Osborn. On Jan. 18, 1839 J. W. Emmerson of Hinds Co. Miss. appointed B. F. Osborne of said Co. his Atty. (Written Emmerson and Emberson.)

EDWARDS, DAVID—BOX 32, PACK 709:
On Mar. 7, 1843 Henry Boozer, Jas. Y. Jones, Wm. Tolbert bound to David Lesly Ord. Abbeville Dist. sum $400.00. Henry Boozer made gdn. David Edwards a minor.

EVANS, MINORS—BOX 32, PACK 710:
On Oct. 29, 1833 Washington Belcher, Edward Collier, Jno. Pressly bound to Moses Taggart Ord. Abbeville Dist. sum $1,000.00. Washington Belcher made gdn. Matilda, Allen, Simpson, Jackson Evans minors of D. Evans decd.

EAKINS, JOSEPH, JR.—BOX 32, PACK 711:
Est. admnr. Nov. 7, 1844 by Thos., Benjamin H. Eakin, Jas. S. Wilson bound to David Lesly Ord. Abbeville Dist. sum $6,400.00. Left a wid. and 4 chn. Thos. Eakins was a brother. Sett. made Jan. 19, 1847. Present, Thos. Eakin admnr., Elizabeth Eakin wid., Geo., Jas., Jno., Eakin. Inv. made Nov 21, 1844 by Geo. Nickles, Benjamin H. Eakin, Jno. Richardson, Robt. C. Richey, Wm. Morrison.

ELLIS, WILLIAM J.—BOX 32, PACK 712:
Est. admnr. Sept. 17, 1844 by J. C. Ellis, Jno. B. Reynolds, Wm. McNary
bound to David Lesly Ord. Abbeville Dist. sum $1,000.00. Left a wid. Nandrana
Ellis and 2 chn. Wm. McNary Ellis, Jno. Vinson Reynold Ellis. Was son of
J. C. Ellis admnr. Nandrana Ellis later married Wm. L. Richey.

EDWARDS, JOHN—BOX 32, PACK 713:
On Oct. 7, 1844 Henry Boozer, Andrew Riley, Jas. M. Edwards bound
to David Lesly Ord. Abbeville Dist. sum $240.00. Henry Boozer made gdn. of
Jno. Edwards minor son of Sarah Edwards.

FRASER, DONALD—BOX 33, PACK 714:
Will dated Aug. 12, 1807 in Abbeville Dist. Rec. April 20, 1812. Exrs:
Wife, Mary Allen Fraser, Brother, Jno. Fraser of Charleston, Geo. Bowie, Jas.
Wardlaw. Wit: Jno. Stuart, Jno. Wilson, Alexr. Ralston. Chn: Jno., Margaret
Fraser. Brothers, Jno., Wm. Fraser. Sis. Isabella. Inv. of David Fraser in same
pack. made Sept. 16, 1797 by Andrew, Jno., Gray, Thos. Keown.

FRANKLIN, WILLIAM B.—BOX 33, PACK 715:
Est. admnr. Jan. 18, 1816 by Sarah Franklin, Francis White, Micajah
Pool, Pleasant Wright bound to Taliaferro Livingston Ord. Abbeville Dist. sum
10,000 lbs. Cit. pub. at Providence Church. Mar. 27, 1818. Paid Sarah Franklin
$140.00. Dec. 20 Paid Jas. Franklin $100.00. 1819 Paid Jno. Smith $120.00.
Feb. 1, 1816 Paid Joseph Cooper legatee $48.50. Mar. 26, 1819 Recd. of Asa
Franklin $130.00.

FREEMAN, HEROD—BOX 33, PACK 716:
Est. admnr. Jan. 1, 1827 by Adam C. Jones, Jno. Donald, Andrew Richey
bound to Moses Taggart Ord. Abbeville Dist. sum $1,000.00. Sale, Jan. 16, 1827.
Byis: Geo. Freeman, Malinda Davis, Nancy Freeman, etc.

FINNEY, BENJAMIN—BOX 33, PACK 717:
Will dated Sept. 19, 1819 in Abbeville Dist. Proved Aug. 7, 1826. Exrs:
Wife, b. ls. Wm., Patrick Calhoun. Wit: Thos. Jones, Joseph Moseley, Sr.,
Joseph Hutton. Wife and chn. ment. but no names given.

FOSTER, ROBERT—BOX 33, PACK 718:
Will dated Aug. 10, 1830 in Abbeville Dist. Proved Aug. 23, 1830.
Exrs: Wife, Elizabeth Foster, Jas. Foster, Jas. McCaslan. Wit: Saml. Pressly,
Herbert Darracott, Jno. C. Darith. Chn: Edward, Susanna, Polly Foster. "Be-
queath land to Jas. McCaslan." Inv. made Sept. 20, 1830 by Jno. C. Dewitt,
Herbert Darracott, Robt. McCaslan.

FORREST, JAMES—BOX 33, PACK 719:
Est. admnr. Feb. 17, 1817 by Elizabeth Forrest, Jas. Sproul, Henry
Burton bound to Taliaferro Livingston Ord. Abbeville Dist. sum 10,000 lbs.
Est. admnr. again Sept. 1, 1820 by Elizabeth Forrest, Beverly, Henry S. Burton
bound to Moses Taggart Ord. sum $10,000.00. Inv. made Mar. 4, 1817 by Jas.
Vaughan, Jas. Carson, Jas. Caldwell.

FOSTER, JEHU—BOX 33, PACK 720:
Will dated Jan. 25, 1810 in Abbeville Dist. Rec. Mar. 6, 1810. Exrs:
Robt., Saml. Perrin Esq., David, Jas. Wardlaw. Wit: Eli Davis, Mary P. Tutt,
Peggy Murdock. Brothers, Jno. Foster of Georgia, Jas. Foster. Chn: Polly Perrin
Foster, Eliza Clopton Foster, Kitty Foster. Note: Jno. Anderson of Edgefield
married Mary Foster. Saml. Marshall married Eliza Foster.

FRANKLIN, MARY—BOX 33, PACK 721:
Est. admnr. Jan. 31, 1827 by Sarah T. Franklin, Geo. Washington
Hodges, Richard Griffin bound to Moses Taggart Ord. Abbeville Dist. sum
$2,000.00. Cit. pub. at Rocky Creek Church. Inv. made Feb. 24, 1827 by
Jesse Beazley, Thos. Haddon, Edmund Caldwell. Byers: Elizabeth Buzbee, Sarah
Franklin. Expend: Nov. 26, 1828 Recd. of Elizabeth Buzbee for son Stephen
$13.75.

FEATHERSTONE, LEWIS—BOX 33, PACK 722:
Est. admnr. Sept. 25, 1805 by Benjamin Johnson of Newberry Dist.
Henry, Edmund Gaines of Abbeville Dist. bound to Andrew Hamilton Ord.
sum $10,000.00. Caty Featherstone was the wid. Paid Wm. Gaines legatee
$143.67. Recd. of Jannet Maddox $40.00. (In same pack. was the following
paper. May have gotten there by mistake. Sarah Wardlaw born April 27, 1794
which makes her 14 yrs. 27th April last. Jno. Wardlaw born Dec. 25, 1795.
Wm. Bowman Wardlaw born Aug. 23, 1802, chn. of Jno. Wardlaw decd.

FOSTER, ROBERT, SR.—BOX 33, PACK 723:
Est. admnr. June 6, 1825 by Ephraim, Joseph Davis, Owen Selby bound
to Moses Taggart Ord. Abbeville Dist. sum $1,000.00. Mar. 5, 1827. Legatees:
Elijah, Saml., Joseph, Hannah, Robt., Sarah Foster. Wid. *Janey* Foster. Marcus
Williams, Jr., legatee.

FOOSHE, CHARLES, SR.—BOX 33, PACK 724:
Will dated Mar. 31, 1820 in Abbeville Dist. Proved Mar. 12, 1823. Exrs:
Sons, Wm., Charles B. Fooshe. s. l. Dudley Richardson. Wit: Zachary Pulliam,
Wm., Nathan Calhoun. Wife, Elizabeth. Chn: Elizabeth Jay, Susannah Allen
2 dtrs. by first wife, Jno., Charles B., Wm. Fooshe, Sarah Payn, Henrietta
Richardson, Fanny Byrd, Patsey Cheatham. Gr. chn: Thos., Elize Payn.
April 27, 1824 Paid Thos. Bird $466.78. Sarah Davis $357.89¼. July 15 Paid
Jno. Cheatham $466.78. Feb. 2, 1825 Paid Wiley Robertson $107.88¾.

FRASER, JOHN—BOX 33, PACK 725:
Will dated Mar. 11, 1807 in Abbeville Dist. Rec. June 1, 1807. Exrs:
Brother, Wm. Fraser, Saml. Mitchell. Wit: Jas. Killough, Saml. Mitchel,
Nathaniel Norwood. Sis. Ester Woods, Mary Jones. Wm. Young son of Esther
Woods. Nov. 17, 1809 Paid Jas. Jones legacy $20.00. Carried to Wm. Fraser's
est. $590.50 being a legacy left him in Jno. Fraser's will.

FOSTER, JOHN, JR.—BOX 33, PACK 726:
Will dated July 1, 1785 in Abbeville Dist. Exrs: Nephew, Saml. Foster
Sr., Saml. Foster, Jr. Wit: Jno. McCurdy, Wm. Foster, Jas. Loosk. Wife, Mary.

Nephews: Saml. Foster, Sr., Alexr., Jas. Foster. Gr. chn: Jno., Jas., Robt., Saml., Elizabeth Foster by son Jas. Foster. Angess, Mary Foster by son Jno. son Jno. Foster. Inv. made May 2, 1786 by Robt. McAlpin, Jno. McElwee, Jas. Foster.

FIELDS, OBADIAH—BOX 33, PACK 727:
Est. admnr. Oct. 30, 1802 by Catharina Fields, wid, Joseph Burton bound to Andrew Hamilton Ord. Abbeville Dist. sum $5,000.00. Inv. made Dec. 22, 1802 by Jas., Capt. Jno. McAdam, Benjamin Osborn.

FULTON, HENRY—BOX 33, PACK 728:
Est. admnr. June 10, 1829 by Lucretia Fulton, Joseph Davis, Hamilton Hill bound to Moses Taggart Ord. Abbeville Dist. sum $1,000.00. Inv. made June 10, 1829 by Jas. Frazier, Hamilton Hill, Robt. Devlin, Andrew Mantz. June 12, 1830 Paid D. Douglass for boarding Elizabeth, Henry, Horatio Fulton 1 yr., all minors under 9 yrs.

FAULKNER, JOHN—BOX 33, PACK 729:
Est. admnr. Oct. 6, 1828 by Wm. Patton, Saml. Young, Jas. Taggart bound to Moses Taggart Ord. Abbeville Dist. sum $2,000.00. Cit. pub. at Long Cane Church. Inv. made Oct. 10, 1828 by Jno. Faulkner, Reuben Weed, Geo. McFarland.

FARRAR, CHESLEY—BOX 33, PACK 730:
Est. admnr. Dec. 8, 1828 by Benjamin Tutt, Wm. Covington, Jas. Hughes bound to Moses Taggart Ord. Abbeville Dist. sum $10,000.00. Inv. made Dec. 29, 1828 by Geo. Palmer, Joseph A. W. Devall, Joseph Mosley. Articles were bought in 1829 for Robt., Saml., Caroline Farrar. Jan. 1, 1830 Recd. of Mrs. E. Farrar $651.00. (Name written Farrow also.)

FINLEY, PETER F.—BOX 34, PACK 731:
Est. admnr. Oct. 19, 1835 by Wm. Lyon, Hiram Moore, Bartholomew Jordon bound to Moses Taggart Ord. Abbeville Dist. sum $4,000.00. Cit. pub. at Asbury Chapel. Inv. made Nov. 3, 1835 by Bartw., Jonatthan Jordon, Hiram Moore, Geo. W. Pressly.

FINLEY, THOMAS—BOX 34, PACK 732:
Will dated 1823 in Abbeville Dist. Proved Jan. 2, 1832. Exrs: Alexr. Hunter, Jno. Clark. Wit: Jas. Hunt, Thos. Brough, Jr., Wm. Clark. Wife, Jane Finley. Niece, Ann Finley. "Bequeath to Reuben Finley of Tenn. wheel wright, whose mother's maiden name was Catherine Kinder." Ment. he was born Feb. 11, 1757 and wife Jane born Nov. 8, 1765. "Bequeath to Thos. Finley Mitchell son of Francis Mitchell." (Jane Finley will in same pack.) Will dated Nov. 26, 1845. Proved Dec. 2, 1845. Exr: Alexr. Hunter. Wit: H. H. Townes, W. Gilbert. Sis. Mary Mackey. Grand Nephew, Thos. Finley Mitchell.

FOSTER, SAMUEL, SR.—BOX 34, PACK 733:
Will dated May 19, 1825 in Abbeville Dist. Proved Dec. 12, 1825. Exrs: Edmond Cobb, Ephraim Davis. Wit: Jno. Slone, Saml. McElwain, Margaret

M. Paul. Gr. chn: Saml., Robt. Foster, sons of Robt. Foster decd., Jno. Slone, Joseph, Elijah, Sarah, Margaret, Francis Foster, chn. of Robt. Foster decd. Alexr. Senclar Foster, Thos. Jordon Foster, sons Saml. C. Foster. Gr. grandson, Saml. Foster Slone, son of Jno. Slone, s. l. Thos. Slone. Dtr. l. Jenny Foster, wife of Robt. Foster decd. Wife, Sarah Foster. Sett. Saml. Foster died in 1825. Sarah Foster died about Feb. 1845. Gr. chn: Sarah Foster in Abbeville, Joseph Foster supposed to be dead, Elijah Foster in Pickens Dist. Margaret Foster married Marcus Williams. Absent, Francis Foster dead (mother Jane is she entitled) Saml., Robt. Foster, 4 chn. of Jno. Sloan, Saml. Sloan and others, names not known, Alexr. S., Thos. Jordon Foster.

FULLER, WILLIAM A.—BOX 34, PACK 734:
      Est. admnr. Dec. 16, 1836 by Hannah Fuller, Wm. Hall, Jno. Holt, Joseph Hughey bound to Moses Taggart Ord. Abbeville Dist. sum $5,000.00. Cit. pub. at Smyrna Church. Notes: Jesse W. Fuller $200.00. Silas Fuller $114.00. Apl. 12, 1839 Recd. from Henry Fuller $75.00.

FURR, HENRY—BOX 34, PACK 735:
      Will dated Mar. 22, 1836 in Abbeville Dist. Proved Aug. 1, 1836. Exr: Jno. Scott. Wit: Wm. T. Duncan, Wiley West, P. J. Downey. Wife, Elizabeth Furr. Chn: Enoch, Susannah Catherine Furr. Cit. pub. at Mt. Zion Meeting House.

FIELDING, THOMAS L.—BOX 34, PACK 736:
      Est. admnr. Oct. 18, 1825 by Wm. Speer Jr., Abraham Bell, Wm. K. Patton bound to Moses Taggart Ord. Abbeville Dist. sum $500.00. Cit. pub. at Rocky Creek Church. Dec. 16, 1824 Paid J. J. Fielder legatee $10.00. Jan. 18, 1825 Recd. of Thos. Anderson schooling due est. $29.96. (Written Fielding and Fielder.)

FRITH, JOSEPH—BOX 34, PACK 737:
      Est. admnr. May 5, 1817 by Geo. Weatherington, Archibald Frith, Wm. Morrison, Jno. Waters bound to Taliaferro Livingston Ord. Abbeville Dist. sum $5,000.00. Cit. pub. at Lomax Meeting House. The wid. Nancy Frith later married Peter Martin. Sale, July 3, 1817. Byrs: Arch. Frith, Nancy Spencer, Jno. Frith, etc.

FOOSHE ,WILLIAM—BOX 34, PACK 738:
      Will dated Oct. 21, 1828 in Abbeville Dist. Proved Nov. 24, 1828. Exrs: Brothers, Jno., Edward Fooshe, Jas. Gillam. Wit: Joseph W. Hill, Jno. Pulliam, Alvek Jay. Wife ment. name not given. Son, Wm. C. Fooshe. Sett. made Nov. 24, 1840. Present, Jno. Charles Fooshe, Wm. Carter who married Martha Fooshe. Absent, Wm. Fooshe a minor, Jas., Daniel Fooshe, Wid. Sarah Fooshe.

FISHER, SAMUEL—BOX 34, PACK 739:
      Est. admnr. Nov. 17, 1820 by Thos., Jas. Fisher, Jno. Clinkscales, Benjamin Griffin bound to Moses Taggart Ord. Abbeville Dist. sum $2,000.00. Legatees, Stephen, Frances, Matilda, Martha, Reuben Fisher, David Cumings.

FOSTER, JOHN EDWARD—BOX 34, PACK 740:
On Mar. 7, 1833 Elizabeth Foster made gdn. of Jno. Edward, Mary C. Foster, minors under 14 yrs. Sept. 11, 1833 Recd. of Jas. McCaslan, Jas. Foster Exrs. of Robt. Foster decd. $1058.00.

FOSTER, ELIZABETH—BOX 34, PACK 741:
Est. admnr. Jan. 24, 1837 by Jas., Moses Oliver McCaslan, Wm. Harris bound to Moses Taggart Ord. Abbeville Dist. sum $20,000.00. Cit. pub. at Hopewell Church. Sett. made Feb. 21, 1837. Present, Jas., Oliver McCaslan, admnrs. whose wives Margaret B. and Larennale C. are distributtes, Jno. Edward Foster, Wm. K. Bradley whose wife Mary C. is also distribute.

FINCHER, ARMAL—BOX 34, PACK 742:
Will dated May 17, 1784 in 96 Dist. Proved July 1784. Exrs: Brother, Aaron Fincher, Henry Millhouse. Wit: Henry, Jno. Clark, Wm. Morgan. Wife, Rebekah Fincher. Chn: Francis, Hester, Rebekah Fincher, Elizabeth Duncan. Inv. made Mar. 7, 1784 by Jno. Wilson, Ralph Hunt, Eli Cook. Jas. Duncan and his wife Elizabeth of Union Dist. were ordered to appear at the Court of Common Pleas at Union Court House with the will of Herman Fincher decd.

FRAZER, WILLIAM—BOX 34, PACK 743:
Will dated Jan. 4, 1809 in Abbeville Dist. Rec. Jan. 13, 1809. Exrs: Esther Woods, Ezekiel Calhoun, Sr. Wit: Thos. Ansley, Ezekiel Calhoun, Sr. Esther Woods. Sis. Mary Jones, Esther Woods. "Bequeath to Wm. Young my bed." Inv. made Feb. 15, 1809 by Walter Ward, Francis Young, Sr., Archibald McKinley.

FIFE, WILLIAM—BOX 34, PACK 744:
Est. admnr. Nov. 29, 1819 by Jas. Fife, Jno. Young, Sr., Wm. Jones, Jno. Glasgow bound to Moses Taggart Ord. Abbeville Dist. sum $2,000.00. Inv. made Dec. 14, 1819 by Jas. Hues, Daniel Thompson, Peter Smith. Byrs: Jas. Fife, Lewis Parks, Wm. Ross, etc.

FRITH, SUSANNAH—BOX 34, PACK 745:
Will dated Dec. 8, 1812 in Abbeville Dist. Rec. April 16, 1813. Exrs: Archibald Frith, Jno. Sprue, Jas. Lomax. Wit: Jas. McKee, Jas. Lomax, Jesse Spencer. Chn: Susannah, Jacob, Joseph, Archey, Jno., Thos. Frith, Avis Brown, Milly Hairston, Nancy Spencer, Rebecca Goselin. Gr. chn: Thos. Brown, Beckey Hairston, Susannah Spencer. Inv. made Jan. 28, 1813 by Jno. Stewart, Joshua Davis, Wm. Martin.

FOSTER, CAPT. HENRY—BOX 34, PACK 746:
Est. admnr. Sept. 12, 1793 by Elizabeth Foster wid. Jno. Sr., Jno. Logan Jr., Dr. Zachary Meriwether bound to Abbeville County sum 500 lbs. Sale, Dec. 6, 1793. Byrs: Elizabeth Foster, Thomas Brightman, Joseph Foster, etc.

FITZGERALD, CHARLES—BOX 34, PACK 747:
Est. admnr. July 12, 1786 by Leonard Nobles, Jno., Thos. Swearington, Jno. Ryan bound to Jno. Thomas, Jr. Ord. 96 Dist. sum $1,000.00. Inv. made in Edgefield Co. Aug. 5, 1786 by Frederick, Vann Swearington, Jr., Wm. Nobles.

FOREMAN, JACOB—BOX 34, PACK 748:
Est. admnr. Jan. 29, 1783 by Rachel, Isaac Foreman, Benjamin Darby bound to Jno. Ewing Calhoun Ord. 96 Dist. sum 14,000 lbs. Inv. made Mar. 24, 1783 by Isaac Foreman, Saml. Walker, Lacon Ryan.

FOSTER, ANDREW—BOX 34, PACK 749:
Will dated Oct. 17, 1780 in 96 Dist. Proved Nov. 11, 1783. Exrs: Jno. Foster, Isaac Patton. Wit: Wm. Patton, Thos. Mayes, Robt. Harris. Was of Fairforest. Wife, Margaret Foster. Dtr., Jane Foster. Other legatees: Joseph Nesbett, Moses, Jno. Foster, Isaac Patton, Wm. McCellan, Geo. Storey.

FROST, JONATHAN—BOX 34, PACK 750:
Est. admnr. Sept. 11, 1783 by Wm. O'Neal, David Smith, Armal Fincher bound to Jno. Thomas Jr. Ord. 96 Dist. sum 2,000 lbs. Wid. Mary Frost. Inv. made Sept. 15, 1783 by Armal Fincher. David Smith, Jno. Clark.

FANT, ABNER—BOX 35, PACK 751:
Est. admnr. June 28, 1841 by Thos., Benjamin Rosamond, Jas. Wright bound to Moses Taggart Ord. Abbeville Dist. sum $300.00. Inv. made July 16, 1841 by Wm. Sr., Wm. Graham, Jr., Jno. Rosamond. Byrs: Widow, G. W. Hodges, Marshall Sharp, etc.

FOOSHE, SARAH—BOX 35, PACK 752:
Est. admnr. Sept. 13, 1843 by Wm., Larkin G. Carter, Meedy Mays bound to David Lesly Ord. Abbeville Dist. sum $15,000.00. Wm. Carter, Downs Calhoun, gdns. of Wm. C. Fooshe a minor. Carter and wife were gdns. of Jas. Fooshe. Sarah Tabitha Ann Carter was a grand dtr.

FOOSHE, JOHN—BOX 35, PACK 753:
Will dated June 8, 1840 in Abbeville Dist. Proved Dec. 12, 1843. Exrs: Sons, Charles W., Jno. W., Joel., Robt. Fooshe. Wit: David Gillam, Jno. Sadler, Nathaniel McCants. Chn: Louisa Logan, Martha Jane Fooshe. b. l., Joel Smith. Sis. Henerietta Richardson. Note: Dr. W. H. Davis married Martha Jane Fooshe. A. J. Logan married Louisa Logan.

FISHER, STEPHEN—BOX 35, PACK 754:
Est. admnr. Jan. 31, 1844 by Caleb, Peter S. Burton, Joshua Ashley, Jno. F. Clinkscales bound to David Lesly Ord. Abbeville Dist. sum $5,000.00. Sett. made Nov. 20, 1846. Present, Caleb Burton, Saml. S., Edny, Stephen M., Wm. Fisher, minors, Jas. D. Murdock in right of wife Martha, Wm. B. Bell in right of his wife Betsey. Absent, Jane Fisher wid., E. Migcah M. Fisher, minor. (One place Migcah was written Amaziah Fisher.)

FINDLEY, JAMES, JR.—BOX 35, PACK 755:
Est. admnr. Nov. 16, 1843 by Jno. W. Hearst, Jno. Chiles, Jno. Cothran bound to David Lesly Ord. Abbeville Dist. sum $1,000.00. Sett. made June 17, 1845. Jno. Carroll married the wid. Elizabeth Findley. Son, Thos. Findley was about 4 or 5 yrs. old.

FRANKLIN, BENJAMIN—BOX 35, PACK 756:
On Nov. 8, 1839 Stanley Crews, Joel Smith, Francis A. Buchanan bound to Moses Taggart Ord. Abbeville Dist. sum $3,000.00. Stanley Crews made gdn. Benjamin Franklin a minor under 21 yrs.

FULTON, MINORS—BOX 35, PACK 757:
On Jan. 26, 1841 Thos. Fulton, Jas. S. Wilson, Isaac Branch bound to Moses Taggart Ord. Abbeville Dist. sum $2,000.00. Thos. Fulton made gdn. Elizabeth A., Jane A., Frances, Richard B., Thos. J., Amanda Fulton, chn. of said Thos. Fulton. Sett. made Dec. 9, 1843 ment. Amanda Fulton now wife of Jesse A. Ingram of Virginia for a small est. left her by her grandfather Benjamin Hill Decd. Jane Augusta Fulton married Thomas Johnson.

FOWLER, MINORS—BOX 35, PACK 758:
On May 4, 1840 Jas. Fisher, Ezekiel Tribble, Robt. Stuckey bound to Moses Taggart Ord. Abbeville Dist. sum $500.00. Jas. Fisher made gdn. Nancy A., Jas. C., Catherine, Sarah, Josephine Fowler minors under 21 yrs. Letters of Admnr. were granted to Jas. C. Fowler of Bibb Co. Geo. on the est. of Sarah J. Senclair decd. in Feb. 1859. Jas. C. Fowler, Virginia V. Scott of Bibb Co. Ga. appointed Jno. G. Baskin of Abbeville Dist. their Atty. to receipt to Robt. Stuckey security of Jas. Fisher gdn. for monies coming to them as heirs at law of Nancy Crowther late of said Dist., decd. on Jan. 16, 1860. Jas. Fisher made gdn. Jas. L., Thos. C., Mary A., Wm. F. Fisher minors under 21 yrs. Nancy A. Fowler married Joshua Buchanan. Catherine Fowler married Cumberland C. Reynolds. Were chn. of Jno. Fowler decd. The Fisher chn. were chn. of Jas. Fisher decd.

FULLER, JESSE W.—BOX 35, PACK 759:
On Oct. 9, 1838 Wm. Hall, Henry Norrell, Francis Atkins bound to Moses Taggart Ord. Abbeville Dist. sum $10,000.00. Wm. Hall made gdn. J. W. Fuller a minor.

FOSTER, JOHN E.—BOX 35, PACK 760:
On Jan. 31, 1837 Bartholomew, Saml. Jordon, Lewis Smith bound to Moses Taggart Ord. Abbeville Dist. sum $20,000.00. Bart. Jordon made gdn. of John Edward Foster a minor. On Mar. 7, 1831 Elizabeth Foster, Wm. Patton, Jno. C. Dewitt bound to Moses Taggart Ord. sum $10,000.00. Elizabeth Foster made gdn. Jno. E., Mary C. Foster, minors. Jno. E. was of age in 1843.

FOSTER, ROBERT—BOX 35, PACK 761:
Est. admnr. Sept. 29, 1802 by Hannah, Saml. Foster, Robt. Griffin, Jno. Shannon, Robt. Gibson bound to Andrew Hamilton Ord. Abbeville Dist. sum $10,000.00. Mar. 1, 1805 Paid Hannah, Elijah Foster for Benjamin Foster $20.00. For Joseph Foster $20.00. For Wm. Foster $20.00. Margaret Foster $20.00. Robt. Foster $20.00. For Robt. Anderson gdn. of Jno. Foster $140.00. For Thos. Nealey $10.00. For Robt. McClellan gdn. of Jas. Foster $37.50. Saml. Foster $24.00. Other heirs were: David Cochran, Wm. McCrone, Robt. Hearst, Andrew Crawford, Ebenezer Foster.

FOSTER, JOHN, SR.—BOX 35, PACK 762:
    Est. admnr. Sept. 12, 1794 by Elizabeth Foster wid. Wm. Huggins, Robt. Thompson bound to Judges Abbeville County sum 500 lbs. Inv. made June 10, 1796 by Saml. Sr., Saml. Foster, Jr., Jas. Devlin, Jas. McConnel.

FARNED, EDWIN—BOX 35, PACK 763:
    Est. admnr. Aug. 16, 1782 by Jno. Rainsford, Jno. Herndon, Herman Gallman bound to Jno. Ewing Calhoun Ord. 96 Dist. sum 14,000 lbs. Cit. pub. at Mrs. Martin's Meeting House. Inv. made Oct. 5, 1782 by W. Jones, Joseph Miller, Thos. Carter. Jno. Rainsford was of Horns Creek. (Written Ferned in one place.)

FORD, PHILIP—BOX 35, PACK 764:
    Admnr. Wm. Prince. Lived in 96 Dist. Inv. made April 23, 1783 by Jas. Jordon Esq., Jno. Ford, Giles Connell. Recd. money of Elishe, Jno., Zadock Ford.

FRANKLIN, ASA—BOX 35, PACK 765:
    Est. admnr. Nov. 2, 1835 by Wm. Barmore, Joseph Richey, Jas. Franklin bound to Moses Taggart Ord. Abbeville Dist. sum $10,000.00. Cit. pub. at Greenville Church. Sale, Nov. 25, 1835. Byrs: Jas., Wm. Franklin, Robt. R. Seawright, etc.

FRAZIER, JAMES—BOX 35, PACK 766:
    Will dated Aug. 20, 1842 in Abbeville Dist. Rec. Sept. 5, 1842. Exr: Thos. Thomson. Wit: A. H. Spence, Jno. C. Red, Sam W. Cochran. Was of Cedar Springs. Wife, Charity Frazier. Chn: Jas. W., Benjamin Frazier, Lucretia S. Devlin. Gr. chn: Henry, Joseph, Jas. A., Sarah A., Allen S. Walker, chn. of decd. dtr. Jane Walker. Martha B., Mary, Rebecca, Charity, Amanda Frazier, Edwin H. Frazier son of Anna Connor, Tallulah H. Frazier. s. l. Robt. Devlin. Nephew, Jno. F. Livingston.

FRANKLIN, JAMES—BOX 35, PACK 767:
    Est. admnr. Oct. 4, 1836 by Stanley Crews, Larkin Griffin, Downs Calhoun bound to Moses Taggart Ord. Abbeville Dist. sum $10,000.00. Susan Franklin, Stanley Crews were gdns. Benjamin, Willison W. Franklin, heirs of Jas. Franklin decd. Sett. made Dec. 21, 1840 ment. Benjamin Franklin a minor about 10 yrs. Benjamin F. Sloan gdn. Eliza Ann, Willison W. Franklin. Wid. Susan Franklin. Deduct on demands of Alexr. W., Elizabeth A. King of whom Jas. Franklin was gdn.

FLEMING, JAMES—BOX 35, PACK 768:
    Est. admnr. June 5, 1822 by Thos. P., Jacob Martin, Geo. Miller, bound to Moses Taggart Ord. Abbeville Dist. sum $1,000.00. Cit. pub. at Upper Long Cane Church.

FINDLEY, JAMES—BOX 35, PACK 769:
    Est. admnr. Jan. 18, 1841 by Saml. Cowan, Hugh G. Middleton, Jno. L. Brown bound to Moses Taggart Ord. Abbeville Dist. sum $2,000.00. Sett. made Feb. 9, 1843. Jerome Cox represents Elizabeth, Elihu, Wm., Benjamin. Jno.

Carroll married Mrs. Jas. Finley who is decd. Absent, Randel Finley, Cela Mitchell, Wm. Brown and wife Matilda.

FORD, RICHARD, SR.—BOX 35, PACK 770:
Will dated April 11, 1809 in Abbeville Dist. Rec. Sept. 28, 1810. Exrs: Wife, Elizabeth, Son, Saml. Ford. Wit: Christopher, Sarah Brooks, Nelly or Milly Ford. Chn: Rebekah Holland, Sally Ann Nelson, Elizabeth Tims, Fanny, Saml., Barrot, Mosey, Milly, Richard Ford. (Written Ford and Foord.)

FRASER, JOHN—BOX 35, PACK 771:
Will dated June 13, 1838 in Abbeville Dist. Proved Sept. 5, 1840. Exr: J. F. Livingston. Wit: J. C. Fowler, Jas. W. McCallister, Jno. Gallaugher. Dtr. Georgianna Fraser. "Other bequests made to Thos. A. Sanders, J. F. Livingston, son of Dr. J. F. Livingston, Clara J. Fraser, dtr. of Jno. Fraser." Wife and mother ment. no names given. Jno. G. Fraser died Aug. 1840. Sett. of trust est. of Eliza A. Davis, wife of Richard D. Davis, in same pack. Eliza Ann Davis died about 31st Dec. 1846 having 2 dtrs. Sarah A., Harriet D. Davis. Harriet D. Davis married Jas. J. Sutton of Pendleton Dist.

FISHER, THOMAS—BOX 36, PACK 772:
Est. admnr. Nov. 25, 1839 by Saml. C. Fisher, Hezekiah, Conrad Wakefield bound to Moses Taggart Ord. Abbeville Dist. sum $10,000.00. Cit. pub. at Little River Church. Sett. made Sept. 22, 1845. Present, S. C. Fisher admnr., Elizabeth Fisher wid., Wilson Ashley and wife Jane, Jno. W. Shirley and wife Lucinda, Jno. Ashley and wife Jemimah, Joshua S. Barnes and wife Nancy, Jno. M. Bryant and wife Elizabeth A. Bryant, Jno., Polly A., Cintha C., Thos. F., Jas. Fisher minors, the first 2 over and the last under 14 yrs.

FURR, SUSANNAH—BOX 36, PACK 773:
On Feb. 13, 1839 Henry Boozer, Jas. Wilson, Peter Rykard bound to Moses Taggart Ord. Abbeville Dist. sum $10,000.00. Henry Boozer made gdn. Susannah Catherine Furr a minor. Mar. 4, 1839 Recd. from Peter Rykard and Elizabeth Furr $1039.00.

FARRAR, MINORS—BOX 36, PACK 774:
On Dec. 5, 1831 Benjamin Tutt, G. W. Huckabee, Jno. Ruff bound to Moses Taggart Ord. Abbeville Dist. sum $2,000.00. Benjamin Tutt made gdn. Caroline, Robt. Farrar, the former over 14 yrs. Benjamin Tutt was b. l. of Caroline Farrar and s. l. of Elizabeth Farrar.

FINNEY, JOHN—BOX 36, PACK 775:
Est. admnr. May 5, 1784 by Robt. Long. Jno. Owens, Robt. McNaire bound to Jno. Thomas Jr. Ord. 96 Dist. sum 1,000 lbs. Inv. made June 12, 1784 by Jas., Joseph Adair, Thos. Ewing. Sale, June 30, 1784. Byrs: Joseph Adair (son of Jas. Adair) Robt. Long, Jno. Robinson, Jas. Polock.

FOYE, PETER—BOX 36, PACK 776:
Est. admnr. Nov. 27, 1783 by Harmatal Foy, Amos Richardson, Jonathan Gilbert bound to Jno. Thomas, Jr. Ord. 96 Dist. sum 2,000 lbs. Inv. made

Jan. 22, 1784 by Jno. Douglass, Amos Richardson, Wright Nicholson.

FAULK, JOHN—BOX 36, PACK 777:
Est. admnr. Oct. 25, 1783 by Benjamin Darby, Isaac Forman, of Horns Creek, 96 Dist. bound to Jno. Thomas Jr. Ord. sum 2,000 lbs. Inv. made Dec. 8, 1783 by Lacon Ryan, Conrad, Jasper Gallman.

FORD, BOLDEN—BOX 36, PACK 778:
On Jan. 11, 1783 Sarah Ford of Indian Creek, 96 Dist. applied for Letters of Admnr. as next of kin. Sale, Feb. 15, 1783. Byrs: Sarah Ford, Saml. Lindsay, Rebeckah Anderson, Francis Strother. Inv. made by Abel Anderson, Wm. Wilson, Wm. Hamilton.

FARIS, ROBERT—BOX 36, PACK 779:
Est. admnr. Jan. 1, 1785 by Dorcas Faris, Hugh Means, Wm. Patton, Andrew Mayes bound to Jno. Thomas Jr. Ord. 96 Dist. sum 2,000 lbs. Sale, Jan. 20, 1785. Byrs: Dorcas Faris, Seth Lewis, Jas. Crawford, etc.

FLANAGAN, BARTHOLOMEW—BOX 36, PACK 780:
Est. admnr. Nov. 25, 1786 by Wm. Turner, Nathaniel Howard, Saml. Uens bound to Jno. Thomas Jr. Ord. 96 Dist. sum 1,000 lbs. Inv. made by Wm. Gould, Nathaniel Haworth, Saml. Uens. Sale, Dec. 2, 1786. Byrs: Wm. Turner, Jno. Maxwell, Joshua Inman, Setch Hatcher.

FOOSHE, MARTHA E.—BOX 36, PACK 781:
On Nov. 10, 1837 Downs Calhoun, Jabez W. H., Jonathan Johnson bound to Moses Taggart Ord. Abbeville Dist. sum $10,000.00. Downs Calhoun made gdn. Martha E. Fooshe a minor.

FOSTER, JOHN W.—BOX 36, PACK 782:
Est. admnr. Feb. 1, 1845 by Jas., Moses O. McCaslan, Jno. E. Foster bound to David Lesly Ord. Abbeville Dist. sum $500.00. Left a wid. and several chn., no names given. Inv. made Feb. 5, 1845 by Jas. McCaslan, Jno. Wideman, Thos. P. Dowten.

FOSTER, JAMES—BOX 36, PACK 783:
Est. admnr. Jan. 6, 1845 by Jas. Foster, Jas. Lesly, Archibald Kennedy bound to David Lesly Ord. Abbeville Dist. sum $4,000.00. Jas. H. Foster was a son to said decd. Wm. A. Pinkerton was gdn. Thos., Jno. Foster, sons. A. P. Lesly recd. $736.43 as a legatee.

FOX, ELIZABETH—BOX 36, PACK 784:
Will date omitted. Proved Mar. 1, 1845 in Abbeville Dist. Exrs: Jas. A. Black, Francis B. Clinkscales. Wit: Jesse Rutledge, Jeney, Joshua Ashley. Single Woman. Niece's son, Washington Green Pruitt. Will to Elizabeth Jesemin Alewine $200.00. Bequeath to Wm. E. Daniel, Wm. C. Able.

GASTON, WILLIAM—BOX 36, PACK 785:
Est. admnr. May 7, 1832 by Jas. Wiley, Wm. Patton, David Lesly bound to David Lesly Ord. Abbeville Dist. sum $3,000.00. Cit. pub. at Ruffs

Church. 1835 Alexr. Gaston recd. $775.70 as his share. Jan. 5, 1836 Paid J. L. Bowies receipt for Jno. Gaston $20.99. Recpt. for Jane Gaston $25.98½.

GOULDEN, JAMES—BOX 36, PACK 786:
    Est. admnr. April 1, 1833 by Wm. Goulden, Jas. Gillam, Reuben, Jno. Goulding, Wm. Carter, Isaac Bunting bound to Moses Taggart Ord. Abbeville Dist. sum $10,000.00. Distributees were: Sarah, Charles, Frances Goulden. (Name written Goulding, Goulden.)

GOLDING, REUBEN—BOX 36, PACK 787:
    Will dated Dec. 20, 1834 in Abbeville Dist. Exrs: Son, Nimrod C. Golding, Wm. Eddins, Wit: Nimrod Overvey, Richard G., Anthony Golding. Wife ment. name not given. Chn: Jas., Nimrod C., Reuben G., Richard A. J. Golding. Expend: Paid Mrs. Lueaney Golding part of her husband's est. $2432.98. Jan. 22, 1835 Paid Richard A. Jackson Golding's part $1266.66½.

GIBSON, PATRICK, ESQ.—BOX 36, PACK 788:
    Est. admnr. Sept. 22, 1836 by Wm. Gibson, Philip Cook, Jno. Kennedy bound to Moses Taggart Ord. Abbeville Dist. sum $2,000.00. Cit. pub. at Tranquil Church. 1837 Paid Rebecca Gibson for tuition of Patrick, Josiah, Elies, Josiah Gibson $3.33. An acct. against Mary Gibson for 2 yrs. board $20.00. Jas. E. Gibson 2 yrs. Board $40.00. Jno. Gibson recd. $93.67 for his share.

GIBERT, DR. EBENEZER PETTIGREW—BOX 36, PACK 789:
    Est. admnr. Dec. 10, 1832 by Sarah B., Jas. F. Gibert, Thos. M. Duncan bound to Moses Taggart Ord. Abbeville Dist. sum $1,000.00. Inv. made Dec. 26, 1832 by Saml. Pressly, T. M. Duncan, Nathaniel Harris.

GILKEYSON, REBECCA—BOX 36, PACK 790:
    Will dated Feb. 25, 1829 in Abbeville Dist. Proved April 9, 1829. Wit: Jas. Johnson, Wm. Ware, Thos. Norwood. Chn: Jerusha Carline, Frances Ellender, Jno. Lewis, Agness Catharine, Eliza Rebecca Gilkeyson, Wm. Downey, Sarah Cook. "My will is that Wm. Pyles of state aforesaid and Jas. Y. Shaw my b. l. living in Alabama after my death to take my 7 chn. home with him and raise them." Gideon Stone married Jerusha Gilkeyson. Johnson Clement married Frances Gilkeyson. Shedrick Farmer married Sarah Gilkeyson. Jas. McDavid married Agness. Eliza, Wm. were minors. Cit. pub. at Friendship Church.

GILKEYSON, WILLIAM—BOX 36, PACK 791:
    Will dated Feb. 19, 1828 in Abbeville Dist. Proved Mar. 10, 1828. Exrs: Wife, Rebecca Gilkeyson, Wm. Pyles. Wit: Geo. Mattison, Geo. W. Reeve, Wm. P. Martin. Chn. ment. names not given. Inv. made Mar. 15, 1828 by Wm. Reeve, Thos. Norwood, Jno. Mattison.

GRAY, JAMES A.—BOX 36, PACK 792:
    Est. admnr. Dec. 19, 1834 by Jas. Wiley, Saml. Houston, Wm. Harris bound to Moses Taggart Ord. Abbeville Dist. sum $12,000.00. Cit. pub. at Bulah Church. Jan. 19, 1836 Paid Hamilton Hill gdn. for Geo. Pauls minor chn. $1212.70¼. Jan. 30, 1836 Paid Elizabeth Gray wid. $1,000.00. Elizabeth Gray

116   ABSTRACTS OF OLD NINETY-SIX AND

gdn. for Egnis D., Margaret M. Gray $400.00. Paid Jno. R. Martin husband of
Mary D. Gray $201.36¾. Paid Alexr. D. Gray gdn. Nancy A. Gray minor
$50.00. Paid Andrew Gray part share $104.48. Paid Jno. Lipscomb for Jno. W.
Gray $80.53. Paid Nancy, Zachariah Gray $350.00.

GRAY, FREDERICK—BOX 36, PACK 793:
    Will dated Nov. 24, 1836 in Abbeville Dist. Proved Oct. 7, 1837. Exrs:
Wm., J. F. Gray. Wit: Williamson Norwood, David F. Cleskey, Alex Hughes.
Wife, Mary Gray. Chn: Geo., Wm., Jno. F., F. Jefferson Gray, Washington R.
Gray decd., Henry Gray decd., Mary Ann Marshall, Cloutte Boyd, Jane Thomas.
Gr. dtr. Eliza Klugh. Sett. made Nov. 13, 1839. Shares recd. by F. G., Timothy
Thomas, Robt. H. Boyd, Thos. J. Gray, Jno. Marshall, Jas. M. Thomas, Z. W.
Arnold and wife, Wm. C. Norwood and wife, W. Wade and wife Elizabeth
Gray, Jno. H. Linch and wife Martha E. Gray.

GUNNIN, JANE—BOX 36, PACK 794:
    Est. admnr. Jan. 27, 1837 by Christian V. Barnes, Ezekiel Gunnion, Jas.
Huey bound to Moses Taggart Ord. Abbeville Dist. sum $5,000.00. Cit. pub.
at Lebanon Church. She died Jan. 14, 1837. Heirs were: Nathan, Ezekiel
Gunnin, Andrew Edwards and wife Hannah W., Jane Gunnin, Margart Gunnin
minor chn. of Benjamin Gunnin, Jr. decd., also Christian V. Barnes and Ann his
wife.

GRAY, JAMES A.—BOX 36, PACK 795:
    Will dated June 6, 1831 in Abbeville Dist. Proved Nov. 14, 1831. Exr:
Thos. Parker. Wit: David Sadler, Robt. Brady, Alexr. Spence. Wife, Elizabeth
E. Gray. Son, Jas. Andrew an infant. Expend: Nov. 29, 1835 Recd. of Arthur
Gray as balance of testator's portion of Alabama lands bequeathed to him by
his father $114.53. Nov. 29, 1833 Paid note to Claudius B. Gray $12.68.

GRAHAM, JAMES, SR.—BOX 37, PACK 796:
    Will dated Nov. 24, 1805 in Abbeville Dist. Proved Mar. 4, 1825. Exrs:
Wife, Anny Graham, Jno., Wm. Graham. Wit: Basil Hallum, Wm., Jno. Owen.
Chn. ment. but names not given. Byrs: Jno. Graham, Jr., Jas. Graham, etc.

GRIFFIN, JAMES—BOX 37, PACK 797:
    Est. admnr. Nov. 20, 1782 by Fanney Griffin, Thos., Jas. Wilson bound
to Jno. Ewing Calhoun Ord. 96 Dist. sum 14,000 lbs. Inv. made Nov. 30, 1782
by Mathew McMullen, Reuben Holloway, Thos. Wilson.

GROVES, JOHN—BOX 37, PACK 798:
    Est. admnr. Aug. 25, 1807 by Lattice Groves wid., Joseph Groves, David
Gillespie, Geo. Patterson bound to Andrew Hamilton Ord. Abbeville Dist. sum
$10,000.00. Sept. 4, 1807 Paid for 2 suits for the 2 sons Sylvanus, Jno. Groves.
Paid Henry Graves Walker who lately married Lettice Groves $130.00. Dated
Sept. 23, 1809. Paid said Walker for Eliza Nicholson Groves an heir of said
est. $1220.80.

GRAY, THOMAS—BOX 37, PACK 799:
    Est. admnr. Feb. 10, 1821 by Sarah Gray, Robt. McCaslan, Adam

Wideman, Jno. Harry bound to Moses Taggart Ord. Abbeville Dist. sum $8,000.00. Inv. made Feb. 13, 1821 by Adam Wideman, Geo. Roberts, Jno. Harry.

GILMER, ROBERT—BOX 37, PACK 800:
Est. admnr. Nov. 28, 1834 by Jas. S., Langdon Bowie, Jas. J. Gilmer, Saml. Irwin bound to Moses Taggart Ord. Abbeville Dist. sum $20,000.00. Sale, Jan. 6, 1835. Byrs: Jas. J., R. A., Mrs. Nancy Gilmer, etc.

GRANT, JOHN—BOX 37, PACK 801:
Est. admnr. Jan. 1, 1821 by Jas., Jno. Jr., Francis Carlile Sr. bound to Moses Taggart Ord. Abbeville Dist. sum $2500.00. Sale, Sept. 28, 1819. Byrs: Wid. Grant, Robt. Shackelford, Jno. Folkenberry, etc.

GRAY, MATHEW—BOX 37, PACK 802:
Est. admnr. Nov. 8, 1833 by Wm. T. Johnson, Jas. Weir, Jno. Cunningham, M. T. Miller bound to Moses Taggart Ord. Abbeville Dist. sum $3,000.00. Cit. pub. at Shilo Church. April 11, 1836 Recd. of Margaret Gray $40.00. To letter postage to old country for communication with the legatees of said est. $.25. To $40.00 for expenses due by est. of Mathew Gray in case of Alexr. Gray to C. G. Memminger of Charleston. Recd. from Memmenger for est. A. Gray in Charleston $339.42.

GLOVER, WILLIAM H.—BOX 37, PACK 803:
Will dated June 15, 1830 in Abbeville Dist. Proved Oct. 4, 1830. Exrs: Wade S. Cochran, Wm. Harris. Wit: Lewis S. Simmons, Jno. Besteder, Hugh Robinson. Wife, Sally Glover. Chn: Willis Jones, Jno. J. Glover. Inv. made Dec. 17, 1830 by Lewis S. Simmons, Saml. Caldwell, Vincent Griffin.

GAINES, HIRAM—BOX 37, PACK 804:
Est. admnr. Dec. 31, 1829 by Elizabeth Gaines, Jno. C. McGehee, Jno. H. Waller bound to Moses Taggart Ord. Abbeville Dist. sum $10,000.00. Cit. pub. at Siloam Church. Property was sold in Cambridge. Est. of Hiram Gaines to Jas. Chiles 1830. Amt. my services bringing negroes from Alabama to this country $35.00.

GUNNIN, BENJAMIN—BOX 37, PACK 805:
Est. admnr. Oct. 9, 1826 by Christian V. Barnes, Isaiah Johnston, Wm. E. Kennedy bound to Moses Taggart Ord. Abbeville Dist. sum $2,000.00. Cit. pub. at Lebanan Church. Ezekiel Gunnin, etc. bought at sale.

GLOVER, WILLIS—BOX 37, PACK 806:
Est. admnr. Mar. 14, 1823 by Susan Glover, Lewellen Goode, Bartlette Bullock, David Griffin bound to Moses Taggart Ord. Abbeville Dist. sum $14,000.00. Cit. pub. at Rehobeth Church. Accts. Nov. 3, 1815 Willis Glover with Nathan Lipscomb. Paid Wm. Holliday for a saddle for Willis Glover $10.00. The above article was struck out of the acct. current with the est. of Wiley Glover decd. by the Comr. in Equity and directed to be charged to Willis

Glover only as Betsey Harris was not liable to pay for anything for Willis after her marriage. Dec. 25, 1817 Paid Wm. H. Glover for making a coat $10.50.

GRAY, HENRY—BOX 37, PACK 807:
Est. admnr. April 16, 1831 by Jno. F., Wm., Frederick, Thos. Jefferson Gray, P. D. Klugh bound to Moses Taggart Ord. Abbeville Dist. sum $75,000.00. Inv. made April 18, 1831 by Owen Selby, Ephraim Davis, Thos. Hinton.

GLOVER, ALLEN—BOX 38, PACK 808:
Est. admnr. Dec. 6, 1823 by Silas Glover, Benjamin McGaw, Wm. Giles, Mathew Brown bound to Moses Taggart Ord. Abbeville Dist. sum $600.00. Sale, Dec. 23, 1823. Byrs: Silas, Lydia Glover, etc.

GRAHAM, ANNA—BOX 38, PACK 809:
Est. admnr. April 11, 1826 by Wm. Graham, Thos. Moore, Wm. H. Jones bound to Moses Taggart Ord. Abbeville Dist. sum $2,000.00. Cit. pub. at Providence Church. Sett. made Jan. 27, 1840. Present, Wm. Graham admnr., Josiah Carlile gdn. of 4 chn. Jas., Jno., Graham, Jno., Gafford husband of Martha Ann Graham. Dec. 10, 1834 Paid Mary Graham for Martha Ann $4.05. Jan. 9, 1835 Paid Zachariah Graham $12.50.

GREER, DAVID—BOX 38, PACK 810:
Will dated Sept. 15, 1819 in Abbeville Dist. Proved Mar. 24, 1820. Exrs: Richard Robinson of Little River, Alexr. Stevenson of Pendleton Dist. Wit: Stephen C. Durrum, Stephen Durrum. Wife, Hannah Greer. Inv. made May 5, 1820 by Wm. Anderson, Jno. McMahan, Wm. Brownlee, Thos. Herron.

GIBERT, STEPHEN B.—BOX 38, PACK 811:
Est. admnr. Dec. 20, 1822 by Sarah B. Gibert, Stephen Lee bound to Moses Taggart Ord. Abbeville Dist. sum $10,000.00. Cit. pub. at Hopewell Church. Paid to the treasurer of Willington Church. Inv. made Jan. 10, 1823 by Uel, Joshua Hill, Charles Britt.

GROVES, HENRY L.—BOX 38, PACK 812:
Est. admnr. Mar. 8, 1824 by Saml. Gilmer, Jr., Saml. Evans, Jno. Gilmer bound to Moses Taggart Ord. Abbeville Dist. sum $300.00. Cit. pub. at Upper Long Cane Church. Inv. made Mar. 10, 1824 by Jno. Gilmer, Saml. R. Evans, Wm. Newell.

GRANT, WILLIAM—BOX 38, PACK 813:
Est. admnr. Nov. 6, 1820 by Mordeica Shackelford, Stephen Jones, Jno. White bound to Moses Taggart Ord. Abbeville Dist. sum $1,000.00. Cit. pub. at Bowies Meeting House. Oct. 29, 1819 Paid to Francis Carlile admnr. est. of Jno. Grant decd. $30.50. Sett. of est. Wm. Grant decd. with Jno. H. Grant distributee and Jno. W. and Allen Shackelford, Exrs. of Mordecai Shackelford who was admnr. Wm. Grant decd.

GILMER, JAMES—BOX 38, PACK 814:
Est. admnr. Feb. 7, 1820 by Saml., Robt. Gilmer, Wm. McClinton bound

to·Moses Taggart Ord. Abbeville Dist. sum $2,000.00. Sale, Mar. 7, 1820. Byrs: Mrs. Gilmer, Saml. Gilmer, etc

GILES, JACOB—BOX 38, PACK 815:
Est. admnr. Oct. 18, 1826 by Mary Giles, David, Joseph McCrery bound to Moses Taggart Ord. Abbeville Dist. sum $1,000.00. Inv. made Nov. 7, 1826 by Jno. Hearst, Jr., Wm. Chiles, Jacob Baughman.

GHENT, JOHN—BOX 38, PACK 816:
Est. admnr. Nov. 13, 1826 by Jas. Hunt, David Lesly, Jno. Gray bound to Moses Taggart Ord. Abbeville Dist. sum $1,000.00. Inv. made Nov. 30, 1826 by Jonathan Johnston, Banister Allen, R. Smith. Byrs: Jno. B. Gent, Lucy Gent, etc.

GRIFFIN, IRA—BOX 38, PACK 817:
Will dated Feb. 4, 1830 in Abbeville Dist. Proved Feb. 9, 1830. Exrs: Brothers, Richard, Joseph, Larkin Griffin. Wit: Leroy Watson, Vincent, Melissa Griffin. Wife, Susannah Griffin. Chn. ment. names not given. May 26, 1832 Paid David Griffin in sett. $19.17. J. F. Griffin for money advanced to Martha $8.00. Dec. 29, 1832 Paid Thos. Stallworth, Sr. for boarding Martha, Augustus $66.62. Dec. 27, 1833 Paid Wm. C. Black in right of wife Martha $1813.63½. Wm. C. Black gdn. Sarah Griffin $4813.63½. Paid Madison C. Livingston in right of wife *Areana* $4813.63.½.

GRIFFIN, MARGARET—BOX 38, PACK 818:
Est. admnr. Dec. 3, 1821 by Jno. L. Griffin, Charles Pitts, Geo. J. Heard bound to Moses Taggart Ord. Abbeville Dist. sum $2,000.00. Cit. pub. at Rocky Creek Church. Inv. made Dec. 28, 1821 by Jas. A. Ward, Charles Maxwell, Nathaniel Marion. Byrs: Robt., Vincent, Richard Griffin, etc.

GORDON, ROBERT—BOX 38, PACK 819:
Will dated April 10, 1813 in Abbeville Dist. Proved Sept. 7, 1814. Exr: Jas. son of Jno. Caldwell. Wit: Jno. Caldwell, Jno., Elizabeth A. Spier. "Request to be buried in the tomb yard of Jno. Caldwell Esq." Sons, Saml., Wm. Gordon. Bequeath to Jno. G., son of Jno. Caldwell Esq. Owned property in the town of Slego, Market St. Ireland, also in village of Tully *Nigrackan*, Ireland. Also ment. Jno. Gordon.

GIBERT, JOHN LEWIS—BOX 38, PACK 820:
Est. admnr. Dec. 22, 1825 by Jane Gibert, Peter B., Jno. Moragne, Edward Collier bound to Moses Taggart Ord. Abbeville Dist. sum $12,000.00. Cit. pub. at Willington Church. Jno. Gideon, Caroline Jane, Hannah Adeline Gibert, gdn. ship was taken for them on Dec. 22, 1835. Accts: Wm. J. Houston in right of wife *Drucilla* W. Houston. Jane Gibert wid.

GRAY, JAMES—BOX 38, PACK 821:
Will dated Feb. 12, 1821 in Abbeville Dist. Probated June 9, 1821. Exrs: Gr. sons, Jas., Thos., Beatty. Wit: Wm. Bond, Henry Wideman, Jno. Beatty. Chn: Anne Beatty, Margaret Gilmore, Geo., Wm., Jas. Gray, Thos. Gray

deed. Gr. chn: Elizabeth, Wm., Mary, Margaret, Sarah Gray, chn. of Thos. Gray deed. Inv. made June 15, 1821 by Adam Wideman, Wm. Bond, Edward Carter, Jno. Beatty.

GRAY, MARY—BOX 38, PACK 822:
Est. admnr. May 6, 1827 by Alexr. D., Jas. A. Gray, Jas. Weems Esq. bound to Moses Taggart Ord. Abbeville Dist. sum $20,000.00. Inv. made June 11, 1827 by Barthw., Jonathan Jordon, Abraham Lites. Sale, June 12, 1827. Byrs: Jno., Robt. D. Gray, Mathew Burt, etc.

GILLESPIE, ELIZABETH—BOX 38, PACK 823:
Est. admnr. Aug. 14, 1818 by Mathew Gillespie, Jas., Thos., Vernon, Wm. Morris bound to Taliaferro Livingston Ord. Abbeville Dist. sum 5,000 lbs. Feb. 2, 1820 Paid Jas. Gillespie $15.83 Nov. 27, 1820 Paid Mathew Gillespie for Abraham Gillespie $15.83. Paid Margaret Buford $15.83.

GRUBBS, RICHARD—BOX 38, PACK 824:
Est. admnr. Sept. 6, 1819 by Elizabeth Grubbs, Nathaniel Shirley, Wm. Blain, Reuben Kay bound to Moses Taggart Ord. Abbeville Dist. sum $8,000.00. Property was advanced to Nathaniel Shirley, Reuben Kay during his life time. Sale, Oct. 28, 1819. Byrs: Elizabeth Grubbs, Wm. Grubbs, Benjamin, Nathan Shirley, etc.

GOWDY, WILLIAM ALFRED—BOX 38, PACK 825:
Est. admnr. Oct. 18, 1819 by Thos., David Gillespie, Nathan Strickland bound to Moses Taggart Ord. Abbeville Dist. sum $3,000.00. Feb. 14, 1819 Recd. of Jno. Thompson of North Carolina on a sett. $400.00. Recd. on acct. of his Robt. Thompson $800.00. A horse was sold to Richard Murray of Alabama for $95.00.

GILES, ROBERT—BOX 38, PACK 826:
Will dated Mar. 27, 1817 in Abbeville Dist. Proved June 2, 1818. Exr: Andrew Giles. Wit: Saml. Pressly, Wm. Giles. Wife and chn. ment. names not given. Inv. made July 1, 1817 by Wm. Giles, Allen Glover, Jas. McClain.

GUNNIEN, BENJAMIN—BOX 38, PACK 827:
Will dated Oct. 6, 1811. Proved Nov. 4, 1811. Exrs: Jas. Wardlaw, Gilbert Mann. Wit: Jno. Mann, Wm. McGaw, Allen M. Gillespie. Wife, Jean Gunnien. Chn: Hannah W., Isabella, Mary, Jas. Gunnien. Andrew Edwards was a distributee.

GRAY, ANDREW—BOX 38, PACK 828:
Est. admnr. Nov. 4, 1817 by Mary, Jas. Gray, Jno. Donald bound to Taliaferro Livingston Ord. Abbeville Dist. sum 10,000 lbs.

GIBSON, ROBERT—BOX 38, PACK 829:
Will dated Jan. 23, 1816 in Abbeville Dist. Proved Jan. 27, 1816. Exrs: Son, Jno. Gibson, s. l. David Taggart. Wit: Saml. C., Saml. Foster, Sr. Wife ment. name not given. Chn: Jno., Prudence Gibson, Mary McCain, Elizabeth Taggart, Jane Conn.

GIBERT, PETER, ESQ.—BOX 39, PACK 830:
Will dated June 8, 1815 in Abbeville Dist. Rec. July 3, 1815. Exrs:
Wife, Elizabeth B. Gibert, Sons, Lewis, Joseph B. Gibert. Wife, Elizabeth Buname
Gibert. Chn: Stephen, Lewis, Joseph B., Lucy, Mary, Susan, Harriet, Elijah
Gibert, Elizabeth C. Lee.

GREEN, ROBERT—BOX 39, PACK 831:
Est. admnr. June 7, 1805 by Catharine Green, Francis Young, Jno. Calhoun, Andrew Hamilton bound to Andrew Hamilton Ord. Abbeville Dist. sum
$10,000.00.

GASTON, JOHN—BOX 39, PACK 832:
Est. admnr. Sept. 3, 1806 by Mary, Wm. Gaston, Jas. Hawthorne, Saml.
Leard bound to Andrew Hamilton Ord. Abbeville Dist. sum $5,000.00.

GRIFFIN, ANTHONY—BOX 39, PACK 833:
Est. admnr. April 15, 1786 by Mary Griffin, Robt. McNeir, Jno. Hunter
bound to Jno. Thomas Jr. Ord. 96 Dist. sum 5,000 lbs.

GIBSON, SAMUEL—BOX 39, PACK 834:
Est. admnr. Sept. 21, 1782 by Mary Gibson, Joseph Dawson, Wm.
Carson bound to Jno. Ewing Calhoun Ord. 96 Dist. sum 14,000 lbs. Mary Gibson
was of Hardlabor Creek. Sale, Dec. 12, 1782. Byrs: Mary Gibson, Thos. Carson, Jno. Hearst, Saml. Bell.

GEORGE, DAVID—BOX 39, PACK 835:
Est. admnr. Nov. 14, 1782 and dated at Fort Boone by Rebecca, Wm.
George, Jas. Hogans, David Hutson bound to Jno. Ewing Calhoun Ord. 96 Dist.
sum 14,000 lbs. Rebecca George was of Tagger River.

GRAY, ELIZABETH—BOX 39, PACK 836:
Inv. made April 16, 1840 by Thos. E. Owen, Jno. Tennent, Wm. P.
Paul. Sale, April 17, 1840. Byrs: Jas. McCree, Jno. E. Williams, Jno. A.
Hamilton, etc. (No more papers.)

GLOVER, JANE—BOX 39, PACK 837:
Will dated July 19, 1822 in Abbeville Dist. Proved Aug. 14, 1822. Exrs:
Sons, Jno., Jas. H. Caldwell. Wit: Jno. Lipscomb, Stephen Witts, Hugh Ward-
law. Gr. son. Jno. Bowman.

GILL, DANIEL—BOX 39, PACK 838:
Will dated Nov. 7, 1796. Proved April 19, 1803. Exrs: Son, Jno. Gill,
Dr. Handy Harris, Saml. Black, Joseph Black, nephew of Wm. Black. Wit:
Daniel McKinzie, Wm. Bole, Ephraim Pursley. Chn: Phany wife of Saml.
Slaughter "give to them land in Edgefield Dist." Peter, Jno., Zekiel Gill, Sarah
Butler, Mary Slaughter. Wife, Susannah Gill. Another will of a Daniel Gill
in same pack: Will dated Dec. 5, 1800, was of Rocky River Congregation. Rec.
June 11, 1802. Exrs: Saml. Linton, Jno. Caldwell Esq., Thos. Shanklin. Wit:
Jno. Baskin, Wm. Bole. Wife, Susannah Gill. Chn: Jno., Fanney, Peter, Ezekiel,
Sarah, Polly Gill.

122   ABSTRACTS OF OLD NINETY-SIX AND

GOLDING, WILLIAM—BOX 39, PACK 839:
Will dated Sept. 4, 1777 in 96 Dist. Probated Sept. 23, 1782. Exrs: Sons, Jno., Reuben Golding. Wit: Jas. Griffin, Laughlin Leonard, Peggy Golding. Chn: Jno., Reuben, Richard, Wm., Robt. Golding, Milley Griffin, Sarah Foster, Elizabeth Tinsley, Mary Leonard.

GILLAM, JOHN—BOX 39, PACK 840:
Est. admnr. Sept. 6, 1783 by Robt. Gillam Esq., Robt. Richey bound to Jno. Thomas Jr. Ord. 96 Dist. sum 2,000 lbs. Byrs: Robt. Gillam, Robt. Richey, Joseph Armstrong, Isaac Dyson, Robt. Dunlap, Joshua Gillam, Thos. Pitts.

GRIFFIN, OWEN—BOX 39, PACK 841:
Will dated Nov. 11, 1806 in Abbeville Dist. Rec. Jan. 9, 1807. Exr: Peter Knop. Wit: Jno. Peter Knop, Jas. Adamson. Chn: Jas., Elizabeth Griffin.

GOLIGHTLY, WILLIAM—BOX 39, PACK 842:
Will dated Jan. 18, 1782. Proved July 31, 1782. Exrs: Wife, Amey Golightly, Brother, David Golightly. Wit: Moses, Jno. Foster, Charles James. Was of Fairforest, 96 Dist. Chn: Wm., Christopher, David, Clarimon, Mary Golightly.

GABEL, HARMON—BOX 39, PACK 843:
Will dated May 23, 1796 in Abbeville Dist. Proved July 23,1802. Exrs: Wife, Margaret Gable, Henry Gable. Wit: Wm. Dorris, Robt. Bradford, George B. Con. Chn: Henry, Jacob, Jno., Harmon Gable.

GRASTY, CHARSHELL—BOX 39, PACK 844:
Est. admnr. July 12, 1782 by Ann Grasty, Nathaniel Spragins, Randel Robinson bound to Jno. Ewing Calhoun Ord. 96 Dist. sum 14,000 lbs. Ann Grasty was of Broad River.

GORDON, WILLIAM—BOX 39, PACK 845:
Will dated April 19, 1781 in 96 Dist. Proved Nov. 7, 1782. Exrs: Wife, Elizabeth Gordon, Thos. Gordon, Gabriel Anderson. Wit: Wm. Cureton, Thos., Penelope Perey. Chn: Wm., Posey, Cassey Gordon.

GUTMAN, JOHN—BOX 39, PACK 846:
Est. admnr. Dec. 6, 1800 by Jno. Gray, Andrew Weed, Wm. Miller bound to Andrew Hamilton Ord. Abbeville Dist. sum $500.00. Cit. pub. at Rocky River Church. Byrs: Jno. Gray, Andrew Jones, Elizabeth Scott, Wm. Miller.

GANTT, DR. BENJAMIN—BOX 39, PACK 847:
Will dated Mar. 17, 1803. Rec. May 16, 1803. Exr. Wife, Fanny Gantt. Wit: Thos. Casey, Jno. Oliver, Leroy Pope. Lived in Petersburg, Georgia. "Will to my natural dtr. Eveline by Hetty S. Sterns." Brothers, Richard, Daniel, Charles Gantt. Nephew, Robson Mewburn.

GRIFFIN, RICHARD—BOX 39, PACK 848:
Est. admnr. Sept. 12, 1794 by Elizabeth Griffin wid., Jas. Eddins, Sr., Jas. Campbell, Sr. bound to Judges Abbeville Co. sum 500 lbs. Cit. pub at

Buffalo Church. Byrs: David Waters, Capt. Jno. Irwin, Wm. Wedgeworth, Elizabeth Griffin, Jas. Steele, etc.

GAINES, DAVID—BOX 39, PACK 849:
Est. admnr. Mar. 6, 1804 by Larkin Reynolds, Jas. Goudey, Jas. Watson bound to Andrew Hamilton Ord. Abbeville Dist. sum $5,000.00. Sale, Mar. 26, 1804. Byrs: Jas., Peggy, Richard, Wm. Gaines, etc.

GRIFFIN, JOHN—BOX 39, PACK 850:
Est. admnr. Feb. 10, 1808 by Lydia Griffin, Jno. Conner, Lewis Mitchel bound to Andrew Hamilton Ord. Abbeville Dist. sum $10,000.00. Wm. Lummus, gdn. of Jno. Griffin a minor legatee of Jno. Griffin Sr. decd., to issue against Jno. Hackney, admnr. by virtue of his marriage with Lydia Griffin Admnr.

GROCE, EDMOND—BOX 39, PACK 851:
Est. admnr. April 21, 1806 by Saml. Cowan, Jas. Hughes, Jas. Harris bound to Andrew Hamilton Ord. Abbeville Dist. sum $5,000.00. Saml. Cowan was next of kin. Sale, June 4, 1806. Byrs: York Rachel, Shepperd Groce, etc.

GLENN, COL. JOHN—BOX 39, PACK 852:
Est. admnr. Sept. 15, 1797 by Joseph Sanders, Toliver Bostick, Richard Andrew Rapley Esq. bound to Judges Abbeville Co. sum $10,000.00. Cit. pub. at Upper Long Cane Church. On Sept. 14, 1797 Major Wm. Glenn stated that before his brother's death, the late Col. Jno. Glenn, he made his will at Lumenburg Court House, Virginia between 17 or 18 yrs. ago.

GREEN, SARAH—BOX 39, PACK 853:
Will dated Jan. 11, 1809 in Abbeville Dist. Rec. Feb. 13, 1809. Exrs: Sons, Jas., Geo. Green. Wit: Bartholomew, Dudley Mabrey, Natn. Rosamond. Chn: Jas., Geo., Thos. Green, Frances Cullins, Elizabeth Sims, Nancy Shirley.

GUTTREY, THOMAS—BOX 39, PACK 854:
Will dated Mar. 18, 1797 in Abbeville Dist. Rec. Mar. 27, 1797. Exrs: Jas. Hamigar, Alexr. Clark, Jr. Wit: Wm. McGaw, Margaret Hamegar. Chn: Alenor, Jean, Jennet, Jno. Guttrey, Margaret Thomson, Jean Huston.

GREEN, SION—BOX 39, PACK 855:
Est. admnr. Jan. 27, 1802 by Elizabeth Green, Nimrod Overbey, Robt. Sample, Jno. Wilson bound to Andrew Hamilton Ord. Abbeville Dist. sum $10,000.00. Sale, Feb. 17, 1802. Byrs: Elisha Weatherford, Daniel Mitchel, Elizabeth Green, Wm. Meek, Jas. Chiles, etc.

GARRETT, ROBERT—BOX 39, PACK 856:
Will dated June 21, 1781 in Granvill Co. Proved Sept. 27, 1783. Exrs: Wife, Mary. Son, Jno. Garrett, s. l. Thos. Huey. Wit: Jno. Garrett, Lucy Lowry, Frances Longmire. "Give wife land at the mouth of Loyeds Creek." Chn: Peggy, Wm., Stephen, Jas., Marey, Patsey, Thos., Jno., Betsey, Jno. Catlett Garrett, Frances Huey, Ann Good.

GRIGG, BENJAMIN—BOX 39, PACK 857:
Est. admnr. Jan. 7, 1785 by Jno. Owens, Jas. Adair, Jno. Jones bound
to Jno. Thomas Jr. Ord. 96 Dist. sum of 2,000 lbs. Inv. made April 6, 1785 by
Jas. Adair, Jas. Craiege, Jno. Jones.

GOUEDY, ROBERT—BOX 39, PACK 858:
Will dated July 2, 1775 in 96 Dist. Proved Sept. 10, 1790. Exrs: Wife,
Mary Gouedy, Robt. Waring, Robt. Dickie. Wit: Wm. Moore, Hector, Susana
Dickie. Chn: Jas., Sarah Gouedy. "Bequeath unto my three Indian dtrs. viz.
Peggy, Kiunague, Nancy Gouedy. Robt. Gouedy was a Merchant at Cambridge.

GRIFFIN, BUCKNER—BOX 39, PACK 859:
Est. admnr. June 9, 1794 by Nathan Sims, Capt. Richard, Robt. Pollard
bound to Judges Abbeville Co. sum 500 lbs. Nathan Sims next of kin. Sale, Oct.
21, 1794. Byrs: Sarah Griffin wid. Nathan, Jno., Sterling Sims, etc.

GILKEYSON. WILLIAM—BOX 39, PACK 860:
Will dated Nov. 30, 1807 in Abbeville Dist. Rec. Feb. 5, 1808. Exr:
Robt. C. Gordon. Wit: Wm. Lesly, Ezekiel Evans, Rebecca Gordon. Wife ment.
name not given. Chn: Jno., Wm., Jane, Jincey, Eloner, Mary Elizabeth Gilkeyson.

GREEN, THOMAS—BOX 39, PACK 861:
Est. admnr. Oct. 1, 1784 by Elisha Green, Joseph West, Wm. Piumer
bound to Jno. Thomas Jr. Ord. 96 Dist. sum 2,000 lbs. Inv. made Oct. 13, 1784
by Jno. Birdsong, Alexr. McDogle, Obediah Howard. Sale, Nov. 1, 1784. Byrs:
Tabitha, Elisha Green, Jno. Pool, Jonathan Burson.

GLAZE, JOSEPH—BOX 39, PACK 862:
Est. admnr. July 7, 1786 by Jane Hardy, Thos. Gafford, Jas. Saxon bound
to Jno. Thomas Jr. Ord. 96 Dist. sum 1,000 lbs. Inv. made July 1786 by David
Burn, Thos. Gafford, as. Henderson.

GRIFFIN, ROBERT—BOX 39, PACK 863:
Will dated Feb. 9, 1809 in Abbeville Dist. Rec. April 8, 1809. Exrs:
Thos. Brightman, Isaac Logan, Geo. Heard. Wit: Armstrong Heard, Sr., Armstrong Heard, Jr. Wife, Margaret Griffin. Dtr. Elizabeth decd. Other chn. ment.
names not given. Gr. chn: Wiley, Leuana, Peggy McMillen. Inv. made April
22, 1809 by Armstrong Heard, Sr., Richard Heard, Jas. Wardlaw.

GLOVER, FREDERICK—BOX 39, PACK 864:
Will dated Dec. 31, 1796 in Edgefield Dist. Rec. Sept. 15, 1798. Exr:
Benjamin Glover. Wit: Wm. Hagood, Jno. McKellar. Chn: Jno., Wiley, Allen,
Benjamin Glover, Willey Harris. Gr. dtr. Caroline Young. Inv. made Sept.
30, 1797 by Patrick McDowall, Jas. Gouedy, Jas. Wilson.

GARRETT, JOHN—BOX 39, PACK 865:
Will dated Oct. 23, 1784 in 96 Dist. Proved Jan. 1, 1785. Exrs: Henry
Ward of Ga., Henry Ward, Jr., of S. C. Wit: Jas. Rivers, Nicholas Ware,
Jno. King. Chn: Robt. Garrett, Frances Longmire, Elizabeth Long of Virginia,
Martha Ware of Georgia, Lucy Lowry, Dolley Ware. Gr. dtr. Sukey Longmire.
Inv. made Jan. 6, 1785 by Capt. Geo. Cowan, Hezekiah Oden, Mathew Stocker.

GANTT, FREDERICK—BOX 39, PACK 866:
Will dated May 5, 1814. Rec. Jan. 24, 1815. Exrs: Wife, Elizabeth
Gantt. Brother, Cador Gantt. Wit: Fracins Cunningham, Cador Gantt, Benjamin
Griffin. Inv. made Jan. 24, 1815 by Eli Norris, Thos. Branyan, David Cummings.

GRAY, WILLIAM—BOX 39, PACK 867:
Will dated Dec. 2, 1809 in Abbeville Dist. Rec. Oct. 28, 1814. Exrs:
Major Andrew Weed, Col. Joseph Hutton, Jno. Gray Sr. Wit: Wm. Baldy,
Jno. Culbertson, Elice Baldy. Wife, Rosannah Gray. Chn: Wm., Jas., Arthur,
Rebecca, Anne Gray. Will was proved in Beaufort Dist. Legatee: Saml. Spence,
Robt. Pettigrew, Robt. Davis, Reuben Roberts, Wm. Sims, Jas. Craig.

GRAY, WILLIAM—BOX 40, PACK 868:
Est. admnr. Feb. 6, 1826 by Polly G. Gray, Andrew McClane, Jas.
Campbell, Daniel Weed bound to Moses Taggart Ord. Abbeville Dist. sum
$1,000.00. Cit. pub. at Hopewell Church. Inv. made Feb. 16, 1826 by Saml.
McClane, Jno., Daniel Weed.

GRAY, WILLIAM—BOX 40, PACK 869:
Est. admnr. June 1, 1818 by Jesse Gray, Jno. Cochran bound to Taliaferro
Livingston Ord. Abbeville Dist. sum $2,000.00. Cit. pub. at Smyrna Church.
Inv. made June 10, 1818 by Benjamin Adams, Saml. Thompson, Jno. H.
Spruce. Byrs: Wm., Jinney, Jno., Jas., Gray, etc.

GARNER, LEWIS—BOX 40, PACK 870:
Est. admnr. May 2, 1816 by Jno. Garner, Wm. Nibbs, Robt. Marsh bound
to Taliaferro Livingston Ord. Abbeville Dist. sum $10,000.00. Inv. made May
24, 1816 by Jno. C. Mayson, Jno. McBryde, Jno. McKellar, Jr. Lewis Garner
lived at Cambridge.

GAINES, EDMOND—BOX 40, PACK 871:
Will dated May 18, 1802 in Newberry Dist. Rec. Jan. 21, 1815. Exrs:
Father, Henry Gaines, Brothers, Richard, Henry Mayo Gaines. Wit: Larkin,
Richard, Robt. Gaines. Wife, Susannah Gaines. Chn. ment. names not given.
Inv. made Nov. 23, 1809 by Edward McCraw, Wm. Arnold, Jordon Moseley.

GRAY, ROBERT—BOX 40, PACK 872:
Est. admnr. April 1, 1811 by Nancy, Andrew Gray, Jno., West Donald
bound to Taliaferro Livingston Ord. Abbeville Dist. sum $10,000.00. Aug. 28,
1811 Paid Elizabeth Morrow $3.13½. Mar. 25, 1810 Paid Pheby Hearst $20.00.

GLANTON, JOHN—BOX 40, PACK 873:
Est. admnr. Dec. 2, 1785 by Nancy, Benjamin, Christopher, Jno. Glanton
bound to Jno. Thomas, Jr. Ord. 96 Dist. sum 1,000 lbs. Inv. made Jan. 26, 1786
by Henry Key, Thos. Pennington, Christopher Glanton.

GILLIAM, CHARLES—BOX 40, PACK 874:
Est. admnr. Nov. 29, 1783 by Jemima Gilliam, Wm. Caldwell, Gibeon
Jones bound to Jno. Thomas, Jr. Ord. Abbeville Dist. sum 2,000 lbs. Inv. made
Feb. 19, 1784 by Jno. Satterwhite, Thos. Turner, Jno. Caldwell.

GANTT, WILLIAM—BOX 40, PACK 876:
Will dated May 1, 1809 in Abbeville Dist. Rec. May 15, 1809. Exrs:
Frederick, Cador Gantt. Wit: Wm. Shirley, Wm. Curton, Jas. P. Conner. Chn:
Frederick, Cador, Jno., Tyre, Levina, Sally, Nancy, Amey Gantt. s. l. Jacob
Loller. Inv. made May 23, 1809 by Wm. Curton, Andrew Jones, Stephen
Durrum.

GRAY, JAMES—BOX 40, PACK 877:
Will dated Feb. 23, 1796. Rec. Mar. 28, 1797. Exrs: s. l. Robt. Ellis,
Robt. Lindsay. Wit: Jno. Murphy, Jno. Lindsay, Jas. Ellis. Dtr. Margaret Gray
Ellis. Gr. sons, Jas. Gray Ellis, Jno. Lindsay Ellis. Inv. made June 6, 1797 by
Jno. Murphy, Andrew, Ebenezer Miller.

GLYN, DAVID—BOX 40, PACK 878:
Est. admnr. April 28, 1786 by Rosanna Glyn, Jno. Lindsay, Robt. Lusk,
Thos. Dugan bound to Jno. Thomas, Jr. Ord. 96 Dist. sum 1,000 lbs. Inv. made
June 14, 1786 by Wm. Hamilton, Wm. Murry, Wm. Wilson. Sale, July 6,
1786. Byrs: Rosannah Glyn, Jno. Blalock, Patrick Lowry, Sims Brown, Jno.
Clark, Charles Crenshaw.

GREEN, PETER—BOX 40, PACK 879:
Will dated Dec. 16, 1794 in Abbeville Dist. Rec. Mar. 27, 1797. Exrs:
Sons, Sion, Philemon Green. Wit: Thos. Anderson, Jno. Bell, Jr. Wife, Thamar
Green. Chn: Philemon, Wm., Sion Green, Sarah, Polly Bell, Martha Moore,
Rebecca Eddins. Inv. made Sept. 8, 1797 by Jas., Nimord Chiles, Robt. Sample.

GILLESPIE, MATHEW—BOX 40, PACK 880:
Est. admnr. Mar. 25, 1793 by Frances Gillespie wid., Jas. Gillespie, Wm.
McCleskey, Sr. bound to Judges Abbeville County sum 1,000 lbs. Cit. pub.
at Rocky River Church. Inv. made May 1, 1793 by Jno. Pattersson, Aaron
Steele, Jno. Caldwell.

GILLESPIE, MATHEW P.—BOX 40, PACK 881:
Est. admnr. Oct. 19, 1825 by Saml., Archibald Scott, Jno. White bound
to Moses Taggart Ord. Abbeville Dist. sum $2,000.00. Cit. pub. at Smyrna
Church. Inv. made Nov. 4, 1825 by Robt. Davis, Wm. Buford, Jno. R. Cozby,
Archibald Scott. Byrs: Isabella H. Gillespie.

GILLESPIE, JAMES—BOX 40, PACK 882:
Est. admnr. Nov. 10, 1795 by Elizabeth Gillespie, wid., Lowry Gillespie,
Andrew Pickens, Jno. Harris of Flatwoods bound to Judges Abbeville Co. sum
1,000 lbs. Cit. pub. at Rocky River Church.

GRIMES, HUGH—BOX 40, PACK 883:
Est. admnr. July 31, 1784 by Margaret, Jas. Galley bound to Jno. Thomas
Jr. Ord. 96 Dist. sum 2,000 lbs. "Due to the est. of Hugh Graham decd. 18 lbs.
5 shillings 3 pence, being all the just debts due to my knowledge this Oct. 21,
1784." Margaret, Jas. Galley, Wm. Black appraised the est. (Note: In bond the
name was written Hugh Grimes, but in other papers written Hugh Graham.)

GREEN, SARAH—BOX 40, PACK 884:
Sale, Mar. 15, 1809. Byrs: Geo., Jas. Green, Wm. Henderson, Delilah
Mabray, Robt. Robertson, Charles, Joshua, Wm. Cullens, Richey Stone, Benjamin
Jones, Jno. Sims, Jno. Gains. (No other papers.)

GRIGSBY, JAMES—BOX 40, PACK 885:
Est. admnr. Mar. 13, 1783 by Richard Corley, Bartlett Bledsoe, David
Nicholson bound to Jno. E. Calhoun Ord. 96 Dist. sum 14 lbs. Richard Corley
of Little Saludy married the wid. Inv. made April 17, 1783 by Bartlett Bledsoe,
Wm. Lisson, Jno. Davis.

GREER, JOSEPH—BOX 40, PACK 886:
Est. admnr. Mar. 12, 1783 by Thos. Murphey, Robt. Neel, Isaac Mathews,
Benjamin Kilgore bound to Jno. Ewing Calhoun Ord. 96 Dist. sum 14,000 lbs.
Inv. made May 23, 1783 by Andrew Cunningham, Jno. McClinton, Jno. Hall.

GAINS, WILLIAM—BOX 40, PACK 887:
Will dated Mar. 30, 1804 in Abbeville Dist. Rec. April 13, 1804. Exrs:
Wife, Jas. Gaines, Jno. Meriwether. Wit: Dabney, Jas. Puckett. Wife and chn.
ment. names not given. Inv. made April 17, 1804 by Joseph Meriwether, Dabney
Puckett, Jas. Johnson.

GEE, JOHN—BOX 40, PACK 888:
Est. admnr. July 3, 1826 by Jno. Hearst, Jno. McComb, Jno. Pressly
bound to Moses Taggart Ord. Abbeville Dist. sum $2,000.00. Mar. 14, 1827
Recd. of Jas. Puckett for land sold by Robt. Gee Atty. to said Puckett. Inv.
made July 22, 1826 by Jonathan Arnold, Jno. Chiles, Saml. Mouchet.

GENRY, WILLIAM D.—BOX 40, PACK 889:
Est. admnr. Jan. 17, 1829 by Gen. Edmund Ware, Wm. Kyle, J. W.
Taggart bound to Moses Taggart Ord. Abbeville Dist. sum $2,000.00. Inv. made
Feb. 5, 1829 by Wm. Pyles, Jno. Mattison, Augusta Maddox. Sale, May 5,
1829. Byrs: Elizabeth Genry, etc.

GOFF, AUGUSTUS—BOX 40, PACK 890:
Est. admnr. Feb. 2, 1838 by Saml. Goff, Thos. Jackson, Robt. Cochran
bound to Moses Taggart Ord. Abbeville Dist. sum $200.00.

GILES, MARY—BOX 40, PACK 891:
Est. admnr. April 17, 1835 by Jno., Jas. S. Baskin, Jas. F. Cook bound
to Moses Taggart Ord. Abbeville Dist. sum $3,000.00. Cit. pub. at Glovers
Chapel. Sett. made June 6, 1845. Present the admnrs. Parties in interest, Jno.
Baskin and wife Jane, Jno., Saml. Young, Francis Young decd. David and
Susannah Carr both decd. Martha Mitchell decd. her heirs, Isabella McGill
decd. her heirs, Mary Giles wife of Wm. Giles died without chn. was a dtr.
of Francis Young.

GILLIBEAU, ANDREW—BOX 40, PACK 892:
Will dated Feb. 18, 1806 in Abbeville Dist. Rec. Feb. 21, 1815. Exr:
Son, Peter Gillibeau. Wit: Charles Hathorn, Peter, Elizabeth Covin. Wife,

Jean Gillibeau. Chn: Jas., Peter Gillibeau, Susannah Bouchillon. "Will unto Eliser Gillibeau supposed to be the dtr. Jas. Gillibeau, begotten by Liddy Bellot $70.00."

GIBERT, DR. JOHN J.—BOX 40, PACK 893:
     Est. admnr. June 12, 1818 by Jas. Pettigrew, Geo., Alexr. Bowie bound to Taliaferro Livingston Ord. Abbeville Dist. sum $15,000.00. Inv. made June 15, 1818 by Dale Palmer, Stephen Gibert, Joshua Hill.

GIBERT, SARAH B.—BOX 40, PACK 894:
     Est. admnr. Oct. 5, 1836 by Jas. F. Gibert, Dyonitus Rogers, Jas. Taggart bound to Moses Taggart Ord. Abbeville Dist. sum $30,000.00. Sett. of est. Stephen and Sarah B. Gibert immerged in one. After death of Stephen Gibert, Sarah B. Gibert admnr. Legatees were: Jas. F., Elizabeth H., Stephen F., Peter L., Jno. A. Gibert. Dated Dec. 1, 1841.

GRAY, JOHN—BOX 40, PACK 895:
     Will dated Sept. 1, 1826 in Abbeville Dist. Proved Aug. 23, 1827. Exrs: Sons, Allen, Jas. Gray, Alexr. Houston, Esq., Jno. Pressley. Wit: Jas., Anna C. Gray, Andrew McClane. Chn: Jas., Mary, Claudius, Joseph, Anna. Allen, Lewis, Patsey Gray. "Owned land in Green County, Ala." (Another will of Jno. H. Gray in same pack.) Will dated May 18, 1862 in Abbeville Dist. Rec. June 26, 1862. Exrs: Son, Jno. Gray, wife. Wit: Robt. Palmer, Wm. H. Brooks, Thos. J. Mabry. Son. Jno. Gray now in the army of the Confederate States. Wife and other chn. ment. no names given.

GRAY, JOHN—BOX 40, PACK 896:
     Est. admnr. July 18, 1812 by Alexr., Benjamin Houston bound to Taliaferro Livingston Ord. Abbeville Dist. sum $5,000.00. Cit. pub. at Willington Church. July 25, 1812 One quire of paper for Armenta Gray $.31½. Sale, Sept. 7, 1812. Byrs: Elizabeth Gray, Margaret Hemphill, Catherine Green, Frances Carlile, Jas. Crage, etc.

GAINES, JAMES—BOX 40, PACK 897:
     Est. admnr. Oct. 22, 1819 by Richard, Thos. Gaines, Saml. Davis bound to Moses Taggart Ord. Abbeville Dist. sum $2,000.00. Cit. pub. at Silom Church. Sale, Nov. 17, 1819. Byrs: Richard, Patsey, Reuben, Thos. Gaines, Chesley Davis, Nathaniel Marion, etc.

GALPHIN, GEORGE—BOX 40, PACK 898:
     Will dated April 6, 1776. Exrs: James Parsons, John Graham, Lauchlin McGillvery, Esq., John Parkinson Merc. Wit: Michael Meyer, John Sturzenegger, David Zubly. Ment: Lived in 96 Dist. "Will that my mulatto girl named Barbara be free. I give to my mulatto girls Rachael and Betsy (daughters of a mulatto woman named Sapho) their freedom. Give to my halfbreed Indian girl, Rose (daughter of Nitehuckey) her freedom. I Give to Thomas Galphin, son of Rachel Dupee, and his sister, Cowpen, in Ogechee, horses, cattle, etc. Also grist mill and saw mill situated on the north side of Town Creek. Also land from Mr. Shaw's lower line upon Savannah River at the Spanish Cutoff,

down the said river to Mr. McGillvery's lower line, containing about 1300 acres in the Province of Georgia. Also 350 acres of land upon Ogechee, which I bought of Patrick Dennison. Give to Martha Galphin, daughter of Rachel Dupee, 500 acres of land above Augusta, in Georgia. Also cattle, etc. at Ogechee. Give to George, son of Metawney (an Indian Woman), stock of cattle with his own, his sister Judith's and brother John's mark and brand. Also the old brick house, in S. C., land above the Spanish Cutoff on Savannah River in Georgia. Give to John, son of Metawney, cattle with his own, his sister Judith's and brother George's mark. Also land upon Ogechee, in Georgia, called the Old Town. Give unto Judith, daughter of Metawney, land and dwelling at Silver Bluff, where she now lives, in S. C. Give unto Barbara, daughter of Rose, decd., land at Silver Bluff in S. C. Give unto Thomas slaves, etc. Give to David Holms land in Georgia. Give to Judith Galphin, my sister, 150 pounds sterling. I leave Catherine Galphin, living in Ireland, 150 pounds sterling. To my sister, Margaret Holms, 50 pounds sterling. To each of her children, now in Ireland, 50 pounds sterling. To her son Robert, now living here, 50 pounds sterling. Give to Mrs. Taylor 50 pounds sterling, etc. To my cousin George Rankin, in Ireland, 70 pounds sterling, to him or his children. Leave to George Nowlan 50 pounds sterling. I leave to my Aunt Lennard's daughter in Ireland, to her and her children, 50 pounds sterling. Leave to my cousin John Trotter, 50 pounds, to him and his children. I leave to Rachel (daughter to Sapho) two negro men and two negro women to be bought out of the first ship that comes in with negroes. Give to Thomas, son of Rachel Dupee, and his children to be maintained and schooled on the plantation. Leave to Betsey Callwell, daughter of Mary Callwell, land at the Three Runs, at the Old Stomp, above Tims Branch. Also 50 pounds Carolina currency. I leave to all the poor widows and fatherless children within thirty miles of where I live in the Provinces of South Carolina and Georgia 50 pounds sterling. I leave 50 pounds sterling to be shared among the poor of Eneskilling and 50 pounds sterling to be shared among the poor of Armagh in Ireland. Leave to Timothy Barnard 200 pounds sterling. Leave to all the orphan children I brought up 10 pounds sterling each and Billey Brown to be bound out to a trade. I leave John McQueen and Alexander, his brother, each a good riding horse. Leave to Mr. Netherclif and his wife each a ring. Leave to Mr. and Mrs. Wylly each a ring. Leave to their daughter Sucky Wylly 50 pounds. Leave to Mrs. Campbell a ring. Leave to Mr. Carlan a ring. Leave to Mrs. Fraisier a ring. Leave to Mr. Newman a ring. Give to the widow Atkins, 20 pounds sterling. To her son William, a riding horse. Give to Parson Seymour and his wife, each a ring. Give to George Parsons, a likely negro boy to be bought him out of the first ship that comes in. Leave to Quintin Tooler 500 acres of ceded land and to all the rest of my Cousin Toolers (men and women) each a ring. I leave my sister Young, in Ireland, 50 pounds sterling, and to each of her children 50 pounds. Give to Clotworthy Robson 500 acres, to his and his heirs. Give to my sister Martha, wife of William Crossley, slaves, etc. GROVES, ELIZA N.—BOX 41, PACK 899:

On Oct. 19, 1809 Henry G. Walker and wife Lattice of Georgia, Jno. Martin, Thos. B. Creagh bound to Andrew Hamilton Ord. Abbeville Dist.

sum $5,000.00. Henry G. Walker made gdn. Eliza N. Groves a minor. Sept. 23, 1809 Recd. of Joseph Groves, Exr. of Jno. Groves, on acct. of said minor $500.00.

GIBERT, MINORS—BOX 41, PACK 900:
On Dec. 22, 1835 Peter B. Moragne, Dyomytius N. Rogers, Wm. J. Houston bound to Moses Taggart Ord. Abbeville Dist. sum $20,000.00. Peter B. Moragne made gdn. of Gideon Jno., Caroline Jane, Harriet Adalnie Gibert minors. Wm. G. Darracott married Caroline Jane. Joseph Noble married Adeline Gibert. Sett. of Jno. Lewis Gibert decd. made Sept. 3, 1842. Mr. Gibert died in 1825. 1837 Paid Benjamin E. Gibert $3.75.

GRIFFIN, JAMES—BOX 41, PACK 901:
On Mar. 18, 1816 Randal Hagood, Bennett McMillan, Benjamin F. Whitner bound to Taliaferro Livingston Ord. Abbeville Dist. sum $5,000.00. Randal Hagood made gdn. Jas. Griffin a minor under 14 yrs. 1817 Recd. of Jas. Griffin, admnr. of Wm. Griffin decd, $73.00. Paid Ord. of Edgefield $1.50.

GRAHAM, MINORS—BOX 41, PACK 902:
On April 13, 1826 Josiah Carwile, Wm. Graham, Jno. Clinkscales bound to Moses Taggart Ord. Abbeville Dist. sum $2800.00. Names of minor chn. not given. 1831 Recd. of Jas. Moore $37.81½ being the balance of a $70.00 note given for rent of plantation belonging to Jas. Graham a minor. Dec. 20, 1830 Paid Zachariah Graham $32.70 in full of est. of Jas. Graham decd.

GLOVER, JOHN—BOX 41, PACK 903:
On June 25, 1833 Wm. Harris, Leroy Watson, Jno. Lipscomb bound to Moses Taggart Ord. Abbeville Dist. sum $10,000.00. Wm. Harris made gdn. of Jno. J. Glover a minor. Feb. 9, 1833 Recd. from est. of Wm. H. Glover being his part $111.26. July 5, 1833 Paid Willis Glover $87.00. Dec. 29, 1833 Recd. from his mother Sarah Glover being his portion of the money produced at Columbia at which place she died $245.33½.

GRAY, MINORS—BOX 41, PACK 904:
Recd. from Andrew Weed, Exr. of Wm. Gray decd., one fourth part of the price of two negroes by said Wm. to his wife for life. Remainder to her 4 sons $502.62½. From Rosanna Gray $25.32. Paid Mary C. Gray for board of her minor chn. Mary, Allan, Lucinda, Hannah Gray.

GRAY, MINORS of Wm. Gray, Jr.—BOX 41, PACK 905:
On Jan. 22, 1831 Jno., J. B. Pressly, Jas. Conner bound to Moses Taggart Ord. Abbeville Dist. sum $1,000.00. Jno. Pressly made gdn. of Wm., Jno., Lucinda, Eliza, Amanda, Hannah Gray minors under 14 yrs. On Dec. 3, 1828 Geo. Cochran made gdn. Wm. A., Jno. G., Martha Ann, Jas. A. Gray minors under 14 yrs.

GRAY, MINORS—BOX 41, PACK 906:
On Dec. 12, 1835 Alexr. D. Gray, Fenton Hall, Wm. Tucker bound to Moses Taggart Ord. Abbeville Dist. sum $1,000.00. Alexr. D. Gray made gdn.

of Zachariah, Nancy Augustine Gray. Nancy A. was of age Nov. 1851. Jan. 2, 1835 Recd. from est. of Jas. A. Gray $310.67. Feb. 11, 1837 Paid Elizabeth Gray $30.00. Chn. of Jas. A. Gray decd.

GRAY, MINORS—BOX 41, PACK 907:
   On Nov. 30, 1835 Elizabeth Gray, Jas. C. Wharton, Jas. S. Wilson bound to Moses Taggart Ord. Abbeville Dist. sum $5,000.00. Elizabeth Gray made gdn. Margaret M., Agness D. Gray, minors Jas. A. Gray decd. Elizabeth wid. of Jas. A. Gray. Had 8 chn. 2 were twins.

GRAY, ROBERT D.—BOX 41, PACK 908:
   On May 14, 1825 Sealy Walker, West, Jas. Donald bound to Moses Taggart Ord. Abbeville Dist. sum $7,000.00. Sealy Walker made gdn. Robt. Douglass Gray. Jan. 1, 1827 Note on Mary Gray $45.00.

GASTON, MINORS—BOX 41, PACK 909:
   On Sept. 16, 1837 Jno. Norwood, Wm. Lyon, Charles Dendy bound to Moses Taggart Ord. Abbeville Dist. sum $3,000.00. Jno. Norwood made gdn. Jane, Jno. Gaston minors.

GASTON, ALEXANDER—BOX 41, PACK 910:
   On Feb. 1, 1836 Andrew Mantz, Hamilton, Saml. Hill bound to Moses Taggart Ord. Abbeville Dist. sum $10,000.00. Andrew Mantz made gdn. Alexr. Gaston a minor.

GILL, EZEKIEL—BOX 41, PACK 911:
   On Oct. 29, 1800 Jno. Gill, Wm. Kerr, Milton Paschal bound to Andrew Hamilton Ord. Abbeville Dist. sum $5,000.00. Jno. Gill made gdn. of Ezekiel Gill a minor. Green Co. Georgia. "Personally came from before me Wm. Browning Justice for said county, Mr. Jno. Gill saith that the acct. is true . . . Dated Dec. 3, 1807." 1804 Cash paid Mary Gill minor by her gdn. Milton Paschall for schooling $5.00. Nov. 19, 1803 Recd. from Jno. Caldwell Esq. Exr. of Daniel Gill decd. $224.58.

GROVES, SYLVANUS—BOX 41, PACK 912:
   On Oct. 20, 1807 Joseph Groves, Nathaniel Alston, Jas. Foster bound to Andrew Hamilton Ord. Abbeville Dist. sum $10,000.00. Joseph Groves made gdn. Jno., Sylvanus Groves minor chn. of Jno. Groves decd. Oct. 12, 1810 Paid Jno. Groves expenses to Augusta 2nd time to get in business as storekeeper. $6.00. Oct. 18, 1808 Paid Sylvanus Groves by his factors Barna, Joseph McKinne in Savannah for expenses and accommodations paid in the hands of Aunt Eleanor King $25.00.

GRAY, REBECCA—BOX 41, PACK 913:
   Gdn. Jno. Gray. Nov. 1, 1814 Recd. $300.00 from the est. of her grand mother Rebecca Hutton decd. Dec. 9, 1816 to removing Rebecca Gray and her property from Union Dist. $22.75. Dec. 2, 1819 Paid in advance for her boarding at Yorkville Female Academy $25.00. Paid Gen. Joseph Hutton for sundries purchased in Petersburgh $19.87½.

GAINES, MINORS—BOX 41, PACK 914:
On Jan. 9, 1835 Seaborn O., Dawson B. Sullivan, Jno. Bowie bound to Moses Taggart Ord. Abbeville Dist. sum $2,000.00. Seaborn O. Sullivan made gdn. Joanna N., Margaret Ann Gaines, chn. of Hiram Gaines decd.

GIBERT, DR. JOSEPH B.—BOX 41, PACK 915:
Est. admnr. Sept. 1, 1828 by Alexr. Hunter, Archibald McMullen, Hudson Prince bound to Moses Taggart Ord. Abbeville Dist. sum $10,000.00. Cit. pub. at Rocky River Church. Sale, Dec. 4, 1828. Byrs. Mrs. Jane Gibert, etc.

GUARIN, JOHN J.—BOX 41, PACK 916:
Est. admnr. Sept. 20, 1823 by Charles Goodman, Jas. Tatom, Jno. L. Pamplin bound to Moses Taggart Ord. Abbeville Dist. sum $500.00.

GIBERT, ELIJAH—BOX 41, PACK 917:
Est. admnr. April 10, 1823 by Joseph B. Gibert, Peter B. Rogers, Wm. Gray bound to Moses Taggart Ord. Abbeville Dist. sum $1,000.00. Cit. pub. at Bethelehem Church.

GRAHAM, MARGARET—BOX 41, PACK 918:
Expend: Mar. 4, 1824 Paid Jane Parker $20.00. Oct. 24, Paid David Parker $26.75. Nov. 1, Paid Stephen Jones $22.75. Sale, Nov. 22, 1824. Byrs: Wm., Jno., Jas. Graham, Jr., Mary Jones, Margaret Parker, etc.

GILLESPIE, JAMES C.—BOX 41, PACK 919:
Est. admnr. July 27, 1829 by Jno. Speer Esq., Stephen Jones of Abbeville Dist., Freeman Wiles of Anderson Dist. bound to Moses Taggart Ord. sum $2,000.00. Cit. pub. at Providence Church. Paid Mary Strickland for the est. as per receipt $5.56. Paid Mrs. Gillespie for tuition of Mary $3.00.

GLASGOW, JOHN—BOX 41, PACK 920:
Est. admnr. Sept. 15, 1828 by Giles W. Glasgow, Joseph, J. T. Williams bound to Moses Taggart Ord. Abbeville Dist. sum $2,000.00. Sale, Oct. 8, 1828. Byrs: Elizabeth, Giles W. Glasgow, Simeon Clay, etc.

GRAY, WILLIAM—BOX 41, PACK 921:
Sale, 1826. Byrs: Polly, Mary Gray, Jas., Jno. W. Gray, Abram Outon, etc. (No more papers.)

GRAY, ELIZABETH—BOX 41, PACK 922:
Will dated Feb. 14, 1840 in Abbeville Dist. Rec. April 17, 1840. Exr: Saml. L. Hill. Wit: Wm. P. Paul, Jas. Edwards, Jno. J. Edwards. Chn: Agness D., Margaret M. Gray, Elizabeth J. Paul, Andrew Paul. Sett. made Jan. 27, 1842 between Saml. L. Hill Exr. and Geo. W. Pressly, gdn. of Agness and Margaret M. Gray, David Wardlaw and wife Elizabeth.

GRAY, ROBERT—BOX 41, PACK 924:
Est. admnr. June 10, 1839 by Jno. A. Andrew J. Donald, Andrew J.

Weems bound to Moses Taggart Ord. Abbeville Dist. sum $10,000.00. Nancy Gray the wid. was admnr. but at her death these were appointed.

GILLAM, DAVID—BOX 41, PACK 925:
Will dated Mar. 12, 1838 in Abbeville Dist. Proved Feb. 14, 1842. Exrs: Jas., Robt. C. Gillam. Wit: R. Boulware, Jas. Owens, Jas. Gillam. Wife ment. name not given. Chn: Harris, Rebecca Gillam.

GRAHAM, MINORS—BOX 41, PACK 927:
The petition of James Graham showeth that on Mar. 25, 1842, he married Mary Young, daughter of V. Young decd. That the said V. Young died and that afterwards the wife of your petr. died leaving two children viz: Cela M. and Valentine Graham. Expend: The State of Mississippi, Itawamba County. On March 6, 1848, James Graham made application in courts to be appointed guardian of Cely Ann and Valentine Graham, minors. (Note: The first petition was made March 25, 1842 in Abbeville District, S. C.) On one paper was written Sarah M. and Valentine Young.

GOLDING, RICHARD A.—BOX 41, PACK 928:
Est. admnr. Nov. 2, 1842, by Reuben G. Golding, Charles B. Fooshe, Harris Y. Gillam, bound to David Lesly Ord. Abbeville Dist. in sum $4000.00. Sett. made June 25, 1845, to ascertain the share of Nimrod C. Goulding of Louisiana. The said R. A. G. Golding was a minor. April 30, 1844, John M. Golding recd., $573.77, as his share. Other parties interested were: R. G. Golding, Wiley D. Mounce and his Lavenia. R. G. Golding was a brother to the decd

GLASGOW, JOHN—BOX 41, PACK 929:
Will dated Dec. 2, 1842. Proved Oct. 23, 1843. Exrs: Wife, Eliza Ann Glasgow, Richard A. Martin. Wit: Robert McComb, George Cochran, M. A. Smith. Lived in Abbeville Dist. Wife, Eliza Ann Glasgow. Sister, Jane Mc-Callister. Sett. ment. widow had a child born just before his death.

GALLIGLY, JAMES—BOX 41, PACK 930:
Est. admnr. March 18, 1844, by John Morgan, Benjamin F. Roberts, Henry Riley bound to David Lesly Ord. Abbeville District in sum $2000.00. He left a widow, Rebecrah and several children. In Aug. 1845, John Morgan recd. $31.72 of his share of estate. Thomas Morgan recd. $31.72 his distributive share. G. W. Butle, Rachel Galligly, Mary Galligly, and William Galligly were also legatees.

GOLDEN, WILLIAM—BOX 41, PACK 931:
On Jan. 19, 1843, Charles B. Goulden, Reuben Golden, J. Maddison Golden bound to David Lesly Ord. Abbeville Dist. in sum $100.00. The petition of Charles B. Golden on Jan. 19, 1843 showeth that his brother William Golden died intestate, leaving no wife or children, but mother, brothers and sister.

GRAHAM, WILLIAM, JR.—BOX 41, PACK 932:
Est. admnr. Jan. 11, 1845 by Jno. Smith of Laurens Dist., Jno. White,

Jno. Taggart of Abbeville Dist. bound to Moses Taggart Ord. sum $500.00. Mar. 5, 1845 J. G. Traynham recd. in full his portion $33.66. Albert M. Graham recd. for coffin $12.94. Wm. Graham died in Abbeville Dist. but most of his property was in Laurens Dist. Polley, Jas. Graham bought at sale.

GLASGOW, JOHN DAVID—BOX 41, PACK 933:
On Jan. 1, 1845 Archibald Kennedy, Jas. H. Foster, Jas. Lesly bound to David Lesly Ord. Abbeville Dist. sum $2,000.00. Was a minor of Jno. Glasgow decd. and Elizabeth A. Glasgow.

GAMBLE, SAMUEL—BOX 41, PACK 934:
Will dated Oct. 19, 1800 in Abbeville Dist. Rec. June 28, 1804. Exr: Wife, Jane Gamble. Wit: Jas., Alexr. Keown, Wm. Adams. Chn: Jno., Robt., Saml. Gamble. "Bequeath to Harris Jones one mare."

HUGHEY, LYDIA—BOX 42, PACK 935:
Est. admnr. Jan. 2, 1837 by Jno. L. Bowman, Francis Atkins, Wm. S. Ansley bound to Moses Taggart Ord. Abbeville Dist. sum $10,000.00. Inv. made Jan. 4, 1837 by Owen Selby, Edmund Cobb, Ephraim Davis, Jas. Partlow. Vachel Hughey bought at sale, etc.

HADDON, ANDREW—BOX 42, PACK 936:
Est. admnr. Nov. 15, 1828 by Saml. Reid, Andrew, Allen Miller, Hugh Kirkwood, bound to Moses Taggart Ord. Abbeville Dist. sum $10,000.00. Cit. pub. at Upper Long Cane Church. Sale, Dec. 5, 1828. Byrs: Andrew Hagan, Robt. Crawford, Wm. McComb, Robt. Richey, etc.

HAMILTON, CAPT. ALEXANDER C.—BOX 42, PACK 937:
Est. admnr. Mar. 21, 1835 by Jas. S. Wilson, Wm. Tennent, Thos. Eakins, Gen. Jno. Bowie bound to Moses Taggart Ord. Abbeville Dist. sum $30,000.00. Cit. pub. at Sharon Meeting House. Saml. S. a son was of age in April 27, 1849. Harriet E. D. of age Aug. 14, 1846. Statement for sett. of Robt. B. Hamilton decd. in same pack. Made May 3, 1847. Present, Jas. Giles admnr. and notified Dr. Lynch who married the wid. and A. F. Posey, admnr. of B. Posey and agent of Dr. Lynch and wife. One half of est. due Mrs. Lynch to be divided among brothers and sis. of Robt. B. Hamilton decd. viz. Mrs. Jane Bowie, Jno. Hamilton, Susan Wilson, Mrs. Anna Giles, Jas. A., Alexr., Saml., Harriet, Richard A. Hamilton.

HUGHEY, JOHN—BOX 42, PACK 938:
Est. admnr. Aug. 27. 1830 by Joseph Hughey, Owen Selby, Ephraim Davis, Michael Peaster bound to Moses Taggart Ord. Abbeville Dist. sum $10,000.00. Cit. pub. at Long Cane Church. Sale, Sept. 14, 1830. Byrs: Jno., Lidia, Jas. Hughey, Robt. Croson, etc.

HILL, JOHN, SR.—BOX 42, PACK 939:
Will dated Oct. 15, 1812 in Abbeville Dist. Rec. April 16, 1813. Exrs: Susannah Hill, Thos. Wilson. Wit: Dudley Mabry, Saml. Rosamond, Saml. Hill. Wife, Susannah Hill. Chn: Saml., Wm., Jno., Joseph, Bluford, Betsey, Nancy,

Sally, Susannah, Fanny, Rebecca, Polly Hill. A drt. Frances married a Rosamond.

HILL, JOSEPH—BOX 42, PACK 940:
Est. admnr. Nov. 15, 1828 by Richard Gaines, Wm. Barmore, Edmond Ware bound to Moses Taggart Ord. Abbeville Dist. sum $3,000.00. May 19, 1832 Paid Jno. Graham and wife Eliza for support of Susan J., Frances E. Hill for 1 yr. $40.00.

HACKETT, ELIJAH—BOX 42, PACK 941:
Est. admnr. Oct. 24, 1828 by Martin, Robt. Hackett, Jno. H. Waller bound to Moses Taggart Ord. Abbeville Dist. sum $20,000.00. Cit. pub. at Mount Moriah Church. Had no family but left 6 brothers and sisters. One, Wm. Hackett decd. had 4 chn. now living and a wid., but Wm. died before Elijah. Elijah C. son of Wm. Hackett of age July 8, 1845.

HUNTER, COL. JAMES—BOX 42, PACK 942:
Est. admnr. Aug. 5, 1833 by Joseph, Hugh Dickson, David R. Caldwell bound to Moses Taggart Ord. Abbeville Dist. sum $25,000.00. Cit. pub. at Rehoboth Church. Sett. made Mar. 4, 1836. Present, Mary A. Hunter wid., Jas. Lawrence Calhoun and wife Nancy M. Hunter, Jno. B. Hunter by his gdn. Wm. Mills, Jas. Hunter by his gdn. Saml. Hunter, Wm. C. Hunter by his gdn. Joseph Dickson. Jas. Hunter the intestate died April 1833. Jno. B. Hunter recd. a legacy under the will of Jno. Hunter his grandfather.

HUEY, JOHN B.—BOX 42, PACK 943:
Will dated Dec. 1, 1833 in Abbeville Dist. Proved Dec. 10, 1833. Exrs: Wife, Ruth R. Huey, Jas. Huey, Jno. Gray. Wit: Wm. H. Caldwell, Wm. Tennent, Robt. Davis. Chn: Jno. Thos., Jane C., Louisa C. Huey. Nov. 8, 1836 Paid Jno. H. Gray legatee $700.00.

HEARST, JOHN—BOX 42, PACK 944:
Will dated Sept. 9, 1780 in Long Cane Sett. 96 Dist. Probated Aug. 23, 1782. Exr: Wife, Mary Hearst. Wit: Charles Teulon, Rob Wilson, Rob Erwin. Chn: Robt., Mary, Jno., Joseph, Thos., Geo., Wm., Christian, Elizabeth, Margaret Hearst. Sept dtr. Eloner O'Bryan. (On bottom of page written Mary Cox alias Hearst.) Will of William Hearst in same pack. Will dated Jan. 8, 1823. Exr: Jno. Hearst. Wit: Saml., Wm. B., Jno. T., Jno. S. Pressly. Lived in Abbeville Dist. Chn. ment. names not given. "Willed property to Jno. Hearst, Ebenezer Pressly." Sett. made Dec. 8, 1834 of Wm. Hearst. Gr. chn. living entitled to a share. Brothers and sisters of testator. Joseph Hearst had 8 chn. Thos. Hearst 8 chn. Eliza Hearst married Wm. Pressly. had 4 chn. Christian Hearst Wilson 1 child. George Hearst had 5 chn.

HICKMAN, RICHARD—BOX 42, PACK 945:
Est. admnr. Oct. 24, 1825 by Barbara D. Hickman, Wm. Pursell, Jno. J. Barratt, Geo. A. Miller bound to Moses Taggart Ord. Abbeville Dist. sum $3,000.00. Cit. pub. at Upper Long Cane Church. Sale took place at the residence of Wm. Pursell Nov. 11, 1825. Byrs: Barbara D. Hickman, etc.

HILL, UEL—BOX 42, PACK 946:
Will dated Aug. 22, 1832 in Abbeville Dist. Executed Nov. 3, 1832.
Exrs: Joshua, Wm. P. Hill, Abner Perrin. Wit: Jacob B. Britt, R. W. Corley,
A. M. McCraven. Niece, Sarah Ann Hartsfield. "Give to Miriam, Sarah Harts-
field a chest made by their father Alsa Hartsfield." Nephew, Wm. P. Hill. Dtr.
Elizabeth wife of Jas. Hughes. Gr. chn: Ann wife of Willis Palmer, Catherine
wife Singleton Hughes, July wife of W. G. Williams. Other legatees, Thos.,
Frances, Pamealy, Jas. Hughes, Jr.

HOWLET, STETH—BOX 42, PACK 947:
Est. admnr. Feb. 20, 1836 by Aaron Lomax, Paschal D. Klugh, Nathaniel
Cobb bound to Moses Taggart Ord. Abbeville Dist. sum $2,000.00. Cit. pub. at
Beulah Church. Sale, Feb. 27, 1836. Byrs: Mary Howlet, Wm. Butler, Sr., etc.

HAMILTON, MAJOR ANDREWS, SR.—BOX 42, PACK 948:
Est. admnr. Feb. 9, 1835 by Jno., Andrew Hamilton, E. S. Davis, Fanney
Calhoun, F. Branch, Jas. S. Wilson bound to Moses Taggart Ord. Abbeville
Dist. sum $20,000.00. Est. admnr. again Dec. 5, 1840 by Jno. A. Hamilton,
Jas. S. Wilson, Johnson Ramey bound to Moses Taggart Ord. sum $2,000.00.
Jno. Cooper of Christian County, Kentucky appointed Hugh C. Cooper of same
county his Atty. to receive his part as heir of Andrew Hamilton of Abbeville
Dist. thru his marriage with Margaret Carr, formerly Margaret Pickens and dtr.
Jno. Harris and gr. dtr. of Andrew Hamilton. Margaret and Jno. Cooper were
parents of Hugh Cooper. Feb. 11, 1836 Paid Archiblad Hamilton leg. $141.09.
Aug. 1, 1836 Paid Lindsay Harper leg. of Sarah Harris decd. in right of his wife
$140.00. J. C. Oliver and wife Sarah dtr. Sarah Harris decd. $140.00. April
1836 Paid Jno. Harris son of Sarah Harris decd. $140.00. Oct. 3, 1836 Paid
Ezekiel Harris son of Sarah $140.00. Aug. 9, 1836 Paid W. L. Beauford and
wife Sarah dtr. of Wm. Harris decd. $28.00. Paid gdn. of Hyram G. Harris,
Marther W. Harris dtr. Wm. Harris decd. $28.00. Charles M., Job W. were sons
Wm. Harris. Aug. 9, 1837 Paid note of hand on M. Megehee, Jas. Alston in
favor of Margaret Kerr, Mary Shannon dtrs. Sarah Harris decd. $380.00 Feb.
11, 1836 Paid Fanny Calhoun legacy $49.00. Andrew Hamilton legacy $46.29.
Nov. 18, 1835 Paid E. L., Jane Davis legacy $199.76.

HAMILTON, WILLIAM—BOX 43, PACK 949:
Est. admnr. Oct. 18, 1832 by Sophia C. Hamilton wid. Jas. Houston,
Jno. Davis bound to Moses Taggart Ord. Abbeville Dist. sum $4,000.00. Inv.
made Nov. 5, 1832 by Saml. Shaw, Jonathan Shirley, Peter S. Burton.

HAGAN, EDWARD—BOX 43, PACK 950:
Est. admnr. Jan. 16, 1834 by Thos., Wm. Hagan, Henry Ruff, Thos.
Gordon bound to Moses Taggart Ord. Abbeville Dist. sum $3,000.00. Cit. pub.
at Upper Long Cane Church. Sett. made April 5, 1847. Alexr. G. Hagan, son
of Andrew Hagan decd. and gr. son of Edward Hagan, for whom Wm. Hagan
was gdn.

HAGAN, ANDREW—BOX 43, PACK 951:
Est. admnr. Dec. 27, 1833 by Wm., Edward Hagan, Thos. McIlwain

bound to Moses Taggart Ord. Abbeville Dist. sum $2,000.00. Cit. pub. at Upper Long Cane Church. Wid. Mary Hagan. Sale, Jan. 14, 1834. Byrs: Mary, Edward, Wm. Hagan, etc.

HAMILTON, JOHN—BOX 43, PACK 952:
Sett. of Jno. Hamilton who died Dec. 1839 made Jan. 23, 1841. Present, Moses Hamilton Ord., Jno. A. Hamilton Exr, Mrs. McMillan Exr, Catherine Douglass, Rachel Laner, Jas A. Hamilton not present. Legattees under will: Mrs. McMillan, Jno. A. Hamilton in trust for Mrs. Kennedy, Catherine Douglass, Rachel Laner, Jno. A., Jas. A. Hamilton. Jno. A. Hamilton in trust for Eliza A. Douglass. (Will missing.)

HUGGINS, WILLIAM A.—BOX 43, PACK 953:
Est. admnr. Jan. 2, 1832 by Dr. Jno. P. Barrett, Jno. Lipscomb, Wesley Brooks bound to Moses Taggart Ord. Abbeville Dist. sum $500.00. Inv. made Jan. 7, 1832 by Richard Henderson, Sr., Richard Henderson, Jr., Nathan Henderson. Byrs: Mrs. Huggins, etc.

HAWTHORN, JAMES—BOX 43, PACK 954:
Est. admnr. Jan. 6, 1834 by Saml. Irwin, Jno. Donald, Andrew Robison, Jno. Goudy bound to Moses Taggart Ord. Abbeville Dist. sum $2,000.00. Cit. pub. at Upper Long Cane Church. Sale, Jan. 24, 1834. Byrs: Wid. Hawthorn, Jno. Lather, Wm. McCrone.

HENDERSON, ISAAC—BOX 43, PACK 955:
Est. admnr. Oct. 25, 1813 by Jinsey Henderson, Alexr. Harrilson, Joseph Stallworth bound to Taliaferro Livingston Ord. Abbeville Dist. sum $2,000.00. Cit. pub. at Mount Moriah Church. Sale, Nov. 12, 1813. Byrs: Jinsey, Nathan, Richard Henderson, etc.

HEMMENGER, JAMES—BOX 43, PACK 956:
Est. admnr. Nov. 26, 1832 by Thos. M. Duncan, Jno. Hemmenger, Wm. Hanvey bound to Moses Taggart Ord. Abbeville Dist. sum $500.00. Inv. made Dec. 10, 1832 by Saml. Cowan, Charles Britt, Wm. Hanvey.

HODGES, MAJOR JOHN—BOX 43, PACK 957:
Will dated Mar. 20, 1834 in Abbeville Dist. Proved Jan. 2, 1835. Exrs: Wife, Frances Hodges, Sons, Geo. W., Gabriel Hodges. Wit: Saml., Jas. L., Jno. G. Anderson. Chn: Jno., Armstead Jones, Matilda, Geo. Washington, Gabriel, Drusilla Hodges, Elizabeth Bowie, Sarah, Margaret, Mary, Saml. Anderson, Frances, Hulda, Absalom Turner, Robt. Wardlaw, Jas., Benjamin, Lucy Wardlaw. Gr. chn: Rhoda, Frances, Gracy, Matilda, Jno., Jas., chn. of Elizabeth Bowie. Sett. made Nov. 15, 1845. Wm. N. McKellar and wife share $61.79½.

HUNTER, WILLIAM—BOX 43, PACK 958:
Will dated May 2, 1832 in Abbeville Dist. Proved May 7, 1832. Exrs: Jno. Donald, A. C. Hawthorn. Wit: Andrew, Enoch Agnew, Larkin Barmore. Chn: Jas., Wm., Margaret, Louisa Hunter.

HARRIS, JOHN—BOX 43, PACK 959:
    Will dated Dec. 5, 1831 in Abbeville Dist. Proved Dec. 12, 1831. Exrs:
Son, Wm. Harris, Robt., Jas. McCaslan. Wit: Patrick Gibson, Joseph S. Wide-
man. Wife, Milly Harris. Chn: Wm., Robt., Elizabeth, Polly, Jno., Sarah,
Caroline, Peggy, Milly, Leuisa Catherine, Thos. S. Harris.

HALL, FLEMING—BOX 43, PACK 960:
    Est. admnr. Feb. 18, 1832 by David, Fenton Hall, Jno. Davis bound
to Moses Taggart Ord. Abbeville Dist. sum of $1,000.00. Nov. 2, 1843. "This is to
certify that David Hall desposited in this post office Storeville, S. C. a letter
inclosing the right end of $50 bill of the bank of Hamburg. I mailed for him
to Jno. Ward Riply in Miss. A. Thomson." On Mar. 1, 1843 Margaret Hall
appeared in court at Ripley, Tippah County, Miss. along with Nathaniel Hobson.
Wm. Shetley into bond in sum $200.00. as gdns. of Fenton B., Laurel V. Hall,
minor heirs of Fleming Hall decd. formerly of Abbeville Dist. and late of
Carroll County, Tenn. Cit. pub. at Rocky River Church. Letter written to
David Hall Esq. Storeville, Anderson Dist. S. C. Ripley, Miss. Dec. 7, 1846.
In letter from Margaret Hall she inquired about her sister Elizabeth Hall of
Anderson Dist. On June 7, 1844 Jno., Mary Ann Ward of Ripley, Miss. wrote
a letter to her brother David Hall Esq. at Anderson, S. C. On Jan. 23, 1843
Zachariah Hall of Tippah County, Miss. appointed David Hall his Atty. to
collect his part of the est. of Fleming Hall, his father, who died intestate in
Tenn. Sett. 7 legatees, only one was given, Jesse M. Hall.

HARRIS, THOMAS—BOX 43, PACK 961:
    Est. admnr. Jan. 13, 1836 by Wade S., Jno. Cothran, Thos. C. Perrin
bound to Moses Taggart Ord. Abbeville Dist. sum $10,000.00. Cit. pub. at
Rehoboth Church. Sale, Jan. 28, 1836. Byrs: Wm. Glover, Sarah Williams,
Jacob Young, etc.

HALL, SARAH—BOX 43, PACK 962:
    Will dated Oct. 13, 1834 in Abbeville Dist. Proved June 3, 1834. Exrs:
Son, Jno. Hall, Jno. Pratt. Wit: Saml. Young, Bennett McAdams, Wm. Pratt
Sr. Chn: Jno., Elizabeth, Sarah Ann, Ursula, Joseph B., Caleb Hall. Inv. made
Mar. 9, 1836 by Jno. R. Wilson, Lydall Williams, Robt. Ellis.

HARRIS, JOHN—BOX 43, PACK 963:
    Will dated Nov. 20, 1817 in Abbeville Dist. Filed April 26, 1819. Exrs:
Benjamin Glover, Wm. Harris. Wit: Allen Glover, Geo. Holleway, Elihu
Bullock. Wife, Milly Harris. Nephews, Jno. G., Wm. Harris, Jno. O. Glover.
"Bequeath to Wiley Harris son Wm. Harris, bequeath to Sarah Glover dtr.
Allen Glover, bequeath to Frederick Glover, to Benjamin Glover, Jr.

HUSTON, HUGH—BOX 43, PACK 964:
    Est. admnr. Dec. 26, 1834 by Geo. Huston, Bailey Fleming, Wm. Coving-
ton bound to Moses Taggart Ord. Abbeville Dist. sum $1200.00. Sale, Jan.
29, 1835. Byrs: Lacy, Sterling Bowen, Geo., Martha Huston, etc.

HOPPER, SAMUEL J.—BOX 43, PACK 965:
    Est. admnr. Dec. 7, 1829 by Joel, Thos., Wm. Smith bound to Moses

Taggart Ord. Abbeville Dist. sum $10,000.00. Cit. pub. at Rocky Creek Church.
Feb. 3, 1832 Elizabeth Hopper recd. $237.43¾ her share of est. Also recd.
$474.92 for the shares of Saml. Y., Catharine M., Elizabeth Hopper.

HODGES, JAMES, SR.—BOX 43, PACK 966:
Will dated Feb. 27, 1826 in Abbeville Dist. Proved Sept. 1, 1828. Exr.
Son, Thompson Hodges. Wit: Jas. Wilson, Robt. Gaines, Jas. Burnside. Wife,
Nancy Hodges. Chn: Betsey, Polly, Martha Weatherall, Nicholas, Ezekiel,
Thompson, Reuben, Jas., Elizabeth Jones. Inv. made Oct. 28, 1828 by Jno.
C. Waters, Thos. A., Benjamin Rosemond, Geo. Weatherall.

HARRIS, JAMES A.—BOX 43, PACK 967:
Est. admnr. Jan. 27, 1816 by Thos. P. Martin, Thos. Heron, Wm.,
Robertson bound to Taliaferro Livingston Ord. Abbeville Dist. sum 10,000 lbs.
Cit. pub. at Rocky River Church. Sale, Mar. 4, 1816. Byrs: Wm., Ester Harris,
Solomon Blackwell, etc.

HENDERSON, JAMES, SR.—BOX 43, PACK 968:
Est. admnr. Feb. 22, 1817 by Saml. Porter, Jno. Adams, Jas. E. Glenn,
Adino Griffin bound to Taliaferro Livingston Ord. Abbeville Dist. sum 10,000
lbs. Cit. pub. at Rehobeth Church. Legatees: Thos., Jas. L., Mathew Henderson,
Jehu Roden, Saml. Porter. Sale, Mar. 12, 1817. Byrs: Ellender, Richard, Sr.,
Lee Henderson, etc.

HILL, THOMAS—BOX 43, PACK 969:
Will dated Aug. 25, 1821 in Abbeville Dist. Proved Nov. 14, 1823.
Exrs: Archey Mayson, Saml. Hensley. Wit: Nathan Chancy, Thos. H. Casen,
Beaufort Chiles. Wife ment. name not given. Chn: Wm., Thos., Willis, Jas.
Hill, Elizabeth Pollard decd. "Bequeath to Martial Pollard." Aug. 9, 1841 Money
recd. by Frances Hencely, admnr. of est. of Saml. Hencely decd., for est. of Thos.
Hill decd. Recd. of Nathan Chaney $38.00. On Nov. 30, 1841 Willis Hill
states that his father Thos. Hill died 1821; that he was an infant then and that
Saml. Hencely is since dead leaving a wid.; and that Frances Hencely has recd.
funds belonging to est. and that she now resides near Cambridge in Edgefield
Dist.

HEARD, RICHARD—BOX 43, PACK 970:
Will dated Mar. 11, 1816 in Abbeville Dist. Proved Mar. 18, 1816. Exrs:
Brother, Isaac Heard, Zachariah Meriwether. Wit: Austin Pollard, Robt.
Griffin, Charles Maxwell. Wife, Nancy Heard. Chn: Salinda, Bailey Heard.
b. 1. Zachariah Meriwether. Capt. Zachariah Meriwether, Bailey Heard was
later of Pam County, Ala.

HARPER, HENRY—BOX 44, PACK 971:
Est. admnr. Sept. 20, 1819 by Lindsay Harper. Saml. Scott, Alexr. C.
Hamilton bound to Moses Taggart Ord. Abbeville Dist. sum $1,000.00. Inv.
made Oct. 4, 1819 by Jas. Toland, Saml. Scott, Jno. C. Oliver. Byrs: Lindsay,
Marthew Harper, etc.

HENDERSON, WILLIAM—BOX 44, PACK 972:
    Est. admnr. Dec. 22, 1826 by Saml., Richard, Jno. Henderson bound
to Moses Taggart Ord. Abbeville Dist. sum $10.000.00. Feb. 9, 1830 Paid
Nathaniel Henderson $200.00. Feb. 8, 1830 Ann Henderson $60.00. Jas. Henderson $30.00. Jan. 12, 1829 Richard Henderson $49.59. Feb. 12, 1829 Jno.
Henderson $72.75. Jan. 10, 1827 To boarding Shadrack son of Wm. Henderson
$30.00. July 23, 1827 Acct. of Eleanor Henderson $75.00. Jan. 9, 1827 For
Sarah dtr. Wm. Henderson $17.25.

HENCELY, MARY—BOX 44, PACK 973:
    Will dated Nov. 18, 1822 in Abbeville Dist. Proved Feb. 28, 1823. Exr:
Saml. Hencely. Wit: Thos., Nancy, Thos. Hill, Sr. Chn; Frances Proctor, Sarah
Sadler, Enoch, Saml. Hencely and his wife Frances.

HUTCHISON, JAMES—BOX 44, PACK 974:
    Will dated May 10, 1822 in Abbeville Dist. Proved Aug. 21, 1822.
Exrs: Joseph C. Mathews, Philip Leroy, Jr. Wit: Jno., Jane McElhenney. Wife,
Jane Hutchison. Chn: Martha, Mary Ann, Isabella, Jane Hutchison. Ment.
Wm. Hutchison gr. father of Mary Ann. Inv. made Sept. 2, 1822 by Joseph
Calhoun, Vincent McElhenney, Jno. Scott.

HENDERSON, JOHN—BOX 44, PACK 975:
    Est. admnr. Nov. 26, 1827 by Nancy Henderson, Elias Lake, Dr. Jno.
Barratt, Thos. Stallworth bound to Moses Taggart Ord. Abbeville Dist. sum
$3,000.00. Cit. pub. at Mount Moriah Church. Jan. 9, 1830 Paid Peper McKeller
for tuition of Nathaniel, Thos. Henderson $16.00. Paid Elener Henderson
$15.00. July 1830 Paid Saml. Henderson $3.12½. 1829 Elizabeth Henderson
$38.35.

HOLT, JOHN—BOX 44, PACK 976:
    Est. admnr. Oct. 20, 1837 by Henry Cannon, Wm. Hall, Thos. W. Pace
bound to Moses Taggart Ord. Abbeville Dist. sum $1200.00. Cit. pub. at Mount
Prospect Church. Dec. 16, 1837 Paid Israel Holt for 3 days service as clerk
$6.00. July 15, 1838 Paid A. Holt $7.00. Wid., Elizabeth Holt.

HILL, WILLIAM—BOX 44, PACK 977:
    Est. admnr. Oct. 9, 1821 by Robt., Adam Hill, Wm. Patton, Saml.
Morris bound to Moses Taggart Ord. Abbeville Dist. sum $5,000.00. Sale, Oct.
31, 1821. Byrs: Jas., Robt., Anne, Wm., Adam Hill, etc.

HENDERSON, ELENOR—BOX 44, PACK 978:
    Est. admnr. Mar. 25, 1825 by Saml. Caldwell, Saml. Cothran, Andrew
Redmond bound to Moses Taggart Ord. Abbeville Dist. sum $3,000.00. Cit. pub.
at Swamp Meeting House. Inv. made April 7, 1825 by Robt. Gillam, Thos.
Harris, Jacob Slappy. Byrs: Jesse, Wm. Henderson, etc.

HENDERSON, MARGARET—BOX 44, PACK 979:
    Est. admnr. Jan. 22, 1829 by Henry Gray, Geo. W. Hodges, Wm. Hunter
bound to Moses Taggart Ord. Abbeville Dist. sum $3,000.00. Cit. pub. at Asbury

Meeting House. On April 5, 1827 Margaret Henderson promised to pay Jas. Devlin, admnr. est. of Jno. Henderson decd. $304.00. Sale, Feb. 3, 1829. Byrs: Jane Henderson, etc.

HILL, SAMUEL—BOX 44, PACK 980:
Est. admnr. Mar. 14, 1825 by Wm. Barmore, Hugh Morrah, Andrew Hawthorn bound to Moses Taggart Ord. Abbeville Dist. sum $2,000.00. Sept. 22, 1826 Recd. from the est. of Jno. Hill decd. $120.68¾, being the legacy that fell to the est. of Saml. Hill decd. from est. Jno. Hill, Jr.

HACKETT, WILLIAM—BOX 44, PACK 981:
Est. admnr. Jan. 30, 1826 by Anna, Elijah Hackett, Jno. Ramsey bound to Moses Taggart Ord. Abbeville Dist. sum $20,000.00. Jan. 23, 1827 Saml. Leak recd. of Richard Griffin $5.00 for Anna Hackett tuition. Wm. Barker recd. $16.00. for Wm. H. Hackett. For Elizabeth F. Hackett $12.00. Peter McKeller recd. $16.00. for tuition of Henry M. Hackett.

HAMMOND, WILLIAM—BOX 44, PACK 982:
Est. admnr. Dec. 12, 1828 by Henry Zimmerman, Philip Cook, David Walker bound to Moses Taggart Ord. Abbeville Dist. sum $3,000.00. Cit. pub. at Swamp Meeting House. Inv. made Dec. 29, 1828 by Jacob Slappy, Thos. Whitlock, Robt. Gibson.

HARRIS, GEORGE—BOX 44, PACK 983:
Est. admnr. Oct. 16, 1829 by Michail Peaster, David H. McClesky, Wm. Hall bound to Moses Taggart Ord. Abbeville Dist. sum $2,000.00. Cit. pub. at the Deadfall. Cit. to acct. to Thos. Joshua Harris, Elizabeth Fisher, the chn. of Jenny Smith decd., the chn. of Wm. Harris decd., the chn. of Jno. Harris decd., and the distributees of Geo. Harris.

HOGAN, RICHARD, SR.—BOX 44, PACK 984:
Est. admnr. Mar. 1, 1837 by Independence L. Pearson, Jno. Cothran, Anthony Caldwell bound to Moses Taggart Ord. Abbeville Dist. sum $1,000.00. Cit. pub. at Rehobeth Church. Mar. 15, 1837 Had 1 note signed by Willis Hogan Jan. 28, 1829. Byrs: Richard, Elizabeth Hogan, etc.

HARRIS, ROBERT—BOX 44, PACK 985:
Will dated Mar. 12, 1812 in Abbeville Dist. Rec. April 13, 1812. Exrs: Wife, Elenor Harris, Son, Jas. Harris, Brother, Jno. Harris. Chn: Jas., Margaret Harris. (4 sons ment. only 1 named.) Wit: Jno., Jas. Caldwell, Jas. Carlile. Sale, May 27, 1812. Byrs: Jno., Wm. Harris, etc.

HILL, DAVID—BOX 44, PACK 986:
Est. admnr. June 27, 1812 by Elizabeth, Jno. Hill, Benjamin, Saml. Rosamond bound to Taliaferro Livingston Ord. Abbeville Dist. sum $1,000.00. Inv. made Aug. 7, 1812 by Jas. Hodges, Jno. Williams, Thos. Wilson. Byrs: Betsey, Elisha, Thos., Jno. Hill, Sr., Major Jno. Hodges. Josey Hill was an heir of David Hill.

HOSKISON, JAMES H.—BOX 44, PACK 987:
Est. admnr. Feb. 16, 1826 by Oswell, Moses Houston, Mathew McNeal

bound to Moses Taggart Ord. Abbeville Dist. sum $5,000.00. Cit. pub. at Hope-well Church. Admnr. Bond of Lucretia Hoskison alias McKittrick decd. Est. admnr. May 21, 1845 by Jas. F. Hoskison, Benjamin McKittrick, Jno. Mouchet bound to David Lesly Ord. Abbeville Dist. sum $1,000.00. July 24, 1826 Recd. of judgment in Elbert County, Georgia vs. Jas. H. Hoskison against Jno. Harris $298.00.

HINTON, JAMES—BOX 44, PACK 989:
    Est. admnr. Sept. 3, 1827 by Thos. Cobb, Jr. Archibald Arnold, Owen Selby bound to Moses Taggart Ord. Abbeville Dist. sum $1,000.00. Cit. pub. at Shiloah Church. Inv. made Nov. 13, 1827 by Jno. Gray, Robt. Morrah, Wm. Grubbs. Byrs: Sopha, Jeremiah Hinton, etc.

HARRIS, JOHN G.—BOX 44, PACK 990:
    Est. admnr. Mar. 3, 1828 by Rachel Harris, Saml., Thos. Atkins, Jas. Patterson bound to Moses Taggart Ord. Abbeville Dist. sum $5,000.00. Sale, Mar. 12, 1828. Byrs: Rachel, Wm. Jr., Wm. Harris, Sr., Eliza Hacket, etc.

HASLET, JOHN—BOX 44, PACK 991:
    Est. admnr. Oct. 21, 1823 by Joseph B. Gibert, Wm. Speer, Peter B. Rogers bound to Moses Taggart Ord. Abbeville Dist. sum $3,000.00. Cit. pub. at Glovers Chapel. Inv. made Nov. 21, 1823 by Edward Tilman, Thos. Montgomery, Geo. Haslet. Byrs: Mrs. Haslet, etc.

HOGG, SHADRACK—BOX 44, PACK 992:
    Est. admnr. Oct. 18, 1826 by Alexr. Hunter, Robt. Smith, Wm. T. Drennan bound to Moses Taggart Ord. Abbeville Dist. sum $2,000.00. Inv. made Oct. 25, 1826 by Dabney Wanslow, Jonathan Johnson, Wm. Smith. Sale, Feb. 14, 1827. Byrs: Wid. Louisa Hogg, Reuben Lowry, etc.

HASLET, GEORGE—BOX 44, PACK 993:
    Will dated Sept. 7, 1817. Proved May 17, 1827. Exr: Alexr. Hunter. Wit: Joseph Vernon, A. Hunter, S. T. Shanklin. Wife, Nancy Haslet. Chn. ment. names not given. Sis. Phebe Haslet. Had 1 note on David C. Haslet $5.00. Ment. son Wm. Haslet and Wm. Morrow as the father and gr. father.

HADDON, JANE—BOX 44, PACK 994:
    Will dated June 25, 1859. Exr. b.l. J. G. E. Branyon. Wit: Seuy, M. D. Branyon, S. H. Tribble. Lived in Abbeville Dist. Sis. Sarah, wife of J. G. E. Branyon. On Jan. 29, 1830 Ebenezer, Saml. Smith, Robt. Dunn were bound to Moses Taggart Ord. Abbeville Dist. sum $700.00. Ebenezer Smith made gdn. Lewis, Jane Haddon minors under 14 yrs.

HADDON, MINORS—BOX 44, PACK 995:
    On Jan. 29, 1830, Andrew, Ebenezer Miller, Saml. Reid bound to Moses Taggart Ord. Abbeville Dist. sum $1700.00. Andrew Miller made gdn. of Wm. Haddon minor over 14 yrs, David Haddon minor under 14 yrs. 1830 Recd. shares of A. Haddon's est. $40.88.

HADDON, WILLIAM—BOX 44, PACK 996:
Est. admnr. Oct. 9, 1826 by Elizabeth, Andrew Haddon, Saml. Reid, Ebenezer Miller bound to Moses Taggart Ord. Abbeville Dist. sum $15,000.00. April 14, 1828 paid Hugh Gaston distributee $285.00. Jan. 6, 1828 paid Ebenezer Miller share $46.00. Sale, Oct. 26, 1826. Byrs: Mrs. Haddon, Andrew, Lucinda Haddon, etc.

HEARD, THOMAS—BOX 44, PACK 997:
Est. admnr. Feb. 15, 1808 by Jas., Elizabeth C. Heard, Dr. Zachary Meriwether, Mathew Gayle Sr. bound to Moses Taggart Ord. Abbeville Dist. sum $10,000.00. Jan. 17, 1808 paid Armstrong Heard, Sr., acct. $10.82. Nov. 19, 1808 paid Mary Heard $111.08. Cit. to acct. Isaac T. Heard, heir of Thos. Heard, made suit for cit. against Jas. P. Heard, Elizabeth C. Heard (now White) and Jno. M. White in right of wife, and his brother Jno. W. Heard.

HAWTHORNE, DAVID H.—BOX 45, PACK 998:
Est. admnr. Aug. 12, 1815 by Hugh Morrah, Isaac Cowan, Abraham Haddon, Joseph Hathorne bound to Taliaferro Livingston Ord. Abbeville Dist. sum $20,000.00. Inv. made Oct. 24, 1815 by Robt. C. Sharp, Abram Haddon, David Taggart. Byrs: Wm. Sharp, etc.

HEMPHILL, MARGARET—BOX 45, PACK 999:
Est. admnr. Feb. 6, 1826 by Wm. Hemphill, Alexr., Jas. A. Houston bound to Moses Taggart Ord. Abbeville Dist. sum $8,000.00. Cit. pub. at Hopewell Church. Wm. Hemphill next of kin. Mar. 1826 Paid Jno. Hemphill legatee $397.89. Alexr. Hemphill $397.89.

HILL, JOSEPH—BOX 45, PACK 1000:
Will dated June 13, 1825 in Abbeville Dist. Proved Nov. 29, 1825. Exrs: Sons, Wm., Wiley Hill, Jas. Gillam. s. l. Isaac Bunting. Wit: Peter Cheatham, Wm. Fooshe, Wiley Corley. Chn: Wm., Wiley, Joseph, Milton, Isaac Mitchel Hill, Helen Bunting. Wife ment. name not given. April 4, 1851 Eliza Smith recd. $1610.46 in full of her brother's portion of est.

HAGOOD, RANDOLPH—BOX 45, PACK 1001:
Est. admnr. Nov. 18, 1820 by Rebecca Hagood, Garland, Benjamin Chiles, Thos. Marsh, Thos. Livingston bound to Moses Taggart Ord. Abbeville Dist. sum $4,000.00. Cit. pub. at Cambridge. Sale, Dec. 15, 1820. Byrs: Richard, Geo. Hagood, etc.

HATTER, BENJAMIN—BOX 45, PACK 1002:
Will dated Nov. 21, 1820 in Abbeville Dist. Probated May 14, 1821. Exrs: Sons, Wm., Zery Hatter, Thos. Sr., Joseph Hill, Abner Piles. Wit: A. Mayson, Thos., Nancy Hill. Chn: Wm., Zery, Polly, Belinda, Susannah, Elizabeth, Richard, Milly, Mahaly Hatter.

HENDERSON, DAVID—BOX 45, PACK 1003:
Est. admnr. April 20, 1811 by Mary, Jas. Henderson, Geo. Rievs,

Thompson Hodges bound to Taliaferro Livingston Ord. Abbeville Dist. sum $2,000.00. Sale, May 9, 1811. Byrs: Wid., Wm., Jas., Mary Henderson, etc.

HOUSTON, ALICE—BOX 45, PACK 1004
    Est. admnr. Dec. 5, 1825 by Jas. R. Houston, Jas. Hughes, Jno. Ferguson bound to Moses Taggart Ord. Abbeville Dist. sum $3,000.00. Jas. R. Houston next of kin. Inv. made Dec. 20, 1825 by Joseph C. Matthews, Jno. Dickson, Philip Leroy. Byrs: Jas. R., Nancy, Alexr. Houston, etc.

HARRIS, SAMUEL—BOX 45, PACK 1005:
    Est. admnr. Dec. 4, 1811 by Titus Murry, Abraham Livingston, Gibson Wooldridge bound to Taliaferro Livingston Ord. Abbeville Dist. sum $20,000.00. Cit. pub. at Rocky River Church. Sale, Dec. 28, 1811. Byrs: Nathaniel, Mary, Nancy, Richard Harris, Sr., etc.

HARRIS, TURNER—BOX 45, PACK 1006:
    Est. admnr. Oct. 19, 1803 by Jno. Harris, Isham, Nathaniel Norwood bound to Andrew Hamilton Ord. Abbeville Dist. sum $1,000.00. Inv. made by Wm. Watson, Saml. Ramsay, Nathaniel Norwood. Byrs: Jno. Harris, Jno. Lively, etc.

HAMILTON, JAMES—BOX 45, PACK 1007:
    Est. admnr. July 6, 1789 by Jane Hamilton, wid., Jas. Hamilton, Jno. Nicholson bound to Judges Abbeville County sum 500 lbs. Admnr. again Oct. 20, 1804 by Isabel, Archibald Hamilton, Alexr. Foster, Thos. Jordon in sum $2,000.00. Inv. made Dec. 21, 1789 by Daniel Ship, Jno., Jas. Wilson.

HUGHES, JAMES—BOX 45, PACK 1008:
    Est. admnr. Mar. 21, 1804 by Benjamin Shirley, Henry Sharp, Thos. Beaty bound to Andrew Hamilton Ord. Abbeville Dist. sum $7,000.00. Sale, April 10, 1804. Byrs: Wm. Hughes, Rachel Hughes, wid., etc.

HAMILTON, ISABEL—BOX 45, PACK 1009:
    Est. admnr. Jan. 24, 1805 by Jehu Foster, Wm., Andrew Hamilton Ord. Abbeville Dist. sum $700.00. Paid Alexr. Hamilton legatee $14.00. Paid schooling for Jenny, Alexr., Billy Hamilton $18.00. Byrs: Jane, Archibald Hamilton, etc.

HEMPHILL, JOHN—BOX 45, PACK 1010:
    Est. admnr. Dec. 24, 1803 by Margaret Hemphill, Robt. Foster, Alexr. Clark bound to Andrew Hamilton Ord. Abbeville Dist. sum $5,000.00. Sale, Jan. 13, 1804. Byrs: Margaret Hemphill, etc.

HAWTHORNE, ROBERT—BOX 45, PACK 1011:
    Est. admnr. Mar. 17, 1812 by Mary Hathorn, Henry, Wm. Sharp bound to Taliaferro Livingston Ord. Abbeville Dist. sum $1,000.00. Sale, Aug. 25, 1812. Byrs: Thos., Polly, Joseph J., Jas. Hawthorn, etc.

HALL, JOHN—BOX 45, PACK 1012:
    Est. admnr. Nov. 6, 1797 by Sarah Hall, wid., Thos., Francis Hodge,

Wm. Dunlap bound to Judges Abbeville County sum $5,000.00. Was a Merchant. Inv. made Dec. 29, 1797 by Dunken Campbell, Thos. Pringle, Francis Hodge. Byrs: Robt. George, Michael Cain, Wm. Holmes, etc.

HEARD, JOHN—BOX 45, PACK 1013:
Est. admnr. Mar. 2, 1807 by Thos. Heard, Thos. Herron, Alexr. Stuart bound to Andrew Hamilton Ord. Abbeville Dist. sum $5,000.00. Wid. was Rebekah Heard. Thos. Heard of Cambridge was a brother. Inv. made Mar. 11, 1807 by Levi Rich, Benjamin Hatter, Jas. Johnson.

HUBBARD, JAMES—BOX 45, PACK 1014:
Est. admnr. Feb. 4, 1811 by Hudson Prince, Charles Miller, Martin Loftis bound to Taliaferro Livingston Ord. Abbeville Dist. sum $500.00. Inv. made Feb. 22, 1811 by Wm. Covington, Saml. McBride, Joseph Prince.

HAMILTON, CAPT. JOHN—BOX 45, PACK 1015:
Will dated Nov. 26, 1805 in Abbeville Dist. Rec. Dec. 26, 1805. Exrs: Wife, Mary Anne Hamilton, Jno. Caldwell, Esq. Wit: Francis Carlile, Wm. Davis. Chn: Thos. Twining, Mary, Isabella, Elizabeth Anne Hamilton, Sarah Waddel.

HANNAH, JEAN—BOX 45, PACK 1016:
Will dated Dec. 30, 1801 in Abbeville Dist. Rec. Feb. 17, 1802. Exr: Niece, Flender McRay. Wit: Nathaniel Bailey, Robt. Evans. Sis. Agness McRay. Nieces, Mary, Jenet McRay. Nephew, Jno. McRay.

HAIRSTON, WILLIAM—BOX 45, PACK 1017:
Sale, May 4, 1808. Byrs: Peter, Jas., Robt., Ann, Wm. Hairston, etc. (No more papers.)

HOUSTON, BENJAMIN—BOX 45, PACK 1018:
No will date given. Rec. Aug. 5, 1816. Exrs: Brother, Alexr. Houston, Son, Jas. Houston, Jno. Gray. Wit: James Hutcheson, Susanna Houston. Wife, Betsy Houston. Chn: Alice, Alexander Pleasant, Amsey, Jas., Benajah Houston. Inv. made Sept. 25, 1816 by A. Houston, Jas. Hutcheson, Joseph Calhoun.

HUGHES, FRANCES—BOX 45, PACK 1019:
Est. admnr. Aug 24, 1812 by Williamson Norwood, Saml. Young, Joshua Dubose bound to Taliaferro Livingston Ord. Abbeville Dist. sum $5,000.00. Est. admnr. again Aug. 24, 1812 by Jas. Hughes, Saml. Cowan, Moses Tullis bound to Taliaferro Livingston Ord. sum $5,000.00. Inv. made Aug. 29, 1812 by Charles Britt, Leonard Wideman, Moses Tullis.

HOWARD, BENJAMIN—BOX 45, PACK 1020:
Will dated Aug. 10, 1813 in Abbeville Dist. Rec. Sept. 18, 1813. Exr: s.l. Wm. Carson, Wit: Robt. Carson, Thos. Lindsay. Chn: Martin Howard, Sally Nelson, Catty Norris, Nancy Carson. Inv. made Oct. 2, 1813 by Thos. Lindsay, Robt. Carson, Wm. Martin.

HILLEN, NATHANIEL—BOX 45, PACK 1021:
Will dated Sept. 20, 1779. Proved Aug. 22, 1783. Exrs: Wife, Mary
Hillin, Son, Jno. Hillin. Wit: Moses Buffington, Jno. Couch, Jno. Devaux.
Was of Eneree, 96 Dist. Chn: Lewis, Jno. Hillen. "Bequeath to Lazarus Bent-
lon, Jno. Cammel."

HAMMOND, JOHN—BOX 45, PACK 1022:
Est. admnr. Nov. 28, 1783 by Joshua Hammond, Abraham Richardson,
Jas. Christopher bound to Jno. Thomas, Jr. Ord. 96 Dist. sum 2,000 lbs. Ann
Hammond resigned as admnrx. Jan. 7, 1783. Inv. made Nov. 15, 1783 by
Charles Banks, Wm. Tarrance, Wm. Murphey.

HEARD, ISAAC—BOX 45, PACK 1023:
Will dated Mar. 20, 1804. Rec. April 9, 1804. Exrs: Wife, Mary Heard,
Thos. Heard, Wm. Wardlaw. Wit: Thos., Wm. Brightman, Jno. Wardlaw. Son.
Elijah Heard. Inv. made April 16, 1804 by Larkin Reynolds, Archibald Frift,
Benjamin Chiles. Richard Heard bought 1 stud colt $93.00.

HILL, JAMES—BOX 45, PACK 1024:
Est. admnr. Sept. 12, 1797 by Adam Hill, Saml. Sr., Jas. Foster, Jr. bound
to Judges Abbeville County sum $1,000.00. Cit. pub. at Cedar Springs Church.
Sale, Dec. 12, 1797. Byrs: Mary Hill, wid., Wm., Adam Hill, Jno. White, etc.

HANKS, LUKE—BOX 45, PACK 1025:
Will dated May 1, 1789 in Pendleton County. Exrs: Wife, Ann Hanks,
Jno. Haynie. Wit: Blake Mauldin, Jno. Reves. Chn. ment. names not given.
Inv. made Aug. 6, 1792 by Stephen Willis, Jas. Nash, Jno. Read Long.

HAYS, WILLIAM—BOX 45, PACK 1026:
Est. admnr. Nov. 10, 1795 by Robt. Hays. Wm. McKeen, Andrew
English bound to Judges Abbeville County sum 1,000 lbs. Wid. Elizabeth Hays.
Inv. made Dec. 7, 1795 by Jno. Wilson, Robt. Kirkwood, Jno. Simpson.

HENDRIX, JAMES, SR.—BOX 45, PACK 1027:
Est. admnr. April 27, 1785 by Margaret Hendrix, Geo. Anderson, Wm.
Harris bound to Jno. Thomas Jr. Ord. 96 Dist. sum 2,000 lbs. Will dated Oct.
18, 1781. Exrs: Wife, Frances Hendrix, Son Wm. Hendrix. Wit: Wm. Crow,
Jas. Hendrix, Jr. (Name worn) Barnett. Was of Two Mile Creek, 96 Dist.
Chn: Wm., Anne, Jno., Elijah, Elizabeth, Jas., Milly, Abner, Frances, Larkin
Hendrix. Inv. made Aug. 4, 1783 by Jno. Pennington, Wm. Crow, Issac Hendrix.

HAYS, COL. JOSEPH—BOX 45, PACK 1028:
Est. admnr. Nov. 8, 1782 by Alice Hays, Henry Pearson, Jas. Waldrop
bound to Jno. Ewing Calhoun Ord. 96 Dist. sum 14,000 lbs. Cit. read at house
of Richard Griffin. Alice Hays the wid. lived between Little River and Bush
River. Paid $15.00 to moving the family from Virginia. April 29, 1786 Henry
Pearson maketh oath that Alice Hays, now wife of Wm. Stewart, sold property
to Stewart's father in N. C.

HAYS, JACOB—BOX 46, PACK 1029:
Est. admnr. Oct. 1783 by Wm. Wood, Jno. Golightly of Fairforest bound
to Jno. Thomas, Jr. Ord. 96 Dist. sum 2,000 lbs. Inv. made Oct. 9, 1783 by
Jno. Golightly, Wm. Prince, Rowland Cournelous.

HENDERSON, JAS. AND DAVID—BOX 46, PACK 1030:
Est. admnr. May 2, 1786 by Wm., Robt., Saml. Foster, Jr. bound to
Jno. Thomas, Jr. Ord. 96 Dist. sum 500 lbs. Inv. made May 2, 1786 by Saml.,
Jas. Foster, Henry McMurdy.

HIGHTOWER, JOSEPH, SR.—BOX 46, PACK 1031:
Est. admnr. Feb. 8, 1786 by Joseph Hightower, Abraham Richardson,
Allen Hinton bound to Jno. Thomas, Jr. Ord. 96 Dist. sum 1,000 lbs. Inv.
made Feb. 7, 1786 by Wm., Jno. Covington, Allen Hinton who appeared before
Leroy Hammond, a Justice of Edgefield Dist.

HAMILTON, ARCHIBALD, SR.—BOX 46, PACK 1032:
Will dated Aug. 31, 1793 in Abbeville Dist. Rec. Nov. 10, 1795. Exrs:
Nephew, Andrew Hamilton, Saml. Green. Wit: Francis Cummins, Robt., Jno.
Green. Sis. Margaret Burney, Mary Karr. Brothers, Jno., Joseph Hamilton.
Cousins, Margaret Benson, Mary Karman, Ann Garner, Joseph Karr. Niece,
Agness Hamilton. Nephew, Saml. Karr. Mary Karr and dtr. Margaret Benson
of Roan Co., N. C. also Exrs.

HUGHES, RICHARD—BOX 46, PACK 1033:
Will dated April 5, 1781. Probated Feb. 13, 1783. Exrs: Joshua Palmer,
Jas. Bogan. Wit: Jno. Albritten, Jeptha Hollingsworth, Jas. Bogan. Wife, Mary
Hughes. Chn: Richard, Jno., Joseph, Thos., Wm. Hughes. Brother Wm. Hughes.
Inv. made April 11, 1783 by Isaac Gregory, Hugh Nelson, Jas. Thomas.

HEWS, JOHN—BOX 46, PACK 1034:
Est. admnr. Feb. 28, 1783 by Elizabeth Hews, Joseph Able, Moses Braford
bound to Jno. Ewing Calhoun Ard. 96 Dist. sum 14,000 lbs. Sale, Mar. 20,
1783. Byrs: Andrew, Rachel Cokran, Jas. Patterson, Elizabeth Hews.

HOSKISON, PEGGY—BOX 46, PACK 1035:
Est. admnr. May 27, 1805 by Sml., Jno., Alexr. Harris bound to Andrew
Hamilton Ord. Abbeville Dist. sum $10,000.00 Sale, June 24, 1805. Byrs: Saml.,
Alexr., Thos. W. Harris, Jno. W. McKinley, etc.

HAYS, ELIZABETH—BOX 46, PACK 1036:
Est. admnr. Feb. 7, 1806 by Jas. Killough, Jno. Gamble, Jas. Hutchison
bound to Andrew Hamilton Ord. Abbeville Dist. sum $5,000.00. Byrs: Wm.,
Robt., Sarah, Elizabeth Hays, Jno. Dickey, etc.

HAWTHORN, ANN—BOX 46, PACK 1037:
Will dated July 24, 1795 in Abbeville Dist. Rec. Nov. 10, 1795. Exrs:
Alexr. Hamilton, Robt. Gilmore. Wit: Jas. Hathorn, L. L. Cunningham,
Andrew Hamilton. (Ann Hawthorn otherwise Ellis.) Gr. chn. David Hazle

Hathorn "land in Pendleton County." Jas., Robt. Nicholson Hathorn, **Ann** Hathorn, Robt. Campbell Gordon. Inv. made Dec. 30, 1795 by Jno. Murphey, Wm. Ross, Joseph Kolb.

HARTLEY, GEORGE—BOX 46, PACK 1038:
Est. admnr. Jan. 22, 1787 by Peter Willhelm, Wm. Houseal, Michael Kinard bound to Jno. Thomas Ord. 96 Dist. sum 500 lbs. Charlotte Willhelm was also admnr. Inv. made Jan. 31, 1887 by Andrew Bowers, Jno. Kinard, Christian Hoyt.

HALL, JAMES—BOX 46, PACK 1039:
Est. admnr. Nov. 8, 1782 by Mary, Wm. Hall. Thos. Cunningham of Enoree bound to Jno. Ewing Calhoun Ord. 96 Dist. sum 14,000 lbs. Inv. made Nov. 19, 1782 by Jno. McClinton, Henry Hamilton, Isaac Hendricks.

HALLUM, WILLIAM—BOX 46, PACK 1040:
Will dated Jan. 9, 1782 in 96 Dist. Probated Sept. 6, 1782. Exrs: Wife, Jenny Hallum, Son, Jno. Hallum. Wit: Saml. Rosamond, Josiah Downen, Jno. Preter. Chn: Wm., Jas., Josiah, Thos. Hallum, Robt. Pickens Hallum and his wife Darkos Hallum, Marsha Hallum. Wife's chn: Wm., Margaret Griffith. "Bequeath to Joseph Smith and Elizabeth his wife."

HOLMES, WILLIAM—BOX 46, PACK 1041:
Est. admnr. Sept. 7, 1802 by Jean Holmes, Jno. Lowry, Ezekiel Calhoun, Jas. D. Anderson bound to Andrew Hamilton Ord. Abbeville Dist. sum $10,000.00. Est. admnr. again Jan. 9, 1807 by Jane, Charles, Jno. Miller, Joseph Black Esq. to Andrew Hamilton Ord. sum $10,000.00. June 9, 1807 Paid tuition of Wm. Holmes $7.00. Dec. 10, 1804 For tution of Robt., Matty Holmes $12.00. Mar. 15, 1807 For tuition of Robt., Betsy, Sally Holmes $5.00.

HAWKINS, PINKETHAM—BOX 46, PACK 1042:
Est. admnr. Sept. 13, 1782 by Michael Harvey, Jas. Christopher, Allen Hinton bound to Jno. Ewing Calhoun Ord. Abbeville Dist. sum 14,000 lbs. Cit. ment Michael Harvey of Savannah River next of kin. Dec. 10, 1779 Boarding Saml. Hawkins $40.00. Sarah Hawkins $40.00. Elizabeth Hawkins her acct. against said est. $44.26. Boarding Mathew, Thos. Hawkins $80.00. Paid David Leach for teaching Stephen Hawkins $7.00.

HENCOCK, SOLOMON—BOX 46, PACK 1043:
Will dated Oct. 2, 1782 in 96 Dist. Probated Nov. 23, 1782. Exr: Jno. Gorre, Sr. Wit: Daniel Gorre, Noah, Richard Bonds. Chn: Wm., Richard, Sarah, Daniel Hencock, Ann Hill, Elizabeth Case. Gr. son: Elisha Hill. Inv. made Nov. 29, 1782 by Daniel Goore, Richard Bonds, Williamson Liles.

HAIRSTON, THOMAS—BOX 46, PACK 1044:
Est. admnr. Nov. 20, 1782 by Wm. Hairston, Jno. McCord, Robt. Maxwell bound to Jno. Ewing Calhoun Ord. 96 Dist. sum 14,000 lbs. Wm. Hairston next of kin. Inv. made Dec. 10, 1782 by Jno. Irwing, Jno. Calhoun, Saml. McMurtey.

HOSKISON, NINIAN—BOX 46, PACK 1045:
     Est. admnr. Feb. 1, 1805 by Margaret Hoskison, Charles Johnson, Wm.
Caldwell, Saml. Harris bound to Andrew Hamilton Ord. Abbeville Dist. sum
$10,000.00. Inv. made June 3, 1805 by Thos. Shanklin, Wm. Davis, Wm. H.
Caldwell.

HAIRSTON, WILLIAM SR.—BOX 46, PACK 1046:
     Will dated Mar. 18, 1808 in Abbeville Dist. Rec. April 9, 1808. Exrs:
Jas. Lomax Sr., Jno. Brannan. Wit: Jas. Lomax, Jr., Steth Howlet, Elijah
Thomas. Wife, Ann Hairston. Chn: Peter, Jas., Jno., Wm., Thos. Hairston,
Jane Brown, Agness Martin. Inv. made April 13, 1808 by Jno. Hairston,
Archibald Douglass, Wm. Bell.

HUTTON, WILLIAM—BOX 46, PACK 1047:
     Will dated June 9, 1806 in Abbeville Dist. Rec. Sept. 4, 1809. Exrs:
Son, Joseph Hutton, Jno. Gray, Sr. Wit: Jno. Morrow, Isaac Boles, Jas. Nelson.
Wife, Rebeccah Hutton. Chn: Joseph, Mary, Rebeccah Hutton, Martha Gaston.
Ment. Rebeccah Dickson, Mary Gray. Sept. 10, 1809 Paid Saml. H. Dickson
part dividend $100.00. Oct. 11, 1810 Paid Joseph Gaston his share $1000.22.
Nov. 7, 1810 Paid Daniel Gray his share $699.50½.

HACKLEMAN, MICHAEL—BOX 46, PACK 1048:
     Est. admnr. Nov. 25, 1808 by Conrad, Geo. Hackleman, Jno. W. Adams,
Esq. bound to Andrew Hamilton Ord. Abbeville Dist. sum $10,000.00. May 19,
1809 Paid Jacob Hackleman $400.00.

HODGES, WILLIAM JR.—BOX 46, PACK 1049:
     Est. admnr. Oct. 19, 1824 by Wm., Richard, Jas. L. Hodges bound to
Moses Taggart Ord. Abbeville Dist. sum $700.00. Inv. made Oct. 29, 1824
by Geo. Weatherall, Thos. Cummins, Charles Hodges. Sale, Nov. 6, 1824.
Byrs: Richard A., Jno. W., Wm. Hodges Sr., Jas. A. Cummins, Thos. Young,
Moses Drummond.

HARRIS, RICHARD—BOX 46, PACK 1050:
     Est. admnr. Jan. 25, 1826 by Alexr. Hunter, Wm. T. Drennan bound to
Moses Taggart Ord. Abbeville Dist. sum $1,000.00. Inv. made Feb. 9, 1826 by
Robt. Smith, Edward Bailey, Dabney Wanslow.

HALLUM, BASIL—BOX 46, PACK 1051:
     Will dated July 25, 1816. Rec. June 10, 1817. Exrs: Joel Lipscomb, Jno.
Y., Suckey Hallum, Thos. Wilson. Wit: Henry, Jno. Wilson, F. Connor.
Wife ment. name not given. Chn: Rapley, Mary Hallum. "Wife now pregnant
with child." Inv. made une 21, 1817 by Nicholas Overby, Geo. Shotwell,
Lewis Mitchel.

HILL, JAMES—BOX 46, PACK 1054:
     Will dated Nov. 6, 1829. Proved Dec. 7, 1829. Exrs: Wife, Katharine
Hill, son, Jacob Hill. Wit: Jas. A. Black, A. W. Lynch, Richard Ashley.
Chn: Jacob, Jno., Saml., Thos., Jas., Caroline, Daniel, Henry H., Margaret

Hill. "And whereas I lived as man and wife with a certain woman Margaret Dorrah for several years and had by her 5 illegimate chn. viz. Jesse, Eleanor, Larsey, Manes, Malinda Hill after which time she eloped from me without any known cause and took up with another man." Inv. made Dec. 14, 1829 by Jas. A., Jno. B. Black, David Russell.

HERRON, THOMAS—BOX 46, PACK 1055:
Will dated June 2, 1821 in Abbeville Dist. Proved Aug. 15, 1822. Exrs: Wife, Frances Herron, Moses Taggart Sr., Wm. Anderson Sr. Wit: Charles C. Yancey, Jas. A. Black, Joshua Pruitt. Chn: Jas. B., Adaline S., Bethethland, Jno. S., Mary T. Herron. Aug. 29, 1848 Jno. H. Miller reed. $118.25 in right of his wife. Geo. W. Wilson recd. $246.65. in right of his wife.

HATTER, BENJAMIN—BOX 46, PACK 1056:
The yr. 1827. (Nothing important in pack.)

HARDEN, RALPH—BOX 46, PACK 1057:
Will dated April 17, 1832 in Abbeville Dist. Proved Feb. 11, 1834. Exrs: Wife, Isabella G. Harden. s.l. Jas. Adams. Wit: Thos. Bigbie, Lyndsey Harper, Toliver Flowers. Chn: Jane D., Jno. G., Ralph L., Arabella G. Harden, Elizabeth W. Adams, Susana C. Donald. Inv. made Feb. 18, 1834 by Elijah Hunt, David B. DeFoor, Nathan Strickland.

HOUSTON, JOHN—BOX 46, PACK 1058:
Will dated Dec. 26, 1802 in Abbeville Dist. Rec. Jan. 1, 1803. Exrs: Saml. Houston, Robt. M. Mann, Abraham Livingston. Wit: Joseph Randolph, S. W. Crawford, A. Crawford. Chn: Jno., Saml., Wm., Jas., Elizabeth. Nancy, Jencey Houston. Nephew, Hugh Houston. s.ls., Jas. Armstrong and Robt. M. Mann. "Give unto Jean Houston who was my late wife." Inv. made Jan. 4, 1803 by Daniel Gillespie, Jas. B. English, Jno. Mann.

HOUSTON, JOHN SR.—BOX 46, PACK 1059:
Will dated June 1, 1778. Exrs: Wife, Else Houston. Wit: Wm. Calhoun, Henry Geddes, Sarah Calhoun. Chn: Robt., Alexr., Jno., Joseph, Benjamin, Catharine Houston. Inv. made Aug. 16, 1793 by Alexr., Jas. Noble, Wm. Hutton.

HEARST, MAJOR JOHN—BOX 47, PACK 1060:
Est. admnr. Feb. 6, 1808 by Robt. Hearst, Josiah Patterson Esq., David Wardlaw bound to Andrew Hamilton Ord. Abbeville Dist. sum $10,000.00. Est. admnr. again Jan. 9, 1807 by Phebe Hearst, Andrew, Jno. Gray to Andrew Hamilton Ord. sum $10,000.00. Sept. 24, 1815 Paid the following: Lewis, Jno., Robt., Geo. Hearst $1200.05. Jane McMillian $1200.05. Jno. Gallaugher $1200.05. Jas. Cochran $1200.05. Jacob Clark $1200.05. Jno. McMillian $3346.91.

HENDERSON, ROBERT—BOX 47, PACK 1062:
Est. admnr. Nov. 23, 1810 by Margaret Henderson, Joseph Sanders, Wm. Paul, Jno. Brannan bound to Jno. Hamilton Ord. Abbeville Dist. sum $5,000.00

Inv. made Dec. 13, 1810 by Charles Caldwell, David Cochran, Wm. Norris.

HUNTER, SOLOMON ALSTON—BOX 47, PACK 1063:
Est. admnr. Sept. 13, 1799 by Elizabeth Hunter, Will Stoutly Harris.
Uel Hill. Joseph Barksdale bound to Andrew Hamilton Ord. Abbeville Dist.
sum $10,000.00. Inv. made Nov. 11, 1799 by Capt. Wm., Edward Collier,
Major Uel Hill. Sale made at house of Robt. Terry decd.

HARWICK, JAMES—BOX 47, PACK 1064:
Est. admnr. Nov. 21, 1782 by Jno. Townes Sr. of Tyger River, Wm.
Wright bound to Jno. Ewing Calhoun Ord. 96 Dist. sum 14,000 lbs. Jno. Towns
of Tyger River applied for Admnr. in behalf of his wife, Margaret Towns.
Inv. made Dec. 1, 1782 by Thos. Smith, Joseph Franklin, Capt. Daniel McKee,
Jno. Gormon.

HOGG, JOHN—BOX 47, PACK 1065:
Will dated June 14, 1781 in 96 Dist. Probated Nov. 8, 1782. Exrs: Wife,
Sarah Hogg, Son, Lewis Hogg. Wit: Thos. Wafer, Wm. Darby, Wm. Sparks.
Chn: Lewis, Thos., Stephen, Jno., Joseph, Zachariah, Jas. Hogg. Gr.son,
Francvis Hogg. "Owned land on Enoree River." Inv. made Dec. 27, 1782 by
Robt. Raderford, Wm., Dawkins, Daniel Johnson.

HEWS, WILLIAM—BOX 47, PACK 1066:
Cit. dated April 26, 1782 ment. Mary Hews of Broad River, 96 Dist., next
of kin. Admnr. Joseph Hews. Inv. made Jan. 4, 1783 by Thos. Brandon, Charles
Sims, Col. Wm. Farr.

HUGHS, DEMPSEY—BOX 47, PACK 1067:
Est. admnr. Oct. 11, 1782 by Reuben, Thos., Russell Beckum bound to
Jno. Ewing Calhoun Ord. 96 Dist. sum 14,000 lbs. Reuben Beckum of Horns
Creek, next of kin. Inv. made Nov. 29, 1782 by Thos. Beckum, Michael
Buckhatter, Jno. Pursell. Wid., Mary Hughes.

HARVEY, THOMAS—BOX 47, PACK 1068:
Est. admnr. Aug. 5, 1782 by Jno. Harvey, Israel Pickens, Jas. Saxon
bound to Jno. Ewing Calhoun Ord. 96 Dist. sum 14,000 lbs. Jno. Harvey
near Little River, next of kin.

HARRIS, WILLIAM—BOX 47, PACK 1069:
Will dated Mar. 12, 1796 in Abbeville Dist. Rec. Mar. 26, 1798. Exrs:
Wife, Margaret Harris, Jno. Caldwell. Wit: Henry Long, Henry Harris.
Chn: Jno., Mary, Lesley, Robt., Alexr., Saml., Wilson., Margaret Harris.
Gr. dtr. Margaret Lesley. "Gave Bulltown plantation to Robt. Harris." Inv. made
April 26, 1798 by Jas. Caldwell Sr., Joseph McCleskey, Saml. Mitchell.

HAMILTON, THOMAS—BOX 47, PACK 1070:
Will dated Nov. 1, 1797 in 96 Dist. Rec. Mar. 26, 1798. Exrs: Margaret,
Jno. Hamilton, David Pressly Jr. Wit: Jas. Oliver, Fredrick Stricklin, Jas.
McCedy. Chn: Jno., Margaret Hamilton. "Among my legal heair, Jno., Thos.

Hamilton, Saray Turner, Margaret Ray." Bequeath to Hamilton Turner. Inv. made April 16, 1798 by Anthony Elton, Robt. Smith, Wm. Carrithers.

HUGGINS, WILLIAM—BOX 47, PACK 1071:
Will dated May 12, 1799 in Abbeville Dist. Rec. June 11, 1799. Exrs: Wife, Martha Huggins, Jas. Gouedy. Wit: Leonard Waller, Isaac, Mary Ray. Chn: Elizabeth, Mary, Wm. Andrew Huggins.

HEMPHILL, ANDREW—BOX 47, PACK 1072:
Will dated Mar. 1, 1800 in Abbeville Dist. Rec. April 7, 1801. Exrs: Jane Hemphill. Wit: Jas. Hutcheson, Thos. Potter, Jas. Milligan. Byrs. at sale. Jno., Susanna, Saml. Hemphill, etc.

HUTCHESON, WILLIAM—BOX 47, PACK 1073:
Will dated Mar. 22, 1806 in Abbeville Dist. Rec. April 4, 1806. Exrs: Son. Jas. Hutcheson. Wit: Jas. Adamson, Jno. Pressly, Daniel Whiteman. Chn: Jas., Agness, Wm. Hutcheson, Jane Caldwell, Mary Brown, Margaret Robinson. Gr. chn: Mary Ann Hutcheson and the 4 chn. of Anny Foster. Paid Geo. Creswell, heir of Jane Creswell decd., his wife's legacy $50.00. (In will written Caswell.) Paid Nancy Hutcheson $50.00. Inv. made April 5, 1806 by Robt. Smyth, Jno. Chastain, Hugh Porter. Inv. of another Wm. Hutcheson made May 17, 1797 by Capt. Jno. McCarter, Wm. Scott, Alexr. Clark.

HATCHER, BENJAMIN—BOX 47, PACK 1075:
Jno. Hatcher a son was admnr. Lived in 96 Dist. Inv. made Nov. 15, 1786 by Vann Swearington Sr., Jesse Roundtree, Thos. Beckum.

HERNDON, WILLIAM—BOX 47, PACK 1076:
Est. admnr. April 29, 1784 by Jno. Herndon, Benjamin Joyner, Adams Purdue bound to Jno. Thomas Jr. Ord. 96 Dist. sum 2,000 lbs. Inv. made June 28, 1784 by Wm., Drury Murphey, Seth Howard at the house of Elender Herndon the wid. Jno. Herndon Esq. was a brother.

HAMPTON, EDWARD—BOX 47, PACK 1077:
Est. admnr. Sept. 2, 1783 by Salley Hampton, Wm. Prince, Ephraim Ruse bound to Jno. Thomas Jr. Ord. 96 Dist. sum 2,000 lbs. Est. admnr. again June 28, 1786 by Bayles Earle, Thos. Wadsworth, David Goodlet to Jno. Thomas Ord. sum 500 lbs. Inv. made June 20, 1786 by Jno. Green, Charles McKnight, Jas. Bates. 1788 Paid Wm. Hampton $20.00. By one negro boy in possession of Col. Henry Hampton 590.17.6. Recd. of Edward, Richard Hampton.

HANNAH, ROBERT—BOX 47, PACK 1078:
Will dated Jan. 8, 1787 in Newberry Dist. Proved Jan. 25, 1787. Exrs: Charles Burton. Wit: Robt. Moore, Charles Thompson. Wife, Jenney Hannah. Dtr. Nancy Chapman. s.l. Charles Burton. Paid Sam Chapman for the land. "Bequeath a calf to little Jean Oiens." Nov. 15, 1808 Paid L. B. Bostick his wife's legacy $644.86. Dec. 8, Paid Thos. Chapman $15.50. (Note: The Expend: of Jno. Chapman decd. to Nathan and Benjamin Chapman admnr. in same pack.)

HUTTON, REBECCA—BOX 47, PACK 1079:
Will dated May 16, 1814 in Abbeville Dist. Rec. Sept. 1, 1814. Exrs:
Jno. Gray, Joseph Hutton. Wit: Anna C. Gray. Chn: Polly, Joseph Hutton,
Martha Gaston, Rebecca Disckson. Gr. chn: Rebecca Gray, Acquilla Hutton.
Expend: Aug. 29, 1815 Paid Saml. H. Dickson legacy $155.00. Oct. 8 Joseph
Gaston legacy $100.00. June 6, 1816 Paid Rev. Daniel Gray by the hands of
Jno. Gray $74.00. July 26, 1816 Paid Rebecca Gray by Jno. Gray her gdn.
$326.25. Sept. 1, 1814 Paid Rev. Daniel Gray legacy $30.00.

HADDEN, ROBERT SR.—BOX 47, PACK 1080:
Est. admnr. Sept. 12, 1791 by Jane Haddon wid. Jno. Lindsay, Wm. Ross
bound to Judges Abbeville County sum 500 lbs. Inv. made 1791 by Jas.
Stevenson, Wm. Ross, Jno. Cowan. An inv. of Robt. Haddon Jr. made Nov.
1, 1788 by Jas. Stevenson, Wm. Ross, Ezekiel Evans. Sept. 24, 1793 Paid
Esther Haddon 7.17.8. Wm. Haddon 7.17.8. June 3, 1795 Paid Wm. Haddon
on acct. of Jean, Mary Haddon 15.15.4. Cash advances to Jean Hallon, alias
Mayn, and her third of est. 50.19.1. Wm. Mayn was admnr. of Robt. Haddon Jr.

HILES, ADAM—BOX 47, PACK 1081:
Will dated Sept. 5, 1783 in New Windsor Township. Proved April 29.
1786. Exrs: Wm. Shinholser, Peter Turkenetz, Jno. Stare. Wit: Jno. Sturzeneg-
ger, Francis Carlile, Casper Nail Jr. Wife, Mary Sophia Hiles. "Bequeath to
Wm. Sr., Susannah Shinholser. To the chn. of Peter Turkenetz Sr., Mary Stare."
Inv. made May 18, 1786 by Jonathan Meyer, Nathaniel Howell, Casper Nail Jr.

HORSEY, DANIEL—BOX 47, PACK 1082:
Will dated Aug. 8, 1763. Wife, Sarah Horsey. Stepsons, Thomas Jones,
Abel Jones. Brother, Isaac Horsey. Daniel and John, sons of Issac Horsey. Wit:
Mary Jones, J. Curry, C. King. Lived at fork of Broad and Seludy Rivers, Berke-
ley County, Williams Creek. Inv. made May 12, 1783 by Lewis Hogg, Ephrain
Cannon, Gabriel Anderson.

HILL, WILLIAM C.—BOX 47, PACK 1083
Jas. Calvert made a petition that he be appointed gdn. Wm. C. Hill a
minor. April 8, 1838 Recd. from Jesse Calvert $700.00.

HAMMONDS, MINORS—BOX 47, PACK 1084:
On Dec. 21, 1830 Wm. Reynolds, Brooks Elmore, Jno. Little, Jno. Gray
bound to Moses Taggart Ord. Abbeville Dist. sum $3,000.00. Wm. Reynolds
made gdn. Henry, Booklin, Evaline, Franklin Hammonds minors. Jan. 2, 1837
Paid J. Lipscomb for Jackson Hammond a minor $48.46. Nov. 15, 1845 J. B.
Hammond recd. $242.50.

HUEY, JOHN—BOX 47, PACK 1085:
On Nov. 30, 1836 Ruth R. Howie, Andrew Gillespie, Sr., Wm. Brooks
bound to Moses Taggart Ord. Abbeville Dist. sum $10,000.00. Ruth R. Howie
made gdn. Albertine E., Frances R., Jno. T. Huey minors under 14 yrs.
(Note. In the bond name written Howie but at singing written Huey.) On
Feb. 24, 1843 Huth R. Boyd and husband Jno. L. Boyd, Andrew Gillespie,

Jas. Huey bound to David Lesly Ord. Abbeville Dist. sum $10,000.00. Sett: Jan 26, 1847 of Albertine E. Huey, dtr. of Jno. B. Huey decd. Present, Jno. L Boyd joint gdn. and wife Ruth R. Huey, the mother of Albertine E. Huey being of age. Jno. T. of age in 1853. Frances R. Huey married Jas. Giles.

HUEY, LOUISA C.—BOX 47, PACK 1086:

On Nov. 30, 1836 Jno., Jno. H. Gray, Joseph T. Baker bound to Moses Taggard Ord. Abbeville Dist. sum $3,000.00. Jno. H. Gray made gdn. of Louisa C. Huey a minor over 14 yrs. Was of age in 1843. Child of Jno. B. Huey.

HOGG, SARAH—BOX 47, PACK 1087:

On Aug. 1, 1836 Wm. Smith, Jonathan Johnson, Alexr. Oliver bound to Moses Taggart Ord. Abbeville Dist. sum $3,000.00. Wm. Smith made gdn. of Sarah Hogg a minor under 14 yrs., child of Shadrack Hogg decd. (Written Salley in one place.) Was of age in June 1847. Dec. 31, 1840 Paid the trustees of the Loundesville Female School for 8 months $15.14.

HILLS, JOSEPH (MINORS)—BOX 47, PACK 1088:

On Nov. 24, 1830 Charles Cullins made gdn. Susan Jane, Frances E. Hill, minor chn. of Joseph Hill decd. under 14 yrs. Feb. 19, 1847 Jno. Graham appointed gdn. Jan. 2, 1832 Paid Eliza Graham, formerly Eliza Hill, wid. for maintenance of Susan J. and Frances E. Hill for 2 yrs. $80.00. Jan. 23, 1837 Recd. of Moses Taggart $26.50 being their share from est. of Jno. Hill Sr. decd. Return of Albert M. Graham, admnr. of Jno. Graham decd., who was gdn. of said minors. A. M. Graham married Frances E. Hill, had 1 child that died. On Jan. 15, 1847 Richard Gaines who acted as gdn. for a number of yrs., desired to be released from gdn. ship as he expected to move to Georgia.

HAMILTON, A. C. (MINORS)—BOX 47, PACK 1089:

On Oct. 28, 1835 Jas. S. Wilson, Joseph Eakins, Thos. Graves bound to Moses Taggart Ord. Abbeville Dist. sum $12,000.00. Jas. S. Wilson made gdn. Joseph A., Alexr., Saml. S., Harriet E. D. Hamilton minors. Expend. of Saml. S. Hamilton: Feb. 12, 1839 Paid Augusta for a draft for use at Randolph College Macon $150.00. July 5, 1838 Recd. amt. of share of brother Richard A. Hamilton personal est. on sett. $177.86. July 2, 1838 Paid Jno. Logan Treasurer of Greenwood Academy $18.00. Aug. 15 Paid stage passage from Abbeville to Milton, N. C. $21.00. Expend. of Alexr. Hamilton Jan. 8, 1838 Paid Jas. Shackleford Treasurer of Cokesbury School $48.00. Expend. of Joseph A. Hamilton: Jan. 6, 1836. Paid J. V. Shanklin Treasurer of Board of Directors of Manual Labor School in Pendleton $27.50. Anna A. minor of Alexr. Hamilton decd. married Jas. H. Giles. On Oct. 3, 1837 Jno. Bowie recd. his share thru a martial right.

HILL, NANCY—BOX 47, PACK 1090:

On Aug. 1, 1825 Wm. Barmore, Ezekiel Rasor, Andrew C. Hawthorn bound to Moses Taggart Ord. Abbeville Dist. sum $2,000.00. Wm. Barmore made gdn. Nancy Elizabeth, Susan Elvira Hill minors under 14 yrs. Paid R. C. Richey, husband of Nancy Hill, $1109.68.

HAMILTON, WILLIAM (MINORS)—BOX 47, PACK 1091:

On May 9, 1836 Luke Hamilton, Jas. D. Houston, Jas. H. Taylors bound to Moses Taggart Ord. Abbeville Dist. sum $2,000.00. Luke Hamilton of Anderson Dist. made gdn. Wm. Hamilton, minor under 14 yrs. On May 2, 1836 Jas. D. Houston, Geo. W. Liddell, Hudson Prince bound to Moses Taggart Ord. sum $2,000.00. Jas. Houston made gdn. Jas., Luke, Elizabeth, Sarah Hamilton minors.

HAWTHORNE, BETSEY—BOX 47, PACK 1092:
On Feb. 1, 1828 Alexr. Foster, Enos Crawford, Jno. Pressly bound to Moses Taggart Ord. Abbeville Dist. sum $1,000.00. Alexr. Foster made gdn. Betsey Hawthorne, minor under 14 yrs.

HENDERSON, WILLIAM (MINORS)—BOX 47, PACK 1093:
On Nov. 12, 1830 Nathaniel, Richard, Thos. Henderson bound to Moses Taggart Ord. Abbeville Dist. sum $3,000.00. Nathaniel Henderson made gdn. Sarah, Wm., Jas., Shadrack, Elizabeth, Jno., Nathan, Saml. Henderson minors. Nathaniel was their brother. Elizabeth married Jno. Moushan. Were chn. of Wm. Henderson decd.

HUGHEY, JEFFERSON—BOX 48, PACK 1094:
Expend. of Jefferson E. Hughey a minor with Joseph Hughey the gdn. 1832 Paid Wm. Russell tutition $7.53. Paid Owen Selby for boarding $30.00.

HOSE, JOHN—BOX 48, PACK 1095:
Will dated Mar. 10, 1806 in Abbeville Dist. Rec. Aug. 25, 1806. Exrs: Wife, Elizabeth Hose, Sons, Henry, Wm. Hose. Wit: Frederick, Jno. P. Knop, Chn: Henry, Saml., Wm. Hose. (Letter) "Perry 17 Feb. 1851. Mr. John Zinamon. Dear Sir: My brother John H. Hose will visit your state you will please to pay over to him the amount of money that may be coming to me from Grandmothers Hose estate he will receipt you for the same in my name and shall be as binding on me as though I was present in person. Our family is all well. Mother wishes to be remembered to you and family. I am yours very respectively, Robert E. Hose." Sett. of Henry Hose made to get share of Charles A. Thompson and Mary F. out of said est. Oct. 2, 1848. Feb. 7, 1840 Paid Joseph Cook for teaching Robt. Hose $10.10. For teaching Frances Hose $10.15. For teaching Elizabeth Hose $2.34. Beresheba Hose also recd. a share.

HARRIS, HARRIET—BOX 48, PACK 1096:
On Dec. 24, 1811 Jno. Gray, Nathaniel, Richard Harris bound to Taliaferro Livingston Ord. Abbeville Dist sum $5,000.00. Jno. Gray made gdn. of Harriet Harris a minor under 14 yrs. On Feb. 7, 1814 Alexr. Hunter, Edward Tilman, Thos. Shanklin bound to Taliaferro Livingston Ord. Abbeville Dist. sum $10,000.00. Alexr. Hunter made gdn. Harriet Harris minor over 14 yrs. Jan. 17, 1813 Paid $5.50 for taking her to Newberry.

HENDERSON, HARRIET—BOX 48, PACK 1097:
On Nov. 20, 1826 Isaac, Archibald Kennedy, Wm. Patton bound to Moses Taggart Ord. Abbeville Dist. sum $4,000.00. Isaac Kennedy made gdn. of Harriet Henderson minor over 14 yrs. 1825 Paid Issac Kennedy for boarding Harriet 12 months $50.00.

HOWARD, MARTHA—BOX 48, PACK 1098:
On Dec. 13, 1822 Robt. Key, Thos. Livingston, Marshall Weatherall bound to Moses Taggard Ord. Abbeville Dist. sum $2,000.00. Robt. Key made gdn. Martha Howard minor.

HOWLETT, FRANKLIN B.—BOX 48, PACK 1099:
On Feb. 15, 1838 Franklin Branch, Wm. Bowie, Saml. Reid bound to Moses Taggard Ord. Abbeville Dist. sum $2,000.00. Franklin Branch made gdn. Franklin Branch Howlet, a minor child of Steth Howlet. 1839 Paid Jno. Calvert for one bed for ward bought at sale of Mary Howlet. Aaron Lomax was admnr. of est. of Steth Howlet decd.

HOLMES, WILLIAM—BOX 48, PACK 1100:
Est. admnr. Oct. 19, 1824 by Luke M. Holmes, Allen Holes of Tenn., Uel Hill, Francis Tompkins of Edgefield Dist. bound to Moses Taggart Ord. Abbeville Dist. sum $6,000.00. Dec. 3, 1824 Isaac Holmes receipts for bonds $126.00. Jno. Holmes legatee $98.59. Geo. D. Mann one half third $49.29. Allen Holmes recd. $60.38½.

HOUSTON, WILLIAM—BOX 48, PACK 1101:
Est. admnr. Jan. 7, 1822 by Nathan, Downs, Wm. Calhoun, David Stewart bound to Moses Taggart Ord. Abbeville Dist. sum $10,000.00. Cit. pub. at Providence Church. Inv. made Jan. 28, 1822 by Jas. Franklin, Alexr. Sample, Alexr. Stuart, Jesse, Wm. Beasley.

HEARST, PHEBE—BOX 48, PACK 1102:
Admnr. Andrew Gray. Expend: 1811 Paid Jno. Cochran legatte $10.14. Daniel Cochran $18.50. Wm. Cochran $104.87½. Robt. Cochran $25.12½. Wm. Norris legatee $14.61.

HAWTHORNE, JAMES—BOX 48, PACK 1103:
Will dated Feb. 10, 1807 in Abbeville Dist. Rec. Oct. 22, 1811. Exrs: Sons, Jas., Thos. Hathorn. Wit: Jno. Murphy, Edward, Robt. C. Sharp. Chn: David H., Robt. N., Jas., Thos., Sarah, Joseph J. Hathorn, Anne Haddon. Gr. chn: Andrew C. son of David H. Hathorn, Eloner A. dtr. of Robt. N. Hathorn. Feb. 3, 1813 Paid Sarah Wilson $91.31. Paid Mary Hawthorn admnr. Robt. N. Hathorn $91.31.

HILL, HAMILTON—BOX 48, PACK 1104:
Will dated May 4, 1839 in Abbeville Dist. Proved May 19, 1839. Exr: Saml. Hill. Wit: G. J. Cannon, Jno. H. Armstrong, R. Hill. Wife, Peggy Hill. "Negroes originally disposed of to the issue of my first wife by their Grandfather Paul." Wid. was Margaret B. Hill.

HADDON, JOHN SR.—BOX 48, PACK 1105:
Will dated Aug. 5, 1836 in Abbeville Dist. Exrs: Jno. Stephenson, Jno. L. Ellis. Wit: Albert Johnson, Enoch Agnew, Joseph Ellis. Wife ment. name not given. Chn: Abram, Jno., Zachariah, Sally, Jane Haddon. Six chn. ment. only five named. Sept. 9, 1837 Paid Ann Ross $2.42. Dec. 28, Paid

Lilly Haddon $36.89. Sally Haddon $36.89. Thos. Banister $36.89. Jane Haddon $36.89. Mar. 20, 1837 Recd. from est. of Zachariah Davis $372.12.

HILL, BENJAMIN—BOX 48, PACK 1106:
Est. admnr. June 23, 1839 by Richard Hill, Jas. Williams, Johnson Ramey bound to Moses Taggart Ord. Abbeville Dist. sum $10,000.00. Will dated July 18, 1838 in Abbeville Dist. Exr: Son, Hamilton Hill. Wit: Frederick S. Lucius, Jno. H. Armstrong, Saml. Hill. Chn: Charity Fulton, Elizabeth Mantz, Christiana Davis, Lucretia Hamilton, Richard, Saml., Frances Hill. Gr. son, Richard B. Fulton. On Jan. 6, 1844 Joseph A. Hamilton recd. of Sarah Hill, Extrx. of Richard Hill decd., $40.00, the interest of his wife in a note on Wm. Davis belonging to est. of Benjamin Hill decd. Andrew Mantz recd. $37.50. Jan. 12, 1845 Frances Burton recd. $65.00. (One place written Frances, formerly Mrs. Mantz, wife of Wm. Mantz.) Hamilton Hill, Charity Fulton died after execution of will but before the testator. Joseph Davis died after testator. Chn. of Hamilton Hill were: Elizabeth wife Thos. McDill, Jane Amanda, Sarah Catharine, Saml. Albert, Lewis Hamilton, Jas. Warren (the last a child of the second marriage.) Chn. of Charity Fulton: Benj. H., Richard B., Catharine F. Fulton. Saml. Hill gdn. Sarah Catharine.

HAIRSTON, JAMES R.—BOX 48, PACK 1107:
Will dated July 5, 1827 in Abbeville Dist. Proved Jan. 2, 1834. Exrs: Wife, Jane Hairston, Jno. Keller. Wit: G. Lomax, B. Johnson, S. Williams. Inv. made Jan. 24, 1835 by W. B. Arnold, Jesse C. Beasley, B. Johnson.

HAGOOD, ELIZA ANN BOX 48, PACK 1108:
Will dated May 9, 1839. Proved June 31, 1839. Exrs: Jno. McGowan, Henry Chiles. Wit: Wm. P. Anderson, Wm. B. Smith, Margaret McGowan. Aunt, Eliza McGowan. Uncle, Richard Hagood. Cousins: Henry, Mary, Robt. Chiles, Caroline Eliza McGowen. (On one paper written Miss Eliza Hagood.)

HOWARD, MARTHA (MINOR)—BOX 48, PACK 1109:
Jan. 7, 1823 Paid Geo. Howard $4.50. Robt. Key gdn. (No other papers.)

HARRISON, NATHANIEL—BOX 48, PACK 1110:
Will dated Sept. 7, 1820 in Abbeville Dist. Proved Feb. 26, 1821. Exr: Wife, Rebecca Harrison. Wit: Robt. Harrison, Jno. Morris, R. W. Washington. Chn: Elizabeth, Heartwell, Hubbard, Alfred, Bradford, Eaton, Gilbert Harrison. "Owned property in Virginia."

HAMILTON, RICHARD A.—BOX 48, PACK 1111:
On May 16, 1837 Jas. S. Wilson, Geo. Lomax, Isaac Branch bound to Moses Taggart Ord. Abbeville Dist sum $3,000.00. Oct. 3, 1837 Amt. of Richard A. Hamilton's share of his father's est. due him $1606.57. One paper stated there were 9 chn. no names given.

HOUSTON, JAMES—BOX 48, 1112:
Est. admnr. Sept. 12, 1834 by Jas. D. Houston, Jno. Swilling, Francis Clinkscales bound to Mses Taggart Ord. Abbeville Dist sum $10,000.00.

Cit. pub. at Shilo Church. Sett. Belinda Anna Scott, late Houston, in acct. with J. D. Houston, late gdn., on final sett. Feb. 13, 1852 due $1453.00. Andrew G., Laura B. Scott consented to the gdn.

HILL, THOMAS—BOX 48, PACK 1113:
        Est. admnr. Nov. 19, 1824 by Saml. Hill, Robt. Gaines, Wm. Henderson bound to Moses Taggart Ord. Abbeville Dist sum $500.00. Druscilla, Washington Hill were chn. of Thos Hill. Inv. made Nov. 25, 1824 by Henry, Jonathan Johnson, Jno. Fooshe.

HENDERSON, JOHN—BOX 48, PACK 1114:
        Est. admnr. Nov. 11, 1816 by Jas. Devlin, Wm. Lesly, Wm. Norris bound to Taliaferro Livingston Ord. Abbeville Dist. sum $10,000.00. Jan. 30, 1818 Paid Robt. Devlin for 1 yr. tution, Sally Henderson $8.00. For boarding Harriet Henderson $60.00. Dec. 25, 1819 Paid Margaret Henderson for loss of Pomps time when hired to her and her attendance on him $55.00.

HOLLAMAND, JOSEPH WHITFIELD—BOX 48, PACK 1115:
        Will dated Sept. 27, 1840. Proved Oct. 5, 1840. Exrs: Brothers, E. P., R. S. Hollamand. Wit: E. Tribble, S. W. Walker, F. B. Millford. Wife, Sarah S. Hollamand. Brothers, Edmund P., Richard S. Hollamand. Sarah S. later married Archibald D. Gailliard.

HOUSTON, HUGH M.—BOX 48, PACK 1116:
        Est. admnr. Nov. 16, 1840 by Ezekiel Tribble, Joseph F. Black, Sterling Bowen bound to Moses Taggart Ord. Abbeville Dist. sum $500.00. Jas. B. Gillespie on Feb. 6, 1813 appointed gdn. of Hugh Houston a minor under 14 yrs.

HAMILTON, ROBERT B.—BOX 48, PACK 1117:
        On Jan. 23, 1841 Jas. H. Giles, Jas. S. Wilson, Benj. Y. Martin bound to Moses Taggart Ord. Abbeville Dist. sum $2,000.00.

HEALY, JEREMIAH—BOX 48, PACK 1118:
        The petition of Walter C. Anderson on Nov. 1, 1841 sheweth that Jeremiah Healy died intestate. Inv. made Nov. 23, 1841 by Daniel Ligon, P. W. Connor, S. A. Hodges.

HODGES, REVD. N. W.—BOX 48, PACK 1119:
        Will dated Oct. 1, 1841 in Abbeville Dist. Rec. Oct. 27, 1841. Exrs: Adna Johnson of Fairforest Dist., Larkin Griffin, Leroy Watson. Wit: Joseph Wardlaw, Thos. J. Coleman, Thos. S. Whitlock. Chn: Edward, Charles, Mary H., N. W., Belton O., Jas., Margaret, A. J. Hodges. Inv. made Nov. 30, 1841 by Wm., Jno. Shedd, Jno. Deleney. Margaret J. Hodges died Aug. 10, 1849. Sis. name, Mary Hasseltine Hodges.

HENRY, FRANCIS—BOX 48, PACK 1120:
        Will dated Nov. 25, 1841 in Abbeville Dist. Proved Mar. 22, 1842. Exrs: Son, Wm. Henry, Saml. Reid. Wit: Joseph Lyon, Saml. Reid, Jas. B. Baley. Wife, Mary Henry. Chn: Wm., Peter, Margaret Henry. Sett. Francis Henry died about Jan. 1842. Margaret marriel a Brown.

HILL, RICHARD—BOX 48, PACK 1121:
Will dated Jan. 19, 1841 in Abbeville Dist. Proved Mar. 28, 1842. Exrs:
Wife, Sarah Hill, Thos. Thompson. Wit: H. H. Penney, Andrew Monroe,
Blassongim Hodges. Son, Andrew M. Hill. Other chn. ment. names not given.
Jan. 2, 1844 Paid A. Ramey legatee $84.75. Thos. McDill $84.75. Thos. McDill
for S. A. Hill $84.75. Saml. Hill $84.75.

HANDLEY, PETER—BOX 48, PACK 1122:
Will dated Sept. 27, 1842 in Abbeville Dist. Proved Nov. 1, 1842. Exr:
Jno. Romans. Wit: Saml. Turner, Jas. Smith Jr., Wm. E. Caldwell. "Bequeathed
est. to Jno. Romans." Inv. made Nov. 11, 1842 by Wm. F. Caldwell, Saml.
Turner, Jas. Smith Jr.

HARRIS, WILLIAM—BOX 48, PACK 1123:
Est. admnr. Jan. 27, 1840 by Elizabeth Harris, Jemima Lipscomb, Jno.
Ruff bound to Moses Taggart Ord. Abbeville Dist. sum $200,000.00. Sett.
made May 15, 1844. Present, Elizabeth Harris wid., Jno. Harris, Geo. A.
Addison and wife Rebecca, Col. Marshall Fraser and wife Sarah A. Absent,
Wiley G. Harris and the minors Willis, Elizabeth Ann J., Mary F. decd. Wm.
Harris. Wm. Harris died Nov. 11, 1839.

HARRIS, WILLIAM—BOX 48, PACK 1124:
Est. admnr. Mar. 24, 1844 by Jas. C. Willard, Jas. McCaslan, Joshua
Wideman, Braxton Cason bound to David Lesly Ord. Abbeville Dist. sum
$5,000.00. Died having no wife or chn. Sett. of est. or shares of Milly, Catherine,
Thos. S. Harris, minor legatees of Jno. Harris decd. made Feb. 12, 1846.
Present, Jas. McCaslan Exr. of Jno. Harris decd., who is now admnr. of Wm.
Harris decd. Sett. of Wm. Harris decd. Present, Jas. McCaslan, Jno. Harris,
Wade Cowan who married Margaret Harris. Absent from state, Robt. R. Harris,
Braxton Cason who married Elizabeth Harris, Martha, Milly, Mary wife of Jas.
T. Hertin decd., Joshua Wideman and wife Sarah.

HARMON, THOMAS—BOX 49, PACK 1125:
Est. admnr. Dec. 5, 1842 by Jno., Emanuel Harmon, Pleasant Scarls,
Charles Freeman bound to David Lesly Ord. Abbeville Dist. sum $36,000.00.
Mary Harmond wid. John and Emmanuel Harmon, sons. Had 10 children.
William, Augusta, Ann and Cornelia Harmon recd. a share of Luke Harmon
decd. Thomas Harmon was their grandfather. Legatees, John, Emanuel Harmon,
Charles Freeman and wife Centha, Alexander and wife Esther Laramore,
Stephen Willis and wife Susan, Frances Harmon.

HAMILTON, MARTHA—BOX 49, PACK 1126:
Est. admnr. Feb. 21, 1843 by Barthw. Jordon, Geo. W. Pressly, Jno.
E. Foster bound to David Lesly Ord. Abbeville Dist. sum $1,000.00. Left one
child. Inv. made Feb. 24, 1843 by Charles Sproull, Jno. Martin, Isaiah Mc-
Cormick, Jno. Norwood.

HEARST, JOHN—BOX 49, PACK 1127:
Est. admnr. April 8, 1843 by Jno. W., Jno. Hearst, Jno. Chiles bound

to David Lesly Ord. Abbeville Dist. sum $50,000.00. Left widow, 1 son Jno. W. Hearst. Exp: Jan. 1, 1845 Paid Saml. *Lasiter,* legatee $448.60. June 11, 1850 Sarah Ann McCwen, wid. of Jno. Hearst, and her husband, P. C. McCwen, recd. $242.00.

HILL, MINORS—BOX 49, PACK 1128:
On May 13, 1843 Saml. L. Hill, Johnson Ramey, Charles H. Allen bound to David Lesly Ord. Abbeville Dist. sum $300.00. Saml. L. Hill made gdn. of his 3 chn., Armstead B., Permelia E., Benjamin A. Hill minor chn. by former wife, Mary E., dtr. of Luke Mathis, decd.

HARDY, MILES—BOX 49, PACK 1129:
Will dated May 30, 1843 in Abbeville Dist. Proved July 17, 1843. Exrs: Wife, Eliza Hardy, Bro. Jno. Hardy, b.l., Jno. C. Speer. Wit: Jas. M. Latimer, Nathaniel Norwood, Jno. W. Connor. Wife, Eliza Hardy. Chn. ment. no names given. Sett: Catharine Hardy wife of Rufus Sadler in 1857. Miles, Frances, E. W. F., Jno. J. Hardy.

HORTON, JAMES T.—BOX 49, PACK 1130:
Est. admnr. July 24, 1843 by Wm. Harris, Jas. McCaslin, Joshua Wideman bound to David Lesly Ord. Abbeville Dist. sum $6,000.00. Sett. made Aug. 19, 1845. Present: Jas. McCaslan, Uriah Blackman gdns., appointed by the court of Equity for Lancaster Dist. of Mary Ann, Margaret Eugenia Horton and Atty. under letters for Burwell Jones and Elizabeth wife, Mary Horton, wid. of decd. Absent: Jas. Thomas and Willis Hollis Horton minors. Jas. T. Horton died June 30, 1843. Wm. Harris admnr. died about Feb. 29, 1844. Burwell Jones and Harriet Elizabeth Jones were of Kershaw Dist.

HENDERSON, MARY—BOX 49, PACK 1131:
Est. admnr. Oct. 17, 1843 by Littleberry B. Freeman, Levi Fulmon, Jno. Brown bound to David Lesly Ord. Abbeville Dist. sum $2400.00. Sett: made Dec. 14, 1846. Present: Charles Freeman, J. P. Self, gdn. of Frances Eliza, Obediah T., Hulda Henderson minors, Jas. S. Holloway and wife Martha, Thos. S. Price and wife Mary Ann.

HILL, BLUFORD—BOX 49, PACK 1132:
Est. admnr. Nov. 20, 1843 by Thos. Rosamond, Geo. W. Youngblood, Jno. Rosamond bound to David Lesly sum $1,000.00. Bluford Hill was son of Jno. Hill decd.

HAWTHORNE, THOMAS—BOX 49, PACK 1133:
Will dted Aug. 8, 1843 in Abbeville Dist. Proved Nov. 27, 1843. Exrs: Sons, Jno. M., Jas. Robt., David O. Hawthorne. Wit: Johnson H., R. C. Sharp, A. H. Miller. Wife, Mary Hawthorne. Chn: Jno., Elizabeth Caroline, Polly Ann, James Robert, William Andrew Jackson, Nancy Aveline, David O. Hawthorne.

HODGES, RICHARD A.—BOX 49, PACK 1134:
Est. admnr. Nov. 28, 1843, by Andrew, Robt. Dunn, Robt. Martin bound to David Lesly Ord. Abbeville Dist. sum $1300.00. Left wid. Phebe Hodges and 3 chn.

HARRIS, MARY F.—BOX 49, PACK 1135:
Est. admnr. Dec. 5, 1843 by Jno. Harris, Jas. H. Cobb, Johnson Ramey bound to David Lesly Ord. Abbeville Dist. sum $10,000.00. Jno. Harris was bro. Elizabeth Harris, mother. Wm. Harris decd. was father.

JOHNSON, JOHN—BOX 50, PACK 1149:
Est. admnr. Jan. 26, 1837 by Francis B., Geo. B. Clinkscales, Jno. Cowan, bound to Moses Taggart Ord. Abbeville Dist. sum $2,000.00. Elizabeth Johnson bought at sale.

IRWIN, ROBERT B.—BOX 50, PACK 1150:
Es. admnr. Mar. 6, 1796 by Agness Irwin wid., Josiah Patterson, Thos. McBride bound to the Judges of Abbeville County sum 1,000 lbs. Inv. made April 20, 1796 by Geo. Conn, Andrew McCormick, Thos. Hearst.

IRWIN, CAPT. JOHN—BOX 50, PACK 1151:
Est. admnr. Mar. 13, 1813 by Humphrey Klugh, Robt. Roman bound to Taliaferro Livingston Ord. Abbeville Dist sum $1,000.00. Cit. pub. at Tabernacle Meeting House. Sale April 2, 1813. Byrs: Rachel, Jas. Irwin. Sale Jno. Irwin made Aug. 9, 1796. Byrs: Jno., Martha, Jas. Irwin.

JEFFRIES, NATHANIEL—BOX 50, PACK 1151:
Will dated Mar. 23, 1794. Rec. Mar. 25, 1794. Exrs: Jno. Brannan, Thos. Edwards. Wit: Jas., Susannah, Mary Lockridge. Son, Thos. Jeffres a tract of land on South Edisto. Chn: Batsey, Mary Jeffres. Wife ment. no name given. Bro. Thos. Jeffres.

JONES, BENJAMIN SR.—BOX 50, PACK 1153:
Est. admnr. Nov. 19, 1839 by Benjamine F. Jones, Wm. H. Kirkpatrick, T. C. P. Jones bound to Moses Taggart Ord. Abbeville Dist. sum $2500.00.

JACKSON, JAMES—BOX 50, PACK 1154:
Est. admnr. Sept. 12, 1791 by Elizabeth Jackson wid., Capt. Jno. Calhoun, Nathan Sims bound to Judges of Abbeville County sum 500 lbs. Sale Oct. 7, 1791. Byrs: Elizabeth Jackson, Jno. Calhoun, Jno. Williams, Jno. Logan, Wm. Miller, Alexr. Sample, Wm. Logan, Andrew Porter, Peter Green, Wm. Heard.

JONES, ANDREW—BOX 50, PACK 1155:
Est. admnr. May 4, 1802 by Catherine, Moses Jones, Johthan Essery bound to Andrew Hamilton Ord. Abbeville Dist. sum $5,000.00. Expend: 1800 for schooling Saml., Catharine, Sarah Jones.

JAMES, JOHN LASHLY—BOX 50, PACK 1156:
Lived in 96 Dist. Charles James admnr. Inv. made Jan. 12, 1785 by Jno. Smith, Joseph Barnet, Jas. Lusk. (No other papers.)

JOLLY, JOHN—BOX 50, PACK 1157:
Lived in 96 Dist. Inv. made Aug. 22, 1786 by Isaac Gregory, Isaac Hawkins, Saml. McJunkins, Henry Travilla. John, Sarah Savage were admnrs. (No other papers.)

JACKSON, RALPH—BOX 50, PACK 1158:
Est. admnr. Sept. 20, 1783 by Ralph Jackson Jr., Thos. Scales bound to
Jno. Thomas Jr. Ord. 96 Dist. sum 2,000 lbs. Inv. made Oct. 4, 1783 by Thos.
Greer, Archy Smith, Thos. Jackson. (No other papers.)

JOHNSON, DANIEL—BOX 50, PACK 1159:
Will dated Jan. 8, 1783 in 96 Dist. Proved Sept. 19, 1783. Exrs: wife,
Ann Johnson, Son, Bartholomew Johnson. Wit: Wm. Malone, Elizabeth Jones,
Rachel Hampton. Wife, Ann Johnson. Chn: Bartholomew, Levy, Thos. decd.,
Sarah, Geo. Johnson. Gr. son, Daniel, son of Thos. Johnson decd.

JOHNSON, FRANCIS—BOX 50, PACK 1160:
Est. admnr. Nov. 8, 1783 by Margaret Johnson, Alexr. Vernon, Nathaniel
Miller bound to Jno. Thomas Jr. Ord. 96 Dist. sum 2,000 lbs. Inv. made
Nov. 1783 by Jno. Lesly, Jas. Seawright, Jno. Miller.

ISSOM, EDWARD—BOX 50, PACK 1161:
Est. admnr. July 12, 1782 by Robt. Bond, Aaron Steel, Thos. Harris,
Abidien Issom bound to Jno. Ewing Calhoun Ord. 96 Dist. sum 14,000 lbs.
Robt. Bond, Abidien Issom next of kin.

IRBEY, GRIEF—BOX 50, PACK 1162:
Est. admnr. Sept. 24, 1785, by Lucy, Thos. Elliot, Wm. Irbey, Thos
Dendy of Laurens County bound to Jno. Thomas Ord. 96 Dist. sum 1,000 lbs.
Inv. made by Thos. Dendy, Jno. Milam, Thos. Cargill. (Name also written
Yerby.)

JACOBS, JOHANAS—BOX 50, PACK 1163:
Est. admnr. May 1, 1784 by Syntha Jacobs, Gibeon Jones, Benjamin
Wood bound to Jno. Thomas Jr. Ord. 96 Dist. sum 2,000 lbs. Inv. made May 15,
1784 by Geo. Goggins, Gibeon Jones, Wm. Burton.

JONES, THOMAS—BOX 50, PACK 1164:
Est. admnr. July 30, 1783 by Elizabeth, James Jones, Solomon Langston,
Ralph Smith bound to Jno. Thomas Jr. Ord. 96 Dist. sum 2,000 lbs. Inv. made
Jan. 3, 1787 by Jno. Thurmond, Jessey Scrugs, Nathan Talley of Edgefield
County.

JOHNSON, JAMES—BOX 50, PACK 1165:
Est. admnr. July 7, 1786 by Luke, Mary Waldrop, Jas. Saxon, Thos.
Gafford bound to Jno. Thomas Ord. 96 Dist. sum 1,000 lbs. Cit. pub. at
Hammonds Store on Bush River. Inv. made July 17, 1786 by Henry Pearson,
Charles Griffin, Jas. Waldrop of Newberry County. Nancy Martin's request
that Luke Waldrop be admnr. said est.

JAPP, JOHN—BOX 50, PACK 1166:
Est. admnr. Mar. 21, 1837 by Jno. Fooshe, Isaac Bunting, Jas. Gillam,
bound to Moses Taggart Ord. Abbeville Dist. sum $1,000.00. Cit. pub. at Mt.
Prospect Meeting House.

JONES, JOHN—BOX 50, PACK 1167:
    On Oct. 23, 1818 Joseph Conn, Wm. Cowan, Jno. Love bound to
Taliaferro Livingston Ord. Abbeville Dist. sum $1,000.00. Joseph Conn made
gdn. of Jno. Jones, a minor under 14 yrs.

JONES, JOHN—BOX 50, PACK 1168:
    Will dated Aug. 2, 1829 in Abbeville Dist. Proved Dec. 7, 1829. Exrs:
Robt., Saml. Cowan. Wit: Thos. Cunningham, Abraham Bell, Jno. Harris. Wife,
Mary Jones. Chn: Edward F., William P., Damarish, Mariah Jones. Gr.dtr:
Elizabeth J. Jones. "Allow Robt. and Saml. Cowan $15.00 each. Allow Robt.
L. Edwards and Garret Morris $1.00 each."

JONES, JOHN—BOX 50, PACK 1169:
    Est. admnr. April 7, 1789 by Edward Jones of Laurens County, Thos.
Butler, Charles Davenport bound to Judges of Abbeville County sum 1,000 lbs.
Cit. pub. at Rocky Creek Church.

JONES, JOHN—BOX 50, PACK 1170:
    Est. admnr. May 5, 1784 by Patrick Bryan, Alexr. Fairburn, Jno.
Adair bound to Jno. Thomas Jr. Ord. 96 Dist. sum 2,000 lbs. Inv. made by
Jas. Adair, Tho. Ewing, Joseph Adair.

JONES, JOHN—BOX 50, PACK 1171:
    Will dated May 24, 1803 in Abbeville Dist. Rec. Oct. 17, 1809. Exrs:
Son, Jno. Jones, Jas. S. Baskin. Wit: Elizabeth, Robt. F., Jno. Jones. Wife,
Elizabeth Jones. Chn: Jas., Jno., Joseph, Harris, Agnes Jones. Gr. son: John
Jones.

JONES, JOHN—BOX 50, PACK 1172:
    Est. admnr. Oct. 12, 1816 by Mary Jones, Andrew McCombs, Bartholomew
Jordan bound to Taliaferro Livingston Ord. Abbeville Dist. sum $10,000.00.
Mary Jones gdn. of Wm., Isaac, Rosey Ann Jones. Legatees: Mary, Andrew
McComb, Betey, Sam. Cowan, Jno,, Robt., Joseph Jones.

IRONS, JOHN—BOX 50, PACK 1173:
    Est. admnr. May 2, 1814 by Jno. Wright, Jno. Stuart, Joshua Davis
bound to Taliaferra Livingston Ord. Abbeville Dist. sum $1,000.00.

JOHNSON, CHARLES—BOX 50, PACK 1174:
    Will dated Sept. 22, 1818. Proved Oct. 4, 1819. Exrs: Son, Warren
Johnson, Alexr. Hunter. Wit: Stephen Crenshaw, Asa Richardson. Wife,
Alse Johnson. Chn: Benjamin T. J., Elizabeth Catharine Johnson, by last wife.
By first wife, Sarah Agnes decd., Polly, Loocey, Warren Johnson.

JOHNSON, BENJAMIN—BOX 50, PACK 1175:
    Est. admnr. Oct. 19, 1814 by Elizabeth, Henry G. Johnson, Clement T.
Latimer, Richard Gaines bound to Tailaferro Livingston Ord. Abbeville Dist.
sum $5,000.00.

JONES, MARY—BOX 50, PACK 1176:
Will dated Oct. 14, 1826 in Abbeville Dist. Proved Oct. 18, 1826. Exrs: Saml. Young Esq., Wm. Chiles. Wit: Wm. Dale, Charles Varnan, J. McCreery. Niece, Jane Adams. "Give to Ebenezer Wideman, son of Jacob Wideman. To Saml. E. Adams, Robt. E. Young son of Saml. Young Esq." Nephews: Wm. H., Jno. Adams. Expend: Nov. 4, 1826 Katharine Adams, property willed to her $53.75.

JOHNSON, THOMAS—BOX 50, PACK 1177:
Will dated Sept. 16, 1836. Proved Oct. 5, 1836. Exrs: Wife, Elizabeth L. Jabes W. Johnson. Wit: Wm. Eddins, Jno. N. Sample, Willis Sadler. Lived in Abbeville Dist. Wife, Elizabeth L. Johnson. Chn: Mahulda Ann, James W. Johnson.

JONES, JOSEPH P.—BOX 50, PACK 1178:
Will dated Sept. 20, 1844 in Abbeville Dist. Proved Nov. 11, 1844. Exrs: Wife, Mary Ann Jones. Wit: Thos. Fulton, Franklin Branch, J. A. Ramey. Wife, Mary Ann Jones. Dtr. Mary Margaret.

JOHNSON, GIDEON H.—BOX 50, PACK 1179:
Est. admnr. Oct. 15, 1827 by Wm., Richard Covington, Jacob Martin bound to Mises Taggart Ord. Abbeville Dist. sum $20,000.00.

JONES, ELIZABETH—BOX 50, PACK 1180:
Est. admnr. March 1, 1838 by Robt. Waters, Wm. A. Moore, David McCants bound to Moses Taggart Ord. Abbeville Dist. sum $10,000.00. Cit. pub. at Walnut Grove Meeting House.

JUNK, JAMES—BOX 51, PACK 1181:
Est. admnr. Nov. 3, 1828 by Jno. Lipscomb, Ira Griffin, Wm. Hamilton bound to Moses Taggart Ord. Abbeville Dist. sum $2,000.00. Cit. pub. at Rehoboth Church.

JOHNSON, BENJAMIN—BOX 51, PACK 1182:
Est. admnr. Dec. 19, 1836 by Geo. Lomax, Jas. S. Wilson, Thos. J. Douglass bound to Moses Taggart Ord. Abbeville Dist. sum $15,000.00. Sale, Jan. 5-6, 1837. Byrs: Elizabeth, Toliver Johnson.

JOHNSON, SARAH—BOX 51, PACK 1183:
Est. admnr. Jan. 13, 1832 by Jas., Archibald Fair, Jno. Osburn bound to Moses Taggart Ord. Abbeville Dist. sum $20,000.00. Cit. pub. at Upper Long Cane Church. 1833 Paid Wm. T. Johnson, admnr. of Henry Johnson decd., amt. due by Sarah Johnson decd. to est. of Henry Johnson $1211.24. Inv. made Jan. 27, 1832 by Jno. Osborn, Daniel Norwood, Allen T. Miller.

JAY, SUSANNAH F.—BOX 51, PACK 1184:
Est. admnr. Oct. 17, 1821 by Barzilla G. Jay, Matthew, Charles Wilson, bound to Moses Taggart Ord. Abbeville Dist. sum $300.00. (Note. In bond written Charles Wilson but the signing Charles Pitts.) Cit. pub. at Greenville Church. Inv. made Nov. 16, 1821 by Robt. Robertson, Benjamin Jones, Henson

Norris. Nov. 19, 1821 Due B. G. Jay $107.00. By proved acct. due Jno. Jay $55.68¾.

JOICEY, WILLIAM—BOX 51, PACK 1186:
Est. admnr. June 2, 1806 by Thos. Heard, Jas. Kyle, David Wardlaw bound to Andrew Hamilton Ord. Abbeville Dist. sum $2,000.00. Inv. made June 11, 1806 by Jas. Gouedy, Jas. McCracken, Jno. C. Mayson.

JONES, HARRIS—BOX 51, PACK 1187:
Will dated Feb. 3, 1800 in Abbeville Dist. Rec. May 2, 1801. Exrs: Wife, Margaret Jones. f.l. Saml. Gamble. Wit: Jno. Barksdale, Jno. Gamble, Robt. Fraser Jones. Sis. Agness.

JACK, DR. THOMAS B.—BOX 51, PACK 1188:
Est. admnr. May 6, 1806 by Geo. Bowie, Jas., Wm. Lesly, Jas. Wardlaw bound to Andrew Hamilton Ord. Abbeville Dist. sum $10,000.00. Cit. pub. at Upper Long Cane Church. Sale, June 3, 1806. Byrs: Jno. B. Jack, Dr. Thos. Casey, Major Jno. Calhoun, Major Jno. Bowie, etc.

JARRET, THOMAS—BOX 51, PACK 1189:
Will dated July 29, 1806. Rec. Sept. 30, 1806. Exrs: Peter Jarret, Basil Hallum, Henry Fleming. Wit: Jno. Callaham, Wm., Margaret Fleming. Wife, Sucky Jarret. Chn. ment. names not given. Inv. made Oct. 28, 1806 by Stephen Jones, Jas. Graham, Charles Collins.

JOHNSON, JOHN, ESQ.—BOX 51, PACK 1190:
Est. admnr. Dec. 2, 1782 by Sarah Johnson, Saml. Otterson, Daniel Ruff, Chandler Aubry bound to Jno. Ewing Calhoun Ord. 96 Dist. sum 14,000 lbs. Jno. Johnson was of Tyger River. Sarah Johnson, Saml. Otterson next of kin. Inv. made Jan. 3, 1783 by Wm. Murray, Thos. Gordon, Thos. Brandon.

JOHNSON, JOHN—BOX 51, PACK 1191
Est. admnr. June 28, 1786 by Thos. Johnson, Joseph Kelso, Jas. McElwain bound to Jno. Thomas Jr. Ord. 96 Dist. sum 500 lbs. Inv. made Aug. 16, 1786 by Wm. Hamilton, Edward Finch, Joseph Hamton.

JOHNSON, ISAAC, SR.—BOX 51, PACK 1192:
Est. admnr. Jan. 11, 1830 by Jacob M. Johnson, Ebenezer Hammond, Moses Jacobs bound to Moses Taggart Ord. Abbeville Dist. sum $500.00. Cit. pub. at Willington Church.

JACK, CAPT. JOHN—BOX 51, PACK 1193:
Est. admnr. June 2, 1806 by Mary Jack, Charles Caldwell, Saml. Feemster bound to Andrew Hamilton Ord. Abbeville Dist sum $10,000.00. Inv. made June 6, 1806 by Wm. Lesly, Jas. Wardlaw, Saml. Feemster.

JACKSON ABEL—BOX 51, PACK 1194:
Will dated Mar. 3, 1806 in Abbeville Dist. Rec. Mar. 29, 1806. Exrs:

Josiah Patterson, Robt. Foster. Wit: Robt., Wm. Clark, Jno. Moore. Chn: Mathew, Hezekiah, Robt., Patsey Jackson.

JAY, JOSEPH, SR.—BOX 51, PACK 1195:
    Est. admnr. Sept. 5, 1806 by Jesse Reagin, Wm., Jno. Jay bound to Andrew Hamilton Ord. Abbeville Dist. sum $5,000.00. Cit. ment. Jesse Reagin next of kin. Sale, Sept. 26, 1806. Byrs: Jno., Wm. Jay, Joseph Lively, Jesse Reagin, Miss Jay, etc.

JONES, JOSEPH—BOX 51, PACK 1196:
    Will dated June 15, 1809 in Abbeville Dist. Rec. Sept. 20, 1809. Exrs: Jno. Jones, Francis Young Jr. Wit: Francis Young Sr., Thos. Ansley, Francis Young. Chn: Harris, Saml., Agness, Elloner Jones. Sis. Agness Jones and her dtr. Sally.

JOHNSON, JAMES—BOX 51, PACK 1197:
    Will dated Mar. 28, 1812 in Abbeville Dist. Rec. June 27, 1812. Exr: Son, Patrick Johnson. Wit: Hannah Cochran, Esther Newel, Wm. Lesly. Wife, Abbegil Johnson. Son, Patrick Johnson. Other Chn. ment. names not given.

JONES, ISAIAH—BOX 57, PACK 1198:
    Will dated July 12, 1831 in Abbeville Dist. Proved Aug. 3, 1831. Exrs: Wife, Elizabeth Jones, Son, Wm. Jones. Wit: Benjamin, Rial, Stephen Jones Jr. Chn: Wm., Wiley, Derotha F., Emley G. Jones, Nancy Greyham, Milly Watson, Polly Glover, Jeuly F. Morgin, Sarah Waters.

JENNINGS, CALEB—BOX 51, PACK 1199:
    Will dated Aug. 13, 1816 in Abbeville Dist. Proved Oct. 2, 1816. Exrs: Wife, Mary Jennings, Sons, Jno., Robt. T. Jennings. Wit: Drury Breazeale, Thos. Mann. Chn: Robt. T., Jno. Jennings, Catharine Medlin. Inv. made Oct. 30, 1816 by Jno. L. Gibert, Joseph Richardson, Michael Medlin.

JAY, WILLIAM—BOX 51, PACK 1200:
    Est. admnr. Oct. 27, 1829 by Wade S. Cothran, Lewis S. Simmons, Jno. Hearst Jr. bound to Moses Taggart Ord. Abbeville Dist. sum $1400.00. Cit. pub. at Damascus Meeting House. Wm. Jay died Oct. 1, 1829. Son, Jesse Jay recd. $88.06. Abigail Jay, wid., recd. $176.11. Joseph Jay recd. $88.06. Tiry Jay recd. $88.06.

JACKSON, WILLIAM—BOX 51, PACK 1201:
    Est. admnr. Dec. 13, 1823 by Saml. Spence, Wm. Dale, Wm. Morrow bound to Moses Taggart Ord. Abbeville Dist. sum $1,000.00. Cit. pub. at Smyrna Church. Est. admnr. again Nov. 1, 1824 by Robt., Jas., Joseph Conn bound to Moses Taggard Ord. sum $2,000.00. Sale, Jan. 8, 1824. Byrs: Nancy Jackson, Mary Briskey, Wm. McCree, etc.

JOHNSON, RACHEL AND THOMAS—BOX 51, PACK 1202:
    On Nov. 13, 1839, Toliver Johnson, John A. Burton, James Burton bound to Moses Taggart Ord. sum $3,000.00. Toliver Johnson made gdn. of Rachel and Thomas Johnson minors. (Letter).

Mexico National Palace,
December the 8, 1848
Dear Brother and Sister: I imbrace this opportunity of writing you a few lines to let you know that we are in good health at this time hopeing that these few lines, may reach you and family injoying the same blessing from God I have nothing of importance to write to you more than we are hear driling every day. It is a lazy waresome life and there are a grate manny getting substitutes and going hom this train I would like to go with them very well but the reason more dont go they have not the money to get substituts and have enough money to go home with and to be a soldier for seven dollars a month he never will get enough for he lives very hard except he buys some little things every day and with that he draws it will take twenty five cents far a day and that takes all he makes for he gese gets twenty five cts per day I thought you would have written to me before now it possible that you have writien to me before now if you have I have not recieved them I have written five or six and have not got an answer to one of them as yet I would like to get one from you very mutch Dear Brother I am tiared of this ware and of a soldiers life I want you to send me a check on some good Bank in new orleans for one hundred Dollars if I can get that check soon I can get the money from the pay master and I will get a substitute and I come home next spring Dear Brother N. B. do attend to this mutch as soon as you get this letter for it will take a long time for a letter to get hear attend to that without fail Dear Brother I am tyred of serving Uncle Sam for seven dollars per month and living hard at best every third night to stand guard six or hours I am tyred of such a life I will assure you thares eight of ten of our mess mates has got substitutes for fifty dollars and is going home with this train you may be sure that casts a dark meloncoly feling on me that I cannot go with them the news of the army has become old to me and to out in the street I cannot understand the Mexician language Dear Brother I have nothing of importance to write to you written so often to you and Brother has written and neither of us has recieved any answer I cannot tell the (word) I have received too from H. Martin and one from T. L. Painter Brother received one from you when we was at publeo dated some time in June I dont recollect Dear Brother I want you to write to me and Brother boath as soon as you get this and tell Tidens to write so nothing more than to give my best respects to all enquireing friends write to me about Aunt Hearston whether she is still on the land of the living or not so nothing mor at this time remains your affectionate Brother

Thos. Johnson

JONES, ELENOR—BOX 51, PACK 1203:
On Nov. 19, 1825 Garret, Wm. Morris, Robt. Bigger, Wm. H. Caldwell bound to Moses Taggart Ord. Abbeville Dist. sum $600.00. Garret Morris made gdn. Elenor Jones minor over 14 yrs. Oct. 22, 1827 Recd. of Jno. Jones, Exr. of Joseph Jones decd., $43.03 in full of her legacy.

JONES, ALBERT W.—BOX 51, PACK 1204:
On Mar. 1, 1838 Robt. Waters, Wm. A. Moore, David W. McCants bound to Moses Taggart Ord. Abbeville Dist. sum $10,000.00. Was a minor. Dec. 8,

1840. Recd. from est. of Isaiah, Elizabeth Jones decd. $208.04.

JONES, JAMES D.—BOX 51, PACK 1205:
On Jan. 2, 1832 Stephen, Rial Jones, Thos. Reddin bound to Moses Taggart Ord. Abbeville Dist. sum $500.00. Stephen Jones made gdn. Jas. D. Jones, a minor under 14 yrs.

JACKSON, MINORS—Box 51, Pack 1206:
Josiah Patterson was the Exr. of Abel Jackson decd. and gdn. of Robt., Patsey, Mathew, Hezekiah Jackson all minors in 1823.

JONES, MASON—Box 51, Pack 1207:
Est. admnr. Mar. 4, 1839 by Jno. C., Benjamin Y. Martin, Thos. Graves bound to Moses Taggart Ord. Abbeville Dist. sum $20,000.00. Cit. ment. Benjamin Y. Martin made suit for admnr. in the effects of Mason Jones late of Lincoln County, Georgia.

IRWIN, JAMES—Box 51, Pack 1208:
Will dated Sept. 16, 1838 in Abbeville Dist. Proved Oct. 9, 1838. Wit: Jno. H. Ward, Addison McGehee, W. T. Motte. "Give all my property to my nephew Jno. Irwin, son of J. Irwin decd., and after his death to his 2 sons, Archibald McMullan Irwin, Jas. Wm. Irwin. Inv. made Nov. 3, 1838 by P. D. Klugh, Addison McGehee, Wm. Buchanan.

IRWIN, FRANCIS—Box 51, Pack 1209:
Will dated Dec. 25, 1827 in Abbeville Dist. Exr. Jno. Hearst. Wit: Saml. Pressly, Jas. P. Smith, Francis Cook. Wife, Nancy Irwin. Chn: Jno., Robt. Irwin. Sis. Elizabeth Irwin. Inv. made Feb. 26, 1828 by Saml. Pressly, Wm. Robinson, Richard Smyth.

JOHNSON, DR. SAMUEL—Box 52, Pack 1210:
Will dated Dec. 7, 1838 in Abbeville Dist. Exrs: David Robison, Jas. Carson. Wit: Jas. McCree, Jas. Carson, David Robison. Chn: Jas., Saml. Johnson, Mary Heatherington, Sarah McIlwain. On Aug. 6, 1840 in the County of Randolph, Illinois Wm. Heatherington was made gdn. of Jas. Heatherington a minor over 14 yrs. Geo., Margaret, Saml. Heatherington, Margaret McIlwain minors under 14 yrs. On Aug. 29, 1840 Jane Ann Heatherington appointed Wm. Heatherington her gdn. Jno. Hunter of said county appointed Wm. Heatherington his gdn. Sett. made Feb. 6, 1846. Present, Jas. Carson Exr. and Jno. Donald Atty. for Jas. Hunter in right of his wife, Sally.

IRWIN, ELIZABETH—Box 52, Pack 1211:
Will dated Jan. 5, 1835 in Abbeville Dist. Exr: Jno. Hearst. Wit: Jas. Smith, Frederick, Francis Cook. Neice, Soffronia Cook. Nephew, Frederick Cook. Mary dtr. of Frederick Cook. Sis. Mary Cook. Brother, Francis Irwin. Will to Saml. Cook $30.00. s.l. Nancy Irwin. Sett. made Jan. 1, 1836. Legatees, Mary wife of Philip Cook, Saml., Jno., Joseph, Wm., Jacob, Henry, Sophronia Cook.

JOHNSON, SAMUEL W.—Box 52, Pack 1212:
    The petition of David F. Cleckley sheweth that Saml. Johnson died intestate. That your petr. is b.l. of said decd. and has but one brother a minor and that his parents has declined to admnr. Sett: made Jan. 13, 1844. J. L. Lesly married the wid. No name given.

JOHNSON, JAMES—Box 52, Pack 1213:
    On Nov. 2, 1840 Grigsby Appleton, Joel Smith, Wm. Buchanan bound to Moses Taggart Ord. Abbeville Dist. sum $2,000.00. Grigsby Appleton made gdn. of Jas. Johnson a minor under 21 yrs.

JOHNSON, FRANCES ANN ELIZABETH—Box 52, Pack 1214:
    On Nov. 13, 1839 Wm. C. Cozby, Francis B. Clinkscales, Newton Davis bound to Moses Taggart Ord. Abbeville Dist. sum $2,000.00. Wm. C. Cozby made gdn. of F. E. Johnson a minor under 21 yrs. Nov. 13, 1839 Recd. $1,009.91 from Francis B. Clinkscales admnr. of Jno. Johnson decd.

JOHNSON, ISAIAH—Box 52, Pack 1215:
    Will dated Aug. 17, 1841 in Abbeville Dist. Proved Sept. 24, 1844. Exr. Son, Leroy T. Johnson. Wit: Nathaniel Moore, Geo. A. Ruff, Jno. Link. Chn: Leroy T., Jane, Caroline, Amanda, Martha, Israel P., Robt. D., Henry O. Johnson, Frances Bowie.

JONES, SAMUEL, SR.—Box 52, Pack 1216:
    Will dated June 22, 1844 in Abbeville Dist. Proved Mar. 11, 1845. Exrs: Sons, Clayton, Charles S. Jones. Wit: Peter Burton, Jno. L. Wright, R. D. Tucker. Chn: Charles S., Wm. J., Mary Ann, Clayton Jones.

IRWIN, SUSANNAH—Box 52, Pack 1217:
    Est. admnr. Jan. 6, 1845 by Jas. J. Gilmer, Robt. Cary, Archibald McCord bound to David Lesly Ord. Abbeville Dist. sum $200.00. Left no husband or chn. but sisters and a brother. Petr. is a b. l. viz. Jane Hunter, Matilda wife of Jas. Gilmer. Isabella McIlhernon, Agness McMullan, Mary, Charlotte, Jas. Irwin, Rebecca Hagerty.

KIDD, GEORGE—Box 52, Pack 1218:
    Will dated Mar. 22, 1927 in Abbeville Dist. Proved Dec. 3, 1827. Exrs: Son, Wm. Kidd. s.l. Jno. Bradley. Wit: Jno. Devlin, Isaac, Sarah Kennedy. Wife, Elizabeth Kidd. s.ls. Jno., Archibald Bradley, Saml. Coleman, Saml. Foster. Chn: Archibald, Wm. Kidd, Jane Patterson. Gr. son: Geo. Foster.

KEOWN, ALEXANDER—Box 52, Pack 1219:
    Est. admnr. Oct. 25, 1822 by Elizabeth Keown, Joseph C. Matthews, Alexr. Houston Esq. bound to Moses Taggart Ord. Abbeville Dist. sum $500.00. Sale, Nov. 15, 1822. Byrs: Elizabeth, Jas., Mary Ann, Wm. Keown, Mary Ann Young, Jane Hutchison, Martha Calhoun, etc.

KOON, ADAM—Box 52, Pack 1220:
    Est. admnr. Jan. 22, 1837 by Henry, David Atkins, Wm. Wharton

bound to Moses Taggart Ord. Abbeville Dist. sum $10,000.00. Cit. pub. at
Asbury Church. Sale, Jan. 30, 1837. Byrs: Wid. Koon, Geo. Cannon, Martin
Shoemaker, etc.

KING, DAVID—Box 52, Pack 1221:
    Est. admnr. Sept. 5, 1825 by Jas. Sample, Charles Neely, Elijah Smith
bound to Moses Taggart Ord. Abbeville Dist. sum $2,500.00. Cit. pub. at
Providence Church. On Nov. 3, 1838 personally appeared Mrs. Susan Franklin
wid. Jas. Franklin decd. and made oath that Mr. Franklin agreed previous to
their marriage never to make any charges against her first husband's chn.; neither
did Mr. Franklin make any charges during his life time. Adjustments of the
accts. of Jas. Franklin decd. gdn. of Alexr., Elizabeth Ann King. Jas. Franklin
gdn. recd. from est. of David King $676.80. Alexr. W. King share one half.

KIRKPATRICK, WILLIAM—Box 52, Pack 1222:
    Est. admnr. Oct. 8, 1818 by Jno., Edmond Clay, Jordon Ramey bound
to Taliaferro Livingston Ord. Abbeville Dist. sum $4,000.00. Inv. made Nov.
14, 1818 by Jno., Andrew Gillespie, Isaiah Johnson. Byrs: Lydia, Wm., Nelly
Kilpatrick, etc. (Written Kirkpatrick and Kilpatrick.)

KERR, DAVID—Box 52, Pack 1223:
    Will dated Oct. 23, 1830 in Abbeville Dist. Proved Jan. 4, 1836. Exr:
Son, Jno. Y. Kerr. Wit: Joseph, Mary, Mary Black Sr. Wife, Sarah Kerr. Chn:
Francis Y., Jno. Y. Kerr, Martha Van Landingham, Rachel E. Sims. Inv. made
Jan. 21, 1836 by Andrew Giles, Jas. Cook, Alexr. Hunter.

KIRKPATRICK, MARGARET—Box 52, Pack 1224:
    Est. admnr. Aug. 9, 1837 by Jno. E. Ellis, Thos. Kirkpatrick, Wm.
McAdams bound to Moses Taggart Ord. Abbeville Dist. sum $20,000.00. On
June 24, 1839 Wm. Kirkpatrick waved his right in the sett. concerning his
mother's est. July 25, 1839 Wm. McAdams recd. his share $16.89½ Aug. 22,
1840 Saml. Buchanan recd. his share $16.89. Wm., Thos. Kirkpatrick, Ann
Ross were also distributees.

KLUGH, HUMPHREY—Box 52, Pack 1225:
    Est. admnr. Nov. 6, 1837 by Paschal D. Klugh, Jno. Cochran, Wm.
Norwood bound to Moses Taggart Ord. Abbeville Dist. sum $20,000.00. Cit.
pub. at Providence Church. Sale, Nov. 22, 1837. Byrs: Martha, Zelinda, W. C.
Klugh, Thos. B. Bird, Mathew Campbell, etc.

KYLE, JAMES—Box 52, Pack 1226:
    Est. admnr. Feb. 1, 1815 by Mary Kyle, Saml. L. Watt, Patrick Noble,
Wm., Robt. H. Lesly bound to Taliaferro Livingston Ord. Abbeville Dist.
sum $20,000.00. May 4, 1816 Paid Louisa Kyle by Mary Kyle when going to
Mrs. Gregories' school $7.37½. Jan. 31, 1817 Paid Hunter Kyle $1.00. Mar.
3, 1817 Paid Jas. Curry tuition for Jas. Kyle $5.00. "June 30, 1817 by $40.00
with which I charge myself being the valuation assessed me by 3 men for
about 3½ acres Jews land near Abbeville Villageto which Mr. Kyle had a claim
by men occupation. Lived there 5 yrs. and by no written title and which

claim was given up to Moses Taggart who got into posseession of after Mr. Kyles' death and was unwilling to give it up but consented to give 9/10th of an acre in another in exchange for this claim and which latter land I took in my own name and assumed to pay the est. whatever the former might be valued at." Dec. 2, 1817 Paid Uriah Barron shoes for Jane Kyle $1.75. Saml. Houston tuition for Margaret Kyle $4.00. For 2½ yds. apron checks for Eliza Kyle $93¾. Paid tuition for Wm. Hunter Kyle $2.57¾.

KEOWN, JAMES, JR.—Box 52, Pack 1227:
Est. admnr. Mar. 26, 1798 by Wm. Richards merchant, Jas. Colhoun, Robt. Messer bound to Andrew Hamilton Ord. Abbeville Dist. sum $1,000.00. Cit. pub. at Rocky River Church. Sale, April 27, 1898. Byrs: Wm. McKun, Jas. Keown Sr., etc.

O'KEEFE, HUGH, ESQ.—Box 52, 1228:
Est. admnr. Sept. 26, 1797 by Mary Ann O'Keefe, Richard Andrew Rapley Esq., Charles J. Colcock, Capt. Oswell Eve bound to Judges Abbeville County sum $3,000.00. Cit. pub. at Rocky Creek Church. ment. Miss Mary Anne O'Keefe next of kin. Inv. made Sept. 26, 1797 by Charles J. Colcock, Thos. Livingston, Jas. Gouedy, Jno. Hearst.

KERR, WILLIAM, SR.—Box 52, Pack 1229:
Will dated Sept. 9, 1795 in Abbeville Dist. Rec. Mar. 27, 1798. Wit: Jas. Sr., Jas. Caldwell Jr., Alexr. Foster. Nephew, Wm. Kerr Jr. s. l. Mary Kerr. Bequeath to Andrew, David, Jno. Kerr.

KENNEDY, EDMUND—Box 52, Pack 1230:
Inv. made July 24, 1805 by Saml. Sr., Jas. Sr., Jas. Foster Jr. June 9, 1809 Paid Nancy Kennedy $12.76. Jean Kennedy her third of est. $122.07. To her 4 chn. each $22.00. Paid Elizabeth Camp $5.75. Wm. Kennedy $10.00. Edmond Kennedy $22.76. Elijah Ragsdale in right of wife $8.00. Wilson Kennedy $22.76. Robt. Kennedy $22.76.

KERR, MARY—Box 52, Pack 1231:
Will dated Jan. 21, 1805 in Abbeville Dist. Rec. Feb. 12, 1805. Exrs: Andrew Norris Esq., Jno. Green, Geo. Bowie Esq. Wit: Saml. Savage Jr. A. Hunter, J. Pringle. Chn: Ruth, Jno. Kerr, Catharine McLain, Jane Green. "Bequeath to Ruth Kerr all my right of dower to the land I got by Saml. Kerr. Also $100.00 note due to me by Jas. Vernon."

KERNON, JAMES—Box 52, Pack 1232:
Est. admnr. Nov. 22, 1813 by Nathaniel, Jas. Henderson, Jno. Sanders bound to Taliaferro Livingston Ord. Abbeville Dist. sum $10,000.00. Inv. made Dec. 4, 1813 by Joseph Stalworth, Richard, Wm. Henderson.

KIRKPATRICK, JAMES—Box 52, Pack 1233:
Est. admnr. Oct. 23, 1809 by Wm. Mayn, Robt. C. Gordon, Wm. Crawford, Ezekiel Evans bound to Andrew Crawford Ord. Abbeville Dist. sum $5,000.00. Sale, Nov. 14, 1809. Byrs: Andrew Kirkpatrick, Thos. Cunningham, Dr. Jno. Miller, etc.

KELSO, JOHN—Box 52, Pack 1234:
    Est. admnr. Aug. 23, 1785 by Joseph, Saml. Kelso, Jno. Foster bound
to Jno. Thomas Jr. Ord. 96 Dist. sum 500 lbs. Inv. made by Hugh Means,
Andrew Mayes, Aaron Jackson.

KERNELL, BARNET—Box 52, Pack 1235:
    Will dated April 15, 1785 in 96 Dist. Proved May 1, 1786. Exrs:
Jno. Turner, Patrick Kernall. Wit: Wm., Anne Moore. Wife, Grace Kernell.
Chn. ment. names not given. Inv. made June 1, 1786 in Edgefield County by
Ward Taylor, Joseph Dawson, Jesse Scruggs.

KING, ISAAC—Box 52, Pack 1236:
    Est. admnr. Nov. 12, 1785 by Benjamin, Priscilla, Henry Long, Jesse
Mabrey bound to Jno. Thomas Jr. Ord. 96 Dist. sum 1,000 lbs. Inv. made
Jan. 25, 1786 by Henry Long, Thos., Saml. Lindsay.

KIRKPATRICK, ANDREW—Box 52, Pack 1237:
    Est. admnr. Nov. 2, 1810 by Margaret Kirkpatrick, Jno. Miller, Robt. C.
Gordon bound to Jno. Hamilton Ord. Abbeville Dist. sum $3,000.00. Dec. 30,
1813 Paid Oliver Martin legatee $171.00. Jno. Kirkpatrick $59.00. Thos. Kirkpatrick $59.00.

KOLB, JOSEPH—Box 53, Pack 1238:
    Will dated Nov. 10, 1820 in Abbeville Dist. Proved Jan. 5, 1824. Exrs:
Col. Isaac Cowan, Capt. Jno. Stevenson. Wit: Alexr. McKinney, Wm.,
Josiah Beaty. Wife, Mary Kolb. Nephews: Silas, Joseph Kolb, Jas., Saml. Alexr.
Joseph, Jonathan, Jno. Stevenson. Neice, Elizabeth Clifford Batey. "Give to
my wife's son Thos. Batey." Stepsons, Henry Sharp, Thos. Batey.

KENNEDY, HUGH—Box 53, Pack 1239:
    Est. admnr. Sept. 7, 1807 by Saml., Jas. Hutchison, Alexr. Houston
bound to Andrew Hamilton Ord. Abbeville Dist. sum $5,000.00. Cit. pub. at
Hopewell Church. Mar. 9, 1815. Legatees, Sarah, Jas., Elizabeth, Nancy, Hugh,
Garet, Margaret, Kennedy, Jas. Hutchison.

KENNEDY, DAVID—Box 53, Pack 1240:
    Will dated Mar. 13, 1814 in Abbeville Dist. Rec. April 6, 1814. Exrs:
Wife, Hannah Kennedy, Jas. Foster. Wit: Jas., Jas. Foster Sr., David Cochran.
Chn: Elizabeth, Martha, Jean, Hannah, Jno., David Kennedy, Jas. Morrow.
Gr. son, David.

KEYS, MALCOM—Box 53, Pack 1241:
    Will dated Nov. 29, 1819 in Abbeville Dist. Proved Feb. 4, 1822.
Exrs: Henry, Jno., Thos. Fulton. Wit: Jas. Frazier, Jas. Richey, Henry Wiley.
Wife, Elizabeth Keas. Chn: Jean, Betsey Keas. Inv. made Feb. 16, 1822 by
Alexr. Deall, Jas. Fell, Henry Wiley. (Name written also Keas.)

KNOPT, CHARLES—Box 53, Pack 1242:
    Est. admnr. Feb. 16, 1807 by Geo. Henry Casper, Frederick Knopt,
Robt. Brooks bound to Andrew Hamilton Ord. Abbeville Dist. sum $5,000.00.

Feb. 16, 1809 Recd. from Philip Knop $5.12. Jan. 17, 1811 Recd. of Peter Knop $5.95. Jan. 1, 1824 Betsey Stanfield late Betsey Knop recd. $315.78 from est. of her father, Charles Knop. (Name written Knopt and Knop.)

KERR, HENRY—Box 53, Pack 1243:
Est. admnr. Dec. 18, 1826 by Jno. Donald, Saml. Irwin, Jas. Hawthorne bound to Moses Taggart Ord. Abbeville Dist. sum $1,000.00. Cit. pub. at Smyrna Church. Inv. made Jan. 3, 1827 by Saml., Jno. Miller, Wm. Henderson. Oct. 29, 1827, Paid Jas. Kerr's recpt. $330.00.

KILLINGSWORTH, MARK—Box 53, Pack 1244:
Est. admnr. Oct. 14, 1840 by Nancy, Jas. Killingsworth, Wm. Ware, Thos. S. Wilks bound to Moses Taggart Ord. Abbeville Dist. sum $40,000.00. Died about the 29th July, 1840. Chn: Jas., Wm., Sarah Lockhart. Due to est. Jas. W. Black and wife, $211.08. Saml. H. Lockhart and wife, $659.04. W. J. Killingsworth, $190.70. Jas. Killingsworth, $177.38. Martha Killingsworth, $2,024.09. Wid. Nancy Killingsworth.

KENNEDY, AMELIA—Box 53, Pack 1245:
Est. admnr. Oct. 1, 1838 by Jno., Jno. Hearst Sr., Thos. W. Chiles, bound to Moses Taggart Ord. Abbeville Dist. sum $10,000.00. Cit. pub. at Cedar Springs Church.

KILLINGSWORTH, NANCY—Box 53, Pack 1246:
Petition of Jas. W. Black sheweth that Mark Killingsworth died, leaving a wid. and chn. That the wid. and her son, Jas. Killingsworth, admnr. on est. That your petr. has married Susan E. Killingsworth, their dtr. Sett., Aug. 10, 1843. Present, Jas. W. Black and wife, Saml. H. Lockhart, Wm. G., Jas., Martha Killingsworth.

KAY, ROBERT H.—Box 53, Pack 1247:
Will dated Nov. 25, 1841 in Abbeville Dist. Proved April 4, 1843. Exrs: Wife, Ebby Kay, son, Geo. Kay, Saml. Donald. Wit: W. Bigby, Jas., Robt. H. Kay. Chn: Emily Richey, Elizabeth Caroline, Isabella Luticia, Geo. H., Jno. B., Jas. H., Charles W. Kay. (One paper ment. Isabella Kay, wid.)

KEY, ROBERT—Box 53, Pack 1248:
Est. admnr. Feb. 25, 1842 by Thos. G. Key, Robt. H. Hunter, (other name not plain) bound to David Lesly Ord. Abbeville Dist. sum $500.00. On Feb. 9, 1842 Thos G. Key of Hamburg wished to obtain Letters of Admnr. on est. of his father, Robt. Key, decd.

KLUGH, ELIZA C.—Box 53, Pack 1249:
On Jan. 8, 1844, Westly C., Paschal D. Klugh, Thos. Jackson bound to David Lesly Ord. Abbeville Dist. sum $1,800.00. Westly C. Klugh made gdn. Eliza C. Klugh, dtr. of Westly C. and Emily A. Klugh. Harriet Robeson decd. was an aunt. Later married W. L. Hudgens.

KEELAND, EDMOND—Box 53, Pack 1250:
Est. admnr. May 22, 1844 by Jereusha Keeland, Jno. Nash, Thos. P.

Spierin bound to David Lesly Ord. Abbeville Dist. sum $200.00. Wid. Jerusha Keeland. No chn. Inv. made June 5, 1844 by Philip Keeland, Jas. Edwards.

KING, MINORS—Box 53, Pack 1251:
On Nov. 8, 1839 Stanley Crews, Joel Smith, Francis A. Buchanan bound to Moses Taggart Ord. Abbeville Dist. sum $3,000.00. Stanley Crews made gdn. Alexr., Ann King, minors under 21 yrs. Dec. 21, 1840 Recd. on sett. of Jas. Franklin's est. who was gdn. Alexr. King, $585.03, and Elizabeth Ann King, who later married Thos. Stacy.

KEOWN, THOMAS—Box 53, Pack 1252:
Est. admnr. Jan. 13, 1845 by Nancy Keown, Wm. Wilson or Nelson, Robt. McKinney bound to David Lesly Ord. Abbeville Dist. sum $300.00. Left a wid. Nancy and 9 chn. No names given.

KINGSMON, JOHN C.—Box 53, Pack 1253:
Est. admnr. April 4, 1845 by Agnus M. Kingsmon, wid. Timothy D. Williams, Jas. S. Wilson bound to David Lesly Ord. Abbeville Dist. sum $1,000.00. Clarage H. Kingsmon was a son.

LONG, JOHN READ—Box 53, Pack 1254:
Will dated Jan. 12, 1819 in Abbeville Dist. Filed Mar. 15, 1819. Exrs: Wife, Sarah Long, son, Reuben Long, Joel Lipscomb, Esq. Wit: Jno. Pulliam, Robt. Young, Alexr. Sample. Chn: Harrison, Reuben, Nicholas Long, Elizabeth Shirley, Lucy Swanzy, decd., Nancy Greenlee, Alcey Sample. Aug. 31, 1822, paid Jno. N. Sample $100.00. Joshua Shirley, $678.25. Lewis W. Greenlee, $1,000.37½.

LESLY, WILLIAM—Box 53, Pack 1255:
Will dated Sept. 26, 1817 in Abbeville Dist. Proved Jan. 23, 1822. Exrs: Robt. H. Lesly, Rev. Wm. H. Barr, Saml. L. Watt, Robt. Wilson, Patrick Noble, Esq., Alexr. Bowie, Esq., Col. Wm. H. Caldwell. Wit: Thos., Ann Lesly, R. Cunningham. Chn: Jno. H., Ann, Wm., Thos., David, Saml. Lesly. Gr. dtr. Frances Caroline Lesly. d.l. Polly Lesley. Dec. 1826. Paid for a bedstead for Peggy Lesly $2.50. Jan. 1, 1827 paid Ann McCurdy taking care of Hugh Lesly $251.50.

LOGAN, COL. JOHN, SR.—Box 53, Pack 1256:
Est. admnr. Sept. 20, 1820 by Dr. Jno. Logan, Jas. A., Joseph Black, Richard Griffin bound to Moses Taggart Ord. Abbeville Dist. sum $50,000.00. Est. admnr. again Mar. 6, 1822 by Jno. Logan, Richard Griffin, Jas. Pulliam bound to Moses Taggart Ord. sum $50,000.00. Cit. pub. July 23, 1807 ment. Jas. C. Logan next of kin. 1833 paid Sarah Black, Jno., Andrew Logan est. due them from est. of Col. Jno. Logan, $995.44. Sale, Jan. 3, 1821. Byrs: Barbara, Andrew, Jno. Logan, Jas. Black, Robt. Young, Abram Pool, etc.

LAINEY, JOHN—Box 53, Pack 1257:
Will dated Mar. 28, 1806 in Abbeville Dist. Rec. June 2, 1806. Exrs: Wife, Isbal Lainey, son, Jas. Lainey. Wit: T. W. Smith, Jno. Baird. Chn:

Jas., Andrew Lainey, Easter Smith, Ann *Frazier*. "Bequeath to Robt. Alexander." Inv. made June 24, 1806 by Jno. Gray, Robt. Gibson, Jno. Baird.

LINK, ROBERT—Box 53, Pack 1258:
Est. admnr. Feb. 12, 1814 by Wm. Link, Robt. McCaslan, Robt. McKinney bound to Taliaferro Livingston Ord. Abbeville Dist. sum $1,000.00. Cit. pub. at Long Cane Church. Recd. from Thos. Gray, Exr. of est. of Thos. Link, in full of a legacy left to Robt. Link by last will of Thos. Link decd. $25.00. Recd. at the hands of Thos. Gray the balance due him at his decd. for his services done in the United States as a soldier $34.60. Paid Thos. Gray going to Charleston to collect money owing him when he died in service, $12.00.

LAWSON, WILLIAM—Box 53, Pack 1259:
Will dated Dec. 3, 1807. Rec. Dec. 12, 1807. Exrs: Wife, Mathew Lawson, David, Jas. Lawson. Wit: George Foreman, J. or *W. Mackney*, Douglass. (Name Douglass all that was written, on another paper, name, Archibald Douglass written.) Dtr., Ann Lawson. Sale, Jan. 11, 1808. Byrs: Nancy, Jno., David Lawson, etc.

LANE, SAMUEL—Box 53, Pack 1260:
Will dated June 6, 1805 in Abbeville Dist. Rec. Nov. 2, 1805. Exrs: Wife, Charity Lane, m.l. Charity Fickling, Benjamin Hill. (No names signed as wit. but at the proving ment. Benjamin Hill, Wm. Devlin.) s.l. Lucretia Schultz. "Bequeath to my wife late the property of Benjamin Hill" an acknowledgement or instrument of writing left in the hands of Mr. Jas. W. Cotten of Charleston giving from Miss Millecent Colcock to Saml. Lane for the sum of $936.00.

LOWRY, JOHN—Box 53, Pack 1261:
Est. admnr. Mar. 18, 1806, by Sarah Lowrey, William H. Caldwell, Donald Fraser, Ezekiel Calhoun Sr., bound to Andrew Hamilton Ord. Abbeville Dist. sum $10,000.00. Expend: Nov. 20, 1806, Elizabeth Lowry, $42.00, Dec. 29, 1806, Charles Martin, $35.00, Jan. 31, 1807, Elizabeth Lowry, $25.00, Feb. 14, 1807, Sarah Lowry, wid. $400.00, Thos. Cummins, $340.00, Jane Caldwell, $351.00.

LANEY, JAMES—Box 53, Pack 1262:
Est. admnr. Jan. 15, 1816, by Andrew Laney, Wm. Smith, Adino Griffin, Jas. Martin, bound to Taliaferro Livingston Ord. Abbeville Dist. sum 10,000 lbs. Cit. pub. at Smyrna Church. Inv. made Jan. 24, 1816, by Adino Griffin, Jno. Donald, J. F. Glover.

LIVINGSTON, JANE—Box 53, Pack 1263:
Will dated Sept. 4, 1813, in Abbeville Dist. Rec. Sept. 25, 1813. Exrs: Jno. Clark, Duke Bell. Wit: Thos., Jno. L. Finley, Sarah Clark. Sis., Esther Clark. Nephews, Jno., Benjamin Boyd. "Bequeath to Catharine Green." Inv. made Jan. 3, 1814 by Thos. Finley, Joseph Simson, Jno. Simpson.

LIVINGSTON, GEORGE—Box 53, Pack 1264:
Will dated May 14, 1798 in 96 Dist. Rec. June 11, 1798. Exrs: Dtr.

Catharine Green, s:l., Robert Green. Wit: Saml. Green, Saml. Patterson, Jonathan Wood. Wife, Jane Leviston. Dtr. Catharine Green. Gr. son. George Leviston Green. Inv. made July 9, 1798, by Francis Carlile, Benjamin Terry, Thomas Ramsay. (Name written Livingston and Leviston.)

LARGENT, THOMAS—Box 53, Pack 1265:
    Est. admnr. Nov. 29, 1785, by Darcus Largent, Wm. Anderson, Gibeon Jones, bound to Jno. Thomas Ord. 96 Dist. sum 1,000 lbs. Inv. made Dec. 30, 1785 by Joseph Williamson, Hopkins Williams, Daniel Dyson.

LITTLE, WILLIAM, JR.—Box 53, Pack 1266:
    Est. admnr. Sept. 27, 1782, by Elizabeth, Jas. Little, Jno. Norris, Jno. McCord, bound to Jno. Ewing Calhoun Ord. 96 Dist. sum 2,000 lbs. Inv. Jas. Little in same package made April 25, 1785, by Charles Thomson, Charles Clanton.

LIPSCOMB, WILLIAM—Box 54, Pack 1267:
    Est. admnr. Dec. 1, 1802, by Nathan, Smith Lipscomb, Nathaniel Burdine, bound to Andrew Hamilton Ord. Abbeville Dist. sum $10,000.00 Expend: May 4, 1806, Mrs. Henderson, attending Leucy as midwife $2.00, Oct. 26, 1806, recording titles from Jas. Smith to heirs of Wm. Lipscomb, $1.68¾, Dec. 4, 2 blankets for Leucy and Isaac $5.00, Jan. 19, 1803, Thos. McCool for attending Spartanburg, $2.00.

LIVINGSTON, THOMAS—Box 54, Pack 1268:
    Will dated July 9, 1809 in Abbeville Dist. Rec. Aug. 25, 1809. Exrs: Sons, Wm., Taliaferro, Thos., Livingston, Archey Mayson. Wit: J. Ward, James Gouedy, Thompson Chiles. Wife ment., no name given. Chn: Madison, Thomas, Taliaferro, Wm., Jno., Jas. Livingston. Two dtrs. ment. but no names given. Inv. made Oct. 10, 1809, by Henry Chalmers, Robert Pollard, Charles Fooshe.

LONG, HARRISON—Box 54, Pack 1269:
    Est. admnr. Oct. 4, 1830, by Joel Smith, Wm. Smith, Grigsby E. Appleton, bound to Moses Taggart Ord. Abbeville Dist. sum $1,000.00. Cit. pub. at Rocky Creek Church. Inv. made Oct. 19, 1830, by Charles Neely, Robt. Bartrim, Downs Calhoun.

LARK, JOHN—Box 54, Pack 1270:
    Rachel Lark, admnr. Lived in 96 Dist. Inv. made May 27, 1823, by Levy Manning, Joseph Jay, Daniel Pickens. (In same pack was the following paper): Jeremiah Dutton, Irby Duberry, Jno. Dennard, Wm. Wofford Jr., were appraisers of est. of Jno. Losson, of 96 Dist. Reuben Losson was admnr. Name also written Lawson.

LIGHTNERS, GEORGE MICHAEL—Box 54, Pack 1271:
    Est. admnr. Sept. 12, 1791, by Jas. Wilson, Wm. Huggins, Dr. Timothy Russell, bound to Judges of Abbeville County in sum 500 lbs. Jas. Wilson was of Cambridge. Inv. made Nov. 5, 1791, by Elijah Moore, James Gouedy, Thos. Livingston.

LAWSON, JONAS—Box 54, Pack 1272:
Will dated April 11, 1806 in Abbeville Dist. Rec. April 28, 1806. Exrs: Jas. Jassey, Robt. Lawson. Wit: Andrew Bradley, Jas. Weems, Jno. Cochran. Chn. James, Robt., Jesse, Jonas, Arthur, Elizabeth Lawson, Margaret Nash. Inv. made June 6, 1806, by John Burton, William Bell, John Calvert.

LINK, THOMAS—Box 54, Pack 1273:
Will dated Dec. 17, 1808, Rec. Mar. 6, 1809. Exr: Thos. Gray. Wit: Saml. Patterson, Wm. Link, Thos. Gray. Chn: Ginney, wife of Geo. Roberts. Peggy, Sally, Robt., Wm., Johnston, Betsy, Fanney, Kitty, Nancy Link. *Milly* Sons, Wm., Taliaferro, Thos. Livingston, Archey Mayson. Wit: J. Ward, or *Nelly*, wife of Jno. Harris. Inv. made Mar. 7, 1809 by Robt. McCaslan, Geo. McFarland, Andrew McComb Sr.

LUCAS, CHARLES—Box 54, Pack 1274:
Est. admnr. Nov. 30, 1784, by Sarah Lucas, Thos. Farrar, David Goodlet bound to Jno. Thomas Jr. Ord. 96 Dist. sum 2,000 lbs. Byrs: Sarah, Jno., Nancy Lucas, Jas. Jordon, Jeremyah Dutton.

LAWSON, JOHN—Box 54, Pack 1275:
Inv. made May 14, 1783. Names not plain. No other records.

LINDSAY, EZEKIEL—Box 54, Pack 1276:
Est. admnr. Feb. 21, 1784, by Betty Lindsay, Henry Hamilton bound to Jno. Thomas Jr. Ord. 96 Dist. sum 2,000 lbs. Inv. made May 10, 1784 by Jno. Lindsay, Patrick Laffaty, Isaiah Vines.

LANGSTON, JOHN—Box 54, Pack 1277:
Est. admnr. Sept. 24, 1785, by Wm., Lydia, Jas., Jno. Bennett, Thos. Blassingham bound to Jno. Thomas Jr. Ord. 96 Dist. sum 400 lbs. Inv. made Nov. 1, 1785 by Thos. Weaver, Wm. Blackstock, Bennett Langston.

LIDDELL, JAMES—Box 54, Pack 1278:
Will dated Mar. 12, 1823, in Abbeville Dist. Proved Feb. 6, 1824. Exrs: Wife, Sarah Liddell. Brother, Washington Liddell, Alexr. Bowie. Wit: Jas. Thomson, Jno. Martin, Jno. Liddell. Chin: Geo. Washington Liddell, Jas. Thomson Liddell, Rachel Lucinda Liddell, Eliza Ann Davis. Stepson, Joseph J. *Perkins*. Recept. "Hinds Co., Miss. Recd. Sept. 20, 1851 of my father, Jno. Swilling, of Abbeville Dist. by Jas. D. Houston of Hinds Co., Miss. his agent the sum $585.00 of est. of Jas. Liddell late of S. C. by us the said G. W. and Belinda Osborn." Sett. made July 2, 1850 ment. Joseph Dickson married Rachel Lucinda Liddell. Belinda, wife of Geo. W. Osborn, formerly wife of G. W. Liddell and as gdn. of Frances C. Liddell, only surviving child of Geo. W. Liddell. Jas. Y. Sitton married Harried D., a gr. dtr. of Eliza A. Davis. Sarah Davis, her other dtr., represented by Joseph Dickson.

LESLY, SAMUEL—Box 54, Pack 1279:
Est. admnr. Nov. 1, 1802, by Elizabeth, Jno. Lesly, Revd. Alexr. Porter, Andrew English, Jas. Young bound to Andrew Hamilton Ord. Abbeville

Dist. sum $5,000.00. Sale, Nov. 13, 1802. Byrs: Elizabeth, Wm., Jno. Lesly, Jas. Morrow, etc.

LEOPARD, THOMAS—Box 54, Pack 1280:
Est. admnr. July 17, 1784 by Wm. West, Jacob Pope, Nathan Melton bound to Jno. Thomas Ord. 96 Dist. sum 2,000 lbs. Inv. made July 17, 1784 by Jacob Pope, Nathan Melton, Joseph Cunningham.

LESLY, JAMES—Box 54, Pack 1281:
Will dated Aug. 6, 1808 in Abbeville Dist. Rec. Aug. 22, 1808. Exrs· Wife, Eliza Lesly, Benjamin Yancey, Esq. Wit: Jas., Moses, Moses Taggart Jr. Father, Wm. Lesly, Esq. Inv. made Aug. 23, 1808 by Geo Bowie, Esq., Jas. Wardlaw, Esq., Moses Taggart.

LILLY, EDMOND B.—Box 57, Pack 1282:
Est. admnr. Oct. 11, 1820 by Wm., Thos. W. Chiles, Saml. Perrin bound to Moses Taggart Ord. Abbeville Dist. sum $5,000.00. Cit. pub. Sept. 29, 1820 at Cambridge. Feb. 25, 1822, Paid Elihu Lipscomb in behalf of his wife, formerly H. W. Lilly, $750.00. Jan. 7, 1823 paid Ord. fees for Inv. of J. A. Lilly est. $.87½.

LILES, JAMES—Box 54, Pack 1283:
Est. admnr. Sept. 5, 1783 by Arramanos, Jno., Williamson Liles, Jno. Gorey bound to Jno. Thomas Ord. 96 Dist. sum 2,000 lbs. (Written also Lyles.)

LIPSCOMB, NATHAN—Box 54, Pack 1284:
Est. admnr. Feb. 9, 1830 by Jno. Lipscomb, Esq., Vincent Griffin, Wesley Brooks bound to Moses Taggart Ord. Abbeville Dist. sum $20,000.00. Inv. made Feb. 18, 1830 by Wesley, Stanmore Brooks, Martin Hackett, Abraham P. Pool.

LIPSCOMB, NATHAN—Box 54, Pack 1285:
Will dated April 26, 1820 in Abbeville Dist. Proved Sept. 29, 1820. Exrs: Sons, Thos., Jno., Nathan Lipscomb. Brothers, Joel Lipscomb, s.l., Wesley Brooks. Wife, Jemima Lipscomb. Chn: Nathan, Thos., Jno. Lipscomb, Polly Griffin, decd., Betsy Griffin, *Tahpones* Brooks. Gr. sons: Nathan, Jas. F., sons of Polly, decd. Feb. 1, 1821 Paid Willis S. Glover on sett. $84.34. Feb. 2, 1822 Paid Vincent Griffin legacy $148.00.

LEARD, ANDREW—Box 54, Pack 1286:
Est. admnr. Dec. 2, 1822 by Jane Leard, Wm. Marsh, Jno. L. Cooper, Jno. F. Yarbrough bound to Moses Taggart Ord. Abbeville Dist. sum $2,000.00. Cit. pub. at Cedar Springs Church. Oct. 7, 1825 Paid Saml. Leard boarding $14.87½. To Jno. Leard Sr. est. $3.80.

LEARD, MINORS—Box 54, Pack 1287:
On Aug. 7, 1826 Isaac Dansby, Henry Nelson, Jno. Drennan bound to Moses Taggart Ord. Abbeville Dist. sum $5,000.00. Isaac Dansby made gdn. of Saml., Nancy Leard, minors under 14 yrs. Sett. Sept. 22, 1840 ment. Nancy Leard, wife of Wm. Holt.

LIPFORD, ASA—Box 54, Pack 1288:
Will dated Aug. 12, 1825 in Abbeville Dist. Proved Dec. 28, 1825.
Exrs: Brother, Dewy E. Lipford, Jas. Murray. Wit: T. P. Martin, Jno. F.
Livingston, Bristow Charters. Mother, brothers and sisters ment. only one
named Wm. Lipford. Inv. made Jan. 17, 1826 by Jas. Murray, Wm. Yar-
brough, David Armstrong. Byrs: Joel, Dewey, Obedience Lipford, Jno. Boyd,
Jno. Yarbrough.

LILLY, JOHN A.—Box 54, Pack 1289:
Est. admnr. Mar. 13, 1821 by Jno. Ross, Dr. Jno. Logan, Wm. White
bound 'to Moses Taggart Ord. Abbeville Dist. sum $5,000.00. Est. admnr.
again May 1, 1820 by Wm., Wm. A. Mays, Archey Mayson to Moses Taggart
Ord. sum $1,000.00. Cit. pub. at Cambridge. Wm. Chiles was gdn. of H. A.
and Julia Lilly. Rev. David Lilly, decd., was father of Jno. A. Lilly.

LILLY, REV. DAVID—Box 54, Pack 1290:
Will dated Nov. 8, 1807 in Abbeville Dist. Rec. Nov. 23, 1807. Exrs:
Thos., Wm. Chiles, Robt. Marsh. Wit: Nathan Lipscomb, Geo. White, Richard
Griffin, "Minister of the Gospel." Chn: Edmund B., Jno. A., Harriet W., Julia
A. Lilly. Feb. 19, 1819 cash furnished Harriet Lilly with carriage and expenses
to N. C. and back again $15.00.

LOGAN, BARBARA—Box 55, Pack 1291:
Est. admnr. Dec. 13, 1830 by Bennett, Larkin Reynolds, Charles Fooshe
bound to Moses Taggart Ord. Abbeville Dist. sum $20,000.00.

LESLY, JAMES—Box 55, Pack 1292:
Will dated June 19, 1818 in Abbeville Dist. Rec. Oct. 25, 1818. Exrs:
Jno Devlin, Wm. Lesly. Wit: Jas. Devlin Jr., Peggy, Martha Devlin. Wife
ment. no name given. Chn: Jas., Mathew Lesly. Jan. 7, 1821 paid Betsy Lesly,
wid. $125.81¼. Saml. Lesly legatee $18.00. Anna Lesly $24.15½. Robt. F.
Lesly $6.94.

LOVELESS, NOAH—BOX 55, PACK 1293:
Will dated Aug. 8, 1826 in Abbeville Dist. Proved May 23, 1829. Exr:
s.l. Jno Matthews. Wit: Humphrey Klugh, Jesse Calvert, Agripa Cooper. Wife,
Jemima Loveless. Gr. dtr. Sarah Loveless. Expend: Micajah and Ann Elizabeth
Petty, recd. of Jno Mathis $42.00, their part of est. On Aug. 28, 1843,
Sophronia Loveless recd. $6.00, Mary Loveless $6.00. On Nov. 30, 1843, Thos.
Campbell recd. $6.00, his part of est.

LIPFORD, DEWEY—BOX 55, PACK 1294:
Est. admnr. Feb. 15, 1837 by Charles Sproull, Wade S. Cothran, Abram
Lights bound to Moses Taggart Ord. Abbeville Dist. sum $10,000.00. Tinsa
Lipford appointed gdn. Mary Jane, Elizabeth Caroline, Martha Ann, Miriam
Frances, Duey Ellington Lipford.

LINDSAY, ROBERT—BOX 55, PACK 1295:
Est. admnr. Jan. 31, 1834 by Sarah, Jno. Pratt, Jas. Fair, Robt. N. Ellis

bound to Moses Taggart Ord. Abbeville Dist. sum $10,000.00. Cit. pub. at Due West Corner. Inv. made Feb. 3, 1834 by Jno. Lindsay, Jno. L., Robt. N. Ellis.

LYON, B. FRANKLIN—BOX 55, PACK 1296:
    Est. admnr. Mar. 21, 1837 by Jas. Gray, Robt. Brady, Herbert Darracott bound to Moses Taggart Ord. Abbeville Dist. sum $500.00. Cit. pub. at Lebanon Church.

LOMAX, JAMES, JR.—BOX 55, PACK 1297:
    Will dated Sept. 5, 1835 in Abbeville Dist. Proved Oct. 15, 1835. Exrs: Wife, Matilda V. Lomax. Brother, Geo. Lomax. Wit: A. B. Arnold, Jesse S. Adams, W. W. Knight. Chn: Wm., Jas., Lucian Haregroves, Geo. Warren Lomax. Inv. made Nov. 17, 1835 by D. Douglass, Jno. F. Gray, Aaron Lomax, Jno. Cochran.

LOMAX, WILLIAM, ESQ.—BOX 55, PACK 1298:
    Est. admnr. July 2, 1834 by Geo., Jas. Jr., Jas. Lomax Sr. bound to Moses Taggart Ord. Abbeville Dist. sum $20,000.00. Sett. made Feb. 6, 1838 of Wm. Lomax decd., so far as to ascertain how est. stands in relation to est. of Jas. Lomax, of which Wm. Lomax est. Jas. Lomax was admnr. Thos. Graves, appointed admnr. of est. of Wm. (until his death) Lomax decd., was a distributee in right of his wife and was gdn. of minor chn. of Wm. Lomax.

LOMAX, JAMES—BOX 55, PACK 1299:
    Will dated Dec. 12, 1832 in Abbeville Dist. Proved Aug. 13, 1835. Exrs: Sons, Geo., Jas. Lomax. Wit: G. H. Hodges, Seyburn, Sidney Lomax. Wife, Lucy Lomax. Chn: Geo., Wm., Jas., Rachel Lomax. Gr. chn: Nancy, Margaret, Jas., son of Absalom Lomax.

LANIER, NATHANIEL—BOX 55, PACK 1300:
    Est. admnr. Oct. 24, 1836 by Rachel A. Lanier, Jno. Hamilton, Harmon Stevenson bound to Moses Taggart Ord. Abbeville Dist. sum $3,000.00. Inv. made Oct. 26, 1836 by Jno. Crawford, Jno. Charles, Jno. F. Livingston.

LIPFORD, SCRUGGS—BOX 55, PACK 1301:
    Est. admnr. Sept. 28, 1825 by Jno. Cochran, Geo. Washington Hodges bound to Moses Taggart Ord. Abbeville Dist. sum $1,000.00. Inv. made Oct. 28, 1825 by Jno., Hart P. Arnold, Charles Cobb.

LONG, JAMES—BOX 55, PACK 1302:
    Will dated Aug. 28, 1807 in Abbeville Dist. Rec. Oct. 20, 1807. Exrs: Wife, Margaret Long, Jno. Weatherall, Hugh Dickson. Wit: Jno. Hodges, Geo., Marshal Weatherall. Chn: Betsey Long, Frankey Hodges, Lucy Anderson. Gr. dtr. Lucy Hodges. Paid Robt. Wardlaw for Lucy Hodges now Lucy Wardlaw. Paid Wm. Long for his wife, Betsey Long, one of the legatees, $1,864.67. Paid Wm. Hodges for his wife Frances, $1,864.67. Richard Anderson for his wife Lucy, $1,864.67.

LEWIS, WILLIAM B.—BOX 55, PACK 1303:
Est. admnr. Feb. 19, 1827 by Elizabeth Lewis, Ira Griffin, Jas. Chiles bound to Moses Taggart Ord. Abbeville Dist. sum $2,000.00. Sale, Mar. 8, 1827. Byrs: Mary Crawford, Andrew Logan, Elizabeth Lewis, Jas. Chiles, Tyler Logan, Jamima Sims, Wesley Brooks.

LINTON, ELIZABETH—BOX 55, PACK 1304:
Est. admnr. Dec. 3, 1830 by Wm. F. Baker, Thos. Jones, Hiram Tilman bound to Moses Taggart Ord. Abbeville Dist. sum $10,000.00. Cit. pub. at Rocky River Church. Sale, Jan. 4, 1831. Byrs: Thos. J., Hamden S., Dr. Jno. N. Linton, etc.

LEONARD, LAUGHLIN—BOX 55, PACK 1305:
Est. admnr. Nov. 8, 1782 at White Hall by Mary Leonard, Henry Pearson, Jas. Waldrop bound to Jno. Ewing Calhoun Ord. 96 Dist. sum 14,000 lbs. Cit. men. Mary Leonard of Little River Saluda, next of kin. Inv. made Dec. 27, 1782 by Richard Griffin, Richard, Reuben Golding.

LOVE, JOHN—BOX 55, PACK 1306:
Est. admnr. Jan. 4, 1791 by Elizabeth Love, wid. Jas., Jno. Caldwell, Wm. Lesly, Wm. Hutton, bound to Judges of Abbeville Dist. sum 1,000 lbs. Inv. made Feb. 4, 1791 by Moses Davis, Wm. McKinley, Wm. Harris, Wm. Love. Byrs: Elizabeth, Jas., Charles, Jas. Love Sr., Thos. Cook, Jas. Caldwell, Alexr. Davis, Joseph Lemaster, Saml. Black, Wm. Barnes, Wm. Harris, David McCleskey, Robt. Bell, Jno. Caldwell, Wm. Pickens.

LACEY, ZILPHA—BOX 55, PACK 1307:
Will dated Oct. 18, 1804 in Abbeville Dist. Rec. Jan. 7, 1805. Exrs: Jno. Oakley, Jno. Cunningham. Wit: Wm. Paris, Douglass Burton. Chn: Nancy, Elizabeth, Charles, Caleb, Stephen, Fields Lacey. Inv. made Jan. 31, 1805 by Thos. Ozburn, Jeremiah McWhorter, Bennet Michael.

LINDSAY, JAMES—BOX 55, PACK 1308:
Est. admnr. Oct. 15, 1816 by Jno. Lindsay, Joseph Miller, Wm. Hadden, bound to Taliaferro Livingston Ord. Abbeville Dist. sum $10,000.00. Inv. made Oct. 28, 1816 by Saml. Pruitt, Joseph Lindsay, Geo. Brownlee Jr. Sale, Nov. 15, 1816. Byrs: Saml. McKinney, Alexr. White, Wm. Wray, Joseph, Jno., Wid. Lindsay, Saml. Lindsay, Col. Isaac Cowan.

LINCOLN, JAMES, ESQ.—BOX 55, PACK 1309:
Est. admnr. Jan. 1, 1808 by Dr. Mathew O. Driscoll, Jno., Wm. Boone Mitchell, all of Collenton Dist. bound to Andrew Hamilton Ord. Abbeville Dist. sum $10,000.00. James Lincoln was of Abbeville Dist. Sale, May 27, 1793. Byrs: Capt. Branson, Jesse Harris, Pleasant Thurmond, Robt. Smith, Andrew Cohon, Wm. O'Keefe, Wm. Dorres, Joseph Creswell, Saml. Patterson, Jno. Brannan.

LEWIS, BENJAMIN—BOX 55, PACK 1311:
Est. admnr. Sept. 30, 1783 by Eleanor Lewis, Jno. Edwards, Jno.

Dalrimple bound to Jno. Thomas Ord. 96 Dist., no sum given. Inv. made Nov. 21, 1783 by Jno. Dalrimple, Joshua Teague.

LUSK, WILLIAM—BOX 55, PACK 1312:
Est. admnr. Oct. 31, 1804 by Mary Lusk, Wm. Neilson, Jas. Foster Sr., Joseph Covey bound to Andrew Hamilton Ord. Abbeville Dist. sum $2,000.00. Inv. made Nov. 12, 1804 by Benjamin Hill, Jno. Lesly, Jas. Foster Sr.

LOVE, WILLIAM—BOX 55, PACK 1313:
Est. admnr. Mar. 27, 1797 by Sarah Love, wid., Jeremiah, Aaron McWhorter bound to Judges of Abbeville Dist. sum $2,000.00. Inv. made May 31, 1797 by Gen. Jno. Norwood, Jno. Miller, Jno. Carrick. Sale, Aug. 15, 1797. Byrs: Sarah, Jas. Love Jr., Zediah Woods, Joseph Pratt.

LYNCH, JOHN—BOX 55, PACK 1314:
Est. admnr. Mar. 22, 1786 by Wm. Lynch, Jno. Gowen, Wm. Smith, bound to Jno. Thomas Ord. 96 Dist. sum 200 lbs. Byrs: Jno. Gowen, Jesse Nevel, Jones Dawson, Wm. Lynch, Mary Campbell, Jno. Clayton.

LYNE, JAMES P.—BOX 55, PACK 1315:
Est. admnr. Sept. 14, 1804 by Daniel New, Henry Mouchet, Andrew McCormick bound to Andrew Hamilton Ord. Abbeville Dist. sum $2,000.00. Inv. made Nov. 7, 1804 by Saml. Perrin, Philip Stiefel, Rhoday Eves.

LANGSTON, ABSOLAM—BOX 55, PACK 1316:
Est. admnr. Sept. 22, 1783 by Christian Langston, Thos. Williams, Jno. Smith, bound to Jno. Thomas Ord. 96 Dist. sum 2,000 lbs. Inv. appraised in Virginia currency by Nehemiah Howard, Wm. Smith, Peter Renfro. Byrs: Christian, Nathan, Caleb, Daniel Langston.

LESLY, JOHN—Box 55, PACK 1317:
Est. admnr. Nov. 2, 1807 by Jannet, Jas., Wm. Lesly, Saml. Wilson bound to Andrew Hamilton Ord. Abbeville Dist. sum $5,000.00. An Inv. dated Aug. 15, 1788 in same package made by Wm. Lesly, Ezekiel Evans, Saml. Houston. Expend: Oct. 11, 1817. Mary Ann, legatee $33.41. Wid. for Jno., Keziah Lesly, legatees $66.82. Betsy Lesly, legatee $33.41.

LIVINGSTON, MARTIN—BOX 56, PACK 1318:
Est. admnr., no dates given, 1784 by Sarah Livingston, Jno. Hipp, Jacob Sligh, bound to Jno. Thomas Ord. 96 Dist. sum 2,000 lbs. Inv. made Jan. 13, 1784 by Jno. Hipp, Jacob Sligh, Peter Hare.

LOTT, JESSE—BOX 56, PACK 1319:
Est. admnr. Dec. 3, 1782 by Sarah Lott, Jno., Jas. Fedrick, near the Ridge, bound to Jno. Ewing Calhoun Ord. 96 Dist. sum 14,000 lbs. Inv. made Jan. 11, 1783 by Jas., Jno. Fedrick, Howell Johnston.

LYON, SAMUEL—BOX 56, PACK 1320:
Will dated Oct. 18, 1806. Prov. April 12, 1815. Exrs: Wife, Jane

Lyon Geo. Bowie. Wit: Jno. Lipscomb, Thos. Purvis, Adam Richards. Lived in Abbeville Dist. Wife, Jane Lyon. Chn: Joseph, Jas., Saml. Wilson and Thos. Ross Lyon, Nancy, Jennet, Margaret Lyon.

LIPSCOMB, THOMAS—BOX 56, PACK 1321:
Will dated Jan. 16, 1823 in Abbeville Dist. Proved Mar. 18, 1823. Exrs: Brothers, Jno., Nathan Lipscomb. Wit: Jno. W. Williams, Grigsby Appleton, *Tappenes* Brooks. Wife, Elizabeth Lipscomb. Chn: *Tahpenis,* Mary Benjamin, Agness, Thos., Leonard Lipscomb. Inv. made Mar. 21, 1823 by Joseph Wardlaw, Vincent Griffin, Albert Waller, Robt. Cheatham.

LOMAX, ABSOLEM—BOX 56, PACK 1322:
Est. admnr. Mar. 1824 by Jas., Wm., Jas. Lomax Jr., bound to Moses Taggart Ord. Abbeville Dist. sum $6,000.00. Inv. made April 21. 1824 by David, Jno. Keller, Jas. Hairston.

LILES, DEBORAH—BOX 56, PACK 1323:
Est. admnr. Oct. 3, 1825 by Joseph Liles, Rice Mills, Saml. Pressly bound to Moses Taggart Ord. Abbeville Dist. sum $3,000.00. Sale, Nov. 24, 1825. Byrs: Mary Cochran, Westley, Isom Liles, etc. Legatees: Westley, Isom, David Liles, Jas. Stuart, Saml. Ross, Peninah Herbert, Elizabeth Adkison.

LIVINGSTON, BRUCE—BOX 56, PACK 1324:
Est. admnr. Jan. 14, 1825 by Jno. C. Livingston, Andrew, Jno. L. Gillespie, Isaiah Johnson bound to Moses Taggart Ord. Abbeville Dist. sum $5,000.00. Cit. pub. at Upper Long Cane Church. March 20, 1826 Recd. of Agness Livingston $45.62.

LOVELESS, JAMES—BOX 56, PACK 1325:
Est. admnr. Jan. 17, 1824 by Wm. Loveless, Elijah Smith, Jno. Stevens bound to Moses Taggart Ord. Abbeville Dist. sum $1,500.00. Sale, Feb. 5, 1824. Byrs: Wm., Jona Loveless, Elizabeth Busby, etc. Returns: Ethel Loveless against est. $2.35. Elizabeth Adams against said est. $2.85.

LEARD, JOHN—BOX 56, PACK 1326:
Est. admnr. Dec. 3, 1821 by Jno. Leard, Archibald Campbell, Saml. Morris bound to Moses Taggart Ord. Abbeville Dist. sum $1,000.00. Cit. pub. at Cedar Springs Church. Inv. made Jan. 22, 1822 by Jesse, Baley Reagin, Archibald Campbell. 1821 Paid Andrew Leard $67.50.

LINTON, CLOTILDA—BOX 56, PACK 1327:
On April 16, 1830 Hampden S., Jno. N., Thos. J. Linton bound to Moses Taggart Ord. Abbeville Dist. sum $10,000.00. Hamden Linton made gdn. Clotilda Linton, minor under 14 yrs.

LOMAX, WILLIAM J.—BOX 56, PACK 1328:
On May 8, 1835 Geo., Jas. Jomax Jr., Geo. W. Hodges bound to Moses Taggart Ord. Abbeville Dist. sum $10,000.00. Jas. Lomax Jr. made gdn. Wm. Lomax, a minor. On June 17, 1835 Thos. Graves made gdn. Tennent Lomax, a minor under 14 yrs. "Recd. from Thos. Graves gdn. by note under seal $2,212.47

in full of est. of my father, Wm. Lomax and of est. of Jas. Lomax Sr. my grandfather, recd. by me said Tennent Lomax." Wm. J. Lomax of age Nov. 19, 1839 and recd. $900.00. from est. his father, Wm. Lomax and Jas. Lomax Sr., his grandfather.

LOMAX, MINORS—BOX 56, PACK 1329:
    On May 7, 1827 Geo. Lomax, Donald Douglass, Jesse S. Adams bound to Moses Taggart Ord. Abbeville Dist. sum $4,000.00. Geo. Lomax made gdn. of Jane, Jas., Nancy, Margaret, Geo. Washington Lomax.

LIVINGSTON, MINORS—BOX 56, PACK 1330:
    On Jan. 1, 1830, Jno. F. Livingston, Jno. Allen, Wm. H. Kyle bound to Moses Taggart Ord. Abbeville Dist. sum $3,000.00. Jno. F. Livingston made gdn. Mary Adaline, Wm. Lewis Livingston, minors.

LESLY, MINORS—Box 56, PACK 1331:
    On Jan. 19, 1831 Isaac, Archibald Kennedy, Saml. Foster bound to Moses Taggart Ord. Abbeville Dist. sum $500.00. Isaac Kennedy made gdn. of Jno. D., Jane Lesly, minors under 14 yrs. On Aug. 1, 1825 Jas. Devlin made gdn. Jas., Ann, Peggy, Hugh Lesly, minor chn. Wm. Lesly decd. On Mar. 4, 1826 Jas. Lesly made gdn. Robt., Jane Lesly, minors

LILLY, MINOR—BOX 56, PACK 1332:
    On Oct. 19, 1814 Wm. White, Charles McGehee, Jno. Shotwell bound to Taliaferro Livingston Ord. Abbeville Dist. sum $5,000.00. Wm. White made gdn. Jno. A. Lilly, minor over 14 yrs. Inv. of a Jno. L. Lilly (same pack.) made July 12, 1821 by Joseph Griffin, Reuben Cooper. Admnr. E. B. Lilly. Harriet, Julia Lilly were ment.

LITTLE, JOHN—BOX 56, PACK 1333:
    On Sept. 22, 1815 Archibald McFerrin, Jno. Shanks bound to Taliaferro Livingston Ord. Abbeville Dist. sum $1,000.00. Archibald McFerrin made gdn. Jno. Little, minor over 14 yrs. Jan. 5, 1817 Paid Jno. Little his share of est. Margery Frazer decd. $83.37½.

LOW, MINORS—BOX 56, PACK 1334:
    On Jan. 14, 1837 Ephraim McLain, Caleb, Peter S. Burton bound to Moses Taggart Ord. Abbeville Dist. sum $2,000.00. Ephraim McLain made gdn. of Caleb B., Sarah Ann Low, minors over 14 yrs., chn. of Sally Hall decd. On May 19, 1847 Caleb B. Low of Wilcox Co., Ala., appointed Geo. Howard of Anderson Dist. S. C., his Atty. to collect all money due him from est. of Sarah Hall decd. of S. C. Caleb B. Low was of age Jan. 25, 1837. His gdn. along with himself removed to Ala. (Letter) The State Of Alabama, Wilcox County July 12, 1847. To Mr. George Howard.
Dear Brother:
    I avail myself of the opportunity of writing to you informing you that I am well and I hope this letter may find you and your family enjoying the same blessing. Sir I recd. a letter from father some time this year and I was much gratified to hear from you all and if my business would permit me to

come I would be quite happy to visit that state once more. Mr. George Howard
sir will ask you to collect some money for me from the estate of mother (Sarah
Hall) and in order that you could settle with the estate I have procured a
Power of Atty. from the Clerk and County Judge of this County which I
enclose in this letter. E. McClain was chosen my gdn. and Uncle Caleb Burton
and Peter S. Burton securities when McClain left this state Caleb Burton kept
a part of the money that was coming and gave his bond for the payment of said
money which bond I have in possession now which E. McClain delivered to
me in payment as he has not settled with me yet but has paid a part the payments are as follows, April 2, 1837 $8.00. Dec. 23, 1837 $53.00. 16 January
1838 $5.50. 17 January 1838 $50.00, Jan. 27, 1842 $70.00, Jan. 13, 1844
$100.00, Nov. 15, 1845 $60.00. The above are receipted which E. McClain has
paid me which receipts and bond I hold in my possession to make a settlement myself for McClain now if Caleb Burton will settle by the authority I send in this
letter you can receipt and make the settlement as well as I can myself but if
he will not please employ an attorney and collect by law for I cannot do without
my money any longer; now Brother G. Howard if you will attend to my business
for me you can pay yourself when you collect the money; send it to Allenton
Wilcox County, Ala., by mail by taking the postmaster receipts for the money
the amounts which I copy from receipts are not payments on the bond but
payments on my part of the legacy left by Sarah Hall estate my name is not
endorsed Caleb B. Low but that is my proper name you can ask a Lawyer
whether to enter the suit Caleb Low or Caleb B. Low. I hope you will understand my statement and attend to my business as I cannot come at this time
myself. I am doing very good business peddling my goods in this county and
design continuing probably for several years. Give my respects to Father John
Hall, Sarah Ann. all my friends in old South Carolina. Tell them to write
to me for it is very seldom I get a letter from any of my relatives so nothing
more at present but write as soon as you can. I remain your brother until
death. Caleb B. Burton. P. S. Please keep the bond and this letter yourself
and let no person have them unless a settlement is made. (This letter was
bacled to Mr. George Howard, Temple of Health Postoffice, Anderson District,
South Carolina. One paper stated that Ephraim McLane was of Bobb Co.,
Ala. Name written McClain and McLane.)

LESLY, AGNESS—BOX 56, PACK 1335:
        Will dated April 11, 1837 in Abbeville Dist. Proved May 9, 1834. Exrs:
s.l. Nathaniel Moor, Saml. Reed. Wit: Elizabeth A., Saml. Reed, Elizabeth C.
Gilmer. Chn: Betsy, Peggy, Wm. Lesly. Sett. made Mar. 31, 1842 named
Nathaniel Moor and wife Margaret, Alexr. Gordon and wife Elizabeth.

LIPFORD, ROYAL N.—BOX 56, PACK 1336:
        Will dated Mar. 11, 1818 in Abbeville Dist. Rec. Mar. 17, 1818. Exrs:
Wm. Yarbrough, Jas. Murray. Wit: Beauford, Moses Yarbrough. Wife, Obedience
Lipford. Chn: Asa, Dewy, Joel, Patsy, Fanny, Polly, Henly, Wm. Lipford. Inv.
made April 14, 1818 by Jno. J. Barnett, Jacob Martin, Thos. Tinsley.

186   ABSTRACTS OF OLD NINETY SIX AND

LOGAN, ISAAC, SR.—BOX 56, PACK 1337:
Will dated June 16, 1823 in Abbeville Dist. Proved Mar. 7, 1825. Exr:
Wyley McMillan. Wit: Jas. P. Heard, Jonathan Johnston, Saml. S. Ward.
Wife, Jane Logan. "Bequeath to Wyley McMillan, son Wm. McMillan." Inv.
made April 30, 1825 by Jno. A., Jas. P. Heard, Saml. S. Ward.

LEROY, PHILIP, SR.—BOX 56, PACK 1338:
Will dated Sept. 27, 1828 in Abbeville Dist. Proved Feb. 10, 1829.
Exrs: Sons, Philip, Charles LeRoy. Wit: P. B. Rogers, Joseph C. Mathews,
Jacob Bellott. Wife, Elizabeth LeRoy. Chn: Peter C. decd., Jno., Philip, Isaac,
Charles LeRoy, Mary Hemphill, Elizabeth Legard. Gr. chn: Philip, Susan.
chn. Peter C. LeRoy. Inv. made Feb. 13, 1829 by Isaac Bouchillon. Jno., Jacob
Bellott, Jno. Hemmenger.

LINDSAY, THOMAS, SR.—BOX 56, PACK 1339:
Will dated May 25, 1820 in Abbeville Dist. Proved Dec. 27, 1821.
Exrs: Wife, Grizel Lindsay. Sons, Jno., Jas. Lindsay. Wit: Patrick Gibson, Wm.
Bond, Hugh Coughran. Chn: Joseph C., Grizel, Polly, Jas., Jno. Lindsay. "My
desire that they pay Ann Boyd $25.000 each." Inv. made Jan. 12, 1822 by
Alexr., Jas. Patterson Jr., Patrick Bradley, Wm. Bond.

LINTON, SAMUEL, ESQ.—BOX 56, PACK 1340:
Est. admnr. Jan. 1, 1827 by Elizabeth Linton, wid., Alexr. Hunter, Wm.
Covington, Jacob Martin, Jno. Power Sr. bound to Moses Taggart Ord. Abbeville
Dist. sum $10,000.00. Cit. pub. at Rocky River Church. Feb. 26, 1829 Paid
Dr. Alexr. B. Linton, son, of Green County, Ga. $400.00. Paid Dr. W. B.
Johnson tuition for Rebecca $144.87½. Mar. 14 Paid Hamden S. Linton
$100.00. Paid Jno. S. Allen, Esq., Atty and Clerk's fees case in Pendleton
$10.40. Paid Jno S. Allen, his wife Ruth's part of est. $1,002.29¼. Moses W.
Linton $73.09. Jas. Wray's wife per recept. $100.00. H. S. Linton gdn. for
Margaret Linton $307.46. Jas. Sloan's wife Rebecca $600.00. Mar. 3, 1820
Paid Wm. F. Baker, Esq., his chns. share as gdn, $1,013.96.

LOMAX, LEWIS—BOX 56, PACK 1341:
Est. admnr. Nov. 7, 1828 by Mary Lomax, Robt. Yeldell, Jonathan
Jordon bound to Moses Taggart Ord. Abbeville Dist. sum $10,000.00. Est.
admnr. again April 4, 1832 by Micajah, Michael Piester, Robt. Yeldell sum
$10,000.00. Inv. made Dec. 10, 1828 by Wm. P. Paul, Malon Morgan, Robt.
Yeldell.

LAWRENCE, WILLIAM—BOX 56, PACK 1342:
Est. admnr. Jan. 23, 1834 by Joel Smith, Jno. White bound to Moses
Taggart Ord. Abbeville Dist. sum $1,000.00. Cit. pub. at Rocky Creek Church.
Inv. made Feb. 1, 1834 by Jas. Franklin, Jas. Sample, Robt. Y. Jones.

LOMAX, PETER—BOX 56, PACK 1343:
Est. admnr. Jan. 16, 1837 by David Raburn, Wm. Lomax, David Atkins
bound to Moses Taggart Ord. Abbeville Dist. sum $3,000.00. Cit. pub. at

Upper Long Cane Church. Inv. made Feb. 3, 1837 by Jno. Keller, Wm. Lomax, David Atkins. Mary Lomax, the wid.

LATIMER, BENJAMIN—BOX 56, PACK 1344.
Est. admnr. July 5, 1830 by Jas. Latimer, Saml. W. Tribble, Archibald Fair bound to Moses Taggart Ord. Abbeville Dist. sum $1,500.00. Inv. made July 6, 1830 by Jas. Kay, Larkin Latimer, Nathaniel Shirley. Sale, Oct. 16, 1830. Byrs: Wm. McAdams, Zachary Carwile, Robt. Wright, Robt. Wallace, Larkin Mitchell, Geo. Grubbs, Larkin, Jas. Latimer.

LINDSAY, JOHN—BOX 56, PACK 1345:
Will dated Feb. 9, 1841 in Abbeville Dist. Exrs: Sons, Jas., Jno. Lindsay. Wit: Abram Haddon, Lydall Williams, Robt. Ellis. Chn: Jas., Jno. Lindsay. Mary, wife of Jas. Martin, Elizabeth wife of Joseph Fields, Nancy, wife of Jno. Murphy, Jane, wife of Alanson Nash, Margaret, wife of Larkin Latimer, Alley, wife of Daniel Pruitt. Gr. son: Abner A. Nash.
(Letter)
State of Mississippi, Attala County
Mr. James Lindsay, Executor of the estate of John Lindsay decd., of Abbeville District, South Carolina.
Dear Brother:
    Thro mercy we are all well and do most prayerfully hope this will reach you and your dear family enjoying life's great blessing we refer you to John, for particularly Dear Brother the bearer of this, viz John T. Nash, our son, is hereby authorized and fully empowered by us as legatees of the estate of the said John Lindsay Snr. deceased, to recover our legacy and part of the said estate of John Lindsay deceased, and to make full and final settlement with you as acting executor of said estate as may be possible and to receipt to you accordingly, which shall and will be satisfactory to us. Therefore, dear brother, we expect and wish you to fully compensate yourself for your trouble, also receive and pay yourself out of said legacy any demand or account which you may have up to this time against our son, Abner A. Nash, and any account he may be owing in the neighborhood also reserve to yourself out of the said legacy what you may require and think the mare worth, which John brought to this country, when out last the creature has been and is yet an expense to us she cannot be rode or used; her hoof is coming off after the foregoing deductions if any please pay over the remainder to John T. Nash and his receipt will and shall be valid and good as given by ourselves and in so doing you will much and ever oblige ever loving and affections to brother and sister. Given from under our hand this ninth day of December AD 1842. Alamon Nash, Jane Nash, Legatees of estate of John Lindsay Senr. decd.

LATIMER, MINORS—BOX 56, PACK 1346:
    On Feb. 25, 1840 Lemuel, Ezekiel Tribble, Hugh N. Huston bound to Moses Taggart Ord. Abbeville Dist. sum $2,000.00. Lemuel W. Trible made gdn. Richard T., Catharine C., Jas. N. Latimer, minors under 21 yrs. On Sept. 6, 1830 Jas. Latimer, Lemuel Trible, Lydell Williams bound to Moses Taggart

Ord. Abbeville Dist. sum $1,000.00. Jas. Latimer made gdn. Thaddeus, Caroline, Jas. Latimer, minors under 14 yrs. Chn. of Benjamin Latimer decd. One place ment. Catharine C. Latimer alias Shirley.

LYON, ELIJAH—BOX 56, PACK 1347:
Will dated Nov. 15, 1842 in Abbeville Dist. Proved Jan. 7, 1843. Exr: Stepson, Jno. Norwood. Wit: Nathan Gunnin, Wm. J. Hammond, Lewis Rich. Wife, Phebe Lyon. Chn: Wm., Elisha Lyon, Mary Norwood. Gr. chn: Jas. F., Mary Ann N., Nathaniel N. Lyon, Franklin Norwood. Sett. made Jan. 8, 1846. Present, Nathaniel Norwood, Wm. Lyon, legatees: Lewis Smith, Nathaniel Norwood. Exrs: of Jno. Norwood decd. Jno. Norwood Exr. of Elijah Lyon decd. was gdn. minor chn. of Isom Norwood decd. Isom Norwood's est. was disposed of before Jno. Norwood became the Exr. of Elijah Lyon, by Elijah Lyon himself in his lifetime, except a bal. due Elizabeth, wife of J. Lipford.

LOMAX, GEORGE—BOX 57, PACK 1348:
Will date left out. Rec. Nov. 17, 1843 in Abbeville Dist. Exrs: Sons, Geo. W., Jas. N., Wm. A. Lomax. Wit: Thos. Thomson, Geo. Lomax, Franklin Branch. Wife, Barbara H. Lomax. Chn: Jno. W., Wm. A., Geo. W., Wm. A. Lomax, Matilda, wife of Thos. J. Douglass.

LIDDELL, MINORS—BOX 57, PACK 1349:
On Nov. 14, 1843 Jno. Swilling, Jas. D. Houston, Robt. McNair bound to David Lesly Ord. Abbeville Dist. sum $7,000.00. Jno. Swilling made gdn. Frances E., Sarah M. Liddell, minors of G. W. Liddell decd. On Sept. 22, 1842 Belinda Osburn nominated her father, Jno. Swilling gdn. for her 2 chn. Frances E., Sarah M. Liddell. On Sept. 4, 1851 Frances, F. A. Mellon recd. from their grandfather Jno. C. Swilling left in trust by their Uncle Jno. C. Swilling decd. to their mother, Belinda Liddell's chn: $1,500.00.

LAGROON, MARY—BOX 57, PACK 1350:
On Jan. 16, 1844, Robt. R. Tolbert, Wm. McDill, Thos. McDill. bound to David Lesly Ord. Abbeville Dist., sum $1,000.00. Robt. R. Tolbert made gdn. of Mary Lagroon, minor. The petition of R. R. Tolbert sheweth that many years since one Robt. Red did make a deed of a certain tract of land lying in Edgefield Dist., S. C. of about 70 acres, adjoining Jacob Thornton and others, to Mrs. Mary Lagrone and her two chn. Rebecca and Mary and at the death of their mother to be equally divided between the said two chn. That Andrew Lagrone, the hsbnd. and his wife, Mary, are both dead. It is said that Andrew Lagrone is in debt, that the said deed of land is rec. in Edgefield Dist. Your Petr. further states there is but one of the chn. residing in this dist., Mary, who is under 14 yrs. That Rebecca in Newberry Dist., is over 14 yrs. Dated this Jan. 16, 1844. Mary Lagroon later became the wife of George Horn of Edgefield Dist. (Name written Lagrone and Lagroon.)

LESLY, JANE—BOX 57, PACK 1351:
Settlement of est. made Oct. 9, 1843. Jane Lesly later married James McCarthy. Isaac Kennedy was gdn. (No other papers.)

LYON, JAMES F.—BOX 57, PACK 1352:
On May 27, 1845, Wm. Lyon, Lewis Smith, Nathaniel Norwood, bound to David Lesly Ord. Abbeville Dist., sum $500.00. Wm. Lyon app. gdn. of his infant son Jas. F. Lyon, minor, under 14 yrs. On Jan. 14, 1865, Jas. F. Lyon recd. several negroes from his father that were willed to him by his Gr. f., Elijah Lyon, decd.

LATIMER, JAMES M., JR.—BOX 57, PACK 1353:
On Feb. 17, 1845, Jas. M. Sr., Clement T., L. Latimer, bound to David Lesly Ord. Abbeville Dist., sum $700.00. Jas. M. Latimer Sr., made gdn. of Jas. M. Latimer Jr. Jas. M. Latimer sheweth that he is entitled to a small est. from his father Benjamin Latimer, decd. which fell in hands of L. W. Tribble, his former gdn. That your petr. is now over 14 yrs. and desires to choose his uncle, Jas. M. Latimer to be his gdn. Dated this Feb. 17, 1845.

LOMAX, JAMES N.—BOX 57, PACK 1354:
Est. admnr. Oct. 7, 1844 by Wm. A., Geo. W. Lomax, Wm. H. Ritchey, to David Lesly Ord. Abbeville Dist., sum $2,000.00. Wm. A. Lomax on Oct. 9, 1844 sheweth that his bro., Jas. N. Lomax, died having no wife or children. Inv. made Oct. 31, 1844, by Aaron Lomax, B. W. Stewart, Thos. Strawhorn, W. H. Ritchie. Sett. made Aug. 25, 1844. Present: Wm. A. Lomax, Jefferson Douglass, who married Matilda Lomax, sister of decd.. and John W. Lomax. Absent, Geo. W. Lomax.

LINDSAY, ISABELLA BOX 57, PACK 1355:
On Jan. 15, 1842 Isabella Lindsay, minor over 14 yrs. sheweth that she is entitled to a small est. bequeathed to her from her aunt, Isabella Bradly, decd. amt. about $50.00. Desirous that Adam Wideman Jr. should be aptd. her gdn.

LIDDELL, GEORGE WASHINGTON—BOX 57, PACK 1356:
Est. admnr. Oct. 13, 1840, by Belinda Liddell, John Swilling, Jas. D. Houston, bound to Moses Taggart, sum $6,000.00. Belinda Liddell Relect of said decd. Belinda Liddell later married Geo. Washington Osborn. Inv. made Nov. 13, 1840, by Wm. Means, Samuel Gilmer, Geo. B. Clinkscales. "Hinds Ct., Miss. Recd. Sept. 20, 1851, of my father, John Swilling, of Abbeville Dist., S. C. by Jas. D. Houston, of Hinds Ct., Miss. his agent, the sum $1,300.00, from the est. of Geo. W. Liddell, decd. of S. C.   G. W. Osborn and Belinda Osborn."

LOCKHART, JAMES—Box 57, PACK 1357:
Will dated May 2, 1843, in Abbeville Dist. Proved July 8, 1843. Exr: Son, Joel Lockhart. Wit: Van A. Lawhorn, Martin A. Bowie, Wm. A. Pressly. Chn: Joel Lockhart, Nancy Ashworth. "Bequeath that my son Joel Lockhart pay to John Green Clay, as trustee for his mother, Polly Clay $400.00. Will to my beloved son, Joel Lockhart, as trustee for my dtr., Nancy Ashworth, the tract of land lying in Elbert Ct., Ga." s.ls., Simon Clay, Noah Ashworth.

McCRACKEN, JAMES—BOX 57, PACK 1358:
Will dated July 11, 1818, in Abbeville Dist. at Cambridge. Rec. Oct. 28, 1818. Exrs: Wm. Wilson, Isham Robinson, of Chestnut Hill, Edgefield Dist. Wit: Robt. Marsh, John McBryde, Archibald Cameron. Mother, Mary McCracken, late of Greenfield, near Stranrace, in the Shire of Galloway, Scotland. Nephew, James Hannay, of Stoneykirk near Stranrace, Galloway,' Scotland. "That my stock of mdse. on hand at my death may be taken into possession by Wm. Wilson and Isham Robinson of Chestnut Hill, Edgefield Dist. Wife, Elizabeth McCracken. Chn: Wm., Mary Ann McCracken. Also, I will that the legacy coming to me from the est. of James Wilson, decd. at the death of his widow, Tabitha Wilson. Chn: Elizabeth McCracken, Rebecca McCracken. "Or eithei of my chn. out of the Dist. of Abbeville, Edgefield, Newberry and Laurens." Sons: Jas., Wm., Alex. McCracken.

MATHIS, WILLIAM—BOX 57, PACK 1359:
Est. admnr. Aug. 24, 1832, by Jas. E. Ellis, W. B. Arnold. John Cochran bound to Moses Taggart Ord. Abbeville Dist., sum $600.00. Inv. made Sept. 10, 1832, by Jesse S. Adams, John V. Reynolds, Archibald Arnold, Wm. Cochran. Sale. Sept. 11, 1832. Byrs: Jas. Arnold, Lewis Mathis, John Cochran, Jesse S. Adams, Frances Matthews, John McCool, John Robertson, John Waller, Joshua Davis, Thomas Perry, Seaborn Lomax.

MONTGOMERY, THOMAS—BOX 57, PACK 1360:
Will dated July 29, 1835 in Abbeville Dist. Exr: Wm. Covington. Wit: John Y. Kerr, Wm. Covington, Lavinia S. Kerr. Bro., Robt. Montgomery. Sis: Mary Hillhouse, Ann Montgomery, decd. Nephew, Joseplus Langdon Mont-gomery, son of sister, Ann Montgomery decd. Inv. made Aug. 19, 1835, by J. H. Baskin, John A. Baskin, Alex. McCallister.

MORROW, JANE—BOX 57, PACK 1361:
Est. admnr. Nov. 13, 1835, by Thos. M. Morrow, Jas. Spence, Thos. Griffin, bound to Moses Taggart, sum $4,000.00. Cit. pub. at Upper Long Cane Church. On April 9, 1832, Jane Morrow, Jas. Spence, Thos. Griffin, bound to Taggart, sum $2,000.00. Jane Morrow made gdn. of Thos. M., Jas. W., Anne J. Morrow, minors. Recd. Sept. 4, 1845, of Thos. M. Morrow, admnr. of John and Jane Morrow, decd. $1,596.82. James W. Morrow. Mrs. Jane Morrow died June 27, 1832.

McCORD, JOSEPH—BOX 57, PACK 1362:
Est. admnr. Dec. 23, 1816, by Mary McCord, Wm., Andrew Paul, bound to Taliaferro Livingston, sum 1,000 lbs. Inv. made Dec. 31, 1816, by Wm. Paul, John Downey. Byrs: Jas. Farguson, Martha Rebon, Wm. Gray, Hugh Wardlaw, Thos. McFerren, Mary McCord Sr., Wm. Gilmore. Expend: Sept. 27, 1817, Paid John McCord, on proven acct. $6.87.

McMAHAN, JOHN—BOX 57, PACK 1363:
Est. admnr. Aug. 1, 1831, by Jas. H., John A. Baskin, Wm. Covington bound to Moses Taggart Ord. Abbeville Dist., sum $2,000.00. Cit. pub. at

Providence Ch. Inv. made Aug. 9, 1831, by Alex. McCallister, John A. Baskin, Wm. Covington. Sarah McMahan was wid. Expend: Recd. Feb. 8, 1834, of Sarah McMahan, part note $32.25, Recd. Dec. 4, 1835, of John Campbell, his note by agreement of the legatees $19.37½. Recd. Jan. 21, 1836, of Alex. McMahan, balance his note $87.65½. Dec. 24, 1834, Paid Fergus McMahan $20.75. Dec. 8, 1834, Paid John R. McMahan, $100.00, Recd. March 3, 1832, of the sheriff, the cost and fees of the decd. in the case of Mary Linning and others vs. Wm. Crofford $15.14. Recd. Oct. 3, 1832, of sheriff of Anderson Ct., the decd. fees in case of Jas. Stuart vs. John McGill $23.00, Recd. of Wm. McMahan $71.25, Recd. of Margaret McMahan $68.06¼.

McCALLISTER, ALEXANDER—BOX 57, PACK 1364.
Will dated Nov. 28, 1809. Rec. Jan. 13, 1810. Exrs: Sons: Francis and John McCallister. Wit: Stephen Levit, Henry Milford, Wm. Milford. Wife: Sarah McCallister. Chn: Francis, Jno., Wm., Nathan, Andrew, Elizabeth, Rosey, Thos. McCallister. Heirs: Wm., Alex., Sarah, John, Thos., Francis, Nathan, Elizabeth, Jean, Fanny McCallister. Wm. Lashly, Margaret, Sarah, Jas., Mary, Elizabeth, Samuel, Rosey Ann, Barbara Emeson. Mary *Blair* or *Linly*, Margaret, Elizabeth, Anney, John Blair, A. Washington McCallister, Barbara, Marthew and John Sr. McCallister.

McCLANE, JAMES—BOX 57, PACK 1365:
Est. admnr. Nov. 24, 1821, by Wm. Patton, Wm. McDonald, John F. Yarbrough, bound to Moses Taggart Ord. Abbeville Dist., sum $3,000.00. Cit. pub. at Cedar Springs Ch. Inv. made Dec. 10, 1821 by Wm. McDonald, Robt. McBryde, Jas. Patton. Sale, Dec. 11, 1821. Byrs: Sally McClane, Wm. Cameron, Wm. Patton, Wm. Cowan, Robt. McCaslan, Wm. Mantz, Benjamin McGaw, Jas. Hanvey, Jas. M. Foster, John McClelland, Archd. Kennedy, Thos. McClane, Ben Trotter, Martha Hill, David Robertson, Robt. Margy Jr., John Weed, Mathew Shanks, Wm. Giles, John McComb, David McClellan. John Pressly. (Name written McClane and McLane.)

McMEANS, WILLIAM—BOX 57, PACK 1366:
Est. admnr. March 28, 1825, by Joseph, James B. English, Alex. Spence, Margaret McMeans, Andrew Gillespie Sr., bound to Moses Taggart Ord. Abbeville Dist., sum $5,000.00. Cit. pub. at Upper Long Cane Ch. Expend: Nov. 3, 1826, Paid Margaret McMean $12.12. Paid Mary McMean, $350.07½. Jos. McMeen $350.07½. May 3, 1827 paid Margaret McMeen, board of Jane Amanda, a minor, $24.00. Oct. 16, 1827, Paid Margaret McMeen, for boarding Rachel McMeen, $17,50. Margaret McMeen for boarding Margaret McMeen, going to school 7 months $17.50, March 11, 1829, Paid Mary A. McMeen, $364.26, Andrew Gillespie Sr., gdn. for Robt. C., Matilda R., Margaret A. and Jane Amanda McMeens, $1,181.13½. Joseph S. McMeens, $364.26. (Name written McMean and McMeens.)

McCRONE, WILLIAM—BOX 57, PACK 1367:
Will dated Feb. 12, 1835 in Abbeville Dist. Exr: John Donald. Wit: John, Alex. H. Miller, Wm. Hill. Nephews: John Donnald, Alexander, Robert

Samuel, Wm. Sims. Nieces: Betty Irwin, Anna Hawthorne. "Bequeath unto my niece's son, John, Wm. Hetherington. To Geo. Hetherington $5.00. Cousin: Jane Miller. Bequeath to James Irwin. Inv. made March 10, 1836, by John Seawright, Robt. Dunn, John Miller. Sett. of Margaret Sims, of whom John Donnald decd. was Exr: Gdn. made Dec. 17, 1835. Margaret is now of age and represented by her husband Newton Scott. Expend: March 30, 1836, Paid Samuel Miller for boarding $43.00. Mrs. Jane Miller's legacy $500.00. May 6, Paid Mrs. Elizabeth Irwin's legacy $500.00. May 17, Paid Mrs. Ann Hawthorne's legacy $1,000.00. Oct. 8, Paid James McFerin's legacy $250.00. Thomas Hawthorne's legacy $250.00. Oct. 10, Paid Alex. Sims $1,500.00, Oct. 17 Paid Wm. Hawthorne $200.00, Jan. 13, 1837, Paid John Hetherington $525.00, Paid Wm. Hetherington $300.00 April 1, Paid Reuben Latimer's legacy $477.00, Paid John Donald's legacy $2,000.00. April 20, Paid Samuel Donnald $477.00. April 24, Paid John Sims' legacy $477.00. Nancy William and Hugh Sims $1,431.00. Paid Wm. Hoge, David White $954.00. Larkin Barmore $477.00. May 1, Paid Robt. Brownlee, $477.00. June 2, Paid Wm. Hill, $477.00.

MAXWELL, CHARLES—BOX 57, PACK 1368:
Est. admnr. Feb. 13, 1832, by John Marshall Maxwell, Isaac Bunting, Wm. Eddins, Jas. Gillam, bound to Moses Taggart Ord. Abbeville Dist., sum $3,000.00. Cit. pub. at Independent Light Infantry. Inv. made Feb. 29, 1832 by Wm. Eddins, Jas. Gillam, Geo. Holloway. Expend: 1832, Paid Sarah F. Maxwell $57.30½. Paid bill of cost for taking interogitairies in Ga. $7.20. 1833 Paid board, tuition of Charles D. Maxwell $17.00.

McCARTNEY, JOHN—BOX 58, PACK 1369:
Est. admnr. Dec. 28, 1827, by Wm. Robinson, Jas. Patterson, bound to Moses Taggart Ord. Abbeville Dist., sum $2,000.00. Inv. made Jan. 14, 1828, by Benjamin, Hamilton Hill, Robt. McBryde, Geo. W. Pressly. Sale, Jan. 25, 1828. Byrs: Wm., Mary, Polly, Jane McCartney, Geo. W. Pressly, Wm. Cowan, Capt. Jas. Cochran, Enos Crawford, Robt. McBryde, Andrew Canady, Maj. John McComb, David Cowan, Benjamin Hill, Wm. Kidd, John B. Foster.

McILWAIN, THOMAS—BOX 58, PACK 1370:
Est. admnr. March 6, 1837, by Jane, John McIlwain, John Logan, Wm. Hagan, bound to Moses Taggart, sum $3,000.00. Cit. pub. at Upper Long Cane Ch. Inv. made March 16, 1837, by John Logan, John Robertson, Thos. Eakins. On Feb. 23, 1846, Wm. McIlwain, recd. $709.47 as his share of est. On Dec. 7, 1839, John M. Hawthorne and wife Nancy, daughter of decd. recd. $468.56, their share. On Feb. 23, 1846, Jas. McIlwain, recd. $84.47, his share in full of the unapportioned part of his brother Edward, decd. Jane McIlwain, the wid. recd. $152.57.

McMILLAN, WILEY—BOX 58, PACK 1371:
Est. admnr. Oct. 26, 1830, by Robt. Crawford, Richard Griffin, Robt. Bartrim, bound to Moses Taggart Ord. Abbeville Dist., sum $2,000.00. Cit. pub. at Mount Moriah Ch. Inv. made Dec. 7, 1830, by John W. Wilson, Jas. F. Watson, Wm. Prichard, Expend: Sept. 25, 1833, John White, boarding Jas.

Franklin McMillan, $35.00. Sale, Dec. 7, 1830. Byrs: Robt. Crawford, D. V. Wade, Drury Wade, Thos. Stallsworth, Willis Ross, A. R. Falkner, John W. Wilson, Amon Stallsworth, Jas. Adams.

MAXWELL, JANE—BOX 58, PACK 1373:
Est. admnr. March 17, 1819, by Chas. Maxwell, John Talbert, John Logan, bound to Moses Taggart Ord. Abbeville Dist., sum $3,000.00. Inv. made March 27, 1819, by Robt. Young, Micajah Poole, Francis White, Wm. Wier.

McMURTRY, JOHN—BOX 58, PACK 1374:
Will dated Aug. 26, 1823 in Abbeville Dist. Prov. Nov. 5, 1823. Exr: Son, Robt. McMurtry. Wit: John Cameron, Chas. Johnson, Mary McMurtry. Wife, Sarah McMurtry. Chn: Samuel, Robt. Mary, Jane, Margaret, James, Elizabeth, John, Chas. and Wm. McMurtry.

MOORE, WILLIAM H.—BOX 58, PACK 1375:
Est. admnr. Jan. 1, 1827, by Philip Leroy, Capt. Joseph Calhoun, Robt. McBride, bound to Moses Taggart Ord. Abbeville Dist., sum $8,000.00. Inv. made Jan. 30, 1827, by Joseph C. Mathews, Jas. R. Houston, John P. Holt, Capt. Joseph Calhoun. Sale, Jan. 31, 1827. Byrs: Isabella Moore, John Calhoun, Jas. R. Houston, Joseph Mathews, Philip Leroy Jr., Emanuel Wiss, Daniel A. Weed, Wm. Reid, Philip Leroy Sr., Robt. H. Houston, Wm. Drennan, Henry Manor, etc.

MARTIN, GEORGE—BOX 58, PACK 1376:
Est. admnr. Dec. 5, 1820, by Sarah Martin, Wm. Thompson, Jacob Thornton, bound to Moses Taggart Ord. Abbeville Dist., sum $1,000.00. Cit. pub. at Hopewell Ch. Sale, Dec. 22, 1820. Byrs: Mrs. Sarah Martin, Geo. Creswell, Nancy Martin, Sarah Martin Jr., Samuel Wideman, Jacob Thornton, Geo. Martin, Jr., Wm. Patton, Robt. Margy Jr., Patrick Bradly Sr.

MATHIS, LUKE—BOX 58, PACK 1377:
Est. admnr. Oct. 20, 1837, by Benjamin, Samuel L. Hill, Andrew Mantz, bound to Moses Taggart Ord., sum $20,000.00. Cit. pub. at Upper Long Cane Ch. Est. admnr. again Aug. 25, 1840, by Samuel Hill, N. J. Davis, Johnson Ramey, in sum $20,000.00. Isabella Mathis, wid. Sett. made Jan. 5, 1839, between Samuel Hill admnr., Isabella Mathis, wid., Charles B. Griffin and wife Jane, a distributee of said est. Isabella Mathis gdn. of her chn: Luke, Sarah, Lewis, Wm., Thomas E. Mathis, Charles B. Griffin and Jane, his wife. Samuel Hill married Mary A. Mathis, who died after her father Luke Mathis, leaving 3 chn. who yet live and after her death he inter-married with *Pamelia,* another of the intestate, who died leaving a ch.; this ch. died when around 8 weeks old.

MANPIN, ROBERT M.—BOX 58, PACK 1378:
Est. admnr. July 12, 1838, by Franklin Branch, John C. Kingsmore, Thos. E. Owens, bound to Moses Taggart Ord. Abbeville Dist., sum $500.00. Inv. made July 13, 1838, by Oliver Taggart, Zachariah W. Arnold, John H. Mundy.

McADAMS, CAPT. JAMES—BOX 58, PACK 1379:
Est. admnr. Dec. 8, 1821, by Charlotte, John McAdams, Sr., John Wright, bound to Moses Taggart Ord. Abbeville Dist., sum $10,000.00. Inv. made Dec. 31, 1821, by Isaac Cowan, Cador Gantt, Thos. Beatty. Sale, Jan. 1, 1822. Byrs: Charlotte McAdams, Bennet McAdam, Capt. John Simson, Moses Ashley, Sr., Capt. Benjamin Griffin, Moses Ashley, Jr., Benjamin West, Samuel Shaw, James Snell, Joseph Burton, John McAdam, Esq., etc.

MOORE, WILLIAM—BOX 58, PACK 1380:
Est. admnr. Oct. 23, 1837 by Nathaniel Moore, Pollard Brown, Wm. Lesly, bound to Moses Taggart Ord. Abbeville Dist., sum $300.00. Cit. pub. at Hopewell Ch. Inv. made Oct. 28, 1837, by Wm. Lesly, Pollard Brown, Geo. A. Ruff. Sale, Oct. 30, 1837. Byrs: Jane Moore, Wm. Lesly, John Moore, Geo. Ruff, C. V. Barns, Andrew Edwards, Harris Alexander.

McGEE, ANNA—BOX 58, PACK 1381:
Will dated Sept. 25, 1837 in Abbeville Dist. Exr: Son, John Magee. Wit: Wm. Barmore, Washington Youngblood, Isaac Agnew. Chn: Jane Dodson, Elizabeth S. Sims, Polly Dunn, John, Burrel, Michael, Abner H., Wm. Magee, Nancy Barmore, decd., Gr. chn: Michael Magee, Sr., Malinda Brownly, Margaret Barmore. Inv. made Nov. 26, 1838, by Benjamin Smith, Ezekiel, John Rasor.

MITCHELL, NIMROD—BOX 58, PACK 1382:
Est. admnr. Nov. 13, 1837, by John Weatherall, James H. Kay, Noah Reeves, bound to Moses Taggart Ord. Abbeville Dist., sum $1,000.00. Cit. pub. at Turkey Creek Ch. Expend: Oct. 28, 1842, Legatees: John Mitchell $17,75, Mathew Bell $17.75, Alanson Lord $17,75, Wm. Mitchell $19.00, A. W. Mitchell $17.75, A. W. Mitchell, gdn. for minors, Geo., Dicey Mitchell $35.90.

McCLINTON, JAMES—BOX 58, PACK 1383:
Est. admnr. April 13, 1835, by Samuel B., John McClinton, Alex. Spence, bound to Moses Taggart Ord. Abbeville Dist., sum $1,200.00. Cit. pub. at Hopewell Ch. Inv. made April 27, 1835 by Dr. Robt. Devlin, Jas. W. Frazer, John, Samuel McClinton. Rosannah McClinton bought at the sale.

McCREARY, JAMES—BOX 58, PACK 1384:
Est. admnr. Sept. 12, 1828, by Downs, Wm., Nathan Calhoun, bound to Moses Taggart Ord. Abbeville Dist., sum $5,000.00. Inv. made Dec. 20, 1828, by Chas. Neely, Robt. A. Cunningham, Walter Anderson. Distributees: Milly, wid., James McCraddy, infant, Mary Frances McCraddy, chn. of decd. Jabez W. H. Johnson, of Laurens Dist., was gdn. of Mary Frances McCraddy. (Name written McCreary and McCraddy.)

McCOOL, ISAAC—BOX 58, PACK 1385:
Est. admnr. Jan. 9, 1826 by Samuel Davis, Thos. Spragins, Zachary Meriwether, bound to Moses Taggart Ord. Abbeville Dist., sum $1,000.00. Inv. made Jan. 26, 1826, by Robt. Turner, Wesley Brooks. Byrs: Elizabeth McCool,

Ira Griffin, Jas. Watson, Lewis Simmond, Robt. Turner, Lavinia Watson, Stanmore Brooks, Samuel Henderson, Samuel Mitchell, Wm. L. Blake, Jas. Chiles, Richard Henderson, Jr., Stephen Witt, Wm. Watson, Wesley Brooks.

MOORE, ALLEN—BOX 58, PACK 1386:
Est. admnr. Oct. 30, 1826, by Robt., Joseph R., John McComb, John Chevis, bound to Moses Taggart Ord. Abbeville Dist., sum $1,000.00. Sale, Nov. 9, 1826. Byrs: A. Laughlan, Robt. McComb, Philip Leroy, Margaret Moore, Wm. Calhoun, John Glasgo, John Johnson, Adam Cole, Geo. Crawford, Levi Hilbern, John McCelvy, Dyonetias Rogers, Wm. H. Moore, Jas. Hogan.

MARTIN, ALEXANDER—BOX 58, PACK 1387:
Will dated Jan. 30, 1814, in Newberry Dist. Prov. Jan. 3, 1832. Exrs: John Martin, Jas. Caldwell. Wit: John M. Morris, W. M. Rutherford, Thos. Gordon. Wife, Agnus Martin. Chn. Ment., no names given. Inv. made Jan. 4, 1832, by Samuel Watt, Wm. Lesly, Samuel A. Jack. Expend: Recd. from Gordon Martin $11.00. From Jas. P. Martin $8.00. From Richard Martin $7.38.

MATTISON, WILLIAM—BOX 58, PACK 1388:
Will dated Mar. 3, 1837, in Abbeville Dist. Prov. Aug. 6, 1838. Exrs: Wife, Eliza, Uriah Jackson Mattison. Wit: James H. Wyatt, Gabriel M. Mattison, C. T. Latimer. Wife, Eliza. Chn. ment., no names given. Legatees: Mary Shirley, Luvinia Kay, U. J., Benjamin W., G. W., Jas. M., G. P., M. E., John R., W. N. Mattison. Nancy Elizabeth, a dtr., married Wm. H. Crawford. Mary married Richard Shirley. Share of B. Nathaniel Shirley, $318.93.

McCOY, ARCHIBALD—BOX 58, PACK 1389:
Est. admnr. Oct. 1, 1827, by Margaret McCoy, John J. Barnett, David Armstrong, bound to Moses Taggart Ord. Abbeville Dist., sum $2,000.00. Inv. made Oct. 22, 1827, by John J. Barnett, Wm. Pursell, Mathew Wilson. Sale, Oct. 23, 1827. Byrs: Margaret, Enos McCoy, Jas., Samuel Huston.

MORROW, JOHN BOX 58, PACK 1390:
Est. admnr. Sept. 1, 1828, by Jane Morrow, wid., Robt. Spence, Alex. Hunter, Wm. H. Caldwell, bound to Moses Taggart Ord., sum $5,000.00. Cit. pub. at Rocky River Ch. Inv. made Oct. 29, 1828 by Joseph Moseley, Thos. Jones, Meridith McGehee. Left wid., Jane, and 3 chn. No names given.

McCRAVEN, JOHN, ESQ.—BOX 58, PACK 1391:
Est. admnr. Nov. 12, 1828, by Jas. McCraven, Samuel Young, Wm. Calhoun, bound to Moses Taggart Ord. Abbeville Dist., sum $10,000.00. Cit. pub. at Hopewell Ch. Inv. made Nov. 28, 1828, by Alex. Bowie, Wm. Lomax, David Lesly. Expend: May 28, 1929, Loaned Robt. McCraven, Sr., on note $100.00. Loaned Dr. Wm. McCraven, on note $100.00.

MUNSON, LEMUEL—BOX 58, PACK 1392:
Est. admnr. Apr. 9, 1823, by John Logan, Peter B. Rogers, John McCraven, bound to Moses Taggart Ord. Abbeville Dist., sum $700.00. Cit. pub.

at Upper Long Cane Ch. Inv. made May 5, 1823, by Samuel Watt, Jas. Tatom, John Bowie, Jr.

McELHENNY, VINCIENT—BOX 58, PACK 1393:
Est. admnr. Dec. 16, 1825, by John McCelvy, Meridith McGehee, Henry A. Mouchett, bound to Moses Taggart Ord. Abbeville Dist., sum $7,000.00. Cit. pub. at Willington Ch. Inv. made Jan. 9, 1826, by Meredith McGehee, John Gray, Wm. Robinson, Henry A. Mouchett. Byrs: Mary, John McElhenny, etc. (Name written McElhaney also.)

McCLURGE, JAMES—BOX 59, PACK 1394:
Est. admnr. Jan. 6, 1812, by Josiah Patterson, Jr., Wm. H. Caldwell, bound to Moses Taggart, Ord. Abbeville Dist., sum $2,000.00. Cit. pub. at Rocky River Ch. Inv. made Jan. 30, 1812, by Chas. Johnson, David Kerr, Isaac C. Bole. Byrs: Margaret McClurge, Robt. Nichols, Ephraim Nichols, Jacob Martin, etc.

McGAW, SARAH—BOX 59, PACK 1395:
Will dated May 19, 1817, in Abbeville Dist. Rec. Dec. 4, 1820. Exrs: Son, Samuel McGaw, Bro., Josiah Patterson. Wit: Samuel, John T. Pressly. Chn: John, Samuel, Wm., Jas., Moses, Agness, Benjamin, Josiah, Mary McGaw. Sale, Dec. 22, 1820. Byrs: Mary Giles, Allen Glover, Benjamin McGaw, Josiah McGaw, Jane Pressly, James Patton, Samuel McGaw, Josiah Patterson, John Pressly, Mathew Shanks, Robert Shanks, Archibald Little.

MOORE, NICHOLAS, BOX 59, PACK 1396:
Est. admnr. Apr. 13, 1821, by Jacob, Geo. Washington Martin, Andrew Giles, bound to Moses Taggart Ord. Abbeville Dist., sum $6,000.00. Cit. pub. at Little Mountain Ch. Inv. made Apr. 27, 1821, by Alex. Hunter, G. W. Martin, Andrew Giles. Expend: Feb. 22, 1822, a hat for Wm. Moore, $2.00, 1829, John Pressly, for W. F. Moore's schooling $6.00, for Rebecca Moore's schooling, $12.00, for Elizabeth Moore's schooling $9.00. For Frances Moore, $9.00. March 1, 1824 Recd. of John Ellington, for tuition of Titus Murry, Jr., $7.00. Mrs. Frances Moore was wid.

McKEE, ADAM—BOX 59, PACK 1397:
Est. admnr. Sept. 4, 1820, by John, Elenor McKee, Isaac Cowan, bound to Moses Taggart Ord. Abbeville District., sum $3,000.00. Inv. made Sept. 19, 1820, by Eli Bowie, Robt. Brackenridge, Michael McKee. Sale, Sept. 20, 1820. Byrs: John Richey, Thos. Hawthorn, Archibald Fair, Wm. Martin, John, Michael, McKee, Adam Bailey, Thos. Perry, Joseph Johnston, John Burton, Francis Sharp, Gabriel Hodges, etc.

MITCHELL, WILLIAM—BOX 59, PACK 1398:
Will dated Mar. 10, 1821, in Abbeville Dist. Prov. Nov. 15, 1821. Exrs: Sons: John, Ephraim, Jas. Mitchell. Wit: James, Nimrod Mitchell. Wife, Chole Mitchell. Chn: Sarah, Nancy, John, Ephraim, Wm., Jas., Polly, *Calous*, Benjamin, Elizabeth Mitchell. Inv. made Dec. 13, 1821, by Jas. Mitchell, Reuben Nash, Wm. Long.

MARTIN, JOHN—BOX 59, PACK 1399:
Will dated Dec. 20, 1821, in Abbeville Dist. Prov. Feb. 9, 1822. Exrs: Wife, Nancy Martin, Dr. Elihu L. Cartledge, Edward Collier, Sr. Wit: B. H. Saxon Joseph L. Bouchillon, Mackerness G. Williams. Wife: Nancy. Chn: Betsey, Julia Thompson, Wm., John Martin, Polly Freeman, Sally David or Davis, Milly Edwards, Phares, Caty, Sabra Key Hessabeth Lee, Edmond Cartledge, Jas., Eli, Caroline Matilda Martin. Inv. made Feb. 19, 1822, by Allen Barksdale, Meridith McGehee, J. L. Gibert, Isaac Moragne. Expend: Jan. 17, 1829, Paid Thos. Edward's legacy $80.00.

MARTIN, JOHN—BOX 59, PACK 1400:
Est. admnr. Nov. 21, 1834, by Robt. A. Martin, Samuel Morris, Dewey E. Lipford, bound to Moses Taggart Ord. Abbeville Dist., sum $20,000.00. Inv. made Dec. 13, 1834, by Samuel Morris, John Chiles, John Ruff. Sett: May 23, 1842. Present: Robt. A. Martin, admnr., Mary Ann Martin, wid., John R., Geo. P., Jas. C. Martin. John Martin died Oct. 1834. Had 4 chn.

MANN, JOHN—BOX 59, PACK 1401:
Will dated Mar. 1, 1830, in Abbeville Dist. Prov. June 21, 1830. Exrs: Alex. Spence, Michail S. Mann, Moses Mann. Wit: Gilbert, Robt. Mann, A. Spence. Wife: Margaret Mann. Chn: John G., Pamela, Wm. R., Margaret, Ann, Michael Mann.

McGAW, MARY—BOX 59, PACK 1402:
Est. admnr. Dec. 9, 1836, by John Link, Robt. Brady, Thos. Parker, bound to Moses Taggart, sum $10,000.00. Cit. pub. at Lebanon Ch. Inv. made Dec. 24, 1836, by Jas. Taggart, Robt. Brady, Robt. Vernon. Expend: Aug. 3, 1936, Paid Robt. Taylor, heir $10.00. Nov. 14, paid Josiah McGaws, acct. for Mrs. McGaw's burial clothes, $5.12½, Nov. 20, paid Wm. Cook for schooling James J. McGaw during Mrs. McGaw's life time. $9.10¾. Paid Samuel C. McGaw part of his mother's, Mrs. Mary McGaw's, estate $15.75. Paid Jane C. McGaw, $1.50. Sett. made Nov. 30, 1839. 6 heirs ment. John McGaw, now decd. was the 7th heir. Hugh McKelvey recd. $40.00. Samuel Link's part $123.94½, John Links' part $123.94½.

McGEHEE, CARR—BOX 59, PACK 1403:
Est. admnr. 1820, by Charlotte McGehee, Richard Griffin, E. Calhoun, John Logan, bound to Moses Taggart, sum $20,000.00. Cit. pub. at Rocky Creek Ch. Inv. made Jan. 15, 1830, by Richard Griffin, Dr. John Logan, John McGehee, Grigsbey E. Apelton, E. R. Calhoun. Expend: Jan. 20, 1830, Addison McGehee, $343.17, Nov. 30, 1831, paid Joel Smith, gdn. Emma Tinsly $670.00, paid note on Wm. Tinsly $200.00. Distributees: Charlotte, Addison McGehee, David. Belinda Ransom, wife and Joel Smith, gdn. of Mary Ann Emma Tinsley's est.

McBRIDE, JAMES, BOX 59, PACK 1405:
Est. admnr. Jan. 10, 1829, by Robt., Thos. McBride, Wm. Robinson, bound to Moses Taggart, sum $1,200.00. Cit. pub. at Long Cane Ch. "Know

that I, John Buck, of Preble County, Ohio, gdn. of Mary, Wm., Jas., Sarah McBride, heirs of James McBride, late of Abbeville Dist., S. C. James McBride died Dec. 25, 1828 leaving 103 acres of land on the waters of Long Cane on or near Reedy's Branch in Abbeville Dist., do appoint Moses Taggart our atty. Dated this Oct. 14, 1835." Sarah McBride was the wid.

(Letter) Mr. A. Burt, Esq.:

Sir Mr. John Buck of Ohio state who will hand you this is out here trying to settle the estate of James McBride, Robert McBride the admnr. of said estate is in Alabama and Thomas McBride is one of his securities and he is in Alabama. William Robinson is the other; he is living here. James McBride died here and his effects were sold by the admnr. The family of James McBride has moved to Ohio state this Mr. John Buck is appointed guardian for the children of James McBride the estate has to be settled in law or by law. Dated Feb. 15, 1836 Hamilton Hill.

In the Court of Common Pleas for the Term of March 1835, Preble County, Ohio, stated that William McBride son of James McBride aged 16 yrs. James McBride aged 12 yrs. Sarah McBride age 7 yrs. At the Oct. Term stated that Mary McBride age 20 yrs.

(Letter) Wilcox, Dec. the 10th 1836.

Dear Friend:

We are all in good health and was glad to hear that health was in some degree returning to yourself & family your letter came to hand respecting the mill tract of land about the same time by our minister one came from T Creswell stating that $6 was offered for it the Dr and myself had frequent *confabs* on the subject and as he had all the trading to do I autheresed him to offer $200 cash but it would take and we finally concluded to give the 6 dollars rather than you should not get the land and Saturday last was appointed to meet at my house to confirm the contract but lo on monday morning I called to tell the Dr that nothing less than $8 per acre would take the land and he would not be bound to that longer than the 25th of this month and the Dr would have been willing even to given that rather than you should not get it but the price was so beyond our limitation I would not yeled to it and concluded to await further advice from you which you will forward with as little duty as possibly after this comes to hand the money is ready for settlement with Mr. Taggart but I have retained it until I get an answer about the land and if you conclude not to purchase I will make an exchange with the Dr the amt of

Sarah purchased at sale $96.08¾.
Cash paid to Wm. Patton at her going away $23.81¼.
Cash paid to Jas C Willard at her going away $6.43¾.
Cash paid John Robinson shoeing horse $1.12½.
Cash paid by R McBryde sugar & coffee at Augusta $3.00.
Cash paid William Cowan Ironing trough $1.00.
Cash paid James Patterson for leather $1.00.
Cash paid Wm. McCartney for waggon $34.50.

The trough and the leather was two dollars each and Mrs. Stuart paid half the you will recollect was 65 dollars and Mrs. Stuart paid half but sally was indebted her mother two dollars for which she is charged the 2 dollars extra the enclosed paper from Mr. Taggart will show that she is indebted to estate $23.87 the money that I borrowed from McCravan I entirely neglected to return but your voucher will be good the amount I have forgotten but that added to the amount 23.87 will be the amount that she will be endebted to me and I request Mr. Taggart to give them a statement by letter as soon as possible and know if they will permit the amount to be deducted and remain in his or your hands or inform him how I am to be repaid there is some mistake in relation to the acct of $41.81 you have paid to Wm. Patton on acct of the estate as you will see by the rect enclosed if a mistake you will have the money refunded I would be glad to get a good light 4 horse waggon if John would make one and have her will (word) and an opportunity would offer for sending her on by same speculation or mover coming any where in reach of this section in the course of the next year I contemplate starting on thursday next to take a *view* of the Chiskasaw *notes* and if it comes up to the representation that I have got of it I think I will move there next winter I understand that very unfavorable accounts of the place have reached your section if spared to return I will give you my opinion of it frankly Oliver & Henry had the measles after I wrote you last but were not much the worse Betsey had a son last night our cotton market has had a great fall within a few days mine was sold this day at 16½ I have just heard it is down to $13 in consequence of the derangement in the banks from the war made on them by our reform administrator to effect the humbug circulation of gold and silver mother and the friends all well you will receive a letter from Jas your friend

                                                    Robert McBryde
(Name written McBride and Mcbryde.)

McFARLAND, GEORGE—BOX 59, PACK 1406:
    Will dated June 2, 1934 in Abbeville Dist. Prov. Sept. 1, 1834. Exrs: John Kennedy, Esq., Archibald Bradly. Wit: Josiah McGaw, Patrick McCaslan, Jas. C. Willard. Wife: Peggy McFarlin. Ch: Jas., Archibald, Rosey, Sally McFarlin. Gr. S. Geo. Weed. Inv. made Sept. 1, 1834 by Robt. McCaslan, Josiah McGaw, John Bradley. Expend: Nov. 21, 1836, paid Geo. Weed $10.63¾. Elizabeth Weed $1.00. Sarah McFarlin $8.50.

McQUEARNS, ALEXANDER—Box 59, PACK 1407:
    Est. admnr. Feb. 18, 1832 by Agness McQuearns, Abram Thompson, Douglass Gray, Col. Jas. Devlin, bound to Moses Taggart, sum $3,000.00. Sale, Feb. 28, 1832. Byrs: Agness McQuearns, John Hearst, Dewi Lipford, Vincent Griffin, Stephen. Wit: Robt. Martin, Samuel Atkins. Expend: Dec. 30, 1832, Recd. of Miss E. McQuearns $3.60.

McCORMICK, JAMES—BOX 59, PACK 1408:
    Est. admnr. Oct. 5, 1829 by Lewis S. Simmons, Wade S. Cothran, Samuel Caldwell, Esq., bound to Moses Taggart, sum $300.00. Inv. made Oct. 22, 1829 by Wade S. Cothran, Samuel Caldwell, Hugh Roberson. Byrs: Jas.

Patterson, Wade S. Cothran, Geo. J. Cannon, Alex. McQurns, Thos. Harris, John Donald, Washington Stover, Wm. Saddler, Saml. Caldwell, Joseph Foggison, Hiram Jay, Wm. Glover, Luellin Oliver, Elijah Lion.

McCRAVEN, ROBERT, SR.—BOX 59, PACK 1409:
    Est. admnr. Dec. 20, 1833 by Robt. McCraven, Dyonetius N. Rogers, John Rogers, bound to Moses Taggart, sum $6,000.00. Cit. pub. at Willington Ch.

McQURNES, MINORS—BOX 59, PACK 1410:
    On May 3, 1847 Capt. Wm. Sanders, Bartw. Jordon, Eli Branson, bound to David Lesly, sum $2,400.00. Capt. Wm. Sanders made gdn. of Samuel McQurnes, minor. On Jan. 1, 1847 Wm. Sanders, Eli Branson, Bartw. Jordon, bound to Lesly, sum $3,000.00. Wm. Sanders made gdn. of Jas. and John McQurnes est. partly arising from sales of land of Agnus C. McQurnes. The petition of Jas. and John A. McQurnes sheweth that their father Alex. McQurnes some years since died intestate and their mother Agnus C. McQurnse, admnr. on the est. also died intestate, and that our bro., Samuel, is about 20 yrs. of age, in Alabama. John A. McQurnes was of age March 8, 1853 when the sett. was made, Samuel McQurnes of age in 1849, Jas. McQurnes of age in 1851.

McMULLAN, JAMES—BOX 59, PACK 1411:
    Will dated Oct. 17, 1822 in Abbeville Dist. Prov. June 10, 1824. Exrs: Robt. McCashlen, Robt. Foster. Wit: Edward W. Collier, John Chambers, John Yong. Chn: Andrew, Sarah. Gr. ch: Jas. McMullin, son of Andrew, Jas. McFarland, son of Sarah McFarland, Margaret, dtr. of Andrew. Expend: Dec. 24, 1827 paid Wm. McMillan $75.74½, his share. Paid Samuel Wideman, one feather bed left his wife. Dec. 5, 1826, paid Jas. McFarlon, Sr., on power of atty, for heirs of est. $60.23. Paid Jas. McFarlan for John, Rosannah McFarlan by power of atty. $106.00.

McCREARY, JOSEPH—BOX 59, PACK 1412:
    Est. admnr. Nov. 5, 1827 by David H. McCreary, John McComb, Robt. McBride, bound to Moses Taggart Ord. Abbeville Dist., sum $10,000.00. Sale, Nov. 21, 1827. Byrs: Mary McCrery, Peggy McCrery, John Stover, John C. McCrery, etc.

McDONALD, WILLIAM—BOX 60, PACK 1413:
    Will dated Aug. 27, 1839 in Abbeville Dist., Prov. Feb. 23, 1848. Exrs: Dr. Geo. W. Pressly, Samuel Morris. Wit: Mathew, Robt. Shanks, Samuel Morris. Chn: Nancy Calhoun, Wm. McDonald. S.l., Wm. Calhoun. Gr. s., John McDonald. "Bequeath to Mathew McDonald." Inv. made Nov. 26, 1840 by Samuel Jordan, A. Kennedy, Geo. W. Pressly.

McCOMBS, MAJ. JOHN—BOX 60, PACK 1414:
    Est. admnr. Nov. 12, 1829 by John Anderson, Saml., Geo. Marshall, A. Perrin, bound to Moses Taggart, sum $30,000.00. Inv. made Dec. 5, 1829 by

Patrick Gibson, Robt. McCaslan, Robt. McBryde. Sale, Dec. 8, 9, 1829. Byrs: Wm. McComb, Abner Perrin, John Anderson, Jas. Hughs, Robt., Kitty McComb.

MADDOX, AUGUSTA—BOX 60, PACK 1415:
Est. admnr. Jan. 11, 1833 by John McCord, Jr., Saml. Watt, Joseph Richey, bound to Moses Taggart, sum $14,000.00. Cit. pub. at Greenville Ch. Expend: Jan. 27, 1834. Recd. of Andrew Robertson, admnr. of Jane Robertson's est. Augusta Maddox full share of est. $347.24. Feb. 15, 1834 paid Letty Maddox her share, $2,350.00. Larkin Maddox his share $1,318.43¾. Wm. *Moseley* his wife's share $1,585.68¾. John Padgette his wife's share $1,585.68¾. (Name written Maddox and Mattocks.)

McCULLOUGH, JOHN—BOX 60, PACK 1416:
Will dated May 2, 1831 in Abbeville Dist. Prov. Mar. 13, 1833. Exrs: Wm. Richey, Sr., Robt. Dunn, John Donnald. Wit: G. W. Sims, Robt. Dunn, John Donnald. Wife: Elizabeth McCullough. Chn: John, Mary, Nancy, Eliza McCullough, Elener Walace, Jane Jay. Inv. made Mar. 27, 1833 by Wm. Richey, Robt. Dunn, John Seawright, Jas. Drake.

MARTIN, THOMAS P.—BOX 60, PACK 1417:
Will dated Jan. 5, 1826 in Abbeville Dist. Prov. Aug. 23, 1827. Exrs: Bro., Jacob Martin, David Lesly, Esq. Wit: John F. Livingston, Thos. Botts, Wm. Armstrong. Son, John C. Martin. Nephews: Thos. S. or L. Martin of Augusta, Ga., Washington B. Martin, Chas. and Thos. P. Martin, sons of Jacob, John A. Martin. Nieces: Indiana Martin, Eliza Martin of Augusta, Ga. Inv. made Oct. 4, 1827 by Geo. A. Miller, John Swillen, Robt. McNarr.

MORGAN, THOMAS—BOX 60, PACK 1418:
Est. admnr. Dec. 3, 1827 by Nancy Morgan, Henry Gray, Thos. Riley, bound to Moses Taggart, sum $3,000.00. Inv. made Dec. 19, 1827 by John Blake, Sr., Henry Boozer, Thos. Wier. Sale, Dec. 21, 1827. Byrs: Joseph Hughey, Stanley Crews, Thos. Riley, Joshua Teague, Mrs. Nancy Morgan, John Marshall, Wm. Morgan, Elijah Teague, John Turner, Jr., Chesley Davis, G. E. Appleton, Malen Morgan, Thos. Morgan, John Morgan, Mary Morgan, etc.

MOSELEY, RICHARD H.—BOX 60, PACK 1419:
Est. admnr. Aug. 27, 1831 by Mary Moseley, John Power, Jr., E. Calhoun, Charlotte, Addison McGehee, bound to Moses Taggart, sum $2,000.00. Cit. pub. at Salem Ch. Inv. made Dec. 27, 1831 by Abraham Bell, Orville Tatom, Jonathan Johnston. Expend: Oct. 11, 1834 paid Thos. Hearn, Medical attention to dtr. Charlotte $16.00. Feb. 27, 1836 cash paid John A. Young board for Phililp for 1832 to 1835 $280.00.

MILLER, JOHN AND RACHEL—BOX 60, PACK 1420:
Will dated July 25, 1811 in Abbeville Dist. Rec. Dec. 28, 1811. Exrs: Wife, Rachel Miller, son, Andrew Miller, Benjamin Yancey, Esq. Blacksmith. Wife, Rachel Miller. Chn: Andrew, Mathew Tompson, Geo., John, Esther,

Mary, Isabella, Jas., Allen Tompson, Wm., Lucinda Miller. Stepson, Washington Liddle. "Give son Andrew 200 acres situated in Pendleton Dist. on waters of 23 Mile Cr." Est. of Rachel Miller admnr. Dec. 2, 1836 by Allen T. Miller, Saml. Reid, Jas. T. Liddell bound to Moses Taggart, sum $2,000.00. Byrs: Joseph Dickson, Sarah Liddel, A. T. Miller, G. W. Liddell, Jas. Todd, Robt. Crawford, Wm. Kirkpatrick, etc. Cit. pub. at Upper Long Cane Ch.

McGAW, JAMES—BOX 60, PACK 1421:
Will dated May 22, 1820 in Abbeville Dist. Prov. June 5, 1820. Wife: Elenor McGaw. Wit: Samuel Pressly, Sr., Mary Giles. Wife: Elenor McGaw. Sis., Mary. Inv. made June 30, 1830 by Rev. John T. Pressly, Dr. Saml. Pressly, Capt. John Hearst.

MERIWETHER, ROBERT H.—BOX 60, PACK 1422:
Will dated Dec. 30, 1827 in Abbeville Dist. Prov. Mar. 28, 1828. Exrs: Wife, Martha. Bros., Wm., Thos. Meriwether. Wit: Wyatt W. Starke, Wm. Tennent, J. W. McKinley. Wife, Martha. Chn: Frances Ann, Martha Elizabeth. Inv. made June 16, 1828 by Jos. Moseley, Thos. Jones, Hiram Tilman. Expend: 1832, paid A. Burt for gdn. of Frances, Martha $10.00. At top of page was written Isaac S. Whitten and Martha, his wife, Exrs. in acct. with est. of Robt. Meriwether.

MERIWETHER, JOHN—BOX 60, PACK 1423:
Will dated Oct. 11, 1819 in Abbeville Dist. Prov. Feb. 7, 1820. Exrs: Sons, John H., Jos. Meriwether, Wm. Tinsley. Wit: Chas. Harris, Jas. Tinsley, Frederick Meriwether. Wife, Ann Meriwether. Chn: Robt., Zachary, John H., Jos. Meriwether. Gr. D., Caroline Meriwether dtr. my son Robt. decd. Inv. made Feb. 22, 1829 by Jas A. Ward, Jas. A. Heard, David Cunningham, Hugh M. Pettis. Byrs: Capt. Zachary Meriwether, Hugh M. Pettus, Benj. Holt, Wm. Cochran, Kennedy H. Blake, Jas. Pert, Jos. Meriwether, Dabney, John McGehee, Nicholas Meriwether, Newton Whitner, Mary R. Meriwether, John Marsh, Stephen Ross, Thos. Brightman, Jonathan Swift, Lewis Conner, John Griffin, Jos. Foster, Joel Lipscomb, Nathaniel Marion.

MAYSON, JOHN C.—BOX 60, PACK 1424:
Will dated Nov. 29, 1817 in Abbeville Dist. Rec. Dec. 23, 1817. Exrs: Bros., Willis, Chas. C. Mayson, Jas. Shackelford, Catlet Conner. Wit: Jas. Hubbard, John W. Keller, W. D. Moore. Sis., Frances Marsh. Wife, Nancy Mayson. "The remaining two thirds to be equally divided between James M. Cowdrey, Harriet Shackelford, William C. Cowdrey." Nancy Mayson bro. Washington Bostick decd. Son, Henry Mayson. John Cowdrey first husband of Nancy. Dtr., Henrietta Mayson. Sons, Washington, John. "Interested in the Mills at Edisto in which Willis Bostick and John Brook are concerned with myself." Expend: Jan. 1822, Paid John G. Bleweron third tax on joint prop. in Orangeburg Dist. for 4 yrs., $5.43.

MOSELEY, WILLIAM—BOX 60, PACK 1425:
Est. admnr. Oct. 26, 1821 by Owen Selby, Marcus Williams, Ephraim

Davis, bound to Moses Taggart, sum $500.00. Inv. made Mar. 1819 by John McGaw, Jos. Calhoun, Patrick Calhoun.

McCANN, JAMES—BOX 60, PACK 1426:
Est. admnr. Oct. 3, 1823 by Edward McCann, Jas. Hawthorn, Wm. Morrison, bound to Moses Taggart, sum $1,000.00. Inv. made Oct. 7, 1823 by Wm. Morrison, Thos. McIlwain, John Hill, Jas. Hawthorn.

MERIWETHER, NICHOLAS—BOX 60, PACK 1427:
Will dated Nov. 30, 1809 in Abbeville Dist. Prov. Feb. 6, 1826. Exrs: Wife, Mary Meriwether, John Bickley, Jr., John Scuddy. Wit: Jos. Meriwether, Lewis Conner, Andrew Logan. Wife, Mary Meriwether. Chn: Mary Ragland, Sally Meriwether, dtrs. by my first wife, Sarah Meriwether. Chn: by Mary Meriwether my 2nd wife, Wm. Bickley, John Lewis, Evaline, Nicholas, Chas. Waller Meriwether. Cit. pub. at Providence Ch.

MORROW, MARY—BOX 60, PACK 1429:
Will dated Jan. 12, 1819 in Abbeville Dist. Prov. Aug. 12, 1822. Exrs: Sons, Geo. M., Jas. Morrow. Wit: Jos. Hutton, Patrick Calhoun, Enos Crawford. Chn: Geo. Mecklin, Jas. Morrow, Margaret Brown. Gr. dtr. Elizabeth Brown. Inv. made Nov. 21, 1822 by Saml. McGaw, John Deall, Jas. Calhoun.

McGAW, SAMUEL—BOX 60, PACK 1430:
Est. admnr. Dec. 6, 1823 by John, Jr., Benjamin McGaw, Jas. Calhoun bound to Moses Taggard sum $3,000.00. Cit. pub. at Hopewell Church. Inv. made Dec. 24, 1823 by Jas. Taggart, Patrick Calhoun, J. Calhoun. Sale, Dec. 30, 1823. Byrs: Mrs. McGaw, John McGaw, Jr., Jas. Alexander, Enos Crawford, John Gray, Jas. R. Houston, Wm. Taylor, Josiah McGaw, Jas. Calhoun, Jas. Taggart, John Martin.

MAYN, WILLIAM—BOX 61, PACK 1431:
Will dated Aug. 12, 1819. Prov. Sept. 6, 1819. Exrs: Ebenezer Miller, Wm. Haddon. Wit: John Given, Samuel Murry, Isaac Hadden. Chn: Anny, Jas. Mayn, Elizabeth Stephenson, Molly M. Williams or McWilliams.

MATHEWS, JANE—BOX 61, PACK 1432:
Admnr. bond missing. On Oct. 30, 1798, Josiah Crammer, Margaret Chevis applied for Letters of Admnr. as next of kin. Pub. at Rocky Springs Church. Inv. made April 13, 1799 by Andrew Weed, John Pettigrew, Wm. Gray.

MADDOX, JENNET—BOX 61, PACK 1433:
Will dated Mar. 1, 1813 in Abbeville Dist. Rec. Feb. 7, 1815. Exrs: David P. Posey, Wm. Norris. No wit. given. Chn: Hebbert, David P. Posey, Peggy decd., Masa Posey, Augusta, Richard, Samuel Maddox.

MITCHELL, BENJAMIN—BOX 61, PACK 1434:
Will dated Mar. 28, 1816. Prov. May 6, 1816. Exrs: Lewis Mitchell, Basil Hallum. Wit: Nicholas Overby, Joseph Joiner, Elsey Buntin. Wife, Judith Mitchell. Chn: Susanna Hallum, Lewis, Randal Mitchell, decd., Elizabeth Adams. Gr. chn: Polly Hail Mitchell; Benjamin R., Morris R. Mitchell. Est. of

Benjamin Mitchell, Sr., in same package. Admnr. Nov. 30, 1808 by Keziah, Lewis, Benjamin Mitchell, Basil Hallum bound to Andrew Hamilton Ord. Abbeville Dist. sum $10,000.00.

MARSHALL, JOHN—BOX 61, PACK 1435:
    Est. admnr. Dec. 16, 1816 by Isabella, Geo., Saml. Marshall, Jno. P. Major bound to Taliaferro Livingston Ord. Abbeville Dist. sum 20,000 lbs. On April 3, 1823 Rachel Atchison, a bound girl of decd., now Rachel, wife of Drury V. Wade, recd. $485.00 from est.

McCONNEL, JOHN—BOX 61, PACK 1436:
    Est. admnr. June 9, 1794 by Elenor McConnel wid., Col. Jno. Quay, Capt. Jno. Norwood bound to Judges Abbeville County sum 1,000 lbs. Inv. made Aug. 21, 1794 by Wiley Glover, Thos. Livingston, Joseph Burton.

MADDOX, JOHN—BOX 61, PACK 1437:
    Est. admnr. Oct. 15, 1810 by Elizabeth Maddox, Geo. Reeves, Jas. Gaines, Wm. McGraw bound to Jno. Hamilton Ord. Abbeville Dist. sum $3,000.00. Byrs: Elizabeth, Lawson, Chandler, Benjamin Maddox Jr., Edmond Ware, etc.

MECKLIN, HUGH, SR.—BOX 61, PACK 1438:
    Will dated Nov. 15, 1800 in Abbeville Dist. Proved Jan. 27, 1818. Exr. Son, David Mecklin. Wit: Jas. D. Anderson, Hugh Mecklin. Wife, Charity Mecklin. Chn: David, Hugh, Elizabeth, Mary Mecklin.

MALROY, WILLIAM—BOX 61, PACK 1439:
    Will dated Sept. 22, 1803 in Abbeville Dist. Rec. Dec. 26, 1803. Exrs: Saml. Milroy, Thos. Wilson, Jno. Weatherall. Wit: Thos. Moore, Mathew, Jno. Wilson. Chn: Saml., Ann, Mary, Hannah, Peggy, Jno. Malroy.

MOORE, JOHN—BOX 61, PACK 1440:
    Est. admnr. Jan. 5, 1782 by Peter Stubbs, Willis Breazeale, Sarah Moore bound to Jno. Ewing Calhoun Ord. 96 Dist. sum 1500 lbs. Inv. made Jan. 5, 1782 by Willis Breazeale, Peter Stubbs, Alexr. Clark.

MATTISON, SUSANNAH—BOX 61, PACK 1441:
    Will dated April 15, 1831 in Abbeville Dist. Proved Feb. 27, 1836. Exrs: Wm. Pyles, Wm. Barmore. Wit: Benjamin, Geo. Mattison, Chester Kingsley. Brothers: Wm., Jno., Allen, Macklin, Asa, Reuben, Jas. Mitchell. Sis: Elizabeth Mitchell, Patcy Box.

MORRAH, HUGH—BOX 61, PACK 1442:
    Will dated Feb. 2, 1837 in Abbeville Dist. Proved Feb. 9, 1837. Exrs: Son, Saml. Morrah, Patrick Noble, Aaron Lomax. Wit: Wm. Hill, Wesley C. Norwood, M. T. Stewart. Wife, Jane Morrah. Chn: Sarah, Jane, Elenor, Mary, Robt., Jno., Saml., David, Geo. Morrah. Sarah was wife of Jno. Richardson.

McFARLAND, JOHN—BOX 61, PACK 1443:
    Will dated May 11, 1830 in Abbeville Dist. Proved Nov. 17, 1832. Exrs: Patrick Noble, Moses Taggart. Wit: M. B. Clark, Wm. Marsh, Jno. Taggart.

"Leave all my est. to Col. Patrick Noble my friend. To Benjamin McFarland who is reputed to be my son."

MORGAN, MALON—BOX 61, PACK 1444:
Will dated Aug. 30, 1836 in Abbeville Dist. Proved Oct. 4, 1836. Wit: Jno. D. Adams, Jno. Devlin, Elijah Teague. Wife, Sarah Morgan. 10 chn. ment. names not given. Sett: Leagtees: Alfred, Davis, Benjamin, Thos., Malon, Jno., Joel Morgan, Geo. Graham and wife Caroline, A. J. Donald and wife Amanda, A. Burton and wife, Joel Graham and wife Isabella.

McCONNEL, JOHN—BOX 61, PACK 1445:
Est. admnr. Mar 20, 1835 by Wm. Sr., Jno. Pratt, Jr., Thos. Crawford bound to Moses Taggart Ord. Abbeville Dist. sum $3,000.00. Cit. pub. at Little River Church. Sale, Jan. 1, 1836. Byrs: Elizabeth McConnel, Elizabeth, Jno. Pratt Jr., Peter S. Burton, Jno. Algier.

McQUEARNS, JAMES—BOX 61, PACK 1446:
Est. admnr. Sept. 15, 1821 by Archibald, Jas. Fair, Alexr. McQuearns bound to Moses Taggart Ord. Abbeville Dist. sum $4,000.00. Had notes on Elizabeth McQuearns. Paid est. $29.16 part of est. of Charles McQuearns decd.

McCORD, MARY—BOX 61, PACK 1447:
Will dated May 8, 1820 in Abbeville Dist. Proved Oct. 1821. Exrs: Son, Jno. McCord, Saml. Irwin. Wit: Hugh Huston, Andrew Hamilton. Chn: Jno., Archibald, Nancy McCord.

MOSELEY, TARLETON—BOX 61, PACK 1448:
Will dated Aug. 25, 1826 in Abbeville Dist. Proved Sept. 12, 1826. Exrs: Wife, Rosena Moseley. Brothers, Henry, Richard Moseley, L. Z. C. DeYampert. Wit: R. H. Lester, J. Calhoun. Chn. ment. names not given. "Owned land on Rocky River." 1829 Recd. of Joseph Mosley $14.00. Inv. made Sept. 16, 1826 by Thos. Parker, Jas. Taggart, Jas. Calhoun.

McALLISTER, JAMES G.—BOX 61, PACK 1449:
Will dated Nov. 30, 1816. Rec. Dec. 30, 1816. Exrs: Francis, Andrew McAllister. Wit: Thos., Robt. Russell. Wife, Elizabeth McAllister. Chn. ment. no names given. Sale, Jan. 16, 1817. Byrs: Wm., Francis, Elizabeth, Thos., Andrew McAllister, Robt., Joseph Black, etc.

McGILL, WILLIAM—BOX 61, PACK 1450:
Will dated Feb. 24, 1837 in Abbeville Dist. Proved Oct. 22, 1838. Exrs: Jas. Fair, Saml. Reid. Wit: Isabella Miller, Saml., Mary, Lemuel, Elizabeth Reid. Nephew, Franey Henry. Inv. made Oct. 30, 1838 by Wm. Gordon, Allen T. Miller, Wm. Hagan.

MARSH, WILLIAM—BOX 61, PACK 1451:
Est. admnr. Nov. 21, 1817 by Elizabeth Marsh, Catlet Conner, Wm. Burris bound to Taliaferro Livingston Ord. Abbeville Dist. sum $2,000.00. Inv. made Nov. 29, 1817 by Henry B. Lightfoot, David Cunningham, Jas.

Anderson. Sale, Dec. 4, 1817. Byrs: Laban C., Elizabeth Marsh, Daniel Rogers, etc.

MONTGOMERY, ANN—BOX 61, PACK 1452:
Est. admnr. Dec. 1, 1823 by Thos. Montgomery, Alexr. Hunter, Thos. Hodge bound to Moses Taggart Ord. Abbeville Dist. sum $500.00. Cit. pub. at Rocky River Church. Inv. made Dec. 22, 1823 by Jas. Gamble, A. Hunter, Matthew McNeil. Sale, Dec. 23, 1823. Byrs: Thos., *Maelin* Montgomery, Revd. Jas. Gammel, etc.

McMURTREY, SAMUEL—BOX 61, PACK 1453:
Est. admnr. Mar. 31, 1796 by Joseph, Jane Montgomery wid. Col. Jno. Glenn, David Strain bound to Judges Abbeville County sum $1500.00. Cit. pub. at Greenville Church. Sale, Aug. 26, 1796. Byrs: Joseph, Jno., Jean, Wm. McMurtrey, etc.

MATTISON, BENJAMIN—BOX 61, PACK 1454:
Est. admnr. Jan. 9, 1830 by Wm., Geo. Mattison, Charles Kay, Chester Kingsley bound to Moses Taggart Ord. Abbeville Dist. sum $12,000.00. Cit. pub. at Greenville Church. Inv. made Jan. 21, 1830 by Patrick Johnson, Wm. Pyles, Jno. Seawright. (Written at bottom of page) "The above schedule consists partly of such property as the said Susannah owned and possessed at the time of her marriage in 1805 with said decd." Sale, Jan. 26, 1830. Byrs: Susannah, Jno., Olley, Geo. Mattison, Jno. Gains, etc.

MILLER, JOHN—BOX 61, PACK 1455:
Est. admnr. Oct. 6, 1828 by Wm. Patton, Saml. Young, Jas. Taggart bound to Moses Taggart Ord. sum $5,000.00. Inv. made Oct. 18, 1828 by Daniel Chambers, Michael Talbert, Saml. Cowan.

MELOY, WILLIAM—BOX 62, PACK 1456:
Est. admnr. Feb. 20, 1830 by Enos Crawford, Jno. Pressly, Alexr. Foster bound to Moses Taggart Ord. Abbeville Dist. sum $200.00. Sale, Mar. 5, 1830. Byrs: Apelton Meloy, Jas. Morrow, Enos Crawford, Elias Chapel, etc.

McCORMICK, HUGH, SR.—BOX 62, PACK 1457:
Est. admnr. Dec. 12, 1827 by Hugh McCormick, Isaiah Johnston, Elijah Lyon bound to Moses Taggard Ord. Abbeville Dist. sum $8,000.00. Jan. 1, 1829 Paid Martha McCormick wid. $632.00.

MARK, CONRAD—BOX 62, PACK 1458:
Est. admnr. Jan. 6, 1817 by Wm., Joseph, Jno. Hearst Jr. bound to Taliaferro Livingston Ord. Abbeville Dist. sum 5,000 lbs. Cit. pub. at Capt. Hearst's Muster Ground.

MADDOX, THOMAS—BOX 62, PACK 1459:
Est. admnr. Dec. 23, 1805 by Cloe Maddox, Francis, Jno. Colbert, Jno. Brown bound to Andrew Hamilton Ord. Abbeville Dist. sum $5,000.00. Sale, Feb. 7, 1806. Byrs: Cloe, Wm., Losson, Lanty, Benjamin Maddox Jr, Chandler Maddox, etc.

MATHISON, JOHN—BOX 62, PACK 1460:
Est. admnr. Jan. 8, 1806 by Frances Matheson, Joshua Hill, Joseph Barksdale bound to Andrew Hamilton Ord. Abbeville Dist. sum $15,000.00. Sale, Feb. 13, 1806. Byrs: Frances Matheson, Allen, Joseph Barksdale, Wm. Lee, Daniel New, Wm. Cain, Isaac Haws, etc.

MOORE, SAMUEL—BOX 62, PACK 1461:
Est. admnr. Nov. 28, 1785 by Eliab Moore, Jno., Wm. Calhoun bound to Jno. Thomas Jr. Ord. 96 Dist. sum 1,000 lbs. Pendleton County Court Term, 1795, On application of Eliab Moore Esq., admnr. of said est., appointed Robt. Dowdle, Jas. Dobbins, Jas. Brice appraisers.

MASON, JOHN—BOX 62, PACK 1462:
Will dated June 29, 1781 in Barkley County, on Waters of Indian Creek, 96 Dist. Proved Nov. 8, 1783. Exrs: Wife, Elener Mason, Sons, David Mason, Joshua Teague. Wit: Joseph Wood, Prudence Williams, Stephen Emmory. Chn: David, Jno., Jobe, Rachel, Judah, Rae Mason.

McDAVID, PATRICK—BOX 62, PACK 1463:
Est. admnr. Mar. 28, 1783 by Benjamin Kilgore, Geo. Berry, Wm. Fowler bound to Jno. Ewing Calhoun Ord. 96 Dist. sum 14,000 lbs. Cit. ment. Benjamin Kilgore was of Duncans Creek. Rosane McDavid wid. Inv. made by Basil Holland, Thos. Murphy, Robt. Hanna.

McMAHAN, PETER—BOX 62, PACK 1464:
Est. admnr. April 13, 1814 by Jas. Peart, Wm. Wardlaw (son of Joseph) bound to Taliaferro Livingston Ord. Abbeville Dist. sum $1,000.00. Inv. made May 4, 1814 by Wm. Wardlaw, the son of Jno. Wardlaw, Robt. Hackett.

MATTISON, HENRY—BOX 62, PACK 1465:
Est. admnr. Oct. 29, 1804 by Elizabeth, Thos. Mattison Sr., Wm., Edmund Ware bound to Andrew Hamilton Ord. Abbeville Dist. sum $5,000.00. Wm. Ware Esq. gdn. of Strother, Hulda, Leroy Mattison, minors. Inv. made Nov. 14, 1804 by D. Mitchell, Henry Johnson, Robt. A. Cunningham.

MITCHELL, JOHN—BOX 62, PACK 1466:
Est. admnr. Sept. 12, 1792 by Wm. Cameron, Patrick Mullin, Arthur Morrow bound to Judges of Abbeville County sum 500 lbs. Wm. Cameron next of kin. Jno. Mitchell was a shoemaker. Inv. made Oct. 12, 1792 by Andrew Weed, Andrew Jones, Wm. Martin.

McKEE, THOMAS—BOX 62, PACK 1467:
Will dated Oct. 20, 1796 in Abbeville Dist. Rec. Mar. 26, 1798. Exrs: Jas. Reid, Robt. Gilmore. Wit: Saml. Reed, Jno. Wardlaw, Daniel Mcantire. Wife, Martha McKee. Chn: Jean, Thos., Wm., Jno., Jas. McKee. Inv. made June 4, 1798 by Jno. Wardlaw, Edward Sharp, Wm. Blain. Sale, July 20, 1798. Byrs: Martha, Margaret, Sarah, Wm., Jno. McKee, Jno. Shirley, etc.

MORRIS, SAMUEL—BOX 62, PACK 1468:
Will dated Mar. 29, 1815 in Abbeville Dist. Rec. April 25, 1815. Exrs:

Wife, Margaret Morris, Wm. Hill. Wit: Andrew Leard, Robt., Wm. Hill Jr. Chn: Saml., Wm., Mariah, Richard Morris, Mary Hathorn, Lucy White, Alis Calhoun. "Bequeath to my wife's sons, Adam, Wm. Henderson. To Adam Henderson's chn., viz. Lucy, Margaret, Jno., Alis Henderson. Gr. chn: Jno. Henderson, son of my dtr. Alis Calhoun, Alexr. Morris, son Geo. Morris. My son Saml. shall receive legacy left to him by his grandfather in England."

McCURDY, JAMES—BOX 62, PACK 1469:
Est. admnr. Mar. 25, 1794 by Adam Hill, Saml. Foster Sr., Saml. Young bound to Judges Abbeville County sum 500 lbs. Inv. made April 26, 1794 by Wm. Hill, Alexr. White, Jno. Baird.

MOUCHET, SAMUEL—BOX 62, PACK 1470:
Will dated 1799 in Abbeville Dist. Rec. May 17, 1800. Exr: Barbara Mouchet. Wit: Wm., G. H. Perrin, Thos. Littleton. Chn: Mary, Catherine, Elizabeth, Eve Barbara, Henry, Ann, Doratha, Geo., Saml., Jacob Mouchet.

MANNING, WALTER—BOX 62, PACK 1471:
Est. admnr. June 17, 1805 by Nancy, Geo. Manning, Jno. Sharp, Francis Clinkscales bound to Andrew Hamilton Ord. Abbeville Dist. sum $10,000.00. Inv. made July 8, 1805 by Saml. Rosamond, Jas. Watts, Christian Rasor. Byrs: Richard, Geo., Ann Manning, wid., Theophlias White, Jno. Brownlee, etc.

MORRISON, ROBERT—BOX 62, PACK 1472:
Est. admnr. Nov. 18, 1811 by Margaret Morrison, David Wiley, Michael Keas, Henry Fulton bound to Taliaferro Livingston Ord. Abbeville Dist. sum $2,000.00. Inv. made Dec. 3, 1811 by Thos. Wyly, Jas. Fell, Wm. Cochran. Sett. Jan. 14, 1834 between Archibald Morrison, son of decd., and Hezekiah Gray, husband of Nancy, a dtr. of decd.

MARS, JAMES—BOX 62, PACK 1473:
Est. admnr. Nov. 4, 1826 by Creswell, Jno. C. Moore, Roger McKinney bound to Moses Taggart Ord. Abbeville Dist. sum $1,000.00. Inv. made Nov. 13, 1826 by Wm. Stallworth, Elbert Henderson, Russel Vaughn. Sale, Nov. 17, 1826. Byrs: Elizabeth Mars, Drury V. Wade, Robt. Walker, Tyra Jay, etc.

McCORMICK, HUGH—BOX 62, PACK 1474:
Est. admnr. June 1, 1835 by Isaiah McCormick, Wm. J. Thompson, Saml. S. Baker bound to Moses Taggart Ord. Abbeville Dist. sum $10,000.00. Cit. pub. at Asbury Chapel.

MATTHEWS, RICHARD—BOX 62, PACK 1475:
Est. admnr. Nov. 17, 1823 by Lyttleton Myrick, Saml. Watt, Jno. Bowie Jr. bound to Moses Taggart Ord. Abbeville Dist. sum $1,000.00. Inv. made Nov. 18, 1823 by Garland Chiles, Wm. Collier, Jno. W. Williams, Richard Todd. Sale, Mar. 10, 1824. Byrs: Jane Matthews, Jno. Sale Jr., Jas. Creswell, Jas. Bullock, etc.

MERIWETHER, FRANCIS—BOX 62, PACK 1476:
Will dated June 7, 1793 in 96 Dist. Proved Sept. 12, 1793. Exrs: Sons,

Jno., Zachary, Nicholas Meriwether. Wit: Jno. Logan Jr., Wm. Gains. Wife, Mary Meriwether. Chn: Jno., Zachary, Nicholas Meriwether, Ann McGehee of Virginia, Mary Conner decd., wife of Jno. Connor, Betty McGehee. Inv. made Nov. 1, 1793 by Jno. Chiles, Thos. Livingston, Leonard Waller.

MOSELEY, RICHARD—BOX 62, PACK 1477:
Will dated April 3, 1829 in Abbeville Dist. Proved Oct. 24, 1831. Exrs: Sons, Henry, Richard Moseley. Wit: A. E. Scuddy, Jno. Baker, Jno. English. Gr. chn: Martha, wife of Charles Johnson, Judith, Emaline Ball. Inv. made Dec. 26, 1831 by Wm. Speer Esq., Wm. Clark, Jno. McCalla, Jas. McCalla. Acct. acknowledged by Mary Moseley, wid. of Richard Moseley Jr., for money borrowed from testator $10.00.

MOORE, THOMAS—BOX 62, PACK 1478:
Est. admnr. Oct. 26, 1821 by Agness, Wm. Moore, Thos. Gordon, Thos. Cunningham bound to Moses Taggart Ord. Abbeville Dist. sum $500.00. Cit. pub. at Upper Long Cane Church. Expend: Oct. 14, 1824. David Moore, a infant, to Nancy Moore, for boarding $30.00. Ann Moore, infant, for boarding $60.00. Wm. Moore, a infant to Nancy Moore, for boarding $30.00.

McNEIL, JOHN, SR.—BOX 62, PACK 1479:
Will dated Jan. 13, 1818 in Abbeville Dist. Proved Mar. 17, 1818. Exr: Andrew Giles. Wit: Jno. Power Sr., A. Giles. Wife, Jane McNeil. Chn: Jno., Matthew, Sarah McNeil. "Bequeth to Robt. Spence." Jan. 13, 1819 Paid Dr. Jno. McNeil $29.12.

McGEHEE, CAPT. CHARLES—BOX 62, PACK 1480:
Will dated July 29, 1815 in Abbeville Dist. Rec. Feb. 5, 1816. Exrs: Wife, Joanne McGehee, Wm. Waller. Wit: Thos. B. Waller, Thos. Purvis, Hyram Gains. Chn: Almera, Nancy, Joanna McGehee. Inv. made Feb. 9, 1816 by Joseph Wardlaw, Gibson Wooldridge, Leonard Waller.

MIMS, SAMUEL S.—BOX 62, PACK 1481:
Est. admnr. Nov. 10, 1826 by Mary Ann Mims, Ephraim R. Calhoun, Jno. C. McGehee bound to Moses Taggart Ord. Abbeville Dist. sum $4,000.00. Sett: May 18, 1843. Present, Tully Boling, who married the wid., Mary Ann. One child Sarah married Jas. Sullivan.

MAXWELL, ELIZABETH—BOX 62, PACK 1482:
Est. admnr. Dec. 17, 1825 by Jno. McGaw Jr., Jas. Taggart, Nathaniel Cameron bound to Moses Taggart Ord. Abbeville Dist. sum $300.00. Cit. pub. at Hopewell Church. Inv. made Jan. 4, 1826 by J. Calhoun, Thos. Parker, Jas. Taggart.

MAYSON, WILLIAM—BOX 62, PACK 1483:
Est. admnr. June 12, 1797 by Jas. Robt. Mayson, Isaac Logan, Jonathan Chiles bound to Judges Abbeville County sum $5,000.00. Jas. R. Mayson next of kin. Inv. made July 19, 1797 by Oswell Eve, Henry Smith, Dennit Hill. Byrs: Jas. Robt., Archey, Jas. Mayson, Berry Bostick, etc.

McELWEE, JOHN—BOX 62, PACK 1484:
Will dated Feb. 9, 1787 in Abbeville Dist. Proved Oct. 2, 1787. Exrs: f. l. Jno. Cochran, Saml. Foster Sr. Wit: Jno. Cozby, Mary, David Cochran. Wife, Sarah McElwee, now pregnant. Dtr, Agness. Sis: Elenor, Martha.

MOTE, ANDREW—BOX 62, PACK 1485:
Will dated Aug. 19, 1787 in Abbeville Dist. Proved Jan. 8, 1788. Exrs: Jno. Lesly, Ezekiel Evans, Saml. Watt. Wit: Jams., Saml. Evans. Wife, Elizabeth Mote. "Bequeath to Jno. Jr., Margaret, Esther Miller, chn. of Andrew Miller decd." Inv. made Jan. 15, 1788 by Jno. Miller, Nathaniel Bailey, Joel Thacker, Wm. Strain. (Written Mote and Moat.)

McKINLEY, MARY—BOX 62, PACK 1486:
Will dated Dec. 4, 1805 in Abbeville Dist. Rec. Dec. 23, 1806. Exrs: Hugh Mecklin Sr., Francis Carlile. Wit: Nathaniel Norwood, Joseph Irving, Francis Carlile. Chn: Mary, Robt. Mecklin, Jane, Esther, Jno. Willson, Archibald Carlile, Jas. Beaty McKinley. "Give to Wm. M., Mary Ann Barksdale, Mary B. McKinley each $50.00. Leave Jno. Montgomery $1.00." Cit. on petition of Henry Moseley and Jane his wife, late Jane McKinley, a distributee of said decd. and ward of Francis Carlile.

MORAGNE, PETER, SR.—BOX 62, PACK 1487:
Will dated Aug. 20, 1807 in Abbeville Dist. Rec. Dec. 9, 1807. Exrs: Son, Peter Moragne Jr., Peter Gibert Sr. Wit: P. Gibert, C. Gibert, J. B. Gibert. Chn: Peter, Francis, Mary, wife of Peter Roger, Jno., Isaac Moragne, Wife, Cecile Bayle. m. l. Mary Bayle.
Will of Peter Moragne Jr. dated May 11, 1813 in Abbeville Dist. Rec. May 22, 1813. Exrs: Peter Gibert Esq., Jno. Bouchillon, Jno. L. Gibert. Wit: Isaac Moragne, Jno. Martin, Lazarus Couven. Chn: Peter Boyer Moragne, Jeanne, wife of Jno. Lewis Gibert.

McCLINTON, SAMUEL—BOX 63, PACK 1488:
Will dated May 1, 1807. Rec. Dec. 7, 1807. Exrs: Robt. Gilmore, David Pressly. Wit: Saml. Gils, Wm. Covey, Saml. Pressly. Chn: Robt., Saml., Jas., Susannah McClinton, Margaret, Mary Gilmore. Gr. son, Saml., son of Robt. McClinton. Inv. made Dec. 15, 1807 by Saml. Leard, Jno. Giles, Jno. Foster, son of Saml. Foster.

MITCHEL, SAMUEL—BOX 63, PACK 1489:
Est. admnr. Feb. 22, 1809 by Martha Mitchel, Saml., Francis Young, Jno. Baskin bound to Andrew Hamilton Ord. Abbeville Dist. sum $10,000.00. Inv. made Aug. 26, 1809 by Benjamin, Jeremiah Tearry, Ezekiel Calhoun Sr. Byrs: Jas. McKinley, Aaron Jones, Saml., Francis Young Sr., Martha Mitchel, Thos. Finley.

MULLAN, PATRICK—BOX 63, PACK 1490:
Will dated Aug. 4, 1824 in Abbeville Dist. Proved June 6, 1825. Exr: Dorcas Frazier. Wit: David Lesly, Wm. Lyle, Jas. Wardlaw. Wife, Barbara Mullan. Dtr. Dorcas Frazier. "Bequeath to Mary Goodwin, wife of Jas. Goodwin,

$20.00." Inv. made June 11, 1825 by Enos, Robt. Crawford Sr., Lewis Arnold, Nathaniel Cameron.

McKINLEY, WILLIAM—BOX 63, PACK 1492:
Est. admnr. June 11, 1798 by Jno. W. McKinley, Major Francis Carlile, Peter Brown boun to Judges Abbeville Co. sum $20,000.00. Mary McKinley appointed her son, Jno. W. McKinley, admnr. Inv. made Aug. 10, 1798 by Major Francis Carlile, Wm. Hutton, Joseph Trimble. Sale, Oct. 12, 1798. Byrs: Mary, Elizabeth, Jno. W., Archibald, Robt., Jean, Mary McKinley Jr., etc.

MONTGOMERY, JOHN—BOX 63, PACK 1493:
Will dated Jan. 4, 1777 in 96 Dist. Proved Dec. 13, 1782. Exrs: Wife, Jean Montgomery, Jas. Finley, Joseph Pickens. Wit: Saml., Jas. Finley, Joseph Pickens. Chn: Margaret, Agness, Jennet, Jeane, Jno. Montgomery. (Part of the Inv., the other part of said Inv. destroyed when Saml. Finley's house was burned by the enemy.)

McCORD, JOHN SR.—BOX 63, PACK 1494:
Will dated Oct. 30, 1806 in Abbeville Dist. Rec. Nov. 25, 1806. Exrs: Sons, Jas., Joseph McCord. Wit: Jno. Hairston, Josiah Chambers, Andrew Paul. Chn: Jno., Jas., Wm., Robt., Joseph, Margaret, Eleanor, Elizabeth McCord, Agness McFarlin, Isabel, wife of Wm. McCracken. Gr. son: Wm. Stuard McCord. Inv. made Jan. 20, 1807 by Jno. Downey, Charles Wilson, Andrew Paul.

MECKLIN, REV. ROBERT—BOX 63, PACK 1495:
Est. admnr. Oct. 6, 1788 by Agness Mecklin wid., Jno., Wm. Harris, Jas. Caldwell bound to Judges Abbeville County sum 1,000 lbs. Expend: Had 1 note on Hugh Mecklin. Paid to Rocky River Congregation for 1786, 28.8.1. Jas. Mecklin on note 4.8.8. David Mecklin 45.3.10. On Mar. 29, 1788 Robt. Mecklin was indebted to Wm. Jackson of Orange Co., N. C., State of Ga., Wilkes Co. July 6, 1798 Moses Trimble made oath that the acct. was true.

McCLUER, WILLIAM—BOX 63, PACK 1496:
Est. admnr. Dec. 28, 1781 by Jno. Wardlaw, Wm. Brown, Alexr. Noble bound to Jno. Ewing Calhoun Ord. 96 Dist. sum 1,000 lbs. Inv. made Mar. 9, 1782 by Jno. Irwin, Wm. Brown, Jno. Logan. Byrs: Jas. Childs, Jno. Irwin, Eliab Moore, Edward Forbis, Jno. Calhoun, Jno. Wardlaw.

MAYSON, JAMES ROBERT—BOX 63, PACK 1497:
Will dated Jan. 22, 1805 in Abbeville Dist. Proved May 6, 1805. Exrs: Wife, Nancy Mayson, Elihu Criswell, Thos. Chiles. Wit: Robt. Cheatham, Thos. Chiles. Chn. ment. names not given.

McNEIL, EDWARD—BOX 63, PACK 1498:
Will dated Aug. 1, 1776 in 96 Dist. Exr: Jno. McDonald. Wit: Jno. Cain, Jas. Johnston, Joseph Polson. Wife, Ann McNeil alias Ann Lambeth. "Give her plantation whereon I now dwell by Broad River." Dtr. Margaret, "Bequeath to her and Wm. Steen near Tyger River." Chn: Jno., Mary, Ann, Fanny McNeil.

ABSTRACTS OF OLD NINETY-SIX AND

MOSS, JOSEPH—BOX 63, PACK 1499:
Est. admnr. Mar. 26, 1792 by Henry, Jas. Chiles, Wyley Glover bound to Judges Abbeville County sum 500 lbs. Inv. made April 2, 1792 by Jno. Bell Sr., Jno. McConnel, Jas. Wilson. Sale, April 24, 1792. Byrs: Jno. Waters, Thos. Dixon, Capt. Calhoun, Henry Chiles, Jno. Calhoun. Joseph Moss lived at Cambridge.

MITCHELL, RANDOLPH—BOX 63, PACK 1500:
Will dated Nov. 4, 1802 in Abbeville Dist. Rec. Dec. 20, 1802. Exrs: Wife, Rebecka Mitchell, Basil Hallum, Christopher Watson. Wit: Stephen, Isaiah Jones, Jas. Graham. Chn: Benjamin, Moris, Polly Hail Mitchell. Est. of Randall Mitchell admnr. Jan. 7, 1786 by Henry, Jas., Jno. White bound to Jno. Thomas Jr. Ord. 96 Dist. sum 1,000 lbs.

McCULLOCH, ROBERT—BOX 63, PACK 1501:
Est. admnr. Oct. 16, 1790 by Margaret McCulloch, Jno. Tulloch, Moses Thompson bound to Judges Abbeville County sum 500 lbs. Est. admnr. again June 1792 by Moses Thompson, Jno. Tulloch, David Edmiston sum 500 lbs. Sale, Oct. 29, 1790. Byrs: Margaret, Hugh, Frances McCulloch, Josiah Patterson, Joseph Carswell, etc.

McCONNEL, JAMES—BOX 63, PACK 1502:
Est. admnr. Oct. 5, 1790 by Rebecca McConnel, Arthur Morrow, Saml. Foster Jr. bound to Judges Abbeville County sum 100 lbs. Rebecca McConnel owned 200 acres in Pendleton County. On Oct. 28, 1790 Eleanor Blackburn appeared before Richard Andrew Rapley, Justice of Peace for Abbeville Co., duly sworn saith that her decd. husband, Jno. Blackburn, before his death, sold his plantation to Jas. McConnel.

MORGAN, JOHN—BOX 63, PACK 1503:
Will dated July 25, 1811 in Abbeville Dist. Rec. Nov. 23, 1811. Exrs: Jno. Gray, Thos. Morgan. Wit: Olleyman Sr., Jas. Dodgen, Saml. Teague. Wife, Elizabeth Morgan. Chn: Thos., Jas. Washington Morgan. Inv. made Jan. 6, 1812 by Britian Osborn, Edmond Cobb, Jno. Hughey.

McCARTER, ROBERT—BOX 63, PACK 1504:
Est. admnr. Mar. 26, 1792 by Jno. McCarter, Fleming Bates, Andrew Jones bound to Judges Abbeville County sum 500 lbs. Inv. made June 12, 1792 by Alexr. Clark, Joel Braziel, Jas. Bonner. Sale, Sept. 21, 1792. Byrs: Moses, Jas., Jno. McCarter, Joel Breazeale.

McELVENNEY, JOHN—BOX 63, PACK 1505:
Est. admnr. Aug. 31, 1807 by Ruth McElvenney, Alexr. Hunter, Robt. Smith, Jno. Howie bound to Andrew Hamilton Ord. Abbeville Dist. sum $10,000.00. Cit. pub. at Rocky River Church. Dec. 31, 1808 Paid Mrs. McElvanney for boarding Robt. McElvanney $25.00. For Margaret, Narcissa McElvanney $40.00. Elizabeth McElvanney $8.00. (Written McElvenney, McElvanney.)

MITCHELL, GEORGE—BOX 63, PACK 1506:
Est. admnr. Feb. 15, 1817 by Nancy Mitchell, Geo., Wm. Reeves, Lang-

ford Hughes bound to Taliaferro Livingston Ord. Abbeville Dist. sum 5,000 lbs. Cit. pub. at Turkey Creek Church. Inv. made Mar. 6, 1817 by Henry G. Johnson, Wm. McCraw, Wm. Long. Larkin W., Ellender H. Mitchell minor chn.

MITCHELL, MARTHA—BOX 63, PACK 1507:
Est. admnr. Mar. 5, 1814 by Saml., Francis Young, Jas. Caruthers bound to Taliaferro Livingston Ord. Abbeville Dist. sum $2,000.00. Cit. pub. at Rocky River Church. Inv. made Mar. 28, 1814 by Ezekiel Calhoun, Andrew Cowan, Thos. Finley.

MOSELEY, CHARLES—BOX 63, PACK 1508:
Will dated Dec. 28, 1808 in Abbeville Dist. Rec. Dec. 7, 1809. Exrs: Wife, Charlotte Moseley, Jno. N., Philip Montague. Wit: Jas. Wilson, Saml. Wimbish, Joel Vic. Chn: Charlotte, Thos. Franklin Moseley. Expend: 1810 Paid Henry Moseley $13.66½. Richard Moseley $2.37½.

McHARG, JOHN—BOX 63, PACK 1509:
Est. admnr. Sept. 20, 1783 by Susannah Mcharg, Adam Goudalock, Robt. Bolt bound to Jno. Thomas Jr. Ord. 96 Dist. sum 2,000 lbs. Inv. made Nov. 1783 by Robt. Bolt, Robt., Jno. Woods.

MORROW, JOHN, SR.—BOX 63, PACK 1510:
Will dated Oct. 3, 1802 in Abbeville Dist. Proved Dec. 8, 1802. Exrs: Wife, Sarah Morrow, Jas. Cooper. Wit: Wm., Jno. Morrow Jr., Jas. Cooper. Chn. ment. names not given. Sale, Sept. 3, 1807. Byrs: Sarah, Joseph, Geo. Criswell, Jas. Wilson, Wm. Dale, Margaret Cooper, Wm., Arthur Morrow Jr., etc.

MORRIS, GEORGE—BOX 63, PACK 1511:
Est. admnr. April. 21, 1806 by Catharine, Saml., Wm. Morris, Alexr. White bound to Andrew Hamilton Ord. Abbeville Dist. sum $5,000.00. Inv. made May 6, 1806 by Jno. Giles, Nathaniel Weed, Saml. Herron.

McKINLEY, ESTHER—BOX 63, PACK 1512:
Will dated July 4, 1789 in Abbeville Dist. Proved Feb. 5, 1791. Exr: Wm. McKinley. Wit: Elijah McCurdy, Wm. Callahan. Chn: Wm. McKinley, Esther Trimble, Susana Woods, Martha Bell, Sarah Baskins. Gr. chn: Jno. Trimble, Esther, Jno. Woods, Esther W., Jno. McKinley Bell. Inv. made July 5, 1791 by Francis Carlile, Ebenezer Pettigrew, Elijah McCurdy Esq.

MOORE, JOHN—BOX 63, PACK 1513:
Est. admnr. Nov. 19, 1814 by Jemima Moore, Alexr., Joseph Houston bound to Taliaferro Livingston Ord. Abbeville Dist. sum $3,000.00. Cit. pub. at Hopewell Church. Inv. made Dec. 5, 1814 by Jno. Blain, Robt. McCravan, Joseph Houston. Sale, Dec. 6. 1814. Byrs: Jemima Moore, Merideth McGehee, Jas. Conner, Caleb Jennings, Jno. Winfield, etc.

MITCHELL, TANNER—BOX 63, PACK 1514:
Will dated Jan. 12, 1791 in Abbeville Dist. Proved June 10, 1793. Exrs. Sons, Solomon, Jno. Mitchell. Wit: Zeri Rice, Stephen Buzbee, Lewis Mitchell.

Chn: Solomon, Lewis, Mason, Jno., Morris, Robt., Rebecca, Thos Mitchell. Gr. chn: Jas. Griffin, Jno., son of Thos. Mitchell. Inv. made Oct. 26, 1793 by Levi Rice, Robt. Sample, Micajah Stevens.

MOORE, QUINTON—BOX 63, PACK 1515:
Est. admnr. June. 15, 1791 by Phebe Norwood, Jas., Ezekiel Evans Sr. bound to Judges Abbeville County sum 1,000 lbs. Cit. pub. at Long Cane Church. Inv. made July 19, 1791 by Jno. Connor, Jno. Lumbus, Benjamin Mitchel. Byrs: Andrew Mooer, Charles Davenport, Saml. Leathers, etc.

MEBAN, JOHN—BOX 64, PACK 1516:
Will dated Sept. 1, 1796 in Abbeville Dist. Rec. Mar. 27, 1797. Exrs: b. l. Thos. Gray, Andrew McComb. Wit: Wm. McBride, Jno. Batty, Jas. Gray. Wife and chn. ment. no names given. Inv. made June 12, 1797 by Jno. Patterson, Jno., Jno. Beatty Sr. Sale, Aug. 12, 1797. Byrs: Margaret Meban, Hardy Cornet, Jno., Josiah Patterson, Jno. Bennet, etc.

MAXFIELD, SUSANA—BOX 64, PACK 1517:
Will dated Sept. 10, 1793. Rec. Mar. 28, 1794. Exrs. Jno., Peter Herston. Wit: Wm. Hutton, Andrew McBride, Margaret Forsythe. Lived on Calhoun's Creek. Chn: Jeen, Agness, Elizabeth, Nancy, Wm. Maxfield. Inv. made May 16, 1794 by Wm. Pettigrew, Benjamin Howard, John Simpson.

MORRIS, WILLIAM, SR.—BOX 64, PACK 1518:
Est. admnr. July 9, 1788 by Eleanor Morris, Wm. Black, Jas. Hamilton, Jeremiah Files bound to Judges Abbeville Co. sum 500 lbs. Inv. made June 6, 1789 by Joseph Black, Jno. Lawrence, Jas. Young. Byrs: Jno. Morris, Thos. Coil, Israel Pickens, Henry Sharp, etc.

McCARLEY, JOHN—BOX 64, PACK 1519:
Est. admnr. July 21, 1783 by Elizabeth McCarley, Geo. Briton, Wm. Smith, Richard Nalley bound to John Thomas Ord. 96 Dist. sum 2,000 lbs. Elizabeth McCarley was of Tyger River. Inv. made Aug. 22, 1783 by Joseph Wofford, Benjamin Roebuck, Wm. Smith. At a Co. Court, held for the Co. of Spartanburg on the 3rd. Mon. in June, 1788, ordered that Col. John Thomas Jr. make a full sett. of the est. of John Carley, whereof Geo. Brition was admnr. (Written McCarley, Carley.)

MILLER, ANDREW—BOX 64, PACK 1520:
Est. admnr. Oct. 6, 1802 by Ebenezer, Joseph Miller, Andrew Bowie bound to Andrew Hamilton Ord. Abbeville Dist. sum $5,000.00. Wid. Elizabeth Miller. Sett. made Oct. 6, 1818. Paid Robt. Miller $132.21½, John S. Miller $132.21½, Jane Miller $264.42, Margaret Miller $264.42.

MILLER, MARTHA—BOX 64, PACK 1521:
Will dated April 13, 1806 in Abbeville Dist. Rec. Sept. 1, 1806. Exr. Rob. Smyth. Wit: Jno., Mathew, T. W. Smyth. Son, David Miller. "Give Nancy Smyth my loom." Inv. made Sept. 3, 1806 by Jno. Foster, Geo. McBeth, Hugh Porter.

McKEEN, WILLIAM—BOX 64, PACK 1522:
Est. admnr. Dec. 7, 1804 by Robt., Wm. Hays, Jas. Herron, Jno. Simpson, Robt. Allen bound to Andrew Hamilton Ord. Abbeville Dist. sum $10,000.00. Cit. pub. at Rocky Springs Church. Robt. Hays, Jas. Herron next of kin. Inv. made Jan. 24, 1805 by Wm. Adams, Saml. Young, Pleasant Waid.

McCULLOUGH, JAMES—BOX 64, PACK 1523:
Will dated Feb. 20, 1804 in Abbeville Dist. Rec. Mar. 11, 1805. Exrs: Jno. Devlin, Jas. Stinson, Jno. Pressly. Chn: Wm., Elizabeth, Nancy, Hannah, Mary McCullough. S. l. Jno. Blair. Est. also admnr. Feb. 13, 1805 by Agness McCullough, Jno. Cowan, Wm. Crawford in sum $5,000.00.

MOORE, FRANCIS—BOX 64, PACK 1524:
Est. admnr. Nov. 22, 1806 by Sarah Moore, Jeremiah, Benj. Terry, Francis Carlile, Esq. bound to Andrew Hamilton Ord. sum $10,000.00. Inv. made Dec. 2, 1806 by Benjamin Terry, Jos. Bickley, Saml. Young. Sale, Dec. 12, 1806. Byrs: Sarah Moore, Jno. Calhoun, Thos. Ward, Jno. Bickley, Andrew Defur, Benj. Terry, Mary Howland, Aley Bass, Thos. B. Cofer, Andrew Cowan, Jno. Beasley, Fras. Carlile, Jno. Cain, Thos. B. Creagh, Abner Brown.

MOORE, DR. JAMES—BOX 64, PACK 1525:
Will dated July 26, 1809 in Abbeville Dist. Proved June 4, 1810. Exrs: Bro. Johathan Moore, Archy, John C. Mayson, Washington Bostick. Wit: Taliaferro Livingston, Thos. Chiles, Jas. Coleman. Wife, Frances Moore. Chn: Edward, James, Frances, Louisa Moore. "My part of Est. of Wm. Anderson, decd., go to my chn."

MARTIN, PETER—BOX 64, PACK 1526:
Est. admnr. Mar. 27, 1797 by Robt. Martin Jr. of Savannah River, Jehu Foster, Robt. Vernon, bound to Judges sum $1,000.00. Inv. made June 20, 1797 by Jeremiah Beall, Richard Posey, Wm. Adams. (Note: This following article was written by someone in tracing this line and left in the box for others to read. Robt. Martin was Peter Martin's father. Robt's. father was John Martin who died in Farmville, Va. in 1787. Robt. Martin, of Savannah River, moved to Abbeville, S. C. from Farmville, Va., with his family in 1788. John of Farmville had a brother, Abraham, who came to S. C. and was killed by the Indians in 1773. Records to the above note were found in Farmville, Va.)

McBRIDE, THOMAS—BOX 64, PACK 1527:
Will dated Apr. 21, 1798 in Abbeville Dist. Rec. June 11, 1798. Exrs: Bro., Hugh McBride, Br. l., Jas. Hutchinson. Wit: Jas. McBride, Mickeal Mclemans, Andrew McComb. Wife, father and 2 chn. ment. no names given. Neph. Tommey McBride, Bro. Hugh McBride, Br. l. Jas. Hutchinson. Inv. made July 3, 1798 by Capt. Jno. Calhoun, Adam Hill, Archibald Thompson.

McGILL, JOHN—BOX 64, PACK 1528:
Est. admnr. Feb. 9, 1785 by Margaret McGill, Geo., Jos. Reed bound to John Thomas Ord. 96 Dist. sum 2,000 lbs. Inv. made Apr. 27, 1785 by Francis Carlie, Wm. McCune, Jas. Ponder.

McILROY, JAMES—BOX 64, PACK 1529:
Will dated Sept. 22, 1780 in 96 Dist. Proved May 3, 1783. Exrs: Wife, Dinah McIlroy, Archer Smith. Wit: Thos. Davis, Jno. Pearson. Wife, Dinah McIlroy. Chn: Rachel, Frances Blassingham, Abigal Beardin, Mary Rentfro, Sarah Bratcher, Comfort Cleaton, Esther Bogan, Jas., Wm., Archibald McIlroy.

MILROY, JAMES—BOX 64, PACK 1530:
Est. admnr. May 9, 1807 by Jno. Cameron, Jas. B. English bound to Andrew Hamilton Ord. sum $1,000.00. This was of James Milroy (Taylor). Cit. pub. at Rocky River Church. Inv. made June 25, 1807 by Wm. H. Caldwell, Saml. Harris. Byrs: Jno. Cameron, Saml. Harris, Jas. B. McKinley, Peter Mabery. Wm. Davis Esq., Andrew McBride, Wm. H. Caldwell, Andrew Griffin.

MOORE, WILLIAM, ESQ.—BOX 64, PACK 1531:
Est. admnr. Jan. 4, 1791 by Davis Moore, Julius Nichols Jr., Nathan Sims, John Wardlaw, Robt. Swanzy, Benj. Mitchel, Jno. Calhoun bound to Judges Abbeville Dist. sum 4,000 lbs. Cit. ment. that Davis Moore, Julius Nichols Jr. next of kin. Wm. Moore was of Cambridge. Richard, a bro. to Wm. and next of kin, but his reason for not admnr. that he was getting old and incapable of undertaking such an arduous task. Inv. made Mar. 4, 1791 by Elijah Moore, Jas. Wilson, Jos. Burton.

McELVANEY, SAMUEL—BOX 64, PACK 1532:
Est. admnr. Jan. 12, 1813 by Margaret McElvaney, Alexr. Hunter, Benj. Houston bound to Taliaferro Livingston sum $5,000.00. Inv. made Jan. 30, 1813 by Chas. Parker, Robt. Smith, W. Carithers. Sale, Feb. 5, 1813. Byrs: Daniel Whitehead, Robt. Smith, Banister Allen, Jno. A. Allen, Chas. Miller, Alexr. Hunter, Nathan Strickland, Jno. Cameron, Jno. Hemming, Benj. Summers, Jno. Grant, Francis Drinkard, Jas. Crawford, Saml. Linton Esq., Robt., Margaret, Wid. Elizabeth McElvaney, etc.

MAYFIELD, JOHN—BOX 64, PACK 1533:
Mary Mayfield the admnr. Lived in 96 Dist. Inv. made July 31, 1783 by Wm. Williams, John Sisson, Lawlot Porter. (No other papers.)

MOFFETT, JOHN C.—BOX 64, PACK 1534:
Est. admnr. Nov. 28, 1783 by Wm. Moffett, Jno. Dalrymple, Ephriam Canon bound to John Thomas Ord. 96 Dist. sum 2,000 lbs. Inv. made Dec. 22, 1783 by Ephairm Cannon, Jno. Riley.

McDONALD, WILLIAM—BOX 64, PACK 1535:
Est. admnr. Nov. 22, 1783 by Jas. Abercrombie, Wm. Baugh, Richard Pugh bound to John Thomas 96 Dist. sum 2,000 lbs. Inv. made Feb. 7, 1784 by Jno. Baugh, Wm. Baugh, Chas. Bradey.

McCREERY, GILBERT—BOX 64, PACK 1536:
Est. admnr. June 8, 1795 by Jas. Hawthorn Sr., Thos. McBride, (Blacksmith), Jno. Brannon, Anthony Yeldall bound to Judges Abbeville Dist. sum 500 lbs. Cit. pub. at Hopewell Church. Ment. Jas. Hawthorn Sr., Thos. McBride

next of kin. On June 5, 1795 Margaret McCreery (alias Margaret Ryley) relinquished her right as admnr. of her decd. husband's est., the late Gilbert McCreery. Inv. made Aug. 4, 1795 by Alexr. White, Jno. Anderson, Hugh McBride. Sale, Jan. 14, 1796. Byrs: Mary McCreery, Hugh McBride, Wm. Buck, Jas. Hawthorn.

McMASTER, JOHN AND PATRICK—BOX 64, PACK 1537:
Es. admnr. Jan. 11, 1782 by Wm. McMaster, Wm. McKinley, Wm. Hays bound to Jno. Ewing Calhoun Ord. 96 Dist. sum 2,000 lbs. Cit. pub. at Long Canes, ment. Wm. McMaster, next of kin. Inv. made Aug. 10, 1782 by Wm. McKinley, Robt. Boyd, Capt. Jas. Little.

MARSHALL, JOHN—BOX 64, PACK 1538:
Will dated Mar. 10, 1784. Exrs: Wm. White, Grant Allen. Wit: John, Amos, Winneford Satterfield. Ment. was of Warren Co., N. C. Bro. Dixon Marshall. "Bequeath to Wm. White, Wm. Mathew, Chas., Peggy Marshall, Grant Allen, Richard Moore."

MOSS, WILLIAM—BOX 64, PACK 1539:
Will dated Nov. 22, 1785 in 96 Dist. Prov. July 7, 1786 by Leroy Hammond of Edgefield Co. Exr. Joseph Dick. Wit: Alexr. Newman, Jno. Broom, Wid. Mary Moss. Chn: Thos., Elizabeth Moss.

MATTISON, WILLIAM—BOX 64, PACK 1540:
Est. admnr. May 8, 1809 by Peggy, Thos. Mattison, Zachariah Davis, Reuben Nash Esq. bound to Andrew Hamilton Ord. sum $10,000.00. Inv. made May 25, 1809 by Wm. Long, Wm. Mitchel, Jas. Kay. Expend: June 2, 1810 Paid Geo. B. Mattison $15.75. Sale made May 26, 1809. Byrs: Peggy, Archibald, John, Matilda, Olley Mattison.

McDONALD, ADAM—BOX 64, PACK 1541:
Est. admnr. Nov. 17, 1807 by Wm. McDonald Sr., Wm. McDonald Jr., Jas. Patton bound to Andrew Hamilton Ord. Abbeville Dist. sum $5,000.00.

McCRONE, ROBERT—BOX 64, PACK 1542:
Est. admnr. Mar. 8, 1803 by Wm. McCrone, John Spruill, Jas. McAdams bound to Andrew Hamilton Ord. Abbeville Dist. sum $1,000.00. Cit. pub. at Greenville Church. Inv. made at the home of Saml. Miller April 2, 1803 by Jas. Richey, Saml. Miller, John Shannon.

McCORMICK, DAVID W.—BOX 64, PACK 1543:
Est. admnr. May 4, 1807 by Andrew McCormick, Geo. Conn bound to Andrew Hamilton Ord. Abbeville Dist. sum $5,000.00. Sale, May 25, 1807. Byrs: Geo. Conn, Stephen Chambers, Andrew McCormick, John Saint, John Chiles, Saml. McClinton, John Laird, Andrew McComb, etc.

McCARTER, MOSES—BOX 64, PACK 1544:
Will dated Feb. 25, 1787 in Abbeville Dist. Prov. Jan. 9, 1788. Exrs: John McCarter, Fleming Bates. Wit: Mary McCarter, Margaret Bates, Jos. Crawford. Wife, Catren McCarter. Chn: Robt., Moses McCarter Jr., Anne York, Catren Evans, John, Wm., Mary, Agness, Jennet, Jas. McCarter, Margaret Bates.

218   ABSTRACTS OF OLD NINETY-SIX AND

McLEAN, JOHN—BOX 64, PACK 1545:
    Est. admnr. Oct. 6, 1789 by Jas. Morrow, Chas. Spence., Saml. Agnew, Saml. Houston bound to Judges of Abbeville Co. sum $1,000.00. Was a blacksmith. Archibald McLean ordered these to admnr. Inv. made Nov. 7, 1789 by Saml. Houston, John Wilson, Jas. Wilson.

McGAW, JOHN—BOX 64, PACK 1546:
    Will dated Feb. 15, 1805 in Abbeville Dist. Rec. Aug. 6, 1805. Exrs: Wife, Sarah McGaw, Son, Saml. McGaw, Saml. Patterson. Wit: Andrew, Robt. Taylor, Rebecca Patterson. Wife, Sarah McGaw. Chn: Wm., Jas., Saml., Mary Agness, Sally, Moses, Benj., Josiah, John McGaw. Expend: Aug. 16, 1810 Paid Robt. Giles and wife Mary McGaw $100.00.

MURPHY, SIMON—BOX 64, PACK 1547:
    Est. admnr. Nov. 8, 1783 by Sarah, Mark Murphy, Jas. Duncan bound to John Thomas Ord. 96 Dist. sum 2,000 lbs. Inv. made Nov. 28, 1783 by Nehemiah Howard, Wm. Woolbanks, Wm. Losson.

MARTIN, CHARLES—BOX 64, PACK 1548:
    Will dated June 28, 1808 in Abbeville Dist. Rec. Oct. 25, 1808. Exrs: Wife, Polly Martin, Jacob, Geo. W. Martin. Wit: Wm. Drinkard, Saml. Linton, Nathaniel Bolen. Wife, Polly Martin. Chn: Jacob, Geo. Wash., Wm. Martin. Suckey Moore, Salley Nichols. Gr. chn: Jas., Thos. Cobb, Patsey Bibb.

MARTIN, GEN. JOHN—BOX 64, PACK 1549:
    Est. admnr. Dec. 11, 1813 by Benj. Glover, Andrew Milligan, Saml. B. Shields bound to Taliaferro Livingston Ord. sum $20,000.00. Inv. made Dec. 27, 1813 by Geo. Robertson, Wm. Calhoun Jr., Nathaniel Norwood, John Moragne. Byrs: Mary Ann, John Sr., Wm. D. Martin, Thos. Saxon, Maj. Richard Griffin, Saml. Cole, etc.

MATTHEWS, VICTOR—BOX 64, PACK 1550:
    Will dated Dec. 31, 1795 in Abbeville Dist. Rec. Mar. 25, 1796. No. Exrs. Wit: Moses Edmiston, Saml. McNeily, Wm. Wedgworth. Wife, Isable Matthews. Chn: Jos., John, Jas., Isaac, Esther, Ann, Elizabeth, Rebekah. Inv. made Apr. 26, 1796 by Wm. Wedgworth, John Lumbas, John Irwin.

McGREER, DANIEL—BOX 65, PACK 1551:
    Will dated June 20, 1817 in Abbeville Dist. Rec. May 4, 1818. No. Exrs. Wit: Saml. R. Evans, Johathan Pressly, Elley Pressly. Sis., Betsey Fife, wife of Hugh Fife. Nephew, Daniel.

MITCHELL, ISAAC—BOX 65, PACK 1552:
    Will dated June 29, 1789 in Abbeville Dist. Filed Oct. 6, 1789. Exrs: Wife, Mary Mitchell, Son, Isaac Mitchell, Nathan Sims, Robt., Richard Pollard. Wit: Zachary Meriwether, Benj. Mitchell, Rosana Swansy. Wife, Mary Mitchell. Chn: Ursula, Catharine, Mary, Sarah Mitchell. Sett: Legatees: Jas. Cook, Robt. Pollard, Wm. Mitchell, Levi Rice, Elisha Mitchell, Richard Pollard, Isaac, Daniel, Martha, John, Jas. Mitchell.

McBRIDE, JOSEPH—BOX 65, PACK 1553:
Est. admnr. Nov. 23, 1805 by Elizabeth McBride, Andrew McCombs, Jno., Saml. Young, David Fife bound to Andrew Hamilton Ord. sum $5,000.00. Cit. pub. at Cedar Springs Church. Expend: Dec. 20, 1805 Paid Betsey McBride legatee, $73.30. Paid David Campbel for carrying 3 chn. of the family to their friends at Winnsborough $8.00. Apr. 25, 1806 Paid Jas. Bailey, schoolmaster, for 8 weeks schooling to Billy McBride, a minor of the family $8.00. Paid John Young for boarding Francis McBride $4.00. Jan. 14, 1808 Paid Betsey McBride (alias Harvey) $158.47. June 20, 1808 Paid Thos. Russell, gdn. of Jas. and Wm. McBride, minors, $243.00.

MAYNE, JOHN—BOX 65, PACK 1554:
Est. admnr. Sept. 19, 1823 by Jno. Donald, Jas. Hawthorne, Wm. Morrison bound to Moses Taggart Ord. sum $1,000.00. Cit. pub. at Greenville Church. Sale. Dec. 5, 1823. Byrs: Elizabeth Mayne, Michel Wilson, Wm. Rhodes, Saml. Porter, Archibald McCord, Wm. Lomax, etc.

MAGILL, JAMES—BOX 65, PACK 1555:
Will dated Feb. 8, 1779 in 96 Dist. Probated Aug. 24, 1782. Exrs: Anthony Golding, Robt. Cunningham, Wm., Henry O'Neal. Wit: Jno., Catren Johnson, Geo. Potts or Botts. Gr. chn: Jas., Anthon, Wm. Golding. S. l. Anthony Golding. Nephew, Wm. Lowrey. Ment. nephews in Ireland but no names given. "Give to my 3 grandsons 207 acres on Hoges Creek in Frederick Co., Va."

McWHORTER, ROBERT—BOX 65, PACK 1556:
Lived in 96 Dist. Adam Goudalock was admnr. Inv. made June 13, 1783 by Robt. Lusk, Jno. Montgomery, Francis Lattimore. (No other papers.)

MURRAY, TITUS—BOX 65, PACK 1557:
Will dated Mar. 19, 1813 in Abbeville Dist. Prov. Oct. 4, 1815. Exrs: Stephen Crenshaw, Wm. Yarbrough. Wit: Abraham Livingston, Jacob Holland, Alexr. Gammill. Chn: Jas., David, Edward, Titus, Frances, Nancy, Polly, Betsy, Bedy Murray.

McGOWAN, JAMES—BOX 65, PACK 1558:
Will dated Dec. 4, 1802 in Abbeville Dist. Prov. Dec. 20, 1802. Exrs: Wife, Elizabeth, S. L., Wm. Carothers. Wit: Jos. Chipman, Hannah McGowen, Mary Carothers, Saml. Scott, Mordeaci Shackelford. Wife, Elizabeth. Chn: Elijah M., Mary, Wm., Robt., John, Jas., Susannah McGowen.

McILWAIN, ANDREW—BOX 65, PACK 1559:
Est. admnr. Jan. 22, 1803 by Jannet McIlwain, Jno. McIlwain, Nathaniel Bailey, Nathaniel Johnson bound to Andrew Hamilton Ord. sum $5,000.00. Inv. made June 3, 1803 by Andrew Bowie, Nathaniel Bailey, Jno. Burton.

McCALL, COL. JAMES—BOX 65, PACK 1560:
Will dated May 20, 1770 in 96 Dist. Prov. Apr. 28, 1784. Exrs: Wife, Elizabeth, Br. l. John Luckie. Wit: Thos. Holland, Jas. Long, Randal Lockhart, Joel Doss. Wife, Elizabeth. Chn: Jas. Harris, Thos., Hugh McCall, Janet Harris.

MECKLIN, DAVID—BOX 65, PACK 1561:
Will dated Nov. 24, 1790 in Abbeville Dist. Prov. Mar. 25, 1796. Exr:
Hugh Mecklin Jr. Wit: Hugh Mecklin, Benj. Montgomery, Hugh Mecklin Jr.
Wife, Agness. Chn: Jas., Hugh Mecklin, Martha Tate. Gr. chn: Martha, John
Linch. Owned land in Guilford Co, N. C.

MINTER, JOSEPH—BOX 65, PACK 1562:
Will dated Apr. 18, 1774. Prov. Apr. 24, 1784. Exrs: Wife Annamariah
Minter, Son Jno Minter, Rowland Gooch. Wit: Jno, Thos. Butler, Wm. Berry.
Lived in Granville Co., N. C. Wife, Annamariah. Chn: Jno., Mary, Salley,
Annamariah, Merry Minter. Owned land on Island Ck.

MORRISON, WILLIAM—BOX 65, PACK 1563:
Est. admnr. Feb. 6, 1815 by Wm. Thompson, Jno. Jay, Thos. Mayho
bound to Taliaferro Livingston Ord. sum $1,000.00. Late of the Army of the
U. S. Cit. pub. at Hopewell Church. Margaret Morrison bought at sale.

MARTIN, JANET—BOX 65. PACK 1564:
Will dated Dec. 4, 1811. Prov. Dec. 14, 1811. Exr. David Pressly. Wit:
Joseph Scott, Ann, Easter Pressly. Lived on Rocky River, Abbeville Dist. "My
will that David Pressly take care of my chn." Cit. pub. at Diamond Hill. Wm.
Gaston gdn. of Jane, Mary Martin legatees.

MULHERN, CHARLES—BOX 65, PACK 1565:
Will dated Mar. 17, 1789 in Abbeville Dist. Prov. Apr. 7, 1789. Exrs:
Jno. Jr., Andrew Logan. Wit: Jno., Zachry Meriwether, Wm. Heard. Chn: Jean,
Jas., Jno Mulhern, Sarah Askins. Gr. dtr. Elizabeth Askins, dtr. to Sarah and
Geo. Askins. "Bequeath to Margaret, Sarah, dtrs. to Jno. Logan, to Jno. Logan Sr.,
to Jno. Logan Jr."

MOSELEY, ARTHUR—BOX 65, PACK 1566:
Will dated Jan. 11, 1804 in Abbeville Dist. Rec. Feb. 6, 1804. Exrs: Bro.
Richard Moseley, Wm. Moseley, Nephew Richard Moseley, son of Richard
Moseley. Wit: Joseph Moseley, Jno., Wm. Bass. Dtr: Rosena. Nephew, Tarleton
Moseley, son of Richard Moseley, Richard Moseley, son of Wm. Moseley of Va.

McINTIRE, DANIEL—BOX 65, PACK 1567:
Will dated Dec. 4, 1805 in Abbeville Dist. Rec. Oct. 21, 1806. Exrs:
Wife, Mary; Son, Samuel. Wit: Thos. Wilson, Wm. Robertson, Richard Marley.
Wife, Mary. Chn: Joseph, Archibald, Saml., Jas., Rebecca McIntire.

MAXWELL, JOHN—BOX 65, PACK 1568:
Will dated Aug. 25, 1792 in Abbeville Dist. Prov. Dec. 16, 1806. Exrs:
Robt., Jane Maxwell, Robt. Sloane. Wit: Jno. Stephens, Robt. Sloane, Thos.
Shirley, Margaret Stephens. Wife, Jane. Owned land near Golden Grove in Green-
ville Co. Chn: Robt., Chas., Wm., Sarah. Nancy, Jno., Hugh, Geo., Sally Max-
well. Gr. s. Jon, son to Robert Maxwell. Give Chas. land in Laurence Co.

MITCHELL, DANIEL—BOX 65, PACK 1569:
Est. admnr. Feb. 10, 1785 by Isaac, Mary Mitchell, Gabriel Smithers,

Jas. Wilson bound to Jno. Thomas Ord. 96 Dist. sum 2,000 lbs. Inv. made Apr. 12, 1785 in Edgefield Co. by Chas. Bussey, Wm. Harvey, Jno. Cunningham.

MANN, SAMUEL—BOX 65, PACK 1570:
Est. admnr. Mar. 31, 1783 by Wm., Margaret Simpson, Francis Sutherland, Wm. Manson bound to Jno. Ewing Calhoun Ord. 96 Dist. sum 14,000 lbs. Wm. Simpson and Margaret, his wife, formerly Mann, next of kin.

MESSER, JAMES—BOX 65, PACK 1571:
Est. admnr. July 19, 1784 by Jno. Messer, Nathaniel Austin, Holloway Power bound to Jno. Thomas Ord. 96 Dist. sum 2,000 lbs. Inv. made Sept. 12, 1784 by Nathaniel Austin, Wm. Gilbert, Martin C. Williams.

MORROW, JAMES—BOX 65, PACK 1572:
Est. admnr. July 9, 1788 by Thos. Morrow, Jas. Foster, Fleming Bates bound to Judges of Abbeville Co. sum 1,000 lbs. Inv. made Dec. 3, 1788 by Fleming Bates, Alexr. Clark, Geo. Morrow.

MURRAY, CAPT. JOHN—BOX 65, PACK 1573:
Est. admnr. Dec. 2, 1786 by Jas. Gray, Jno. Ryan, Jas. Vessels bound to Jno. Thomas Ord. 96 Dist. sum 1,000 lbs. Inv. made Dec. 27, 1786 in Edgefield Co. by Jesse Roundtree, Wm. Shinholser, Jonathan Meyers.

McGARITY, JOHN—BOX 65, PACK 1574:
Will dated Apr. 18, 1785 in 96 Dist. Prov. Sept. 27, 1785. Exrs. Jno. Gooden, Thacker Vivion. Wit: Jonathan, Peter Pennell. Wife, Mary. Chn: Clemmons, Michael, Sally, Roby, Patrick, Moley, Elizabeth, Nancy McGarrity. (Name also written Mackgarrethe.) Inv. made by Jas. Blassingham, Jno. Putman, Nehemiah Howard.

MOORE, JAMES ESQ.—BOX 65, PACK 1575:
Will dated Jan 12, 1780 in 96 Dist. Prov. Sept. 23, 1782. Exrs: Wife, Anne, Wm., Jno., Richard Moore. Wit: Wm. Neal, Wm. Wilson. Wife, Anne. Chn: Davis, Jas., Jonathan, Wm., Drayton Moore. Mother, Susanna Moore.

MOORE, PATRICK—BOX 65, PACK 1576:
Lived in 96 Dist. Anne Moore, Wm. Tate Admnrs. Inv. made June 20, 1783 by Wm. Thomson, David Allen, Geo. Taylor. (No other papers.)

McCORD, JAMES—BOX 65, PACK 1577:
Est. admnr. Dec. 20, 1785 by Wm. Moore and wife Sarah, Jas. Hughes, Jeremiah Silman bound to John Thomas Ord. 96 Dist. sum 500 lbs. Inv. made Mar. 30, 1786 by Aaron Moore, Jas. Miller, Jos. Fowler.

MORROW, ELIZABETH—BOX 65, PACK 1578:
Will dated July 6, 1816 in Abbeville Dist. Prov. Oct. 4, 1816. Exrs: Son, Jno.: s. l. Jas. Cochran. Wit: Jno. M. Cochran, Arthur Morrow. Chn: Mary Cooper Stuart, Margaret Cochran, Elizabeth Cooper, Arthur, Elizabeth Morrow.

McGOWAN, DRURY—BOX 65, PACK 1579:
Est. admnr. Sept. 18, 1807 by Wm. Moore, Jas. Cobb bound to Andrew

Hamilton Ord. sum $1,000.00. Inv. made Sept. 26, 1807 by Wm. **Waller, Wm.** Todd, Richard Henderson.

MELVILLE, ROBERT—BOX 65, PACK 1580:
Will dated Sept. 12, 1782 in 96 Dist. Prov. Mar. 24, 1783. Exrs: **Wife,** Mary, Robt. John Maxwell. Wit: Nicolas, Wm. Maxwell. Wife, Mary. **"Bequeath** to Robt. Maxwell, Jno. Miller, Jno. McFatvick."

MARTIN, ROBERT—BOX 65, PACK 1581:
Will dated May 9, 1810 in Abbeville Dist. Rec. Sept. 3, 1810. Exr. **Wife** Jannet. Wit: David Pressly, Thos. Anny Gillespie. Wife, Jannet. Chn: Jas., Jean, Mary Martin.

McCURDY, JOHN, SR.—BOX 65, PACK 1582:
Will dated Apr. 28, 1784 in 96 Dist. Exrs: Thos. Weems, Wm. **Alexander,** Patrick Calhoun. Wit: Wm. Alexander, Mathew, Janet Young. Wife, **Margaret.** Chn: Jno., Sarah McCurdy, Margaret Weed, Agness Cunningham, Jennet Young. Inv. made Aug. 4, 1789 by Nathan Loosk, Saml. Porter, Jas. Watt.

MUSGROVE, JOHN—BOX 65, PACK 1583:
Est. admnr. May 1, 1784 by Arramenta Wilson, Jno. Musgrove, **Dannett** Abney, Wm. Abney bound to Jno. Thomas Ord. 96 Dist. sum 2,000 lbs. **Sale,** June 10, 1784. Byrs: Minty Wilson, Jno. Wm. Musgrove.

McKINLEY, JAMES—BOX 65, PACK 1584:
Will gone. Wm. McKinley, Wm. Burrows, Francis Carlisle Exrs. **Lived** in 96 Dist. Inv. made Aug. 9, 1777 by Jno. Bell, Jas. Caldwell, Jno. Bole.

MILES, WILLIAM JR.—BOX 65, PACK 1585:
Will dated Dec. 4, 1779 in 96 Dist. Prov. June 14, 1783. Exrs: **Joseph** Barnett, Edward Nash. Wit: Wm. Nash, Ann Hendrix, Joseph Barnett. **Wife,** Sarah. Dtrs: Nicey Miles, "plantation on 2 Mile Creek." Lucy Miles. **Father, Wm.** Miles, Sr.

MATTHEWS, JOHN—BOX 65, PACK 1586:
Will dated Oct. 21, 1793. Rec. Mar. 25, 1794. Exrs: Bro. **Isaac** Mathews, Alexr. Noble. Wit: Nancy, Sr., Wm. Calhoun. "Bequeath to **wid.** Agness Calhoun." Son, Isaac Mathews. Inv. made Apr. 18, 1794 by **Alexr.** Noble, Jas. Noble, Jas. Mulligan.

MOORE, CAPT. DAVIS—BOX 65, PACK 1587:
Est. admnr. June 11, 1799 by Jas. Moore of Charleston, Jas. **Gouedy,** Leonard Waller bound to Andrew Hamilton Ord. Abbeville Co. sum $10,000.00. Jas. Moore next of kin.

MOUCHET, CHARLES, SR.—BOX 65, PACK 1588:
Est. admnr. Oct. 3, 1834 by Saml. M. Bradford, Philip Cook, Henry **Rush** bound to Moses Taggart Ord. sum $1,000.00. Cit. pub. at Bethany Church. Est. admnr. again Oct. 17, 1838 by Isam Mouchett, Chas. M. Pelot, Jas. Williams.

McGEE, MICHAEL, SR.—BOX 66, PACK 1589:
Est. admnr. Nov. 10, 1834 by Burrell, Abner H. McGee, Wm. Barmore, Ezekiel Rasor bound to Moses Taggart Ord. sum $20,000.00. Cit. pub. at Turkey Creek Church. Expend: Sept. 22, 1835 Paid Polly Dunn for Saml. Dunn on Pow. of Atty. $600.00. Nov. 25, 1835 Paid Wm. Magee $335.00. Paid Michael Magee $545.00. Paid Jno. Bagee $250.00. Paid G. H. Brownlee $360.00. Paid Thos. Dodson $598.84. Paid Wm. Barmore, for his dtr. Margaret, $395.00.

MOORE, WILLIAM—BOX 66, PACK 1590:
Will dated Mar. 25, 1783 in 96 Dist. Prov. June 7, 1783. Exrs: Wife, Ann Moore, Wm. Wright. Wit: Nathaniel Abney, Thos. Chiles, David Childers. Wife, Ann Moore. Chn: Jno., Martha, Mary, Elizabeth, Sarah, Ann, Esther Moore. Dtr. l. Susannah Moore. "Give to Wm. Malone a tract on Broad River." (This will was badly torn.)

MOORE, WILLIAM—BOX 66, PACK 1591:
Will dated Mar. 16, 1811, in Abbeville Dist. Prov. Feb. 3, 1812. Exrs: Sons, Jno., Robt. Moore. Wit: Thos. Wilson, Jno. Hinton, Wm. Gafford. Chn: Thos., Jno., Robt. Moore. Legatees: Wm. and Mary McAlpin, Elbert Moore, Elijah Moore, Moses Moore. Mar. 23, 1812 Paid Solomon McAlpin $2.02½.

MOORE, WILLIAM—BOX 66, PACK 1592:
Will dated Oct. 10, 1803 in Abbeville Dist. Rec. April 10, 1806. Exrs: Nephew, John Moore, son to Jos. Moore, Solomon McAlpin. Wit: Wm. Hamilton, Saml., Jas. William McBride. Nephew John Moore, commonly known by the name of Little River John Moore. Cousin, Elijah Moore, now living on Vans Creek in Elbert Co., Ga. Nephews: Jas. Moore, son to Jos., living on Vans Creek, Elbert Co., Ga.; Lewis Moore. Sister, Mary McAlpin. Bequeath to Moses, Albert Moore, sons to Jos. Moore, living on Vans Creek, Elbert Co., Ga.

MOORE, WILLIAM, ESQ.—BOX 66, PACK 1593:
Sale made May 20, 1791. (Nothing of importance in pack.)

McKOWN, JOSEPH—BOX 66, PACK 1594:
Est. admnr. Nov. 3, 1834 by Robt., Jos. McCown, Robt. C. Sharp, Saml. Agnew bound to Moses Taggart Ord. sum $4,000.00. Cit. pub. at Little Hope. Expend: Apr. 30, 1835 Catharine, Mary, Margaret A. and Sarah McKown, Jno. Wear legatees. (Name written McCown, McKown.) Sale, Nov. 18, 1834. Byrs: Robt., Katharine, Jos., Wid. McKown, etc.

MARTIN, THOMAS—BOX 66, PACK 1595:
Est. admnr. Nov. 20, 1819 by Saml. Robison, Jas. Hawthorne, Wm. Martin, Jno. Wilson bound to Moses Taggart Ord. sum $2,000.00.

MERIWETHER, FRANCIS—BOX 66, PACK 1596:
Will dated Jan. 10, 1819 in Abbeville Dist. Prov. July 26, 1819. Exrs: Bros. Jos., Zachary Meriwether. Wit: Dabney, Esther McGehee. Wife, Mary R. Meriwether. Chn. ment. names not given.

McKELLAR, JOHN, SR.—BOX 66, PACK 1597:
Est. admnr. Mar. 28, 1817 by Jas. McCracken, Donald, Peter McKellar bound to Taliaferro Livingston Ord. sum $50,000.00. Cit. pub. at Silom Church. Formerly of Abbeville Dist. but late of Augusta, Ga.

McKELLAR, JOHN, JR.—BOX 66, PACK 1598:
Est. admnr. Oct. 18, 1819 by Mrs. Nancy McKellar, Chas. C. Mayson, Jas. M. Cowdrey Esq. bound to Moses Taggart Ord. sum $500.00.

MAYSON, COL. JAMES, ESQ.—BOX 66, PACK 1599:
Will dated Dec. 29, 1796 in 96 Dist. Rec. Mar. 3, 1800. Exrs: Sons, Jas., Jno., Robt. Mayson, Chas. Jones Colcock. Wit: Richard Shackleford, Saml. Savage, Standmore Butler. Present Wife, Henrietta Mayson. Chn: Jno., Louisa, Merriam, Jas. Robt. Mayson. Gr. chn: Jonathan Swift, Addeaney Mayson.

MILLER, JOHN—BOX 66, PACK 1600:
Will dated Apr. 14, 1793 in 96 Dist. Exrs: Robt. Henderson, Jas. White. Wit: Jas., David Cochran, Mary Miller. Chn: Thos., Agness Miller. Bro. Wm. Miller:

MILLER, WILLIAM—BOX 66, PACK 1601:
Est. admnr. Dec. 21, 1832 by Allen T. Miller, Wm. P. McCord, Saml. Reid, Geo. Wash. Liddell bound to Moses Taggart Ord. sum $1,000.00. Cit. pub. at Upper Long Cane Church.

MORGAN, RICHARD A.—BOX 66, PACK 1602:
On Jan. 7, 1839 Jos., Henry Norrell, Jno. D. Adams bound to Moses Taggart Ord. sum $10,000.00. Joseph Norrell made gdn. of Richard Alfred Morgan, a minor.

McQUEARNS, MINORS—BOX 66, PACK 1603:
On Nov. 20, 1833 Agness C. McQuearns, Wm. Sanders, Jno. Besteder, bound to Moses Taggart Ord. sum $3,000.00. Agness C. McQuearns made gdn. of Saml. Jas., Jno. A. McQuearns, minors of Alexr. McQuearns decd.

McKINLEY, JANE—BOX 66, PACK 1604:
On Jan. 6, 1807 Francis Carlile Esq., Archibald McKinley bound to Andrew Hamilton Ord. sum $10,000.00. Francis Carlile Esq. made gdn. of Robt. Mecklin McKinley, Jean McKinley, minors.

McMILLAN, MINORS—BOX 66, PACK 1605:
On Jan. 15, 1833 Josiah McGaw, Jno. Bradley, Jno. Kennedy bound to Moses Taggart Ord. sum $1,082.00. Josiah McGaw made gdn. of Sarah, Mary, Andrew, Randal, Susannah McMillan, minors of Andrew McMillan decd.

McGEHEE, CARR—BOX 66, PACK 1606:
On Dec. 8, 1807 Carr McGehee, Joel Lipscomb, Reuben Chiles Esq. bound to Andrew Hamilton Ord. sum $10,000.00. Carr McGehee made gdn. of Belinda, Addison, Mary Ann McGehee, minors under 14 yrs.

McMILLAN, MINORS—BOX 66, PACK 1607:
On Oct. 23, 1830 Hamilton Wiley, Archibald Kennedy, Saml. Pressly, bound to Moses Taggart Ord. sum $1,000.00. Hamilton Wiley made gdn. of Elizabeth, Sarah, Mary, Andrew, Randal, Susannah McMillan, minors.

McELVANEY, ANDREW PICKENS—BOX 66, PACK 1608:
On Jan. 31, 1812 Wm. Oliver, Nathan M. Strickland, Jas. Pringle, bound to Taliaferro Livingston Ord. sum $1,000.00. Wm. Oliver made gdn. of Andrew Pickens McElvaney, minor under 14 yrs. 1812 recd. of A. Hunter, admnr. of est. of Jno. McElvaney decd., his part of est. $210.89.

MORRAH, MINORS—BOX 66, PACK 1609:
On Jan 11, 1830 Aaron Lomax, Jno. S. Adams, Jas. S. Wilson bound to Moses Taggart Ord. sum $20,000.00. Aaron Lomax made gdn. of Mary Morrah, a minor. On Jan. 11, 1839 Aaron Lomax made gdn. of Geo. B. Morrah, a minor. Was a bro. to Saml. R. Morrah. In 1845 Mary Morrow was wife of Ed. L. Murray. (Name written Morrah and Morrow.)

McCONNEL, MINORS—BOX 66, PACK 1610:
On Nov. 18, 1835 Thos. Crawford, Jno. L. Ellis, Wm. Pratt bound to Moses Taggart Ord. sum $6,000.00. Thos. Crawford made gdn. of Mary Ann Catherine McConnel, Wm. Thos. McConnel, minors. In 1844 Mary Ann was wife of Robt. J. Winn.

MATTISON, HENRY, MINORS—BOX 66, PACK 1611:
Bond gone. Expend: June 10, 1812 Paid Jas. Kyle for Strother, Hulda Mattison $4.50. May 7, 1814 Paid Wm. Mattison for tutition $7.00. Wm. Ware Esq. was gdn. of Strother, Mahulda, Leroy Mattison, minors of Henry Mattison decd.

MOORE, MINORS—BOX 66, PACK 1612:
On Aug. 10, 1818 Andrew McGill, Jas. Cochran, Geo. Hearst bound to Taliaferro Livingston Ord. Abbeville Dist. sum $2,000.00. Andrew McGill made gdn. of Wm., Sarah, Elizabeth Moore, minors under 14 yrs. In 1807 Sarah Moore gdn. of Jno. F., Susan F. Moore.

MATHEWS, MINORS—BOX 66, PACK 1613:
On Mar. 6, 1826 Joseph N. Boyd, Jas., Christopher Conner bound to Moses Taggart Ord. sum $1,000.00. Jas. Conner made gdn. of Esther Anne, Sarah, Elizabeth, Jno. Matthews, minors under 14 yrs. Chn. of David Mathis. (Name written Matthews and Mathis.) Entitled to a share from their grandfather's est., Geo. Crawford.

MOSELEY, MINORS—BOX 66, PACK 1614:
On June 23, 1837 Tarlton P., Mary Moseley, Jno. Power Jr. bound to Moses Taggart Ord. sum $3,000.00. Tarlton P. Moseley made gdn. of Philip H., Charlotte M. Moseley, minors. Charlotte M. Was about 17 yrs. Mary Moseley was mother. Tarleton Moseley, brother.

McGAW, MINORS—BOX 66, PACK 1615:
On Mar. 15, 1833 Mary McGaw, Jas. Calhoun boud to Moses Taggart Ord. sum $2,000.00. Mary McGaw made gdn. of Elizabeth, Saml. C., Jas. J., Jane E. McGaw, minors of Saml. McGaw decd.

McCREADY, JAMES WILLIAM—BOX 66, PACK 1616:
On Jan. 12, 1836 Wm. S. Smith, Downs Calhoun, Willison B. Beazley bound to Moses Taggart Ord. sum $2,000.00. Wm. S. Smith made gdn. of Jas. Wm. McCready, a minor. On Dec. 8, 1829 Permelia McCrady, Wm., Downs Calhoun bound to Moses Taggart Ord. sum $2,000.00. Milly McCrady made gdn. of Jas. W. McCrady, a minor under 14 yrs.

MORRAH, DAVID—BOX 66, PACK 1617:
On Jan. 16, 1839 Saml. R., Jane Morrah, Johnson H. Sharp bound to Moses Taggart Ord. sum $20,000.00. Saml. R. Morrah made gdn. of Elenor, David Morrah minors. Hugh Morrah, who died Feb. 4, 1837, was father of minors.

MORROW, ANNA J.—BOX 66, PACK 1618:
On Nov. 24, 1835 Thos. M. Morrow, Jas. Spence, Thos. Griffin bound to Moses Taggart Ord. sum $2,000.00. Thos. M. Morrow made gdn. of Ann J. Morrow, a minor. Thos. M., Jas. W. Morrow, minors over 14 yrs. Anne J. Morrow, a minor under 14 yrs. Chn. of John Morrow decd.

MORGAN, MINORS—BOX 66, PACK 1619:
On Feb. 19, 1828 Nancy Morgan, Wm. B. Arnold, Thos. Wier bound to Moses Taggart Ord. sum $3,000.00. Nancy Morgan made gdn. of Jno., Thos. Morgan, minors over 14 yrs.

McMEANS, AMANDA—BOX 66, PACK 1620:
On July 14, 1831 Wm. Smith, Margaret McMeens, Jno. Evans bound to Moses Taggart Ord. sum $800.00. Wm. Smith made gdn. of Jane Amanda Mc-Meens, minor under 14 yrs.

McMEANS, MINORS—BOX 66, PACK 1621:
On Mar. 11, 1829 Andrew, Daniel Gillespie, Jos. S. English, Margaret McMeans bound to Moses Taggart Ord. sum $10,000.00. Andrew Gillespie made gdn. of Robt. C., Margaret E., Rachel M. McMeans, minors over 14 yrs. Jane A. McMeans, a minor under 14 yrs. Minors of Wm. McMeans decd.

MOORE, MINORS—BOX 66, PACK 1662:
On Jan. 18, 1833 Henry Bentley, Jos. Calhoun, Hugh H. Stewart bound to Moses Taggart Ord. sum $2,500.00. Henry Bentley made gdn. of Jas. Wash. Moore, Jane Moore, minors of Wm. H. Moore decd.

MARION, NATHANIEL—BOX 66, PACK 1623:
Will dated May 2, 1836 in Abbeville Dist. Prov. July 27, 1829. Exrs: Wife, Jane Marion, Jas. Shackleford, s. l. John R. Torrent. Wit: F. Connor, O. A. Williams, W. C. Anderson. Wife, Jane Marion. Chn: Nathaniel Peter, John Samuel, Jane Elizabeth Marion. "Bequeath to E. M. W. Tarrant." Sett. made Feb. 9, 1842. Nathaniel Marion died July 11, 1839. Dr. John Holland married

Jane Elizabeth. Louisa Charlotte Fishro Marion was a decd. dtr. Legatees: Nathaniel McCants, Mary Louisa and husband Geo. H. Round, Nathaniel Olin Holland, by his father, Dr. John Holland, Allen G. McCants, Victoria Jane, wife of D. Sanders, Amanda L. and husband Chas. Winter, Lois R. and husband Dr. Asa W. Greggs, Robt. G., John J., and Allen G. McCants. Jane Marion was Jane McCants before marriage and by a deed made Nov. 26, 1818 made in contemplation of marriage, Nathaniel Marion and Jane McCants conveyed to Robt. McCants, certain ests. in trust. Marriage between the two was solemnized after execution.

MERIWETHER, ROBERT—BOX 67, PACK 1624:
Est. admnr. July 2, 1810 by John, Jos. Meriwether, Dabney McGehee bound to John Hamilton Ord. sum $5,000.00. 1818 Paid Zachary Meriwether for Caroline Meriwether $21.75.

MORRIS, MARGARET—BOX 67, PACK 1625:
Will dated Nov. 27, 1817 in Abbeville Dist. Proved Nov. 22, 1826. Exr: Wm. Hill. Wit: Wm., Adam McDonnell, Robt. Hill. Chn: Saml. Morris, Wm., Adam Henderson. Step chn: Alis Colhoun, Lucy White, Alis Henderson, Mary Hawthorne, Sarah Henderson, Richard, Wm. Morris. Gr. chn: Alis, Lucy, Margaret, John Henderson. Est. admnr. July 2, 1827 by Saml. Morris, John Martin, Wm. Cowan bound to Moses Taggart Or. Abbeville Dist. sum $1,000.00. Cit. pub. at Cedar Springs Church.

McCALLA, JOHN—BOX 67, PACK 1626:
Will dated Aug. 17, 1836 in Abbeville Dist. Exrs: Sons, Isaac H., Geo. R. McCalla. Wit: Wm. N. Martin, Enos Campbell, Sarah C. Giles. Wife, Susan McCalla.

McCELVEY, JAMES, SR.—BOX 67, PACK 1627:
Will dated June 11, 1824 in Abbeville Dist. Proved Feb. 22, 1833. Exrs: Sons, John, Jas. McCelvey. Wit: Thos. Dickson, Ezekiel, Joseph C. Mathews. Wife, Elizabeth McCelvey. Chn: John, Elizabeth, Margaret, Agnes, Jas., Geo., Hugh McCelvey. Inv. made May 13, 1833 by Joseph C. Mathews, John Gray, Philip LeRoy.

McCOMB, ANDREW, SR.—BOX 67, PACK 1628:
Est. admnr. Dec. 11, 1819 by John, Rebecca, Andrew McComb bound to Moses Taggart Ord. Abbeville Dist. sum $8,000.00.

MORAGNE, FRANCIS—BOX 67, PACK 1629:
Will dated Feb. 24, 1818 in Abbeville Dist. Proved Mar. 4, 1818. Exrs: Wife, Jane Moragne, John Moragne, Peter Gillibau. Wit: Isaac Moragne, Mackerness G. Williams, Jas. Sheperd. Son, Peter Moragne. "Bequeath to Jas., John, Joseph Bouchillon. My son Peter after decd. of my wife live with his Uncle Peter Gillibau."

McCAW, DR. WILLIAM—BOX 67, PACK 1630:
Est. admnr. Jan. 8, 1833 by Frances McCaw, Wm., Patrick Calhoun

bound to Moses Taggart Ord. Abbeville Dist. sum $100,000.00. Inv. made Jan. 21, 1833 by Reuben Starke, Andrew Giles, Edward Tilman. Feb. 3, 1836 paid Wm. H. McCaw $3.00. Paid him at Athens $20.00.

MORROW, WILLIAM—BOX 67, PACK 1631:
    Will dated July 16, 1824 in Abbeville Dist. Proved Aug. 4, 1828. Exr: Alexr. Hunter. Wit: Sterling Williams, Robt., Alexr. Foster. Wife, Sarah Morrow. Chn: Jas., Andrew, John Morrow, Polly Buchanan. Gr. chn: Wm., son of John Morrow, Sarah, Mary Buchanan, Wm., son of Jas. Morrow, Mary, dtr. of John Morrow. "Give to my son John's dtr. Nancy Haslet and the chn. of my decd. dtr. Polly Buchanan."

MOUCHETT, SAMUEL—BOX 67, PACK 1632:
    On Oct. 6, 1838 Isam C. Mouchett made suit for Letters of Admnr. Cit. pub. at Hopewell Ch. Sett. made Dec. 23, 1843. Present, Isham Mouchett, admnr., Jas. Williams who married Elizabeth and gdn. of Wm. Mouchett a minor. Saml., *Kesamy* Mouchet by letter. Geo. Mouchett.

MALLERY, WILLIAM D.—BOX 67, PACK 1633:
    Est. admnr. Mar. 20, 1839 by Joel Smith, Jonathan Jordon, John White bound to Moses Taggart Ord. Abbeville Dist. sum $5,000.00. Cit. pub. at Long Cane Church. Inv. made April 12, 1839 by Downs Calhoun, Jas. Smith, Wm. Buchanan.

McGEHEE, JOANNA—BOX 67, PACK 1634:
    Will dated July 30, 1828 in Abbeville Dist. Proved Nov. 12, 1834. Exrs: s.ls. Seaborn O. Sullivan, Wm. B. Brooks. Wit: Dr. Ephraim R. Calhoun, W. P. Hatter, John C. McGehee. Gr. chn: Guilford, son of John H. Waller, Joanna, dtr of Hiram Gaines, Margaret Gaines. Chn: Almina Brooks, Nancy Sullivan.

MATHISON, WILLIAM A.—BOX 67, PACK 1635:
    Est. admnr. Jan. 13, 1830 by Josiah Sibley, Jas. Hubbard, Laurance Brock bound to Moses Taggart Ord. Abbeville Dist. sum $20,000.00.

MULLAND, MARY—BOX 67, PACK 1636:
    Will dated Mar. 31, 1817 in Abbeville Dist. Prov. July 7, 1817. Exr: Fanny Thornton. Wit: Andrew McCombs Sr., Abraham Outon, Saml. Young Jr. Neice, Fanny Thornton, mother of grand neice, Emely Thornton. Inv. made Aug. 16, 1817 by John Young, Francis McBride, Jas. McAllister.

MATTISON, JOHN—BOX 67, PACK 1637:
    Will dated Mar. 1, 1834 in Abbeville Dist. Exrs: John Magee, Gabriel M. Mattison, Wm. P. Martin. Wit: Chester Kingsley, Philip Lee, Wm. P. Martin. Chn: Nancy, Gabriel M. Mattison, Mary, Theodosha Gaines. Gr. son. Benjamin, son of Benjamin Mattison decd. "That Richard, Jas. Gaines, John Mitchell do acct. etc." Wife, Gracy Mattison. Owned land in Anderson Co. Sett. made Nov. 30, 1840. Legatees: Jas. Johnson who married Julia Ann. Saml. Hodges who married Nancy. Richard Gaines who married Mary. Jas. Gaines who married Theodosha. John Magee who married Harriet C. John Mitchell who married Lucretia. John Mattison died Feb. 25, 1839.

MACKLIN, JAMES—BOX 67, PACK 1638:
Will dated Nov. 21, 1818. Proved April 19, 1820. Exrs: Son, Wm. A. Macklin, Wm. Bumpass. Wit: Geo. Rowlan, Abner Wasson. Was of Rutherford Co., Tenn. Chn: John A., David, Robt., Wm. A., Jas. S., Unice Macklin, Peggy F. Bumpass, Catharine S. Rone, Jane Overall. Est. also admnr. Sept. 19, 1820 by Capt. Hugh Macklin Sr., Wm. Ward, Jonathan Johnson bound to Moses Taggart Ord. Abbeville Dist. sum $3,000.00.

McCLINTON, ROBERT—BOX 67, PACK 1639:
Will dated Jan. 10, 1833 in Abbeville Dist. Prov. May 6, 1833. Exrs: Son, Mathew McClinton, John Chiles. Wit: Jas. M. Chiles, Franklin Norwood, Josiah Drinkwater. Chn: Mathew, John McClinton, Elizabeth Stover. Expend: Nov. 27, 1838 paid John Stover $4.00.

McMILLAN, ANDREW—BOX 67, PACK 1640:
Will dated Feb. 24, 1832 in Abbeville Dist. Proved April 12, 1832. Exrs: Wife, Susannah. Son, Robt. Mathews McMillan. s.l. Hamilton Wiley. Wit: Washington Belcher, Wm. Harris, Adam Wideman. Chn: Andrew, Randolph, Robt. M. McMillan.

McCOMB, ROBERT, SR.—BOX 67, PACK 1642:
Will dated Nov. 15, 1833 in Abbeville Dist. Proved April 1, 1834. Exrs: Sons, Joseph, Robt. McCombs, John Pressly. Wit: Andrew Weed, John Glasgow, Elizabeth McComb. Wife, Mary McComb. Chn: Joseph, Robt., Polly McComb, Martha Laughlin. Cit. ment. legatees: Ann, Rebecca, Mary, Elizabeht, Joseph, Robt. McComb, Alexr. Laughlin and wife, Martha.

McADAMS, JOHN—BOX 67, PACK 1643:
Est. admnr. Jan. 12, 1835 by John McAdams, Lemuel W. Tribble, Lydall Williams, John E. Ellis bound to Moses Taggart Ord. Abbeville Dist. sum $10,000.00. Cit. pub. at Turkey Creek Church. Heirs: John, Robt., James Jones McAdams, Jas. Fisher and wife Polly, Lemuel W. Tribble was gdn. of Nancy, Emily, Jas. R., Stephen, Saml. W., Ezekiel, John Tribble. Geo. Grubbs and wife Polly Ann. John Wright and wife, Drusilla. Archibald Mattison and wife Sarah. Masten Shirley and wife Rachel. Thos. Davis and wife Jane, Elizabeth, Rebecca, and wid. Sarah McAdams.

McGREGOR, JANE—BOX 67, PACK 1644:
Est. admnr. Sept. 6, 1836 by Joseph Foster, Leroy Watson, Joseph Norrel bound to Moses Taggart Ord. Abbeville Dist. sum $1,000.00. Cit. pub. at Rocky Creek Church. Joseph Foster next of kin.

McDERMONDS AND WINTERS—BOX 67, PACK 1645:
On Nov. 12, 1819 Dr. Nathaniel Harris made suit for Letters of Admnr. on estates of Daniel McDermond and Adolphus Winters decd. Est. admnr. Nov. 14, 1819 by Dr. Nathaniel Harris, Wm., Alexr. Noble bound to Moses Taggart Ord. Abbeville Dist. sum $800.00.

McCOMB, WILLIAM—BOX 67, PACK 1646:
Will dated Jan. 13, 1837 in Abbeville Dist. Proved July 25, 1837. Exrs:

Wife, Hannah McComb, Thos. Crawford, Saml. Reid. Wit: Saml., Mary Mc-
Ilwain, Elizabeth Stevenson. Chn: Jas., Mary Ann, Nancy, Rebecca, Eliza,
Hannah, Mariah, Wm., John McComb.

McMASTER, WILLIAM—BOX 67, PACK 1647:
Will dated Nov. 24, 1823. Proved Mar. 18, 1824. No. Exr. Wit: Jona-
than Thornton. Wife, Rebecca McMaster. Chn: Rachel, Martha B., Susannah
T. Thornton. Sanford Thornton was a legatee.

McNEIL, JANE—BOX 67, PACK 1648:
Will dated May 14, 1824 in Abbeville Dist. Proved June 7, 1824. Exr:
Son, John McNeil. Wit: Frances More, John, Matthew McNeil. "My first
husband's chn. Wm., Andrew, Jeon, Thos., Elizabeth, Mary. My chn: John,
Mathew McNeil, Maria Spence, Jane Meanes decd., Margaret, Jane, Sarah
McMillin." Inv. made June 22, 1824 by Wm. Covington, Thos. Montgomery,
Geo. Haslet.

MERIWETHER, JOHN L.—BOX 67, PACK 1649:
Est. admnr. Sept. 5, 1831 by John Bowie, Saml. Watt, Alexr. C. Hamilton
bound to Moses Taggart Ord. Abbeville Dist. sum $3,000.00. Cit. pub. at
Damascus Church.

MAXWELL, DR. GEORGE—BOX 67, PACK 1650:
Est. admnr. Mar. 21, 1821 by Col. Edmond Ware, Robt. Kay, Larkin
Gaines bound to Moses Taggart Ord. Abbeville Dist. sum $1,000.00. Inv. made
April 1822 by Thos. Moore, Wm. Robinson, Wm. Henderson Sr.

McDOW, ROBERT—BOX 67, PACK 1651:
Est. admnr. April 24, 1829 by Andrew Gillespie Sr., Joseph S. English,
Jas. Huey bound to Moses Taggart Ord. Abbeville Dist. sum $2,000.00. Cit.
pub. at Lebanon Church. June 16, 1830 paid Thos. McDow share of his
brother's est. $14.57¾. Jas. McDow $14.57¾. Wm. McDow, Jane McMeen
their share $29.15½. Mrs. Agness Livingston's share $14.57¾. John McDow
his share $15.04½.

McILWAIN, SAMUEL—BOX 67, PACK 1652:
Est. admnr. May 3, 1830 by Thos. McIlwain, Wm. Morrison, Edward
Haggan bound to Moses Taggart Ord. Abbeville Dist. sum $1,000.00. Cit. pub.
at Upper Long Cane Church. Sale, Jan. 1, 1831. Byrs: Thos., Wm., Hugh Mc-
Ilwain, Wm. Morrison, John Logan.

McDONALD, WILLIAM—BOX 68, PACK 1653:
Will dated Oct. 11, 1825 in Abbeville Dist. Proved Nov. 4, 1825. Exr:
Wm. Patton. Wit: Jas., Wm. Patton, A. Kennedy. Brother, Robt. McDonald.
Sisters: Molly Falkner, Jean, wife of John Brady. "Bequeath to Wm. McDonald
Patton, son of Jas. Patton, to Wm. McDonald, son of John McDonald, to Wm.
Patton, son of John Patton decd., to Molly wid of John McDonald."

MARTIN, REVD. CHARLES W.—BOX 68, PACK 1654:
Est. admnr. Oct. 5, 1840 by Jacob, Benjamin Yancey Martin, Andrew

Giles bound to Moses Taggart Ord. Abbeville Dist. sum $20,000.00.   Brother to
Benjamin Y. Martin.

McCURRY, STEPHEN—BOX 68, PACK 1655:
Will dated Dec. 29, 1840 in Abbeville Dist. Proved Jan. 4, 1841. Exr:
Sterling Bowen. Wit: Joseph F. Bell, J. H. Baskin, John McCurry. Wife, Gincy
McCurry. Chn. ment. no names given.

MOTT, WILLIAM S.—BOX 68, PACK 1656:
Est. admnr. April 5, 1841 by John Irwin, Mathew Campbell, Thos. A.
Cobb bound to Moses Taggart Ord. Abbeville Dist. sum $500.00. Sett. ment.
that the decd. was an illegitimate and left no wife or chn.

MATHEW, MINORS—BOX 68, PACK 1657:
On July 12, 1830 David, John Mathews, Saml. Cowan bound to Moses
Taggart Ord. Abbeville Dist. sum $600.00. David Mathis made gdn. of Easter
Ann, Sarah Mathis minors of David Mathis over 14 yrs. (Written Mathew,
Mathis.)

MAYS, MINORS—BOX 68, PACK 1658:
On Oct. 14, 1840 Benjamin, John Rosamond, Felix Rogers bound to
Moses Taggart Ord. Abbeville Dist. sum $2,000.00. Benjamin Rosamond made
gdn. of Lethe, Jessy, Abner Mays minors of Abner Mays decd. 1841 Recd. of
Mathew Mays, admnr. of S. Whitty decd., who was gdn. of above chn.

MURPHEY, MARGARET—BOX 68, PACK 1659:
Will dated Oct. 19, 1841 in Abbeville Dist. Proved Mar. 19, 1842. Exrs:
John E. Ellis, Abram Haddon. Wit: Geo. Brownlee, Lydell Williams, Ebenezer
E. Pressly. Chn: John, Wm., Mary, Easther Murphey. Expend: Legatees: Jas.
Rodgers, Jas. Cooper, Robt. Smith, Henry Leland Murphey, John Mason Mur-
phey. On Sept. 4, 1843 Henry L. Murphey was living in Shelby Co., Tenn.
(Letter)
State of Tennessee, Typton County August 12th 1844
Dear brother it is with great pleasure I take this present privilege of
addressing you with these lines to let you know that my self and Margaret are
well at this time hoping these few lines may find you enjoying the same blessing
your letter came to hand on the 6th of this instance their is very little sickness
in the neighborhood there is some cases of chills and fever the friends are generally well Mason was hear about three weeks ago he is now teaching school I
saw Clarinda last saturday she was well John *Hamrcks* family is well he is gone
to marry at this time with Jane S. *Abnrmother* and family is well there is fine
crops of corn and wheat made in this neighborhood cotton is not so good on
account of the rust the Mississippi river have been very high for some time
higher than it has ever been known it has fell some there has been a great
destruction of crops and property and dwellings swept away and lives of people
destroyed Parson J. Wilson is well and sends his respects to you nothing more
at present but remains your brother until death give my respects to my aunts
and Margaret the same and receive the same yourself and to John McCann and

all enquiring frieds. Jas. A. Cooper, Margaret Cooper.

Margaret Murphey was the grandmother of Clarinda Smith, Mahalah, Jos. Rodgers.

MORGAN, NANCY—BOX 68, PACK 1660:

Est. admnr. Oct. 24, 1842 by John Morgan, Wm. Buchanan, John Turner bound to David Lesly Ord. Abbeville Dist. sum $3,200.00. Mother of John Morgan. Sett. Jan. 18, 1844. Present, John, Thos. Morgan. M. Morgan is in Miss. Martin Setzler who married Mary Morgan who is dead leaving 2 chn.

MAYS, MATHEW—BOX 68, PACK 1661:

On June 24, 1842 Medy Mays sheweth that his father Mathew Mays decd. left a wid., Lucretia Mays, and 13 living chn. Sett. made Feb. 7, 1845. Present: Medy, Henry, Larkin, Lucretia Mays wid. Thos. Rosamond and wife, Sarah. Elihu Campbell who married Emeline, she died leaving no chn. Stephen Whitty and wife Elizabeth. Elias T. Graham and wife Caroline. Enoch Carter and wife Nancy. Daniel, Abner, Jane, Tibitha, Lucretia Mays were minors.

MARTIN, NANCY—BOX 68, PACK 1662:

Will dated June 3, 1842. in Abbeville Dist. Proved June 8, 1842. Exr: Dr. Franklin Branch. Wit: Peter Gibert, Thos. A. Benning, F. Branch. Wid. of Geo. Washington Martin decd. Chn: Wm. Bird Martin of Ala., John Benning Martin, Martha Sarah Ann Chiles, America Rowenna Eliza Haddon, Indiana Martin. Gr. dtr. Arabella Frances Chiles.

MORAGNE, PETER F.—BOX 68, PACK 1663:

On April 7, 1842 Mary Ann Moragne. Joseph Bouchillon Sr. were admnrs. Sett. made Jan. 31, 1844. Present: Joseph Bouchillon, Mary Ann Moragne wid. and gdn. of Wm. Francis, Emma, Caroline. Placedia Moragne. Peter F. Moragne died Feb. 21, 1842.

MOSELEY, BENJAMIN—BOX 68, PACK 1664:

Est. admnr. Oct. 31, 1842 by Gabriel M. Mattison, Noah R. Reeves, Wm. Moseley bound to David Lesly Ord. Abbeville Dist. sum $3,000.00. Left 2 sons but no wid. Sale, Nov. 17, 1842. Byrs: Marinda, John E., Wm. Moseley, Lewis Pyles, etc.

MANN, GILBERT M.—BOX 68, PACK 1665:

Est. admnr. Jan. 26, 1843 by Robt., John G. Mann, David Robison bound to David Lesly Ord. Abbeville Dist. sum $100.00. Left no wife. Was father of Robt. Mann.

McGILL, JOHN—BOX 68, PACK 1666:

Est. admnr. Feb. 11, 1843 by David Robison, Jas. S. Wilson, Thos. Gordon bound to David Lesly Ord. Abbeville Dist. sum $400.00. Wid. Jane McGill. s.l. of David Robison. On Jan. 23, 1846 Jane McMill recd. $11.43 of a note on Jas., Wm. McGill.

McGILL, JOHN T.—BOX 68, PACK 1667:

On Feb. 13, 1844 Jane McGill, David Robison, Johnson E. Sharp bound

ABBEVILLE DISTRICT WILLS AND BONDS   233

to David Lesly Ord. Abbeville Dist. sum $215.58. Died in 1842 leaving a wid.
Jane and a posthumous child John Thos. McGill.

MOORE, ROSA—BOX 68, PACK 1668:
    Will dated Mar. 12, 1839 in Abbeville Dist. Proved Aug. 24, 1843. Exr:
Son, Wm. A. Moore. Wit: David W. McCants, Saml., Wm. Graham Sr. Chn:
Joseph, Wm. A., John Moore, Mary Roland, Nancy Arnold, Jane Davenport,
Caroline Graham, Rosa Ann Holloway. Gr. chn: Jane, Joseph, John T. Hollo-
way.

McDILL, THOMAS—BOX 68, PACK 1669:
    Will dated April 8, 1843 in Abbeville Dist. Proved July 14, 1843. Exr:
Son, Thos. McDill. Wit: David M. Wardlaw, Geo. J. Cannon, *Vina* or *Nina*
Anderson. Wife, Jane McDill. Chn: Wm., Thos. R., Jane McGill, Molly Lagron
decd. Gr. chn: Rebecca, Mary Lagron. Sett. made Jan. 5, 1847 named John H.
Hutchison only son of Jane.

McCORMICK, MARTHA—BOX 68, PACK 1670:
    Will dated July 18, 1843 in Abbeville Dist. Proved Oct. 24, 1843. Exr:
Son, Isaiah McCormick. Wit: Saml. Marshall, Charles Sproull, John R. Martin.

MOORE, WILLIAM A.—BOX 68, PACK 1671:
    Will dated July 17, 1843 in Abbeville Dist. Proved Nov. 15, 1843. Exrs:
Son, John W. Moore. s.l. David W. McCants. Wit: Joel Smith, Williston W.
Franklin, Wm. Graham. Wm. Andrew, Jane Elizabeth, John Washington,
Oliver Jas., Augustus Wesley Moore, Telitha Ann McCants, Lucinda Calvert,
Docitheras Clayton. Wife, Lucy Moore. He died Oct. 1843. May 6, 1845 Recd.
by sett. of Rosa Moore decd. the legacy of Wm. A. Moore decd. $184.53.

MARS, MINORS—BOX 68, PACK 1672:
    On Dec. 9, 1843 John A. Mars, John, Adam Wideman bound to David
Lesly Ord. Abbeville Dist. sum $600.00. John A. Mars made gdn. of *Lodeski*
Adeline, Mary E. Mars minors of John A. Mars. Gr. father, Adam Wideman.
Feb. 16, 1847 Alfred R. Roberts and wife Mary E. Mars recd. $187.27 from
est of Adam Wideman. Oct. 7, 1844 Wm. Gray and wife L. Adeline Mars recd.
$166.26. Dec. 9, 1843 John A. Mars states that his wife was Elizabeth Wideman
now decd.

MARTIN, JOHN—BOX 68, PACK 1673:
    Est. admnr. Jan. 2, 1843 by Robt. Martin, Jas. Cowan, Wm. Dunn
bound to David Lesly Ord. Abbeville Dist. sum $1,000.00. Wid. Sarah Martin.
Chn: Robt., Wm., Jas., Elizabeth, Saml., Nancy Martin. Sally married Andrew
Webb had 2 chn. and since dead, and also John. Wm. Richey Sr. a distributee.

McDOWELL, DR. PATRICK—BOX 68, PACK 1674:
    Est. admnr. June 3, 1844 by Joel, Charles Smith, Robt. Y. Jones bound
to David Lesly Ord. Abbeville Dist. sum $16,000.00. Wid. Nancy N. Mc-
Dowell. Chn: Jas. A., Geo. M., Patrick H., Edwin H. McDowell.

MORRIS, SAMUEL—BOX 68, PACK 1675:
Will dated July 30, 1841 in Abbeville Dist. Proved Aug. 17, 1841. Exrs: Archibald Kennedy, Dr. Geo. W. Pressly. Wit: Henry Fosbrook, John Ruff, John Riley. Wife, Margaret Morris. Chn: Louisa M., Jas. H., Elizabeth, Sarah Jane, Saml. Morris, Mariah N. C. Martin. Sett. 1845. Mary Louisa was wife of Wm. Gibson. Saml. Morris in Ala. Robt. A. Martin married Caroline.

MATTISON, MINORS—BOX 68, PACK 1676:
On Dec. 26, 1840 Archibald Mattison, John E. Ellis, Jas. Wright bound to Moses Taggart Ord. Abbeville Dist. sum $500.00. Archibald Mattison made gdn. of Polly Ann Catharine, Peggy M., Archibald N. Mattison minors under 14 yrs. On Dec. 21, 1846 made gdn. of Jas A., Olley N., Geo. F. Mattison minors over 14 yrs. Nancy Crowther decd. left a small est. to said minors.

MATHISON, HICKERSON—BOX 68, PACK 1677:
Est. admnr. Feb. 16, 1841 by Major Armstead Burt, John F. Livingston, Thos. Thompson bound to Moses Taggart Ord. Abbeville Dist. sum $1,000.00.

McILWAIN, THOMAS—BOX 68, PACK 1678:
On Nov. 14, 1840 John, Wm., Jas. McIlwain bound to Moses Taggart Ord. Abbeville Dist. sum $2,000.00. John McIlwain made gdn. Wm., Edward, Jane, Mary, Andrew McIlwain minors of Thos. McIlwain decd. Mrs. Jane McIlwain's share $1,874.22. Sett. ment. 8 distributees, no names given.

MORGAN, THOMAS M.—BOX 68, PACK 1679:
On Jan. 1, 1838 Francis Atkins, Wm. Anderson, Abraham Lites bound to Moses Taggart Ord. Abbeville Dist. sum $5,000.00. Francis Atkins made gdn. of Thos. Morgan a minor. Jan. 22, 1838 Recd. from John Morgan $918.58.

MILLER, SAMUEL—BOX 69, PACK 1680:
Will dated Sept. 21, 1840 in Abbeville Dist. Proved Mar. 5, 1845. Exrs: John, Alexr. Miller, John Webb. Wit: John, Saml. Donald, Wm. Hill. Chn: John, Robt. Miller, Elizabeth, wife of John Webb, Margaret decd. wife of John Brown. Gr. chn: Emily, Saml. Webb, Alexr. Miller, Elizabeth, dtr. of my gr. son, Alexr. Miller, Jane Brown. Power of Atty. Stephen Davidson and wife, Catharine Brown, dtr. of Margaret Brown decd., Jas. H. McQuern and wife, Nancy, dtr. of Margaret Brown late wife of John Brown of Clinton Co., Indiana sheweth that Margaret Brown decd. was a dtr. of Saml., Jane Miller of Abbeville Dist. Stephen, Catharine Davidson was of Fulton Co. Dated this June 17, 1847. Saml. M. Brown, Joseph, Elizabeth D. Fickle, his wife formerly Elizabeth D. Brown, dtr. of Margaret Brown decd. were of Clinton Co., Indiana. On May 25, 1846 Saml., Wm. M. Miller recd. of his father Robert M. Miller $100.00 from their gr. father's est. Saml. Miller. Were of Mercer Co., Ill. Robt. M. Miller had 8 chn: Jane wife of Isaac Fickle, Nancy B. D. wife of John W. Deal, John R., Saml., Margaret, Robt., Mary E., Wm. McCrone Miller.

MILLER, SAMUEL—BOX 69, PACK 1681:
Est. admnr. Dec. 2, 1844 by Lewis D. Merryman, John R. Tarrant,

Tarleton P. Moseley bound to David Lesly Ord. Abbeville Dist. sum $1,000.00. Left a wid. Susan and several chn. of Cokesburry, S. C. Inv. made Dec. 27, 1844 by Gabriel Hodges, Charles Smith, Thos. W. Williams.

McCALISTER, JAMES W.—BOX 69, PACK 1682:
Est. admnr. Oct. 24, 1844 by Lydia W. McCalister, Wm. McWhorter bound to David Lesly Ord. Abbeville Dist. sum $200.00. Left a wid. Lydia McCalister and several chn.

MOORE, JAMES—BOX 69, PACK 1683:
Est. admnr. Dec. 23, 1844 by Saml. Donnald, Wm. Hill, J. W. Agnew bound to David Lesly Ord., sum $500.00. Left a wid. Mary and several chn.

MOORE, JANE E., MINOR—BOX 69, PACK 1684:
Est. admnr. Jan. 25, 1845 by Wm. A., John W. Moore, David W. McCants, bound to David Lesly Ord. sum $2,000.00. Was a minor legatee to Wm. A. Moore decd. and a sis. to Wm. A. Moore. Sett. made Dec. 18, 1846 named 8 distributees vis. Wm. A., John, A. W., Jas. M. Calvert, O. J., D. C., Lucy Moore, David McCants, Jas. W. Calvert.

MOSELEY, BURREL—BOX 69, PACK 1685:
Est. admnr. Oct. 21, 1844 by G. M. Mattison, Geo. Richey, Robt. Wood, bound to David Lesly Ord., sum $3,000.00. Left a wid. Jane and 5 chn.

MOTES, TYLER—BOX 69, PACK 1686:
Est. admnr. Feb. 11, 1844 by Thos. C. Lipscomb, Saml. McGowan, John White, bound to David Lesly Ord., sum $500.00. Left no wife or chn. but a mother and bros.

MAYS, LUCRETIA—BOX 69, PACK 1687:
Est. admnr. Mar. 1, 1845 by Larkin, Medy, Jr., Mays, Thos. Rosamond, bound to David Lesly Ord., sum $5,000.00. Mother of Medy Mays, Jr.

MORRIS, MINORS—BOX 69, PACK 1688:
On Nov. 1, 1844 Margaret Morris, Archibald Kennedy, Geo. W. Pressly, bound to David Lesly Ord., sum $6,000.00. Margaret Morris made gdn. of Elizabeth, Jas. H., Sarah J. Morris, minors of Margaret Morris and Saml. Morris decd. On Oct. 24, 1860 Sarah J. was wife of J. A. Myers.

MANN, JONATHAN C.—BOX 69, PACK 1689:
Est. admnr. Mar. 17, 1845 by Gilbert C. Mann, Isaac Hobart, bound to David Lesly Ord., sum $100.00. "He died upwards of 20 yrs. ago but no admnr. had taken place until now."

McBRIDE, JANE—BOX 69, PACK 1690:
Will dated May 29, 1839 in Abbeville Dist. Proved July 1, 1839. Exrs: Archibald Bradley, Josiah McGaw. Wit: John Kennedy, Jas. Richey, Saml. Young. Bro. 1., Thos. C. McBride and wife Jane McBride. "Give to John Faulkner and wife, Mary, my sis. niece, Margaret Hutchson McBride." Expend. Recd. of Saml. McBride $3.12½.

MAYS, ABNER—BOX 69, PACK 1691:
On Feb. 7, 1845, Medy, Jr., Larkin Mays, Felix Rogers, bound to David Lesly Ord., sum $370.00. Medy Mays made gdn. of Abner Mays minor, under 14 yrs.

MAYS, JESSE—BOX 69, PACK 1692:
On Feb. 7, 1845 Felix Rogers, Wm. Hodges, Medy Mays, Jr., bound to David Lesly Ord., sum $370.00. Felix Rogers made gdn. of Jesse Mays a minor.

MANN, MINORS—BOX 69, PACK 1693:
On Nov. 2, 1840 Ezekiel Tribble, John B. Black, Sterling Bowen bound to Moses Taggart Ord., sum $2,000.00. Ezekiel Tribble made gdn. of Rhoda Elizabeth, Evan Whitfield Mann minors under 21 yrs.

McCLANE, MARY—BOX 69, PACK 1694:
Est. admnr. May 5, 1845 by Andw. McClane, Jos. C. Mathews, N. M. Strickland bound to David Lesly Ord., sum $80.00. Andw. McClane states that his sis. Mary McClane died many years ago a lunatic without issue.

McKITRICK, LUCRETIA—BOX 69, PACK 1695:
On May 8, 1845 the petition of Jas. F. Hoskison states that his father, Jas. Hoskison died many yrs. ago. That afterwards his mother, Lucretia, married Benj. McKitrick.

NELSON, HENRY—BOX 69, PACK 1696:
Est. admnr. Jan. 2, 1837 by Wm., Enoch Nelson, Saml. Jordon, Dewie E. Lipford, bound to Moses Taggart Ord., sum $50,000.00. Cit. pub at Long Cane Ch.

NOBLE, REBECCA—BOX 69, PACK 1697:
Est. admnr. Mar. 16, 1831 by Wm. P., Patrick Noble, bound to Moses Taggart Ord., sum $7,000.00. Sett. made Mar. 21, 1831. Andw. A. Noble's sh. $463.76. Saml. Noble's sh. $463.76. Ezekiel and Jos. Noble's sh. $463.76.

NASH, DR. JOHN J.—Box 69, PACK 1698:
Est. admnr. Feb. 15, 1833 by John Weatherall, Sr., Joel Smith, John F. Gray, bound to Moses Taggart Ord., sum $10,000.00. Mrs. Margaret Nash bought at sale.

NORRIS, ANN—BOX 69, PACK 1699:
Est. admnr. Feb. 17, 1829 by Barthw. Jordan, Jos. Davis, Esq., Col. Jas. Devlin, bound to Moses Taggart Ord., sum $10,000.00. Cit. pub. at Cedar Springs Ch. Legatees: Elisa, Ezekiel, Robt. Norris.

NIX, THOMAS—BOX 69, PACK 1700:
Est. admnr. Nov. 30, 1833 by Dearest Nix, wid., John A. Donald, Andw. J. Weems, bound to Moses Taggart Ord., sum $2,000.00. Cit. pub. at Asbury Chapel. On Aug. 24, 1846 Lucy West Carter and husband, Asa Carter, Mary, Edward Nix of Jasper Co., Miss. appointed John D. Nix their Atty. to collect their shares of Thos. L. Nick's est. in Abbeville, S. C.

NORTHCUT, BENJAMIN—BOX 69, PACK 1701:
Will dated Mar. 22, 1832 in Abbeville Dist. Prov. Dec. 8, 1834. Exrs:
Wm. Mattison, Noah Cobb. Wit: Elijah Wyatt, Geo. Mattison, Alexr. E. Kary.
Wife, Lettice Northcut. Chn: Syntha, Matilda, Mahala, Priscilla Posey, Lettice
Petty, Polly Smith, Malinda Donaldson, wife of Jacob Donaldson. s.l: Noah
Cobb, Andw. Richey.

NORRELL, JACOB—BOX 69, PACK 1702:
Est. admnr. Feb. 23, 1832 by Jas. Gillam, Wm. P. Hatter, John Bowie,
bound to Moses Taggart Ord., sum $1,000.00. John Norrell bought at sale.

NOBLE, MAJOR ALEXANDER—BOX 69, PACK 1703:
Est. admnr. Feb. 13, 1804 by Wm. Noble, Geo. Bowie, Esq., bound to
Andw. Hamilton Ord., sum $10,000.00. Expend: Apr. 23, 1802 paid Rev.
Moses Waddel for tuition of Patrick Noble $21.25. For tuition of Jos. Noble
$13.12½. Mar. 8, 1808 paid Ezekiel Noble $130.91. Sale, Oct. 22, 1804. Byrs:
Wm., Jane, Jas. Ezekiel Noble, Wm. Calhoun, etc.

NOBLE, DR. JOHN L.—BOX 69, PACK 1704:
Will dated May 26, 1816. Prov. Sept. 23, 1816. Exrs: Patrick Calhoun,
John Baskin. Wit: Patrick Noble, Esq., Jas. Calhoun, Jos. Hutton. Sis: Mary,
wife of Thos. S. Baskin, Sarah Baskin. Nephew: Jas. Noble. Sis: 1, Betty Noble.

NORWOOD, ISHAM—BOX 69, PACK 1705:
Est. admnr. Oct. 10, 1817 by Allen Glover, Harrison Waites, Thos.
Harrison, bound to Taliaferro Livingston Ord., sum 10,000 lbs. Sett. made
Nov. 8, 1843. Elizabeth Norwood now wife of J. J. Lipford.

NOBLE, ALEXANDER—BOX 70, PACK 1706:
Est. admnr. Apr. 13, 1821 by Nathaniel Harris, Patrick, Ezekiel, Wm.
Noble, bound to Moses Taggart Ord., sum $20,000.00. Cit. pub. at Willington
Ch. Expend. Oct. 18, 1822 paid Mary H. Noble $200.00.

NOBLE, JAMES, SR.—BOX 70, PACK 1707:
Will dated Nov. 5, 1796 in Abbeville Dist. Rec. Nov. 8, 1796. Exrs:
Bro. Alexr. Noble, Jos. Calhoun. Wit: Fleming Bates, Wm. Noble, Nancy
McFarland. Wife, Mary Ann Noble. Chn: Jas., John, Mary, Sarah Noble.

NOBLE, JAMES L.—BOX 70, PACK 1708:
Est. admnr. Aug. 30, 1814 by Elizabeth, Dr. John L. Noble, Jas. Pat-
rick Calhoun, bound to Taliaferro Livingston Ord., sum $15,000.00. Inv. made
Sept. 29, 1814 by Patrick, Wm., Jos., Calhoun, Jos. Hutton.

NORRELL, JAMES—BOX 70, PACK 1709:
Will dated Aug. 12, 1779, in 96 Dist. Probated Apr. 26, 1782. Exrs:
Wife, Mary Norrell, Nathaniel Spraggins, Esq., Son, Isaac Norrell. Wit:
Richard Allison, Wm. Anderson, Saml. Abney. Wife, Mary Norrell. Chn:
Isaac, Levy, Jacob, Jas., Martha, Elizabeth, Mary Norrell.

NORWOOD, SAML.—BOX 70, PACK 1710:
Will dated Nov. 16, 1789 in 96 Dist. Prov. Oct. 5, 1790. Exrs: Adam
Crain Jones, Esq., Jas. Watts. Wit: Adam Crain Jones, Jr., John Jones,
John Langerds. Wife, Elizabeth Norwood. Chn: John, Thos., Blakely, Wm.,
Robt., Jos., Theophilus Norwood, Elizabeth Porter, Agnes Watts, Mary Watts.
Gr. chn: Saml., John, Richard Norwood, sons of Theophilus Norwood. "Owned
land in Pendleton Co."

NORRIS, WILLIAM—BOX 70, PACK 1711:
Will dated Feb. 10, 1781 in 96 District. Prov. Oct. 18, 1782. Exrs:
Wife, Agness Norris, John Fedrick. Wit: Howell Johnston, Elizabeth Norris,
Jos. Abel. Wife, Agness Norris. Chn. ment., no names given.

NORRIS, WILLIAM—BOX 70, PACK 1712:
Will dated Feb. 7, 1818 in Abbeville Dist. Prov. June 1, 1818. Exrs:
Wife, Mary Norris, Jas. Devlin, Jr. Wit: John Devlin, John Eales, John Hender-
son. Wife, Mary Norris. Chn: Betey, John, Jean Norris. "Will that Jean T.
Lesley live with my wife until she comes of age, etc."

NORRIS, WILLIAM—BOX 70, PACK 1713:
Est. admnr. May 21, 1827 by Jesse S. Adams, Chas. Neely, Luke Mathis,
bound to Moses Taggart Ord., sum $10,000.00.

NORRIS, WILLIAM—BOX 70, PACK 1714:
Will dated Oct. 27, 1803. Rec. Dec. 30, 1803. Exrs: Wife, Athaiah
Norris, Walter Manning. Wit: Henry Gaines, Walter Manning, Wm. Sims.
Chn: Hesikiah, Eley, Alexr. Norris.

NOBLE, JOHN—BOX 70, PACK 1715:
Est. admnr. Apr. 27, 1782 by Benj. Tutt, Wm. Moore, Jos. Towles,
bound to John Ewing Calhoun Ord., 96 Dist., sum $2,000.00. Benj. Tutt was
of Cuffetown.

NEELY, WILLIAM—BOX 70, PACK 1716:
Will dated Sept. 6, 1821. Prov. Feb. 4, 1822. Exrs: Wife, Polly Neely,
sons, Chas., Wm. L. Neely. Wit: Jas. Franklin, Alexr. Sample, Robt. Bartrim.
Wife, Polly Neely. Chn: Jubelous, Sanders, Beauford, Oswell, Judah, Chas.,
Wm. L. Neely. "Sally Samuels shall have bed and furniture."

NASH, COL. REUBEN—BOX 70, PACK 1717:
Est. admnr. June 3, 1822 by John, Valentine Nash, Wm. Ware, Henry
Delph, bound to Moses Taggart Ord., sum $5,000.00. Inv. made July 25, 1822
by Wm. Long, Esq., Edmond Ware, Esq., Wm. Mattison, John Seawright,
Wm. Richey.

NORRIS, JAMES—BOX 70, PACK 1718:
Est. admnr. Feb. 12, 1816 by John E. Norris, Jas. Cochran, Esq., Jos.
Cooper, bound to Taliaferro Livingston Ord., sum 10,000 lbs. Sale, Feb. 29,
1816. Byrs: Anna Norris, Saml. H. Owen, etc.

NICHOLS, JULIUS—BOX 70, PACK 1719:
Will dated Jan. 23, 1803 in Abbeville Dist. Rec. Mar. 8, 1804. Exrs: Wife, Patty Nichols, Son, Julius Nichols. Wit: Zachary Pulliam, Jas. Johnson, Gillam Sale. Wife, Patty Nichols. Chn: Julius, Wm., Sally Nichols, Lucy Marshall. Gr. ch. the chn. of Sukey Moore, Betsey Cooper, Molley Jones, Lucy Marshall, Julius Nichols, Bobby Hunt, Wm., Thos. Nichols.

NASH, JOHN—BOX 70, PACK 1720:
Will dated Oct. 20, 1794 in Abbeville Dist. Rec. Mar. 25, 1795. Exrs: Wife, Polly Harrison, Sons, Reuben, Abner, Ezekiel Nash. Wit: Wm., John White, Jas. Smith. Wife, Polly Harrison. Chn: Reuben, Abner, Ezekiel, Nimrod, Theodoshe, Melinda, Lucinda, Mertilday Nash, Betty Evans. Inv. made July 8, 1795 by Robt. Elgin, Nicholas Long, Jas. Kay.

NORWOOD, THEOPHILUS—BOX 70, PACK 1721:
Will dated Apr. 13, 1787. Prov. July 9, 1789. Exrs: John Middleton, Saml. Porter. Wit: Saml. Norwood, John Middleton. Wife, Elener Norwood. Chn: Saml., Richard, John Middleton Norwood.

NORWOOD, GENL. JOHN—BOX 70, PACK 1722:
Will dated Jan. 22, 1798 in Abbeville Dist. Rec. Mar. 26, 1798. Exrs: John Miller, Hugh Reid, Wm. Cunningham. Wit: Robt. Wilson, Jas. Watts, Wm. Russell. Wife, no name given. Chn: Andw., Daniel, Wm., Theophilus, John, Saml. Norwood, Jean Gutherie.

NIXON, EDWARD—BOX 70, PACK 1723:
Inv. made Feb. 20, 1786 by Nathaniel Davis, Philip Anderson, John Inlow. (No other papers.)

NICHOLS, JOHN—BOX 70, PACK 1724:
Est. admnr. Apr. 3, 1784 by Joshua Petty, Zachariah Bullock, bound to John Thomas Ord. 96 Dist., sum 2,000 lbs. Inv. made May 31, 1804 by Jas., Zachary Pulliam, Jas. Johnson.

NEALE, ANDREW—BOX 70, PACK 1725:
Wm. Beneson was admnr. Lived in 96 Dist. Inv. made Aug. 16, 1783 by Thos. Watt, Jas. Mulwee, Robt. Gibson. (No other papers.)

NAIL, JOHN—BOX 70, PACK 1726:
Est. admnr. Apr. 26, 1784 by Geo. Miller, Leonard Nobles, Wm. Nichols, bound to John Thomas, Jr. Ord. 96 Dist., sum 2,000 lbs. Inv. made June 25, 1784 by Wm. Nichols, Leonard Nobles, Frederick Tillman.

NICHOLS, GEORGE—BOX 70, PACK 1727:
Est. admnr. Oct. 10, 1786 by Jas. Lee, Wm., John Smith, bound to John Thomas Ord., sum 1,000 lbs. Inv. made Oct. 14, 1786 by Wm. Plummer, Raney Belue, Geo. Harland Hatter. Sale, Nov. 7, 1786. Byrs: Margery, Nancy, Elenor Nichols, etc.

NORRIS, WILSON—BOX 70, PACK 1728:
Will dated Mar. 30, 1812 in Abbeville Dist. Rec. Oct. 3, 1812. Exrs:
Bro., Wm. Norris, Wm. Barmore. Wit: Wm. Cullins, Jas. S. Kenrick, Alexr.
Norris. Wife, Delila Norris. Son, Henson Norris. Other chn. ment. no names
given.

NELSON, ROBERT—BOX 70, PACK 1729:
Est. admnr. May 9, 1814 by Wm. Crump, Jas. Henrick, bound to
Taliaferro Livingston Ord., sum $1,000.00. Sale, May 25, 1814. Byrs: Wm.
Crump, Jos. Nelson, etc. Money recd. from government for militia service
$26.07¼.

NORWOOD, ELIZABETH—BOX 70, PACK 1730:
Will dated Dec. 29, 1806 in Abbeville Dist. Rec. Dec. 19, 1812. Exrs:
Sons, Thos., Wm. Norwood. Wit: Jas., Sally Watts, Hugh, John Porter. Chn:
Thos., Blakely, Wm., Jos. Norwood, Betsey Porter, Anne Watts.

NIX, THOMAS decd. (MINORS)—BOX 70, PACK 1731:
On Dec. 5, 1836 John A. Donald, John Martin, Dewi E. Lipford,
bound to Moses Taggart Ord., sum $10,000.00. John Donald made gdn. of
John, Mary, Edward, Lucy, Emeline Nix, minors. On Mar. 1, 1855 Emeline
Catharine Rebecca Nix, wife of G. B. Carter, was living in Augusta, Perry Co.,
Miss. rec. $150.00 from her decd. father's est. Dearest Nix wid. of Thos.
Nix decd. Mary, Edward Nix. Asa Carter and wife Lucy were living in Jasper
Co., Miss.

NELSON, HENRY H.—BOX 70, PACK 1732:
On Jan. 22, 1838 Enoch, Wm. Nelson, Peachman Alford, bound to
Moses Taggart Ord., sum $10,000.00. Enoch Nelson made gdn. of Henry
Harvey Nelson, a minor. Son of Henry Nelson decd. Was of age in 1845.

NOBLE, PATRICK—BOX 70, PACK 1733:
Est. admnr. Apr. 27, 1840 by Wm. P., Andw. A., Ezekiel Pickens
Noble, Wm. Calhoun, bound to Moses Taggart Ord., sum $50,000.00. Patrick
Noble the father of Ezekiel Pickens Noble. Sett. made Mar. 17, 1842. Ezekiel
P. Noble was gdn. of Ed., Alexr., Saml. Noble. John Cunningham in right
of wife Floride and gdn. of Elizabeth Noble, minor. Patrick Noble died Apr. 7,
1840.

NICHOLS, WILLIAM—BOX 70, PACK 1734:
Est. admnr. Dec. 2, 1839 by Benj. Y., Jacob, John C. Martin, bound
to Moses Taggart Ord., sum $10,000.00. Expend: Nov. 10, 1839 paid expenses
in removing negroes from Athens, Ga., to Abbeville $8.00. March 1, 1841 paid
Mathew Young, Treas. of Mineral Springs $28.17.

NELSON, WILLIAM F.—BOX 70, PACK 1735:
Est. admnr. Nov. 25, 1839 by Enoch Nelson, Henly M. Lipford, Wm.
Sims, bound to Moses Taggart Ord., sum $30,000.00. Sett. made Nov. 29,

1842. J. P. Neel married Caroline M. wid. of Wm. Nelson. Mary Nelson was only child.

NOBLE, JOSEPH—BOX 71, PACK 1736:
Est. admnr. Jan. 18, 1844 by Wm. P., Andw. A., Ezekiel P. Noble, bound to David Lesly Ord., sum $12,000.00. Jos. Noble a bro. to Wm. P. Noble. Left a wid. and 1 child. Feb. 23, 1844 Recd. from E. P. Noble in full of land sold Henry Hunter of Ala. $134.42.

NICHOLS, JULIUS—BOX 71, PACK 1737:
Inv. made Aug. 6, 1842 by Geo. Marshall, Jas. F. Edwards, S. D. Ashe. Lived in Abbeville Dist. Eliza Nichols wid.

NOBLE, WILLIAM—BOX 71, PACK 1738:
Est. admnr. Apr. 30, 1824 by Rebecca, Ezekiel, Patrick Noble. bound to Moses Taggart Ord., sum $20,000.00. Inv. made July 15, 1824 by Arthur Slaughter, Thos. M. Nathaniel Harris, Meridith McGehee.

NORRIS, ELI—BOX 71, PACK 1739:
Will dated Oct. 26, 1837 in Abbeville Dist. Prov. Dec. 12, 1838. Exr: Son, Washington Norris. Wit: Wm., Mary, Enoch Barmore. Wife, Olly Norris. Chn: Huldy Blain, Westley, Washington, Tildy, Frances, Henry, Willis, Sanford, Olly, Eli Norris.

NOBLE, HARRIET A.—BOX 71, PACK 1740:
Est. admnr. May 19, 1845 by Wm. P., Andw. A. Noble, Alexr. Houston, bound to David Lesly Ord., sum $4,000.00. Harriet Adeline Noble wid. of Joseph Noble decd.

NORWOOD, JOHN—BOX 71, PACK 1741:
Will dated May 13, 1844 in Abbeville Dist. Rec. May 5, 1845. Exrs: Bro., Nathaniel Norwood, Lewis Smith, Esq. Wit: Wm. Chiles, Wm. Lyon, John Davis. Wife, Elizabeth A. Norwood. Chn: Jos., Franklin Norwood. Sett. made Sept. 15, 1846. A. J. Weems married the wid. Elizabeth A Norwood.

NORWOOD, FRANKLIN W.—BOX 71, 1742:
On May 27, 1845 the petition of Elizabeth A. Norwood sheweth that some time since Elijah Lyon departed this life leaving a will whereby he appointed John Norwood his stepson his sole Exr. who qualified and took upon himself the execution of said will; but before the provisions of the same were fully performed the said John Norwood also departed this life leaving a will in which he left his friends N. Norwood, L. Smith, Exrs.; and your petr. his wid. and infant son, Franklin W. Norwood has been left a legacy of a negro boy Ellis, which by reason of his tender years he is incapable of managing. Your petr. prays that she may become his gdn.

OSBORNE, JOHN—BOX 71, PACK 1743:
Est. admnr. Sept. 5, 1836 by Jas. Fair, Wm. Pratt, Sr., John L. Ellis, John Swilling, bound to Moses Taggart Ord., sum $10,000.00. Cit. pub. at

Little Mountain Ch. Sett. made Jan. 5, 1842. Present, the wid. Hannah Osborne, Wm. P. Hawkins and wife Caroline, Jacob M., John. Benj. F. Osborn. Absent, Wm., Jas., Geo. W. Osborn, the chn. of Sarah decd. who married Josiah Burton; the chn. of Susan Emline decd. who married John H. Emmerson. Mrs. Osborn present being gdn. of her chn: Margaret L., Martha L., Eliza B. Osborn.

OAKLEY, JOHN—BOX 71, PACK 1744:
Est. admnr. Nov. 4, 1815 by Wm. Wray, Jas. McAdams, Thos. Beaty, bound to Taliaferro Livingston Ord., sum $1,000.00. Wm. Oakley bought at sale.

OLIVER, JAMES—BOX 71, PACK 1745:
Will dated June 19, 1799. Rec. Mar. 4, 1803. Exrs: Wife, Mary Oliver, Hugh Mecklin, son of David, Wm. Woods. Wit: Anthony Malcom Elton, Wm. Curry. Wife, Mary Oliver. Chn: Jas., John, Wm., Thos., Alexr., Andw., Saml. Oliver. Dtrs. ment. no names given. Expend: Aug 1, 1807 paid John C. Oliver's legacy $52.00. Feb. 17, 1809 paid Saml. McElvaney his wife's legacy $214.28. Nathan M. Strickland and wife Mary, gdns. of Saml., Jane, and Robt. Oliver.

OWENS, JOHN—BOX 71, PACK 1746:
Will dated Aug. 19, 1774 in 96 Dist. Prov. Sept. 14, 1797. Exrs: Wm. Stuart, Jas. Seawright. Wit: Saml. Agnew, Ed. Williams, Pershanna Williams. Wife ment., no name given. Chn: Heliner Blain, Rosey, Mary, Wm., Jane, Elizabeth, Margaret Owens. (Note: When the will was prov. Ed. Williams and wife Pershanna lived in Oglethorp Co., Ga.)

ORR, WILLIAM—BOX 71, PACK 1747:
Est. admnr. Mar. 15, 1783 by Mark Love, Andw. Ross, Jas. Caldwell, Sr., bound to John Ewing Calhoun Ord., 96 Dist., sum 14,000 lbs. Mark Love of Tagger River next of kin.

OSBURN, SAMUEL—BOX 71, PACK 1748:
Est. admnr. Feb. 6, 1827 by John Lipscomb, Simon S. Bonham, bound to Moses Taggart Ord., sum $4,000.00. Cit. pub. at Mount Moriah Ch. Expend: Jan. 1, 1832 paid Elizabeth Redmond wid. of Saml. Osborne $136.50. Paid Milton Osborne $68.34. Jan. 15, 1833 paid Willis B. Cason for his wife, Parthena $73.10. Mar. 4, 1834 paid Emily Osborne $75.78.

OVERBY, ABSOLEM—BOX 71, PACK 1749:
On May 7, 1804 John Shotwell made suit for Letters of Admnr. Cit. pub. at Rocky Ck. Ch.

OWEN, JOHN—BOX 71, PACK 1750:
Will dated Feb. 28, 1826 in Abbeville Dist. Prov. Mar. 6, 1826. Exrs: Wife, Sarah Owen, Sons, Travis, Wm. Owen. Wit: John Cochran, Wm. Rowland, Jas. J. Richardson. Wife, Sarah Owen. Chn: Travis, Wm., Nancy, Martha Owen. "Eleven chn. ment. but only these given."

O'MARGY, ROBERT—BOX 71, PACK 1751:
Will dated Sept. 11, 1823 in Abbeville Dist. Prov. Jan. 5, 1824. Exrs.

Son, Robt. Margy, Harris Tiner. Wit: Saml., John Young, Daniel Faris. Wife, Martha Margy. Chn: Robt. Margy, Jean McColluch, Nancy W. McDonnald.

OSTIN, WILLIAM H.—BOX 71, PACK 1752:
On Jan. 6, 1845 Jas. Lindsay, Andw. C. Hawthorne, Saml. E. Pruitt, bound to David Lesly Ord., sum $1,000.00. Jas. Lindsay gdn. of Wm. H. Ostin a minor. His father, Saml. Ostin, died about 1828. (Name written Ostin and Austin.)

PAUL, WILLIAM—BOX 71, PACK 1753:
Est. admnr. June 11, 1824 by Jos., Robt. Foster, Jos. Conn, bound to Moses Taggart Ord., sum $3,000.00. Inv. made June 27, 1824 by Andw., Geo. Paul, David H. McClesky.

PORTER, JOHN—BOX 71, PACK 1754:
Will dated Sept. 19, 1824 in Abbeville Dist. Prov. Dec. 6, 1824. Exrs: Wife, Mary Porter, Bro.; Hugh Porter, Capt. Daniel Norwood. Wit: C. B., Andw. S., Hugh Porter, Jr. Wife, Mary Porter. Bro., Hugh Porter.
Will of another John Porter in same package. Will dated Dec. 27, 1798 in Abbeville Dist. Prov. Dec. 20, 1803. Exrs: Wife, Elizabeth Porter, James Watts. Wit: Jas. Jones, Benj. Simson, Thos. Winn. Wife, Elizabeth Porter. Chn: Saml. Norwood Porter, Hugh, John Porter. "Owned land in Winston Co. in Orangeburgh Dist. near the White Pond lying on the waters of Pond Branch and Yarrow Branch."

PUCKETT, RICHARD—BOX 71, PACK 1755:
Will dated Sept. 20, 1826. Exrs: Wife, Frankey Puckett. Son, Thos. Redin Puckett, Walter Anderson. Wit: Waid, Roberson S. Puckett. Wife, Frankey Puckett. Chn: Agness Johnson, Thos. R., Wiat W., Roberson Luland Puckett, Polly Abercrombie. S.l., Jas. McCrady. Gr. dtr. Mary Frances McCrady. Niece, Gilley Henderson.

PATTERSON, ROBERT—BOX 71, PACK 1756:
Est. admnr. Feb. 27, 1826 by Anna Patterson, Andw. Anderson, John McComb, Matthew Shanks, bound to Moses Taggart Ord., sum $1,000.00. Cit. pub. at Battallion Muster Ground near Wideman's. Inv. made Mar. 15, 1826 by Robt. McCaslan, Josiah McGaw, John Kennedy. Sale, Mar. 16, 1826. Byrs: Anna, Mary Patterson, John Young, John Stover, etc.

PATTERSON, ROBERT—BOX 71, PACK 1757:
Will dated Oct. 11, 1782 in 96 Dist. Prov. July 7, 1789. Exrs: Son, Geo. Patterson. Wit: Pierre Regnier, Peter, Elizabeth Gibert. Wife ment., no name given. Chn: Geo., Jas., Robt., Sally, Annie Patterson. Inv. made May 12, 1790 by Thos. Hughes, John R. Ragland, John Sharp.

PITMAN, BURGESS—BOX 71, PACK 1758:
Est. admnr. Nov. 19, 1819 by John, Jas. Glasgow, Wm. McDonnald, Sr., Jas. McAlister, bound to Moses Taggart Ord., sum $7,000.00. Cit. pub. at

Hopewell Ch. Expend: Dec. 18, 1826 paid Burgess Pitman for Mary Pitman $12.50. 1827 paid Burgess Pitman, Jr. $16.00. Paid Dr. Pressly for use of est. of Mary Pitman $105.75. By a note on Peter, H. M. Pitman $8.06¼.

PATTERSON, WILLIAM—BOX 72, PACK 1759:
    Est. admnr. Jan. 4, 1830 by Wm. Harris, Vincent Griffin, Leroy Watson bound to Moses Taggart Ord., sum $5,000.00. Cit. pub. at Damascus Ch. Sale, Jan. 14, 1830. Byrs: Ona, Jas. Patterson, Wm. Pinchback, etc.

PYLES, WILLIAM—BOX 72, PACK 1760:
    Est. admnr. Feb. 1, 1836 by Jas. F. Wyatt, Wm. Mattison, Redmon G. Wyatt, bound to Moses Taggart Ord., sum $20,000.00. Legatees: Nancy dtr., wife of Jas. F. Wyatt, Matilda, wife of Lemuel Johnson, Sally, wife of Joel Stone, Elizabeth, Lewis, Saml. Pyles, Robt. R. Seawright and wife.

PAUL, ANDREW, SR.—BOX 72, PACK 1761:
    Will dated Oct. 8, 1822 in Abbeville Dist. Exrs: Son, Geo. Paul, Hamilton Hill, John Hearst Jr. Wit: A. C. Hamilton, Hugh, Jas. Wardlaw. Chn: Geo., Wm. Pressly, Andw., Eliza, Mary Paul, Jenny Hill.

PULLIAM, ZACHARY—BOX 72, PACK 1762:
    Will dated Dec. 4, 1820 in Abbeville Dist. Prov. Jan. 2, 1826. Exrs: Son, John Pulliam, Robt. A. Cunningham, Robt. Turner. Wit: John Pulliam, John Brown, Margaret Cunningham. Chn: John, Robt. Pulliam. Sis., Anna Cooper. Inv. made Jan. 31, 1826 by Wm. Calhoun, Wm. Fooshe, Elihu Creswell, John N. Sample.

POLLARD, AUSTIN—BOX 72, PACK 1763:
    Est. admnr. Feb. 9, 1819 by John Roberson, Robt. Pollard Sr., Elihu Creswell, bound to Moses Taggart Ord., sum $40,000.00. Sale, Feb. 19, 1821. Byrs: Thos. B., Richard, Robt. Pollard, etc.

PURSELL, WILLIAM—BOX 72, PACK 1764:
    Est. admnr. Apr. 3, 1834 by John H. Pursell, David Lesly, Donald Douglas, bound to Moses Taggart Ord., sum $10,000.00. Cit. pub. at Upper Long Cane Ch.

PORTER, ANDREW S.—BOX 72, PACK 1765:
    Est. admnr. Dec. 11, 1830 by Jas. Casper, Thos. Bigby, Richard Porter, Hugh M. Prince, bound to Moses Taggart Ord., sum $4,000.00. Cit. pub. at Smyrna Ch.

PRATT, JOSEPH—BOX 72, PACK 1766:
    Will dated Jan. 27, 1826. Prov. Apr. 1826. Exrs: Sons, Wm., Thos., Jos. Pratt. Wit: Cador Gantt Esq., Jas. Pratt, John Given. Wife, Elizabeth Pratt. Chn: Emma, Sarah, Wm., Thos., Jos., John, Elizabeth, Nancy Pratt. Niece, Caroline. Inv. of Thos. Pratt in same pack. Made Nov. 25, 1826 by Ebenezer Miller, Daniel Norwood, John Osborn.

PATTON, WILLIAM—BOX 72, PACK 1767:
Est. admnr. July 27, 1833 by Jane Patton wid., Jas. Foster, Henry Nelson, John Bradley, Jas. C. Willard, John, Isaac, Archibald Kennedy, Chas. Dendy, bound to Moses Taggart Ord., sum $85,000.00. Mar. 2, 1839 John F. Patton to A. Kennedy admnr. 1 horse to ride to Ohio $50.00. Wm. W. Patton 1 horse to ride to Ohio $75.00. Notes in the hands of Chas. L. Williams of Habersham, Ga. $1,201.98¾.

PACE, JOHN—BOX 72, PACK 1768:
Est. admnr. Dec. 7, 1828 by Henry, Wm., John F. Gray, bound to Moses Taggart Ord., sum $20,000.00. Est. admnr. again July 29, 1831 by Sarah Pace, Jas. Jr., Geo., Wm. Lomax, bound to Moses Taggart Ord., sum $10,000.00. Cit. pub. at Long Cane Ch. Inv. made Jan. 3, 1829 by Patrick Noble, John F. Gray, Wm. Morrison, Joshua Davis. Byrs: Mrs. Pace, Richard Pace, Andw. Prewett, Andw. Agnew, etc.

PITMAN, MARY—BOX 72, PACK 1769:
Will dated Nov. 15, 1826 in Abbeville Dist. Prov. Dec. 1, 1826. Exrs: Son, Burgess Pittman, bro., John Glasgow. Wit: Patrick Gibson, Isaac Evans, A. Perrin. Chn: Jas., Saml. Thompson. Mary Glasgow, wife of Jas. Glasgow, Burgess Pitman. Gr. dtr. Elizabeth Glasgow.

PATTERSON, JOSIAH, SR.—BOX 72, PACK 1770:
Est. admnr. Dec. 19, 1825 by Jas., Wm. Patterson, Abner Perrin, bound to Moses Taggart Ord., sum $40,000.00. Albert F. Traylor a distributee.

PRESSLY, DR. SAMUEL—BOX 72, PACK 1771:
Est. admnr. Dec. 21, 1837 by Chas. Dendy, Geo. W. Pressly, Henly Lipford, bound to Moses Taggart Ord., sum $30,000.00. Cit. pub. at Cedar Springs Ch. Expend: Feb. 26, 1844 paid Jane Brown legatee in Creswell est. $118.85. Apr. 13, 1844 paid Jos. Pressly's tuition at Erskine College $16.00. June 3, 1844 paid John C. Pressly's tuition at Erskine College $16.00. Wid., Elizabeth Pressly. Sent to Ala. by son Jos. in answer to a letter recd. from Ala. 1 carriage price $325.00. 1839 paid Saml. Cornelius Pressly on going to Chester $5.00. Eliza a dtr. married A. M. Cook. Sarah, a legatee, married John Miller. Oct. 24, 1838 paid Jas. Brown, a legatee in Creswell's est. $85.00. Apr. 14, 1840 paid David Pressly on going to Ala. $50.00. On Aug. 11, 1847 A. M. Cook and wife, Eliza were living in Camden, Wilcox Co., Ala.

PULLIAM, LUCK L.—BOX 72, PACK 1772:
Will dated Sept. 12, 1833. Exrs: Son, Robt. Swanzy, Jabez W. H. Johnson. Wit: Nimrod Overbey, J. W. Anglin, Walter Anderson. Chn: Robt. Swanzy, John, Elizabeth Beazly, Tabitha Sims, Polly, Mahala, Rody, Eliza Ann Pulliam. To John's chn: Lucy L., Jas. R., Robt. W. Swanzy. Expend: Nov. 27, 1837 Recd. of Franklin Beazley $9.12½. Dec. 28, 1838 paid Lewis Busby, husband of Mary Pulliam $100.00.

246   ABSTRACTS OF OLD NINETY-SIX AND

PUCKETT, JAMES—BOX 73, PACK 1773:
Will dated Sept. 29, 1829 in Abbeville Dist. Prov. Oct. 28, 1829. Exrs:
Wife, Margary Puckett, Dr. Saml. Pressly, John Chiles, Patrick Gibson. Wit:
John W. Foster, Abraham Russell, John White. Wife, Margary Puckett. Chn:
Jas., D. C., Richard M., Wm. C., Caroline, Elizabeth, Archa Shippy Allen
Puckett, Patcy, wife of Greenberry Crawford. Expend: Jan. 1830 paid Dabney
Puckett in Ala. $124.87½.

PORTER, DAVID—BOX 73, PACK 1774:
Est. admnr. Mar. 15, 1836 by Jas. Devall, Peter B. Moragne, Nathaniel
Harris, bound to Moses Taggart Ord., sum $10,000.00. Cit. pub. at Willington
Ch. Sett. made Feb. 5, 1840. Pharis Martin married Catherine wid. of decd.
Distributees: J. O. Devall, Jas. H. Carter married Mary Ann, Jas. W., Madin
Porter, Wm. Wilson married Frances, David S. Porter.

PATTERSON, ROBERT SMITH—BOX 73, PACK 1775:
Est. admnr. June 16, 1834 by Josiah Patterson, John Lipscomb, John
Hearst Sr., bound to Moses Taggart Ord., sum $20,000.00. Mary D. Patterson
wid. Inv. made Sept. 10, 1835 by Vincent Griffin, Stephen Witt, John Hearst Sr.

PRESSLY, JOHN BROWN—BOX 73, PACK 1776:
Est. admnr. Feb. 4, 1833 by Dr. Geo. W. Pressly, Jos. Davis Esq., Saml.
Morris, bound to Moses Taggart Ord., sum $20,000.00. Cit. pub. at Upper
Long Cane Ch. Inv. made Feb. 20, 1833 by Meredith McGehee, John Turnbull,
Robt. Vernon.

PASCHAL, JOHN G.—BOX 73, PACK 1777:
Est. admnr. May 5, 1835 by Dr. Alexr. B., Archibald Arnold, Milton
Paschal, bound to Moses Taggart Ord., sum $7,000.00. Cit. pub. at Smyrna Ch.
Expend: June 22, 1838 paid Mrs. Eliza Paschall $200.00. Paid Mrs. E. Paschall
for Sarah A. E. Paschall $36.02½. Paid Mrs. Paschall for Mary F. A. Paschall
$29.87½. Paid John F. Paschall $4.67½. Recd. of Wm. Paschall on acct.
$77.81½. Recd. of Daniel G. Paschall on acct. $27.81. Recd. of Saml. Paschall
$142.00.

PETTIS, JAMES W.—BOX 73, PACK 1778:
Est. admnr. Sept. 9, 1831 by John S. Stone, Wm. S. Jones, Zachariah
W. Arnold, bound to Moses Taggart Ord., sum $2,000.00. Cit. pub. at Provi-
dence Ch. Elizabeth Pettis wid. Inv. made Oct. 14, 1831 by John Cochran,
Chas. Cobb, Stanley Crews.

PATTERSON, ANDREW—BOX 73, PACK 1779:
Est. admnr. Mar. 19, 1819 by Jane Patterson, Geo., Archibald Kidd,
bound to Moses Taggart Ord., sum $800.00. Inv. made Apr. 1, 1819 by Andw.
McComb Sr., John Patterson, Patrick Bradley. Byrs: Jane, John, Rachel Patterson, etc.

POSTELL, COL. JAMES—BOX 73, PACK 1780:
Will dated Mar. 12, 1824 in Abbeville Dist. Prov. June 14, 1824 in

Beaufort Dist. Exrs: Gr. s. by marriage. Jas. Louis Petigru. Wit: John L. Seabrook, Jas. L. Postell, Wm. P. Pelott. Wife, Jane Postell. Chn: Jas. Postell, Mary S. Jenkins, "Paid to her son, John F. Pelot." Gr. s., Charles Pelot. Inv made Aug. 5, 1824 by Chesley Daniel, Jos., Wm. Calhoun.

PULLIAM, JAMES—BOX 73, PACK 1781:
    Will dated Mar. 1823 in Abbeville Dist. Prov. Jan. 4, 1833. Exrs: Wife, Rhoday Pulliam, Zachary Pulliam. Wit: Harrison Long, Peter Wason. Wife recd. est. Expend: Apr. 28, 1834 Recd. of Wiley Pulliam $100.00.

PASCHALL, SAMUEL—BOX 73, PACK 1782:
    Will dated July 18, 1805 in Abbeville Dist. Rec. Nov. 2, 1805. Exrs: Sons, Saml., Milton Paschall. Wit: Archibald C. McKinley, Jas., Saml. McBride. Wife, Fereby Paschall. Chn: Mary Chadwick, Rachel Cole, Sarah Glover, Susan Lofties, Nancy Bell, Mildred Cothran, Bettey Balandingham, Fereby Lofties, Wm., John, Saml., Milton Paschall. Gr. chn: Saml. son of Milton Paschall; Saml., Wm., John, Elijah, Paschall Hammock. S. l., John Hammock.

POOLE, MICAJAH—BOX 73, PACK 1783:
    Will dated Sept. 3, 1819. Prov. Dec. 20, 1819. Exrs: Alexr. W. Adams, Francis White. Wit: Joel Lipscomb, Alexr. Stuart, W. Wier. Chn: Robt. Poole, Nancy Young wife Robt. Young. Inv. made Jan. 12, 1820 by Jas. Pulliam, John Logan, Alexr. Stuart, Wm. Neely.

POOLE, CAPT. THOMAS—BOX 73, PACK 1784:
    Est. admnr. June 28, 1806 by Leah, Micajah Poole, Robt. White, John Gayle, bound to Andw. Hamilton Ord., sum $10,000.00. Cit. pub. at Fellowship Ch. near Cambridge. Jan. 22, 1808 Recd. of Abraham Poole on note $6.37½. Sale, Nov. 27, 1806. Byrs: Leah, Elizabeth, Micajah, Abram Poole, Park Eddins, etc.

PAUL, GEORGE—BOX 73, PACK 1785:
    Est. admnr. Dec. 18, 1825 by Elizabeth Paule, Saml. Pressly, John Martin, bound to Moses Taggart Ord., sum $3,000.00. Cit. pub. at Upper Long Cane Ch. Sale. Jan. 6, 1826. Byrs: Elizabeth, Wm. P., Nancy Paul, Rebecca Sanders, Martha Tennant.

POOLE, ABRAHAM P.—BOX 73, PACK 1786:
    Est. admnr. Mar. 18, 1819 by John T. Coleman, Thos. Chiles Esq., John Logan, bound to Moses Taggart Ord., sum $2,000,00. Cit. pub. at Mount Garrison. Sale, May 15, 1819. Byrs: Seth, Benj. Poole, Col. John Logan, etc.

PARKER, CHARLES—BOX 73, PACK 1787:
    Est. admnr. Aug. 4, 1823 by Alexr. Hunter, Hudson Prince, Wm. Harkness, bound to Moses Taggart Ord., sum $3,000.00. Cit. pub. at Rocky River Ch. Inv. made Sept. 23, 1823 by Robt. Smith. Hugh Macklin, Dabney Wansly. Nancy Parker wid.

PARKER, WILLIAM J.—BOX 73, PACK 1788:
    Will dated July 20, 1819. Prov. July 23, 1819. Exrs: John, Louis B.

Holloway. Wit: Jas. Gowdy, J. Tolbert. "After death exrs. to deliver up his affairs to Dr. W. O. Bickley, then proceeds to be addressed to John Thoburn Esq. of Phila., who will then pay over to Saml. Huston or the next surviving heir of Wm. J. Parker, or to the Orphan Soc. at Phila." Inv. of Dr. Wm. J. Parker of Phila. Pa. made Aug. 12, 1819 by Thos. Chiles, J. M. Cowdrey, L. Myrick.

POLLOCK, JAMES—BOX 73, PACK 1789:
    Est. admnr. Sept. 14, 1822 by Ninian Thomson, Wm. McCulloch, Ebenezer Pollock, Andw. McClane, bound to Moses Taggart Ord., sum $500.00. Cit. pub. at Hopewell Ch.

POSEY, RICHARD—BOX 73, PACK 1790:
    Will dated Oct. 10, 1820 in Abbeville Dist. Prov. Oct. 20, 1820. Exr: Andw. Milligan. Wit: Joshua Dubose, Nicholas Harvick, John H. Cofer. Chn: Harrison, Richard, John H., Behethlom Posey, Precious Shepard, Dianna Gray, Ann Wade Shepard.

POLLARD, ROBT., SR.—BOX 73, PACK 1791:
    Will dated Feb. 1, 1820. Rec. Sept. 25, 1820. Exrs: Jos., Thos. Hill, Thos. Braxton Pollard. Wit: Peter Cheatham, Wm. Sadler, Isaac Pollard. Chn: Robt., Thos. Braxton Pollard, Polley Hill, Elizabeth Hopper. Gr. chn: Chas. Davenport, Jas. Madison, Mary Pollard.

POLLARD, JAMES—BOX 73, PACK 1792:
    Will dated Mar. 15, 1815. Rec. May 16, 1815. Exrs: Wife, Rebekah Pollard, father, Robt. Pollard Sr., Uncle, Jos. Hill, Bro., Robt. Pollard. Wit: Chas. Maxwell, Thos. Cheatham, John Pollard. Wife, Rebekah Pollard. Chn: Chas. Davenport Pollard, Jas. Madison Pollard. "Child that wife is now pregnant with." Nephew, Thos. Norris. "That the graveyard where Chas. Davenport, Esq., and his first wife are buried be pailed in."

POOLE, ROBERT—BOX 73, PACK 1793:
    Est. admnr. Dec. 30, 1821 by Nancy Poole, Jas. Sample, Alexr. Sample, Alexr. Stuart, bound to Moses Taggart Ord., sum $2,500.00. Cit. pub. at Providence Ch.

PATTERSON, JOHN—BOX 73, PACK 1794:
    Est. admnr. Jan. 24, 1820 by Robt. Patterson, Robt., Hugh McBride, John McComb, bound to Moses Taggart Ord., sum $2,000.00. Sale, Feb. 10, 1824. Byrs: Robt. McCaslan, John, Robt. McBride, Margaret Robinson, Mary, Rachel, Jas. Patterson, etc.

PORTER, SAMUEL—BOX 74, PACK 1795:
    Will dated May 4, 1833 in Abbeville Dist. Exrs: Sugar Bonds, Saml. W. Beaty. Wit: Jas. Casper, F. Y. Baskin, Thos. Crawford. Wife, Susannah Porter. Est. to be divided into 6 shares; viz., Jane L. Brownlee, Susannah Beaty, Susannah M., Sinthy M., Saml. P., Eliza A. Dobins. Wid. Nancy Porter. To

ABBEVILLE DISTRICT WILLS AND BONDS   249

the heirs of Andw. R. Porter decd. To my Chn: Saml., Hugh, John, Richard E.
Porter. Sugar Bonds later moved to Ga. as a letter was written to him there by
David Lesly Ord. in care the Jefferson Court House, Jackson Co., Ga.

PRITCHARD, WILLIAM S.—BOX 74, PACK 1796:
Est. admnr. Oct. 28, 1835 by Curry, Josiah Patterson, Wm. Harris,
bound to Moses Taggart Ord., sum $500.00. Cit. pub. at Mount Moriah.

PRINCE, WINKFIELD—BOX 74, PACK 1797:
Est. admnr. Oct. 3, 1836 by Hugh M., Hudson M. Prince, Robt. F.,
Jas. A. Black, bound to Moses Taggart Ord., sum $2,000.00. May 16, 1841 paid
Louiza Prince $218.56¼.

PEARSON, JAMES—BOX 74, PACK 1798:
Will dated Mar. 22, 1817 in Abbeville Dist. Prov. July 17, 1817. Exrs:
Son, John Pearson, Ephraim Nichols. Wit: Jas. Nickels, Wm. Moore, John
Speer. Wife, Mary Pearson. Chn: John, Jas,. Henry, Wm., Alexr. Polly, Sally,
Cynthia Pearson. "Owned plantation in Franklin Co., Ga."

PULLIAM, JOHN, SR.—BOX 74, PACK 1799:
Will dated May 2, 1798. Rec. June 11, 1798. Exrs: Wife, Sarah Pul-
liam, Son, Zachary Pulliam, S.l., Chas. Fooshe. Wit: Elisha Weatherford,
Daniel Mitchell, Fielder Wells. Wife: Sarah Pulliam. Chn: Thos., John, Martha
Fooshe, Betsey Gholson decd. (Her 3 chn: Nancy, Zachariah, Benj. Gholson)
Nancy Ball, Mary, Rhoda, Judy Lewis Chiles, Fanny, Anna, Zachary Pulliam.
Expend: June 10, 1813 paid Meek or Nick Sisson his wife's legacy $8.56¼.
Sept. 20, paid Peter H. Cochran his wife's legacy $17.57¼. Paid John Pulliam
admnr. of Thos. Pulliam decd. legacy $17.57¼. Paid Jas. Pulliam a balance
of his wife's legacy $17.57¼. Oct. 16 paid Agrippa Cooper his wife's legacy
$17.57¼. Oct. 18 paid John Chile's wife's legacy $17.57¼. Paid Zachary Pulliam admnr. Mary Pulliam decd. legacy $17.57¼. Paid Fanny Coleman
$730.43½. Paid Anny Cooper $750.43½.

PETERSON, ANDREW—BOX 74, PACK 1800:
Est. admnr. Dec. 13, 1786 by Theophilus Goodwin, John Rodgers,
Abraham Neighbours, bound to John Thomas Ord. 96 District., sum 1,000 lbs.
Inv. made by Jos. Parsons, John McClintock, Wm. Fowler.

PURDY, HENRY—BOX 74, PACK 1801:
Will dated July 30, 1816 in Abbeville Dist. Prov. Sept. 3, 1816. Exrs:
Agness, Jas. Purdy, Hugh Morrah Esq. Wit: John Thomson, Alexr. Gammell,
Henry Purdy. Wife, Agness Purdy. Chn: Wm. N., Margaret, Agness, Mary,
Sarah, Jane, Jas., Henry, Leroy Purdy. "Bequeath to Elizabeth Brooks, Grizzelah
Gillespie, Ann Ritchey." "When Wm. Norrel comes of age."

PICKETT, THOMAS—BOX 74, PACK 1802:
Will dated May 26, 1782 in 96 Dist. Probated Feb. 24, 1783. Exrs:
Wife, Mille Pickett, Wm. Runolds. Wit: Thos. Rennolds, Wm. Goode. Wife,

Mille Pickett. Chn: names not given. Inv. made Apr. 16, 1783 by Chas. Ashley, Ed. Morris, Thos. Dalton.

PETTIGREW, JOHN—BOX 74, PACK 1803:
Will dated Feb. 3, 1803 in Abbeville Dist. Rec. Dec. 1, 1806. Exrs: Son, Robt. Pettigrew, John Gray, Sr. Wit: Thos. Finley, Robt., Wm. Pettigrew. Wife, Sarah Pettigrew. Chn: Jas., Geo., Robt., Betsey, Wm. Pettigrew, Polly Wilson. Sis. 1, Anne Pettigrew. Inv. made Dec. 11, 1806 by Sterling Dickson, John, Wm. Gray.

PORTER, ELIZABETH—BOX 74, PACK 1804:
Will dated 1806 in Abbeville Dist. Rec. July 1, 1806. Exrs: Reuben Weed, Hugh McBride. Wit: Nathaniel Weed, Robt. McBride. Chn: Rev. Alexr., Martha Porter, Saml., Elizabeth Lesly. Bequeath to Andw., Hugh, Nancy English, Sarah Porter, Sarah Weed Jr. Inv. made July 4, 1806 by Saml. Leard, Jas. Hathorn.

PRESSLY, JANE—BOX 74, PACK 1805:
Est. admnr. Dec. 3, 1805 by John Pressly, Jos., Geo. Hearst, Jos. McCord, Greggery Caudle, Joseph, John McCord Sr., bound to Andw. Hamilton Ord., sum $10,000.00. Expend: July 18, 1807 paid Geo. Hearst legatee $576.00. John Pressly legatee $576.00. Andw. Paul legatee $561.56. Jos. McCord legatee $561.61. John Pressly Jr. was son.

PULLIAM, THOMAS—BOX 74, PACK 1805:
Est. admnr. Apr. 15, 1801 by John Pulliam, Wm. Calhoun, Jos. Cooke, bound to Andw. Hamilton Ord., sum $3,000.00. Legatees: John, Sarah, Zachary, Polley, Jas. Pulliam, John Chiles, Dabney Gholston, Agrippa Cooper.

PARKER, JAMES—BOX 74, PACK 1807:
Will dated May 26, 1820. Prov. Feb. 15, 1823. Exr: Wife, Jane Parker. Wit: Wm. Buchanan Sr., Wm. Buchanan Jr., Wm. McCrea. Chn: Margaret, Mary, Isabell, Sally, Rebecah, Jas., Elizabeth, John Parker. "Owned land on Wilson's Ck. in Pendleton Dist."

PHELPS, AARON—BOX 74, PACK 1808:
Est. admnr. Feb. 28, 1818 by Mary Ann Phelps, Chas. C. Mayson, Wm. Nibbs, bound to Taliaferro Livingston Ord., sum $2,000.00. Inv. made at Cambridge Mar. 9, 1818 by John McBride, Jas. McCracken, Robt. Marsh.

PARKER, HENRY—BOX 74, PACK 1809:
Est. admnr. Feb. 8, 1785 by Jas. Rosamond, Gabriel Smithers, John Harris, bound to John Thomas Ord. 96 Dist., sum 2,000 lbs. Inv. made Apr. 16, 1785 by Wm. Anderson, Lewis Banton, Nimrod Williams.

PAUL, NANCY—BOX 74, PACK 1810:
Est. admnr. Nov. 7, 1825 by Jas., West Donald, Sealy Walker, bound to Moses Taggart Ord., sum $3,000.00. Inv. made Nov. 28, 1825 by Barton Jordon, Abraham Lites, Thos. Edwards, Luke Mathis. Expend: Nov. 20, 1825 recd. of Wm. P. Paul for est. of Nancy Paul $21.66.

PETTUS, CAPT. JAMES—BOX 74, PACK 1811:
    Will dated May 11, 1817. Prov. July 1, 1820. Exrs: John, Geo. Shotwell,
Wm. P. Arnold. Wit: Harrison Monday, John P., Jas. Arnold, Jas. Eddins.
Wife, Anna Pettus. Chn: Elenor Lipford, Polly Hart, Lucy Overton, Jas. Wm.,
Louisa Ann, Susannah Graves, Virginia, Clotilda Pettus. Sett. made Feb. 7, 1843.
Jas. A. Jay married Clotilda. Ed. Lipford married Ellenor. H. Owen married
Louisa and lived in Miss. John Stone married Susan. Wm. Jones married Lucy.
Mary wid. of Peter Lomax decd. John Foster married Virginia.
(Letter) St. Clair, Alabama, June 22nd 1842
        Dear brother when I wrote my first I did not know that I should see
Mr. Young though he did not leave as soon as I expected & he is with us at
this time. We are all well this morning and we hope this will find you &
yours all well you requested me in your letter to give you my onest views with
respect to this country. I have not been here long enough to know how things
will operate & will be particular to state nothing but what I really know. first
I can say that this country abounds with provision such as corn and meat wheet
fat hogs & cows & here the poorest class can get plenty bread & meat milk and
butter if they will work for it. this country has been healthy so far, but owing
to situation of the country you might not like as such you would do well to look
for yourself unless you are willing to take it better for worse I know I can live
better here than I could on Sandtuck once I can get a start yes my prospects
are better now than I ever had before there is joining me 80 acres of land with
a small farm open & good hewed log house with a stone chimney that I can get
for $200. I think the owner offered it to me on monday last at 2,50 and be-
lieve situated as he is can buy it for 200. I have not been over the land though
I think it low there is allso 40 acres joining it that can be bought that has 12
acres open on it the man that lived on the 40 acres last year made 180 bushels
of corn and 14 hundred wt of cotton on the 12 acres Mr. Thomas Jones will be
out you can write to me I think if you can sell your land to advantage you
would do well to sell & move I know this that I would rather live here & there
are better places than this. Major   Shotwell and Brother W. H. Shotwell &
family are well if I can superseede the nessaty of my coming to S. C. I want
to do so if not I will have to come I send you some accounts do the best you
can with them. I would like to hear Esq Lomax is like cannot tell him he
has my consent to setle the estate of Mrs. Pettus I will abide by a setleme before
the ordinary & you can testify that I represent Jones I am yours
                                                      J. J. Stone
        Written to Mr. James A. Jay, Abbeville, S. C.

PATTERSON, JAMES—BOX 74, PACK 1812:
    Will dated Aug. 7, 1795. Rec. Nov. 10, 1795. Exrs: Son, Josiah Patterson,
Wm. McGaw, John Patterson. Wit: Wm. Carson, John Beaty, Robt. Howard.
Was of Long Canes in Abbeville Dist. Chn: Jenet Carswell, Alexr., Josiah Pat-
terson. Gr. chn: Jean McCormice dtr. of Jenet Carswell, Agness Mills, Kathrine
Graves, Jas. son of Josiah Patterson. "Leave Mr. Dickson preacher of the gospel
a cow and calf."

PAUL, JOHN—BOX 74, PACK 1813:
Est. admnr. Apr. 12, 1824 by Robt., Anthony Yeldell, John Adams, bound to Moses Taggart Ord., sum $1,000.00. Cit. pub. at Smyrna Ch. Sale, Apr. 30, 1824. Byrs: Polly Paul, Elenor, Agness McCord, etc.

PETTIGREW, EBENEZER, ESQ.—BOX 74, PACK 1814:
Will dated Mar. 10, 1821. Probated Aug. 5. 1821. Exr: Bro., John Pettigrew. Wit: Alexander Hunter, Jos. F. Bell, C. Stark. Wife, Nancy Pettigrew. Chn: Lewis Franklin, Harriet Gibert Pettigrew. Expend: June 20, 1798 paid John Dunlap Esq. the costs of a nonsuit obtained against Mrs. Pettigrew now Mrs. Finley in Pendleton Court $10.00. Sarah Pettigrew was admnr. of est. June 11, 1801 paid John Frazer for teaching Jackey and Ebenezer Pettigrew, Sally, Sarah B. Pettigrew.

PORTER, JAMES—BOX 74, PACK 1815:
Est. admnr. June 11, 1798 by Sarah Porter wid., John Gray, Thos. Brightman Sr. bound to Moses Taggart Ord., sum $1,000.00. Inv. made June 30, 1798 by John Leaney, John, Andw. Gray.

PRESSLY, JOHN—BOX 74, PACK 1816:
Est. admnr. Oct. 13, 1826 by Martha Pressly, John Devlin, Jas. Drennan bound to Moses Taggart Ord., sum $1,500.00. Cit. pub. at Cedar Springs Ch. Inv. made Oct. 31, 1826 by Wm. Chiles, John Hearst Jr., John Lindsay, Jas. Drennan.

PRESSLY, JOHN—BOX 74, PACK 1817:
Will dated Nov. 6, 1808. Rec. Mar. 20, 1809. Exrs: Wife, Nancy Pressly, John Shattien. Wit: Jas. Lydia Adamson, Fanny Shatten.

PARKER, JOHN—BOX 74, PACK 1818:
Will dated Apr. 12, 1784. Prov. May 27, 1784. Exrs: Wife, Charity Parker, Jas. Hollingsworth. Wit: John Robinson, Wm. Young, Jas. Hollingsworth. (In one place his name is written Jonathan Parker.)

PACE, SILAS—BOX 74, PACK 1819:
Est. admnr. Feb. 22, 1811 by John Pace, Jas. Lomax Sr., Peter Hairston bound to Taliaferro Livingston Ord., sum $6,000.00. Inv. made Apr. 24, 1811 by Jas. Lomax Sr., Benj. Adams, Geo. Connor.

PASCHALL, MILTON—BOX 75, PACK 1820:
Will dated July 10, 1832 in Abbeville Dist. Prov. Mar. 3, 1834. Exrs: Sons, Saml., Milton Paschall. Wit: Abraham Bell, John Smith, Wm. Speer. Wife, Sarah Paschall. Chn: Milton, Daniel, Jesse, Thos., Amanda, Louisa, Elizabeth, Saml., John Paschall, Ferreby Thomas.

PETTIGREW, SAMUEL—BOX 75, PACK 1821:
Est. admnr. Mar. 25, 1795 by Anney Pettigrew wid., Reuben, Andw. Weed, Benj. Howard, bound to Judges of Abbeville Co., sum 500 lbs. Inv. made Apr. 4, 1795 by John, Wm. Gray, Robt. Crawford. Sale May 7, 1795. Byrs: Ann, John, Jas. Pettigrew, etc.

ABBEVILLE DISTRICT WILLS AND BONDS   253

PATTON, SAMUEL—BOX 75, PACK 1822:
Est. admnr. Apr. 22, 1782 by Arthur Patton, Jas. Noble, Wm. Hays of Long Cane Setl. 96 Dist. bound to John Ewing Calhoun Ord., sum $14,000.00. Arthur Patton next of kin. Inv. made Sept. 3, 1782 by Peter Stubs, Jas. Noble, Wm. Hays.

PRINGLE, JAMES—BOX 75, PACK 1823:
Est. admnr. Mar. 28, 1797 by Thos. Pringle, Francis Hodge, Jos. Black, John Hall, bound to Judges of Abbeville Co., sum $2,000.00. Cit. read at Duewest Corner. Ment. Thos. Pringle, Francis Hodge next of kin. Inv. made May 22, 1797 by Gen. John Norwood, Jos. Black, John Hall. Nov. 5, 1800 cash paid Martha Pringle $27.00. Oct. 22, 1800 paid Eliza Pringle $73.52. May 29, 1801 paid on acct. of Alexr. Pringle decd. legatee $86.00. Paid Eliza Pringle legatee $25.82¼. James Pringle legatee $27.61¼. Martha Pringle legatee $71.94¼. Sale, July 13, 1797. Byrs: Thos. Pringle, Jesse Kenady, Eliza Pringle, Henry Watt, Robt. Chesnut, Zadeciah Woods, Wm. Ashley, Wm. Cunningham, Jas. Young, David Russell, Jas. McCurry, Saml. Shaw, Francis Hodge, Mathew Robertson, Margaret McNear, Saml. Norwood, Jas. Gilmore, Robt. Green, John Liddell, Andw. Pickens, Thos. Wilson, Ebenezer Miller, Wm. Dunlap, Wm. Boles.

PULLIAM, BENJAMIN—BOX 75, PACK 1824:
Est. admnr. Oct. 16, 1816 by Mary Pulliam, Alexr., Robt. Sample, Pleasant Wright. All of Abbeville Dist., sum $10,000.00 bound to Taliaferro Livingston Ord. Cit. pub. at Providence Ch. Inv. made Oct. 19, 1816 by Jas. Pulliam, John Read Long, David Stuart. Jan. 3, 1820 paid Jas. Franklin for tuition of Wyly, Willis Pulliam $15.00. Saml., Mary Davis the gdns. of 3 chn. of decd.

PLESS, JOHN M.—BOX 75, PACK 1825:
Est. admnr. Nov. 24, 1810 by Alexr. Jos., Benj. Houston of Abbeville Dist. bound to John Hamilton Ord., sum $1,000.00. Inv. made Dec. 7, 1810 by Jas. Hutcheson, Jos., Benj. Houston. Dec. 15, 1810 cash paid Phillip Pless $24.02. Sale byrs: Robt. Smith, Alexr. Houston, Jas. Conner, Robt. Foster, Wm. Smith, Francis Carlile, Jos. Trimble, Wm. Basse, Leonard Bell, Jas. Hutcheson, David Boyse, Jas. Stewart, Saml. Blair, Jas. Thompson, etc.

PARK, JOHN—BOX 75, PACK 1826:
Will dated Aug. 13, 1779. Prov. Jan. 23, 1784. Exr: son, Jos. Park. Wit: Roger Smith, Wm. Simmons, Elizabeth Smith. Ment. was of Craven Co. Farmer. Wife, Ann Park, Chn: Jos., Mary, Margaret, John, Saml., Wm. Park. Bro., Jos. Park. Chn. of Jos. Park, Margaret, Wm., Thos., Jean Park. Uncle, Saml. Noble. Inv. made Feb. 10, 1784 by Robt. Harris, Andw. Mayes, Daniel McBride.

PERSELL, JOHN—BOX 75, PACK 1827:
Est. admnr. Oct. 30, 1786 by Farrell Riley, Mathew Brooks, Mathew Wells of 96 Dist., sum 1,000 lbs., bound to John Thomas Jr. Ord. Est. appraised by Hugh O'Neal, Wm. Cason, Saml. Akin, Mathew Brooks.

PARK, JOSEPH, JR.—BOX 75, PACK 1828:
Est. admnr. Nov. 21, 1783 by Wm. Thomson, Daniel McBride of Fair
Forest, sum 2,000 lbs., bound to John Thomas Ord. of 96 Dist. Also Rachel
Thomson, wife of Wm. Thomson. Inv. made Dec. 10, 1783 by Robt. Harris,
Andw. Mayes, John Davidson Sr. Sale, Dec. 22, 1783. Byrs: Wm. Thomson,
Eleanor Harper, Jas. Crawford, Andw. Thomson, Daniel Jackson, Thos., Mar-
garet Park, Andw. Mayes, Daniel McBride, Hugh Means, Geo. Storey.

PEAK, NATHANIEL—BOX 75, PACK 1829:
Will dated Sept. 20, 1758. Prov. June 14, 1783. Was of Orange, Co.,
N. C. Exr: Jos. Birchfield. Wit: Geo. Sims, Jos., Diesa Birchfield, Ed. Cantreel.
Sons: John, Jas. Peake. Inv. made July 24, 1783 by Jas. Birchfield.

PRINCE, EDWARD—BOX 75, PACK 1830:
Will dated Dec. 3, 1827. Prov. Dec. 17, 1827. Exrs: Son, Hugh M.
Prince, Alexr. Hunter. Wit: John C. Martin, Wm. B. Scott. Wife, Rebecca
Prince, Chn: Hugh M., Polly Clay, Jonathan, Sylvanus, Loocey Prince. Inv.
made Feb. 23, 1831 by John Power Jr., Geo. N. Sims, John Black.

PRINCE, EDWARD S.—BOX 75, PACK 1831:
Est. admnr. Dec. 2, 1828 by Alexr. Hunter, John McComb, Robt. F.
Black, bound to Moses Taggart Ord. of Abbeville Dist., sum $2,000.00. Cit. pub.
at Smyrna Ch.

PRINCE, EDWARD, SR.—BOX 75, PACK 1832:
Will dated Sept. 28, 1816. Rec. Oct. 3, 1818. Exrs: Joseph Black, Geo.
W. Martin. Wit: Andrew, Jas. Morrow, Francis Drinkard. Wife, Lucy Prince.
Chn: Joseph, Edward Prince. Gr. dtr. Susan Black. s.l. Hudson Prince. Ment.
7 gr. chn. by the name Clerk. "Give unto Sally Bevel $100.00." Sale, Feb. 25,
1831. Byrs: Hudson, Hugh M., Silvus, Payton Prince, John, Robt. F., Joseph
Black, etc.

PERRIN, SAMUEL—BOX 75, PACK 1833:
Will dated Aug. 20, 1828. Prov. Nov. 3, 1828. Exrs: Sons, Henry
Wm., Thos. Chiles Perrin. Wit: John F. Pelot, John Chiles, Saml. Pressly. Wife,
Eunice Perrin, Chn: Henry Wm., Mary Ann, Agness, Saml., Jas., Thos. Chiles
Perrin. Expend: Dec. 1835. Left with Lewis Perrin when going to Spartanburg
for Saml. $25.00. July 1 paid to H. W. Perrin at Mount Vernon $496.67.
Sett. made Jan. 26, 1839. Present, Thos. C. Perrin surviving. Exr. (Henry W.
Prince, decd.) and gdn. of Jas., Eunice, Elizabeth L., Lewis Perrin. Baron B.
Foster who married Mary Ann. Saml. Perrin, Agnes W. Quarles.

PORTER, JAMES—BOX 75, PACK 1834:
Est. admnr. Mar. 4, 1818 by John, Isaac Moragne, Edward Collier
bound to Taliaferro Livingston Ord. Abbeville Dist. sum $2,000.00. Cit. read
at Liberty Meeting House. Inv. made Mar. 6, 1818 by Isaac Moragne, Mackerness G. Williams, John L. Gibert. Sale, Aug. 8, 1818. Byrs: David Porter, John
Moragne, John Furgeson, Wm. Cain.

PUGH, MARY—BOX 75, PACK 1835:
Est. admnr. Mar. 17, 1824 by Col. John Cochran, Joseph Davis, Owen Selby bound to Moses Taggart Ord. Abbeville Dist. sum $2,000.0.. Inv. made May 8, 1824 by Wm. Mantz, Benjamin Hill, Adam, Wm. Stuart.

PATTERSON, SAMUEL, SR.—BOX 75, PACK 1836:
Will dated Mar. 30, 1821. Prov. Oct. 8, 1824. Exrs: Son, John Patterson, John C. Covey. Wit: Andrew McCombs, John Bradley, Wm. Link. Wife, Rachel Patterson. Chn: Andrew decd. John, Robt., Saml. Patterson. s.l. Wm. Ross. Dtr. Law, Jenny, wife of Andrew Patterson decd. Gr. son, Saml., only son of Andrew Patterson decd. Sale, Oct. 28, 1824. Byrs: Robt., Mary, Alexr. Patterson, Jas. Glasgow Sr., etc.

PERRIN, WILLIAM—BOX 75, PACK 1837:
Est. admnr. Jan. 3, 1829 by Thos. C. Perrin, John McComb bound to Moses Taggart Ord. Abbeville Dist., sum $2,000.00. Admnr. again Nov. 13, 1811 by Robt., Saml. Perrin, Geo. Sullivan bound to Taliaferro Livingston Ord. Abbeville Dist. sum $2,000.00. Inv. made by John Chiles, Henry W., Abner Perrin, Jr.

PRINCE, JOHN, ESQ.—BOX 75, PACK 1838:
Will dated Feb. 7, 1782 in 96 Dist. Prov. Dec. 20, 1785. Wit: Stephen Vaughan, Nevil Wayland, Richard Lewis. Wife, Mary Prince. Ment. Robt., Patty, Henry, Wm., Francis, Robt., John (son Henry Prince) Mary, wife of Baylis Earls, Thos., Margaret Farrar. Patty Prince recd. 20 lbs. Va. Currency. (Did not give relationship.)

PRINCE, JOHN W.—BOX 75, PACK 1839:
Will dated Nov. 17, 1825. Exrs: Jas. A., Robt. F. Black, Francis B. Clinkscales, John Swilling. Wit: John Cunningham, R. M. Montgomery, John Barksdale. "My 6 legal heirs" viz. Hudson Prince of Pendleton Dist.; Rebeckah, wife of Edward Prince; Geo. Prince of Georgia; Silvanus, son of my brother Silvanus Prince; Susan wife of Robt. F. Black, dtr. my sis. Sarah Prince; Elizabeth Mims dtr. my sis. Polly Prince. Jan. 2, 1826 paid Wright Mims legatee $600.00.

PRINCE, JOHN—BOX 75, PACK 1840:
Will dated July 15, 1806. Rec. Oct. 6, 1806. Wit: Jeremiah Strother, Edward Prince, John Haslet. Wife, Sary Prince. "Est. divided between Susannah, Hudson, John Prince, and the child that is expected from my wife." Inv. made Oct. 6, 1806 by Donald Fraser, Joseph Franklin, A. Hunter. Inv. of Sarah Prince decd. made Oct. 8, 1806 by Donald Fraser, Thos. Shanklin, Alexr. Hunter, John McNeel.

POSTELL, RACHEL—BOX 75, PACK 1841:
Will dated Mar. 8, 1816. Rec. April 11, 1818. Exrs: Husband, Colo. Jas. Postell, Charles J. Jenkins. Wit: Dr. Edward W. North, Jas. L. Pettigrew. Will proven April 11, 1818 in Beaufort Dist. before Robt. G. Norton Ord. of

256 ABSTRACTS OF OLD NINETY-SIX AND

Beaufort Dist. Was of *Coosawhatchie* in Beaufort Dist. "After death of my husband est. to be in trust of Charles J. Jenkins for use of my adopted chn. viz. Wm. Henry, Eliza Mary Hay. Nieces, Mrs. Eliza Postell, wife of Capt. Jas. Postell. Mrs. Rachel Sweet, wife of Rev. Jas. D. Sweet." Inv. made June 29, 1818 by Thos. Finly, Joseph C. Mathews, Joseph Calhoun.

PRESSLY, DAVID—BOX 75, PACK 1842:
   Est. admnr. Feb. 12, 1819 by Saml., Rev. John T. Pressly, John Devlin, John Hearst bound to Moses Taggart Ord. Abbeville Dist. sum $20,000.00. Acct. of expenses with the admnr. Oct. 1837 sent to Oxford College at Ohio $325.00. Nov. 1839 on leaving for Due West $20.00. 1841. On leaving for Allegheny $45.00. 1842 on leaving for Mississippi $20.00 A. M. Cook was a legatee.

PERRYMAN, DR. SAMUEL—BOX 75, PACK 1843:
   Will dated May 7, 1838. Proved Aug. 17, 1838. Exrs: Wife, Sarah A. Perryman, Zebulon Rudolph Jr., Dr. John P. Barratt, Richard Watson. Wit: Edna Caldwell, Margaret A. Holloway, Simon Patterson. Chn: Wm., Saml., Richard Mumford Perryman. "Plantation in Lounds Co., Alabama owned by Dr. J. P. Barratt and myself be sold and divided between my wife and chn. That the amt. owe me by Jas. Hagood of Lounds Co., Alabama, formerly of Edgefield Dist., S. C. be given back to said Hagood. Unto Hardy White my colt." Brothers and sisters: Alexr., Milton T. Perryman, Martha Gallaugher, Nancy Medlock. "My business in the hands of Beckham Vaughan of Lounds Co., Ala. be closed by him at least by Jan. 1841." Feb. 8, 1841 paid Edna Caldwell gdn. Ann Caldwell $1,139.52. H. H. Creswell and wife part of Sett., was a child's part there being 3 chn.

PAXTON, NAPOLEON B.—BOX 75, PACK 1845:
   Will dated Jan. 27, 1838 in Abbeville Dist. Proved Mar. 5, 1838. Exr: Brother, Josiah Carson Patterson. Wit: Wm. Harris, John Hearst Sr. A. V. (last name worn) "My brother Josiah Patterson shall give education to Jas., Arthur Moseley Patterson, sons of Jas. Patterson, my father, by his last wife."

PUCKETT, MARGARET—BOX 75, PACK 1846:
   Est. admnr. Dec. 30, 1805 by John Ealls, Jas. Huston, Geo. Conn, Joseph Creswell, Andrew McCormick, Abraham Russell bound to Andrew Hamilton Ord. Abbeville Dist. sum $10,000.00. Est. admnr. again Feb. 15, 1806 by John, Wm. Chiles, Jas. Pucket, Saml. Perrin, Jas. Adamson bound to Andrew Hamilton Ord. sum $10,000.00. Inv. made Jan. 6, 1806 by Wm. McGough, Elias Gibson, Saml. Young.

PETTIGREW, JAMES, SR.—BOX 76, PACK 1847:
   Will dated Dec. 18, 1784 in 96 Dist. Wit: Handy Harris, Jas., Wm. Pettigrew. Wife, Mary Pettigrew. Chn: John, Jas., Geo., Ebenezer, Wm. Pettigrew, Martha Witherspoon, Mary Verner. Inv. made Aug. 14. 1789 by Wm. McKinley, Handy Harris, Moses Davis.

POLLARD, RICHARD—BOX 76, PACK 1848:
   Will date left out. Rec. Jan. 9, 1804 in Abbeville Dist. Wife, Sary Pol-

lard, John *Walls*, Wm. Pollard. Son, Austin Pollard. Wit: John Ball, Elisha Weatherford, Robt. A. Cunningham. Chn: Pamelar, Austin, Isaac, Richard Pollard. Inv. made Jan. 27, 1804 by John Ball, Joseph Hill, Harry Smith.

PULLIAM, MARY—BOX 76, PACK 1849:
Est. admnr. Oct. 18, 1809 by Zachary Pulliam, Joseph Hill, Robt. Cunningham bound to Andrew Hamilton Ord. Abbeville Dist. sum $5,000.00. Expend: Oct. 11, 1811 paid Nancy Ball legatee $50.00. Dec. 28, paid Zachary Gholston legatee $80.50. Paid Richard M. *Sisson* wife's legacy $80.50. April 21, 1812 paid Jas. Pulliam balance of his wife's legacy $41.50. April 22 paid Sarah Pulliam legacy $41.50. April 20, paid Agrippa Cooper balance of his wife's legacy $41.50. April 30, paid Benjamin Gholston legacy $80.50. May 2 paid John Chiles wife's legacy $41.50. May 30 paid John Pulliam legacy $41.06. May 31, 1811 paid Peter H. Coleman wife's legacy $200.44.

PIERSON, JOHN—BOX 76, PACK 1850:
Est. admnr. Jan. 2, 1808 by Jas. Pierson, Phillmon Buford, John Cain bound to Andrew Hamilton Ord., Abbeville Dist. sum $5,000.00. Wid. Sarah Pierson. Oldest son, Jas. Pierson. Feb. 1808 paid Sally Pearson otherwise called Sally Mason $37.60. Paid Jeremiah Dobbs legatee $34.75.

PAUL, MINORS—BOX 76, PACK 1851:
On Feb. 15, 1826 Hamilton, Benjamin Hill, Joseph Davis bound to Moses Taggart Ord. Abbeville Dist. sum $10,000.00. Hamilton Hill made gdn. of Eliza, Andrew Paul, minors over 14 yrs. Mary Ann Paul an infant under 14 yrs. Dec. 22, 1831 paid a legacy to Jas. J. Devlin, husband of Mary Ann Paul $1,208.75.

PAUL, MINORS—BOX 76, PACK 1852:
On Jan. 25, 1832 Jas. A. Gray, Jas. Donald, Thos. Lyon bound to Moses Taggart Ord. Abbeville Dist. sum $2,000.00. Jas. A. Gray made gdn. of Elizabeth, Andrew Paul, minors of Geo. Paul decd. under 14 yrs.

PRATT, JOHN—BOX 76, PACK 1853:
On Feb. 4, 1828 Wm., Jas. Pratt, Saml. Young bound to Moses Taggart Ord. Abbeville Dist. sum $20,000.00. Wm. Pratt made gdn. of John Partt a minor over 14 yrs.

PRESSLY, JOHN—BOX 76, PACK 1854:
On Nov. 23, 1827 Martha Pressly, John, Jas. Devlin bound to Moses Taggart Ord. Abbeville Dist. sum $2,000.00. Martha Pressly made gdn. of John E. Pressly a minor under 14 yrs.

POOLE, SARAH UGENIA—BOX 76, PACK 1855:
On Sept. 6, 1836 Abraham P. Poole, Larkin Griffin, John M. Cain bound to Moses Taggart Ord. Abbeville Dist. sum $2,000.00. Abraham Pool made gdn. of Sarah Pool minor under 14 yrs. "April 1, 1850 Recd. of Abraham P. Pool $2,164.69 by me J. W. Lipscomb in right of my wife Sarah E. Lipscomb. Recd. of John D. Williams Exr. of Col. Jas. Williams $957.80 her part of est."

PORTER, MINORS—BOX 76, PACK 1856:
    On Sept. 26, 1836 Israel N., Robt. M., Marion J. Davis bound to Moses
Taggart Ord. Abbeville Dist., sum $2,000.00. Israel N. Davis made gdn. of
Hugh L., Jane E. Porter, minors under 14 yrs. Return of Robt. N. Davis gdn.
Jane Porter a minor ward now resident for last 6 yrs. with Israel N. Davis her
former gdn. in Monroe Co., Miss. Made Jan. 12, 1847. Sett. of Jane E. Porter
decd. minor made Dec. 21, 1852. Chn: of Andw. R. Porter decd.

PORTER, MINORS—BOX 76, PACK 1857:
    On Jan. 5, 1835 Jas. S. Harris, Jas. H. Baskins, Jas. Wileythe, bound
to Moses Taggart Ord., Abbeville Dist. sum $1,400.00. Jas. S. Harris made
gdn. of John Harris Porter, Saml. S., Hugh L., Robt. M., Jane E. Porter, chn.
of Andw. R. Porter decd.

PORTER, H. (MINORS)—BOX 76, PACK 1858:
    On Mar. 18, 1828. John, Wm. Brownlee, Robt. F. Black, bound to
Moses Taggart, Ord. Abbeville, Dist. sum $20,000.00. John Brownlee gdn. of
Susan, Wm. B., Sarah Ann, John Ewen, Saml. A. Porter, minors under 14.
Chn. of Hugh Porter decd. Sett. of S. A. Porter decd. made June 25, 1843.
Present John Porter gdn. he having notified M. J. D. and wife Sarah A., the
surviving legatee residing without the state.

PENALL, THOMAS E.—BOX 76, PACK 1859:
    Est. admnr. June 27, 1839, bound to Moses Taggart Ord., Abbeville
Dist., sum $2,000.00, by Robt. A. Pennall, Jas. W. Frazier, Robt. Devlin. Cit.
pub. at Asbury Chapel.

PATTERSON, SAMUEL, (Dumb Man)—BOX 76, PACK 1860:
    On Jan. 3, 1839 Alexr. P. Robinson, John Faulkner, Henry Bentley,
bound to Moses Taggart Ord., Abbeville Dist. sum $20,000.00 Alexr. P. Robinson
made gdn. (He was deaf and dumb.) Sett. made June 26, 1854 of Saml. Patterson a mute as managed by John Faulkner who acted as agent of John C. Cowey.
I, the said Cowey being Exr. of est. Saml. Patterson decd., father of said mute.
Present Wm. K. Bradley who represents Saml. Patterson of Tenn., a nephew
of said mute. State of Ala. Butler Co. John Patterson recd. $913.51 dist. sh. of
est. Sept. 15, 1854. Wm., Nancy Ross of Monroe Co., Ala. recd. $913.51. dist.
sh. of Dumb Saml. Patterson decd. est. Sept. 15, 1854. 4 distributees, Mrs. Margaret Robertson, Mrs. Nancy Ross, John P., Saml. Patterson.

PATTERSON, JOSIAH C.—BOX 76, PACK 1861:
    Will dated July 1, 1839. Prov. Aug. 7, 1839. Exrs: Wife, Mourning
Patterson, Bros., Jas., Arthur M. Patterson, Wm. Harris. Wit: R. F. Gray,
Wm. A. Smith, A. Burt. Inv. made Dec. 26, 1839 by Geo Marshall, John
Hearst Sr., Vincent Griffin.

PORTER, HUGH, SR.—BOX 76, PACK 1862:
    Will dated May 2, 1808. Rec. July 18, 1808. Wit: John Donald, Alexr.
Spence, Hugh Porter Jr. Chn: Jas., Philip, Margery, Wm., Mary, Hugh, John,

Martha, Saml. Porter. Gr. dtr., Mary Chiles Brightman. Inv. made Aug. 1, 1808 by Robt. Smyth, Andw. Gray, John Donald. Another inv. of Rev. Hugh Porter made Aug. 25, 1813 by Wm. Chiles, John Harris, Jas. Henderson. Sale, Nov. 16, 1813. Byrs: Vincent Griffen, Mary E. Porter, John Conner Esq., Saml. Porter, Joab Wilson, Pleasant Thurman, Saml. Caldwell, Jas. Wedgeworth, John Hearst, David Rush, Robt. Foster. Jos. Walker, Wm. Lummus, Garret E. Groce, etc.

PORTER, HUGH—BOX 76, PACK 1863:
Will dated Dec. 15, 1824 in Abbeville Dist. Prov. June 6, 1825. Exrs: Wife, Sarah Porter, John B. Black, Wm. Brownlee, Wit: Richard E. Porter, Moses Rutherford, Hugh Porter, II. Chn. names not given. Inv. made July 9, 1825 by Thos. Patterson, Stephen Jones, David Pressly. Sale, Aug. 12, 1825. Byrs: Archibald Mauldin, David Robertson, Richard Porter, Jesse Goodwin, Caldwell Howie, Col. W. Caldwell, Lee Branton, Andw. Porter, Wm. Brownlee, W. K. Patton.

PADGETT, JOHN—BOX 76, PACK 1864:
Est. admnr. Nov. 4, 1839 by Ezekiel, John Rasor, Abner H. McGee, Enoch Barmore, sum $20,000.00. Bound to Moses Taggart Ord., Abbeville Dist. Cit. pub. at Bethesda Meeting House. Inv. made Nov. 26, 1839 by Albert N. Ware, Gabriel M. Mattison, Robt. Smith, Jas. Killingsworth. John Padgett died Sept. 1839. His wid. Malinda later married John R. McCord. Dist. were 2 infant chn., Mary Ann, Louisa Padgett. Ecily Padgett a ch. died March 1840.

PRATT, WILLIAM—BOX 76, PACK 1865:
Est. admnr. Mar. 28, 1797. Mary Pratt wid., Jos. Pratt, Gen. John Norwood, Cader Gantt bound to Judges of Abbeville Dist., sum $6,000.00. Cit. pub. at Due West Corner. Inv. made May 3, 1797 by Genl. John Norwood, John Lindsay, Capt. John McAdam. Sale, July 6, 1797. Byrs: Thos. Taylor, Robt. Greene, Jas. Russell, Jos. Burton, John Robertson, Mathew Fox, Wm. Drennan, Jos. Pratt, John Sullivan, Francis Cunningham, Mary Pratt, John Shirley, Josiah Burton, Wm. Beck, John Miller, Jas. Gilmore, Wm. Tyner, Austin Smith, Jos. Ellis, etc.

PRESSLY, ROBERT—BOX 76, PACK 1866:
Est. admnr. Oct. 12, 1831 by John S., Saml. Pressly, Wm. Patton, sum $500.00, bound to Moses Taggart Ord. Abbeville Dist. Cit. pub. at Hopewell Ch. Inv. made Oct. 31, 1811 by Saml. Pressly, Thos. McBryde, John Chiles.

PRATT, JAMES—BOX 76, PACK 1867:
Will dated Sept. 7, 1828 in Abbeville Dist. Prov. Sept. 25, 1828. Exrs: Robt. Lindsay, John Pratt. Wit: Saml., Wm. Young, Jas. Lindsay. Wife, no name given, Chn: John, Wm., Robt. Pratt. Inv. made Oct. 11, 1828 by Jas. Lindsay, John L. Ellis, Saml. Young. Sett. made Jan. 5, 1843. Present, John Pratt Exr. who represents two minor chn.: Elizabeth, Sarah A. Pratt. Louisa Pratt wid. of Wm. Pratt decd. and admnrx.; Timothy Thomas, Wm. N. Cunning-

ham, Jas. B. Ky. and wife, Robt., John, Elizabeth, Sarah A. Pratt. 8 distributees in all.

PRATT, SARAH—BOX 76, PACK 1868:
Est. admnr. Nov. 16, 1804 by Wm. Jr., John Pratt Sr., Jas. Lindsey Sr., Saml. Young, bound to Moses Taggart Ord. Abbeville Dist., sum $10,000.00. Sett. made Jan. 5, 1843. Present, John Pratt, Admnr. who represents 2 minors. Elizabeth, Sarah Pratt. Louisa Pratt wid. admnrx. of Wm. Pratt a decd. bro. Timothy Thomas, W. N. Cunningham, Jas. B. Kay, Robt. Pratt. Inv. made Dec. 1, 1840 by Bennet McAdams, Lydall Williams, John E. Ellis. Sarah Pratt mother of Wm., John Pratt.

PELOT, JOHN F.—BOX 76, PACK 1869:
Will dated Jan. 23, 1841. Filed Oct. 26, 1841. Exrs: Ed. M. Burton, Henry J. Pope. Wit: Miss Harriett N. Clark, Miss Elvira A. Smith, Robt. A. Toombs. Was of Wilkes Co., Ga. Wife, Harriett L. Pelot to receive house and lot in the Town of Washington whereon I now reside. To friend Mary Minton one negro girl. Sons, Francis L., Wm. L. Pelot. Owned property in Ga. and S. C. Inv. made Oct. 27, 1841 by A. Houston, Robt. Brady, Dr. John S. Reed.

PETERSON, CONRAD—BOX 76, PACK 1870:
Est. admnr. Oct. 29, 1829 by Dr. Saml., John Pressly, Patrick Gibson, bound to Moses Taggart Ord. Abbeville Dist., sum $200.00. Inv. made Nov. 18, 1829 by Abner Perrin, Rice Mills, Col. John Hearst.

PRINCE, EDWARD S.—BOX 76, PACK 1871:
Inv. made Jan. 7, 1829 by A. Maulding, Silvanus Prince. Another Inv. made Jan. 15, 1828 by A. Giles, Jas. Morrow, G. W. Martin. Sale, Jan. 17, 1828 of Ed. Prince Jr. Byrs: John H. Riley, Dr. John Linton, John C. Martin, Hugh M. Prince, Sylvanus Prince, Edwin W. Hunter, Hudson Prince, Robt. F. Black, Elijah Turnbull, Alexr. Russell, Jonathan Prince, David McCallister, Archibald McMullen, Thos. Shanklin, John Russell, Edward Tilman.

PERRIN, ABNER, SR.—BOX 76, PACK 1872:
Est. admnr. Mar. 31, 1835 by Abner Perrin, Albert T. Traylor, Saml. Zimmerman, sum, $10,000.00, bound to Moses Taggart Ord., Abbeville Dist. Inv. made Apr. 16, 1835 by Saml. Zimmerman, A. T. Traylor, Josiah Patterson. Byrs: Abner Perrin, Wm. Cowen, A. T. Traylor, Saml. Zimmerman.

PURSLEY, HIRAM—BOX 76, PACK 1873:
Est. admnr. Dec. 2, 1839 by Jas. Pursley, Christian V. Barns, Jos. Lyon, sum $500.00, bound to Moses Taggart Ord. Abbeville Dist. Inv. made Dec. 12, 1839 by C. V. Barns, Josiah Patterson, John Moore. Power of Atty: Margaret A. L. Norris formerly Margaret A. L. Pursley of the Co. of Onachita, State of Arkansas, appointed Jas. Norris of same Co., for her as heir of est. of Hiram Pursley, Jan. 3, 1856. Sett. of Hiram Pursley est. made Jan. 6, 1842. Wife of James Norris. Present: Jas. Pursley admnr., Andw. Gillespie in right of his wife Jenny, David, Betsey, Mary Pursley, Mrs. Margaret Pursley mother

of decd. Sett. of est. as far as regards the int. therein of the family of David Pursley decd. David Pursley survived Hiram and died leaving a wid. and 9 chn.

PATTERSON, WILLIAM—Box 76, PACK 1874:
Est. admnr. Dec. 27, 1837 by Josiah C., Napoleon B. Patterson, Benj. F. Lipscomb, sum $40,000.00, bound to Moses Taggart Ord. Abbeville Dist. Cit. pub. at Mt. Pleasant Ch. Inv. made by David Gillam, John Hearst Sr., Cary Patterson. Byrs: Mrs. Black, Josiah C., N. B. Patterson, John White, G. B. Crawford, John Hearst, Francis Arnold, W. D. Partlow.

PENNELL, ALEXANDER—BOX 76, PACK 1875:
Est. admnr. by Jos. C. Matthews, Hugh Stuart, Thos. Keown, sum $500.00, bound to Moses Taggart Ord. Abbeville Dist., Jan. 6, 1840. Sett. made Jan. 10, 1844. Present J. C. Matthews, admnr., Wm. Pennell, distributee. Wid. and 3 chn. Sale, Jan. 25, 1840. Byrs: Jane Pennell, H. H. Stewart, Wm. Pennell, H. Bentley, J. B. Speed, H. Darracott.

PATTERSON, ALEXANDER, SR.—BOX 76, PACK 1876:
Will dated Apr. 27, 1835. Prov. July 1839. Exrs: John Kennedy, Josiah McGaw. Wit: Archibald, John, Sally Ann Bradley. Chn: Jane, Josiah, Saml., Alexr. Patterson, Gr. chn: John, Jane, Mary Patterson chn. of decd. son Jas. Patterson. Malcom Patterson son of Alexr. Patterson. Archibald Bradley married Jane Patterson. Inv. made July 17, 1839 by W. Bradley, A. Bradley, Jas. C. Lindsay.

PAULE, ANDREW, JR.—BOX 76, PACK 1877:
Est. admnr. Sept. 1, 1828 by Hamilton, Benj. Hill, John Devlin, sum, $10,000.00, bound to Moses Taggart Ord. Abbeville Dist. Cit. pub. at Cedar Springs Ch.

PAUL, WILLIAM P.—BOX 77, PACK 1878:
Will dated Jan. 25, 1841. Rec. Feb. 27, 1843. Exrs: Jas. S. Willson merchant at Abbeville Village, Jas. J. Devlin, Saml. S. Hill. Wit: Jas. Edwards, David Atkins, Chas. H. Wilson. Wife, Agness Elvira Paul. Chn: Sarah Frances, Agness Amanda, Elvira Jane, Mary Lydia Paul. "After Mary's death her part to be divided between the heirs of my bro. Geo. Paul and Jane Hill that is now decd. and my sis. Mary Devlin." Inv. made Mar. 11, 1843 by N. Jefferson Davis, Jas. Edwards, David Atkins. Sale, Mar. 13, 1843. Byrs: Isaac Hobert, David Keller, Franklin Branch, Wm. Sales, Archibald McCord, John Wilson, Jas. A. Hamilton, Elijah N. Wilson, Jas. Moore, etc.

PATTERSON, JAMES N.—BOX 77, PACK 1879:
Est. admnr. Mar. 22, 1843 by Larkin Reynolds, Jas. C. Sproull, Milton W. Coleman, bound to David Lesly Ord. Abbeville Dist., sum $30,000.00. Petition of Larkin Reynolds sheweth that Jas. N. Patterson departed this life intestate at about age of 10 yrs., that he was the stepson of your petr. Sett. made Oct. 8, 1844. Present, Larkin Reynolds and wife, Mary D. Reynolds distributees.

PETTIGREW, ROBERT—BOX 77, PACK 1880:
Est. admnr. Aug. 17, 1843 by Dr. Isaac Branch, Jas. H. Cobb, Johnson Ramey, Jas. Huey, sum $8,000.00, bound to David Lesly Ord. Abbeville Dist. Left a wid. and several chn. 1844 Pd. J. L. Pettigrew legacy $388.90. E. A. Pettigrew was the wid.

PETTIGREW, GEORGE—BOX 77, PACK 1881:
Will dated Mar. 1, 1839. Prov. Aug. 9, 1843. Exrs: son, Robt. Pettigrew, s. l., John Brownlee. Wit: Joel Lockhart, John Robinson, F. Y. Baskin. Chn: Sarah Oliver, Margaret Robison, John Even, Robt. H. Pettigrew, Rosa Ann Brownlee, Gr. chn: Mary Emely dtr. of Margaret Robison, Mary T., Sarah J. Paskel. "Their part to be left in hands of John Brownlee". Sons, Geo. P., Perry Pettigrew. Sett. made Aug. 21, 1851. Wid. Mary Pettigrew. Due R. P. Oliver $866.58. (On another page part of a will was written.) Ment. dtr. Jane Paskel, son, Robin Pettigrew. Inv. made Dec. 14, 1849 by John C. Mauldin, Joel Lockhart.

PAUL, WILLIAM P. (MINOR CHILDREN)—BOX 77, PACK 1882:
Andrew J. Weems, Saml. Hill, N. J. Davis bound to David Lesly Ord. Abbeville Dist. sum $500.00. Andw. J. Weems made gdn. of Sarah F., Agness A., Elvira J. Paul. Sett. of Sarah F. Paul made May 19, 1852 who married John R. Adair. Sett. of Elvira J. Paul made Nov. 7, 1857 who married Wm. W. Godfrey. Petition of Andw. Weems sheweth that many yrs. since Andw. Paul died leaving a will in which he willed a certain tract of land to Wm. P. Paul and his bodily heirs, that the said Wm. P. Paul, his son, also died leaving a will and Saml. Hill qualified as Exr. Wm. Paul left a wid., Agnes E. Paul and the following chn. by a former wife Mary L. and by his present wid. three chn: Sarah F., Agnes A., Elvira J. Paul, all under 14 yrs. Agnes A. Paul married S. Keller.

PARKER, JANE—BOX 77, PACK 1883:
Est. admnr. Oct. 17, 1843 by Jas. Parker of Anderson Dist., Mathew Pool, Zachariah Graham of Abbeville Dist. bound to David Lesly Ord. sum $200.00. Petition of Jas. Parker sheweth that about 1820 his father, Jas. Parker, died leaving a will which his wid. Jane was exr., that lately the mother of Jas. Parker died having a number of chn. all of age, but one, (Sarah) in the State Asylum. On July 16, 1844 Margaret, Rebecca Parker, Mathew Pool, Zachariah Graham recd. $41.37 each of the est. Inv. made Nov. 22, 1843 by Wm. Buchanan Jr., Wm. Buchanan Sr., Jos. Milford, John Morgan.

POSEY, BENJAMIN L.—BOX 77, PACK 1884:
Est. admnr. Nov. 25, 1843 by Addison F. Posey, Jas. H. Cobb, Johnson Ramey, John A. Martin, John Cunningham bound to David Lesly Ord. Abbeville Dist. sum $70,000.00. Benj. Posey left several chn., one admnr., Addison F. Posey. Expend: for Charlotte E. Posey in 1844 amt. $43.88. Sarah S. Posey $85.75. Recd. from A. F. Posey, Exr. of Martha C. Posey decd., $698.24. Our distributee sh. of est. Apr. 20, 1847. W. B. Traynham, Eliza Traynham, A. W.

Lynch and wife Elizabeth recd. part of est. $489.56. (In one place name appeared
to be Benj. L. then in another Benj. S. Not positive.)

PRATT, SARAH A.—BOX 77, PACK 1885:
    On Feb. 16, 1843 John, Robt. Pratt, Jas. Lindsay bound to David Lesly
Ord. Abbeville Dist. sum $1,854.00. John Pratt made gdn. Sarah Ann Pratt.
Setl. made Jan. 25, 1845 of Sarah Ann Pratt, a minor, now wife of John T.
Miller, recd. $1,026.13 from est. of Jas. Pratt decd. Recd. $932.21 from est.
of Sarah Pratt decd. John Pratt, gdn., was a bro. to Sarah Ann Pratt.

PRATT, ELIZABETH O.—BOX 77, PACK 1886:
    On Jan. 8, 1843 Robt., John Pratt, Jas. B. Kay bound to David Lesly
Ord. Abbeville Dis. sum $1,864.00. Robt. Pratt gdn. of Elizabeth O. Pratt, a
minor. Robt. Pratt was a bro. to Elizabeth O. Pratt. dtr. of Sarah Pratt. Elizabeth
O. Pratt later married Lewis C. Clinkscales.

PRATT, WILLIAM—BOX 77, PACK 1887:
    Est. admnr. Dec. 23, 1842 by Louisa Pratt, Wm. Robertson, John Donald,
Robt. Smith bound to David Lesly Ord. Abbeville Dist. sum $13,000.00. Louisa
Pratt, the wid. Had 4 minor chn. Wm. Robertson was bro. of Louisa Pratt. Inv.
made Feb. 24, 1842 by Lydall Williams, Wm. Pratt Sr., Robt. Ellis.

PUCKETTS, JAMES (MINORS)—BOX 77, PACK 1888:
    On Feb. 5, 1844 Wm. C. Puckett, Andw. J. Weed, Wm. Brady bound to
David Lesly Ord. Abbeville Dist. sum $480.00. Wm. C. Puckett made gdn. of
Eliza E., Allen S., and Louisa Puckett. Louisa Puckett of age Feb. 20, 1857
when the setl. was made. Wm. C. Puckett, their gdn., was a bro.

PARKER, THOMAS—BOX 77, PACK 1889:
    Will dated Jan. 24, 1844 in Abbeville Dist. Prov. Apr. 11, 1844. Exr.
Wife, Ellen L. Parker. Wit: Dr. John S. Reid, Jas. Taggart, A. T. Hamilton.
Chn. ment. names not given. Inv. made July 3, 1844 by Moses O. Talman,
Jas. Taggart, F. A. Calhoun, Robt. Brady.

PARTLOW, CAPT. JOHN—BOX 77, PACK 1890:
    Will dated Aug. 10, 1839 in Abbeville Dist. Prov. June 19, 1844. Exrs:
Sons, Wm. D., Jas. Y. L., John A. Partlow. Wit: Thos. S. Henderson, John
Scott, S. or L. White. Chn: Wm., Jas. Y. L., John A. Partlow, Ophela S.,
wife of Joshua W. Jones, Emily G., wife of Sampson Cain (John Wm. Cain, only
chn. of Emily and Sampson Cain) Elizabeth Ann Partlow. Inv. made Oct. 31,
1844 by Jos. Wardlaw, Milton W. Coleman, Thos. C. Lipscomb.

PENNY, MINORS—BOX 77, PACK 1891:
    On Apr. 3, 1841, Henry, John W. Penny, John Ruff bound to Moses
Taggart Ord. Abbeville Dist. sum $2,000.00. Henry H. Penny made gdn. of
Thos. H. Penny, a minor over 14 yrs., Martha G. Penny, a minor under 14
yrs. Setl. of Thos. Penny, now of age, made Dec. 2, 1845. By the will of Elizabeth
Cromer recd. $372.84. Setl. of Martha G. Penny also recd. $372.84. from the
will of Elizabeth Cromer. She later married a Hawthorne.

PATTON, WILLIAM (MINORS)—BOX 77, PACK 1892:
In July 15, 1839 Isaac Kennedy, Geo. J. Cannon, John Kennedy, Jane Patton bound to Moses Taggart Ord. Abbeville Dist. sum $30,000.00. Isaac Kennedy made gdn. of Rebecca A., Edmond L., Sarah C. Patton. Setl. of Sarah C. Patton, now of age, made Mar. 27, 1852. Setl. of Rebecca A. Patton, now of age, made Feb. 17, 1847. Setl. of Wm. W. Patton, now of age, made Mar. 22, 1845. John Franklin Pratton was a minor.

PEASTER, MATILDA—BOX 77, PACK 1893:
On Feb. 9, 1833 Micajah H. Piester, Geo. Lomax, John McCord Jr. bound to Moses Taggart Ord. Abbeville Dist. sum $2,000.00. Micajah Piester made gdn. of Matilda Piester, his dtr. She recd. $770.75 from land that was sold in Newberry Dist., that had been given to her by her grandfather Jacob Cromer. Frances Atkins states that she had been long acquainted with M. H. Peaster and that his dtr., Matilda, is somewhat of a lunatic . . . Expend: Jan. 28, 1833. Recd. from admnr. Adam Cromer on est. of Jacob Cromer decd. $857.44. The gdn. married Hannah Cromer, dtr. of decd. The ward Matilda is the only dtr. by Hannah, the wife of the gdn. (Name written Peaster and Piester.)

PATTERSON, MINORS—BOX 77, PACK 1894:
On Feb. 18, 1841 John Patterson, Archibald K. Patton, Saml. Cowan bound to Moses Taggart Ord. Abbeville Dist. sum $2,000.00. John Patterson made gdn. of Jane K., Mary Patterson minors over 14 yrs. Expend: 1841 recd. of John Kennedy Exr., Alexr. Patters on decd. for my two wards Jane, Mary Patterson $166.67.

PATTON, JANE—BOX 77, PACK 1895:
Will dated Sept. 16, 1844 in Abbeville Dist. Filed Oct. 2, 1844. Exrs: Archibald, Isaac Kennedy. Wit: Robt. Devlin, Margaret Morris, John A. Brown. Chn: John Franklin, Wm. Washington, Rebecca Amanda, Edmond Lewis, Sarah C. Patton. Gr. dtr., Margaret Jane Patton. "The other half of a child's part to A. Kennedy to be held in trust for the use of Nancy C. Patton during her natural life, at her death the property in trust to decend to her dtr., Margaret Jane Patton." Jane Patton died Sept. 15, 1844. Inv. made Dec. 6, 1844 by S. B. McClinton, Jas. H. Foster, Saml. Jordon.

PAUL, WILLIAM A.—BOX 77, PACK 1896:
Est. admnr. Sept. 17, 1844. by Francis Atkins, Barthw. Jordan, Abraham Lights, bound to David Lesly Ord. Abbeville Dist., sum $1,000.00. Inv. made Oct. 4, 1844 by Barthw. Jordan, Abraham Lites, John D. Adams. Wm. A. Paul died having no wife or chn. State of Ala., Burten Co. A negro boy Dave was sold in said state in 1845 that belonged to est. of Wm. A. Paul decd. late of S. C.

POSEY, MARTHA CRENSHAW—BOX 77, PACK 1897:
Will dated Aug. 17, 1844 in Abbeville Dist. Prov. Sept. 21, 1844. Exrs: Bro., Addison F. Posey. Dr. Isaac Branch. Wit: Ann R. Jackson, Melissa A. Sample, Mary A. Allen. Left $500.00 to the M. E. Ch. at Abbeville to pay the debts hanging over it from which the trustees of said ch. are responsible. Left

$250.00 to the education of my cousin, Margarett Matilda Posey, dtr. of the late Charles Posey now residing in Laurens Dist. Rest of est. be divided equally among bros. & sis. (no names given.) On Apr. 20, 1847 her bro. B. L. Posey recd. $698.25 from her est. A. W. Lynch recd. $698.25 in right of wife Elizabeth who was a sis. of said Martha C. Posey (On one paper it stated that Martha C. Posey was not quite 19 yrs. old when she died) Letter found in package. Franklin, Miss. 9 April 1846.

Dear Sir:

Yours of the 24 has just been read, in answer to which, I would say that I am willing to recieve and accept notice through the Medium of yours without publication. You and all parties conderned can therefore preceede as though notice of publication had been made through the medium of the Abb Banner. I am respectfully yours obb servt.

W. B. Traynham

PHILLIPS, WILLIAM—BOX 77, PACK 1898:

Est. admnr, Oct. 21, 1844. by Thomas Rosemond, Medy Mays, W. W. Anderson, bound to David Lesly Ord. Abbeville Dist., sum $100.00. Sale, made Nov. 14, 1844. Byrs: Wesley Robertson, Wm. Graham Sr., Elizabeth Phillips, Larkin Mays, W. T. Jones, Jos. Bingham. Jane, Mary Phillips both decd. were ment. in the accts.

PRINCE, SARAH W., (MINOR)—BOX 77, PACK 1899:

On Jan. 9, 1846 Robt. McNair, John Swilling, Geo B. Clinkscales, bound to David Lesly Ord. Abbeville Dist., sum $1,229.00. Robt. McNair made gdn. of Sarah Prince a minor about 9 yrs. old. Of age when the setl. was made Mar. 29, 1858. Expend: Jan. 1, 1857 Recd. from est. of Hutson Prince, legacy $180.00. The petition of Robt. McNair respectfully sheweth that on Apr. 15, 1845 H. M. Prince presented a petition to this court for the gdnship. of Sarah Prince a minor under age of choice. Your petr. being dissatisfied with that appointment and with the consent of the mother of said minor who is now about 9 yrs. your petr. prays that in as much as he is the grandfather of said Sarah, and her father W. Prince is dead and as she has an est. given her from her grandfather Hudson Prince of $614.56, etc . . . Louisa Prince was the mother of Sarah. She was the dtr. of Winkfield Prince.

PRINCE, HUDSON, JR.—BOX 77, PACK 1900:

The petition of Dr. Linch sheweth that Hudson Prince Jr. died intestate leaving neither wife or chn. That he has been dead more than 6 months. Dr. A. W. Lynch made the admnr. on Dec. 2, 1844. Sale, Dec. 17, 1844. Byrs: Mrs. Russell, Jas. Russell, Hugh Prince.

PRICE, JAMES B.—BOX 77, PACK 1901:

Est. admnr. July 30, 1844 by Nancy, Abraham Price bound to David Lesly Ord. Abbeville Dist., sum $1,000.00.

PENNALL, MINORS—BOX 77, PACK 1902:

On Jan. 25, 1845, Wm. Pennel, Henry Simpson, Wm. H. Calhoun, bound to David Lesly Ord. Abbeville Dist., sum $196.00. Wm. Pennel made gdn. of Esther, Robt. Pennell. Chn. of Alexr. Pennell Decd. Their gdn., Wm. Pennell was an uncle.

PASCHALL, MINORS—BOX 77, PACK 1903:
    On Mar. 19, 1838 Thos. Jr., Thos. Anderson Sr., Littleton Yarbrough, M.D., bound to Moses Taggart Ord. Abbeville Dist., sum $20,000.00. Thos. Anderson Jr., made gdn. of Sarah Ann Elizabeth, John Thos. Franklin, Mary Frances Amelia Paschal minors under 14 yrs.

QUARLES, JOHN—BOX 78, PACK 1904:
    Est. admnr. July 14, 1823 by Richard Quarles, Luke Matthews, Jos. Davis, sum $3,000.00. Bound to Moses Taggart Ord. Abbeville Dist. Inv. made Aug. 7, 1823 by Amos Edwards, Jas. Edwards, Luke Mathis. Byrs: Wm. Quarles, Dr. Arnold, Robt. Richey, Saml. A. Wilson, Saml. Quarles, Thos. Osborn, Luke Mathis, Alphus Baker, Jas Wilson, Wm. H. Giles, Richard Qaurles, Henry Livingston, Elias Morgan, etc.

QUEEN, PATRICK—BOX 78, PACK 1905:
    Est. admnr. Mar. 26, 1798 by Jenny Queen wid. Saml Foster Esq., Adam Hill, sum $1,000.00, bound to Judges Abbeville Dist. Inv. made Apr. 26, 1798 by Alexr. White, John Foster, Wm. Cochran. Sale, May 1, 1798. Byrs: Wm. McDonnald, Jenny Queen, Saml. Morris, Alexr. White, John Foster, John Briscoe, David Pressly, Robt. McMichal, Saml. Morris, Rowlin Kown, John Brachenridge.

REYNOLDS, BENJAMIN—BOX 78, PACK 1906:
    Est. admnr. April 18, 1816 by Jas. Arnold, John Connor, Jas. Pettus, John Downey bound unto Taliaferro Livingston Ord. Abbeville Dist. aum $20,000.00. Cit. pub. at Cambridge. Inv. made May 17, 1816 by Gibson Wooldrige, Jas Wardlaw, Jas. Shackleford. Expend: June 5, 1816 Paid for 1 pr. slippers for Hulda Reynolds $1.87½. Jan. 5, 1817 Paid J. V. Reynolds for superintending the plantation 1 yr. $200.00. Dec. 22, 1817 Paid John McGhee for boarding Bennet, Larkin Reynolds for 1817, $157.06¼. Paid Wm. Smith on probate money Mr. Reynolds recd. for him in Virginia $115.77. Jan. 10. 1818 Recd. of Jas. Reynolds on note $11.57.

ROMAN, ABRAHAM—BOX 78, PACK 1907:
    Est admnr. July 24, 1813 by Grissilla, John Roman, Jas Smith bound to Taliaferro Livingston Ord. Abbeville Dist. sum $2,000.00. Cit. pub. at Tabernacle Meeting House. (Letter) To Mr. John Roman, Stoney Point, P. O. Abbeville, South Carolina.
Columbus, Mississippi Oct. 12th. 1845
Dear Uncle,
    I write to inform you that I am married a short time since to Mr. Jesse Aiken and we are well at present I wish you to inform us concerning the money that is due me from my fathers estate as we need it very much whether it is ready or not we wish you to write soon and give a full stament concerning the money and when it will or can be ready and also inform me how my brothers are doing and

where they live and whether they are well. We have nothing more at the time but times are hard and crops are stored hoping the lines may find you and family well we subscribe our names. Jesse Aiken Elizabeth Aiken formerly Elizabeth Roman. Jan. 16, 1846 Jesse, Lydia Elizabeth Aiken dtr. of Abraham Roman both of Lowndes County, Miss, recd. $200.00 from her father's est. in Abbeville, S. C. June 4, 1827 Recd. of Malinda Roman $4.81¼.

REGAN, JOHN—BOX 78, PACK 1908:
Est. admnr. Oct. 17, 1823 by Jesse Regan, Robt., Thos. McBride bound to Moses Taggart Ord. Abbeville Dist. sum $500.00. Cit. pub. at Asbury Chappel. Dec. 23, 1823 Paid Elizabeth Regan $64.37½. Nov. 4, 1824 Recd. of Bailey Regan $19.93¾. Byrs. at sale. Jesse, Bailey, Young, Elizabeth Regan, Nathaniel Robinson, Wm. Chiles, etc.

RAMEY, DR. JAMES—BOX 78, PACK 1909:
Est. admnr. May 25, 1826 by Jonathan Johnston, Alexr. Hunter Esq., Geo. W. Martin bound to Moses Taggart Ord. Abbeville Dist. sum $3,000.00. Inv. made May 27, 1826 by Ephraim R. Calhoun, Joseph S. Talbert, John McLerman.

RAMSAY, SAMUEL—BOX 78, PACK 1910:
Est. admnr. Oct. 20, 1824 by Jonathan Johnston, Saml. Davis, Harrison Long bound to Moses Taggart Ord. Abbeville Dist. sum $1,000.00. Cit. pub. at Providence Church. April 2, 1827 Paid Isaac Ramsay $20.00. Paid to est. of Wm. Ramsay $20.00. Reserved to myself Jonathan Johnston as an heir of est. $20.00.

RUSSELL, ROBERT—BOX 78, PACK 1911:
Est. admnr. Aug. 15, 1825 by Jane Russell, Saml. Houston, Patrick Johnston, Joesph Lyon bound to Moses Taggart Ord. Abbeville Dist. sum $3,000.00. Cit. pub. at Upper Long Cane Church. Jan. 1, 1827 Paid John Russell in part $15.00. Mar. 6 Paid Robt. Russell his share $100.00 May 7, Paid John Brown his share $192.60. June 29, Paid John Wier for Jas., Margaret Smyley $160.00. Dec. 25 Paid Jane C. Russell part share $25.00. April 14 Paid John Richey part share $25.00. April 14, Paid Alexr. Russell part share $25.00. Oct. 18, 1826 Paid John, Jane Brown part share $1166.68¾.

RICHEY, JAMES S.—BOX 78, PACK 1912:
Est. admnr. Sept. 3, 1827 by Wm. Richey, John Donnald, John Miller bound to Moses Taggart Ord. Abbeville Dist. sum $1,000.00. Cit pub. at Greenville Church. Inv. made Sept. 10, 1827 by John Donnald, John Seawright, Robt. Dunn, Benjamin Moseley, John McCullough. Sale, Oct. 11, 1827. Byrs: Robt., Geo., Wm. Jr., Mrs. Richey, John Robertson.

RICH, JAMES—BOX 78, PACK 1913:
Est. admnr. Mar. 24, 1817 by John Davidson of the est. of Jas. Rich of the State of Connecticut, but late of Abbeville Dist. bound to Taliaferro Livingston Ord. Abbeville Dist. sum 1,000 lbs. Mary C. Rich his wid. sheweth that her husband died on Sept. 27th. last. That he was possessed of about 64 acres on water of Long Cane Creek bounded by lands of John Lyon, Jas. C. Lites, John

Patterson upon which he died and where your Petr. and her chn. now live. Heirs, Mary C. Rich wid. Alice wife of Lew Sprouse aged about 16 yrs. Martha age about 10 yrs. Mary Elizabeth age about 5 yrs.

RUSSELL, JAMES—BOX 78, PACK 1914:
Est. armnr. Oct. 26, 1827 by John, Wm. Cunningham, Saml. Houston bound to Moses Targgart Ord. Abbeville Dist. sum $5,000.00. Nov. 1832 Recd. of Wm. Russell note in full $111.44. Recd. of Jas. C. Russell $128.72. Recd. of Martha Russell $53.85. Recd. of Miss Jane Russell $53.88. Recd. of Betsey Ann Russell $11.06¼.

RHUSON, THOMAS—BOX 78, PACK 1915:
Est. admnr. May 4, 1832 by Wm. Sadler, Jas. Gillam, Wm. Eddins bound to Moses Taggart Ord. Abbeville Dist. sum $500.00. Inv. made May 14, 1832 by Robt. Cunningham, Nathan Calhoun, John N. Sample. Sale, May 15, 1832. Byrs: Mrs. Rhuson, Chas. B. Fooshe, Braxton Smith, Wm. Carter, Pleasant Sadler, etc.

ROBERTSON, JOHN, SR.—BOX 78, PACK 1916:
Est. admnr. July 2, 1827 by Andrew Robison, Wm. Ware, John Donald bound to Moses Taggart Ord. Abbeville Dist. sum $40,000.00. Cit. pub at Scuffle-town. Legatees: Jane Robison wid. Peggy wife of Richard Maddox. Lettice wife of Augusta Maddox. Andrew, John Robison Jr. Jane wife of Joseph Richey, Elizabeth wife of John McCord. Mary Stone wid. (Written Robertson, Robison).

RAVLIN, WILLIAM—BOX 78, PACK 1917:
Est. admnr. April 28, 1831 by Bartholomew Jordon, Abraham Lites. John Devlin bound to Ord. sum $2,000.00. Inv made April 29, 1831 by David, John Ravlin, Jas. Devlin.

ROBISON, JANE—BOX 78, PACK 1918:
Est. admnr. Dec. 19, 1831 by Andrew Robison, Augustin Maddox, John Donald bound to Moses Taggart Ord. Abbeville Dist. sum $20,000.00. Legatees: John, Andrew Robison, John McCord, Augustine Maddox, Joseph Richey. Sale, Jan. 5, 1832. Byrs: Augusta, Richard Maddox, Nancy Robestson, Wm. Kay, etc

RITCHEY, NANCY—BOX 78, PACK 1919:
Est. admnr. Nov. 16, 1812 by John Weatherall, Hugh Dickson, Joseph Ritchey bound to Taliaferro Livingston Ord. Abbeville Dist. sum $10,000.00. Cit. pub. at Greenville Church. Sett. of John Ritchie est. made Nov. 24, 1808. Legacy recd. from est. of Jas. Ritchie Senr. $250.00. There were 10 shares, no names given. Sale of Nancy Ritchie made Dec. 10, 1812. Byrs: Margaret, John, Wm., Jas., Joseph Ritchey, etc. (Name written Richie, Ritchie, Ritchey).

RAMSAY, NEWTON—BOX 78, PACK 1920:
Est. admnr. Dec. 28, 1827 by Saml. Ramsay, John Cothran, Jas. Patterson bound to Moses Taggart Ord. Abbeville Dist. sum $6,000.00. Dec. 10, 1828 Paid John Ramsey $9.00. Dec. 5, 1828 Articles bought for Anny Ramsay $54.26. Sale, Jan. 15, 1828. Byrs: Ann, Saml. Ramsay, Jacob Slappy, Roger McKinney, Joseph Rushton, etc.

RAY, ZACHARIAH—BOX 78, PACK 1921:
Est. admnr. Oct. 20, 1824 by Henry Gray, J. Weens, Dudley Brooks bound to Moses Taggart Ord. Abbeville Dist. sum $1,000.00. Sale, Feb. 1, 1828. Byrs: Silas, Jas., Mrs. Sarah Ray, David Thomas, Henry Gray, etc.

ROBISON, HENRY—BOX 78, PACK 1922:
Est. admnr. Dec. 15, 1824 by Wm., Wm. Robinson Senr. Robt. McBride bound to Moses Taggart Ord. Abbeville Dist. sum $2,000.00. Inv made Jan. 4, 1825 by Francis McBride, Mathew, John Shanks. April 8, 1826 Paid Wm. Robinson Jr. $20.00. Paid Margaret Robinson $3.50. (Written Robison, Robinson).

ROBERTSON, WILLIAM—BOX 78, PACK 1924:
Est. admnr. Nov. 5, 1819 by John, Andrew Robertson, Joseph Richey, John McCord Jr. bound to Moses Taggart Ord. Abbeville Dist. sum $20,000.00. Cit. pub. at Greenville Church.

ROBINSON, GEORGE—BOX 78, PACK 1925:
Will dated Oct. 15, 1817 in Abbeville Dist. Prov. Dec. 15, 1817. Exrs: Wife, Mary Robertson, John McCalla. Wit: John, Hickerson Barksdale, Saml.. Cole. Chn: Jas Miscampbell, Mary Elizabeth, Martha Ann, Jane Brownlee. "Wife pregnant with child." April 1820 Paid taxes for land lying in Orangeburg Dist. $1.39. April 4, 1820 Recd. from John Roberson admnr. of Saml. Robertson est. $44.79. July 14, Recd. from Wm. Brownlee $100.00. Jan. 1829 Paid Mary E. Robertson $10.00 Oct. Paid Martha A. Robertson $10.00 Jane B. Robertson $10.00. Nov. 20, 1826 Paid Mary Collier Extrx. said to be for use of Mary E. Robertson $100.00. June 12, 1827 Paid Edward Collier and wife $350.75.

REGAN, JESSE—BOX 79, PACK 1926:
Est. admnr. Nov. 24, 1826 by Young Regan, John Leard, Robt. McBride bound to Moses Taggart Ord. Abbeville Dist. sum $2,000.00. Cit. pub. at Hopewell Church. Jan. 26, 1828 paid Baley Reagin $2.25. Feb. 2, 1828 paid Allen Reagin $8.25. Sale, Dec. 13, 1826. Byrs: Rachel, Allen, Baley, Young Ragan, etc. (Written Regan, Reagin.)

RICHEY, WILLIAM—BOX 79, PACK 1927:
Will dated 1779 in 96 Dist. Rec. May 16, 1783. Exr: Sis. Mary Ritchey. Wit: Ebenezer, Aaron Starns, John Field. Parents, Robt., Margaret Richey. One paper ment. Mary Goodman Exr. Inv. made by Saml. Wharton, Saml. Weathers, John Carter. (Written Ritchey, Richey.)

RAY, ISAAC—BOX 79, PACK 1928:
Est. admnr. May 2, 1805 by Mary Ray, John Stevens, Thos. Heard bound to Andrew Hamilton Ord. Abbeville Dist. sum $5,000.00. Inv. made May 16, 1805 by Michael Taylor, Benjamin Chiles, John Logan. Sale, May 22, 1805. Byrs: Mary Ray, Hannah Osbrone, Bird Martin, etc.

RUSSELL, ROBERT—BOX 79, PACK 1929:
Est. admnr. Dec. 13, 1805 by Alexr. White, Jas. Gray bound to Andrew Hamilton Ord. Abbeville Dist. sum $5,000.00. Inv. made Jan. 3, 1806 by John, Saml. Foster, Sr., Andrew White.

RAPLEY, RICHARD ANDREW—BOX 79, PACK 1930:
Est. admnr. Mar. 14, 1823 by Jas. Nicholson, Patrick Duncan, Thos. *Lehre* bound to Moses Taggart Ord. Abbeville Dist. sum $75,000.00. Cit. pub. at Upper Long Cane Church.

RICE, ZERI—BOX 79, PACK 1931:
Est. admnr. Jan. 29, 1824 by Jas., Saml. Sills, Robt. Buchanan bound to Moses Taggart Ord. Abbeville Dist. sum $1,000.00. Cit. pub. at Siloam Church. Feb. 13, 1826 paid Garland Rice $2.00. Pinckney Rice $2.00. May 16, 1827 paid Caroline Rice $1.62½.

RUSHTON, JOHN—BOX 79, PACK 1932:
Est. admnr. Jan. 16, 1826 by Jas. Carson, Saml. Marshall, John Hearst bound to Moses Taggart Ord. Abbeville Dist. sum $10,000.00. Cit. pub. at Smyrna Church. Inv. made Feb. 8, 1826 by Saml., G. F. Caldwell, Jacob Slappy. Sale, Feb. 9, 1826. Byrs: Priscilla Rushton, Jacob Slappy, Leroy Wason, Richard Pollard, Hugh Robinson.

RUSHTON, PRISCILLA—BOX 79, PACK 1933:
Est. admnr. Feb. 26, 1827 by Jas. Carson, Luke Mathis, Donald Douglass bound to Moses Taggart Ord. Abbeville Dist. sum $5,000.00. Cit. pub. at Rehobeth Church. Sale, Mar. 8, 1827. Byrs: Nathan Rushton, etc.

ROBERTS, BENJAMIN—BOX 79, PACK 1934:
Est. admnr. July 18, 1823 by Paschall D. Klugh, Henry Gray, Jas. Arnold bound to Moses Taggart Ord. Abbeville Dist. sum $10,000.00. Nancy wife of Benjamin Roberts relinquished her right of admnr. to her brother, Paschall D. Klugh. Oct. 10, 1826 paid Thos. J. Roberts $9.00. Jan. 11, 1827 paid tuition of Benjamin F. Roberts $5.00. To John B. Roberts for boarding $66.00.

RICHEY, WILLIAM—BOX 79, PACK 1935:
Est. admnr. Jan. 3, 1820 by Joseph Richey, Jas. Agnew, Wm. Blain bound to Moses Taggart Ord. Abbeville Dist. sum $6,000.00. Recd. 1820 of John Richey for rent of land $15.50. Recd. of Margaret Richey for rent $17.00. Recd. of Robt. Richey on note $44.74. Mar. 12, 1821 paid Jas Richey, Jr. $5.00.

RICHEY, WILLIAM—BOX 79, PACK 1936:
Est. admnr. Nov. 24, 1821 by Col. Isaac Cowan, John Wier, Robt. Richey, Saml. R. Evans bound to Moses Taggart Ord. Abbeville Dist. sum $2,000.00 Cit. pub. at Upper Long Cane Church. Inv. made Dec. 6, 1821 by Robt. Richey, Joseph Lyons, Wm. Cochran. Betsey Richey the wid. later married Joseph Lyon.

ROBERTSON, ROBERT—BOX 79, PACK 1937:
Will dated Nov. 5, 1819 in Abbeville Dist. Prov. Feb. 4, 1825. Exrs: Hugh Morrah, Jas Wardlaw, Esq., Barzilla G. Jay. Wit: Augustine Arnold, Wm. McIlwain, Jr., Henson Norris. Chn: Reuben Robertson, Jean, Susanna, Elizabeth Greer. Bro. John Robertson. Sett. made July 16, 1833 ment. Henson Norris, Sanders Williamson, legatees in right of their wives.

RICHARDSON, DUDLEY—BOX 79, PACK 1938:
Est. admnr. May 27, 1826 by Thos. B. Byrd, Elihu Creswell, Robt.
Turner bound to Moses Taggart Ord. Abbeville Dist. sum $20,000.00 Cit. pub.
at Siloam Church. Sale, Dec. 20, 1826. Byrs: Chas. B. Fooshe, Thos. Long,
Chesley Davis, Henry Richardson, etc.

RYKARD, PETER—BOX 79, PACK 1939:
Will dated Feb. 1, 1826 in Abbeville Dist. Prov. Feb. 6, 1826. Exrs:
Sons, David, Jacob Rykard. Wit: Jas. P. Darby, Thos. Hinton, John Blake.
Wife ment. no name given. Chn: Adam, Peter, Jacob Rykard, Mary Magdelane Keller. Sett: Feb. 23, 1859. Present: Jacob, Peter Rykard, Sarah C. wife
of Wm. P. Level, Walter G. Keller in right of wife Mary Magdelane. Gr. son:
S. P. Rykard. Joel W. Townsend who represented Martha M. Townsend a gr.
dtr. and sis. of S. P. Rykard. Absent, Mary wid. of Peter Rykard. At this
time Adam Aykard was dead.

ROMAN, SMITH—BOX 79, PACK 1940:
Est. admnr. Jan. 20, 1837 by John Roman, John Buchanan, Joel Smith
bound to Moses Taggart Ord. Abbeville Dist. sum $10,000.00. Feb. 12, 1838
paid Jas. Shackelford trustee Cokesbury School $96.31¼. Cit. pub. at Rocky
Creek Church.

RUSSELL, JANE—BOX 79, PACK 1941:
Est. admnr. Nov. 26, 1833 by Saml. Huston, Hudson Prince, Robt.
McNair bound to Moses Taggart Ord. Abbeville Dist. sum $2,000.00. Cit. pub.
at Upper Long Cane Church. Wife of Jas. Russell decd. Mar. 17, 1835 paid
Jas. C. Russell $135.00. Dec. 2, 1835 paid E. A., Mary Russell $19.75. Byrs:
Margaret Carlisle, Jas. C., Alexr., Martha Russell, Sarah Liddell, etc.

RYAN, LACON—BOX 79, PACK 1942:
Will dated Aug. 14, 1784 in 96 Dist. Prov. Nov. 30, 1785. Exrs:
Brothers, John, Benjamin Ryan, Arthur Simkins. Wit: Saml. Walker, Conrad
Gallman, Robt. Bartlett. Wife, Margaret Ryan. Chn: Benjamin, Sarah Ryan.
Father, Benjamin Ryan, Sr. Ment. mother, no name given. "Bequeath to Peter
Hillard two chn. Nancy, Wm. Hillard." Margaret Ryan later married Wm.
Harden. Inv. made Feb. 8, 1786 by Isaac Forman, Saml. Walker, Conrod
Gallman. Inv. of a Thos. Ryan in same pack. made Oct. 25, 1784 by John Hail,
Jacob Folk, John Bogin.

RUSSELL, JAMES—BOX 79, PACK 1943:
Est. admnr. July 5, 1806 by Elizabeth, Robt. Russell, Alexr. Stuart,
Chas. Spence, Wm. McGreer, Robt. Ritchey bound to Andrew Hamilton Ord.
Abbeville Dist. sum $10,000.00. Inv. made July 10, 1806 by Wm. Lesly, Joseph
Gaston, Andrew Bowie. Sale, July 29, 1806. Byrs: Elizabeth, Robt., Mathew
Russell, Wm. Young, Wm. Yarbrough, etc.

RAY, THOMAS—BOX 79, PACK 1944:
Will dated Sept. 19, 1788 in Abbeville Dist. Prov. Mar. 26, 1792. Exrs:
Wife, Susannah Ray, Jas. McMillian, Wm. Moore. Wit: Wm., Wm. Moore,

Jr., John Bradnerd. Chn. ment. no names given. Sale, June 13, 1792. Byrs: Susannah, Isaac, John Ray, Wm. Huggins, Elijah Moore, Robt. McCombs, etc.

ROBERTS, HENRY—BOX 80, PACK 1945:
Est. admnr. Nov. 1, 1784 by Geo. Roberts, John Garrett, Robt. Burns bound to John Thomas Jr. Ord. 96 Dist. sum 2,000 lbs. Inv. made April 13, 1785 by Wm., John Lofton, John Ryan.

RAVLIN, JOHN—BOX 80, PACK 1646:
Est. admnr. May 4, 1783 by Jas. Johnston, Chas. Caldwell, Saml. Foster Sr. bound to Judges Abbeville County sum 2,000 lbs. Will dated Sept. 8, 1792 in Abbeville Dist. Exrs: Jas. Johnston, Chas. Caldwell. Wit: Richard Brown, Thos. Jordon, Chas. Devlin. Wife, Mary Ravlin. Chn: John, Wm., Nancy, Elizabeth, Margaret Ravlin, Abigail Caldwell. Gr. son. Jas. Caldwell. Inv. made June 8, 1793 by Capt. Saml. Reid, Capt. Thos. Weems, Robt. Foster.

ROGERS, JEREMIAH—BOX 80, PACK 1947:
Will dated Feb. 9, 1808 in Abbeville Dist. Rec. Feb. 16, 1808. Exrs: Son, John Rogers, Josiah Patterson Jr. Wit: Peter B., Anne Rogers, Phillip LeRoy. Chn: John, Sarah, Rebeckah Rogers, Mary wife of Jacob Devall. Inv. made Mar. 2, 1808 by Geo. Crawford, Adam Wideman, Uel Hill.

RED, JOSEPH—BOX 80, PACK 1948:
Inv. made April 29, 1783 by Ralph Smith, Capt. John Blassingame, Wm. Blackstock. Sale, May 20, 1783. Byrs: Holland Sumner, Jas. Hughes, John Roebuck, Thos. Blossomgale, Mills Sumner, John Lancaster, Austin Clayton. Anna Red, now Sumner, recd. a legacy.

ROSEMOND, JAMES—BOX 80, PACK 1949:
Will dated July 15, 1795 in Abbeville Dist. Rec. July 10, 1806. Exrs: Saml. Rosemond, Jas. Watts. Wit: Jas. Watts, Wm. Norwood, Robt. Ingram. Chn: Nathaniel, Thos., Benjamin, Saml., Mary Rosemond. "To my wife's son Jas *Lahorty* I leave a horse and saddle." Owned 947 acres of land in Laurens Co. on the waters of Saludy, Reedy River. Wife ment. no name given.

REDD, KEZIA—BOX 80, PACK 1950:
Est. admnr. Jan. 15, 1821 by Robt. H., Wm. H. Woolfolk, Hugh M. Pettus bound to Moses Taggart Ord. Abbeville Dist. sum $2,000.00. 1822 Expend: of Keziah Redd to Wm. M. Woolfolk. Paid Hugh M. Pettus $95.69 to my expenses. Paid $20.00 my coming out to South Carolina from Virginia to settle up est.

RUSS, OR REES, DAVID—BOX 80, PACK 1951:
Est. admnr. Mar. 10, 1786 by Elizabeth *Russ or Rees,* John Jastis, Nathaniel Hayworth, Solomon Rees bound to John Thomas Ord. 96 Dist. sum 5,000 lbs. Inv. made April 24, 1786 by Jas. Abernathy, John Richardson, John Crumly. (Name appears Rees or Rees, Russ, not positive.)

ROBERTS, ABSALOM—BOX 80, PACK 1952:
Est. admnr. Jan. 5, 1813 by John Scudday, Wm. Robertson bound to
Taliaferro Livingston Ord. Abbeville Dist. sum $2,000.00. April 20, 1820
Letters of Admnr. granted to Thos. Roberts. Inv. made by Jeremiah Bell,
Wmson. Norwood, Joseph Turnbull, Sale, Mar. 6, 1813. Byrs: Thos. White,
Mrs. Roberts, John Scudday.

REYNOLDS, LARKIN—BOX 80, PACK 1953:
Est. admnr. July 20, 1809 by Benjamin, Jas. Arnold, Jas. Pollard bound
to Andrew Hamilton Ord. Abbeville Dist. sum $10,000.00. Benjamin, Beven,
Nancy, Caswell, Mahaly Reynolds chn. of Larkin Reynolds by their gdn.
Joseph Foster for a cit. against Benjamin Reynolds admnr. to shew cause why
he should not settle the est. Feb. 9, 1812 paid Wm. Cochran part legacy
$20.31¼. Paid Joseph Foster part legacy $19.35½.

RICHEY, JAMES—BOX 80, PACK 1954:
Will dated May 8, 1832 in Abbeville Dist. Prov. June 7, 1833. Exrs:
Brother, Wm. Richey, Robt. Dunn, Jas. Wilson. Wit: John McCullough Jr.,
Wm. Hill, Hezekiah Elgin. Chn: Nancy, Peggy, Wm., Saml., John, Betty, Sally
Richey. Gr. Chn: Jas., son of Jas. Richey, Polly dtr of Jas. Richey. "Direct that
a certain note which I hold on Wm. Lord be given to my dtr. Mary his wife."
Inv. made June 12, 1833 by Wm. Barmore, Robt. Dunn, Alexr. Elgin.

ROBINSON, JOSEPH—BOX 80, PACK 1955:
Est. admnr. Feb. 13, 1783 by Ann Robinson, Joshua Palmer, Jas. Bogan,
yeoman, bound to John Ewing Calhoun Ord. 96 Dist. sum 14,000 lbs. Cit.
ment. Ann Robinson, Moses Cherry of Browns' Creek near Broad River, 96
Dist., next of kin. Inv. made April 6, 1783 by Thos. Ward, Joshua Palmer,
Jas. Savage.

RAMBO, LAWRENCE—BOX 80, PACK 1956:
Will dated June 11, 1775 in Granvill Co., 96 Dist. Rec. Aug. 16, 1782.
Exrs: Son, Laurance Rambo, John Herendon. Wit: John Rainsford, John Roe-
buck, Rebecca Adames. Chn: Reuben, Laurence, Beneja, Joseph, Elender,
Elizabeth, Rebecca, Margaretta Rambo, Ruth Herendon. Wife, Mary Rambo. Inv.
made Sept. 30, 1782 by Wm. Jones, Joseph Miller, Thos. Carter.

ROSS, ROBERT—BOX 80, PACK 1957:
Will dated July 12, 1790 in Abbeville Dist. Prov. Oct. 5, 1790.
Exrs: Jas. McBride, Andrew McComb. Wit: Andrew McComb, Saml. Young,
Hugh McBride. Wife ment. name not given. "Leave s. l. Hugh McBride and
my dtr. Martha a horse." Gr. Chn: Robt., Jas. McBride.

ROEBUCK, GEORGE—BOX 80, PACK 1958:
Will dated Feb. 6, 1781 in 96 Dist. Prov. July 5, 1783. Exrs: Sons,
Geo., Benjamin Roebuck. Wit: John Winn, Jas. Oliphant, Esq., Aubrey
Noland. Wife, Mary Roebuck. Inv. made by John Blassingame, Jonathan
Lennard. (Name not plain.)

HACKETT, RICHARD—BOX 80, PACK 1959:
Est. admnr. Feb. 10, 1785 by Jas. Carson, Wm. Brookes, Moses Walton bound to John Thomas Jr. Ord. 96 Dist. sum 2,000 lbs. Inv. made by Wm. Stringer, John Hitt, Geo. Delaughter.

RICE, JOSEPH—BOX 80, PACK 1960:
Est. admnr. Aug. 16, 1782 by Gasper, Harmon Gallman, Wm. Brown, John Rainsford bound to John Ewing Calhoun Ord. 96 Dist. sum 14,000 lbs. Cit. ment. Harmon Gallman, Wm. Brown of Horns Creek were next of kin. Read at Horns Creek Church. Inv. made Oct. 3, 1782 by John Gray, Conrad Gallman, Saml. Walker.

ROEBUCK, COL. BENJAMIN—BOX 80, PACK 1961:
Will dated Feb. 12, 1785 in 96 Dist. Sett: of Tyger River. Prov. May 25, 1785. Exrs: Brothers, Geo., John Roebuck. Wit: Peter Brooks. Mother ment. name not given. Bro. Obediah Roebuck. Sisters: Franky, Katety, Sally, Betsey, Mary, Roahdy Roebuck. Inv. made July 8, 1785 by Wm. Clayton, Jonathan Sinard, Christopher Casey.

RAY, JAMES—BOX 80, PACK 1962:
Est. admnr. Jan. 20, 1783 by Abraham Richardson, Joshua Hammond, Jas. Christopher bound to John Ewing Calhoun Ord. 96 Dist. sum 14,000 lbs. Jas. Ray was a brick layer near Cherokee Ponds.

ROSS, THOMAS—BOX 80, PACK 1963:
Est. admnr. Dec. 19, 1806 by Wm. Ross, Wm. Garett, Jas. Gilmore, Henry Livingston bound to Andrew Hamilton Ord. Abbeville Dist. sum $10,000.00. Mar. 14, 1809 paid Jane Ross on note $11.62½. Inv. made Dec. 26, 1806 by Robt. Lindsay, Robt. Ellis, Thos. Beaty.

ROGERS, PETER—BOX 80, PACK 1964:
Will dated Nov. 9, 1789 in Hillsborough Township, Abbeville Dist. Rec. Oct. 7, 1801. Exr: Wife, Anna Beraud. Wit: Peter Gibert, Susanne David, Ann Bouchillon. Chn. ment. names not given. Est. admnr. Mar. 3, 1803 by Peter Rogers, Isaac, Dr. John Moragne bound to Andrew Hamilton Ord. Abbeville Dist. sum $5,000.00. Cit. pub. at Vienna ment. Peter Rogers next of kin.

ROBERTS, LUCY—BOX 80, PACK 1965:
Est. admnr. July 18, 1834 by Geo., Jas. Lomax, Jr., Isaac Branch bound to Moses Taggart Ord. Abbeville Dist. sum $2,000.00. Cit. pub. at Beaulah Church. Inv. made Sept. 6, 1834 by Aaron Lomax, Jesse S. Adams, John Stuart, Robt. Carlile, Nathaniel Cobb.

ROSS, WILLIAM—BOX 80, PACK 1966:
Will dated Aug. 27, 1796 in 96 Dist. Rec. Mar. 28, 1797. Exrs: Wife, Martha Ross, Wm. Ross, Robt. Ellis. Wit: Robt. Gilmor, John Lindsay, Joseph Kolb. Chn: Wm., Thos., Martha, Jean, John Ross. Gr. son: Wm. Ross Jr., s. l. Wm. Garrett. Inv. made June 8, 1797 by John Lindsay Sr., John, Isaac Cowan.

ROUNDTREE, JETHRO—BOX 80, PACK 1967:
Est. admnr. Nov. 26, 1782 at Cuffetown by Jesse Roundtree, Daniel Shaw, Simeon Cushman bound to John Ewing Calhoun Ord. 96 Dist. sum 14,000 lbs. Inv. made Dec. 16, 1782 by Benjamin Harris, Daniel Shaw, John Sturrenegger.

ROBINSON, JOHN—BOX 80, PACK 1968:
Est. admnr. July 19, 1805 by Sarah Robinson, Alexr. Sherard, Wm. Dickey, the first of Abbeville Dist., the last 2 of Pendleton Dist. bound to Andrew Hamilton Ord. Abbeville Dist. sum $10,000.00. Inv. made July 30, 1805 by Hugh Maxwell, Geo. Patterson, Jas. Carlile.

ROBERTSON, JOHN—BOX 80, PACK 1969:
Est. admnr. Oct. 8, 1810 by Wm., Henry Robertson, Jas. Hutcheson bound to John Hamilton Ord. Abbeville Dist. sum $5,000.00. Inv. made Oct. 30, 1810 by Jas. Hutcheson, Wm. Robinson, Hugh McBride (Written Robertson, Robinson.)

ROBERTSON, JOHN, SR.—BOX 80, PACK 1970:
Will dated May 30, 1787 in Abbeville Dist. Filed July 1787. Exrs: Sons, Wm., Robt. Robertson. Wit: Adam Crain Jones, Saml. Rosamond, Jas. Watts. Wife, Jean Robartson. Chn: Wm., Robt., John, Andrew Robartson. Inv. made Aug. 3, 1787 by Saml. Rosamond, Jas. Watts, Josiah Downey. (Written Robertson, Robartson.)

ROBINSON, JOHN D.—BOX 80, PACK 1971:
Est. admnr. Mar. 21, 1820 by John Robertson, Elihu Creswell, John Pulliam bound to Moses Taggart Ord. Abbeville Dist. sum $4,000.00. Cit. pub. at Little River Church. Sale, April 5, 1820. Byrs: Patsey, John, Isham Roberson, etc. (Written Robinson, Roberson, Robertson.)

ROBINSON, JOHN—BOX 80, PACK 1972:
Est. admnr. Sept. 20, 1833 by Caleb, Peter, Wm. Burton bound to Moses Taggart Ord. Abbeville Dist. sum $3,000.00. Inv. made Oct. 15, 1833 by Cador Gantt, Peter S. Burton, Joshua Ashley.

ROBERTS, LEROY—BOX 80, PACK 1973:
Will dated May 12, 1816 in Abbeville Dist. Prov. Aug. 5, 1816. Wit: Jas. Lomax Sr., John Williams. Wife, Lucy Roberts. Son, Leroy Roberts. Est. admnr. July 18, 1834 by Geo., Jas. Lomax Jr., Isaac Branch bound to Moses Taggart Ord. Abbeville Dist. sum $2,000.00.

ROBISON, JAMES—BOX 80, PACK 1974:
Est. admnr. May 27, 1803 by Jas., John Robison, John Eager bound to Andrew Hamilton Ord. Abbeville Dist. sum $2,000.00. Cit. ment. John Robertson next of kin. Sale, June 17, 1803. Byrs: John, Geo. Robison, Wm. Lang, Thos. McKeddy, David Boyse, etc.

RICHARDSON, WILLIAM—BOX 80, PACK 1975:
Est. admnr. Jan. 18, 1812 by Chas. Johnson, Josiah Patterson Jr. bound

to Taliaferro Livingston Ord. Abbeville Dist. sum $1,000.00. Cit. pub. at Rocky River Church. Mar. 1813 paid Rebecca Richardson $82.69. John G. Richardson $20.67¼. Ann D. Richardson $20.67¼. Green C. Richardson was a son of Wm. Richardson. Inv. made Feb. 1, 1812 by Christopher Brooks, David Kerr, Isaac C. Bole.

RAMSAY, JAMES—BOX 80, PACK 1976:
Est. admnr. May 17, 1838 by Tyra Jay, John Ruff, Jas. Patterson bound to Moses Taggart Ord. Abbeville Dist. sum $1,000.00. Est. admnr. again Dec. 27, 1827 by Saml. Ramsay, John Cothran, Jas. Patterson to Moses Taggart Ord. sum $2,000.00. City pub. at Tranquil Church. Inv. made June 5, 1838 by Hugh Roberson, David Walker, Alexr. Deale, Manoah Weatherington.

REIGHLEY, WILLIAM—BOX 81, PACK 1977:
Will dated 1795 in Abbeville Dist. Rec. June 9, 1795. Exrs: Jas. Ponder, Robt. Black Sr. Wit: Saml. Linton, Wm. Black, Andrew McMullan. Wife. Elizabeth Reighley. Son, Wm. Reighley. Other chn. ment. names not given. "Owned land in Pendleton Co." Inv. made July 10, 1795 by Joseph, Wm. Black, Aaron Alexander.

RITCHEY, JOHN—BOX 81, PACK 1978:
Est. admnr. Nov. 4, 1808 by Nancy Ritchey wid., Rev. Hugh Dickson, John Weatherall, Hugh Morrah, John Hodges, Esq., bound to Andrew Hamilton Ord. Abbeville Dist. sum $10,000.00. Legatees: Joseph, Jas., John, Robt., Richey, Wm. Dunn. Sale, Nov. 24, 1808. Byrs: Joseph, Nancy, Ann, Betsey, Peggy, Robt. Richey Sr. (Written Ritchey, Richey.)

RALSTON, JAMES—BOX 81, PACK 1979:
Will dated Oct. 10, 1793. Rec. Mar. 25, 1795. Exrs: Wife, Martha Ralston, Wm. Russell. Wit: John Cunningham, Mary Fox. Chn. ment. no names given. Inv. made May 8, 1795 by Wm. Harris, Jas. Caldwell, Joseph McCleskey.

RICHEY, ROBERT—BOX 81, PACK 1980:
Est. admnr. Mar. 17, 1787 by John Richey, John Rodgers, Jas. McLaughlin bound to John Thomas Jr. Ord Abbeville Dist. sum 1,000 lbs. "John Richey states that his father Robt. Richey about 14 yrs. ago made a will while living in Virginia, that the said will is lost or mislayed or concealed by some person, that this deponent from all circumstances and information he verly believes that Wm. Goodman has consented or sent the said will out of this country and this deponent further saith that the said decd. made no other will that he knows of. Dated Mar. 17, 1787." Lived in Laurens Co. Inv. made by Saml. Scott, Wm. Anderson, David Alexander.

RICHARDSON, JOHN—BOX 81, PACK 1981:
Est. admnr. April 17, 1807 by Joseph Hill, Chas. Fooshe, Daniel Mitchell bound to Andrew Hamilton Ord. Abbeville Dist. sum $10,000.00. Inv. made May 10, 1807 by Robt. Pollard, Nimrod, John Chiles. Sale, May 15,

1807. Byrs: Wm., Lucy, Dudley Richardson, Lewis Youngblood, Richard Owen, Henry Johnson, Austin, Robt. Pollard, etc.

RUSSELL, THOMAS—BOX 81, PACK 1982:
Est. admnr. Mar. 22, 1803 by Sarah Russell, Thos. Blair, Robt. Foster bound to Andrew Hamilton Ord. Abbeville Dist. sum $5,000.00. Jan. 10, 1804 Recd. from Mary Russell $21.25. From Wm. Russell $3.50. From Agness Russell $3.00. Byrs: Mrs. Sarah Russell, Mary, Wm., Agnes Russell, Moses McCarter, John Leard, Robt. Clark, John Prince, etc.

RAMEY, JORDON—BOX 81, PACK 1983:
Est. admnr. Jan. 2, 1837 by John W. Ramey, Jas. S. Wilson, Saml. Branch bound to Moses Taggart Ord. Abbeville Dist. sum $2,000.00. Cit. pub. at Lebanon Church. Had 5 minor chn. Sett. ment. John Jordaon A., Sarah Ann, Polly G., John W. Ramey, admnr.

ROBISON, ALEXANDER S.—BOX 81, PACK 1984:
Will dated May 14, 1827 in Abbeville Dist Exrs: Brothers, John, Jas., Hugh Robison. Wit: Jas. Turner, Jas. Sherard, John White Jr. Sisters: Ann Scott, Jean Sherard, Sarah Downs. Inv. made Sept. 15, 1827 by Geo. Pettigrew, Geo. Patterson, David Pressly Sr.

RENNOLDS, THOMAS—BOX 81, PACK 1985:
Will date left out. Lived in 96 Dist. Exrs: Wife, Elizabeth Rennolds, Wm. Rennolds. Wit: John Herndon, Francis Moore, Jas. Booth. Chn: Fielding, John, Thos., Jas., Benjamin, Sarah, Nancey Rennolds. Inv. made Sept. 18, 1786 by John Herndon, Phill May, Leonard Nobles.

ROWAN, WILLIAM—BOX 81, PACK 1986:
Est. admnr. Aug. 5, 1805 by Jas., John Carson, Wm. McGough bound to Andrew Hamilton Ord. Abbeville Dist. sum $500.00. Cit. pub. at Long Cane Church. Ment. Jas. Carson next of kin. Inv. made Aug. 10, 1805 by Wm. McGough, John Hearst, John Gray.

RODEN, THOMAS—BOX 81, PACK 1987:
Hugh Freeman the admnr. Lived in 96 Dist. Inv. made July 28, 1783 by Alexr. Kilpatrick, John McGrew, John McCarroll. Name also written Rhoden. No other papers.

ROGERS, JOHN—BOX 81, PACK 1988:
Est. admnr. July 14, 1835 by Patrick S., Dyonysus Rogers, Isaac S. Whitten bound to Moses Taggart Ord. Abbeville Dist. sum $4,000.00. Patrick S. Rogers was gdn. of Simeon, Sophia, Midleton, Eliza, Caroline Rogers, minors.

ROBISON, HUGH—BOX 81, PACK 1989:
Will dated Aug. 1, 1835 in Abbeville Dist. Exrs: Wife, Peggy Robertson, Jas. Robertson. Wit: Geo. Pettigrew, Geo. Patterson, Robt. Hawks. Son, John Robertson. Other chn. ment. no names given. John's grandmother, Sarah Robertson. Sett: Feb. 23, 1847. Wid. Margaret Robison, John C. Robison. Martha a

dtr. married Arthur A. Bowie. John, Sarah, Emily Robison the 2 latter minors. Rosa died in infancy.

RAMSAY, ELI—BOX 81, PACK 1990:
    Est. admnr. Oct. 2, 1822 by Wm. Ramsay Jr., John McBride, Wesley Brooks bound to Moses Taggart Ord. Abbeville Dist. sum $1,000.00. Cit. pub. at Siloam Church. Inv. made Oct. 5, 1822 by Ira Griffin, David Cunningham, Wm. Hackett. Sale, Oct. 25, 1822. Byrs: Jonathan Swift, Wm. Ramsay Jr., Jonathan Johnson, Mrs. Ramsay.

RAMPAY, JOHN—BOX 81, PACK 1991:
    Will dated Dec. 30, 1811 in Abbeville Dist. Rec. Jan 17, 1812. Exrs: Peter, Nicholas Rampay, Jas. Stiefle, John Liveley. Wit: Saml. Perrin, Wm. Mantz, John Rampey. Chn: Margaret, John, Daniel, Jas. Rampey. Inv. made Jan. 29, 1816 by Philip Stiefle, Wm. Dorris, Saml. Zimmerman.

ROGERS, ROBERT—BOX 81, PACK 1992:
    Est. admnr. July 2, 1784 by Mary Rogers, David, Dudley Pruitt bound to John Thomas Jr. Ord. 96 Dist. sum 2,000 lbs. Inv. made July 24, 1784 by Henry King, Dudley Pruitt, Jesse Jernigin

RIDDLE, JOSEPH—BOX 81, PACK 1993:
    Will dated Dec. 30. 1811 in Abbeville Dist. Rec. Jan. 17, 1812. Exrs: dtrs. Margaret, Elizabeth Riddle. Patrick Calhoun. Wit: Jas. Calhoun Jr., Jas. Noble. Wm. Jones, Wm. T. Shackelford. Wife, Elizabeth Riddle. Chn: Margaret, Elizabeth Riddle, Mary McCombes, Martha Chevis. "Owned land in the neighborhood of Willington." Inv. made Feb. 6, 1812 by Jas. Calhoun Jr., Jas. Noble, Joseph Hutton.

RUSSELL, DR. TIMOTHY—BOX 81, PACK 1994:
    Will dated July 1, 1794 in Abbeville Dist. Rec. Mar. 25, 1799. Exr: Wife, Margaret Russell. Wit: Benjamin Howard, John Hall, Jas. Galleher. Nephew, Abraham Russell. "Will tract of land in Edgefield Co. to my son Robt. Russell son of Martha Russell." Inv. made May 23, 1799 by Wm. Robinson, Andrew McComb, Robt. Carson, Saml. Young.

RABUN, DAVID—BOX 81, PACK 1995:
    Will dated Jan. 14, 1815. Prov. Nov. 28. 1815. Exrs: Wife, Martha Rabun. Son, David Rabun. Wit: Jas., Joseph McCord, Wm. Young. Chn: David, Jane Rabun.

ROUNDTREE, JOB—BOX 81, PACK 1996:
    Est. admnr. Nov. 29, 1783 by Jesse Roundtree, John Sturzneger, Leonard Myers bound to John Thomas Jr. Ord. 96 Dist. sum 2,000 lbs. Inv. made Dec. 4, 1783 by Leonard Meyers, Daniel Shaw, Jas. Richard.

ROBERTSON, HENRY—BOX 81, PACK 1997:
    Est. admnr. Jan. 29, 1787 by Nathaniel, Mary Robertson, John Ross bound to John Thomas Jr. Ord. 96 Dist. sum 200 lbs. Sale, Mar. 25, 1787.

Byrs: Mary Robertson, Daniel Kelly, Saml. Earles, Saml. Weaver, John Blithe, John Chastain, Solomon Murphee, etc.

REGAN, TALITHA—BOX 81, PACK 1998:
On Jan. 2, 1832 John Roberson, John Leard, Bailey Regan bound to Moses Taggart Ord. Abbeville Dist. sum $500.00. John Robinson Jr. made gdn. of Talitha Regan a minor. July 19, 1832 Recd. of Young Reagin $187.56. July 24, Rec. of Bailey Reagin $118.76. Jan. 25, 1832 paid Patrick Gibson for surveying land belonging to est. of Jesse Reagin her part $.87½. (Name appeared to be Tabitha or Talitha.)

RUSHTON, GAINES F.—BOX 81, PACK 1999:
On April 4, 1832 John, Wade S. Cothran bound to Moses Taggart Ord. Abbeville Dist. sum $4,712.00. On the 2nd July 1827 Jas. Carson, Esq., made gdn. of Gaines F. Rushton a minor under 14 yrs.

RUSHTON, ELLAPARE—BOX 81, PACK 2000:
Only July 2, 1827 Geo. F. Caldwell, Jas. Carson, Chas. Sproull bound to Moses Taggart Ord. Abbeville Dist. sum $500.00. Geo. F. Caldwell made gdn. of Ellapare Rushton a minor under 14 yrs. May 20, 1830 Recd. of Jas. Carson, Esq., admnr. of est. of John, Priscilla Rushton decd. $200.00.

RAMEY, JORDON, MINORS—BOX 81, PACK 2001:
On Sept. 9, 1837 John Ramey, Jas. S. Wilson, Jas. Huey bound to Moses Taggart Ord. Abbeville Dist. sum $2,000.00. John Ramey made Gdn. of Asberry R., Lucius D., Elizabeth N., Leonidas, Bachman Ramey minors under 14 yrs. On Sept. 11, 1837 Christian V. Barns made gdn. of Jordon Allen Ramey a minor. Nov. 1838 paid John W. Ramey for expenses to Covington, Georgia $9.87½. (Written also Beckham Ramey.)

RICHEY, WILLIAM, MINORS—BOX 81, PACK 2002:
On Dec. 4, 1831 John Wier, Joseph, Thos. Lyons bound to Moses Taggart Ord. Abbeville Dist. sum $2,000.00. John Wier made gdn. of Robt. C., Isaac C., Elizabeth D., Margaret D. Richey minors of Wm. Richey decd. Heirs: Jane C. Dunn, Polly Ann Hathorn, Robt. C., Isaac C., Margaret D., Elizabeth D. Richey. 1832 paid John Dunn $118.00. Paid Thos Hathorn $118.00.

RICHARDSON, OSWELL—BOX 81, PACK 2003:
On June 24, 1814 David Gillam, Thos. B. Waller, Chas. McGehee bound to Taliaferro Livingston Ord. Abbeville Dist. sum $1,000.00. David Gillam made gdn. of Oswell Richardson a minor of John Richardson decd. under 14 yrs.

RABUN, JANE—BOX 81, PACK 2004:
On Nov. 24, 1819 David H. McCleskey, Jas. Conn, Hugh Wardlaw bound to Moses Taggart Ord. Abbeville Dist. sum $3,000.00. David H. McCleskey made gdn. of Jane Rabun a minor under 14 yrs.

ROBERTSON, SAMUEL—BOX 81, PACK 2005:
Will dated April 11, 1830 in Abbeville Dist. Prov. Feb. 12, 1831. Exrs:

Son, John Robertson, Thos. P. Spierin, David Robertson. Wit: Moses Taggart, Thos. P. Spierin, John W. McCool. Chn: Eliza, John, Wm. Robertson, Rosey Ann wife of Jas. Burnett. "Jinny my wife's unfortunate dtr. be supported." Wife's name not given. One paper ment. a Jane Robertson.

ROGERS, JEREMIAH—BOX 81, PACK 2006:
Mar. 27, 1809 paid Sarah Rogers $6.00. Nov. 25 paid Rebeckah Rogers $10.00. May 1, 1809 Recd. from John Rogers $1.50. Sept. 4, Recd. Peter B. Rogers $25.00. No other papers.

RAMEY, JOHN—BOX 81, PACK 2007:
Will dated Feb. 1, 1826 in Abbeville Dist. Exrs: Jonathan, Sugar Johnson. Wit: W. F. Baker, Christian V. Barns, John Gray. Wife, Sarah Ramey. Chn. ment. names not given. "Will to my wife 147 acres of land lying in Lancaster Dist." Sett. Dec. 1, 1840 between Jonathan Johnson Exr., Richard Hill, Johnson Ramey, Wm. Thompson, Edward Moseley, Jas. H. Cobb legatees by marriage. Inv. made Dec. 4, 1839 by Henry Brooks, Andrew Gillespie, Sr., Jas. Pursley.

RAMSAY, RICHARD—BOX 82, PACK 2008:
Est. admnr. Dec. 28, 1827 by Saml. Ramsey, John Cochran, Jas. Patterson bound to Moses Taggart Ord. Abbeville Dist. sum $2,000.00. Inv. made Mar. 27, 1829 by Wm., Leroy Watson, Robt. Tolbert. Sale, Mar. 27, 1829. Byrs: Saml., John Ramsey, Thos. Carson, John Casey.

REID, HUGH—BOX 82, PACK 2009:
Will dated May 15, 1829 in Abbeville Dist. Prov. Aug. 7, 1829. Exrs: Son, Saml. Reid. s. l. Robt. C. Wilson. Wit: Mary G. Lesly, Hugh Kirkwood, Wm. Bowie. Chn: Geo. Reid, Margery wife of Ebenezer Miller. Margaret wid. of Joseph Miller decd., Elizabeth Wilson, Rebecca wife of Rev. W. H. Barr, Jas. Reid of Indiana, Union Co., Saml. Reid. Inv. made Oct. 9, 1829 by Jas. Fair, Allen T. Miller, Hugh Kirkwood. One paper stated that Margaret Miller was of Mississippi.

RICHEY, ROBERT—BOX 82, PACK 2010:
Will dated Aug. 4, 1824 in Abbeville Dist. Prov. Aug. 15, 1828. Exrs: Son, Jas. Richey, John Wier, John Seawright. Wit: Margaret Wier, John L. Gillespie, Hugh H. Stewart. Wife, Mary Richey Chn: Elizabeth, Jas., Robt. Richey, Margaret Seawright, Wm. Richey decd., Jennet Seawright, Anny Brownlee, Nancy Pursly. Inv. made Nov. 20, 1828 by Joseph Lyon, Wm. Cochran, John L. Gillespie.

ROBERTS, GEORGE—BOX 82, PACK 2011:
Will dated June 29, 1828 in Abbeville Dist. Prov. Aug. 23, 1828. Exrs: Sons, Geo., Alfred Roberts. Wit: Sarah Gray, John McComb, Saml. Pressly. Wife, Jenny Roberts. Chn: Ryland, Reuben, Geo., Alfred, Rebecca Roberts, Betsey Gray, Franky Wideman, Sally wife of Robt. Brady. Gr. son: Geo. son of Ryland Roberts. Inv. made Sept. 11, 1828 by Robt. McCaslan, John McComb, John Wideman.

RASOR, JAMES—BOX 82, PACK 2012
Nuncaptive Will of Jas. Rasor. On the 26th Jan. 1821 Jas. Rasor stated that he wanted Ezekiel Rasor "to take all my property except my wearing apparel my wife to take such of them as she pleases and my brothers to wear the balance and to sell it and give to my wife Sally one half of proceeds." Spoken by Jas. Rasor on Feb. 8, 1821 in presence of Ezekiel, Sally, Permelia Rasor. Lived in Abbeville Dist.

RED, ROBERT, ESQ.—BOX 82, PACK 2013:
Will dated Jan. 11, 1840 in Abbeville Dist. Prov. Jan. 25, 1840. Exrs: Sons, John C., Jas. H. Red. Wit: Geo. W. Pressly, Geo. Red, John McCrery. Chn: John C., Jas. H., Nancy A. Red, Margaret C. McClinton. "Bequeath to Rebecca J. Red $10.00 for purpose of buying mourning. Bequeath to the Presbytery of S. C. $200.00 for the pious purposes of aiding the American Parent Bible Society and the Assemblys Foreign Missionary Society. Contribute $100.00 for the support of the gospel at Rehobeth Church or to that church to which most of my chn. shall be attached." Margaret C. Red married S. B. McClinton.

RODGERS, GEORGE—BOX 82, 2014:
Est. admnr. Oct. 11, 1838 by Ezekiel Tribble, Sterling Bowen Sr., Oliver Taggart bound to Moses Taggart Ord. Abbeville Dist. sum $10,000.00. Cit. pub. at Shiloh Church. Oct. 12, 1841 paid Joseph Roberts legatee $53.62. H. E. Rodgers recd. $379.00 of his father's est. Geo. Rodgers decd. Sale, Oct. 18, 1838. Byrs: Miss Matilda, Mrs. Caroline Rodgers, etc.

RICHARDSON, HENRIETTA—BOX 82, PACK 2015:
Est. admnr. July 22, 1839 by Jas. W. Richardson. David Gillam, Chas. B. Fooshe bound to Moses Taggart Ord. Abbeville Dist. sum $10,000.00. Cit. pub. at Siloam Church. John W. Fooshe married Martha Richardson. Mary Richardson married John P. Coleman. Aug. 1844 Recd. of admnr. $40.57 share of Frances Sample, now Frances Lissey.

RICHARDSON, MARY—BOX 82, PACK 2016:
Est. admnr. Sept. 3, 1838 by John Richardson, Hugh Boyd, John Cochran bound to Moses Taggart Ord. Abbeville Dist. sum $10,000.00. Inv. made Sept. 15, 1838 by Thos. Cobb, Benjamin Adams, John Thompson.

RICHARDSON, WILLIAM—BOX 82, PACK 2017:
Est. admnr. Nov. 4, 1799 by Stephen Bostick, Ann his wife, Littleberry Bostick bound to the Judges Abbeville Co. sum $6,000.00. Heirs: John, Wm., Turner, Dudley Richardson. John Robinson was gdn. Thos. Hill married Polly a dtr. of Wm. Richardson. Nancy a dtr. married Stephen Bostick. Paid Stephen Bostick and wife's expenses to Virginia to settling the est. belonging to Wm. Richardson in Virginia 2 months, $100.00.

RED, GEORGE—BOX 82, PACK 2018:
Will dated Aug. 15, 1827 in Edgefield Dist. Exrs: Wife, Nancy Red, Robt. Red. Wit: Russell Vaughan, Joseph Aiton, Jas. Sheffer. Chn. ment. names

not given. Sept. 24, 1840 Nancy Red the wid. gave up her admnr. on est. as Robt. Red the other admnr. was dead, wanted David J., Jas. W. Red to admnr. Jan. 25, 1843 Miss M. L. E. Red a minor recd. $1,495.19. Wm. C. Red a minor.

ROBINSON, HARRIET LAVINA—BOX 82, PACK 2019:
Est. admnr. Oct. 15, 1840 by Wm. Jr., Wm. Pratt Sr. Thos. Crawford bound to Moses Taggart Ord. Abbeville Dist. sum $10,000.00. Wm. Pratt Jr. was a relation of said Harriet L. Robinson. Nancy Robinson recd. a child's part of est. Jackson Robinson recd. a part.

ROBINSON, ANDREW—BOX 82, PACK 2020:
Will dated June 9, 1840. Prov. Sept. 1840. Exr: Son, Wm. Robertson. Wit: Wm. Barmore, Benjamin Moseley, Robt. Smith. Wife, Nancy Robertson. Chn: Andrew, Jackson, Wm., Harriet Lavina Robertson, Louisa Pratt. Sett: Eliza Klugh recd. $50.45 in right of her mother Emily. Mar. 29, 1864 Louisa Haynie and Mrs. Hudgens the only child of Emily Robertson recd. a share. (Written Robinson, Robertson.)

ROBINSON, WILLIAM—BOX 82, PACK 2021:
Will dated Jan. 8, 1840 in Abbeville Dist. Prov. Aug. 17, 1840. Exrs: Dr. Geo. W. Pressly, John Robinson. Wit: Wm. David, Wm. Cowan, Saml. Young, Saml. Morris. Chn: Mary, Martha, Jiney, David P., Wm. H., Alexr. T., Frederick B., John, Henry Robinson. b. l. Saml. Boags. s. l. Rebecca Boags. Sett: Mar. 11, 1842. Wm. Davis in right of wife Martha. Saml. B., Henry Robinson in Mississippi. Jas. Robinson in Alabama.

ROBERTS, GEORGE—BOX 82, PACK 2022:
N. J. Davis sheweth that Geo. Roberts died without a will leaving a est. in this state and Mississippi, that your petr. is a b. l. The wid. and chn. residing in Mississippi.

ROBERTSON, WILLIAM—BOX 82, 2023:
Will dated April 26, 1815 in Abbeville Dist. Rec. July 3, 1815. Exrs: Wm. Robison Jr., Thos. Wilson. Wit: Thos. Moore, Mathew, Thos. Wilson. Wife, Elizabeth Robertson. Chn: Thos., Wm., Jas., Elijah Reuben, Betsey, Sally Robertson. Set.t Jan. 6, 1844. 7 legatees, Jas., Thos. Robison, Reuben and wife Sally, Peter Philips and wife Elizabeth in Pickens Dist. Elijah Robison in Alabama, Wm. Robison dead had 4 chn. Reuben Robison dead 5 chn. and wid. Lindy in Alabama. Thos. P., Adam C. Robertson heirs of Reuben Robertson decd. On Dec. 11, 1843 Sarah, Mary, Wm. Robertson heirs of Wm. Robertson decd. of Alabama, Tuskaloosa Co. "do appoint Wm. Moore of said Co. our Atty. to receive from Jas. Robertson the legacy bequeathed unto the said Wm. Robertson from the will of Wm. Robertson of S. C." Mahala Combs (late Mahala Robertson) Wm. Robertson of Tuscaloosa Co. appointed John S. Moore of Fayette Co. Alabama their Atty. to receive their share of Wm. Robertson's est. in Abbeville Dist., she being a dtr. of Reuben Robertson decd. and gr. dtr. of said Wm. Robertson. Daniel Swindle and Jerusha Caroline Swindle his wife,

late Jerusha Caroline Robertson of Walker Co. Ala. appointed John S. Moore their Atty., she being a dtr. of Reuben Robertson decd. and gr. dtr. Wm. Robertson decd. On Dec. 11, 1842 Wm. Moore made gdn of Thos. Perry Robertson, Adam Crane Robertson minors under 21 and chn. of Reuben Robertson decd. (Written Robison, Robertson.)

ROSS, STEPHEN—BOX 82, PACK 2024:
Will dated Dec. 18, 1841 in Abbeville Dist. Prov. Dec. 13, 1842. Exr: Wife, Elizabeth Ross. Wit: Peter McKellar, John P. Baratt. Chn: Martha Jane, Moses Glenn, Isabella Ann Ross. Inv. made Dec. 14, 1842 by Peter McKellar, Henry H. Creswell, Wm. Butler Brooks.

ROBERSON, CHRISTANNA—BOX 82, PACK 2025:
Will dated Jan. 20, 1842 in Abbeville Dist. Prov. Nov. 7, 1842. Exrs: Son, Wm. Roberson, John B. Bull or Ball. Wit: Andrew Weed, Jas. Richardson, A. Houston. Son, Wm. Roberson. Gr. dtr: Rosanna Caroline Roberson. Inv. made Jan. 21, 1843 by Saml. R. Morrah, Wm. C. Mills.

RODEN, JAMES AIKEN—BOX 82, PACK 2026:
Est. admnr. Feb. 6, 1843 by Jas. C. Sproull, John Cothran, Richard Watson bound to David Lesly Ord. Abbeville Dist. sum $500.00. Died leaving no wife or chn. Sale, Feb. 22, 1843. Byrs: Jehu Roden, Amon Stallworth, C. B. Gabriel, Jacob Thornton, etc.

ROBERTSON, ROBERT—BOX 82, PACK 2027:
Jan. 6, 1844 Wm. Moore of Tuscaloosa Co. Ala., Jas. Robison, A. J. Moore of Abbeville Dist. bound to David Lesly Ord. Abbeville Dist. sum $168.00. Wm. Moore made gdn. Robt. Robison a minor over 14 yrs., son of Wm. Robison Jr. decd. the son of Wm. Robison Sr. decd. Jan. 6, 1844 Robt. Robison was about 20 yrs.

ROBISON, JOHN W.—BOX 82, PACK 2028:
Est. admnr. May 24, 1843 by John, Jas. McClinton, Michael McGee bound to David Lesly Ord. Abbeville Dist. sum $500.00. Left no wife or chn.

ROBINSON, SAMUEL—BOX 83, PACK 2029:
Will dated July 17, 1841 in Abbeville Dist. Prov. Mar. 22, 1843. Exrs: Son, David Robertson, Wm. Hill, David Robison. Wit: Archibald McCord, Jas. J. Gilmer, Wm. Hill. Chn: Jane, Eliza Robinson. Wife ment. name not given. On April 4, 1854 Geo. A. Ruff, Mary his wife of Itawamba Co. Mississippi appointed Jas. Pursley of Abbeville Dist. their Atty. to obtain their part of their late father Saml. Robertson decd. John Robinson son of Saml. recd. $511.91. David, Saml., Geo. Robison recd. a part. Eliza married Jesse Carlisle.

ROMANS, SMITH, MINORS—BOX 83, PACK 2030:
Dec. 9, 1839 Paschal D. Klugh, John Roman, Thos. Jackson bound to Moses Taggart Ord. Abbeville Dist. sum $3,000.00. P. D. Klugh made gdn. John A., Robt. S., Stephen W., Daniel S. Romans minors under 21 yrs. (Letter)

Oct. 28th 1847 Mississippi
Dear Brother,
      I now take my seat to dropy you a few lines to inform you and the rest
of my brothers and friends that I am now in good health. I have had a few
chills this fall but now in good health hope that these few lines will reach you
in dew season and find you all enjoying the same blessing. Brother William I
rec. a letter from Uncle Paschal inst. stating that he wished to pay me in
Mississippi if I had no objection I have none atall and that I must get you
or some of my friends to go with him to the court house Brother William I must
get you to go with him as you are his choice and mine two. Just tell Uncle
Paschal I wrote to him 2 or 3 days before I got his letter and I did not think
it worth while to write again Also I rec. a letter from Stephen at the same
time stating that you all was well and he was a going to get married but I
know it aint so but Ah Alas when have I received one from you about the
first of June If I mistake not Brother it seems to me that you have got Georgia
in your head so strong I have wished a thousand times since I heard you was a
going there it was to this great country Miss. but tho next I hear from you I
hope you have changed and are bound for Mississippi. Dear Brothers and Sister
I want to see you all very much indeed but also when shall I have that pleasure
no man can tell but if ever it will be heare. William I want Daniel to come out
here with Mr. Klugh next spring and live with me I will do as good a part by
him as any person can do and more than I know that he had rather be heare
than there. I did think I would come back this fall but it is out of my power
to come for I am a going to marry in Dec. about the last to Miss Sarah Ann
Dubard and cannot come certain. William I bought Dr. Klugh's horse when he
was about to start back I gave him my note to the amount of $82½ for him
that will be deducted out when the settlement is made there also I borrowed
$10 from the old man when we first moved out here That is all so fare as I know.
I am overseeing for Dr. Peete he gives me $12½ per month and find my horse
to ride. I have been offered $100 for him and wont take it such horses cant be
bought in Kentucky for less than that. Dr. Peete works 10 hand and will make
80 or 90 Bags weighing 45 lbs and corn plenty I have got out 5000 lbs now my
hands picks from 200 to 300 lbs every day. I expect to by land and go to
farming to my self next year on my own hook. I feel a little large I am a
going to marry I must tell you what I weigh 154 lbs neat and I think my
darling love Miss Sally will weigh the same if not more I must tell you her
age she will be 17 the 6th of Dec. next. And I 21 the 3 of November. William
I want you to send me a Reckord of Fathers and Mothers ages when they was
born when they was married and when they departed this life and as many
more of my friends as you please I have nothing more that I can think of at
present I must come to a close give my best respects to all enquiring friends
To Wm. B. Roman and wife 11 oclock at night by Robert S. Roman. N. B.
Direct your letter to Smiths Mills, *Tallehacha* Cty. This Oct. 28th 1847.

ROBERTSON, ANDREW A., JR.—BOX 83, PACK 2031:
      Est. admnr. Jan. 27, 1846 by Wm., Jackson, Nancy Robertson bound to

David Lesly Ord. Abbeville Dist. sum $10,000.00. Wm. Robertson a bro. to Andrew Robertson for whom he was gdn. Had no wife or chn. but a mother, brothers and sisters. Andrew A. Robison a minor over 14 yrs. entitled to about $400.00 from est. of his decd. sis. Harriet L. Robison of whom Wm. Pratt Jr. was admnr. Sett: Mar. 8, 1848. Present, Wm. Roberson, admnr. Nancy Robison the mother, Louisa Pratt for self and legatee of Jackson Robison to his share of Andrew's est. Absent, W. C. Klugh gdn. for Eliza C. Klugh a minor child of Emily Robison decd.

RAIFORD, WILLIAM P.—BOX 83, PACK 2032:

Will dated Jan. 30, 1840 near Rocky River, Abbeville Dist. Prov. Jan. 15, 1845. Exrs: Son, John Raiford. Wife, Susan C. Raiford. Wit: Joseph T., Wm. T., T. G. Baker. Gr. chn: John Wm, Louisa Raiford Power, Susan Caroline Raiford. On May 8, 1854 John W. Raiford of *Barboun* Co. Alabama appointed G. H. Wilson, Esq., his Atty. to demand of Henry F. Power, Robt. Hodges his part of his gr. f. est. Wm. P. Raiford decd. John Logan on Mar. 3, 1858 recd. from G. W. Huckabee admnr. of Henry Power decd. $19.64 "being the shares of the minor chn. of Louisa R. Logan of whom I am gdn."

RUFF, CHRISTIAN—BOX 83, PACK 2033:

Will dated Mar. 31, 1830 in Abbeville Dist. Prov. Dec. 19, 1844. Exr: Bro. John Ruff. Wit: Geo. Penny, David Brackenridge, *Harry or Hany* Ruff. Wife, Lucretia Ruff. Chn. ment. no names given. Est. admnr. Mar. 20, 1845 by Henry H. Penny, Andrew Gillespie, Christian V. Barnes bound to David Lesly Ord. Abbeville Dist. sum $20,000.00. Sett: Dec. 5, 1855. Present, H. H. Penny admnr. W. O. Pursley who married Narcissa Ruff. D. E. Pursley who married Emeline Ruff. David, Luana Ruff recd. shares. Feb. 1, 1849. Recd. from admnr. of Mrs. Cromer the mother of Christian Ruff decd. $2,624.55. Recd. from admnr. of Eliza Cromer decd. Philip Cromer legacy $89.97.

RUSSELL, JOHN, SR.—BOX 83, PACK 2034:

Will dated Feb. 20, 1796 in 96 Dist. Rec. April 24, 1800. Exrs: Son, John Russell. Dtr. Ann Russell. s. l. Saml. Armstrong. Wit: John Hairston, Richard A. Rapley, Esq., John Richmond. Chn: Ann, Jas., John Russell Jr., Mary wife of Saml. Armstrong, Martha wife of Jas. Miller. Gr. son. Wm. Russell. Inv. made June 4, 1800 by Wm., John Hairston, Joseph Sanders.

SCOTT, JOHN, ESQ.—BOX 83, PACK 2035:

Est. admnr. July 10, 1837 by Joseph C. Matthews, Wm., Joseph Calhoun Sr. bound to Moses Taggart Ord. Abbeville Dist. sum $10,000.00. Cit. pub. at Willington Church. Feb. 4, 1839 Recd. of Eleanor Scott for land rent $100.00. Sett: Feb. 8, 1842. Present, Joseph C. Matthews admnr. Thos. B. Scott, Mrs. E. Scott gdn. of Joseph A. Scott, Wm. T. Drennan gdn. of John Scott.

SEAWRIGHT, ANDREW—BOX 83, PACK 2036:

Est. admnr. Feb. 22, 1835 by John Collins, Andrew, Wm. Richey bound to Moses Taggart Ord. Abbeville Dist. sum $3,000.00. Sett: Oct. 20, 1835.

Margaret Seawright legatee and ward of Jas. Richey. Mar. 17, 1835 paid Jas. W. Richey $76.42. April 11 paid Eleanor A. Seawright $50.00.

STONE, POLLY—BOX 83, PACK 2037:
    Est. admnr. Jan. 20, 1832 by John Donald, Wm. Richey, Benjamin Moseley bound to Moses Taggart Ord. Abbeville Dist. sum $3,000.00. Cit. pub. at Greenville Church. Sett. of Polly Stone est. "so far a negro man Crawford is concerned, who was willed by Jane Robertson to John Robertson and at his death (he died in 1851) the said boy was to be divided amongst Polly Stone and her heirs." Distributees, Benjamin McFarlin and wife Nancy, Benjamin S. Owens and wife Jenny, Wm. Stone, Reuben Cummins chn., John Cummins and wife Malinda, John Stone's chn. Filed Nov. 23, 1852. On Sept. 22, 1853 John Cummings and wife Malinda of Oklibheha Co. Miss. Wm. Richey was gdn. Wm., Nancy, Polly Ann Stone minor chn. of Polly Stone decd.

STEVENSON, ANDREW—BOX 83, PACK 2038:
    Est. admnr. Mar. 17, 1832 by Elizabeth, John Stevenson, Wm. Pressly McCord, Hugh Kirkwood bound to Moses Taggart Ord. Abbeville Dist. sum $2,000.00. Cit. pub. at Upper Long Cane Church. Sale, April 6, 1832. Byrs: Jas., John, Elizabeth, Capt. John Stevenson, Robt. Crawford, etc. Minor chn: Sarah, Rebecca, Andrew T. Stevenson.

SIMMONS, CHARLES S.—BOX 83, PACK 2039:
    Est. admnr. Feb. 7, 1833 by Lewis S. Simmons, Robt. S., Josiah Patterson bound to Moses Taggart Ord. Abbeville Dist. sum $2,000.00. Cit. pub. at Rehoboth Church.

STARK, JEREMIAH—BOX 83, PACK 2040:
    Will dated Feb. 23, 1824 in Abbeville Dist. Prov. June 7, 1824. Exr: Son, Chas. Stark. Wit: Robt., Wm. C. Cozby, Elijah Hunt. Wife, Mary Stark. Chn. were written but only son Chas. Stark ment. Dec. 30, 1826 paid Benjamin Osburn's legacy $216.00. Aug. 20, 1827 Thos. Smith's legacy $303.00. Nov. 29, 1827 paid Jas Stark's legacy $206.00. Nov. 29, 1827 paid Charity Vernon's legacy $218.00.

SADLER, NATHANIEL—BOX 83, PACK 2041:
    Est. admnr. Nov. 15, 1828 by John Matthews, Robt. Buchanan, Wm. Taggart bound to Moses Taggart Ord. Abbeville Dist. sum $1,000.00. Inv. made Dec. 2, 1828 by Robt. Buchanan, Smith Romans, Stephen Watson.

SHIRLEY, LINDSAY—BOX 83, PACK 2042:
    Est. admnr. Mar. 6, 1829 by Wm. Ward, John N. Sample, Wm. Eddins bound to Moses Taggart Ord. Abbeville Dist. sum $1,000.00. Cit. pub. at Rocky Creek Church. Sept. 22, 1829 paid John Shirley $20.00. Recd. of Joshua Shirley on sett. $60.00. Richard Wood was a legatee.

STIEFLE, PHILIP—BOX 83, PACK 2043:
    Est. admnr. Dec. 1, 1821 by Mary Stiefle, Wm. Mantz, John Hearst

bound to Moses Taggart Ord. Abbeville Dist. sum $10,000.00. Jan. 7, 1832 paid
Philip H. Stiefle $14.50. Wm. Stiefle $11.00. Geo. F. Stiefle $14.50.

SHILLITO, GEORGE—BOX 83, PACK 2044:
    Est. admnr. Nov. 15, 1833 by Pamelia C. Shillito wid., Isaac, Saml.
Branch, Jas. Moore bound to Moses Taggart Ord. Abbeville Dist. sum $1,000.00.
Inv. made Dec. 4, 1833 by Thos. S. Spierin, Saml. Branch, Jas. S. Wilson.

SAMPLE, WASHINGTON—BOX 83, PACK 2045:
    Est. admnr. Oct. 15, 1834 by John N., Isaac Sample, Walter Anderson
bound to Moses Taggart Ord. Abbeville Dist. sum $10,000.00. Cit. pub. at
Siloam Church. Nov. 4, 1835 paid John N. Sample $604.18½. Paid Francis
Sample $740.18¾. Sept. 20, 1836 paid Daniel B. Sample $25.50. Sale, Nov. 4,
1834. Byrs: John N., Fanny, Isaac, Jas. Sample, etc.

SIMPSON, POLLY—BOX 83, PACK 2046:
    Est. admnr. Oct. 17, 1823 by Andrew Milligan, Jas. Calhoun, Jas. Tag-
gart bound to Moses Taggart Ord. Abbeville Dist. sum $1,000.00. Cit. pub. at
Willington Church. Feb. 19, 1824 paid John Simpson $6.25. Inv. made Oct. 30,
1823 by Robt. McKinley, Jas. Wilson, Francis Mitchel.

SMITH, AUSTIN—BOX 83, PACK 2047:
    Will dated June 11, 1834 in Abbeville Dist. Prov. Sept. 1, 1834. Exrs:
Wife, Abigail Smith, John B. Black, David Pratt. Wit: John, Jas. Young,
Jas. A. Black. Gr. Dtr. Almina Pratt. Inv. made Oct. 2, 1834 by Thos. Fisher,
John, Jas. Young.

SMITH, RICHARD—BOX 83, PACK 2048:
    Est. admnr. Feb. 25, 1831 by John G. Mouchet, Philip Cook, Entriken
Ramey bound to Moses Taggart Ord. Abbeville Dist. sum $1,000.00. Cit. pub.
at Mills Meeting House. Mar. 23, 1832 Recd. of Frederick Smyth $5.37½.
Sale, Mar. 15, 1831. Byrs: Miss Elizabeth, Peter, John Smyth, Pleasant
Searls, etc.

SHANNON, JAMES—BOX 83, PACK 2049:
    Will dated April 10, 1822. Prov. July 16, 1822. Exrs: Wm. Richey Sr.,
John Donnald. Wit: Jas., Wm. Richey, John Donnald. Bro. Robt. Shannon.
Sis: Polly Shannon otherwise Polly Fields. John, Elizabeth Fields, chn. of Polly
Shannon.

SAMPLE, JOHN B.—BOX 83, PACK 2050:
    Est. admnr. Jan. 7, 1833 by John N., Jas. Sample, Downs Calhoun
bound to Moses Taggart Ord. Abbeville Dist. sum $20,000.00. Dec. 21, 1833
paid Barbary Sample $92.22. Jan. 21, 1834 paid Susannah C. Sample
$2,708.15¾. Cit. pub. at Providence Church.

SALE, JAMES—BOX 84, PACK 2051:
    Will dated Mar. 25, 1826 in Abbeville Dist. Prov. May 19, 1828. Exrs:
Wife, Elizabeth Sale, Albert, John H. Waller. Wit: Joel Etheridge, Margaret

Watson, Maxmilian Hutchison. Chn. ment. names not given. Admnr. of Jonathan Sales in same pack. Made Aug. 4, 1823 by Wm., Jas. Sales, Jas. Johnston bound to Moses Taggart Ord. Abbeville Dist. sum $500.00. Inv. made Aug. 13, 1823 by Criswell Moore, Martin Bullock, Jas. Griffin. Sale, Aug. 22, 1823. Byrs: Wm., John Sale, Jas. Griffin.

STALLWORTH, THOMAS—BOX 84, PACK 2052:
Will dated Mar. 18, 1824 in Abbeville Dist. Prov. April 24, 1824. Exrs: Edmund, Jas., Amon Stallworth. Wit: Edward C. Roden, Wm. Stallworth, Nathan Henderson. Chn: Amon, Sarah, Edmund, Jas. Stallworth, Mary Wilson. "Bequeath to Sanders McMillan bed and furniture." Inv. made Dec. 18, 1824 by Wm. Stallworth, Albert Waller, Wm. Hackett.

SMITH, DAVID—BOX 84, PACK 2053:
Est. admnr. Dec. 14, 1825 by Joab Wilson, Robt. Key, Wm. Lomax bound to Moses Taggart Ord. Abbeville Dist. sum $1,000.00. Cit. pub. at Rehoboth Church. Inv. made Jan. 2, 1826 by Jas. Sales, Saml. Henderson, Saml. Ramsey. Byrs: Mary, J. W. Wilson, Joel Etheridge, etc.

SMITH, JOHN—BOX 84, PACK 2054:
Est. admnr. Jan. 1, 1826 by Henry Gray, Chas. Neely, Paschal D. Klugh bound to Moses Taggart Ord. Abbeville Dist. sum $4,000.00. Sett: Oct. 5, 1832. Legatees: Craven, John, Geo., Jonathan, Mary Ann, Martha, Joshua, Saml., Joseph Smith, Elizabeth Murphey and husband.

SPROULL, JAMES—BOX 84, PACK 2055:
Will dated May 6, 1825 in Abbeville Dist. Prov. June 18, 1825. Exrs: Wife, no name given, Geo. F. Caldwell. Bro: Chas. Sproull. Wit: Saml. Caldwell, W. J. Cothran, W. C. Ralls. Chn: Elizabeth, Mary Ann, Harriet, Jas., Wm. Sproull. Inv. made Aug. 10, 1825 by Saml. Caldwell, Jas. Carson, C. W. Mantz.

STALLWORTH, JOHN—BOX 84, PACK 2056:
Est. admnr. Feb. 13, 1835 by Elias Lake, Robt. R. Tolbert, Amon Stallworth bound to Moses Taggart Ord. Abbeville Dist. sum $2,000.00. Feb. 4, 1841 paid Lemuel Bell for Margaret Stallworth $27.22. 1836 paid L. J. White for Sarah Stallworth $5.87½.

SPEIRIN, PATRICK—BOX 84, PACK 2057:
Est. admnr. May 15, 1835 by Jas. Moore, Thos. P. Speirin, Alpheus Baker bound to Moses Taggart Ord. Abbeville Dist. sum $1,000.00. Inv. made July 16, 1835 by John A. Calhoun, Jas. Alston, Henry Hendrix.

SMITH, WILLIAM—BOX 84, PACK 2059:
Est. admnr. Aug. 30, 1824 by Thos., Joel Smith, Jesse Calvert, John Fooshe, John Logan, Richard Griffin bound to Moses Taggart Ord. Abbeville Dist. sum $150,000.00. Cit. pub. at Tabernacle Meeting House. Legatees: Thos., John, Robt., Wm. Lewis Smith. Joel Smith gdn. of Chas. Smith, John Fooshe and wife, Geo. Anderson and wife, Wm. L. Gary, Dr. Isaac Teague and wife, Lucy Smith, Nancy Gary.

SMITH, MOSES—BOX 84, PACK 2060:
Will dated Feb. 10, 1837 in Abbeville Dist. Prov. Oct. 8, 1837. Exrs:
Wm. Barmore, Saml. Agnew Sr. Wit: Enoch Barmore, Richard P. Bowie,
Washington Drummond. Chn: Geo., Wm., Robt., Joseph Ebenezer, Saml.,
Benjamin Smith. "Give to my dtr. Jane Cullins all my interest in a tract of
land she now lives on in the State of Indiana." Gr. chn: Jas., Moses Dunn chn.
of dtr. Feby Dunn decd. Expend: Dec. 18, 1837 paid Michael Magee
Legatee, Power of Atty. $200.00. Nov. 2, 1837 paid Wm. Gaines auctioner $3.00.

STIEFLE, JAMES—BOX 84, PACK 2061:
Est. admnr. Sept. 14, 1797 by Philip Stiefle, Henry Zimmerman, Wm.
McBride bound to Judges of Abbeville Co. sum $5,000.00. Mary Stiefle the
wid. Philip was a son. June 7, 1799 paid Jacob Shibley legatee $28.00. Jan. 9,
1800 paid John Shibley legatee $47.00. Sale, Nov. 21, 1797. Byrs: Mary, Geo.,
Jas., Philip Stiefle, Garret Longmire, John Shibley, etc.

STALLWORTH, WILLIAM—BOX 84, PACK 2062:
Will dates Sept. 28, 1821 in Abbeville Dist. Prov. Feb. 14, 1831. Exr:
Wife, Sarah Stallsworth. Wit: Wm. Chipley, Jas. Walker, Joseph Stallworth.
Chn. ment. names not given. "A legacy left to Jane Pope." Inv. made Mar.
14, 1831 by Albert Waller, Maxmilian Hutcheson, John Barratt.

STUART, WILLIAM—BOX 84, PACK 2063:
Est. admnr. Dec. 5, 1831 by Hamilton Hill, John Devlin, Esq., Joseph
Davis, Esq., bound to Moses Taggart Ord. Abbeville Dist. sum $2,000.00. Cit.
pub. at Lebannon Church. Dec. 30, 1833 paid John Stewart Jr. $1,12½. Sale,
Dec. 7, 1831. Byrs: Elizabeth, John Stewart Sr., John Norris, Andrew
Stewart, etc.

SANDERS, REBECCA—BOX 84, PACK 2064:
Est. admnr. Oct. 18, 1825 by Jas. Wiley, Saml. Pressly, Enos Crawford
bound to Moses Taggar Ord. Abbeville Dist. sum $3,000.00. Cit. pub. at Upper
Long Cane Church. Luke Mathis gdn. of Joseph H., Catharine Sanders minors.
June 1, 1829 Receipt of Robt. Key by Wm. Sanders $6.37½.

SMITH, ELIJAH—BOX 84, PACK 2065:
Est. admnr. April 13, 1830 by Jas., Robt. Smith, Jas. Franklin bound
to Moses Taggart Ord. Abbeville Dist. sum $1,000.00. Cit. pub. at Providence
Church. Sale, April 17, 1830. Byrs: Robt., Jas., Patsey Smith, John Stone,
Jas. W. Pettus, Abraham Dyson, etc.

SKINNER, JOHN—BOX 85, PACK 2066:
Est. admnr. Sept. 16, 1837 by Tiry Jay, John Ruff, John Donald bound
to Moses Taggart Ord. Abbeville Dist. sum $3,000.00. Cit. pub. at Mt. Pleasant
Church. Francis Walker left 2 chn. John, Frances. John died without wife or
chn. and his mother being dead made Frances the sole heir. Frances married
Robt. Walker. Mariah Skinner recd. $112.23 in Feb. 1840 as her part. Inv. made
Oct. 3, 1837 by John Ruff, Saml. Morris, Young Reagin.

SAMPLE, ROBERT—BOX 85, PACK 2067:
Will dated Oct. 6, 1813 in Abbeville Dist. Rec. Feb. 3, 1817. Exrs:
Wife, Barbary Sample. Bro. Alexr. Sample. Son, John Sample. Wit: Joel Lip-
scomb, Benjamin Gaines, Geo. Heard. Chn: Polley Pulliam, John, Permelia,
Catharine, Jamimie Sample. Expend: June 9, 1823 paid Permelia Calbert
legatee $453.00. Nov. 29, 1822 paid Wm. Sample legatee $453.00. Dec. 29,
1819 paid Daniel Sample legatee $453.00. Jan. 14, 1820 paid Saml. Davice for
Mary Davice legatee $53.00. Nov. 9, 1829 paid Jemimah Ellis formerly
Jemimah Sample $453.00. Mar. 14, 1832 Henry Johnson recd. $500.00 in
right of his decd. wife late Pamela Sample. Jemimah married Robt. N. Ellis.

SHEPPERD, DR. WESLEY—BOX 85, PACK 2068:
Est. admnr. Oct. 19, 1813 by Thos., Walter Chiles bound to Taliaferro
Livingston Ord. Abbeville Dist. sum $10,000.00. Lived at Cambridge. Sale,
Nov. 5, 1813. Byrs: Sally Shepperd, Jared E. Groce, etc.

STEVENS, MARTHA—BOX 85, PACK 2069:
Will dated Dec. 28, 1826 in Abbeville Dist. Prov. Oct. 26, 1827. Exr:
Son, Jas. Stevens. Wit: D. E. Davenport, Jared Burt, John W. Williams. Chn:
Jas., Pamela Stevens, Wm. Andrew Huggins, Elizabeth Anderson, Ann Turner.
Inv. made Nov. 9, 1827 by Stephen Ross, John Chatham, Robt. Turner.

STEPHENS, JAMES—BOX 85, PACK 2070:
Est. admnr. Oct. 22, 1823 by John, Saml. Cothran, Charlotte Stephens,
Geo. Marshall bound to Moses Taggart Ord. Abbeville Dist. sum $9,000.00.
Cit. pub. at Rehobeth Church. Sale, Dec. 30, 1823. Byrs: Charlotte Stephens,
John Kary, Joseph Conn, Thos. Harris, Wm. B. Lewis, etc.

SAMPLE, ALEXANDER—BOX 85, PACK 2071:
Est. admnr. Sept. 19, 1825 by John N., Jas. Sample, Wm. S. Campbell,
Alexr. Stuart bound to Moses Taggart Ord. Abbeville Dist. sum $40,000.00.
Dec. 11, 1827 paid Isaac Sample $111.10. Paid Washington Sample $335.68¾.
Dec. 7, 1827 Recd. of Permelea Sample $107.00.

SPRAGINS, WILLIAM—BOX 85, PACK 2072:
Will dated Oct. 23, 1821 in Abbeville Dist. Prov. Jan. 15, 1827. Exrs:
Son, Thos. Spragins, John Meek. Wit: Richard, Thos. Gaines, John W. Anglin.
Wife, Martha Spragins. Chn: Wm. now living in Alabama, Thos. Spragins,
Tabitha Adkinson, Sarah Meek.

SPENCE, SAMUEL—BOX 85, PACK 2073:
Will dated Jan. 30, 1824 in Abbeville Dist. Prov. Mar. 17, 1824. Exrs:
Wife, Mary Spence. Son, Wm. Spence. Wit: Joseph McCrery, Margaret, Sarah
Wiley. Chn: Wm., Rosey, Mary, Nancy, Jane, Anny, Alexr. Spence.

SPILLERS, JOHN—BOX 85, PACK 2074:
Est. admnr. Nov. 20, 1835 by Jas. S. Gilmer, Wm. Morrison, Benjamin
McFarlin bound to Moses Taggart Ord. Abbeville Dist. sum $2,000.00. Cit.
pub. at Upper Long Cane Church. Sett: Feb. 4, 1842. Present, Jas. S. Gilmer
admnr.; Wm. N. Purdy who married the wid.

SPENCE, ALEXANDER—BOX 85, PACK 2075:
Est. admnr. Dec. 11, 1815 by Saml. Spence, Hugh McCormick, Jas. Miller bound to Taliaferro Livingston Ord. Abbeville Dist. sum $5,000.00. May 5, 1817 paid Rosey Spence $368.62½. Paid Mary McCrery $66.87½. Paid Chas. Spense $72.87½. Paid Alexr. Spence $57.87½. Paid Agnes Spence $122.87½. Paid Sarah Spence $122.87½. Paid Saml. Spence $64.12½. Cit. pub. at Smyrna Church.

SANDERS, ANN—BOX 85, PACK 2076:
Est. admnr. July 10, 1820 by Joseph, Eli S. Davis, Luke Matthews bound to Moses Taggart Ord. Abbeville Dist. sum $3,000.00. Sale, July 28, 1820. Byrs: Rebecca, Agness Sanders, Selah Walker, Lewellen Good, etc.

SIMPSON, JOSEPH—BOX 85, PACK 2077:
Est. admnr. Mar. 21, 1820 by Polly Simpson, Andrew Milligan, Joseph Moseley, Wm. Calhoun bound to Moses Taggart Ord. Abbeville Dist. sum $1,200.00. Cit. pub. at Rocky River Church. Sale, April 6, 1820. Byrs: Polly Simpson, Thos. Finley, Geo. Whitefield, Jas. Shoemaker, etc.

STUART, ADAM, SR.—BOX 85, PACK 2078:
Will dated Nov. 14, 1822 in Abbeville Dist. Prov. Dec. 20, 1822. Exrs: Son, Adam Stuart, Joseph C. Matthews. Wit: Elizabeth, John Stuart Jr., Joseph C. Mathews. Wife, Jane Stuart. Chn: Thos. Clark, Jas., Mary, Ann, Elizabeth, Adam, John, Wm., Isaac, Andrew Stuart. Expend: Feb. 2, 1824 paid Jas. Foster legacy $172.50. Jane. 29, 1828 paid Peter Stuart legacy $172.50. Paid Catharine Stuart legatee $2.00.

SAMPLE, WILLIAM—BOX 85, PACK 2079:
Est. admnr. Sept. 3, 1832 by John B., John N. Sample, Saml. Davis bound to Moses Taggart Ord. Abbeville Dist. sum $3,000.00. Cit. pub. at Siloam Church. Inv. made Sept. 18, 1832 by John N. Sample, Jonathan, Henry Johnson.

SHIRLEY, BENJAMIN—BOX 85, PACK 2080:
Est. admnr. Aug. 20, 1824 by Jas. Richey, Weldon Pearman, John Seawright, Reuben Kay bound to Moses Taggart Ord. Abbeville Dist. sum $10,000.00. Cit. pub. at Greenville Church. Jan. 5, 1827 paid Mastin Shirley $59.08. June 2, paid Nathaniel Shirley $53.50. Paid John Shirley $53.50.

STUART, ALEXANDER—BOX 85, PACK 2081:
Will dated Aug. 26, 1830 in Abbeville Dist. Filed April 21, 1840. Exrs: Wife, Peggy Stuart, Jesse Beazley, Thos. C. Stuart. David Stuart. Wit: John B. Davis, Wm. Crawford, Willison B. Beazley. Chn: John, Mary Ann Stuart, Margaret Harrison, Thos. Caldwell, Caroline Calvert. Step Dtr: Sarah Caldwell. Sis: Mary McKinney. Caroline married Hudson Calvert. Margaret married John Harrison. Dec. 15, 1836 paid John Stuart's tuition at Greenwood $30.00.

SCOTT, WILLIAM, SR.—BOX 85, PACK 2082:
Will dated Jan. 19, 1830 in Abbeville Dist. Prov. June 30, 1830. Exrs. Wife, Mary Scott. Son, John Scott. Wit: Henry Furr, John, Thos. Hemmenger.

ABSTRACTS OF OLD NINETY-SIX AND

Chn: John, Jas., Susannah, Alexr., Mary, Nancy, Sarah, Davis, Clark, Amanda, Martha Scott. "Susannah have negro girl Judy that she carried away with her to Georgia when she married." Nov. 23, 1840. Legatees: Thos. Dickson and wife, Wm. T. Drennan and wife, Wm. McCaslin and wife, Wm. A. Brownlee.

SHEPPERD, ANNE—BOX 85, PACK 2083:
Will dated Aug. 19, 1818 in Abbeville Dist. Prov. Nov. 6, 1818. Exr: Son, Jas. Shepperd. Wit: Thos. Mann, Dale Palmer, Wm. Pettigrew. Chn: Jas. in his 22nd, Wm. in his 19th, Oct. 22 Wilson will be 15, Tinson was 13 yrs. 24th July last. Inv. made Dec. 2, 1818 by Leonard Wideman, Dale Palmer, Wm. Pettigrew.

SALES, JOHN, SR.—BOX 85, PACK 2084:
Will dated June 5, 1819 in Abbeville Dist. Prov. Nov. 24, 1823. Exrs: Sons, Jas., Wm. Sales. Wit: Thos. Chiles, Wm. Todd, Lewis Mathews. Wife, Rebecca Sales. Chn: Sarah, Johnson, Gilliam, Jas., Gideon, Jonathan, John, Thos., Wm. Sales. Expend: Jan. 22, 1824 paid Rev. Jas. Doggens for preaching mother's funeral sermon $5.00. Feb. 6, paid Smith Scogins his wife's dividend of est. $50.00.

SANDERS, JOSEPH—BOX 85, PACK 2085:
Will dated Mar. 20, 1805 in Abbeville Dist. Rec. May 6, 1805. Exrs: Wife, Sarah R. Sanders, Donald Fraser. Wit: John Lowry, Wm. Baird, A. Hunter. Chn: Thos. Adams, Donald Fraser, Joseph, Polly Sanders. Inv. made May 18, 1805 by Edward, Alexr. Prince, Saml. Savage. Mar. 24, 1806 paid for preaching the child Joseph's funeral sermon $2.00.

SANDERS, DONALD F.—BOX 85, PACK 2086:
Will dated Aug. 14, 1822 in Abbeville Dist. Prov. Sept. 2, 1822. Exr: Thos. P. Martin. Wit: Jacob Martin, E. S. Murray, Henry Power. Mother, Sarah Brooks. Bro. Thos. A. Sanders. Half Sis: Amanda Brooks.

SMITH, MARGARET—BOX 85, PACK 2087:
Will dated Sept. 29, 1822 in Abbeville Dist. Prov. Jan. 6, 1823. Exrs: s. l. Jas. Pennall, John Martin. Wit: John McComb, Wm. McDonald, Wm. Martin. "Was late of the City of Charleston." Dtr: Eliza Catharine Pennall. Gr. Dtr: Eliza Margaret Pennall, "bequeath 9 shares which I hold in the Union Insurance Office in Charleston." Gr. Son: Wm. S. Pennall. "Owned land on Reedy Branch and Saint Johns Parish."

SHANKS, MATHEW—BOX 86, 2088:
Est. admnr. Nov. 5, 1836 by Mathew Shanklin Sr., Mathew Jr., Robt. Shanks bound to Moses Taggart Ord. Abbeville Dist. sum $1,000.00. Cit. pub. at Hopewell Church. Mathew Shanks states that Mathew Shanks Sr. left as heirs, Mathew, Robt. Shanks, Jas. Shanks since dead leaving chn: Robt. M., Matthew, Alexr., Margaret, Anna Shanks and chn. of his dtr. Margaret who married Abram Outon viz. John, Wm., Sarah, Anna Outon and perhaps others. John Shanks chn. of another decd. dtr. Martha, wife of John McFerrin, viz.

Anna, Isabella, Nancy, Dolly McFerrin. Jenny, wife of J. Anderson, who is since dead leaving chn. viz. Mathew, Mary A., Martha, Margaret. John Shanks was of Mississippi. Martha McFerrin and family in Alabama.

SHANKLIN, DR. SAMUEL T.—BOX 86, PACK 2089:
Est. admnr. Jan. 11, 1822 by Richard, Wm. Covington, Josiah Patterson bound unto Moses Taggart Ord. Abbeville Dist. sum $8,000.00. Aug. 25, 1823 paid Mrs. H. C. Shanklin $10.00. June 26, 1823 Recd. from Capt. Thos. Shanklin $130.00. The wid. (no name given) and Martha Shanklin recd. a legacy due Dr. Shanklin from *Moors* est. in Edgefield.

SIMS, ANDREW—BOX 86, PACK 2090:
Est. admnr. Aug. 8, 1823 by Jas., John, Jas. Foster Sr. bound to Moses Taggart Ord. Abbeville Dist. sum $500.00. Cit. pub. at Lebanon Church. Jan. 1, 1825 Recd. of Catharine Sims $6.03. Sale, Aug. 26, 1823. Byrs: Mary Ann, Catharine, Jas. Sims, etc.

STONE, RICHARD—BOX 86, PACK 2091:
Est. admnr. Jan. 2, 1824 by Col. Edmond Ware, Chas. Cullums, Cador Gantt bound to Moses Taggart Ord. Abbeville Dist. sum $1,000.00. Inv. made Feb. 5, 1824 by Jordon, Benjamin Moseley, Capt. John Mattison, Robt. V. Posey. Sale, Feb. 23, 1824. Byrs: Mrs. Polly Stone, etc.

STUART, DAVID, JR.—BOX 86, PACK 2092:
Est. admnr. Dec. 11, 1822 by Alexr., David Stuart Sr., Jesse Beazley bound to Moses Taggart Ord. Abbeville Dist. sum $1,000.00. Inv. made Dec. 17, 1822 by Wm. Beazley, Robt. Bartrim, Cas. Neely. Sale, Dec. 18, 1822. Byrs: Alexr. Stuart, Lewis Cobb, Benjamin Smith, etc.

SWAIN, JOHN—BOX 86, PACK 2093:
Will dated Mar. 7, 1821 in Abbeville Dist. Prov. Sept. 11, 1823. Exrs: Sons, Jesse, John Swain. Wit: John Weatherall, Robt. Swain, Wm. Hodges. Wife, Anna Swain. Chn: Jas., Jane, Jesse, Nancy, Mary, John, Wm., Peggy Swain, Betsy Smith. Distributee, Silas Smith. Inv. made Nov. 5, 1823 by Jas. Wilson, John Weatherall, Michael Magee, Moses Smith.

SMITH, NELSON P.—BOX 86, PACK 2094:
Est. admnr. Mar. 18, 1828 by Edmund Cobb, Ephraim Davis, Edmund Cobb Jr. bound to Moses Taggart Ord. Abbeville Dist. sum $2,000.00. Cit. pub. at Smyrna Church. Paid board for the following: Mattison, Satira, Wiley, Willis Smith. Feb. 8, 1832 paid Joseph Crawford $50.00 for Satira Smith now Crawford.

SHARP, EDWARD—BOX 86, PACK 2095:
Will dated Feb. 28, 1812 in Abbeville Dist. Rec. Mar. 17, 1812. Exrs: Sons, Henry, Robt. C., Wm. Sharp. Wit: Hugh Dickson, John Shirley, Jas. McKee. Chn: Wm., Edward, Nelly, Clement Sharp. Inv. made April 9, 1812 by Robt. C. Sharp, Christian Rasor, Andrew Agnew.

SANSOM, JOHN—BOX 86, PACK 2096:
Est. admnr. Nov. 29, 1780 by Jane Sansom, David Edmiston, David,

294   ABSTRACTS OF OLD NINETY-SIX AND

Alexr. Logan bound to John Ewing Calhoun Ord. Abbeville Dist. sum 14,000 lbs. Inv. made Jan. 18, 1783 by Alexr., John, David Logan.

SHIELDS, MAJOR THOMAS B., ESQ.—BOX 86, PACK 2097:
Est. admnr. May 2, 1803 by Saml. B. Shields, Geo. Bowie, Dr. Jesse C. Bouchell bound to Andrew Hamilton Ord. Abbeville Dist. sum $5,000.00. Cit. pub. at Upper Long Cane Church. Saml. B. Shields next of kin.

SCOTT, WILLIAM—BOX 86, PACK 2998:
Est. admnr. Jan. 6, 1806 by Isabel Scott, Wm. Douglass, Saml., Lewis Youngblood bound to Andrew Hamilton Ord. Abbeville Dist. sum $5,000.00. Inv. made Jan. 15, 1806 by Alexr. Turner, John Gentry, Andrew Shelnut.

STEVENSON, THOMAS—BOX 86, PACK 2099:
Est. admnr. June 11, 1785 by Margaret Stevenson, John McKee bound to John Thomas Jr. Ord. 96 Dist. sum 2,000 lbs. Inv. made July 22, 1785 by John Grisham, Joseph Culton, Robt. Stevenson.

SAWYER, JOHN—BOX 86, PACK 2100:
Will dated Oct. 2, 1784 in 96 Dist. Prov. Oct. 13, 1784. Exrs: Wife, Priscilla Sawyer, Elkanok, Geo. Sawyer. Wit: John Thos. Fairchild, Benjamin, Lewis Powell. Chn: John, Lewis, Sarah, Cader, Debony, Elkanok, Geo., Sevility Sawyer. Inv. made Feb. 7, 1785 by John T., Abraham Fairchild, John Frederick.

SCOTT, SAMUEL—BOX 86, PACK 2101:
Est. admnr. Dec. 25, 1816 by Jane Scott, Bruce Livingston, Jas. Morrow bound to Taliaferro Livingston Ord. Abbeville Dist. sum $2,000.00. Inv. made Dec. 28, 1816 by Bruce Livingston, Chas., Robt. Spence. Robt. Richey Jr. Sale, Feb. 2, 1817. Byrs: Jane, Rachel, Saml. D. Scott, etc.

SANDERS, ADAM—BOX 86, PACK 2102:
Will dated Aug. 29, 1805 in Abbeville Dist. Rec. Oct. 21, 1805. Exr: Wife, Jenny Sanders. Wit: Dr. Thos. B. Jack, Jehu Foster, Jenny Hamilton. Nephew, Thos. Adams Sanders. Cousin, Joseph Sanders. "After death of wife my est. to go to my wife's bros. and sisters all my real and personal est. which I wish to be equally divided and to my dear friend Wm. Hamilton 2 shares." Inv. made Feb. 20, 1807 by Joseph Reynolds, John Downey, Andrew Paul.

SAXON, BENJAMIN THOMAS—BOX 86, PACK 2103:
Will dated Jan. 19, 1832 in Abbeville Dist. Prov. April 16, 1832. Exr: Alexr. Houston. Wit: Wm. H. Barr, Alexr. Hughes, Mary Perrin. Wife, Matilda W. Saxon. "Appointed neighbor Benjamin H. Saxon gdn. of his chn." Sale, April 21, 1832. Byrs: B. H., Sophia, B. M. Saxon, etc.

SCOTT, ANDREW W.—BOX 86, PACK 2104:
Est. admnr. Dec. 1, 1817 by Peyton Bibb, Jacob Martin, Saml. Savage bound to Taliaferro Livingston Ord. Abbeville Dist. sum $5,000.00. Archibald H. Scott of Georgia owed a note of $150.00. Inv. made Oct. 6, 1817 by A. Giles, R. Covington, Thos. A. Sanders.

STEELE, DAVID—BOX 86, PACK 2105:
Will dated May 31, 1827 in Abbeville Dist. Prov. Sept. 25, 1827. Exrs:
Wife, Mary Steele, John McCullough Sr. Wit: Jas. H., Chas. Stark, Wm.
P. Allen. Chn: Wm., Larkin, Sarah, Jane, Lucinda, Permelia, Cynthia, Katharine,
Elizabeth, Mary, Nancy Steele.

SWANZEY, DR. SAMUEL—BOX 86, PACK 2106:
Est. admnr. Oct. 6, 1817 by Jas. Swanzey, Jas. Hodges, Joseph Eakins
bound to Taliaferro Livingston Ord. Abbeville Dist. sum $10,000.00. Cit. pub.
at Siloam Church. Wm. Wier gdn. Sarah Ann, Robt. W., Rosanna, Eliza Caroline, Mary Ann, Louisa Swanzey minor chn. of Dr. Saml. Swanzey. Paid David
Stewart for raising of one child Lucy L. Swanzey $201.94½.

SMYTHE, ROBERT, JR.—BOX 86, PACK 2107:
Will dated Aug. 31, 1816 in Abbeville Dist. Prov. Sept. 6, 1816. Exrs:
Wife, Martha Smythe, Jas. Patterson. Wit: Dr. John H. Miller, Geo. Bowie,
John F. Glover. Chn: Robert Smythe being the child which I have had by
my present wife. Nancy wife of Jas. Patterson.

SMYTHE, MARTHA—BOX 86, PACK 2108:
Will dated Jan. 24, 1827 in Abbeville Dist. Prov. Feb. 1, 1827. Exrs:
John Devlin Esq., Wm. McClinton. Wit: John R. McBride, Dewi E. Lipford,
Jas. Drennan, Jas. McCreary. Nephew, Wm. McClinton. b. l. John Devlin and
his chn. by my sis., Mary Esther McCullough. Sis. Charlotte McCullough.
"Give unto Jas. Patterson whose hand is shot off $50.00. Bequeath to Andrew
Dale, Robt. Crawford, Elizabeth B. Lesly, John C., Gilbert McCrery. John,
Joseph sons of Joseph McCrery, Dewi Lipford."

SAXON, BENJAMIN—BOX 86, PACK 2109:
Will dated Jan. 4, 1784 in 96 Dist. Prov. Sept. 13, 1785. Exrs: Wife,
no name given. Sons, Jas., Saml. Saxon. Wit: Jean Quinton, Nicholas Curry,
Gabriel Patrick. Chn: Wm., Benjamin, John, Jas., Saml. Saxon. Gr. Chn: Saml.
Barkesdel, Mary Saxon.

STUART, WILLIAM—BOX 86, PACK 2110:
Est. admnr. Nov. 4, 1799 by Martin Stuart, Archibald Hamilton, Saml.
Houston bound to Andrew Hamilton Ord. Abbeville Dist. sum $2,000.00. Was
a Constable. Martin Stuart next of kin. Inv. made Nov. 18, 1799 by Wm.
Lesly Esq., John Pickens, Mathew Reid.

SMITH, WILLIAM—BOX 87, PACK 2111:
Est. admnr. April 5, 1791 by Wm. Russell, Jas. Stevenson, Saml. Reid,
John Miller bound to Judges Abbeville Co. sum 500 lbs. Inv. made July 11,
1791 by Wm., Joseph, Saml. Black Sr. Sale, July 12, 1791. Byrs: John Caldwell, Hugh McLine, Mary Smith, etc.

STUART, WILLIAM—BOX 87, PACK 2112:
Will dated June 7, 1794 in Abbeville Dist. Exrs: Wife, Jennet, Alexr.
Stewart. Wit: Mathew Wilson, David Robinson, Saml. Armstrong. Chn: Alexr.,
Wm., John, Mary, Elizabeth Stuart. Gr. son: John Wier.

SMITH, ROBERT, SR.—BOX 87, PACK 2113:
Will dated Oct. 25, 1783 in 96 Dist. Prov. Nov. 29, 1783. Exr: Wm. Anderson. Wit: Jas. Hollingsworth, Cornelius Dendy, Thos. Ross. Nephews, Thos. Turk, Robt. Smith, Wm. Thomas and Omey Carter's two eldest chn. Inv. made Dec. 22, 1783 by Thos. Anderson, Abraham Little, John Caldwell.

SPARKS, ZACHARIAH—BOX 87, PACK 2114:
Est. admnr. Sept. 1, 1786 by Frances, Mary Luffrey, Edward Giddeon, Alexr. Menary bound to John Thomas Jr. Ord. 96 Dist. sum 500 lbs. Inv. made Sept. 29, 1786 by Adam Gordon, Joseph Glenn, Andrew Endsley.

STUCKEY, THOMAS, JR.—BOX 87, PACK 2115:
Est. admnr. Oct. 6, 1804 by Elizabeth Stuckey, John Hadden, Jas. Agnew bound to Andrew Hamilton Ord. Abbeville Dist. sum $5,000.00. Sale. Nov. 15, 1804. Byrs: Thos. Stuckey Sr., Robt. Black, etc.

STEEN, COL. JAMES—BOX 87, PACK 2116:
Will date torn. Prov. Jan. 9, 1782. Exrs: Saml. McJunkins Esq., Major Thos. Brandon, Wm. Steen. Wit: Jas. Lusk, Saml. Bailey, John Kelley. Lived in 96 Dist. Wife's name not plain. Chn: Jean, John, Wm., Jas., Richard Steen, Anabel Davis. (Will badly torn.)

SCOTT, JOHN—BOX 87, PACK 2117:
Will dated Jan. 4, 1780 in Granville Co. Prov. Nov. 23, 1782. Exrs: Sons, Saml., Jas. Scott. Wit: John Douglass, Saml., John Boyd, John Sharpton. "Bequeath to Saml. Scott 300 acres in Richmond Co., Georgia granted in my name May 4, 1773, to Jas. Scott bequeath 200 acres on Savannah River in Georgia granted to me July 5, 1774." Inv. made Dec. 5, 1782 by Jas., Joseph Thomas, Wm. Rennalds. Jas. D. Scott was a son.

SPENCE, JAMES—BOX 87, PACK 2118:
Est. admnr. Feb. 13, 1808 by Agness, Saml. Spence, Jas. Hutchison, John Robinson bound to Andrew Hamilton Ord. Abbeville Dist. sum $5,000.00. Inv. made Mar. 1, 1808 by Jas. Hutcheson, Wm. Gray, John Robinson.

SMITH, HARRY—BOX 87, PACK 2119:
Will dated Mar. 24, 1804 in Abbeville Dist. Rec. May 7, 1804. Exrs: Wife, Fanney Smith, Major Richard Watts of Laurens Dist., Capt. John Watts of Laurens Dist. Wit: Thos., Davil Hill, John Ball. Chn: Thos. Hobson Smith, Sarah Scrugs, Wm. Burley, Elizabeth Gains, Alsey Abseley. Inv. made May 26, 1804 by Chas. Fooshe, Joseph Hill, Robt. Pollard.

SWANZEY, ROBERT—BOX 87, PACK 2120:
Will dated June 20, 1795. Rec. June 13, 1796. Exrs: Wife, Rosannah Swanzey. Son, Saml. Swanzey. Wit: Mcmn. Walker, Alexr. Welch, Jacob Ege, Thos., Daniel Gratton. Chn: Jenn, John, Saml. Swanzey. (At a Court held for Greenbrier Co. in Va. Sept. 27, 1795. The last will and testament of Robt. Swanzey was proved by John Stuart, Clerk of Court.) Inv. made July 30, 1796 by Alexr. Sample, Walter Anderson, Nathan Sims.

SMITHERS, GABRIEL—BOX 87, PACK 2121:
Est. admnr. March 29, 1797 by Robt. McCoombs of Cambridge, Wm. Calhoun, undersheriff, Robt. Smith unto the Judges of Abbeville County sum $5,000.00. Inv. made Sept. 12, 1797 by Thos. Livingston, Jas. Wilson, Jas. Gouedy.

SMITH, ANNE—BOX 87, PACK 2122:
Est. admnr. July 4, 1814 by Wm. Smith, Wm. Norris unto Taliaferro Livingston Ord. Abbeville Dist. sum $2,000.00. Cit. pub. at Siloam Church. Inv. made July 14, 1814 by John, Jas. Smith, Wm. Phillips. Expend: Sept. 29, 1814. Robt. Roman in his own right and for Daniel Smith, James Sims who is entitled to 3/4 of said est.

STRAIN, ROBERT—BOX 87, PACK 2123:
Est. admnr. Nov. 30, 1824 by Robt., Mathew Wilson, Saml. Houston unto Moses Taggart Ord. Abbeville Dist. sum $1,000.00. Cit. pub. at Upper Long Cane Church. Expend: Dec. 18, 1825 paid Mary Strain $20.00. Inv. made Dec. 14, 1824 by Saml. Kidd, Allen T. Miller, Hugh Kirkwood. Byrs: Mathew Wilson, Robt. Crawford, Hugh Kirkwood, Saml. Houston, Robt. Wilson.

SMITH, SMALLWOOD—BOX 87, PACK 2124:
Inv. made May 20, 1783 by Enoch Grigsby, John Davis, Russell Wilson. Lived in 96 Dist. Expend: July 23, 1785 paid Jacob Smith gdn. to the children of Smallwood Smith. May 20, 1784 paid Frederick Sisson husband to the decd. wid. for her dowry.

STRAIN, JAMES—BOX 87, PACK 2125:
Est. admnr. Jan. 7, 1783 by Saml., John, David Strain unto John Ewing Calhoun Ord. 96 Dist. sum 14,000 lbs. Inv. made Feb. 1, 1783 by John, Wm. David Strain.

STOKES, JOHN, SR.—BOX 87, PACK 2126:
Est. admnr. March 19, 1816 by Mary, John, Jacob Stokes, Wm. Lummus unto Taliaferro Livingston Ord. Abbeville Dist. sum $10,000.00. Inv. made April 2, 1816 by Wm. Cochran, W. Bradley Lewis, Joseph Culpepper.

SWANCY, JOHN WILSON—BOX 87, PACK 2127:
Will dated Jan. 6, 1804 in Abbeville Dist. Exrs: Wife, Lucy, Saml. Swancy, Saml. Anderson. Wit: John H., Henry H. Marable, Burnal Russell. Son, Robt. Swancey. (State of North Carolina, Northampton County) March Sessions 1804. This the will was exhibited into court and duly proved by the oath of John H. Marable one of the witnesses. Sale, April 13, 1804. Byrs: Dr. Saml., Lucy Swanzy, Walter Anderson Sr., Capt. John Hodges, Thos. Pinson, Elisha Weatherford, Jas. Campbell, David Steel, etc.

SMITHERS, CHRISTOPHER—BOX 87, PACK 2128:
Will dated Feb. 17, 1781. Probated Sept. 2, 1782. Exrs: John Sturzenegger, Lud Williams. Wit: John Nail, John Tobler Sr., Wm. Shinholser. Lived in New Windsor Township, carpenter. 96 Dist. Wife, Catharine Smithers, Son, Jas. Smithers.

SLAPPY, JACOB—BOX 87, PACK 2129:
Est. admnr. Dec. 7, 1829 by John G. Slappy, Jas. *Shibley*, Geo. F. Caldwell unto Moses Taggart Ord. Abbeville Dist. sum $15,000.00. Inv. made Jan. 9, 1830 by Jas. Carson, Geo. F. Caldwell, Lewis Simmons. Sale, Jan. 13, 1830. Byrs: Saml. Caldwell, Wm. Harris, Lewis Simmons, Geo. Caldwell, David Williams, Hugh Robeson, Wm. Dorn, Tyra Jay, Washington Walsh, John Casey, John Conner, etc.

STEDMAN, JOHN—BOX 87, PACK 2130:
Est. admnr. Sept. 12, 1797 by Jas. Stedman, Robt. Martin, Jas. Tannehill unto the Judges of Abbeville County sum $3,000.00. Inv. made Nov. 11, 1797 by Joseph, John Trimble, Peer Brotwn. Cit. pub. at Cedar Springs Church.

SHINHOLSER, JOHN—BOX 87, PACK 2131:
Est. admnr. Sept. 13, 1782 by Wm. Shinholser, Joachim Bulow, David Zubly unto John Ewing Calhoun Ord. 96 Dist. sum 14 lbs. Inv. made Dec. 30, 1782 by John Sturzenegger, John Tobler Sr., Adam Files. Wm. Shinholser was of Beach Island.

STRICKLAND, JACOB—BOX 87, PACK 2132:
Will dated Feb. 21, 1814 in Abbeville Dist. Rec. April 13, 1814. Exr: Brother, Isaac Strickland. Wit: Thos. Oliver, Howel Vick, John Cameron. Brothers, Joseph, Isaac Strickland. (Now stationed at Camp Alston.) Inv. made April 23, 1814 by Nathan Sr., Frederick Strickland.

SUMMERLIN, JACOB—BOX 87, PACK 2133:
Est. admnr. May 4, 1785 by Ann Summerlin, Thos. Ray, Edward Vann unto John Thomas Jr. Ord. 96 Dist. sum 1000 lbs. Inv. made by Jas. King, Edward Vann, Drury Mims.

SUBER, GEORGE—BOX 87, PACK 2134:
Est. admnr. Oct. 17, 1783 by Conrod, Rachel Suber, Daniel Gartman, unto John Thomas Jr. Ord. 96 Dist. sum 2,000 lbs. Inv. made Dec. 12, 1783 by Michael Dickert, Conrad Suber, Christian Ruff.

SWAIN, ROBERT—BOX 87, PACK 2135:
Will dated Oct. 2, 1812 in Abbeville Dist. Rec. Nov. 16, 1812. Exrs: Sons, John, Robt. Swain. Wit: John Weatherall, Wm. Richey, Wm. Hodges. Chn: Jane Norriss, Mary, John, Robt. Swain, Elizabeth Reevs, "a tract of land lying in Pendleton District." Inv. made Dec. 22, 1812 by John Weatherall, Gabriel Long, Hugh Dickson.

SMITH, AARON—BOX 87, PACK 2136:
Inv. made June 13, 1783 by John Smith, Abraham Moore, Thos. Compton. Byrs: Wm., Zophar, Sarah Smith, Joseph Howel, John, Ralph Smith. Lived 96 Dist. (No other papers.)

STRAIN, THOMAS—BOX 87, PACK 2137:
Est. admnr. Dec. 31, 1781 by John Strain, Robt. Bond, Wm. Drennan.

Saml. McMurtrey unto John Ewing Calhoun Ord. 96 Dist. sum 1,000 lbs. Inv. made Jan. 9, 1782 by Wm. Drennan, Robt. *Delfudg*, Saml. McMurtrey.

SHURGION, JOHN—BOX 87, PACK 2138:
Est. admnr. Nov. 8, 1783 by Elizabeth Shurgion, Ebenezer Moss, John Pennington unto John Thomas Jr. Ord. 96 Dist. sum 2,000 lbs. Inv. made Dec. 27, 1783 by Thos. Childers, Edward *Mitichuson*, William *Mitichuson*. (Not positive whether the name was Shurgion, or Spurgeon. Written so dim.)

SMITH, JOSEPH—BOX 87, PACK 2139:
Est. admnr. Sept. 19, 1783 by Mary Ann Smith, Wm. Malone, Bartholomew Johnson unto John Thomas Jr. Ord. 96 Dist. sum 2,000 lbs. Inv. made Oct. 13, 1783 by Alexr. Dickey, Geo. Montgomery, Bartholomew Johnson.

SMITH, GIDEON—BOX 87, PACK 2140:
Will dated Aug. 20, 1779 in 96 Dist. Proven Aug. 23, 1783. Exrs: Jas. Steen, John, Abraham Smith. Wit: Robt. Lusk, Joseph Jolly, John Jeffries. Wife, Jean Smith. Son, Jas. Smith.

SAMUEL, ELISHA—BOX 87, PACK 2141:
Est. admnr. Nov. 20, 1782 by Mary Beal, Thos., James Wilson unto John Ewing Calhoun Ord. 96 Dist. sum 14,000 lbs. Mary Beal next of kin. Inv. made Nov. 30, 1782 by Thos. Wilson, Mathew McMillian, Wm. Hagood.

SWEARINGEN, JOSEPH VAN—BOX 87, PACK 2142:
Will dated July 14, 1794 in Abbeville Dist. Rec. Nov. 10, 1794. Exrs: Wife, Mary Swearingen, s. l. Thos. Shanklin. Wit: Saml. Linton, Henry Sharp, John Glenn, Jacob Clearman. Chn: Sarah Pickens, Hannah Shanklin, Mary Elizabeth Thompson, Elizabeth Barrett. Gr. chn: Robert Shanklin, Mathew, Joseph, John Thompson. Inv. made Jan. 5, 1795 by James Ponder, Aaron Alexander, Wm. Black.

SHANNON, JOHN—BOX 87, PACK 2143:
Est. admnr. Mar. 4, 1806 by Elizabeth Shannon, Robt. Gibson, John Pinkerton, Jas. Richey, Saml. Foster unto Andrew Hamilton Ord. Abbeville Dist. sum $10,000.00. Expend: Feb. 16, 1813 paid $1.25 for a hat for Robt. Shannon. Nov. 24, 1809 paid for boarding Jas., Robt. Shannon $13.12. Sale, Mar. 24, 1806. Byrs: Elizabeth Shannon, Saml. Miller, Benjamin Northcutt, Alexr. McKinney, Wm. Anderson, John Pinkerton, Wm. McIlwain, Robt. Gibson, William McKain, John Gibson, Dr. John Miller, Jas. Richey Jr., Wm. Norris, John Brown, etc.

STANFIELD, WILLIAM—BOX 87, PACK 2144:
Will dated July 9, 1805 in Abbeville Dist. Rec. Aug. 15, 1806. Exrs: Peter Hitt, John *Mills*. Wit: Henry Beasly, John Milton, Wm. Link. Wife, Sarah Stanfield, Son, John Stanfield. Legatees: Robt. Stanfield, Jane Hitt, Peggy Miles, Milley Link. "Give Thos. Link five shillings." Inv. made Sept. 18, 1806 by Andrew Crozier, Leonard Wideman, John Carr. Paid Thos. Gray legacy left to Thos. Link. Paid John Harris legatee $727.49½.

STANFIELD, JOHN—BOX 87, PACK 2145:
Est. admnr. Dec. 12, 1805 by Richard, Sarah Stanfield, Edward Collier unto Andrew Hamilton Ord. Abbeville Dist. sum $5,000.00. Inv. made Jan. 2, 1806 by Joshua Hill, Leonard Wideman, Andrew Crozier. Sale, Jan. 3, 1806. Byrs: Sarah Stanfield Jr., Edmond Brown, John Talbert, Sarah Stanfield Sr. Lewis Free, Jesse Barker, Richard Stanfield, Joshua Hill, Richard Beazley.

STEELE, AARON—BOX 87, PACK 2146:
Inv. made Dec. 14, 1795 by Wm. Pickens Sr., Jas. Carlile, Robt. Davis. Expend: 1801 paid Jean Steel legacy $85.78. 1802 paid Aaron Steel Jr. legacy left him by his grandfather and Wm. Steel $43.95. Paid Jas. Steel legacy $41.20. Paid Abner Steel legacy $41.20. Exrs: Elizabeth Steele, John Caldwell.

SHANKLIN, PHEBE—BOX 87, PACK 2147:
Will dated Mar. 12, 1807 in Abbeville Dist. Rec. Sept. 15, 1807. Exrs: Thos. Shanklin, Saml. Savage Esq. Wit: Jas. Powell, Elizabeth Douglass, A. Hunter. Chn: Nancy Fugua, Richard, Wm. Covington, Former husband, Wm. Covington, Gr. Dtr: Harriet Moore. Inv. made Sept. 19, 1807 by John McNeil, Hudson Prince, Henry Hester.

SPRUILL, JOHN—BOX 87, PACK 2148:
Will dated Jan. 25, 1808 in Abbeville Dist. Rec. Feb. 2, 1808. Exrs: Son, Simeon Spruill, s. l. William Welden. Wit: Reuben Nash, Geo., Stephen Mitchell. Wife, Ruth Spruill. Chn: Wm., Geo., Luke, Simeon, John, Polly, Saml., Jepter or Jester, Nancy, Sally, Thos., Gabriel. Also heirs of daughter Peggy, no names given. Inv. made Feb. 5, 1808 by Abner Nash, Wm. Mitchell, Moses Hughes.

SIMS, LEWIS B.—BOX 87, PACK 2149:
Est. admnr. Dec. 7, 1807 by Lucy L. Sims, Pleasant Wright, John Hodges, Saml. Thompson unto Andrew Hamilton Ord. Abbeville Dist. sum $5,000.00. Inv. made Dec. 18, 1807 by John Sims, Eli Bowie, Thos. Davis. Sale, Jan. 2, 1808. Byrs: Wm. Sims, Pleasant Wright, Daniel Ward, Smith Bolin, Robt. White, Nicholas Overbey, Robt. Sample, Jas. Campbell, Jack Sims, Lucy L. Sims wid., Wm. Neely, Wm. Campbell, David Brown, Jack Pulliam Jr., Stephen Busbee.

SIMS, NATHAN—BOX 87, PACK 2150:
Will dated Dec. 15, 1802 in Abbeville Dist. Rec. Jan. 20, 1803. Exrs: Sons, Martha, John, Leonard Sims. Wit: John Sims, Saml. Swanzy, Z. Rice. Wife, Mary Sims, Chn: Pamelia Griffin, Leorana Calhoun, Sarah Smith, Susannah Bond, Agness Smith, Downs, Martin, John, Geo., Starling, Leonard, Wm. Sims. Inv. made Feb. 12, 1803 by Alexr. Sample, John Pulliam, John R. Long.

SHAW, SAMUEL—BOX 88, PACK 2151:
Est. admnr. July 25, 1805 by Mary Shaw wid., Wm. Ashley, Stephen Garrison unto Andrew Hamilton Ord. Abbeville Dist. sum $5,000.00. Cit. pub. at Greenville Church. Inv. made by Thos. Ashely, Josiah Burton, John Ashely.

Sale, Aug. 16, 1805. Byrs: Moses Clark, Thos. Tramble, Saml. Shaw, Jas. McAdams, Hugh Blair, Mary Shaw, Jas. Henry Sr., Alexr. Ervin, Benjamin West, Caleb Burton, Wm., Nancy McCurry, Richard Robinson, Thos. Russell, Washington Russell, John Randolph, Jean, Archibald Shaw, etc.

SKELTON, MARK—BOX 88, PACK 2152:
Est. admnr. Feb. 7, 1784 by Josiah Tanner, Wm. Wilkins unto John Thomas Jr. Ord. 96 Dist. sum 2,000 lbs. Inv. made May 21, 1785 by Wm. Lipscomb, Wm. Thomson, Littleton Napp.

SPRAGGINS, NATHANIEL—BOX 88, PACK 2153:
Est. admnr. Mar. 15, 1784 by Wm. Spraggins, Jacob Brooks, Michael Abney unto John Thomas Jr. Ord. 96 Dist. sum 2,000 lbs. Inv. made April 28, 1784 by Thos. Spraggins, Jas. Carson, Dennitt Abney.

SEAWRIGHT, JAMES—BOX 88, PACK 2154:
Will dated Oct. 29, 1789 in Abbeville Dist. Proven, April 6, 1790. Exrs: Saml. Agnew, Hugh Wardlaw. Wit: Andrew Seawright, Jas. Gray, Saml. Lindsay. Chn. ment., names not given. Inv. made July 14, 1791 by Saml., Joseph Reid, Edward Sharp, Sale, Aug. 10, 1790. Byrs: Henry Peacock, Jas. Hathorn, Andrew Kirkpatrick, David Crawford, Geo. Wilder, John Weatherall, Andrew Seawright, Henry Purdy, Moses Smith, John Wilson.

SAFOLD, WILLIAM—BOX 88, PACK 2155:
Will dated Aug. 11, 1784. Proven Oct. 16, 1784. Exr: Wife, Temperance Safold. Chn: Anne, Daniel, Saml., Isham, Wm., Reuben, Elizabeth, Sarah Safold. Inv. made Oct. 28, 1784 by John Watson, Littleton Napp, Wm. Thomson.

STRAIN, JOHN—BOX 88, PACK 2156:
Will dated June 26, 1798 in Abbeville Dist. Rec. Nov. 5, 1798. Exrs: David Strain, Jas. Watt. Wit: Robt. Wilson, Mathew Reed, Joseph Robison. Wife ment., no name given. Sons, John, James Strain. Inv. made Dec. 27, 1798 by John McMurtray, Robt. Thornton, Saml. Lyon.

STRAIN, CAPT. WILLIAM—BOX 88, PACK 2157:
Est. admnr. June 13, 1796 by Margaret wid., David Strain, Saml. Houston unto the Judges of Abbeville County sum $2,000.00. Inv. made July 13, 1796 by Joseph Gaston, John Johnson, Mathew Wilson. Sale, Aug. 9, 1796. Byrs: Margaret Strain, Chas. Holland, Robt. Bradford, Wm. Lesly Esq., Saml. Armstrong, David Robinson, John Pickens, Wm. Finney, John Strain Jr., Wm. Miller, Martin Shoemaker, Margaret McCord, John Montgomery, Wm. Russell, Wm. Garrett.

SANDERS, THOMAS—BOX 88, PACK 2158:
Will dated May 9, 1780 in 96 Dist. Proven April 14, 1785. Wit: Robt. Pulliam. Chn: Joseph, Wm., Jerusha Sanders. Wife ment., no name given. "Now being called out to the field of battle." (State of Georgia, Wilks County. Proven April 14, 1785.) Est. admnr. Feb. 1785 by Mary Sanders, Gabriel Smithers, John Lockridge unto John Thomas Jr. Ord. 96 Dist. sum 2,000 lbs.

SHAW, DANIEL—BOX 88, PACK 2159:
Est. admnr. Oct. 3, 1783 by Patrick Shaw, Robt. Harris, Adam Potter unto John Thomas Jr. Ord. 96 Dist. sum 2,000 lbs. Inv. made Oct. 21, 1783 by David Brown, Wm. Thomson, Adam Potter. Sale, Oct. 27, 1783. Byrs: Col. John Thomas Jr. Esq., Saml., Parick, Wm. Shaw, Daniel Jackson, Gilbert Shaw, Saml. Pattan, Gracy Turnbull, Catharine Shaw.

SLOAN, JOHN—BOX 88, PACK 2160:
Will dated Nov. 23, 1806 in Abbeville Dist. Rec. April 15, 1807. Exrs: John Jones, Robt. McClellan, Thos. Sloan. Wit: Thos. Wilson, Wm., Wm. Moody Jr., Wife, Jane Sloan. Chn: Thos., Molley, John Sloan, Jean Martin. "Owned land on Little Mulberry Creek." Inv. made July 8, 1807 by Henry Mitchell, Robt. Foster, Sias Cogburn.

SHAW, WILLIAM—BOX 88, PACK 2161:
Will dated Dec. 11, 1787 in Abbeville Dist. Rec. Oct. 7, 1788. Exrs: Patrick Calhoun Esq., Mr. Houskinson. Wit: Patrick Calhoun, Felix Hughes, Elizabeth Conner. "Bequeath 21 pounds due me from William Stephens of the Chiocas to my mother now living in Maryland." No name given. Ment. Robt. Shaw. "Owe the sum 9 shillings and one penny to one Count a Taylor in Bladessburgh." Inv. made Aug. 13, 1788 by Fleming Bates, Wm. Hutton, John McCarter.

SCOTT, JAMES D.—BOX 88, PACK 2162:
Est. admnr. July 18, 1814 by Saml. Jr., Saml. Sr., Archibald Scott unto Taliaferro Livingston Ord. sum $2,000.00. Inv. made Aug. 9, 1814 by Wm. Buford, Joseph Scott, Jas. Caldwell. Byrs: Saml., Archibald, Agness, Joseph Scott Sr.

SPENCE, JAMES—BOX 88, PACK 2163:
Will dated April 26, 1834 in Abbeville Dist. Proven Oct. 20, 1834. Exrs: Sons, Jas., John Spence. Wit: Patrick Gibson, Rice Mills, Saml. Zimmerman. Wife, Ann Spence. Chn: Jas., John, Wm., Nelly, Sarah, Ann Spence, Jane, wid. of Geo. Young, Peggy, Mary Creswell. S. ls: Joseph, Thos, Criswell. Gr: Dtr: Sarah Young. Inv. made Dec. 19, 1834 by Rice Mills, Saml. Zimmerman, John Robinson.

STALSWORTH, JOSEPH—BOX 88, PACK 2164:
Will dated July 19, 1796 in Abbeville Dist. Rec. Nov. 7, 1796. Exrs: Wife, Grace Stalsworth. Brothers: Wm., Thos. Stalsworth. Wit: Isaac Logan, Robt. Griffin. Dtr: Elizabeth Dial, s. l. Jas. Dial, Gr. Chn: Hasting Dial, Joseph Stalsworth Dial, (Letter found in package.)
Laurens C. H. June the 6th 1866
Dear Sir, The result of the war having settled the *monezed* interest of the estate of Joseph Stalsworth of which I am the admnr. and in order to ballance accounts you will please take the necessary steps to settle the said estate in your office as soon as possible. Joseph and Isaac Dial resides beyond the limits of the state would be legatees. I made a return before the ordinary

at Laurens the first of the year and forwarded the same inclosing two dollars to you but have not had an acknowledgement of the recpt. of it, I have had no little trouble & considerable expense in management of the estate for the last five years and had I not obtained an order from you for the sale of a negro would have suffered loss. As it is I do not suppose that there will be much money handled the negro was sold the 1st of Jan. 1863 and the expenses paid up to that time and the remainder of the funds amounting to about $400 was invested in Confederate bonas I do not recollect whether I returned that investment to your office or not. Please write me what showing will be necessary for me to make in this matter. I can give the certificate of Col. Simpson depostive at Laurens that the above stated funds was invested in bonas in the name of the said estate. In as much possible as I expect to be looser in the matter it will be desirable to settle it up with as little expense as possible. I do not remit any funds not knowing what amount it will take but will forward them immediately on receipt of a note from you. Your early attention and any advice that you may think propper to give will greatly oblige. June the 6th 1866.

Your friend,
Albert Dial

Hasting Dial was father of Albert Dial. Inv. made Nov. 16, 1796 by John, Benjamin Waller, Robt. Griffin.

STEELE, AARON—BOX 88, PACK 2165:
Will dated Aug. 5, 1794 in Abbeville Dist. Rec. Nov. 9, 1795. Exrs: John Caldwell, Wife, Elizabeth, Robt. Harris. Wit: John Caldwell, Jas. Cozby, Robt. Harris. Wife, Elizabeth Steele. Chn: Jas., Abner, Aaron, Jain Steele. Sale, Dec. 15, 1797. Byrs: Elizabeth, Abner, Jas. Steel, Joseph LeMaster, Robt. Harris, Abram Pickens, Robt. Patterson, Saml. Scott, John Caldwell, Robt. Bond, Jane Steel, Thos. Gillespie, Andrew Kennedy, Fortune Dobbs, Robt. Davis, Watson Cook, Wm. Mobley, etc.

STOREY, ANTHONY—BOX 88, PACK 2166:
Est. admnr. Sept. 12, 1783 by Sarah, Geo., Henry Storey, Robt. Farris, unto John Thomas Jr. Ord. 96 Dist. sum 2,000 lbs. Inv. made Sept. 30, 1783 by Hugh Means, Wm. Patton, Robt. Farris. Sale, Oct. 20, 1783. Byrs: Sarah, Geo. Jr., John, Geo. Sr., Henry Storey, Hugh Means, Wm. Elders.

SIMPSON, JAMES—BOX 88, PACK 2167:
Est. admnr. Nov. 11, 1793 by John McFall of Pendleton Co., merchant, Capt. John Q. Quay, Wm. Calhoun unto the Judges of Abbeville Co. sum 500 lbs. Cit. pub. at Due West Corner. Paid Wm. McCrone as Atty. for the heirs $85.75. Inv. made Nov. 30, 1793 by John George, Robt. Dodwle, Alexr. McAllister.

SMITH, RALPH—BOX 88, PACK 2168:
Will dated July 24, 1781 in 96 Dist. Prov. Oct. 8, 1784. Exrs: Wife, Ann Smith. Sons, Zophar, Nathan Smith. Wit: Edmund Bearden, Saml. Lancaster, John Wofford. Chn: Wm., Aaron decd. and his wife Sarah, Zophar Smith,

Rachel Crumpton, Nathan, Joel, Saml., Ralph, Joseph, Martha, Ann, Rebecca Smith. Gr. chn: Jonathan, Joab, Mercy, chn. of Aaron, Sarah Smith. Inv. made Oct. 25, 1784 by Saml Lancaster, John Shands, Brittain Millsford.

STUART, MARY—BOX 88, PACK 2169:
John Weir, Robt. Richey bound unto Moses Taggart Ord. Abbeville Dist. sum $3,500.00. Dated Oct. 27, 1825. John Weir made gdn. of Mary, John W. Stuart minors. Expend: Jan. 21, 1829, Amt. H. H. Stewart's note $2.50. Jan. 3, 1827—Cash sent by A. Stewart for John, $17.10. Jan. 12, 1829 Mary Stuart of Newton Co. Georgia appointed Saml. Stewart of Co. and State aforesaid her Atty. to receive money due her from John Ware of the State of South Carolina, Abbeville Dist.

STEWART, WILLIAM, MINORS—BOX 88, PACK 2170:
Hamilton, Saml. L. Hill, John H. Armstrong bound unto Moses Taggart Ord. Abbeville Dist. sum $15,000.00. Hamilton Hill made gdn. of Adam Leoo or Levi, John Lewis, Mary Stewart minors.

SALE, JAMES—BOX 88, PACK 2171:
Susan, Benjamin Sale minors in 1831. (Nothing else of importance).

SEAWRIGHT, MINORS—BOX 88, PACK 2172:
On Nov. 10, 1834 Jas. W. Richey, John Donnald, John Seawright bound to Moses Taggart Ord. sum $6,000.00. Jas. W. Richey gdn. of Nancy A., Vashti, Amanda, Robt., Wm. W., Margaret C. Seawright minors of Andrew Seawright decd.

SMITH, NELSON P., CHILDREN—BOX 88, PACK 2173:
In 1835 Willis, Wiley Smith were minors. Edmund Cobb gdn. Joseph, Satira Crawford legatees. Legatees of Wm. Anderson: Margaret, Edmund, Mary, Wm., John, Nathaniel Anderson. (This last could have been in package by mistake.)

STEWART, DAVID—BOX 88, PACK 2174:
Will dated Oct. 11, 1837 in Abbeville Dist. Prov. Jan. 23, 1838. Exr: Jabez W. H. Johnson. Wit: Wm. Buchanan, John Caldwell, W. H. Green. Chn: Thos., John Alexander Stewart. Inv. made Jan. 31, 1838 by Downs Calhoun, Willison B. Beazley, Walter Anderson.

STONE, MALINDA—BOX 88, PACK 2175:
On Jan. 20, 1852, Benjamin Moseley, John Donald, Wm. Richey bound to Moses Taggart Ord. Abbeville Dist. sum $2,000.00. Benjamin Moseley gdn. of Melinda Stone minor under 14 yrs. Cit. ment. Melinda Stone (now Cummins.)

STEVENSON, MINORS—BOX 88, PACK 2176:
Sept. 4, 1834 John Stephenson, Mathew T. Miller, Francis H. Carlile bound to Moses Taggart Ord. Abbeville Dist. sum $1,000.00. Sept. 4, 1834 John Stephenson made gdn. of Sarah M., Rebecca, Andrew T. Stephenson, minors of Andrew Stevenson decd. (Name written Stephenson also.)

SMITH, MADISON—BOX 88, PACK 2177:
Oct. 31, 1832 Wm., Thos., Hugh B. Campbell bound unto Moses Taggart Ord. Abbeville Dist. sum $500.00. William Campbell gdn. of Madison Smith minor.

SAMPLE, MINORS—BOX 88, PACK 2178:
On June 5, 1837 Thos. B. Byrd, Robt. Turner, Ephraim R. Calhoun bound unto Moses Taggart Ord. Abbeville Dist. sum $20,000.00. Thos. B. Byrd gdn. of Louisa, Sarah, Mellisa, John B. Sample minors. Sarah married Isaac Logan. Louisa married John Wilson. Expend: July 20, 1851 Recd. from est. of Barbara Sample $168.75. Chn. of Susannah C. Sample.

SMITH, MINORS—BOX 88, PACK 2180:
On Oct. 20, 1834 Rice Mills, Jas., John Spence bound unto Moses Taggart Ord. Abbeville Dist. sum $300.00. Rice Mills gdn. of Mary Ann Mills Smith minor. dtr. of Stephen Smith decd. Expend: Jan. 1835 paid Alsey C. Mills for nursing his wife $3.50.

SIMPSON, POLLY, MINORS—BOX 88, PACK 2181:
On Nov. 10, 1829 Andrew Sr., Daniel Gilespie, Beauford Yarbrough bound unto Moses Taggart Ord. Abbeville Dist. sum $3,000.00. Andrew Gillespie Sr., gdn. of Thos., Joseph, John, James, minors over 14 yrs.; Henry, Jemima, David Simpson also chn. of Polly Simpson decd.

SKINNER, MINORS—BOX 88, PACK 2182:
On Aug. 12, 1837 John Skinner, Tyra Jay, John Ruff bound unto Moses Taggart Ord. Abbeville Dist. sum $500.00. John Skinner gdn. of Frances, John Richard Skinner, minors. Expend: 1839 paid Moriah Skinner for boarding Frances Skinner, $8.25.

STUART, MARGARET—BOX 88, PACK 2183:
Will dated Nov. 20, 1838 in Abbeville Dist. Prov. Jan. 15, 1839. Exrs: Son, John Stuart, Dr. E. R. Calhoun. Wit: Williston B. Beazley, Jas. F. Pinson, Philip Waite. Chn: Mary Ann, John Stuart, Sarah Buchanan, Susan Calhoun. Gr. chn: Emily Turner, Louisa, Sarah, Mellisa, John Sample children of dtr. Susan Calhoun. Margaret Stuart died Jan. 9, 1839. Sett. made June 27, 1842. Present: Dr. E. R. Calhoun, Wm. Buchanan in right of his wife Sarah Caldwell, John A., Mary Ann Stuart by her guardian E. R. Calhoun, minor children of John B. Sample, two of these of age. Capt. Bird was gdn.

SIMS, GEORGE N.—BOX 88, PACK 2184:
Will dated Jan. 23, 1835. Prov. Mar. 30, 1835. Exrs: Wife, no name given. Alexr. Hunter, Robt. F. Black. Wit: Joseph Black, Oliver Taggart, A. W. Lynch. Chn., no names given. Inv. made by Robert McNair, Nelson Norris, Hugh Prince.

SANDERS, JOHN—BOX 89, PACK 2185:
Will dated Jan. 7, 1818 in Abbeville Dist. Rec. Jan. 21, 1818. Wit: Wm. S. McCord, Rowland Burges, Joseph Davis. No Exrs. given. Wife, Anna

Sanders. Chn: Aggy Cook Sanders, Francis Dickeson Sanders. Sarah Ann, Thos., Wm., Eliza Malvener, John Sanders. Inv. made Feb. 17, 1818 by John Cochran Sr., Joseph Davis, Rowland Burges. Inv. of John Sanders same package made Sept. 3, 1784 by Thos. Weems, John Cochran, John Lockridge, Esq.

STARKE, CHARLES—BOX 89, PACK 2186:
Will dated Oct. 6, 1838 in Abbeville Dist. Prov. Feb. 4, 1839. Exrs: s. l. Abner E. Fant, Col. A. Rice. Wit: Blackman Burton, John, Philip P. Milford. Wife, Keziah Stark. Chn: Saml. C., Sarah Ann, Jas. H. Stark, Mary Madison, Elizabeth Fant. Grandson: Saml. J. H., son of Saml. C. Stark. Inv. made Feb. 11, 1839 by Blackman Burton, Robt. D. Johnson, Wm. Hampton, Zachariah Hall. (Note: Inv. of Patrick McDavid made April 26, 1783 by Basil Holland, Thos. Murphy, Robt. Hanna found in same package. Could have gotten there by mistake.)

STARKE, DR. NEWMAN—BOX 89, PACK 2187:
Est. admnr. Jan. 6, 1829 by Wyatt W., Reuben Starke, Wm. McCaw bound unto Moses Taggart Ord. Abbeville Dist. sum $5,000.00. Inv. made by Jas., Dr. Elijah Hunt, Hugh Mecklin. Sale, Jan 15, 1829. Byrs: Richard Covington, Reuben Starke, W. L. Gary, Milton Paschal, Silas Glover, F. Y. Baskin, Edward Bailey, Jas. H. Scott, R. Starke, etc.

STEWART, JOHN—BOX 89, PACK 2188:
Will dated Nov. 4, 1826 in Abbeville Dist. Prov. Jan. 1, 1827. Exrs: Son, Joseph Stewart, Charles Drennan. Wit: James Wiley, Robt. Drennan, John Coughran. Wife, Elizabeth Stewart. Chn: Joseph, Wm., Robt., Jas., Archibald D., Elizabeth, Agnes, Jane, Ann, Fanny Stewart. Gr: dtr: Elizabeth Morrow. Inv. made Jan. 12, 1827 by Alexr. Wiley, Francis Wilson, West Donald.

SANDERS, WILLIAM M.—BOX 89, PACK 2189:
Est. admnr. Jan. 28, 1828 by Luke Mathis, Marshal Weatherall, Richard Hill bound unto Moses Taggart Ord. Abbeville Dist. sum $2,000.00. Inv. made Feb. 9, 1828 by Jas. Alston, John Taggart, Marshal Weatherall. Expend: Feb. 1, 1830 Recd. of Jas. Wiley, admnr. of Rebecca Sanders decd., part Wm. M. Sander's share $39.12½.

SANDERS, THOMAS—BOX 89, PACK 2190:
Est. admnr. Jan. 3, 1825 by John, Archibald Tittle, Alexr. Jordon unto Moses Taggart Ord. Abbeville Dist. sum $1,000.00. Cit. pub. at Asbury Chapel. Inv. made Jan. 18, 1825 by Abram Thompson, A. Tittle, Jas. A. Gray.

SHIRLEY, WILLIAM—BOX 89, PACK 2191:
Will dated May 13, 1827 in Abbeville Dist. Prov. Oct. 1, 1827. Exrs: Wife, Jemimay Shirley; Brother, John Shirley. Wit: Jas. A. Black, Lankford Hughes, Jas. Griffin. Chn. ment., names not given. Inv. made Nov. 2, 1827 by Cador Gantt, Hezekiah Wakefield, Stephen Fisher.

SMITH, STEPHEN—BOX 89, PACK 2192:
Est. admnr. April 3, 1830 by Saml., John B. Pressly, Thos. McBride

unto Moses Taggart Ord. Abbeville Dist. sum $100.00. Inv. made April 10, 1830 by Rice Mills, Abner Perrin, Jas. Traylor.

STEVENSON, JAMES—BOX 89, PACK 2193:
Will dated Feb. 24, 1820 in Abbeville Dist. Prov. June 3, 1822. Exrs: Andrew, John Stevenson. Wit: Wm. Hadden, Henry Sharp, Alexr. Fife. Chn: Mary Seawright, Margaret Carrick, Jane Hamilton, James, Andrew, John Stevenson. Gr. chn: Margaret Seawright, Jas. Stevenson. Expend: April 1, 1822 paid Jas. Seawright legacy $15.00.

SHIRLEY, ELIZABETH—BOX 89, PACK 2194:
Will dated March 27, 1826. Prov. April 21, 1826. Exrs: Son, Nathaniel Shirley, s. l. Jas. Richey. Wit: John Donnald, John, Andrew Seawright. Chn: Nathaniel, Mastin, John Shirley, Lety Peerman, Armond Kay, Julines Richey, Rhody Cullins, Lettice Wilson, s. l. John Wilson. Inv. made May 12, 1826 by Jas. Lattimore, John Kay, John Branyon, John McClain. Heirs of Lettice. John Wilson, Jas. W., Elizabeth Wilson, Reuben D. Adams and wife Margaret, Benjamin Wilson. Sett. of est: Rena Letty Adams who before her marriage was a Wilson entitled to a share of est. of Elizabeth Shirley in right of her father John Shirley. Made Jan. 8, 1851. Alfred, Reney Adams recd. $141.90 for their share. William N., Richard C. Wilson legatees.

SIMMS, ENOCH—BOX 89, PACK 2195:
Est. admnr. Feb. 2, 1826 by Robt. W., John Wilson, Donald Douglass unto Moses Taggart Ord. Abbeville Dist. sum $2,000. Inv. made Feb. 4, 1826 by John Wilson, John McLaren, Donald Douglass. Sale, Feb. 6, 1826. Byrs: John Wilson, Francis Young, Wm. Herston, Lewis Howlan, Pinkney White.

SALES, WILLIAM—BOX 89, PACK 2196:
Will dated Aug. 7, 1828 in Abbeville Dist. Prov. Dec. 2, 1828. Exrs: Bro., Johnson Sale, Robt. Burns. Wit: Tebitha Sale, John M. Moore, Catlett Conner. Wife, Rebecca Sale. Chn: Sarah Elmira, Smith Burton, Wm., Elvira Ann Sale. Expend: Jan. 1, 1828, paid board of Josephine for 2 yrs, 5 mo. $144.90. Paid for Julia's board, $24.00.

SPEED, ROBERT—BOX 89, PACK 2197:
Will dated Jan. 2, 1826 in Abbeville Dist. Prov. Jan. 13, 1826. Exrs: Wade Speed, John E. Calhoun. Wit: Thos. Dickson, Saml. Calhoun, H. McCoy. Wife, Elizabeth Speed. "Bequeath unto the following, Mary, John, Jas. Speed, Rebecca Kemp, Betsey Tyler, Wade, Florence, Terrel, Wm. Speed, John E. Calhoun."

SPENCE, MARY—BOX 89, PACK 2198:
Inv. made Mar. 7, 1826 by David H. McCrery, Alexr. Wiley, Wm. Dale. Sale, Mar. 8, 1826. Byrs: Wm. G. Spence, West Donald, Wm. Dale, David, Joseph McCrery, Rosannah, Mary Spence, etc.

SHANKLIN, THOS.—BOX 89, PACK 2199:
Will dated Jan. 19, 1829. Prov. Mar. 2, 1829. Exrs: Son: Joseph V.

Shanklin, Alexr. Hunter. Wit: Archibald McMullan, Wm. M. Johnson, A. Hunter. Chn: Elizabeth Harris, Polly Crawford. Joseph V. Shanklin. Gr. Chn: Thos., son of Elizabeth Harris, Edward, Caroline, Stanhope Harris, Thos., Wm., Polly, Drucilla Crawford, Polly Riley, Sarah McKinley, Margaret Scott, Saml., Joseph, Thos., Wm., Elizabeth Caldwell, Martha Shanklin. (Dtr. of Saml.).

(Letter) Pendleton 27th March, 1829:

Dear Sir, I take this liberty of requesting you to file this in your office as my renunciation of my trust as Exes. of the late will & testament of my father. The distance at which I live renders it very inconvenient to me to attend to the execution of the will. I think more ever that Mr. A. Hunter fully qualified to discharge the duties imposed by the will & have no doubt that he will do so to the interest satisfaction of all concerned. Mr. Hunter being so convenient to the property would necessary impose upon him the (word) of executorship & my qualifying as Exr. would there fore be only for forms sake. My situation not enabling me to take my share in the duties incident to the trust I do not wish to incur any of its responsibilities. Yours with much esteem & respect, Jos. V. Shanklin. Sale, Mar. 18, 1829. Byrs: Ed. Tilman, John Boyd, John Riley, Alexr. Hunter, G. W. Huckebee, Wm. Lesley, John W. McKinley, Joseph Caldwell, etc.

STEELE, WILLIAM L.—BAX 89, PACK 2200:

Est. admnr. Mar. 6, 1840 by Geo. Holloway, Martin Hackett, Hardy Clark unto Moses Taggart Ord. Abbeville Dist. sum $2,000.00. Heirs, David Steel an uncle and Sarah Steele, now Sarah Lummus. Left no parents, or sis. or bro. as far as is known. Bibb County, Ga. In person came before me David Waters who being duly sworn says that Sarah Lummus dtr. of Chas. Steel is now living and is a sis. of Wm. Steel and he further states that he saw the parents of Sarah Lummus married. Sworn to and subscribed before me this 10th of Nov., 1841.

Nathan C. Williamson, J. P.   David Waters

21 Mar. 1842 Recd. from Geo. Holloway admnr. of Wm. L. Steel decd. $241.00 in full of personal est. of David Steel, presented and which will be rec. in Ord. office in Edgefield Dist. Wm., Robt., Sarah Lummus of Jasper County, Ga. appointed their son Wm. Lummus now of Newton County, Ga. their Atty. to receive their part of est. of Levy or Lucy Steel of Abbeville Dist., S. C. Dated this Nov. 17, 1840.

SAXON, MATILDA W.—BOX 89, PACK 2201:

Est. admnr. Feb. 19, 1839 by B. H. Saxon, Jas. Taggart, Francis A. Calhoun unto Moses Taggart Ord. Abbeville Dist. sum $3,000.00. Cit. pub. at Episcopal Church in Abbeville. (Letter) Columbia 13 May 1839 Moses Taggart Esq. Dear Sir, Inclose I send you a return of est. of Matilda W. Saxon, decd. probated before James Guignard Esq. Ordy. of Richland Dist., agreeable to my promise when I saw you last which I hope will come safe to hand and prove satisfactory. My health is not good and I shall be obliged to retreat to the up country, in which it is probable I may have the pleasure of seeing you at Abbeville with since wishes for your health and happiness I remain, Your friend and humble servant. B. H. Saxon. Col. Benj. H. Saxon was gdn. of Sarah M. J. Saxon a minor. Expend: Feb. 3, 1838 paid Jackson Wright for coffin $18.00.

SHIRLEY, JOHN—BOX 89, PACK 2203:
Est. admnr. July 31, 1832 by Obadiah, Benj. Shirley, Jas. Armstrong, John Branyan unto Moses Taggart Ord. Abbeville Dist. sum $3,000.00. Inv. made Oct. 25, 1832 by L. W. Trible, Nathaniel Shirley, John Kay. Robt. Chamblee married Elizabeth A. Shirley.

STRAIN, MARY—BOX 89, PACK 2204:
Will dated Feb. 7, 1833 in Abbeville Dist. Prov. Feb. 26, 1833. Exr: Bro. Hugh Wilson. Wit: Mathew, Elizabeth Wilson, Franklin Branch. Chn., Jas., Mathew Strain. 3 oldest chn. ment. but only 2 named. Bro., Jas. Wilson. Inv. made Mar. 11, 1833 by John J. Barnett, Wm. Pursell, Mathew Wilson. Byrs: Mathew Wilson, Hugh Kirkwood, Hugh, Nancy Armstrong, Wm. Mc-Allister, Wm. Pursell, Jane Strain, J. S. Lamb, Joseph Lyon, Elizabeth Strain, etc.

SPEER, WILLIAM, SR.—BOX 89, PACK 2205:
Will dated Aug. 28, 1826 in Abbeville Dist. Prov. April 26, 1830. Exrs: Sons, John, Wm. Speer. Wit: Abraham Bell, Wm. Ward, Jas. L. McBride. Wife, Martha Speer. Chn: John, Wm., Alexr. Speer, Margaret Rucker. Inv. made April 28, 1830 by Dr. E., Jas. Hunt, John McCalla.

SMITH, PETER—BOX 89, PACK 2206:
Will dated Dec. 30, 1831 in Abbeville Dist. Prov. June 14, 1832. Exrs: Sons, Peter, Wm. H., Chas. A. Smith. Wit: Wm. A. Bull, E. Hammond, Henry Evans. Chn: Peter, Charles, Wm. Smith, Mary Collins, Betsy Parnell. Ment. in Sett: John Parnell, M. B. Collins, Frederick Smith. Wife ment., no name given in will. One paper named the wid. as Susannah Smith. Inv. made Aug. 9, 1832 by John Chastain, Isaac Hawes, Thos. Harman.

SHACKLEFORD, MORDECAI—BOX 89, PACK 2207:
Will dated Sept. 16, 1839 in Abbeville Dist. Prov. Sept. 26, 1839. Exrs: Sons, John W., Allen Shackelford. Wit: S. Y., Isaac, R. E. Carlile. Chn: John W., Allen, Thos., Howard, Stephen, Wiley Shackleford. "Legally to my children namely John W., Robt. Shackelford, John H. Grant in the place of Mary McCaslin his mother." Gr. Son, John Howard Grant. Inv. made Oct. 1. 1839 by Lindsay Harper, Alexr. Oliver, Geo. Patterson.

SPILLARS, ELENOR JANE (MINOR)—BOX 89, PACK 2208:
On Dec. 2, 1837 Jane Spillars, Wm. Morrison, Jas. Gilmer bound unto Moses Taggart Ord. Abbeville Dist. sum $10,000.00. Jane Spillars, gdn. of Elenor Jane Spillars a minor, married Wm. Taylor. Mar. 27, 1857 both recd. $927.77 from Wm. A. Purdy a gdn.

SKINNER, MINORS—BOX 89, PACK 2209:
On Aug. 6, 1838 Tiry Jay, John Ruff, G. Cannon bound unto Moses

Taggart Ord. Abbeville Dist. sum $500.00. Tiry Jay made gdn. of Wm., Nathan T., Patience A., Thos. T. Skinner minors. Patience A. Skinner of age when sett. was made July 7, 1855. Thos. Skinner of age when sett. made Dec. 7, 1857. Were children of John Skinner decd.

SPEED, MARTHA S.—BOX 89, PACK 2210:
Will dated Sept. 14, 1840 in Abbeville Dist. Prov. Oct. 5, 1840. Exrs: Bro., Wm. Calhoun, Jas. Taggart. Wit: S. L. or S. Baker, Thos. Lee, A. Armistead, J. S. Reid. "Bequeath watch belonging to my husband John B. Speed to his father." Sis., Anna Eliza Holt and her 2 chn., Martha, Elizabeth Holt. Sis, Mary Jane Calhoun. Inv. made Nov. 9, 1840 by M. O. Talman, Joseph C. Mathews, A. R. White.

STUART, JOHN A.—BOX 90, PACK 2211:
June 27, 1842 John A. Stuart recd. $256.08 from est. of Alexr., Margaret Stuart decd. (Letter) Mr. David Lesly, Dear Sir, As it is not convenient for me to attend at your office in person I take the liberty of saying by letter that I am eighteen years of age that I have property coming to me from the estate of my father Alexr. Stuart and also from my mother Margaret Stuart both decd. and desire that you grant Letters of Guardianship for my person and property to my friend Dr. E. R. Calhoun by so doing you will accomodate yours. Both ests. worth $500 cash. Mary A. Stuart Expend: June 27, 1842. Paid Thos. C. Stuart $22.51. Nov. 1844 Mary A. Stuart recd. $299.90 from est. Was wife of L. Coleman Griffin.

STEPHENS, JOHN—BOX 90, PACK 2212:
Est. admnr. Aug. 19, 1841 by Robt. M. Davis, Martin Bowie, Lyle Stephens unto Moses Taggart Ord. Abbeville Dist. sum $5,000.00. Mary Stephens wife of John Stephens decd. Inv. made Aug. 26, 1841 by Joel Lockhart, Wm. C. Cozby, Mathew Young. Dtr., Sarah J. Stephens. Expend: 1843 Paid Thos. Stephens $10.00.

SLOAN, SAMUEL F. (MINOR)—BOX 90, PACK 2213:
Saml. F. Sloan sheweth that he is a minor over 14 yrs. and entitled to one fourth part of his father, John Sloan's est. and that Edward Vann of Abbeville Dist. be appointed his gdn. this Nov. 9, 1841. Nov. 22, 1845 he was now of age.

SMITH, DR. WILLIAM A.—BOX 90, PACK 2214:
Est. admnr. Mar. 18, 1844 by Richard B., Isaac Smith, Richard A. Martin, Saml. Jordon; the first two of Spartanburg Dist., the others of Abbeville Dist. unto David Lesly Ord. Abbeville Dist. sum $7,000.00. Richard B. Smith was a bro. Interstate died leaving no wife or chn., but a father, bros. etc. Heirs: Isaac, E. P. Jr., Aaron M. Smith, C. P. Littlejohn, S. F. Smith, Laban C. Chappell, Anthony R. Golding.

SMITH, ISRAEL—BOX 90, PACK 2215:
Est. admnr. Nov. 6, 1843 by Wm. T. Drennan, Robt. Brady, Alexr. Scott unto David Lesly Ord. Abbeville Dist. sum $1,000.00. Wm. T. Drennan

sheweth that Israel Smith, a stranger, lately departed this life at the residence of your petr. interstate. The said decd. had been working for a few years in this country and was working for your petr. where he was taken with his last illness. Your petr. could not ascertain precisely where he was from, nor who his kindred was and his friends but has (word not plain) report that he had two bros.; their place of res. not known. Dated this 19th Oct. 1843. Inv. made Nov. 24, 1943 by Joseph C. Mathews, Lewis Covin, Robt. Brady.

SPENCE, JAMES—BOX 90, PACK 2216:
John Spence on Jan. 6, 1842 sheweth that his bro., Jas. Spence, departed this life interstate leaving no wid. but infant children. Inv. made Feb. 21, 1842 by Wm. Robinson, Adam Wideman, Rice Mills. Sett. made Oct. 23, 1843. Legacy due Sarah M. Young from Saml. Young's est. in the hands of Jas. Spence, admnr. of Geo. Young $57.05.

SELBY, OWEN—BOX 90, PACK 2217:
Est. admnr. Nov. 27, 1842 by Martha Selby, Henry, Thos. Riley, Jas. Hughes unto David Lesly Ord. Abbeville Dist. sum $9,000.00. Sett. made July 27, 1844. Present, Henry Riley to ascertain share of Jas. Edwards who married Pamela Selby; Edmond Anderson who married Sarah. Sett. of Wm. A. Selby a minor and Owen Selby his gdn. who recd. his est. Jane. 23, 1838 in the sett. of Lidia Hughes' est. $533.33. Martha Selby the wid. and gdn. of Elizabeth, Martha, John Edmond, Vachail Hughey acting as gdn. of Wm. Selby.

STINSON, JOHN—BOX 90—PACK 2218:
Est. admnr. May 16, 1843, by Jas. Foster, Archibald K. Patten, Archibald Kennedy unto David Leslic Ord. Abbeville Dist. sum $200.00. Inv. made June 2, 1843 by John W. Foster, Ferdick Conner, Geo. Sayner. Sale: June 2, 1843. Byrs: J. S. Foser, July A. Stinson, Richard A. Martin, Dr. W. S. Smith, Samuel Bradford, John Spence, Ferdeick Conner, John Wideman, Robert McKinney, Jas McCallester, Thos. Lenk, John Glasgow, Phebe Drennen, Wm. Alexander, Jas. Foster, Ninian Thomson.

STEWART, JOHN—BOX 90, PACK 2219:
Will dated July 7, 1838 in Abbeville Dist. Prov. Aug. 10, 1843. Exrs: Sons, Mark, Benton, Shepherd Stewart. Wit: Aaron, Jesse, Saml. Lomax. Chn: Chas., Mark, John, Redman, Benton, Lieuana, Shepherd, Jas. Stewart. Legatees: Wm. Russell, Shepherd G., Chas., Jas., Mark T,, R. G., Benton W., John Stewart. Wm. Russell married Leuana Stewart.

SWILLING, JOHN C.—BOX 90, PACK 2220:
Will dated July 17, 1837 in Abbeville Dist. Prov. Oct. 7, 1837. Exrs: Father, John Swilling. Wit: Franklin Branch, J. Cunningham, Francis B. Clinkscales. Mother, name not given. Sis., Belinda Liddell. Niece, Belinda Houston. Sis., Lucinda Houston. Bro., Jas. Swilling. "State of Miss., Hinds County. Recd. of my father John Swilling of Abbeville Dist., S. C. Sept. 20, 1851 by James D. Houston of Hinds County, Miss. sum $350 legacy left to Belinda Liddell's children by John C. Swilling, late of S. C." G: W. Osborn, Belinda Osborn

SADLER, WILLIAM—BOX 90, PACK 2221:
Will dated June 4, 1842 in Abbeville Dist. Prov. June 10, 1842. Exrs:
Son, John Sadler, Son-in-law, Robt. Chatham. Wit: John L. Cheatham, C. B.
Fooshe, N. Nathinal McCants. Chn: Mary Ann, Willis C., John Sadler,
Francis Cheatham. Inv. made July 26, 1842 by John, C. B. Fooshe, Jas. Gilliam.
Robt. Cheathman married Frances Sadler Feb. 19, 1845. Susan D. Sadler a wid.

STRICKLAND, STUTELY—BOX 90, PACK 2222:
Est. admnr. Mar. 11, 1843 by David, Wm., David C. McWhorter unto
David Lesly Ord. Abbeville Dist. sum $50.00. Stutely Strickland son-in-law of
David McWhorter. Left a wid. and an infant child. Inv. made Mar. 27, 1843
by Jas. Hawkins, Wm. McAdams, Basil Callaham.

SHELL, FRANCIS A.—BOX 90, PACK 2223:
"Know that we G. W. Curtiss, Thos. L. Whitlock, H. A. Latimer bound
to David Leslie Ord. Abbeville Dist. sum $1,000.00 this Sept. 4, 1843." G. W.
Curtiss made gdn. of Francis A. E. Shell, minor.

STARKE, S. J. H.—BOX 90, PACK 2224:
"Know that we, Ezekiel, Saml. W. Tribble, John B. Black bound to David
Leslie Ord. Abbeville Dist. sum $4,000.00 this 4th day of Sept. 1843." Ezekiel
Tribble made gdn. S. J. H. Stark minor. Jan. 7, 1839 Ezekiel Tribble, John B.
Black, Hudson Price were bound to Moses Taggart Ord. Abbeville Dist. sum
$10,000.00. Ezekiel Tribble made gdn. of S. J. H. Starke. Feb. 22, 1830 Chas.
Starke, Wm. Covington, John McNeil bound to Moses Taggart Ord. Abbeville
Dist. sum $2,000.00. Chas. Starke made gdn. of S. J. H. Starke, minor, under
14 yrs.

SETZLER, MINORS—BOX 90, PACK 2225:
"Know that we Martin Setzler, John Miller, Adam Epting of Newberry
Dist. bound to David Lesly Ord. Abbeville Dist. sum of $500.00 on 16th of
Oct. 1844." Martin Setzler made gdn. of Mary Ann B., Jacob T. Setzler, minors.
Martin Setzler sheweth that Nancy Morgan departed this life interstate, that
John Morgan is the Admnr., that your ptr. married Mary, her dtr. and has by
her two children under the age of 14 yrs. That Mary is dead. Martin Setzler
resides in Newberry Dist. and father of the two minors.

SHARPE, HENRY—BOX 90, PACK 2226:
Will dated Mar. 13, 1844 in Abbeville Dist. Prov. June 3, 1846. Exrs:
A. C. Hawthorne, John Cowan, Son, Henry Sharpe. Wit: John, Wm. J.
Stevenson, G. W. Brownlee. Wife, Eady Sharpe. Chn: Joseph Sharpe, Elenor
wife of George Shirley, Edward, Henry, Thos., Francis, Mary Ann, Caroline,
Bennett Sharpe. Gr. Chn., Jarmina, Zimry. Inv. made June 7, 1844 by Saml.
Reid, Jas. Lindsy. Sale, Nov. 14, 1844. Byrs: G. W. Brownlee, Bennet, Eady
Sharpe, Robt. H. Winn, John Cowan, Henry Sharpe, Geo. Shirley, Joseph
Sharpe, etc. July 11, 1848, D. Wright received $395.89 in right of his wife,
Caroline.

SHIRLEY, MASTIN—BOX 90, PACK 2227:
Ezekiel Tribble, Mastin, Nathaniel Shirley, bound to Moses Taggart Ord.·Abbeville Dist. sum $2,000.00. Martin Shirley made gdn. of John F., Margaret J., Mary Ann, Nancy C., Newton N. *Lettic-e* A. Shirley, minors under 14 yrs. Jan. 28, 1841, Mastin Shirley, Ezekiel Tribble, Nathaniel Shirley, bound to Moses Taggart Ord. Abbeville Dist. sum $2,000.00. Martin Shirley made gdn. of Benj. H., Elizabeth, Sarah C. Shirley, minor chn. of Mastin Shirley.

SHARP, WILLIAM—BOX 90, PACK 2228:
Will dated Sept. 4, 1844 in Abbeville Dist. Prov. Sept. 2, 1884. Exrs: Wife, Ann Sharpe. Son, Wm. Sharpe, John L. Sims. Wit: Hugh Dichson, Saml. W. Agnew. Chn: Robt., Wm. Sharpe. Inv. made Dec. 18, 1844 by Saml. Agnew, John M. Hawthorn, Edward Hagan. Sale, Dec. 18, 1844. Byrs: John Hagan, Wm. H., Bennet, Joseph, R. C. Sharpe, D. O. Hawthorn, J. E. Branion, John Cowan, Wm. Wood, Andrew Pruitt, Geo. Penny, J. L. Sims.

SPEED, JOHN—BOX 90, PACK 2229:
Will dated Sept. 11, 1840 in Abbeville Dist. Exr: Wife, Martha Speed. Wit: Thos. Lee Stephen, A. R. White.

SALE, GILLIAM—BOX 90, PACK 2230:
Est. admnr. Jan. 24, 1845 by Wm. M., John M. Sale, Godfrey Chas. Bowers, unto David Lesly Ord. Abbeville Dist. sum $2,000.00. Gilliam Sale the father of Wm. M. Sale, died about a year ago.

SALE, THOMAS—BOX 90, PACK 2231:
Est. admnr. Jan. 24, 1845, by Wm. M., John M. Sales, Godfrey M. Bowers unto David Lesly Ord. Abbeville Dist. sum of $600.00. Wm. M. Sale sheweth that his uncle Thos. Sale departed this life about 17 or 18 yrs. ago having neither wife or chn. or lineal descendant and leaving no property but entitled to 7 or 8 hundred dollars due him from his father's est. John Sale, decd. Dated 27 of Dec. 1844.

SKINNER, FRANCES—BOX 90, PACK 2232:
John Ruff sheweth that Francis, John Skinner are entitled to an est. but due to their minority are incapable of managing. Expend: Paid Frances Skinner, wife of Robt. Walker, $8.50. For 1841, paid Moriah Skinner for 1843, $49.34.

THACKER, MARTIN—BOX 90, PACK 2233:
Est. admnr. Aug. 3, 1835 by Wm. F., Joseph T. Baker, John C. Livingston, unto Moses Taggart, Ord. Abbeville Dist. sum $300.00. Inv. made Aug. 18, 1835 by Henry Brooks, Christian Barns, Ezekiel Gunnon. Cit. pub. at Cokesberry Camp Meeting. Sale, Aug. 18, 1835. Byrs: Christiam Barnes, Jr., John W. Ramey, Joseph Baker, Freeman Dixan, John Shillito, Wm. Brooks, Jas. Dixon, etc.

THOMAS, DAVID—BOX 90, PACK 2234:
Est. admnr. Oct. 13, 1828 by Henry Gray, Pascail D. Klugh, Thos. Riley

unto Moses Taggart Ord. Abbeville Dist. sum $6,000.00. Inv. made Dec. 20, 1828 by D. H. McCleskey, P. D. Klugh, Fleming Wiley, Thos. Hinton, F. G. Thomas. Sett: Distributees. Wm., John Thomas, Saml. Thompson hus. of Peggy, Daniel Malone hus. of Elizabeth, Wm. McCree hus. of Harriett, Henry Ammonds, hus. of *Kambabhude*, Mrs. Jane Hughes ommitted. Aug. 20, 1830, Thos. Edwards recd. $39.00 as one heirs of said est. and on account of Matilda Waters whose discharge of promise to procure for Henry Gray, Admnr. when she becomes of age, this sum, we receive as the heirs of Kitty Waters who was the dtr. of David Thomas, decd. State of Ala., Montgomery County. Wm. Patterson an acting justice for said county who saith that he was personally acquainted with Kitty Thomas, who married John Waters, who formally lived in Abbeville Dist. S. C. was the dtr. of David Thomas of said Dist. and that he was also acquainted with Susan Waters, the dtr. of Kitty Waters, who married Thos. Edwards. Dated 26 of July, 1830.

TERRY, CAPT. JEREMIAH S.—BOX 90, PACK 2235:
    Est. admnr. Nov. 22, 1823 by Sarah, Benj. Terry, Francis Young, unto Moses Taggart Ord. Abbeville Dist. sum $10,000.00. Inv. made April 7, 1824 by Henry Hester, Williamson Norwood, John Harris.

TODD, ELIZABETH—BOX 90, PACK 2236:
    Est. admnr. Nov. 15, 1833 by Saml. Cowan, Peter F. Moragne, Paul Rodgers unto Moses Taggart Ord. Abbeville Dist. sum $10,000.00. Cit. pub. at Buffalo Church. Inv. made Dec. 9, 1833 by John Clay, Jas. Laremore, M. G. Williams. Sale, Dec. 10, 1833. Byrs: C. W. Vaughn, Archibald Todd, Wm. Chastain, Wm. Goodman, Jas. Laremore, John Clay, Jas. Hughes.

TULLIS, AARON—BOX 90, PACK 2237:
    Est. admnr Dec. 25, 1826 by Judy C. Tullis, Joseph N. Boyd, Pleasant Thurmond, John McCraven unto Moses Taggart, Ord. Abbeville Dist. sum $10,000.00. Cit. pub. at Hopewell Church. Inv. made Jan. 17, 1827 by Wm. Carson, John McCelvy, Jas. Thomson. Sale, Jan. 18, 1827. Byrs: Thos. Hollanshead, J. R. Huston, Wm. T. Drennan, Moses B. Rogers, David Mathis, Jas. Conner, Jr., Geo. Crawford, John Young, Moses Jacobs, Edward McCan, Jas. Thompson.

TILLMAN, EDWARD—BOX 91, PACK 2238:
    Will dated uly 15, 1814 in Abbeville Dist. Rec. Jan. 18, 1815. Exrs: Sons, Hiram, Edward Tilman, Alexandra Hunter. Wit: John Boyd, V. Clary, A. Hunter. Chn: Hiram, Edward, Daniel Tillman, Lucy Smith, Polly Hendley. "Owned land in Union Dist. on Fannings Creek to be divided between my gr. chn. of Lucy Smith, Polly Hendley. I have a mortgage on Jas. Smith land for $480.00 due the heirs of John Hendley, decd." Inv. made Jan. 28, 1815 by Chas. Johnson, Thos. Shanklin, John Boyd.

THACKER, ISAAC—BOX 91, PACK 2239:
    Will dated Dec. 29, 1811 in Abbeville Dist. Rec. Feb. 11, 1812. Wit: Wm. Lesly, Andrew McAllister, Joseph Johnson. Exr: Wife, Mary Thacker,

Robery C. Gordon. Chn: Betsy, Catherine, Mary, Rachel, Peggy, Rosy Ann, Isaac, Sally, Genicy, Wm. Lesly, Jemimey. "Unto my Gr. Chn. of Mary, leave 1 dollar." Inv. made Feb. 14, 1812 by Joseph Johnson, John Perry, Nathaniel Baley.

TOLAND, HUGH—BOX 91, PACK 2240:
    Est. admnr. Jan. 18, 1809 by John Toland, Joseph Eakins, Thos. Jordon unto Andrew Hamilton Ord. Dist. sum $10,000.00. Inv. made by John Cason, John Gibson, Joseph Eakins. Expend: March 13, 1815, paid Mary Toland, wid. $200.00. Paid James Toland legatee, $229.24. March 12, 1811, paid Joseph Toland, legatee, $200.00. Paid Andrew Toland, $200.00. Hugh Toland $200.00. Joseph Lowry, $200.00.

THORNTON, ABRAHAM—BOX 91, PACK 2241:
    Est. admnr. Feb. 24, 1826 by Richard, Jessie Henderson, Wm. A. Huggins, unto Moses Taggart Ord. Abbeville sum $1,000.00. Cit. pub. at Mount Moriah Church. Sept. 25, 1832, Lydia Thornton wanted Moses Taggart to settle with Richard Henderson. Inv. made by Geo. F. Caldwell, Wm. Henderson, John Cothran. Byrs: Geo. F. Caldwell, Wm. Terry, Vincent Griffin, Lidy, Jacob, Job Thornton.

TOLBERT, MAJOR JOHN—BOX 91, PACK 2242:
    Will dated May 5, 1822 in Abbeville Dist. Prov. May 18, 1823. Exrs: Bro., Anslem Tolbert. Sons: Joseph L., John C. Tolbert. Wit: Garland Walker, Jas. Gouedy, Ezekeil Evans, Jr., B. F. Whitner. Wife, Nancy Tolbert. Chn: Louisa Harrison, Joseph S., John C., Pamela, Hillery, Jeremiah Tolbert, Harriett Sollier. Son-in-law, Sterling Harrison. Inv. made June 10, 1823 by David Cunningham, Issac Bunting, Thos. Goodman.

TERRY, BENJ.—BOX 91, PACK 2243:
    Est. admnr. Feb. 6, 1823 by Alex. Hunter, John B. Huey, Wm. H. Caldwell unto Moses Taggart Ord. Abbeville Dist. sum $3,000.00. Cit. pub. at Rocky River Church. Will dated Aug. 9, 1830. Wit: John, Judith Hall, Elizabeth B. Gibert. Lived in Abbeville Dist. Gr. dtr. Jane, wife of Alex. Hunter. Gr. son, Joseph Gibert.

TILLET, JAMES—BOX 91, PACK 2244:
    Est. adnmr. Oct. 25, 1783 by John Ford of Inoree, Henry White, Josiah Culbertson, unto John Thompson Ord. 96 Dist. sum 2,000 pounds. Inv. made Jan. 2, 1784 by Jesse Connell, Thos. Compton, Geo. Connell.

THOMAS, DANIEL—BOX 91, PACK 2245:
    Inv. made July 16, 1783 by Chas. Sims, Jacob Brown, Nathaniel Abney. (Not any papers in pack.)

THOMSON, CHAS.—BOX 91, PACK 2246:
    Est. admnr. Oct. 16, 1784 by Margaret Thomson, Wm. Blackstock, Wm. Clayton unto John Thomas Jr. Ord. 96 Dist. sum 2,000 pounds. Inv. made Nov. 9, 1784 by Benj. Roebuck, Wm. Blackstock, Wm. Skelton. Byrs: Margaret, Abby Thomson.

THOMSON, WM.—BOX 91, PACK 2247:
Est. admnr. Oct. 6, 1801 by Wm. Dorris, John Anderson, John Chiles unto Andrew Hamilton Ord. Abbeville Dist. sum $5,000.00. Inv. made Oct. 6, 1801 by John Anderson, Geo. Conn, John Chiles. Cit. pub. at Cedar Springs Church.

THOMPSON, PETER—BOX 91, PACK 2248:
Est. admnr. March 25, 1795 by Lamentation Thompson wid., Wm. Adams, Wm. Dunlap unto the Judges of Abbeville County sum 1,000 pounds. Inv. made April 25, 1795 by Jeremiah, Duke Bell, Robt. Kirkwood. Sale, July 1, 1795. Byrs: Wm. Goodman, Lamentation Thompson, Peter, Robt. Martin, Thos. Ward, Daniel Garven. etc.

TAYLOR, JOHN—BOX 91, PACK 2249:
Est. admnr. July 12, 1782 by Haney Taylor, John Liles, Randel Robinson unto John Ewing Calhoun Ord. 96 Dist. sum of 14,000 pounds. Inv. made Aug. 24, 1782 by Jas. Hogin, Wm. Hill, John Gorman. John Taylor lived at Broad River, near the mouth of Tigger River.

TERRY, JEREMIAH—BOX 91, PACK 2250:
Est. admnr. Jan. 19, 1804 by Nathaniel Terry, Josiah Chambers, John Sanders unto Andrew Hamilton Ord. Abbeville Dist. sum $5,000.00. May 15, 1794. Robt., Susanna Terry his wife, applied for letters of Admnr. Cit. pub. at Hopewell Church. Inv. made March 4, 1795 by Capt. Uel Hill, Drury Brazele, Wm. Collier. Sale, May 10, 1796. Byrs: Wm., Fanny Terry.

THOMAS, WALTER—BOX 91, PACK 2251:
Est. admnr. Nov. 22, 1792 by Patrick McDowall, Henry Wilson, James Mayson Esq., Thos. Wilson Senr. to the Judges of Abbeville Co. sum 2,000 pounds. Admnr. took place at the house of Henry Wilson of Cambridge. Inv. made Dec. 5, 1792 by Frederick Glover, Gabriel Smihers, Thos. Wilson Jr. (Letter)

Charleston
Oct. 23, 1792

Dear Sir,

I received a few days ago your very friendly letter which gave us the first information of the death of Mr. Thomas and should have given you an answer respecting the disposal of his effection before this time but deferred it till I should see Mr. Wilson or Mr. McDowall. I have called several times at their lodgings but have not yet had the pleasure of meeting with them it is however probable that I shall see them before they leave town. From what you mention of Mr. Wilson and McDowall altho unacquainted with either of the gentlemen, Mrs. Thomas and myself as relatives of the deceased are quite satisfied that they should proceed to administer on his effects. Our only wish on this subject is that justice may be done and that all his creditors should be paid if his effects are sufficient for that purpose as I presume they are. And if any thing considerable should remain after satisfying all legal demands we only wish it might be put into a way of being sent to his father or sisters in Europe. His private papers can be of no use to his administrators and are a kind of property probably of no value except to his friends we think therefore it is not improper to request that they may be sent to us as the only relatives of the deceased in this country, as soon as a suitable conveyance and opportunity shall offer. If it should appear that there are effects sufficient to answer all legal demands and pay necessary expenses without selling his wearing apparel, we would also rquest that his clothes may be sent us, that they with any thing else that may remain if any thing should remain, may be sent to his relatives in Europe. Will you be bbliging as to communicate to those gentleman who are about to administer on Mr. Thomas property the substance of this letter. Please to accept of my thanks with those of the family for your politeness and friendly offer of your aid in this business. With much esteem I am Dr. sir Your sincere friend and humble servant.

Samuel Beach

(This letter was written to Ephraim Ramsay Esq. Councellar at Law at Cambridge, 96 Dist.)

Cambridge
1st Nov., 1792

Sirs

I understand that some of the Cambridge people perhaps Wilson and McDowall intend to apply for adminstration on the estate of the late Walter Thomas, Pres. of Cambridge College this application I oppose as I have reason to believe that their damands are very inconsiderable against his estate from receipts I saw amongst his papers. Mr. Thomas had a number of poor relations in Wales who are best intitled to the small pittance of property he has left behind him and who I am determined shall receive the benefit of it if in my power to secure it for them. Besides he has near relations in Charleston, his bros. children who by law have a preferrence if they think proper and to whom I have wrote but suppose my letter has miscaried not having had an answer on their behalf. Sir as next of kin to the deceased I have entered a Caveat with the Clerk of course as the right of administration is disputed you cannot by law determine it until the meeting of the common Law Court at which time the next of kin will either appear or renounce their right if they should do the latter I have nothing more to say against these gentlemens administering and will contend myself with having discharged my duty as a friend to the deceased whilst he was living after this inlimation I expect you will refuse granting my administration until the next of kin makes known to you their intentions. I am sir,

Your Mo obl.
W. Shaw

THOMPSON, MOSES—BOX 91, PACK 2252:

Est. admnr. Oct. 12, 1831 by John, Saml. Pressly, Wm. Patton unto Moses Taggart Ord. Abbeville Dist. sum $500.00. Cit. pub. at Asbury Church. Inv. made Oct. 29, 1831 by Abner Perrin, Alex. Pressly, Timothy Russell. Byrs: Alex. Pressly, Phillip Cook, Saml. Pressly. Had notes on Wm. Thomson.

TUTT, JAMES AND TABITHA—BOX 91, PACK 2253:

Est. admnr. Nov. 28, 1834 by Henry S. Black, Zeri Hatter, Stephen

Whitley unto Moses Taggart Ord. Abbeville Dist. sum $2,000.00. Sett: James H. Wells in right of wife Rebecca Tutt, Wm., Frances, Benj., John, Robt. Tutt, Henry S. Black in right his wife Martha Tutt Black, all above heirs being chn. of said Jas. Tabitha Tutt. Inv. made Dec. 9, 1834 by Richard C. Griffin, Zeri Hatter, John Child.

THOMPSON, ROBERT—BOX 91, PACK 2254:
Est. admnr. Sept. 25, 1806 by Saml., Margaret Thompson, John Gentry, Daniel McDonald unto Andrew Hamilton Ord. Abbeville Dist. sum $10,000.00. Inv. made Oct. 7, 1806 by Andrew Logan, Robt. Anderson, Alex. Turner. Sale: Oct. 16, 1806. Byrs: Margaret Thompson, Jas. Strother, David Thomas, Jas. Brooks, Archibald Frith, Thos. Herd, Larkin Reynolds, John Foster, Jas., Saml. Thompson, etc

TEULON, CHARLES—BOX 91, PACK 2255:
Will dated Oct. 4, 1812 in Abbeville Dist. Prov. Oct. 3, 1814. Exrs: Wife, Christianna Teulon, Son, Wm. Teulon. Wit: Robt. Carson, Edward Carey. Chn: Wm. Teulon "give 200 acres lying in Saint Mathews Parish near Santee River", Peter, Ann, Mary, Sarah, Elizabeth, Rebecca. Gr. dtr. Christianna Carey. Inv. made Oct. 24, 1814 by Robt., Wm. Carson, Benj. Finley.

TULLOCK, SAMUEL—BOX 91, PACK 2256:
Est. admnr. Feb. 5, 1810 by Jemmima Tullock, Hugh McBride, Wm. Henderson unto Andrew Hamilton Ord. Abbeville Dist. sum $5,000.00. Inv. made Feb. 9, 1810 by Robt. McComb, Wm. Roberson, John Foster. Sale, Mar. 3, 1810. Byrs: Jemmima Tullock, Peter Harbart, Robt. McComb, Wm. Henderson, John McFerren, David Fife, John McClelin, Andrew McComb Sr., John Logan, John Berry, Wm. McDonald, Hugh McBride, John Roberson, Simon Berry, Thos. Burnett.

TURNER, ABEDNIGO—BOX 91, PACK 2257:
Est. admnr. Nov. 5, 1802 by Phebe Turner, Benj. Waller, Joseph, Thos. B. Waller unto Andrew Hamilton Ord. Abbeville Dist. sum $10,000.00. Inv. made Nov. 13, 1802 by John Chiles Sr., Thos. B. Waller, Armstrong Heard. Byrs: Phebe Turner, Benj. Glover, Walter Chiles, Robt. Foster.

THOMPSON, LAMENTATION—BOX 91, PACK 2258:
Est. admnr. Nov. 5, 1798 by Wm. Adams, Jeremiah Bealle, Robt. Hays unto Andrew Hamilton Ord. Abbeville Dist. sum $4,000.00. Inv. made Nov. 13, 1798 by Jeremiah Bealle, Saml. Gamble, Richard Posey. Cit. read at Poseys Meeting House. Expend: April 15, 1807 Paid Farlow Thompson $216.50. Paid Wm. Thompson $190.31. Sale, Dec. 6, 1798. Byrs: Andrew McBride, Wm. Smih, Richard Posey, Wm. Adams, Robt. Allen, Patrick Cane, John Bosdel, Hugh Sexton, Wm. Fletcher, Francis Young, Farley Thompson, Wm. Winbush, Jas. Brough, John Cofer, Peter Ward, Joseph Dickes, Arch Claton, Issac Boles, Robt. Messes, Thos. Wilson, Andrew Brown, Lewis, Wm. Thompson.

TUTTON, PETER—BOX 91, PACK 2259:
Est. admnr. March 4, 1819 by Mary, John, Jas. Tutton unto Moses Taggart

Ord. Abbeville Dist. sum $10,000.00. Inv. made Mar. 9, 1819 by John Gray, John Pressly, Robt. Pettigrew. Byrs: Mary Tutton, Jas. Patton, Simon Beard, Jas. Morrow, Andrew Crawford, Saml. Foster Sr., Enos Crawford, John Pressly, Robt. Pettigrew, James, Polly, Wm. Tutton, Mary Gray.

TODD, WILLIAM—BOX 91, PACK 2260:
Will dated Sept. 11, 1822 in Abbeville Dist. Prov. Oct. 18, 1822. Exrs: Wife, Elizabeth Todd, Creswell Moore. Wit: Roger McKinney, Jas. Ross, Lewis Gwyn. Chn: Archibald, Wm. Todd, "Bequeath to Wm. a plantation or tract of land lying in Edgefield Dist." Tirza, Mary Ann, Sereny Todd. "Bequeath to my 3 daughters, Tirza, Mary Ann, Sereny Todd, 370 acres lying in Edgefield Dist., 100 acres lying in Pendleton Dist." Inv. made Oct. 24, 1822 by Roger McKinney, Lewis Gwyn, Wm. Stallworth, Thos. Ross.

TAGGART, ALEXANDER—BOX 91, PACK 2261:
Est. admnr. March 1, 1819 by Sarah Taggart relict, Joseph Conn, Thos. Hawthorn unto Moses Taggart Ord. Abbeville Dist. sum $10,000.00. Est. admnr. again Dec. 13, 1822 by Saml. C. Jones in right of his wife, Wm. Anderson, John Burton, sum $7,000.00. Sarah Taggart married Saml. Jones. (Letter)

Johnston Creek
Dec. 30, 1834

Moses Taggart
Dear Sir,
Mr. Jones talks of a meeting of the legatees for to close a settlement of the est. of Alex. Taggart before he leaves the state, this is to authorize you to enter into a sett. with him if I am not present as tho I were present.

James M. Thomas

Inv. made Mar. 8, 1819 by Issac Cowen, Abram Haddon, Robt. C. Sharp. Sale, April 10, 1819. Byrs: Mrs. Sarah Taggart, Thos. Hawthorn, Col. Isaac Cowan, John Singley, Wm. Sharp, Joseph J. Hawthorn, John Donnald, Mases Taggart, Saml. McKinney, Thos. Kirkpatrick, Alex. McKinney. Expend: Nov. 7, 1833 Cash advanced Mary Ann Thomas $155.90¾.

THOMSON, JOHN—BOX 91, PACK 2262:
Will dated Aug. 24, 1817 in Abbeville Dist. Prov. Oct. 26, 1817. Exrs: Sarah Thomson, Wm. H. Caldwell, Wm. McMullan. Wit: Jas. Richey, Jas. Purdy. Wife ment. no name given. Chn. ment. no names given. Sett. made Apr. 21, 1830 between Col. Caldwell Exor. and wife Extrx. Jas. Huey, Saml. Baker, Wm. Thompson, Susan J. Thompson, Isaaiah Johnson gdn. Elvira, Julia Ann Thompson. S. Baker gdn. of Saml. Thompson. Sale, Jan., 1818. Byrs: Robt. Richie, John Hodges, Wm. Boyd, Hutson M. Pitman, Wm. Norris, Thos. Vernon, Wm. McMullen, Andrew English, Jas. Scott, Jane Scott, Saml. Evans, etc.

TATOM, WILLIAM, ESQ.—BOX 91, PACK 2263:
Will dated Mar. 14, 1803. Rec. Feb. 15, 1804. Exrs: Wife, Polly Tatom, Donald Fraser, John Hughes. Wit: John N. Newby, Williamson Norwood, A. Tatom. Was of Town of Vienna, Abbeville Dis. Son, Orval Tatom. Inv. made Feb. 20, 1804 by John N. Newby, Jas. Calhoun Jr., Williamson Norwood.

TINSLEY, ISAAC—BOX 92, PACK 2264:
Est. admnr. at White Hall Nov. 8, 1782 by Elizabeth Golding Tinsley, Henry Pearson, John Richey unto John Ewing Calhoun Ord. 96 Dist. sum 14,000 pounds. Elizabeth Tinsley, wid. was of Carsons Creek in 96 Dist. Inv. made Nov. 28, 1782 by Richard Griffin, Anthony, Reuben Golding.

TURNER, STERLING—BOX 92, PACK 2265:
Est. admnr. Nov. 27, 1783 by Jas. Spann, Amos Richardson, Jonathan Gilbert unto John Thomas Jr. Ord. 96 Dist. sum 2,000 lbs. Inv. made Jan. 10, 1784 by Amos Richardson, Wright Nicholson, John Duglass. Inv. of Absolum Turner decd. found in same pkg., made July 10, 1783 by Wm. Jay, Daniel Richardson, John Cox.

THOMSON, JOHN—BOX 92, PACK 2266:
Will dated Dec. 28, 1780 in 96 Dist. Prov. Nov. 1, 1783. Exrs: Wife, Ann Thompson. Bro., Wm. Thompson. Wit: John Davidson, Nicholas, Robt. Harris, Geo. Park. Chn: Richard, Ephraim, Andrew, John, Wm., Margaret, Mary, Ann Thompson. Mother, Elenor Harper. Inv. made Dec. 13, 1783 by Robt. Harris, Andrew Mayes, John Davidson. Sale, Dec. 29, 1783. Byrs: Ann Thomson, Elenor Harper, Jas. Crawford, Andrew, Richard Thomson, Andrew Mayes, Danield Jackson, Thos. Mayes, Patrick Shaw, Saml. Jackson, Wm. Shaw. (Name written Thompson, Thomson)

TINSLEY, THOMAS—BOX 92, PACK 2267:
Will daed Jan. 4, 1797. Rec. March 25, 1799. Exrs: Son, John Tinsley, Wm. McKinley. Wit: John Actkinson, Joseph Hutton. Chn: John, Wm., Elijah Tinsley, Elizabeth Spencer, Eloner, Thos., Jas. Tinsley, Joannah Roberts, Diadame, Delilah Tinsley. Wife ment. name not given in will but on another page written Sarah Tinsley.

TRIMBLE, JAMES—BOX 92, PACK 2268:
Est. admnr. Mar. 27, 1797 by Esther Trimble wid., John Hamilton of Savannah, Alex. Clark Jr. unto the Judges of Abbeville Co. sum $2,000.00. Bond ment. Jas. Trimble was the son of Esther Trimble. Cit. pub. at Hopewell Church. Inv. made July 1, 1797 by Peter Brown, Archibald McMullan, Caleb W. Baker.

THOMAS, EDWARD—BOX 92, PACK 2269:
Est. admnr. Jan. 5, 1791 by John Norwood, John Miller, Jas. Stevenson unto the Judges of Abbeville Co. sum 500 lbs. Inv. made April 5, 1791 by John Miller, Wm. Cunningham, Aaron McWhorter. Inv. of Robt. Thomas found in same pkg. made Aug. 9, 1783 by Hugh Means, Saml. Culbertson, Matthew Patton as shewn to them by Martha, Wm. Thomas admnrs. of said est.

THACKER, JOEL—BOX 92, PACK 2270:
Will dated Feb. 5, 1805 in Abbeville Dist. Rec. Mar. 2, 1805. Exrs: Andrew Stephenson, Andrew Bowie, son, Ezekiel Thacker. Wit: Robt., Jas. McAlister, Robt. Brackenridge. Chn: Nathaniel, Ezekiel, Rose, Mary Thacker. Wife ment. no name given. Inv. made Mar. 21, 1805 by Hugh Reid, John Miller,

Wm. Garrett. Expend: Nov. 6, Paid Jennett Thacker $8.00. Mar. 13, 1805 Recd. of Isaac Thacker note $100.84.

TAYLOR, DR. RICHARD H.—BOX 92, PACK 2271:
Est. admnr. May 15, 1800 by Jas. Wardlaw, Jehu Foster unto Andrew Hamilton Ord. Abbeville Dis. sum $800.00. Cit. pub. at Upper Long Church. Sale, June 7, 1800. Byrs: Jehu Foster, Andrew Bowie, Ezekiel Calhoun, Andrew Hamilton Esq., John McCord Jr., Jas. Wardlaw, Joseph Downey, John Bowie Esq., Jesse C. Bouchell, Mrs. Livingston, John Tucker.

TWEED, JAMES—BOX 92, PACK 2272:
Est. admnr. Dec. 15, 1786 by Duncan O'Bryant, Thom. Boyce, Richard Hancock unto John Thomas Jr. Ord. 96 Dist. sum 1,000 lbs. Inv. made Jan. 19, 1787 by Andrew Rogers Jr., Zachariah Bailey, Saml. Hall.

THOMAS, JONATHAN—BOX 92, PACK 2273:
Inv. made Dec. 14, 1779 by Benj., Carter, John Sealy. Sale, Dec. 15, 1779. Byrs: Capt. Peter, Wm. Nance, Joseph Brown, Robt. Glover, Francis Jenkins, Thos. Martin, John Jenkins, Wm. Berry, John McColping, Thos. Stokes, Thos. Hays, Jas. Lindsay, Sarah Canady, Joseph Thomas. (No other papers)

TINSLEY, JAMES—BOX 92, PACK 2274:
Est. admnr. Aug. 1, 1783 by Nancy Tinsley, Isaac Williams unto John Thomas Jr. Ord. 96 Dist. sum 2,000 lbs. Inv. made Aug. 19, 1783 by Harv Pearson, Richard, Anthony Golding.

TIMMONS, THOS.—BOX 92, PACK 2275:
Est. admnr. May 21, 1785 by John Timmons, James Jordon unto John Thomas Jr. Ord. 96 Dist. sum 2,000 lbs. Inv. made June 13, 1785 by Jas. Jordon, Alex. Vernon, Francis Dodds. Sale, June 13, 1785. Byrs: Ruth, Abner, Saml., John Timmons, Israel Morris.

TINSLEY, MENOAH—BOX 92, PACK 2276:
Est. admnr. Oct. 6, 1785 by Betty Tinsley, Thos. Cargill, David Baley of Laurens Co., bound to John Thomas Jr. Ord. 96 Dist. sum 1,000 lbs. Inv. made Oct. 18, 1785 by Thos. Dendy, John Milam, Thos. Cargill.

THOMAS, ROBT.—BOX 92, PACK 2277:
Inv. made Aug. 9, 1783 by Hugh Means, Mathew Patton, Saml. Culbertson. Sale, Jan. 26, 1784. Byrs: Martha, Wm. Thomas, Josiah Culbertson. (No other papers.)

THOMSON, GEO.—BOX 92, PACK 2278:
Est. admnr. Aug. 11, 1783 by Lucy, Burwell Thomson, Jechonias Langston, Thos. Williams unto John Thomas Jr. Ord. 96 Dist. sum 2,000 lbs. Inv. made by Saml. Lemaster, Moses Spann, Jechonias Langston. Sale, Nov. 12, 1783. Byrs: Lucy, Burrel, Saml., Fanney, Geo., Selah, Stephen, Balam Thompson, Moses Spann, Wm. Bratcher. (Name written Thompson also.)

TOBLER, JOHN, JR.—BOX 92, PACK 2279:
Est. admnr. July 1, 1786 by Charlotte Tobler, Wm. Shinholster, Isaac Ardis bound to John Thomas Jr. Ord. 96 Dist. sum 500 lbs. Inv. made by Isaac Ardis, Wm. Shinholster, Casper Nail Jr.

TEDDARS, JOHN—BOX 92, PACK 2280:
Est. admnr. Feb. 19, 1803 by Mary Teddars, David Bell, Devenport Lawson untc Andrew Hamilton Ord. Abbeville Dist. sum $5,000.00. Inv. made Feb. 21, 1803 by Jesse Harrison Sr., John Chastain, Jas. Sanderford. Sale, Mar. 7, 1803. Byrs: Mary Teddars, Jesse Harrison, Isom Hopkins, Jas. Watson, Jas. Hall, Benj. Evens, Devenport Lawson, Jas. Campbell, Jas. Croe, John Wait, Robt. Bell, Jas. Holland, John Thorton.

TANYHILL, JAMES—BOX 92, PACK 2281:
Est. admnr. July 19, 1803 by Catharine Tanyhill, Wm. Calhoun Sr., Ezekiel Calhoun unto Andrew Hamilton Ord. Abbeville Dist. sum $10,000.00. Inv. made July 19, 1803 by Isaac Bole, Jeremiah Bell, Col. Joseph Calhoun. Expend: Aug. 4, 1803 Paid Jas. Tannehill $64.63½. Paid Rachel Tannehill $39.13. Sale, Aug. 4, 1803. Byrs: Jacob Clark, Fleming Bates, Catharine Tanne-hill, John Robertson, Jas. Tannehill, Phillip King, Rachel, Jack Tannehill, John Hemphill, etc. (Name also written Tannehill.)

TROTTER, MAJOR JOHN, ESQ.—BOX 92, PACK 2282:
Est. admnr. June 10, 1799 by Richard Andrew Rapley Esq., Joseph San-ders Jr., Geo. Bowie Esq. unto Andrew Hamilon Ord. Abbeville Dist. sum $5,000.00. John Trotter was of Cambridge. Inv. made June 20, 1799 by Jas. Gouedy, Patrick McDowal, Thos. Livingston, Robt. McCoombs. Esq.

TAYLOR, ANDREW—BOX 92, PACK 2283:
Will dated Jan. 13, 1818 in Abbeville Dist. Prov. Feb. 12, 1818. Exrs: Andrew and son John McComb. Wit: Robt. McCaslan, Archibald Bradley, Geo. McFarlin. Wife, no name given. Chn: Jane Moragne, Robt. Taylor (dead). Gr. chn: Andrew, Jane Anderson, David, Robt. Taylor, Polly Anderson, James Taylor, Shuson Sims. Inv. made Feb. 14, 1818 by Robt. McCaslan, John Taylor, Henry Wideman, Andrew Sims Jr.

TAGGART, MOSES—BOX 92, PACK 2284:
Est. admnr. Nov. 19, 1822 by Jas. Taggart, Robt. McCaslan bound unto Moses Taggart Sr. sum $2,000.00. Inv. made Jan. 15, 1823 by E. S. Davis, H. C. Hamilton, Saml. L. Watt.

TILLMAN, HIRAM—BOX 92, PACK 2285:
Will dated Mar. 28, 1837 in Abbeville Dist. Prov. Feb. 7, 1838. Exrs: Wife, Nancy Tilman, Ed. Tilman, Wm. F. Baker. Wit: John Ramey, Andrew Gillespie Jr., Wm. J. Thompson. "Bequeath to Hiram Tilman Jr., son of Edward Tilman, bequeath unto Iwanowna Tilmon one negro girl, bequeath unto Edward Tilman Jr., son of Edward Tilman, bequeath unto Kitty Tilman, dtr. of Edward Tilman, bros: Edward, Daniel Tilman, sis., Lucy and sis. Pollys chn. Inv. made Feb. 20, 1838 by A. Giles, Jacob Martin, Thos. Graves. Expend: I certify that I

witnessed Edward Tillman enclose in a letter and deposit $50 in the Post Office at Abbeville Court House on the 12th June, 1846 to the address of Wm. Henley, Columbia Maury Co., Tennessee. Wm. Hill. Nancy Tillman, the wid. later married James Tate. (Letter)

Greene County, Alabama
April 25, 1846

Dear brother

I rec'vd. a letter from your son Hiram dated the 15th of January last and *ascten* by your request. In the letter he states that my bro. Hiram Tilman had left some land to be disposed of after the death of his wife for the benefit of my children and others that the land had been sold and that the money would be paid at any time by deducting the interest my chn. are all willing to receive their distribution shares now and have sent on receipts in this letter with a request that you sent the money by mail in a letter directed to me and to *Erie*, Greene County, Alabama. If you should not think yourself justified in sending the money on these vouchers please til us know what course will be necessary to get the money. Your relations in Alabama and Mississippi are all well as far as I know.

Your affectionate Sit.,
Lucy Smith

(Another Letter)

MACON, MISS.
4th Feb., 1846

Edward Tilman
Dear Sir,

I received a letter from your son Hiram Tilman giving me an account of the provisions of the will of Hiram Tilman decd. and informing me that I had an interest in the est. of said decd. to the amount of $50 or $60 and that the purchaser of the land would pay by deducting the legal interest. Hirams letter also informed me that you have qualified as Executor. I hereby authorize you to collect the amount coming to me by allowing (Mr. Allen the purchaser of the land) a deduction of the lawful interest and remit the same by mail and by doing this shall be a receipt to you for the same, receive our best respects.

Yours,
A. J. Colbert

(On the back of Lucy Smiths letter were the names of the ones who received their distributive shares of Edward Tilmans est. on April 25, 1846. Mary T. Foster, H. L. *Kannan*, J. Hendly, Sarah P. *Torgie or Forbie*. Recd. of Ed. Tilman Exr. of H. Tilman decd. $48.92 in full the share of Allen Foster decd. of the real est. sold by Ed. Tilman Exr. in Abbeville Dist., South Carolina. Aug. 10, 1846. L. or S. J. Foster. Wm. D. Hendly also recd. $48.92 the share of G. Hendley decd. (On the back of this was where a letter had been written but was destroyed all but the following.)

Write you a few lines informing you that on the 5 day of June, Allen Foster (my B. L.) was found up stairs on the hearth dead and the worst is his death was caused by his own hands by cuttin of his throat with his own razor he made seven licks three on one side. (No more to the letter, rest had been destroyed.)

TATOM, ORVILLE—BOX 92, PACK 2286:
Will dated Sept. 4, 1837. Wit: A. B. Arnold, Thos. Graves, Wm. Tennant, Wm. Bradshaw. Wife, Caroline S. Tatom, Son, Wm. T. Tatom. Exrs: Wm. Tennant, Jas. A. Norwood. Inv. made Nov. 28, 1838 by Wm. Gray, Littleton Yarbrough, Thos. Graves.

TURPIN, DR. THOMAS—BOX 92, PACK 2287:
Est. admnr. Oct. 18, 1813 by John Stuart, Billups Gayle bound unto Taliaferro Livingston Ord. Abbeville Dist. sum $10,000.00. Dr. Thomas Turpin was of Georgia, but he died in S. C. Admnr. Gen. John Stuart was of Georgia.

TURNBULL, JOHN—BOX 92, PACK 2288:
Will dated Sept. 3, 1818 in Abbeville Dist. Rec. Jan. 11, 1821. Exrs: Wife, Jane Turnbull. Son, Elijah Turnbull. Wit: Williamson Norwood, John Gray, Andrew Norris. Other chn. ment., no names given. Jane Turnbull was gdn. of Jane, Nancy, Theodore, Mary, Martha Turnbull minors. Jane married Thos. J. Linton. Nancy married W. H. Kyle. John Turnbull died Dec. 13, 1820. Left 9 chn.

TURNBULL, JANE—BOX 92, PACK 2289:
Will dated Mar. 15, 1833 in Abbeville Dist. Exrs: Sons, John Sheridan, Jas. Theodore Turnbull. Wit: R. Livingston, P. T., Mary A. Tullis. Inv. made Nov. 16, 1833 by Wm. F. Baker, Jas. W. Prather, Dr. H. H. Townes. Jane Turnbull gdn. of Nancy, James T., Mary R., John S., Martha Turnbull minors under 21 years on Feb. 11, 1822.

TRIMBLE, ESTHER—BOX 92, PACK 2290:
Will dated Nov. 13, 1818 in Abbeville Dist. Prov. April 26, 1819. Exrs: Son, John Trimble, s. l., Robert Smith. Wit: Thos. Finley, Francis Mitchel, Wm. Clark. Chn: Esther Smith, Sarah Shannon, John, Joseph Trimble. Sale, May 13, 1819. Byrs: John Glover, Saml. Drinkwater, Archibald McMullin, Robt. Smith, John Tommis, Robt., John W. McKinley, Lewis Sims, John Trimble, Dudley Jones, Joseph Trimble, Moses Martin.

TAGGART, JOHN—BOX 92, PACK 2291:
Est. admnr. Jan. 5, 1807 by Moses, David Taggart, Robt. Smyth, Robt. Gibson unto Andrew Hamilton Ord. Abbeville Dist. sum $10,000.00. Inv. made Jan. 8, 1807 by Robt., John Gibson, Joseph Eakins. Elenor Taggart the wid. and the mother of David Taggart. Moses Taggart was b. l. Expend: Feb. 8, 1813 Paid for note for Wm., Alex. Taggart $10.00. Jan. 31, 1810 Paid for a saddle for Rebecca Taggart $12.00.

TULLIS, AARON DECD. MINORS—BOX 92, PACK 2292:
On April 7, 1830 Judith C. Tullis, Jas. Conner or Cowen unto Moses Taggart Ord. Abbeville Dist. sum $2,000.00. Judith C. Tullis made gdn. of Martha W., over 14 yrs., Wm. B., Jane Eliza, Aaron W., Thos. E., Elizabeth J. Tullis minors under 14 yrs.

TURNER, MINORS—BOX 92, PACK 2293:
On June 23, 1828 Robt., Wm. Turner, Thos. B. Boyd bound to Moses Taggart Ord. Abbeville Dist. sum $2,000.00. Robt. Turner gdn. of Matilda, John, Judith, Robt. Turner, minors under 14 yrs. Sett. of Judith Major decd. formerly Judith Turner, made Sept. 14, 1837. She left one dtr. John W. Major recd. $210.17, balance in his own right. Matilda Turner married Saml. B. Major. Robt. Turner the gdn. was the father of John C., Robt. H. Turner, Matilda, Judith Major. Gr. chn. of John Chiles decd.

THOMAS, DAVID—BOX 92, PACK 2295:
Sale made Dec. 22, 1828. No other papers in pkg.

TRAMMELL, JOHN—BOX 93, PACK 2296:
Est. admnr. July 26, 1784 by Chas., John McKnight bound unto John Thomas Jr. Ord. 96 Dist. sum 2,000 lbs. Inv. made Aug. 12, 1784 by Alex. Kilpatrick, Robt., Wm. McMullen.

TOLBERT, DANIEL—BOX 93, PACK 2297:
Est. admnr. Nov. 2, 1840 by Andrew Riley, Wm., Jas. Tolbert, Henry Boozer bound unto Moses Taggart Ord. Abbeville Dist. sum $20,000.00. Sett: Mary Tolbert wid. Chn: Elizabeth Hall, now dead, left 2 chn., Margaret, Mary Hall. Jane Wilson, now dead, leaving 2 chn. Nancy married John Livingston, Martha Jane Wilson under age. John Tolbert in Ga., Jas., Wm. Tolbert, Mary, wife of Andrew Riley, Elender, wife of James Martin, Ann Hughey, wife of Vachail Hughey, Rachel Tolbert, an idiot. Elizabeth Hall, wife of John Hall of Newberry Dist.

TAGGART, MOSES—BOX 93, PACK 2298:
Will dated July 9, 1841 in Abbeville Dist. Prov. Oct. 8, 1841. Wit: John H. Wilson, John F. Livingston, Thos. P. Spierin. Wife, Anna Taggart. Chn: John, Jas. Taggart, Margaret Tallman, Mary Perrin, Ann Owen, Oliver, Robt., Lewis Taggart, b. l. John Donnald. Exrs: John Donnald, Robt. Lewis, John Taggart. Had one note on M. O. Tallman. Inv. made Nov. 2, 1841 by Thos. Jackson, Johnson Ramey, Chas. Dendy.

TURNER, SAMUEL Y. MINOR—BOX 93, PACK 2299:
Nov. 9, 1843, Saml. Turner, John Wilson, Wm. Buchannan bound unto David Lesly Ord. Abbeville Dist. $1,388.00. Saml. Turner made gdn. of Saml. Y. Turner a minor. Saml. Turner on Nov. 9, 1843 sheweth that some time since Wm. Young departed this life intestate leaving no wife or chn., but a mother Elizabeth Hopper, a bro., James Young., a sis., Lucinda, wife of Robt. Y. Jones, Robt. J. Young a bro., (supposed to be dead), and a sis., Emiline dead, who married the petr. Saml. Turner, left one child Saml. Y. Turner under 14 yrs.

TENCH, MARGARET—BOX 93, PACK 2300:
James A. Norwood on Mar. 29, 1843 sheweth that John Tench died intestate about the year 1826 leaving a widow Margaret and two sets of chn., and that no admnr. was taken on his est., that lately his wid. Margaret also died. (Letters)   Mississippi Carrol County

July 13, 1844
Dear Brother.
     I now take my pen in hand to informe you that we have had to part with
our second daughter Nancy A. which died June the 28 which it is the firs
death that we have witnessed in our family but very little sickness since we have
been together but thanks be to God for his kindness to us for our lives helths
strength and being here we are all at present intolerable health at present we hope
that these few lines will meet you all in good health but it is necessary that we
should thing allwise on that grate goodness power of that great and merciful
God that directs and manages all things as he pleases and where them do we
then object that will of our heavenly father that is so good and merciful to us
that this will be done I beseach you bros. and sis. pray for us I will inform you
that there a good deale of sickness in our secsion of country this summer and
joining countyes and very fatel what cause we can't tell we have had fine
seasons fine crops here I have had a hard years work so far I have cultivated
near about 40 acres with one horse and two little sones Henry and Wm. with there
horses. Bro. I received your leater that you sent by cousin thomas harris which
informed me you would indever to do what you could for me pervid I would
give you some authority to do and act for me so here I try to send you this power
to collect that little morsel which is due me of my fathers estate If I have any rigt
there including all of you bros. and sis. I hope Samuel you will manage it with
any difficulty which I never received one pennys worth but som thirty or forty
dollars but I care nothing about that Samuel I wish you to arang this matter
with James in peace and qiteness as bros. ato do I hope bro. James you will
studdy my right and claim to be just as well as your own bro. Samuel I wish
you to git this amount let it be little or much as I have an opertunity of gitting
it brought to me this fawl or witer by Cousin Wm. Harris the preacher of the
gospel if you can posable make this collection for me send it by Mr. Wm. Harris
and he will receipt for me nothing more but remanes your bro. and sis. until
death.
                    Wm. and Nancy Walker, Sam'l. W. and Mary Ann Walker
          Written to Sam'l. W. Walker, Abbeville Dist., South Carolina. (Wm.
Walker decd. was his father,)
          Letter to Mr. John Tench at Newman, Ga.
                              Noxabee County, Mississippi, Cooksville
                                             Nov. 22, 1843
My dear Bro.,
     I expect by the time you receive this letter you will think that I am
getting to be very negligent as regards the answering of your letters, I must confess that I am rather ashamed of not answering your other letter, but if you do
not receive this as soon as you anticipated you have received it do not atribute
it to my neglect. I received your letter on last thursday evening after it had been
at the more than a week I am gratified to write you that my family has enjoyed
extreme good health this year and was very sorry to hear of the affliction of your
family which I hope will not be there by the time you receive this you wrote
for me to come which is entirely out of my power, you wrote also for me to have

Aggy and her child appraised and send you the bill of appraisement, which I think entirely useless as you and Mr. Lyon are as well acquainted with the value of the two negroes as I am or any person else, you also know her to be the most indifferent of any of the negroes named in the deed, though not with standing what ever the price you and Mr. Lyon puts on her within reason I will abide by, I have appointed you my attorney I have had the power of attorney wrote by an acting magistrate of the beat and approved of by the Clerk of the probate court which you will find inclosed in this letter if the negroes are sold I wish you to purchase Dannel, (name) mary or *clary* and her either of the four mentioned will do if you get either of the boys which I rather you would if they (word) the negro that you purchase for me bring it on with you I will pay the expenses from carolina to your home and when you git it home write to me and I will send after it, if Mr. Lyon concludes to move to Perry County Al. you can send the negro on with him as the distance will not be so great, as the boys will not want to lose any time from school. my children are all going to school except John he started the first of the month with his (word) to attend the lectures at Louisville, Kentucky. Rheuben, Henry and John Gray was well when I heard from them a fortnight ago Henry lost his youngest child a short time before I heard from him the chn. send their respects to you and family. I will pay you when I sell the crop the account you have against the est. Eliz. wishes to be remembered to her Aunt Gray bro. do come and see me nothing on earth would give me more pleasure than to see you.

Sincerely your -sis.,
Eliz. B. Gray

(letter)

State of Alabama, Perry County
Feb. 24th, 1845

Dear Sir,

Your letter of the first came safely to hand in which you say the estate of my mother after paying all demands will leave a balance in your hands of some $3,500 whatever part is coming to me I wish you to receive for me and I do hereby appoint you my att. in fact and in law to do all things in that matter that I myself could if I were present. I wish you to purchase for me two negro girls should there be a sufficency for that purpose and give them to my sis. Keziah McKinly and Margaret Tate You must take the bill of sail in my name and have them recorded as I am aware that (word) McKinly and Tate are both involved should there not be enough to purchase two please purchase one and give her to Mrs. Tate and the balance of the money you can loan to *Mrs.* McKinly and take their note signed by Mr. McKinly and wife I should be pleased if the est. could be sett. without difficulty. I shall ever consider myself under the greatest obligation to you for your kindness I recollect seeing you twice when I was small and be asured that I esteem and respect you as a gentleman in whom I can place the most implicit confidence. You will find enclose my account against the est. for my bed and furniture trunk etc. I am with proper and dire respect yours,

R. Patton

Written to David Lesly Ord. Abbeville Dist. The petition of Robt. M. McKinly sheweth that John Tench died Aug. 1826 intestate leaving a wid.

Margaret Tench who was the wid. of John Denton having by the said Denton viz Keziah B., now the wife of one of your petitioners Robt. M. McKinly, Rebecca H., the wid. of James Patton decd. Margaret C., now the wife of Daniel Tait, also by her last husband John Tench the following chn. viz Eliz. Gray the wid. of Wm. Gray in Miss., Susan Creagh, Lyon wife of John Lyon, John Tench, Thos. *Creah* was a bro. to Margaret Tench. (letter)

> South Canebreak, Perry County, Ala.
> Aug. 25, 1845

Dear Sir,

I wish you to pay to my son Thos. W. Patton my full share of my mothers est. Margaret Tench decd. and this shall be your receipt in full for the same. I have given my son directions how to dispose of it. Rebecca H. Patton to David Lesly Ord. Abbeville Dist., S. C.

TOLBERT, ROBERT—BOX 93, PACK 2301:
Will dated June 7, 1837 in Abbeville Dist. Prov. Feb. 23, 1844. Exrs: Son, Robt. Talbert, John P. Barratt. Wit: Saml. Rambo, Dr. John, Levina Barratt. Wife, Nancy Talbert. Gr. son: John Robt. Talbert. Nancy Talbert and infant child name not known. Mrs. Mary Ryleys chn. viz. Wm., Ann, Mary Ryley. Legatees J. Pealor, James H. Red. Inv. made March 19, 1846 by Esme Jones, Willis Ross, Maximillan Hutchison.

TRIBBLE, MINORS—BOX 93, PACK 2302:
Feb. 15, 1841 Lemuel W. Trible, Ezekiel Trible bound unto Moses Taggart Ord. Abbeville Dist. sum $300.00. Lemuel W. Tribble made gdn. of Stephen M., Lemuel W. Trible minors over 14 yrs. I petition Moses Taggart Ord. to be appointed gdn. for my minor chn. in the est. of Nancy Crowther decd. Feb. 15, 1841. L. W. Trible.

TILLMAN, MINORS—BOX 93, PACK 2303:
Mar. 5, 1838 Edward Tilman, Langdon Bowie, Oliver Taggart bound unto Moses Taggart Ord. Abbeville Dist. $10,000.00. Edward Tilman made gdn. of Hiram, Edward Alexander, Kitty C., Iwanawna Tilman minors chn. of Edward Tilman, the gdn. Ed. A. Tilman died Oct. 16, 1838. James G. Stuart of Macon, *Noxabee* County, Miss. leg. recd. of E. Tilman Exr. of Hyrum Tilman decd. formerly of Abbeville Dist., S. C. his share of said est.

> Noxabee City, Miss.
> Feb. 6, 1847.

To Mr. Ed. Tilman
Dr. Sir,

Enclose I send you Mr. Stuarts Recpt. you will please forward the amt. due him, to me as soon as convenient. This leaves us all well and hope you and family are enjoying the same blessing. Please present our best respects to your son Hiram and accept for yourself and family the same.

> I remain yours,
> A. J. Colbert

N. B. Mr. Stuart has moved this winter to Louisanna, Claiborn Parish near *Minden* and was all well a few weeks ago. A. J. C. Jan. 5, 1848 Be it remembered that this day I saw Ed. Tilman deposite in the Post Office of Abbeville Dist., S. C. $56.00 and sent the same to Hiram D. Tilman, Hopewell Post Office, Alabama.

Isaac Branch

TURNER, JOHN—BOX 93, PACK 2304:
Est. admnr. Dec. 10, 1844 by Saml., Patsy Turner, John Morgan, John Buchanan unto David Lesly Ord. Abbeville Dist. sum $4,000.00. Patsy Turner wid. of John Turner. Saml. Turner a bro. Left no chn. Inv. made Dec. 24, 1844 by Wm. Buchanan, John Morgan, Wm. Roman. Sett. made Jan. 12, 1847. Present, Martha Turner wid. who left no chn., Rebecca *Gallegby*, Wm. Turner by power of atty, Wm. Taggart, Mary his wife, also by power of atty. Eliz. Buchanan representing Wm. Buchanan her son, Alex., Saml. Turner. Jan. 12, 1847 John R. Turner recd. $149.66.

TATE, ENOS—BOX 93, PACK 2305:
Will dated Mar. 6, 1841. Rec. Feb. 10, 1845. Exrs: Son, Uriah O. Tate, Thos. J. Heard. Wit: Richard Bennett, John A. Verdel, John Nunnelee. Lived in Elbert County, Ga. Wife, Mary Tate. Gr. son: Enos Asbury Tate, d. l., Sarah S. Tate. Decd. uncle, Enos Tate. Inv. made Feb. 1845 by John Senr., John Power, Jr., F. B. Clinkscales. Late of Abbeville Dist.

TINER, HARRIS—BOX 93, PACK 2306:
Will dated Mar. 25, 1844 in Abbeville Dist. Prov. Sept. 6, 1844. Exr: Wife, Jane Tiner. Wit: Robt. Brady, J. J., E. Y. Shanks. Sis-in-law, Louisa Wiseman. Inv. made Sept. 17, 1844 by Jas. Gray, Henry Bently, Ninian Thomson.

VERNON, RICHARD—BOX 93, PACK 2307:
Est. admnr. Nov. 1, 1821 by Christopher, James, Frederick Conner unto Moses Taggart Ord. Abbeville Dist. sum $1,000. Christopher Conner made admnr. in right of his wife. This was the 2nd admnr. bond, first one gone from pkg. Inv. made June 1814 by Thos. Ward, Wm. Vernon, Andrew Mc-Bride, Geo., Robt. Vernon as shewn to them by Rebecca Vernon, Ezekiel Calhoun admnrs. Expend: Oct. 3, 1829. Paid S. N. W. Vernon $225.

VERNON, RICHARD—BOX 93, PACK 2308:
Es. admnr. June 6, 1814 by Rebecca Vernon, Ezekiel Calhoun, Thos. Ward, Saml. Scott unto Taliaferro Livingston Ord. Abbeville Dist. sum $1,000. Inv. made June 24, 1814 by Thos. Ward, Robt., Geo. Vernon. Sale, June 25, 1814. Byrs: Rebecca Vernon, Peter Brown, Wm., Geo., Vernon, Ezekiel Calhoun, Wm. Davis, Esq., Geo. Kirkwood, Thos., Sarah Ward, Luke Burns, Isiah Johnston, John H. Lesly, Israel Davis, Joseph Irving, Thos. Lee, Joseph Moseley. Expend: 1816 paid Sarah Ward $7.97½. Paid Peter Ward $12.70. 1821 paid Christopher Conner in right of wife $152.96.

VANHAZLET, WM. H.—BOX 93, PACK 2309:
Est. admnr. Jan. 20, 1807 by Saml., Benj. H. Saxon, Isaac Moragne

unto Andrew Hamilton Ord. Abbeville Dist. sum $10,000.00. Inv. made Jan.
28, 1808 by Saml. Saxon, Andrew, Thos. Lee. Sale, Jan. 30, 1808. Byrs:
B. H. Saxon, A. Lee Jr., Geo. Whitefield, Robt. McClinton, Wm. Calhoun,
Peter Gibert Esq., Drury Breazeal, Lewis Gibert, M. D. Griffin, Thos. Lee Sr.,
Delany Carroll.

VERNON, JAMES, JR.—BOX 93, PACK 2310:
Will dated Sept. 1, 1787 in Abbeville Dist. Exrs: Bros., Joseph, Richard
Vernon. Wit: Felix Hughes, Robt. Houston, Mary Kerr. Bros., Nehemiah,
Isaac, Robt., Joseph, Richard Vernon. Sis., Sarah, Hannah Vernon. Nephew,
John Vernon. "Bequeath to Jane Kerr a mare." (Will of James Vernon Sr. in
same pkg.) Will dated Feb. 8, 1802 in Abbeville Dist. Rec. June 10, 1802.
Exrs: Sons, Joseph, Nehemiah Vernon. Wit: Elizabeth, Saml., Handy Harris.
Wife ment. no name given in will, on another paper name ment. as Elenor
Vernon. Chn: Richard, Nehemiah, Joseph Vernon, Hannah, wife of John
Hazelet, Robt. Vernon. Gr. Son: John Vernon (son of Mary.) "Give son
Richard now in North Carolina a tract of land provided he settles my affairs
in N. C. at his own expense." Expend: Nov. 1803 paid James Tinsley of Thos.
Vernon's est. $10.06¼.

VICK, FATHA—BOX 93, PACK 2311:
Will dated Sept. 3, 1810 in Abbeville Dist. Rec. Jan. 7, 1811. Exrs:
Sons, Jonas, Cullen Vick. Wit: Ethel Tucker, James Nickels, Delila Hall.
Chn: "Jonas Vick a tract of land on the west side of the Cherokee road,"
Cullen, Sarah, Will, Howel Vick. "Leave John Cain $1.00." Paid Joseph
Vick legacy $4.58¾. Joal Vick $4.58¾. Benjamin Vick $4.58¾. Wilson Vick
$4.58¾. Sarah Vick $4.58¾. Howel Vick $4.58¾. Cullen Vick $4.58¾. Inv.
made Jan. 12, 1811 by Saml. Wimbish, Ethel Tucker, Nathan Strickland.

VERNON, SARAH—BOX 93, PACK 2312:
Est. admnr. Jan. 29, 1831 by John Pressly, Enos Crawford, Thos. W.
Vernon unto Moses Taggart Ord. Abbeville Dist. sum $600.00. Inv. made
Feb. 8, 1831 by Joseph T. Baker, Robt. Vernon, John McGaw. Expend: Feb.
17, 1831. Recd. of est. of T. W. Vernon $49.00. Sale, Feb. 9, 1831. Byrs:
Robt. Vernon, John B., Joseph Williams, Andrew English, Capt. John McGaw,
Thos. Ward Vernon, Moses Vernon, Wm. Kirkpatrick, Freeman Dixon,
Abraham Outen, Richard Hill, Andrew Smith, John Houston, etc.

VERNON, THOS.—BOX 93, PACK 2313:
Will dated May 26, 1830 in Abbeville Dist. Prov. Aug. 14, 1830. Exrs:
John Pressly Esq., Thos. W. Vernon. Wit: Oswald Houston, Zachariah Ford,
M. W. Vernon. Wife, Sarah Vernon. Chn: James, T. W., Elizabeth, R. H.
Vernon. Expend: Feb. 7, 1831. Recd. cash of Moses W. Vernon $11.00. Inv.
made Aug. 27, 1830 by Robt. Vernon, Elijah Brown, J. C. Livingston. Sale,
July 9, 1831. Byrs: Robt. Vernon Sr., Jas. Conner, Jr., Joseph Baker, John
Pressly Esq., Thos. W. Vernon, John McFarland, Jas. Dixon, Robt. Spence,
Robt. Crawford, Daniel Jacobs, Moses Vernon, etc.

VERNON, ALEX—BOX 93, PACK 2314:
Will dated Jan. 5, 1787 in Spartanburg Co. Exrs: Son, Jas. Vernon, Jas. Jordan Esq., Wm. Benson. Wit: Margaret Barry, Wm. McDowall, Mary Vernon. Wife, Margaret Vernon. Chn: Nancy wife of Michael Miller, Margaret Vernon, "Give to her son Andrew 20 pounds," Mary, Jas. Vernon. Inv. made by John Nicholl, Alex: Ray, Nevil Wayland.

VERNON, ELENOR—BOX 93, PACK 2315:
Est. admnr. Feb. 8, 1813 by Joseph Vernon, Thos. Tinsley, John Spence unto Taliaferro Livingston Ord. Abbeville Dist. sum $2,000.00. Cit. pub. at Rocky River Church. Inv. made March 11, 1813 by Thos. Tinsley, John Boyd, Ed. Tilman. Sale, March 12, 1813. Byrs: Joseph Vernon, Robt. Vernon, Isaac Vernon, Josiah Patterson, Thos. Tinsley, John, Geo. Haslett, Thos. Montgomery, James Tinsley. Expend: Paid Wm. Vernon's acct. $6.19. Paid attorney's fees in case Robt. Vernon vs. Joseph Vernon $15.00. Paid Robt. Vernon his part of said est. $125. Paid Richard Vernon part of his share per Geo. Vernon, March 28, 1819 $33.37½. Paid Isaac Vernon in full $125. Paid John Haslett his part $125. Paid Jas. Tinsley his part $125. 7 legatees: Robt. Vernon, John Haslett, Jas. Tinsley, Isaac, Richard, Joseph, Nehemiah Vernon. Feb. 10, 1813 paid traveling expenses to Greenville $7.25.

VAUGHAN, JAMES—BOX 93, PACK 2316:
Est. admnr. Sept. 2, 1825 by Matilda Vaughan, Saml., Geo. F. Caldwell, Richard Pollard unto Moses Taggart Ord. Abbeville Dist. sum $4,000.00. Cit. pub. at Mt. Moriah Church. Expend: Oct. 7, 1825. Recd. of Russel Vaughan for cotton sold in Augusta $200.00. Oct. 9, Recd. of the Sheriff of Edgefield Dist. $164.12½. Recd. of Drury Vaughan $75. Byrs: Mrs. Matilda Vaughan, Russel Vaughan, Elias Herd, Joseph Thornton, Joseph Holliway, Leroy Watson, Craven Smith, Saml. Caldwell, etc.

VICKERY, WILLIAM—BOX 93, PACK 2317:
Will dated Jan. 14, 1804 in Abbeville Dist. Rec. Mar. 6, 1804. Exrs: Benj. Howard, Andrew McComb. Wit: John Glasgow, Andrew McComb Sr., Wm. Fife. Chn: Wm. Vickery of Ga., Nancy Davis, Ruth, wife of Francis Hunter, Betty Vickery. "To Zackrias Ford for whom I stood in baptism for bed, etc., also reserving that Miss Fanney Ford had a free maintenance as long as she remains single." Inv. made Mar. 16, 1804 by Saml. Patterson, Wm. Fife, John Glasgow. Byrs: Mrs. Mary Mullin, Mrs. Atward, Andrew McComb, Francis Hunter, Wm. Fife, Augustin Davis, Joseph McBride, John Stanfield. Abraham Outon and his wife Fanny Ford were leg. Cit. pub. at Fraziers near Cedar Springs.

VERNON, JAMES T. W. (MINOR)—BOX 93, PACK 2318:
On Mar. 7, 1832 Joseph T. Baker, Robt., Thos. W. Vernon bound unto Moses Taggart Ord. Abbeville Dist. sum $3,000.00. Thos. W. Vernon made gdn. of Jas Thos. Ward Vernon minor under 14 yrs. and Elizabeth Rebecca Harper Vernon a minor. Chn. of Thos. Vernon decd. (Letter) Anderson C. H. Jan. 28, 1847 Dr. Sir: Mr. James T. W. Vernon is disatisfied with the state-

ment for settlement which his gdn. Robt. Vernon has produced, and desires you to make an est. from the papers in your office returns and see whether he has received from the Exr. as cash and which he has failed to collect. The original amt. of which was $40.00 and also says that the gdn. is not entitled to commissions in as much as he failed to make his annual returns since 1839. We will compensate you for any services rendered, if you comply with his desires, write & send the statement to him to this office. Whitner Harrison. To David Lesly, Abbeville C. H. Ord.

VERNON, ROBERT ALEXANDER B.—BOX 93, PACK 2319:
Est. admnr. Nov. 30, 1840 by Robt. Vernon, John Link, Jas. N. Dixon unto Moses Taggart Ord. Abbeville Dist. sum $1,000.00. Inv. made Dec. 18, 1840 by Andrew Gillespie Sr., John Link, Jas. N. Dixon. Elizabeth A. Vernon, the wid. and one child living Mary T. Vernon. Two of the chn. died since intestate. Name, Mary Tercy Pleasant Vernon. (Letter) To Mr. John Link. "Stated that Wm. H. Bolmon has been legally appointed by the Ord. of Anderson Dist. the gdn. of Mary Vernon and also understand that Old Mr. Vernon now resides in Ga."

VESSELS, SUSANNA—BOX 93, PACK 2320:
Est. admnr. Nov. 8, 1843 by Alexr., Joseph D. Scott, Wm. T. Drennan unto David Lesly Ord. Abbeville Dist. sum $500.00. Expend: 1844 Alexr. Scott stated that in Feb. he recd. from Thos. Lyles Exr. of est. of Joicey Lyles on a legacy coming from said Joicey to Susanna Vessels $90.00. Chas. M. Vaughan sheweth that his mother-in-law Susanna Vessels died leaving a hus. and chn. That her sister Mary Liles of Newberry Dist. died having no hus. or chn. but a will in which she gave to her sis. and her bodily heirs a legacy.

VAUGHANS, MINORS—BOX 93, PACK 2321:
On Dec. 6, 1839 Anthony G. Campbell, Jas. Goodman, John Vance of Laurens Dist. bound unto Moses Taggart Ord. Abbeville Dist. sum $5,000.00. Anthony G. Campbell made gdn. of Mary B., Jas. N. Vaughn minors under 21 yrs. Joseph Philpot, b.l. of Mary B. Vaughan.

WHITLOW, SAMUEL—BOX 94, PACK 2322:
Est. admnr. Feb. 16, 1819 by Sarah Whitlow, Benj. Hatter, Wm. Spragins unto Moses Taggart Ord. Abbeville Dist. the sum $5,000.00. Inv. made Feb. 19, 1819 by Elihu Creswell, John, Chas. Fooshe, Joseph Hill.

WARD, DR. JAMES A.—BOX 94, PACK 2323:
Will dated Jan. 14, 1827 in Abbeville Dist. Prov. Jan. 25, 1827. Exrs: Wife, Rebecca Ward, Jubar S. Neely. Wit: Chas. Neely, Chas. B. Fooshe, O. Richardson, M. Walker. Chn: Caroline Loretta Neely, Sarah Ann, Martha S. Ward. "That Jubar L. Neely shall have the management of Sarah Ann's est." Inv. made Dec. 18, 1827 by Dr. John Logan, Thos. B. Boyd, Chas. B. Fooshe, Maj. Wm. Eddins.

WALLER, SARAH—BOX 94, PACK 2324:
Est. admnr. Dec. 28, 1820 by Wm. White, Wm. Chiles, Wm. Bullock

unto Moses Taggart Ord. Abbeville Dist. sum $12,000.00. Inv. made Jan. 11, 1821 by Littleton Myrick, Jas. Coleman, David Cunningham, Wm. Bullock. Wm. Chiles was Exr. of Wm. White late admnr. of Thos. B. Waller decd. Sale, Jan. 16, 1821. Byrs: Wm. White, Grigsbey Appleton, Richard Plunket, Jordan Peters, Wm. Mitchell, Hugh Oliver, Robt. Chatham, John Lightfoot, Martin Hacket, James Griffin, David Cunningham, Wm. Stallsworth, Wm. Hargrove, Amelia Waller, Thos. Brightman, Vincent Lester, John Marsh, John L. Robinson, Wm. Bullock, James Coleman, Hiram Gaines, Leonard Waller, John Talbert, Nathaniel Marion, Joseph Wardlaw, James P. Heard, Washington Glover, C. C. Mayson, Edward Collier, Richard Griffin, Jacob Anderson, Wm. Hacket.

WALLER, LEONARD—BOX 94, PACK 2325:
Will dated Jan. 4, 1826 in Abbeville Dist. Prov. Mar. 6, 1826. Exrs: Jas. Coleman, Albert, John H. Waller. Wit: Thos. Whitlock, Saml. Ramsey, Henry Breazeale. Chn: Wm. Waller, Nancy wife of -Jas. Coleman, Pamelia, wife of Jas. Foster, Mary Groce decd. late wife of Jared E. Groce, Elizabeth wife of Thos. Lipscomb decd., Annis Groce decd. late wife of Jared E. Groce, Silyra Waller. "Will to Leonard J. White son of Nancy Coleman." Wife, Frances Waller. Inv. made Mar. 14, 1826 by Wesley, Stanmore Brooks, Maximillian Hutchison, Martin Hacket, Robt. Cheatham.

WILSON, ANDREW—BOX 94, PACK 2326:
Est. admnr. Feb. 3, 1823 by Eldred, Wm. Smith, Andrew Milligan unto Moses Taggart Ord. Abbeville Dist. sum $3,000.00. Inv. made Feb. 18, 1823 by Jeremiah Bell, Wm. Smith, John Tench. Sale, at res. of Wm. Smith Sr., Feb. 21, 1823. Byr: Charity Wilson.

WALKER, RICHARD—BOX 94, PACK 2327:
Est. admnr. Oct. 27, 1832 by Thos. Ferguson, A. F. or T. Traylor, Pleasant Searls unto Moses Taggart Ord. Abbeville Dist. sum $1,000.00. Cit. pub. at Republican Meeting House. Expend: Dec. 21, 1832 by legacy from est. of John, Mary Walker, $203.54. To Elizabeth Walker for boarding and clothing Frances a minor 9 yrs. old from June 2, 1834 to Jan. 2, 1835, $25.00. For boarding Mary a minor 5 yrs. old, $25.00. For boarding Manda a minor 4 yrs. old, $25.00. For boarding Willard Walker a minor 7 yrs. old, $25.00.

WATKINS, ROBERT—BOX 94, PACK 2328:
Will dated Dec. 7, 1822, in Abbeville Dist. Prov. July 24, 1828. Exrs: Dr. Wm. N. Richardson, Bro. John Watkins. Wit: Peter B. Moragne, J. L. Gibert, John McMullen. Chn: Geo. Watkins "bequeath land lying in Lauderdale County, Ala." Alfred, Robt., Lyric, Augustus Peyton, Augustus Lyrick Watkins. Inv. made July 31, 1828 by Lewis Covin, W. A. Bull, Edward Collier.

WINN, LEWELLEN—BOX 94, PACK 2329:
Est. admnr. Feb. 4, 1828 by John Hearst Jr., Saml., Geo. W. Pressly unto Moses Taggart Ord. Abbeville Dist. sum $30,000.00. Set: Nov. 8, 1838.

Present Warren F. Winn, Burrel E. Hobbs who married Julia E. Winn dtr. of decd. Sarah Winn married O. A. Williams, Elizabeth married Arthur Freeman, Moriah married Stephen J. Blackwell, Susan married George *Price.*

WOODS, SUSANNAH C.—BOX 94, PACK 2330:
Will dated June 6, 1829 in Abbeville Dist. Prov. June 22, 1829. Exrs: Jonathan Johnson, Wm. Covington. Wit: Hugh Mecklin, Ralph Hardin, J. S. Allen. Chn: Martha Bell Drinkwater, Jas., Michael, Andrew C., Robt. W., John Woods, Isabella G. Harden. Inv. made June 29, 1829 by Hugh Mecklin, Jonathan Johnson, R. Smith.

WALLER, JOHN H.—BOX 94, PACK 2331:
Est. admnr. Dec. 10, 1830 by Jas. F., Leroy Watson, Martin Hacket, Jas. F. Watson, Stanmore Brooks, Vincent Griffin unto Moses Taggart Ord. Abbeville Dist. sum $10,000.00. Expend: Dec. 5, 1831 paid Albert Waller $30.12½. Inv. made Dec. 21, 1830 by Albert Waller, Stephen Ross, Stanmore Brooks. Sale, Dec. 22, 1830. Byrs: Nancy Waller, James F. Watson, John P. Barratt, Seaborn O. Sullivan, Stephen Witt, John Casey, James W. Child, etc.

WILLSON, ROBERT W.—BOX 94, PACK 2332:
Est. admnr. April 16, 1830 by Susan E. Willson, Geo. Red, Russel Vaughan unto Moses Taggart Ord. Abbeville Dist. sum $3,000.00. Russel Vaughan was of Edgefield Dist. Inv. made Dec. 30, 1830 by David Lesly, Wm. Lomax, Jas. Alston, Robt. Richey. Sale, May 4, 1830. Byrs: Mrs. Susan Wilson, John Wier, Saml. A., John Wilson, James Spence, Thos. Jackson, James McCraven, James Moore, etc.

WILSON, JAMES—BOX 94, PACK 2333:
Est. admnr. Mar. 9, 1836 by Nathaniel Banks, Robt. H. Green, Orville Tatom unto Moses Taggart Ord. Abbeville Dist. sum $2,000.00. Cit. pub. at Glovers Chapel. Expend: Jan. 1, 1832 paid Margaret Wilson board $65.00. Inv. made Mar. 23, 1830 by Joshua Dubose, John Clark, Thos. W. Williams. Sale, Mar. 26, 1830. Byrs: Margaret Wilson, Wm. McRandall, Robt. H. Greene, Geo. W. Speed, Lewis Howland, Thos. Brough, Wm. Walker, John Turnbull, Joseph Mathews, John Gallaugher, Henry Maynor, Noah Lyon, Meredith McGehee, Chas. A. Pelot, Peter Bevill, Nathaniel Banks, John McKinley.

WILLIAMS, ROBERT—BOX 94, PACK 2334:
Est. admnr. Aug. 9, 1823 by Joseph, John Williams, Stephen Henderson unto Moses Taggart Ord. Abbeville Dist. sum $700.00. Cit. pub. at Providence Church. Inv. made Sept. 1, 1823 by Thos. Cummins, Richard L. Anderson, Wm. Henderson. Sale, Sept. 19, 1823. Byrs: Miss Sarah Williams, Thos., Stephen Henderson, Elizabeth Williams, John Williams, Harrison Monday, Richard Anderson, Jesse Cummins.

WARD, WILLIAM—BOX 94, PACK 2335:
Will dated Dec. 14, 1805 in Abbeville Dist. Rec. Dec. 20, 1805. Exrs: Walter Ward, Ezekiel Calhoun Sr. Wit: Francis Carlile, Walter Ward. Wife,

Mary Ward. Chn: Peggy, Jas., Peter Ward. Inv. made by Jeremiah S. Terry, John Barksdale, Nathaniel Norwood. Expend: Oct. 31, 1821 paid J. C. Ward $399.47¾. Paid Mary McCleskey $132.12½. Paid Margaret Ward $506. Sale, June 22, 1811. Byrs: Isaac C. Boles, Wm. Davis 'Esq., David McCleskey, Walter, Peter Ward, Joseph Brown, Robt. Allen, Archilaus Walker, Archibald McKinley, Geo. Loftis, Ezekiel Calhoun, Jeremith S. Terry, John Young.

WILSON, NANCY—BOX 94, PACK 2336:
Will dated Jan. 16, 1825 in Abbeville Dist. Prov. April 30, 1825. Exrs: Son, Saml. A. Wilson, dtr., Nancy Wilson. Wit: Moses, Robt. L. Taggart, Nancy C. Wilson. Chn: Saml. A., Robt. C., Grizzilla, Nancy, Elizabeth Wilson, Jane McKinley Wilson, "Owned a tract of land in Pendleton Dist." Inv. made May 19, 1825 by John McCord Sr., Michael Wilson Sr., Andrew W. Shillite. Byrs: Nancy Wilson, Hugh English, Wm. Russell, Robt. C. Wilson, Richard D. Davis, David Holeman, Saml. A., Elizabeth Wilson, Chas. Dendy, John McCord Sr., Benj. McFarland, Marshall Weatherall, Jane Wilson, James Smith, Benj. Adams Sr., Saml. Robertson, Joseph Davis Esq., Nathaniel Cameron, John Hill, Grizzilla Wilson.

WARDLAW, HUGH, ESQ.—BOX 94, PACK 2337:
Will dated Nov. 9, 1802 in Abbeville Dist. Rec. Jan. 10, 1803. Exrs: Son, James Wardlaw, Rev. Hugh Dickson, Col. John Weatherall. Wit: Thos. B. Jack, John, Glover Wardlaw. Wife, Polly Wardlaw. Chn: Robt., David Wardlaw, "a tract of land lying on Beaver Dam Creek in Pendleton Dist." Joseph, Peggy Wardlaw tract of land lying in Pendleton Dist., Hugh Hutson, Elizabeth, Nancy Wardlaw, Jenny wife of Jesse Colbert. Expend: Jan. 9, 1804. Paid Jean Calvert legacy $60. Sett. April 13, 1835. Legatees: Wm., David, Joseph, Margaret Wardlaw wife of James Wardlaw, of Anderson to her chn., John, Elizabeth, Eliab Allen Wardlaw, Nancy, wife of Elijah Majors, Hugh Hutson Wardlaw, Polly wife of Jesse H. Ballentine. Jane Calvert decd. late wife of Jesse Calvert had 7 chn. who were: Jesse, Hugh Hutson, Frances, Jane wife of Wm. Smith, Elizabeth Wardlaw, wife of Wm. B. Leak, Nancy Caroline, wife of James Dunn, Mary Elizabeth Calvert, John Bayles Calvert, Lucy Evaline Calvert. Robt. Wardlaw decd. had 2 chn. who were: Hugh Marshall Wardlaw, Elizabeth Ann wife of David Robt. Caldwell. Hugh Hutson Wardlaw decd. had one dtr. Mary Ann, wife of Benj. Hodges. Share of Elizabeth Wardlaw decd. $932.58. Nancy Wardlaw decd. $932.58.

WEATHERALL, COL. JOHN—BOX 94, PACK 2338:
Will dated Nov. 2, 1824 in Abbeville Dist. Prov. Nov. 16, 1824. Exrs: Sons, Geo., Marshall Weatherall. Wit: Saml. Anderson, Hugh, Joseph Dickson. Wife, Betsey Weatherall. Chn: Geo., Marshall Weatherall, Polly wife of James Hodges Jr., James, Adm. C. J., Sarah, John, Betsey, Peggy L., Joseph S. D., Frances E. Weatherall. Gr: Son: Saml. son of Marshall Weatherall. Sett. ment. James Hodges and wife Elizabeth, Sarah M. Means, Frances Evlina Weatherall. Inv. made Nov. 23, 1824 by Saml. Anderson, Wm. Barmore, Saml. Agnew, Wm. Dunn.

WILEY, THOMAS—BOX 95, PACK 2339:
Est. admnr. Oct. 17, 1826 by James Wiley, Samuel Young, Wm. Patton, Alexr. Foster unto Moses Taggart Ord. Abbeville Dist. sum $10,000.00. Cit. pub. at Hopewell Church. Margaret Wiley the wid. Expend: May 26, 1832 paid John Coughran att. of James Wiley of Tenn. gdn. minor chn. of said decd., $700. State of Ala., Wilcox County. Personally came Saml. Young who on oath saith that the above return of Expend of est. of Thos. Wiley as it is stated is true. Sworn this July 27, 1832. Saml. Young.

WHITE, JOHN, JR.—BOX 95, PACK 2340:
Est. admnr. Oct. 4, 1836 by Nathan, Robt. McAlister, John Robison unto Moses Taggart Ord. Abbeville Dist. sum $3,000.00. Inv. made Nov. 3, 1836 by Francis Young, John Robison, Wiley Shackelford. May 15, 1841 his wid. charged the est. with boarding 2 chn., Alexr. White about 7 yrs. old, Rosannah White about 3 yrs. old. Sarah White was wid., Nathan McAllister was her bro. Paid Mr. A. T. or J. McCurry and wife $5.93.

WEST, JOHN F.—BOX 95, PACK 2341:
Est. admnr. Oct. 12, 1837 by Thos. S. Wilkes, Andrew Winn, Robt. Crawford unto Moses Taggart Ord. Abbeville Dist. sum $3,000.00. Inv. made Dec. 15, 1837 by Lewis Rodgers, James McCalister, Jacob Hill. Left a wid. Caroline West, 2 chn. Laura, Frances F. West.

WIDEMAN, LEONARD—BOX 95, PACK 2342:
Will dated Feb. 3, 1830 in Abbeville Dist. Prov. Oct. 7, 1831. Exrs: Sons, Henry, Leonard, Saml. Wideman. Wit: Patrick Gibson, Hiram Palmer, Joseph A. W. Devall. Wife, Savil Wideman. Chn: Lucy Devaul, Edward, Francis, Henry, Leonard, Saml., Katharine Wideman, Sooky Mosely. Inv. made May 26, 1832 by Robt. McCaslan, Abner Perrin, John Wideman. Another paper stated Merideth Wideman was an heir.

WILLIAMS, JAMES—BOX 95, PACK 2343:
Est. admnr. Nov. 23, 1836 by Wm. Hill, John, Saml. Donnald unto Moses Taggart Ord. Abbeville Dist. sum $10,000.00. Inv. made Dec. 19, 1836 by Saml., David Robison, James Gilmer. Expend: May 23, 1837 paid Mary Williams $52.19. Cit. pub. at Sharon Church. Sett. made Jan. 6, 1838 between Wm. Hill admnr. Mary Williams wid. and gdn. of her chn: Sarah, John, Margaret, James, Saml., Wm. Williams. John Johnson in right of his wife Patsey Williams, David Robinson in right of his wife Elisa Williams, Thos. Hamilton in right of his wife Caroline Williams. John B. Williams was a son.

WARD, THOMAS—BOX 95, PACK 2344:
Est. admnr. July 2, 1814 by Wm. Ward, Abraham Bell, Jordan Ramey unto Taliaferro Livingston Ord. Abbeville Dist. sum $2,000.00. Cit. pub. at Rocky River Church. Inv. made July 21, 1814 by James Alston, Robt. Jones, Jordon Ramey. Sale, Aug. 15, 1814. Byrs: Margaret Ward, Robt. Jones, Wm. Ward, John Allen, Abraham Bell, Dempsey Perkerson, Robt. Ward, Thos.

Caldwell, Wm. Harris, Wm. Ezel, Isaac Ward, Wm. Beuford, Chas. Parker, Richard Moseley, Wm. Raiford, John S. Crawford, John Barksdale, Thos. Tinsley, A. E. Scudday. Expend: April 16, 1819 paid Agness Cook $60. Paid Sarah Ward $195. Paid Rebecca Vernon $32.13½. Paid Ann Ward $10. Paid Mary Caldwell $10. Walter H. Ward $11.10. Robt. Vernon $108.38½. Jas. C. Ward $225.04½.

WILSON, JOHN—BOX 95, PACK 2345:
    Will dated Aug. 30, 1796 in Abbeville Dist. Rec. Mar. 27, 1797. Exrs: Wife, Ruth Wilson, Jacob Clark. Wit: John, Saml. Shepard. Chn: John, James, Jacob, Betsey Wilson. Inv. made June 10, 1797 by Robt. Kirkwood, Thos. Cooper.

WILSON, JOHN—BOX 95, PACK 2346:
    Will dated June 9, 1783 in 96 Dist. Exrs: Wm. Clark, Willis Breazeale. Wit: James Foster, Daniel O'Keef, Hugh Wilson. Wife, Catharine Wilson. Chn: Ann, Jean Wilson. Step dtr. Sarah Lockhart. (Will badly torn.) One paper ment. Ruth Wilson as wid. Inv. made Dec. 6, 1785 by Robt. Harkness, Robt. McAlpin, James Bonner.

WARDLAW, ROBERT—BOX 95, PACK 2347:
    Est. admnr. June 22, 1812 by David, James Wardlaw unto Taliaferro Livingston Ord. Abbeville Dist. sum $5,000.00. Inv. made June 27, 1812 by Hugh Morrah Esq., John Burton, Jesse Calvert, Richard L. Anderson. Cit. pub. at Greenville Church. Expend: Jan. 2, 1819. Paid Mary Wardlaw for boarding $50. Paid James Wardlaw $1.50. Paid Betsey Wardlaw $15. Marshall Wardlaw $2.25. Sale, Nov. 17, 1812. Byrs: Lucy Wardlaw wid., Joseph Wardlaw, Major John Hodges, Dr. John H. Miller, Pleasant Wright Esq., Abner McQuire, John Wardlaw, Moses Taggart, Wm. Bowman, Saml. Robinson, Saml. Anderson, Thos. Cunningham, Edward Foster, Alexr. Sims, Wm. McIlwayn Jr., Geo. Lomax, Wm. Mathews, Malon Morgan, H. Wardlaw, Harrison Monday, Oliver Martin, Arthur Rhodes, John Freeman, John Hill, Joseph Burton, Saml. Agnew, John Wright.

WILSON, SAMUEL—BOX 95, PACK 2348:
    Will dated Feb. 19, 1830 in Abbeville Dist. Exr: Wife, Permely Wilson. Wit: Wm. A. Moore, Wm. S. Jones, Robt. Watters. Chn: Wm., Louisa Elizabeth Wilson, Thos. Jackson Wilson. Inv. made Nov. 17, 1835 by James Colbert, David W. McCants, Wm. Moore. Est. admnr. Oct. 28, 1835 by Joel, Chas. Smith, John White unto Moses Taggart Ord. Abbeville Dist. sum $5,000.00. Cit. pub. at Providence Church.

WAIT, AARON—BOX 95, PACK 2349:
    Est. admnr. Oct. 13, 1834 by Stephen Whitley, Daniel Carter, Henry S. Black unto Moses Taggart Ord. Abbeville Dist. sum $1,000.00. Inv. made by Mathew Mays, John L. Cheatham, Richard White. Sett. made Sept. 10, 1844. Stephen Whitley the admnr. died in Dec. 1839. Aaron Wait left a wife Nancy Wait and 6 chn: John, David, Henry, Saml., Catharine, Ann Wait.

WIDEMAN, JACOB—BOX 95, PACK 2350:
Est. admnr. Nov. 7, 1836 by Wade S. Cothran, Chas. Sproull, Bartholomew Jordon unto Moses Taggart Ord. Abbeville Dist. sum $3,000.00. Inv.
made Dec. 8, 1836 by Lewis Simmons, John Zimmerman, Lewis Perrin, Richard
P. Quarles. Expend: Dec. 25, 1838 paid Mary Wideman $43.22. Jane Wideman,
Mary A. E. Wideman now Mary A. E. Rush, Henry E., James Wideman,
Margaret Wideman married Joseph Clark. Left a wid. A. Catharine Wideman
and 5 chn.

WINN, LETTICE—BOX 95, PACK 2351:
Est. admnr. Jan. 7, 1828 by Jas. W. Prather, Alexr. Scott, Andrew Smith
unto Moses Taggart Ord. Abbeville Dist. sum $2,000.00. Cit. pub. at Glovers
Chapel. Est. admnr. again May 21, 1824 by Henry Graves Walker of Ga.,
Lincoln County, Joseph B. Gibert, Meredith McGehee of Abbeville Dist. unto
Moses Taggart Ord. sum $10,000.00. Cit. pub. at Rocky River Church.
Expend: June 8, 1825 paid Jas. R. Baird for his wife's receipt $15.03¾. Recd.
April 7, 1826 of est. of Robt. Winn decd. $23.24 as heir also the portions to
which my bros. Abner, Elisha Winn, also the portion claimed by Littleton Hunt
thru his wife and also the portion claimed by Salvadore Thompson in his right
and that of his mother Elizabeth Thompson by Lemuel Winn. Legatees:
Richard Winn, a bro. to Robt. Winn decd., Simon Berry in right of his wife
Sally, formerly Thompson, Peter, Farley, Allen Thompson representatives by
Elizabeth Thompson a decd. sis. of Robt. Winn. Henry Graves Walker in
right of his wife Lettice Winn. Eliza N. Groves, a legatee.

WILSON, THOMAS—BOX 95, PACK 2352:
Est. admnr. Feb. 27, 1826 by Wm. H., Benj. Jones, Robt. P. Delph unto
Moses Taggart Ord. Abbeville Dist. sum $4,000.00. Cit. pub. at Upper Long
Cane Church. Inv. made by John Williams, John C. Waters, John R. Hodges.
Expend: Mar. 2, 1827 recd. of Hannah Wilson $147.50. Mar. 14, 1828 recd.
of Robt. Wilson $4.31½. Sale, Mar. 16, 1826. Byrs: Hannah Wilson, Wm. H.
Jones, Robt. P. Delph, Henry Wilson, Benj. Rosamond, John Donnald, John
Moore, Jas. Graham, Robt. W. Wilson, etc.

WILLIS, RACHEL—BOX 95, PACK 2353:
Est. admnr. Sept. 19, 1834 by John A. Mars, Jas. C. Willard, Thos.
P. Dowton unto Moses Taggart Ord. Abbeville sum $12,000.00. Cit. pub. at
Hopewell Church. Inv. made Oct. 24, 1834 by Robt. McCaslan, Peter B.
Rogers, A. Houston Esq., Herbert Darricott. Will dated July 16, 1834. Exrs:
Dionyseous N. Rogers, Valentine Traylor. Wit: Cecilia B. Devall, P. B.
Rogers, (One name not eligible to read.) Chn: Julia F. Traylor, Martha W.
wife of John Mars, Milly Drucilly, Thos. Jefferson, Mary Elizabeth, Sarah
Catharine Willis. Julia F. married Valentine Traylor. Were chn. of Joshua
Willis decd.

WILLIS, JOSHUA—BOX 95, PACK 2354:
Will dated Sept. 23, 1830 in Abbeville Dist. Prov. Oct. 13, 1832. Exrs:
Wife, Rachel Willis. s. l. John A. Mars. Wit: Adam Wideman, Wyatt A. Taylor,

Hugh Cochran. Chn: Julia Franklin Willis, Martha W. Mars, Milly Ann D. Willis, Thos. J., Mary E., Sarah C. Willis. Inv. made Nov. 8, 1830 by Robt. McCaslan, John Harris, John Wideman. Sale, Nov. 15, 1830. Byrs: John A. Mars, John Harris, Singleton Hughes, John, Robt. McDonnald, John Goodwin, Wyatt A. Taylor, Robt. A. Martin, Adam Wideman, John Houston, Jas. Drennan, David D. Marvin, Jas Findley, John Shanks, Abner Campbell, David Porter.

WILSON, CHARLES—BOX 95, PACK 2355:
Will dated Nov. 20, 1809 in Abbeville Dist. Rec. Mar. 27, 1811. Exrs: John Brownlee, John Wilson, John Armstrong, John Walls. Wit: John Wilson, Thos. Robinson, John Armstrong. Chn: Michael, Jas., John, Elizabeth, Margaret Wilson. Inv. made April 12, 1811 by Joseph McCord, Andrew, Wm. Paul.

WELLS, MOSES—BOX 95, PACK 2356:
Est. admnr. Oct. 28, 1831 by John W. Anglin, Walter Anderson, Washington Sample unto Moses Taggart Ord. Abbeville Dist. sum $5,000.00. Pub. at Mount Prospect Church. John W. Anglin next of kin. Inv. made Nov. 12, 1831 by Washington Sample, Robt. Swancy, Jas. Caldwell. Permely Wells a dtr. Mary Wells desire that John W. Anglin should admnr. on said est.

WILSON, JAMES—BOX 96, PACK 2357:
Will dated Mar. 10, 1812 in Abbeville Dist. Rec. Oct. 12, 1812. Exrs: Son, Wm. Wilson, Isham Robinson, Jas. McCracken. Wit: Abraham Giles Dozier, Jas. Cowdrey, John Gayle. Wife, Tabitha Wilson. Chn: Jas. Henry Wilson (a minor) Elizabeth McCracken, Mary Robinson, Nancy, Wm. Wilson. "Owned land in Edgefield Dist., and house and lot at Cambridge." Inv. made Dec. 21, 1812 by John C. Mayson, David Cunningham. Sett. made June 20, 1845. Heirs: Wm. Wilson, Elizabeth Todd, James H. Wilson, Nancy Ghent, heirs of Mary Brown decd. Leroy Brown, Caroline Grigsly or Grissly, Robt. Robinson decd., Whitfield Brown and wife, T. Todd and wife, Sims and wife, M. Walton and wife, Albert Robinson, T. J. Jame and wife. Expend: Oct. 9 1816. Recd. of R. Fitchet of Va. being the residue of a legacy from est. of Thos Wilson decd. father of James Wilson, $203.60. Sale took place at the late residence of Tabitha Wilson decd. in Edgefield Dist.

WILLS, JOHN—BOX 96, PACK 2358:
Will dated May 3, 1807. Rec. Nov. 10, 1807. Exrs: not ment. Wit: Saml., Meriah Herron. Wife, Kezia Wills. Dtr., Polly Wills. "Wife now pregnant." Sale, Nov. 25, 1807. Byrs: John Calhoun, Thos. Burnett, Wm. Hill, Andrew Gray, Wm. Smyth, Kezia Wills, Wm. Hughes, John Conn, Andrew McComb, Chas. Wilson, Enos Crawford, Wm. McDonald Sr., Andrew English, etc.

WALKER, HENRY GRAVES—BOX 96, PACK 2359:
Est. admnr. Dec. 3, 1827 by Lettice Walker, Jas. W. Prather, Alexr. Scott unto Moses Taggart Ord. Abbeville Dist. sum $1,000.00. Cit. pub. at Vienna. Inv. made Dec. 6, 1827 by Andrew Rembert, Wm. Gray, Mathew

Young. Agreement: We Andrew Rembert Exor. of Robt. Winn decd. and H. G. Walker admnr. of Lettice Winn decd. came to an agreement, with all the stock which was willed by the said Robt. Winn to his mother Lettice Winn decd. belonging to the said Robt. and Lettice Winn it being a part of the property of Robt. Winn decd. etc. Expend: Dec. 20, 1827 paid John H. Walker $566.21. Sale, Dec. 13, 1827. Byrs: Robt. Howard, Alexr. Scott, Capt. Wm. Drennan, Chas. B. Herrod, Wm. Gray, James R. Houston, Peter Bevel, John Scott, Jas. Rembert, Saml. Cole, Thos. T. Hamilton, John H. Walker, Jeremiah G. Walker, Phares C. Walker, James V. Oalds, Thos. Jones, John S. Turnbull, Letty Walker, Wm. Walker, John Holt, Andrew Rembert, Adolpus Sailers.

WARDLAW, ISAAC—BOX 96, PACK 2360:
Est. admnr. Mar. 30, 1835 by Thos. B. Byrd, Saml. Davis, Bennett Reynolds unto Moses Taggart Ord. Abbeville Dist. sum $3,000.00. Inv. made April 25, 1835 by John B., Saml. Davis, Robt. Turner, Joseph Foster.

WILSON, ELIZABETH—BOX 96, PACK 2361:
Est. admnr. Dec. 3, 1821 by Alexr. Stuart, Jesse Beasley, Hugh Wardlaw unto Moses Taggart Ord. Abbeville Dist. sum $3,000.00. Cit. pub. at Providence Church. Expend: Dec. 18, 1821 paid Drewry Wilson legatee $22.36. John L. Davis $22.36. Elizabeth Watson $22.36. Martin Wilson $22.36. Saml. Wilson $22.36. Obadiah Wilson $22.36. Feb. 12, 1822 paid Jane Wilson gdn. $22.12½. Feb. 12, 1823 paid Patsy Watson $21.37½. Feb. 14, 1825 paid Elizabeth Bell gdn. $120.00. Sale, Dec. 18, 1821. Byrs: John L. Davis, Alexr. Caldwell, Mrs. Patsy Watson, Martin, Saml., Jane Wilson, Saml. Hopper, Ephraim Banks, Hugh Porter, Thos. Smith, Jochonias Wilson.

WALKER, JOHN—BOX 96, PACK 2362:
Est. admnr. Feb. 7, 1831 by Thos. Ferguson, Ebenezer Hammond, Levi Ferguson unto Moses Taggart Ord. Abbeville Dist. sum $4,000.00. Cit. pub. at Plumb Branch Church. Expend. Mar. 16, 1832 paid Nancy Walker $9.75. Inv. made Mar. 7, 1831 by Peter Smith Jr., Wiley Freeman, John Martin. Sale, Mar. 16, 1831. Byrs: Mary Walker, Elizabeth Brown, Nancy Walker, Stephen Medling, Abner Campbell, Thos. Ferguson, Jas. Findley, Richard Walker, Phillip Cook, Ebenezer Hammond, Pleasant Searles, Robt. Jennings, Wm. McKinney, Toliver Martin, Sanders Walker, Phares Martin, Edward Jones.

WALKER, MARY—BOX 96, PACK 2363:
Est. admnr. Aug. 30, 1831 by Thos. Ferguson, Isaac *Hawes*, E. Hammond unto Moses Taggart Ord. Abbeville Dist. sum $1,200.00. Cit. pub. at Plumb Branch Church. Inv. made Dec. 21, 1831 by Cutberth Price, James Findley, John Martin. Sale, Dec. 20, 1831. Byrs: Nancy Walker, Elizabeth Brown, Wm., Jas. Findley. Expend: Dec. 6, 1832 paid Nancy Walker legacy $60.18¾. Paid Elizabeth Brown legacy $10.37¼.

WATSON, WILLIAM—BOX 96, PACK 2364:
Will dated Feb. 23, 1837 in Abbeville Dist. Prov. Sept. 14, 1837. Exrs:

ABBEVILLE DISTRICT WILLS AND BONDS   341

Saml. Perryman, LeRoy, Richard, Edward Watson. Wit: John P. Barratt, Jas. F., LeRoy Watson. Gr: Chn: Richard, Edward Watson, Sarah A. Perryman, Elizabeth M. Rudolph decd. John B. Rudolph son of Elizabeth M. Rudolph decd. Inv. made Nov. 22, 1837 by LeRoy Watson, Vincent Griffin, Wm. Harris. Sale, Nov. 23, 1837. Byrs: Vincent Griffin, Richard, Jas. F. Watson, Donald McKellar, Saml. Perryman, John Cresswell, John P. Barratt, Geo. Red, Willis Smyth, Seaborn O. Sullivan, Saml. Leak, Francis Arnold, Anderson Turner, Richmond Still, Thos. Henderson.

WALLER, BENJAMIN—BOX 96, PACK 2365:
Est. admnr. Oct. 15, 1821 by Marshall, Leonard Waller, Thos. Lipscomb, unto Moses Taggart Ord. Abbeville Dist. sum $8,000.00. Inv. made Nov. 25, 1822 by Joseph Wardlaw, Thos. Lipscomb, Wm. Cochran. Expend: Nov. 17, 1824 paid Saml. Marshall $267.55. Paid Leonard Waller $671.73¾. Paid A. Waller act. $15.04½. Sale, Nov. 27, 1822. Byrs: Marshall, Mary Waller, Thos. Lipscomb, Lewis Simmons, Dr. Saml. Marshall, Robt. Hacket, Elijah Hacket, James Whitlock.

WALLER, BENJAMIN—BOX 96, PACK 2366:
Will dated Mar. 1, 1804 in Abbeville Dist. Rec. April 19, 1804. Exrs: Jas. Watson, Nathan Lipscomb, Abraham Marshall. Wit: Ann Conner, Joseph Wardlaw, Wm. Meaks. Wife, Joanna Waller. Chn: Betsy Thompson Waller, Matilda, John Harvy, Guilford, Hulda Waller. (wife now pregnant with child.) Inv. made May 3, 1804 by Wm., Thos. B. Waller, Geo. White. Expend: May 14, 1805. Paid Thos. B. Waller for est. of John N. Waller decd. on a sett. $144.98¾. Nov. 12, 1805 paid Jas. Goudy for Doratha Waller's acct. agreeable to contract $27.64½.

WEEMS, JAMES—BOX 96, PACK 2367:
Est. admnr. Aug. 17, 1827 by Agnes Weems, Sealy Walker, Jas. A. Gray unto Moses Taggart Ord. Abbeville Dist. sum $10,000.00. Inv. made Dec. 18, 1827 by Bartw. Jordon, Malon Morgan, Wm. Reynolds. Expend: Due from est. Emly Weems decd. $9.11½. From Jas. M. Weems $100. Nov. 28, 1832 paid Saml. Weems $215.00. Sale, Dec. 19, 1827. Byrs: Agnes, Jefferson Weems, John Devlin, J. Adams, Madison Weems, Jonathan Jordon, Wm. Smyth, John Gray, etc.

WAKEFIELD, THOMAS—BOX 96, PACK 2368:
Est. admnr. Sept. 5, 1825 by Hezekiah Wakefield, Jas. A. Black, John Osburn unto Moses Taggart Ord. Abbeville Dist. sum $4,000.00. Inv. made Sept. 15, 1825 by Richard Robinson, Archibald Maddison, John Calahan. Expend: Nov. 6, 1827 paid Abel Wakefield $712.91. John Davis $712.91. Saml. Wakefield $712.91. Jane Wakefield 19.56¼. Byrs: John, Hezekiah Wakefield, etc.

WILEY, ANDREW—BOX 96, PACK 2369:
Est. admnr. Sept. 3, 1822 by Jas. Wiley, Matthew Wilson, Saml. Houston unto Moses Taggart Ord. Abbeville Dist. sum $5,000.00. Cit. pub. at

Upper Long Cane Church. Byrs: Elizabeth, Jas. Wiley, Christopher Conner, Andrew Smith, Benj. Finney. Notes due est. $60.00 made by Mary, Elizabeth Wiley. $3.00 made by Hugh, Wm. Wiley.

WHARTON, NANCY—BOX 96, PACK 2370:
Est. admnr. Jan. 6, 1823 by Jonathan Bartholomew Jordon, Wm. Patton, unto Moses Taggart Ord. Abbeville Dist. sum $1,000.00. Inv. made Jan. 16, 1823 by John L. Cooper, John, David Cochran. Sale, Jan. 17, 1823. Byrs: Nancy Wharton, Abram Lites, John Foster, Jas. McClinton, Jacob C. Kitchens, Robt. Hill, etc.

WATSON, MORTON—BOX 96, PACK 2371:
Est. admnr. Feb. 10, 1816 by Mary Watson, John Arnold, Geo. Lomax unto Taliaferro Livingston Ord. Abbeville Dist. sum $10,000.00. Inv. made Feb. 27, 1816 by Thos. Edwards, Jas. Pettus, Jas. Cobb, John Buchanan. Sale, Feb. 28, 1816. Byrs: Polly Watson, Jas. Cobb, John Arnold, Wm. Wiley, Ellerson Cobb, Geo. Wiley, John Moseley, John Spruce, Wm. McWain, Jas. Ware, Geo. Connor, Geo. Hambrick, Josiah Cotton, etc.

WHITE, RICHARD M.—BOX 96, PACK 2372:
Will dated Mar. 25, 1824 in Abbeville Dist. Prov. April 17, 1824. Exrs: Wm. Chiles, Jas. Coleman Sr. Wit: Thos. L. Eskridge, Thos. W. Chiles, Joseph McCrery, b. l., Wm. Chiles. Bro. Geo. White decd. and his chn. Wm. White, Agnes, wife of Wm. Bullock, John, Mary Ann, Leonard, Richard M. White, Nancy Coleman wid. of Geo. White. Inv. made May 1, 1824 by John Martin, Henry Wyley, Thos. L. Eskridge. Sale, May 3, 1824. Byrs: Pink White, Wm. Chiles, John Martin, Jas. Donnald, Nathanial Weed, Jas. Foster, Thos. Adkins, Saml. Jordon, Alexr. Dale, Ira Griffin, David McCrary, Conrod Peterson, Saml. Perrin, Thos. Chiles, Wm. Crow, Young Ragan, Wm. Mantz, etc.

WILSON, HUGH—BOX 96, PACK 2373:
Est. admnr. July 27, 1836 by John Wilson, Clement T. Latimer, Wm. Richey unto Moses Taggart Ord. Abbeville Dist. sum $3,000.00. Cit. pub. at Moseley's Meeting House. Inv. made Sept. 7, 1836 by Clement T. Latimer, Jesse Gent, Chas. Kay, Lemuel Johnson. Sale, Sept. 8, 1836. Byrs: B. G. Jay, Wm. Wilson, Wm. P. Martin, Wm. Richey, Lewis Pyles, Hugh Wilson, Elijah Wyatt, Joel Stone, Silas Gains, Warren Bagwell, Thos. Kirkpatrick, etc.

WATSON, JAMES—BOX 96, PACK 2374:
Will dated Oct. 26, 1822 in Abbeville Dist. Prov. Dec. 20, 1823. Exrs: Son, Leroy Watson, Wm. Harris. Wit: Wm. Watson, John Henderson, Jas. Burns. Wife Mary Magdalene Watson. Chn: Leroy, Jas., Dorothy Jean Watson. Inv.' made Jan. 6, 1824 by Saml. Cothran, David Griffin, John G. Harris. Sale, Jan. 15, 1824. Byrs: Wm. Sadler, Jarrot H. Glover, Beverly Burton, Jas. F., Wm. Watson, John Ramsey, Thos. Stallworth Sr., John Johnson, Wm. Hammonds.

WALKER, WILLIAM—BOX 96, PACK 2375:
Est. admnr. Jan. 24, 1826 by Jas. A. Walker, Wm. Anderson, Geo. Huston unto Moses Taggart Ord. Abbeville Dist. sum $2,000.00. Inv. made July 15, 1826 by Wm. Anderson Sr., Wm. Brownlee, Joseph Pulliam, Stephen Durham.

Mississippi Carroll County
July 13, 1844

Dear Bro.

I now take my pen in hand to inform you that we have had to part with our second daughter Nancy A. which died June 28 which it is the first death that we have wit. in our family but very little sickness since we have been together but thanks be to God for his kindness to us for our lives helth strength and being here we are all at present in tolerable health at presence we hope that these few lines will meet you all in good health but it is necesery that we should think all wise on that grate goodness power of that good and merciful god that directs and manages all things as he pleases and who then do wheter object that will of our heavenly father that is so good and merciful to us that his will be one I beseash you bros. and sis. pray for us I will inform you that there a good deal of sickness in our secsion of contry this summer and joining countys and very fatil what cause we cant tell we have had seasons of fine crops here I have had a hard year work so far I have cultivated near about 40 acres with one horse and· two little sones, Henry and Wm. with there hoing. Bro. I received your leater that you sent by cousin thos harris which informed me you would indever to do what you could for me *pervid* I would give you some athority to do and act for me so here I try to send you this power to collect that little morsel which is due me of my fathers estate. If I have any right there including all of you brothers and sisters I hop Saml you will manedy it with out any difaculty which I nevei recieved one pennys worth but was som thirty or forty dollars lowser I wish you to arang this matter with Jas. in peace and qiteness as brothers a to do I hope Bro. Jas. you will study my right and clame to be justus as well as your own bro. Saml I wish you to git this amount let it be little or much as I have an opertunity of gitting it brought to me this fawl or winter by Cousin Wm. Harris the preacher of the gospel if you can posable mak this collection for me send it by Mr. Wm. Harris and he will recept for me nothing more but remaines your brother and sister until death Wm. and Nancy Walker Saml. W. and Mary Ann Walker.

Written to Saml. W. Walker Abbeville Dist. South Carolina. Mar. 19, 1846 Wm. H. Harris recd. of Saml. W. Walker Sr. $260.25 in full of est. Wm. Walker decd. late of Abbeville Dist. to the heirs of Wm. Walker late of Carrol County, Mississippi. Expend: Jan. 16, 1830 recd. of Jas. Walker $20.87¼. Recd. of John Walker $34.50. Recd. of Robert G. Walker $5.37¼. Recd. of Mary Walker $8.20. Recd. of Nancy Walker $343.57¼.

WALKER, WILLIAM—BOX 97, PACK 2376:
Will dated Mar. 28, 1777 in Camden Dist. Prov. Feb. 4, 1784. Exrs: Wife, Mary Walker, Jas. Wilkinson Sr., Jas. Wilkinson Jr. Wit: Lewis

Standley, Archibald Steel. Chn: Jonathan, Geo., Mary, Martha, Susannah Walker. Inv. made by Daniel McClary, John Ross, Jesse Tate.

WHITE, ALEXANDER—BOX 97, PACK 2377:
Will dated July 4, 1819 in Abbeville Dist. Prov. Oct. 18, 1819. Exrs: Wife, Elizabeth White, Hugh Porter, Son, John White. Wit: Hugh Porter, John Jr., Jas. White. Chn: John, Nancy, Jas., Catarena, Martha White. Inv. made Oct. 27, 1819 by Saml. Scott, Hugh Porter, Jesse Camel.

WEED, ELIZABETH—BOX 97, PACK 2378:
Will dated Oct. 14, 1826 in Abbeville Dist. Rec. Dec. 20, 1826. Exrs: John Pressly Esq., Son, Nathaniel Weed. Wit: Jas. Richey, Saml. Morris. Son Nathaniel Weed. Gr: Son: Jas. son of Nathaniel Weed s. l. John Pressly Esq., Alexr. Davison. "Held notes on Geo. Penny, Jas. C. Nathaniel Weed. Sale, Jan. 12, 1827. Byrs: Jas. C., Nathaniel Weed. Thos. Eskridge, Saml. Jordon, Penny, Saml. Young Esq., John, Jas. Patton, John Pressly, Saml. Morris, Wm. Chiles. Est. admnr. Dec. 29, 1826 by Nathaniel Weed, John Pressly, Harris Tiner unto Moses Taggart Ord. Abbeville Dist. sum $500.00. Cit. pub. at Hopewell Church.

WOODS, ARCHIBALD—BOX 97, PACK 2379:
Est. admnr. April 30, 1819 by Jas. Woods, Saml. Drinkwater, Wm. Covington unto Moses Taggart Ord. Abbeville Dist. sum $7,000.00. Inv. made May 19, 1819 by Robt. Cozby, Stephen Jones, John A. Baskin, John White, Mathew T. Caldwell. Expend: June 30, 1820 paid Susan C. Woods $494.00. Sale, Nov. 10, 1819. Byrs: Wm. Simpson, Linsey Harper, John White, Robert Smith, John Harris, Jas. Woods, John Steward, Saml. Patterson, Wm. Carothers, G. W. Simpson, Jas. Simpson, John Moffet, Jane David, Rachel W. Woods, etc.

WATSON, RICHARD—BOX 97, PACK 2380:
Est. admnr. Dec. 23, 1824 by John Wesley Brooks, Jas. Dozier, Albert Waller unto Moses Taggart Ord. Abbeville Dist. sum $30,000.00. Expend: Jan. 5, 1825 paid Leroy Watson $321.00. Paid 2 trips to Columbia for Sarah A. Watson $15.00. For Mary E. Wason tuition at Columbia $100.00. Sale, Jan. 6, 1825. Byrs: Lavinia Watson, Thos. Saml. Henderson, James Watson, Abraham Light, Robt. Turner, Saml. Cochran, Isaac McCool, Lewis S. Simmons, Wm. Hammond, Saml. Caldwell, Wm. Watson.

WILSON, JOHN—BOX 97, PACK 2381:
Est. admnr. May 15, 1815 by Grisilla, Robert C., Wm. Wilson, Jas. Taggart unto Taliaferro Livingston Ord. Abbeville Dist. sum $2,000.00. Inv. made May 23, 1815 by Moses Taggart, Oliver Martin, Wm. Wilson. Sale, June 16, 1815. Byrs: Moses Taggart, Michael, Wm., Saml. A. Wilson, Jas. Lewis, Mrs. Grisilla Wilson, Alexr. Bowie, John Lathers, Robt. C., Nancy Wilson, Robt. Richey.

WATSON, CHRISTOPHER—BOX 97, PACK 2382:
Will dated Aug. 17, 1802 in Abbeville Dist. Rec. Nov. 30, 1808. Exrs:

Stephen Watson, Lewis, Randolph Mitchell. Wit: Benjamin Mitchell, Basil Hallum, Chas. Cobb. Wife Elizabeth Watson. Dtr. Susanna Watson. Inv. made Dec. 2, 1808 by Geo. Connor, Ambrose, Thos. Edwards. Sale, Dec. 3, 1808. Byrs: Benjamin Mitchell, Chas. Collins, Jas. Loveless, John Connor, John Wilson, John Philips, Jas. Hagood, Lewis Mitchell, Stephen Watson, Joseph Foster, Geo. Connor.

WARDLAW, JOSEPH—BOX 97, PACK 2383:
    Will dated Oct. 5, 1795 in Abbeville Dist. Rec. Nov. 10, 1795. Exrs: Wife, Agness Wardlaw, Bro., Hugh Wardlaw. Wit: Zachary Meriwehter, Isssac Heard, Jas. Douglass. Chn: Wm., John, Alis, James, Mary Wardlaw. Inv. made Feb. 2, 1796 by John Meriwehter, Robt. Griffin, Thos. Brightman.

WILSON, ROBERT—BOX 97, PACK 2384:
    Est. admnr. Sept. 6, 1783 by Bursheba Wilson wid., Wm. Farr Esq. unto John Thomas Jr. Ord. 96 Dist. sum 2,000 lbs. Inv. made Sept. 28, 1793 by Sisson, Chas., Parten, Barratt Travis.

WHITE, GEORGE, CAPT.—BOX 97, PACK 2385:
    Est. admnr. Feb. 7, 1814 by Wm. Esq., Leonard Waller unto Taliaferro Livingston Ord. Abbeville Dist. sum $10,000.00. Cit. pub. in the Villiage of Cambridge. Inv. made Feb. 21, 1814 by Joseph Wardlaw, Nathn, Thos. Lipscomb. Expend: Feb. 23, 1815 Recd. of Nancy White $996.35. Sale, Feb. 23, 1814. Byrs: Alexr. Travis, Joseph Wardlaw, Nathan Henderson, Jas. Coleman, Nelson P. Jones, Thos. Stallworth, Garland Burt, Creswell Moore, Wm. Stallworth, David Cunningham, Robert Walker, Jenry J. Chalmers, Jas. Sale, Jas. Ward, Thos. B. Waller, Walter Chiled, Catlett Conner, Walter O. Beckley, John G. Blewer, Thos. Brightman, Wm. Spikes, Willis Bostick, Billips Gayle, Chas. McGehee, Wm. White, Ira Griffin Esq., Armstrong Heard, John Walker, Jesse Loveless, John C. Mayson, Jas. Thornton, Richard Watson, Chas. Barker, John Scott, Thos. Lipscomb, Lew Goode, Michael Cauley, Leonard Waller, Jas. Matthews, Jas. Henderson, Joab Wilson, Nancy White, etc.

WRIGHT, ROBERT—BOX 97, PACK 2386:
    Est. admnr. Feb. 1, 1832 by Anne Wright, Jas. Armstrong, Wm. Cowan, the last 2 of Anderson Dist. unto Moses Taggart Ord. Abbeville Dist. sum $2,000.00. Inv. made Feb. 16, 1832 by L. W. Trible, Lydall Williams, Jas. Latimer. Sale, Feb. 16, 1832. Byrs: Stephen, Jas. Latimer, Anne, John Wright, Jas. Dixon, Jas. Cowan, Jas. Armstrong, Jonathan Pearman, Mastin Shirley, Jas. Webb, John Armstrong, Saml. Shirley, John Pratt, etc.

WILSON, WILLIAM, ESQ.—BOX 97, PACK 2387:
    Est. admnr. Feb. 5, 1811 by Jas., David H. Hawthorn, John P. Arnold unto Taliaferro Livingston Ord. Abbeville Dist. sum $4,000.00. Inv. made Feb. 18, 1811 by Joseph Hackney, John P. Arnold, Carr McGehee. Expend: March 6, 1811 Paid Joseph Hathorn $3.00. Sale, Feb. 21, 1811. Byrs: Mrs. Salley Wilson, Jas. Hathorn, Wm. Buchanan, Dabney McGehee, Joseph Hackney, John P. Arnold, John Wyly, John Arnold Sr., Benjamin Mitchell, Thos. Weir, Alexr.

Turner, Carr McGehee, Jas. Cobb, Robert Gibson, Jessee Gray, John Cochran, Zachariah Ray, Jas. Patterson, Felix Patterson, Jas. Pettus, John Turner, Micajah Petty, Benjamin Johnston, Joseph Cooper, Perry Anderson, Eli Dodson, Charles Cobb, Elijah Teague, Jas C. Logan.

WILSON, THOMAS—BOX 97, PACK 2388:
Est. admnr. Dec. 13, 1807 by Joel Lipscomb, Carr McGehee, Reuben Chiles unto Andrew Hamilton Ord. Abbeville Dist. sum $5,000.00. Inv. made April 5, 1808 by Robt. White, Alexr. Sample, John Caldwell. Expend: April 1, 1809 paid Wm. Wilson $16.64. Oct. 21, paid Martin Wilson $18.37¼. June 7, 1813 paid John Wilson legatee $4.00. Drury Wilson legatee $9.39. Nov. 21 paid John Davis legatee $5.16. Jan. 21, 1818 paid Jeconias Wilson legatee $501.00. Paid Elizabeth Wilson the wid. $575.27½. Paid Mathew Watson legatee $96.55. Paid Susanna Wilson legatee $102.87½. Feb. 20, 1811 paid Obadih Wilson $55.14. Paid Saml. Wilson $270.24.

WHITE, MARGARET—BOX 97, PACK 2389:
Will dated Sept. 6, 1812 in Abbeville Dist. Rec. Sept. 9, 1812. Exr: Jas. Cochran Esq. Wit: Jas. Devlin Jr., David Cochran. "Property to be divided between Sally McCollum's chn., John Henderson's chn., Robert Henderson's chn." Inv. made Nov. 5, 1812 by Jas. Jr., John Devlin, Chas. Caldwell, Wm. Norris, John W. Cochran. Byrs: Thos. Cobb, Thos. Jeffries, John Henderson, John McCollam, Joseph Sanders, Jamimah Tullock, John L. Cooper, Jas. Cochran, Wm. Norris, Pleasant G. Wharton, Toliver Livingston, Wm. Frazier, Alexr. Wilson, John Love, etc.

WRIGHT, JOHN—BOX 97, PACK 2390:
Est. admnr. Mar. 13, 1813 by Patsey Wright, Moody, Armstead Burt unto Taliaferro Livingston Ord. Abbeville Dist. sum $10,000.00. Cit. pub. at Smyrna Church. Inv. made April 7, 1813 by Wm. Hall, Wm. McDonald, Jas. Cochran, John Devlin. Byrs: Patsey Wright, Joseph Jones, Martin Palmer, John, Mathew Burt, Wm. McDonald, Allen Glover, Martha Wright, etc.

WARDLAW, POLLY—BOX 97, PACK 2391:
Will dated Nov. 6, 1813 in Abbeville Dist. Rec. Nov. 15, 1813. Exr: David Wardlaw. Wit: Hugh Wardlaw, Robt. Dowdle, Elizabeth Wilson. Wid. of Saml. Wardlaw decd. Chn: Geo., Betsey, Jenny W. Wardlaw. Other papers name written Mary ardlaw. Inv. made Dec. 1, 1813 by John Finley, Andrew Stevenson, Ebenezer, Jas. Miller. Sale, Dec. 2, 1813. Byrs: Wm. H. Barr, Wm. Bowman, Andrew Stevenson, John Finley, John S., Rachel Miller, Hugh Reid, Wm. Mayn, Jas. Leonyard, Jas. Liddle, Jas. Bailey, John Gilmore, Robert Roddom, Daniel Norwood, Thos. Kirkpatrick, Martin Thacker, Mary Gantt, John Wardlaw, Wm. Crawford, Agnes Lesly, David Christopher, John Gantt, Wm. P. Brooks, John Osburn, John T. Davis, Wm. Wray.

WINN, ROBERT—BOX 97, PACK 2392:
Will dated April 11, 1824 in Abbeville Dist. Prov. April 15, 1824. Exr: Andrew Rembert. Wit: Jas. W. Prather, Robt. Howard. Mother ment. name

not given. Neice, Eliza N. Groves. "Bequeath riding horse to Andrew Rembert." Inv. made April 22, 1824 by Joshua Dubose, etc.

WOOLDRIDGE, ROBERT—BOX 97, PACK 2393:
Est. admnr. Nov. 13, 1820 by Susannah W. Wooldridge, Saml. Linton Jr., Dr. Eli S. Davis unto Moses Taggart Ord. Abbeville Dist. sum $3,000.00. Cit. pub. at Little Mountain Church. Inv. made Nov. 20, 1820 by Jas. Crawford, Wm. McCalister, Archibald McMullan. Sale, Jan. 13, 1821. Byrs: John S. Allen, John Boyd, Jas. Ball, Joseph T. Baker, Jas. Crawford, Richard Fulton, H. M. Pitman, Jas. Harris, Susannah W. Wooldridge, etc.

WHITMAN, CHRISTIAN—BOX 97, PACK 2394:
Est. admnr. Feb. 26, 1830 by Jacob Whitman, David Martin, Jas. F. Griffin unto Moses Taggart Ord. Abbeville Dist. sum $400.00. Cit. pub. at Siloam Church. Inv. made Mar. 15, 1830 by Chas. B. Fooshe, Philip Day, Jas. Pert. Byrs: Mrs. Margaret Mitchell, Capt. Thos. B. Bird, Jacob Whitman, Stephen Ross, John Cothran, John Day, etc.

WHITE, FRANCES—BOX 97, PACK 2395:
Est. admnr. May 8, 1822 by Jas. Franklin, Thos. Edwards, Alexr. Sample unto Moses Taggart Ord. Abbeville Dist. sum $10,000.00. Cit. pub. at Providence Church. Expend: 1925 paid Daily L. White $1,471.58. Sale, Dec. 19, 1822. Byrs: Daily White, Joel Lipscomb, Wm. Beasley, John P. Gaines, Wm. Smith, Nathan Calhoun, Wm. Turner, etc. Inv. made May 20, 1822 by Alexr. Sample, Wm. Beasley, Jas. Smith, Robt. Young.

WIMBISH, SAMUEL—BOX 97, PACK 2397:
Est. admnr. Jan. 4, 1791 by Mildred, Saml., Jas. Wimbish, Wm. Hutton, Jas. Caldwell unto the Judges of Abbeville County sum 3,000 lbs. Est. admnr. again Feb. 10, 1816 by Saml. B. Shields, Benjamin Glover, Andrew Milligan unto Taliaferro Livingston Ord. Abbeville Dist. sum 20,000 lbs. Inv. made Jan. 26, 1791 by Wm. McKinley, John Harris, Joseph Turnbull. Byrs: Jas., Alexr. Wimbish, John Harris, Mrs. Mildred Wimbish, Saml. Wimbish. Another sale bill made Feb. 26, 1816. Byrs: Didanna Wimbish, etc.

WALLER, JOHN—BOX 98, PACK 2398:
Will dated Dec. 11, 1801 in Abbeville Dist. Rec. Oct. 8, 1802. Exrs: Wife, Elizabeth Waller. Sons, John Nickodeemus, Thos. Baxter Waller, Benj. Waller. Wit: Nathan Lipscomb, John Scogin, Thos. Heard, Benj. Chiles. Baptist Minister. Chn: Ann Marshall, Benj., John Nickodeemus, Thos. Baxter, Dorothy, Frances Jane Waller, Phebe Turner, Mary Magdalene Watson, Elizabeth Chiles. (Will of John N. Waller in same pack.) Will dated Sept.14, 1802 in Abbeville Dist. Exrs: Brothers, Benj., Thos. B. Waller. Wit: David Lilly, Abednego, Phebe Turner. Wife, Rhoda Waller "now pregnant with child." Son, Albert Waller.

WHITE, ANDREW—BOX 98, PACK 2399:
Est. admnr. June 11, 1798 by Jane White wid., Wm. White of Calhouns Creek, Wm. Garrett, Alexr. White bound to Andrew Hamilton Ord. Abbeville

Dist. sum $1,000.00. 1799 Recd. of Thos. White $4.00. Inv. made June 30, 1798 by Christopher Brooks, Joseph Brown, Jacob Clearman. Byrs: Wm. White Jr., Andrew Holland, Francis Drinkard, Jas. Nelson, etc.

WATSON, STEPHEN—BOX 98, PACK 2400:
Will dated 1807 in Abbeville Dist. Rec. Feb. 17, 1807. Exrs: Bro. Wm. Watson, John McGehee. Wit. names left out. Wife, Joanna Watson. Dtr. Peggy Watson. Inv. made Feb. 20, 1807 by Geo. White, John Chiles, Jas. Watson. Joanna Watson later married Charles McGehee. Sale, Mar. 10, 1807. Byrs: Joanna, Anthony, Saml. Youngblood, Robt. Finny, etc.

WEEMS, THOMAS, SR.—BOX 98, PACK 2401:
Est. admnr. May 21, 1806 by Martha, Moses Weems, John Sanders bound to Andrew Hamilton Ord. Abbeville Dist. sum $10,000.00. Inv. made May 29, 1806 by Major Chas. Caldwell, Josiah Chambers, Wm. Paul. Inv. of Capt. Thomas Weems (same pack.) made Dec. 12, 1794 by John McCord Sr., Jas. Foster Sr., Jas. Cochran. Wid. Elizabeth Weems. Sale, Dec. 11, 1794. Byrs: Thos. Weems Jr., Capt. Jas. Chalmers, Henry, John Weems Jr. Sale of Thos. Weems Jr. made June 20, 1806. Byrs: Marha, Moses, Wm., Thos. Weems, Jas. Wardlaw, etc.

WOOLDRIDGE, MAJOR GIBSON—BOX 98, PACK 2402:
Will dated Oct. 24, 1816 in Abbeville Dist. Rec. Nov. 2, 1816. Exrs: Sons, John, Thos. Wooldridge. Wit: Jas. Ball, David F. Hudson, Royall N. Lipford. Chn. ment. no names given. Admnr. bond of John Wooldridge (same pack.) made Mar. 3, 1817 by Thos., Robt. Wooldridge, Saml. Linton bound to Taliaferro Livingston Ord. Abbeville Dist sum $10,000.00. Inv. of John Wooldridge made Mar. 7, 1817 by Geo. Patterson, Ethel Tucker, Lindsay Harper. Sale, Jan. 8, 1818. Byrs: Mrs. P. Wooldridge, Patsy Wooldridge, Benj. Murray, Jas. Caldwell. Mrs. Leah Wooldridge bought at sale of Gibson Wooldridge.

WEED, MARTHA—BOX 98, PACK 2403:
Will dated Sept. 22, 1809 in Abbeville Dist. Rec. Oct. 2, 1809. Exrs: Jas. Cochran, Robt. Crawford, John Devlin. Wit: Wm., Margaret McCree, Ebenezer Cooper. Chn: Andrew, Nathaniel, Reuben, Martha Weed. Gr. Son: Reuben son of Reuben Weed. s. l. Jas. Cochran. Martha's chn: Jas., John, Reuben. 3 dtrs. ment. no names given. Inv. made by Nov. 22, 1809 by Thos. Jordon, Enos Crawford, Jas. Devlin Jr.

WHITE, JAMES—BOX 98, PACK 2404:
Will dated Dec. 6, 1797 in Abbeville Dist. Rec. Mar. 27, 1798. Exr: Wife, Margaret White. Wit: Mathew Edwards, John Henderson, Ezekiel Evans. Inv. made April 11, 1798 by Mathew Edwards, John Brannan, Joseph Sanders Sr. Sale, April 12, 1798. Byrs: Margaret Douglass, John Richmond, Wm. McIlwain, Jas. Russell, Benj. Gunnin, etc.

WEBB, JAMES—BOX 98, PACK 2405:
Will dated Aug. 12, 1794 in Abbeville Dist. Rec. Sept. 12, 1794. Exrs:

Andrew Webb, John McAdam. Wit: Wm., Agness Fullerton, Katren Jones. Chn: Elizabeth, Jas., Mary, Sarah, Agness, Andrew Webb. Inv. made Oct. 6, 1794 by John Murphey, John Lindsay, Wm. Brownlee. Sale, Oct. 21, 1794. Byrs: Jas., Elizabeth, Andrew Webb, Wm. Tyler, Robt. Gibson, Nancy Peacock, Saml. Miller, Leonard Saylors, etc.

WEST, WILLIAM, JR.—BOX 98, PACK 2406:
Will dated Feb. 14, 1785 in 96 Dist. Exrs: Wife, Jane West, Jacob Pope, Andrea Lea. Wit: John, Nancy Wood, Elizabeth Marsh. Chn: Thos., Jane, Elizabeth West, Mary Chiles. Inv. made 1786 by Nathan Melton, Daniel Parkins, Alexr. McDougal.

WEEKS, WILLIAM—BOX 98, PACK 2407:
Will dated Feb. 2, 1783 in Berkley County. Exrs: Benjamin Heaton, Mercer Babb. Wit: Saml. Pearson, John Ellemon. Dtr. Mary Coley. Other chn. ment. no name given. Gr. Dtr: Charata Weeks. Inv. made Nov. 28, 1785 by Wm. Weeks, Saml. Cannon, Jacob Chandler.

WILEY, JOHN—BOX 98, PACK 2408:
Est. admnr. Dec. 17, 1807 by Jas., Richard Gains, Jas. Johnson bound to Andrew Hamilton Ord. Abbeville Dist. sum $5,000.00. Cit. ment. Jas. Gains next of kin. Inv. made Jan. 19, 1808 by John Meriwether, Jas. Pulliam, Dabney Puckett. Sale, Feb. 6, 1809. Byrs: John, Mary, Geo., Wm. Wiley, Thos. King, Aaron Moore, Nancy Lawson, Andrew McFarran, etc.

WADDEL, ROBERT—BOX 98, PACK 2409:
Est. admnr. May 3, 1800 by Elizabeth Waddell, John Crawford, John Stuart bound to Andrew Hamilton Ord. Abbeville Dist. sum $500.00. Inv. made May 27, 1800 by Robt. Caldes, Jas. Robinson, Jas. Brough. Byrs: Saml. Gamble, Elizabeth Waddel, John Warden, Kesiah Patterson, Thos. Brock, etc. Feb. 25, 1807 Recd. from Jas. McElvey. One paper stated Elizabeth McElvey (alias Waddell.)

WIDEMAN, HENRY—BOX 98, PACK 2410:
Will dated June 25, 1803 in Abbeville Dist. Rec. Nov. 22, 1806. Exrs: Son, Adam Wideman, Thos. Grey. Wit: Joshua Hill, Robt., Jean McCravan. Chn: Adam, Jacob Wideman, Elizabeth Benton, Lucy, Sally Pruit. Gr. Chn: Jas. son of Lucy Pruit that goes by the name Jas. Davis; Clary, Leonard, Margaret, Sally, Jas. Couch heirs of Jas. Couch decd. Other legatees: Leonard, John, Thos., Mark Wideman, Clary Wilson. Inv. made Nov. 24, 1806 by Andrew McComb Sr., Capt. Wm. Gray, Joshua Hill, John Patterson.

WEEMS, HENRY, SR.—BOX 98, PACK 2411:
Est. admnr. May 14, 1814 by Thos. Weems, Jas. Stevenson, Geo. Conn bound to Taliaferro Livingston Ord. Abbeville Dist. sum $1,000.00. Thos. Weems next of kin. Sale, June 3, 1814. Byrs: Thos., Henry, Wm., Nancy Weems, etc.

WILSON, HENRY—BOX 98, PACK 2412:
Will dated Nov. 8, 1807 in Abbeville Dist. Rec. Dec. 15, 1807. Exrs:
Wife, Betsey Wilson, Meredith McGehee, Benjamin Glover, Joseph Bickley.
Wit: Thos. Casey, Geo. Patterson, Wm. Hyman. Chn. ment. no names given.
Inv. made by Ezekiel Noble, Henry Barksdale, Wm. Noble. Sale, Jan. 1. 1808.
Byrs: Wm. S. Wilson, Saml. Saxon, Eliza Wilson, Saml. Young, etc.

WARDLAW, NANCY—BOX 98, PACK 2413:
Est. admnr. Dec. 7, 1805 by Jos. Wardlaw (son of Joseph) Thos. Brightman, Wm. Wardlaw (son of Joseph) bound to Andrew Hamilton Ord. Abbeville Dist. sum $5,000.00. Cit. pub. at Siloam Church., ment. Jas. Wardlaw
next of kin. Sale of Joseph and Agness Wardlaw decd. made Jan. 1806. Byrs:
Hugh, Jas. Wardlaw Jr., Thos. Brightman, Eliab Wardlaw, etc.

WITTS, ELIJAH—BOX 98, PACK 2414:
Inv. was to be made 60 days from Feb. 21, 1785. Lived in 96 Dist.
(No other papers.)

WIDEMAN, JOHN—BOX 98, PACK 2415:
Est. admnr. Feb. 29, 1804 by Rhoda Eves, John Chiles, Geo. McBeth
bound to Andrew Hamilton Ord. Abbeville Dist. sum $2,000.00. Inv. made
Mar. 13, 1804 by Larkin Cason, Andrew McCormick, Edward (name not
plain.) Byrs: Mrs. Rhoday Eves, John Clem, Zachariah Posey, Henry Mouchet,
Polly Clark, Peter Fritz, etc.

WATT, SAMUEL, ESQ.—BOX 98, PACK 2416:
Est. admnr. Dec. 11, 1802 by Jannett Watt, Andrew, John Bowie, Wm.
Lesly bound to Andrew Hamilton Ord. Abbeville Dist. sum $10,000.00. Oct. 9,
1806 Mary, Elizabeth Watt recd. $623.51¼ of the est. of Jennet Watt
decd. Inv. made Jan. 4, 1803 by Wm. Lesly, Geo. Bowie, Ezekiel Evans.

WEAVER, AARON—BOX 98, PACK 2417:
Est. admnr. Nov. 14, 1782 by Jane Weaver, John Douglass, Lewis Clark
bound to John Ewing Calhoun Ord. 96 Dist. sum 14,000 lbs. Cit. ment. Jenney
Weaver of Nine Creek next of kin. Inv. made Nov. 14, 1782 by Russell Wilson,
Lewis Clark, John Douglass.

WOOD, JOHN—BOX 98, PACK 2418:
Est. admnr. Jan. 1, 1783 by Rebecca Wood, Martin Armstrong, Joseph
Venable bound John Ewing Calhoun Ord. 96 Dist. sum 14,000 lbs. Rebecca
Wood of Lawson's Fork next of kin. Inv. made Jan. 2, 1783 by David Lewis,
John Young, John Connor.

WOODS, WILLIAM—BOX 98, PACK 2419:
Will dated Nov. 8, 1802 in Abbeville Dist. Rec. Feb. 20, 1804. Wit:
Wm. Carrithers, Jeremiah Robinson, Hugh Mccklin. Wife, Susanna Carathina
Woods. Inv. made by Robt. Smith, Jeremiah Robinson, Wm. Carrithers.

WATSON, MATHEW—BOX 98, PACK 2420:
Est. admnr. Jan. 14, 1815 by Stephen, Morten Watson bound to Talia-

ferro Livingston Ord. Abbeville Dist. sum $1,000.00. Cit. pub. at Rocky Creek Church. Inv. made Jan. 19, 1815 by Humphrey Klugh, Wm. P. Arnold, Jas. Wedgeworth, Wm. Phillips, Robt. Roman.

WILSON, MATHEW—BOX 98, PACK 2421:
Will dated Nov. 3, 1834 in Abbeville Dist. Prov. Dec. 10, 1834. Exrs: Wife, Elizabeth Wilson. Son, Hugh Wilson. Wit: Robt. Gilmer Sr., Hugh Kirkwood, Saml. Houston. Chn: Elizabeth Ann Reid, John H., Jas., Hugh, Leroy C., Matthew Harvey Wilson, Matilda Vashti Branch. Gr. Chn: Jas., Matthew H. Strayn, Wm. Hadden, Wm. C. Kirkwood. "In consequence of my son Hugh Wilson going to move to Alabama my will that my son Mathew Wilson be Exr." Jan. 18, 1836 paid F. Branch legacy $150.00.

WRIGHT, WILLIAM—BOX 98, PACK 2422:
Will dated June 2, 1805 in Abbeville Dist. Rec. Aug. 2, 1805. Exrs: Wife, Elendor Wright. Son, John Wright, s. l. Jas. Wims. Wit: Saml., Mary Watson, Leuisey McCoy. Chn: John, Wm., Jas., Nancy, Eliza Wright, Jane Wims, Sarah Loson. Sale, Feb. 30, 1805. Byrs: Robt., John, Jones Lawson Jr., Jas., John, Elizabeth Wright, etc.

WADDELL, JOHN—BOX 98, PACK 2423:
Est. admnr. Jan. 13, 1812 by Joseph, Benjamin, Alexr. Houston bound to Taliaferro Livingston Ord. Abbeville Dist. sum $1,000.00. Ci. pub. at Hopewell Church. Inv. made Jan. 14, 1812 by Peter Brown, Archibald McMullan, Benjamin Houston, Joseph Brown.

WHITE, FRANCIS—BOX 99, PACK 2424:
Will dated Nov. 21, 1802 in Abbeville Dist. Rec. Dec. 10, 1802. Exrs: Son, Robt. White, Thos. Edward. Wit: John Connor, John Shotwell, Jas. Eddins. Chn: Francis, Robt., Wm., Durret, Caty White, Elizabeth Edwards, Judea Eddins. Gr. Son: Francis White Bostick.

WARDLAW, JANE—BOX 99, PACK 2425:
Est. admnr. Nov. 7, (no other date) by Jas. Devling, Jr., Jas. Cochran Esq., John Henderson bound to Andrew Hamilton Ord. Abbeville Dist. sum $5,000.00. Expend: May 1, 1810 paid Jas. Wardlaw Esq. for est. of John Wardlaw Esq. $101.03. April 8, 1813 paid Jas. Devlin and wife legatees $477.63½. Paid John Hearst and wife legatees $477.63½. Paid John, Wm. B. Wardlaw minor legatees each $477.63½. Paid Sally Wardlaw $49.50.

WHITE, CHARLES—BOX 99, PACK 2426:
Est. admnr. Dec. 26, 1812 by Wm. White, Jared E. Groce bound to Taliaferro Livingston Ord. Abbeville Dist. sum $5,000.00. Cit. pub. at Fellowship Church ment. Wm. White next of kin. Inv. made Jan. 20, 1813 by Jared E. Groce, John Chiles, Jas. Shackelford. Byrs: Wm., Geo. White, Wm. Bostick, Saml. Whitlow, Nathan Lipscomb, etc.

WOODIN, REBECCA—BOX 99, PACK 2427:
Will dated Nov. 20, 1784. Prov. Feb. 7, 1789. Exr: Dr. John Dela-

howe. Wit: Wm., Elizabeth Sophia Cunnington, Michail O'Brien. Was of St. Phillips Parish in the City of Charleston. "If I should die in Charleston to be buried as near the remains of my parents and sis. in St. Michails Church Yard. Bequeath est. to Dr. John Delahowe practitioner of Physic in the City of Charleston. To Daniel Bourdeauxa valuable rose diamond ring set round with 12 brilliants. Bequeath to Miss Eliza Bourdeaux, to Mrs. Matthews." Inv. made July 4, 1789 by Peter Gilbert, John Eymerie, Pierre Rogers.

WEDGEWORTH, WILLIAM—BOX 99, PACK 2428:
Will dated April 27, 1798 in Abbeville Dist. Rec. June 11, 1798. Exrs: Son, Jas. Wedgeworth, Joseph Matthis, Jas. Buchanan. Wit: John Lumbus, Zeri Rice, John Irwin. Wife, Ester Wedgeworth. Chn: Wm., Joseph, John Richard, Jane Wedgeworth. "Give to Jas. an orphan child living with me 5 lbs."

WILSON, ROBERT—BOX 99, PACK 2429:
Est. admnr. Mar. 27, 1798 by Jas., Matthew Shanks, John Waddell bound to Judges Abbeville County sum $1,000.00. Cit. pub. at Long Cane Church ment. Jas. Shanks next of kin. Inv. made June 2, 1798 by Matthew Shanks, Agness Massey, Wm. Hillhouse.

WARD, DANIEL—BOX 99, PACK 2430:
Est. admnr. July 7, 1809 by Benjamin, Lewis Mitchell unto Andrew Hamilton Ord. Abbeville Dist. sum $1,000.00. Inv. made July 8, 1809 by Ambrose Edwards, Lewis Mitchell, Basil Hallum. Sale, July 28, 1809. Byrs: Wm. Smith, Lewis Mitchell, Robt. White, Nicholas Overby, Pleasant Wright, Daniel Lafoy, Benjamin Mitchell.

WORTHINGTON, SAMUEL—BOX 99, PACK 2431:
Will dated April 20, 1781 in 96 Dist. Exrs: Saml. Pearson, Saml. Cannon, Marcer Babb. Wit: Thos. Burton, Jas. Holt, Solomon Martin. Chn: Mary, Martha, Robt. Worthington. Seven chn. ment. only 3 named. Byrs: David Martin, John Rachel, Sarah, Elijah Worthington, Jacob Chandler, Matthew Brooks. Inv. made in Newberry County Jan. 16, 1786 by Jacob Chandler, Matthew Brooks, Saml. Cannon.

WEED, NATHANIEL, SR.—BOX 99, PACK 2432:
Will dated Dec. 18, 1797 in Abbeville Dist. Rec. Mar. 27, 1798. Wit: John Young, Mary Hill, John Huston. Wife's name not given. "One half of est. to daughter Margaret Weed, Robt. Crawford Sr., Jas. Young Sr. Est. admnr. Mar. 27, 1798 by Margaret Weed, Robt. Crawford, Jas. Young, John Lesly, David Kennedy unto the Judges of Abbeville County sum $1,000.00. Inv. made Oct. 5, 1798 by Benjamin Hill, Jas. Foster Sr., David Kennedy. Sale, Oct. 10, 1798. Byrs: Jas. Cochran, Robt. Crawford, Jehu Foster, Robt. Jones, Jas. Young, John Douglass, Benjamin Hill, Saml. Morris, David Kennedy, Thos. Weams, Robt. Crawford, Robt. Henderson, Jas. Forbes, Jas. Calhoun.

WILLIAMS, SAMUEL—BOX 99, PACK 2433:
Expend: Nov. 2, 1802. Paid Richard Williams $5183. Est. admnr. April

27, 1782 by Benjamin Tutt, Wm. Moore, Joseph *Towles* unto John Ewing Calhoun Ord. 96 Dist. sum 14,000 lbs. Inv. made by Wm., Jas. Watson, Richard Henderson. Sale, Jan. 5, 1803. Byrs: Shadrick Henderson, Robt. Marsh, Nathan Anderson, Cresswell Morre, John Stephens, John Goudy, Jas. Forrest, Wm. McCrea, Wm. Harrison, John McCool, Benjamin Chiles, Joseph Williams, Joseph Conn, David Thompson, Peter Ball, Capt. Lewis Matthews, Richard Williams, etc.

WILLIAMSON, JOSEPH—BOX 99, PACK 2434:
Est. admnr. Dec. 8, 1804 by Jas. Collier, Jehu Foster, unto Andrew Hamilton Ord. Abbeville Dist. sum $5,000.00. Cit. pub. at Buffalo Church. Onv. made Nov. 30, 1804 by Uel Hill, John Prince, Josiah Patterson. Sale, Dec. 28, 1804. Byrs: Ann Williamson, Alexr. Houston, Alexr. Clark, Christian Barnes, Dale Palmer, Delinah Carl, David Boyse, Geo. Palmer, Jas. Conner Sr., Jas. Collier, Joseph Houston, Mary Pharr, Richard Terry, Susanna Bushelon, etc.

WILLIAMS, SIMEON—BOX 99, PACK 2435:
Will dated April 8, 1801 in Abbeville Dist. Rec. Sept. 23, 1801. Wit: Chas. Dodson, John Williams. Wife, Eaduf Williams. Chn. ment. names not given. My wife's son Isaac Sherodine to have an equal part with my chn. Owned 100 acres of land in Greenville County. Receipts: Dec. 15, 1802 Reuben D. Williams recd. $65.00. Inv. made Nov. 14, 1801 by John Hairston, John Sims, Jas. Lomax. Sale, Oct. 23, 1802. Byrs: Eduff Williams, Partain Hagood, Jas. Read, John Wilson, John Adams, John Willson, Jas. Lomax, Wm. Brown, Larkin Butler.

WALLACE, ROBERT—BOX 99, PACK 2436:
Est. admnr. April 29, 1782 by Isobel Wallace, Benjamin Tutt, David Maxwell bound to John Ewing Calhoun Ord. 96 Dist. sum 2,000 lbs. Isobel Wallace was of Cuffetown Creek. Inv. made June 22, 1782 by Jas. Harrison, Benjamin Glanton, Saml. Anderson.

WELLS, THOMAS—BOX 99, PACK 2437:
Est. admnr. May 12, 1792 by Ann Wells wid., Joel, Isaac Thacker, Nathaniel Bailey unto the Judges of Abbeville County sum 500 lbs. Cit. pub. at Upper Long Cane Church. Inv. made June 6, 1792 by Jas. Evans, Ezekiel Evans Sr., Isaac Thacker.

WILLIAMS, JOHN—BOX 99, PACK 2438:
Est. admnr. Dec. 11, 1782 by Israel Pickens, Wm. White, Alexr. Noble unto John Ewing Calhoun Ord. 96 Dist. sum 14,000 lbs. Israel Pickens was of Little River. Inv. made Apr. 30, 1783.

WEEMS, BARTHOLOMEW—BOX 99, PACK 2439:
Est. admnr. Jan. 22, 1801 by Margaret, Saml., Bartholomew Weems, Robt. Keown unto Andrew Hamilton Ord. Abbeville Dist. sum $5,000.00. Inv. made Feb. 13, 1801 by Robt. Foster, Robt. McClellan, Jas. Cochran. Cit. pub. at Smyrna Church. Expend: 1802. Paid Robt. Ferguson legacy $80.50.

Paid John Weems legacy $18.00. Paid Bartholomew Weems legacy $50.50. Sarah Weems legacy $50.50. Robt. Keown $50.50. Paid Emily Weems $131.00. Sale, Feb. 17, 1801. Byrs: Margaret, Jas., Saml. Weems, Saml. Stuart, etc.

WIMBISH, ALEXANDER—BOX 99, PACK 2440:
Will dated Sept. 16, 1817 in Abbeville Dist. Prov. Oct. 20, 1817. Exr: Bro. Wm. Wimbish. Wit: John Wimbish, Jordan Ramey, Peter Wimbish. Wife, Frances Wimbish. Chn. names not given. Expend: May 7, 1823 paid John C. Wimbish for corn for the family for year 1822, $40.00. Jan. 11, 1819 paid Sarah A. Wimbish $30.00. Paid Nancy F. Wimbish $35.00. Apr. 22, 1819 paid Lucy Wimbish $15.00. Paid Peyton C. Wimbish $20.56¼.

WOOD, JAMES—BOX 99, PACK 2441:
Est. admnr. Jan. 1, 1783 at Lawsons Fork by Mary Wood, Martin Armstrong, Joseph Vonable unto John Ewing Calhoun Ord. 96 Dist. sum 14,000 lbs. Inv. made Jan. 1, 1783 by John Timmons, Wm. Benson, Wm. Thomson.

WALLER, THOMAS B.—BOX 99, PACK 2442:
Est. admnr. Mar. 4, 1816 by Wm. White, Wm. Chiles, Nathan Lipscomb Jr. unto Taliaferro Livingston Ord. Abbeville Dist. sum 10,000˙ lbs. Expend: Feb. 10, 1818 paid Jas. Young gdn. for A. Waller $1,100.00. Paid Thos. Livingston for copying papers relative to the est. of John N. Waller $6.50. Sale, Mar. 7, 1816. Byrs: Sarah Waller, Chas. Maxwell, Jacob Anderson, Robt. Marsh, Chesley Davis, Zachary Meriwether, David Cunningham, Thos. Lipscomb, Andrew Huggins, Hyram Gains, Joanna McGehee, Edmund Lilly, Wm. White, Leonard Scott, John G. Bluer, Joseph Wardlaw, etc.

WALTON, JOHN—BOX 99, PACK 2443:
Est. admnr. Apr. 30, 1784 by Moses Walton, John Wyld, Jas. Carson unto John Thos. Ord. 96 Dist. sum 2,000 lbs. Inv. Apr. 1784 by Abraham Little, Thos. Baker, John Webb. Sale, June 25, 1784. Byrs: Moses, Nelly Walton, Michail Kay, Saml., Jas. Carson, Thos. Baker.

WILSON, JAMES—BOX 99, PACK 2444:
Est. admnr. Oct. 25, 1826 by Jas. Esq., Jas. Foster, Jas. R. Miller unto Moses Taggart Ord. Abbeville Dist. sum $2,000.00. Cit. pub. at Smyrna Church. Sale, Feb. 22, 1826. Byrs: Jane C. Wilson, Joseph Conn, Jas. Foster, John Morrow, Hugh English, Christian Ruff, Luke Mathis, J. L. Cooper, Andrew McGill, Jane Lesly, etc.

WHARTON, PLEASANT G.—BOX 99, PACK 2446:
Will dated Sept. 18, 1819 in Abbeville Dist. Prov. Nov. 16, 1819. Exrs: Wife, Nancy Wharton, Bartholomew Jordan. Wit: John Devlin, John L. Cooper, David Cochran. Chn. Sarah, Jas. C., Wm. L. Wharton. Inv. made Dec. 27, 1819 by Jas. Devlin, John, David Cochran, John L. Cooper, Jas. Cochran.

WARDLAW, JOHN—BOX 99, PACK 2447: •
Est. admnr. Jan. 21, 1834 by Wm., Joseph Wardlaw, David Thomas unto Moses Taggart Ord. Abbeville Dist. sum $3,000.00. Wm., Joseph Ward-

law was of Laurens Dist. Inv. made Feb. 12, 1824 by Robt. Hackett, John T.
Coleman, Jas. Shackelford. Sale took place at the residence of David Gilliams
Feb. 1824. Byrs: Thos. Marsh, Elijah, Robt. Hackett, Harrison Monday, Jesse
Henderson, Ann Pert, Wm. Wardlaw, Jas. Pert, John V. Reynolds, Zachary
Meriwether, Jas. Henderson.

WARDLAW, JOHN, SR., ESQ.—BOX 100, PACK 2448:
    Will dated Feb. 6, 1791 in Abbeville Dist. Prov. Apr. 5, 1791. Exrs:
Wife, Lydda Wardlaw, Joseph Wardlaw, John Meriwether. Wit: Wm. Logan,
Wm. Wardlaw, A. C. Mastin. Chn: Jas., Saml., Hugh, Mary, Lydda, Peggy,
Hannah, Nancy, Betty Wardlaw, Isbel Heard. Est. admnr. Oct. 22, 1804 by Jas.
Wardlaw Esq., John Burton, John Hodges, David Esq., Wm. Wardlaw unto
Andrew Hamilton Ord. Abbeville Dist. sum $10,000.00. Inv. made Nov. 3, 1804
by John Logan, Saml. Anderson, David, Robt. Wardlaw. Sale, Nov. 10, 1804.
Byrs: Jane Wardlaw wid. Peggy, Jas. Wardlaw, Wm. Forgay, John Wardlaw,
Hugh Morrah Esq., Geo. Bowie Esq., John Wright, Wm. McIlwain, Capt. John
Hodges, Saml. Anderson, Terry Lomax, Chas. Mitchel, John Davison, Archibald
Hamilton, Hugh Wardlaw, Jas. Heard, Thos. Heard, etc.

WARDLAW, JOHN—BOX 100, PACK 2449:
    Est. admnr. Feb. 4, 1826 by Margaret Wardlaw, Bartholomew, Alexr.,
Saml. Jordon unto Moses Taggart Ord. Abbeville Dist. sum $8,000.00. John
Edward Foster married Jane Wardlaw a dtr. Inv. made Feb. 8, 1826 by Col.
John Hearst, Jas. Devlin, Saml. Jordon, Hiram Moore. Wm. A. Moore married
Margaret L. Wardlaw.

WARE, GEN. EDWARD—BOX 100, PACK 2450:
    Will dated Mar. 8, 1833 in Abbeville Dist. Prov. Apr. 17, 1833. Exrs:
Sons, Thos. E., Albert N. Ware, s. l., Jas. S. Rodgers. Wit: Wm. Ware, Jas. H.
Baskin, Thos. P. Spierin. "Desire to be burried in Turkey Creek Church yard
where some of my chn. are buried." Chn: Albert N. Ware by my first marriage,
Louisa Catharine, Jas., Henry, Nimrod Washington Ware, Emily R. wife of
Jas. Rodgers, Thos. Edwin, Peregine P., Edmund P. Ware. Wife, Peggy Ware.

WHITE, WILLIAM—BOX 100, PACK 2451:
    Expend: Sept. 19, 1809 paid Stephen Bostick gdn. of Francis W.
Bostick legacy $111.02½. Nov. 27, paid Stephen Bostick legacy $14.00. Dec. 3,
paid Francis White legacy $39.00. Apr. 2, 1810 paid Durret White $58.18¾.
Robt. White the admnr. No other papers.

WHITE, WILLIAM—BOX 100, PACK 2452:
    Will dated Apr. 19, 1819 in Abbeville Dist. Prov. July 23, 1819. Exrs:
Alexr. White, Wm. H. Caldwell. Wit: Wm. Norris, Jas. B. Gillespie, Martha
White. Wife, Jane White. Chn: Alexr. White, Mary McCarley. Gr. Chn:
Martha dtr. of Alexr. White, Andrew White. "Bequeath to Wm. son of Thos.
White." Inv. made Jan. 9, 1808 by Pleasant Wright, Alexr. Sample, Micajah
Poole. (This inv. must be of another Wm. White.) Sale, Nov. 18, 1819. Byrs:
Martin Shoemaker, Geo. Green, Jas. Pursley, John Sims, Andrew Smith, Hudson

Pitman, Jas. T. Williams, John Sigman, Abraham Woton, Abraham Outon, Joseph Simpson, Jane, Jas., Alexr. White, etc.

WHITE, WILLIAM—BOX 100, PACK 2453:
Will dated May 16, 1821 in Abbeville Dist. Probated June 11, 1821. Exrs: Wm. Chiles, Richard M. White, Joseph N. Whitner. Wit: Robt. H. Woolfolk, Jas. Payne, Catlett Conner. Nephews: John, Wm. Waller. Neice, Susannah Waller, chn. of my sis. Sarah Waller decd. Bro., Richard M. White. Sis: Elizabeth Pollard wid. of Wm. Pollard decd. B. l., Jas. Coleman, my sis. Nancy Coleman his present wife. "Give negroes to the chn. of my said sis. Nancy by former marriage with Geo. White with the exception of Agness Bullock to wit, Wm., John, Mary Ann, Leonard, Richard." B. l. Wm. Chiles. Husband of my sis. Tabitha Chiles. Neices: Caroline, Mary Ann Waller. Nephew, Wm. Waller chn. of Wm. Waller and my sis. Susan Waller. Neice, Agness wife of Wm. Bullock. Neice, Susan wife of Ira Griffin. Neice, Sarah wife of Jas. Hubbard. Inv. made July 2, 1821 by Robt. H. Woolfolk, David Cunningham, John Johnson.

WOOLRIDGE, PATSEY—BOX 100, PACK 2454:
Est. admnr. Sept. 5, 1824 by Alexr. Hunter, John Power Sr., Robt. F. Black unto Moses Taggart Ord. Abbeville Dist. sum $5,000.00. Cit. ment. Geo. Palmer next of kin. Inv. made Feb. 9, 1807 by Joshua Hill, Jas. Foster, Chas. Britt.

WALLACE, RICHARD—BOX 100, PACK 2455:
Est. admnr. Jan. 30, 1807 by Geo., Dale Palmer, John Hays unto Andrew Hamilton Ord. Abbeville Dist. sum $5,000.00. Cit. ment. Geo. Palmer next of kin. Inv. made Feb. 9, 1807 by Joshua Hill, Jas. Foster, Chas. Britt.

WHITE, JOHN—BOX 100, PACK 2456:
Est. admnr. Nov. 19, 1839 by Robt. H., David, Wm. Lesly, Jas. Thompson, unto Moses Taggart Ord. Abbeville sum $3,000.00. Cit. pub. at Providence Church. Inv. made Dec. 17, 1809 by J. H. Baskin, Wm. C. Cozby, Mathew Young, T. Shackelford, John G. Caldwell, Elizabeth White the wid.

WHITE, JOHN—BOX 100, PACK 2457:
Will dated Sept. 23, 1785 in Abbeville Dist. Rec. Mar. 25, 1794. Exrs: Ezekiel Evans, Wm. Lesly Sr. Wit: Saml. Watt, Saml. Houston, Henry Purdy. Wife, Agness White. Chn. and gr. chn: Jas., Sarah, Margaret, Jannet White. Inv. made May 1794 by Robt. Simmons, John Brannan, John McCord Sr.

WHITE, JOHN—BOX 100, PACK 2458:
Will dated Feb. 9, 1827 in Abbeville Dist. Prov. June 4, 1832. Exrs: Wife, Margaret White, son, Wm. White. Wit: Patrick Gibson, Abraham, Timothy Russell. Chn: Wm., Sarah White, Letty wife of Joseph Ashney, Frederick, Polly, Jas., John, Anny White. Inv. made July 18, 1832 by Abraham Russell, Young Reagin, Thos. McBride.

WHITE, JOHN—BOX 100, PACK 2459:
Will dated Feb. 9, 1827 in Abbeville Dist. Prov. Feb. 16, 1827. Exrs:

Wife, Isabella White, John White Jr. Wit: David Pressly Sr., Nathan Bowie, Henry Bowen. Inv. made Feb. 17, 1827 by David Pressly Sr., John Robison, Arthur Bowie.

WEEMS, MARGARET—BOX 100, PACK 2460:
Will dated Aug. 7, 1821 in Abbeville Dist. Prov. Dec. 22, 1823. Exrs: Son, Jas. Weems, s. l., Thos. Jordan. Wit: John, Martha Devlin. Legatees: Thos. Jordan, John, Bartholomew Weems, Isabella Keown, Saml., Jas. Weems. Gr. dtr: Nancy Ferguson, s. l. Robert Ferguson. "Bequeath $5.00 to the Missionary Society of the Presbyterian Church." Expend: 1 note on Robt. Keown $39.56½.

WEEMS, EMILY—BOX 100, PACK 2461:
Est. admnr. Aug. 6, 1827 by Henry Gray, Geo. Lomax, Henry Norrell unto Moses Taggart Ord. Abbeville Dist. sum $2,000.00. Will dated Mar. 2, 1827. Prov. Mar. 24, 1827. Exrs: Jas. Wardlaw Simeon Bonom. Wit: Jas., A. E., Jane Weems. Gr. chn: John B. Weems, Emily, Jane McDonnal. Expend: Paid Jas. Weems $159.85.

WATSON, ARTIMAS—BOX 100, PACK 2462:
Est. admnr. Dec. 5, 1786 by Daniel Bullock, Barrett Traverse, Joseph Nunn, David Collier unto John Thomas Jr. Ord. 96 Dist. sum 500 lbs. Inv. made Dec. 5, 1786 by Nicholas Lewis, Wm. Butler, Frederick Sisson. One paper ment. Hannah Bullock admnr.

WATSON, MICHAEL—BOX 100, PACK 2463:
Will dated May 26, 1782 in 96 Dist. Probated July 22, 1782. Exrs: Wife, Martha Watson, Arthur Watson, Robt. Stark. Wit: Robt. Stark, Wm. R. Withers, Richman Watson. Chn: Elijah Watson. Other chn. names not given.

WILSON, MICHAEL—BOX 100, PACK 2464:
Will dated Apr. 16, 1784 in 96 Dist. Rec. Mar. 25, 1784. Exr: Wife, Margaret Wilson. Wit: John McCord, Matthew Donalson, Saml. Houston. Chn: Chas., John Wilson.

WORRILL, AMOS—BOX 100, PACK 2465:
Est. admnr. Dec. 30, 1811 by Lucy, Solomon Worrill, Augustin E. Scudday, Wm. P. Raiford unto Taliaferro Livingston Ord. Abbeville Dist. sum $5,000.00. Following recd. property at different times. Mary Hammonds after her marriage by A. Worrill decd. and Lucy Worrill, Richard, Solomon, Ramain Worrill. Sale, Jan. 16, 1812. Byrs: Lucy Worrill, Job Hammond, Solomon, Sarah Worrill, Wm. P. Raiford, Saml. Scott, Joseph Bickley, Jas. Ball, John Montgomery, Robt. Baird, etc.

WINN, THOMAS—BOX 100, PACK 2466:
Will dated Oct. 31, 1796 in Abbeville Dist. Rec. Mar. 28, 1797. Exrs: Wife, Letice Winn, John N., Jas. Carter. Wit: Geo. Whitefield, Wm. Adams, Saml. McCleskey. Chn: Lettice, Robt., Abner, Elemuel, Thos. Winn. "Bequeath to my son Elisha Winn the money due me out of my bro. Washington Winn's

est. in *Luninburgh* County in Virginia." Inv. made Apr. 1797 by Jeremiah Beall, Richard Posey, Duke Beall.

WALLER, ELIZABETH—BOX 100, PACK 2467:
    Will dated Aug. 1, 1803 in Abbeville Dist. Rec. Jan. 29, 1804. Exrs: Sons, Benjamin, Thos. B. Waller. Wit: Leonard Waller, Polley Hill. Chn: Dorothy Waller, Ann Marshall, Benjamin, Thos. B. Waller, Pheba *Coliler*, Mary M. Watson, Elizabeth Chiles, Frances Jean Wardlaw. Inv. made by Geo. White, Leonard Waller, Richard Griffin.

WILLIAMS, CHARLES—BOX 100, PACK 2468:
    Est. admnr. Aug. 30, 1782 by Celia Williams wid., Joshua Gray, Ebenezer Starnes unto John Ewing Calhoun Ord. 96 Dist. sum 14,000 lbs. Was of Stevens Creek. Inv. made Sept. 3, 1782 by Ebenezer Starnes, Joshua Gray, Saml. Stalnaker, Thos. Freeman.

WOODS, ESTHER—BOX 100, PACK 2469:
    Will dated Feb. 4, 1815 in Abbeville Dist. Rec. Feb. 10, 1816. Exrs: Francis Young Jr., Thos. Finley. Wit: Sarah A. Clark, Catharine Green. Son, Wm. Young. "Bequeath to Ruth Wilson, Catharine Green. Desire that Francis Young Jr. take care of my son Wm. Young. Inv. made Mar. 1, 1816 by Saml. Young, Thos. Ansley, Aaron Jones. Sale, Apr. 1, 1816. Byrs: Francis Young Jr., John Baskin, Saml. Young, Geo. Wilson, Aaron Jones, Catharine Green, John Young, James Wilson, Thos. Dickie, Johnson Martin, Jas. Harris, Geo. L. Green, Francis Young Sr., Thos. Caldwell.

WATKINS, WILLIAM—BOX 100, PACK 2470:
    Will dated Oct. 22, 1805. Rec. Nov. 18, 1805. Exrs: Wife, Sarah Watkins, John Watkins. Wit: John Ball, Elisha Weatherford, Micajah Stevens. Chn: Willis, Henry, Ester Watkins. Inv. made Dec. 10, 1805 by John Ball, Jas. Campbell, Wm. Grubs. Byrs: Henry Johnson, John Crafford, John Ball, John Calhoun, Robt. White, Micajah Pool, John Watkins, Micajah Stephens, Jas. Campbell, Geo. Heard, John Gooshe, Jas. Eddins, Robt. Sample.

WEEMS, WILLIAM—BOX 100, PACK 2471:
    Est. admnr. Jan. 22, 1801 by Wm. Jr., Emily Saml. Weems, John Row unto Andrew Hamilton Ord. Abbeville Dist. sum $1,000.00. Sale, Feb. 20, 1801. Byrs: Wm. Weems, Robt. Hairston, Jas. Cochran Andrew Calhoun, David Pressly, John Row, Jas. McCool, Jeney H., Saml. Weems, Jas. Stephenson, Thos. Jordon, Jas. Baker.

WILSON, GEORGE—BOX 100, PACK 2472:
    Est. admnr. June 9, 1795 by Anne Wilson wid., Jas. Richey Jr., John Martin, Robt. Gibson, Henry Purdy unto the Judges of Abbeville County sum 2,000 lbs. Geo. Wilson was an innkeeper. Sale, July 14, 1795. Byrs: Edward Sharp, Saml. Lindsey, Chas. Cullons, Henry Gotcher, Rev. Peter McMullan, Chas. Hulsey, Wm. Ross, Pleasant Wright, John Lindsey, Wm. Tyner, John Pruitt, Wm. Tyler, Joseph Brown, Saml. Miller, Wm. McCrone, Wm. Dickson, Wm. Pratt, Wm. Maddon, Ann Kelley, Henry Purdy, Caleb Conaway, etc.

WATKINS, HENRY—BOX 101, PACK 2473:
Est. admnr. Mar. 26, 1793 by Seleter Watkins wid., Jas. Watkins, John
Nash, Thos. Shirley unto the Judges of Abbeville County sum 1,000 lbs. Inv.
made June 1, 1793 by Herod Freeman, Reuben Nash, Wm. White. Sale, Oct.
10, 1793. Byrs: Wm. Putman, Jas., Seleter Watkins, Jas. Barmore, Robt. Gibson,
Pressly Owens, John Rutledge, John Brownlee, Thos. Watts, John Mitchell,
Wm. Davis, Wm. Reeve, Wm. Woods.

WALLIS, JOHN—BOX 101, PACK 2474:
Will dated 1781. Prov. Sept. 19, 1785. Exr: Wife, Mary Wallis. Wit:
John Crozier, Daniel Hogan, John Roberts. Was of the Province of Georgia
and Parish of St. Mathew. Chn: *Miche*, Jesey, Jonathan Wallis. "Owned land
in South Carolina on the waters of Enoree." Inv. made Oct. 29, 1785 by Alexr.
Harper, Jacob Roberts, Joseph Barten.

WARE, NICHOLAS—BOX 101, PACK 2475:
Will dated Feb. 7, 1787 in Abbeville Dist. Prov. Apr. 26, 1787. Exrs:
Wm. Ware, John Nash, Joseph *Reden*. Wit: John Hall, Archibald Shirley, C.
Matthews. Chn: Frances, Wm., Thos., Jas., Betsey, Edmond, Nathaniel Ware,
Nancy wife of Jas., Geo. Wilder the husband of Frances. Inv. made May 2,
1787 by Chas. Davenport, Saml. Rosamond, Thos. Foster.

WATT, JENNET—BOX 101, PACK 2476:
Will date left out. Rec. Mar. 2, 1805. Exrs: Jas. Wardlaw Esq., Jas.
Kyle, Andrew Bowie. Wit: Robt. Wilson, Geo., Andrew Bowie, Ezekiel Evans
Jr. Chn: Polly, Elizabeth, Nancy, Jenny, Saml. Lesly Watt, Rosey Ann Bowie.
Nephews, John, Saml. Watt Bowie. "To Jennet Lesley Miller, Peggy Miller
$8.00 each." Inv. made April 20, 1805 by Geo. Bowie, Ezekiel Evans, Robt. C.
Gordon.

WARD, JOSEPH—BOX 101, PACK 2477:
Will dated Mar. 13, 1796 in Abbeville Dist. Rec. Mar. 26, 1798. Exrs:
Wm. Ward. Francis Carlile. Wit: Thos. Adams, David Welch. Wife, Agness
Ward. Bro., Peter Ward. Chn. names not given. Inv. made April 7, 1798 by
Francis Young, Jas. Caldwell, John Harris. Expend: Mar. 23, 1799. Paid Mary
Ward on pro. acct. $9.00. Apr. 20, 1799 recd. of Thos. Ward $3.25. Sale,
Mar. 22, 1799. Byrs: Peter Brown, Wm. Ward, John Drinkwater, Henry
Bole, John Bole, Robt. Patterson, John Tillman, Francis Carlile, Wm. Bole, John
Baskin, Carey Evins, Lewis Howland, Isaac Bole, Saml. Young, David Maddin,
Robt. Denham, John Baker, Richard Grier, Jas. Trimble, Peter Wimbish.

WARDLAW, JOHN (MINORS)—BOX 101, PACK 2478:
On Sept. 17, 1827 Margaret Wardlaw, Bartholomew Jordan, Jas. Devlin
bound unto Moses Taggart Ord. Abbeville Dist. sum $3,000.00. Margaret
Wardlaw made gdn. of Jane, David, Margaret Wardlaw minors under 14 yrs.
On Jan. 27, 1827 Margaret Wardlaw made gdn. of Wm. Wardlaw a minor
under 14 yrs. Est. of John Wardlaw decd. made Feb. 9, 1847, to ascertain the
share of David Wardlaw now of age. After examining the papers containing

the accts. and taking as the basis of the one between Foster and Wife and Wm. A. Moore and wife etc.

WELLS, ELIZABETH (MINOR)—BOX 101, PACK 2479:
On Dec. 2, 1811 Jeremiah Burnett, John Chiles, Jas. Cochran bound unto Taliaferro Livingston Ord. Abbeville Dist. sum $5,000.00. Jeremiah Burnett made gdn. of Elizabeth Wells a minor under 14 yrs. Expend: Jan. 1, 1813 recd. of Thos. Burnett Exr. of John Wells decd. $305.67¾.

WELLS, MARY (MINOR)—BOX 101, PACK 2480:
On Dec. 2, 1811 John Donald, Thos. Lyon, Jas. Cochran bound to Taliaferro Livingston Ord. Abbeville Dist. sum $5,000.00. John Donald made gdn. of Mary Wells minor under 14 yrs. The est. of John Wells decd. to John Donald.

WELLS, PAMALA—BOX 101, PACK 2481:
On Nov. 18, 1833 Walter Anderson, Jabez W. H. Johnson bound unto Moses Taggart Ord. Abbeville Dist. sum $540.00. Walter Anderson made gdn. of Pamelia Wells a minor. On Oct. 28, 1831 John W. Anglin, Walter Anderson, Washington Sample bound unto Moses Taggart Ord. Abbeville Dist. sum $1,000.00. John W. Anglin made gdn. of Pamelia Wells minor over 14 yrs. Expend: July 7, 1834 recd. from est. Moses Wells $279.91½. Was the minor of Moses Wells decd.

WILLIS, (MINORS)—BOX 101, PACK 2482:
On July 18, 1835 Jas. C. Willard, Jas. Cason, Thos. P. Dowtin, D. M. Rogers bound unto Moses Taggart Ord. Abbeville Dist. sum $1,000.00. Jas. C. Willard made gdn. of Thos. J., Mary E., Sarah C. Willis minors. Apr. 17, 1845 W. N. Traylor recd. $4,026.35 in right of his wife Sarah C. Willis due her from est. of Joshua, Rachel Willis.

WILLIAMS, (MINORS)—BOX 101, PACK 2483:
On Nov. 13, 1837 Mary Williams, Jas. Gilmer, David Robinson bound unto Moses Taggart Ord. Abbeville Dist. sum $3,000.00. Mary Williams made gdn of Sarah M., Margaret S., Jas. N., Saml. L. Williams minors of Jas. Williams.

WATSON, MARGARET (MINOR)—BOX 101, PACK 2484:
On Oct. 24, 1809 Chas. McGehee, and Joanna his wife, Geo. White, Thos. B. Waller bound unto Andrew Hamilton Ord. Abbeville Dist. sum $5,000.00. Chas., Joanna McGehee made gdn. of Peggy Watson a minor 3 yrs. old the 18th of Mar. last.

WILSON, (MINORS)—BOX 101, PACK 2485:
On Oct. 4, 1836 Jabez W. H. Johnson, Downs Calhoun, John B. Davis bound unto Moses Taggart Ord. Abbeville Dist. sum $3,000.00. Jabez W. H. Johnson made gdn. of John W., Louisa E. Wilson minors. Wilson died in 1835 and Joel Smith admnr. with the will annexed. By the will the family

consisted of the wid. Pamela, Wm., Louisa E. Wilson. Wm. Wilson became of age in Aug. 1839 and left this country and has been absent ever since. Louisa Wilson of age in May 1843.

WILSON, WILLIAM & LUCINDA—BOX 101, PACK 2486:
On Nov. 2, 1829 Wm. H. Jones, Hannah Wilson, Lorenzo D. Wright bound unto Moses Taggart Ord. Abbeville Dist. sum $500.00. Wm. H. Jones made gdn. of Wm., Lucinda Wilson minors over 14 yrs.

WADE, JUDITH—BOX 101, PACK 2487:
On Dec. 21, 1811 Thos. Chiles, Richard Eskridge bound unto Taliaferro Livingston Ord. Abbeville Dist. sum $5,000.00. Thos. Chiles made gdn. of Judith Wade a minor over 14 yrs.

WARDLAW, HANNAH—BOX 101, PACK 2488:
On Mar. 8, 1802 Isaac Logan, Robt. Griffin, bound unto Andrew Hamilton Ord. Abbeville Dist. sum $5,000.00. Isaac Logan made gdn. of Hannah Wardlaw a minor.

WYLEY, (MINORS)—BOX 101, PACK 2489:
On Mar. 3, 1828 Saml. Young, John McComb, Andrew Bonner bound unto Moses Taggart Ord. Abbeville Dist. sum $6,000.00. Saml. Young made gdn. of Jane, John Wyley minors over 14 yrs., Elizabeth, Jas., Nancy, Sally, Polly Wyley minors under 14 yrs., Chn. of Thos. Wyley decd. Expend: Feb. 12, 1827 paid Margaret Wiley wid. of Thos. Wiley $282.12½.

WILLIAMS, CORNELIUS BROWN—BOX 101, PACK 2490:
Guardianship bond missing. One paper stated that Joseph Hutton was the gdn in July 1796. Expend: Nov. 4, 1796 recd. of Peter Brown for C. B. Williams schooling 7 shillings. On Nov. 23, 1796 Cornelius Brown Williams recd. a legacy left to him by the last will of Cornelius Brown decd.

WEEMS, JAMES, ESQ. (MINORS)—BOX 101, PACK 2491:
On Aug. 15, 1829 Agnes Weems, Bartholomew Jordan, Thos. Jefferson Weems bound unto Moses Taggart Ord. Abbeville Dist. sum $4,000.00. Agnes Weems made gdn. of Jas. Madison, Agnes Alvira, Jane Ann Weems minors over 14 yrs., Mary Malvina, Saml. Westley, David Weems minors under 14 yrs. Sett. made Nov. 26, 1844 to ascertain the share of Jas. Morris and wife Mary M. and also the portion of David Weems decd. who died a minor in Sept. 1844.

WILSON, THOMAS—BOX 101, PACK 2492:
On Mar. 22, 1815 Richard, Ira Griffin bound unto Taliaferro Livingston Ord. Abbeville Dist. sum $5,000.00. Richard Griffin made gdn. of Thos. Wilson a minor over 14 yrs.

WALKER, (MINORS)—BOX 101, PACK 2493:
On Oct. 8, 1838 Thos. Ferguson, Peter Smith, Ivy Taylor bound unto Moses Taggart Ord. Abbeville Dist. sum $5,000.00. Thos. Ferguson made gdn. of Frances, Willard, Mary, Amanda Walker minors.

WALLER, WILLIAM W.—BOX 101, PACK 2494:
On Jan. 5, 1829 Ira, Joseph Griffin, John Logan bound unto Moses Taggart Ord. Abbeville Dist. sum $5,000.00. Ira Griffin made gdn. of Wm. W. Waller a minor over 14 yrs. Expend: Feb. 6, 1832 recd. of A. Waller, L. Griffin admnrs. of est. of Jas. Coleman decd. $400.00.

WARDLAW, WILLIAM B.—BOX 101, PACK 2495:
On Mar. 18, 1818 John, John Hearst Sr., Jas. Devlin bound unto Taliaferro Livingston Ord. Abbeville Dist. sum $2,000.00. John Hearst made gdn. of Wm. Boman Wardlaw a minor over 14 yrs. On Dec. 4, 1809 Jas. Devling Jr., John Henderson, Jas. Cochran Esq. bound unto Andrew Hamilton Ord. Abbeville Dist. sum $5,000.00. Jas. Devling made gdn. of Wm. Boman Wardlaw a minor. Will of Wm. B. Wardlaw dated Mar. 22, 1826. Exrs: Col. John Hearst, Col. Jas Devlin. Wit: Thos. C. Perrin, John T. Pressly. Lived in Abbeville Dist. Neice, Jane Hearst. Nephews, John W. Hearst, Jas., Wm. B. Devlin, Wm. Wardlaw. Sis. Margaret Devlin. "Bequeath land to Col. John Hearst." S. l., Peggy Hearst. Bro. John Wardlaw decd. "Bequeath to Col. Jas. Devlin." Prov. June 27. 1826. Inv. made Aug. 12, 1826 by John Pressly, Thos. M. Downey, Bartholomew Jordan.

WIMBISH, PETER—BOX 101, PACK 2496:
Est. admnr. Nov. 13, 1819 by Joseph B. Gibert, Saml. Young, Andrew Milligan unto Moses Taggart Ord. Abbeville Dist. sum $200.00. Inv. made Nov. 27, 1819 by Richmond Harris, Benjamin, Jeremiah S. Terry.

WRIGHT, ROBERT—BOX 101, PACK 2497:
Will dated Mar. 24, 1813 in Abbeville Dist. Prov. Apr. 24, 1813. Exrs: Wife, Mary Wright, Suger Wright, John McAdam. Wit: Edward Hill, John Lanyard. Chn: Waddeys and her two sons, Thos. and Robt. Davis. Cattys, and her 3 chn., Joseph, Clement, Salley Woodward. Jared, John, Suger Wright, Latty dtr. of Jared Wright my son, Robt. Wright, Betsey, Polly, Daniel, Thornton, Lorenzo Wright. Inv. made June 19, 1813 by Isaac Cowan, John Lindsay, Zachariah Davis.

WILSON, JOHN—BOX 101, PACK 2498:
Est. admnr. Jan. 21, 1839 by Jas. W. Richey, John Seawright, John R. Shirley unto Moses Taggart Ord. Abbeville Dist. sum $10,000.00. Cit. pub. at Little River Church. Inv. made Feb. 2, 1839 by Weldon Pearmon, John R. Shirley, John Kay. Paper for 1844 ment. that Jas. Richey was gdn. for Wm. Wilson a minor.

WILSON, ELIZABETH—BOX 101, PACK 2499:
Est. admnr. Aug. 27, 1838 by Leroy C. Wilson, Wm. Bowie, Wm. Lesly unto Moses Taggart Ord. Abbeville Dist. sum $7,000.00. Sett. made Sept. 8, 1841. The admnr. Leroy Wilson with his council J. Wilson appeared at the instance of David Lesly attorney in fact of Jas. W. Lyle, for himself and as gdn. of Robt. Wilson to settle as to the shares of Jas. W. Kyle and Mary R. his wife, Robt. Wilson. Ment. 6 chn. but all names not given. Wm.

H. Barr gdn. of Susan Wilson a minor. Inv. made Oct. 31, 1838 by John Ware, Wm. Lesly, Saml. Gilmer.

WILSON, HENRY—BOX 101, PACK 2500:
Est. admnr. Feb. 2, 1835 by Jas. Y., Wm. H. Jones, Joel Smith, unto Moses Taggart Ord. Abbeville Dist. sum $1,000.00. Cit. pub. at Providence Church.

WELLS, SENA—BOX 101, PACK 2501:
Est. admnr. Dec. 5, 1831 by John W. Anglin, John N. Sample, Johnson L. Sims unto Moses Taggart Ord. Abbeville Dist. sum $2,000.00. Cit. pub. at Mt. Prospect Church ment. that Sena Wells had been absent about 10 yrs. On Nov. 5, 1831 Clement Wells relinquished his claim as admnr. on Sena Wells property to John W. Anglin. Sale took place at the late residence of Moses Wells decd.

WILSON, ROBT.—BOX 101, PACK 2502:
Est. admnr. Dec. 14, 1832 by Elizabeth Wilson, Saml. Reid, Allen T. Miller, Alexr. Bowie unto Moses Taggart Ord. Abbeville Dist. sum $3,000.00. Cit. pub. at Upper Long Cane Church. Expend: Jan. 4, 1836 recd. of Elizabeth Wilson $25.75. Dec. 3, 1834 paid on note to Jas. Wilson $231.59. Inv. made Jan. 9, 1833 by Robt. Gilmer Sr., Saml. A. Jack, Hugh Kirkwood.

WARDLAW. HUGH—BOX 101. PACK 2503:
Est. admnr. Feb. 25, 1833 by Nancy Wardlaw. Bartholomew Jordan. Jas. Devlin unto Moses Taggart Ord. Abbeville Dist. sum $2,000.00. Inv. made Mar. 11, 1833 by Bartw. Jordan, Hamilton Hill, Col. John Hearst.

WATSON. HEZEKIAH—BOX 102, PACK 2504:
Est. admnr. Oct. 27, 1828 by John W. Swanzy, Richard Anderson, Geo. W. Hodges bound to Moses Taggart Ord. Abbeville Dist. sum $1,000.00. Cit. pub. at Greenville Church. Inv. made Nov. 21, 1828 by Wm. Dunn, Jas. Hodges, A. C., Edward Weatherall. Sale, Nov. 27, 1828. Byrs: Gilla Watson, Rosannah Moore, Saml., Richard L. Anderson, etc.

WALLACE, ROBERT—BOX 102, PACK 2505:
Will dated Aug. 16, 1837 in Abbeville Dist. Exrs: Larkin Barmore, Saml. Donald. Wit: John Donald, Richard P. Bowie, Wm. Barmore. Wife, Nancy Wallace. Son, Geo. Wallace. "Est. to be divided between Allen McCullough, Reuben Richey of Anderson Dist. my wife's son and dtr., Elizabeth Drennon. May 17, 1841 paid John Donald Atty. for John, Elenor McCullough $261.84¾.

WARE, JANE—BOX 102, PACK 2506:
Will dated Mar. 24, 1832 in Abbeville Dist. Exrs: John E. Ellis Esq., Jas. Pringle. Wit: Thos., Martha, Mathew Hodge. Chn: Wm., Jas., Robt., Nancy Ware. Gr. Dtr: Jane Ware, Dec. 26, 1834 paid John Smith legatee $224.96¼.

WHITLEY, STEPHEN—BOX 102, PACK 2507:
Est. admnr. Dec. 27, 1839 by Mathew Mays, Larkin G. Latimer, Daniel

Carter bound to Moses Taggart Ord. Abbeville Dist. sum $20,000.00. Stephen Whitley was a half bro. to Meedy Mays Sr. who died without wife or child. Sett. Feb. 5, 1845. Present, Meedy Mays Sr., Meedy Mays Jr. The admnr. Matthew Mays decd. Wiley Culbreath gdn. of minor chn. of Abney Mays decd. Absent, John Mays and wife both lunatics, the said John not having been heard from in 7 yrs. His wife Nancy served with notice and child Frances represented by Wm. Mays. Catharine Perkins wid. of Abney Mays decd. Nancy Mays married Benjamin Broadway neither heard from in 10 yrs. Frances Mays was 10 yrs. old. Catharine Perkins was wife of Milton Perkins.
(Letter)
Wiston Asylum Jan. 15, 1845.
Dear Sir,
    Yours of the 6th inst. reached me in due course of mail & I avail myself of the earliest leisure to inform you that an individual answering the description given of your brother who calls himself John Mays, is a patient in this institution. He was brought here from the County of Franklin December 14th 1841. His mind is seriously (2 words can't make out) but he is certainly harmless & altogether inoffensive. He is occasionally disposed to wander off & within the last 10 days succeeded in doing so & was absent for two or three days. Generally however he walks at pleasure about the grounds. And for his disposition to wander would not even require the supervision of an attendant. His bodily health is quite good, and altho his mind will probably never be restored, he seems to be capable of appreciating comforts. Should his friends desire to remove him to South Carolina they will of course be permitted to do so. Indeed it would be proper that the authorities of the Lunatic Asylum in So. Carolina should be (word) where he is & that steps should be taken for his return. With respect,
                                Fras. T. *Shilling*
    (Written to Meedy Mays Sr. Abbeville Dist. Looked like letter was mailed at Staunton, Va. not positive.)

WATSON, STEPHEN—BOX 102, PACK 2508:
    Will dated Mar. 13, 1832 in Abbeville Dist. Prov. Nov. 8, 1839. Exrs: Robt. Buchanan, Joel Smith. Wit: Jas., Robt. Buchanan, Stephen Buzby. Chn: Morten, Matthew Watson, Sarah Cobb. s. ls. Steth Howlet, Jas. Jonsten. "Gave Steven Pulliam a negro." Sett: May 3, 1842. Sarah Cobb in Miss. Her chn. were: Thos. A., Lewis B. Cobb, Elizabeth *Leak*. Mathew Watson's chn; Eliza McCants, Elizabeth Jane Buchanan. Morten Watson's chn: Matilda, Hulda Pulliam, Belinda, John A., *Jabel*, Nancy Watson. Represented by Esq. McCants, Robt. E. Buchanan, Larkin Pulliam, John, *Jabel* Watson.

WATSON, RICHARD & EDWARD—BOX 102, PACK 2509:
    On Nov. 6, 1837 Dr. John P. Barratt, Stanmore B. Brooks, Griggsbey Appleton bound to Moses Taggart Ord. Abbeville Dist. sum $20,000.00. John P. Barratt made gdn. Richard, Edward Watson minors. Est. of Wm. Watson decd. in acct. with John Barratt gdn. of Richard Watson. April 16, 1838 cash on going to Alabama $81.50.

WARD, WILLIAM—BOX 102, PACK 2510:
Will dated May 13, 1837 in Abbeville Dist. Prov. Sept. 4, 1837. Exrs:
Wife, Martha Ward, Jonathan Johnson. Wit: John English, Jas. E. G. Bell,
Thos. Anderson. Son, Robt. Ward. Other chn. ment. names not given. Inv.
made Oct. 6, 1837 by Henry Moseley, Sugar Johnson, John English.

WALLACE, ROBERT—BOX 102, PACK 2511:
Est. admnr. Mar. 15, 1841 by Larkin, Wm. Barmore, Marshal Sharp
bound to Moses Taggart Ord. Abbeville Dist. sum $10,000.00. Sett: Distributees
Wid. Jane Wallace. Nancy, Geo., Elizabeth, Robt. R., Mary Jane, Ellenor,
John T., Dulinda, Ebenezer, Joanna, Luticia Wallace.

WILSON, JAMES—BOX 102, PACK 2512:
Est. admnr. May 29, 1782 by John, Martha Wilson, Col. Geo. Reid,
Capt. John Calhoun bound to John Ewing Calhoun Ord. 96 Dist. sum 14,000
lbs. Cit. pub. at Johns Creek ment. John, Martha Wilson of Long Cane. Sett.
next of kin. Inv. made July 16, 1782 by Alexr. Boyse, Geo. Reid, Jas. Seawright.

WITTS, STEPHEN—BOX 102, PACK 2513:
Will dated Sept. 10, 1840 in Abbeville Dist. Prov. Oct. 15, 1840. Exrs:
John Lipscomb, Bartholomew Jordon. Wit: Vincent Griffin, Leroy Watson,
Geo. Marshall. Wife, Parthena Witts: Chn: Lucinda Wetherford, Susan
McElwee, Mary, Franklin, Rachel, Phebe, Jefferson, Elizabeth, Thos., Wm.,
Smallwood, Williamson Witts. Inv. made Dec. 8, 1840 by Joseph Norrell, Geo.
Marshall, John Hearst Sr.

WOOD, DAVID—BOX 102, PACK 2514:
David Wood died Sept. 11, 1841. A brother to Jas. Wood Jr. Owned
house and lot in Cambridge. John Grand b. l. of Jas., David Wood made admnr.
after Jas. Wood died. Dated Sept. 13, 1843. Inv. made Jan. 27, 1842 by Wm.
B. Smith, N. W. Griffin, Thos. Scurry.

WOOD, JAMES—BOX 102, PACK 2515:
Est. admnr. Nov. 6, 1843 by John Grant, Jabez W. H. Johnson, Jas.
Wood, the 1st of Laurens Dist. unto David Lesly Ord. Abbeville Dist. sum
$1,000.00. Inv. made Nov. 21, 1843 by Jabez W. H. Johnson, Jas. Wood,
A. J. Patterson. Sale, Nov. 21, 1843. Byrs: John Grant, Elizabeth Wood,
Reubin Golding, A. J. Patterson, Nimrod Stuart, John Sadler, Isaiah Ramsey,
Angus Campbell.

WILLIS, THOMAS J.—BOX 102, PACK 2516:
Est. admnr. Oct. 16, 1843 by John, Adam, Leonard Wideman unto
David Lesly Ord. Abbeville Dist. sum $8,000.00. Thos. J. Willis died leaving
a wid. Was s. l. of John Wideman. Sett. April 2, 1844 of Thos. J. Willis
minor ward of Jas. C. Willard his gdn. for money from est. of Joshua, Rachel
Willis. Thos. J. Willis departed this life before age, leaving a wid. and a
postthumoruras child. Was son of Joshua Willis. Since his death he has a child
living. Martha T. Willis the minor and gr. child of John Wideman Esq. Sett.
of John Wideman admnr. of Thos. J. Willis decd. with Wm. K. Bradley who
married Sarah the wid. of T. J. Willis.

WARDLAW, JAMES—BOX 102, PACK 2517:
Will dated June 6, 1840 in Abbeville Dist. Prov. Apr. 26, 1842. Exrs:
Sons, David Lewis, Robt. Henry Wardlaw. Wit: Chas. H. Allen, John F.
Livingston, Jas. H. Cobb. Chn: David Lewis, Robt., Henry, Mary Caroline,
Hannah Margaret, Elizabeth Amanda, Joseph Jas., Wm. Alfred, Francis Hugh,
Jane Eliza Wardlaw. S. 1., Thos. C. Perrin. "$300.00 in trust for Mary Anne
wife of Benjamin Hodges." Gr. Dtr: Hannah Bonham. Sett. ment. Jane F.
Perrin, Joseph J. Wardlaw, Elizabeth A. Ramsey, H. Margaret Patterson. Inv.
made July 12, 13, 1842 by Benjamin Y. Martin, John Wier, Robt. Richey,
Wm. Brooks.

WAKEFIELD, HEZEKIAH—BOX 102, PACK 2518:
Est. admnr. Dec. 21, 1843 by Conrad, John Wakefield, Saml. C. Fisher,
John F. Clinkscales, Jas. A. Gantt unto David Lesly Ord. Abbeville Dist. sum
$20,000.00. John Wakefield was son of Hezekiah Wakefield. Inv. made in
Anderson Dist. by Silas W. Kay, Walter C. Dickson, John Grubbs. Sett. made
Feb. 23, 1847. Present, John Wakefield son and admnr. Cynthia Ann Wake-
field the wid. Saml. C. Fisher who married Rhoda a dtr., Jonathan Pearmon
who married Lete a dtr., Conrad Wakefield, John F. Clinkscales who married
Elizabeth C. a dtr., Jas. A. *Garret* or *Gannt*, gdn. of Isabella E., Jas. A.,
Benjamin F., Martin F., Eleanor A. Wakefield. Absent, Thos. A., Andrew J.
Wakefield.

WILLIAMSON, JOHN—BOX 102, PACK 2519:
Est. admnr. June 26, 1841 by Polly Williamson, Benjamin F. Jones,
John Vance unto Moses Taggart Ord. Abbeville Dist. sum $300.00. Polly Wil-
liamson was wid. Inv. made July 21, 1841 by John Vance, Austin Arnold,
B. F. Jones.

WRIGHT, ROBERT (MINORS)—BOX 102, PACK 2520:
On Dec. 7, 1840 John Wright, Ezekiel, Richardson Tribble bound unto
Moses Taggart Ord. Abbeville Dist. sum $2,000.00. John Wright made gdn.
of John W., Thos. L., Sarah Ann, Margaret Wright minors of Robt. Wright.

WRIGHT, SUSAN (MINOR)—BOX 102, PACK 2521:
On Feb. 11, 1841 Daniel S. Beacham, Chas. Dendy, Thos. R. Gray
bound unto Moses Taggart Ord. Abbeville Dist. sum $1,000.00. Daniel S.
Beacham made gdn. of Susan Wright a minor over 14 yrs.

WHITE, ALEXANDER & ROSANNA—BOX 102, PACK 2522:
Petition of Andrew J. McCurry on Mar. 18, 1844 sheweth that John
White decd. left a wid. Sarah and chn., both under 14 yrs. Alexr., Rosanna
White. Nathan McCalister, Sarah's bro. admnr. on est. of John White. Sarah
married Andrew J. McCurry. Rosanna White lived at the home of said McCurry
until 1851 when she left his house and never returned. Was of age in July 1858.

WILLIAMSON, DR. THOMAS G.—BOX 102, PACK 2523:
Will dated Mar. 28, 1841 in Abbeville Dist. Prov. June 7, 1841. Exrs:
F. 1., Jas. Gillam, b. 1., Robt. C. Gillam. Wit: Sarah C. Gillam, Jas. R.

Boulware, Jas. R. Fooshe. Wife, Susan C. Williamson. Son, Jas. Williamson. Sept. 1842 Susan C. Rudd recd. $2,218.94 from est. Sale, July 8, 1841. Byrs: Richard C. Griffin, John Holland, Dabney Calhoun, B. R. Worthington, John Simpson, Wm. Eddins, John Foy, Allen Vance, J. P. Watts, Jas. Gillam, Richard White, Susan Williamson, Elijah Witts, Capt. T. Nickolls, Susan C. wife of Daniel Rudd. Inv. made July 7, 1841 by Wm. Eddins, Jas. R. Boulware, David Gillam.

WALKER, SELAY—BOX 103, PACK 2524:
    Est. admnr. Oct. 15, 1842 by Jas. J., Robt. Devlin, John F. Livingston, unto David Lesly Ord. Abbeville Dist. sum $3,000.00. Left Mary Walker the wid. Chn: Robt. M., Sarah J., Joseph, Allen C. Walker. Jefferson Thomas married Mary Walker. There were 5 chn. in all. Sale, Nov. 23, 1843. Byrs: Mary Walker, Jas. Foster, Lewis Smith, G. J. Cannon, Jas. Wharton, Wm. Lyon, Robt. Walker, J. J. Devlin, Margaret Wardlaw, etc.

WILLIAMS, JOHN E.—BOX 103, PACK 2525:
    Est. admnr. Jan. 12, 1843 by Esther Williams, Wm. E. Dunn, Isaac Branch, Thos. Jackson unto David Lesly Ord. Abbeville Dist. sum $2,000.00. Left a wid. Esther Williams and 3 infant chn. Two were Saml., John Williams. Sale, Jan. 27, 1843. Byrs: Esther, T. D. Williams, B. Y. Martin, etc.

WIDEMAN, ADAM—BOX 103, PACK 2526:
    Will dated June 24, 1840 in Abbeville Dist. Prov. Oct. 7, 1842. Exrs: Sons, John, Adam Wideman. Wit: John Kennedy, Wm. Harris, Robt. McCasland. Chn: John, Saml., Joshua, Adam, Uel Wideman, Henry Wideman decd. Rachel Willis decd. Elizabeth Mars decd.

WEATHERALL, ELIZABETH—BOX 103, PACK 2527:
    Est. admnr. May 9, 1843 by Joseph S. D. Weathcrall, Joseph Dickson, Jas. Murray bound to David Lesly Ord. sum $6,000.00. Was mother of Joseph Weatherall. John Weatherall a son was in Franklin, Holmes Co. Miss. in Jan. 1845. Legatees in Pontotoc, Miss. Viz. Marshall, Geo., A. C. J. Weathcrall, Jas, Betsey J., Mary S. Hodges. Other legatees, John, F. E. Weatherall, Sarah M. Means.

WARE, JANE—BOX 103, PACK 2528:
    On Dec. 12, 1843, Jas., Wm. Ware, Ann Smith bound to David Lesly Ord. sum $300.00. Jas. Ware made gdn. of Jane Ware his dtr. a minor over 14 yrs. old who had a legacy left her by Jane Wire.

WARE, NIMROD W.—BOX 103, PACK 2529:
    In 1842 the petition of Thos. Edwin Ware sheweth that the said decd. died in Louisiana having no wife or chn., but bros. Was a son of Ed. Ware decd.

WEBB, ANDREW (MINORS)—BOX 103, PACK 2530:
    On Oct. 24, 1857 John Webb, Robt. Martin, Thos. R. Cochran bound to Wm. Hill Ord. sum $160.00. John Webb made gdn. of John M. Webb a minor. On Mar. 14, 1845 Andrew Webb, John Kav, Wm. W. Green bound

to David Lesly Ord. Abbeville Dist. sum $65.00. Andrew Webb made gdn. of
Manerva Jane, John Marshall Webb minors of Andrew Webb. Entitled to a
legacy from will of John Martin decd. Minerva J. Webb of age in 1857 and
wife of Mathew Williamson.

WALKER, WILLIAM F.—BOX 103, PACK 2531:
        On Jan. 15, 1845 Mary Walker, Robt. Devlin, Robt. M. Walker bound
to David Lesly, Ord. sum $300.00. Mary Walker gdn. of Wm. F. Walker a
minor under 14 yrs. Mary Walker sheweth that her husband Sila Walker died
leaving a wid. and 8 chn. that she has had an infant child by her said husband
Wm. F., who is an infant; the other chn. are her step chn.

WALKER, MINORS—BOX 103, PACK 2532:
        On Jan. 15, 1845 Robt. Devlin, John F. Livingston, Jas. Devlin bound
to David Lesly Ord. Abbeville Dist. sum $1,000.00. Robt. Devlin made gdn.
of Sarah J., Joseph T., Allen Sila, Henry H., Jas. A. Walker minors.

WATSON, LEROY—BOX 103, PACK 2533:
        Will dated Jan. 17, 1844 in Abbeville Dist. Prov. Oct. 10, 1851. Exrs:
Bro. Jas. F. Watson, Albert Waller. Son, Jas. Leonard Watson. Wit: Milton W.
Coleman, Wm. P. Hill, Tandy Turner, Thos. S. Henderson. Chn: Jas. Leonard,
Frances Mary, John Waller, Leroy, Wm. Henry, Alfred Wayne, Chas. Edward,
Joseph Benjamin, Frances Mary Watson.

YOUNG, JAMES—BOX 104, PACK 2549:
        Will dated Nov. 26, 1797 in Abbeville Dist. Rec. Mar. 27, 1798. Exr:
Wife, Jean Young. Wit: Wm. Crawford, Saml., Archibald Shaw. Chn: Nancy,
Mary, Jean, Wm., Saml., John Young. Inv. made Aug. 28, 1798 by Wm.
Crawford, John Lindsay, Wm. Mayn. Sale, Nov. 1, 1798. Byrs: Jas. Langham,
Robt. Guttery, Andrew Miller, Robt. Green, Thos. Taylor, Wm. Gready,
Zedikiah Woods, Thos. Russell, Damey Sanders, Wm. Ashley.

YOUNG, FRANCIS—BOX 104, PACK 2550:
        Will dated Feb. 3, 1822 in Abbeville Dist. Prov. Aug. 5, 1822. Exrs:
John, Francis, Saml. Young. Wit: John Cameron, John McClelland, John C.
Harris. Chn: Isabella MaGill, Mary, Saml. Young, Margaret Young Baird,
Francis, John Young, Jane Baskin, Martha Mitchell decd., Susannah Kerr decd.
Joseph Young. Gr. chn: Francis, Thos., Saml., Jane Mitchell chn. of Martha
Mitchell decd., Martha Vanlandingham, Rachel Simms, Francis, John, David
Kerr chn. of Susannah Kerr decd. "Leave $50.00 to John Baskin." Expend:
Sept. 27, 1825 Paid Elihu Beard legatee $156.00. Paid George N. Sims legatee
$50.00. Inv. made Sept. 24, 1822 by Alexr. Speer, Thos. Jones, John Cameron.

YELDELL, ROBERT, SR.—BOX 104, PACK 2551:
        Will dated June 29, 1789 in Abbeville Dist. Prov. Oct. 6, 1789. Exrs:
S. L. Peter Hairston, Son, Robt. Yeldell. Wit: Elizabeth Wilson, Joseph Hasel
Sr., Alexr. Smith. Wife name not given. Chn: Jas. Yeldell decd., Jean Yedell,
Sarah White, Mary Hairston, Robt., Anthony Phebe Yeldell. Gr. chn: Robt.
Yeldell, Robt. Hairston, Ment. dtr. of Joseph Dennis, no name given.

YORK, JOHN—BOX 104, PACK 2552:
Est admnr. Feb. 21, 1785 by Jas. Jr., Jas. Allison Sr., unto John
Thomas Jr. Ord. 96 Dist. sum 2,000 lbs. Inv. made by Holloway Power, John
Brockman, Edward Pugh. Sale, May 11, 1785. Byrs: Jas. Allison Jr., Jas. Allison
Sr.

YOUNGBLOOD, LEWIS—BOX 104, PACK 2553:
Est. admnr. Sept. 5, 1808 by Larkin Reynolds, Wm. Wilson, Joseph
Motes unto Andrew Hamilton Ord. Abbeville Dist. sum $5,000.00. Inv. made
Sept. 13, 1808 by Andrew Logan, Archy Frith, David Thomas. Byrs: Rachel
Youngblood, Nathan Lipscomb, Larkin Reynolds, Bird Martin, Peter Youngblood,
Robt. Foster, Benjamin Johnson, Peter Arnold, John Turner, Wm. Douglass,
John H. Spruce.

YAWN, LEWIS—BOX 104, PACK 2554:
Est. admnr. Nov. 6, 1837 by Thos. Rosemond, Dudley Maybrey, Wm.
Wilson unto Moses Taggart Ord. Abbeville Dist. sum $1,000.00. Inv. made
Nov. 24, 1837 by Wm. T. Jones, Marshal Sharp, Dudley Mabrey. Byrs: Sanders
Williamson, Benjamin Johnson, Reuben Robertson, Wm. Wilson, Jackson An-
derson, Wm. T. Jones, Elias Cook, John Porterfield, Henson Norris, Elizabeth
Foolmore.

YARBROUGH, WILLIAM D.—BOX 104, PACK 2555:
On Dec. 9, 1836 Littleton Yarbrough, Nicholas H. Miller, Jas. Murray
bound unto Moses Taggart Ord. Abbeville Dist. sum $20,000.00. Littleton
Yarbrough made gdn. of Wm. D. Yarbrough a minor. Nov. 19, 1833 Wm.,
Moses Yarbrough bound unto Moses Taggart Ord. Abbeville Dist. sum $3,000.00.
Wm. Yarbrough made gdn. of Wm. D. Yarbrough. Expend: 1839 recd. of Jas.
Murray, Exr: of Wm. Yarbrough decd. $656.62½.

YOUNG, ISAAC—BOX 104, PACK 2556:
Will dated July 8, 1841 in Abbeville Dist. Prov. Aug. 1841. Exr:
Ezekiel Rasor. Wit: Wm. Barmore, John Rasor, Valentine Young. Wife, Moriah
Young. Bro. Valentine Young. Wife now pregnant with child. "My desire to
be buried at the Mulburry Meeting House." Inv. made Sept. 8, 1841 by Jas.
W. Blain, Wm. Barmore Esq., Joseph Weatherall. Sale, Jan. 21, 1842. Byrs:
Mariah P. Young, Ezekiel Rasor, Wm. Barmore, Dr. Bowen, Isaac Richey, A. H.
Magee.

YOUNG, WILLIAM—BOX 104, PACK 2557:
Est. admnr. Nov. 7, 1842 by Jas. Young, Elizabeth Hopper, T. J. Neely
unto David Lesly Ord. Abbeville Dist. sum $3,000.00. Wm. Young a bro. to
Jas. Young. Inv. made Nov. 10, 1842 by Wm. A. Moore, Jas. Smith, T. Neely.
May 1, 1845 Elizabeth Hopper recd. $660.48 as her share. Sett. made Oct. 22,
1844. Present, Jas. Young admnr., Robt. Y. Jones a distributee in right of wife
Lucinda. Elizabeth Hopper wid. Robt. P. Young supposed to be dead. Saml.
Turner in right of wife Emeline and infant son Saml. Y. Turner.

YOUNG, ISAAC (MINORS)—BOX 104, PACK 2558:
On Oct. 10, 1846 Jas. Graham, now of *Mawamba* County, Miss., Valentine Young and Marshal Sharp of Abbeville Dist. bound unto David Lesly Ord. sum $452.00. Jas. Graham made gdn. of Selah M., Valentine Graham minors under 14 yrs. Mar. 19, 1839 Ezekiel Rasor, Enoch Barmore, Saml. Agnew bound unto Moses Taggart Ord. Abbeville Dist. sum $10,000.00. Ezekiel Rasor made gdn. of Isaac Young a minor under 21 yrs. Feb. 5, 1844 Ezekiel, John, Jas. C. Rasor bound unto David Lesly Ord. Abbeville Dist. sum $457.92. Ezekiel Rasor made gdn. of Sarah Jane Young a minor. Dtr. of Maria P. Young. Nancy Sims the gr. mother. Valentine Young the gr. father of Sarah Young.

YOUNG, JAMES R—BOX 104, PACK 2559:
Est. admnr. Dec. 7, 1841 by Saml. J. Young, John (last name not clear) of Kershaw Dist. bound unto David Lesly Ord. Abbeville Dist. sum $500.00. (Letter)
4 Oct. 1841
Camden
Dear Sir:
On the other page is my petition for letter of administration to granted to me. Observe or shew to Mr. Jno. F. Livingston this letter. Will you have the goodness to drop me a few lines when you will be able to grant the titles, so I can go over to your dist. Your early attention to this matter will be accepted.
Your Ob Sevt.
Saml. J. Young
South Carolina
Abbeville Dist. To the Ord. of Abbeville Dist.
Whereas Jas. R. Young late of the Dist. and State afore said, departed this life on the 22nd day of August in the yr. of our Lord 1841, intestate, having whilst he lived divers goods and chattels, rights and credits. Therefore your Petitioner Saml. J. Young a son of the said decd. prays that letters of administration of the goods and chattels rights & cerdits of the said decd. may be granted.
Oct. 4, 1841
Saml. J. Young

YOUNG, GEORGE—BOX 104, PACK 2560:
Est. admnr. May 2, 1823 by Jane Young, Jas. Sr., Jas. Spence Jr., Joseph Creswell, unto Moses Taggart Ord. Abbeville Dist. sum $500.00. Inv. made May 16, 1823 by Rice Mills, Wm., Wm. Robinson Sr., Elias Gibson. Byrs: Jas., Jr., Jas. Spence Sr., Jane Young, Thos. Jr., Joseph Creswell Jr., Rebecca Mc-Comb, Rice Mills, John Young.

ZIMMERMAN, PHILIP—BOX 104, PACK 2561:
Est. admnr. July 25, 1809 by John Zimmerman, Jesse Thornton, Nathaniel Harrison unto Andrew Hamilton Ord. Abbeville Dist. sum $5,000.00. Est. admnr. again Mar. 16, 1847 by W. W. Belcher, John Zimmerman unto David Lesly Ord. Abbeville Dist. sum $5,000.00. Left a wid. and an infant

child. Inv. made Aug. 4, 1809 by Robt. Perrin, Philip Stiefel, Jacob Casper. Sale, Aug. 11, 1809. Byrs: Gregory Caudle, John, Saml. Zimmerman, David Jay, Jas. Stiefel, Robt. Gillam, Nicholas Stalsworth, Mary Stiefel, Polly Zimmerman, etc.

ZIMMERMAN, MARY—BOX 104, PACK 2562:
Will dated Apr. 20, 1799. Rec. Feb. 27, 1801. Wit: John Boker, Robt. Bradford, Jas. Stuart. Was of Hardlabor in Abbeville Dist. Chn: Mary Zimmerman, Elizabeth Mantz. Had one note on Jas. Stiefel.

ZIMMERMAN, CAPT. PETER—BOX 104, PACK 2563:
Est. admnr. Mar. 25, 1796 by Elizabeth Zimmerman wid., Capt. Patrick Gibson, Stephen Mantz unto the Judges of Abbeville County sum 1,000 lbs. Inv. made May 24, 1796 by Wm. Dorris, Joseph Hearst, Jas. Stiefel. Sale, Nov. 29, 1796. Byrs: Elizabeth Zimmerman, John Wideman, Nicholas Rambay, Stephen Mantz, Henry Dilbon, Jas. Henderson, Saml. Carter, David Rush, John Hose, Abner Perrin, Geo. Perrin, Wm. Perrin, Wm. Wade, John Scoggins, Jesse Harris, Jas. Yeldell, Thos. McBride, Philip Stiefel, etc.

ZIMMERMAN, HENRY—BOX 104, PACK 2564:
Will dated May 28, 1834 in Abbeville Dist. Prov. Apr. 24, 1835. Exrs: Wife, Catharine Zimmerman, John Zimmerman. Wit: W. Lomax, R. Hill, S. Hill. Chn: John H., Albert B., Caroline, Jane Zimmerman. "Owned land in Edgefield Dist. on branches of Reedy Creek." Caroline Zimmerman later married Lemuel O. Shoemaker. John H. Zimmerman later became a Minister of the Methodist E. Church. Jane married Alpheus E. Barnes. Inv. made April 25, 1835 by Richard Hill, Saml. A. Wilson, Henry Brooks.

ADAMS, JAMES—BOX 105, PACK 2565:
Will dated Oct. 14, 1781 in 96 Dist. Probated Apr. 26, 1782. Exrs: Sons, Drury, Thos. Adams. Wife, Sarah Adams. Wit: John Herndon, Benjamin, Hannah Moseley, John Golding. Chn: Drury, Thos., Littlebury, Benjamin, Sarah, Elizabeth, Rachel, Jas. decd., Rebecka Adams.

ADAMS, JAMES—BOX 105, PACK 2566:
Est. admnr. May 1, 1804 by Nipper Adams, Reuben Putman, Wm. Martin, Wm. Lord unto Andrew Hamilton Ord. Abbeville Dist. sum $5,000.00.

ANDERSON, COLBERT—BOX 105, PACK 2567:
Will dated Nov. 20, 1782 in 96 Dist. Prov. Nov. 29, 1785. Exrs: Wife, Mary Anderson. Son, Jas. Anderson. Wit: Wm., Molly Mathis, Elizabeth McCrae. Chn: Jas., John, Jane, Colbert Anderson. Bros. Jas., Stephen Anderson.

ADAMS, LUCINDA—BOX 105, PACK 2568:
On Jan. 13, 1834 Joseph, Henry Norrell, John D. Adams bound unto Moses Taggart Ord. Abbeville Dist. sum $500.00. Joseph Norrell made gdn. of Lucinda Adams a minor over 14 yrs.

ADAMS, JOHN L. & WILLIAM H. (MINORS)—BOX 105, PACK 2569:
On Feb. 15, 1830 Catharine Adams, Alexr. Foster, John B. Pressly bound

unto Moses Taggart Ord. Abbeville Dist. sum $1,000.00. Catharine Adams made gdn. of Wm. H., John L. Adams minors.

ATCHISON, JANE—BOX 105, PACK 2570:
On Nov. 4, 1817 Andrew McGill, John Donald, Jas. Gray bound unto Taliaferro Livingston Ord. Abbeville Dist. sum $10,000.00. Andrew McGill made gdn. of Jane Atchison a minor over 14 yrs.

ATCHISON, JANE—BOX 105, PACK 2571:
On Dec. 16, 1816 Joseph Eakins, Geo., Saml. Marshall bound unto Taliaferro Livingston Ord. Abbeville Dist. sum $1,000.00. Joseph Eakins made gdn. of Jane Atchison a minor under 14 yrs.

ATCHISON, SAMUEL & RACHEL (MINORS)—BOX 105, PACK 2572:
On Apr. 3, 1815 Geo., John Marshall bound unto Taliaferro Livingston Ord. Abbeville Dist. sum $2,000.00. Geo. Marshall made gdn. of Saml., Rachel Atchison minors over 14 yrs. Expend: June 3, 1816 paid Jas. Johnson gdn. for Sarah Atchison. $242.28. Nov. 25 paid Jas. Johnson $30.54 for Mary Atchison. May 16, 1817 paid Wm. Runnels gdn. for Wm. Atchison $30.56. July 16, paid Jas. Johnson $28.00 in full of all demands against Elizeyan Atchison decd. for funeral expenses and other charges. Nov. 25, 1816 recd. of est. of Saml. Atchison decd. from Thos. King $8.93.

ATCHISON, SARAH—BOX 105, PACK 2573:
On Sept. 16, 1816 Jas. Johnson, Thos. King, John Connor bound unto Taliaferro Livingston Ord. Abbeville Dist. sum $10,000.00. Jas. Johnson made gdn. of Sarah Atchison a minor under 14 yrs.

ALLEN, CHARLES—BOX 105, PACK 2574:
Est. admnr. by Chas. Smith, Marshall Franks, Andrew Rodgers unto John Thomas Ord. 96 Dist. sum (Note: There were no dates or sum written to this except in one place was 178. This was all to it.)

ANDREWS, JAMES A.—BOX 105, PACK 2575:
On June 23, 1839 John Jr., John Wilson Sr., Saml. Branch bound unto Moses Taggart Ord. Abbeville Dist. sum $2,000.00. John Wilson Jr. made gdn. of Jas. A. Andrews.

ATCHISON, WILLIAM—BOX 105, PACK 2576:
On Apr. 3, 1815 Wm. Reynolds, Edmond Stephens bound unto Taliaferro Livingston Ord. Abbeville Dist. sum $1,000.00. Wm. Reynolds made gdn. of Wm. Atchison a minor over 14 yrs.

ALLEN, (MINORS)—BOX 105, PACK 2577:
On July 7, 1784 Jacob Smith, Enoch Grigsby bound unto John Thomas Jr. Ord. 96 Dist. sum 2,000 lbs. Jacob Smith made gdn. of Young, Milly, Polly, Nancy, Drury Allen minors.

AGNER, (MINORS)—BOX 105, PACK 2578:
On Aug. 13, 1831 Saml. Morris, Wm. Sr., Wm. McDonnell Jr. bound

unto Moses Taggart Ord. Abbeville Dist. sum $2,000.00. Saml. Morris made gdn. of Saml., Polly, Lucy, John Agner minor chn. of John Agner decd.

ARMSTRONG, JOHN—BOX 105, PACK 2579:
On Dec. 7, 1827 Saml. Huston, Robt. Wilson, John H. Armstrong bound unto Moses Taggart Ord. Abbeville Dist. sum $1,000.00. Saml. Huston was gdn. of John Armstrong a minor over 14 yrs.

ARMSTRONG, (MINORS)—BOX 105, PACK 2580:
On Feb. 24, 1827 Saml. Huston, John Power, Patrick Johnson bound unto Moses Taggart Ord. Abbeville Dist. sum $2,000.00. Saml. Huston was gdn. of Matilda Vasti, Amanda Zena Armstrong minors under 14 yrs.

ARNOLD, (MINORS)—BOX 105, PACK 2581:
On Oct. 23, 1838 Zachariah W. Arnold, Timothy, F. G. Thomas bound unto Moses Taggart Ord. Abbeville Dist. sum $500.00. Z. W. Arnold was gdn. of Martha Ann, John W. Arnold minors.

ANDERSON, (MINORS)—BOX 105, PACK 2582:
On Dec. 14, 1835 Edmund Beazley, Edmund Cobb, Robt. Anderson bound unto Moses Taggart Ord. Abbeville Dist. sum $2,000.00. Edmund Beazley made gdn. of Mary, Wm., John, Nathaniel Anderson minors.

ANDERSON, (MINORS)—BOX 105, PACK 2583:
On Jan. 6, 1840 Laban T., Landy G., Andrew J. Shoemaker bound unto Moses Taggart Ord. Abbeville Dist. sum $500.00. Laban T. Shoemaker made gdn. of Saml., Nancy, Mary, Laban Anderson minors.

ARNOLD, (MINORS)—BOX 105, PACK 2584:
On Aug. 15, 1838 Wm. B., Francis Arnold, John A. Calhoun bound unto Moses Taggart Ord. Abbeville Dist. sum $3,000.00. Wm. B. Arnold was gdn. of John, Mary, Francis Arnold minors.

ATKINS, JOHN—BOX 105, PACK 2585:
Will dated Oct. 1, 1777. Exrs: John F. Smith, Jas. Atkins. Wit: John, Sarah Smith. Wife, Christian Atkins. Chn: Robt., Barlet Atkins.

AGER, JOHN, SR.—BOX 105, PACK 2586:
Will dated July 7, 1817 in Abbeville Dist. Prov. Mar. 1, 1819. Exr: Son, Adam Ager. Wit: Alexr. Houston Esq., Robt. Waddell, Susannah Houston. Wife ment. no name given. Chn: John, Adam, Sarah, Margaret, Jane, Elizabeth Ager.

ABBET, JAMES—BOX 105, PACK 2587:
Cit. pub.. May 11, 1805 Wm. Cummins made application for Letters of Admn. of est. of Jas. Abbet decd. as next of kin. Pub. at Greenville Church. (No other papers.)

ANDERSON, JAMES—BOX 105, PACK 2588:
Will dated May 18, 1782 in 96 Dist. Prov. May 6, 1783. Exrs: Geo.

Anderson, John Hunter. Wit: Jas., Answorth Middleton, Thos. *Antuckin.* Chn: Wm., Alexr., Geo. Anderson, Answorth Middleton, Robt. Yung, John Miller, Andrew Anderson. Wift ment. name not given.

ADAMSON, JAMES—BOX 105, PACK 2589:
Will dated Sept. 6, 1811 in Abbeville Dist. Rec. July 25, 1814. Exr: Son, Jonathan Adamson. Wit: John Hearst Jr., Henry, Mary Gable. Wife, Lydia Adamson. Chn: Margaret, Rutha, Sally, Harriot, Jonathan Adamson.

ANDREWS, (MINORS)—BOX 105, PACK 2590:
On June 25, 1832 Alexr., John, John Wilson Sr. bound unto Moses Taggart Ord. Abbeville Dist. sum $1,000.00. Alexr. Wilson made gdn. of Margaret, Jane, Alexr., Benjamin Andrews minors.

AUSTIN, JOHN—BOX 105, PACK 2591:
On Aug. 2, 1813 Joseph Cooper, Jas. Hodges, Benjamin Rosamond bound to Taliaferro Livingston Ord. sum $1,000.00. Joseph Cooper made gdn. of John Austin a minor over 14 yrs. and son of Cornelius Austin.

ABBET, JAMES—BOX 105, PACK 2592:
Est. admnr. Aug. 5, 1805 by Wm. Cummins, Chas. Mitchell, Nancy Rasor unto Andrew Hamilton Ord. Abbeville Dist. sum $1,000.00.

BASKIN, JAMES H.—BOX 105, PACK 2593:
On Sept. 7, 1805 Anne Baskin, Thos. Shanklin, Geo. Bowie Esq. bound unto Andrew Hamilton Ord. Abbeville Dist. sum $3,000.00. Anne Baskin made gdn. of Jas. Hall Baskin a minor.

BREEDLOVE, JOHN WATKINS—BOX 105, PACK 2594:
On Mar. 24, 1809 Julius Esq., Lettice Nichols, Chas. Caldwell, John Hairston Sr. bound unto Andrew Hamilton Ord. Abbeville Dist. sum $5,000.00. Julius, Lettice Nichols his wife made gdn. of John Watkins Breedlove a minor.

BAIRD, JOHN & NANCY (MINORS)—BOX 105, PACK 2595:
On Jan. 28, 1804 John, Moses Taggart, (other name not clear) bound unto Andrew Hamilton Ord. Abbeville Dist. sum $3,000.00. Jas. Taggart made gdn. of John, Nancy Baird minors.

BAIRD, (MINORS)—BOX 105, PACK 2596:
On Feb. 9, 1804 Martha Baird, Alexr., Andrew White bound unto Andrew Hamilton Ord. Abbeville Dist. sum $5,000.00. Martha Baird made gdn. of Mary, Kitty, Andrew, Simeon Baird minors.

BENDER, GEORGE—BOX 105, PACK 2597:
On Jan. 24, 1783 Adam Hiles, John Sturzenegger, Lud Williams, David Bowers, John Clark bound unto John Ewing Calhoun Ord. 96 Dist. sum 14,000 lbs. Adam Hiles, John Sturzenegger made gdns. of Geo. Bender minor about 14 yrs. Son of the late Geo. Bender of said dist.

BUZBEE, (MINORS)—BOX 105, PACK 2598:
On Nov. 1, 1813 Elizabeth Buzbee, John Jackson bound unto Taliaferro Livingston Ord. Abbeville Dist. sum $1,000.00. Elizabeth Buzbee made gdn. of Melinda, Benjamin, Stephen, Micajah, John, Lewis Buzbee minors under 14 yrs., Jane Buzbee a minor over 14 yrs.

BUZBEE, LEWIS—BOX 105, PACK 2599:
On Nov. 24, 1830 Benjamin Buzbee, John Caldwell bound unto Moses Taggart Ord. Abbeville Dist. sum $200.00. Benjamin Buzbee made gdn. of Lewis Buzbee a minor over 14 yrs.

BALL, BURWELL—BOX 105, PACK 2600:
On May 3, 1813 Wm. Davis, Geo. Heard, Lewis Ball bound to Taliaferro Livingston sum $2,000.00. Wm. Davis made gdn. of Burwell Ball a minor over 14 yrs.

BARTEE, WILLIS W.—BOX 105, PACK 2601:
On Mar. 20, 1815 Peter H. Coleman, Jas. Pulliam bound unto Taliaferro Livingston Ord. Abbeville Dist. sum $2,000.00. Peter H. Coleman was gdn. of Willis W. Bartee a minor over 14 yrs.

BALL, WILLIAM—BOX 105, PACK 2602:
On June 7, 1811 Lewis Ball, Benjamin Pulliam, Wm. Davis bound unto Taliaferro Livingston Ord. Abbeville Dist. sum $1,000.00. Lewis Ball made gdn. of Wm. Ball a minor over 14 yrs.

BALL, ANNA—BOX 105, PACK 2603:
On July 31, 1815 Wm., Lewis Ball, Wm. Glover, bound unto Taliaferro Livingston Ord. Abbeville Dist. sum $2,000.00. Wm. Ball made gdn. of Anna Ball a minor over 14 yrs.

BUSHELL, NICHOLAS—BOX 105, PACK 2604.
Est. admnr. April 9, 1789 by Kathrine Bushell wid., Christopher Conner, Josiah Patterson bound unto the Judges of Abbeville County, sum 1,000 lbs.

BROWN, THOMAS—BOX 105, PACK 2605:
On Feb. 14, 1825 Donald, John Douglass, Geo. Washington Hodges, bound unto Moses Taggart Ord. Abbeville Dist. sum $1,000.00. Donald Douglass made gdn. of Thos. Brown a minor.

BULLOCK, ELIZABETH AND REBECCA—BOX 105, PACK 2606:
On Mar. 2, 1831 Vincent Griffin, Patrick Noble, John Lipscomb bound unto Moses Taggart Ord. Abbeville Dist. sum $20,000.00. Vincent Griffin made gdn. of Elizabeth, Rebecca Bullock minors, one over 14 yrs. and the other under 14 yrs.

BROOKS, JACOB WARRIN—BOX 105, PACK 2607:
On April 2, 1804 John Brooks, Wm. Yarbrough, Jeremiah Strother bound unto Andrew Hamilton Ord. Abbeville Dist. sum $5,000.00. John Brooks made gdn. of Jacob Warrin Brooks a minor 17 yrs. of age last June.

ABSTRACTS OF OLD NINETY-SIX AND

BEAUFORD, EZEKIAL AND JAMES—BOX 105, PACK 2608:
On Oct. 12, 1818 Margaret, Wm. Beauford, Jas. Gillespie bound unto
Taliaferro Livingston Ord. Abbeville Dist. sum $5,000.00. Margaret Beauford
made gdn. of Ezekiel P., Jas. S. or L. Beauford minors under 14 yrs.

BICKLEY, JOHN—BOX 105, PACK 2609:
On Dec. 28, 1801 John Nelson Newby, Jas. Bickley, Wm. Tatom
bound unto Andrew Hamilton Ord. Abbeville Dist. sum $10,000.00. John N.
Newby made gdn. of John Bickley a minor.

BICKLEY, WALTER O.—BOX 105, PACK 2610:
On Dec. 28, 1801 Jas. Bickley, John N. Newby, Joseph Bickley bound
unto Andrew Hamilton Ord. Abbeville Dist. sum $10,000.00. Jas. Bickley made
gdn. of Walter O. Bickley a minor.

BRADLEY, ELIZABETH DOOLY—BOX 105, PACK 2611:
On Oct. 20, 1810 John Calvert, Archibald Douglass bound unto John
Hamilton Ord. Abbeville Dist. sum $3,000.00. John Calvert made gdn. of
Elizabeth Dooly, John E., Lewis W., Lew Kelly W. Bradley minors under 14
yrs. Sept. 7, 1812 John, Jesse Calvert, David Wardlaw bound unto Taliaferro
Livingston Ord. Abbeville Dist. sum $1,000.00. John Calvert made gdn. of
Elizabeth Dooly Bradley a minor over 14 yrs.

BALL, JUDITH—BOX 105, PACK 2612:
On July 31, 1815 Wm. Glover, Wm. Ball, Wm. W. Davis bound unto
Taliaferro Livingston Ord. Abbeville Dist. sum $5,000.00. Wm. Glover made
gdn. of Judith Ball a minor over 14 yrs.

BANKS, (MINORS)—BOX 105, PACK 2613:
On Sept. 7, 1813 Benjamin Glover, Wm. Robinson bound unto Taliaferro Livingston Ord. Abbeville Dist. sum $2,000.00. Benjamin Glover made
gdn. of Peter Smith, Polly, Melinda Banks minors under 14 yrs., Lucy Banks
a minor over 14 yrs.

BURDEN, ABRAHAM—BOX 105, PACK 2614:
On Feb. 3, 1820 Valentine Young, Chas. Hodges, Benjamin Rosemond
bound unto Moses Taggart Ord. Abbeville Dist. sum $500.00. Valentine Young
made gdn. of Abraham Burden a minor over 14 yrs.

BANKS, MELINDA—BOX 105, PACK 2616:
On Feb. 12, 1821 Pyrum, Jas. Olds, Peter Downey bound unto Moses
Taggart Ord. Abbeville Dist. sum $300.00. Pyrum Olds made gdn. of Melinda
Banks a minor under 14 yrs.

BASKIN, ROBERT M.—BOX 105, PACK 2617:
On July 25, 1805 Thos. S., John A. Baskin, Agrippa Cooper, bound
unto Andrew Hamilton Ord. Abbeville Dist. sum $2,000.00. Thos. S. Baskin
made gdn. of Robt. McKinley Baskin a minor over 14.

BROUGH, GEORGIANNA C.—BOX 105, PACK 2618:
On Jan. 4, 1836 Benjamin McKittrick, Alexr., John Scott bound unto
Moses Taggart Ord. Abbeville Dist. sum $10,000.00. John Scott made gdn. of
Georgianna Catharine Brough a minor.

BARMORE, (MINORS)—BOX 105, PACK 2619:
On Dec. 30, 1834 Wm. Barmore, Ezekiel, John Rasor bound unto Moses
Taggart Ord. Abbeville Dist. sum $7,000.00. Wm. Barmore made gdn. of
Elizabeth, Mahala, Nancy, Larkin Barmore minors of Peter Barmore decd.

BOUCHILLON, (MINORS)—BOX 105, PACK 2620:
On Apr. 2, 1804 Susannah Bouchillon, Peter Guillebaw, Deleany Carrel
bound unto Andrew Hamilton Ord. Abbeville Dist. sum $5,000.00. Susannah
Bouchillon made gdn. of John Bouchillon 4 yrs. of age last May, Joseph Leonard
Bouchillon 3 yrs. old, Jenny Bouchillon 1 yr. old last May minors.

BYRD, AGNES SIMPSON—BOX 105, PACK 2621:
On July 24, 1784 Wm. Simpson, Jas. McElawyne, Arthur Simpson
bound unto John Thomas Ord. Abbeville Dist. sum 2,000 lbs. Wm. Simpson
made gdn. of Agnes Simpson Byrd a minor.

BOWMAN, WILLIAM—BOX 105, PACK 2622:
On Mar. 27, 1806 Jean Caldwell, Jehu Foster, John Brannan bound
unto Andrew Hamilton Ord. Abbeville Dist. sum $5,000.00. Jean Caldwell
made gdn. of Wm. Bowman a minor.

BELL, THOMAS—BOX 105, PACK 2623:
Est. admnr. Mar. 25, 1795 by Robt. Bell, John McCord Sr., Wm.
Russell unto the Judges of Abbeville County sum 500 lbs.

BANKS, ELIAS—BOX 105, PACK 2624:
Cit. pub. at Zion Church. Ment. David Mathews applied for Letters of
Admnr. Dated Nov. 21, 1834. (No other papers).

BROWN, MARY—BOX 105, PACK 2625:
Est. admnr. Dec. 7, 1812 by Wm. Hutchison, Amos Anderson, John
Sanders unto Taliaferro Livingston Ord. Abbeville Dist. sum $1,000.00. Cit.
Pub. at Rehobeth Church ment. Wm. Hutchison next of kin.

BELL, MATTHEW—BOX 105, PACK 2626:
Est. admnr. May 19, 1824 by Wm. Bell, Daniel Brooks, John Williams
unto Moses Taggart Ord. Abbeville Dist. sum $1,000.00. Cit. Pub. at Greenville
Church.

BASDON, JOHN—BOX 105, PACK 2627:
Est. admnr. Apr. 26, 1784 by Milley Basden, Chas. Ward, Chapman
Ward Taylor, unto John Thomas Ord. 96 Dist. sum 2,000 lbs.

BARRON, THOMAS—BOX 105, PACK 2628:
Est. admnr. Mar. 8, 1784 by Mary Barron, Gilbert, Saml. Shaw unto
John Thomas Ord. 96 Dist. sum 2,000 lbs.

BRYAN, JOHN—BOX 105, PACK 2629:
Est. admnr. Aug. 9, 1783 by Mary Bryan, John, Wm. Elder unto John Thomas Ord. 96 Dist. sum 2,000 lbs.

BUGG, NICHOLAS H.—BOX 105, PACK 2630:
Est. admnr. Apr. 17, 1809 by Charlotte Bugg, Joseph, Jas. Bickley unto Andrew Hamilton Ord. Abbeville Dist. sum $5,000.00.

BARKSDALE, JOHN, SR.—BOX 105, PACK 2631:
Will dated Dec. 20, 1790 in Abbeville Dist. Exrs: Son, Richard Barksdale, Higgerson Barksdale. Wit: Archibald Cowan, Jas. *Alliwine,* Charity Ogle. Chn: Thos. Barksdale, Anna Davis alis Williamson, Clevues Barksdale, Unity Martin, Polly Carter alias Sharp, Frances Mathison, Higgerson Barksdale. Gr. dtr: Mary Ann Mathison. Est. admnr. Nov. 7, 1796 by John Mathison, John Martin, Joshua Hill unto the Judges of Abbeville County sum $5,000.00. Cit. Pub. at Hopewell Church. One paper ment. Susanna Barksdale the wid. Legatees ment. in sett. Wm., John Martin, Polly Freeman, Sally David chn. of John Martin.

BOGGS, ROBERT—BOX 105, PACK 2632:
Est. appraised Dec. 27, 1802 by Wm. Lesly, Wm. Garret, Mathew Wilson. Joseph Gaston, Jas. Johnson, John McMurtrey or any 3 or 4 of you. (No other papers.). Lived in Abbeville Dist.

BASDON, JOHN—BOX 105, PACK 2633:
Inv. made May 26, 1784 by Wm. Moss, Wm. Jones, Daniel *Wallicon.* Milley Basdon, Chas. Ward were the admnrs. Was of Beech Island in 96 Dist.

BONNER, JOHN—BOX 105, PACK 2634:
Est. admnr. Apr. 6, 1790 by Jas. Bonner, Willis Breazeale, Arthur Patton unto the Judges of Abbeville County sum 500 lbs.

BREAZEALE, JOHN—BOX 105, PACK 2635:
Est. admnr. Feb. 4, 1822 by Wm. Breazeale, Joseph, Jas. A. Black unto Moses Taggart Ord. Abbeville Dist. sum $700.00.

BROWN, JAMES—BOX 105, PACK 2636:
Est. admnr. Sept. 1, 1817 by Josiah Sr., Jas. Patterson unto Taliaferro Livingston Ord. Abbeville Dist. sum $500.00. Cit. Pub. at Buffalo Church.

BELL, JAMES—BOX 105, PACK 2637:
Est. admnr. May 11, 1816 by Arthur Mathew, Wm. Bell unto Taliaferro Livingston Ord. Abbeville Dist. sum $1,000.00. Cit. Pub. at Hopewell Church ment. Jas. Bell was late of the Army of the United States.

BELL, PATRICK—BOX 105, PACK 2638:
Cit. Pub. at Duewest Corner ment. Wm. Agnew applied for Letters of Admnr. as next of kin. Dated Jan. 23, 1794. Jas. Bell also applied for Letters of Admnr. as next of kin on Jan. 8, 1793.

BENNET, JOHN—BOX 105, PACK 2639:
Est. admnr. Mar. 12, 1800 by Mary Bennet, John Wilson, Lewis Bailer unto Andrew Hamilton Ord. Abbeville Dist. sum $2,000.00. Petition of Jas. Bennet one of the legatees of John Bennet decd. for a cit. to issue against Caleb, Mary Nipper admnrs. of est. of John Bennet decd. Datd Mar. 17, 1812.

BURDEN, WILLIAM—BOX 105, PACK 2640:
Est. admnr. Sept. 17, 1830 by Abram Burden, Dudley Mabrey, Valentine Young unto Moses Taggart Ord. Abbeville Dist. sum $500.00.

BARTEE, WILLIS—BOX 105, PACK 2641:
Cit. Pub. at Turkey Creek Church Dec. 1, 1823 ment. Chas. Pitts applied for Letters of Admnr. (No other papers.)

BOWIE, ANDREW—BOX 105, PACK 2642:
Est. admnr. Feb. 15, 1808 by Rosey Ann, Geo. Esq., John Bowie Sr. unto Andrew Hamilton Ord. Abbeville Dist. sum $5,000.00.

BARKSDALE, POLLY—BOX 105, PACK 2643:
Est. admnr. Mar. 22, 1814 by Saml., Benjamin H. Saxon Esq., unto Taliaferro Livingston Ord. Abbeville Dist. sum $10,000.00.

BREAZEALE, DRURY—BOX 105, PACK 2644:
Est. admnr. Feb. 2, 1829 by Benjamin H. Saxon, Jas. Patterson, Thos. P. Spierin unto Moses Taggart Ord. Abbeville Dist., sum $2,000.00. Cit. Pub. at Hopewell Church. Inv. made Mar. 7, 1829 by Pierre Guilleban, Jacob Bellott, Isaac Bouchillon. Byrs: Benjamin McKittrick, Willis Breazeale, B. H. Saxon, Paul Rogers. Will dated Sept. 7, 1820 in Abbeville Dist. Prov. Mar. 1, 1822. Exr: Wife, Mary Breazeale. Wit: Mary Robertson, Dale Palmer, John L. Gibert. Chn. ment. named not given.

BRIGHTMAN, THOMAS, JR.—BOX 105, PACK 2645:
Nathaniel Marion the admnr. Lived in Abbeville Dist. Appraisers: John McBride, Jas. P. Heard, Littletin Myrick, Chas. C. Mayson Esq. Dated May 6, 1822. (No other papers.)

BANKS, JAMES—BOX 105, PACK 2646:
Est. admnr. June 9, 1794 by Thos. Banks, Geo. Patterson, John Cowan unto the Judges of Abbeville County sum 500 lbs. Cit. Pub. at Hopewell Church.

BOUCHILLON, JOSEPH—BOX 105, PACK 2647:
Est. admnr. Jan. 18, 1804 by Elijah, Drury Breazeale, Abraham Campbell unto Andrew Hamilton Ord. Abbeville Dist. sum $5,000.00.

BAILEY, JEAN—BOX 105, PACK 2648:
Will dated Feb. 14, 1780 in 96 Dist. Prov. Sept. 12, 1792. Exr: Nathaniel Bailey. Wit: Saml. Watt, John Middleton, Thos. Wells. Chn: Joseph, Nathaniel, Isabel Bealey. Gr. dtr: Jean Thaker.

BURGESS, WILLIAM, SR.—BOX 105, PACK 2649:
Will dated May 15, 1775 in 96 Dist. Prov. July 1, 1783. Exrs: Wife,

Olive Burgess, John Evans. Wit: John, Wm., Sarah Evans. Chn: John, Jas., Jacob, Wm., Delilah, Elizabeth, Jemima Burgess, Rhoda Williams.

BAIRD, THOMAS—BOX 105, PACK 2650:
Will dated May 3, 1797 in Abbeville Dist. Rec. Sept. 12, 1797. Exrs: Wife, Jennet Baird, Bro., Alexr. Baird. Wit: John Boles, Allen Doyle, Francis Cummins.

BUZBEE, JOHN—BOX 105, PACK 2651:
Will dated Mar. 26, 1778 in 96 District. Exrs: Wife, Jane Buzbee. Son, John Buzbee. Wit: No names given. Chn: John, Jesse, Jacob, Moses, Benjamin, Mary, Stephen, Jane Buzbee.

BOWMAN, WILLIAM—BOX 105, PACK 2652:
Will dated Nov. 4, 1789 in Abbeville Dist. Prov. Apr. 6, 1790. Exrs: Saml. Reid, John Jr., Hugh Wardlaw. Wit: Saml. Agnew, Alexr., Geo. Reid. Gr: Sons: Wm. Bowman, Saml. Moore Wardlaw. Dtr. 1. Jean Bowman. Chn. ment. names not given.

BLACK, PETER—BOX 105, PACK 2653:
No will date given. Prov. Dec. 22, 1784 in 96 Dist. Exrs: Wife, Rachel Black, Daniel Perkins. Wit: Joseph Wright, Thos. Black, David McConnel. Chn: Thos., Jas., John, Wm., Mary, Rachel, Ruth Black.

BAYLE, MARY—BOX 105, PACK 2654:
Will dated Aug. 11, 1777. Rec. Mar. 25, 1795. Wit: P. Gibert, Joseph, Jean Bouchillon. Ment: "I Mary Sayral wid. of John Bayle of Hills-borough Township." Chn: Peter Bayle, Cecille wife of Peter Moragne, Francis Bayle Taylor in Charlestown.

BATES, FLEMING—BOX 105, PACK 2655:
Will dated Mar. 12, 1801. Rec. July 2, 1804. Exrs: Wife, Margaret Bates, Col. Joseph Calhoun, John McCarter, Robt. Alexr. Bates, John McCarter Bates. Wit: Wm. Hutton, Hamilton Wilson, Wm. Henderson. Chn: Robt. Alexr. Bates, John McCarter Bates, Catharine Hicks, Sally Grimes, Ann Clark, Betsey Fleming.

BRYSON, JAMES—BOX 105, PACK 2656:
Will dated Oct. 1, 1777 in 96 Dist. Prov. Oct. 1, 1782. Exrs: Bro. Wm. Bryson. Sis., Martha Bryson. Wit: John Hunter, Jonathan Downs, Mat. Hunter. Sis., Mary Flemming, Agnes Hunter. "To my Sis's. in the Kingdom of Ireland, Margaret, Jane, 2 lbs." Bros., Robt., Wm. Bryson.

BAIRD, MARY—BOX 105, PACK 2657:
Will dated Apr. 14, 1818 in Abbeville Dist. Probated May 7, 1821. Exrs: Sons, Wm. P. Raiford, Jas. R. Baird. Wit: Stephen Crenshaw, Saml. Savage, Welcom Whipple. Chn: Jas. R. Baird, Wm. P. Raiford, Rebecca Rowe. Gr. chn: John M. Raiford, John Batts Baird, Mary, Luiza Baird. Mary Baird was wid. of Batts Baird.

BELL, JOHN—BOX 105, PACK 2658:
Chas. Fooshe, Robt., Austin Pollard were appraisers. Dated Sept. 22, 1813. Lived in Abbeville Dist. John Meriwether, Lewis Bell were the Exrs. (No other papers in package.)

BECK, WILLIAM—BOX 105, PACK 2659:
Will dated Mar. 25, 1811 in Abbeville Dist. Rec. May 29, 1811. Exrs: Joseph Kolb, Wm. Ellis. Wit: Wm. Mayn, Abraham Haddon, Wm. Roberts. Chn: Sally, Catharine Beck. Wife, Hannah Beck. "Bequeath to John Perry my s. l., bequeath to Wm. Roberts."

BAIRD, JOHN BATTS—BOX 105, PACK 2660:
Will dated June 22, 1803 in Abbeville Dist. Rec. Aug. 27, 1803. Wit: Wm. Moore, Wm. Carithers, Wm. W. Bibb. Wife ment. name not given. Son, Jas. Baird.

BUCHANAN, MARY—BOX 105, PACK 2661:
Will dated Sept. 19, 1796 in Abbeville Dist. Rec. Mar. 27, 1797. Exr: Dtr., Margaret Buchanan. Wit: Thos., John Ramsay. Chn: Margaret Buchanan, Mary McMullin, Henry Buchanan. Gr: son: Henry Givens Ramsay. The Rev. McMullin was also ment.

BAKER, JOHN—BOX 105, PACK 2662:
Will dated Nov. 17, 1812 in Abbeville Dist. Rec. Aug. 9, 1814. Exr: Wife, Rebecca Baker. Wit: Jas. Adamson, Jas., Catharine Stiefel. "After her death property to go to John Rampy Sr."

BAKER, JOHN—BOX 105, PACK 2663:
Will dated May 3, 1823 in Abbeville Dist. Prov. Feb. 13, 1824. Exr: Son, John Baker. Wit: John Ramey. John Baker. Wife, Elizabeth Baker. "Bequeath to Mary Wallace, Keziah McClennen, Rosannah Wallace." Property divided between my son John, Elizabeth, Wm., Joseph Baker.

BAKER, CALEB—BOX 105, PACK 2664:
Will dated Apr. 7, 1803 in Abbeville Dist. Rec. Apr. 28, 1803. Wit: Joseph Moseley, Handy Haris. Wife, Margaret Baker. Chn. ment. names not given.

BOUCHILLON, JOHN—BOX 105, PACK 2665:
Will dated Apr. 14, 1778. Prov. July 7, 1789. Exr: Bro., Joseph Bouchillon. Wit: John Beraud, Pierre Roger, Pierre Regneir. Live in Hillsborough Township, Abbeville Dist. Give to son John, 100 acres situated above the French Mill on Little River, at the mouth of Mill Creek. Wife, and other chn. ment. names not given. In the French will his name was written Jean Bouchillon.

BARKSDALE, JOHN—BOX 105, PACK 2666:
On Apr. 25, 1803 Wm. Martin recd. from John Martin Sr. the sum 14 lbs 13 shillings as his share from his gr. father, John Barksdale decd. est. John Martin the father of the said Wm. Martin. On Sept. 30, 1805 Isaac Davids

recd. $391.00 for his wife, Sally Davids part from her gr. father John Barksdale decd. est. Jas. Freeman recd. $187.25 his wife's legacy from her gr. father's est. John Barksdale decd. On July 9, 1803 John Martin Jr. recd. 14 lbs. 15 shillings from his gr. father's est. John Barksdale decd.

BUFORD, WILLIAM—BOX 105, PACK 2667:
    Will dated Mar. 29, 1827 in Abbeville Dist. Prov. Oct. 27, 1828. Exrs: Wife, Sarah D. Buford, Elijah Hunt. Wit: Jas. Hunt, Wm. P. Raiford, John W. Scudday. Chn: Wm. L., Martha D., Susan S. Buford. Daniel Anderson later married Martha D. Buford.

POWERS, BENJAMIN—BOX 105, PACK 2668:
    Will dated June 15, 1786. Exrs: David Bowers, Isaac Ardis. Wit: John Sturzenegger, Jacob Tim., Cradk. Burnell. Will prov. Dec. 18, 1786 in Edgefield Dist. Was of Beech Island in 96 Dist. Wife, Sarah Bowers. "At my wife's death my property to go to Mary her dtr." Owned land also in Georgia.

BOGGS, ELIZABETH—BOX 105, PACK 2669:
    Will dated Sept. 12, 1815 in Abbeville Dist. Prov. Dec. 3, 1821. Exrs: John Devlin Esq., Robt. Smyth. Wit: Andrew Sr., Andrew McComb Jr., Peter Herbert. Bequeath to Robt. son of John Foster and my dtr. Elizabeth, to Wm. son of Robt. McClinton and my dtr. Ann, to Robt. son of John Devlin and my dtr. Mary, to Robt. son of Hugh McColough and my dtr. Esther, to John Mathew Smyth son of Robt. Smyth and my dtr. Martha, to John son of Saml. Patterson and my dtr. Sarah, to Robt. son of Jas. McColough and my dtr. Charlotte. On back of will written Elizabeth Boggs died Sept. 7, 1821.

BECK, HANNAH—BOX 105, PACK 2670:
    Will dated Mar. 31, 1813 in Abbeville Dist. Rec. July 12, 1813. Exrs: Joseph Kolb, Wm. Ellis. Wit: Robt. Ellis, Jonathan Stevenson, Wm. Roberts. Chn: Catherine, Sarah Beck. "Bequeath to John Perry, Wm. Roberts." Will ment. 4 chn. only 2 given unless John Perry, Wm. Roberts were the other 2. (Name written Beck and Beack.)

BROWN, JOHN—BOX 105, PACK 2671:
    Will dated Sept. 27, 1785 in 96 Dist. Prov. Nov. 30, 1786: Exr: Son, Wm. Brown. Wit: Wm. Carson, John Betty, Joseph Turnbull. Wife, Mary Brown. Chn: Elizabeth, Louisa, Sarah, Edy, Mary, Wm. Brown. Gr. Dtr: Anna Brown.

BURGESS, SAMUEL—BOX 105, PACK 2672:
    Will dated Sept. 23, 1785 in 96 Dist. Prov. Jan. 3, 1786. Exr: Son, John Burgess. Wit: Moses Weldon, Saml. Cooper, Saml. McJunkin. Wife and 2 dtrs. ment. no names given.

BOLE, JOHN—BOX 105—PACK 2673:
    Will dated Oct. 31, 1795 in Abbeville Dist. Rec. Mar. 25, 1796. Exrs: Jas. Carlile, Wm. Bole. Wit: Francis Carlile, Wm. McKinley Esq., J. W. McKinley. Wife, Anne Bole. Chn: Henry, Isaac Bole. "Bequeath to John Carlile,

Isaac C. Bole, Andrew Wilson, Mary Ward and to the rest of my sons and son in laws 5 shillings each."

BOLE, JOHN—BOX 105, PACK 2674:
Will dated May 18, 1830 in Abbeville Dist. Prov. Mar. 26, 1831. Exrs: Wife, no name given. Jas. Caldwell. Wit: Jas. Carlile Sr., Jas. L. Bole, Geo. Cornett. Chn: Polly, Jas., Walker Bole.

BUTERMAN, JOHN—BOX 105, PACK 2675:
Will dated July 9, 1765. Exr. Stepbro., Frederick *Prissack*. Wit: Names worn from page. "To my dearly beloved step bro. named Frederick *Prissack* whome I dearly do love, being he is my dearly beloved bro. and has come of the same womb as I have come, altho we had not one earthly father." Land originally granted to my father *Joham Bietermann* on Broad River. (Will so badly worn and torn could not make all out. Name looked like Buttermann and Bietermann.)

BROWNLEE, JAMES—BOX 105, PACK 2676:
Will dated July 21, 1789 in 96 Dist. Rec. June 12, 1798. Exrs: Joseph Brownlee, John Richey. Wit: Andrew Webb, Joseph Brownlee, Alexr. Elgin. Chn: Wm., Elizabeth, Jas., Geo. Brownlee.

BARKSDALE, ELIZABETH—BOX 105, PACK 2677:
Will dated May 28, 1798 in Abbeville Dist. Rec. Mar. 26, 1799. Exr: Bro. l., Joseph Barksdale. Wit: Wm. Williamson, Molley Walker, John Bogs. "Bequeath to my sis. chn. Patsey Barksdale."

CALHOUN, MARTHA M.—BOX 106, PACK 2678:
On June 14, 1836 Sarah A., Wm. M. Calhoun, Wade Speed bound unto Moses Taggart Ord. Abbeville Dist. sum $10,000.00. Sarah A. Calhoun made gdn. of Martha M. Calhoun a minor.

CALHOUN, (MINORS)—BOX 106, PACK 2679:
On Dec. 2, 1826 Wm. M. Sims, Richard H. Lester, John McGaw Jr. bound unto Moses Taggart Ord. Abbeville Dist. sum $1,000.00. Wm. M. Sims gdn. of Rebecca H. and Wm. M. Calhoun minors over 14 yrs.

CALHOUN, (MINORS)—BOX 106, PACK 2680:
On Jan. 6, 1834 Downs Calhoun, Saml. Crawford, Chas. Smith bound unto Moses Taggart Ord. Abbeville Dist. sum $1,000.00. Downs Calhoun made gdn. of Mary L., Lavinda, Willis B., Wm. D., Levinia minors under 14 yrs.

CALHOUN, LEROY (MINOR)—BOX 106, PACK 2681:
On May 2, 1831 Geo. Palmer, Isaac S. Whitten, Singleton Hughes bound unto Moses Taggart Ord. Abbeville Dist. sum $2,000.00. Geo. Palmer made gdn. of Leroy Calhoun a minor.

CRAWFORD, (MINORS)—BOX 106, PACK 2682·
On July 3, 1815 Jas. Hutchison, Robt. A. Bates, Jas. Craig bound unto

Taliaferro Livingston Ord. Abbeville Dist. sum $1,000.00. Jas. Hutchison made gdn. of Ebenezer, Rhoda C. Crawford minors under 14 yrs.

CRAWFORD, JAMES C.—BOX 106, PACK 2683:
On Oct. 4, 1813 Jas. Hutchison, Alexr. Houston, John McGaw bound unto Taliaferro Livingston Ord. Abbeville Dist. sum $2,000.00. Jas. Hutchison made gdn. of Jas. C. Crawford a minor over 14 yrs.

CUNNINGHAM, (MINORS)—BOX 106, PACK 2684:
On Oct. 13, 1834 John Cunningham, Andrew R. Johnson, Wm. C. Norwood bound unto Moses Taggart Ord. Abbeville Dist. sum $300.00. John Cunningham made gdn. of Benjamin F. Cunningham a minor over 14 yrs. Martha V., Joel J. Cunningham minors under 14 yrs.

CRAWFORD, JOHN (MINOR)—BOX 106, PACK 2685:
On Oct. 3, 1814 Jas., Wm. Hutchison, Robt. A. Bates bound unto Taliaferro Livingston Ord. Abbeville Dist. sum $2,000.00. Jas. Hutchison made gdn. of John M. Crawford a minor over 14 yrs.

CHILES, MARIAH—BOX 106, PACK 2686:
On Mar. 21, 1810 Wm., John Chiles, Saml. Perrin, bound unto John Hamilton Ord. Abbeville Dist. sum $5,000.00. Wm. Chiles made gdn. of Mariah Chiles a minor.

COCHRAN, WILLIAM—BOX 106, PACK 2687:
On July 9, 1803 John, Jas. Patterson bound unto Andrew Hamilton Ord. Abbeville Dist. sum $2,000.00. John Patterson made gdn of Wm. Cochran a minor.

CALDWELL, SOPHIA—BOX 106, PACK 2688:
On Jan. 27, 1830 John R., Jas. H. Caldwell, Wm. P. Paul, bound unto Moses Taggart Ord. Abbeville Dist. sum $500.00. John R. Caldwell made gdn. of Sophia Caldwell a minor over 14 yrs.

CALVERT, WILLIAM C. HILL—BOX 106, PACK 2689:
On Feb. 6, 1832 John, Jesse Calvert, A. C. Hamilton bound unto Moses Taggart Ord. Abbeville Dist. sum $3,000.00. John Calvert made gdn. of Wm. C. Hill Calvert a minor.

CALVERT, JOHN & LUCY—BOX 106, PACK 2690:
On Dec. 20, 1833 Jesse Calvert, Joseph, Robt. H. Wardlaw bound unto Moses Taggart Ord. Abbeville Dist. sum $1,000.00. Jesse Calvert made gdn. of John B., Lucy Calvert minors.

CALAHAN, THOMAS—BOX 106, PACK 2691:
On Jan. 4, 1820 Robt. Perrin, Jas. Taggart, John McCraven bound unto Moses Taggart Ord. Abbeville Dist. sum $2,000.00. Robt. Perrin made gdn. of Thos. Calahan a minor over 14 yrs.

CHRISTOPHER, (MINORS)—BOX 106, PACK 2692:
On Apr. 6, 1818 David Christopher, John Davis, Jas. Cobb bound unto Taliaferro Livingston Ord. Abbeville Dist. sum $2,000.00. David Christopher made gdn. of Wm., Buckner Griffin Christopher minors under 14 yrs.

COBB, (MINORS)—BOX 106, PACK 2693:
On Sept. 19, 1808, Mina Ann Cobb, Benjamin Mitchell, Basil Hallum bound unto Andrew Hamilton Ord. Abbeville Dist. sum $5,000.00. Mina Ann Cobb made gdn. of Sarah Qualls Cobb, Nancy Walton Cobb minors. On Sept. 19, 1808 Mina Ann Cobb, Benjamin Mitchell, Basil Hallum bound unto Andrew Hamilton Ord. Abbeville Dist. sum $10,000.00. Mina Ann Cobb was gdn. of John, Polly, Jas., Harvey, Patsey, Chas., Temperance Cobb minors.

CROZIER, ELIZABETH—BOX 106, PACK 2694:
On Feb. 3, 1836 Wm. A. Crozier, Saml. Cook, Jas. Rarden bound to Moses Taggart Ord. Abbeville Dist. sum $1,000.00. Wm. A. Crozier made gdn. of Elizabeth Crozier a minor.

COLLINS, MINORS—BOX 106, PACK 2695:
On Nov. 22, 1834 John, Wm. Collins, Andrew Richey bound to Moses Taggart Ord. Abbeville Dist. sum $4,000.00. John Collins made gdn. of Wm. F., Margaret R. Collins minors.

CHILES, FANNY—BOX 106, PACK 2696:
On Mar. 20, 1811 Austin Pollard, Benjamin Chiles, Zachry Meriwether Sr. bound to Moses Taggart Ord. Abbeville Dist. sum $2,000.00. Austin Pollard made gdn. of Fanny Chiles a minor under 14 yrs.

CAMERON, JOHN—BOX 106, PACK 2697:
Est. admnr. April 9, 1789 by Alexr. Cameron of Charleston, Saml. Houston, Jas. Hawthorne of Abbeville Dist. unto the Judges of Abbeville County, sum 1,000 lbs.

CRAWFORD, JAMES—BOX 106, PACK 2698:
Est. admnr. Joseph, Geo. Reed, Gabriel Smithers bound unto John Thomas Ord. 96 Dist. sum 2,000 lbs. (No dates given in bond.)

CRESWELL, GEORGE—BOX 106, PACK 2699:
Cit. Pub. at Asbury Church. John Gray made suit for Letters of Admnr. Dated June 10, 1830 (No other papers in package.)

COLEMAN, CHRISTOPHER—BOX 106, PACK 2700:
Est. admnr. Oct. 15, 1784 by Wm. White, Abner, Wm. Coleman bound unto John Thomas Ord. 96 Dist. sum 2,000 lbs.

CARLISLE, FRANCIS—BOX 106, PACK 2701:
Cit. Pub. Jan. 15, 1815 ment. John Carlisle applied for Letters of Admnr. Jeremiah S. Terry, Ezekiel Calhoun, Thos. Cunningham were sworn to appraise the est. Dated Feb. 1, 1815. (No other papers.)

CHALMERS, WILLIAM—BOX 106, PACK 2702:
Cit. Pub. Oct. 4, 1790 ment. Jas. Chalmers applied for Letters of
Admnr. Lived in Abbeville Dist. (No other papers.)

CARSON, JOSEPH—BOX 106, PACK 2704:
Est. admnr. Oct. 5, 1790 by Moses, Andrew Carson, Wm. Baskin Esq.,
Geo. Crawford unto the Judges of Abbeville County sum 200 lbs.

CARSON, WILLIAM—BOX 106, PACK 2705:
Est. admnr. Aug. 6, 1803 by Elizabeth, John Carson, John Hearst unto
Andrew Hamilton Ord. Abbeville Dist. sum $10,000.00.

CLARK, JOHN—BOX 106, PACK 2706:
Will dated 1839. (Month left out.) Exrs: Joshua DuBose, Thos. Cun-
ningham. Wit: A. Houston, J. Bouchillon Sr., Robt. T. Jennings. Lived in
Abbeville Dist. "Bequeath to John Clark Scott son of Wm. Scott." Sis: Nancy
Clark, Hannah Goodman. "Bequeath to Celia D., Esther C. Boyd dtrs. of John
Boyd decd. of Fairfield Dist. "Bequeath to Katharine, Joseph, Saml., Jas. Wilson
chn. of Jas. Wilson decd. of Abbeville Dist. Est. admnr. Nov. 28, 1803 by Sarah
Clark, Abraham Hadden, Wm. Beck unto Andrew Hamilton Ord. Abbeville
Dist. sum $5,000.00. (This bond must be of another John Clark.) Sett. for
Sept. 12, 1850 ment. Katharine Hanway formerly Katharine Wilson died leav-
ing a husband and 2 chn. Celia D. Boyd married Geo. *Leitner* of Fairfield
Dist. Jan. 10, 1848 Geo. *Leitner* of Fairfield Dist. appointed Dr. Thos. R.
Center of Richland Dist. his attorney to collect legacy that was left to Celia D.
Boyd by will of John Clark of Abbeville Dist.

CLARK, JOHN—BOX 106, PACK 2706:
(This is the same Clark as above). Sett. made Jan. 14, 1848 ment. Esther
C. Boyd married Dr. T. R. Center of Richland Dist. Inv. made Dec. 21, 1839
by Henry Hester, Williamson Norwood, Robt. E. Belcher.

CALDWELL, JAMES, JR.—BOX 106, PACK 2707:
Est. admnr. Mar. 12th, 1805 by Jane, Wm. Caldwell, John Lowry, Jas.
Foster unto Andrew Hamilton Ord. Abbeville Dist. sum $5,000,00.

CALDWELL, JAMES—BOX 106, PACK 2708:
Est. admnr. July 29, 1803 by Jenny Caldwell, Jas. Warlaw, Geo. Bowie
unto Andrew Hamilton Ord. Abbeville Dist. sum $10,000.00.

CALDWELL, HENRY NICHOLS—BOX 106, PACK 2709:
Est. admnr. Mar. 23, 1809 by Julius Nichols Esq., John Martin, Joseph
Bickley unto Andrew Hamilton Ord. Abbeville Dist. sum $10,000.00.

CHAMBERS, WILLIAM—BOX 106, PACK 2710:
Est. admnr. Mar. 27, 1792 by Stephen Chambers, John Hearst, Jas.
C. Edwards, Patrick Gibson Jr. unto Judges of Abbeville County sum 500 lbs.
Est. admnr. again Mar. 27, 1792 by Josiah, Stephen Chambers, John Hearst,
Patrick Gibson unto the Judges of Abbeville County sum 500 lbs. Cit. ment.

Stephen Chambers next of kin. Inv. made by Capt. Thos. Weems, John Norris, Thos. Edwards, Mathew, and Jas. C. Edwards. Dated Mar. 27, 1792. (One paper Stephen Chambers signed his name as Chalmers.)

CHALMERS, MAJOR JAMES—BOX 106, PACK 2711:
Est. admnr. Mar. 28, 1799 by Elizabeth Chalmers wid., Wm. Callahan, Thos. Weems Jr., Saml. Morris unto Andrew Hamilton Ord. Abbeville Dist. sum $5,000.00.

COVEY, JOHN—BOX 106, PACK 2712:
Inv. made Apr. 23, 1803 by Jas. Hathorn, Geo. Conn, Wm. Robinson. (No other papers in package.)

COWDREY, JOHN—BOX 106, PACK 2713:
Est. admnr. Oct. 28, 1818 by Jas. M. Cowdrey, Walter O. Bickley, Chas. C. Mayson unto Taliaferro Livingston Ord. Abbeville Dist. sum $2,000.00.

CASHADEY, MICHAEL—BOX 106, PACK 2714:
Est. admnr. Oct. 9, 1788 by Thos. Weems, John Norris, Wm. Lesly Jr. unto the Judges of Abbeville County sum 1,000 lbs. Inv. made Jan. 6, 1789 by John Chalmers, John Norris, Robt. Waddell.

COLE, JOHN—BOX 106, PACK 2715:
Est. admnr. Oct. 10, 1788 by Saml. McMurtrey, Wm. Martin, Andrew Watt unto Judges of Abbeville County sum 1,000 lbs. Cit. Pub. at Long Cane Church.

CLIZLER, SAMUEL—BOX 106, PACK 2716:
Cit. pub. at Little Mountain Church Mar. 4, 1821 ment. Timothy Clizler applied for Letters of Admnr. of est. of Saml. Clizler late of the State of Ga. Inv. made Mar. 8, 1821 by Alphues Baker, Jacob Martin, Thos. Botts.

CROOKS, ANDREW—BOX 106, PACK 2717:
Est. admnr. Oct. 15, 1783 by Andrew Russell, John Riley, Geo. Montgomery unto John Thomas Ord. 96 Dist. sum 2,000 lbs.

CROZIER, JAMES—BOX 106, PACK 2718:
Est. admnr. Oct. 16, 1790 by John Tullock, Francis Sutherland. Wm. McDonnell unto the Judges of Abbeville County sum 1,000 lbs.

CLEM, JOHN—BOX 106, PACK 2719:
Es. admntr. Oct. 27, 1818 by Robt., Jas., Ebenezer Foster unto Taliaferro Livingston Ord. Abbeville Dist. sum $1,000.00.

CODELS, RICHARD—BOX 106, PACK 2720:
Cit. pub. Oct. 8, 1788 ment. Barsheba Baker applied for Letters of Admnr. of est. of Richard Coddel.

CALHOUN, JAMES—BOX 106, PACK 2721:
Est. admnr. June 9, 1794 by Wm. Calhoun Sr., John Logan Jr., Capt. John Norwood unto the Judges of Abbeville County sum 500 lbs. Jas. Calhoun

was of Corn Acre. Wm. Calhoun next of kin. Mar. 24, 1794 Margaret Calhoun wid. of Jas. Calhoun gave up her admnr. to his father Wm. Calhoun.

CALHOUN, JAMES—BOX 106, PACK 2722:
Est. admnr. Nov. 3, 1804 by Jas. Hutchinson, John Scott, Alexr. Clark unto Andrew Hamilton Ord. Abbeville Dist. sum $2,000.00.

CAMPBELL, JAMES—BOX 106, PACK 2723:
Est. admnr. Feb. 3, 1785 by Margaret Campbell, Gabriel Smithers, Adam Crane Jones Jr. unto John Thomas Ord. 96 Dist. sum 2,000 lbs.

CAMPBELL, JOHN—BOX 106, PACK 2724:
Est. admnr. May 17, 1814 by Elizabeth, Wm. Campbell, Wm. McCurry unto Taliaferro Livingston Ord. Abbeville Dist. sum $1,000.00. June 11, 1814 Wm. Brownlee, Wm. Campbell, Wm. McCurry appointed to appraise the est.

COOK, ROBT. JONES—BOX 106, PACK 2725:
Est. admnr. June 3, 1811 by Joseph Hackney, Jas. Arnold, Leroy Roberts unto Taliaferro Livingston Ord. Abbeville Dist. sum $2,000.00. Cit. pub. May 13, 1811 ment. Joseph Hackney next of kin.

COLLINS, PETER, JR.—BOX 106, PACK 2726:
Est. admnr. June 27, 1785 by Campbell, Margaret Kennedy, John Neale unto John Thomas Ord. 96 Dist. sum 1,000 lbs. Est. admnr. again Apr. 29, 1786 by John Ballenger, Wm. McKinley, Andrew Pickens unto John Thomas Ord. 96 Dist. sum 1,000 lbs.

COBB, CALEB—BOX 106, PACK 2727:
Est. admnr. May (date left out) 1806 by Archibald Douglass, John Gray, John Hairston unto Andrew Hamilton Ord. Abbeville Dist. sum $5,000.00.

CARUTHERS, MARTHA—BOX 106, PACK 2728:
Will dated Dec. 5, 1791 in Abbeville Dist. Rec. Mar. 25, 1796. Exr: Son, Jas. Caruthers. Wit: Benjamin Terry, Son, Jas. Caruthers. "Bequeath to Francis Young, Benjamin Terry." Chn: Saml., John, Margaret, Martha Caruthers. "Bequeath to my said chn. the money that is due to me in North Carolina from Philip Gates and Jacob Whiworth. My son Jas. to go to N. C. to collect this." Also appoint Francis Carlile and John Harris to appraise my est.

CRAWFORD, ENOS—BOX 106, PACK 2729:
Will dated Aug. 9, 1816 in Abbeville Dist. Prov. Mar. 6, 1820. Exrs: Son, Andrew Crawford, s. l., Robt. Foster. Wit: John Devlin, John M. Cochran, Peggy Devlin. Chn: Andrew, Betsey Crawford, Martha W. Foster, Sarah Martin. Wife ment. name not given.

CARMICHAEL, WILLIAM—BOX 106, PACK 2730:
Will dated June 28, 1798 in Abbeville Dist. Rec. Dec. 27, 1800. Exr: Wife, Sarah Carmichael. Wit: Josiah Patterson Sr., John Thomson, Margaret Patterson. "Bequeath to Wm. Carmichael son of Daniel Carmichael decd. Also Joseph, Wm., Robt. Carmichael." "That if my wife should depart this life before John Tidwell is become of age that he should have his freedom."

CAIN, JOHN—BOX 106, PACK 2731:
Will dated Mar. 12, 1839. Prov. Aug. 5, 1839: Exrs: Dr. S. V. Cain, Wm. B. Smith. Wit: Paul Rogers, Benjamin McKittrick, Mary E. Moragne. Bro., Dr. S. V. Cain. Bro. l., Dr. N. Harris.

COUCH, THOMAS—BOX 106, PACK 2732:
Will dated Feb. 12, 1776. Prov. Jan. 30, 1784. Exrs: Wife, Mary Couch. Son, John Couch. Wit: Nathaniel Hillin, Ann Stone, John Stroud. Was of Enoree, 96 Dist. Chn: Wm., Thos., Judith, Elizabeth, Pattey, John, Drewey, Joseph Couch.

COLLONS, SUKEY—BOX 106, PACK 2733:
Will dated Feb. 14, 1784 in 96 Dist. Prov. June 6, 1784. Exrs: Wm. Burton, mother, Lucy Colings. Wit: Jas. Johnson, Wm. Burton Jr., Phebe Burton. Owned land on Thickety Creek. "Am the dtr. of Joseph Collons."

CARSON, WILLIAM—BOX 106, PACK 2734:
Will dated Sept. 15, 1828 in Abbeville Dist. Prov. Dec. 11, 1837. Exrs: Son, Martin Carson, John McComb. Wit: Stephen Lee, Joseph Hillhouse, John McDonnald. Chn: Jas., Jane Caroline, Wm., Robt., Martin, John Carson, Elizabeth, Margaret Houston, Benjamin, Mary H., Lucinda D. Carson.

CALDWELL, ELIZABETH—BOX 106, PACK 2735:
Will dated Mar. 2, 1808 in Abbeville Dist. Rec. Oct. 17, 1816. Exr: Joseph Black. Wit: John B., Joseph Black. Wid. of John Caldwell. Chn: Jas., Andrew Caldwell, Jane Hamilton, Isabela Pickens. "My little Negro girl now in possession of Joseph Hamilton in the State of Ga."

CHAMBERS, JOHN, SR.—BOX 106, PACK 2736:
Will dated Feb. 25, 1792 in Abbeville Dist. Prov. Mar. 28, 1792. Exr: Wife, Agness Chambers. Sons, Josiah, Stephen Chambers. Wit: Thos. Weems, John Norwood, Jas. Leany. Chn: John Chambers, Elizabeth Kile, Mary Patterson, Keziah Pankey, Stephen, Josiah, Sally, Pie, Anne Chambers. "Give to son Stephen 90 pounds Virginia money due to me from Jas. Cooker." (John wrote his name Chalmers, Chambers.)

CRAWFORD, JAMES, SR.—BOX 106, PACK 2737:
Will dated Nov. 7, 1780. Probated Feb. 4, 1783. Exrs: s. l., Jesse Campbell, Joseph Turnbull. Wit: John Sprott, John Cochran, Wm. Alexander. Was of Long Cane Sett., 96 Dist. Wife, Elizabeth Crawford. Chn: Thos., Wm. Crawford, Margaret Campbell, John Crawford, Martha Lang, Jas. Crawford, Elizabeth Turnbull. Inv. made May 3, 1783 by Andrew Hamilton, Wm. Alexr., Thos. Weems.

CONNOR, JOHN—BOX 106, PACK 2738:
Will dated July 6, 1822. Exrs: Son, Lewis Connor, Dr. Francis Connor. Wit: Jas. E. Glenn, Hart P. Arnold, Wm. Rowland. Chn: Lewis Connor, Fanney wife of John Swilling, Molley Johnson, Betsy Nash.

CONN, GEORGE—BOX 106, PACK 2739:
Will dated Apr. 20, 1819 in Abbeville Dist. Prov. June 7, 1819. Exrs:
Wife, Esther Conn. Son, Jas. Conn. Wit: Joseph Norrell, Abner Watson, Wm.
Robinson: Chn: Mary, Catharine, Jas. Conn. "Bequeath to Wm. Jackson
plantation whereon he now lives." Oct. 6, 1819 Benjamin Adams, David H.
McCleskey, Malon Morgan, Wm. Smith appointed to appraise the est.

CAMPBELL, JAMES—BOX 106, PACK 2740:
Will dated Oct. 15, 1810 in Abbeville Dist. Exrs: Joseph Black, Joseph
Bell. Wit: Thos., Martha Hodge, Joseph F. Bell. Chn: Moley Campbell. Gr.
son: Absolom Campbell son of John Campbell.

CAMPBELL, JAMES—BOX 106, PACK 2741:'
Will dated June 28, 1784. Prov. Fev. 3, 1785. Exr: Jas. Seawright. Wit:
Adam Crain Jones Jr., Adam Crain Jones, Jas. Seawright. Was of Granvill
County, of Long Cane. Chn: Jas., Rachel, Mary, Rebecky, Esther, Margaret,
Isabell Campbell. Wife, Margaret Campbell. Gr. son: Francis Sharp.

CAMPBELL, JOHN—BOX 106, PACK 2742:
Will dated July 13, 1786 in 96 Dist. Rec. Mar. 28, 1798. Exrs: Geo.
Conn, Adam Hill, Robt. Smith. Wit: Jas. Cox, Rowley McMullan. Chn:
Esther, Mary Campbell. Ment. 3 sons no names given.

CHILES, JAMES—BOX 106, PACK 2743:
Will dated May 28, 1784 in 96 Dist. Prov. June 15, 1784. No exrs:
Wit: Jas. Heard, John Edmistin, Henry Chiles. Wife ment. name not given.
Chn: Nancy, Jas., Henry Chiles. Est. admnr. July 2, 1784 by Jas. Chiles Jr.,
Wm. Huggins, Geo. Heard unto John Thomas Ord. 96 Dist. sum 2,000 lbs.

CROWTHER, JAMES, SR.—BOX 106, PACK 2744:
Will dated Dec. 26, 1827 in Abbeville Dist. Prov. Nov. 16, 1829. Exr:
Wife, Nancy Crowther. Wit: Jas. H. Stark, Joshua Pruitt, C. Stark.

CUNNINGHAM, JAMES—BOX 106, PACK 2745:
Will dated Jan. 13, 1798 in Abbeville Dist. Rec. Mar. 30, 1799. Exr:
Wife: Jean Cunningham. Wit: Thos. Ramsay, Jas. Cunningham, John Edwards.
Chn: Jean Carson, John, Jas., Sara, Saml. Cunningham.

CUNNINGHAM, JANE—BOX 106, PACK 2746:
Will dated Sept. 1, 1810 in Abbeville Dist. Prov. Dec. 24, 1817. Exrs:
Chn: David, Pamela Cunningham. Wit: John Cunningham, Robt. A. Cun-
ningham, Cornelus Cargill. Chn: David, Pamela Cunningham, Betsey Durrett.
Polly Davenport decd.

CUNNINGHAM, JANE—BOX 106, PACK 2747:
Will dated July 24, 1806 in Abbeville Dist. Rec. Feb. 15, 1811. Exr:
Francis Carlile Esq. Wit: Francis Carlile, Francis Moore, John M. Carlile.
Chn: Jas., John, Saml. Cunningham, Jane Moore, Sarah Fleming.

COX, WILLIAM—BOX 106, PACK 2748:
Will dated Mar. 7, 1809 in Abbeville Dist. Rec. Aug. 17, 1809. Exrs:

s. l., Jas. Young. Major David Anderson of Laurens Dist. Wit: Geo., Elender Shotwell, Alexr. W. Adams. Wife, Margaret Cox. Chn: Rhoda wife of Jas. Young. Albert Walker my said dtrs. son. (Another paper ment. the chn. of Jas. Young of Laurens Dist. Viv: Gallatin, Wm. A., Keturah, Phebe, Susannah C., Rhoda E. C. Young.)

COWEN, MAJOR JOHN—BOX 106, PACK 2749:
Will dated Sept. 18, 1804 in Abbeville Dist. Rec. June 22, 1805. Exrs: Bros., Isaac, Wm. Cowen, John Shannon. Wit: Jas., Joseph, Saml. Lindsey. Mother, Ann Cowan. Bro., Wm.'s 2 chn., Ann, Wm. Cowan. B. ls., Wm. Brownlee, David Hawthorne, Saml. Snoddy.

COWAN, HANNAH—BOX 106, PACK 2750:
Will dated July 21, 1815 in Abbeville Dist. Prov. July 29, 1819. No Exrs: Wit: Wm. Bole, Elizabeth H., John Baskin. Chn: Hiram, John Cowan, Dusilla Baskin.

CLARK, WILLIAM—BOX 106, PACK 2751:
Will dated July 3, 1790. Prov. Apr. 5, 1791. Exrs: Wife, Mary Clark. Son, Alexr. Clark. Wit: Saml. Blair, Wm. Scott, Alexr. Clark. Chn: Alexr., Jane, Mary, Susanna, Robt., Wm., John Huston Clark.

CUNNINGHAM, JOHN R.—BOX 106, PACK 2752:
On Oct. 16, 1810 Jeremiah S. Terry, Williamson, Nathaniel Norwood bound unto John Hamilton Ord. Abbeville Dist. sum $2,000.00. Jeremith S. Terry made gdn. of John R. Cunningham a minor.

DICKISON, (MINORS)—BOX 106, PACK 2753:
On Nov. 26, 1827 John McFarland, John Deall, David Anderson bound unto Moses Taggart Ord. Abbeville Dist. sum $2,000.00. John McFarland made gdn. of Mary E., Freeman Dickison minots over 14 yrs.

DAVIS, CATHARINE—BOX 106, PACK 2754:
On July 20, 1819 Sugar, John Wright, Vincent Ratcliff bound unto Moses Taggart Ord. Abbeville Dist. sum $2,000.00. Sugar Wright made gdn. of Catharine Davis a minor.

DRENNAN, ELIZA & JOHN—BOX 106, PACK 2755:
On Dec. 2, 1831 John Devlin, Wm. H., Robt. Drennan bound unto Moses Taggart Ord. Abbeville Dist. sum $2,000.00. Robt. Drennan made gdn. of Eliza J., John Drennan minors over 14 yrs.

DOUGLASS, THOMAS JEFFERSON—BOX 106, PACK 2756:
On May 27, 1819 John Cochran, Geo. Washington Hodges, Donald Douglass bound unto Moses Taggart Ord. Abbeville Dist. sum $6,000.00. Donald Douglass made gdn. of Thos. Jefferson Douglass a minor over 14 yrs.

DOUGLASS, DONALD—BOX 106, PACK 2757:
On July 31, 1815 Wm. Cochran, Joseph Foster, Wm. Lummus bound unto Taliaferro Livingston Ord. Abbeville Dist. sum $10,000.00. Wm. Cochran made gdn. of Donald Douglass a minor over 14 yrs.

DILBON. GEORGE—BOX 106, PACK 2758:
On Jan. 2, 1832 David, John Walker, Wade Esthridge bound unto Moses Taggart Ord. Abbeville Dist. sum $300.00. David Walker made gdn. of Geo. Dilbon a minor over 14 yrs.

DAVIS, (MINORS)—BOX 106, PACK 2759:
On Feb. 6, 1809 Wm. Davis Esq., Ezekiel Calhoun Sr., Wm. H. Caldwell bound unto Andrew Hamilton Ord. Abbeville Dist. sum $10,000.00. Wm. Davis made gdn. of Moses, Jas. C., Rebecca, Alexr. Davis minors.

DOWTIN, CATHARINE—BOX 106, PACK 2760:
On Feb. 7, 1831 Thos. P. Dowtin, Jas. C. Willard, Jas. Cason bound unto Moses Taggart Ord. Abbeville Dist. sum $1,000.00. Thos. P. Dowtin made gdn. of Catharine Dowtin a minor over 14 yrs.

DRUMMOND, MOSES—BOX 106, PACK 2761:
On Dec. 7, 1804 Thos., John Chatham bound unto Andrew Hamilton Ord. Abbeville Dist. sum $3,000.00. Thos. Chatham made gdn. of Moses Drummond.

DOWNEY, JOHN—BOX 106, PACK 2763:
Est. admnr. July 13, 1784 by Frances Downey, John Lockridge, Jas. Compton unto John Thomas Ord. 96 Dist. sum 1,000 lbs.

DAVIS, ABSOLOM—BOX 106, PACK 2764:
On Dec. 26, 1811 Abraham Livingston, Wm. Yarbrough, Titus Murry appointed to appraise est. of said Absolom Davis.

DAVISON, ELIZABETH—BOX 106, PACK 2765:
Est. admnr. Apr. 11, 1812 by Wm., John Davison unto Taliaferro Livingston Ord. Abbeville Dist. sum $2,000.00.

DOUGLASS, HUGH—BOX 106, PACK 2766:
Est. admnr. July 2, 1807 by Capt. John Meriwether, Jas. Cobb bound unto Andrew Hamilton Ord. Abbeville Dist. sum $10,000.00. Cit. pub. at Providence Church ment. Capt. John Meriwether next of kin.

DAMEWOOD, HENRY—BOX 106, PACK 2767:
Cit. pub. July 28, 1791 ment. Andrew Hamilton Esq. applied for Letters of Admnr. (No other papers.)

DONALD, MARY ANN—BOX 106, PACK 2768:
Cit. pub. Apr. 28, 1838 at Asbury Church ment. John A. Donald applied for Letters of Admnr. (No other papers.)

DEAL, JOHN—BOX 106, PACK 2769:
Est. admnr. June 14, 1791 by Rebeckah, Wm. Jr., Wm. Deal, Saml. Foster Sr. unto the Judges of Abbeville Dist. sum 1,000 lbs.

DUNLAP, JOHN—BOX 106, PACK 2770:
Est. admnr. Nov. 24, 1783 by Margaret Dunlap, Wm. Millwee, Jas. Millwee of Bush River unto John Thomas Ord. 96 Dist. sum 2,000 lbs.

DAVIS, ELIZABETH—BOX 106, PACK 2771:
Amount of negro hire and rent of plantation belonging to est. of
Elizabeth Davis decd. Jan. 1, 1829. Negro man Jim, Wm. Calhoun $60.00.
Lidda, Patsey, Robt. McComb $54.00. Plantation, Wm. Carson $35.00. (No
other papers.)

DOZEN OR DOZIER, JAMES—BOX 106, PACK 2772:
Will dated June 26, 1813 in Abbeville Dist. Prov. Sept. 24, 1813. Exr:
Bro., Abram Giles. Wit: John C. Mayson, Jeptha Dyson, Jas. Shackelford.
Bros., Abram Giles Dozen, John Dozen. Sis., Elizabeth Godfrey. Owned land
in Marion Dist. South Carolina. (Not positive if name was Dozen, Dozier as
writing wasn't so good.)

DONALDSON, JENNY—BOX 106, PACK 2773:
Will dated Sept. 19, 1809 in Abbeville Dist. Rec. Nov. 18, 1809. Exrs:
Robt. C. Gordon, John C. Calhoun, Wm. Wilson. Wit: Jas. Curry, Ezekiel
Sr., Elizabeth Evans. (In will name was written Gennet and Jenny Donaldson.)
Sis., Jane Fee now residing in the Kingdom of Ireland. Neices, Nancy wife of
Jas. Drake. Jenny Brackenridge. Nephew, Robt. Brackenridge. Bro., John
Brackenridge. Property was left to her by the last will of Mathew Donaldson.

DRUMMON, DANIEL—BOX 106, PACK 2774:
Will dated Feb. 7, 1822 in Abbeville Dist. Prov. July 16, 1822. Exr:
Aaron Clov—. Wit: Wm. Barmore, Moses Drummond, Chas. Cullins.
Wife, Rebecca Drummon. Chn: Jas. Mattison, Susannah, Aaron, Washington,
Elizabeth, Mason Drummon. Owned land in Laurens Dist.

DONALD, ALEXANDER—BOX 106, PACK 2775:
Will dated July 5, 1803 in Abbeville Dist. Rec. Mar. 2, 1806. Exrs:
John Donald, Andrew Gray. Wit: Wm., Deborah Norris, Jas. Edmiston. Gr.
sns: West, Jas. Jr., Andrew Donald. "A tract of land lying in Chester County
which my son Jas. Donald had in possession when he decd. after their
mother's decease or marriage." Gr. s., Geo. Donald. Give my son John Donald a
tract of land lying on Sandy River in Chester County, also a tract of land in
Richland County. Chn: Mary wife of Andrew Gray, Nancy wife of Robt. Gray,
Hezekia Donald. Gr. son: Archibald Douglass land lying on Bever Creek in
Fairfield County. Great gr. son. Donald Douglass land in Bever Creek in Fairfield County.

DOUGLASS, WILLIAM A.—BOX 106, PACK 2777:
Will dated Jan. 13, 1807 in Abbeville Dist. Rec. Jan. 29, 1807. Exrs:
John Meriwether, Jas. Gouedy. Wit: Zachary Meriwether Jr., Larkin Whitton,
Esther McGehee. Sis: Barbara wife of Robt. Meriwether. Wife, mother ment.
no names given. Inv. made Jan. 31, 1807 by Joseph Meriwether, Benjamin
Hatter, Nicholas Meriwether. Byrs: Dabney McGehee, Thos. Brightman,
Nicholas Meriwether, Carr McGehee, John Meriwether, Wm. Douglass, Wm.
Sample, Wm. Young, Robt. Meriwether, Jas. Pollard, John Wardlaw, Zachary
Meriwether, John McFarlin, Chas. Maxwell, Amon McMilan, Richard Hatter,
Jane Douglass, Francis Meriwether, Elizabeth Douglass, etc.

DUNLAP, WILLIAM—BOX 106, PACK 2778:
Will dated Oct. 20, 1810 in Abbeville Dist. Rec. Jan. 7, 1811. Exrs: Joseph Black Esq., Donald Fraser, Alexr. Hunter. Wit: Jas. Pringle, Wm. McMullan, Alexr. Hunter. Chn: Margaret Sullivan, Sarah Dunlap, Rachel Leonard, Hannah Maddison. Gr. chn: Wm. McMullan, Wm. Garvin. "Leave to the heirs of Wm. Reighley decd. vsz Mary, Wm., Anne, Jincey Reighley."

DELISHAW, SAMUEL—BOX 106, PACK 2779:
On Oct. 21, 1846 Jacob Delishaw Exr. of Saml. Delishaw ordered the sale to take place at residence of said decd. (No other papers.)

DELISHAW, SARAH ROBERSON—BOX 106, PACK 2780:
Will dated Aug. 16, 1781. Rec. Mar. 26, 1793. Exr: Husband, Jacob Delishaw. Wit: Peter Gibert Esq., Pierre Elie Bellot, Jacques Langel. "I leave my husband Jacob Delishaw all the money that is due me in the Bank of England."

ELLINGTON, MARY—BOX 106, PACK 2781:
On Jan. 4, 1830 John G., Wm. H. Caldwell, David Lesly, bound unto Moses Taggart Ord. Abbeville Dist. sum $2,000.00. John G. Caldwell made gdn. of Mary Ellington a minor over 14 yrs.

EMMERSON, ROBERT & SARAH—BOX 106, PACK 2782:
On Dec. 3, 1823 Geo. A. Miller, Jas. Sr., Jas. S. Russell bound unto Moses Taggart Ord. Abbeville Dist. sum $200.00. Geo. A. Miller made gdn. of Robt., Sarah Emmerson minors of Mary Emmerson decd.

EMMERSON, WILLIAM McCURDY—BOX 106, PACK 2783:
On Dec. 3, 1823 Henry Emmerson, Jas. Russell bound unto Moses Taggart Ord. Abbeville Dist. sum $100.00. Henry Emmerson gdn. of Wm. McCurdy Emmerson a minor.

ELMORE, (MINORS)—BOX 106, PACK 2784:
On Mar. 19, 1838 Simeon Chaney, Jas. Gillam, Wm. Whitley bound unto Moses Taggart Ord. Abbeville Dist. sum $500.00. Simeon Chaney made gdn. of John, Elizabeth, Emily Elmore minors.

EDWARDS, JAMES—BOX 106, PACK 2785:
On Sept. 17, 1838 Franklin, Jas. P. Bowie, Jas. Cobb bound unto Moses Taggart Ord. Abbeville Dist. sum $500.00. Franklin Bowie made gdn. of Jas. Edwards a minor. Sett. made Jan. 2, 1849 ment. Jas. Edwards now of age was son of Randel Edwards decd.

EDWARDS, AMOS & JAMES—BOX 106, PACK 2786:
On Mar. 29, 1811 Jane Edwards, Gilbert C. Smith bound unto Taliaferro Livingston Ord. Abbeville Dist. sum $500.00. Jane Edwards made gdn. of Amos, Jas. Edwards minors over 14 yrs.

EDWARDS, (MINORS)—BOX 106, PACK 2787:
On Feb. 24, 1801 Abraham Livingston, John Mann bound unto Andrew

Hamilton Ord. Abbeville Dist. sum $1,500.00. Abraham Livingston made gdn. of Matthew, Betsey, Andrew Edwards minors.

EVANS, ISOM—BOX 106, PACK 2788:
Est. admnr. May 25, 1784 by Nancy Evans, John McElhenney, Saml. Nesbett unto John Thomas Ord. 96 Dist. sum 2,000 lbs.

EDWARDS, THOMAS—BOX 106, PACK 2789:
Est. admnr. Mar. 26, 1796 by Jane Edwards wid., John Brannan, Robt. Smith, Josiah Chambers unto the Judges of Abbeville County sum 1,500 lbs.

ELMORE, MARTHA—BOX 106, PACK 2790:
Est. admnr. Apr. 1, 1829 by Stephen Witts, Jas. Patterson, Archibald Tittle unto Moses Taggart Ord. Abbeville Dist. sum $1,000.00.

EASTON, JAMES—BOX 106, PACK 2791:
Will dated Mar. 19, 1810. Prov. Feb. 11, 1812. Exrs: Henry Potter of Raleigh, John Kennedy near Washington, Joel Dickinson of Washington, Marshall Dickinson, of *Greenville*. Son, John S. Eaton (No Wit.) "Was of County of Pitt in State of N. C." Chn: Elizabeth Hardee Simpson Kennedy, John Simpson Easton. Wife ment. name not given. Give to my wife property which her mother Elizabeth Simpson gave unto us." Give all my debts due me in the western country to the chn. of Henry Potter and his wife Sylvia Potter."

EVANS, JOHN—BOX 106, PACK 2792:
Will dated Sept. 16, 1779. Prov. Feb. 8, 1785. Exr: Wife, Sarah Evans. Wit: Mary Edwards, Martha, Jas. Puckett. Chn: Josiah, Frances, Miriam. Rachel, Wm., John Evans, Mary Edwards.

ELGIN, CATY—BOX 106, PACK 2793:
Will dated Dec. 12, 1828 in Abbeville Dist. Prov. May 15, 1829. Wit: Jas. Latimer, Jas. Kay, Catharine Lattimer. "Bequeath land whereon Wm. Reeves now lives unto him provided he pay $54.00 to Alexr. Elgin. Bequeath property also to Ann Elgin, Elizabeth Hughs."

FRAZER, JOHN B.—BOX 107, PACK 2794:
On Jan. 19, 1820 Dorcas Frazer, John L. Livingston, David Lesly bound unto Moses Taggart Ord. Abbeville Dist. sum $1,000.00. Dorcas Frazer made gdn. of John B. Frazer a minor over 14 yrs.

FORESBROOK, HENRY—BOX 107, PACK 2795:
On Oct. 3, 1803 Saml. Morris, Saml. Foster, John Leard bound unto Andrew Hamilton Ord. Abbeville Dist. sum $5,000.00. Saml. Morris made gdn. of Henry Foresbrook a minor.

FOLK, ELIZA & JACOB—BOX 107, PACK 2796:
On Dec. 17, 1784 Peter Stockman, Henry Coone, Henry Stockman bound unto John Thomas Ord. 96 Dist. sum 2,000 lbs. Peter Stockman made gdn. of John, Elizabeth, Jacob Folk minors.

FIELDS, HETTY—BOX 107, PACK 2797:
On June 5, 1815 Wm. Wray, David H. Hathorn, Jas. McAdams bound unto Taliaferro Livingston Ord. of Abbeville Dist. sum $1,000.00. Wm. Wray made gdn. of Hetty Fields a minor over 14 yrs.

FIELDS, JOSEPH—BOX 107, PACK 2798:
On June 5, 1815 Wm. Wray, David H. Hathorn, Jas. McAdams bound unto Taliaferro Livingston Ord. Abbeville Dist. sum $1,000.00. Wm. Wray made gdn. of Joseph Fields, Olive Wray minors under 14 yrs.

FOSTER, POLLY ANN—BOX 107, PACK 2799:
On Oct. 25, 1834 Jas. M., Thos., John B. Foster bound unto Moses Taggart Ord. Abbeville Dist. sum $100.00. Jas. M. Foster made gdn. of Polly Ann Foster a minor under 14 yrs.

FURCHES, JOHN—BOX 107, PACK 2800:
Est. admnr. Oct. 18, 1816 by Elizabeth Furches, Jas. Russell, John Brannan unto Taliaferro Livingston Ord. Abbeville Dist. sum $10,000.00. Was late of Vienna in said dist.

FOSTER, JOHN—BOX 107, PACK 2801:
On June 5, 1826 Joseph Foster, Jas. Pulliam, Thos. B. Byrd bound unto Moses Taggart Ord. Abbeville Dist. sum $3,000.00. Joseph Foster made gdn. of John Foster a minor over 14 yrs.

FORD, JAMES—BOX 107, PACK 2802:
Est. admnr. Feb. 22, 1785 by John, John Jr. Steen unto John Thomas Ord. 96 Dist. sum 2,000 lbs. This bond was also for Elijah Wells, Jas. Ford.

FERGUSON, JOHN—BOX 107, PACK 2803:
Est. admnr. Mar. 13, 1787 by Wm. Simpson, Wm. Fowler, Andrew Park of the County of Laurens and Dist. of 96 unto John Thomas Ord. sum 1,000 lbs.

FOSTER, ANDREW—BOX 107, PACK 2804:
Est. admnr. Aug. 7, 1786 by Moses, Henry Foster, Saml. Kelso unto John Thomas Ord. 96 Dist. sum 200 lbs.

FRAZIER, DAVID—BOX 107, PACK 2805:
Est. admnr. Sept. 13, 1797 by John Frazier, John Gray, John Leany unto the Judges of Abbeville County sum $2,000.00.

FOOSHE, CHARLES—BOX 107, PACK 2806:
Est. admnr. Dec. 7, 1814 by Benjamin, Alexr. Houston unto Taliaferro Livingston Ord. Abbeville Dist. sum $2,000.00. Cit. pub. at Harmony Church. Sale, Dec. 22, 1814. Byrs: Elizabeth, Elijah Fooshee, Joseph Houston, John B. Winfield, Saml. Pursley, Jas. Hutchison, Wm. Moseley, John Gray.

FALAW, LEWIS—BOX 107, PACK 2807:
Est. admnr. Jan. 6, 1789 by John Wilson for myself and wife late Winney Falaw, John Miller, John Lindsay unto the Judges of Abbeville County

sum 1,000 lbs. Winney Wilson the wid. of said Lewis Falaw. Cit. pub. at Long Cane Church. Inv. made Jan. 31, 1789 by John Miller, Wm. Mayne, Saml. Lindsay.

FRITTES, CATREENA—BOX 107, PACK 2808:
Will dated May 7, 1805 in Abbeville Dist. Rec. Oct. 7, 1805. Wit: Wm. Dorris, John Basken, John Rampey. Chn: Elizabeth Rampey, Mary Martin. Gr. chn: Mary, Cattey, Margaret Rampey.

FOX, MARY—BOX 107, PACK 2809:
Will dated Feb. 19, 1828. Prov. Nov. 18, 1828. Exrs: Joseph Esq., Jas. A. Black Esq. Wit: Thos. Tinsley, Edmund P. Hollaman, Geo. W. Tinsley. Wid. of John Fox. Chn: Elizabeth, Catharine Fox, Mary Ann *Lucreery* Posten, Elenor wife of Jas. Able, Mathew Fox. Gr. chn: Mary Able, Mary Posten.

FORMAN, GEORGE—BOX 107, PACK 2810:
Will dated May 20, 1786 in Edgefield Dist. Exrs: Son, Isaac Forman. Dtr. Mary Forman. Wit: Jonathan Gouldsbrough, Benjamin Harvy, Athanathan Thomas. Wife, Charity Forman. Chn: Jacob Forman to his heirs lands in Crackers Neck on Savannah River. Geo. decd., Mary, Sarah, Martha, Judah, Nancy, Isaac, Verly, Olive, Gilpah Forman. Inv. made in Edgefield County Jan. 13, 1787 by Benjamin Ryan Jr., Nathaniel White, Gasper Gallman.

FOSTER, JAMES—BOX 107, PACK 2811:
State of South Carolina
96 Dist.
Be it remembered that in the night of the 4th day of this instant we to wite John Foster, John Cozby and Margaret McCarter being eacho of us present in the dwelling hous of Jas. Foster in the Long Cane Settl. in said dist, the said Jas. Foster being then in his last sickness of which he died on Monday night following being the 6th instant. That in the night first mentioned the said Jas. Foster then appeared to us to be of perfect memory and understanding. The Jas. Foster told the said John Foster that he would wish to settle his affairs as he believed it was death that was working with him & therefore desired his father, said John Foster to bring the above John Cozby present that he might deliver before them both how he would desire his affairs to be ordered, the above Margaret McCarter being also present with us & in the presence of the said Jas. Foster, who desired his lands might be devided between his four sons viz. John Foster, Jas. Foster, Robt. & Saml. Foster to wit, 100 acres of land to each of his sons. That his eldest son John was to have 100 acres of a place called The Five Springs. That his son Jas. was to have 100 acres at a place called the spring, which the said witnesses understood to be next adjoining to the 5 springs above mentioned, but did not direct how the remaining 200 acres of land where his dwelling house was how it should be divided between his two youngest sons viz. Robt. & Saml., the said Jas. Foster being desired by his father John Foster to consider how he would order matters between & concerning his wife and daughter made a (word) for sometime but that his sickness so increased that afterwards he the said Jas. Foster was not so

composed as to be capable to proceed farther in ordering how his other parts of property should be settled or disposed of. In witness whereof we the said John Foster, John Cozby and Margaret McCarter have hereunto signed our names in the presence of each other this 10th day of May 1782.

FORT, PHILIS—BOX 107, PACK 2812:
Will dated Jan. 25, 1781. Prov. Mar. 31, 1791. Exr: B. l. John Rivers, Lewis Holloway. Wit: Will. Reed, Phens. Alexander. Lived in Mecklenburg County, N. C. "Bequeath unto Jas. Son of John Rivers, bequeath unto Nancy dtr. of John Rivers, Thos., and Jones Rivers sons of John Rivers. Bequeath unto my sis. Mason Fort now in Va., money which lies in Co. David Mason's hand in Va., Sis. Frances For. Will was Prov. in Mecklenburg County, N. C. Mecklenburg Co. N. C. Agreeable to a dedimus to us directed from the Court of Common Pleas of the Dist. of 96. We Hezekiah Alexander & Wm. Folk Justices in the county aforesaid have caused to appear Wm. Wilson Esq. before us and him having sworn did put the following interogatories to which he answered in manner following. viz. First. Did you know Jas. Rivers a boy almost blind who passed as the son of John Rivers decd. Yes. I knew a boy who lived in the family of John Rivers & whom I then did conceive to be his son, he appeared to be about 10 yrs. of age, of a fair complexion & very near sighted, fair hair. This boy was so generally believed by people who lived in Rivers neighborhood to be his son & Wm. Reed or Rud who wrote Philis Fort well told me that he in writing Philis Forts will told me that in writting in said will had mistaken the name of Jas. Fort & inserted Jas. Frivers, this was done by the donor's telling him that she gave Jas. a negro. 2. Did you know Philis Fort, sis. of John Rivers wife, where did she live & where did she die? I knew Philis Fort said to be John Rivers wifes sis. that she lived in the house & with said John Rivers & that I believe she died at the house of Said Rivers. 3. What was done with the boy Jas. Rivers after the death of John Rivers? After the death of John Rivrs, which was some time after that of Philis Fort, Jones Rivers came into this county & by virtue of the will of John Rivers he Jas. became Exr. on said John's est. & took into charge the property by her given incharge of John Rivers. Jones Rivers becoming the Exr. of John Took into care the boy Jas. Rivers & not having sufficient horses as he said to carry him into Va. to his friends at the time he went there himself, left him in care of a certain Geo. Dean, with whom Jas. Rivers the boy lived sometime, when he taken to Va. by a certain Benjamin Maberry. Charlotte Oct. 4, 1791 Then did the aforementioned Wm. Wilson Esq. sign his name to the within interogatories before & in presence of us. Hezekiah Alexander, Wm. Filk. At the time that Jas. Rivers lived with John Rivers he as about 8 or 10 yrs. old in the years 1778 & 1779. On July 12, 1790 in Edgefield County, S. C. Jas. Fort came into court being 20 yrs. old and chose Edward Mitchell as his guardian.

GAINES, WILLIAM H.—BOX 107, PACK 2813:
On Jan. 31, 1852 Elizabeth Gaines, Stanmore Brooks, Reuben Hutchison bound unto Moses Taggart Ord. Abbeville Dist. sum $2,000.00. Elizabeth Gaines made gdn. of Wm. H. Gaines a minor. Son of Hiram Gaines decd.

Elizabeth Gaines his mother.

GAINES, SARAH ANN—BOX 107, PACK 2814:
On Feb. 1, 1830 John Ramsey, Thos. Carson, Lewellen Goode the 1st 2 of Anderson Dist. bound unto Moses Taggart Ord. Abbeville Dist. sum $1,000.00. John Ramsey made gdn. of Sarah Ann Gaines a minor over 14 yrs.

GLASSGO, SAMUEL—BOX 107, PACK 2815:
On Oct. 13, 1800 Andrew Cochran, John Beatty, Saml. Patterson bound unto Andrew Hamilton Ord. Abbeville Dist. sum $500.00. Andrew Cochran made gdn. of Saml. Glasgo a minor.

GLASGOW, (MINORS)—BOX 107, PACK 2816:
On Dec. 14, 1830 John Deall, David Anderson, John Pressly bound unto Moses Taggart Ord. Abbeville Dist. sum $500.00. John Dale made gdn. of Polly, Rebecca Mazena, John Harper Glasgow minors under 14 yrs.

GRAY, (MINORS)—BOX 107, PACK 2817:
On Aug. 9, 1836 Jas. Conner, Robt., Thos. W. Vernon bound unto Moses Taggart Ord. Abbeville Dist. sum $2,000.00. Jas. Connor made gdn. of Wm. A., Jas. A., John A., Martha Gray minors.

GUNNIN, (MINORS)—BOX 107, PACK 2818:
On Aug. 21, 1813 Jane Gunnin, Bruce Livingston bound unto Taliaferro Livingston Ord. Abbeville Dis. sum $2,000.00. Jane Gunnin made gdn. of Ann Patterson Gunnin, Nathan, Benjamin, Ezekiel Gunnin minors over 14 yrs.

GRAY, CHARLOTTE—BOX 107, PACK 2819:
On Jan. 9, 1836 Margaret, Martha M. Gray, Wm. Wire, bound unto Moses Taggart Ord. Abbeville Dist. sum $5,000.00. Margaret Gray made gdn. of Charlotte Gray a minor over 14 yrs.

GUNNIN, HANNAH WARDLAW—BOX 107, PACK 2820:
On Feb. 14, 1816 Jane Gunnin, Bruce Livingston, Wm. McMeen bound unto Taliaferro Livingston Ord. Abbeville Dist. sum $10,000.00. Jane Gunnin made gdn. of Hannah Wardlaw Gunnin a minor over 14 yrs.

GRIFFIN, JOHN—BOX 107, PACK 2821:
On Oct. 3, 1814 Wm. Lummus, Wm. Cochran, Dabney McGehee bound unto Taliaferro Livingston Ord. Abbeville Dist. sum $2,000.00. Wm. Lummus made gdn. of John Griffin a minor over 14 yrs.

GLOVER, WILLIS SATTERWHITE—BOX 107, PACK 2822:
On Feb. 14, 1815 Nahtan Lipscomb, Saml. Perrin bound unto Taliaferro Livingston Ord. Abbeville Dist. sum $10,000.00. Nathan Lipscomb made gdn. of Willis Satterwhite Glover a minor over 14 yrs.

GREEN, SAMUEL & WILLIAM—BOX 107, PACK 2823:
On May 3, 1830 Geo. W. Pressly, Robt. McBryde, Saml. Pressly bound unto Moses Taggart Ord. Abbeville Dist. sum $100.00. Geo. W. Pressly made guardian of Saml., Wm. Glover minors over 14 yrs.

GREEN, ROBERT—BOX 107, PACK 2824:
On Oct. 4, 1813 Catharine Green, Joseph Simpson, Ezekiel Calhoun bound unto Taliaferro Livingston Ord. Abbeville Dist. sum $2,000.00. Catharine Green made gdn. of Robt. Green a minor under 14 yrs.

GREEN, GEORGE L.—BOX 107, PACK 2825:
On Oct. 4, 1813 Catharine Green, Joseph Simpson, Ezekiel Calhoun bound unto Taliaferro Levingston Ord. Abbeville Dist. sum $2,000.00. Catharine Green made gdn. of Geo. L. Green a minor over 14 yrs.

GARRETT, STEPHEN & JAMES—BOX 107, PACK 2826:
On Dec. 2, 1786 John Martin, Jones Rivers bound unto John Thomas Ord. 96 Dist. sum 500 lbs. Jones Rivers made gdn. of Stephen, Jas. Garrett minors.

GHENT, JOHN—BOX 107, PACK 2827:
On Dec. 6, 1826 Elijah Hunt, John McCraven bound unto Moses Taggart Ord. Abbeville Dist. sum $3,000.00. Elijah Hunt made gdn. of John Ghent a minor over 14 yrs.

GARRETT, WILLIAM—BOX 107, PACK 2828:
On Dec. 2, 1786 John, Edmond Martin bound unto John Thomas Ord. 96 Dist. sum 1,000 lbs. Edmond Martin made gdn. of Wm. Garrett a minor.

GAINES, SALLY—BOX 107, PACK 2829:
On Mar. 20, 1810 Henry G., Benjamin Johnson, Edmond Ware bound unto John Hamilton Ord. Abbeville Dist. sum $5,000.00. Henry G. Johnson made gdn. of Sally Gaines a minor.

GILL, MARY—BOX 107, PACK 2830:
On Nov. 7, 1803 Milton Paschal, Martin Loftis, Wm. Kerr bound unto Andrew Hamilton Ord. Abbeville Dist. sum $5,000.00. Milton Paschal made gdn. of Mary Gill a minor.

GRIFFIN, SUSANNA & RICHARD—BOX 107, PACK 2831:
On Sept. 15, 1803 John, Jas. Smith, Wm. Stevens bound unto Andrew Hamilton Ord. Abbeville Dist. sum $5,000.00. John Smith made gdn. of Susannah, Richard Griffin minors.

GILLALAND, WILLIAM—BOX 107, PACK 2832·
Est. admnr. Apr. 29, 1785 by Joseph Towles, Jeremiah Williams, Jacob Chandler unto John Thomas Ord. 96 Dist. sum 1,000 lbs

GAINES, BENJAMIN—BOX 107, PACK 2833:
Est. admnr. June 12, 1815 by Elizabeth Gaines, Edmond, Wm. Ware unto Taliaferro Livingston Ord. Abbeville Dist. sum $2,000.00.

GRAY, JOHN—BOX 107, PACK 2834:
Est. admnr. Mar. 16, 1807 by Rebecca, Robt., Alexr. Gray, Archibald Douglass unto Andrew Hamilton Ord. Abbeville Dist. sum $10,000.00.

GRIFFIN, JAMES—BOX 107, PACK 2835:
Est. admnr. Feb. 6, 1815 by John L. Griffin, Edmond Stephens, unto Taliaferro Livingston Ord. Abbeville Dist. sum $1,000.00. Cit. pub. at Cambridge ment. Jas. L. Griffin was late of the Army of the U. S.

GOWEDY, ROBERT—BOX 107, PACK 2836:
Est. admnr. Apr. 5, 1790 by Jas. Gowedy, Wm. Moore, David Cunningham unto the Judges of Abbeville County sum 1,000 lbs.

GOLDING, RICHARD—BOX 107, PACK 2837:
Est. admnr. Oct. 7, 1788 by Susannah Golding wid., John Hallum, David Clark unto the Judges of Abbeville County sum 1,000 lbs. (Written Golding, Goulding.)

GOULDEN, JAMES—BOX 107, PACK 2838:
Cit. pub. Jone 26, 1827 ment. Geo. Bowen applied for Letters of Admnr. (No other papers.)

GILLAM, JAMES—BOX 107, PACK 2839:
Cit. pub. Mar. 25, 1837 at Lowndsville ment. Michael Taylor Applied for Letters of Admnr. (No other papers).

GRIGSBY, JAMES—BOX 107, PACK 2840:
On Dec. 17, 1785 Enoch Grigsby, Jacob Smith bound unto John Thomas Jr. Ord 96 Dist. sum 2,000 lbs. Enoch Grigsby made gdn. of Jas. Grigsby a minor.

GIBSON, GILBERT—BOX 107, PACK 2841:
Cit. pub. Apr. 7, 1788 at Long Cane Church ment. Adam Crain Jones Esq. applied for Letters of Admnr. (No other papers.)

GORLEY, JAMES—BOX 107, PACK 2842:
Will dated Sept. 17, 1788. Prov. July 6, 1790. Exrs: Alexr. Smith, John Logan. Wit: Alecr. Logan, Robt. Yeldin, Margaret McCreery. Was of Cambridge, Abbeville Dist. Bros., Robt. Thos., Hugh Gorley. B. l. Saml. Keown. "Give to David Hawthorn, Margaret McCreery, Andrew Cochran, Jas. Fell." Est. admnr. July 6, 1790 by Andrew Ross, Robt., Thos. Gorley unto the Judges of Abbeville County sum 500 lbs.

GRAY, ARTHUR—BOX 107, PACK 2843:
Will dated Nov. 9, 1826 in Abbeville Dist. Prov. Dec. 1, 1826. Exrs: Wife, Mary Gray, Alexr. Foster. Wit: John Gray, Jane Foster, Mary Spence. Chn. ment. names not given.

GRIMSLY, ELIJAH—BOX 107, PACK 2844:
Will dated Feb. 1, 1786 in Abbeville Dist. Prov. Apr. 28, 1786. Exrs. Saml. Rosamond, Richard Hodges. Wit: Ledford Payne, Robt. Swain, Wm. Hodges. "Give wife a tract of land being in the State of N. C. on Pettening Creek in Dobs County which land is now in the possession of my bro. John Grimsley. Give dtr. Mary Grimsly a tract of land in Washington County, Ga.

Waters of Broad River. Wife's name not given. Sis., Sarah Hodges in Laurens County. Richard, John Hodges sons of said Sarah Hodges.

GLOVER, JOHN F.—BOX 107, PACK 2845:
    Will dated Mar. 4, 1819 in Abbeville Dist. Prov. Nov. 14, 1819. Exrs: Wife, Jean Glover. Son, Jarrot H. Glover. Wit: Elizabeth Caldwell. Wm. T. Drennan, Wm. Robison Jr. Chn: Jarrot H., Sarah Cate, Edwin Atwood, Allen Glover. Owned land on the Five Noch Road.

GLOVER, WILLIAM—BOX 107, PACK 2846:
    Will dated Apr. 24, 1782 in Camden Dist. Prov. Aug. 24, 1782. Exrs: Sons, Drewry, John Glover. Wit: Randel Griffin, Edward Lacey. Wife, Chatrine Glover. Chn: John, Drewry Glover, Elizabeth wife of Philip *Sandefree,* Mary, Jess, Wm. Glover. Give to my son Lowrys son John 10 shillings. Give to my son Isums son Frederich 10 shillings.

GRAHAM, JAMES, SR.—BOX 107, PACK 2847:
    Will dated Aug. 21, 1815 in Abbeville Dist. Rec. Jan. 29, 1816. Exrs: Sons, Jas. Jr., Wm. Graham, Thos. Wilson. Wit: Thos. Moore, Benjamin Rosamond, Henry Wilson. Chn: Wm., Jas. Jr., Jenny, Margaret, Mary Graham. Wife ment. name not given. Gr. sons: Jas. son of Wm. Graham, Jas. son of Jas Graham Jr. and Barzilla Graham.

GILLESPIE, ANDREW—BOX 107, PACK 2848:
    Will dated July 24, 1813. Pro. May 3, 1819. Exrs. Son, Andrew Gillespie. Wit: Jas. B. English, Abraham, Jane Livingston. Wife, Jane Gillespie. Chn: Andrew, Jane, Daniel, John Gillespie.

GLANTON, BENJAMIN—BOX 107, PACK 2849:
    Will dated Mar. 21, 1782 in 96 Dist. Exrs: Wife, Margaret Glanton, Son, John Glanton, Jas. Harrison. Wit: Mary Cochan, Susanna Glanton. Chn: John, Lues, Benjamin Glanton, Fauniah Bryan, Molley Spieer.

HUGHES, JAS. AND PERMELIA—BOX 107, PACK 2850:
    On Oct. 30, 1833 Jas. Sr., Thos. Hughes, John Pursell bound unto Moses Taggart Ord. Abbeville Dist. sum $1,300.00. Jas. Hughes made gdn. of Jas., Permelia Hughes minors. Desire of Jas., Pamelia A. Hughes that their father Jas. Hughes be appointed their gdn. to take charge of the legacy left them by the will of Uel Hill.

HAGAN, MINORS—BOX 107, PACK 2851:
    On Dec. 7, 1835 Wm., Edward Hagan, Wm. Gordon bound unto Moses Taggart Ord. Abbeville Dist. sum $3,000.00. Wm. Hagan made gdn. of Alexr. G., Thos., Andrew B. Hagan minors.

HUBBARD, MINORS—BOX 107, PACK 2852:
    On Sept. 22, 1814 David Richardson, Wm. Sr., John Morris bound unto Taliaferro Livingston Ord. Abbeville Dist. sum $2,000.00. David Richardson made gdn. of Holloway, Mary Hubbard minors over 14 yrs. Elizabeth, Sarah, Dovey, Cynthia Hubbard minors under 14 yrs.

HASLET, MINORS—BOX 107, PACK 2853:
On Jan. 2, 1827 Hannah A. Haslet, Thos. Montgomery, Joseph B. Gibert bound unto Moses Taggart Ord. Abbeville Dist. sum $2,000.00. Hannah A. Haslet made gdn. of Jas. A., Moses W., Hannah C. Haslet the latter under 14 yrs. the 2 former over 14 yrs.

HOPPER, MINORS—BOX 107, PACK 2854:
On Feb. 3, 1832 Elizabeth Hopper, Robt. Y., Wm. S. Jones bound unto Moses Taggart Ord. Abbeville Dist. sum $2,000.00. Elizabeth Hopper made gdn. of Saml. Y., Catharine M., Elizabeth Hopper minors of Saml. J. Hopper. The minor Saml. was written Saml. J. in bond but on another paper written Saml. Y. (Don't know which is right.)

HILL, JAMES. W.—BOX 107, PACK 2855:
On Nov. 28, 1839 Landy G. Shoemaker, Andrew J. Donald, Laban T. Shoemaker bound unto Moses Taggart Ord. Abbeville Dist. sum $3,000.00. Landy G. Shoemaker made gdn. of Jas. W. Hill a minor under 14 yrs.

HEARST, MINORS—BOX 107, PACK 2856:
On Nov. 7, 1827 John Heard, Donald Douglass bound unto Moses Taggart Ord. Abbeville Dist. sum $10,000.00. Col. John Hearst made gdn. of Jane Hearst a minor over 14 yrs., John W., Elizabeth K. Hearst minors under 14 yrs.

HAMILTON, ALEXANDER—BOX 107, PACK 2857:
On Aug. 6, 1810 John Gray, Wm., Jas. Hutchison bound unto John Hamilton Ord. Abbeville Dist. sum $3,000.00. Jas. Hutchison made gdn. of Alexr. Hamilton a minor.

HEARST, MINORS—BOX 107, PACK 2858:
On Nov. 7, 1814 John, Wm., Hearst, John Chiles bound unto Taliaferro Livingston Ord. Abbeville Dist. sum $10,000.00. John Hearst made gdn. of Mary, Sarah Hearst minors over 14 yrs., Isbel Hearst a minor under 14 yrs.

HENDERSON, MINORS—BOX 107, PACK 2859:
On Oct. 29, 1812 Margaret Henderson, Wm. Norris, Henry Livingston bound unto Taliaferro Livingston Ord. Abbeville Dist. sum $2,000.00. Margaret Henderson made gdn. of John, Lucinda, Jane, Nancy, Sally Amanda Henderson minors under 14 yrs.

HENDERSON, MINORS—BOX 107, PACK 2860:
On Oct. 29, 1812 John Henderson, Jas. Devlin, David Cochran bound unto Taliaferro Livingston Ord. Abbeville Dist. sum $2,000.00. John Henderson made gdn. of Sally, Peggy, Harriet, Robt. Lewis Henderson minors under 14 yrs.

HOLLIDAY, WILLIAM E.—BOX 107, PACK 2861:
On June 18, 1827 Geo. W. Hodges, John, Donald Douglass bound unto Moses Taggart Ord. Abbeville Dist. sum $2,000.00. Donald Dougless made gdn. of Wm. E. Holliday a minor over 14 yrs.

HARLAND, EZEKIEL—BOX 107, PACK 2862:
On Dec. 4, 1786 John McCoy, Wm. Carson, Michael Duvall bound unto John Thomas Ord. 96 Dist. sum 500 lbs. John McCoy made gdn. of Ezekiel Harland a minor.

HADDEN, ROBERT JR.—BOX 107, PACK 2863:
Est. admnr. Oct. 8, 1788 by Wm. Mayn, Jas. Stevenson, Wm. Ross unto the Judges of Abbeville County sum 1,000 lbs. Cit. pub. at Greenville Church.

HUDNELL, EZEKIEL—BOX 107, PACK 2864:
Est. admnr. May 9, 1812 by John Hudnell, Robt. Johnson, David Pace unto Taliaferro Livingston Ord. Abbeville Dist. sum $1,000.00. Cit. pub. at Bufflow Church.

HALL, VINCENT—BOX 107, PACK 2865:
Est. admnr. July 3, 1834 by Sarah Hall, Saml. Young, Bennett McAdams unto Moses Taggart Ord. Abbeville Dist. sum $1,000.00. Cit. pub. at Little River Church.

HEARST, JOSEPH, SR.—BOX 107, PACK 2866:
Est. admnr. Oct. 20, 1814 by John Jr., Joseph Hearst, Andrew Paul, Joseph McCord unto Taliaferro Livingston Ord. Abbeville Dist. sum $2,000.00.

HAMILTON, JOHN—BOX 107, PACK 2867:
Est. admnr. June 14, 1791 by John Norwood, Wm. Russell, Benjamin Howard unto the Judges of Abbeville County sum 1,000 lbs. Est. admnr. again Jan. 24, 1791 by John Norwood, Wm. Cunningham, Wm. Shillitoe unto the Judges of Abbeville County sum 1,000 lbs. Cit. pub. at Long Cane Church.

HEWS, WILLIAM—BOX 107, PACK 2868:
Est. admnr. Dec. 23, 1782 by Thos. Brandon, Joseph Hews, Jas. Noble unto John Ewing Calhoun Ord. 96 Dist. sum 14,000 lbs.

HARRIS, BARTON—BOX 107, PACK 2869:
Est. admnr. Dec. 2, 1785 by Rebecca Harris, Edward Couch, John Vardell unto John Thomas Ord. 96 Dist. sum 1,000 lbs. Will dated Nov. 13, 1781. Wit: John *Arters* or *Asters,* Mary *Arter* or *Aster.* Lived in 96 Dist. Wife, Rebecca Harris. Chn: ment. names not given. Wife was Exr.

HOLLOWAY, CHARLES—BOX 107, PACK 2870:
Est. admnr. July 27, 1783 by Vardry McBee of Thickety, John Thomas Esq. of Tyger River unto John Thomas Ord. 96 Dist. sum 2,000 lbs.

HAYS, JOSEPH—BOX 107, PACK 2871:
Est. admnr. Aug. 12, 1786 by John Sunter, Joseph Adair, Lewis Saxon, Lewis Davis Yancey unto John Thomas Ord. 96 Dist. sum 5,000 lbs.

HATCHER, BENJAMIN—BOX 107, PACK 2872:
Est. admnr. Oct. 17, 1886 by John Hatcher, Jesse Roundtree, Vann Swearington unto John Thomas Ord. 96 Dist. sum 1,000 lbs.

HAM, JEREMIAH—BOX 107, PACK 2873:
Est. admnr. Apr. 9, 1785 by Jas. Hamm, Abraham Moore, Thos. Williams bound unto John Thomas Ord. 96 Dist. sum 2,000 lbs.

HARVICK, WILLIAM—BOX 107, PACK 2874:
Will dated May 21, 1824 in Abbeville Dist. Prov. Aug. 2, 1824. Exr. Nicholas Harvick. Wit: Orville Tatom, Williamson Norwood, Major B. Clark. "Leave to my bro. Nicholas Harvick all my lands lying in the Arkensaw Territory. Nephew, Wm. Harvick, Bro., Jacob Harvick, Sis., Polly wife of Andrew Warnick.

HOUSTON, JOHN, JR.—BOX 107, PACK 2875:
Est. admnr. June 10, 1793 by Mary Lemaster formerly Mary Houston wid. of John Houston Jr. decd., Joseph Lemaster, Capt. John, Jas. Calhoun unto the Judges of Abbeville Dist. sum 500 lbs. Cit. pub. at Hopewell Church.

HARRIS, JOHN—BOX 107, PACK 2876.
Est. admnr. Dec. 15, 1786 by John Rodgers, Jas., Chas. Saxon unto John Thomas Ord. Abbeville Dist. sum 1,000 lbs.

HARRIS, ROBERT M.—BOX 107, PACK 2877:
Est. admnr. June 6, 1814 by Martha Harris, Jas., Wm. Hutchison unto Taliaferro Livingston Ord. Abbeville Dist. sum $1,000.00.

HODGES, WILLIAM SR.—BOX 107, PACK 2878:
Est. admnr. Feb. 19, 1838 by John F. Gray, David L. Wardlaw, Thos. C. Perrin unto Moses Taggart Ord. Abbeville Dist. sum $10,000.00. Cit. pub. at Tabernacle and Cokesbury.

HILL, BENJAMIN BOX 107, PACK 2879:
On Feb. 16, 1824 Thos. Goodman, John D. Williams, Wm. Collier were ordered to appraise the est. of Benjamin Hill decd. (No other papers.)

HILL, WILLIAM C.—BOX 107, PACK 2880:
Est. admnr. Nov. 7, 1822 by Jesse, John Calvert, Joshua Davis unto Moses Taggart Ord. Abbeville Dist. sum $2,000.00.

HEARD, ARMSTRONG, JR.—BOX 107, PACK 2881:
Est. admnr. Apr. 13, 1816 by Zachary Meriwether, Jas. P., Isaac Heard unto Taliaferro Livingston Ord. Abbeville Dist. sum $10,000.00. Inv. made Apr. 22, 1816 by Billups Gayle, David Cunningham, Jas. Heard. Sale, Apr. 27, 1816. Byrs: Isaac Heard, Robt. Christy, John Mays, John Carter, Wm. White, Wm. Nichols, Jonathan Swift, Reuben Gains, Washington Bostick, Gibson Wooldridge.

HEARD, TABITHA—BOX 107, PACK 2882:
Est. admnr. Oct. 6, 1807 by Richard Heard, Edward Stephens, Isaac Logan unto Andrew Hamilton Ord. Abbeville Dist. sum $10,000.00. Was the wife of said Richard Heard.

HIGGINS, JOHN—BOX 107, PACK 2883:
Est. admnr. Mar. 26, 1793 by Adam Crain Jones Esq., Patrick McDowall, Saml. Savage unto the Judges of Abbeville County sum 500 lbs.

HAGOOD, REBECCA—BOX 107, PACK 2884:
Will dated June 2, 1824 in Abbeville Dist. Prov. Oct. 7, 1825. Exrs: Catlett Connor, Garland Chiles. Wit: Wm. Caldwell, John C. McGehee, Joseph N. Whitner. Owned land on Cuffetown Creek. Dtr., Eliza Ann Hagood. Sis., Eliza Chiles, Holly Moore Ray.

HODGES, ELIZABETH—BOX 107, PACK 2885:
Will dated May 6, 1799 in 96 Dist. Prov. Oct. 7, 1816. Exrs: Sons, Chas., John Hodges. Wit: Saml. Anderson, Jas. Dougharty, John Hodges.

HEARTLY, GEORGE—BOX 107, PACK 2886:
Will dated at Camden Sept. 20, 1780. Wit: A true copy translated from the German Taken by me, Wm. Houseal this 25th Nov., 1786. Wm. Vanhorn, Lieut., Capt. Livingston, Michael Kinard, Mathew Quatelbaum. Wife, Parlotta Heartly. Give 100 acres of land to my bros. son, Geo. Heartly which I hold over the Baptisim as God-father.

HUGHES, CATHARINE—BOX 107, PACK 2887:
Will dated Oct. 10, 1795 in Abbeville Dist. Rec. Mar. 27, 1797. Wit: Linsay Shewmaker, Andrew McCoy, Andrew Holland. Gr. chn: Caterener, Jean Hanner, Margaret, Wm. Hughes Holland.

HARRIS, JEAN—BOX 107, PACK 2888:
Will dated June 14, 1786. Exrs: Wm. Dawkins, Jas. Liles, Sanvard Cockrell. Wit: Geo., Micajah Harris, Robt. Rutherford. Chn: Jean Dawkins, Cloey Liles, Lettes Cockrell.

HUTCHISON, WILLIAM, JR.—BOX 107, PACK 2889:
Will dated Jan. 13, 1797 in Abbeville Dist. Rec. Mar. 27, 1797. Exrs: Wm. McGaw, Fleming Bates. Wit: Saml., Mary Ann, Agness Hutchison Jr. Mother, Agness Hutchison. Bro., Robt. Hutchison.

HARRIS, BEN OR BURR—BOX 107, PACK 2890:
Will dated Aug. 26, 1783 in 96 Dist. Prov. Mar. 8, 1787. Exrs: Sons, Geo., Cage Harris. Wit: Wm. Riddell, Robt. Rutherford, Thos. Cockrell. Wife, Jean Harris. Chn: Obed, Thos., Geo., Cage Harris. Inv. made May 7, 1787 by Robt. Rutherford, Wm. Dawkins, Wm. Herring.

HARRIS, THOMAS—BOX 107, PACK 2891:
Will dated Sept. 8, 1826 in Abbeville Dist. Prov. Dec. 4, 1826. Exrs: Wm. H. Caldwell, Elijah N. or M. Harris. Wit: Nancy S Cain, Jesse Kennedy, Jas. H. Baskin. Wife ment. name not given. Chn: John, Thos. A., Jas., Wm. P., Elijah Harris.

HOWLET, PINNIX—BOX 107, PACK 2892:
Will dated June 2, 1816 in Abbeville Dist. Rec. May 9, 1817. Exrs:

Rev. Hugh Dickson, Geo. Connor. Wit: John Davison, Wm. Pardue, Jas. Lomax Jr. Wife, Peggy Howlet. Chn: Eliza, Betey, Jerusha, Polly Howlet.

HAMMET, JAMES—BOX 107, PACK 2893:
Will dated May 4, 1781 in 96 Dist. Prov. Mar. 9, 1787. Exrs: Wife, Hannah Hammet. Son, John Hammet. Wit: Wm. Laughlin, Jas. Pinkerton, Elizabeth Hammet. Will was prov. by Elizabeth Harris then Elizabeth Hammet.

HAMMOND, JOHN, SR.—BOX 107, PACK 2894:
Will dated Jan. 22, 1779 in 96 Dist. Exr: Nephew, Chas. Hammond. Wit: John Jr., Saml., Susanna Hammond. Chn: Susanna, Chas., Leroy, John Hammond. Wife, Ann Hammond.

HARRIS, REV. JOHN—BOX 107, PACK 1895:
No will given. Prov. Apr. 5, 1790. Exrs: Wife, Mary Harris. Sons, Handy, John Harris. Wit: Robt. Hall, John Bowie, Joseph Wason. Lived in Abbeville Dist. Minister of the Gospel. Chn: Handy, John Harris, Elizabeth wife of Joseph Erving, Anne Handy McCurdy, Thos. Harris. Gr. dtr: Elizabeth Luerena McCurdy. "Land lying on Keowee River."

HAWKINS, JOHN—BOX 107, PACK 2896:
Will dated July 18, 1797 in Abbeville Dist. Rec. Mar. 25, 1799. Exr: Son, Benjamin Hawkins. Wit: John Cunningham, John Fiske, Tyre Maulden. Wife, Elizabeth Hawkins. Chn: Elizabeth, Rebecca, Mary, Patience, Nancy, Joseph, Jas., Mathew, Benjamin Hawkins.

HOGAINS, JOSEPH BOX 107, PACK 2897.
Will dated Nov. 18, 1779 in 96 Dist. Prov. Feb. 9, 1785. Exr: Wife, Rebecca Hogains. Wit: Sterling Turner, Peter, John Foy. "Bequeath to Jesse, Sarah Gains."

HUSTON, JAMES—BOX 107, PACK 2898:
Will dated Oct. 9, 1799. Rec. Nov. 25, 1802. Exrs: Dtr., Mary Huston, Wm. Sample, John Meriwether. Wit: John Meriwether. S. l. Wm. Sample.

HARRIS, HARRIET—BOX 107, PACK 2899:
On Dec. 14, 1812 Walter H. Ward, Richard, Nathaniel Harris bound unto Taliaferro Livingston Ord. Abbeville Dist. sum $2,000 00. Walter H. Ward made gdn. of Harriet Harris a minor.

JACKSON, WILLIAM (MINORS)—BOX 108, PACK 2900:
On Jan. 1, 1827 Robt. Conn, Wm. Robinson bound unto Moses Taggart Ord. Abbeville Dist. sum $2,000.00. Robt. Conn made gdn. of Peggy, Eliza Jackson minors over 14 yrs.

JACKSON, WILLIAM (MINORS)—BOX 108, PACK 2901:
On Mar. 18, 1831 Wm. Robertson, Patrick Gibson, John Creswell bound unto Moses Taggart Ord. Abbeville Dist. sum $500.00. Wm. Robertson made gdn. of Mary, Thos., Wm. Jackson minors.

JONES, SALLY—BOX 108, PACK 2902:
On Nov. 4, 1811 Andrew Milligan, Robt. Wooldridge bound unto
Taliaferro Livingston Ord. Abbeville Dist. sum $1,000.00. Andrew Milligan
made gdn. of Sally Jones a minor over 14 yrs.

JACKSON, MINORS—BOX 108, PACK 2903:
On Oct. 22, 1806 Josiah Patterson, Robt. Foster, Jas. McCarter, Alexr.
Houston bound unto Andrew Hamilton Ord. Abbeville Dist. sum $10,000.00.
Josiah Patterson made gdn. of Mathew, Hezekiah, Robt., Patsey Jackson minors.

JONES, THOMAS—BOX 108, PACK 2904:
Will dated July 19, 177 (last number torn from page.) Prov. Jan. 20,
1786. Exrs: Wife, Catherin Jones, Joseph Hampton, Capt. Chas. King. Wit:
Isaac, Ann Morgan, Sarah Wood. Lived in 96 Dist. Chn: Elizabeth Jones.
Other chn. ment. no names given.

JAMES, JOHN LASHLY—BOX 108, PACK 2905:
Est. admnr. June 14, 1784 by Chas. James, Wm. Crocker unto John
Thomas Ord. 96 Dist. sum 2,000 lbs.

JOHNSON, JOHN—BOX 108, PACK 2906:
Est. admnr. May 12, 1792 by Elizabeth Johnson wid., Nathaniel Bailey,
Joseph Gouge unto the Judges of Abbeville County sum 500 lbs. Cit. pub. at
Greenville Church.

IRWIN, CAPT. JOHN—BOX 108, PACK 2907:
Est. admnr. Mar. 26, 1796 by Mary Irwin wid., Jas. Irwin, John
Hairston, Thos. Brightman Sr., Jas. Stevenson, John Irwin Jr., Col. John
Norwood unto the Judges of Abbeville County sum 1,500 lbs. Cit. pub. at
Greenville Church.

JOHNSON, JOHN—BOX 108, PACK 2908:
Est. admnr. Apr. 28, 1785 by Moses Lyddle, John Norwood unto John
Thomas Ord. 96 Dist. sum 1,000 lbs.

JONES, ANDREW—BOX 108, PACK 2909:
Est. admnr. Nov. 4, 1799 by Peter Tutton, Reuben Weed, Wm. Deale
Jr. unto Andrew Hamilton Ord. 96 Dist. sum $4,000.00. Cit. pub. at Rocky
Spring Meeting House ment. Reuben Weed, Wm. Deale Jr. next of kin.

JOLLY, JOSEPH, JR.—BOX 108, PACK 2910:
Est. admnr. July 17, 1783 by Thos. Brandon, Joseph Hughes, Turner
Roundtree, Jas. Woodson bound unto John Thomas Ord. 96 Dist. sum 2,000 lbs.

JONES, THOMAS—BOX 108, PACK 2911:
Est. admnr. Nov. 10, 1786 by Henry Parkman, Jas. Coursey, Wm. Terry
unto John Thomas Ord. 96 Dist. sum 1,000 lbs.

JONES, JOSEPH, JR.—BOX 108, PACK 2912:
Est. admnr. Sept. 5, 1783 by Candice, Candice Jones Jr., Wm. Thomas
unto John Thomas Ord. 96 Dist. sum 2,000 lbs.

KENNEDY, ROBERT—BOX 108, PACK 2913:
On June 1, 1807 Wilson Kennedy, Mathew Russell bound to Andrew Hamilton sum $1,000.00. Wilson Kennedy made gdn. of Robt. Kennedy a minor.

KENNEDY, HUGH—BOX 108, PACK 2914:
On May 1, 1815 Jas. Hutchison, Geo. Creswell bound unto Taliaferro Livingston Ord. Abbeville Dist. sum $1,000.00. Jas. Hutchison made gdn. of Hugh Kennedy a minor over 14 yrs.

KIRKWOOD, WILLIAM C.—BOX 108, PACK 2915:
On Nov. 21, 1836 Hugh Kirkwood, Saml. Reid, Leroy C. Wilson bound unto Moses Taggart Ord. Abbeville Dist. sum $100.00. Hugh Kirkwood made gdn. of Wm. C. Kirkwood a minor.

KELLAR, DAVID (MINORS)—BOX 108, PACK 2916:
On July 26, 1833 David, John Keller, J. C. Wharton bound unto Moses Taggart Ord. Abbeville Dist. sum $2,000.00. David Kellar made gdn. of John J., Sarah A., Elizabeth B., Elvira, Angeline Kellar minors.

KEY, WALTER G.—BOX 108, PACK 2917:
Est. admnr. Mar. 27, 1850 by P. D. Klugh, Wm. Hill unto F. W. Sellick Ord. Abbeville Dist. sum $800.00. Sett. made June 15, 1850. The only distributee is Mary E. Key a sis. of the whole blood now in Troup County, Ga. Shares of Walter G., Mary E. Key in the est. of Humphrey Klugh decd. $488.43. On Nov. 6, 1837 Paschal D. Klugh, John Cochran and Wm. Norwood bound unto Moses Taggart Ord. Abbeville Dist. sum $600.00. Paschal D. Klugh made gdn. of Walter, Mary Key minors. (Name written Key and Kee.) On June 4, 1850 Alexr. A. Roberts of Troup County, Ga. appointed John H. Wilson of Abbeville Dist., S. C. his attorney to receive from Paschal D. Klugh who was admnr. of Walter Key late of Edgefield Dist. his part of said est.

KENNEDY, HUGH—BOX 108, PACK 2918:
On Aug. 27, 1814 Jas. Kennedy, John Winfield, Jas. Karr bound unto Taliaferro Livingston Ord. Abbeville Dist. sum $1,000.00. Jas Kennedy made gdn. of Hugh Kennedy a minor under 14 yrs.

KAISE, MARIA ELIZABETH—BOX 108, PACK 2919:
Will dated Sept. 9, 1791. Rec. Mar. 25, 1801. Wit: Jas. Stiefel, (Name not plain.) Lived on Hard Labor Creek in Edgefield County. Dtr., Elizabeth Margretha Caise.

KELLY, MICHAEL—BOX 108, PACK 2920:
Will dated Dec. 18, 1834 in Abbeville Dist. No Exr. Wit: Joel Lockhart, Israel Desernett, Arthur Bowie. Wife, Hannah Kelly. Chn. ment. names not given.

KENNEDY, JOSEPH, DR.—BOX 108, PACK 2921:
Will dated Aug. 1, 1795 in Abbeville Dist. Rec. Mar. 25, 1796. Exrs:

Sons, Wm., Josiah Kennedy. Wit: John, Susannah Connor. Wife, Mary Kennedy. Chn: Wm. C. Kennedy, Mary Barr, Josiah, Andrew, Elizabeth, Joshua, Joseph, Maxfield Kennedy. Owned land on Broadmouth Creek. "Give to son Maxfield Kennedy 100 acres in Ga."

KIRKWOOD, HUGH—BOX 108, PACK 2922:
    Will dated Oct. 10, 1779. Prov. Apr. 27, 1785. Exr: Major John Bowie. Wit: John Caldwell, John Moore, Bennet Crafton. "Serjeant of the 2nd Co. of Independants in the Service of the State of S. C. being to all appearance at the point of death occasioned by a wound I recd. the 9th Inst. in an attack made on the Town of Savannah." Order my Exr. to make titles of land to General Andrew Williamson Esq. on the waters of Little River. Ment. 3 chn. names not given.

KIRKWOOD, SALLY—BOX 108, PACK 2923:
    Est. admnr. Feb. 2, 1808 by Geo. Bowie Esq., Jas. Kyle unto Andrew Hamilton Ord. Abbeville Dist. sum $2,000.00. Cit. pub. at Upper Long Cane Church ment. Geo. Bowie Esq. next of kin.

KIRKWOOD, NATHAN—BOX 108, PACK 2924:
    Est. admnr. Feb. 25, 1807 by Sarah Kirkwood, Geo. Esq., John Bowie Esq. unto Andrew Hamilton Ord. Abbeville Dist. sum $5,000.00.

KING, PATRICK—BOX 108, PACK 2925:
    Cit. pub. at Rocky River Church June 13, 1829 ment. Dr. John McNeil applied for Letters of Admnr. (no other papers.)

KEOWEY, JOHN—BOX 108, PACK 2926:
    Est. admnr. Apr. 11, 1803 by Eleanor Keowey, Saml. Young unto Andrew Hamilton Ord. Abbeville Dist. sum $5,000.00.

KERR, LATTICE—BOX 108, PACK 2927:
    Est. admnr. Dec. 13, 1805 by David Kerry, John Robinson, Martin Loftis, Archillis Walker unto Andrew Hamilton Ord. Abbeville Dist. sum $5,000.00.

KENNEDY, EDMOND, SR.—BOX 108, PACK 2928:
    Est. admnr. May 25, 1805 by Jane Kennedy, Geo., Archibald Kidd, Saml. Foster Jr. unto Andrew Hamilton Ord. Abbeville Dist. sum $3,000.00.

KING, BENJAMIN—BOX 108, PACK 2929:
    Will dated July 1, 1788. Prov. July 8, 1788. Exrs: Wm. Moore, Wm. Swift of Cambridge. Wit: Robt. G. Harper, David, Wm. Moore Jr. merchant of Cambridge, 96 Dist. Chn: Benjamin, John Cogdell King.

LIPSCOMB, (MINORS)—BOX 108, PACK 2931:
    On Mar. 20, 1809 Smith, Nathan, Joel Lipscomb bound unto Andrew Hamilton Ord. Abbeville Dist. sum $10,000.00. Smith Lipscomb made gdn. of John, Salley, Betsey Lipscomb minors.

LIPSCOMB, (MINORS—BOX 108, PACK 2932:
On Mar. 26, 1809 Smith, Nathan Esq., Joel Lipscomb Esq., bound unto Andrew Hamilton Ord. Abbeville Dist. sum $10,000.00. Smith Lipscomb made gdn. of Thos., Wm., David Lipscomb minors over 14 yrs.

LIPFORD, (MINORS)—BOX 108, PACK 2933:
On Apr. 3, 1826 Joel J. Lipford, Geo. A. Miller, Chas. Dendy bound unto Moses Taggart Ord. Abbeville Dist. sum $2,000.00. Joel J. Lipford made gdn. of Polly, Henry, Fanny, Wm. Lipford minors.

LONGMIRE, GEORGE (MINORS)—BOX 108, PACK 2934:
On Feb. 8, 1785 Richard Lowry, Thos. Livingston bound unto John Thomas Ord. 96 Dist. sum 2,000 lbs. Richard Lowry made gdn. of Suckey, Garrett Longmire minors of Geo. Longmire decd.

LESLY, HUGH—BOX 108, PACK 2935:
On Mar. 3, 1837 Jas. Lesly, Jas. Foster, Archibald Kennedy bound unto Moses Taggart Ord. Abbeville Dist. sum $1,000.00. Jas. Lesly made gdn. of Hugh Lesly a minor.

LOWRY, DAVID—BOX 108, PACK 2936:
On Mar. 21, 1808 Wm. H. Caldwell, Wm. Davis, Jas. Foster bound unto Andrew Hamilton Ord. Abbeville Dist. sum $1,000.00. Wm. H. Caldwell made gdn. of Jas. Lowry a minor over 14 yrs.

LOWRY, JAMES—BOX 108, PACK 2937:
On Feb. 4, 1811 Wm. H. Caldwell, Josiah Patterson Jr., John Ellington bound unto Taliaferro Livingston Ord. Abbeville Dist. sum $1,000.00. Wm. H. Caldwell made gdn. of Jas. Lowry a minor over 14 yrs.

LONG, (MINORS)—BOX 108, PACK 2938:
On Jan. 29, 1807 Thos. Baskin, Saml., Wm. Crawford bound unto Andrew Hamilton Ord. Abbeville Dist. sum $10,000.00. Thos. Baskin made gdn. of Nancy M., Martha L., John Long minors.

LOMAX, GEORGE JACKSON—BOX 108, PACK 2939:
Sett. of share of Jackson Lomax, son of Absolem Lomax decd. to ascertain the share of said Jackson to the est. of his father Absolem Lomax. Jas. Lomax the admnr. decd. and W. H. Richey and wife the representatives of Jas. Lomax decd. Dated Feb. 1, 1833. Geo. Jackson Lomax was a gr. son of Jos. Lomax Sr. decd.

LINCOLN, JAMES, ESQ.—BOX 108, PACK 2940:
Est. admnr. July 19, 1792 by Hugh O'Keefe, Wm. Huggins, Timothy Russell unto the Judges of Abbeville County sum 2,000 lbs. Cit. ment. Hugh O'Keefe next of kin.

LONGMIRE, GEORGE—BOX 108, PACK 2941:
Est. admnr. Feb. 8, 1785 by Henry Ware Jr., Thos. Livingston bound unto John Thomas Ord. 96 Dist. sum 2,000 lbs.

412   ABSTRACTS OF OLD NINETY-SIX AND

LUMMUS, ELIZABETH—BOX 108, PACK 2942:
Est. admnr. Oct. 29, 1811 by John Lummus, Jas. Lomax Jr., Humphrey Klugh unto Taliaferro Livingston Ord. Abbeville Dist. sum $10,000.00.

LITTELL, WILLIAM—BOX 108, PACK 2943:
Est. admnr. Apr. 1, 1797 by Isabel, Jas. Little, John McCord Sr., Saml. Lyon unto the Judges of Abbeville County sum $1,000.00. Isabel Little the wid. Cit. pub. at Upper Long Cane Church.

LETCHER, JAMES—BOX 108, PACK 2944:
Est. admnr. Mar. 24, 1783 by Milley Letcher, Wm. Carson, Benjamin Blackey unto John Ewing Calhoun Ord. 96 Dist. sum 14,000 lbs. Milley Letcher of Stevens Creek was next of kin

LESLEY, JOHN—BOX 108, PACK 2945:
Est. admnr. Apr. 5, 1788 by Wm. Jr., Wm. Lesly Sr., Jas. White unto the Judges of Abbeville County sum 2,000 lbs. Cit. pub. at Upper Long Church.

LESLY, WILLIAM—BOX 108, PACK 2946:
Est. admnr. June 6, 1825 by John, Jas. Devlin, Bartholomew Jordan unto Moses Taggart Ord. Abbeville Dist. sum $1,000.00. Cit. pub. at Asbury Chapel.

LINDSAY, JAMES—BOX 108, PACK 2947:
Est. admnr. Sept. 12, 1791 by Elizabeth Lindsay wid., Wm. Ross, Jas. Stevenson unto the Judges of Abbeville Dist. sum 500 lbs. Cit. pub. at Long Cane Church. Inv. made Oct. 8, 1791 by Saml. Lindsay, John Murphey, Wm. Brownlee, Wm. Ross.

LINDSAY, JOHN—BOX 108, PACK 2948:
Est. admnr. Oct. 24, 1808 by Robt. Lindsay unto Andrew Hamilton Ord. Abbeville Dist. sum $2,000.00.

LOGAN, JOHN, SR.—BOX 108, PACK 2949:
Est. admnr. Aug. 6, 1807 by Jas. C., Andrew Logan, David Ansley unto Andrew Hamilton Ord. Abbeville Dist. sum $5,000.00.

LOGAN, THOMAS—BOX 108, PACK 2950:
Est. admnr. June 14, 1791 by John Logan son of Alexr. Logan, Saml. Foster Sr., Wm. Russell unto the Judges of Abbeville County sum 100 lbs. Cit. pub. at Cedar Springs Church ment. John Logan next of kin.

LINVILL, ANN—BOX 108, PACK 2951:
Est. admnr. Oct. 29, 1785 by Elisha Rhodes, Geo. Hughes, Elijah Whitten unto John Thomas Jr. Ord. 96 Dist. sum 200 lbs.

LEE, THOMAS, SR.—BOX 108, PACK 2952:
Will dated Oct. 14, 1815 in Abbeville Dist. Rec. Jan. 22, 1816. Exrs: Benjamin H. Saxon, Benjamin Glover. Wit: Wm., Mary Barksdale, John McCarter. Chn: Margery wife of Wm. McCullock, Ann, Wm., John, Andrew Lee Sr. Wife, Ann Lee.

LOOSK, JAMES—BOX 108, PACK 2953:
Will dated Jan. 3, 1786 in 96 Dist. Rec. Nov. 5, 1804. Exrs: Sons,
Henry, Nathan Loosk, Wm. Baty, Saml. Foster Sr. Wit: Andrew Weed,
Wm. Foster, Nat. Weed Jr. John McCiddy. Wife, Eleanor Loosk. Chn: Robt.
Loosk, Eleanor Baty, Elizabeth Gray, Nathan Loosk. Gr. son: Wm. Loosk.

LYON, EDWARD—BOX 108, PACK 2954:
Will dated Dec. 13, 1822 in Abbeville Dist. Prov. Mar. 18, 1823. Exrs:
Sons, Thos., Nicholas Lyon. Wit: Sarah Milligan, Rhoda Jones, Andrew Mil-
ligan. Wife, Jemima Lyon. Chn: Thos., Nicholas Lyon.

LIDDELL, JAMES—BOX 108, PACK 2955:
Will dated July 6, 1791. Prov. Nov. 8, 1796. Exrs: Wife, Esther Liddell,
John Liddell, Robt. Anderson Esq. Moses Liddell. Wit: Joseph Bell, Hugh
Macklin, Robt. Black. Chn: John Liddell, Ellener Jerrats Liddell. "Leave to Geo.
Liddell son Jas., to Mathew Robinson son Jas., to Moses Liddell's son Jas., to
Daniel Keith, Andrew, Moses Liddell, Jas. Martin."

LITTLE, JAMES—BOX 108, PACK 2956:
Will dated Mar. 20, 1785 in 96 Dist. Prov. Apr. 14, 1785. Exrs:
Henry Good, Ephraim Clark. Wit: Hugh Taylor, Jesse Clark, Wm. *Splean.*
Wife, Mary Little. Chn: Mary, Thos. Little.

LITTLE, WILLIAM—BOX—108, PACK 2957:
Will dated Sept. 4, 1788 in Abbeville Dist. Exr: Son, John Little.
Wit: John, Handy, Thos. Harris. Was a weaver. Chn: Anne, John Little.
"Bequeath to Mary Little, alias Smith."

LIDDELL, GEORGE—BOX 108, PACK 2958:
Will dated Dec. 28, 1789. Exrs: Moses Liddell, Capt. John Norwood.
Wit: Robt. *Watt* or *Hall*, H. Reid, Andrew Liddell. Wife, Rachel Liddell. Chn:
Jas., Geo. Washington Little have plantation by Seneca River. Wife pregnant
with child.

LESLEY, SAMUEL—BOX 108, PACK 2959:
Will dated Nov. 7, 1784 in 96 Dist. Exrs: Bro., John McCurdey, Jas.
Loosk. Wit: Sally Lesly, Jas. Turner, Mathew Young. Wife, Anne Lesly. Ment.
3 chn. names not given.

LOGAN, ANDREW—BOX 108, PACK 2960:
Will dated Aug. 25, 1788 in Abbeville Dist. Prov. Oct. 10, 1788. Exrs:
Wife, Lydia Logan, John Wardlaw. Wit: Wm. Heard. Elizabeth Wardlaw,
(name) Wardlaw. Chn: John, Isaac Logan. Nephew, Wm. Heard.

LOGAN, ANDREW—BOX 108, PACK 2961:
Will dated Nov. 18, 1810 in Abbeville Dist. Rec. Mar. 4, 1811. Exr:
Col. John Logan. Wit: Zachary Meriwether, Joseph Foster. Sis., Lydia Slater,
Mary Norwood, Jamine Tullock, Ellinor Harwick. Bros., Wm., Henry Logan.
"Bequeath to John, Sally Logan chn. of Col. John Logan."

LEWALLEN, RICHARD M.—BOX 108, PACK 2962:
    No will date given. Rec. Nov. 21, 1803. Wit: Wm. Wyatt Bibb, Andrew
M. Goocher. Lived in Abbeville Dist. Wife, Lettice Lewallen. Bro., Mays
Lewallen. Sis., Lettice Lewallen. Est. admnr. Nov. 21, 1803 by Latice Lew-
allen, Jas. Baird, Andrew M. Goocher unto Andrew Hamilton Ord. Abbeville
Dist. sum $10,000.00.

McGAW, JANE CAROLINE—BOX 108, PACK 2963:
    On Dec. 5, 1836 Thos. Parker, Jas. Calhoun, Jas. Taggart bound unto
Moses Taggart Ord. Abbeville Dist. sum $2,000.00. Thos. Parker made gdn.
of Jane Caroline McGaw a minor.

McCLEANE, ELIZA AND JAMES—BOX 108, PACK 2964:
    On Dec. 30, 1837 David McClean, Jas. Foster, Archibald Kennedy
bound unto Moses Taggart Ord. Abbeville Dist. sum $10,000.00. David McClean
made gdn. of Elizabeth, Jas. McClean minors. Mar. 11, 1846 Elizabeth McClean
recd. $97.77 from her father Jas. McClain est. Jas. McClain recd. the same.
(Name written McClean, McClain.)

MOSELEY, ROSANNA—BOX 108, PACK 2965:
    On Feb. 11, 1804 Richard, Joseph, Henry Moseley bound unto Andrew
Hamilton Ord. Abbeville Dist. sum $10,000.00. Richard Moseley made gdn. of
Rosanna Moseley a minor.

McCRAVEN, ANDREW M.—BOX 108, PACK 2966:
    On Dec. 8, 1828 Wm. Calhoun, Wm., Jas. McCraven bound to Moses
Taggart sum $2,000.00. Wm. McCraven made gdn. of Andrew M. McCraven
a minor over 14 yrs.

McCRAVEN, ANN—BOX 108, PACK 2967:
    On Dec. 8, 1828 Paul Rogers, W. A. Bull, Benjamin McKittrick bound
unto Moses Taggart Ord. Abbeville Dist. sum $5,000.00. Paul Rogers made
gdn. of Ann McCraven a minor over 14 yrs. Wm. M. Rogers a minor under
14 yrs

MIDDLETON, HEZEKIAH—BOX 108, PACK 2968:
    On July 17, 1810 John, Jas. Carr, Thos. Patterson bound unto John
Hamilton Ord. Abbeville Dist. sum $1,000.00. John Carr made gdn. of
Hezekiah Middleton a minor.

MOUCHET, WILLIAM—BOX 108, PACK 2969:
    On Jan. 29, 1840 Jas. Williams, Richard Hill, Jas. H. Cobb bound unto
Moses Taggart Ord. Abbeville Dist. sum $1,000.00. Jas. Williams made gdn.
of Wm. Mouchet a minor under 21 yrs.

MEEK, (MINORS)—BOX 108, PACK 2970:
    On June 6, 1828 John Meek, Thos. J. Spraggins, Wm. Payne, John
Chappell, (John Meek resides in the state of Ala.) bound unto Moses Taggart
Ord. Abbeville Dist. sum $2,000.00. John Meek made gdn. of Wm. S., Jas. M.,
Tabitha F. A. Meek minors under 14 yrs.

McCOLLUM, (MINORS)—BOX 108, PACK 2971:
On Jan. 5, 1818 Peggy McCollum, Thos, Bartholomew Jordon bound
unto Taliaferro Livingston Ord. Abbeville Dist. sum $2,000.00. Peggy Mc-
Collum made gdn. of Sally, Thos., John McCollum minors. (At signing of the
bond Margaret McCollum was written.)

McELRATH, MICHAEL—BOX 108, PACK 2972:
On Apr. 1, 1785 Saml. Nisbett, John McElrath, Jas. McElwayne, Thos.
Penny bound unto John Thomas Ord. 96 Dist. sum 2,000 lbs. Saml. Nisbett
made gdn. of Michael McElrath a minor. John McElrath sheweth that Michael
McElrath by a fall from his horse is rendered thereby, unable to transact his
own business, by an injury to his head.

McELVANEY, (MINORS)—BOX 108, PACK 2973:
On Mar. 18, 1812 Alexr. Hunter, Joseph Black bound unto Taliaferro
Livingston Ord. Abbeville Dist. sum $3,000.00. Alexr. Hunter Esq. made gdn.
of Margaret, Narcissa, John Taylor McElvaney minors under 14 yrs.

McCORD, STUART—BOX 108, PACK 2974:
On Mar. 10, 1783 Jas. Kyle, Wm. Richards, Martin Stuart bound to
Andrew Hamilton Ord. Abbeville Dist. sum $15,000.00. Jas. Kyle made gdn.
of Wm. Stuart McCord a minor

McCORD, JOSEPH A.—BOX 108, PACK 2975:
On Jan. 7, 1835 Mary, Wm. P., John P. McCord bound unto Moses
Taggart Ord. Abbeville Dist. sum $10,000.00. Mary McCord made gdn. of
Joseph A. McCord a minor.

MITCHELL, SAMUEL—BOX 108, PACK 2976:
On Sept. 1, 1817 Francis Mitchell, Meridith McGehee, Geo. Green
bound unto Taliaferro Livingston Ord. Abbeville Dist. sum $2,000.00. Francis
Mitchell made gdn. of Saml. Mitchell a minor over 14 yrs.

MITCHELL, JOHN—BOX 108, PACK 2977:
On Feb. 26, 1800 Daniel Mitchell, Joseph Hill, Jas. Chiles bound unto
Andrew Hamilton Ord. Abbeville Dist. sum $8,000.00. Daniel Mitchell made
gdn. of John Mitchell a minor.

MITCHELL, FRANCIS AND THOMAS—BOX 108, PACK 2978:
On Mar. 5, 1814 Saml. Young, Jas. Caruthers, Francis Young bound
unto Taliaferro Livingston Ord. Abbeville Dist. sum $2,000.00. Saml. Young
made gdn. of Francis, Thos. Mitchell minors over 14 yrs.

MORROW, WILLIAM MUNROE—BOX 108, PACK 2979:
On Oct. 26, 1829 Jas. Morrow, Wm. Brownlee, John B. Black bound
unto Moses Taggart Ord. Abbeville Dist. sum $1,000.00. Jas. Morrow made
gdn. of Wm. Munroe Morrow a minor over 14 yrs.

MOORE, JOHN AND SUSAN—BOX 108 PACK 2980:
On Jan. 7, 1811 Sarah Moore, John Callahan, Thos. B. Creagh bound

unto John Midlton Gaines, Commander in Chief and Ord. of Abbeville Dist. sum 2,000 lbs. Sarah Moore made gdn. of John, Susan Moore. Chn. of Francis Moore decd.

MOORE, THOMAS—BOX 108, PACK 2981:
On Aug. 17, 1838 John S., Nathaniel, John Moore Jr. bound unto Moses Taggart Ord. Abbeville Dist. sum $5,000.00. John Moore Sr. gdn. of Thos. Moore a minor.

McKINLEY, JEAN—BOX 108, PACK 2982:
On Dec. 5, 1808 Nathaniel Norwood, Saml. Young, Walter H. Ward bound unto Andrew Hamilton Ord. Abbeville Dist. sum $2,000.00. Nathaniel Norwood made gdn. of Jean McKinley a minor.

MARTIN, MINORS—BOX 108, PACK 2983:
On Dec. 27, 1831 Jas., John Martin, Joseph Evans bound unto Moses Taggart Ord. Abbeville Dist. sum $2,000.00. Jas. Martin made gdn. of Margaret, Mary, Elizabeth, Alexr., Ezekiel, Oliver Martin minor chn. of Alexr. decd. Nancy Martin the wid. of Alexr. Martin decd.

MARTIN, JANE AND MARY—BOX 108, PACK 2984:
On Dec. 14, 1811 Wm. Gaston, Wm. Dale, John Foster bound unto Taliaferro Livingston Ord. Abbeville Dist. sum $2,000.00. Wm. Gaston made gdn. of Jane, Mary Martin minors under 14 yrs.

McADAMS, ROBINSON—BOX 108, PACK 2985:
On Feb. 28, 1831 John Clinkscales, Bennet, Charlotte McAdams bound unto Moses Taggart Ord. Abbeville Dist. sum $1,000.00. Charlotte McAdams made gdn. of Robinson McAdams a minor over 14 yrs.

McADAMS, REBECCA—BOX 108, PACK 2986:
On Feb. 18, 1836, Sarah McAdam, Jas. Hadden bound unto Moses Taggart Ord. Abbeville Dist. sum $500.00. Sarah McAdam made gdn. of Rebecca McAdams a minor over 14 yrs.

McMASTER, DIANNA—BOX 108, PACK 2987:
Es. admnr. Feb. 5, 1806 by Wm. McMaster, Jeremiah Bell, John H. Cofer bound unto Andrew Hamilton Ord. Abbeville Dist. sum $5,000.00.

McCOY, MARTHA—BOX 108, PACK 2988:
Est. admnr. May 6, 1833 by Alexr. McCoy, Jas. A., Robt. F. Black unto Moses Taggart Ord. Abbeville Dist. sum $8,000.00. Cit. pub. at Shiloh Church.

McELWAYN, JAMES—BOX 108, PACK 2989:
Est. admnr. Nov. 11, 1793 by Wm. McElwayn, Wm. McCrone, Saml. Houston unto the Judges of Abbeville County sum 500 lbs. Cit. read at Due West ment. Wm. McElwayn next of kin.

ABBEVILLE DISTRICT WILLS AND BONDS   417

McKINNEY, ELI—BOX 108, PACK 2990:
On Feb. 27, 1837 Wm. R. Reid applied for Letters of Admnr. Cit. pub. at Willington Church.

MILLER, ANDREW—BOX 108, PACK 2991:
Est. admnr. Nov. 8, 1783 by Alexr. Vernon, Mary, Nathaniel Miller bound unto John Thomas Ord. Abbeville Dist. sum 2,000 lbs.

MILLS, GERARD—BOX 108, PACK 2992:
On Sept. 9, 1826 Saml. Branch applied for Letters of Admnr. (No other papers.)

McCOLLOUGH, ROBERT—BOX 108, PACK 2993:
Cit. pub. at Cedar Springs Church on Mar. 7, 1792 ment. Moses Thompson of Abbeville Dist. applied for Letters of Admnr. as next of kin.

MORGAN, JOSHUA—BOX 108, PACK 2994:
Est. admnr. Sept. 30, 1786 by Wm. Jackson, Benjamin Rainey, Wm. Gilbert bound unto John Thomas Ord. 96 Dist. sum 300 lbs.

MOSELEY, WILLIAM—BOX 108, PACK 2995:
Est. admnr. Mar. 17, 1819 by John Archer, Lewis Mitchell, Chas. Maxwell bound unto Moses Taggart Ord. Abbeville Dist. sum $7,000.00.

MAYS, THOMAS, JR.—BOX 108, PACK 2996:
Est. admnr. Oct. 16, 1815 by Thos. Mays Sr., Wm. Thompson, David Fife unto Taliaferro Livingston Ord. Abbeville Dist. sum 1,000 lbs. Cit. pub. at Hopewell Church ment. Thos. Mays Jr. was late of the Army of the U. S.

MAXWELL, JOHN, SR.—BOX 108, PACK 2997:
Est. admnr. Jan. 6, 1818 by Chas. Maxwell, Edmond Ware, Joseph Cooper unto Taliaferro Livingston Ord. Abbeville Dist. sum $5,000.00.

McCURDY, JOHN—BOX 108, PACK 2998:
Est. admnr. Oct. 7, 1789 by John Harris, Elijah, Rhoda McCurdy unto the Judges of Abbeville County sum 1,000 lbs. Est. admnr. again on July 7, 1789 by Wm. McCurdy, Arthur Morrow, Saml. Foster unto the Judges of Abbeville County sum 1,000 lbs. Cit. pub. at Long Cane Church.

MITCHELL, STEPHEN—BOX 108, PACK 2999:
Est. admnr. Feb. 1, 1825 by Rev. Jas. E. Glenn, Robt. Key, Donald Douglass unto Moses Taggart Ord. Abbeville Dist. sum $3,000.00.

MITCHELL, ROBERT—BOX 108, PACK 3000:
Est. admnr. Oct. 9, 1789 by John Mitchell, Elijah McCurdy, Richard M. Grill or McGrill unto the Judges of Abbeville County sum 1,000 lbs. Cit. pub. at Long Cane Church ment. John Mitchell next of kin. Robt. Mitchell was a shoemaker.

McALISTER, WILLIAM—BOX 108, PACK 3001:
Est. admnr. Nov. 15, 1791 by Robt. McAlister, Saml. McMurtrey, Thos.

Coil unto the Judges of Abbeville County 500 lbs. Robt. McAlister next of kin.

MONTGOMERY, ELIZABETH—BOX 108, PACK 3003:
Est. admnr. Feb. 11, 1804 by John Montgomery, Robt. Green, Alexr. C. Hamilton unto Andrew Hamilton Ord. Abbeville Dist. sum $5,000.00.

MONTGOMERY, JOHN—BOX 108, PACK 3004:
Est. admnr. June 11, 1798 by Jas. Thornton, John Johnston, Wm. Garrett, Henry Long unto the Judges of Abbeville County sum $1,000.00. Cit. pub. at Upper Long Cane Church ment. Jas. Thornton, John Johnson next of kin.

MOORE, JAMES—BOX 108, PACK 3005:
Inv. made Nov. 4, 1836 by Wm. Stalsworth, Roger McKinney, Albert Henderson, Joseph M. Holloway, Russell Vaughn. Creswell Moore was admnr. (No other papers.)

MOORE, GEORGE—BOX 108, PACK 3006:
Est. admnr. Apr. 23, 1814 by Sarah Moore, John Love, John Frazer, unto Taliaferro Livingston Ord. Abbeville Dist. sum $1,000.00. Inv. made May 20, 1814 by John Frazer, Robt. Atkins, John Love.

McCULLOCK, JAMES, JR.—BOX 108, PACK 3007:
Es. admnr. Mar. 4, 1816 by Wm., John McCullock, John E. Norris, Andrew Gillespie unto Taliaferro Livingston Ord. Abbeville Dist. sum 10,000 lbs. Cit. pub. at Hopewell Church.

McFARLAND, AGNESS—BOX 108, PACK 3008:
Est. admnr. July 2, 1827 by Jas. N. Dickson, Nancy, Robt. Douglass, John McFarland, Thos. Cunningham unto Moses Taggart Ord. Abbeville Dist. sum $2,000.00. Cit. pub. at Lebanon Church.

McWHIRTER, DAVID—BOX 108, PACK 3009:
Cit. pub. at Long Cane Church Oct. 3, 1789 ment. Mary McWhirter the wid. applied for Letters of Admnr. Another cit. pub. Dec. 17, 1790 at Greenville Church ment. Joseph Hawkins applied for Letters of Admnr.

MADDOX, JANE—BOX 108, PACK 3010:
Inv. made Oct. 15, 1816 by Jas. Gaines, Henry, Benjamin Johnson, Clement T. Lattimore. Elizabeth Maddox, Geo. Reeve the admnrs.

MADDOX, HENRY—BOX 108, PACK 3011:
Cit. pub. at Upper Long Cane Church May 26, 1839. Polly Maddox the admnr.

MARTIN, JANE—BOX 108, PACK 3012:
Cit. pub. Nov. 5, 1832 ment. Alexr. McKinney, Richard W. Martin applied for Letters of Admnr. as next of kin.

MARTIN, ARABELLA—BOX 108, PACK 3013:
Est. admnr. Jan. 1, 1827 by Thos. P., Jacob Martin, Alexr. B. Arnold

unto Moses Taggart Ord. Abbeville Dist. sum $30,000.00. Cit. pub. at Hopewell Church ment. Thos. P. Martin next of kin.

MARTIN, THOMAS—BOX 108, PACK 3014:
Est. admnr. July 26, 1785 by Saml. Rosamond, Elijah Grimsley, Saml. Agnew unto John Thomas Ord. 96 Dist. sum 1,000 lbs.

MARTIN, WILLIAM—BOX 108, PACK 3015:
Est. admnr. Apr. 30, 1784 by Jonathan Downs, John, Grace, Edmond Martin bound unto John Thomas Ord. 96 Dist. sum 2,000 lbs.

MILIGAN, JAMES—BOX 108, PACK 3016:
Will dated Mar. 12, 1805 in Abbeville Dist. Rec. Mar. 22, 1809. Exrs: Joseph Calhoun, Robt. Hays. Wit: Wm., Mary Harris, P. Gibert. Chn: Andrew Milligan, Mary Aston, Rachel, Catharine White. "Bequeath to Thos. White's chn."

MORRISON, ARCHIBALD—BOX 108, PACK 3017:
Will dated May 22, 1800 in Abbeville Dist. Rec. June 18, 1807. No Exrs: Wit: Jas. Cooper, John Morrow Sr., David Wyly. Chn: Robt., Mary, Elizabeth, Rachel Morrison.

MULLIN, JOHN—BOX 109, PACK 3018:
Will dated Oct. 10, 1805 in Abbeville Dist. Rec. Nov. 23, 1808. Exr: Wife, Mary Mullin. Wit: Francis, Elizabeth Hunter. Bro., Patrick O. Mullin.

MERIWETHER, MARY—BOX 109, PACK 3019:
Will dated June 19, 1807 in Abbeville Dist. Rec. Aug. 3, 1807. Exrs: Sons, John, Zachary, Nicholas Meriwether. Wit: Ann Nealy, John Hatter. Chn: John, Zachary, Nicholas Meriwether, Ann McGehee of State of Va. Gr. dtr: Mary Lewis Meriwether. "Bequeath to Sarah M. wife of Joseph Foster."

MATTHEWS, JOSEPH—BOX 109, PACK 3020:
Will dated Nov. 15, 1823 in Abbeville Dist. Prov. Dec. 4, 1826. Exrs: Sons, John, David Matthews. Wit: Jesse Calvert, Jas. E. Glenn, Robt. Buchanan. Wife, Rachel Matthews. Chn. David, John, Rachel, Elizabeth, Ann Matthews.

McLAREN, JOHN, SR.—BOX 109, PACK 3021:
Will dated June 6, 1837 in Abbeville Dist. Prov. June 19, 1837. Wit: Jas. S. Wilson, Joseph Wardlaw, Jas. H. Cobb. "Bequeath to Agness McLaren wid. of my bro." Nephew, John McLaren Jr. Neice, Jenet H. McLaren.

MILLER, JOHN—BOX 109, PACK 3022:
On Feb. 1, 1812 Hugh Reid, Andrew Stevenson, Wm. Haddon appointed to appraise est. of John Miller decd. Exrs: Benjamin C. Yancey, Rachel Miller. (No other papers.)

MILLER, ROBERT—BOX 109, PACK 3023:
Will dated Apr. 24, 1809 in Abbeville Dist. Prov. Jan. 23, 1822. Exrs: Wife, Kety Miller, Jas. Morrow. Wit: Jas. Sr., Jas. Foster, David Kennedy.

"At her death property to go to John Brough son to Margaret Brough and Jas. Foster son of Jas. Foster Sr.

MILLER, ELIZABETH STEAD—BOX 109, PACK 3024:
    Will dated Nov. 15, 1825. Prov. Sept. 30, 1831. Wit: Henry Trescot, Edward McCrady, John R. Ludlow. Was of Charleston, S. C. Chn: Wm. C., John, Elizabeth Miller. Lived at No. 212 Meeting St. Recd. property from her mother Susannah Cox and bro., Joseph. D. Cox's est. Wm. *Rudd* recd. one fourth part. Died in Abbeville. Cit. pub. at Little Mountain Church. Est. admnr. Oct. 12, 1831 by Wm. C. Miller, Thos. Parker, Geo. W. Wilson unto Moses Taggart Ord. Abbeville Dist. sum $20,000.00.

McCULLOCH, JAMES—BOX 109, PACK 3025:
    Will dated Oct. 5, 1817 in Abbeville Dist. Prov. Jan. 5, 1818. Exrs: Wife, Mary McCulloch, Saml. Morris. Wit: Matthew McDonnell, Robt., Adam Hill. Chn: Saml., May, Robt., Ann, Elizabeth McCulloch, Margaret Morris. "Bequeath to gr. son, Jas. S. M. McCulloch, 3 acres of land from Isaac McCulloch still, house, and benefit of the spring."

McQUERANS, SAMUEL—BOX 109, PACK 3026:
    Will dated Nov. 7, 1818 in Abbeville Dist. Prov. Jan. 3, 1820. Exrs: Wife, Elizabeth McQuerans. Son, Jas. McQuerans. Wit: Robt., Mary Drennan. Chn: Easter, Alexr. McQuerans, Margaret Hill, Chas., Saml McQuerans.

McKEE, ADAM—BOX 109, PACK 3027:
    Will dated July 13, 1805 in Abbeville Dist. Rec. Jan. 5, 1807. Exrs: Wife, Jean McKee. Sons, Michael, Adam McKee. Wit: Wm., Jas. McKee, Joseph Harris. Chn: Grisel, Micheal, Adam McKee, Jean Lindsay, Elijah, John, Mary, Wm. McKee. "To my dtr. Margaret's chn. I leave $2.00."

McILWAIN, JOHN, SR.—BOX 109, PACK 3028:
    Will dated Dec. 1, 1806. Rec. Dec. 27, 1806. No Exrs: Wit: Alexr. Sims, Hugh Huston, John, Ann McIlwain, Saml. Logan. These witnesses wrote and certified that John McIlwain of Abbeville Dist. on Nov. 21, 1806 that his est. should be divided between his wife and chn. The witnesses signed their names to this effect Dec. 1, 1806. (No wife or chn. names given.) Est. admnr. Dec. 29, 1806 by Anne, Wm. McIlwain, Saml. Houston, Wm. Wilson bound unto Andrew Hamilton Ord. Abbeville Dist. sum $10,000.00.

McCRAW, SAMUEL—BOX 109, PACK 3029:
    Will dated Apr. 23, 1810 in Abbeville Dist. Rec. Oct. 19, 1812. Exr: Son, Edward McCraw. Wit: John Morrison, Nancy Mitchell. Chn: Edward, Stephen, Wm. McCraw, Lucy wife of David Owen, Frances Heard, Mary Owen, Betsey McCraw. Gr. son: John son of John Hughes decd.

MILLS, GILBERT—BOX 109, PACK 3030:
    Will dated Nov. 3, 1789. Prov. Apr. 7, 1790. Exrs: Wm. McGaw. Wife, Marthew Mills. Wit: Wm. Clark, Alisboh Hokens. Lived in the sett. of Little River. Sons, Alexr., Wm. Mills.

ABBEVILLE DISTRICT WILLS AND BONDS 421

MEYER, MICHAEL—BOX 109, PACK 3031:
Will dated Nov. 23, 1784 in 96 Dist. Prov. May 27, 1785. Exrs: Sons, John, David, Jonathan Meyer, Casper Nail Sr. Wit: John Clarke, John Savage, Zachariah Johnston. Chn., John Meyer, "Bequeath to the said John Meyer a tract of land which we 3 bros. took up together under one grant in the yr. 1737, which tract was willed to me by said bros., Leonard and Wlrich Meyers." Catherina, David, Jonathan Meyers, bequeath to the last 2 sons each 130 acres of a tract of land of 390 acres in Beach Island on Horseshoe Pond. Give 130 acres to Grace, Sally and Leonard chn. of my son Leonard decd. Elezabeth Meyers.

MARK, JOHN BALTHASER—BOX 109, PACK 3032:
Will dated Mar. 21, 1789. Prov. Apr. 5, 1790. Exrs: Philip Zimmerman, Chas. Fredrick Frolick. Wit: Chas. Friedrich Frolich or *Frolick*, Philip Zimmerman. Son, Henry a tract of land between Mile Branch and Coffetown. Dtr., Elizabeth wife of Nicholas Brisky 100 acres between Herman Gable and her sis. Philipine. Dtr., Elizabeth Margaretha Mark, Conrad Mark. Wife ment. name not given. On Dec. 24, 1834 John Kennedy, John Faulkner, Archibald Kennedy bound unto Moses Taggart Ord. Abbeville Dist. sum $1,000.00. John Kennedy made gdn. of Peggy Ann, Rachel M. C. Patterson minors. (This bond could have gotten in this package by mistake.)

MORROW, ARTHUR—BOX 109, PACK 3033:
Will dated June 4, 1807 in Abbeville Dist. Rec. Oct. 20, 1807. Exrs: Son, John Morrow. s. l., Jas. Morrow. Wit: Jas. T. Gray, Jas. Cochran Sr., Alexr. Porter. Wife, Elizabeth Morrow. Chn: John, Wm., Arthur Morrow, Mary Cooper Morrow. Gr. chn: Jas. Linn Morrow, Arthur Blain Morrow sons of Arthur Morrow.

McKINNEY, SUSANNAH—BOX 109, PACK 3034:
Will dated Nov. 2, 1824 in Abbeville Dist. Prov. June 4, 1827. Wit: Criswell, Mary, John C. Moore. "Leave to my half sis. Sarah Teddard's chn. Bequeath my right of land that David Teddard now lives on to said chn."

MORROW, GEORGE—BOX 109, PACK 3035:
Will dated Mar. 10, 1790 in Abbeville Dist. Prov. Apr. 6, 1790. Exrs: Wife, Mary Morrow, Wm. Hutton, Ebenezer Pettigrew. Wit: Wm. Deall, Wm. Deall, Jane Foster. Chn: Hugh, John, Jane, Margaret, Mary Ann, Jas., Geo. Mecklin Morrow.

McCORMICK, WILLIAM—BOX 109, PACK 3036:
Will dated June 30, 1807 in Abbeville Dist. Rec. Jan. 25, 1808. Exrs: Wife, Eleanor McCormick, Thos. Brough. Wit: Francis Sutherland, Peter Hemmenger, John Morrow. Chn: Mary, Elizabeth McCormick. In the Codicil written to the will dated Oct. 22, 1807 ment. "Bequeath to Maria McCormick who if alive now lives in Fairfield Dist. of this state, whom I acknowledge to be my dtr. receive $20.00."

MURPHY, JOHN—BOX 109, PACK 3037:
Will dated Aug. 15, 1817 in Abbeville Dist. Prov. June 5, 1820. Exrs:
Wife, Margaret Murphy. Son, Wm. Murphy. Wit: Jas. C., John E., Margaret
Ellis. Chn: Wm., Esther, Margaret, Mary, John Murphy. s. l., Mathew
Strickland.

MADDOX, HENLY—BOX 109, PACK 3038:
Will dated May 29, 1806 in Abbeville Dist. Rec. July 11, 1806. Exrs:
Wife, Jenet Maddox, Edmund Gaines, Edward McCraw. Wit: John Finley,
Jas. Watkins, Archibald Cameron. Chn: Augustin, Richard, Saml. Maddox,
Caty Nolin Freman. "Bought land lying on Turkey Creek from Thos. Shirley."

MARTIN, CHARLES—BOX 109, PACK 3039:
Will dated July 1819. Prov. Aug. 14, 1819. Exr: Wife, Prudence B.
Martin. Wit: Richard Covington, Jas. Cobb, John W. Prince. Son, John Allen
Scott Martin. "Owned land on Savannah River and Stevens Creek. Edmond
Bacon Esq. owes me $1,000.00."

MARTIN, WILLIAM—BOX 109, PACK 3040:
Will dated Jan. 25, 1793 in Abbeville Dist. Rec. Mar. 27, 1798 Exrs:
Saml. Watts, Wm. Lesly. Wit: Robt. McCrone, Mathew Wilson, Robt. Simmons. Gr. sons: Wm., Joseph, John, Jas. McMurtry. S. l., Jas. McMurtry. Gr.
dtrs., Sarah Watts, Jenny McMurtry. Dtr., Jean.

MARTIN, WILLIAM—BOX 109, PACK 3041:
Will dated Dec. 4, 1817 in Abbeville Dist. Prov. Jan. 15, 1818. Exr:
Bro., Geo. Washington Martin. Wit: Andrew Smith, Thos. McMillan. Nephews,
Wm. Marshall Moore, Wm. Bird Martin son of Nancy, Geo. W. Martin.

NOBLE, SARAH AND JOHN—BOX 109, PACK 3042:
On Nov. 19, 1806 Jas. Noble, Patrick, Ezekiel Calhoun bound unto
Andrew Hamilton Ord. Abbeville Dist. sum $10,000.00. Jas. Noble made gdn.
of Sarah, John Noble minors over 14 yrs.

NORRIS, EZEKIEL B.—BOX 109, PACK 3043:
On Nov. 7, 1831 Robt. Stuckey, Jas. A. Black, Jas. Spence bound unto
Moses Taggart Ord. Abbeville Dist. sum $1,400.00. Robt. Stuckey made gdn.
of Ezekiel B. Norris a minor over 14 yrs.

NORWOOD, SAMUEL—BOX 109, PACK 3044:
On Apr. 27, 1785 John Norwood, Benjamin Lawrence, John Wardlaw
bound unto John Thomas Ord. 96 Dist. sum 100 lbs. John Norwood made gdn.
of Saml. Norwood a minor.

NEALE, WILLIAM—BOX 109, PACK 3045:
Est. admnr. Sept. 16, 1785 by Daniel, Thos., Saml. Jackson unto John
Thomas Ord. 96 Dist. sum 500 lbs.

NIXON (No name given)—BOX 109, PACK 3046:
Est. admnr. Jan. 4, 1785 by Thos. Brandon, Jas. McElwayne Sr. unto

John Thomas Ord. 96 Dist. sum 2,000 lbs.

NEELEY, WILLIAM—BOX 109, PACK 3047:
Will dated Nov. 6, 1783 in 96 Dist. Prov. Jan. 26, 1785. Exrs: Geo., John Neeley. Wit: Mary Edwards, Agnes Love. Chn: John Neeley land on Little River, Joseph, Wm., Elizabeth, Sarah, Mary Neeley. S. l., Archible Sawyers. Jas. Sawyer son of said Archible Sawyers.

NORRIS, ANDREW—BOX 109, PACK 3048:
Will dated July 15, 1824 in Abbeville Dist. Prov. Oct. 19, 1824. Exrs: Wife, Anna E. Norris, Ezekiel Noble. Wit: Richard B. Carter, Rebecca Dale, Mary H. Noble, Rebecca Harris. "Bequeath my law books to Patrick Noble."

OLIVER, (MINORS)—BOX 109, PACK 3049:
On Apr. 11, 1807 Nathan M., Mary, Nathan Strickland Sr., Anthony Wm. Elton bound unto Andrew Hamilton Ord. Abbeville Dist. sum $10,000.00. Nathan, Mary Strickland appointed gdns. of Saml., Jenny, Robt. P. Oliver minors.

OWENS, (MINORS)—BOX 109, PACK 3050:
On Mar. 19, 1784 John Wallace, Robt. Gillam, Isaac Mitchell bound unto John Thomas Ord. 96 Dist. sum 2,000 lbs. John Wallace made gdn. of Wm., Elizabeth, Mary Owens minors.

OAKLEY, JOHN AND FIELDING—BOX 109, PACK 3051:
On June 5, 1815 John Oakley, Wm. Wray, Jas. McAdams bound unto Taliaferro Livingston Ord. Abbeville Dist. sum $1,000.00. John Oakley made gdn. of John, Fielding Oakley minors over 14 yrs.

OWENS, JOHN—BOX 109, PACK 3052:
Est. admnr. Sept. 24, 1785 by Ann Owens, John, Andrew Rodgers Jr. unto John Thomas Ord. 96 Dist. sum 500 lbs. In one place Ann Owens was written Ann Owing.

O'NEAL, JOHN—BOX 109, PACK 3053:
Est. admnr. Apr. 24, 1786 by Wm., Grace Cosby, Jas. Jordon, Jas. Hamilton unto John Thomas Ord. 96 Dist. sum 500 lbs.

PYLES, REUBEN AND LEWIS—BOX 109, PACK 3054:
On Oct. 21, 1816 Wm. Pyles, John Freeman, Abner Nash bound unto Taliaferro Livingston Ord. Abbeville Dist. sum $5,000.00. Wm. Pyles made gdn. of Reuben, Lewis Pyles minors over 14 yrs.

PENNELL, ELIZA MARGARET—BOX 109, PACK 3055:
On Jan. 15, 1838 Saml., Bartholomew Jordon, Wm. Paul bound unto Moses Taggart Ord. Abbeville Dist. sum $20,000.00. Saml. Jordon made gdn. of Eliza Margaret Pennal a minor. June 27, 1839 Robt. A. Pennal, Jas. W. Frazier, Robt. Devlin bound unto Moses Taggart Ord. Abbeville Dist. sum $20,000.00 Robt. A. Pennal made gdn. of Eliza Margaret Pennal a minor under 21 yrs.

PERRIN, MARGARET CAROLINE—BOX 109, PACK 3056:
On Mar. 3, 1828 Lewis Pyles, Isaac Cowan, John Clinkscales bound unto Moses Taggart Ord. Abbeville Dist. sum $3,000.00. Lewis Pyles made gdn. of Margaret Caroline Pyles a minor.

PERRIN, HENRY W.—BOX 109, PACK 3057:
Est. admnr. (month left out) 23, 1834 by Thos. C. Perrin, Jas., Robt. H. Wardlaw unto Moses Taggart Ord. Abbeville Dist. sum $10,000.00. Cit. Pub. at Tranquil Church.

PORTER, WILLIAM B.—BOX 109, PACK 3058:
On Oct. 22, 1836 Wm. C. Cozby, John Brownlee, Patrick Noble bound unto Moses Taggart Ord. Abbeville Dist. sum $1,000.00. Wm. C. Cozby made gdn. of Wm. B. Porter a minor over 14 yrs.

PATTON, ARCHIBALD K.—BOX 109, PACK 3059:
On July 15, 1839 Jane Patton, Jas. Foster, Archibald Kennedy bound unto Moses Taggart Ord. Abbeville Dist. sum $10,000.00. Jane Patton made gdn. of Archibald K. Patton a minor under 21 yrs.

PAUL, (MINORS)—BOX 109, PACK 3060:
On Feb. 9, 1828 Ephraim Davis, Edmund Cibb, Owen Selby bound unto Moses Taggart Ord. Abbeville Dist. sum $1,000.00. Ephraim Davis made gdn. of Geo., Wm. Jackson, Andrew Paul minors under 14 yrs. of Wm. Paul decd.

PENNINGTON, (MINORS)—BOX 109, PACK 3061:
On July 22, 1784 Levi Casey, Chas. King, Henry White bound unto John Thomas Ord. Dist. sum 2,000 lbs. Levi Casey made gdn. of Ruth, Jacob, Naomi Pennington minors.

PRESSLY, WILLIAM P.—BOX 109, PACK 3062:
On June 20, 1831 Saml., John B. Pressly, Bartholomew Jordon bound unto Moses Taggart Ord. Abbeville Dist. sum $2,000.00. Saml. Pressly made gdn. of Wm. P. Pressly a minor.

POPE, WILEY AND REBECCA—BOX 109, PACK 3063:
On Oct. 18, 1813 Moses Smith, Ezekiel, Abner Nash bound unto Taliaferro Livingston Ord. Abbeville Dist. sum $5,000.00. Ezekiel Nash made gdn. of Wiley Martin Pope a minor under 14 yrs., Rebecca Miller Pope a minor over 14 yrs.

PETTIGREW, ROSANNAH G. AND JAMES R.—BOX 109, PACK 3065:
On Feb. 9, 1829 Wm. Pettigrew, John McFarland, Jas. N. Dickson bound unto Moses Taggart Ord. Abbeville Dist. sum $1,000.00. Wm. Pettigrew made gdn. of Rosannah G., Jas., Robt. Pettigrew minors.

PETTIGREW, JOHN M.—BOX 109, PACK 3066:
Cit. pub. Sept. 11, 1813 ment. John M. Pettigrew now of age. (No other papers.)

PORTER, MARY ANN—BOX 109, PACK 3067:
On June 11, 1814 John Porter bound unto Taliaferro Livingston Ord. Abbeville Dist. sum $10,000.00. John Porter made gdn. of Mary Ann Porter a minor under 14 yrs. (Letter)
Brick House
10 June 1814
To T. Livingston Esq.
Dear Sir:
Should the Court of Ordinary be disposed to appoint the Rev. Jno. Porter gdn. for Ann Porter the dtr. of Hugh Porter decd. I will at any time when requested become his security for his gdn. ship and also be the means of getting approved security with myself to join him in a necessary bond for that purpose & untill the same is done this my letter shall stand binding on me for that end and purpose. I am with esteem.

Yr. Ob. Sevt.
Benj. Glover.

POLLARD, PAMELA—BOX 109, PACK 3068:
On Mar. 20, 1810 Saml. Whitlow, Chas. Fooshe, Wm. Wilson bound unto John Hamilton Ord. Abbeville Dist. sum $5,000.00. Saml. Whitlow made gdn. of Pamela Pollard a minor.

PARKER, JONATHAN—BOX 109, PACK 3069:
Est. admnr. Jan. 4, 1784 by Aaron Fincher, Wm. Plumer, Moses Collyer bound unto John Thomas Ord. 96 Dist. sum 2,000 lbs. Dated at Spartanplian in said dist. Esther Parker the wid.

PRUIT, JACOB—BOX 109, PACK 3070:
Est. admnr. Feb. 7, 1814 by Moses, Joshua, John Pruit bound unto Taliaferro Livingston Ord. Abbeville Dist. sum $1,000.00. Cit. ment. Jacob Pruit was late of the Army of this State.

PARSONS, JOHN—BOX 109, PACK 3071:
Est. admnr. June 20, 1812 by John L. Brown, Andrew McComb bound unto Taliaferro Livingston Ord. Abbeville Dist. sum $1,000.00. Cit. ment. John Parsons was late of the City of Charleston. John L. Brown next of kin.

PERRY, WILLIAM—BOX 109, PACK 3072:
Est. admnr. Apr. 1, 1829 by Stephen Witt, Jas. Patterson, Archibald Tittle unto Moses Taggart Ord. Abbeville Dist. sum $1,000.00.

PICKENS, JAMES—BOX 109, PACK 3073:
Est. admnr. Sept. 18, 1823 by Jas. Cobb, John Power Sr., Alexr. C. Hamilton unto Moses Taggart Ord. Abbeville Dist. sum $200.00.

PARK, JOSEPH—BOX 109, PACK 3074:
Est. admnr. Feb. 9, 1784 by John, Geo. Park, John David Davidson unto John Thomas Ord. 96 Dist. sum 2,000 lbs. Joseph Park was son of John Park.

PACK, JOHN—BOX 109, PACK 3075:
Est. admnr. July 12, 1785 by Hannah Pack, John Gibbs unto John Thomas Jr. Ord. 96 Dist. sum 500 lbs. (Note: In the bond the name Pack looked like Park in some places, but am not positive which would be correct.)

PAMPLIN, JOHN—BOX 109, PACK 3076:
Est. admnr. Dec. 15, 1786 by Silvanus Walker, Geo. Anderson, John Rodgers unto John Thomas Jr. Ord. 96 Dist. sum 1,000 lbs.

PARKER, WILLIAM HENRY—BOX 109, PACK 3077:
Est. admnr. Mar. 2, 1829 by Thos. Esq., Chas. Parker, Edward Frost of the City of Charleston, the two latter, the former of Abbeville Dist. unto Moses Taggart Ord. Abbeville Dist. sum $20,000.00. Cit. pub. at Hopewell Church.

PATTERSON, THOMAS W.—BOX 109, PACK 3078:
Est. admnr. Sept. 4, 1820 by John M. White, Jas. Hubbard, John Marsh unto Moses Taggart Ord. Abbeville Dist. sum $500.00. Cit. pub. at Mount Garrison Camp ground was read at Fellowship Church.

PETTIGREW, DR. EBENEZER P.—BOX 109, PACK 3079:
Est. wa to be appraised on or before Feb. 10, 1833 by Dr. Saml. Pressly, Thos. M. Duncan, John Hays Sr., Dr. Andrew Harris. Mrs. Sarah B. Gibert was admnr. (No other papers.)

PARNELL, WILLIAM—BOX 109, PACK 3080:
Est. admnr. Nov. 12, 1819 by Wm. Barksdale, Matthew Robinson, John Burnett unto Moses Taggart Ord. Abbeville Dist. sum $2,000.00. Cit. pub. at Little Mountain Church.

PARKER, ROBERT—BOX 109, PACK 3081:
Est. admnr. Feb. 25, 1805 by Hugh Porter, John Brannon, John Sanders unto Andrew Hamilton Ord. Abbeville Dist. sum $5,000.00.

PORTER, REV. HUGH—BOX 109, PACK 3082:
Est. admnr. Aug. 2, 1813 by Mary Elizabeth, John Porter, Thos. Chiles, Benj. Glover unto Taliaferro Livingston Ord. Abbeville Dist. sum $20,000.00. Est. admnr. again May 14, 1814 by John Tarrant, John Power, John Downey unto Taliaferro Livingston Ord. Abbeville Dist. sum $15,000.00. Cit. pub. at Rehobeth Church.

PRINCE, SARAH—BOX 109, PACK 3083:
Est. admnr. Oct. 6, 1806 by John, Hudson Prince, John McNeil, unto Andrew Hamilton Ord. Abbeville Dist. sum $10,000.00. Cit. ment. Hudson Prince next of kin.

PRINCE, JOSEPH—BOX 109, PACK 3084:
Est. admnr. Jan. 8, 1833 by Alexr. Hunter, G. N. Sims, Geo. W. Wilson unto Moses Taggart Ord. Abbeville Dist. sum $2,000.00. Cit. pub. at Rocky River Church.

PETTIGREW, WILLIAM—BOX 109, PACK 3085:
Est. admnr. June 6, 1814 by Jas., John M. Pettigrew, John T. Davis
unto Taliaferro Livingston Ord. Abbeville Dist. sum $1,000.00. Cit. pub. at
Rocky River Church.

PETTIGREW, EBENEZER, ESQ.—BOX 109, PACK 3086:
Est. admnr. Mar. 27, 1795 by John Pettigrew unto the Judges of Abbe-
ville County sum 2,000 lbs. Est. admnr. again Mar. 25, 1795 by Sarah Pettigrew
the wid., Col. Joseph Calhoun, Benjamin Howard unto the Judges of Abbeville
County sum 2,000 lbs. Est. admnr. again on Nov. 7, 1797 by Thos. Findley,
John Quay, Wm. Dunlap unto the Judges of Abbeville County sum $8,572.00.

POLSON, JOSEPH—BOX 109, PACK 3087:
Inv. made June 7, 1783 by Zachariah Bullock, Wm. Pool, Lawrence
Easterwood. (No other papers.)

POLLARD, ROBERT—BOX 109, PACK 3088:
Will dated June 22, 1822 in Abbeville Dist. Prov. June 9, 1823. Exrs:
Wm. Hill, Wiley Hill of Laurens Dist. Wit: Sterling Tucker, Jas. Hunter Jr.,
Hamilton Hill. Wife, Helena Pollard. Dtr., Martha Catharine Pollard. Inv.
made June 9, 1823 by Elihu Creswell, Jas. Mitchell, Peter Cheatham. Sale,
Nov. 20, 1823. Byrs: Joseph Hill, Wm. Eddins, Alexr. Sample, Wm. Turner,
Wm. Beasley, Nathan Calhoun, Stephen Ross, Jas. Mitchell, Mrs. Whitlow,
Thos. Cobb, Isaac Bunting, Chas. Patterson, Thos. Chiles, John A. Heard,
Chas. Cooper, Wm. Collier, Helena Pollard, Simeon Chaney, John Logan,
Richard Pollard, Jas. A. Ward, Mansfield Day, Wm. Fooshe, Marshall Pollard,
Isaac McCool, Wiley Hill, Larkin Chiles, Wm. Atwood, Reuben Drake, John
Watts, Jonathan Swift, John N. Sample, Richard Cook, Robt. Hackett, John
Creswell, Hiram Gaines, John Franks, Robt. Turner, Sarah Whitlow.

PULLIAM, SARAH—BOX 109, PACK 3089:
Will dated Aug. 4, 1812 in Abbeville Dist. Rec. Sept. 1812. Exrs:
sons in law, Jas. Pulliam, Peter II. Coalman. Wit: Robt. A. Cunningham,
Dudley Richardson, Champress Turner. Chn: John Pulliam, Martha Fooshe,
Betsey Gholston decd. her 3 chn. viz. Nancy, Zachariah, Benjamin Gholston.
Nancy Ball, Rhoda, Zachary Pulliam, Juda L. Chiles, Fanny Coalman, Anny
Cooper. "Bequeath to John Coalman son of Fanny Coalman."

PALMER, DALE—BOX 109, PACK 3090:
Will dated June 10, 1815 in Abbeville Dist. Prov. Jan. 11, 1821. Exr:
Wife, Mary Palmer. Wit: Joshua Hill, John Hays, Geo. Palmer. Heirs ment.
names not given.

PATTERSON, SAMUEL—BOX 109, PACK 3091:
Will dated Mar. 3, 1791 in Abbeville Dist. Rec. Sept. 13, 1794. Exrs:
Wm., John McGaw. Wit: Thos. Clark, Wm. Carson, Alexr. Patterson. Wife,
Mary Patterson. Chn: Saml., Josiah, Jas., Margaret, John, Mary, Sarah, Jean
Patterson.

PETTIGREW, LOUISE—BOX 109, PACK 3092:
    Will dated June 16, 1819 in Abbeville Dist. Prov. Nov. 13, 1826. Exrs: Sons, Jas. L., Thos. Pettigrew. Wit: Stephen Gibert, Thos. Carter, Daniel New. Chn: Jas. L. Pettigrew of Coosawhatchie, Thos. of the Navy of the U. S., Chas., John G. Pettigrew. Husband, Wm. Pettigrew. Father, the late Rev. Jean Louis Gibert. Bro., John Joseph Gibert decd. Dtrs: Jane G., Mary, Louise, Adaline, Harriett Pettigrew.

RYKARD, MINORS—BOX 109, PACK 3093:
    On Jan. 28, 1835 Thos. Rykard, John, David Keller bound unto Moses Taggart Ord. Abbeville Dist. sum $10,000.00. Thos. Rykard made gdn. of Levi Harrison Rykard, Mary Ann Rykard, Mary Margaret Seigler minors.

ROSS, MINORS—BOX 109, PACK 3094:
    On Feb. 8, 1820 Ann Ross, Margaret, John, Wm. Kilpatrick bound unto (Ord. name not plain) sum $2,000.00. Anne Ross made gdn. of Margaret, Martha, Jas., Abner, John Ross minors under 14 yrs.

RED, MINORS—BOX 109, PACK 3096:
    On (no dates given) Wm. Smith, John Blassingame, Henry, Jas. White bound unto John Thomas Ord. 96 Dist. sum 1,000 lbs. Wm. Smith made gdn. of John, Wm., Elizabeth Red minors.

REIGHLEY, POLLY AND WILLIAM—BOX 109, PACK 3097:
    On Oct. 8, 1802 Wm. Richards, Capt. John Calhoun bound unto Andrew Hamilton Ord. Abbeville Dist. sum $5,000.00. Wm. Richards made gdn. of Polly, Wm. Reighley minors.

REIGHLEY, ANNE AND JENNY—BOX 109, PACK 3098:
    On Oct. 8, 1802 Wm. Richards, Jacob Clark bound unto Andrew Hamilton Ord. Abbeville Dist. sum $5,000.00. Wm. Richards made gdn. of Anne, *Jenny Reighley minors.

RUSSELL, MINORS—BOX 109, PACK 3099:
    On Sept. 19, 1812 Robt. Russellfi Chas. Spence bound unto Taliaferro Livingston Ord. Abbeville Dist. sum $5,000.00. Robt. Russell made gdn. of Alexr., John, Jas. Russell minors under 14 yrs. Sept. 19, 1812 Robt. Russell, Chas. Spence bound unto Taliaferro Livingston Ord. Abbeville Dist. sum $5,000.00. Robt. Russell made gdn. of Jane C., Elizabeth, Wm., Robt. Russell minors over 14 yrs.

RUSSELL, MINORS—BOX 109, PACK 3100:
    On Mar. 7, 1831 Saml. Houston, Robt. F., Thos. P. Black bound unto Moses Taggart Ord. Abbeville Dist. sum $3,000.00. Saml. Houston made gdn. of Mary, Elinor Russell minors over 14 yrs. Nancy C. Russell minor under 14 yrs.

RICHARDSON, TURNER—BOX 109, PACK 3101:
    On Nov. 13, 1804 John Archie or Archer Elmore Esq., John Robinson, David Caldwell of Laurens Dist. bound unto Andrew Hamilton Ord. Abbeville

Dist. sum $5,000.00. John A. Elmore made gdn. of Turner Richardson a minor over 14 yrs.

RICHARDSON, MINORS—BOX 109, PACK 3102:
On Oct. 1, 1816 Rebecca Richardson, Saml. Buchanan, Geo. Haslet bound unto Taliaferro Livingston Ord. Abbeville Dist. sum $1,000.00. Rebecca Richardson made gdn. of Asa D., Mildred G., Rebecca G. Richardson minors over 14 yrs. Oct. 1, 1816 Rebecca Richardson, Saml. Buchannan, Geo. Haslet bound unto Taliaferro Livingston Ord. Abbeville Dist. sum $1,000.00. Rebecca Richardson made gdn. of Elizabeth T., Green C. Richardson minors under 14 yrs.

RICHARDSON, DUDLEY—BOX 109, PACK 3103:
On July 3, 1804 John Robinson, Wm. Wilson, Thos. Hill bound unto Andrew Hamilton Ord. Abbeville Dist. sum $5,000.00. John Robinson made gdn. of Dudley Richardson a minor.

ROGERS, MINORS—BOX 109, PACK 3104:
On Nov. 5, 1838 Ezekiel Trible, Sterling Bowen, Wm. Anderson bound unto Moses Taggart Ord. Abbeville Dist. sum $10,000.00. Ezekiel Trible gdn. of Elizabeth M., Gilbert E., Nelson B., Caroline A. R. Rodgers minors under 21 yrs. Sett. Jan. 20th, 1855 ment. Nelson B. Rodgers was of age Aug. 23, 1842 Mrs. E. M. Roberts and her husband Joseph Roberts recd. $109.96.

ROGERS, MINORS—BOX 109, PACK 3105:
On Nov. 20, 1835 Patrick S., Dyonisius M., Paul Rogers bound unto Moses Taggart Ord. Abbeville Dist. sum $6,000.00. Patrick S. Rogers made gdn. of Simeon, Sophia, Eliza, Middleton, Caroline Rogers minors.

ROBISON, JANE BELL—BOX 109, PACK 3106:
On July 1, 1832 Wm. Sr., Wm. Robison Jr., Wm. Cowan bound unto Moses Taggart Ord. Abbeville Dist. sum $1,000.00. Wm. Robison made gdn. of Jane Bell Robison a minor over 14 yrs.

ROMAN, DANIEL—BOX 109, PACK 3107:
On Nov. 28, 1817 John H. Miller, Saml. L. Watt, Alexr. B. Arnold bound unto Taliaferro Livingston Ord. Abbeville Dist. sum $10,000.00. John H. Miller made gdn. of Daniel S. Roman a minor under 14 yrs.

ROMAN, NANCY—BOX 109—PACK 3108:
On Nov. 2, 1835 John Roman, John White, Joel Smith bound unto Moses Taggart Ord. Abbeville Dist. sum $300.00. John Roman made gdn. of Nancy Roman a minor.
(Letter)
Stoney Point So. Ca.
Nov. 2nd 1835
Moses Taggart Esq.
Dear Sir:
Mr. John Roman informs me that he about to be appointed gdn. for his

dtr. Nancy and wants security.

Joel Smith.

RYAN, SARAH—BOX 109, PACK 3109:
On Dec. 2, 1786 John Ryan, John Watson, John Swearinggen bound unto John Thomas Ord. 96 Dist. sum 500 lbs. John Ryan made gdn. of Sarah Ryan a minor. John Ryan on Dec. 4, 1786 sheweth that Sarah Ryan a minor was about 7 yrs. old.

RODEN, LEANNER—BOX 109, PACK 3110:
Will dated Dec. 10, 1832 in Abbeville Dist. Prov. Mar. 6, 1837. Exr: Wm. Harris. Wit: Leroy Watson, Thos. Whitlock, Wm. Harris. Son, John Roden. Gr. son: Jas. Aiken Roden.

RIDDLE, ELIZABETH—BOX 109, PACK 3111:
Will dated Nov. 24, 1815 in Abbeville Dist. Prov. Mar. 21, 1823. Exrs: Dtr. Margaret Riddle, Patrick Calhoun. Wit: Andrew Norris, H. Edwards, Wm. Shackelford.

RICHEY, JAMES, SR.—BOX 109, PACK 3112:
Will dated Dec. 16, 1807. Exrs: Sons, John, Jas. Richey. Wit: Geo. Brownlee, Wm. McCrone, Jas. Richey Jr. Was of Chickasaw in Abbeville Dist. Chn: John, Jas., Robt. Richey, Agness Purdy, Wm., Andrew Richey. Gr. chn: John, Margaret, Jas. Wilson, Robt. Morrah, Margaret dtr. of my son Jas. Richey, Margaret dtr. to my son Andrew Richey, Jas. son to Wm. Richey, Margaret Seawright dtr. to Robt. Richey, Margaret dtr. to my son John Richey.

ROSAMOND, JEAN—BOX 109, PACK 3113:
Will dated Jan. 11, 1793 in Abbeville Dist. Prov. Mar. 25, 1793. Wit: Jas. Watts, Matthew, Agness Wilson. Bro., Saml. Rosamond and Sarah Rosamond his wife. Sis. Margaret Weems, Sarah Hodges. Bro., Jas. Rosamond. Cousin, Matthew Wilson.

RAGLAND, SAMUEL—BOX 109, PACK 3114:
Will dated Jan. 16, 1796 in Abbeville Dist. Rec. June 10, 1799. Exr: 'Vife, Serah Ragland. Wit: Andrew Adams, Thos. Morgin. "Give tract of land in Newberry County." Chn: Nancy, Nathaniel Ragland, "all debts due in Va." Benjamin Ragland.

RUSSEL, DAVID—BOX 109, PACK 3115:
Will dated July 20, 1805 in Abbeville Dist. Prov. Oct. 18, 1815. Exrs: Joseph Black, Matthew Russel. Wit: Wm., Robt., Robt. Black. Wife, Milly Russell. Sons, David, John Russel. "Should my wife now be with child it to receive share, or to the survivor excluding my first wifes' chn."

ROBINSON, JAMES—BOX 109, PACK 3116:
Will dated Dec. 20, 1811 in Abbeville Dist. Rec. Oct. 18, 1814. Exrs: Wife, Christiana Robinson, John Guthrie, Thos. Brough. Wit: Alexr. Spier, Jas. J. Cosby, John W. Newby. (Note: name written Robinson, Robertson in the will.)

ROGER, ANN LESPINE—BOX 109, PACK 3117:
Will dated Feb. 17, 1776. Prov. May 6, 1800. Exrs: Patrick Calhoun Esq., Jas. Roemore, Peter Moragne, John Eimery, John Beraud, Joseph Bouchillon. Wit: P. Moragne, Peter B. Bayle, Peter Roemore, Jacob Bailand, John Eimery. Ment. Wid. Chn: Peter, Jeremiah Roger, Mary Roger to receive land in the Town of New Bourdeaux.

ROBERTSON, MATILDA—BOX 109, PACK 3118:
Will daed July 21, 1832. Prov. Oct. 1, 1832. No Exrs: Wit: Robt. Young, Mary Maddox, Nancy Stone. Ment: Parents, bros., sis., no names given. Est. admnr. Oct. 3, 1862 by Wm. Robertson, Jas. Seawright, Wm. Donnald unto Wm. Hill Ord. Abbeville Dist. sum $4,000.00. Sett. made Mar. 29, 1864. Ment: 6 shares viz. Wm. Robertson, Louisa Haynie, Emily Klugh, A. Jackson Robertson, Harriet L., Andrew Robertson. By the will of Andrew J. Robertson his sis. Louisa Haynie was to receive share. Mr. Burt represents Mr. Tollison and wife. Chn. of J. L. Pratt decd. share.

REID, GEORGE—BOX 109, PACK 3119:
Will dated Nov. 23, 1786 in 96 Dist. Prov. Apr. 6, 1790. Exrs: Major John Bowie Esq., Capt. Hugh Wardlaw, Capt. Wm. Baskin Esq. Wit: Jas. Reid, John Bowman, John Wardlaw Jr. Chn: Rose wife of John Bowie Esq., Ann wife of Capt. Wm. Baskin Esq., Margaret wife of Hugh Reid, Saml., Alexr., Joseph Reid. "I recommend Polly McGee to the care of my sons Alexr., Joseph Reid."

ROSS, WILLIAM—BOX 109, PACK 3120:
Est. admnr. Feb. 10, 1818 by Ann Ross, Margaret, Andrew Kirkpatrick unto Taliaferro Livingston Ord. Abbeville Dist. sum $5,000.00.

ROSS, MOSES—BOX 109, PACK 3121:
Est. admnr. Nov. 11, 1815 by Mary Ross, Joseph Black, bound unto Taliaferro Livingston Ord. Abbeville Dist. sum $2,000.00.

RUSSELL, JAMES—BOX 109, PACK 3122:
On July 5, 1806 Wm. Lesly Esq., Joseph Gaston, Andrew Bowie, Saml. Lyon, David Strain appraised the est. Robt. Russell, Alexr. Stuart were admnrs. (No other papers.)

RUSSELL, ROSEY ANN—BOX 109, PACK 3123:
On Nov. 14, 1828 Saml. Branch made suit to grant him Letters of Admnr. Cit. pub. at Upper Long Cane Church. (No other papers.)

RUSSELL, JAMES—BOX 109, PACK 3124:
Est. admnr. Nov. 1, 1824 by Rosey Russel, Henry Gray, Henry Weems bound unto Moses Taggart Ord. Abbeville Dist. sum $1,500.00. Cit. ment. Rosannah Russell as admnr. Pub. at Lomaxs Meeting House.

ROBINSON, THOMAS—BOX 109, PACK 3125:
Est. admnr. Nov. 10, 1813 by Benjamin C. Yancey, Moses Taggart bound unto Taliaferro Livingston Ord. Abbeville Dist. sum $1,000.00.

ROBERTSON, JAMES M.—BOX 109, PACK 3126:
Est. admnr. May 7, 1834 by John N. Waddel, A. Burt, D. Wardlaw bound unto Moses Taggart Ord. sum $3,000.00. Cit. pub. at Hopewell Church.

ROBERTS, ABSOLEM, SR.—BOX 109, PACK 3127:
Est. admnr. Apr. 20, 1820 by Thos. Roberts, Thos. B. Creagh, Jas. Bickley bound unto Moses Taggart Ord. Abbeville Dist. sum $200.00.

ROBISON, JOHN D.—BOX 109, PACK 3128:
Cit. pub. at Siloam Church ment. John Robison applied for Letters of Admnr. on Mar. 14, 1820. (No other papers.)

ROMAN, ABRAHAM—BOX 109, PACK 3129:
Est. admnr. Apr. 7, 1826 by Smith Roman, Jesse Calvert, bound unto Moses Taggart sum $700.00.

RYAN, THOMAS—BOX 109, PACK 3130:
Will dated July 19, 1781 in 96 Dist. Prov. Oct. 7, 1783. No Exrs. Wit: Thos. Greer, John Bogan, Obediah Howard. Wife: Sarah Ryan.

RICHARDSON, WILLIAM—BOX 109, PACK 3131:
Est. admnr. Mar. 27, 1797 by Anne Richardson, Harry Smith, Capt. John Meriwether, Dennitt Hill. Alexr. Deall bound unto the Judges of Abbeville County sum $6,000.00. Est. admnr. again June 10, 1799 by John Norwood Sr. of Edgefield County unto Andrew Hamilton Ord. Abbeville Dist. sum $6,000.00. Stephen Bostick, Anne Bostick his wife were admnrs. Est. admnr. again Mar. 28, 1798 by Jonathan, Jas. Chiles, Col. Jas. Mayson unto the Judges of Abbeville Co. sum $6,000.00.

RAMSAY, WILLIAM—BOX 109, PACK 3132:
Est. admnr. Apr. 3, 1827 by Jonathan, Henry Johnston, G. W. Hodges bound unto Moses Taggart Ord. sum $500.000. Cit. pub. at Rocky Creek Church.

SPENCE, MINORS—BOX 110, PACK 3133:
On Oct. 23, 1827 Jas., John Gray, Jas. Taggart bound unto Moses Taggart Ord. Abbeville Dist. sum $4,000.00. Jas. Gray made gdn. of Jane Spence, a minor over 14 yrs. Alexr., Anne Spence minors under 14 yrs.

SCOTT, MINORS—BOX 110, PACK 3134:
On Oct. 20, 1818 Wm. Beauford, Saml., Jane Scott bound unto Taliaferro Livingston Ord. Abbeville Dist. sum $1,000.00. Jane Scott made gdn. of Saml., Wm. Reece, Archibald Scott minors over 14 yrs. Elizabeth Scott a minor under 14 yrs.

SMITH, MINORS—BOX 110, PACK 3135:
On Dec. 17, 1784 Jacob Smith, Enoch Grigsby bound unto John Thomas Ord. 96 Dist. sum 2,000 lbs. Jacob Smith made gdn. of Polly, Mastin, Wylly Smith minors.

SMITH, MINORS—BOX 110, PACK 3136:
On Jan. 7, 1833 John G. Mouchett, Phillip Cook, Jas. Stiefel bound

unto Moses Taggart Ord. Abbeville Dist. sum $400.00. John G. Mouchett made
gdn. of Saml., Wm., Laurence, Mary M. Smith minors of Richard Smith decd.

SMITH, MARY ANN AND MARTHA—BOX 110, PACK 3137:
On Dec. 21, 1826 Robt. Crossan, Jas. Weems Esq., Joseph Smith bound
unto Moses Taggart Ord. Abbeville Dist. sum $10,000.00. Robt. Crossan made
gdn. of Mary Ann, Martha Smith minors under 14 yrs.

SMITH, MINORS—BOX 110, PACK 3138:
On Jan. 8, 1827 Henry Gray, Joseph Davis, Jonathan Smith bound
unto Moses Taggart Ord. Abbeville Dist. sum $10,000.00. Henry Gray made
gdn. of Saml., Elizabeth, John Smith minors over 14 yrs., Joshua Smith minor
under 14 yrs.

STEWART, MINORS—BOX 110, PACK 3139:
On Jan. 8, 1830 Jas. S. Harris, Jas. Wiley, M. B. Clark bound unto
Moses Taggart Ord. Abbeville Dist. sum $1,000.00. Jas. Harris made gdn. of
Francis T., Jane M. Stewart minors over 14 yrs.

SWAIN, MINORS—BOX 110, PACK 3140:
On July 20, 1819 John Sr., Robt. Swain, Chas. Hodges bound unto
Taliaferro Livingston Ord. Abbeville Dist. sum $1,000.00. John Swain made
gdn. of John Jr., Wm., Peggy Swain minors under 14 yrs.

STONE, MINORS—BOX 110, PACK 3141:
On Feb. 7, 1832 Wm. Richey, John Donald, Wm. Ware bound unto
Moses Taggart Ord. Abbeville Dist. sum $1,500.00. Wm. Richey made gdn.
of Wm., Nancy, Polly Ann Stone minors over 14 yrs.

SHIELDS, MINORS—BOX 110, PACK 3142:
On Mar. 19, 1806 Saml. B. Shields, Andrew Bowie, Alexr. C. Hamilton
bound unto Andrew Hamilton Ord. Abbeville Dist. sum $2,000.00. Saml. B.
Shields made gdn. of Theodore C., Wm. Franklin Shields minors.

SHIRLEY, MINORS—BOX 110, PACK 3143:
On Oct. 4, 1832 Obadiah, Benjamin Shirley, John Armstrong bound
unto Moses Taggart Ord. Abbeville Dist. sum $2,000.00. Obadiah Shirley made
gdn. of Loving, Catharine, Annis, Elizabeth Ann Shirley minor chn. of John
Shirley decd.

SHANNON, MINORS—BOX 110, PACK 3144:
On Jan. 2, 1815 Joseph Hawthorn, Alexr., David Taggart bound unto
Taliaferro Livingston Ord. Abbeville Dist. sum $10,000.00. David Taggart
made gdn. of Jas., Robt., Mary Shannon minors over 14 yrs.

SIMS, MARIA P.—BOX 110, PACK 3145:
On Mar. 22, 1837 Ezekiel, Christian, John Rasor bound unto Moses
Taggart Ord. Abbeville Dist. sum $3,000.00. Ezekiel Rasor made gdn. of Maria
P. Sims a minor over 14 yrs.

SWANZY, MINORS—BOX 110, PACK 3146:
On Feb. 2, 1818 John R. Long, Alexr. Sample, Wm. Grubbs bound unto Taliaferro Livingston Ord. Abbeville Dist. sum $15,000.00. John R. Long made gdn. of Rosanna, Eliza Caroline, Mary Martha, Louiza Lucy Swanzy minors under 14 yrs. Sarah Ann, Robt. W. Swanzy minors over 14 yrs. Minors of Dr. S. Swanzy.

STIEFLE, MARY H.—BOX 110, PACK 3147:
On Oct. 15, 1835 Phillip Horatio Mantz of the State of Ga., Mary Stiefle, Thos. C. Perrin bound unto Moses Taggart Ord. ·Abbebille Dist. sum $6,000.00. Philip H. Mantz made gdn. of Mary H. Stiefle a minor.

STIEFLE, MINORS—BOX 110, PACK 3148:
On Oct. 14, 1835 Mary Stiefle, Andrew Mantz, Catharine Zimmerman bound unto Moses Taggart Ord. Abbeville Dist. sum $10,000.00. Mary Stiefle made gdn. of Geo. F., Wm. M. Stiefle minors over 14 yrs.

SELBY, WILLIAM ANDERSON—BOX 110, PACK 3149:
On Feb. 8, 1827 Saml., Owen Selby, Ephraim Davis bound unto Moses Taggart Ord. Abbeville Dist. sum $2,000.00. Saml. Selby made gdn. of Wm. Selby a minor under 14 yrs. (Letter to David Leslie)
Ga. *Conela* County
Jan. 10th 1846
D. Leslie Esq.
Sir:
This will be handed to you by Mr. Geo. H. Gray who comes to Abbeville to receive the funds due me as gdn. for W. A. Selby.
John H. Tench
Wm. A. Selby was child of Isabella Selby who was Isabella Hughey the dtr. of Lidia Hughey decd. of whom Owen Selby was appointed gdn.

SAMPLE, WILLIAM—BOX 110, PACK 3150:
Est. admnr. Feb. 4, 1833 by Saml. Davis, Robt. Turner, Thos. B. Boyd bound unto Moses Taggart Ord. Abbeville Dist. sum $4,000.00. Cit. pub. at Rocky Creek Church.

SMITH, JOHN—BOX 110, PACK 3151:
Est. admnr. Dec. 12, 1834 by John Hearst, Dewy E., Henry M. Lipford bound unto Moses Taggart Ord. Abbeville Dist. sum $1,000.00. Cit. pub. at Mt. Pleasant Church.

SMITH, JOHN—BOX 110, PACK 3152:
Est. admnr. Jan. 5, 1807 by John B. Smith, Robt. Brown, Phillamon Beuford bound unto Andrew Hamilton Ord. Abbeville Dist. sum $10,000.00. Cit. pub. at Rocky River Church.

SCOTT, WALTER—BOX 110, PACK 3153:
Est. admnr. Sept. 30, 1794 by Edward Adair, Wm. Dunlap, Saml. Houston unto the Judges of Abbeville County, sum 1,000 lbs. Walter Scott was an Indian Trader. Cit. pub. at Upper Long Cane Church.

SAUNDERS, JOHN—BOX 110, PACK 3154:
Est. admnr. July 13, 1784 by Thos. Downey, John Lockridge, Jas.
Compton Edwards unto John Thomas Ord. 96 Dist. sum 1,000 lbs.

SHOTWELL, JOHN—BOX 110, PACK 3155:
Will dated Apr. 1, 1816 in Abbeville Dist. Rec. Aug. 1, 1818. Exrs:
Capt. Geo. Shotwell, Jared E. Groce. Wit: Richard Stephens, Wm. Wier, Nancy
White. Sis., Susannah Shotwell. Mother, Hannah Shotwell. Other bros., sis.
ment. no names given. Est. admnr. Mar. 15, 1819 by John Burdine, Alexr.
Sample, Saml. L. Watt unto Moses Taggart Ord. Abbeville Dist. sum $20,000.00.
Cit. pub. Aug. 1, 1818 ment. John Shotwell decd. was late of the Ala. Terri-
tory. Geo. Shotwell of Greenville Dist. refused to act as Exr.

SMYTH, ROBERT—BOX 110, PACK 3156:
Est. admnr. May 19, 1826 by Martha Smyth, John Devlin, Wm. Chiles
unto Moses Taggart Ord. Abbeville Dist. sum $20,000.00. Cit. pub. at Asbury
Church ment. Martha B. Smyth next of kin.

SMITH, ELIZABETH—BOX 110, PACK 3157:
Est. admnr. Jan. 6, 1823 by Robt. W., Thos. Smith, Richard Griffin
unto Moses Taggart Abbeville Dist. sum $2,000.00.

STUART, PETER—BOX 110, PACK 3158:
Est. admnr. Feb. 4, 1785 by Jas. Stuart, Geo. Reid unto John Thomas Jr.
Ord. 96 Dist. sum 2,000 lbs. Name written Stuart, Stewart.

SHILLITTO, NANCY—BOX 110, PACK 3159:
Est. admnr. Dec. 13, 1825 by Geo. Shillitto, Thos. E. Owen, John W.
Laren bound unto Moses Taggart Ord. Abbeville Dist. sum $1,000.00. Cit. pub.
at Long Cane Church.

SPEED, JAMES W.—BOX 110, PACK 3160:
Est. admnr. Nov. 12, 1819 by Michael Speed, Williamson Norwood,
Ezekiel Calhoun bound unto Moses Taggart Ord. Abbeville Dist. sum $10,000.00.

SAXON, YANCY—BOX 110, PACK 3161:
Est. admnr. Sept. 14, 1785 by Jas., Chas., Saml. Saxon, Wm. Millwee,
bound unto John Thomas Ord. 96 Dist. sum 1,000 lbs.

SCOTT, WILLIAM—BOX 110, PACK 3162:
Est. admnr. Jan. 5, 1827 by John, Jas., Alexr. Scott bound unto Moses
Taggart Ord. Abbeville Dist. sum $2,000.00. Inv. made Jan. 20, 1827 by Henry
Furr, Peter Hemmenger, Wm. T. Drennan.

STARK, REUBEN—BOX 110, PACK 3163:
Will dated Nov. 24, 1830. Prov. June 21, 1837. Exrs: Son, Wyatt W.
Starke, Elijah Hunt, Edmund Tillman, Abram Bell, Jas. Casper. Wit: Nathan
M. or W. Strickland, Patrick Noble, Jas. Grant. Wife, Elizabeth G. Starke. Gr.
chn: Pinkney, Reuben, Catharine Jane chn. of Wyatt W. Starke. "After Wyatt's
death property to go to chn. of Saml. C. Starke then living except Mary Martin."
Owned land in the State of Ala., also in the town of Pensacola.

SPENCE, ANN—BOX 110, PACK 3164:
Will dated Mar. 23, 1808 in Abbeville Dist. Exrs: Son, Joseph Spence, John Wardlaw. Wit: John Martin, Mary Ann Wardlaw, Isabel T. English. Chn: Polly, Saml., Joseph Spence.

SALES, JAMES—BOX 110, PACK 3165:
On Aug. 3, 1826 Saml. Henderson, Maximilian Hutchison, Jas., Leroy Watson were ordered to appraise the est. by Elizabeth Sales the admnrx.

SCOT, ALEXANDER—BOX 110, PACK 3166:
Will dated Jan. 18, 1806 in Abbeville Dist. Rec. Mar. 17, 1806. Exrs: Wife, Jan Scott, Son Alexr. Scott. Chn: Wm., Jas., Alexr. Scott, Agnes Highnot, Sariah Cambel, Benjamin, Belford, Newd Scot. Wit: Andrew Calhoun, Larkin Reynolds.

SCOTT, ARCHIBALD—BOX 110, PACK 3167:
Will dated Feb. 1, 1808 in Abbeville Dist. Rec. July 4, 1808. Exrs: Sons, Saml., Archibald Scott. Wit: John Caldwell, Joseph, Jas. H. Scott. Wife, Agnes Scott. Chn: Peggy, Saml., Polly, Archibald, Betsy, Jas. Scott.

SCOTT, JOSEPH, SR.—BOX 110, PACK 1368:
Will dated Apr. 2, 1818 in Abbeville Dist. Rec. Oct. 20, 1818. No Exrs. Wit: Johnsone Newell, John McMahan. Wife ment. no name given. Chn: Jas., Joseph Jr., Nancy Scott.

SANDERS, JOSEPH—BOX 110, PACK 3169:
Will dated Apr. 21, 1813 in Abbeville Dist. Rec. June 29, 1813. Exrs: Wife, Rebecka Sanders. Wit: John, Jas. E. Brannan, John Sanders. Chn: Joseph Hall Sanders, John, Wm. Muckelwee, Nancy Sanders.

SMITH, JANE—BOX 110, PACK 3170:
Will dated Feb. 10, 1807 in Abbeville Dist. Rec. May 17, 1811. No Exrs. Wit: Gilbert, Robt. M. Mann, Wm. Huston. Chn: Geo., Gilbert, Michael, Albert Smith, Jane Edwards, Margaret, Elizabeth Mann, Anne Shoemaker.

SMITH, MICHAEL—BOX 110, PACK 3171:
Will dated June 9, 1803 in Abbeville Dist. Rec. May 17, 1811. No Exrs. Wit: Abraham Livingston, Gilbert Mann. Wife, Jean Smith. Chn: Michael, Gilbert Smith.

STURRENEGGER, DR. JOHN JACOB—BOX 110, PACK 3172:
Will dated Mar. 1, 1775. Prov. Aug. 9, 1784. Exr: Son, John Sturrenegger. Wit: John Tobler, John Starr, John Shinholser. Lived in New Windsor Township, 96 District. Wife, Elizabeth Sturrenegger. Chn: John, Cathrina Sturrenegger. (Name written Sturzenegger.)

SMITH, GEORGE—BOX 110, PACK 3173:
Will dated Oct. 1, 1794 in Abbeville Dist. Exrs: John Jones, John Bell. Wit: John Pinkerton, Elizabeth Bell, Robt. Wallace. Wife: Elizabeth Smith. Chn: Elizabeth, Jane, S. Is: Robt., Joshua Wallace.

SKELLY, AGNESS—BOX 110, PACK 3174:
Will dated Mar. 15, 1790. Prov. Apr. 6, 1790. Exrs: Joseph Crawford,
Wm. White. Wit: Joseph Milligan, John Swanzy, Mary White. Child ment.
no name given. Sis., Margaret Skelly.

SHAW, WILLIAM, SR.—BOX 110, PACK 3175:
Will dated Sept. 8, 1793. Rec. Sept. 15, 1794. Exrs: Sons, Jas., Wm.
Shaw. Wit: not plain. Lived in Cambridge, Abbeville Dist. Chn: Jas., Wm.,
Mary, Elizabeth Sted, Ann, Matilda Smith, Margaret Elin. Gr. son: John, son
of Jas. Shaw.

SHAFFER, FREDERICK—BOX 110, PACK 3176:
Will dated Jan. 31, 1784. No Exrs. Wit: Ulrick Mayer, John————?
John Swingtenberg. Wife, Maria Elizabeth Shaffer. Son ment. no name given.
"land on the branches of Wateree. Give 3 single dtrs. (names not given) 150
acres lying and joining Jas. McMasters land Fork of Saludy and Broad River."

TURNER, HAMILTON—BOX 110, PACK 3177:
On Feb. 7, 1803 John Hamilton, John Harris, David Gillespie bound
unto Andrew Hamilton Ord. Abbeville Dist. sum $5,000.00. John Hamilton
made gdn. of Hamilton Turner a minor.

THACKER, MINORS—BOX 110, PACK 3178:
On Oct. 21, 1839 Christian Barns, Johnson Ramey, Wm. F. Baker bound
unto Moses Taggart Ord. Abbeville Dist. sum $1,000.00. Christian Barns made
gdn. of John F., Jane Elizabeth Thacker minors.

TILMAN, DANIEL WHITE—BOX 110, PACK 3179:
On Jan. 6, 1817 Edward, Hyram Tilman, Jas. Murray, bound unto
Taliaferro Livingston Ord. Abbeville Dist. sum $20,000.00. Edward Tilman
made gdn. of Daniel White Tilman a minor over 14 yrs. Mar. 1, 1819 General
Joseph Hutton, John Devlin, Chas. Spence bound unto Moses Taggart Ord.
Abbeville Dist. sum $20,000.00. General Joseph Hutton made gdn. of Daniel
White Tilman a minor.

TUTTON, PETER—BOX 110, PACK 3180:
On May 5, 1820 Mary, Wm. Tutton, John Pressly Sr. bound unto Moses
Taggart Ord. Abbeville Dist. sum $1,000.00. Mary Tuttom made gdn. of Peter
Tutton a minor over 14 yrs.

TRAYLOR, WINSTON N.—BOX 110, PACK 3181:
On Oct. 26, 1835 Edward Collier, Abner Perrin, Albert T. Traylor bound
unto Moses Taggart Ord. Abbeville Dist. sum $5,000.00. Edward Collier made
gdn. of Winston N. Traylor a minor.

TEAGLE, NATHANIEL—BOX 110—PACK 3182:
On Jan. 7, 1833 John Teagle, Jacob Richard, John Sloan bound unto
Moses Taggart Ord. Abbeville Dist. sum $300.00. John Teagle made gdn. of
Nathaniel Teagle a minor under 14 yrs.

THOMPSON, ROBERT—BOX 110, PACK 3183:
On Mar. 17, 1818 Wm. Reynolds, Bartholomew Jordon, Joseph Conn bound unto Taliaferro Livingston Ord. Abbeville Dist. sum $1,000.00. Wm. Reynolds made gdn. of Robt. Thompson a minor over 14 yrs.

TENNENT, CHARLES M.—BOX 110, PACK 3184:
Est. admnr. Dec. 23, 1826 by Dr. Wm. Tennent, Wm. Lomax bound unto Moses Taggart Ord. Abbeville Dist. sum $1,000.00. Cit. pub. at Upper Long Cane Church.

TENNENT, LAVINIA—BOX 110, PACK 3185:
Est. admnr. Dec. 23, 1826 by Dr. Wm. Tennent, Wm. Lomax unto Moses Taggart Ord. Abbeville Dist. sum $2,000.00. Cit. pub. at Upper Long Cane Church.

TURNER, GILBERT—BOX 110, PACK 3186:
Est. admnr. July 7, 1783 by Wm. Turner, Michael Abney, John Edwards bound unto John Thomas Ord. 96 Dist. sum 2,000 lbs. Cit. ment. he was of Saluda in the Dist. aforesaid.

THACKER, BARTHOLOMEW—BOX 110, PACK 3187:
Est. admnr. Apr. 6, 1790 by Rev Daniel Thacher, Saml., Joseph Reed bound unto the Judges of Abbeville County sum 500 lbs. Cit. pub. at Long Cane Church ment. Rev. Daniel Thatcher next of kin. Daniel Thatcher was a cousin to the decd.

TANE, JOHN, SR.—BOX 110, PACK 3188:
Est. admnr. Mar. 17, 1812 by Archibald Douglass, Wm. Cochran bound unto Taliaferro Livingston Ord. Abbeville Dist. sum $1,000.00. Cit. pub. at Providence Church. (Not positive whether the name was Tane or Tune.)

TERRY, JEREMIAH—BOX 110, PACK 3189:
Est. admnr. Sept. 12, 1794 by Robt., Susannah Terry his wife, Joseph Sr., Joseph Sanders Jr. unto the Judges of Abbeville County sum 500 lbs. On Sept. 13, 1803 Nathaniel Terry applied for Letters of Admnr. as next of kin in place of Robt. Terry decd. the former admnr. Mar. 4, 1795 Capt. Uel Hill, Wm. Collier, Drury Breazeale were ordered to appraise the est.

TEASDALE, ISAAC—BOX 110, PACK 3190:
Est. admnr. Sept. 1, 1817 by Elizabeth Teasdale, Robt. Finney, Adino Griffin bound unto Taliaferro Livingston Ord. Abbeville Dist. sum $1,000.00.

TINSLEY, PHILIP—BOX 110, PACK 3191:
Est. admnr. Apr. 27, 1784 by Ann Tinsley, Richard Golding, Chas. Brice bound unto John Thomas Ord. 96 Dist. sum 2,000 lbs.

TITTLE, PETER—BOX 110, PACK 3192:
Est. admnr. Oct. 31, 1812 by Jas. Edwards, Wm. Harris bound unto Taliaferro Livingston Ord. Abbeville Dist. sum $1,000.00. Cit. ment. Jas. Edwards made suit for Letters of Admnr. as next of kin of est. of Peter Tittle late of the State of Ky.

TOWLES, STOKELY—BOX 110, PACK 3193:
Est. admnr. Feb. 7, 1785 by Martha, Joseph Towles, Joshua Gillam bound unto John Thomas Ord. 96 Dist. sum 2,000 lbs.

TOWLES, OLIVER—BOX 110, PACK 3194:
Est. admnr. Apr. 28, 1784 by John Towles, John Ritchey, Saml. *Tayton* bound unto John Thomas Ord. 96 Dist. sum 2,000 lbs. (Tayton or Taylor.)

TOLER, JOHN—BOX 110, PACK 3195:
Est. admnr. Oct. 20, 1813 by Joseph Bickley, Milton Paschal, bound unto Taliaferro Livingston Ord. Abbeville Dist. sum $1,000.00. Cit. pub. at Rocky River Church.

TAYLOR, ROSANNA—BOX 110, PACK 3196:
Est. admnr. July 17, 1835 by Alexr. McKinney, Mathew, Robt. Shanks bound unto Moses Taggart Ord. Abbeville Dist. sum $800.00. Cit. pub. at Hopewell Church.

TEDDARDS, JOHN—BOX 110, PACK 3197:
Est. admnr. Oct. 19, 1815 by Partin Hagood, Richard Turner bound unto Taliaferro Livingston Ord. Abbeville Dist. sum 1,000 lbs. Cit. ment. John Teddards late of the army decd.

THORNTON, WILLIAM—BOX 110, PACK 3198:
Cit. pub. June 26, 1789 ment. John Strain applied for Letters of Admnr. Read in Long Cane Church. (No other papers.)

THOMPSON, ROBERT—BOX 110, PACK 3199:
Est. admnr. May 28, 1814 by Burges Pitman, Isaac Evans, Jas. McAllister unto Taliaferro Livingston Ord. Abbeville Dist. sum $1,000.00. Cit. pub. at Long Cane Church.

THOMPSON, JOHN—BOX 110, PACK 3200:
Est. admnr. Jan. 3, 1820 by Moses A. Bates, Edward Collier, Meridith McGehee bound unto Moses Taggart Ord. Abbeville Dist. sum $1,000.00. Cit. pub. at Willington Church. Name Bates written Moses E. Bates in cit.

TODD, ARCHIBALD—BOX 110, PACK 3201:
Est. admnr. Nov. 15, 1839 by Peter F. Moragne, Michael R. Breazeale, Jas. Devall bound unto Moses Taggart Ord. Abbeville Dist. sum $7,000.00. Cit. pub. at Buffalo Church.

TENNENT, WILLIAM, ESQ.—BOX 110, PACK 3202:
Est. admnr. Sept. 13, 1817 by Martha Tennent, Wm. Lomax, Alexr Speer bound unto Taliaferro Livingston Ord. Abbeville Dist. sum 10,000 lbs.

TAYLOR, THOMAS—BOX 110, PACK 3203:
Will dated 1787. Exrs: Wm. Miles, John Taylor. Wit: Micajah Stevens, Herod Freeman. Was of Culpeper County. (Probable Va.) Wife, Johannah Taylor. Chn. ment. names not given.

TURK, JOHN—BOX 110, PACK 3204:
Will dated July 21, 1794 in Abbeville Dist. Rec. Mar. 26, 1795. Exrs:
Wife, Jean Turk, Joseph McMurtrey. Wit: Saml. McMurtrey, Jas. McAllister
John Strain. Jean's mother ment. no name given.

THORNTON, SAMUEL—BOX 110, PACK 3205:
Will dated Aug. 10, 1796 in Abbeville Dist. Rec. June 13, 1797 Exrs:
Jas., Robt. Thornton. Wit: John Montgomery, John, Thos. Strain. Wife, Mary
Thornton. Chn: Jas., Margaret, Magdolene, Robt. Thornton.

VAUGHN, CHARLES—BOX 110, PACK 3206:
On Oct. 19, 1813 Jas. Hutchison, Robt. McBride, Henry Robinson bound
unto Taliaferro Livingston Ord. Abbeville Dist. sum $1,000.00. Jas. Hutchison
was gdn. of Chas. Vaughn a minor over 14 yrs.

VINES, JAMES—BOX 110, PACK 3207:
On Sept. 24, 1835 Nelia, David Vines, Wm. R. Swain bound unto
Moses Taggart Ord. Abbeville Dist. sum $1,000.00. Neely (written Nelia and
Neely) Vines made gdn. of Jas. Vines a minor.

VAUGHAN, JAMES—BOX 110, PACK 3208:
Cit. pub. at Rehobeth Church on Aug. 2, 1824 ment. Mrs. Matilda
Vaughan, Saml. Caldwell applied for Letters of Admnr. (No other papers.)

WILLIAMS, WILLIAMSON—BOX 110, PACK 3209:
On Oct. 2, 1804 Lewallen Goode, Jas. Gowdy, Jas. McCracken bound
unto Andrew Hamilton Ord. Abbeville Dist. sum $5,000.00. Lewallen Goode
made gdn. of Williamson Williams a minor. On Mar. 7, 1803 Joseph Williams,
Alexr. Stuart, Thos. Brightman bound unto Andrew Hamilton Ord. Abbeville
Dist. sum $5,000.00. Joseph Williams made gdn. of Williamson Williams a
minor.

WARD, JENNY YOUNG—BOX 110, PACK 3210:
On Mar. 4, 1805 Saml. Young, Mordecai Shackelford, Archelous Walker
bound unto Andrew Hamilton Ord. Abbeville Dist. sum $2,500.00. Saml. Young
made gdn. of Jenny Young Ward who was 9 yrs. old the 1st May last.

WRIGHT, MINORS—BOX 110, PACK 3211:
On Feb. 1, 1832 Anne Wright, Jas. Armstrong, Wm. Cowan of Anderson Dist. Anne Wright of Abbeville Dist. bound to Moses Taggart Ord. Abbeville Dist. sum $2,000.00. Ann Wright made gdn. of Vincent, Turner Thornton
Wright minors under 14 yrs.

WARDLAW, JOHN—BOX 110, PACK 3212:
On Nov. 24, 1808 Wm., Jas. Jr., Hugh Wardlaw bound to Andrew
Hamilton Ord. Abbeville Dist. sum $5,000.00. Wm. Wardlaw made gdn. of
John Wardlaw a minor.

WORRILL, MINORS—BOX 110, PACK 3213:
On Jan. 6, 1812 Solomon Worrill, Joseph Bickley bound unto Taliaferro

Livingston Ord. Abbeville Dist. sum $2,000.00. Solomon Worrill made gdn. of Nancy, Temperance Worrill minors over 14 yrs.

WALLER, MARSHALL—BOX 110, PACK 3214:
On Dec. 14, 1815 Leonard Waller, John Chiles, Thos. Livingston bound to Taliaferro Livingston Ord. Abbeville Dist. sum $10,000.00. Leonard Waller made gdn. of Marshall Waller a minor over 14 yrs.

WALLER, WILLIAM W.—BOX 110, PACK 3215:
On July 5, 1830 Sanley Crews, Grigsby Applcotn, Joel Smith bound unto Moses Taggart Ord. Abbeville Dist. sum $6,000.00. Stanley Crews made gdn. of Wm. W. Waller a minor over 14 yrs.

WRENCH, LEWIZA MARGARET—BOX 110, PACK 3216:
On Mar. 2, 1807 Sarah Wrench, Andrew Norris Esq. bound unto Andrew Hamilton Ord. Abbeville Dist. sum $10,000.00 Sarah Wrench made gdn. of Lewiza Margaret Wrench a minor. (Name written Louisa Margaret Wrench in one place.)

WOOLDRIDGE, WILLIAM & ELIZABETH—BOX 110, PACK 3217:
On Mar. 16, 1819 Patsy Wooldridge relict of John Wooldridge decd., Dudley Jones, Geo. Patterson bound unto Moses Taggart Ord. Abbeville Dist. sum $10,000.00. Patsy Wooldridge was gdn. of Wm., Elizabeth Wooldridge minors over 14 yrs. Matilda, Lucy, Nancy, Sally, Susanna, Harriet Wooldridge minors under 14 yrs.

WIMBISH, MARIA & ELIZABETH—BOX 110, PACK 3218:
On Feb. 24, 1816 Joshua Dubose, Williamson Norwood, John H. Cooper bound unto Taliaferro Livingston Ord. Abbeville Dist. sum $10,000.000. Joshua Dubsoe made gdn. of Maria Wimbish a minor over 14 yrs., Elizabeth Wimbish a minor over 14 yrs.

WILSON, MINORS—BOX 110, PACK 3219:
On Feb. 22, 1812 Joseph, Jas. Bickley bound unto Taliaferro Livingston Ord. Abbeville Dist. sum $10,000.00. Joseph Bickley was gdn. of John, Thos., Susan W., Amelia, Francis Wilson minors under 14 yrs., Chas. Wilson a minor over 14 yrs. Cit. of Elizabeth Wilson in same pack. Pub. Aug. 26, 1838 at Upper Long Cane Church.

WILSON, LEMUEL—BOX 110, PACK 3220:
On Jan. 25, 1822 Benjamin, Wm. Bell, Sampson Pope bound unto Moses Taggart Ord. Abbeville Dist. sum $500.00. Benjamin Bell made gdn. of Lemuel Wilson a minor under 14 yrs.

WILSON, MINORS—BOX 110, PACK 3221:
On Dec. 5, 1831 Wm. H. Jones, John Wilson, Loranzo Wright bound unto Moses Taggart Ord. Abbeville Dist. sum $2,000.00. Wm. H. Jones made gdn. of Betsey, Jane, Robt. Wilson minors under 14 yrs.

WILSON, MINORS—BOX 110, PACK 3222:
    On Apr. 5, 1839 Jas., Alexr. P. Conner, Henry Bently bound unto Moses Taggart Ord. Abbeville Dist. sum $5,000.00. Jas. Conner made gdn. of Catharine R., Joseph N., Saml., Jas. Wilson minors under 21 yrs. Chn. of Jas. Wilson decd.

WARD, POLLY & ANN—BOX 110, PACK 3223:
    On Mar. 4, 1805 Peter Brown, Jeremiah Terry, Benjamin Gunnin bound to Andrew Hamilton Ord. Abbeville Dist. sum $5,000.00. Peter Brown made gdn. of Polly Harbert Ward 15 yrs. last Dec. Anne Pole Ward 8 yrs. old last Oct.

WILLARD, JOHN—BOX 110, PACK 3224:
    Est. admnr. Oct. 10, 1785 by Elizabeth Willard, Thos. Cargill, Chas. Saxon, John Rodgers Jr. bound unto John Thomas Ord. 96 Dist. sum 500 lbs. Inv. made Dec. 10, 1785 by David Bailey, Wm. Cargill, Cornelius Tinsley.

WEST, WILLIAM—BOX 110, PACK 3225:
    Es. admnr. Dec. 3, 1785 by Jane West, Daniel Parkins, Alexr. McDougel bound unto John Thomas Ord. 96 Dist. sum 1,000 lbs.

WITZEL, DR. JOHN—BOX 110, PACK 3226:
    Est. admnr. Jan. 6, 1789 by Eleanor Witzel, Norwood, Gabriel Smithers bound unto the Judges of Abbeville County sum 1,000 lbs. Eleanor Witzel the wid.

WATERS, JANE—BOX 110, PACK 3227:
    Est. admnr. Feb. 3, 1812 by David Waters, Wm. Bell, John Cochran bound unto Taliaferro Livingston Ord. Abbeville Dist. sum $2,000.00.

WARE. MARGARET—BOX 110, PACK 3228:
    Est. admnr. May 14, 1833 by Thos. Edwin Ware, Thos. P. Spierin, Mark M. Johnson, Wm., Albert N. Ware bound unto Moses Taggart Ord. Abbeville Dist. sum $10,000.00. Cit. pub. at Turkey Creek Church.

WILEY, JOHN—BOX 110, PACK 3229:
    Est. admnr. Aug. 22, 1812 by Saml. Mosely, John Scogin bound to Taliaferro Livingston Ord. Abbeville Dist. sum $1,000.00. Cit. pub. at Johns Creek Meeting House.

WHITE, JAMES—BOX 110, PACK 3230:
    Est. admnr. Oct. 8, 1810 by Jas. Forrest, Robt. Lindsay, Sylvanus Adams bound to John Hamilton Ord. Abbeville Dist. sum $1,000.00.

WEEMS, CAPT. THOMAS—BOX 110, PACK 3231:
    Est. admnr. Nov. 18, 1794 by Elizabeth Weems, Saml. Sr., Robt. Foster, John Hearst, Bartholomew Weews Sr. bound unto the Judges of Abbeville County sum 1,500 pounds. (Was a blacksmith.) Cit. pub. at Long Cane Church ment. Elizabeth Weems the wid.

WILLIAMS, DR. FRANKLIN—BOX 110, PACK 3232:
    Est. admnr. Jan. 30, 1836 by Vincent Griffin, John White, John Allen

bound unto Moses Taggart Ord. Abbeville Dist. sum $10,000.00. Cit. pub. at Mount Moriah Church.

WILLIAMS, ROBERT—BOX 110, PACK 3233:
Est. admnr. Oct. 10, 1786 by Leonard Nobles, John Swearingen, Edward Couch, John Randol bound unto John Thomas Ord. 96 Dist. sum 500 lbs. Letters of admnr. pub. in Edgefield County.

WILLIAMS, SAMUEL—BOX 110, PACK 3234:
Est. admnr. July 5, 1802 by Catharine, Joseph Williams, Thos. Brightman, Alexr. Stuart bound unto Andrew Hamilton Ord. Abbeville Dist. sum $10,000.00.

WILLIAMS, SAMUEL—BOX 110, PACK 3235:
Est. admnr. Oct. 2, 1804 by Lew Allan Goode, Jas. Gowdy, Jas. McCracken bound unto Andrew Hamilton Ord. Abbeville Dist. sum $10,000.00. Cit. ment. Lew Goode next of kin.

WILSON, WILLIAM—BOX 110, PACK 3236:
Est. admnr. Oct. 5, 1815 by Gilbert Wilson, Joseph Cowie. John Stuart bound unto Taliaferro Livingston Ord. Abbeville Dist. sum $1,000.00. Wm. Wilson was late of the Army of the U. S.

WILSON, WILLIAM—BOX 110, PACK 3237:
Est. admnr. Dec. 1, 1783 by Mary Wilson, Zachariah, Nathaniel Bullock bound unto John Thomas Ord. 96 Dist. sum 2,000 lbs. Inv. made by John Bullock, Caleb Holloway, Wm. Mathis. No date given on Inv.

WALKER, LATTICE—BOX 110, PACK 3238:
Will dated Jan. 22, 1829 in Abbeville Dist. Prov. Sept. 7, 1829. Exr: Adolpus J. Sale. Wit: Elizabeth W., A. Scott, J. W. Prather. Wid. of Henry G. Walker. "Bequeath to the Heirs of Eliza N. Sales." No names given.

WILSON, ARABELLA—BOX 110, PACK 3239:
Will dated Oct. 9, 1824 in Abbeville Dist. Prov. Dec. 31, 1824 or 1825. Exrs: Sis., Margaret Wilson. Bro., Wm. Wilson. Wit: Wm. Lesly, Margaret Wilson, J. Morrow. Neice, Betsy Beard wife of Jas. Caldwell. "Bequeath to my sis. Margaret Wilson, my bro. Wm. Wilson an equal share in a house and lot in the town of Natchez of the est. of Patrick Wilson decd. and my share of my sis. Elizabeth's part decd. of the same. My wish to be buried in the same grave of that of my father and bro. Hamilton. Also that there shall be a decent head stone procured with my father John Wilson, Brother Hamilton Wilson and my own name engraved on it and set at the head of my grave."

WATSON, MICHAEL—BOX 110, PACK 3240:
Will dated May 26, 1782 in 96 Dist. Probated July 22, 1782. Exrs: Arthur Watson, Robt. Stark. Wit: Wm. R. Withers, Robt. Stark, *Richman* Watson. Wife, Martha Watson. 4 dtrs. ment. no names given. "Give to my son Eliga

Watson tract of land on Clouds Creek joining land of Warren, Cusack, Allen Containing 550 acres."

WARD, THOMAS—BOX 110, PACK 3241:
Will dated Nov. 1, 1815 in Abbeville Dist. Rec. Mar. 2, 1818. Exr: Ezekiel Calhoun Sr. Esq. Wit: Geo. Bowie, Wm. Fleming, Mary Calhoun. Chn: Peter Ward, Betsey, Rebecca Vernon, Sally Ward, Rachel Gillespie. Gr. Chn: Jas., Peter Ward, Nancy Cook, Walter H., Margaret Ward chn. of Wm. Ward decd. Mary Caldwell Ward, Jean, Anney Ward chn. of Joseph Ward decd.

WATERS, MARY—BOX 110, PACK 3242:
Will dated July 4, 1792 in 96 Dist. Sept. 14, 1798. Exrs: Son, David Waters, Joseph Wardlaw. Wit: Chas. Davenport, Thos. Butler. Chn: David Watters, Elizabeth Lombes, Rachel Beel, Sarah Porter. Marthew Burne, Gennet Watters. "To my dtr. Elizabeth Lombesone bolt of lining cloth No. 1 her dtrs. Mary, Sarah Steel to be divided between them. Give Gennet Watters lining cloth to be divided, giving one gown pattern of her part to Gennet Beel." Gr. son: Wm. Steel.

WARDLAW, ELIAB—BOX 110, PACK 3243:
Will dated Feb. 15, 1808 in Abbeville Dist. Rec. Mar. 8, 1808. Exrs: Bro. Jas. Wardlaw. Cousin, David Wardlaw. Wit: John Griffin, Wm. Hackett, Edmund Stephens. Bros. Jas., Wm., John Wardlaw. Sis: Mary, Jenny, Peggy, Betsy, Nancy Wardlaw. "Leave $1,500.00. to Lucy Hackett son Joseph. Leave $200.00 to John McFarlane son Eliab G. McFarlane."

WAITE, JOHN—BOX 110, PACK 3244:
Will dated Sept. 7, 1805 in Abbeville Dist. Rec. Nov. 27, 1805. Exrs: Sons, Henry, Francis Waite. Wit: Reuben Chiles, Grigary Cordol, John Pressly. Wife, Anne Waite. Chn: Francis, Aagon Waite "113 acres on Hard Labor Creek and Martin's Branch, Henry Waite 125 acres lying in Edgefield County on Little Saluda and Big Creek where he now lives, Thos. Waite 50 acres lying on Little Saluda and Big Creek in Edgefield County." Saphire, Robt., John, Nelly Betty, Peggy Waite. (Name Saphire looked like Sophire in one place.)

WHITE, JOHN—BOX 110, PACK 3245:
Will dated Feb. 7, 1786 in Spartanburg Co. Prov. Mar. 2, 1787. Exrs: Wife, Anne White, Alexr. Walker, Richard Harrison. Wit: Alexr. Walker, Henry Walden. Chn: Mary, Lecy, Ursula, John, Susannah White.

WADLINGTON, THOMAS, SR.—BOX 110, PACK 3246:
Will dated Feb. 11, 1777 in 96 Dist. Prov. Dec. 20, 1777. Exrs: Wife, Sarah Wadlington. Sons, Wm., Thos. Wadlington. Wit: Abraham Ethell, Thos., Penelope Perry. "Give her plantation on Collins Creek." Chn: Wm., Thos., Jas., Ann, Edward, Sarah Johnston, Geo. Wadlington.

WALLACE, WILLIAM, SR.—BOX 110, PACK 3247:
Will dated Oct. 9, 1815 in Abbeville Dist. Prov. May 6, 1816. Exrs: John McAdam, Benjamin Shirley. Wit: Sugar Wright, John McLain. Wife, Eleanor Wallace. Chn: Mary, Wm., Cattey, Jas. Wallace. "Give to my son Jas. Wallace the price of the mare I let him have when he left this Country."

WALLACE, JAMES—BOX 110, PACK 3248:
Will dated Feb. 9, 1795 in Abbeville Dist. Rec. Mar. 25, 1795. Exrs: Geo. Brownlee, Andrew Webb. Wit: John Murphy, Wm. Brownlee, Andrew Webb. Wife, Eleanor Wallace. Chn: Joshua, Robt., Wm. Wallace. "Leave to John McClean etc."

WEED, NATHANIEL—BOX 110, PACK 3249:
Will dated Mar. 16, 1818 in Abbeville Dist. Prov. Aug. 3, 1818. Exrs: Wife, Elizabeth Weed, Joseph McCreary Esq. Wit: Wm. Dale, Jas. Cochran, C. Ruff. Chn: Jas. Cooper Weed, Marhta Crawford Weed, Reuben C. Weed, Sarah Jones Weed, Andrew, Nathaniel Weed. s. l., John Pressly. Inv. made Sept. 19, 1818 by Wm. Dale, Jno., Alexr. Martin, Wm. Gaston, Henry Wiley.

WEBB, ANDREW—BOX 110, PACK 3250:
Will dated Apr. 2, 1806 in Abbeville Dist. Rec. Oct. 18, 1808. Exrs: Saml. Pruitt Jr., John McAdam. Wit: Saml. McKinney, Andrew Richey, John McAdam. Chn: John, Robt., Jas. Webb. Wife, Egness Webb.

WILLIAMS, JAMES—BOX 110, PACK 3251:
Will dated Aug. 11, 1836 in Abbeville Dist. Prov. Aug. 26, 1837. No Exrs. Wit: Andrew Edwards, Jas. Pursley, Pollard Brown. Son, Jas. Williams. Est. admnr. Sept. 7, 1837 by Jas. Williams, Pollard Brown, Nathaniel Moore unto Moses Taggart Ord. Abbeville Dist. sum $10,000.00.

WHITE, NANCY—BOX 110, PACK 3252:
Will dated Nov. 10, 1819 in Abbeville Dist. Prov. Jan. 4, 1820. Exr: Dtr. Jenny White. Wit: Nancy Wilson, Lucinda Henderson, Jas. Wardlaw, Andrew Hamilton Sr. Other chn. ment. names not given. Codicil written to the will Nov. 10, 1819 signed her name as Agness White. Named her dtr. Jenny Cameron Extrx., John Cameron Exr.

WHITE, ROBERT & ANDREW—BOX 110, PACK 3253:
On Sept. 8, 1810 John, Jean Strain, Robt. Thornton, Saml. Paxton bound unto John Hamilton Ord. Abbeville Dist. sum $1,000.00. John, Jean Strain were gdns. of Robt., Andrew White minors.

WILSON, HUGH—BOX 110, PACK 3254:
Will dated Aug. 11, 1795 in Abbeville Dist. Rec. Nov. 7, 1796. Exr: Wife, Christian Wilson. Wit: John Crawford, John Giles, P. Gibert. Lived on Mill Creek. Dtr. Elenna. Wife now pregnant with child.

WILSON, NATHANIEL—BOX 110, PACK 3255:
Will dated July 28, 1797 Rec. Sept. 12, 1797. Exrs: Easter Wilson,

Duke Bell. Wit: Saml. Patterson, Wm., John Frazier. Sis., Jane, Sarah, Mary, Easter Wilson. "Leave Duke Bell my gun."

WILSON, WILLIAM—BOX 110, PACK 3256:
Will dated Feb. 19, 1800 in Abbeville Dist. Rec. July 18, 1802. Exrs: Wife, Rebecca Wilson. Son, John Wilson, Robt. Foster Sr. Wit: John, Saml. Youngblood, John Baker, Jr., Richard Edwards. Chn: John, Robt., Elizabeth Wilson. Inv. made Aug. 10, 1802. Saml., Robt. Thompson, John Baker Jr. Sale, Aug. 28, 1802. Byrs: Rebekah Herd, Thos. Brightman, Henry Weems, John Wilson, Saml. Youngblood, Wm. Wilson, Luis Youngblood, Thos. Perry, John Adams.

YOUNG, JAMES, R N. OR M.—BOX 110, PACK 3257:
On Mar. 6, 1839 Robt. Young of Ala., Franklin Branch, Chas. Dendy of Abbeville Dist. bound unto Moses Taggart Ord. Abbeville Dist. sum $10,000.00. Robt. Young made gdn. of Jas. R. M. or N. Young a minor.

YARBROUGH, BEAUFORD—BOX 110, PACK 3258:
Est. admnr. July 6, 1835 by John, Wm. Moses Yarbrough bound unto Moses Taggart Ord. Abbeville Dist. sum $3,000.00. Cit. pub. at Sharon Church.

YOUNGBLOOD, JOHN Y.—BOX 110, PACK 3259:
On Apr. 27, 1826 John Marshall, John Burnett, Benjamin Johnston, John, Wm. Thomas were ordered to appraise the est. David Thomas the admnr. (No other papers.)

YOUNGBLOOD, LEWIS—BOX 110, PACK 3260:
On Mar. 20, 1810 Rachel Youngblood, John Meriwether, Jackson Tyner bound unto John Hamilton Ord. Abbeville Dist. sum $5,000.00.

YELDELL, ANTHONY—BOX 110, PACK 3261:
Est. admnr. Jan. 12, 1827 by Robt. Yeldell, Jas. Adkins, Abraham Lites bound unto Moses Taggart Ord. Abbeville Dist. sum $6,000.00. Cit. pub. at Cedar Springs Church.

YOUNG, SAMUEL, SR.—BOX 110, PACK 3262:
Will dated Nov. 28, 1822 in Abbeville Dist. Prov. Mar. 3, 1823. Exrs: Robt. McBride, John Covey. Wit: Saml. Young, Joseph Creswell, Douglas Robinson. Chn: Saml., John Young. "Bequeath to Jane my dtr. 1., Geo's wid., also his child Sally." Dtrs. ment. no names given. (Name Covey written Coway on other papers.)

YOUNG, SAMUEL—BOX 110, PACK 3263:
Will dated Apr. 19, 1817 in Abbeville Dist. Prov. Sept. 1, 1817. Exrs Wife, Elizabeth Young, Jas. Young. Wit: Robt. Pollard, Joseph, Nancy Neely. Chn: Robt., Wm., Jas., Lucinda, Elly, Ammiline Young.

YOUNG, JEAN—BOX 110, PACK 3264:
Will dated Oct. 8, 1814 in Abbeville Dist. Rec. Jan 2, 1815. Exrs: Son, Wm. Young, Moses Taggart. Wit: Wm. Crawford, Aaron Ashley, John Neely. Chn: Saml., Wm., John Young, Mary Shaw, Jean Leonard. S. l., Wm. Shaw.

ALEXANDER, ANDREW—BOX 111, PACK 3265:
Est. admnr. Sept. 1, 1845 by Wm. Alexr., Jas. C. Willard, Jas. McCalister bound unto David Lesly Ord. Abbeville Dist. sum $500.00. Wm. Alexr. sheweth that his Father Andrew Alexander left a wid. and some minor chn. Andrew Alexander died about June 26, 1845. Sett. ment. wid. and 5 chn. no names given.

ALEXANDER, WILLIAM— BOX 111, PACK 3266:
Est. admnr. Feb. 12, 1846 by Archibald, Isaac Kennedy, Jas. Foster bound unto David Lesly Ord. Abbeville Dist. sum $400.00. Sale, Feb. 27, 1846. Byrs: John, Jane Alexander, etc. Petition ment. he left a wid. no name given.

ARTHUR, WILLIAM E. H.—BOX 111, PACK 3267:
Est. admnr. Nov. 15, 1845 by Dr. Feedrick G. Thomas, Thos. W. Williams, Isaac Branch bound unto David Lesly Ord. Abbeville Dist. sum $8,000.00. Sett. made Jan. 5, 1846. Present Dr. F. G., Thos. S. Arthur only heirs of said decd. Dr. Thomas gdn. of said decd. made his returns in Lexington Dist. Inv. made Dec. 29, 1845 by Elihu Watson, Larkin Griffin, Dr. Thomas R. Gary, Chas. Smith.

BEACHUM, DR. JAMES—BOX 111, PACK 3268:
Est. admnr. Apr. 6, 1846 by Daniel S. Beachum, David W. McCants, John Vance unto David Lesly Ord. Abbeville Dist. sum $1,000.00. Will dated Feb. 6, 1846. Exor: father, Daniel Beachum. Wit: Welley C. Norwood, David W. McCants. Lived in Abbeville Dist. Bro. Thos. Jefferson Beachum. (Name written Beachum and Beacham). July 1, 1849 the following distributees recd. each $157.00 viz. Larkin Mays, H. or W. Higgins or Wiggins, M. or N. Elliott Beacham. Sett. made Apr. 23, 1849 stated Jas. H. Beachum died Mar. 1846 having no wife or chn. but father, D. S. Beacham, and 3 sis. and 1 bro. No names given.

BUCHANAN, ROBERT E.—BOX 111, PACK 3269:
Will dated Feb. 4, 1844 in Abbeville Dist. Rec. Sept. 3, 1845. Exr: Wife, Elizabeth Buchanan. Wit: Mm., Francis A. Buchanan, L. V. Cobb. Chn. ment. no names given. Est. admnr. July 6, 1860 by Francis A., Wm. Buchanan, Wm. C. White unto Wm. Hill Ord. Abbeville Dist. sum $25,000.00

BEARD, ELIHU—BOX 111, PACK 3270:
Est. admnr. Jan. 19, 1846 by John Baskin, Alexr. F. Wimbish, Wm. S. McBride bound unto David Lesly sum $400.00 Left a wid. no chn. Inv made Jan. 31, 1846 by Saml. Hill, Oliver Taggart, A. F. Wimbish, Lyttleton Yarbrough.

BROWN, MATHEW—BOX 111, PACK 3271:
Est. admnr. Dec. 1845 by John Brown, Andrew J. Weed, Wm. Bradly, Alexr. Robinson unto David Lesly sum $2,000.00. John Brown on Nov. 22, 1845 sheweth that Matthew Brown died about Apr. last, leaving no wid, but your petr. and 2 chn. Matthew Brown had 4 chn. by his first wife and 3 by his last wife the wid. Giles by whom the real est. comes. Sett. made Mar. 29, 1851. Present John, Saml. Brown, Jas. Brown absent in Ind., Saml. Henry McDonald a minor, Andrew, Rosanah, Mary E. Brown also absent.

CRAWFORD, WADE—BOX 111, PACK 3272:
On Feb. 10, 1846 Anthony Harmon, Stephen W. Willis, Alexr. Laramore bound unto David Lesly Ord. Abbeville Dist. sum $1,000.00 Anthony Harmon made gdn. of Wade Crawford a minor over 14 yrs. Wade Crawford sheweth that he refuses to live with his mother Vice Banks and his stepfather Jas. Banks. Anthony Harmon gdn. states that Wade has been living 4 or 5 yrs. with Mr. Banks and that he has not schooled him any, has not paid proper attention to his raising, thinks he would be trained up in disatisfaction, Mr. Banks drinks hard, gets drunk. Knows that Wade is about 16 yrs. Geo. Martin is a bro. 1. to the said minor. Anthony Harmon further states that Geo. Crawford died intestate, possessed of a small est. that the wid. had recd. from sett. as also Geo. Martin and wife Martha. That the remaining est. due to Wade and Mary Crawford the only 2 remaining distributees. That the minor Wade had left his mother from disagreement with his stepfather Jas. Banks and is living with your petr. who is a uncle by the mother.

COZBY, ROBERT—BOX 111, JACK 3273:
Will dated Sept. 3, 1842 in Abbeville Dist. Prov. Jan. 22, 1846. Exrs: J. H. Baskin. Wit: Matthew Young, John G. Cladwell, John A. Mecklin. Wife, Temperance Cozby. Chn: Prudence A. Carlile, Wm. C. Cosby, Jane F. Carlile, Sarah B. Christopher, Margaret B. Carlile, Esther S. Porter, Isabella T. Cozby decd. Martha A., John R. Cozby, Elizabeth decd. wife of Robt. P. Oliver. Gr. Chn: Mary Elizsbeth dtr. of Elizsbeth Oliver, now married, but do not recollect the name of her husband, Jas. Smith Cozby son of my decd. son, Rev. Jas. C. Cozby.

CHILD, ROBERT—BOX 111, PACK 3274:
Will dated Jan. 3, 1846 in Abbeville Dist. Prov. Feb. 25, 1846. Exrs: Jas. W. Child, John McLennan. Wit: Z. W. Carwile, John R. Tarrant, Abr. P. Pool. Wife, Sarah Child. Son, Wm. A. Child. Bro., Jas. Wesly Child. Nephew, Robt. Alexr. Child. Bond: Patrick H. Eddins of the County of Tuscoloosa, State of Ala. is firmly bound unto Jas. W. Child Exr. of Robt. Child decd. late of Abbeville Dist. in the sum of $1,000.00. Dated this 23 Oct., 1848. Wid. of Robt. Child was Sarah E. Child.

TAIT, NANCY—BOX 112, PACK 3311:
On Nov. 1, 1845 Andrew Giles sheweth that Nancy Tait formerly of this dist. lately died in Desoto County, Miss. Left a will there of which Jas. M. Tait of Desoto County, Miss. was Exr.

WHALEY, WILLIAM—BOX 112, PACK 3312:
He died May 22, 1845. Elizabeth Whaley the wid. Lewis Whaley the father. (No other papers.)

WRIGHT, JOHN—BOX 112, PACK 3313:
Est. admnr. July 28, 1845 by Aaron Lomax, Wm. Hill, Jas. S. Wilson bound to David Lesly Ord. sum $600.00. Left a wid. and several chn. Sett. Sept. 21, 1847. Named Wid. Catharine, W. Wright, Saml. Fife and wife, Thos. Jester and wife, Jenny, Matilda Wright.

WHITLEY, STEPHEN, JR.—BOX 112, PACK 3314:

Est. admnr. Dec. 23, 1845 by Medy Jr., Larkin, Henry Mays bound to David Lesly Ord. Abbeville Dist. sum $4,000.00. B. l. to Medy Mays. Left a wid. Mary Elizabeth and a child Sarah Whitley.

WILSON, MRS. ELIZABETH M. A.—BOX 112, PACK 3315:

Est. admnr. Aug. 4, 1845 by Francis M. Galbraith, Mathew J., Thos. W. Williams, G. W. Huckabee bound unto David Lesly Ord. Abbeville Dist. sum $8,000.00.

WEBB, JAMES—BOX 112, PACK 3316:

Est. admnr. Sept. 15, 1845 by Wm., Andrew Dunn, Daniel Pruit bound unto David Lesly Ord. Abbeville Dist. sum $1,500.00. Andrew Dunn sheweth that Jas. Webb left no wid. or chn. Inv. made Sept. 1, 1845 by A. C. Hawthorne, Jas. B. Richey, Robt. Martin. Shares were given on Apr. 12, 1847 to Elizabeth Pruitt, John, Hannah Webb, Jane Dunn. Recd. Dec. 27, 1847 of Andrew Dunn $103.08 the share of Robt. Webb of said est.

WILLIAMS, THOMAS W.—BOX 112, PACK 3317:

Will dated Jan. 13, 1846 in Abbeville Dist. Prov. Feb. 5, 1846. Exrs: Wife, Eliza. T. Williams. Nephew, Mathew J. Williams. Wit: Mary Ann Martin, Dr. A. B. Arnold, John C. Martin. Gr. Nephews: Albert H., Jas., John, Thos. Humphreys. Gr. Niece: Mary Ann Humphrey. Niece, Mrs. Frances M. Clark. "Am indebted to Mrs. Ann M. Turpin and her chn., Alfred B., Ann Eliz. Turpin. Owned house and lot in Cokesbury. I hold Jas. H. Baskins bond for titles to the land on which Dr. Giles now lives in the edge of Anderson Dist. that said land be sold and money appropriated to the use of the said Dr. Robt. Giles and his wife Martha and her chn." The following is copy of letter found in package:

Yorkville, S. C.

Dec. 6th.

My Dear Friend:

Your last letter was duly received and I hasten to drop you a line by my earliest opportunity. I regretted exceedingly to find that you inferede by my not sending this receipt that I distrusted you. I assure you there is no one of my entire acquaintance in whom I place more implicit confidence than in yourself. You know when I was last at Cokesbury I expressed myself entirely satisfied with the sett. of the est. I have unfortunately lost or mislaid the receipt you sent me. Consequently I will have to send you a blank and you can fill it up, similar to the old one. Pay Mr. Perrin with ten dollars of Dr. Gary's note, while I am writing the merry drum —— (word) are resounding in out streets, calling for volunteers for the Mexican War. The Chester Co. left Chesterville today, Charleston, Columbia and Winnsboro are all to their post. Where is Abbeville? What has become of the "McDuffies Rifle Guards." I Hope they are at the post of duty. The music of tonight reminds me of tattoo at Westpoint as it is about 1:00. I hope our correspondence will not cease because our business is drawing to a close. Georgiana and Willy ate well. Georgiana desires to be affectionately remembered to Mrs. W and yourself. Remember me to Mrs. W. And accept the assurance of the continued regards of

Your sincere friend

F. M. Galbraith

WIMBISH, ALEXANDER FRANCIS—BOX 112, PACK 3318:
Est. admnr. Nov. 5th, 1845 by Alexr. F. Wimbish, Michael Speed, Jas. E. G. Bell bound unto David Lesly Ord. Abbeville Dist. "No sum given." A. F. Wimbish sheweth that Alexr. Wimbish died many yrs. ago leaving a will and certain property to his wid. Frances during her life. That the said Frances is also dead. Sett. made Feb. 28, 1848. Legatees: Gilbert, Lucy Green, W. M. Bell, Susan, Peyton C., Jas. Wimbish, Joseph Scott, Sarah White.

WILSON, JOHN R.—BOX 112, PACK 3319:
First return of A. J. Weems Exr., Trustee of John Robt. Wilson a minor child of Robt. Wilson decd. and ward of Susan E., now McCraken, his mother, for land willed by John Wilson Sr., decd. John R. Wilson was a minor gr. child of John Wilson Sr. decd.

WIRE, WILLIAM—BOX 112, PACK 3320:
Will dated June 2, 1845 in Abbeville Dist. Exr: Wife, Sarah Wire. Wit: Thos. Hodge, Albert Johnson, Jas Wire. Sis., Ann Smith. Inv. made Jan. 1, 1846 by Albert Johnson, Thos. David, Jno. Cunningham.

WILSON, JOHN, SR.—BOX 112, PACK 3321:
Est. admnr. Feb. 27, 1846 by John E. Nary, Johnson Ramey, John A. Hunter bound unto David Lesly Ord. Abbeville Dist. sum $250.00. John E. Nary sheweth that John Wilson married the wid. Branch who was a dtr. of the decd. Sett. made Apr. 23, 1847. Ment. 5 dist. Wm. Kirkpatrick, Eaton and wife, Nary and wife. Son, Robt. Wilson. Est. of John Wilson.

YOUNG, NANCY—BOX 112, PACK 3322:
Will dated Nov. 29, 1842 in Abbeville Dist. Exr: Son, Francis Young. Wit: Wm. N. Fant, W. B. Shackleford, John W. Conner. Wid. of Francis Young decd. Chn: Mary, Matthew, Jane wife of Elijah Turnbull. Inv. made Sept. 17, 1845 by E. E. Pressly, Robt. Ellis, Lydall Williams.

ABERCROMBIE, JAMES R. & THOS. J., MINORS—BOX 113, PACK 3323:
On Sept. 12th., 1848 Thos. Abercrombie of Perry County, Ala. J. W. H. Johnson, Thos. J. Pinson bound unto David Lesly Ord. Abbeville Dist. sum $866.00. The petition of Abercrombie of Perry County, Ala. in which was decreed to each of his children five in number $186.73 and from the Est. personal of F. Long decd. That 2 of the chn. are minors, viz. Jas. R., Thos. J. Abercrombie.

ABNEY, S. W.—BOX 113, PACK 3324:
Est. admnr. Sept. 29, 1848 by Mary C., Saml. Abney, J. F. Marshall bound unto David Lesly Ord. Abbeville Dist. sum $100.00. (Was late a soldier in the Mexican War.)

ANDERSON, SAMUEL—BOX 113, PACK 3325:
Will dated Feb. 20, 1847 in Abbeville Dist. Prov. Sept. 17, 1848. Exrs:
Wife, Jane P. Anderson. Son, Walter C. Anderson. Wit: R. A., Francis E.
Archer, Rhed Bowie. Chn: Nancy Agnew, Walter C. Anderson, Mary Ann S.
Youngblood, John S., Tobiatha L. Anderson, Rebecca R. Brown. Gr. Son. Saml.
son of John S. Anderson. Inv. made Dec. 20, 1848 by W. C. Anderson, G. W.
Hodges, D. M. Caldwell.

ANDERSON, DAVID—BOX 113, PACK 3326:
Est. admnr. May 28, 1847 by John Link, Robt. Brady, Jas. Martin bound
unto David Lesly Ord. Abbeville Dist. sum $2,000.00. Inv. made June 12, 1847
by Jas. Martin, S. C. McGaw, Thos. Ervin. Power of Attorney State of Ala.,
County of Chambers, given by Martha Taylor to her gr. son Robt. Anderson
Taylor who is over 21 yrs. of age on Feb. 19th, 1848, giving him power to receive
all her portion of Est. of her bro. David Anderson of Abbeville Dist. who died
about the 1st of May last. Power of Attorney for Holmes Co. Miss. ment. that
Jane Shanks received $170.00 from the est. of David Anderson of Abbeville Dist.
Petition of John Link shows that John Anderson died leaving no wife or chn.
Sett. ment. legatees Martha, Robt. A. Taylor, John, Jonathan Anderson, Jane
Shanks the chn. of Mary McGaw.

ASHLEY, WILLIAM SR. AND ANNA—BOX 113, PACK 3327:
Will dated Apr. 7, 1837 in Abbeville Dist. Prov. Sept. 29, 1849. Exr:
Wife, Agnes. Wit: Jas. Black, Addline E., Margaret Burnett. Wid. Anna died
in 1849. John T. Hadden sheweth that Mrs. Anna Ashley died leaving a small est.
which is principally indebted to Mrs. Smith for care and attention for many yrs.
the deceased being helpless. The said Mrs. Smith being her dtr. June 12, 1851
Mrs. Sophia Smith $86.27. Sale, Oct. 20, 1849. Byrs: John Smith, Joshua,
Edward, Wm. Ashley, Jackson Shaw, Moses, Aaron, John Richard Ashley, S. M.
Fisher, etc.

BURTON, JOSEPH—BOX 113, PACK 3328:
Est. admnr. Dec. 23, 1846 by John F. Ellis, Abram, Zachariah Hadden
bound unto David Lesly Ord. Abbeville Dist. sum $2,400.00. Left a wid. and
5 or 6 chn. On Feb. 14, 1848 John E. Ellis, Zachariah Hadden, John Pratt bound
unto David Lesly Ord. Abbeville Dist. sum $650.00. John E. Ellis made gdn.
for Timothy Marion, Joseph Burton minors under 14 yrs. Sett. made Jan. 24,
1850. Ment. Margaret Burton, Sarah wife of Jas. E. Gray, Delila Burton wid.
Mary was a minor child. (In same package.) The pet. David Russel sheweth
that Josiah Burton died in the late Mexican War. Dated this 15 Oct., 1849.

BARMORE, WILLIAM—BOX 113, PACK 3329:
Will dated July 24, 1849. Prov. Nov. 27, 1849. Exr. Sons Enoch, Larkin
Barmore. Wit: Humphrey Jackson, J. H. Wilson, G. M. Jackson. Wife, Mary
Barmore. Chn: Enoch, Larkin Barmore, Margaret Donald, Elizabeth Hodge,
Sally Bradon decd., Polly Hawthorn, Nancy Sharpe, Malinda Brownlee, Pamela
Razor. Gr. son. Wm. Calvin Barmore. Inv. made Dec. 14, 15, 1849 by Saml.
Donald, Joseph Dickson, Benjamin Smith, Saml. Agnew.

BUGG, WILSON—BOX 113, PACK 3330:
(Was a man of color)
Est. admnr. May 8, 1848 by B. V. Posey, Jas. H. Cobb, John McBride
unto David Lesly Ord. Abbeville Dist. sum $200.00.

BROWNLEE, ROBERT—BOX 113, PACK 3331:
Est. admnr. Feb. 18, 1850 by Ira Arnold, Richard Maddox, Geo. French
unto F. W. Selleck Ord. Abbeville Dist. sum $6,000.00. Ira Arnold sheweth that
Robt. Brownlee died sometime since the summer of 1843 intestate without wife
or chn.

BOYD, JANE—BOX 113, PACK 3332:
WM. Campbell on Mar. 19, 1846 sheweth that Jane Boyd died intestate
having no legitimate chn. (No other papers.)

BOTTS, JACOB R.—BOX 113, PACK 3333:
Est. admnr. Aug. 19, 1848 by Thos. Botts, B. Y. Martin, Foster Marshall
bound unto David Lesly Ord. Abbeville Dist. sum $100.00. Jacob R. Botts was late
a soldier in the Mexican War. Admnr. of Wm. P. Botts, made Aug. 19, 1848 by
Thos. Botts, Benjamin Y. Martin, Foster Marshall bound unto David Lesly Ord.
Abbeville Dist. sum $100.00. Wm. R. Botts was late a soldier in the Mexican War.
Thos. Botts on Aug. 5, 1848 sheweth that his 2 sons Jacob R., Wm. P. Botts
both enlisted in the Mexican War under Capt. Marshall and both died in the
service, intestate without a wife or lineal decendant and are entitled to arrears
as also land from the government of the U. S.

BRADLY, MARGARET—BOX 113,, PACK 3334:
Est. admnr. Nov. 30, 1849 by Jas. McClinton, Allen Puckett, W. L. Keller
bound unto David Lesly Ord. Abbeville Dist. sum $100.00. Jas. McClinton
sheweth that his sister Margaret Bradly who was an heir of John McClinton decd.
died in Texas.

BOWEN, WOODY—BOX 113, PACK 3335:
Est. admnr. Nov. 30, 1849 by Geo. Washington Bowen, Sterling Bowen,
Jr., Clayton Jones, Levi Branson bound unto David Lesly Ord. Abbeville Dist. sum
$4,000.00. Power of Atty: S. C. Abbeville Dist. Whereas S. W. Walker and
wife Nancy Bowen, heirs and distributees of the late Woody Bowen decd. in-
tending to remove from this state westward. Know that we, the said Saml. W.
Walker and Mary A. E. Walker his wife who is a dtr. of Woody Bowen decd.
and Nancy Bowen wid. of said Woody Bowen do appoint Ezekiel Tribble our
Atty. Dated Dec. 21, 1859. Sett. made Mar. 9, 1851. Present Geo. W. Bowen,
Sterling Bowen admnrs. assisted by H. A. Jones, Jones Bowen, John S. Carwile
who married Easther a dtr. of said decd. Daniel R. Bowen, E. Tribble representing
by Power of Atty. Nancy Bowen wid. and S. W. Walker who married Mary E.
Bowen. Legatees out of State are: John Bowen, Wm. Bowen, Saml. S. Carwile
who married Susan Bowen, Jas. A., Woody Bowen.

BOGGS, MARY F.—BOX 113, PACK 3336:
On Feb. 26, 1849 Margaret Boggs, Wm. C. Puckett, Tyra Jay bound unto

David Lesly Ord. Abbeville Dist. sum $1,000.00. Margaret Boggs made gdn. of Mary Frances Boggs child of Margaret Boggs and the decd. Saml. Boggs.

BOGGS, REVD. JOHN—BOX 113, PACK 3337:
Will dated Aug. 9, 1848 in Abbeville Dist. Prov. Oct. 2, 1848. Exrs: Capt. Robt. Cunningham, Dr. E. R. Calhoun. Wit: John McLees, John Power Jr., J. N. Reeder. "Was late of Va." Dtr. Mary Ann Boggs. Est. to be used by her for the best interest of herself and young sisters.

BRANYON, THOMAS—BOX 113, PACK 3338:
Est. admnr. Oct. 19, 1846 by Henry, Joseph J., Thos. F. Branyon, Saml. M. Webb, Thos. M. Branyon bound unto David Lesly Ord. Abbeville Dist. sum $12,000.00. Henry, Joseph, Thos. F. Branyon the said Thos. F. residing in Abbeville the other 2 in Anderson Dist. Henry, Joseph, Thos. F. Branyon were sons of said decd. Thos. Branyon left no wid. but several chn. Sett. made Jan. 15, 1850. Stated that Reuben, Abner Branyon, Wm. Jolly recd. $13.33 as their share of sett. Wm. Jolly married Jane Branyon a dtr. of said decd. Saml. Webb married Caroline now decd. the dtr. of Thos. Branyon, by whom he has 3 chn. living, John Thos., Jas. Marion, Hannah Webb. Francis Marion Branyon a minor.

BAKER, DR. EDMOND C.—BOX 113, PACK 3339:
Est. admnr. June 11, 1847 by Grigsby Appleton, Joel Smith, Jas. Bailey bound unto David Lesly Ord. Abbeville Dist. sum $800.00. Est. admnr. again Jan. 8, 1848 by Jas. Bailey, Joel, Jas. Smith bound unto David Lesly sum $500.00. Former admnr. Grigsby Appleton having removed from the state.
(Letter)
Lumpkin, Ga.
May 15, 1847
Dear Sir:
    You will not be surprised at the receiving this letter knowing affliction that has been laid upon me. I have not heard any thing that Courtney said of the family, or if he left a will or made any disposition of his affairs. If he did not I beg of you as a holy charity to take out letters of administration, if it can not be put off until July when Alphnw will visit you and assist in settling the Est. of the decd. bro. I can hardly think coherently. We are all in great distress. Do write immediately and give me any information you can in relation to Courtneys death or how he left his affairs. If you will administer and finally give me such advice as your experience and friendship may enable you to comfort and direct me. Give my love to your kind lady thank her for me for all the attention to Courtney. Oh if he had been at your house, or Capt. Cunninghams. I am with great respect your most obliged and very humble servant.
    A. Baker written to G. Appleton Esq., Stony Point, Abbeville Dist., S. C. Dr. Baker died without wife or chn.

BOZEMAN, SUSANNAH—BOX 113, PACK 3340:
Will dated Sept. 3, 1845 in Abbeville Dist. Prov. Feb. 12, 1849. Exr: John C. Martin. Wit: Wm. M. Smith, S. D. Deal, B. H. Smith. Chn: Elizabeth S. wife of Thos. Taylor of Anderson Dist., Jas. J., Thos. S. Bozeman, Catharine

R. wife of John Smith of Benton County, Ala. "Give to my son Thos. supposed now to reside in the State of Ala. $10.00."

BOGGS, SAMUEL—BOX 113, PACK 3341:
Est. admnr. Nov. 17, 1846 by John W. Hearst, Wm. P. Sullivan, John Cothran bound unto David Lesly Ord. Abbeville Dist. sum $4,000.00. Expend: Dec. 24, 1848 Paid Margaret Boggs $35.14. Inv. made Dec. 17, 1846 by John Robinson, Edmond Walker, Buckly Harris.

BRACKENRIDGE, DAVID—BOX 113, PACK 3342:
Will dated Dec. 4, 1846 in Abbeville Dist. Prov. Dec. 14, 1846. Exr. Nephew, Adam Jackson McKee. Wit: A. C. Hawthorne, Richard P., Rhod Bowie. Nephew, Adam Jackson McKee son of my sis. Elenor McKee. Sis. Elizabeth Bailey decd., Jane Smith decd. Sept. 7, 1849 Jas. B. Baley decd. $123.00 in full of my part and Wm. and Margaret Baleys acting under the power of atty. from them.

BROOKS, WILLIAM—BOX 113, PACK 3344:
Est. admnr. Jan. 18, 1847 by Wm. H., Susannah Brooks, John L. Boyd, Andrew Gillespie bound unto David Lesly Ord. Abbeville Dist. sum $30,000.00. Wm. H. Brooks son of Susannah Brooks and Wm. Brooks decd. Sett. made Feb. 28, 1848. Present, Susannah Brooks wid., Wm. H. Brooks, B. M. Cheatham gdn. of Amelia E., Susan Ann F. Cheatham chn. of Eliz. Amanda dtr. of intestate who is now dead. Warren D. Brooks died since his father; his share distributed amongest his mother and bros. and his 2 neices.

BOWIE, ARTHUR—BOX 113, PACK 3345:
Will dated Dec. (day left out) 1846 in Abbeville Dist. Prov. Nov. 20, 1847. Exr: Arthur A. Bowie. Wit: Benjamin Brown, R. M. Davis, Jas. Baskin. Chn: Martin A., Arthur A. Bowie, Elizabeth, Martha and Mary Stephens. Wife, Sarah Bowie. Gr. dtr: Sarah Jane Stephens. Inv. made Jan. 29, 1848 by Robt. M. Davis, Archibald Mauldin Sr., Benjamin Brown.

BARKSDALE, RICHARD B.—BOX 113, PACK 3346:
Est. admnr. Aug. 19, 1848 by Wm. Barksdale, Moses W. Lackey, Foster Marshall bound unto David Lesly Ord. Abbeville Dist. sum $100.00. Was late a soldier in the Mexican War. Wm. Barksdale sheweth that his son Richard Barksdale entered the service in the Mexican War under Capt. Marshall and died in service intestate without wife or lineal discendant.

BAKER, THEODORE G.—BOX 113, PACK 3347:
Est. admnr. July 19, 1847 by John Davis, Joseph T., Jas. Baker bound unto David Lesly Ord. Abbeville Dist. sum $5,000.00. John Davis sheweth that his s. l. Theodore G. Baker died leaving a wid. and infant chn. S. S. Baker was gdn. of John Joseph, Theodore G. Baker minors. Inv. made Aug. 13, 1847 by Wm. C. Cozby, Oswell McLin, Wm. Barksdale.

BAKER, HENERIETTA—BOX 113, PACK 3348:
On Dec. 7, 1846 Joseph T. Baker, R. M. Davis, W. R. Sanders bound unto

David Lesly Ord. Abbeville Dist. sum $2,000.00. Joseph T. Baker made gdn. of Henerietta Baker a minor over 14 yrs. Henerietta Baker sheweth that she is the dtr. of Joseph T. Baker and that she is the minor of Nancy T. Tait decd. late of Desoto Cty., Miss.

BARMORE, MARY—BOX 113, PACK 3349:
Est. admnr. Aug. 13, 1847 by Jesse W. Norris, G. W. Hodges, Augustus Lomax bound unto David Lesly Ord. Abbeville Dist. sum $4.000.00. Jesse W. Norris was of Anderson Dist. Mary Barmore died July 6, 1847. Inv. made Dec. 7, 1847 by Ezekeil Rasor, Allen Dodson, A. II. Magee.

BLACK, JAMES—BOX 113, PACK 3350:
Will dated Dec. 27, 1844 in Abbeville Dist. Prov. Oct. 14, 1846. Exr: Thos. W. Williams. Wit: Archibald Arnold, J. H. Beachum, Thos. R. Garey. Chn: David Black, Wm. B. Black decd., Jas. R., Maria, John Black who is a lunatic in the Asylum of this state. "To the Commissioners of the poor of Abbeville Dist. I bequeath the sum $200.00." Est. also admnr. Nav. 21, 1846 by Joel W. Townsend, Saml. B. Major, Westly C. Klugh unto David Lesly Ord. Abbeville Dist. sum $2,000.00. Joel W. Townsend married Mariah Black a dtr. of said decd. On Jan. 3, 1848 W. H. Blackmon recd. $31.15 in full of the share of his wife Mary Jane.

BELL, GEORGE—BOX 113, PACK 3351:
Est. admnr. Jan. 1, 1849 by Jas. Lindsay, C. H. Kingsmore, D. O. Hawthorne bound unto David Lesly Ord. Abbeville Dist. sum $200.00.

BURELL, JOHN B.—BOX 113, PACK 3352:
John Burrell died Sept. 16, 1844. Wm. Smith was the admnr. Inv. made Dec. 20, 1844 by Wm. Lomax, Jas. Hughey, Ephraim Davis. Sale made Dec. 20, 1844. Byrs: John Burrell, John Hinton, John D. Adams, Bashti Burell.

COVIN, JOHN P.—BOX 114, PACK 3353:
Est. admnr. Oct. 18, 1848 by Jas. W. Covin, Joseph L. or S. Bouchillon, Alexr. A. Laramore bound unto David Lesly Ord. Abbeville Dist. sum $5,000.00. John P. Covin was the father of Jas. W. Covin. Husband of Delilah Covin. Sett. made Feb. 5, 1850. Present: Jas. W. Covin admnr., Delilah Covin wid., Thos. McAlister who married Mary a dtr. of said decd. Andrew H. McAllister who married Lucinda Jane another dtr. of said decd. Sarah Ann Covin. Absent, Lazarus Covin, David T. Covin, Joseph S. Covin. John P. Covin died in Aug. 1848.

CALLAHAN, MARTHA JANE—BOX 114, PACK 3354:
Est. admnr. Apr. 5, 1850 by Alexr. Scott, J. W. Prather, Wm. T. Drennan bound unto F. W. Selleck Ord. Abbeville Dist. sum $1,060.00. Alexr. Scott sheweth that Martha Jane Callahan died intestate, having no husband or lineal descendant, but a bro. under age Chas. T. and as supposed a father residing in Ala.

COCHRAN, WILLIAM—BOX 114, PACK 3355:
Est. admnr. May 22, 1848 by Nancy Cochran, John H. Mundy, John V.

Reynolds, Wm. McNairy bound unto David Lesly Ord. Abbeville Dist. sum $10,000.00. Nancy Cochran sheweth that her husband Wm. Cochran died Mar. 22, 1848 leaving your petr. his wid. and several chn. Sett. made Jan. 7, 1851. Present Nancy Cochran wid., Smith Sale in right of his wife Amanda, John H. Mundy in right of his wife Mahala decd. and her surviving chn. viz. Wm., Emma, John Mundy. Lewis Matthews in right of his wife Elizabeth. Absent: John, Newton, Benjamin Larkin, Wm. Cochran minors not present.

COLE, ELIZABETH—BOX 114, PACK 3356:
    Was a free woman of color. Did not copy.

CALDWELL, JOHN G.—BOX 114, PACK 3357:
    Est. admnr. Sept. 12, 1846 by Wm. H. Caldwell, John Brownlee, Ezekiel Speed bound unto David Lesly Ord. Abbeville Dist. sum $20,000.00. Power of atty. State of Ala., Russel County. Know that I Elizabeth Caldwell late of Abbeville Dist., S. C. at present residing in Russell County, Ala. have constituted David Lesly Esq. of Abbeville Dist. my atty. to receive from Wm. H. Caldwell admnr. of my decd. husband John G. Caldwell what is belonging to me as a wid., and as gdn. of my 6 minor chn, viz: Thompson, Wm. D., Mary J., Emily J., Jas. E., Henerietta L. or S. Caldwell. Dated Feb. 7, 1848. Sett. made Dec. 17, 1847. Ment. that D. T. Boswell married Frances a dtr. of said decd. Wm. H. Caldwell the admnr. was a bro. to the said John G. Caldwell decd.

CANNON, GEORGE JOHNSTON—BOX 114, PACK 3358:
    Will dated Jan. 13, 1848. Rec. July 18, 1848. Examined July 5, 1848. Exr: Wife, Mary Cannon. Wit: Saml. T. Myrick, Wm. Eating, Geo. Sebzburn. Lived in Newberry Dist. Sis., Mary Wicker and her chn. viz. Adam, Wm., J. H. Epting. Elizabeth Boyd, Anna Lake, D. L. Wicker, Sarah Setzler, S. V. Wicher. Bros., Saml. D. Cannon decd., David M. Cannon. "It is my will that D. L. Wicker be the adviser of my Exrs. ment. within in the bounds of Newberry Dist. My will that B. B. Jordan be the adviser in Abbeville Dist. A paper ment. that Jacob Setzler and John S. or L. Hutchinson were heirs of said decd. Jacob Setzler was a son of Sarah Setzler decd. John Hutchison was a son of Anna Hutchison. Dated July 19, 1850. Mary Wicker died in the spring of 1849. Adam Epting her admnr. Chn. of Wm. Cannon a bro. who died many yrs. ago, moved to Abbeville and from there moved off not known where to. Chn. of Saml. D. Cannon who died about 10 yrs. ago in Newberry Dist. Elizabeth wife of Geo. Sligh both living in Newberry, Nancy B. wife of Cook of Laurens still living, David Cannon in Fla., abt. 21, Harrison Cannon in Newberry abt. 15, Perston Cannon in Newberry abt. 12; Chn. of Thos. Cannon died in Newberry about 6 yrs. ago leaving Levinia a minor abt. 16 in Newberry, chn. of Anna who married Hutchinson died many yrs. ago. 20 or 25 leaving chn. Nancy wife of Wm. Folken or Folker in Newberry.

COWAN, ISAAC F.—BOX 114, PACK 3359:
    Est. admnr. Dec. 11, 1846 by John, Jas. Cowan, Jas. W. Agnew bound unto David Lesly Ord. Abbeville Dist. sum $1,600.00. John Cowen sheweth that his son Isaac F. Cowan departen this life in infancy without wife or chn. The

petition of John Cowan sheweth that his son I. F. Cowan had a negro woman and 3 chn., a gift by his gr. father I. Cowan. Inv. made Jan. 19, 1847 by John Stevenson, Jas. Martin, John Robinson.

CHILD, SARAH E.—BOX 114, PACK 3360:
Will dated Mar. 7, 1846 in Abbeville Dist. Prov. Apr. 12, 1847. No Exrs: Wit: Elizabeth Todd, Jas. A. Pope, Jas. H. Wilson. Son, Wm. Child. Est. also admnr. May 21, 1847 by Patrick H. Eddins, Elizabeth Todd, Sampson V. Cain bound unto David Lesly sum $2,400.00. Patrick Eddins was a b. l. of Sarah E. Child. (Letter.)
Cambridge
May 20, 1847
Mr. Lesly
Dear Sir:
Mr. Eddins has informed me that you wish me to say what I think Mrs. Sarah E. Child's personal est. will amount to. I cannot say particularly what will be the amount, though Mr. Eddins says that he has executed a bond to the amount $12,000.00. which I think will fully cover the amt. of her personal est.
Yours very respectfully
Jas. C. Child

CANNON, LUCINDA JANE—BOX 114, PACK 3361:
On Jan. 19, 1850 Louisa, Sarah, Thos. W. Pace bound unto David Lesly Ord. Abbeville Dist. sum $2,000.00. Louisa Pace was gdn. of Lucinda Jane Cannon a minor. Louisa Pace sheweth that sometime in 1849 Silas Pace died without wife or chn., but a mother and bros. and sis. and a child of a decd. sis. viz. Lucinda Jane Cannon child of H. or W. Cannon and wife, the mother of child, Mrs. Cannon being dead. That she said Lucinda Jane in entitled to a share of the est. of Silas Pace decd. and that she is a minor of about 3 or 4 yrs. Sett. made Oct. 29, 1856 of Lucinda Jane Cannon in hands of Aiken Brazeal and Louisa his wife former gdn. and Philip Cromer present gdn.

CRAWFORD, ESTER—BOX 114, PACK 3362:
Will dated Jan. 30, 1847 in Abbeville Dist. Prov. May 15, 1848. Exrs: A. P. Conner, W. W. Belcher. Wit: Jas. Cason, Philip Zimmerman, Saml. S. Wilson. Chn: Jas., Mathews, Geo., Greenberry Crawford, Isabella Conner, Betty Ann. S. l., Jas. Conner. Gr. chn: Louisa dtr. of Jas. Conner, Mary dtr. of Mathews Crawford, Matilda Hanvey, Rebecca Nichols, Louisa Conner dtr. of Isabella Conner. Jas. son of Mathews Crawford. "Bequeath to Geo. A. C. Hanvey, Wade, Geo. B., Jas. B. Crawford." (Bond) Whereas Geo. B. Crawford a minor left this state in A. D. 1846 and went as was believed to Miss. and thence to Mexico in 1847 and has not been heard from since and is believed to be in fact dead, and whereas the said Geo. B. Crawford has an interest in the est. of his grandmother Esther Crawford decd. in the hands of Alexr. P. Conner her exor. and whereas the said Geo. B. Crawford not having been heard from for more than 7 yrs. is presumed dead, and the said Alexr. P. Conner is willing to acct. for such money as may be in his hands to Jas. B. Crawford a bro. and Mary L. Conner a sis. of said Geo. B. Crawford, are his only heirs. Dated Jan. 30, 1855.

CAIN, MARY—BOX 114, PACK 3363:
Will dated Apr. 7, 1845 in Abbeville Dist. Prov. Sept. 6, 1847. Exr. Dr. Sampson Cain. Wit: Catharine B. Moragne, N. Harris Moragne, J. M. Moragne M. D. Gr. chn: Mary E. Davis, Mary E. Middleton, John E. Cain. Chn: Randolph, Wm. Cain, Bersheba A. Harris, Margaret B. Moragne, Sampson V. Cain. S. ls: Isaac Moragne, Dr. N. Harris. Inv. made Sept. 20, 1847 by Dr. Wm. Tennent, Benjamin McKittrick, Wm. P. Noble.

CALHOUN, WILLIAM M.—BOX 114, PACK 3364:
Est. admnr. Feb. 3, 1849 by J. H., Philip, LeRoy, Peter G. Legard, bound unto David Lesly Ord. sum $10,000.00. (Bond.)
State of Ga., Cobb County
Know that we, John F. McKoy of said state aforesaid and my wife Martha (late Martha E. Holt) one of the dtrs. of John P. Holt and gr. dtr. of Martha Calhoun late of Abbeville Dist. and Elizabeth A. Holt dtr. of John P. Holt and gr. dtr. of the same Martha Calhoun and who are legatees named in the Martha Calhoun's will. Also were heirs of Wm. Calhoun. Dated Dec. 3, 1850. Sett. made Dec. 10, 1850. Present: Jas. H. Leroy admnr. and distributee in right of his wife Elizabeth A. also Jas. L. McCelvey in right of his wife Mary Jane sis. of the decd. John E. Calhoun a minor. Geo. Brown and his wife Martha Calhoun absent. John F. McKay and wife Martha E. Holt and Elizabeth Holt both absent. (In sett. the name was written McKay instead of McKoy. Don't know which is correct.)

DYSON, JAMES—BOX 115, PACK 3382:
Est. admnr. Jan. 25, 1848 by John Sadler, Z. W. Carwile, R. C. Griffin bound unto David Lesly Ord. Abbeville Dist. sum $5,000.00. Mary Dyson of Cambridge, Abbeville Dist. on Jan. 11, 1848 sheweth that it was her desire that Letters of Admnr. should be granted to her bro. John Sadler of the est. of her decd. husband. Sett. made Jan. 9, 1850 ment. that Wm. Thos., Mary Dyson were minors under 14 yrs. Mrs. Dyson later married a Thompson. Sale made Feb. 8, 1848. Byrs: Jas. Creswell, Marshal Thompson, Wm. Thompson, John Perdue, John Sadler, Willis Sadler, John W. Smith, etc.

DEVLIN, COL. JAMES—BOX 115, PACK 3383:
Will dated Feb. 24, 1849 in Abbeville Dist. Prov. July 17, 1849. Exr. Son, John L. Devlin. Wit: Lewis Smith, David Jordan, Martha M. Devlin. Chn: Sarah Wardlaw Kennedy, John L. Devlin, Martha Purdy, Mary A. McCarthy, Jas. M. Devlin, Elizabeth, Caroline Mealy. "Bequeath to Jane Tayler youngest dtr. of *Jannt* Devlin." Martha Purdy married Leroy Purdy. (Elizabeth D. and Amanda C. Mealy.) Mary Devlin married John McCartny. On Apr. 17, 1850 Elizabeth and Caroline Mealy of Holmes County, Miss. dtrs. of said decd. did appoint Jas. H. Devlin also of Miss. their atty. On Aug. 6, 1849 the petition of Sarah, Archibald, Lucretia, Leroy Tittle, Madison Tittle, Mary Tittle are minors under 14 yrs. and that Archibald Tittle their father was their gdn. That they are the gr. chn. of the late Col. Jas. Devlin by his decd. dtr. Jane Tittle who left as her representatives Jas. B. Tittle, John L. Tittle, Martha *Smith* now the wife

of Saml. Agnew, Margaret now the wife of Alexr. Stewart. (In the notice that appeared in the newspaper the name Mealy was written Nealy.)

DARRICOTT, JOHN AND REBECCA—BOX 115, PACK 3384:
Est. admnr. June 18, 1849 by Herbert Darracott, Jas. McCaslan, D. M. Rogers bound to David Lesly Ord. Abbeville Dist. sum $4,000.00. of the estate of John and Rebecca Derricott both decd. Herbert Derricott was a son to John Derricott. Will dated Jan. 22, 1816. Exrs: Thos. Jones of Elbert Co., Ga. Francis Darracott of Wilks Co., Ga. Wit: Thos. Casey, Henry Hester. Lived in Abbeville Dist. Chn: Garland, Louisa, Harbert, Eliz. Jane, Fanny Darracott. Wife, Rebeckah Darracott. Prov. June 25, 1849, Sett. made Dec. 4, 1850. Parties interested were, Moses O. Talman and wife Frances, Louisa Hester, Eliz. Jones, Saml. *Koskogey* and Eliz. his wife, and the chn. of Garland Darracott decd. viz. Francis Darracott now dead leaving heirs whose names are not known, Rebecca the wife of Patrick *Gillen.*

DEASON, (MINORS)—BOX 115, PACK 3385:
On Jan. 25, 1847 Berry, John Deason, Daniel P. Self all of Edgefield Dist. bound unto David Lesly Ord. Abbeville Dist. sum $1,732.00. Berry Deason made gdn. of Martha Ann, Jas. Deason minors under 14 yrs. Berry Deason on Jan. 25, 1847 sheweth that some yrs. ago Joseph T. Price died intestate leaving a wid. Tilda and 4 chn., Elizabeth, Thos., Wm., and Patsy Price. That your petr. intermarried with Elizabeth and has by her 2 infant chn. viz., Martha Ann and Jane Deason. That your petrs. wife Elizabeth died before her Mother the said Tilda, and afterwards Tilda also died.

DIXON, JAMES N.—BOX 115, PACK 3386:
Est. admnr. Jan. 21, 1848 by Leroy J. Johnson, Henry Simpson, Wm. Pennell bound unto David Lesly Ord. Abbeville Dist. sum $1,000.00. Left a wid. and 6 chn. (Names not given.)

DONALD, ROBERT—BOX 115, PACK 3387:
Est. admnr. Mar. 20, 1849 by Saml. Donald, Wm. Hill, Jas. Johnson bound unto David Lesly Ord. Abbeville Dist. sum $2,000.00. Col. Donald sheweth that his bro. Robt. Donald died intestate. Sale made Apr. 13, 1849. Byrs: John Donald Sr., John Donald Jr., Wm. W. Anderson, Thos. Williamson, Dr. Enoch Agnew, W. Y. Blain, A. J. Richey, Saml. Donald, Ira Strain, Thos. Rosamond. Inv. made Apr. 13, 1849 by Enoch Barmore, Wm. Agnew, Joseph Agnew.

DANSBY, ISAAC—BOX 115, PACK 3388:
Est. admnr. Oct. 20, 1848 by Jane M., Geo. W., Isaac W. F. Dansby bound unto David Lesly Ord. Abbeville Dist. sum $10,000.00. On Oct. 4, 1848 the petition of Jane M. Dansby sheweth that her husband Isaac Dansby died intestate leaving your petr. his wid, and 2 sets of chn. One of whom is a minor. Power of Atty. On Jan. 22, 1850 Isaac W. F. Dansby of the County of Shelby, State of Texas appointed his bro. Geo. W. Dansby of Abbeville Dist. his Atty. to receive his share as due him a son of Isaac Dansby decd. late of Abbeville Dist.

There were 4 distributees including the wid. Jane M. Dansby, Reason, Isaac W. F., Martha E. J., Geo. W. Dansby.

DRINKARD, WILLIAM—BOX 115, PACK 3389:
Est. admnr. Aug. 19, 1848 by Geo. S. Drinkard, Isaac Branch, J. Foster Marshall bound unto David Lesly Ord. Abbeville Dist. sum $75.00. (Bond ment. that Wm. Drinkard was late a soldier of the Mexican War.) Geo. S. Drinkard sheweth that his bro. Wm. Drinkard entered in the Mexican War under Capt. Marshall and died in the service with out wife or lineal descendant. That he was a Private in Capt. Marshalls Co., 1st. So. Car. Vds. in Mexico, that he has an interest in th U. S. Land Warrant issued to the heirs at law of the said Wm. Drinkard and Wiley Drinkard and Frank Drinkard 2 of the heirs have been beyond the limits of S. C. more than 5 yrs., in parts unknown, and have never been heard from and are supposed to be dead.

DRENNAN, (MINORS)—BOX 115, PACK 3390:
On Oct. 8, 1847 Wm. O. McKinney, Pheba Brennan, Robt. M. McKinney bound unto David Lesly Ord. Abbeville Dist. sum $108.00. Wm. O. McKinney made gdn. of Mary Ann, Elizabeth E. C. his wife, Nancy A., Martha Jane, Joseph C. W. Drennan minors. Wm. O. McKinney sheweth that Joseph Drennan died intestate and that John Kennedy admnr. on his est. and also died and his admnr. Isaac Kennedy settled up the est. in 1847. Your petr. states that there is a wid. Phebe Drennan and 5 chn. viz. Mary Ann 18 yrs. of age, Elizabeth E. C. now the wife of your petr., Nancy A. 15 yrs. old, Martha Jane 13 yrs., Joseph C. W. Drennan abt. 11 yrs. old.

DOUGLASS, (MINORS)—BOX 115, PACK 3391:
On Feb. 13, 1848 Thos. J. Douglass, Lucin H. Lomax bound unto David Lesly Ord. Abbeville Dist. sum $2,000.00. Thos. J. Douglass made gdn. of his 2 infant chn. Thos., Archibald Douglass. T. J. Douglass sheweth that some time since Geo. Lomax departed this life leaving a will leaving a negro to his dtr. the wife of your petr. The said Matilda also died leaving a husband the petr. and 2 infant chn. Geo. A. Douglass was one of the chn.

DAVIS, JAMES C.—BOX 115, PACK 3392:
Est. admnr. Sept. 5, 1848 by Ephraim Davis, Henry Riley, J. Foster Marshall bound unto David Lesly Ord. Abbeville Dist. sum $100.00. Ephraim Davis sheweth that his son Jas. C. Davis late a soldier in the Mexican War died in the service intestate without wife or chn. He was in Co. E. under Capt. Marshall of the Palmetto Regiment.

DAY, JOHN—BOX 115, PACK 3393:
Est. admnr. June 8, 1847 by Patrick Hefferman, Dr. Isaac Branch, John Lesly bound unto David Lesly Ord. Abbeville Dist. sum $200.00. Patrick Hefferman sheweth that his s. l. John Day died intestate and insolvent, and a wife. Inv. made June 26, 1847 by Thos. Pinson, Downs Calhoun, Nathan Ingram. Byrs. at sale: Elizabeth Day, Patrick Hefferman, Thos. Pinson, Nathan Ingram, Thos. Stewart.

DUNN, JANE—BOX 115, PACK 3394:
Will dated July 22, 1848 in Abbeville Dist. Probated Jan. 20, 1849. Exrs: Sons, Andrew, Wm. Dunn. Wit: John Donnald Sr., Jas. F., Saml. Donnald. Chn: Pheby Hodges, Andrew, Wm. Dunn. Sett. made Feb. 18, 1850. Present, Dr. Andrew Dunn Exr. Jane Dunn died in Jan., 1849. John Dunn, Polly Richey, H. J. Richey, B. F. Mosley all recd. a distributee share. Jane Dunn had a life est. of Robt. Dunn decd.

EDWARDS, ELIZA—BOX 115, PACK 3395:
On Oct. 11, 1848 Wm. B. Bowie, Benjamin H. Eakins, Jas. McConnly, bound to David Lesly Ord. Abbeville Dist. sum $112.00. Wm. B. Bowie made gdn. of Eliz. Edwards a minor. Eliz. Edwards sheweth that there is $56.00 in the hands of the Ord. of the est. of her decd. father Randel Edwards and that she is over 14 yrs. Sett. made Feb. 28, 1857 ment. that Eliz. Edwards was now of age.

EDWARDS, REBECCA AND SAMUEL—BOX 115, PACK 3396:
On Oct. 19, 1847 Ezekiel Martin, Thos. Strawhorn, Agness Martin bound to David Lesly Ord. Abbeville Dist. sum $224.00. Ezekiel Martin made gdn. of Rebecca and Saml. Edwards minors. Minor chn. of Randell Edwards decd. Sett. made Feb. 3, 1857 ment. that Rebecca Edwards married Jas. Henderson.

EDWARDS, SAMUEL—BOX 115, PACK 3397:
On Dec. 3, 1849 John Strawhorn, Thos. Johnson, Wm. A. Lomax bound unto David Lesly sum $100.00. John Strawhorn made gdn. of Saml. Edwards a minor. Son of Randell Edwards decd. Sett. made June 10, 1853 ment. that he was now of age.

EDWARDS, SARAH M.—BOX 115, PACK 3398:
On Feb. 3, 1849 Franklin, Wm. B., Asa Bowie bound to David Lesly Ord. Abbeville Dist. sum $100.00. Franklin Bowie made gdn. of Sarah M. Edwards a minor. Sett. made Jan. 5, 1857 ment. that Sarah M. Edwards decd. was a ward of Franklin Bowie. Was a sis. to Eliz. Edwards.

ELLIS, (MINORS)—BOX 115, PACK 3399:
On Sept. 6, 1847 Wm. L. or S. Richey, John V. Reynolds, John Cochran bound to David Lesly Ord. Abbeville Dist. sum $547.00. Wm. Richey made gdn. of Wm. McNairy Ellis, John V. R. Ellis minors under 14 yrs. Wm. Richey on Sept. 6, 1847 sheweth that Wm. J. Ellis died intestate, leaving a wid. and 2 chn. under 14 yrs. Your petr. has now inter-married with the wid. *Mandarence* Richey. John Vincent Ellis a minor.

ETHRIDGE, JOEL—BOX 115, PACK 3400:
Est. admnr. Jan. 18, 1850 by Robt. R. Tolbert, Jas. C. Williams, Marshall E. Walker bound unto David Lesly Ord. Abbeville Dist. sum $600.00. Joel Ethridge died 1849 leaving a wife and 5 chn.

EAKINS, (MINORS)—BOX 115, PACK 3401:
On Jan. 19, 1847 Thos., Benj. H. Eakins, Andrew Morrison, Wm. C. Hill bound to David Lesly sum $4,236.40. Thos. Eakins made gdn. of Jane,

462   ABSTRACTS OF OLD NINETY-SIX AND

Geo., John, Elizabeth Eakins minors of Joseph Eakins Jr. decd under 14 yrs. Thos. Eakins was an uncle to the said chn.

EAKIN, WILLIAM—BOX 115, PACK 3402
Est. admnr. Dec. 20, 1849 by Thos. Eakin, Jas. McIlwain, Andrew Morrison bound unto David Lesly Ord. Abbeville Dist. sum $4,000.00. Thos. Eakin sheweth that his son Wm. Eakin died intestate leaving an est. and family. Sett. made Feb. 17, 1857. Present, Thos. Eakin admnr. Margaret A. Eakins the wid., Saml. Thos., Wm. Eakins minors.

EAKINS, JOSEPH, SR.—BOX 115, PACK 3403:
Will dated May 15, 1845 in Abbeville Dist. Prov. May 11, 1847. Exrs: Sons, Thos., Benjamin Eakins, S. l., Goe. Nickle. Wit: Henry B., Wm. C. Nickle, Henry W. Sharp, Wife, Sarah Eakins. Chn: Thos. Wm., Saml., Benj., Eliz., Sally, Mary Eakins, Joseph Eakins decd. Power of Atty. Kemper Co., Miss. Whereas I, Saml. Eakin a son of said Joseph Eakin but now of *Rankin* Co., Miss. have appointed Wm. Eakin of Kemper Co., Miss., my lawful atty. to receive my share of said est. Dated Nov. 20, 1849. Sett. made Jan. 22, 1850. Legatees ment. were, Thos., Benjamin Eakin, Geo. Nickles and wife, W. W. Eakin, John Stewart and wife Elizabeth, Saml. Eakin, Sarah Eakin. Power of Atty. Whereas Joseph Eakin late of Abbeville Dist., S. C. did bequeath unto me Elizabeth Stewart formerly Elizabeth Eakin and dtr. of said decd. but now of Kemper Co., Miss., a legacy from his est. have appointed Wm. Eakin of Kemper Co., Miss., my atty.

EDWARDS, T. D. M.—BOX 115, PACK 3404:
Est. admnr. May 19, 1849 by Dr. Isaac Branch, W. Aug. Lee, H. A. Jones bound unto David Lesly Ord. Abbeville Dist. sum $200.00. Dr. Isaac Branch sheweth that Thos. D. M. Edwards died intestate without wife or chn.

EVANS, THOMAS—BOX 115, PACK 3405:
Est. admnr. Nov. 6, 1848 by Saml. Y. Hopper, Jas. Young, Robt. Jones bound unto David Lesly sum $1,000.00. Saml. Y. Hopper was of Stoney Point, Abbeville Dist., S. C. Sett. made Nov. 24, 1848. Present, S. Y. Hopper admnr., B. Y. Goldman who married the wid. Elizabeth Evans. No chn. He died 1847.

FULTON, BENJAMIN H.—BOX 115, PACK 3406:
Est. admnr. Nov. 1, 1847 by Isaac, Archibald Kennedy, John Watson bound unto David Lesly Ord. Abbeville Dist. sum $4,000.00. Jane Fulton the wid. Later married Wiley Burnett. Inv. made Dec. 11, 1847 by A. Kennedy, F. Conner, John F. Patton.

FORTESQUE, THOMAS—BOX 115, PACK 3407:
Est. admnr. Dec. 4, 1847 by Richard A. Martin, John Watt, A. Kennedy bound unto David Lesly Ord. Abbeville Dist. sum $200.00. Thos. Fortesque was a bro. l. to Richard Q. Martin. Inv. made Jan. 24, 1848 by Joseph C. Matthews, Thos. J. Matthews, H. H. Stewart. Byrs. at sale: Syntha Ann, Richard Martin, Mrs. Fortesque.

ABBEVILLE DISTRICT WILLS AND BONDS 463

FOOSHE, WILLIAM—BOX 115, PACK 3408:
Est. admnr. Nov. 6, 1848 by Chas. B., Joel Fooshe, R. G. Golding bound unto David Lesly Ord. Abbeville Dist. sum $50.00. C. B. Fooshe sheweth that his son Wm. Fooshe died in the late Mexican War.

FISHER, (MINORS)—BOX 115, PACK 3409:
On Sept. 22, 1845 Saml. C. Fisher, John F. Clinkscales, John W. Shirley bound to David Lesly Ord. Abbeville Dist. sum $1,816.00. Saml. C. Fisher made gdn. of Catha C., Thos. F., Jas. L. Fisher minors. Sett. made May 23. 1848 ment. that Catha C. Fisher was of age. She recd. $340.00 her distributee share of her father's est. Thos. Fisher. Were the chn. of Thos. and Elizabeth Fisher decd.

FOOSHE, RICHARD—BOX 115, PACK 3410:
Est. admnr. May 7, 1849 by Robt. R. Tolbert, Jas. S., N. Henderson bound unto David Lesly Ord. Abbeville Dist. sum $200.00. Byrs: Peter Rampy, Tilmond Walker, J. Fooshe, R. Fooshe, etc.

FINLEY, REUBEN—BOX 115, PACK 3411:
Thos. M. Finley sheweth that he is the oldest son of Reuben Finley decd. and the admnr. of his est. in the State of Tenn., that your petr. is informed and believes that his father Reuben Finly had a vested interest in certain personality under the will of Thos. Finley decd. passed to his legal representative and your petr. prays that admnr. of said est. of Thos. Finley decd. may be confined to your petr. Dated May 24, 1847.

FOOSHE, CHARLES B.—BOX 115, PACK 3412:
Est. admnr. Feb. 4, 1850 by Jas. W. Richardson, Meedy Mays, John Sadler, John T. Carter, N. W. McCants bound unto David Lesly Ord. Abbeville Dist. sum $20,000.00. Sett. made Feb. 24, 1852. Present, Jas. W. Richardson admnr. Sarah Fooshe wid., Jas., Joel, Washington Fooshe. John Sadler who married Casandara, Rebecca Ann Fooshe, John Fooshe son of Martha Fooshe now decd. Francis A. Buchanan married Mrs. Fooshe.

FARIS, DANIEL—BOX 115, PACK 3413:
Est. admnr. July 1, 1849 by Saml. Link, Jas. McClane, Alexr. P. Robinson bound unto David Lesly Ord. Abbeville Dist. sum $4,000.00. Saml. Link sheweth that Daniel Faris is dead leaving no kindred of any degree as this deponent believes in the U. S. of America. He died at his residence where he had been living for the last 3 yrs. and 2½ mo. entirely. Since when he was unable to attend to his business in consquence of cancer, and also lived with deponent at times or boarded with him before that time. Dated May 30, 1849.

FLINN, DAVID—BOX 115, PACK 3414:
Will dated Feb. 14, 1849 in Abbeville Dist. Prov. Mar. 1, 1849. Exr. Jeremiah T. Gibert. Wit: Joseph C. Mathews, Alexr. Scott, Jas. A. Wilson. Wife, Lucretia Flinn. Chn: John, Martha Flinn. Sett: made Oct. 25, 1854. Ment. that Mrs. Lucretia Flinn married John Bolger on Oct. 1, 1854. The 2 chn. were John W., and Martha C. Flinn.

GILMER, NANCY—BOX 116, PACK 3427:
Will dated Nov. 10, 1849 in Abbeville Dist. Prov. Jan. 9, 1850. Exrs:
David Keller, Esq., David Robison. Wit: David Keller, David, Geo. W. Robison.
Chn: Ann Jane Cary, Jas. J. Gilmer. On June 21, 1852 notice was given to the
absent distributees, particularly to the chn. of Saml. McIlwain and Wm. Gilmer
who reside without the state. There were 5 distributees.

GIBERT, JOHN B.—BOX 116, PACK 3428:
Inv. made Jan. 21, 1846 by Benjamin McKittrick, E. C. Martin, S. F.
Giles. B. E. Gibert the admnr. Mrs. Jane Gibert named in Sett.

HARRIS, RICHMOND—BOX 116, PACK 3429:
Will dated Apr. 21, 1837 in Abbeville Dist. Exrs: Wm. Harris, Henry Hes-
ter, Williamson Norwood. Wit: Wm. Gray, Alex. Hughes, J. W. Dubose. Wife,
Martha Harris. Chn: (Probable Chn:) Wm., Frances, Andrew J., Jane R.,
Leweza J. Harris. (Newspaper notice ment. the following heirs and legattes
who reside without the limits of the state viz. Frances E. Harris, Agnes S. Hunter
Uriah R. Harris, Louisa I. Heard, A. J. Harris.)

HERRON, THOMAS AND FRANCES—BOX 116, PACK 3430:
Est. admnr. Dec. 7, 1846 by Geo. A., Nicholas Miller, Bannister Allen,
bound unto David Lesly Ord. Abbeville Dist. sum $2,500.00. Frances Herron
was the wid. of Thos. Herron. Heirs: Jas. B. Herron, Geo. W. Wilson, John H.
Miller, John Herron, Polly T. Herron, Geo. Wilson and John Miller in right
of their wives.

HOGAN, RICHARD—BOX 116, PACK 3431:
Est. admnr. Nov. 25, 1847 by Thos. R., Chas., Chas. W. Sproull bound
unto David Lesly Ord. Abbeville Dist. sum $2,000.00. Richard Hogan left no
wife or chn. Wyatt Hogan was a bro. Distributees, John Ramsey and wife. John
Hogan absent from state. Wiley Hogan was a bro. also. Power of Atty: On
Dec. 4, 1848 Gincy Ramsey of Madison Co., Fla., appointed Andrew Mantz of
Abbeville Dist. her atty. as an heir of Richard Hogan decd.   (Letter)

Madison, Fla.
Nov. 15, 1848
My Dear Sir:
I have been engaged by Mrs. Nancy Hogan to enquire into the business
of the est. of Richard Hogan lately decd. in Abbeville Dist., So. Car. What property was left by the deceased and how many heirs are there of the Est. and who.
Has Mr. John Hogan claimed any part of sd. est? Are not heirs of John Hogan
the heirs proper of Richard Hogan. If so when will you be ready to distribute
to them their portion? Please write me what is necessary to enable me to receive
for the chn. of John Hogan a distributive share of the Est.
                              Yours truly,
                              S. Spencer
Jane Ramsey was of Madison Co., Fla.   (Letter)

Madison Court House, Fla.
Dec. 4, 1848
David Lesly Esq.
Dear Sir:
    By reference to the books of Moses Taggart you will find where there was $187.00 paid by John Ramsey into his office for Willis Hogan, and placed in the hands of the late Richard Hogan, for the use of said Willis Hogan (he being insane) and the said Willis Hogan being now dead, and not believing that Richard Hogan ever used any of the money there must be something due. Gincy Ramsey. Henry Jones and his wife Elizabeth were also distributees.

HUSKISON, WILLIAM AND MARY ANN—BOX 116, PACK 3432:
    On Mar. 22, 1847 Wm. C., John Graham, Meedy Mays Jr. bound unto David Lesly Ord. Abbeville Dist. sum $160.00. Wm. C. Graham made gdn of Wm., Mary Ann C. Huskison minor chn. of John Huskison decd. Mary Ann was of age in 1855 and the wife of *Effort* Norris.

HOLLOWAY, REBECCA—BOX 116, PACK 3433:
    Est. admnr. Sept. 13, 1847 by Thos. Ferguson of Edgefield Dist., Pleasant Searls, L. or S. Newby bound unto David Lesly Ord. Abbeville Dist. sum $300.00. Edgefield Dist. June 8, 1847. Wm. H. Adams of the Dist. aforesaid being the only bro. residing in the said state of Rebecca Holloway wife of Geo. Holloway decd. both of Abbeville Dist. Sale made Dec. 14, 1847. Byrs: Thos. Nichols, Jas. Richardson, Wm. Buchanan, Allen Vance, Larkin Carter, Robt. Tarrant, Wm. Blake, Stanley Crews, P. D. Klugh, Walter Hamilton, Saml. Baird, etc.

HOLLOWAY, GEORGE—BOX 116, PACK 3434:
    Will dated Aug. 3, 1846 in Abbeville Dist. Filed Oct. 16, 1846. Exrs: Wife, Rebecca Holloway, Dr. Ephraim Calhoun, Hugh A. C. Walker. Wit: John R. Tarrant, Joel W. Townsend, F. G. Thomas. Nephew, John Pool. "Bequeath to Rev. John Carlisle now a traveling member of the S. C. Annual Conference." Geo. Holloway died Aug. 26, 1846. Rebecca his wife later died May 25, 1847.

HENDERSON, SHADRICK—BOX 116, PACK 3435:
    Est. admnr. Dec. 20, 1847 by Nathaniel, John Henderson, McMillan Hutcheson bound unto David Lesly Ord. Abbeville Dist. sum $800.00. Shadrick Henderson recd. property from Wm. Henderson decd. Sarah McDill decd. share was $66.48 now due to her husband Wm. McDill and 2 minor chn. Thos. R., Robt. A. McDill. Saml., Nathan and Jas. Henderson also recd. share.

HUMPHRIES, JAMES L.—BOX 116, PACK 3436:
    Est. admnr. Oct. 4, 1847 by A. H. Humphrys unto David Lesly Ord. Abbeville Dist. sum $416.00. Albert A. Humphreys sheweth that Thos. W. Williams in his last will bequeathed to your petr. and his bros. and sis. $208.00 and among the devises as your petr. bro. Jas. L. Humphries now decd. Your petr. is the gdn. of John, Mary Ann, Thos. Humphries. Jas. L. Humphries died in Ga. (In the bond A. H. Humphries was written, but in the petition A. A. Humphries was written, don't know which is correct.) Jas. L. Humphries died in Oglethrop Co., Ga., having no wife or chn.

HALL, FENTON, SR.—BOX 116, PACK 3437:
    Est. admnr. Nov. 2, 1848 by Jesse W. Norris, Robt. B. Norris, John
Clinkscales, Ezekiel Hall bound to David Lesly Ord. sum $3,000.00. Died Oct.
23, 1848.   (Letter)

Crawfordville, Miss.
August 25, '72.
Dear Mother and Sisters and Brothers:

    I take the present opportunity to write you a few lines to inform you all
that me and Rebecca is well hoping when these few lines come to hand it may
find you all well I received your letter today dated on the 10 August and was glad
to hear from you all Mother you wanted me to let you now what I wood take for
my claim in the land I dont no you do what you think is best and it will be satisfaction with me if you want to sell it you can do so or you can rent out it will
sout me I want bee contrary you say you have written three letters to me and
got no ans I have not received them as for my part I have not ben able to no
whar to write your post office has bin changed I want you to write to me and give
me all the news of the surrounding contry I want to no whar G. W. Hall is
and all his family is and if William Hall is living at the same old place and
whear W. N. Hall and the rest of the family Ward is Sarah is and what she is
doing and be shore and tell them to write to me I will say something about my
crop I think it will mak 8 bags and corn nuff now I am working my self I think
you all could do a little better in framing I want you to write to me how is the
Preachers at first creek and Rocky River and have all the churches is prospering I
am going to for my letter I think I will settle my self here we have good preachers
here give my best respect to Uncle Billy Tucker and Aunt all of the inquiring
friends so I will close for this time as you wrote such a long letter to me I will
give you more in the next letter I remain you sun and brouther untell deathe
                              J. D. Hall
        Written to Miss Mary D. Hall, Centerville, Abbeville County, S. C.

HEARST, JOHN, SR.—BOX 116, PACK 3438:
    Sett. made Oct. 31, 1850. Present John W. Hearst M. D. Exr, and Joseph
Hearst, D. G. Philips who married Mary J. and J. N. McCain who married Sarah
A. John Hearst died about Dec. 24, 1847. W. L. Murphy married Martha A.
Inv. made Jan. 10, 1848 by Geo. W. Pressly, Joseph Wardlaw, Geo. Marshall
Capt., P. W. Bradley. Sale made Nov. 24, 1857. Byrs: Joseph, J. W. Hearst, J.
H. Chiles, etc. No will or bond in package.

HUGHEY, (MINORS)—BOX 116, PACK 3439:
    On Feb. 5, 1847 Vachel, John Hughey, A. J. Logan bound to David Lesly
Ord. Abbeville Dist. sum $225.00. Vachel Hughey made gdn. of Martha E.,
Mary Ann, Elizabeth C., Nancy R., Jas. E., Isabella, Fredrick T. Hughey minors.
chn. of Vachel Hughey. Vachel Hughey on Feb. 5, 1847 sheweth that he
married Anna Tolbert the dtr. of Daniel Talbert. Daniel Talbert died about 1840.
Minors under 14 yrs.

HALL, JOHN H.--BOX 116, PACK 3440:
Est. admnr. Nov. 3, 1848 by Mary Walker, Henry R. Williams, Wm. Leslie Harris bound unto David Lesly Ord. Abbeville Dist. sum $50.00. Mary Walker sheweth that she is the mother of John H. Hall who died at the Isle of *lober* in the service of the U. S.

HOUSTON, ROBERT R.—BOX 116, PACK 3441:
Est. admnr. Aug. 19, 1848 by Lewis J., Jane A., Elizabeth A. Wilson bound unto David Lesly Ord. Abbeville Dist. sum $60.00. Died leaving no wife or chn.

HERNDON, STEPHEN—BOX 117, PACK 3442:
Will dated Aug. 9, 1848 in Abbeville Dist. Prov. Oct. 11, 1848. Exrs: Son, Benjamin Z. Herndon, Revd. Henry W. Ledbetter. Wit: Silas L. Heller, Jas. W. Clinkscales, Elihu Watson. (At the beginning of the will was dated Jan. 19, 1847 while at the signing was written Aug. 9, 1848.) Chn: Sarah P. wife of Hickerson Burnamof, Tallapoosa Co., Ala., Minerva Virginia Herndon a minor decd., Belinda Dorothy wife or Revd. Henry W. Ledbetter, Barbara W. wife of Massillon M. Glenn of Barbour Co., Ala., Benjamin Zechariah Herndon.

HOGAN, (MINORS)—BOX 117, PACK 3443:
On May 7, 1849 Absolem Gray, N. J. Davis, A. R. Ramey bound unto David Lesly Ord. Abbeville Dist. sum $289.00. Absolem Gray made gdn. of Jas. F., John, Wade Hogan minors. Sarah Hogan the mother. Jas. Hogan was of age in Apr. 8, 1858 when sett. was made. John of age in Jan. 1858. Richard Hogan decd. was a bro.

HUNTER, ELIZABETH—BOX 117, PACK 3444:
Will dated Aug. 30, 1839 in Abbeville Dist. Prov. Nov. 17, 1846. Exr. John Kennedy. Wit: John Faulkner, Kitty McComb, John Kennedy. Chn: Polly Ann Porterfield, Wm. Washington Hunter.

HAWTHORN, LANY—BOX 117, PACK 3445:
Will dated May 3, 1849 in Abbeville Dist. Prov. June 26, 1849. Exrs: Sons, Thos., D. O. Hawthorn. Wit: A. H. Miller, C. M. Sharp, J. R. Hawthorn. Chn: D. O., Jas., John Hawthorn, Mary Ann Lindsay, Thos., A. C. Hawthorn. "Bequeath to the chn. of my son Jas. Hawthorn now living in Ga. $50.00 each." Inv. made July 11, 1849 by R. C. Sharp, Daniel Pruitt, J. R. Hawthorn, A. H. Miller.

HOPPER, ELIZABETH—BOX 117, PACK 3446:
Will dated Feb. 13, 1846 in Abbeville Dist. Exr. Son, Jas. Young. Wit: Martha, Louisa, John Watts. Chn: Elizabeth Evans, Saml. Young Hopper, Katherine Crocker at this time residing in Miss., Jas. Young. Gr. dtr. Elenor, dtr. of Lucinda Jones. Sett. ment. Jacob Crocker as the husband of Katharine.

HANVEY, WILLIAM—BOX 117, PACK 3447:
Est. admnr. July 1, 1849 by Wm. Bradley, Jas. McCaslin, A. Kennedy bound unto David Lesly Ord. Abbeville Dist. sum $600.00. Thos., Edward, Geo.,

Wm. Hanvey were the chn. of Wm. Hanvey decd. and Susan Hanvey. On Jan. 7, 1851 Susan Hanvey of Carroll Co., Ga., appointed Geo. M. Hanvey of Abbeville Dist. her atty. Sett. made Jan. 28, 1851. Present, Susan Hanvey wid. Absent parties, Thos., Jas., Edward., Wm., Oliver, Wright, Mary A., and Saml. T. Hanvey.

HOWLET, MARY—BOX 177, PACK 3448:
    Est. admnr. Nov. 13, 1848 by John, Wm. Calvert, Jas. McCool bound unto David Lesly Ord. Abbeville Dist. sum $200.00. Inv. made Nov. 17, 1848 by J. W. Lomax, Jubal W. Warson, Thos. Burt. Sale made Nov. 18, 1848. Byrs: Jno. Calvert, Wm. Cobb, Jas. McCool, Jubal Watson, F. Branch gdn. for Franklin Howlet.

HOWELL, LUCY—BOX 117, PACK 3449:
    Will dated May 18, 1844 in Abbeville Dist. Pro. Oct. 12, 1848. Exr: Saml. Mitchell. Wit: Thos. W. Gantt, J. H. Charpings, J. F. Underwood. Chn: Nancy Walton, Mary Elliot, John Partow, Rebecca Brown, Katharine Howel, Jas. Partow, Lucy B. Mitchell. Gr. Dtr: Sarah Ann Elizabeth Mitchell. "Give to my dtr. Lucy B. Mitchell all the money that was left me by my father in the hands of Wm. Jennings."

JORDON, JAMES—BOX 117, PACK 3450:
    Est. admnr. Sept. 28, 1856 by Harmon Stevenson, Johnson Ramey, Thos. Thompson unto David Lesly Ord. Abbeville Dist. sum $250.00. Harmon Stevenson sheweth that Jas. Jordan died intestate having no lineal descendants or wife, but a father and mother residing beyond this state.

JONES, JAMES Y.—BOX 117, PACK 3451:
    Will dated Feb. 24, 1848 in Abbeville Dist. Pro. Feb. 3, 1849. Exr: Wife, Elizabeth Jones, Son, Robt. Jones. Wit: Lewis Grant, Jas. Graham, P. W. Counts. Chn: Dewitt, Mary, Willy, Jane Jones, Nancy wife of Benj. F. Roberts, Robt. Jones. Sett. made June 27, 1860 ment. Thos. Jones and Mary Miller. Robt. J. Elliis married Willy Jones. A. J. Miller married Mary Jones.

JOHNSON, ELIZABETH—BOX 117, PACK 3452:
    Est. admnr. Nov. 2, 1846 by Tidence Johnson, Aaron Lomax, Benton W. Steward bound unto David Lesly Ord. Abbeville Dist. sum $2,000.00. Tidence Johnson was a son. On Oct. 30, 1850 Willis F. White of Pickens Co., Ala. in right of his wife Ann, (late Ann Johnson) a dtr. of Benjamin and Elizabeth Johnson decd. late of Abbeville Dist., S. C. do appoint Tidence Johnson of Abbeville Dist. my atty. On Feb. 16, 1852, David Perry and Mary his wife a dtr. of Elizabeth Johnson decd. both of Muscogee Co. Ga., appointed J. Foster Marshall Esq. their atty. Sett. made Jan. 15, 1849. Persent. Toliver Johnson, Tidence Johnson, Benj. Johnson, Thos. Johnson, Esq. Cozby (W. C.) gdn. of Frances J. Johnson child of John Johnson decd. Absent David Perry and wife Mary, Jas. H. Willis, F. White and wife Ann, Jas. Martin and wife Rachall.

JONES, MOSES—BOX 117, PACK 3453:
  Will dated Mar. 26, 1849. Pro. Apr. 12, 1849. Exrs: Bro., Edmond Jones,
Thos. Fergerson. Wit: Addison F. Posey, Joseph J. Wardlaw, Saml. McGowan.
Wife, Susan Jones. Chn:Elizabeth S., Caroline Jones. Sett. made Feb. 2. 1857.
Present, Ellington A. Searles admnr. of Thos. Fergerson decd. who was the
exr. of Moses Jones decd. Thos. Jennings who married Caroline Jones.

JENNINGS, ROBERT T.—BOX 117, PACK 3454:
  Will dated Mar. 12, 1848 in Abbeville Dist. Prov. Oct. 3, 1848. Exr.
Wife, ment. no name given. Wit: Thos., Ievi Fergerson, L. Newby. Wife and
chn. ment. but no names given. "Give my wife ⅓ of the balance and then that
all my chn. Coleman and the rest have an equal devide." On another paper
Ellenor Jennings was named as the wife.

JOHNSON, JONATHAN—BOX 117, PACK 3455:
  Est. admnr. Nov. 29, 1847 by Downs, Nathan Calhoun, J. W. H.
Johnson bound unto David Lesly Ord. Abbeville Dist. sum $16,000.00. Will
dated Feb. 27, 1847. Prov. Nov. 2, 1847. Exr. Downs Calhoun. Wit: N. McCants,
Thos. J. Pinson, Thos. Stuart. Lived in Abbeville Dist. Wife, Mary Johnson.
Chn: Mary Ann Sadler, Elizabeth Gilliam, John Thos. Johnson, Cornelia Ann.
Selina Johnson. Owned land in Cherokee Co., Ala. Mary Ann Sadler married
Willis C. Sadler, Elizabeth Gilliam married Harris Y. Gilliam.

KENNEDY, JOHN—BOX 117, PACK 3456:
  Est. admnr. Oct. 22, 1846 by Isaac Kennedy, B. H. Fulton, John Watson
bound unto David Lesly Ord. Abbeville Dist. sum $35,000.00. On Sept. 22, 1846
Sarah Kennedy wid. of John Kennedy desired that his bro. Isaac Kennedy should
admnr. on her husband's est. Sett. ment. wid. Sarah Kennedy, Margaret Sanders,
Margaret, Wm. Watson, John, Isaac, Caroline, Rebecca A., Jas., Sarah C. Kennedy. John Devlin was gdn. of A. B. Kennedy, W. P. Kennedy.

KARY, ROBERT W.—BOX 117, PACK 3457:
  Est. admnr. Jan. 1, 1849 by Jane A. Karey, Archibald McCord, Jas. Gilmer,
Thos. E. Owen bound unto David Lesly Ord. Abbeville Dist. sum $6,000.00.
Jane A. Karey the wid. Sett. made Mar. 7, 1851. Present, Mrs. Jane A. Karey
wid., John E. Martin who married Agness a dtr. of Robt. Carey who died Jan. 4,
1851 leaving a child Emeline Agness, Geo. Washington a distributee who is of
age, absent for sickness. The other chn. minors, Thos., Robt., Wm., Mary Jane,
John, Loura, Jas., Lewis, Saml. Karey. Robt. W. Karey died Dec. 14, 1848.

KAY, LUTITIA—BOX 117, PACK 3458:
  Est. admnr. Sept. 8, 1848 by Geo. H. Kay, Jas., Richey Seawright bound
unto David Lesly Ord. Abbeville Dist. sum $700.00. Lutitia was a minor. Geo.
H. Kay sheweth that his sis. Lutitia Kay died in infancy. Sett. of Isabella L.
Kay decd. in same package made Feb. 4, 1857. Present, Geo. H. Kay, John B.
Kay, Isabella Kay, Jas F. Mattison and wife, Jas. H. , Chas. W. Kay. Sett. made
to ascertain the share going to Geo. Washington Richey in right of his mother,
Emily Richey alias Emily Kay a sis. of the aforesaid Isabella L. Kay. Her name
was Isabella Luticia Kay.)

KIRKPATRICK, THOMAS—BOX 117, PACK 3459:
Est. admnr. Dec. 11, 1848 by Jane Kirkpatrick, Wm., Richard Maddox, G. M. Mattison, Wm. M. Moseley bound unto David Lesly Ord. Abbeville Dist. sum $25,000.00. Jenny Kirkpatrick sheweth that Thos. Kirkpatrick died intestate leaving a wid. and several minor chn. Jane the wid. and 7 chn.

PACK 3460 TO 3474 LEFT OUT—MISNUMBERED

MARTIN, WILLIAM P. (MINORS)—BOX 118, PACK 3475:
On June 4, 1849 Wm. P. Martin, Wm. W. Moseley, G. M. Mattison bound unto David Lesly Ord. Abbeville Dist. sum $418.00. Wm. P. Martin made gdn. of F. C., S. Matilda, Margaret R., N. L., Cordelia Martin. Apr. 28, 1849 Recd. of Mary Blain Extrx. of Wm. Blain decd. by the hands of Wm. P. Martin for her $52.32 in full of all her persl. property sold by her under a covenant and by the will of Wm. Blain. T. Y. Martin, Wm. Long Jr., and Mary A. Long on May 2, 1849 also recd. $52.32. On May 7, 1849 T. or G. Wright and Mahala B. Wright also recd. $52.32. B. M. Martin also recd. $52.32 on May 14, 1849. Elizabeth Jane Martin recd. $52.32 on Sept. 29, 1849. On Sept. 29, 1849 W. P. Martin also recd. $261.60 for himself and 4 minor chn.

MORRAH, JANE—BOX 118, PACK 3476:
Will dated June 12, 1847 in Abbeville Dist. Prov. Oct. 19, 1847. Exr. Son, Saml. R. Morrah. Wit: Wm., Geo. W., Jas. S. Robinson. Chn: Sally Baramore, Jane Sharp, Eleanor Jones, Mary Murray, John Morrah. Saml., David, Geo. Morrah. Sett: ment. Enoch Barmore and wife Sarah, Johnson H. Sharp and wife Jane Caroline Sharp, L. T. C. P. Jones and wife Elenor Jones, Edward L. Murray and wife Mary Murray.

MORRAH, (MINORS)—BOX 118, PACK 3477:
On Sept. 6, 1848 Andrew Morrow, Moses W. Lackey, Wm. Barksdale, Foster Marshall bound unto David Lesly Ord. sum $300.00. Andrew Morrow made gdn. of Amelia Rebecca Morrow, Geo. A. Morrow minors. Andrew Morrow Esq. sheweth that his son Albert G. Morrow was a soldier in the late Mexican War and died without wife surviving him, leaving 2 infant chn. under 14 yrs. who are entitled to pay and Bounty Land from the U. S.

McCELVY, JOHN—BOX 118, PACK 3478:
Est. admnr. May 28, 1847 by Jas. L. McCelvy, H. H. Townes, Jas., Hugh McCelvy bound unto David Lesly Ord. sum $30,000.00. Jas. McCelvy sheweth that his father John McKelvy died intestate. Sett. made Apr. 3, 1849. Present: the admnr. Vincent McCelvy, John H. McCelvy, W. C. Scott. There were 11 distributees viz. Rebecca, Jas. L. McCelvy, W. C. Scott, Wm., V., John H., G. W., Sarah J., H., Margaret A. McCelvy. (Name was also written McKelvy.)

MABRY, WHITFIELD W.—BOX 118, PACK 3479:
Est. admnr. Oct. 18, 1848 by Dudley Mabry, W. W. Anderson, A. J. Moore, Valentine Young bound unto David Lesly Ord. sum $2,000.00. Dudley Mabry sheweth that his son Whitfield W. Mabry died intestate without wife or lineal descendant. Power of Atty., State of Ala., Tuscaloose Co. Whereas Dudley

Mabry of Abbe. Dist., S. C., was empowered to draw certain monies from the est. of Mrs. Elizabeth Hodges decd. and did draw the funds aforesaid and whereas the said D. Mabry was sued to judgment and did confess a judgment to his son Whitefield W. Mabry since decd. Now know that we Geo. W. Tierce, Jas. S. Mabry of the Co. of Tuscaloosa, Ala., being entitled to said funds drawn by the said Dudley Mabry by Power of Atty. from the est. of Mrs. Elizabeth Hodges decd. do appoint Wm. McCombs and Rhoda B. Doyle of Abbe. Dist. oud lawful atty. Whitfield W. Mabry left a father Dudley Mabry and bros., Zachariah S., Jas. S., Geo. M., John W., Wm. W., Andrew Jackson, Elizabeth Mabry. Smith Mabry residing in Miss.

MOSELEY, JANE—BOX 118, PACK 3480:
Est. admnr. Oct. 7, 1847 by Wm., Benj. F. Moseley, G. M. Mattison, John Moore bound unto David Lesly Ord. sum $1,600.00. Wm. and B. F. Moseley sheweth that Jane Moseley wid. of Burrel moseley late decd. died intestate leaving 5 minor chn. Sept. 22, 1847 Mr. Lesly this is to confirm you that we Wm. Richey, H. T. or J. Richey being bros. and next of kin do consent to Benj. F. and Wm. Moseley to admnr. When Sett. was made in June 5, 1849 ment. that Sarah, Sena Margaret, Nancy Moseley were minors.

MARTIN, ROBERT—BOX 118, PACK 3481:
Will dated Sept. 1, 1847. Prov. in Abbeville Dist. Sept. 9, 1847. Exr: David Lesly. Wit: Jas. Taggart, Jas. Spence, Jas. F. Gilbert. Chn. ment. no names given. Est. also admnr. Oct. 16, 1847 by Jas. H. Cobb, Jas. Taggart, Thos. Smith bound unto David Lesly Ord. sum $200.00. Sale made Nov. 2, 1847. Byrs: Thos. Cobb, Sarah Wilson, Robt. Crawford, Chas. Evans, Edw. Robinson, Jane Martin, Mary Martin, Jas. Martin, etc.

MARTIN, GEORGE—BOX 118, PACK 3482:
Est. admnr. Nov. 6, 1848 by Jas. C. Martin, P. H. Bradley, R. W. Lites bound unto David Lesly Ord. Abbeville Dist. sum $3,000.00. Jas. Martin was a bro. to Geo. P. Martin. Inv. made Jan. 6, 1849 by P. H. Bradley, John McClellan, Chas. Sproull.

MAYS, MEEDY, JR.—BOX 118, PACK 3483:
Est. admnr. Jan. 30, 1849 by Larkin, Henry Mays, Thos. Rosamond, Enoch Carter bound unto David Lesly Ord. sum $30,000.00. Larkin Mays sheweth that his bro. Meedy Mays Jr., died intestate leaving a wid. and 3 chn. Sett. made Jan. 10,1852. Present Larkin, Henry, Mary Elezabeth Mays the wid. Leroy J. Johnson their gdn. representing the minors John Mathew Mays, Anna Lucretia Mays. On Mar. 14, 1854 Abna Mays recd. $322.41.

McCASLAN, ROBERT—BOX 118, PACK 3484:
Will dated Oct. 6, 1840. Prov. in Abbeville Dist. Dec. 3, 1849. Exrs: Sons, Jas., Wm., Moses Oliver McCaslan. Wit: W. W. Belcher, Wm. Harris, J. C. Willard. Wife, Margaret McCaslan. Chn: Jas., Wm.. Moses Oliver, Alexr. Lesly, Polly McClane, Patrick Calhoun McCaslan, Elizabeth Ann McCaslan. Sett. made Dec. 5, 1850. Testator died Nov. 27, 1849. David McClane married Mary McCaslan, John Chann married Elizabeth Ann.

MILLS, RICE—BOX 118, PACK 3485:
Est. admnr. Sept. 25, 1848 by Edward R. Mills, A. Bradly, Geo. Sibert bound unto David Lesly Ord. sum $70.00. Edward R. Mills sheweth that Rice Mills died in Fla.

MAYS, JOHN—BOX 118, PACK 3486:
Est. admnr. June 29, 1849 by Meedy Mays, L. G. Carter, L. Burnett bound unto David Lesly Ord. Abbeville Dist. sum $3,500.00. Meedy Mays Sr. sheweth that he was the receiver of John Mays who was a lunatic in the asylum of Va. and had an est. in Abbeville Dist. S. C. Present at sett: Meedy Mays admnr. Wm. Mays gdn. of his only dtr. Frances. John Mays left a wid. Nancy and the child Frances.

MAYS, JAS. MADISON—BOX 118, PACK 3487:
Will dated Aug. 18, 1849. Prov. in Abbeville Dist. Sept. 11, 1849. Exrs: Edna Caldwell, Stanmore Brooks. Wit: E. W. Thornton, Jacob Miller, Jas. Wideman. Dtr: Virginia Pickens Maynard, Bro. Wm. Pinckney Maynard. Stanmore B. Brooks stated that Jas. Maynard and his dtr. Virginia lived at the home of Mrs. Caldwell.

MARTIN, NANCY—BOX 118, PACK 3488:
Will dated July 13, 1840. Prov. Sept. 3, 1849. Exrs: Sons, Edward C., Jas. E. Martin. Wit: Armistead Burt, Moses Jacobs Jr., Gabriel Cox. Was a wid. Chn: Edward C., Jas. E., Caroline M., Hepsabeth Lee Carson, Sarah K. Tullis. Sett. made Jan. 29, 1852 ment. that M. H. Carson was the husband of Hepsabeth Lee Martin. Nancy Martin died Aug. 17, 1849. On Dec. 20, 1852 Catharine Laughton, John M. Tullis, Sabra Tullis each recd. $10.95 of said est. July 23, 1851 Phares Martin recd. $22.85 her part of rent of the plantation of John Martin decd. On Aug. 20, 1853 Wm. A. Crozier recd. $190.31 in full of his interest of said est. On Mar. 24, 1854 Martin H. Carson recd. $190.31. On Jan. 29, 1852 Thos. Edward recd. $105.64 the share of Mildred Edwards his wife in the sett. of John Martin decd. On Nov. 29, 1857 Cartin recd. $108.69.

MATHEWS, JOHN—BOX 118, PACK 3489:
Est. admnr. Nov. 10, 1848 by David Mathews, Williams Truwit, J. C. Willard bound unto David Lesly Ord. Abbeville Dist. sum $500.00. David Mathews sheweth that his son John Mathews died intestate in Miss. without wife or chn. leaving a father and 2 sis. heirs at law. Green Co., Ala. In consideration of A. P. Conner paying as security for Wade Sheblsworth paid the sum of $210.00 to the est. of Green B. Crawford we hereby assign, transfer and sell over to said A. P. Conner all our right and interest in the est. of our deceased bro. and bro. l. John Mathews. Sarah Mathews, Wade Hallesworth. (Note: At the top was written Sade Shelbsworth but at bottom at signing looked like Hallesworth. Not positive.)

MARTIN, NATHANIEL—BOX 118, PACK 3490:
Est. admnr. Dec. 25, 1848 by Z. W. Carwile, S. M., R. C. Griffin bound unto David Lesly Ord. Abbeville Dist. sum $200.00. Zachariah W. Carwile lived

at Cambridge. Inv. made Jan. 19, 1849 by R. C. Griffin, Jas. W. Richardson, S. B. Sale.

MANN, JOHN G.—BOX 118, PACK 3491:
Est. admnr. Nov. 20, 1848 by Dr. Isaac Branch, Benj. Y. Martin, H. A. Jones bound unto David Lesly Ord. Abbeville Dist. sum $3,000.00. Isaac Branch sheweth that John Gibson Mann died intestate leaving a wid. (Letter)

Macon, Ga.
Apr. 2, 1866
To the Probate Judge of Abbeville Dist., S. C.
Dear Sir:

I hasten to make a request of you the Subsistance of it is as follows. I wish for you to search the Records of your office and see if theri was any administration maid on the Est. of John G. Mann and by whom it was administered. See if it was made by one Dr. Isaac Branch and if so pleas give me a copy of the Record of all the Transactions State what the said property of John G. Mann was praised at and also what it brought at administrators sale also pleas give me a copy of the winding up of the said est. and into whose hands the money was paid pleas search out and see if any debts was paid of the Est. and by who and how much the est. was in debt and how particular if Archeyble Scott paid any of the debts and how mutch he had to pay and also the Vouchers by whitch the Est. was wound up in a woura pleas to commit to writing the hole of procedure of the administration and into whos hands the money of the est. was paid by the administrator.

Respectfully your Obt. Servant,
Mr. S. W. or L. W. Bramlet
Macon, Ga.

MILLER, LEWIS J.—BOX 118, PACK 3492:
Est. admnr. Oct. 5, 1846 by Nathaniel J. Davis, Johnson Ramey, Joseph A. Hamilton bound unto David Lesly Ord. Abbeville Dist. sum $4,000.00. Jane Miller the wid. Inv. made Nov. 11, 1846 by Geo. J. Camron, Robt. W. Rary, Thos. Fulton.

MABRY, JOHN W.—BOX 118, PACK 3493:
Est. admnr. Feb. 12, 1849 by Dudly Mabry, H. A. Jones, Wm. McWhorter bound unto David Lesly Ord. Abbeville Dist. sum $600.00. Dudly Mabry sheweth that his son John W. Mabry died intestate leaving no family.

MARTIN, JAMES—BOX 118, PACK 3494:
Est. admnr. Mar. 17, 1849 by Jas. Martin, S. S. C. McGaw, John Link bound unto David Lesly Ord. Abbeville Dist. sum $500.00. Jas. Martin sheweth that his father Jas. Martin died intestate. Jas. Martin mother died shortly after the interstate, Jas. Martin. Inv. made Apr. 7, 1849 by John Link, T. Johnson, Wm. Henderson.

McCORD, MARY E.—BOX 118, PACK 3495:
Est. admnr. June 21, 1849 by Zackeriah McCord of Augusta, Ga., Pleasant

Searls, Jas. Blackwell of Edgefield Dist. bound unto David Lesly Ord. Abbeville Dist. sum $600,00. Zachariah McCord of Augusta, Ga. sheweth that he married Mary E. Collins dtr. of E. W. Collins decd. That by the will of E. Collins decd. made 11 yrs. ago certain slaves and land was given to the said E. W. Collins for his 2 chn. Thos. R., and the said Mary E. that the said E. W. Collins died 1844, Ed. Collins 1847 and the wife of your petr. died Nov. 2, 1848 leaving your petr. and an infant child Mary E. McCord. Dated this Apr. 23, 1849.

MOORE, NATHANIEL—BOX 118, PACK 3496:
Est. admnr. Feb. 14, 1849 by Margaret Moore, Joseph Lesly, Alexr. Gordon bound unto David Lesly Ord. Abbeville Dist. sum $7,000.00. Margaret Moore sheweth that Nathaniel Moore her husband died intestate in Jan. last leaving your petr. his wid. and 5 infant chn. the oldest being about 17 yrs. of age. Chn. were: Margaret, Mary Jane, Wm. Moore, Nancy wife of Henry M. Willbanks, Louisa H. Moore. Sett. to ascertain the share of Louisa H. Moore who lately married John Leroy made Apr. 27, 1860. Sett. made Dec. 18, 1866. Present J. P. Huckabee the husband of Margaret and Wm. Moore who represents Mrs. Moore the admnr.

McBRIDE, WILLIAM—BOX 118, PACK 3497:
Est. admnr. Feb. 24, 1849 by John, Thos. C., Joseph McBride bound unto David Lesly Ord. Abbeville Dist. sum $100.00. John McBride sheweth that his son Wm. McBride died intestate without wife or chn.

MILLER, (MINORS)—BOX 118, PACK 3498:
On Apr. 28, 1847, N. J. Davis bound unto David Lesly Ord. Abbeville Dist. sum $1,500.00 and was appointed gdn. of Jesse, Lewis Miller minors under 14 yrs. and the chn. of Jane Miller. N. J. Davis sheweth that L. J. Miller died intestate leaving a wid. Jane and 2 infant chn., Wm. Jesse, Lewis J. Miller.

MARTIN, THOMAS P.—BOX 118, PACK 3499:
Est. admnr. Jan. 12, 1850 by Jacob, John C. Martin, Andrew Giles Esq. bound unto David Lesly Ord. Abbeville Dist. sum $6,000.00. Jacob Martin was the father of Thos. P. Martin. Sett. of Thos. Peyton Martin who died in the State of La. intestate, leaving a wid. Martha A. Martin and 4 chn. viz. Ann Elizabeth, Leonora C., Chas W., Martha Peyton Martin. Leonora C. Martin died June 24, 1849 in the State of Ala. Thos. P. Martin died July 23, 1848 in *Bossin* Parish, La. Ann Elizabeth married a Peterson.

McCARTNEY, JOHN—BOX 118, PACK 3500:
Est. admnr. Jan. 21, 1850 by John, Jas. J. Devlin, Mary A. McCartny bound unto David Lesly Ord. Abbeville Dist. sum $3,000.00. John Devlin sheweth that his bro. l. John McCartny died leaving a wid. and 1 child. Expend: July 1, 1852 Recd. from E. Noble Esq. money collected in Miss. from Wm. McCartney $111.67. Sett. made July 24, 1852. Present, John B. Richey in right of his wife Mary A. the wid of said decd. and Leroy Purdy gdn. of Emma J. McCartney only child.

MILLER, ALEXANDER—BOX 118, PACK 3501:
Est. admnr. Jan. 18, 1850 by Jas. Cowan, Jasper N., D. O. Hawthorne, Jas. W. Black bound unto David Lesly Ord. Abbeville Dist. sum $12,000.00. Jas. Cowan for himself and the wid. Elizabeth Ann Miller sheweth that Alexr. Miller died intestate without lineal descendant, but leaving a wid. Elizabeth A. and a father John Miller as his only heirs. Sett. made Feb. 9, 1850. Alexr. H. Miller died about the 25th Dec., 1849.

MYERS, NELLY—BOX 118, PACK 3502:
Est. admnr. Jan. 23, 1847 by Abram Lights, A. H. Morton bound unto David Lesly Ord. Abbeville Dist. sum $40.00 Abram Lights sheweth that some yrs. ago Saml. Cummins a Dutchman died intestate leaving a sis. Nelly Myers. Expend: May 1844 Elendor Myers to Benj. White to making Saml. Cummins coffin $5.00.

MARTIN, (MINORS)—BOX 118, PACK 3503:
On Jan. 3, 1850 Jas., Wm. H. Taggart, John F. McComb bound unto David Lesly Ord. Abbeville Dist. sum $852.00. Jas. Taggart made gdn. of Susan, Henry D., Sarah C. Martin minors. Jas. Taggart sheweth that some time since, Robt. Martin and wife of Abbeville Dist. both decd. died intestate leaving 7 chn. The petitioner also states that lately and since the death of said Robt. Martin, his bro. Richard A. Martin of Elbert Co., Ga. died intestate leaving neither wife or chn. There are minors viz. Susan, Henry D., Sarah C., Mary, Wm. Martin.

MITCHELL, WILLIAM, SR.—BOX 118, PACK 3504:
Est. admnr. Dec. 20, 1847 by Saml. Donnald, Wm. Hill, A. C. Hawthorn bound unto David Lesly Ord. Abbeville Dist. sum $500.00. Inv. made Jan. 12, 1848 by John R. Wilson, Stephen Latimer, David Moore. Sale made Jan. 13, 1848. Byrs: Wm. Armstrong, Jno. R. Shirley, Deliley Mitchell, Stephen Latimer, Harrison Latimer, Saml. Donnald, B. F. Shirley, G. W. F. Mitchell, etc.

MITCHUM, JOSHUA—BOX 118, PACK 3505:
Will dated June 5, 1846 in Abbeville Dist. Probated Aug. 19, 1846. Exr. Bro., Jas. Mitchum. Wit: Starling Q. Williams, A. B. Arnold, A. W. Lynch, Sisters, Margaret Jones, Martha Lenhaw or Lenham. Jas. Mitchum was of Muscoge Co., Ga. Then on another paper stated that he was of Harris Co., Ellislie P. Office, Ga. (Name also written Meachum on the papers but in will written Mitchum.)

McDILL, (MINORS)—BOX 119, PACK 3505½:
On Mar. 25, 1848 Wm., Thos. McDill, Jas. Edwards bound unto David Lesly Ord. Abbeville Dist. sum $400.00. Wm. McDill made gdn. of Thos. R., Robt. A. McDill minors. Wm. Henderson their gr. father. Wm. McDill their father. Wm. McDill on Mar. 28, 1848 sheweth that he is the father of Thos. R. over the age of choice and Robt. A. under 14 yrs. That they have an est. due them from their gr. father Wm. Henderson decd of around $200.00. That Shad Henderson a son of Wm. Henderson decd. also died intestate. Sarah Henderson decd. was the wife of Wm. McDill.

MOSELY, DOROTHY—BOX 119, PACK 3506:
Est. admnr. July 9, 1847 by Wm., B. F. Mosely, Timothy Stephens bound unto David Lesly Ord. Abbeville Dist. sum $1,000.00. Benj. F. Mosely sheweth that some time since his father made his will and died leaving your petr. and his bro. Exer. and gdn. of his sis. Dorathy Mosely, who had also died about 34 yrs. of age. That there are minor chn. also of a decd bro. Burrel Mosely decd.

McALLISTER, WILLIAM—BOX 119, PACK 3507:
Will dated Oct. 17, 1846 in Abbeville Dist. Prov. Jan. 27, 1847. Exrs: Son, David McAllister, Archibald Fair. Wit: John H. Wilson, Geo. A., Nicholas H. Miller. Wife, Matilda Frances McAllister. Dtr. Nancy Fair. Gr. son, Wm. E. McAllister. (Name written McCallister and McAllister.)

MORROW, ALBERT G.—BOX 119, PACK 3508:
Est. admnr. Aug. 19, 1848 by Andrew Morrow, Thos. C. Potts, Foster Marshall bound to David Lesly Ord. Abbeville Dist. sum $100.00. Andrew Morrow sheweth that his son Albert G. Morrow entered the service of the Mexican War under Capt. Marshall and died in service having chn. intestate and is entitled to arrears from the government.

McCANTS, DAVID JAS.—BOX 119, PACK 3509:
Est. admnr. Jan. 1, 1850 by Nathaniel McCants, John Saddler, Simeon Chaney bound unto David Lesly Ord. Abbeville Dist. sum $600.00. Nathaniel McCants the father of David J. Sarah E. McCants was the wife of David J. McCants.

PACK 3510: Gone.

MOORE, ROBERT—BOX 119, PACK 3511:
Will dated July 23, 1846 in Abbeville Dist. Prov. Oct. 5, 1846. Exrs: son, Andrew J. Moore, Marshal Sharp, Enoch Barmore. Wit: Wm. Barmore, Saml. Agnew Sr., J. L. Sims. Chn: A. J., Wm., John More, Mahaly Williamson, Nancy Thompson, Thursday Graham. Gr. chn: Jas. A., Margaret Elender Thompson chn. of Nancy and Bolen Thompson. On Aug. 14, 1849 Jas. Graham recd. $924.04 in right of his wife Theresa. (In will her name was written Thursday.) Thos. Williamson recd. $924.04 for his wife Mahala. Power of Atty. On July 20, 1849 Wm. Moore of Tuscaloosa Co., Ala., appointed Jas. Graham her atty. to receive from Marshal Sharp and A. Jackson Exrs. of my decd. father Robt. Moore of Abbeville Dist., S. C., to receive what is due me.

McKELLER, DONALD, SR.—BOX 119, PACK 3512:
Will dated Aug. 17, 1846 in Abbeville Dist. Prov. July 3, 1848. Exrs: Sons, Peter, John McKellar, John McClelland. Wit: Henry H. Creswell, Saml. J. Porter, Jno. McBryde. Chn: Peter, Mary, John McKellar, Nancy Reynolds. Gr. chn. Mary Independence dtr. of Alexr. decd. and his wife Lucy McKellar, Catharine Ann Isabella dtr. of Edward Watson. "Bequeath to my bro. ls., John McDougal, Donald McDougal of Scotland each $100.00." Sett. made Jan. 17, 1850 ment. that Donald McKellar died about June 3, 1848. Mary J. McKellar was a minor. On July 17, 1849 Bennett Reynolds recd. $2,060.00 his share of est.

MOORE,·THOMAS—BOX 119, PACK 3513:
Est. admnr. Nov. 26, 1847 by Alexr., Wm. Moore, Ezekiel Trible, bound unto David Lesly Ord. Abbeville Dist. sum $5,000.00. Alexr. Moore on Nov. 12, 1847 sheweth that his father Thos. Moore died intestate. Sale, Nov. 30, 1847. Byrs: Wm., Seth H., Alexr., John, Jenny Moore, etc.

NORWOOD, NATHANIEL—BOX 119, PACK 3514:
Est. admnr. Aug. 25, 1848 by Mary Norwood, Wm. Lyon, Wm. Harris bound unto David Lesly Ord. Abbeville Dist. sum $10,000.00. Nathaniel Norwood left a wid. Mary Norwood and several infant chn. Distributees: Jas. Wesly, Sarah Virginia Norwood, Ann E., R. F. Moseley, Nannie C., John Harmon, Orran Norwood decd.

NOBLE, JOSEPH A. (MINOR)—BOX 119, PACK 3515:
Est. admnr. Dec. 25, 1848 by Jane Gibert, S. Lee, Benj. McKittrick, D. M. Rogers bound unto David Lesly Ord. Abbeville Dist. sum $20,000.00. Jane Gibert sheweth that her gr. son Joseph A. Noble in minority departed this life intestate. Sett. made Jan. 4, 1849 of Joseph Noble decd. and Harriet A. Noble decd. of whose ests. Wm. P. Noble was the admnr. and afterwards he was appointed gdn. of Joseph A. Noble only child and distributee of Joseph and Harriet A. Noble. Joseph A. Noble having lately died admnr. has been granted to Jane Gibert. Joseph A. Noble at time of his death was about 5 yrs. old, leaving no parents or sis. or bros. Mary H. Noble authorized Dr. Nathaniel Harris to sell a certain tract of land known as the Fort Charlotte place on Savannah River in Abbe. Dist. Dated May 30, 184-. Looked like 6.

NORWOOD, WILLIAMSON—BOX 119, PACK 3516:
Will dated Apr. 17, 1847. Prov. Aug. 2, 1850. Exrs: Son, Jas. A. Norwood, John A. Calhoun, Edmond Belcher. Wit: Nathaniel Norwood, Thos. McByrde, A. B. Arnold, Alexr. Hunter. Chn: Caroline Clark decd., Jas. A. Norwood, Mary A. Belcher decd., Sarah A. Calhoun. Gr. chn: Joseph, Caroline, Mary C. chn. of Caroline Clark decd. and A. B. Clark. "Give land to John A. Calhoun."

NORWOOD, JESSE—BOX 119, PACK 3517:
Est. admnr. Sept. 18, 1848 by Saml., Jas. Agnew, Enoch Barmore bound to David Lesly Ord. Abbeville Dist. sum $50.00 of Jesse Norwood a soldier in the late Mexican War. Saml. Agnew sheweth that Jesse Norwood died in the Mexican War intestate leaving a wid. and chn. Betsey Norwood the wid.

NOBLE, PATRICK JR.—BOX 119, PACK 3518:
1st. Lt. of Dragoons, U. S. A.
Will dated Dec. 25, 1848 in Abbeville Dist. Prov. Jan. 20, 1849. Exr: Edward Nobel. Wit: B. P. Hughes, L. T. Bratton, T. B. Dendy. Sis., Elizabeth Bonneau Noble, Floride C. Cunningham. Bros. Ezekiel Pickens Noble, Edward, Alexr., Saml. B. Noble. "Leave Mary A. Noble wife of Edward Noble." Leave Ezekiel P. Noble $60.00 to purchase for his son Patrick Noble. Leave Lt. John Love 1st. Dragons, U. S. A., my Mexican Mustong in the charge of Lt. Chapman, Ft. Gibson, Ark.

NORRIS, ALEXANDER—BOX 119, PACK 3519:
Est. admnr. Sept. 14, 1848 by Wm. W. Anderson, Robt. W. Norris, H. A. Jones Esq. bound unto David Lesly Ord. Abbeville Dist. sum $350.00. He died without wife or chn. but left bro. and sisters.

NOBLE, JOHN A.—BOX 119, PACK 3520:
John A. Noble died in Ga. Edward Noble was admnr. of his est. in Abbe. Dist. J. W. M. *Branyon* married Catharine Noble. Mary H. Noble the mother of said decd. and Catharine were the only dist. Admnr. was granted in May, 1846.

NICHOLS, GASSAWAY R.—BOX 119, PACK 3521:
Est. admnr. Jan. 3, 1848 by Jas. O. Conner, John E. Foster, Alexr. P. Conner bound unto David Lesly Ord. Abbeville Dist. sum $2,400.00. Gassaway R. Nichols was a bro. l. to Jas. O. Conner. Sett. made July 7, 1849 ment. that the wid. Rebecca C. Nichols had twins born after the death of her husband and that twins are both now dead.

OGLESBY, WM. WESLEY—BOX 119, PACK 3522:
Was a free man of color so I did not copy his est.

OVERBY, ADAM—BOX 119, PACK 3523:
Est. admnr. Dec. 7, 1846 by Z. W. Carwile, Sampson V. Cain, John R. Tarrant bound unto David Lesly Ord. Abbeville Dist. sum $3,000.00. (Letter) Cambridge, S. C.

Oct. 23, 1846
David Lesly Esq.
Dear Sir:
Adam Overby of this Dist. died some few days ago leaving a small est., and having no relations in this state and myself being the highest creditor and may be appointed admnr. Sett. made Apr. 6, 1855. Thos. Thompson Esq. as atty. represents Green Blanton and his chn. claiming to be distributees of said Adam Overby.

PITMAN, FRANCIS—BOX 119, PACK 3524:
Est. admnr. Jan. 23, 1850 by John Douglass, Isaac Branch, Sterling Dean bound unto David Lesly Ord. Abbeville Dist. sum $100.00.

PRATT, JOHN, JR.—BOX 119, PACK 3525:
Will dated June 19, 1849 in Abbeville Dist. Prov. July 2, 1849. Exrs: Thos. Crawford, Nancy N. Pratt. Wit: Robt., Wm., John Pratt Sr. Chn: Phalba N., Thos. R., Permelia H., Stephen L. Pratt. Annual returns of Louisa Pratt now by marriage Louisa Haynie of her minor chn., Jas., Ophelia, Wm. A., Sarah L. Pratt.

PULLIAM, RHODA AND JAS.—BOX 119, PACK 3526:
Est. of Rhoda Pulliam admnr. Oct. 20, 1846 by Thos. B. Byrd, Albert Waller, P. D. Klugh bound unto David Lesly Ord. Abbeville Dist. sum $8,000.00. Wid. of Jas. Pulliam decd. Sett. made Mar. 5, 1852 ment. that Rhoda Pulliam

had no chn. but bros. and sisters. Present: Thos. Thompson representing Zachariah, Benj. Gholston chn. of Elizabeth Gholston a sis. of Rhoda Pulliam and H. A. Jones representing John Pulliam, Jas. A. Warex, and Harriet his wife and Zachariah Pulliam some of the chn. of Zachariah Pulliam a decd. bro. Absent: chn. of John Pulliam to wit, Larkin, Wm., Joseph, Richard, Elizabeth, Sarah Pulliam. Chn. of Zachariah Pulliam to wit, Caroline wife of Mart T. Stewart, Robt. Pulliam. Chas B. Fooshee son of Martha a sis. of Rhoda and Patsy now wid. of John Cheatham, also dtr. of Martha. Chn. of Nancy Ball unknown. Fanny Mitchell and Anna Cooper sisters of Rhoda.

POLLARD, ROBERT—BOX 119, PACK 3527:
Est. admnr. Sept. 3, 1849 by James Young., Downs, W. D. Calhoun bound unto David Lesly Ord. Abbeville Dist. sum $6,000.00. Present at sett: B. Y. Golman hus. of Eliz. one of the chn. of Elizabeth Hopper decd. Robt. T. Jones, S. Y. Hopper. Absent, Jacob Crocker and Caroline his wife, James Young.

PENNELL, JAMES AND EMILY H.—BOX 119, PACK 3528:
Est. admnr. Mar. 22, 1847 by Moses O., Jas. McCaslan, Thos. P. Dowtin, bound unto David Lesly Ord. Abbeville Dist. sum $3,000.00. Bond for both now decd. Philip Zimmerman sheweth that Emily Pennel wid. of Jas. W. Pennel died intestate leaving 2 minor chn., Alexr., Wm. Henry Pennell. The 2 chn. lived with S. Wideman.

PERRIN, EUNICE—BOX 119, PACK 3529:
Est. admnr. Nov. 23, 1846 by John Cothran, James M., Saml. Perrin bound unto David Lesly Ord. Abbeville Dist. sum $6,000.00. John Cothran sheweth that Eunice Perrin died about May 19, last and that he is the son-in-law of said decd. Inv. made Dec. 30, 1846 by John W. Hearst, W. P. Sullivan, Cary P. Patterson, Frederick Cook. Byrs: Saml. Perrin, John Cothran, Thos. C. Perrin, R. P. Quarles, Henry Nelson, B. B. Foster, Harvey Nelson.

PAUL, AGNESS E.—BOX 119, PACK 3530:
Est. admnr. Mar. 12, 1847 by Andrew J. Weems, John A. Donald, Bartw. Jordan bound unto David Lesly Ord. Abbeville Dist. sum $1,000.00. Andrew J. Weems sheweth that his sis. Agness E. Paul died intestate leaving some infant chn.

PATTERSON, JOSIAH—BOX 119, PACK 3531:
Will dated Aug. 22, 1846 in Abbeville Dist. Prov. Dec. 1, 1846. Exrs: Sons, Andrew Giles, James C. Patterson. Wit: James T. Baskin, Robt. Ward, John Moseley. Wife, Elenor Patterson. Chn: Mary A. Campbell, Jane L. Cater, Louisa A. Hamilton, John A. Patterson, Sarah Giles, James C., Josiah B. Patterson. Sett: Mar. 5, 1848. Legatees: R. B. Campbell and wife, R. B. Cater and wife, A. Giles and wife.

PORTER, REVD. JOHN—BOX 119, PACK 3532:
Will dated July, 1838 in Abbeville Dist. Prov. Jan. 25, 1847. Exrs: Wife, E. D. Porter, Dr. T. R. Gary, T. W. Williams, Henry Hester. Wit: Nathaniel Marion, James Shackelford, James B. Clanahan. Wife, E. D. Porter. Chn.,

Martha Matilda, Hugh Francis, Hester Ann, Mary Glover, Catharine Jones, Mary Eliz. Porter. Power of Atty. On Nov. 13, 1852 Hugh L. Porter of Tishamingo County, Miss., the surviving bro. of Jane E. Porter decd. late of Itawamba County, Miss., who died without issue and without any sis. or other bro. surviving her chn. of Andrew R. Porter decd. late of Abbeville Dist., S. C. and Nancy H. Porter alias Nancy H. Davis being now the wife of Israel N. Davis do nominate David Lesly my atty. to ask, demand and receive of and from Robt. M. Davis late the gdn. of said Jane E. Porter decd. Revd. John Porter died about Jan. 19, 1847. His wife was Eliz. D. Porter. Leg: Hester Ann Porter, wife of Robt. M. Davis, Mary G. Porter, James T. Allen and Catharine J., his wife, Hugh F. Porter, Meady Mays and Mary E. his wife, Eliz. D. Porter, Wm. Griffin recd. $37.00 in right of his wife on April 30, 1836.

PORTER, MACLIN—BOX 120, PACK 3533:
Est. admnr. Jan. 22, 1847 by James W. Porter, Phares Martin, A. H. McAllister bound unto David Lesly Ord. Abbeville Dist. sum $300.00. James W. Porter sheweth that his bro. Maclin Porter died having no wife or chn., but a mother, bros. and sisters.

PRINCE, EDWARD S.—BOX 120, PACK 3534:
On Oct. 28, 1848 the petition of Edward S. Prince sheweth that he is about 20 yrs. old, and a bro. of James Prince decd. who was a Soldier in the late Mexican War. I pray that Thos. G. Campbell be appointed my gdn. to receive the arrears of pay and my interest in the land bounty due my decd. bro. James Prince decd. This petition was written at Sandy Ridge, Ga., to David Lesly of Abbeville.

PRINCE, JAMES C.—BOX 120, PACK 3535:
Est. admnr. Oct. 30, 1848 by Thos. G., Wm. Campbell, J. Foster Marshall, bound unto David Lesly Ord. Abbeville Dist. sum $100.00. Thos. G. Campbell sheweth that James Prince died intestate as a soldier in the late Mexican War leaving no wife or chn., father or mother, but 1 bro. and sis., Edw. S., Anna Prince.

PRATT, (MINORS)—BOX 120, PACK 3536:
On Apr. 28, 1851, Wm. Robertson, Wm. W. Moseley, A. F. Posey bound to F. W. Sellick Ord. Abbeville Dist. sum $2,000.00. Wm. Robertson made gdn. of James L., Matilda O., Wm. A., Sarah L. Pratt minors under 14. Louisa Pratt sheweth that her hus. Wm. Pratt died intestate. Louisa Pratt married Patrick C. Haynie.

PRICE, WILLIAM M.—BOX 120, PACK 3537:
On Mar. 15, 1847 John H. Holliway, John Self, James Yeldell, the two latter in Edgefield Dist. bound unto David Lesly Ord. Abbeville Dist. sum $2,000.00. Jno. H. Holliway made gdn. of Wm. M. Price a minor child of Joseph T. Price decd. and Tilda Price decd. who died deaving 4 chn., Eliz., Thos., Patsy and your petr.

PALMER, GEORGE—BOX 120, PACK 3538:
Will dated Jan. 2, 1847 in Abbeville Dist. Prov. April 15, 1848. Exr. Wm.

Trewit. Wit: John Leroy Taylor, Benj. Taylor, Wm. Holsomback. Wife, Rachel Palmer. Chn: Willis, Jas. Hiram, Nineon, Joshua B., Milton, Dale Palmer, Beattics wife of Simeon Brooks decd., Harriet Bell. Gr. chn.: George M., Isabella Brooks. "Owned land on Buffalow Creek."

PURDY, NANCY—BOX 120, PACK 3539:

Est. admnr. Sept. 2, 1847 by Jas. Purdy, Wm. Tucker, Wm. N. Purdy bound unto David Lesly Ord. Abbeville Dist. sum $50.00. Nancy Purdy was mother of Jas. Purdy. Inv. made Sept. 25, 1847 by John L. Boyd, Wm. N. Purdy, Andw. Gillespie.

PURDY, JAMES—BOX 120, PACK 3540:

Est. admnr. Jan. 14, 1850 by Wm. N., Leroy Purdy, Wm. Tucker (the latter of Anderson Dist.) bound unto David Lesly Ord. Abbeville Dist. sum $75.00. Wm. N. Purdy sheweth that his bro. died intestate without wife or chn. Inv. made Jan. 19, 1850 by Capt. John L. Boyd, Andw. Gillespie Esq., Francis Brooks.

PACE, SILAS—BOX 120, PACK 3541:

Est. admnr. Mar. 31, 1849 by Sarah Pace, Silas Ray, John Davis bound unto David Lesly Ord. Abbeville Dist. sum $9,000.00. Sarah Pace sheweth that her son Silas H. Pace died Mar. 10, 1849 without wife or chn. Your petr., 3 sis., and a bro., and the chn. of Richard Pace decd. and 1 child of Lucinda Connor decd. as his only heirs. Sarah Pace shows that some heirs live beyond the limits of the state viz. minor chn. of Richard Pace viz. Sarah Jane, John Pickney Pace, John Thomas and wife Matilda.

PRICE, COLBERTH—BOX 120, PACK 3542:

Est. admnr. Jan. 25, 1845 by Wm. C. Robertson, James Tompkins bound unto David Lesly Ord. Abbeville Dist. sum $1,600.00. Sett. made July 31, 1853. Present: W. C. Robertson, Freeland and Nix admnrs. of est. of Martha, Vicey Price distr. of their father Colberth Price. (Written also Cathbert Price.) Wm. McCain was gdn. of Sarah Weeks. dtr. of Sarah Price and also entitled to a share from est. of Cathbert Price.

POSEY, ROBERT V.—BOX 120, PACK 3543:

Est. admnr. May 14, 1849 by J. W., B. V., A. F. Posey bound unto David Lesly Ord. Abbeville Dist. sum $500.00. J. W., B. V. Posey sheweth that their father Robt. V. Posey a few days since died leaving a wid. and chn. all of whom are grown and of age, evcept a sis. who died having chn. Sett: April 20, 1852. Present, J. W., B. V. Posey admnrs., Harrison, Henson Posey, N. G., A. E. Hughes who married Edny, Sally dtrs. of said decd. and the wid. Massa Posey. James, Robt., Wm. Helmes chn. of Mary Helmes not present.

PATTON, WILLIAM W.—BOX 120, PACK 3544:

Est. admnr. Oct. 15, 1849 by John F., E. L. Patton, Archibald Kennedy bound unto David Lesly Ord. Abbeville Dist. sum $15,000.00. Jno. F. Patton sheweth that his bro. Wm. W. Patton died in St. Louis intestate without wife or chn. Sett: May 4, 1852 ment. the following dist. viz. A. K. Patton, Edmund L.,

Miss L. C. Patton, Dr. A. F. Wideman in right of his wife Rebecca A. Intestate died July 6, 1849 in St. Louis, Missouri.

PENNELL, (MINORS)—BOX 120, PACK 3545:
On June 2, 1847 Moses O., James McCaslin, Thos. P. Dowton bound unto David Lesly Ord. Abbeville Dist. sum $4,000.00. M. O. McCaslin made gdn. of Alexr., Wm. H. Pennell minors under 14 yrs. M. O., Jas. W. McCaslan sheweth that sometime since Jas. W. Pennell died intestate and P. Zimmerman admnr. the est. Shortly afterwards Emily H. Pennell died. Wm. Henry, James Alexr. Pennell their chn.

RED, DR. JOHN C.—BOX 120, PACK 3546:
Est. admnr. Feb. 24, 1848 by N. J. Davis, Adam Wideman, John A. Hamilton bound unto David Lesly Ord. Abbeville Dist. sum $16,000.00. N. J. Davis sheweth that his bro.-in-law John C. Red died intestate and his wid. is your petr's. sis. viz. Frances Red.

REAGIN, JOSEPH—BOX 120, PACK 3547:
Est. admnr. Nov. 2, 1846 by Jesse Reagin, Archibald Bradley, Andw. J. Weed bound unto David Lesly Ord. Abbeville Dist. sum $1,000.00. Sett. made Sept. 5, 1848. Present Jesse Reagin. Joseph Reagin died before his father Young Reagin without wife or chn. Other dist. were: Nicholas Reagin, G. K. Bradley, Elizabeth Bradley.

RUFF, JOHN L.—BOX 120, PACK 3548:
Est. admnr. Nov. 3, 1848 by David F., John, Elizabeth Ruff bound unto David Lesly Ord. Abbeville Dist. sum $1,200.00. David F. Ruff was a bro. to John L. Ruff. Sett. ment. that Daniel W. Reid married the wid. E. A. Ruff. On Jan. 20, 1858 John Ruff recd. from est. $194.91. Inv. made Dec. 4, 1848 by Tiry Jay, Hiram Jay, John Ruff.

ROBERTSON, ANDREW JACKSON—BOX 120, PACK 3549:
Will dated Oct. 9, 1846 in Abbeville Dist. Prov. June 23, 1847. Exr. Wm. Robertson. Wis: Jno. R. McCord, Nimrod Richey, W. P. Martin. Mother, Nancy Robertson. Sis., Louisa Pratt. Bro., A. Robertson decd. "Give to Eliz. C. Klough dtr. of Emily Klough decd." Inv. made Aug. 4, 1847 by Wm. Moseley, Benj. Smith, Ezekiel Rasor.

ROBINSON, WILLIAM H. (MINORS)—BOX 120, PACK 3550:
On Feb. 25, 1847 Archd., Isaac Kennedy, Richard A. Martin bound unto David Lesly Ord. Abbeville Dist. sum $1,234.00. Archd. Kennedy made gdn. of Eliz. Jane, Wm. C., Alexr. T. Robinson minors under 14 yrs. Jane Davis the mother of said minors. On May 3, 1858 Tiry Jay, A. J. Weed, G. A. Davis bound to Wm. Hill Ord. Abbeville Dist. sum $1,137.42. Tiry Jay made gdn. of Thos. A. Robinson a minor. Wm. Robinson was also a minor. On Feb. 25, 1847 the petition of Archd. Kennedy sheweth that Wm. H. Robinson died in 1845, left a widow Jane M. Robinson and 3 infant chn., Eliza. Jane, Wm. C., Alexr. T. the first of whom is about 10 yrs. old. Thos. A. was of age when sett. was made in April 6, 1866. _ _

RASOR, JOHN—BOX 120, PACK 3551:
Est. admnr. Nov. 17, 1846 by Sarah Rasor, Isaac C. Ritchey, Abner H. McGehee, Robt. C. Ritchey bound unto David Lesly Ord. Abbeville Dist. sum $20,000.00. On Oct. 26, 1846 the petition of Isaac Ritchey sheweth the John Rasor died intestate while traveling in Fla. Mary Ann Donald was a dtr. Sett. made Feb. 13, 1848. Present, wid., Isaac Ritchey admnrs., E. Rasor gdn. of Sarah T,. Pamela C. Rasor minors, John Donald gdn. of Geo. Rasor. Absent: R. F. Wyatt and wife Nancy Ophelia.

PACKS MISNUMBERED FROM 3551 TO 3569:

SHOEMAKER, LANDY G.—BOX 121, PACK 3569:
Est. admnr. Sept. 17, 1849 by Lemuel O., Polly M. Shoemaker, G. Zimmerman bound unto David Lesly Ord. Abbeville, Dist. sum $1,000.00. Landy G. Shoemaker was a bro. to L. Shoemaker.

STEIFLE, MARY—BOX 121, PACK 3570:
Will dated July 30, 1847 in Abbeville Dist. Prov. Dec. 24, 1847. Exr. Bro., Andrew Mantz. Wit: Andrew W. Shillito, Wm. Reynolds, Bookter Hammond. Chn: Phillip H., Wm. A., Geo. F. Steifle. Gr. chn: Mary A. *Truslett.*

STEIFLE, WILLIAM M.—BOX 121, PACK 3571:
On Sept. 18, 1848 the petition of G. F. Steifle sheweth that you being the Exr. of my mother Mary Steifle decd. by law as a derelict est. and my bro. Wm. M. Steifle having recently died also. As one of the heirs, I petition that you become the admnr. of his est. To David Lesly. In one place the name G. F. looked G. T. Steifle. Not positive. On Oct. 28, 1851 Elizabeth Mantz recd $40.00 from said est.

STEPHENS, SARAH JANE—BOX 121, PACK 3572:
On Nov. 24, 1846 Robt. M. Davis, Wm. C. Cozby, A. A. Bowie bound to David Lesly Ord. Abbeville Dist. sum $1,280.00. Robt. David made gdn. of Sarah Jane Stephens a minor. On Sept. 10, 1859 Sarah Jane Stephens and her husband Daniel E. Carlile recd. $1,038.64 Robt. M. Davis sheweth that he was the admnr. of John Stephens decd. and that he left a wid. Mary and 1 child Sarah Jane Stephens who is about 7 yrs. of age.

SUMNER, BENJAMIN, SR.—BOX 121, PACK 3573:
Est. admnr. Nov. 2, 1848 by Wm. Campbell, Hugh Prince, James F. Bell bound unto David Lesly Ord. Abbeville Dist. sum $2,000.00. Wm. Campbell on Oct. 30, 1848 sheweth that Benj Sumner died intestate leaving chn. all of whom are married or have left. Sett., Jan. 12, 1850 ment. James Young married Zelpha and J. W. Hodge married Eliz. (Probably chn.) In the return of the est. ment. that John W. Harkness married Eliz. (which is correct I do not know.) Probably Ord. fault. On Jan. 28, 1850 Alexr. Moore recd. his share of $177.00.

SHIRLEY, NATHANIEL—BOX 121, PACK 3574:
Est. admnr. Sept. 28, 1849 by Nancy, Richard, John Shirley, John R. Wilson, Wm., John B. Armstrong bound unto David Lesly Ord. Abbeville Dist.

sum $12,000.00. On Sept. 14, 1849 Richard Shirley sheweth that Nathaniel Shirley died intestate leaving a wid. and eleven chn., 4 of whom are minors. Sett. made Feb. 26, 1851. Present Nancy Shirley, wid., Richd. and John Shirley admnr. and distributees, Wm., James, Geo. Shirley. Absent, Benj. Shirley, Reuben Branyon who married Luvenia a dtr., Polly Ann a minor, Lety M. Shirley a minor, Nancy J. Shirley a minor, A. N. Shirley.

STEWART, BENTON, W—BOX 121, PACK 3575:
    Will dated Dec. 15, 1846 in Abbeville Dist. Prov. Dec. 6, 1847. Exr. Bro, Sheperd G. Stewart. Wit: W. H. Ritchie, W. S. Robertson, T. L. Johnson. "Leave everything to my bro. Sheperd G. Stewart as I am about to leave the United States for the Mexican War." Wm. Russell on Nov. 18, 1848 sheweth that by marriage to Louanna Russell he is a distributee by said marriage. Other heirs were: Chas., James G., Mark. T., Redman Stewart.

SEIGLER, DANIEL M.—BOX 121, PACK 3576:
    Est. admnr. Jan. 26, 1847 by Archibald, Isaac Kennedy, John Free bound unto David Lesly Ord. Abbeville Dist. sum $1,000.00. D. M. Seigler was a b. l. to John E. Wilson. Daniel M. Seigler died in Miss. County of Itawamba. Sarah J. Seigler the wid. married Wm. Gillespie. James N. Yarbrough married Mary Ann half sis. of said decd. Present at the Sett. June 23, 1856 was Miss Martha Caroline Free and the admnr. who married Nancy Jane Free viz. John Free. Martha Caroline Free married Bird Bluford. Eunice H. Seigler, leg. Will dated Oct. 2, 1846. Wit: John B. Sparks, Harry M. Johnson, James R. McMullan. Was of Itawamba Co., Miss. Wife, Sarah Jane Seigler. "Bequeath to my mother Nancy Free and Eunice H. Seigler of Abbeville Dist." Halfsisters, Mary Ann Yarbrough, Nancy Jane, Martha Caroline Free of Abbeville Dist.

STARKEY, ISAIAH—BOX 121, PACK 3577:
    Est. admnr. Aug. 9, 1848 by Elizabeth Starkey wid., J. Foster Marshall, W. A. Wardlaw unto David Lesly Ord. Abbeville Dist. sum $50.00. Late a soldier in the Mexican War. On Aug. 2, 1849 N. J. Davis, Hugh Armstrong, Wm. McWhorter bound unto David Lesly Ord. Abbeville Dist. sum $100.00. N. J. Davis made gdn. of Caroline, Lidia Starkey minors. One paper stated that the oldest child Polly was about 19, Caroline about 17, Lidia about 15.

SMITH, (MINORS)—BOX 121, PACK 3578:
    On Sept. 12, 1848 Hazle Smith, Thos. J. Pinson, J. W. H. Johnson, W. B. Meriwether bound unto David Lesly Ord. Abbeville Dist. sum $1,444.00. Hazel Smith made gdn. of his 2 chn. Elizabeth F., Marshall R. Smith minors under 14 yrs. Sett. made Feb. 14, 1861. Their father now dead. The 2 chn. recd. a distributee share in right of their mother of the est. of Mrs. Francs Long decd.

STERLING, EPHRAIM—BOX 121, PACK 3579:
    Est. admnr. Sept. 2, 1848 by James Sterling, Z. W. Carwile, J. Foster Marshall bound unto David Lesly Ord. Abbeville Dist. sum $50.00. James Sterling sheweth that his bro. Ephraim Sterling died intestate without wife or chn. or father or mother living at the time of his death, that he died in the late Mexican War as a soldier in the Palmetto Regiment Co. E., under Capt. J. F. Marshall.

STRAWTHER, REUBEN—BOX 121, PACK 3580:
Est. admnr. Aug. 1, 1849 by Enoch, H. H. Nelson, John Agner bound unto David Lesly Ord. Abbeville Dist. sum $200.00. (He was a free man of color.)

STEVENSON, CAPT. JOHN—BOX 121, PACK 3581:
Est. admnr. Feb. 6, 1850 by Wm. J. Stevenson, Alexr. G., Wm. Hagen, Wm. Gordon bound unto David Lesly Ord. Abbeville Dist. sum $4,000.00. He died Jan. 20, 1850 leaving a wid. and 6 chn. Sett: Feb. 13, 1851. Present: the admnrs. Wm. J. Stephenson, Alexr. G. Hagen who married Rebecca Ann Stevenson the wid.. J. F. Simpson married Eliza. T. Stevenson who is now dead leaving 2 chn., J. H., J. J. Simpson. Margaret S., Mary Jane, Isabella A. Stevenson a minor. James Hunter, John J. Simpson were the chn. of Eliz. T. Simpson.

STILL, RICHMOND—BOX 121, PACK 3582:
Est. admnr. Nov. 28, 1849 by James F. Watson, Joseph, Hugh W. Wardlaw bound unto David Lesly Ord. Abbeville sum $10,000.00. Sett. April 6, 1852. Present, Jas. H. Wideman, Exr. of Jas. F. Watson admnr. of the est., *Lauronole* Still wid., Saml.A. Wilson and Virginia his wife, Saml. McQuerns who married Eugenia. Richmond Still died Nov. 1849.

SMITH, WILLIAM C.—BOX 121, PACK 3583:
Est. admnr. Nov. 4, 1847 by F. G. Thomas, H. A. Jones, Isaac Branch bound to David Lesly Ord. Abbeville Dist. sum $500.00. Inv. made Dec. 22, 1847 by David W. McCants, Elihu Watson, Gabriel Hodges.

SMITH, LUCY—BOX 121, PACK 3584:
Will dated Feb. 20, 1845 in Abbeville Dist. Prov. July 12, 1847. Exrs: Sons, Joel, Chas. Smith. Wit: Thos. C. Perrin, John A. Wier, B. P. Hughes. Gr. dtr. Lucretia Caroline Teague. Chn: Thos., John, Robt., Joel, Wm., Lewis, Chas. Smith, Milly wife of Geo. Anderson, Lucy wife of John White. "Bequeath $500.00. to the Edgefield Baptist Association." Lucy Smith died about July 3, 1847.

SMITH, ROBERT—BOX 121, PACK 3585:
Will dated Sept. 15, 1846. Prov. Nov. 24, 1846. Exrs: Sons. Wm:, Robt. Jefferson Smith. Wit: Dabney Wanslow, John Wansley, A. Hunter. Wife, Easter Smith. Chn: Robt. J., Wm. J., Jas. J., Margaret Smith. Gr. chn: Sarah Hogg, John James Oliver. Inv. made Dec. 5, 1846 by Bannister Allen, Dabney Wanslow, Jonathan Johnston, John Allen, James Bozeman.

SMITH, BENJAMIN—BOX 121, PACK 3586:
Est. admnr. Oct. 16, 1848 by David, David M., John Smith bound unto David Lesly Ord. Abbeville Dist. sum $8,000.00. On Oct. 14, 1848 Unity Smith relinquished her right of admnr. David Smith sheweth that his bro. Benj. Smith died intestate leaving a wid. and several chn. Sett: Jan 14, 1851. Present, David Smith admnr., Mrs. Unity Smith wid., John W. Smith, David L. Rotten who married Nancy Smith a dtr., Benj. F. Smith. Absent, David, Silas H., Sarah Ann. W. J. Smith, minors, On Jan. 14, 1851 J. Wesley Smith recd. $473.38.

SHARP, ZIMRIE—BOX 121, PACK 3587:
On May 3, 1847 Bennett Sharp, John Cowan, D. O. Hawthorn bound to David Lesly Ord. Abbeville Dist. sum $400.00. Bennett Sharp made gdn. of Zimri Sharp a minor a Gr. Son of Henry Sharp over 14 yrs. Sett. Feb. 3, 1849 ment. that the gdn. of Bennett Sharp was about to remove beyond the limits of this state and that Zimri Sharp was about 20 yrs. old.

TOWNES, DR. H. H.—BOX 121, PACK 3588:
Est. admnr. July 1, 1849 by Dr. Wm. Tennant, Genrl. J. P. Graves, Wm. T. Drennan, Benj. McKittrick bound unto David Lesly Ord. Abbeville Dist. sum $20,000.00. Sett: April 3, 1851. Present, Wm. Tennant, Genl. James P. Graves admnr. the latter a distributee in right of his wife Catharine F., H. A. Jones atty. for Mrs. Lucretia A. Townes wid.

TOLBERT, MARY—BOX 121, PACK 3589:
Will dated Feb. 19, 1842 in Abbeville Dist. Prov. Aug. 13, 1847. Exr., S. l., Andrew Riley. Wit: Owen Selby, Thos. Jr., Thos. Riley Sr. Wid. of Dan Tolbert. Chn: Rachel Tolbert, Elendar Martin. Receipt Aug. 13, 1847. As legatees of Mary Tolbert decd. we consent that Wm. Tolbert admnr. with the will annexed as Andrew Riley has declined to do so. Signed, Andw. Riley, Jas. Tolbert, Vachel Hughey, James P. Martin. Expend: Jan. 3, 1860. Paid Mary Riley toward the support of Rachel Tolbert (idiot) $63.75.

TOLBERT, WILLIAM—BOX 121, PACK 3590:
Will dated Nov. 30, 1848 in Abbeville Dist. Porv. Jan. 3, 1849. Exrs: Son, Jas. Franklin Tolbert, S. l., Thos. Riley. Wit: Vachel Hughey, F. B. Logan, James Tolbert. Wife, Isabella Marshall Tolbert. Chn: Jas. Franklin Tolbert, Mary Ann Riley, Daniel Marshall, Rebecca Jane, Isabell Elizabeth, Martha Eliza., Frances Elvira, Amanda Fletcher, John Wesley Tolbert. Inv. made Feb. 10, 1849 by Vachal Hughey, Henry Riley, S. G. Stewart, Henry Boozer.

TURNER, MARTHA—BOX 121, PACK 3591:
Est. admnr. Sept. 17, 1849 by Nathl. Jeffries, Chas. T. Haskell, H. A. Jones bound unto David Lesly Ord. Abbeville Dist. sum $4,000.00. Nathl. Jeffries was a B. l. to said decd. Sett: Dec. 7, 1850. Present, Nathl. Jeffries admnr., Geo. Paul in right of wife Mary, Saml. S. Hinton represented by Andrew Mantz by power of atty., A. Douglass in right of wife Rebecca, Thos. Hinton the father of said decd., Willis Smith in right of wife Sarah, Emry Vann in right of wife Frances, Jeremiah Hinton, John Hinton, J. J. Hamilton in right of wife Eliza. sis. of decd. Nancy A. Hinton a minor. Power of Atty. State of Fla. Madison Co. Whereas Martha Turner the sis. of said Saml. S. Hinton late of Abbeville Dist. S. C. died intestate leaving property, and Nathl. Jeffries admnr. on est. Now know ye that I the said Saml. Hinton do appoint Andrew Mantz of Abbe. Dist. my atty. to receive my part of said est. Dated this Nov. 25, 1850.

TRUCHLET, MARY AUGUSTA—BOX 121, PACK 3592:
On June 10, 1848 Joseph A. Truchelet, Andrew Mantz, the former of Augusta, Ga bound unto David Lesly Ord. Abbeville Dist. sum $700.00. Joseph

A. Truchlet made gdn. of Mary Augusta Truchelet a minor. Joseph A. Trchelet sheweth that he married Mary H. Steifle dtr. of Mary Steifle decd. and have by the said wife Mary H., a dtr. Mary Augusta Truchelet now about 8 yrs. old and that his said wife has departed this life. That your petr. the father resides in the city of Augusta, Ga.

THOMSON, NANCY—BOX 121, PACK 3593:
Expend: Feb. 20, 1852 Paid Jas. Graham for support of said Nancy Thomson $102.80. Enoch Barmore her trustee. April 1, 1848. Recd. Exrs. of Robt. Moore decd. $591.76.

UPSON, (MINORS)—BOX 122, PACK 3594:
On Jan. 7, 1850 Robt. Drennan bound unto David Lesly Ord. sum $1,000.00. Made gdn. of John D., Eliza. R. Upton minors. On Jan. 9, 1850 Robt. Drennan sheweth that some 4 yrs. ago he paid to one Markus Upson some $450 as the shares of John D., Eliza. R. Upson minors under 14 yrs. That the said Markus Upson was appointed gdn. in Edgefield Dist., and that now the said Markus Upson has left the state. Expend: Jan. 6, 1855 Cash paid John D. Upson on his going to Miss. $75.00. John D. was of age in 1858. On Sept. 1, 1852 Mary Devlin recd. of Robt. Drennan gdn. of Rachel Jane Upson a minor $296.75.

WILSON, TANDY W.—BOX 122, PACK 3595:
Est. admnr. Nov. 3, 1848 by Robt. Wilson, D. Washington Hawthorne, W. Leslie Harris bound unto David Lesly Ord. Abbeville Dist. sum $50.0. Robt. Wilson sheweth that his son was killed in the late Mexican War.

WILSON, ALEXANDER—BOX 122, PACK 3596:
Est. admnr. June 12, 1847 by Jno. G. Wilson, Augustus Lomax, Robt. A. Fair bound unto David Lesly Ord. Abbeville Dist. sum $2,000.00. Alexr. Wilson was the father of John G. Wilson. Legatees ment. in sett. Jan. 12, 1849: John G., Robt. A. Wilson, W. Kennedy, Thos., Joseph Lesly, and the chn. of Andrews, B. A., Mary Andrews.

WILSON, HENRY R.—BOX 122, PACK 3597:
Est. admnr. Dec. 7, 1846 by John R. Wilson, Saml. Reid, James Fair bound unto David Lesly Ord. Abbeville Dist. sum $3,000.00. Sarah D. Wilson the wid. John R. Wilson was a bro. to Henry R. Wilson.

WHITE, JOHN—BOX 122, PACK 3598:
Est. admnr. Jan. 17, 1848 by Bartw., Jonathan Jordan, Lewis Smith bound unto David Lesly Ord. Abbeville Dist. sum $400.00. Legatees: Eliz. White, Jas. Thomson, W. Baskin, Lemuel Reid, J. N., W. R. White.

WILSON, CHARLES—BOX 122, PACK 3599:
Est. admnr. Jan. 26, 1848 by Adison F. Posey, Thos. B. Dendy, Edward Noble bound unto David Lesly Ord. Abbeville Dist. sum $200.00. Chas. Wilson left no wife or chn., but a father and a mother.

WILSON, GRIZZELLA—BOX 122, PACK 3600:
Will dated Oct. 29, 1847 in Abbeville Dist. Prov. Nov. 17, 1847. Exr.

Son, Lewis J. Wilson. Wit: Jas. A. McCord, Jas. M. Carson, Jas. Carson. Chn: Elijah N. Wilson, Nancy C. Richey, Edward B., Jane E., Lewis J., Eliza. Ann Wilson.

WILSON, MATHEW H.—BOX 122, PACK 3601:
Est. admnr. April 25, 1849 by John H. Wilson, Saml., Lemuel Reid bound to David Lesly Ord. Abbeville Dist. sum $2,000.00. He died without wife or chn. Dec. 13, 1847.

WILSON, EDWARD B.—BOX 122, PACK 3602:
Est. admnr. Jan. 26, 1848 by Lewis J., Jane A., Eliz. Ann Wilson bound unto David Lesly Ord. Abbeville Dist. sum $100.00. Lewis J. Wilson a bro. to Edward B. Wilson. Left no wife or chn.

WIER, JOHN—BOX 122, PACK 3603:
Will dated Feb. 13, 1849 in Abbeville Dist. Prov. Feb. 24, 1849. Exrs: Son, John Alexr. Wier, Thos. C. Perrin. Wit: Saml. A. Wilson, Joseph Aiken, Joseph Lyon. Chn: John Alexr., Margaret Isabella Wier. Gr. chn: Wm. Wier Martin, Reallura Martin chn. of my decd. dtr. Ann. Sett. made Mar. 27, 1850. Ment. that John Weir died about the 17th. Feb., 1849.

WIDEMAN, SAMUEL, JR.—BOX 122, PACK 3604:
Est. admnr. Dec. 7, 1849 by Margaret Wideman wid., W. W. Belcher, J. C. Willard, Saml. Cowan, A. P. Conner bound unto David Lesly Ord. sum $35,000.00. Mr. Lesly Nov. 2, 1849. I wish you to appoint Wm. W. Belcher admnr. of my husband est. who died on Sunday last. Signed, Margaret Wideman. Sett. made Jan. 30, 1851. M. O. McCaslan was the gdn. of Jas. A. Pennal and Wm. H. Pennal infant chn. of Emily H. Pennel a dtr. of Saml. Wideman. Frances E. Zimmerman was a dtr. Distrib: Margaret Wideman wid., chn. of E. H. Pennal, Frances E. Zimmerman, Mary S., Wm. H., Jas. A. Wideman. Frances Zimmerman was the wife of Philip Zimmerman decd.   (Letter)

Nov. 19, 1849
Mr. Lesly
Sir:
          I hear that Mr. John Wideman intends objecting to your granting the letters of admnr. today asked by me to Major Belcher. I beg of you for the sake of my interest and my chn. interest not to entertain any objection he may offer for they are groundless He has grossly insulted me in my own house because I would not yeild to his selfish and mercenary motives which I could not doe for I have no confidence in him and I there fore will not consent for him to have any thing to doe with my business. I pray you to grant the letters as requested. I remain under subdued feeling of affliction.
                                        Margaret Wideman

WIDEMAN, LEONARD—BOX 122, PACK 3605:
Est. admnr. Jan. 3, 1848 by Jas. H., Sarah. Wid., John Wideman. Geo. W. Pressly, Adam, Saml. Wideman. Geo. Sibert, Ricd. A. Martin, Dr. John W. Hearst bound unto David Lesly Ord. Abbeville Dist. sum $80,000.00. Dr. Jas. H.

Wideman sheweth that his father Leonard Wideman left a wid. and chn. of whom I am the only son. Sett. made Mar. 29, 1849. Jas. H. Wideman was gdn. of Mary S., Martha A., Sarah J. Wideman, Thos. J. Lyon married Margaret, Anthony Harmon married Catharine. Mary married P. A. Waller.

WATSON, EDWARD—BOX 122, PACK 3606:
Will date Dec. 12, 1846 in Abbeville Dist. Prov. Dec. 7, 1847. Exrs: Henry H. Creswell, Stanmore Brooks, John P. Barratt. Wit: Wm. G. Kennedy, John B. Johnson, Mary McKellar. Dtr. Catharine A. Watson. Sett. made Jan. 5, 1858 ment. that Edward Watson died in the City of Mexico, a soldier in the Mexican War in the fall of the yr. 1847.

WILLIAMS, LYDALL—BOX 122, PACK 3607:
Est. admnr. July 26, 1848 by John C. Williams, Robt. Ellis, Jas. Cowan bound unto David Lesly Ord. Abbeville Dist. sum $10,000.00. Left a wid and 2 chn. Sale, 1848. Byrs: Saml. Smith, Geo. Nickles, A. J.McKee, Andrew Stevenson, Edward Hagen, Wm. Sharp, David Hannah, Jasper N. Hawthorne, Zachariah Haddon, Hno. Donald, Sr., Thos. Cunningham, John Hagen, J. B. Chandler, Jas. Cowan, Wm. Agnew, D. O. Hawthorne, John Hagen.

WITT, (MINORS)—BOX 122, PACK 3608:
On Dec. 20, 1848 B. F. Witt, Barthw. Jordon, David Teddards bound unto David Lesly Ord. Abbeville Dist. sum $600.00. B. F. Witt made gdn. of David Jefferson, Elizabeth Witt minors. Joseph Irwin sheweth that he married Parthena Witt the wid. of Stephen Witts decd. that there are 2 minors David Jefferson Witts is 14 yrs. Pamela Elizabeth Witts is under 14 yrs. Stephen Witt was the father of Benjamin F. Witt ment. in bond. On Dec. 29, 1854 Benjamin Franklin Witt who is now dead.

YOUNG, SAMUEL—BOX 122, PACK 3609:
Will dated Aug. 31, 1846 in Abbeville Dist. Prov. Nov. 2, 1846. Exr. Dr. Geo. W. Pressly. Wit: Wm. K. Bradley, Andrew J. Wier, Richard A. Martin. Sis., Jane B., Margaret Young. "Bequeath my rifle gun to John H. Young."

YOUNG, JOHN—BOX 122, PACK 3610:
Est. admnr. Dec. 11, 1848 by Jno. W. Hearst, Jas. H. Wideman, Saml. Perrin bound unto David Lesly Ord. Abbeville Dist. sum $1,000.00. Sett. made Feb. 4, 1850 ment. Mary, Geo., John H., Abner Young.

ABNEY, ABSOLOM—BOX 122, PACK 3611:
On Oct. 7, 1850 Jas. Drennan, A. P. Connor, W. R. Bradley bound unto F. W. Selleck Ord. Abbeville Dist. sum $100.00. Jas. Drennan gdn. of Absolom Abney a minor. Mary Abner his mother.

AGNEW, MALINDA—BOX 123, PACK 3612:
Est. admnr. Nov. 1, 1851 by Ebenezer E. Pressly, Alfred Agnew, H. A. Jones bound unto F. W. Selleck Ord. Abbeville Dist. sum $30,000.00. Sett. made Feb. 26, 1853. Present, Revd. E. E. Pressly, H. A. Jones, Jas. W. Agnew. Absent dist: Alfred, Dr. Enoch, Saml. W., Wm., Dr. Washington, Malinda Jane, Joseph Agnew. The admnr. married Elizabeth a dtr.

ANDERSON, (MINORS)—BOX 123, PACK 3613:
On Nov. 29, 1850 John Anderson, Henry Riley, Levi H. *Rykard* bound to F. W. Selleck Ord. Abbeville Dist. sum $800.00. John Anderson made gdn. of Wm., Mary, John, Jas., Andrew, Nathl., Margaret, Edmond Anderson chn. of John Anderson. Were the gr. chn. of Edmon Cobb decd. J. L. Smith married Margaret Anderson. Power of atty. State of Fla., Columbia Co. Edmund, Wm. Anderson of said state appointed John H. Tolbert of same place their atty. to receive their part due them from their father John Anderson of Abbeville Dist.

ALSTON, JAMES—BOX 123, PACK 3614:
Will dated Dec. 13, 1850 in Abbeville Dist. Filed Feb. 7, 1851. Exrs: Wife, Catharine Alston, John McIlwain. Wit: Andrew McIlwain, D. M. Ross, J. R. Cunningham. Nephew, Philip Alston son of my bro. Wm. Alston of Columbus, Gr. Dtr., Jane Charity Caball.

ANDERSON, JANE M.—BOX 123, PACK 3615:
Est. admnr. Oct. 21, 1851 by Thos. Chatham, Richard M. White, J. R. Tarrant bound to F. W. Selleck Ord. Abbeville Dist. sum $6,000.00. Was a minor. Left a mother Mary E. now the wife of Thos. Chatham and no bros. or sis. of the whole blood living.

BOWIE, HEZEKIAH—BOX 123, PACK 3616:
Est. admnr. Nov. 6, 1850 by Wm. B. Bowie, Wm. Gordon, Peter Henry bound unto F. W. Selleck Ord. Abbeville Dist. sum $500.00. Sett. made Nov. 2, 1852. Present, W. B. Bowie admnr., David Ruff who married Lucinda, John F., Mary C. Bowie. Widow Lucinda Bowie.

BIGBY, REVD. GEO. M.—BOX 123, PACK 3617:
Will dated May 27, 1851 in Abbeville Dist. Filed June 21, 1851. Exrs: Sons, Geo. M., John W. Bigby, Col. Jas. Robinson. Wit: John Wilson, David Moore, Wm. M. Moseley. Wife, Mary Ann Bigby. Chn: Emily E. Robinson, Geo., Jno. W. Bigby, Mary Ann Fletcher, Wm. A., Martha C., Jas. A., Thos. S., Alcisia E. Bigby. Mary A. F. married Chas. Davis.

BLAKE, JOHN—BOX 123, PACK 3618:
Will dated Sept. 29, 1848 in Abbeville Dist. Filed May 10, 1850. Exrs: Sons, Wm. N., Calleb Blake. Wit: John Logan, John McLees, A. M. Blake. Chn: Kennedy M., Wm. N., Adam B., John M., Jas. M., Jane K. David decd. Mary Ann Kennedy, Sarah Watson, Esther E. "A tract of land in Anderson Dist."

BROWN, ANDREW J.—BOX 123, PACK 3619:
Est. admnr. Dec. 12, 1850 by W. C. Ware, F. A. Rogers, Jas. A. McKee bound unto F. W. Selleck Ord. Abbeville Dist. sum $200.00.

BELCHER, ROBERT E.—BOX 123, PACK 3620:
Will dated Mar. 15, 1847 in Abbeville Dist. Filed Nov. 12, 1850. Exrs: Williamson, Jas. A. Norwood. Bros., Wm. W., Jas. M. Belcher. Wit: J. E. Lyon. Robt. McLees, Lemuel Dowdey. Wife, Rebecca Belcher. Chn: Warren P., Wn W., Williamson H., John H., Henry Clay Belcher, Jas. N., Mary Ann Belcher.

BENTLY, HENRY—BOX 123, PACK 3621:
Will dated Mar. 27, 1851 in Abbeville Dist. Filed Apr. 1851. Exr: R. A. Martin. Wit: P. C. McCaslan, T. F. Lanier, David McClain. Wife, Mary Bently. Chn: Martha Ann, Wm. Henry Bently.

BOWICK, MILLIGAN—BOX 123, PACK 3622:
Est. admnr. Oct. 18, 1851 by Edward Cowan, Henry Cason, John T. Lyon bound unto F. W. Selleck Esq. Ord. Abbeville Dist. sum $500.00. Milligan Bowich died in May 1850 leaving no wife or chn. but a mother and bros.

BURTON, POLLY ANN—BOX 123, PACK 3623:
On Feb. 3, 1851 David Russell, Ezekiel Tribble, J. W. Black bound unto F. W. Selleck Ord. Abbeville Dist. sum $50.00. David Russell made gdn. of Polly Ann Burton a minor. Sophia Burton sheweth that her dtr. Polly Ann Burton is a minor under age and that she is entitled to an interest in a land warrant granted to her father Josiah Burton by the U. S. Government for services rendered during the Mexican War.

BIRDASHAW, JOHN—BOX 123, PACK 3624:
Est. admnr. Sept. 24, 1850 by Thos. Jefferson Lyon, Adam Wideman, R. W. Lites bound unto F. W. Selleck Ord. Abbeville Dist. sum $600.00. Thos. Jefferson Lyon sheweth that John Birdashaw late of this Dist. went recently upon a visit to Ga. and while there was accidently killed by the discharge of a gun. He died in Aug. Sett. made Oct. 20, 1852. Amount of Simpson Birdashaw's note $102.95. On Sept. 9, 1854 Fanney Birdashaw recd. $43.02 in full of the est. (Name was also written Burdeshaw.)

BOWIE, WILLIAM S. OR L.—BOX 123, PACK 3625:
Est. admnr. Oct. 14, 1851 by Robt. H., Joseph J. Wardlaw, Jas. M. Perrin bound unto F. W. Selleck Ord. Abbeville Dist. sum $8,000.00. Sett. made Oct. 22, 1847. Present admnrs. and Pickney G. Bowie as distributee being a bro. of said decd. and also as admnr. with will annexed of Geo. A. Bowie decd. another bro. Jordan E. Allen gdn. of the minor chn. of Luther A. Bowie decd. another bro. Intestate died without wife or chn., never being married. Parents dead.

COBB, RICHMOND S.—BOX 123, PACK 3626:
No bond found in package. Sett. made May 1, 1855 of Richmond S. Cobb a minor now of age. Was son of Edmund Cobb decd. Expend: Apr. 23, 1855 Paid to Elizabeth Cobb $22.50.

CAMPBELL, JOHN—BOX 123, PACK 3627:
Will dated Jan. 9, 1852 in Abbeville Dist. Filed Feb. 2, 1852. Exr. Joseph F. Bell. Wit: Jas. Young, Edmond P. Holleman, P. N. Bell. Wife, Nancy Campbell. Chn: Ment. no names given. Power of Atty. Dec. 21, 1855. Know that we, Archibald Young and Mary Young his lawful wife formerly Mary Campbell of the Co. of Gwinnett, State of Ga. do appoint Thos. D. Young of same place our Atty. to receive from the est. of John Campbell of Abbeville Dist. our share, Mary being a legatee of said est. Sett. made Oct. 25, 1865 ment that Jas. P. Campbell was a legatee. John L. and Thos. P. Campbell were legatees. Mary

Young wife of Archibald Young, Wm. Campbell, Zelpha McMahan wife of A. McMahan. Ann, Jesse Campbell, Fergus Jaran Campbell.

CALLIHAM, CHARLES T.—BOX 123, PACK 3628:
Est. admnr. Apr. 15, 1850 by Alexr. Scott, Jas. W. Prather, Wm. T. Drennan bound unto F. W. Selleck Ord. Abbeville Dist. sum $400.00.

CALDWELL, CAPT. JAS. B.—BOX 123, PACK 3629:
Est. admnr. Jan. 22, 1851 by Geo. R. Caldwell, Wm. B., Stanmore B. Brooks bound unto F. W. Selleck Ord. Abbeville Dist. sum $2,000.00. Geo. R. Caldwell was a bro. to Jas. B. Caldwell. On Jan. 31, 1853 J. T. Webber, Edna Caldwell, Stanmore B. Brooks stated that they were satisfied with the Sett.

COLE, JAMES—BOX 123, PACK 3630:
Sett. made Dec. 6, 1852 of est. of Jas. Cole a minor, by consent, he being of age now, in the Court of Ord. for the satisfaction of A. P. Connor the Exr. of Jas. Connor who was the gdn. of said Jas. Cole. (No other papers.)

CALDWELL, WM. H., JR.—BOX 123, PACK 3631:
Est. admnr. Sept. 10, 1850 by Nathaniel J. Davis, Thos. E. Owens, John A. Hamilton bound unto F. W. Selleck Ord. Abbeville Dist. sum $10,000.00. Recd. Oct. 10, 1853 from Nathaniel Davis admnr. of est. Wm. H. Caldwell decd. $486.71 of my distributive share of my decd. bro. Wm. H. Caldwell. Signed, Saml. Y. Caldwell admnr. of the est. of John Caldwell decd. of Panola Co., Miss.

CALDWELL, JANE Y.—BOX 123, PACK 3632:
Est. admnr. Sept. 1, 1850 by Nathaniel J. Davis, Thos. E. Owens, John A. Hamilton bound unto F. W. Selleck Ord. Abbeville Dist. sum $16,000.00. She died Apr. 1850. Sett. made June 1, 1852. Distributees: John J. Caldwell, the chn. of Mary Ann Harris decd. the wife of Revd. W. H. Harris, Saml. Y. Caldwell, D. O. Mecklin and wife Elizabeth, Thos. F., Agness J., Rebecca R., Sarah Caldwell. On Jan. 4, 1856 Jas. M. Thomson and wife Julia E. Thomson recd. $209.87 coming to Julia E. Thomson from the est. of Wm. H. Caldwell decd. and Jane Y. Caldwell decd. being a distributee.

CUTLER, SAMUEL—BOX 123, PACK 3633:
Est. admnr. Mar. 19, 1851 by Walter B. Meriwether, Allen Vance, Jas. W. Richardson bound unto F. W. Selleck Ord. Abbeville Dist. sum $200.00. Sale, 1857. Byrs: Agnes, Nathan Calhoun, Mrs. Cutler, Jas. Fooshe, John Sadler, etc.

CALHOUN, DOWNS—BOX 123, PACK 3634:
Will dated May 18, 1843 in Abbeville Dist. Prov. July 8, 1850. Exr: Bro., Nathan Calhoun. Wit: John Taggart, John F. Livingston, Addison F. Posey, Johnson Ramey. Wife, Susan Calhoun. Chn: Melissa, John Sample chn. of my wife Susan by a former marriage, Lavinda, Willis Boyd Calhoun, Wm. Downs Calhoun. Gr. chn: Louanie Elizabeth Beazley.

CUNNINGHAM, SARAH—BOX 123, PACK 3635:
Will dated Jan. 16, 1851 in Abbeville Dist. Prov.May 15, 1851. Exrs: Dr.

Ed. Simpson, Thos. Payne. Wit: Nathan Ingram, Joel W. Pinson, T. R. Puckett. "Bequeath to Elizabeth Owen, Rachel, Dr. Ed. Simpson." On Feb. 5, 1852 the minor chn. of Garlington Owens were, Martha Frances, Sarah Catharine Owens.

CLIFTON, JAMES W.—BOX 123, PACK 3636:
    Est. admnr. Sept. 21, 1850 by J. Bailey, Jas. W. Fooshe, David Waid Anderson bound unto F. W. Selleck Ord. Abbeville Dist. sum $400.00.

CALHOUN, FRANCES—BOX 123, PACK 3637:
    Est. admnr. Mar. 19, 1851 by Dr. Ephraim R. Calhoun, Chas. R. Moseley, John Logan bound unto F. W. Selleck Ord. Abbeville Dist. sum $1,600.00. Mother of Ephraim R. Calhoun.

CHEATHAM, JOHN L.—BOX 123, PACK 3638:
    Est. admnr. June 14, 1851 by R. G. Golding, Alfred Cheatham, Washington Fooshe bound unto F. W. Selleck Ord. Abbeville Dist. sum $1,800.00.

COOK, SARAH ELIZABETH—BOX 123, PACK 3639:
    Est. admnr. Nov. 7, 1851 by John H., Jeremiah Cook, David W. Devore bound unto F. W. Selleck Ord. Abbeville Dist. sum $3,000.00. Was the wife of John H. Cook. On Sept. 6, 1854 Thos. J. Permenter of Lean Co., Tex. appointed Thos. Rotten now in the state of S. C. his Atty. to receive his part of said est. On Nov. 20, 1853 Edward C. Permenter of Green Co., Ala. recd. a share. On Nov. 26, 1853 Wm. Carter was trustee for L. G. Carter as a distributee. On Mar. 27, 1854 Jas. Permenter of Macon Co., Ga. appointed Thos. Rotten of S. C. his Atty. for said est. Louicy Rotten appointed her son Wm. Rotten to receive her share.

CONNOR, ANDREW J.—BOX 123, PACK 3640:
    On June 13, 1850 Jas. O., A. P. Connor, Jas. Hanvey bound unto F. W. Selleck Ord. Abbeville Dist. sum $1,200.00. Jas. O. Connor made gdn. of Andrew J. Connor a minor of Jas. Connor decd. and a bro. to said Jas. O. Connor.

DEVLIN, JOHN—BOX 124, PACK 3641:
    Will dated July 1, 1850 in Abbeville Dist. Filed Sept. 18, 1850. Exrs: Sons, Robt., Jas. Devlin. Wit: Barthw. Jordon, Leroy Purdy, A. Kennedy. Wife ment. no name given. Chn: Robt., Jas., Peggy Ann, Betsey, Martha, Mary Devlin. Gr. chn: Mary Bradley, John E. Pressly. "Give unto Erskine Seminary $50.00. Give as much as necessary to put a gravestone to my first wife's tomb." Sett. made Apr. 1, 1852. Present, Robt., Jas. J. Devlin Exrs., Mary Devlin the wid., Robt. Drennan who married Mary Devlin, Mrs. Martha McGaw a dtr., Elizabeth Drennan wife of Wm. Drennan, Jas. Drennan who married Peggy Ann Devlin. Expend: Recd. Apr. 1, 1852 of Dr. Robt. Devlin Exr. of John Devlin Esq. decd. $50.00 the full amount of legacy left to Erskine College. Robt. C. Grier.

DEAN, STERLING—BOX 124, PACK 3642:
    Est. admnr. Oct. 29, 1850 by A. L. Gray, J. W., A. R. Ramey bound unto F. W. Selleck Ord. Abbeville Dist. sum $400.00. Died in Sept. last. Inv. made Dec. 12, 1850 by Wm., Thos. McDill, John Douglass.

DONALD, ALEXANDER—BOX 124, PACK 3643:
Est. admnr. Dec. 2, 1850 by Bartholomew, Jonathan Jordan, A. L. Gray bound unto F. W. Selleck Ord. Abbeville Dist. sum $1,200.00. Sale, Dec. 4, 1850. Byrs: Martha Donald, Jas. McQuarnes, Luis Smith, J. J. Jordon, etc.

DOYEL, WALTER—BOX 124, PACK 3644:
Est. admnr. Sept. 27, 1850 by R. B. Doyel, Geo. Nickles, Andrew C. Hawthorn bound unto F. W. Selleck Ord. Abbeville Dist. sum $500.00. R. B. Doyle on Sept. 5, 1850 sheweth that Walter Doyle died in the month of Mar. many yrs. ago. Sett. made Feb. 6, 1852. Present, R. B. Doyle admnr., Ann, Catharine, Mary F., R. B., R. P. Doyle, Rhoda Bowie, Eli B. Gibbins distributees. (Name written Doyle also.)

DAVIS, NANCY—BOX 124, PACK 3645:
Est. admnr. Feb. 15, 1851 by Jas. H. Foster, Isaac Kennedy, Jas. Lesly bound unto F. W. Selleck Ord. Abbeville Dist. sum $1,000.00. Jas. H. Foster on Jan. 8, 1851 stated that Nancy Davis died several yrs. ago.

DICKSON, (MINORS)—BOX 124, PACK 3646:
Sett. of est. of Saml. J. Dickson now of age made Jan. 18, 1859. John S. Dickson had a legacy coming to him from the est. of his gr. mother Jane Young decd. Expend: Jan. 1, 1841 Left in John Baskin's hand as Exr. of Nancy Young decd. the following amts. of the minor chn. of John Dickson decd. Andrew W. Dickson $111.25. Julia Ann Dickson $111.25. Jane Y. Dickson $111.25. Saml. J. Dickson $111.25.

DENDY, DR. THOS. B.—BOX 124, PACK 3647:
Will dated June 28, 1851 in Abbeville Dist. Filed Aug. 6, 1852. Exrs: Wife, Mary Jane Dendy, John McClellan, Chas. Dendy. Wit: John McBryde, John H. Chiles, John T. Lyon. Chn: Ellen, Jas. N., Thos. McClellan Dendy.

DIXON, (MINORS)—BOX 124, PACK 3648:
On Dec. 19, 1851 Jas. Martin, Leroy J. Johnson, Wm. Pennall bound unto F. W. Selleck Ord. Abbeville Dist. sum $1,000.00. Jas. Martin made gdn. of John Joseph, Freeman Bates Dixon, Martha M., Rost. S., Mary A. E. W. Dixon minor chn. of Jas. N. Dixon decd. and Mary Dixon. The minors had due them real est. of their father in Elbert Co., Ga.

DAVIS, (MINORS)—BOX 124, PACK 3649:
On May 12, 1851 Silas Ray, Robt. Y. Jones, Leroy Purdy bound unto F. W. Selleck Ord. Abbeville Dist. sum $2,400.00. Silas Ray made gdn. of Frances E., Martha Jane Davis minors. Frances E., Martha Jane Davis sheweth that they are entitled to one share of the est. of Silas Pace decd. by virtue of an assignment made to them by their father John Davis of his interest in the est. of Silas Pace decd. On Jan. 11, 1870 a paper stated that Frances E. was the wife of Wm. L. McCord, Martha Jane the wife of G. T. Jackson.

EAKINS, (MINORS)—BOX 124, PACK 3650:
On May 13, 1851 Thos. Eakins, Archibald M. McCord, Jas. McIlwain

bound unto F. W. Selleck Ord. Abbeville Dist. sum $1,300.00. Thos. Eakins made gdn. of Saml. T., Wm. Eakins minor chn. of Wm. Eakins decd. The gdn. Thos. Eakins was their gr. father. On Feb. 17, 1851 Margaret A. Eakins sheweth that her husband Wm. Eakins died June 4, 1849.

ELGIN, ELIZABETH—BOX 124, PACK 3651:
Est. admnr. Sept. 15, 1851 by Hezekiah Elgin, Saml. Martin, N. G., A. E. Hughes bound unto F. W. Selleck. Ord. Abbeville Dist. sum $1,200.00. Sett. made Apr. 7, 1855. Present, the admnr. and Jas. Elgin and John Mitchell a distributee in right of his mother. Legatees: Hezekiah Elgin admnr., Harrison, Jas., Abner Elgin, Chn. of Wm. Stone, Chn. of Larkin Mitchell.

EAKINS, SARAH—BOX 124, PACK 3652:
State of S. C., Co. of Abbeville. To Chas. W. Griffin Esq., Judge of Probate. Benjamin H. Eakins sheweth that your petr. and Thos. Eakins now decd. were the trustees for their sis. Sarah Eakins. That Thos. Eakins in now dead, that his sis. Sarah is an invalid and helpless and needs constant care and attention. That she is now living with your petr. Dated May 28, 1784.

FOSHEE, (MINORS)—BOX 124, PACK 3653:
On Feb. 14, 1852 Marshall E. Walker, Jas. McMillam, Tilman A. Walker bound unto F. W. Selleck Orl. Abbeville Dist. sum $200.00. Marshall E. Walker made gdn. of Mary A. E., Lydia Catharine Foshee minors. Elizabeth A. McMillan on Feb. 9, 1852 sheweth that she is the wid. of Richard Foshee decd. and the mother of said minors.

FRANKLIN, BENJAMIN, JR.—BOX 124, PACK 3654:
Est. admnr. Dec. 22, 1851 by A. A. King, Thos. Stacey, Henry Mays bound unto F. W. Selleck Ord. Abbeville Dist. sum $5,000.00. Sett. made Jan. 4, 1853. Present, Susan Franklin mother of said decd. and only distributee. Intestate had neither wife or chn., bros. or sis. of the whole blood.

GRAHAM, MARTHA S.—BOX 124, PACK 3655:
On Jan. 24, 1851 Chas. N., Wm. Sr., Albert M. Graham bound unto F. W. Selleck Ord. Abbeville Dist. sum $520.00. Chas. N. Graham appointed gdn. of said minor. Sett. made Dec. 31, 1855. Present, C. N. Graham gdn., W. H. Parkerson who married Martha Graham.

GALLAHER, JOHN—BOX 124, PACK 3656:
Est. admnr. Oct. 21, 1851 by Andrew J. Weed, A. B. Boyd, John Brown bound unto F. W. Selleck Ord. Abbeville Dist. sum $150.00. (Name also written Gallaugher.)

GRAHAM, JOHN, SR.—BOX 124, PACK 3657:
Will dated Mar. 29, 1851 in Abbeville Dist. Filed June 7, 1851. No. Exr. Wit: Wm. Jr., Wm. Graham Sr., Enoch Carter. Wife, Mary Graham. Son, Wm. Graham. Est. admnr. June 23, 1851 by Wm. C. Graham, John W. Moore, Albert M. Graham unto F. W. Selleck Ord. Abbeville Dist. sum $500.00. John Graham was the father of Wm. C. Graham. Sale, Oct. 7, 1851. Byrs: Wm. C. Graham,

Jas. Robertson, John W. Moore, Wm. Huskinson, Thos. Rosamond, Enoch Carter, Saml. Graham, Jas. Hill.

GRAHAM, WILLIAM, SR.—BOX 124, PACK 3658:
    Est. admnr. Oct. 8, 1851 by Wm., C. N., Saml., Albert M. Graham bound unto F. W. Selleck Ord. Abbeville Dist. sum $3,000.00. Sett. made May 12, 1854. Present, Wm., C. N. Graham admnrs. and Capt. J. W. Moore who represents John, Sarah Rosamond as one of the distributees of said est. The decd. Wm. Graham was admnr. of the est. of Jas. Graham and there yet remains a share of that est. due to Mary Ann Graham a minor. The decd. also admnr. on est. of Thos. Graham. 8 distributees, Jas., Wm., E. T., C. N., A. M. Graham minors of John Graham, Sarah Rosamond, Saml. Graham.

GRAHAM, THOMAS A.—BOX 124, PACK 3659:
    Est. admnr. Dec. 4, 1851 by Wm. Sr., Albert, Wm. Graham Jr. bound unto F. W. Selleck Ord. Abbeville Dist. sum $150.00. Wm. Graham on Nov. 18, 1850 sheweth that his nephew Thos. A. Graham minor died Apr. last.

GORDON, ROBERT C.—BOX 124, PACK 3660:
    Will dated Jan. 18, 1852 in Abbeville Dist. Filed Jan. 28, 1852. Exrs: Sons, Jas., Robt. Thos. Gordon. Wit: Andrew Winn, Chas. Dendy, Thos C. Perrin. Wife, Rebecca Gordon. Chn: Rosa Ann wife of Jas. McCord, Ezekiel Evans Gordon, Rebecca Eveline wife of Leroy C. Wilson, Jas., Robt. Thos., Mary Watt, Jane Elizabeth Gordon. Gr. dtr: Jane Watt Wilson. Statement for sett. Aug. 20, 1866. Jane Watt Wilson married Thos. Crymes. Elizabeth a dtr. of Robt. Gordon married Hugh Kirkwood. M. Harvey Wilson was a gr. son of said decd. The notice in the paper for Nov. 16, 1852 ment. that Jas. McCord, Ezekiel E. Gordon reside without the state.

MISNUMBERED TO 3679:

KENNEDY, ARCHIBALD—BOX 125, PACK 3679:
    Est. admnr. Oct. 22, 1850 by J. P., Isaac Kennedy, Jas. H. Foster bound unto F. W. Selleck Ord. Abbeville Dist. sum $10,000.00. On Sept. 30, 1850 J. P. Kennedy sheweth that his father Archibald Kennedy died on Sept. 16, 1850. Distributees: J. P., E. G. Kennedy.

KELLER, JOHN—BOX 125, PACK 3680:
    Will dated May 20, 1852 in Abbeville Dist. Filed May 28, 1852. Exrs: S. ls: Philip Cromer, Jas. C. Harper. Wit: A. H. Morton, J. W. W. Marshall, John W. Lomax. Wife, Elizabeth Keller. Chn: John F., Dr. D. C. Keller. Power of Atty. State of Ala., Talladega Co. Know that I David C. Keller of said state do appoint Wm. O. Cromer of Abbeville Dist., S. C. my Atty. to collect what is coming to me from the est. of my father John Keller decd. Dated this Nov. 1783. Sett. made Aug. 2, 1855. Present, Phillip Cromer, Jas. C. Harper. Exrs: Geo. W. Cromer husband of Ann a dtr. of said decd., John F. Keller a son, L. R. A. Harper and wife, Wm. A. Swift and wife, Dr. David C. Keller, J. C. Harper and Rebecca E. his wife, Philip Cromer and Dorthy Ann his wife, Wm. A. Swift and Nancy J. his wife, L. R. A. Harper and Mary C. his wife. Petition for sett:

Nancy Jane Penn, Mary C. Harper, Geo. W. Cromer, Francis E. Davis, Geo. A. Cromer, Cornelia C. Miller, Florence R. Cromer, John D. W. Cromer, Eugenia N. Young, Jas. J. Cromer a minor about 20 yrs. of age. Plantiffs against: Jas. C. Harper, Dorthy A. Cromer, David C. Keller, J. Franklin Keller, Oscar Cromer, Georgia Tate, Rosey Martin, Jennie Heard, John F. Harper, Ready Harper. Nancy Jane Penn resided at Elberton, Elbert Co., Ga. Mary C. Harper resided at Elberton, Ga. Rebecca Harper resides at Elberton, Ga. David Keller resides at Sylocauga Post Office, Talledgo Co., Ala. On May 11, 1874 ment. that Rosey Martin was about 19 yrs. Jennie Heard about 17 yrs. John F. Harper about yrs. Ready Harper about 12 yrs. of age.

LOGAN, ANDREW F.—BOX 125, PACK 3681:
        Est. admnr. May 23, 1850 by Isaac, F. B., Andrew Logan bound unto F. W. Selleck Ord. Abbeville Dist. sum $2,000.00. Inv. made June 8, 1850 by Wm., Caleb A. Blake, Bennett Reynolds. Sett. made Mar. 27, 1852. Distributees: Jane Arnold, John Lewis Logan, Francis, Jas. W., Nancy Logan.

LEITNER, GEORGE E.—BOX 125, PACK 3682:
        Est. admnr. Nov 10, 1851 by Thos. Chatham, Wm. Smith, R. M. White bound unto F. W. Selleck Ord. Abbeville Dist. sum $3,000.00. Geo. Leitner was a s. l. to Thos. Chatham. Sett. made May 13, 1853. Present, Thos. Chatham admnr. and Gilford T. Waller who married the wid. Parthena A. Leitmer. Left also a child but no name given.

LESLY, JOSEPH—BOX 125, PACK 3683:
        Will dated Apr. 23, 1850. Filed Aug. 5, 1850. Exrs: Major John Power, Alexr. McCallister, Alexr. Hunter. Wit: Thos. Hodge, Wm. Campbell, John Power. Ment: Wife, Mary Lesly. Nieces: Betsey, Mary, Ibby Lesley. "Bequeath to Joseph McCallister (son of Jas. McCallister decd.) $100.00. Bequeath to the chn. of Mrs. Margaret Moore and the chn. of Mrs. Betsey Gordon (of Ga.) wife of Alexr. Gordon, the former has 5 chn., the latter 6 chn." Est. also admnr. Feb. 18, 1852 by Alexr. Hunter, Peter Gibert, Thos. Cunningham bound unto F. W. Selleck Ord. Abbeville Dist. sum $9,000.00. Margaret Moore was a gr. dtr. Sheweth that Joseph Lesly died leaving a wid. Mary and 2 chn. of an only son Robt. who had died in his father's lifetime. Robt. the father of your petr. was an only child and left surving him 3 chn., Wm. who died married but without chn. in his gr. father's lifetime. Elizabeth the wife of Alexr. Gordon and your petr. late the wife of Nathaniel Moore and now a wid. Your petr. and said Elizabeth Gordon (Mary Lesly now being of dead) are the only heirs at law of said Joseph Lesly decd. Elizabeth Gordon's chn. were: Nancy, Mary, Nathaniel, Wm., Saml., Joseph Gordon all minors under 21 yrs. Your petr. had family, Nancy married Henry Wilbank, Wm., Louisa, Mary Jane, Margaret all minors. Mrs. Gordon and family live in Cobb Co., Ga.

LONG, WILLIAM, SR.—BOX 125, PACK 3684:
        Will dated Nov. 16, 1847. Filed Jan. 23, 1852. Exrs: Son, Wm. Long, W. P. Martin. Wit: Geo. Mattison, Jesse Gent, Wm. P. Martin. Wife, Elizabeth

Long. Chn: Elizabeth, Margaret, Reuben, Wm. Long. (Wm. Long Sr. died Jan. 18, 1852.)

LOMAX, WILLIAM—BOX 125, PACK 3685:
Est. admnr. Oct. 17, 1850 by David Atkins, David, John Kellar, Abraham Lites bound unto F. W. Selleck Ord. Abbeville Dist. sum $20,000.00. Wm. Lomax died Sept. 1850. F. l. of David Kellar, David Atkins. Sett. made Apr. 7, 1854. Present, David Kellar admnr., Barthw. Jordon who represents Jas. Yeldell. John D. Adams represents the chn. of Jas. Lomax. On Feb. 6, 1865 Lewis Pressly and Mary his wife recd. $50.52 of said est. Nov. 7, 1854 David, Elizabeth Raburn recd. $36.63 for their share. Apr. 7, 1854 Wm., Louisa A. Richardson recd. $33.53 of their share of their gr. father's est., Viz. Wm. Lomax. Apr. 23, 1855 Thos. H., Julia Pressly recd. for their share $329.75. Nov. 4, 1854 David, Sarah Atkins recd. $31.48.

LYON, MARY A. (MINOR)—BOX 125, PACK 3686:
On Feb. 11, 1851 Geo. B. Richey, John A. Weir, B. P. Hughes bound unto F. W. Selleck Ord. Abbeville Dist. sum $2,000.00. Geo. B. Richey made gdn. of Mary A. Lyon a minor. Sett. made Jan. 5, 1852 ment. that Jas. F. Donald had married Mary A. Lyon.

LOGAN, JOHN LEWIS—BOX 125, PACK 3687:
On Mar. 26, 1851 Isaac Logan, Jas. P. Martin, J. F. Tolbert bound unto F. W. Selleck Ord. Abbeville Dist. sum $600.00. Isaac Logan made gdn. of John Lewis Logan minor son of Frances Logan and a bro. to Andrew F. Logan decd.

LOGAN, ANDREW J.—BOX 125, PACK 3688:
No will date. Filed May 25, 1850 in Abbeville Dist. Exr. Fredrick W. Logan. Wit: Dr. John Logan, John McLees, J. S. Marshall. Wife, Louisa Logan. Chn. ment, names not given. Expend: June 20, 1853 Paid Isaac Logan admnr. of Francis Logan $1,134.94.

LYON, SAMUEL—BOX 125, PACK 3689:
Est. admnr. Apr. 19, 1850 by Jas. A., John T. Lyon, B. P. Hughes bound unto F. W. Selleck Ord. Abbeville Dist. sum $3,600.00. Saml. Lyon died Feb. 7, 1850. His wid. and mother each got ½. No names given.

LYON, JOSEPH—BOX 125, PACK 3690:
Will dated Feb. 26, 1850 in Abbeville Dist. Filed Mar. 27, 1850. Exrs: Jas. A., John T. Lyon, Benj. P. Hughes. Wit: Wm. Barr, Thos. B. Dendy, A. L. Gillespie. Chn: Jas. A., John T., Wm., Harvey T, Saml. Lyon. Wife, Elizabeth Lyon. Dtr. in law, Mary Ann Lyon. Joseph Lyon died Mar. 16, 1850.

LIPSCOMB, JEMIMA—BOX 125, PACK 3691:
Will dated Apr. 17, 1849 in Abbeville Dist. Filed Feb. 16, 1850. Exrs: Dtr., Elizabeth Harris, Geo. A. Addison. Wit: Wm. Hill, Thos. C., Jas. M. Perrin. Gr. dtrs: Ann Jemima Harris, Rebecca wife of Geo. A. Addison. Great gr. dtr. Mary Elizabeth dtr. of Marshall Frazier.

LOGAN, (MINORS)—BOX 125, PACK 3692:
  On Jan. 15, 1851 Wm. J., Hart P. Arnold, John H. Mundy bound unto
F. W. Selleck Ord. Abbeville Dist. sum $3,000.00. Wm. J. Arnold made gdn. of
Jas. Wm., Nancy Logan minors. Isaac Logan was an uncle to said minors. Ex-
pend: Mar. 27, 1850 Recd. from Est. Mary Logan $142.90. Recd. from Est. A.
Logan $62.41. Recd. from Francis Logan est. $133.80.

LONG, HENRY S.—BOX 125, PACK 3693:
  On May 28, 1851 Wm. Long, W. P. Martin, W. W. Moseley bound unto
F. W. Selleck Ord. Abbeville Dist. sum $1,400.00. Wm. Long made gdn. of
Henry S. Long a minor of said Wm. Long. He also had a small est. coming to him
from the est. of Henry Johnson decd.

LONG, MIVERVA A. E.—BOX 125, PACK 3694:
  On May 28, 1851 Wm. Long, W. P. Martin, W. W. Moseley bound unto F.
W. Selleck Ord. Abbeville Dist. sum $1,400.00. Wm. Long made gdn. of Min-
ervia A. E. Long a minor of said Wm. Long. She had a small est. coming to her
from the est. of Henry Johnson decd. On Apr. 28, 1855 Joseph R., Minervia A. E.
Latimer recd. $140.00. as the heirs of Mahuldah Long decd.

MARSHALL, GEORGE—BOX 125, PACK 3695:
  Will dated Aug. 19, 1845 in Abbeville Dist. Filed Jan. 19, 1852. Exrs:
Son, Joseph Stien Marshall, S. Is: Jonathan Jordon, Joel Smith. Wit: John Hin-
ton, Lewis Mathis, M. W. Coleman. Chn: Mary Ann Miles Jordon, Isabella Eliz-
abeth Smith, Nancy Narcissa McDowall, Joseph Stien Marshall, Sarah Carson
Marshall, Martha Rebecca Marshall. Wife, Jane Marshall. Gr. chn: Jas. Alexr.,
Geo. Marshall, Patrick Henry, Edwin Holbrook McDowall chn. of Nancy Narcissa
McDowall. Sett. made Feb. 12, 1856. Martha Anderson and Sarah C. Lipscomb
each recd. $3,389.83. Martha was the wife of W. S. Anderson. On Feb. 12, 1856
Thos. C. Lipscomb recd. $971.77 as his share from est.

McDUFFIE, GEORGE—BOX 125, PACK 3696:
  Est. admnr. Nov. 1, 1851 by Mary S. McDuffie, John C., Mathew R.
Singleton bound unto F. W. Selleck Ord. Abbeville Dist. sum $250,000.00. Geo.
McDuffie was the father of Mary McDuffie.

PACKAGES FROM 3697 TO 3715 EITHER GONE OR MISNUMBERED

NORWOOD, JESSE (MINOR)—BOX 126, PACK 3714:
  On May 6, 1850 Saml. Agnew, Benjamin Smith, Abner H. McGee bound
unto F. W. Selleck Ord. Abbeville Dist. sum $300.00. Saml. Agnew made gdn. of
Wm. T., Mary Ann, Elizabeth F. Norwood minors under 14 yrs. chn. of Jesse
Norwood decd. and Elizabeth Norwood.

NORRELL, THOMAS—BOX 126, PACK 3715:
  Est. admnr. Feb. 2, 1852 by John Sadler, Jas. W. Richardson, Joel Fooshe
bound unto F. W. Selleck Ord. Abbeville Dist. sum $300.00. Expend: Aug. 24.
1854 Recd. from Jonathan Norrell on note $112.67.

PORTERFIELD, WILLIS (MINORS)—BOX 126, PACK 3716:
On Nov. 4, 1850 John, Wm. W. Hunter, Wm. W. Belcher bound unto F. W. Selleck Ord. Abbeville Dist. sum $600.00. John Hunter made gdn. of Margaret, John, Mary Porterfield minors of Willis, Mary Porterfield decd.

PATTERSON, SAMUEL—BOX 126, PACK 3717:
Est. admnr. Apr. 8, 1851 by A. P. Robinson, J. J. Shanks, Wm. Davis. Frederick Connor bound unto F. W. Selleck Ord. Abbeville Dist. sum $6,000.00. A. P. Robinson sheweth that Saml. Anderson a mute, late of the state of Ala. died a few months ago. Dated Mar. 22, 1851. Power of Atty. Know that I Saml. Patterson of Tipton Co., Tenn. have appointed Wm. K. Bradley of Abbeville Dist. my Atty. to receive for the share due me of the est. of Saml. Patterson, late of Lowndes Co., Ala. Dated this Aug. 9, 1853. Saml. Patterson. (One paper stated he was a dumb mute.)

PRICE, JOSEPH B.—BOX 126, PACK 3718:
Est. admnr. June 25, 1855 by Thos. Chatham, Wm. Smith, Richard M. White bound unto Wm. Hill Ord. Abbeville Dist. sum $500.00. Nancy Price sheweth that she is the wid. of Joseph Price who died 1844. No admnr. taken out until now. Hartwell H., Abram Price were 2 distributees. On Nov. 12, 1855 T. P., Elizabeth Beasley recd. $39.00 from said est. Amey G. Price a dtr. of Joseph Price.

PATTERSON, JAMES—BOX 126, PACK 3719:
Est. admnr. Apr. 15, 1850 by Jas. H. Wideman, Thos C. Perrin, Saml. McGowen bound unto F. W. Selleck Ord. sum $1,500.00.

PRUIT, DANIEL E.—BOX 126, PACK 3720:
Est. admnr. Oct. 25, 1851 by Jas. Lindsay, Saml. E., Andrew Pruit, A. C. Hawthorne bound unto F. W. Selleck Ord. Abbeville Dist. sum $18,000.00. Sett. made Jan. 10, 1854 ment. the wid. and 8 distributees. No names given.

PORTERFIELD, WILLIS—BOX 126, PACK 3721:
Est. admnr. Sept. 13, 1850 by John, Wm. W. Hunter, Richard A. Martin bound unto F. W. Selleck Ord. Abbeville Dist. sum $250.00. He died about May 12, 1850. Sale, Sept. 28, 1850. Byrs: John, Wm. Hunter, Allen Smith, Margaret Porterfield, Thos. Link, etc.

ROBERTSON, JOHN—BOX 126, PACK 3722:
Will dated June 27, 1851. Filed Sept. 1, 1851. Exr: Wm. Robertson. Wit: Jas. W. Blain, W. P. Martin, B. F. Moseley. Nephew, Wm. Robertson to have my interest in bounty land which I hope to get for my military service. Sale, Dec. 23, 1851. Byrs: Alexr. Padgett, Richard Maddox, Wm. Robertson, John Gaines, Wm. Ware Esq., W. P. Martin, etc.

ROBERTSON, JAMES—BOX 126, PACK 3723:
Est. admnr. June 10, 1851 by R. M. David, Joseph T. Baker, Wm. C. Cozby bound unto F. W. Selleck Ord. Abbeville Dist. sum $25,000.00. Sett. made Jan. 11, 1854. Present, R. M. Davis admnr. and Elijah H. Speer who married

ABBEVILLE DISTRICT WILLS AND BONDS   501

Sarah a dtr. of Jas. Robertson. He died in the spring of 1851. Left a wid., Elizabeth and 2 chn. Sarah C. Speer, Jas. Jr. who is a minor.

ROBINSON, WILLIAM—BOX 126, PACK 3724:
Est. admnr. July 7, 1851 by John W. Hearst, Jas. Wideman, Geo .W. Pressly bound unto F. W. Selleck Ord. Abbeville Dist. sum $1,000.00. Sett. made Aug. 10, 1854. Present, Dr. J. W. Hearst admnr. and Simpson Evans who married Susan Ann a dtr. of Wm. Robinson. Sale, Nov. 5, 1851. Byrs: Nancy, John Robinson, etc.

RUSSELL, JOHN—BOX 126, PACK 3725:
Est. admnr. June 19, 1852 by John Cothran, Jas. M. Perrin, A. G. Caldwell bound unto F. W. Selleck Ord. Abbeville Dist. sum $200.00.

RILEY, ANDREW—BOX 126, PACK 3726:
Will dated Oct. 18, 1848 in Abbeville Dist. Filed Dec. 15, 1851. Exr. Son, John Rutledge. Wit: Thos., Bert Riley, David Edwards. Wife, Mary Riley. Chn: John Rutledge, Dan Talbert, Jas. Harvey, Robt. Russel, Andrew Pinckney, Wm. Newton, Mary Elizabeth, Martha Jane Riley. "My desire that my chn. be educated at Greenwood in the schools under the Presbyterian Demonination."

ROGERS, (MINORS)—BOX 126, PACK 3727:
On Jan. 8, 1852 D. M. Rogers, Jas. McCaslan Esq., Edward Noble bound unto F. W. Selleck Ord. Abbeville Dist. sum $300.00. D. M. Rogers made gdn. of Martha Ann, Virginia Rogers minors under 21 yrs. They were sis. to their gdn. D. M. Rogers. Were the chn. of Peter B. Rogers decd. and entitled to bounty land from the government in the right of their father.

REYNOLDS, (MINORS)—BOX 126, PACK 3728:
On Jan. 6, 1851 Larkin Reynolds, Thos. L. Coleman, J. Foster Marshall bound unto F. W. Selleck Ord. Abbeville Dist. sum $1,800.00. Larkin Reynolds was made gdn. of Benjamin Larkin, John Simmons, Sarah A. Maria Reynolds minors. Larkin Reynolds sheweth that his chn. are entitled to a small est. from that of their Uncle John Simmons of Laurens Dist. Sett. made Nov. 19, 1860 stated that Sarah married John W. Ligon.

SHIRLEY, WILLIAM—BOX 126, PACK 3730:
Will dated Dec. 20, 1851 in Abbeville Dist. Filed Feb. 13, 1852. Exr. Bro., Benjamin Shirley. Wit: J. R. Wilson, Benjamin McLain, Jas. H. Haddon. Mother, Nancy Shirley. "Other bros. and sisters ment. names not given." Had notes on Richard Shirley, John B. Armstrong, Reuben Branyon, Jas. Shirley. Dec. 20, 1856 Paid John Shirley $12.73. Inv. made by L. Y. Trible, Mastin Shirley, Jas. H. Haddon.

SPEED, MICHAEL—BOX 126, PACK 3731:
Will dated Feb. 3, 1847 in Abbeville Dist. Filed July 24, 1851. Exrs: Wife, Eleanor Speed; Sons, Wm. G., Ezekiel P. Speed. Wit: John Cowan, Saml. Hill, O. Taggart. Chn: Wm. G., Ezekiel P., Saml. D. Speed, Leah Paschel, Sarah A., Mary A. Speer. Leah Paschel married Saml. Paschal.

SHEPPARD, (MINORS)—BOX 126, PACK 3732:
    On June 3, 1851 Frances, Geo. Sheppard, Elihu P. Campbell bound unto
F. W. Selleck Ord. Abbeville Dist. sum $2,000.00. Frances Sheppard made gdn.
of Elihu T. Young Shepperd, Jas. Stanmore Shepperd, Wm. A., Geo. R., Martha
Frances Shepperd minors. Frances Shepperd sheweth that she is the mother of
said chn., and their father Wade H. Shepperd is decd. Entitled to a est. in the
hands of Dr. John Watts of Laurens Dist., who was the admnr. of their father's est.

STARKEY, ELIZABETH—BOX 126, PACK 3733:
    Est. admnr. May 20, 1850 by Isaac Branch, H. A. Jones, J. G. Wilson
bound unto F. W. Selleck Ord. Abbeville Dist. sum $50.00. Carolina Starkey was
a distributee.

SPIERIN, THOMAS P.—BOX 126, PACK 3734:
    Est. admnr. Sept. 12, 1851 by Elizabeth Spierin, David Lesley, John Wil-
son bound unto F. W. Selleck Ord. Abbeville Dist. sum $1,000.00. Elizabeth
Spierin the wid.

SAXON, D. T.—BOX 126, PACK 3735:
    Will dated Mar. 23, 1848 in Abbeville Dist. Filed Dec. 10, 1850. No Exr.
Wit: Jas. R. LeRoy, Wm. C. Vaughn, Hugh S. Saxon. Wife, Elizabeth Saxon.
"Give land lying on the west side of the Greenville Road." Bequeath to Jas. L.
McCelvey.

STILL, D. MOODY—BOX 126, PACK 3736:
    Est. admnr. June 21, 1851 by Willis Smith, J. Foster Marshall, Wm. M.
Hughey bound unto F. W. Selleck Ord. Abbeville Dist. sum $400.00. Sett. made
June 7, 1852. Present, Willis Smith admnr., Saml. McQueens who married Eu-
genia Still a dtr. of Richmond Still decd. a bro. of said decd. S. A. Wilson recd.
$8.10 in right of his wife Virginia Distributes viz. Amy, Jeremiah, Elizabeth
John, Polly, Nancy, Pricilla, Richmond, Lucy, Jarusha, Maria Still.

SEAWRIGHT, JOHN—BOX 126, PACK 3737:
    Est. admnr. Apr. 5, 1850 by Jas., Robt. R., John N. Seawright, Jas. B.,
Wm. Richey bound unto F. W. Selleck Ord. Abbeville Dist. sum $20,000.00.
Power of Atty. State of Ga., Chattooga Co. July 14, 1851. Know that I Ebenezer
W. Seawright of said Co. do make John N. Seawright of Abbeville Dist., S. C.
my Atty. to collect from the admnrs. of the est. of my father John Seawright decd.
all that may be due me. Power of Atty. State of Miss. Tippah Co. Mar. 15, 1880.
Know that we, J. C. Seawright, J. A. Welch and his wife M. V. Welch of said
county do appoint J. N. Seawright of Donaldville, S. C. our Atty. to receive what
is due us from the est. of our gr. father John Seawright decd. Sett. made Aug. 9,
1851. Present, Robt. R., John N. Seawright admnrs., Saml. E. Pruit who married
Elizabeth a dtr. of said decd. Also Isaac C. Seawright and Emily C. Seawright
minors over the age choice, unrepresented. Wid. Jane Seawright send her consent.
Wm., Thompson Seawright absent but sent their consent. Power of Atty. Tippah
Co., Miss. Know that I, L. C. Alvis of said Co. do this 3rd July, 1880 appoint J.
N. Seawright my Atty.

SIMPSON, (MINORS)—BOX 126, PACK 3738:
On Feb. 17, 1851 John F. Simpson, Thos. Crawford, Peter Henry bound unto F. W. Selleck Ord. Abbeville Dist. sum $1,500.00. John F. Simpson made gdn. of Jas. H., John J. Simpson minors of John F. Simpson gdn., and are entitled to a share of the est. of John Stephenson decd. in right of their mother Eliza Simpson.

SMITH, THOMAS—BOX 126, PACK 3739:
Est. admnr. Sept. 23, 1850 by Eliza., Joel, Chas. Smith bound unto F. W. Selleck Ord. Abbeville Dist. sum $15,000.00. Eliza. Smith the wid. Thos. Smith died about the middle of Oct. 1849.

SCOTT, JOSEPH—BOX 126, PACK 3740:
Est. admnr. Oct. 17,1851 by Thos, B., John O. Scott, Thos. Brough bound unto F. W. Selleck Ord. Abbeville Dist. sum $9,000.00. Sett. made Aug. 3, 1855 ment. that John F. Brough had married the wid. of Joseph Scott decd. No name given. Wm. T. Drennan gdn. of Joseph Ann Scott only child of said decd

TOMPKINS, BRANTLEY—BOX 126, PACK 3741:
Est. admnr. Oct. 6, 1851 by Thos. Petigrue, Thos. C. Perrin, S. McGowan bound unto F. W. Selleck Ord. Abbeville Dist. sum $12,000.00. Thos. Pettigrew, Capt. in the Navy of the U. S. sheweth that Brantley Tompkins died about the month of Sept. 1850.

VESSELLS, JOHN—BOX 126, PACK 3742:
Est. admnr. Aug. 5, 1850 by Thos. J. Vessells, Alexr. Scott bound unto F. W. Selleck Ord. Abbeville Dist. sum $35.00. Thos. J. Vessells sheweth that he is a son of John Vessells decd. who died in the yr. 1847.

VESSELLS, EPHRAIM—BOX 126, PACK 3743:
Est. admnr. Oct. 10, 1850 by W. C. Ware, M. O. Talman, T. A. Rogers bound unto F. W. Selleck Ord. Abbeville Dist. sum $400.00. On Sept. 25, 1850 W. C. Ware sheweth that Ephriam Vessells was killed Aug. 25 by Geo. McCelvey.

TOLBERT, RACHEL C.—BOX 127, PACK 3744:
Expend: May 7, 1850 Recd. from J. F. Tolbert Exr. of the will of Wm. Tolbert $165.00. Jas. Tolbert was the trustee for Rachel C. Tolbert who was ment. as an idiot.

WALLER, BENJAMIN F.—BOX 127, PACK 3745:
Est. admnr. June 10, 1850 by Gilford, Nancy Waller, Jas. F. Watson bound unto F. W. Seleck Ord. Abbeville Dist. sum $1,200.00. Guilford Waller was a bro. to said decd. Benjamin Waller died May 13, 1850. (Letter)
Pleasant Grove,
Apr. 29, 1851
Mm. F. W. Selleck
Dear Sir:
You will please have the kindness to make the sett. of the est. of Benjamin F. Waller decd. with Gilford Waller the admnr. as we are perfetly willing to abide

by the sett. you and him will make.
Yours very respectfully,
W. W., Nancy, Elizabeth W., Statira Waller.

WILLIAMS, TIMOTHY D.—BOX 127, PACK 3746:
Est. admnr. June 27, 1851 by Saml. A. Dunn, John W. Posey, M. H.
Deale bound unto F. W. Selleck Ord. Abbeville Dist. sum $400.00. Saml. A.
Dunn was a b. l. to T. D. Williams.

WATSON, WILLIAM ELLIS—BOX 127, PACK 3747:
Est. admnr. Sept. 16, 1851 by John Davis, Jas. Shillito, John T. Lyon
bound unto F. W. Selleck Ord. Abbeville Dist. sum $300.00. Sett. made Mar. 15,
1853. Present, Dr. John Davis admnr. and Abner Watson the father. Note: At
this point of sett. Abner Watson presented an acct. of $31.50 for nursing his son
during his last illness which acct. I refused to admit from the fact that the decd.
was at the time of his being taken sick at the house of his employer N. J. Davis
where every comfort would have been administered to him and there was no
necessity of his removal to the house of said Abner Watson.

WATSON, JAMES F.—BOX 127, PACK 3748:
Will dated May 17, 1850 in Abbeville Dist Filed Nov. 4, 1851. Exrs: Wife,
Margaret Watson. Son, Geo. McDuffie Watson, Albert Waller, Jas. H. Wideman.
Wit: Wm. P. Hill, Lemuel Bell, John McNeil. Chn: Wm. Edward, Geo. McDuf-
fie, Jas. Franklin, Thos. Anthony, Dorothy Jane Watson. "My Exrs. shall pay an-
nually to the Deacons of the Baptist Church of Christ at Mount Moriah in the
Dist. of Abbeville for the support of the pastor of said church $25.00. Will that
my mercantile business, my dwelling house, lots in the village of Greenwood,
Abbeville Dist. remain unsold." He died about the 6th Sept, 1850.

WHITE, LEONARD J.—BOX 127, PACK 3749:
Est. admnr. May 4, 1850 by Clestia A. White, Geo. W., Gabriel Hodges,
John Cochran, Thos. Eakins, John Cowan bound unto F. W. Selleck Ord. Abbe-
ville Dist. sum $70,000.00. Sett. made July 18, 1851 ment. that his wid. Celestia
A. had married Jas. N. Cochran Esq.

WEED, ANDREW—BOX 127, PACK 3750:
Will dated Jan. 26, 1850 in Abbeville Dist. Filed Mar. 4, 1850. Exrs:
Wife, Mary Weed, Wm. H. Simpson, Alexr. Houston. Wit: Wm. H., Susan
Simpson, Alexr. Houston. Dtr. Anna Mitchell.

WHATLEY, JOSEPH R.—BOX 127, PACK 3751:
Est. admnr. Sept. 30, 1850 by John D. Adams, John Burnett, Jas. H.
Martin bound unto F. W. Selleck Ord. Abbeville Dist. sum $450.00. He died
July last. Expend: Oct. 15, 1851 Paid Khadyah Whatley $8.00.

WAGNER, WILLIAM—BOX 127, PACK 3752:
Est. admnr. Sept. 15, 1851 by Thos. Chatham, J. Foster Marshall, Wm.
Smith bound unto F. W. Selleck Ord. Abbeville Dist. sum $1,500.00. John R.
Cheatham sheweth that his bro. l. Wm. Wagner died about the 1st. Feb. last.
Dated this 27 May, 1851. N. Stewart gdn. of Mary E. Wagner.

WILSON, JOSEPH N.—BOX 127, PACK 3753:
Est. admnr. Nov. 13, 1851 by B. M. Cheatham, John White, Andrew Gillespie bound unto F. W. Selleck Ord. Abbeville Dist. sum $4,000.00. Sett. made Jan. 11, 1853 ment. the wid. as the only distributee. No name given.

WHITLEY, SARAH—BOX 127, PACK 3754:
On July 4, 1851 Enoch Carter, Elihu Campbell, Henry Mays bound unto F. W. Selleck Ord. Abbeville Dist. sum $800.00. Enoch Carter made gdn. of Sarah Whitley a minor dtr. of Elizabeth Whitley. Expend: Oct. 15, 1851 Recd. from John Hill Ord. Edgefield Dist. from est. of Wm. Mays decd. $9.41. Jan. 1, 1852 Recd. from est. of Meady Mays $332.95.

WARE, NICHOLAS M.—BOX 127, PACK 3755:
Est. admnr. Jan. 30, 1851 by Wm. J. Ware, Abner H. Magee, L. T. C. Jones bound unto F. W. Selleck Ord. Abbeville Dist. sum $2,000.00. Nicholas Ware was the father of Wm. J. Ware. Sale, Feb. 17, 1851. Byrs: Elizabeth, Wm. J., Wm. Ware Esq., etc.

WILLIAMSON, SANDERS—BOX 127, PACK 3756:
Est. admnr. Feb. 22, 1852 by Wm. W. Anderson, Saml. Agnew bound unto F. W. Selleck Ord. Abbeville Dist. sum $400.00. Sale, Mar. 12, 1852. Byrs: Catharine, Thos. Williamson, etc. Had one note on Elizabeth, Wm. J. Ware. Jan. 13, 1854 Recd. from W. Robertson in the matter of Nancy Williamson $7.06. On Dec. 26, 1853 Personally appeared Wm. A. J. Ware before Wm. Higgins Magistrate and made oath that he received a note from John Dial for collection against said est.

WHALEY, LEWIS—BOX 127, PACK 3757:
Est. admnr. Dec. 30, 1850 by Franklin, Wm. B., Henry B. Bowie bound unto F. W. Selleck Ord. Abbeville Dist. sum $1,000.00. He died on Friday, Dec. 7, 1850. Sett. made Nov. 26, 1852. Present: Franklin Bowie admnr., distriutees viz. John, Elizabeth, Damaus A. Whaley.

WHARTON, WILLIAM A.—BOX 127, PACK 3758:
On Jan. 11, 1851 David, John Kellar, David Atkins bound unto F. W. Selleck Ord. Abbeville Dist. sum $2,800.00. David Keller made gdn. of Wm. A. Wharton a minor. On Dec. 17, 1850 Wm. Wharton sheweth that he is nearly 18 yrs. old and that he has a distributee share coming to him from the est. of Wm. Lomax decd. Was of age in 1854.

WIER, THOMAS—BOX 127, PACK 3759:
Will dated Feb. 9, 1850 in Abbeville Dist. Filed July 5, 1851. Exrs: Henry Booser, Wm. N. Blake. Wit: Johua Turner, Wm. Buchanan, J. J. Sharp. Wife: Mary Wier. Chn: John, Elizabeth Wier. He died in June, 1851. His wife Mary died prior to his death. Power of Atty. State of Ala., Chotaw Co. Know that I Thos. Addison gdn. of Ann, Lucy Wier chn. age 16 and 18 yrs. old, of Saml. Wier late of Pickens Co. decd. and heirs of Thos. Wier late of Abbeville Dist., S. C. do appoint Thos. C. Ware of Columbus, Miss. my Atty. to collect what is due my wards from the est. of Thos. Wier of S. C. Dated Feb. 16, 1854. One

paper stated that Wm. Wier of Lowndes Co., Miss. made his will on the 9th Sept. 1853. Thos. Wier's chn. were: Robt., Jas., Wm., Saml., John, Thos., Elizabeth, Stewart, Andrew and Swanzy Wier recd. from me $400.00 to buy land in Ga. Elizabeth Wier married Wm. N. Blake.

WILSON, ELIZABETH—BOX 127, PACK 3760:
Will date left out. Filed July 24, 1851. Exr. Saml. Reed. Wit: Allen T. Miller, S. W. Cochran, A. W. M. Reed. Chn: Elizabeth wife of Saml. Reed, Jemima Huston, Matilda Vashti Branch, Elizabeth Reid.

WILSON, BENJAMIN A.—BOX 127, PACK 3761:
Est. admnr. Nov. 18, 1850 by Saml. A. Jr., R. H. Wilson, Larkin Reynolds bound unto F. W. Selleck Ord. Abbeville Dist. sum $1,500.00. Benjamin A. Wilson died Oct. 24, 1850. Was a bro. to Saml. A. Wilson. Robt. C. Wilson was the father of Benjamin. 9 distributees: Robt. C. Saml. Wilson, Archibald Tittle, R. H., W. W., Nancy C., Jas. L., Thos. J., John S. Wilson.

WITT, BENJAMIN F.—BOX 127, PACK 3762:
Est. admnr. Oct. 31, 1850 by Johnson Sale, W. P. Tedards, Wm. P. Andrews bound unto F. W. Selleck Ord. Abbeville Dist. sum $600.00. He died Aug. Sett. made Feb. 4, 1852. Present, Johnson Sale admnr., Joseph S. Irvin who married Parthenia Witt wid. of Stephen Witt and mother of decd. and Nancy Witt the wid. Amount found due to David Witt a minor, the intestate being his gdn. $139.57. Amt. due Elizabeth $131.69.

ZIMMERMAN, (MINORS)—BOX 127, PACK 3763:
On Nov. 13, 1850 W. W. Belcher, Thos. Thomson bound unto F. W. Selleck Ord. Abbeville Dist. sum $1,300.00. W. W. Belcher made gdn. of Mary C., Philip L. Zimmerman minors of F. E. Zimmerman.

(PACKAGES MISNUMBERED AGAIN)

LOMAX, AARON—BOX 127, PACK 3460:
Will dated Mar. 29, 1848 in Abbeville Dist. Filed Dec. 20, 1848. Exrs: Augustus Lomax, John Foster. Wit: John W., Wm. A. Lomax, W. S. Robertson. Chn: Geo., Saml. R., Jesse Lomax. Savannah L. Foster, Augustus, Geo. Lomax. Wife ment. name not given. Susannah married John Foster. Elizabeth Lomax bought at sale.

LOW, THOMAS—BOX 128, PACK 3461:
Est. admnr. Oct. 19, 1847 by Saml., Bartholomew, Jonathan Jordon bound unto David Lesly Ord. Abbeville Dist. sum $400.00.

LOVELESS, JAS. AND LUCY—BOX 128, PACK 3462:
Admnr. bond of Jas. and Lucy Loveless made Oct. 22, 1846 by Ephraim R. Calhoun, Jas. S. Wilson, John McClellan bound unto David Lesly Ord. Abbeville Dist. sum $100.00. Jas. Loveless died in the spring and his wife Lucy just recently.

LESLY, ROBERT H.—BOX 128, PACK 3463:
Est. admnr. Nov. 1, 1847 by John W., Wm. A., Wm. Lesly bound unto

David Lesly Ord. Abbeville Dist. sum $10,000.00. Robt. H. Lesly was the father of John W. Lesly. Sett. made Jan. 12, 1848. Present: John W.. Joseph L., W., Smal. Thos. Lesly. Absent: Mrs. Lesly wid., J. A. Fraser. Elizabeth Lesly's share was $2,877.23.

LeROY, ISAAC—BOX 128, PACK 3464:
Est. admnr. Feb. 9, 1848 by Jacob B. Britt, J. C. Willard, J. H. Britt bound unto David Lesly Ord. Abbeville Dist. sum $5,000.00. (On back of bond was written Isaac LeRoy alias King decd.) In sett. the following names ment., Susan, C. T., J. P., Margaret E. LeRoy. Left a wid. and chn.

LIDDELL, SARAH—BOX 128, PACK 3465:
Est. admnr. June 5, 1848 by Jas. T. Liddell, Allen T. Miller, Saml. Reid bound unto David Lesly Ord. Abbeville Dist. sum $1,000.00. Sarah Liddell the mother of Jas. T. Liddell. Sett. made July 2, 1850. Present: Jas. T. Liddell admnr., John Swilling agent of Belinda Osborn wife of Geo. W. Osborn formerly wife of Geo. W. Liddell and as gdn. of Frances C. Liddell only surviving child of Geo. W. Liddell, John J. Pickens son of Sarah Liddell, Jas. Sitton who married Harriet D., a gr. dtr. of Sarah Liddell, Joseph Dickson who married Rachel Lucinda a dtr. of Sarah Liddel. Sarah Liddell survived her son Geo. W. Liddell; at her death Frances C. Liddell was the only surviving child. She also survived her dtr. Eliza. A. Davis. Her chn. at Sarah Liddell's death were Harriet D. Sitton, Sarah M. Davis.

LIPFORD, OBEDIENCE—BOX 128, PACK 3466:
Est. admnr. Apr. 5, 1848 by Thos. J. Hill, E. Trible, Jas. W. Black bound unto David Lesly Ord. Abbeville Dist. sum $1,000.00. J. J. Lipford was a son of said decd. Thos. J. Hill was a s. l. Sett. made Apr. 21, 1849. Mrs. Lipford died Feb. 1848. The will of Asa Lipford decd. dated Aug. 12, 1825. Prov. Dec. 28, 1825. Asa Lipford died leaving a mother Obedience Lipford and bros. and sisters as follows: viz. Duey Lipford who died 1857 having a wid. and 4 or 5 chn. Martha Lipford who married D. A. Weed, removed from state. Martha is dead leaving husband and chn. Joel J. Lipford living in Abbeville. Mary wife of John Donald. Present: Henry N. Lipford living in Fla. Frances wife of Thos. Hill. Wm. Lipford in Alabama.

LIPFORD, EDWARD—BOX 128, PACK 3467:
Est. admnr. Dec. 31, 1846 by Chas. A., John W. Cobb, John Cochran, Wm. B. Roman bound unto David Lesly Ord. Abbeville Dist. sum $2,000.00. Left no wife but several chn., his oldest son was John Lipford. Sett. made Nov. 3, 1848 to ascertain the share of Jackson Lindsay and wife Mary.

LIPFORD, ALLEN—BOX 128, PACK 3468:
On Jan. 11, 1848 Thom. Stacy, Susan Franklin, J. Bailey bound unto David Lesly Ord. Abbeville Dist. sum $300.00. Thos. Stacy made gdn. of Allen Lipford a minor. On Jan. 5, 1849 Chas. A., J. W. Cobb, W. B. Roman bound to David Lesly Ord. Abbeville Dist. sum $222.80. Chas. A. Cobb made gdn. of Allen Lipford a minor over 14 yrs. and son of Edward Lipford decd.

LIPFORD, AMOS—BOX 128, PACK 3469:
On Jan. 5, 1849 J. W., Chas. A. Cobb, J. N. Cochran bound unto David Lesly Ord. Abbeville Dist. sum $222.80. J. W. Cobb made gdn. of Amos Lipford a minor son of Edward Lipford. Was of age in 1851.

LIPFORD, (MINORS)—BOX 128, PACK 3470:
On Jan. 5, 1849 Chas. A., John W. Cobb, W. B. Roman bound unto David Lesly Ord. Abbeville Dist. sum $900.00. Chas A. Cobb made gdn. of Frances W., Wm., Clotilda Lipford minors. On Feb. 8, 1854 Anderson, Middleton, Willis Cobb bound unto David Lesly Ord. Abbeville Dist. sum $75.00. Anderson Cobb made gdn. of Wm. Lipford a minor. They were the chn. of Edward Lipford decd. On Nov. 3, 1848 the petition of Frances E. Lipford sheweth that she is a minor about yrs. and is desirous to remove to Senclair Co., Ala. with her sis. Mary Lindsay. Power of Atty. Know that we, Chas. D. Mann and his wife Clotilda Mann of Pontotoc Co., Miss. do appoint Wm. Gresham of said Co. our Atty. to receive what is due us from the est. of Edward Lipford of Abbeville Dist., S. C. Dated this 17th Dec. 1860. Power of Atty. Know that we, Barach Lindsay and his wife Frances E. Lindsay late Frances E. Lipford do appoint Abner P. Jones St. Clair Co., Ala. our Atty. to get what is due us from the est. of Edward Lipford decd. of Abbeville Dist., S. C. Dated Sept. 28, 1852.

LACKEY, THOMAS P.—BOX 128, PACK 3471:
Est. admnr. Aug. 19, 1848 by Moses W. Lackey, W. Barksdale, J. Foster Marshall bound unto David Lesly Ord. Abbeville Dist. sum $50.00. Late a soldier in the Mexican War. Moses W. Lackey on Aug. 5, 1848 sheweth that his son Thos. P. Lackey entered the service in the Mexican War under Capt. Marshall and died in the service intestate without wife or chn.

LATIMER, ALBERT G.—BOX 128, PACK 3472:
Est. admnr. May 21, 1849 by Micajah B., C. T. Latimer, B. M. Lattimore bound unto David Lesly Ord. Abbeville Dist. sum $6,000.00. Left a wid. and 4 minor chn. Sett. ment. wid. no name given. Chn: C. C. A., Jas. S., Mary K., A. G. Latimer. (Name in some places were written Lattimore.)

LOGAN, FRANCIS—BOX 128, PACK 3473:
Est. admnr. Oct. 1848 by Isaac, A. J., Frederick B. Logan, L. H. Rykard bound unto David Lesly Ord. Abbeville Dist. sum $8,000.00. Polly Logan the wid. Francis Logan a bro. to Isaac, Andrew Logan. Left a wid. and chn. Sett. made Nov. 14, 1850. Ment wid. Mary and 6 chn: viz Andrew F. Logan, Mrs. Jane Arnold wife of Wm. Arnold, John L., Francis, Nancy, Jas. W. Logan.

LOGAN, MARY—BOX 128, PACK 3474:
Est. admnr. May 23, 1850 by Isaac, F. B., Andrew Logan bound unto F. W. Selleck Ord. Abbeville Dist. sum $2,000.00. Est. admnr. again Dec. 3, 1849 by Andrew J., F. B., Andrew Logan bound unto David Lesly Ord. Abbeville Dist. sum $2,000.00. Sett. made Mar. 27, 1852 ment. as distributees, Andrew F. Logan, Jane wife of Wm. J., Arnold, John Lewis, Francis, Jas. W., Nancy Logan.

LONG, FRANCES—BOX 128, PACK 3475:
Est. admnr. Nov. 20, 1846 by J. W. H. Johnson, D. Calhoun, Thos. Stewart bound unto David Lesly Ord. Abbeville Dist. sum $8,000.00. Power of Atty. Know that we, Thos. Polly and Mitchel B. Hopper of Perry Co., Ala. have appointed Thos. Abercrombie also of said co. and who is about to go to S. C. to collect our rights from the est. of Frances Long (formerly Francis Pucket while a wid. of Richard Puckett late of Abbeville Dist.) in right of our wives, Permelia F. Polly formerly Permelia F. Abercrombie now wife of said Thos. Polly and Martha A. Hopper formerly Martha A. Abercrombie now wife of Mitchel B. Hopper both dtrs. of Mary Abercrombie formerly Mary Puckett who was the wife of said Thos. Abercrombie and dtr. of said Frances Puckett decd. . Frances Long died Oct. 1846. Sett. made Sept. 12, 1848. Present: J. W. H. Johnson admnr. and legatee in right of his wife, Thos. R. Puckett, Wyatt W. Puckett, Thos. Abercrombie representing under power of Atty. Permelia Frances wife of Thos. Polly, Martha Agness wife of Mitchell B. Hopper, 2 chn. by Mary a dtr. of Mrs. Long and a gdn. under an appointment in Ala. of Jas. Redding and Thos. Jabez, Hazel Smith who married Mary Frances dtr. of Permelia McCrady who was a dtr. of Mrs. Long. Permelia died before Mrs. Long leaving 1 dtr. Mary Frances who survived the gr. mother and died leaving a husband Hazel Smith and 2 chn., Eliza. Frances and Marshall R. J. W. H. Johnson representing under power of Atty. Elizabeth Ramsey. Absent, Robertson L. Puckett residing in Ga.

HODGES, FRANCES—BOX 129, PACK 1136:
Est. admnr. Mar. 19, 1844 by Geo. W. Hodges, Thos. M. Wilson, John Cochran bound unto David Lesly Ord. Abbeville Dist. sum $500.00. Est. admnr. again July 2, 1855 by Gabriel, Geo. W. Hodges, B. C. Hart bound unto Wm. Hill Ord. Abbeville Dist. sum $1,200.00. The mother of Gabriel, G. W. Hodges. Sett. made Aug. 27, 1857 ment. 18 distributees, no names given. On Aug. 27, 1857 Lucy W. Davis recd. $21.10 her share of pension money obtained from the U. S. on acct. of said Frances. For satisfactory consideration I hereby relinquish and grant to Gabriel Hodges of Abbeville Dist., S. C. all my interest and claim under the pension recovered from the U. S. on acct. of the military services of Major John Hodges decd. Signed, A. T. Hodges, Oct. 23, 1855. Kate, Drucilla, Douglass, S. A., R. H. W. Hodges were all distributees.

HASLET, NANCY—BOX 129, PACK 1137:
Will dated Sept. 23, 1842 in Abbeville Dist. Prov. July 15, 1844. Exr. Son, Wm. M. Haslet. Wit: Lyndsey Harper, Richard Ashley, A. Hunter. Chn: Wm. M., John A. Hunter Haslet, Mary Jane Phebe McBride, Sarah N. McCalister. John A. McBride the husband of Mary Jane McBride.

HAMILTON, WILLIAM—BOX 129, PACK 1138:
On Sept. 12, 1843 Jas. D. Houston, John Swilling, Ezekiel Trible bound unto David Lesly Ord. Abbeville Dist. sum $3,000.00. Jas. D. Houston made gdn. of Elizabeth, Luke, Jas., Sarah Hamilton chn. of Wm. Hamilton decd. Sett. of Luke Hamilton made Sept. 11, 1848 ment. he was of age. Elizabeth of age Jan. 29, 1849 stated that she was now Elizabeth Stewart. Sarah A. married Jas. P. Neal.

HARRIS, JOHN— BOX 129, PACK 1139:
Est. admnr. Dec. 26, 1844 by Elizabeth Harris, Marshall Frazer, Wiley G. Harris bound unto David Lesly Ord. Abbeville Dist. sum $20,000.00. Elizabeth Harris sheweth that her son John Harris left a wid. Henretta A. Harris, no chn. Note: In the sett. of Mary F. Harris est., a minor child of Wm. Harris decd., John Harris her bro. was admnr.

HODGES, (MINORS)—BOX 129, PACK 1140:
On Jan. 6, 1845 Andrew, Wm. Dunn, John Miller bound unto David Lesly Ord. Abbeville Dist. sum $724.00. Andrew Dunn made gdn. of Jas. R., John C., Chas. R. Hodges minors of Richard A. Hodges decd. Their mother was Phebe Hodges.

HUSKISON, JOHN—BOX 129, PACK 1141:
On Mar. 17, 1845 Wm. S. Smith, Andrew Cobb, Wm. W. Franklin bound unto David Lesly Ord. Abbeville Dist. sum $600.00. Rebecca Huskison sheweth that her husband John Huskison died leaving 2 chn. by a former wife. Sett. made Jan. 22, 1847 ment. that his wife Rebecca Parker died shortly after her husband.

HESTER, HENRY—BOX 129, PACK 1142:
Est. admnr. Dec. 23, 1844 by Louisa Hester, Herbert Darricott, Moses O. Talman bound unto David Lesly Ord. Abbeville Dist. sum $30,000.00. Left a wid. Louisa and several chn. Sett. made Jan. 15, 1846. Present: Louisa Hester wid., Saml., Thos., Robt. Hester by consent, Jas. Norwood who married Sarah Ann Hester. Louisa Hester was gdn. of Rebecca T., Elijah, John H. Hester minors. Louisa Hester was a sis. to Herbert Darracott. Henry Hester left 2 sets chn. (Letter written to Mrs. Louisa Hester, Abbeville Dist., S. C.)

Elberton, 11th. Jan., 1846

My Dear Mother

I received yours by Abram the other day I was fixing to start over this morning when Tom came with another letter from you postponing the day till Thursday next 15th. It will be out of my power to attend on that day, my objection coming over to day was to make arrangements, (if necessary) so that the business might be settled without me, and return home tomorrow. If you can postpone the time till Thursday week 22nd I will meet you at the court house on that day. If however it cannot be put off you can go on with the matter and I will come over at the time proposed and agree to, or do whatever it may be necessary or proper for me to do. I will be over on Wed. 21st if nothing prevents, and then go on to the court house or ratify what may have been done as may be right. We are all in tolerable health and getting on much as usual Ma Cornelia and the family join me in Love to you and all the family,

Very affectionately,
Robt. Hester

HOUSTON, JOHN—BOX 129, PACK 1143:
Est. admnr. Jan. 4, 1845 by Elenor, Robt. R. Houston, Lewis J. Wilson bound unto David Lesly Ord. Abbeville Dist. sum $100.0. John Houston left a wid. Elenor and several chn.

HAMILTON, JOHN—BOX 129, PACK 1144:
Will dated Oct. 6, 1839 in Abbeville Dist. Prov. Dec. 6, 1839. Exrs: Son, John A. Hamilton. Dtr. Lavinia McMillan. Wit: Wm. Gaines, Thos. E., Ann Owen. Chn: Lavinia McMillan, Jas., John A. Hamilton, Jane Kennedy, Katharine Douglass, Rachel Lenair, Eliza. A. Douglass.

HUEY, JAMES—BOX 129, PACK 1145:
Will dated Feb. 8, 1845 in Abbeville Dist. Prov. May 17, 1845. Exrs: Wid. Martha P. Huey, Thos. C. Perrin, Albert J. Clinkscales, Alexr. Hunter. Wit: Thos. J. Mabry, F. M. Brooks, J. H. Walkup. Wife, Martha P. Huey. Chn: Sarah C. Clinkscales, Martha D. Huey. "Bequeath to my bro. Robert's chn. in Chambers Co., Ala., and my sis. Jane B. Walkup's chn. in Union Co., N. C." (Note: Name Walkup looked like Walkuss in one place.)

JONES, ADAM CRAIN, JR.—BOX 129, PACK 1146:
Inv. made Jan. 20, 1807 by Enoch Dodson, Wm. Ware, Wm. Robertson. Sale, Jan. 21, 1807. Byrs: Margaret, A. C., Sr., Benjamin Jones, Geo. Swindle, Wm. Patterson, Wm. Robinson, Jr., Jas. Barmore, N. J. Rosamond, Thos. Wilson, John Young, Hugh Morrah, Esq., John Brown, John Dyson, Heord Freeman, Saml Miller, R. Posey, as. Campbell. (No other papers.)

JOHNSON, HENRY—BOX 129, PACK 1147:
Will dated May 13, 1826 in Abbeville Dist. Prov. Feb. 15, 1832. Exrs: Sons, Jonathan, Henry Johnson. Wit: John Bartee, Chas B. Fooshe, Barzilla G. Jay. Wife, Frances Johnson. Chn: Thos., Jonathan, Henry, Nancy Johnson, Polly Ramsey, Huldah Johnson. Est. of Frances Johnson admnr. Nov. 8, 1853 by Wm. Long, Wm. P. Martin, S. Latimer bound unto Mathew McDonald Ord. Abbeville Dist. sum $10,000.00. Sett. of Henry, Frances Long made Mar. 20, 1856. Present: Henry Johnson, Elihu Madden gdn. of Cornelia, Margaret Johnson, and trustee for Nancy Ware, Thos., J. W. Johnson, Jas. R. Latimer who married Manerva A. E. Long gr. dtr. of Henry Johnson decd., Harris Y. Gillam. Absent: Wm. M. Callaham, who married Sarah F. Long a' gr. dtr. Henry Long, Willis Sadler who married Mary Ann Johnson dtr. of Jonathan Johnson and Mahulda Ann Cheatham dtr. of Thos. Johnson. Polly Shirley absent, Wm. W. Long. H. Y. Gillam married Elizabeth. (Letter)
Aberdeen, Miss.
Oct. 4, 1853
A. J. Jones, Commissioner in Equity in Abbeville Dist., S. C.
I am the sole surviving Executor of the est. of Henry Johnson deceased, and I have learned this morning that my mother had departed this life, which makes it necessary for me to act as Executor, or resign, and let some one else administer under all the circumstances I choose the latter and this is my resignation and I wish you so to receive it. If it is not out place I would like to reccommend Wm. Long as administrator on said est.

Henry Johnson

JOHNSON, HENRY—BOX 129, PACK 1148:
Est. admnr. Aug. 15, 1828 by Sarah, Wm. T., Isaiah Johnson, Wm. Cun-

ningham bound to Moses Taggart Ord. Abbeville Dist. sum $30,000.00. Cit. pub. at Union School House. Est. admnr. again Feb. 17, 1826 by Sarah, Wm. T. Johnson, Jas. Fair, Thos. P. Martin bound unto Moses Taggart Ord. Abbeville Dist. sum $30,000.00. The following recd. shares: Wid., Wm. T., Albert, Andrew R., Benjamin, Sidney, Geo. W., Margaret, John H., Sarah A. Johnson.

AIKEN, JOSEPH—BOX 130, PACK 3764:
     Est. admnr. Jan. 1, 1853 by John F. Gray, H. A. Jones, John McIlwain, ohn A. Wier bound to F. W. Selleck Ord. Abbeville Dist. sum $40,000.00. John F. Gray sheweth that Joseph Aiken died intestate and that his chn. by his first wife are the only heirs. Sett. made Feb. 8, 1854. Distributees ment: Wm. H. Gray, Robt. S. Hudson thru his wife Nancy E. formerly Gray and niece of intestate, Hugh S. Potts thru his wife Narcissa E. formerly Gray, a niece of intestate. Edward M. Hudson thru his wife Martha formerly Gray, a niece of intestate.

ATKINS, JAMES—BOX 130, PACK 3765:
     Est. admnr. Mar. 9, 1853 by Jas. J. Devlin, Daniel, David Atkins bound to F. W. Selleck Ord. Abbeville Dist. sum $1,000.00. Had wid. Martha Atkins and 3 chn: viz. Wm. D., Thos. J., Daniel Atkins as gdn. of Margaret L. Atkins a minor.

ATCHESON, WINFIELD S.—BOX 130, PACK 3766:
     Est. admnr. Dec. 5, 1853 by Jas. A. Edmunds, Thos. P. Dowtin bound to Mathew McDonald Ord. Abbeville Dist. sum $3,000.00. He died Oct. 26, 1853.

ARNOLD, DR. ALEXR. B.—BOX 130, PACK 3767:
     Will dated Mar. 22, 1851. Prov. Mar. 31, 1853. Exrs: John Speer, Esq., Dr. W. R. Sanders. Wit: Thos. W. Gantt, Saml. Lindsay, H. H. Scudday. Lived in Village of Lowndesville, Abbeville Dist. Wife ment. name not given. Niece, Elizabeth Yancey Arnold Gannt "whom I have raised." Nephew, Alexr. B. Cochran. On Mar. 12, 1854 Elizabeth Y. Arnold stated that she recd. 400 acres of land in Rabun Co., Ga. and the interest of said decd. in a gold mine in Habersham Co., Ga. John Speer was of Wilson Creek. (Letter)

Newman, Ga.
F. W. Selleck, Esq.
Dear Sir:
     I received a day or 2 since, a letter from Capt. Gantt conveying the melancholy intelligence of the death of my old friend Dr. Arnold, also informing me I had been named in his will as one of his Executors, now my dear Sir you must see at once that it is out of the question for me to act however such I might desire to further the wishes of my deceased friend. I must therefore leave the matter to other hands with my best wishes for yourself, I rmain,

                                        Very truly yours,
                                        W. R. Sanders

BOWIE, LOUISA A.—BOX 130, PACK 3768:
     Est. admnr. Dec. 22, 1852 by Andrew T. Strain, John H. Wilson, Nancy J. Bowie bound unto F. W. Selleck Ord. Abbeville Dist. sum $15,000.00. Est.

admnr. again Oct. 30, 1856 by Nancy Jane Bowie, Robt. H. Wardlaw, John H. Wilson bound unto F. W. Selleck Ord. Abbeville Dist. sum $12,000.00. Sett. made Nov. 1865 stated that Andrew T. Strain admnr. has lately died. His sis., Mrs. Nancy Jane Bowie is the admnrx. of the said Strain and also of the said Louisa A. Bowie. There were 3 distributees, mother and 2 bros: Mrs. N. J. Bowie, Robt. E., Andrew Bowie.

BURNET, LITTLEBERRY—BOX 130, PACK 3769:
Will dated Oct. 12, 1852 in Abbeville Dist. Filed Dec. 28, 1852. Exrs: John R. Tarrant, Thos. Nichols, Sr. Wit: N. W. Stewart, Jonathan Norrell, J. L. Fennell. Wife, Sarah Burnet. Chn. ment. names not given. On June 10, 1858 Wm. Wheeler, S. Wheller, Jacob McCartey bound to W. F. Durisoe Ord. Edgefield Dist. sum $550.00. Wm. Wheeler made gdn. of Sumter D., Wm. N. Burnett minors of Littleberry Burnett.

BANKS, ELIZABETH—BOX 130, PACK 3770:
Est. admnr. Mar. 21, 1853 by Jas., Elias Banks, Steven W. Willis, bound to F. W. Selleck Ord. Abbeville Dist. sum $2,000.00. Elizabeth Banks mother of Jas. Banks died Feb. 18, 1853. Sett. made Apr. 26, 1856 named 11 distributees: viz. Jas., Chas., Elias, Saml., Amos, Geo., Wm., Stewart Banks, Synthia Mathews, Chn. of Sally Waters.

BROOKS, HENRY—BOX 130, PACK 3771:
Est. admnr. June 11, 1853 by Jas. M. Carwile, Basil, John L. Callaham bound to F. W. Selleck Ord. Abbeville Dist. sum $5,000.00. Sett. made Jan. 20, 1853. Present: Jas. M. Carwile in right of wife *Eshegenia* L. a distributee, J. W., Wm. D., Jas. M. Brooks, Wm. F. Kennedy and wife Emily. Absent: Ransom A. Brooks, Wm. H. Wilson and wife Frances A. and Emory D. Brooks the latter a minor. Mrs. Nancy E. Pursly wife of John Pursely is dead. Power of Atty. Russell Co., Ala. Know that I Jas. M. Brooks being 21 yrs. old an heir of Henry Brooks of Abbeville Dist., S. C. do appoint Wm. D. Brooks my Atty. Dated this Dec. 28, 1854.

BASKIN, JOHN—BOX 130, PACK 3772:
Will dated Jan. 19, 1853 in Abbeville Dist. Filed Jan. 28, 1853. Exrs: Son, Jas. S. Baskin, Dr. L. Yarbrough. Wit: John E. Uldrick, Jas. W. Porter, A. F. Wimbish. Chn: Jas. S. Baskin, Jane Y. Harkness, Susannah Simpson, Mary, Martha Baskin. Dtr. l. Jane Baskin wife of my decd. son Francis Y. Baskin. Gr. dtrs: Jane E. Baskin, Margaret Cook. "Leave one lot to Isabella McBride, Saml. Simpson." To the chn. of my decd. dtr. Margaret Cook, John, Jas., Jane, Mary, Margaret Cook.

BOWIE, (MINORS)—BOX 130, PACK 3773:
On Nov. 8, 1852 Wm. B. Bowie, Benjamin H. Eakins, Peter Henry bound unto F. W. Selleck Ord. Abbeville Dist. sum $800.00. Wm. B. Bowie made gdn. of Eli W., Zebrah F. Bowie minor chn. of Hezekiah Bowie decd.

BOYD, FRANCES—BOX 130, PACK 3774:
Est. admnr. Apr. 25, 1853 by John L. Boyd, Susannah, Wm. H. Brooks,

John H. Gray bound unto F. W. Selleck Ord. Abbeville Dist. sum $18,000.00. Sett. made Mar. 16, 1855. Present: John L. Boyd, Mrs. Susannah Brooks admnrs., Francis Wilson a distributee in right of wife Sarah A., Andrew Gillespie gdn. for Thos. Boyd a minor child. Distributees: John L. Boyd, Susannah Brooks, chn. of Jas. Boyd decd.: viz. Frances Eliza wife of Dr. T. J. Mabry, Sarah A. wife of F. A. Wilson, Wm. Benjamin Boyd.

BROWN, JOSEPH—BOX 130, PACK 3775:
Will dated Nov. 28, 1850 in Abbeville Dist. Filed Oct. 6, 1853. Exrs: Son, John Brown, Wm. Truwit. Wit: Wm. Harmon, Hezekiah F. Smith, Berry Dison. Wife, Elizabeth Brown. Chn: Uriah, Macklin, John, Joyse Brown afterwards Joyse Corley decd. leaving 3 chn: viz. Clemman, Jas. A., Esekiah Corley. Gr. dtr. Beattus Deason dtr. of my decd. dtr. wife of Joseph Deason. S. ls., Joseph Deason, Henry Baily. Gr. chn: Sarah, Elizabeth chn. of my decd dtr. Delila Bailey. Son, John Brown.

BARKSDALE, BENJAMIN—BOX 130, PACK 3776:
Est. admnr. Mar. 2, 1854 by Benjamin D. Barksdale, Robt. H., J. J. Wardlaw, Wm. Barksdale bound unto Wm. Hill Ord. Abbeville Dist. sum $3,000.00. Benjamin Barksdale was the father of Benjamin D. Barksdale. Those who recd. shares of est: L. B. Guillebeau, David M. Wardlaw, John C. Hayes, John, Fran Adams, John A. Hamilton, M. McDonald.

BASS, DR. D. M.—BOX 130, PACK 3777:
Est. admnr. Oct. 19, 1852 by David Keller, Jas. J. Gilmer, Wm. L. Wharton bound unto F. W. Selleck Ord. Abbeville Dist. sum $2,000.00. Henry Bass was the father of Dr. D. M. Bass.

COCHRAN, ALEXANDER B.—BOX 130, PACK 3778:
Est. admnr. Sept. 5, 1853 by Jas. N. Cochran, Jas. J. Adams, Benjamin Z. Herndon bound to F. W. Selleck Ord. Abbeville Dist. sum $20,000.00. Jas. N. Cochran was a bro. to Alexr. B. Cochran. 4 distributees: viz. J. N., Major John Cochran, Mrs. M. A. McNary, J. W. Cochran.

COWAN, WILLIAM—BOX 130, PACK 3779:
Est. admnr. Dec. 17, 1853 by Thos. F. Lanear, H. A. Jones, Henry S. Kerr bound to Wm. Hill Ord. Abbeville Dist. sum $500.00. Letter to Matthew McDonald. Sir, My. bro. Wm. Cowan has lately departed this life, having as his only distributees, myself his sis., and a bro. Saml. Cowan who resided in *Limestone* Co., Ala., but who has not been heard from for some considerable time. It is my desire that my s. l. Thos. F. Lanier should administer on said est. Signed, Mary McCaryney. Sett. made May 15, 1858. Stated that Saml. Cowan who lived in Ala., that information reached his relations here 2 yrs. ago that he died having no heirs surviving him.

CALHOUN, EDWIN B.—BOX 130, PACK 3780:
On Feb. 15, 1853 W. D. Calhoun, Benjamin L., Benjamin V. Posey bound unto F. W. Selleck Ord. Abbeville Dist. sum $100.00. W. D. Calhoun made gdn. of Edwin B. Calhoun a minor. W. D. Calhoun sheweth that his son Edwin

Broyles Calhoun is a minor entitled to an est. from Robt. Pollard in right of his mother Ellen Calhoun decd.

CALHOUN, (MINORS)—BOX 130, PACK 3781:
On Dec. 6, 1852 M. O. Tallman, W. Alexr. Drennan, D. M. Rogers bound unto F. W. Selleck Ord. Abbeville Dist. sum $300.00. M. O. Tallman made gdn. of John, Frances J. Calhoun minor chn. of Joseph Calhoun decd.

CUNNINGHAM, (MINORS)—BOX 130, PACK 3782:
On Jan. 10, 1860 Jas. Irwin, Wm. McIlwain, Jas. J. Gilmer bound unto Wm. Hill Ord. Abbeville Dist. sum $240.00. Jas. Irwin made gdn. of John W., Robt. F. Cunningham minors. Ann E., Mary J. Cunningham also minor chn. of Jas. S. Cunningham. Robt. F. was entitled to an est. from his gr. father John Goudy decd. Statement to ascertain the amount due by Jas. Irwin gdn. of John and R. W. Cunningham minors and who died in the service of the Confederate States as soldiers during the present war. Jas., Anna E. Cunningham, Mary J. McAllister on July 29, 1863 recd. $149.79.

CUNNINGHAM, BENJAMIN F.—BOX 130, PACK 3783:
Est. admnr. Nov. 30, 1853 by Joel J. Cunningham, John A. Wier, John T. Miller bound unto Matthew McDonald Ord. Abbeville Dist. sum $16,000.00. He died Oct. 19, 1853. Sett. made Oct. 29, 1855. Present: J. J. Cunningham admnr. Was a bro. to said decd. 4 distributees: viz. J., S. W., M. V., J. J. Cunningham.

CHARPING, JOHN H.—BOX 130, PACK 3784:
Est. admnr. Jan. 16, 1854 by Daniel F. Freeland, Jas. T. Baskin, F. W. Davis bound unto Wm. Hill Ord. Abbeville Dist. sum $1,200.00. He died July 23, 1853. Margaret Charping the wid.

CAMPBELL, DANIEL—BOX 130, PACK 3785:
Est. admnr. Feb. 13, 1854 by W. W. Waller, H. W. Wardlaw, W. W. Perryman bound unto Wm. Hill Ord. Abbeville Dist. sum $1,200.00. (Letter.)
New Market
Jan. 26, 1854
Mr. Wm. Hill
Dear Sir:
Mr. Danile Campbell died in this place on last Sunday and we wish you to grant us letters of admnr.
W. W. Perryman, W. W. Waller.

CALDWELL, J. J.—BOX 130, PACK 3786:
Est. admnr. Mar. 25, 1853 by Nathaniel J. Davis, John White, John McLaren bound unto F. W. Selleck Ord. Abbeville Dist. sum $1,000.00. He was late of the State of Miss. Recd. from Nathaniel J. Davis admnr. of est. of Jane Y. Caldwell decd. $629.61 my share of my decd. mother this 10th Oct., 1853. Signed, Saml. L. Caldwell admnr. of est. of John J. Caldwell decd. of Panola Co., Miss.

COOK, JAMES F.—BOX 130, PACK 3787:
Est. admnr. Dec. 15, 1854 by Wm. H. Simpson, Wm. S. McBride, Thos. B. Scott bound unto Wm. Hill Ord. Abbeville Dist. sum $800.00. J. E. Uldrick a distributee, also J. B. Cook.

CALHOUN, ELIZABETH M.—BOX 130, PACK 3788:
Est. admnr. Dec. 5, 1853 by M. O. Talman, Jas. McCaslan, D. M. Rogers bound unto Matthew McDonald Ord. Abbeville Dist. sum $7,000.00. She died on or about Aug. 1853.

CALHOUN, ELLEN—BOX 130, PACK 3789:
Est. admnr. Feb. 15, 1853 by W. D. Calhoun, Benjamin L., Benjamin V. Posey bound unto F. W. Selleck Ord. Abbeville Dist. sum $200.00. Sett. made July 18, 1854 ment. her share of est. of Robt. Pollard decd.

CLECKLEY, DAVID F.—BOX 130, PACK 3790:
Est. admnr. Nov. 5, 1852 by Rufus, Elizabeth Ann Cleckley, Saml. McGowan, Jas. M. Perrin bound unto F. W. Selleck Ord. Abbeville Dist. sum $40,000.00. Rufus Cleckley of St. Mathews Parish, Orangeburg Dist. sheweth that David F. Cleckley died in Abbeville Dist. leaving as his heirs and next of kin, his wid., Elizabeth Cleckley and 6 chn: viz. Wm. J., Alonzo, Addison, Irving, Johnson Cleckley and your petr. Rufus Cleckley.

DAY, MANSFIELD—BOX 131, PACK 3791:
Mansfield Day on Nov. 8, 1853 sheweth that he is a minor child of Philip Day decd. of Abbeville Dist., that he is a minor over the age of choice and requests that Benjamin V. Posey be appointed his gdn.

DOUGLASS, MARY—BOX 131, PACK 3792:
Will dated May 24, 1851 in Abbeville Dist. Filed Nov. 8, 1852. Exr. Dr. Ephraim R. Calhoun. Wit: N. McCants, R. G. Golding, Benjamin Blackerby. Chn: John, Wm., Jas. Douglass, Peggy Anderson, Lurany Pert. Gr. chn: Wm., Lewis, Nancy, Rebecca Pert, chn. of my decd. dtr. Elizabeth Pert. Mary Pert dtr. of Lurany Pert, John Henry Waits son of Mary Waits.

DONALD, JANE—BOX 131, PACK 3793:
Est. admnr. Jan. 24, 1854 by Francis Atkins, Bartw. Jordon, Ermund Cobb bound unto Wm. Hill Ord. Abbeville Dist. sum $6,000.00. Will dated Sept. 14, 1853. Filed Jan. 9, 1854. Exr. Son, Joseph Atkins. Wit: Lewis Smith, Bartw., Thos. Jordon. Wid. of Abbeville Dist. Heirs: Rachel Teague decd., Jas. Atkins decd., John Adams, Abram Lites, David Atkins, Francis, Joseph, Thos. Atkins, Teresa Lipford, Jane Lites. Power of Atty. Benton Co., Ala. July 29, 1856. We the chn. of Rachel Teague decd. learning that we are entitled to an est. from Jane Donald decd. do appoint W. C. Davis of Abbeville Dist. our Atty. to collect what money is coming to us and to make check on Charleston made payable to Abner A. Teague. (Letter)
Rush Co., Ind.
June 13, 1856
Robert Atkins
Sir:

I received your favor of the 27th, May last and have as you will appointed Mr. Davis as I thought he would be a suitable person the time being short and he having the case before him. When the sett. is made I wish you to receive the money and forward it as soon as convenient as directed in a former letter or I might say deposit it some good bank and take up a draft on some N. Y. Bank payable to me or my order and pay yourself for your trouble. The friends are all well as far as known to us at this time we have had a fine spring for business and some crop looks well some wheat corn oats and garden vegestables was badly frosted on the 31st May but are recovering to some extent as my time is up I will close by saying when you write again tell us what you are following for a livelihood.

Thos., Joseph Atkins

Lived in Ga., Henry Co. On Sept. 25, 1865 Abner A. Teague of Benton Co., Ala. recd. $328.28 the amt. due myself, H. B. Johnson and wife, O. D. Whitsides and wife, Elijah Teague, Robt. J. Teague from est. of Jane Donald of Abbeville Dist., S. C.

DUNCAN, THOMAS M.—BOX 131, PACK 3794:
Will dated Feb. 7, 1849 in Abbeville Dist. Filed Dec. 3, 1853. Exrs: Jacob B. Britt, Jas. C. Willard. Wit: Jas. H. Britt, John M. David, Mary A. Hayes. Sis., Nancy Ann Hemminger. Neice, Eleanor Jennet Duncan McGrath. Michael McGrath was present at the Sett.

ENGLISH, DANIEL—BOX 131, PACK 3795:
Will dated Hay 4, 1853 in Abbeville Dist. Filed Dec. 13, 1853. Exrs: Wife, Elizabeth English, S. l's. John Sentell, Thos. Aiton, Jackson English. Wit: Jacob Miller, Joseph Philpot, Jas. M. Harrison. Chn: Hetha Dooly, Rocelia Aiton, Lucinda Jay, Sarah Hardin, Jackson English, Frances Sentell, Elizabeth Morris, Amanda Spikes.

GABLE, WILLIAM—BOX 131, PACK 3796:
Est. admnr. Nov. 16, 1852 by David, Edmund Walker, Tiry Jay bound unto F. W. Selleck Ord. Abbeville Dist. sum $1,000.00. Wm. Gable was the s. l. of David Walker. Left a wid. Margaret Gable and 1 child.

GILLESPIE, ANDREW, SR.—BOX 131, PACK 3797:
Est. admnr. Jan. 4, 1854 by Jas. Pursley, Isaac Branch, B. P. Hughes bound unto Wm. Hill Ord. Abbeville Dist. sum $1,000.00. Left a wid. and 4 dtrs. On Apr. 11, 1857 Grizzilla Gillespie recd. $136.46. Sarah G., Margaret H., Anne E. Gillespie also recd from est.

GILLAM, ELIZABETH—BOX 131, PACK 3798:
Will dated May 2, 1836 in Newberry Dist. Filed Jan. 20, 1853. Exrs: F. B. Huggins, P. C. Caldwell. Wit: M. W. Gracey, L. L. Swindler, Wm. O. Connor. Great gr. dtr: Sarah Schoppert. Gr. chn: Mary B. Schoppert, Elizabeth Gillam dtr. of Wm. Gillam. When the will was prov. ment. that Gracey was in Ala. and Swindler in Tex. L. M. Gillan of Pilot Mountain, N. C. sheweth that he is a son of Wm. Gillam and gr. s. of Elizabeth Gillam decd. Dated this 30th Mar., 1853. Son of Wm. Gillam of Surry Co., N. C.

HAIRSTON, JANE—BOX 131, PACK 3799:
    Will dated June 4, 1853 in Abbeville Dist. Filed Oct. 25, 1853. Exr:
David Keller, Esq. Wit: John W. Lomax, Garlington Owens, Elizabeth B. Lomax.
Nephew, Jas. Wesley Johnstan son of Toliver and Jane Johnston. "Bequeath to,
Thos., Oliver Johnston, Rachel Martin, Wm. son of John Gray decd., Mary Ann
Thompson, Sarah Jane Lomax dtr. of John and Elizabeth Lomax." On July 24,
1855 Thos. Johnson of Panola Co., Miss. appointed John Adams of Abbeville
Dist. his atty. in the est. of Jane Hairston. On Aug. 2, 1856 Jas. H. Martin and
wife Rachel Martin of Tippah Co., Miss. appointed David Keller Esq. their Atty.
in est. of Jane Hairston. On July 9, 1856 Toliver Johnson of Panola Co., Miss.
appointed Tidence Johnson of same Co. his Atty.

HAMILTON, CHRISTIANA—BOX 131, PACK 3800:
    Est. admnr. July 3, 1852 by Nathaniel J. Davis, John Adams, Henry S.
Kerr bound unto F. W. Selleck Ord. Abbeville Dist. sum $100.00.

HELMS, (MINORS)—BOX 131, PACK 3801:
    On Feb. 13, 1854 B. V., B. L., John W. Posey bound unto Wm. Hill Ord.
Abbeville Dist. sum $200.0. B. V. Posey made gdn. of Jas. A., Robt., Wm. Helms
minors of Andrew Helms, minors over the age of choice about 19, 17, 15 yrs.
Also entitled to a small est. from Robt. V. Posey decd.

HARPER, JANE—BOX 131, PACK 3802:
    Will dated Feb. 23, 1853 in Abbeville Dist. Filed May 14, 1853. Exr:
Son, Henry H. B. Harper. Wit: Alexr. Oliver, W. F. Clinkecales, Ezekiel P.
Speed. Chn: Wm. H. Harper, Martha T. Caldwell wid., Jas. C., Lyndsay R. A.,
Henry H. B., John A. H. Harper, Sarah H. McGehee. Will ment. that John A.
H. Harper was of Ga. Dr. Jas. A. McGehee husband of Sarah was also of Ga.

HAGEN, THOMAS—BOX 131, PACK 3803:
    Est. admnr. Feb. 8, 1853 by David Keller, John McIlwain, H. A. Jones
bound to F. W. Selleck Ord. Abbeville Dist. sum $600.00. Sett. made Apr. 7,
1854. Present, David Keller admnr., Martha Hagen sis. of said decd. Ment. 6
distributees but no names given. Sale, Feb. 26, 1853. Byrs: Martha, John,
Mary, Edward, A. G. Hagen, etc.

HACKETT, ELIJAH C.—BOX 131, PACK 3804:
    Est. admnr. Dec. 20, 1853 by America E. Hackett, S. Ann Moore, August
G. Hackett bound to Wm. Hill Ord. Abbeville Dist. sum $20,000.00.

HAMPTON, WASHINGTON E.—BOX 131, PACK 3805:
    Will dated May 18, 1852 in Abbeville Dist. Filed July 24, 1852. Exr: Wm.
J. Milford. Wit: Wm. S. Hampton, John, Wm. J. Milford. Wife, Malinda R.
Hampton. Chn: Thos. E., Wm. H., Jas. B. Hampton. "Wife now pregnant with
child."

IRWIN, SAMUEL—BOX 131, PACK 3806:
    Will dated Sept. 1852 in Abbeville Dist. Day left out. Filed May 9, 1854.
Exr: Son, Jas. Irwin. Wit: Thos. C. Perrin, Wm. H. Parker, Thos. Thomson.

Wife, Elizabeth Irwin. Chn: Jas. Irwin. Wife of Wm. N. Purdy. Gr. chn: Elenor Jane Spillars, Jas. H., Elizabeth A., Saml. A., Margaret A., Sarah G., Wm. Purdy. Saml., Robt. Irwin sons of Jas. Irwin. Sis., Bella Cowan. Elenor Jane Taylor and her husband Wm. Taylor recd. $54.28. Mrs. Jane Purdy was married twice, by her first marriage had 1 child now the wife of Wm. Taylor of Anderson. By the last marriage she left 6 surviving chn. Sett. to ascertain the share of Amaziah Purdy in the hands of the late Jas. Irwin. Present, Amaziah Purdy and Mrs. Charlotte Irwin Extrx. of Jas. Irwin. Amaziah was a bro. to Wm. A. Margaret Ann Purdy married a Hall.

JORDON, DR. SAML. W.—BOX 131, PACK 3807:
Est. admnr. Jan. 24, 1853 by Jonathan, Bartw., David Jordon bound to F. W. Selleck Ord. Abbeville Dist. sum $2,000.00.

KAY, REUBEN—BOX 131, PACK 3808:
Est. admnr. Oct. 26, 1853 by Richard G. Kay, John M. G. Branyan, Stephen M. Tribble, Thos. M. Branyon unto Mathew McDonald Ord. Abbeville Dist. sum $3,000.00. R. G. Kay, J. M. G. Branyan were next of kin.

LAMB, (MINORS)—BOX 131, PACK 3809:
On Dec. 7, 1852 M. G. Ross, John R. Tarrant, R. M. White bound to F. W. Selleck Ord. Abbeville Dist. sum $300.00. M. G. Ross made gdn. of Jas., John, Barrett Lamb minors. M. G. Ross was a cousin to said minors who were the chn. of Jas. Lamb decd. late a soldier in the Mexican War, who served in the Palmetto Regiment of S. C. Vols. as a Pri. in Co. E. commanded by Capt. J. F. Marshall.

LOGAN, FRANCIS—BOX 131, PACK 3810:
On Sept. 5, 1853 Isaac, F. B. Logan, Saml. Turner bound to F. W. Selleck Ord. Abbeville Dist. sum $2,000.00. Isaac Logan made gdn. of Francis Logan a minor son of Francis Logan decd. Sett. made Jan. 25, 1858 stated that he was now of age.

LAMB, JAMES—BOX 131, PACK 3811:
Est. admnr. July 14, 1852 by M. G. Ross, John R. Tarrant, J. W. Lipscomb bound to F. W. Selleck Ord. Abbeville Dist. sum $200.00. Jas. Lamb died in Mexico while in the service of the U. S.

LOGAN, LOUISA R.—BOX 131, PACK 3812:
Est. admnr. Jan. 3, 1853 by Henry F. Power, G. W. Huckabee, Wm. L. Campbell bound to F. W. Selleck Ord. Abbeville Dist. sum $15,000.00.

LOMAX, LUCY—BOX 131, PACK 3813:
Will dated Dec. 16, 1852 in Abbeville Dist. Filed Jan 17, 1853. Exr: Nephew, Warren G. Lomax. Wit: David Keller, John H. Wilson, H. M. Wardlaw. "Bequeath to Nancy Meridith."

LYON, NATHANIEL N.—BOX 131, PACK 3814:
Est. admnr. Jan. 4, 1853 by Tilman A. Walker, Leroy Purdy, Jas. J.

Devlin bound to F. W. Selleck Ord. Abbeville Dist. sum $2,500.00. Elisha Lyon was the father of said decd. Tilman A. Walker sheweth that his bro. l., Nathaniel Lyon died in Cass Co., Ga., leaving a will. Mary Ann, Tilman A. Walker recd. a legacy from said will. (Will dated Oct. 11, 1852. Filed Jan. 4, 1853. Wit: Wm. H. Felton, A. J. Weems, John Felton. Was of Cass. Co., Ga. "Leave entire est. to my only full sis. Mary Ann Walker.")

LOGAN, WILLIAM W.—BOX 131, PACK 3815:
    Est. admnr. Apr. 19, 1856 by G. W. Huckabee, Jas. M. Latimer, John Brownlee bound to Wm. Hill Ord. Abbeville Dist. sum $10,000.00. Est. admnr. again Oct. 20, 1852 by Henry F., John Power, Sr., J. W. Huckabee unto F. W. Selleck Ord. Abbeville Dist. sum $20,000.00. Wm. W. Logan was a son l. to Henry F. Power who was a bro. l. to G. W. Huckabee. Wm. Raiford, Mary Susan Logan were chn.

LESLY, DAVID—BOX 131, PACK 3816:
    Will dated Feb. 3, 1854 in Abbeville Dist. Filed Feb. 11, 1854. Exrs: Wife, Louisa Lesly, Wm. McWorter, John W. Lesly. Wit: Thos. C. Perrin, Wm. M. Hadden, Jas. S. Cothran. S. l. Margaret McWhorter wife of Wm. McWhorter. "Bequeath to Louisa Jane McWhorter dtr. of Wm. McWhorter." Sis. l., Eliza N. Kyle. Nephews: John W., Thos. Lesly; Nieces: Anna Louisa wife of J. W. Norris, Virginia E. Lesly.

LYON, JOHN—BOX 131, PACK 3817:
    Est. admnr. Nov. 11, 1853 by John F. C. Settle, John T., Bartley M. Cheatham bound to Matthew McDonald Ord. Abbeville Dist. sum $25,000.00. John Lyon died Oct. 23, 1853 leaving a wid. Lucy and 1 child now married who with her husband are residents of Floyd Co., Ga.

McNEIL, JOHN—BOX 131, PACK 3818:
    Will dated Nov. 1, 1852 in Abbeville Dist. Filed Nov. 4, 1852. Exrs: Son, Alexr. McNeil, S. S. Marshall. Wit: Wm. F. Moss, W. G. Waller, W. W. Waller. Wife and chn. ment. but only one named, Alexr. McNeil.

McILWAIN, JANE, JR.—BOX 132, PACK 3819:
    Est. admnr. Apr. 22, 1854 by Andrew, Wm. McIlwain, Jr., Geo. Nickles, bound to Wm. Hill Ord. Abbeville Dist. sum $2,500.00. Wm. McIlwain Jr. was a bro. to said decd. She left a mother and 6 bros. and sis. John McIlwain was a bro.

MAGEE, LUCY ANN—BOX 132, PACK 3820:
    On Mar. 9, 1854 Wm. P. Magee Sr., Peter Burton, Abner H. Magee, G. M. Mattison bound to Wm. Hill Ord. Abbeville Dist. sum $1,500.00. Wm. P. Magee Sr. made gdn. of Lucy Ann Magee a minor. Wm. P. Magee sheweth that his dtr. about 7 yrs. of age is entitled to legacy from est. of her Gr. grandfather Benjamin Thornton who lately died in Ga.

MAYNARD, VIRGINIA PICKENS—BOX 132, PACK 3821:
    On July 29, 1852 Edna Caldwell, Stanmore B. Brooks, Jacob Miller bound to F. W. Selleck Ord. Abbeville Dist. sum $6,000.0. Edna Caldwell made

gdn. of Virginia Pickens Maynard minor. Edna Caldwell sheweth that she is the
gr. mother of Virginia Maynard a minor about 7 yrs. and child of Jas. M. Maynard
decd.

McBRYDE, JOHN—BOX 132, PACK 3822:
On Feb. 3, 1854 Andrew J. Weed, Joseph Cirswell, Thos. C. McBryde
bound to Wm. Hill Ord. Abbeville Dist. sum $700.00. Andrew J. Weed made
gdn. of John McBryde a minor about 16 yrs. John McBryde was his gr. father.

McBRYDE, JOHN—BOX 132, PACK 3823:
Will dated Nov. 12, 1852 in Abbeville Dist. Filed Dec. 28, 1853. Exr:
Andrew J. Weed. Wit: Geo. W. Pressly, Simpson Evans, Geo. McYoung. Chn:
Jane, Josiah, Thos., Joseph, Jas., Saml. McBryde. Gr. sons: John, John Andrew
McBride. Sett. made Apr. 12, 1856. Present, Andrew Weed, Thos., Joseph
McBride, Joseph Creswell in right of his decd. wife Jane. Absent: Joseph
McBride in Texas, Saml. McBride in Miss., Jas. McBride. Thos Creswell recd.
a share of $55.25. Power of Atty. Cherokee Co., Texas. Know that I Saml.
McBride of said Co. do appoint Wm. Bradley who resides at Indian Hill,
Abbeville Dist., S. C. my Atty. to receive what is coming to me from my father's
est. John McBride who resided at his death at Indian Hill, Abbeville Dist., S. C.
Dated Oct. 13, 1854.

MATTHEWS, JOSEPH C.—BOX 132, PACK 3824:
Will dated Jan. 2, 1854 in Abbeville Dist. Filed Feb. 21, 1854. Wit: M.
O. Tallman, Jas. MaCelvey, A. Houston. Wife, Margaret Matthews. Chn: Thos.
J., Mary, Lucretia, Ezekiel W., Joseph A. Matthews, Jane A. Christopher, Rachel
C. McCaslan, Elizabeth T. Shanks, Margaret E. McGaw, Martha L. Wilson.

Son l., Geo. A. Christopher.   (Letter)
Clear Springs
24 Feb., 1854
Mr. Wm. Hill
Dear Sir:
I wrote a few line to you but hearing that you had not recd. it. I now write
you a few more on the same business. Mrs. Matthews and the legatees have requested me to Admnr. on the est. of Capt. J. C. Matthews decd. with the will
annexed I wish you to grant a citation, etc. Jas. McCallan.

MALONE, JAMES P.—BOX 132, PACK 3825:
Est. admnr. Oct. 20, 1852 by Nathan L. Lipscomb, Wm. W. Waller.
John M. Keller bound unto F. W. Selleck Ord. Abbeville Dist. sum $700.00. N.
L. Lipscombe later moved to Greenville Dist., S. C.

MABRY, R. L.—BOX 132, PACK 3826:
Est. admnr. Sept. 5, 1853 by Mathew W., Thos. J., Jas. F. Mabry, Jas.
N. Cochran bound to F. W. Selleck Ord. Abbeville Dist. sum $30,000.00.
Mathew Mabry was a son of said decd. Legatees: Wyatt Holmes, Thos J. Mabry,
Jas. F., M. W. Mabry, Mrs. Ross, Saml. Mabry, Caroline, Lucien Mabry.

MARTIN, BEVERLY M.—BOX 132, PACK 3827:
    Est. admnr. Oct. 1, 1853 by Wm. A. Lee, Robt. A. Fair, Wm. H. Parker
bound unto Matthew McDonald Ord. Abbeville Dist. sum $500.00. She was late
of the State of Ga. Left a father and 5 bros. and sis.

McKINNEY, ROBT.—BOX 132, PACK 3828:
    Est. admnr. Feb. 24, 1853 by A. P. Robinson, Robt. McComb, Saml. Link
bound to F. W. Selleck Ord. Abbeville Dist. sum $3,000.00.

McGAWS, (MINORS)—BOX 132, PACK 3829:
    On Jan. 4, 1853 Martha McGaws, Robt., Jas. J. Devlin bound to F. W.
Selleck Ord. Abbeville Dist. sum $7,000.00. Martha McGaws made gdn. of
Martha J., Saml. T., Elizabeth Carrie McGaw minor chn. of Josiah McGaw decd.
and said Martha McGaw. Martha Jane McGaw later married H. P. Helper.

MOSELEY, (MINORS)—BOX 132, PACK 3830:
    On Dec. 2, 1852 Benjamin F. Moseley, Gabriel M. Mattison, Wm. P.
Martin bound to F. W. Selleck Ord. Abbeville Dist. sum $4,100.00. Benjamin F.
Moseley made gdn. of Sarah J., Irene E., Margaret, Nancy, Wm. L. Moseley
minors. On Apr. 27, 1847 Wm., Benjamin F. Moseley, G. M. Mattison, Noah M.
Reeves bound to David Lesly Ord. Abbeville Dist. sum $224.00. Wm. Moseley
made gdn. of Sarah J., Irene E., Margaret, Nancy, Wm. L. Moseley minors under
14 yrs. chn. of Burrel Moseley decd. and Jane Moseley decd. Irene Moseley
married John A. Crawford. Sarah Jane married G. F. Mattison.

McCLINTON, MATTHEW—BOX 132, PACK 3831:
    Will dated Dec. 18, 1848 in Abbeville Dist. Filed June 30, 1853. Exrs:
John Cothran, Tira Jay. Wit: Robt. A., Jas. C. Martin, A. Wideman. Wife,
Margaret McClinton. Bro., John McClinton.

McCAW, WILLIAM H.—BOX 132, PACK 3832:
    Est. admnr. Sept. 22, 1852 by Thos. C. Perrin, E. McCaw, Jas. M. Perrin,
Saml. McCaw bound to F. W. Selleck Or. Abbeville Dist. sum $8,000.00.
Dr. J. J. Wardlaw was gdn. of Julia, Fanny, Mary McCaw minors. L. Yarbrough
was the gdn. of John T., Wm. H. McCaw minors. Dr. W. T. Bailey married
the wid. of said decd. Chn. were: Julia, Fannie, Mary, Wm., John T., Alexr. B.
McCaw.

McCALLISTER, JAMES—BOX 132, PACK 3833:
    Est. admnr. June 1, 1853 by Alexr. L. McCaslan, A. P. Connor, Jas.
Drennan bound unto F. W. Selleck Ord. Abbeville Dist. sum $3,000.00. Sett.
made Oct. 24, 1855. Present: A. L. McCaslan admnr., Nathan McCallister,
Mrs. Margaret Black wid., being 2 distributees.

MEANS, WILLIAM—BOX 132, PACK 3834:
    Will dated Feb. 10, 1852 in Abbeville Dist. Filed May 3, 1852. Exrs:
Wife. no name given, Jas. Means, Jas. McGill. Wit: David Lesly, Lemuel Reid.
W. S. Cothran. Chn: Margaret B. wife of Jas. McGill, Jane C. wife of Jas.
Wilson of Miss., John Means. Had chn. by 2 marriages. Sett. made May 16, 1854
ment. Mrs. Sally Means as the wid, 10 chn. ment. but no names given.

MADDOX, HENRY—BOX 132, PACK 3835:
Est. admnr. Oct. 11, 1853 by Wm. P. Martin, John M. Grier, Wm. Long bound to Mathew McDonald Ord. Abbeville Dist. sum $1,000.00. Matilda M. Maddox was wife of said decd. Sett. ment. wid. and 4 chn. Wm. P. Martin was gdn. for Wm. M., Geo. M., Nancy A., Sarah J., Frances A. Maddox minors.

McKELDON, SUSAN—BOX 132, PACK 3836:
Est. admnr. Jan. 6, 1854 by Andrew Paul, John, Wm. Adams bound to Wm. Hill Ord. Abbeville Dist. sum $400.00.

MAGILL, WILLIAM, SR.—BOX 132, PACK 3837:
Est. admnr. Oct. 4, 1853 by Jas. Magill, Thos. Robinson, Henry S. Kerr bound to Mathew McDonald Ord. Abbeville Dist. sum $2,700.00. Jas. Magill was a son of said decd.

McLENNAN, JOHN—BOX 132, PACK 3838:
Will dated Jan. 3, 1852 in Abbeville Dist. Filed July 11, 1853. Exrs: Jas. Wesley Child, Thos. Thompson. Wit: Daniel Campbell, S. V. Cain, M. B. Hackett. Father, Alexr. McLennan. Mother, Isabella McLennan. Aunt, Nancy McLennan. Sis., Bell Finlayson. "My parents, bros., and sis. reside in the Parish of Lochalsh, Scotland." Gr. dtr. Catharine Ann Watson. (In the evidence of the will.) Stated that Mr. McLennan later went to Fla. That his dtr. Ann McLennan married Edward Watson. Did not approve of their marriage.

MATHIS, ISABELLA—BOX 132, PACK 3839:
Will dated May 19, 1841 in Abbeville Dist. Exr: Jas. Carson. Wit: Franklin Branch, Thos. E. Owens, Jas. Carson. Chn: Jane Griffin, Luke, Sarah Ann, Lewis, Wm., Thos. E. Mathis. "As for my gr. chn. of Saml. Hill and my dtr. Mary Hill I give them nothing as their mother has recd. her portion." Sett: Thos. M. Morrow and wife, Chas. B. Griffin and wife were distributees.

PACKAGES MISNUMBERED AGAIN

ROWLAND, NATHANIEL—BOX 133, PACK 3552:
Est. admnr. Sept. 6, 1847 by David W. McCants, Mary Rowland, John W. Moore, Aaron Lomax bound to David Lesly Ord. Abbeville Dist. sum $42,000.00. Left a wid. Mary Rowland and several chn. Sett. made Nov. 21, 1849. Due to B. F. Johnson and Augustus Roland admnr. of wid. Mary Roland decd. to be divided among B. F. Johnson and wife, Thos. Burnett and wife, Augustus Roland and Malinda Rowland decd. Thos. Burnett's wife was Amanda.

ROWAND, MARY AND MALINDA—BOX 133, PACK 3553:
Est. of Mary Rowland admnr. May 18, 1849 by Benjamin F. Johnson, John Burnett. Augustus Rowland, David McCants bound to David Lesly Ord. Abbeville Dist. sum $20,000.00. Est. of Malinda Rowland admnr. the same day sum $8,000.00. Petr. of Admnrs. sheweth that Mary Rowland wid. of Nathaniel Rowland and Malinda Rowland who was of age and had property are both dead. Sett. of Malinda Rowland made Nov. 21, 1849 to be divided in 3 shares: viz. A. Rowland, B. F. Johnson, Thos. Burnett. The same recd. shares in est. of Mary Rowland.

REAGIN, YOUNG—BOX 133, PACK 3554:
Est. admnr. Nov. 2, 1846 by Jesse Reagin, Archibald Bradley, Andrew J. Weed bound to David Lesly Ord. Abbeville Dist. sum $4,000.00. Jesse Reagin sheweth that Young Reagin and Joseph Reagin his father and bro. died intestate. Had a wid. and 4 chn. On Oct. 1848 Catharine Reagin, G. K., Elizabeth Bradley, Nicholas Reagin all recd. a share of Young Reagin's est.

REAGIN, RACHEL—BOX 133, PACK 3555:
Est. admnr. Dec. 20, 1849 by E. O. Reagin, F. T. White, Walter G. Keller bound to David Lesly Ord. Abbeville Dist. sum $200.00.

REAGIN, EDWIN O.—BOX 133, PACK 3556:
On Sept. 5, 1848 Jesse Reagin, John W. Hearst bound to David Lesly Ord. Abbeville Dist. sum $890.0. Jesse Reagin made gdn. of Edwin O. Reagin a minor. (Name written Edwin and Edward Reagin.) Was a son of Young Reagin decd. Edward O. Reagin of Holmes Co., Miss. sheweth that he is a minor over 16 yrs. Son of Young Reagin and a bro. to Joseph Reagin decd. and Jesse Reagin. "That his bro. Jesse Reagin of Holmes Co., Miss. be appointed his gdn. Dated 11, Sept. 1848.

RICHEY, ROBERT—BOX 133, PACK 3557:
Est. admnr. Jan. 11, 1847 by Elizabeth, John B., Jas. B., Wm. L., Nancy Adeline Richey bound to David Lesly Ord. Abbeville Dist. sum $30,000.00. John B. Richey sheweth that his father Robt. Richey died intestate leaving a wid. Elizabeth and 8 chn.

RICHEY, ROBERT J.—BOX 133, PACK 3558:
Will dated Feb. 1, 1848 in Abbeville Dist. Prov. Feb 19, 1848. Exr: F. l. Jas. Carson. Wit: Jas. M., Mary Carson, Elizabeth Richey. Ment: Late of Fla. but now of Abbeville Dist. Wife, Mary Caroline Richey. Chn: Jas. Augustus, Robt. Alexr. Richey. "Owned real est. in Fla."

ROBISON, ISAAC—BOX 133, PACK 3559:
Will dated Apr. 4, 1848 in Abbeville Dist. Prov. Aug. 7, 1848. Exrs: Jesse, Anna Robison. Wit: John R. Shirley, Reuben Kay, W. Pearman. Sis., Anna Robison. Bro., Jesse Robison. (In will name written Robison and Robinson.)

RASOR, CHRISTIAN—BOX 133, PACK 3560:
Will dated Jan. 26, 1844 in Abbeville Dist. Prov. Dec. 19, 1848. Exrs: Son, Ezekiel Rasor, Revd. Hugh Dickson. Wit: Jas. W., Daniel Blain, T. Y. Martin. Chn: Jas. decd., Sarah, Ezekiel Rasor, Betsey wife of Thos. Phair, Nancy M., wife of Jas. Sims decd., John Rasor. Gr. dtr. Sarah A. J. Rasor dtr. of Jas. Rasor decd. Sett. made Feb. 5, 1850. Present: Ezekiel Rasor admnr., Tya Martin who married Sarah Rasor, Thos. Pharr and Elizabeth his wife, Edward Rouey who married Nancy M. John Rasor died in the lifetime of his father leaving chn: viz. Jane E. wife of Isaac C. Richey, Polly Ann wife of John Donald Jr., Mary wife of R. Wyatt, Geo. W., P. C. Rasor, S. A. J. Conner dtr. of Jas. Rasor decd. and wife of M. L. Conner.

RICHEY, JOSEPH—BOX 133, PACK 3561:
Will dated Aug. 12, 1847 in Abbeville Dist. Prov. May 1, 1848. Exrs:
Enoch Barmore, Geo., Andrew Richey. Wit: T. Y. Martin, Joseph Agnew, Wm.
Barmore. Chn: John R., Nancy, Jinny, Joseph, Wm., Andrew, Geo., Elizabeth,
Robt., Peggy, Jackson Richey. Wife ment. name not given. "Desire to be decently
buried at Greenville Meeting House." Sett. made Feb. 6, 1850 ment. that he died
about Apr. 6, 1848. Chn: Jas. Jackson, John R., Joseph, Wm., Andrew, Geo.,
Robt. Richey, Jenny Smith, Peggy Hughes, Nancy, Elizabeth Richey. Margaret
Hughes was the wife of Wm. W. Hughes.

RICHEY, WILLIAM—BOX 133, PACK 3562:
Will dated Nov. 3, 1846 in Abbeville Dist. Prov. Nov. 20, 1846. Exrs:
Sons, Wm., Nimrod Richey, Gabriel M. Mattison. Wit: Andrew Dunn, Jas.
Stone, Benjamin Owen. Wife, Elizabeth Richey. Chn: Wm., Nimrod, H. J.
Richey, Nancy Hawthorn, Jane Moseley, Margaret Mattison, Robt., Geo. Richey.
Present at sett: Henry J. Richey, John Hawthorne, Wm. Moseley gdn. of Jane
Moseleys' chn. 8 legatees: 1. Geo. Richey, 2. Nimrod Richey, 3. Henry J. Richey,
4. Margaret Mattison, 5. Wm. Richey decd. Had 8 chn: Lutecia Cochran, Elmina
or Elvira McClinton, Ann Maclin, B. A. Richey, Savannah Elberson, W. J.
Richey decd. (had 3 chn., viz. Nanie, Wm., Hannah) Sarah J. Hill decd. 2 chn
Mamie, Jessie Nettie Smith. 6. Nancy Hawthorne decd. 3 chn. names unknown,
Leona Hawthorne, Lane, Mary Hawthorne, J. H., J. O., Consa, Robt. Hawthorne.
7. Jane Moseley decd. had 4 chn. viz. Sarah J. Mathson, Irene Crawford, Wm.
L. Moseley, Margaret Emins. 8. Robt. Richey decd. had 8 chn: 4 unknown, G. H.
Richey, M. A. McKee, M. E. Harvey, C. W. Richey. Transcript. Be it remembered
that on this 15th day Aug., 1887 the Term of Probate Court of Crawford Co.,
Ark. at the courthouse in the town of Van Buren that C. L. Tucker may be
appointed gdn. of his dtr. Bessie Tucker a minor over 14 yrs. who has a small
est. coming to her from the State of Ga.

RANDEN, JOHN W.—BOX 133, PACK 3563:
On Jan. 8, 1847 Andrew J. Weems, Isaac Branch, John A. Hamilton bound
to David Lesly Ord. Abbeville Dist. sum $12,000.00. Andrew Weems made gdn.
of John W. Randen a minor. John W. Randen sheweth that his father John C.
Randen died intestate many yrs. ago, leaving a wid. Rachel, a dtr. Mary M. and
your petr. as his distributees in the Dist. of Edgefield and that J. Holloway
and the wid. admnr. on his est. That his mother has married again, etc. (In one
place name written Rareden.)

RED, JAMES H.—BOX 133, PACK 3564:
Est. admnr. Feb. 1, 1850 by Joseph Pealor, Jasper Yeldell, Daniel Miner
bound to David Lesly Ord. Abbeville Dist. sum $25,000.00. Died without wife
or chn. Was a bro. l. to Joseph Pealor. Jas. Red was never married. Dr. Joseph Pealor and his wife Nancy A. Pealor were distributees.

ROBISON, (MINORS)—BOX 133, PACK 3565:
On Mar. 1, 1848 Robt. M. Davis, Wm. C. Cozby, A. A. Bowie bound
to David Lesly Ord. Abbeville Dist. sum $4,000.00. Robt. M. Davis made gdn. of

Sarah, Emily Robison minors over 14 yrs. Chn. of Hugh Robison decd. Andrew A. was their bro. l. Sett. made Feb. 7, 1850 ment. that Sarah Robison had married Alonzo Prather. Emily married A. Z. Bowman.

RUSSELL, ABRAHAM—BOX 133, PACK 3566:
Will dated June 30, 1835 in Abbeville Dist. Prov. Dec. 26, 1848. Exrs: Son, John Russell, S. l. Josiah Trotter. Wit: Wm. Sr., Mary, F. B. Robinson. "Bequeath est. to wife during her lifetime, then my 4 sons and 2 dtrs. and my great grandson by Martha Boyd." (No names given.) Sett. made Sept. 14, 1850. Present, John Russell Exr., Jacob Baukman who married Rebecca Russell, Henry R., Jas. Russell, Jane Trotter, Wm. Moats a minor. Jacob Baukman was written also Jacob Baughman.

ROBERTS, JANE—BOX 133, PACK 3567:
Will dated June 30, 1847 in Abbeville Dist. Prov. Oct. 1, 1849. Exr: Jas. McCaslan. Wit: J. E. Foster, Robt. A., Elizabeth Jane McCaslan. Chn: Sarah Brady, Elizabeth Gray, Frances, Reuben, Reland, Geo., Alfred Roberts. "Give Margaret Louisa dtr. of Reuben Roberts, to Frances dtr. of Reland Roberts, to Elizabeth Jane dtr. of Geo. Roberts, to Frances Emily dtr. of Sarah Brady, to Robt. Matison son of Alfred Roberts."

ROSS, STEPHEN AND ELIZABETH—BOX 133, PACK 3568:
Est. of Stephen Ross admnr. Jan. 1, 1849 by John R. Tarrant, R. M. White, T. L. Coleman bound to David Lesly Ord. Abbeville Dist. sum $4,000.00. Ets. of Elizabeth Ross admnr. same time in sum $1,500.00. Sett. made Jan. 7, 1851. Present, John R. Tarrant admnr. Moses G. Ross aged 20 yrs. 9 mo. and Henry M. Quattlebum who married Jane a distributee, Isabella Ann a minor.

NOBLE, JOHN A.—BOX 134, PACK 3293:
Est. admnr. May 4, 1846 by Edward Noble, D. M. Rogers, Dr. Nathaniel Harris bound to David Lesly Ord. Abbeville Dist. sum $4,000.00. Edward Noble stated that John A. Noble died intestate in Ga., without wife or lineal descendants.

PITTS, DANIEL—BOX 134, PACK 3294:
Est. admnr. Oct. 22, 1845 by Willis Ross, Wm. Rushton, Johnson Sale all of Edgefield Dist. bound to David Lesly Ord. Abbeville Dist. sum $8,000.00. Left a wid. and 3 chn. Wid., Sarah Pitts. Sett. made Nov. 23, 1855 ment. that *Ariana* E. married Lafayette Bellamy. Dorothy A. Pitts was of age in 1862.

PRICE, JOSEPH T.—BOX 134, PACK 3295:
Est. admnr. July 24, 1846 by L. B. Freeman, Chas. Freeman, Wm. C. Robertson bound to David Lesly Ord. Abbeville Dist. sum $2,500.00. Est. admnr. again Jan. 22, 1846 by L. B. Freeman of Edgefield Dist., Pleasant Searles, Wm. Robertson bound to David Lesly Ord. Abbeville Dist. sum $2,500.00. Sett. made Feb. 9, 1847 named distributees: viz. John H. Holloway and wife, Thos. Price, Wm. a minor, Berry Deason and wife Elizabeth now decd. a dtr. of Tilda Price who left 2 chn. Martha, Jane Deason.

PENNAL, SAMUEL C.—BOX 134, PACK 3296:
Est. admnr. June 12, 1846 by John Cothran, J. W. Hearst, Saml. Perrin bound to David Lesly Ord. Abbeville Dist. sum $1,000.00. Left no wife or chn.

PENNAL, JAMES W.—BOX 134, PACK 3297:
Est. admnr. Dec. 24, 1845 by John S. Wideman, Philip Zimmerman, Saml., Adam Wideman bound to David Lesly Ord. Abbeville Dist. sum $6,000.00. Left a wid. Emily and 3 chn. minors under 14 yrs. (Name also written Pennell.)

PORTER, (MINORS)—BOX 134, PACK 3298:
On June 22, 1846 Wm., Saml. A., Saml. Wilson bound unto David Lesly Ord. Abbeville Dist. sum $242.50. Wm. Wilson made gdn. of Wm. Chappel Porter, Neri B. Porter minors under 14 yrs. Wm. Wilson was a bro. l. to said minors. On Oct. 21, 1854 Jas. W. Porter stated that he was a bro. to Neri Porter who was about to remove to Ark. .

PAUL, MARY S.—BOX 134, PACK 3300:
On Nov. 13, 1843 Wm. S. Wharton, Jas. Devlin, David Wardlaw bound to David Lesly Ord. Abbeville Dist. sum $1,000.00. Wm. Wharton made gdn. of Mary S. Paul a minor. Mary S. Paul sheweth that her gr. father Andrew Paul decd. bequeathed to his son Wm. P. Paul now decd. a tract of land. That the said Wm. P. Paul left by his first wife, your petr. only. Sett. made Nov. 20, 1849 stated that Mary had married Capt. Wm. S. Harris.

RAMSAY, DANIEL—BOX 134, PACK 3301:
Est. admnr. Jan. 5, 1846 by L. B. Freeman, Saml. Cowan, Jas. C. Willard, Joseph Britt bound to David Lesly Ord. Abbeville Dist. sum $50,000.00. Little B. Freeman was of Edgefield Dist. Daniel Ramsay died on or about the 19th Dec., 1845. L. B. Freeman was a relation to the wid. of said decd. Left a wid. Rhoda Ramsay and 2 bros. On Feb. 6, 1847 John Ramsay Sr., of Ala. stated that he had recd. money, etc. from John Ramsey Jr. of Tenn. from the est. of Daniel Ramsey of Abbeville Dist., S. C. On Oct. 5, 1846 Geo. Ramsey of Cleveland, Bradley Co., Tenn. appointed John, Thos. Ramsey of same Co., his agents to collect what was coming to him from the est. of his bro. Daniel Ramsay of Abbeville Dist.

RICHARDSON, JAMES—BOX 134, PACK 3302:
Dr. Nathaniel Harris sheweth that Jas. Richardson died intestate having a wid. Rebecca but no chn., but bros. Est. admnr. Sept. 1, 1845 by Dr. Nathaniel Harris, Wm. McBride, Jas. Baskin bound to David Lesly Ord. Abbeville Dist. sum $500.00.

ROBINSON, WILLIAM H.—BOX 134, PACK 3303:
Est. admnr. Jan. 22, 1846 by Archibald, Isaac Kennedy, Jas. H. Foster bound to David Lesly Ord. Abbeville Dist. sum $1,000.00. Left a wid. and chn. under 14 yrs. Jane M. Rboinson the wid.

SMITH, JAMES—BOX 134, PACK 3304:
Est. admnr. Sept. 22, 1845 by Robt. Smith, John W. Moore, Jas. A.

Jay, John Carter, Wm. Strawhorn bound to David Lesly Ord. Abbeville Dist.
sum $25,000.00. Jas. Smith was the father of Robt. Smith. Sett. made Apr. 20,
1847. Present, Robt. Smith admnr., Nathan Calhoun husband of Amelia a dtr.
of said decd., Wm. S. Smith, Franklin Bowie husband of Belinda a dtr. of said
decd,. Jas. Smith Jr., Mr. Wm. Smith representing Wm. W. Franklin and
Mahulda his wife, Isaac Smith. Absent, Christopher Smith only child of Elijah
Smith a son of said decd.

STALLSWORTH, THOMAS—BOX 134, PACK 3305:
    Will dated Mar. 21, 1846. Prov. June 23, 1846. Exrs: Bro., Amon
Stallsworth, Nathaniel Henderson. Wit: Thos. Lake, Jas. Eathridge, Thos.
Ramsey, Russell Vaughn. Was of Edgefield Dist. "Bequeath to Jas. Leonard
Sales, Martha Elizabeth Sales, Ann Holloway, Thos., Nathaniel Henderson,
Elizabeth Tolbert, Eleanor Lake."

SMITH, FANNY—BOX 134, PACK 3306:
    Est. admnr. Oct. 9, 1845 by Wm. B. Smith, Chas., Thos. B. Dendy
bound to David Lesly Ord. Abbeville Dist. sum $2,000.00. Wm. B. Smith stated
that his mother Mrs. Fanny Smith died in 1842.

SHOEMAKER, LANDY G.—BOX 134, PACK 3307:
    Est. admnr. Nov. 26, 1845 by Geo. J. Cannon, Thos. McDill, L. Thomp-
son Shoemaker bound to David Lesly Ord. Abbeville Dist. sum $800.00. Mary C.
Shoemaker sheweth that Landy G. Shoemaker died leaving your petr. and 4 infant
chn.

SIMMONS, AMELIA—BOX 134, PACK 3308:
    Will adted July 1, 1843 in Abbeville Dist. Prov. Nov. 15, 1845. Exr: Dr.
F. G. Thomas. Wit: Jas. W. Wrightman, John F. Arnold, Wm. E. Arthur. Sis.
Ann Ward decd. of Charleston, S. C. Dtr. Sarah A. J. Wheaton. On May 20,
1847 W. Aug. Lee recd. $42.38 share of Sarah A. J. Wheaton now Mrs. Lee
Saml. Dunwoody, L. D. Merrimon, Chas. Smith, W. H. Blackmon recd. dis-
tributive shares.

SHANNON, MARY—BOX 134, PACK 3309:
    Est. admnr. Mar. 16, 1846 by Lindsay Harper, Caleb Burton, Jas. C.
Harper bound to David Lesly Ord. Abbeville Dist. sum $1,000.00. Lindsay Har-
per sheweth that Major Andrew Hamilton died intestate, that John Hamilton
admnr. on said est., that Sally Hamilton a dtr. of Major Andrew Hamilton married
John Harris both decd. leaving a dtr. Mary Harris who married Saml. H. Shannon
and by him has chn., names not known. (Letter to Mr. Lindsay Harper, Harpers
Ferry, Abbeville Dist., S. C.)
Princeton, Ind.
Oct. 2, 1848
Dear Sir
    Your letter of Sept. 3, is before and it is very strange you have not received
a receipt for the draft, as it was duly received and receipted for some few days
after you received the letter from me dated as you may say the 25th of May. We

are all well and hope this may find you enjoying the same blessing.
Respectfully
S. H. Shannon

    Saml. H. Shannon was gdn. of Weston Garret and Benjamin Franklin Shannon minors. Saml. H. Shannon was of Gibson Co., Ind. Mary Shannon died in Ind. Power of Atty. Gibson Co., Ind. On Nov. 10, 1847 Weston Garret Shannon and Benjamin Franklin Shannon sheweth that they were sons of Saml. H. Shannon, Mary Shannon late Mary Harris, who was a dtr. of Sarah Harris, who was a dtr. and heir of Major Andrew Hamilton decd. of Abbeville Dist. That their mother lately died in Gibson Co. That they are minors over 14 yrs. and entitled to an est. from Andrew Hamilton decd.

SCOTT, MARTHA J.—BOX 134, PACK 3310:

    Est. admnr. Jan. 14, 1846 by Wm. McCaslan, Wm. C. Scott, Wm. T. Drennan bound to David Lesly Ord. Abbeville Dist. sum $3,000.00. Wm. McCaslan sheweth that Wm. Scott died having 2 sets of chn. 3 chn. by his first wife, and 7 by his last wife now being Mary Scott. That a dtr. Martha has lately died. Alexr., Clark, Amanda, Martha Jane Scott were chn. of Wm. Scott decd. Wm. T. Drennan married Mary Scott. Thos. Dixon married Nancy Y. Scott. On Feb. 7, 1843 Wm. and Amanda Brownlee recd. from est. of Wm. Scott Sr.
Letter to Mr. Wm. McCaslan
Abbeville Dist., S. C.

Verrennes 8th 1847

    Mr. McCaslan your letter came duly to hand with your sett. I took my family down as far as mothers on Tuesday and the next day I started to the courthouse and it was so cornday I did not get all the way and at the same time I had had the cold and cough for three weeks and now I have a pain or hurting on my back below my shoulder blade which wrenched me quite unfit for work or any thing else except to set by the fire I think you will have to excuse me for not going to the sett. I am willing to abide by whatever sett. you all agree on some way of decision I dont want my absence to prevent a sett. I except Mr. Dickson to come to my house to night and if I change my notion I will let you know through him if he goes and if you see O. Conner tell him I expect to be down thare in a month or two and I wish him to have the money for me. I have nothing more to whrite to you at this time but remain your friend.
Wm. A. Brownlee

PACKAGES MISNUMBERED AGAIN

McILWAIN, JOHN—BOX 135, PACK 3840:

    Est. admnr. July 16, 1853 by Wm. Hill, Theopilus Alexr. Sale, David Lesly, Robt. H. Wardlaw, John, Saml. Donald bound to F. W. Selleck Ord. Abbeville Dist. sum $60,000.00. Wid. Ellen V. McIlwain. Wm. McIlwain was a bro. to said decd.

NORRELL, (MINORS)——BOX 135, PACK 3841:

    On Oct. 11, 1853 Benjamin V., Benjamin S. Posey bound to Mathew McDonald Ord. Abbeville Dist. sum $66.64. Benjamin S. or L. made gdn. of Sarah

Ann, Mary Jane Norrell minors. Made gdn. also of Isabella, Stephen, John Norrell minor chn. of Jas. M. Norrell decd.

PADGETT, (MINORS)—BOX 135, PACK 3842:
On Oct. 11, 1853 Benjamin V., Benjamin Posey bound to Matthew Mc-Donald Ord. Abbeville Dist. sum $60.00. Benjamin V. Posey made gdn. of Louisa, Mary Ann Padgett minors of John Padgett decd. Also entitled to a share in the U. S. Bounty Land Warrants as heirs of John Padgett decd.

POSEY, MARSA—BOX 135, PACK 3843:
Will dated Mar. 6, 1852 in Abbeville Dist. Filed Mar. 16, 1853. Exr: Son, Benjamin V. Posey. Wit: Benjamin L. Posey, Robt. C. Wilkison, A. A. Williams. Chn: Benjamin V., John W., Henson Posey. Gr. son: Benjamin Williams Posey son of Benjamin V. Posey.

RICHEY, MARGARET—BOX 135, PACK 3844:
Will dated Aug. 16, 1853 in Abbeville Dist. Prov. Nov. 1, 1853. Exrs: Robt., Andrew Dunn. Wit: Joseph Dickson, Isaac C. Richey, T. Y. Martin. Niece, Margaret R. Dunn. Nephew, Wm. Dunn. "Give to Jane W. Dunn dtr. of my nephews Jas. Dunn decd. Between my bros., and sis. viz. the heirs of Joseph Richey decd. Alley Dunn, Jas. Richey, the heirs of John Richey decd. the heirs of Robt. Richey decd. Nancey Haggan, Ann Sharp, Mary Hawthorne." Power of Atty: Know that I Jas. Richey of Lowndes Co., Ala. on this 15, Feb., 1855 do appoint H. A. Jones, Esq., of Abbeville Dist., S. C. my Atty. to collect what is coming to me from est. of my sis., Margaret Richey and Jas. Purdy the bro. of my wife, both of Abbeville Dist. who have lately died. Power of Atty. On Feb. 16, 1855 Wm. M. Hughs of Benton Co., Ala. appointed Robt. Richey of same co. his Atty. to receive what may be coming to him as an heir of the said Margaret Richey. The distributees of Margaret Richey were: John Richey, Nancy, Joseph, Wm., Robt. Richey, Wm. Hughs and wife Margaret, Andrew Richey, Saml. Smith and wife Jane, Geo. Richey, Silas Jones and wife Elizabeth, Jas. Jackson Richey. Power of Atty. On Mar. 1, -1855 Robt. W. Richey of Polk Co., Ga. appointed Johin N. Seawright his Atty. to receive his share of said Margaret Richey. On Feb. 24, 1855 Wm. Richey of Cass Co., Ga. appointed Jas. Albert Richey of Abbeville Dist. his Atty. for his part of said Margaret Richey est. On Dec. 12, 1855 Robt. Richey of Shilly Co., Ala., nephew of Margaret Richey appointed Jas. W. Blain his Atty. . . . Others who recd. share in Abbeville Dist. were: Wm., Ally Dunn, Edward, Nancy Hagan, Mary Hawthorn, Anna Sharp.

RICHEY, JOHN, SR.—BOX 135, PACK 3845:
Est. admnr. Oct. 19, 1852 by Benjamin P. Hughes, John A. Wier, Geo. McD. Miller bound unto F. W. Selleck Ord. Abbeville Dist. sum $5,000.00. He died in Sept. There were 5 distributees viz: Jas. A., Robt., Oliva, Wm. A., Margaret E. Richey.

ROBERTSON, MARGARET—BOX 135, PACK 3846:
Est. admnr. Aug. 6, 1852 by R. M. Davis, Arthur A. Bowie, Wm. C. Cozby bound unto F. W. Selleck Ord. Abbeville Dist. sum $4,000.00. Distributees: A. Bowman, John E. Robertson, A. A. Bowie.

RILEY, THOMAS—BOX 135, PACK 3847:
Will dated May 1, 1852 in Abbeville Dist. Filed Feb. 11, 1854. Exrs: Sons, Henry, Thos., Birt Riley. Wit: Robt., Mary, Thos. Jones. Wife, Elizabeth Riley. Chn: Henry, Birt, Thos., Mary Ann Riley, Elizabeth S. R. Smith child of Mary Smith decd. was a distributee. Willis Smith was her gdn. in 1870.

RICHEY MARGARET—BOX 135, PACK 3848:
On Nov. 22, 1852 Benjamin P. Hughes, John White bound to F. W. Selleck Ord. Abbeville Dist. sum $1,500.00. Benjamin Hughes made gdn. of Margaret Richey a minor of John Richey Sr. decd. Sett. made June 13, 1854 stated that Margaret Richey had married Geo. Dusenberry.

ROBERTSON, REUBEN—BOX 135, PACK 3849:
Was a free man of color. Did not copy.

RANEY, MATILDA P.—BOX 135, PACK 3850:
Est. admnr. Apr. 4, 1853 by John Cothran, Jas. H. Wideman, Jas. M. Perrin bound to F. W. Selleck Ord. Abbeville Dist. sum $5,000.00. Power of Atty. On Aug. 27, 1858 Thos. F. Rainey of Dewitt Co., Tex. appointed John H. Rainey of Abbeville Dist. his Atty. Thos. F., John H. Rainey were the only distributees. (Name written Raney and Rainey.)

STEVENSON, (MINORS)—BOX 135, PACK 3851:
On Dec. 16, 1853 Jas. C. Stevenson, Adam J. McKee, Wm. McComb bound to Wm. Hill Ord. Abbeville Dist. sum $600.00. Jas. C. Stevenson made gdn. of Susan S., Margaret E. Stevenson minors. Jas. C. Stevenson sheweth that his bro. Wm. Stevenson died leaving a wid. and 4 chn.

SMITH, SOPHIA—BOX 135, PACK 3852:
Will dated Oct. 21, 1853 in Abbeville Dist. Filed Nov. 16, 1853. Wit: Joshua Ashley, John T. Haddon, David Russell. Chn: Rebecca, Sophia, Daniel Smith. Inv. made Feb. 4, 1854 by J. W. Black, Thos. Davis, David Russell.

SIMMONS, ENOCH—BOX 135, PACK 3853:
On Feb. 15, 1854 John P. Barratt, Stanmore B., Wm. B. Brooks, John J. G. Barratt bound to Wm. Hill Ord. Abbeville Dist. sum $20,000.00. On Mar. 1, 1854 Stephen Elmore and his wife Ann E. Elmore, J. H. Pinson and his wife Margaret Florentine Pinson. Emily J., Harriet O., Elmire H., Nancy E. Simmons were distributees. Harriet S. Simmons the wid.

STEVENSON, (MINORS)—BOX 135, PACK 3854:
On Dec. 16, 1853 Andrew Stevenson, Peter Henry, Alexr. G. Hagen bound to Wm. Hill Ord. Abbeville Dist. sum $600.00. Andrew Stevenson made gdn. of Mary Louisa, Hamilton O. Stevenson minors. Andrew Stevenson sheweth that his bro. Wm. Stevenson left a wid. and 4 chn. under 14 yrs. Jane E. Stevenson was the wid., 4 chn. were: Mary Louisa, Hamilton O., Susan Sanora, Margaret Elizabeth Stevenson.

SMITH, CHARLES A.—BOX 135, PACK 3855:
Will dated June 7, 1853 in Abbeville Dist. Filed Nov. 7, 1853. Exr:

Bro., Peter Smith. Wit: Wm. H. Smith, Ezekiel Asbel, Lemuel W. Allen. Wife, Mary Smith. Chn. ment: no names given. Sett. made Aug. 1, 1855 named the chn: Frances of age, Alexr. a minor, Sophronia minor, Duett a minor, Maratt and Chas. minors.

STOKES, JOSEPH H.—BOX 135, PACK 3856:
     Est. admnr. Oct. 31, 1853 by Anna R. Stokes, Geo. W., Gabriel Hodges bound to Mathew McDonald sum $15,000.00. Mrs. Anna R. Stokes wid. was a sis. of Washington Hodges.

SMITH, HEZEKIAH F.—BOX 135, PACK 3857:
     Est. admnr. Dec. 6, 1853 by Peter Smith, Williams Trewit, J. W. B. Smith bound to Mathew McDonald Ord. Abbeville Dist. sum $2,800.00. He died Oct. 2, 1853. Sett. made Aug. 1, 1855 stated that the wid. Martha had married Saml. Stewart. Georgiana Smith was an infant about 3 yrs.

STRICKLAND, NATHAN M.—BOX 135, PACK 3858:
     Will dated Oct. 9, 1852 in Abbeville Dist. Filed Jan. 2, 1856. Exrs: John S. Reid, Robt. H. Wardlaw. Wit: Andrew McClane, Rebecca Thornton, Wm. A. Richey. Wife, Polly Strickland. Gr. dtr. Mary Elizabeth Grant. Margaret Cheves my wife's mother.

STEPHENSON, WM.—BOX 135, PACK 3859:
     Est. admnr. Nov. 18, 1852 by Saml. W., W. S., M. R. Cochran bound to F. W. Selleck Ord. Abbeville Dist. sum $1,500.00. Sett. made Oct. 31, 1854. Present: S. W. Cochran admnr., Jane E. Stevenson wid., Andrew, Jas. C. Stevenson gdns. of the 4 minor chn. (Name written Stephenson and Stevenson.)

SIMS, THOMAS—BOX 135, PACK 3860:
     Est. admnr. Feb. 11, 1854 by John R. Wilson, Saml. Donald, Saml. Reid bound to Wm. Hill Ord. Abbeville Dist. sum $10,000.00. On Dec. 19, 1855 Elijah Sims of Jefferson Co., Ala. appointed David McCombs of said Co. his Atty. to receive what was due him as an heir of Thos. Sims est. in Abbeville Dist., S. C. On Nov. 21, 1855 Joshua Tatum and Eliza Ann Tatum his wife, Daniel W. Sandel and Amey Sandel his wife, A. L. Mellown and wife Elizabeth Mellown, Benjamin T. Sims, John H. Coatney and wife Caroline Coatney, Jackson Carter and wife Mary Ann M. Carter, heirs of said Thos. Sims decd. Clovis C. Sims gdn. of the persons and est. of Jas. J. Sims, Nancy S. Sims, Benjamin Sims all heirs of Newton Co., Miss. do appoint Abner H. McGee Sr., their Atty. to collect what is coming to them from the est. of Thos. Sims. decd. Sett. made Jan. 1, 1856 ment: wid, Margaret E. Sims, David McCombs who married Sarah a dtr., John M. Dunlap who married Martha a gr. dtr. of said decd., John M. Greer gdn. of Benjamin Greer who is entitled to a share thru his mother who is decd. Distributees were: Margaret Sims wid., John B. Sims, David Greer and wife Mary decd., Arthur Sims, Mrs. Cox, Micajah Sims. Thos. S. Greer was a gr. s. On Dec. 5, 1856 Nancy Cox of Chotaw Co., Miss. asked that John R. Wilson admnr. of Thos. Sims. est. pay over to her nephew Wm. T. Dean of Chotaw Co., Miss. her amount of $562.03 of her father's est. John B. Dean and Susan his wife of Choctaw Co., Miss. recd. share of her father's est.

TRIBBLE, JOHN——BOX 136, PACK 3861:
Est. admnr. Nov. 3, 1852 by Wm. Clinkscales, Esse, Lemuel Tribble, Hugh Robinson bound to F. W. Selleck Ord. Abbeville Dist. sum $15,000.00. Esse Tribble the wid. Sett. made Mar. 13, 1854 stated that Lemuel N. Tribble a distributee was of age . Margaret A. Tribble a dtr. was the wife of Thos. P. Jones in 1854. Mary E. Tribble a dtr. Her mother Esse Tribble married Christopher Ellis.

TOLBERT, JAMES—BOX 136, PACK 3862:
Est. admnr. Oct. 10, 1853 by Rebecca, John H. Tolbert, J. Foster Marshall, Jas. P. Martin bound to Mathew McDonald Ord. sum $19,000.00. Rebecca, John H. Tolbert was next of kin. Sett. made Feb. 21, 1855. Present: the admnr. and admnrx., Mrs. J. W. Buchanan, John F. Davis who married Mary Isabella Tolbert and Jas. Strawhorn the admnr. of Levi Strawhorn decd. There were 6 distributees: viz. Levi Strawhorn, J. W. Buchanan, F. H. Davis, J. H. Tolbert, W. K., Joseph M. Tolbert. There were 6 chn. including the late Mrs. Levi Strawhorn, who died about 3 wks. before Jas. Tolbert, leaving a husband and a child. The child died about 3 wks. after the testator; the father the said Levi has since died.

TEDARDS, DAVID—BOX 136, PACK 3863:
Will dated Jan. 17, 1853 in Abbeville Dist. Prov. Nov. 1, 1853. Exrs: Sons, Felix, Wiley Tedards. Wit: Thos. Ross, Willis B. Cason, Thos. Mabry Ross. Wife, Sarah Tedards.

THOMPSON, WILLIAM—BOX 136, PACK 3864:
Est. admnr. Apr. 8, 1854 by Jas. W. Richardson, Saml. Beard, Thos. Blake, John Sadler bound to Wm. Hill Ord. Abbeville Dist. sum $600.00. Mary Ann Thompson the wid. (Name written Thompson and Thomson.)

WHITE, FRANCES—BOX 136, PACK 3865:
Will dated Feb. 11, 1851 in Abbeville Dist. Filed June 17, 1853. Exr: Thos. J. Lyon. Wit: Adam Wideman, John P. Quattlebaum, Robt. W. Lites. Son, Jas. M. White decd. Gr. chn: Frances Gillam, Ann Virginia, Mary Longmire, Jas. White Harrison. Codicil dated May 17, 1852 named a dtr. Kesiah Evans. Gr. dtr. Emma Pauline Evans.

WILSON, HUDSON—BOX 136, PACK 3866:
Was a free man of color. Did not copy.

WADE, DRURY V.—BOX 136, PACK 3867:
Est. admnr. Jan. 17, 1854 by Thos. J. Roberts, J. Foster Marshall, Thos. Eakins bound to Wm. Hill Ord. Abbeville Dist. sum $500.00. Ann Wade the wid. Sarah Ann, Mary E., Manley, John R. Wade distributees.

WATSON, JOHN—BOX 136, PACK 3868:
Est. admnr. Oct. 19, 1852 by Wm. Weston, John Faulkner, A. P. Conner bound to F. W. Selleck Ord. Abbeville Dist. sum $7,000.00. Wm. Watson was a bro. to John Watson. Sale, Nov. 25, 1852. Byrs: Mary, Wm., Robt. Watson, etc.

WATSON, DR. A. K.—BOX 136, PACK 3869:
Est. admnr. Nov. 8, 1853 by Johnson, Benjamin W. Sale, Willis Ross

bound to Mathew McDonald Ord. Abbeville Dist. sum $6,000.00. Sale, made Dec. 9, 1853. Byrs: J. R., J. M. Watson.

WILLIAMS, JOSEPH W.—BOX 136, PACK 3870:
Est. admnr. Feb. 16, 1853 by Robt. A., Jas. McCaslan, Wm. E. Link bound to F. W. Selleck Ord. Abbeville Dist. sum $200.00. Was a painter by trade.

WATSON, WILLIAM EDWARD—BOX 136, PACK 3871:
Will dated May 4, 1852 in Abbeville Dist. Filed Dec. 11, 1852. Exr: Larkin Reynolds. Wit: W. P. Hill, Hugh Wardlaw, W. T. Templeton. Mother, Margaret Watson.

WEBB, JOHN—BOX 136, PACK 3872:
Will dated July 21, 1846 in Abbeville Dist. Filed Feb. 19, 1853. Exrs: Bro. l., John Miller, Saml. Donald. Wit: Thos. Branyon, Robt. McAdams, Jas. Elgin. Wife. ment. no name given. Chn: Mary, Permelia H., John Webb. "Exrs: procure a headstone for my dtr. Hannah decd. and also one for her child." Gr. son, John Marshall Webb son of Andrew Webb. Power of Atty. On Mar. 28, 1859 Wm. M. C. Webb of Winston Co., Miss. appointed John Miller of Abbeville Dist. his Atty. to receive what was coming to him from the est. of John and Elizabeth Webb decd. of Abbeville Dist. On Feb. 1, 1859 Andrew Webb of Calhoun Co., Ala. appointed Marion Cullins of the same co. his Atty. to collect what was coming to him from the est. of John Webb decd. of Abbeville Dist., S. C. On July 25, 1859 Hezekiah Elgin and his wife and Saml. M. Webb recd. their share of the est. Mary Webb married Caleb Cullins. John McClain on Aug. 16, 1859 recd. $860.13 the share of Mrs. Peggy McClain decd. who was a legatee of John Webb. Jas. McClain was husband of Peggy.

WEED, REUBEN—BOX 136, PACK 3873:
Est. admnr. May 12, 1853 by Andrew J. Weed, Jas. Young, Jonathan Jordon bound to F. W. Selleck Ord. Abbeville Dist. sum $1,000.00. Reuben Weed died on or about June 30, 1845. Andrew J. Weed sheweth that he was a son of Reuben Weed decd. who was a soldier in the Revolutionary War.

WILSON, (MINORS)—BOX 136, PACK 3874:
On Nov. 1, 1852 John R. Wilson, Saml. Ried, John Donald bound to F. W. Selleck Ord. Abbeville Dist. sum $1,200.00. John R. Wilson made gdn. of Margaret R., Ann S. Wilson minors. John R. Wilson sheweth that he is an uncle of said minors who were chn. of his decd. bro. Henry R. Wilson.

WILSON, (MINORS)—BOX 136, PACK 3875:
On Jan. 29, 1853 Saml. A. Wilson, Archibald Tittle, W. W. Wilson bound to F. W. Selleck Ord. Abbeville Dist. sum $59.74. Saml. A. Wilson made gdn. of Thos. J., John L. Wilson minors of Robt. C. Wilson. John L. Wilson was of age in 1858. Had 2 decd. bros., Benjamin A., W. W. Wilson.

WILSON, FRANCES—BOX 136, PACK 3876:
On Feb. 17, 1853 B. M. Cheatham, John White bound to F. W. Selleck Ord. Abbeville Dist. sum $1,500.00. B. M. Cheatham made gdn. of Frances

E. Wilson a minor. Frances E. Wilson sheweth that she is a minor of age of choice and late the wife of Joseph N. Wilson decd.

WHALEY, JOHN C.—BOX 136, PACK 3877:
On Feb. 15, 1853 W. D. Calhoun, Benjamin L., Benjamin V. Posey bound to F. W. Selleck Ord. Abbeville Dist. sum $200.0. John Whaley sheweth that he is the son of Lewis Whaley decd. and that his father was a soldier in the War of 1812. John Whaley of age in 1855.

WARDLAW, JOSEPH—BOX 136, PACK 3878:
Will dated May 22, 1852. Filed June 7, 1852. Exrs: Son, Hugh W. Wardlaw, Thos. C. Perrin Esq. Wit: Henry H. Creswell, Jas. Douglass, W. L. Templeton, J. R. Ellis. Chn: Hugh Waller Wardlaw, Harriet Whitlock, Benjamin F. Wardlaw. "Bequeath to my dtr. Harriet Whitlock and her chn. all my lands in Fla." Thos. L. Whitlock her husband.

YOUNG, SARAH J.—BOX 136, PACK 3879:
On Feb. 1, 1847 Nancy M. Sims, Valentine Young, Mason C. Henderson bound to David Lesly Ord. Abbeville Dist. sum $740.00. Nancy M. Sims made gdn. of Sarah Jane Isaac Young a minor about 5 yrs. old. Nancy M. Sims later married Edward Roney. Sarah Young was the child of Isaac Young decd. Nancy M. Sims was the gr. mother of Sarah Young. In 1858 Sarah was the wife of Jas. M. Wright. Maria Richey was the mother of Sarah Young.

ZIMMERMAN, JOHN—BOX 136, PACK 3880:
Will dated May 2, 1853 in Abbeville Dist. Prov. Oct. 31, 1853. Exr: J. W. Hearst. Wit: John Cothran, Saml. Perrin, David Walker. Chn: Peter Zimmerman, Mary decd. wife of Jackson Roundtree, Philip Zimmerman decd. "Bequeath to Mary Caroline, Philip LaFayette the surviving chn. of my decd. son Philip Zimmerman."

ATKINS, MARGARET—BOX 137, PACK 3881:
On Nov. 24, 1854 Daniel Atkins, Jas. J. Devlin, Thos. J. Atkins bound to Wm. Hill Ord. Abbeville Dist. sum $148.00. Daniel Atkins made gdn. of Margaret Lucinda Atkins a minor about 12 yrs. Daniel Atkins was an uncle of said minor. Sett. made Feb. 8, 1861. Present, Margaret L. Atkins and her husband David F. Dansby.

ALLEN, JOHN E.—BOX 137, PACK 3882:
Will dated Apr. 2, 1853 in Abbeville Dist. Filed Aug. 23, 1854. Exr: Thos. Thomson. Wit: John F. Livingston, Benjamin A. Hughes, C. H. Selleck. Wife, Sarah A. Allen. Mother, Jane L. Allen. Eugene Allen son of my bro. Chas. H. Allen.

BULL, JOHN B.—BOX 137, PACK 3883:
Will dated Apr. 8, 1843 in Abbeville Dist. Exrs: Wm. P. Noble, Paul Rogers, Edmund C. Martin. Wit: Wm. H. Davis, J. L. Bouchilleon Sr., E. C. Martin. Wife, Sarah Bull. Bro., Genl. Wm. A. Bull. "Give to Jas. Morrow Jr. $5,000.00." He died Jan. 5, 1855.

BRANYON, JOHN M.—BOX 137, PACK 3884:
Est. admnr. Aug. 26, 1854 by Jas. G. E., A. W. Branyon, John R. Wilson bound to Wm. Hill Ord. Abbeville Dist. sum $300.00. John M. Branyon the father of Jas. G. E. Branyon.

BROUGH, THOMAS—BOX 137, PACK 3885:
Will dated Mar. 14, 1854 in Abbeville Dist. Filed Apr. 1854. Exrs: Son, John Fleming Brough, J. W. Jones. Wit: J. L. Brown, Jas. Macelvey, A, Waller. Wife, Eveline Brough. S. l. Albert A. Humphries. Chn: John Fleming Brough, Thos. Jefferson, Frances Ann, Louisa Eveline, Wm. Henry Brough, Jane Elizabeth Humphries.

BOOZER, HENRY—BOX 137, PACK 388c.
Will dated Dec. 16, 1854 in Abbeville Dist. Filed Dec. 29, 1854. Exrs: Son, John Boozer., S. l. Robt. Leavell. Wit: Jas. Hughey, Jas. H. Riley, L. H. Smith. Wife, Mary Boozer. Chn: Elivira Leavell, Hugh Dickson, John Boozer, Simon P., Wm., David, Hamilton Boozer, Barbary Blackburn, Caroline wife of G. W. Blackburn.

BAKER, SAMUEL S.—BOX 137, PACK 3887:
Will dated Jan. 20, 1854 in Abbeville Dist. Exrs: Wife, Jane T. Baker; Son, Thomson Baker, Jas. W. Child, Wm. T. Drennon. Chn: Thomson, Ann, Martha, Caroline, Sarah, Francis, Julia, Eliza, Lucy, Jas. Wm., Harrison Baker. In Oct. 1856 Jas. Taggart Jr. had married Martha Baker. Ann married a Partlow.

BARMORE, ENOCH—BOX 137, PACK 3888:
Est. admnr. Aug. 7, 1854 by David L. Donald, John C. Williams, Joseph Dickson, Saml. Donnald bound to Wm. Hill Ord. Abbeville Dist. sum $40,000.00. He died in June 1854. Sett. made Apr. 24, 1856 ment. 9 chn. viz: D. Donald and wife, Eugenia, Mary Eliza, Wm. C., Robt., Hugh, Jas. L., Margaret W., Frances Barmore now decd. Wid., Sarah Barmore.

BOWIE, RICHARD PRICE—BOX 137, PACK 3889:
Will dated Jan. 12, 1855 in Abbeville Dist. Prov. Mar. 3, 1855. Exr: Wm. B. Bowie. Wit: Edward, Robt., W. A. Hagen. Wife, Jane D. Bowie. Dtr. Martha Jane Bowie.

BASKIN, JAMES S.—BOX 137, PACK 3890:
Will dated Oct. 25, 1854 in Abbeville Dist. Filed Nov. 6, 1854. Exrs: Wm. H. Simpson, Wm. S. McBride. Wit: S. R. Morrah, Octavius T. Porcher, J. S. Robinson. Dtr. Jane E. Baskin.

BEASLEY, WILLIAM—BOX 137, PACK 3891:
Will dated Nov. 20, 1853 in Abbeville Dist. Filed Jan. 6, 1855. Exr: Wife, Mary Beasley. Wit: W. A. Crozier, W. T. Rodgers, W. Q. Martin.

BROOKS, NANCY—BOX 137, PACK 3892:
Will dated Sept. 20, 1879 in Abbeville Dist. Exr: John B. LeRoy. Wit: J. M. White, Jas. Power, *Eslenna* R. LeRoy. Chn: Elizabeth J. Barker, Mary L.

Moore, Forinta C. Wilson, Eliza C. Schroder, Anna J. Daniel, John M. Brooks, Silas H. Brooks. Gr. s: Willie M. Blanchett. (There must have been 2 Nancy Brooks as the dated are different.) Est. admnr. Nov. 6, 1854 by Stanmore B. Brooks, Thos. C. Lipscomb, Larkin Reynolds bound to Wm. Hill Ord. Abbeville Dist. sum $20,000.00. Sett. made Apr. 2, 1855 ment. 8 distributees viz.: Stanmore B. Brooks, Wesley Brooks, John Chappel and wife Elizabeth, John P. Barratt and wife Lavinia. Edna Caldwell. Chn. of Mary S. Watts, Wm. B. Brooks, Geo. Robinson.

BAKER, (MINORS)—BOX 137, PACK 3893:
On Mar. 5, 1855 Saml. S., Joseph T. Baker bound to Wm. Hill Ord. Abbeville Dist. sum $1,500.00. Saml. S. Baker made gdn. of John Joseph, Theodore E. Baker minors of Theodore G. Baker decd. who was a bro. to Saml. S. Baker. On July 31, 1876 the petition of Martha M. Baker sheweth that she is the infant dtr. and only child of John J. Baker decd. who formerly resided in Abbeville Co. but removed to Miss. and died about 1872. (On one paper the minor was written Theodore E. and Theodore G. Baker in another place.)

COWAN, SAMUEL—BOX 137, PACK 3894:
Will dated Dec. 15, 1851 in Abbeville Dist. Filed Sept. 4, 1854. Exrs: Son, Edmund Cowan, Jas. C. Willard. Wit: A. A. Noble, S. J. Willard, J. B. Willard. Wife, Jane Cowan. Chn: Robt. Simpson, Shepperd Groce Cowan, Amanda Tolbert, Wade Cowan, Wm. Nixon Cowan, Edmund Cowan, Chas. Wesley Cowan, Mary Jane Cason. On May 1, 1861 Benjamin Tolbert recd. shares for his chn. viz: Thos., Ansel, Frances Tolbert.

CONNER, JAMES O.—BOX 137, PACK 3895:
Est. admnr. Aug. 7, 1854 by Alexr. P. Conner, Jas. B. Crawford. Saml. Jordon, M. O. Talman bound to Wm. Hill Ord. Abbeville Dist. sum $20,000.00. Mary L. Conner the wid. of said decd. and a sis. to Jas. B. Crawford.

CALHOUN, GEORGE W.—BOX 137, PACK 3896:
Est. admnr. Jan. 1, 1855 by Nathan Calhoun, Jas. W. Richardson, John W. Calhoun bound to Wm. Hill Ord. Abbeville Dist. sum $25,000.00. He left no wife or chn., but a father, bros. and sis. Sett. made Jan. 17, 1859 ment. 7 distributees viz: Nathan Calhoun the father, Thos. M. White and wife, Sarah, J. R. Proffitt and wife Mary E., Jas. S. Calhoun a minor, Virginia Calhoun a minor, Robt. C. Calhoun a minor, B. F. Calhoun a minor.

CLAY, JOHN—BOX 137, PACK 3897:
Est. admnr. Feb. 9, 1855 by Jas. L. McCelvey, Jas. McCelvey, Hugh McKelvey bound unto Wm. Hill Ord. Abbeville Dist. sum $12,000.00. Elizabeth Clay the wid. Sett. made May 13, 1856. Present, the admnr. J. L. McKelvey, the wid. Elizabeth Clay, Elisha, H. W., W. A. Clay, S. O. Speed distributees. Sett. named 7 distributees viz: Shadrack Clay, Jas. T. Clay, Chn. of Josiah Wells, Elisha Clay, H. W. Clay, Mary Speed, W. A. Clay.

CATER, RICHARD B.—BOX 137, PACK 3898:
Est. admnr. June 28, 1854 by Wm. A. Giles, D. F. Freeland bound to Wm. Hill Ord. Abbeville Dist. sum $1,200.00.

COVIN, DELILA—BOX 137, PACK 3899:
Will dated Sept. 28, 1854. Filed Oct. 24, 1854. Exr: Lewis Covin. Wit:
John Harmon, P. L. Guillebeau, J. J. Guillebeau, P. B. Moragne. Ment: Lived
in Abbeville Dist. Chn: Joseph Covin, Mary McAllister wife of Thos. McAllister,
Loucinda J. McAllister wife of Andrew McAllister, Sarah A. Covin. "Bequeath
to my son Lazareth S. Covin and Jas. W. Covin, David T. Covin, Joseph L.
Covin." Grand. dtr. Louisa E. Covin dtr. of Joseph Covin.

COOK, SAMUEL G.—BOX 137, PACK 3900:
Will dated Apr. 29, 1854. Filed June 3, 1854. Exrs: Wife, Louana Cook,
s. l., E. M. Whatley. Wit: Saml. Maxwell, J. T. Webber, S. S. Marshall. Chn:
Mary wife of E. M. Whatley, Eugenia Gemima Cook.

CASON, BENJAMIN A.—BOX 137, PACK 3901:
Est. admnr. Oct. 26, 1854 by Jas. Cason, L. B. Guillebeau, W. W. Belcher
bound to Wm. Hill Ord. Abbeville Dist. sum $5,000.00. Left a wid. Amelia
Cason and 3 chn. It was Amelia Cason's request that her father admnr. on her
husband's est.

DUNWOODY, SAMUEL—BOX 138, PACK 3902:
Will dated May 1, 1849 in Abbeville Dist. Filed Oct. 28, 1854. Exrs: Wife,
Lavinia Dunwoody, Chas. Smith, Dr. F. G. Thos. Wit: Henry Bass, W. A.
Gamewell, Geo. W. W. Stone. Chn: Saml. Hart who has devoted himself to the
Ministry, Susan Esther Dunwoody, Lavinia Ann Frances Dunwoody. "Owned
house and lot at Cokesbury in which I now reside. Also house and lot in St. Matthews Parish, Orangeburg Dist. bounded by Revd. John Wannamaker and others."
Power of Atty. Anderson Co., S. C. Whereas I Victoria Dunwoody am entitled
to a distribute share of real est. of my late father Saml. Dunwoody. Dated this
Feb. 9, 1876. On July 5, 1878 Mrs. Keziah Dunwoody stated that she was the
mother of Lucy E. Dunwoody who was born May 4, 1857 and that she is the dtr.
also of Saml. Dunwoody Jr. decd. Mrs. Lavinia Dunwoody wid. of Saml. Dunwoody died Feb. 10, 1873. On Dec. 7, 1869 Saml. K. Dunwoody died intestate
leaving his wid. Mrs. Keziah K. Dunwoody and 7 chn: viz. Rhoda Ellen 21,
David Paul 19, Victoria Jas. 18, Lucy Elizabeth 15, Chas. Andrew 14, Hubert
Williams 10, and Edgar Whitfield Dunwoody 5 all residing in Anderson Co.
Susan Esther Graydon wife of Sterling E. Graydon, Lovenia Frances Ziegler wife
of M. G. Ziegler were dtrs. of Saml. Dunwoody of Abbeville. Rhoda E. Dunwoody married a Rochester.

DALE, SAMUEL E.—BOX 138, PACK 3903:
Est. admnr. Sept. 12, 1854 by LeRoy J. Johnson, Christian V. Barnes
bound to Wm. Hill Ord. Abbeville Dist. sum $600.00. Margaret Dale the wid.

DOWTIN, THOMAS P.—BOX 138, PACK 3904:
Will dated Sept. 22, 1854 in Abbeville Dist. Filed Jan. 23, 1855. Exrs:
Wife, M. O. McCaslan, John S. Dowtin. Wit: J. A. Gibert, Jas. W. Child, R. A.
F. McCaslan. Chn: John S. Dowtin, Mary Ann Sproull, Drusillah Ray, Jas. C.
Dowtin, Mildred W. Wideman, Thos. A. Dowtin, Nancy L., David, Katharine

Dowtin. Henry D. Ray husband of Drucilla Ray. Wife ment. no name given. Sett. named Mrs. Amelia Dowtin as wid. Catharine married a Womble. Mary Ann married E. H. Sproull.

ELLIS, JOHN R.—BOX 138, PACK 3905:
Est. admnr. Mar. 9, 1855 by Jas. C. Ellis, Silas Ray, Thos. W. Pace bound to Wm. Hill Ord. Abbeville Dist. sum $1,600.00. Left a wid. and 5 chn. On Feb. 17, 1855 Willy Ellis gave her consent to her father in law J. C. Ellis to admnr. on her husband's est. Chn: Mary E., Jane J., Jas. R., Wm., Benjamin W. Ellis.

GIVENS, JOHN—BOX 138, PACK 3906:
Est. admnr. May 8, 1855 by John L., Robt., Joseph Ellis bound to Wm. Hill Ord. Abbeville Dist. sum $8,000.00. Wid., Elizabeth Givens. S. l., Geo. Williams. Sett. made Oct. 14, 1856. Present: John T. Givens of Fla., Geo. W. Williams in right of his wife Malinda, Miss Sally Givens, Jane Givens.

GUILLEBEAU, PIERRE—BOX 138, PACK 3907:
Will dated Sept. 25, 1852 in Abbeville Dist. Filed Dec. 27, 1854. Exrs: Sons, Peter L., John J. Guillebeau. Wit: B. E. Gibert, J. E. Bellot, J. L. Wilhite, A. Houston. Chn: Mary Bouchlong, Martha Hays, Peter L., John J., Lazrus B., Andrew, Susan, Elizabeth C. Guillebeau, Ann LeRoy. (Name also written Gillibo.) On Nov. 21, 1855 Mary, Isaac Bouchillon of Floyd Co., Ga. recd. $155.25 their share of est. Martha was the wife of J. C. Hayes.

GAINES, WILLIAM H.—BOX 138, PACK 3908:
Est. admnr. Nov. 22, 1854 by Elizabeth Gaines, Thos. C. Lipscomb, Martin Hackett bound to Wm. Hill Ord. Abbeville Dist. sum $8,000.00. Elizabeth Gaines the mother of said decd.

GOULDEN, CHARLES B.—BOX 138, PACK 3909:
Est. admnr. Jan. 29, 1855 by John Goulden, Jefferson Floyd, Jas. Gillam bound to Wm. Hill Ord. Abbeville Dist. sum $10,000.00. He died Oct. 8, 1853 without wife or chn. Was a brother to John Goulden. Died while on a visit to Tenn. Left a mother Frances Goulden and bros. and sis., John Goulden, Sarah Burnett wid. of Andrew Jackson.

GORDON, THOMAS, SR.—BOX 138, PACK 3910:
Will dated Dec. 7, 1853 in Abbeville Dist. Filed Oct. 7, 1854. Exrs: Sons, Wm., Thos. Gordon. Wit: David Keller, Andrew Robison, Jas. Cunningham. Wife, Mary Gordon. Chn: Thos., Abraham, Jas., Robt., Nancy Elizabeth Gordon.

GRAY, JOHN—BOX 138, PACK 3911:
Will dated Oct. 21, 1837 in Abbeville Dist. Filed Sept. 23, 1854. Exr: Son, John Harris Gray. Wit: Wm. Brooks, Andrew Gillespie Sr., Henry C. Penney. Wife, Elizabeth Gray. Chn: "Bequeath $50.00. to the Southern Board of Foreign Missions to constitute my son the Revd. Wm. A. Gray a life member that money be sent to the Rev. J. L. Merreck missionary to Persia." Sarah A. Boyd, John H. Gray. Gr. son: Wm. A. G. Boyd.

HUGHES, ELIZABETH—BOX 138, PACK 3912:
Will dated Sept. 12, 1849 in Abbeville Dist. Filed Oct. 18, 1853. Exr: Son, Nathaniel Hughes. Wit: T. Y., Mahala, W. P. Martin. Chn: Mary Ann, Nathaniel, Edward J., Hezekiah, Jas., Geo., Alexr. E. Hughes, Nancy Reeve. Gr. dtr: Polly Malissy Hughes.

HENDERSON, WILLIAM—BOX 138, PACK 3913:
Est. admnr. Dec. 13, 1854 by Thos. J. Mabry, Frank A. Wilson, A. Gillespie bound to Wm. Hill Ord. Abbeville Dist. sum $1,500.00. Jas. A. Hilburn and wife Elizabeth sheweth that Wm. Henderson is a bro. and bro. l. of your petrs. Sett. made Jan. 24, 1856 named 3 distributees viz: Jas. Hilburn and wife, Sarah Henderson, Joseph McKents and wife. On Oct. 2, 1866 J. Harvey Edwards and wife Leonna (then Mrs. McKents) were heirs of said est.

HILBURN, LEVI—BOX 138, PACK 3914:
Est. admnr. Nov. 15, 1854 by Edmund Cobb, John Link, Jas. A. Richey bound to Wm. Hill Ord. Abbeville Dist. sum $10,000.00. Sett. made Aug. 16, 1856. Present: Edmund Cobb admnr., Susan Hilburn wid., John Link gdn. of E. R. Hilburn minor, John H. Carr gdn. of Levi J. Hilburn, the admnr. is gdn. of N. E. Hilburn.

HUNTER, JOHN—BOX 138, PACK 3915:
Will dated Sept. 9, 1854 in Abbeville Dist. Prov. Oct. 21, 1854. Exrs: Wife, Jane Hunter, Wm. W. Hunter. Wit: John, W. K. Bradley, J. F. McComb. Bequeath to Wm. Washington Hunter, Margaret, John H., Mary Porterfield.

HENSCHELL, ALBERT—BOX 138, PACK 3916:
Est. admnr. Sept. 20, 1854 by Moses Winstock, A. C. Hawthorn bound to Wm. Hill Ord. Abbeville Dist. sum $1,000.00. Be it known that in consequence of the reported death of the above named Henschell, it being said that he was murdered in the State of Tenn., Moss Winstock being a large creditor of said Henschell obtained Letters of Admnr. and proceeded to the latter est. in order to take possession of his est. While absent prosecuting the business he met with the aforesaid Henschell alive and well. Admnr. was ceased.

JOHNSON, WALTER G.—BOX 138, PACK 3917:
Est. admnr. Jan. 16, 1855 by Benjamin M. Lattimer, G. M. Mattison, M. B. Lattimer bound to Wm. Hill Ord. Abbeville Dist. sum $12,000.00. Walter G. Johnson was a bro. l. to B. M. Lattimer. Left a wid. Mrs. Harriet C. Johnson and 3 chn.

JACKSON, JOHN M.—BOX 138, PACK 3918:
Est. admnr. Apr. 27, 1855 by Thos. Jackson, Mathew McDonald bound to Wm. Hill Ord. Abbeville Dist. sum $1,000.00. John M. Jackson died in the State of Ga.

JONES, S. T. C. P.—BOX 138, PACK 3919:
Will dated Jan. 16, 1854. Filed Aug. 29, 1854. Exr: Bro., H. A. Jones. Wit: Isaac Branch, W. C. Davis, J. H. Wilson. Was of Mt. Pleasant, Abbeville

ABBEVILLE DISTRICT WILLS AND BONDS 541

Dist. Wife, Hellena Jones. Nieces: Mary Elizabeth Jones dtr. of H. A. Jones Esq., Sarah Fickling Jones 2nd dtr. of my bro. H. A. Jones, Eugneia, Frances Barmore dtrs. of Enoch Barmore Esq., Mary Townes Jones, Calhoun Jones chn. of Dr. N. S. Jones of *Wetumpka*, Ala. Nephew, D. F. Jones. Niece, Sarah Williamson, Mary Traynham also ment.

KEMP, WILEY—BOX 138, PACK 3920:
Will dated Dec. 28, 1853 in Abbeville Dist. Filed Oct. 20, 1854. Exrs John J. Keller. Wit: David Keller, Joseph M., John E. Ellis Jr. Wife, Jamima Kemp.

KAY, MARY E.—BOX 138, PACK 3921:
On Jan. 25, 1855 Richard G. Kay, John M. G. Branyon, Mary Kay bound to Wm. Hill Ord. Abbeville Dist. sum $1,096.00. Richard G. Kay made gdn. of Mary Elizabeth Kay a minor 9 yrs. old. Sett. made Apr. 9. Sett. made Apr. 16, 1866 ment. that she was the wife of W. C. Hall. On Apr. 9, 1866 W. C. Hall and his wife of Carnesville, Ga., stated it was all right for the gdn. to settle the est.

LINDSAY, JAMES—BOX 138, PACK 3922:
Est. admnr. Sept. 11, 1854 by J. Bonner, L. T. Lindsay, A. C. Hawthorne, E. E. Pressly bound to Wm. Hill Ord. Abbeville Dist. sum $60,000.00. He died Aug. 10, 1854. Left a wid. Polly Ann Lindsay and 6 chn: J. Oliver Lindsay, Armathine L. wife of J. J. Bonner, L. T. Lindsay who is now dead leaving neither wife nor child, A. Poinsett Lindsay, W. Winfield Lindasy, A. B. Calvin Lindsay.

LEARD, JOHN—BOX 138, PACK 3923:
Est. admnr. Oct. 4, 1854 by Saml. P. Leard, Thos. J. Lyon, Adam Wideman bound to Wm. Hill Ord. Abbeville Dist. sum $1,300.00. Saml. P. Leard sheweth that his father John Leard died in 1843 and that in his early life was a soldier in the Revolutionary Army. It is believed that the chn. of said decd. by taking the proper steps will recover from the U. S. Government a pension for their father's services. Sett. made Feb. 5, 1855 named 3 distributees: Saml. P., Mary Ann, Ellen Leard. On May 17, 1856 Mary A. Leard and Nelly Leard of Wilcox Co., Ala. recd. from Saml. Leard admnr. $249.24 their full share of the pension of their father John Leard who was a Revolutionary Soldier.

MAGILL, JANE—BOX 139, PACK 3924:
Est. admnr. Nov. 22, 1854 by Thos., David Robison, Jas. J. Gilmer bound to Wm. Hill Ord. Abbeville Dist. sum $1,000.00. Mrs. Jane Magill a wid. was a sis. to Thos. Robison. Sett. made Apr. 28, 1856. Present: Thos. Robison admnr., Wm. Magill a distributee in right of his wife Margaret, Jas. M. Gillam in right of wife Mary Ann and David Robison the father of said decd.

MATTOX, JESSE—BOX 139, PACK 3925:
Est. admnr. Sept. 16, 1854 by Wm. W. Mattox, John Mauldin, G. M. Mattison bound to Wm. Hill Ord. Abbeville Dist. sum $1,000.00. Wm. Mattox was a bro. to Jesse Mattox. Sett. made Mar. 5, 1856. Present: G. M. Mattison who represents the admnr., W. W. Mattox, Saml. Bratcher a distributee in right of his

ABSTRACTS OF OLD NINETY-SIX AND

wife Mary, Wm. Holmes gdn. of the minor chn. of Henry Mattox decd. 7 distributees: Mother, Basil Mattox, Wm. Maddox admnr., Saml. Bratcher and wife, Jabez Richey and wife Fanney, Chn of Robt. Mattox, Chn. of Henry Mattox.

MARSHALL, JOSEPH—BOX 139, PACK 3926:
Will dated Nov. 30, 1853 in Abbeville Dist. Filed Nov. 28, 1854. Exrs: Nephews, Joseph Steene Marshall, Joseph Warren Waldo Marshall. Wit: Jonathan Jordon, Jas. Douglass, Jas. W. Richey. Sis., Jane McWilliams. Nieces: Mary Jane Orr, Mary Isabella Jane Gray. Bros: Hugh, John Marshall. Nephews: Joseph Steene Marshall, Absalom L. Gray, Joseph Warren Waldo Marshall, Geo. Washington Marshall. Sett. made Jan. 1, 1857. Legatees: Dr. S. Marshall, Jane McWilliams, Mary Jane Orr, Isabella Marshall, Mary A. Major, J. S. Marshall, Geo. Marshall. To heirs Nancy Aikens decd.

MORAGNE, EDWARD R.—BOX 139, PACK 3927:
Est. admnr. Dec. 6, 1854 by Wm. H. Davis, Dyonisius M. Rogers, Wm. T. Drennan bound to Wm. Hill Ord. Abbeville Dist. sum $200.00. Benjamin V. Posey made gdn. of Sarah F. McKelden a minor. On Aug. 30, 1854 Sarah F. McKelden sheweth that she is entitled to 160 acres of Bounty Land from the Government from est. of her late mother Susan B. McKelden. That she is about 19 yrs. old. Child of Geo. McKelden decd. Sett. made June 8, 1855 stated that she was the wife of Richard Anderson.

MARTIN, COL. JOHN C.—BOX 139, PACK 3929:
Est. admnr. Oct. 14, 1854 by Benjamin Y., Mary A. Martin, John F. Livingston, John Brownlee, N. H. Miller, Thos. Thomson, Jacob Martin bound to Wm. Hill Ord. Abbeville Dist. sum $225,000.00. Left a wid. Mary A. Martin and 8 chn. all under 21 yrs. Sett. made Dec. 22, 1855. Present: B. Y. Martin admnr., Jacob Martin gdn. of Luther L. Martin, John Brownlee gdn. of John M. Martin, Lemuel Reid gdn. of Saml. S. Martin, B. P. Hughes gdn. of Jas. Martin, Thos. Thomson gdn. of Sally Martin. Mary A. Martin recd. $68.16 for her ward Wm. B. Martin.

McCORD, ELLEN—BOX 139, PACK 3930:
Will dated Mar. 14, 1854 in Abbeville Dist. Filed Apr. 3, 1854. Exrs: Nephew, John W. McCree, Jas. Carson Esq. Wit: D. S. Benson, W. J. Smith, J. A. Allen. Nephews: John W., Jas. H. McCree. Niece: Margaret E. McCree.

McCALLISTER, JOSEPH L.—BOX 139, PACK 3931:
Est. admnr. Oct. 2, 1854 by Jane McCallister, Wm. K. Bradley, A. S. McCaslan bound to Wm. Hill Ord. Abbeville Dist. sum $400.00. He died in La. Left a wid. Jane McCallister and 2 chn: Jas. R., Elizabeth now wife of John L. Farmer, all now of Abbeville Dist.

McCELVEY, HEZEKAIH C.—BOX 139, PACK 3932:
Will dated May 31, 1854 in Abbeville Dist. Filed June 29, 1854. Exrs: Bros., Jas. L. of Abbeville Dist., Geo. W. McCelvey of Texas. Wit: Jas., Hugh McCelvey, M. O. Talman. Bros., Jas. L., Geo. W. McCelvey.

NELSON, HARVEY H.—BOX 139, PACK 3933:
Will dated Mar. 27, 1855 in Abbeville Dist. Filed Apr. 28, 1855. Exr:
Bro., Enoch Nelson. Wit: D. A. Jordon, Saml. McQuerns, Wm. Butler. Wife,
Louisa E. Nelson. (Letter to Mrs. L. E. Nelson, Guincy, Fla.)
So. Car.
Abbeville Dist.
July 9th, '54
Dear Wife:
I have recd. yours of the 22 of June I am anxious that we should again live
together and for that purpose I am willing to make all acknowledgements that are
due and to promise you more to drink to Excess as to moving to another country
and not determined as to where I shall settle for life and I can safely say that it
is not probable that it will be in S. C. or Fla. I design looking to Ga. for a home
provided you are willing to be my wife. My dear wife you no we are both to blame
in a great measure we must forget the past and look to the future. Louisa we must
forgive one another bare and forbare is the golden rule Reply soon as I am anxious
to hear from you the year is drawing to a close and we ought to understand each
other as soon as possible If you *Creceed* to this letter I shall look us out a home
some where in Ga. this fall perhaps Louisa the time is not fare distant I hope
when we can enjoy life as once we did, Reply to your husband soon.
H. H. Nelson
Perhaps you have some choice in the counties if you have I shall look at
your choice Wright me what you think of *Berkeror* Lee or Doly or *Westen*
counties.
Your husband H. H. Nelson
(Letter) So. Car.
Abbeville
May 23rd., '54
Louisa do not get dismade your troubles has been great and so has mine
but I hope there is a better day coming for me and you I do not want you to let
your best friends no what I have written as I expect to come down this summer to
see you Enoch and Louemma and Caroline and Mary and Mr. Lomax I expect to
start on next monday for Fla. and I expect Enoch will use his greatest exertions to
get you to apply for a divorce I have one thing to say I will try you once more as
it appears as if I cannot live without you Louisa keep this to yourself and say
nothing about it I find my best friends are my worst enemies so we will live together again in spite of this world no one noes how I have suffered yes I have
tride to kill my self several times I no your lefe has been a burden since you left
me you feel near and dear to me I have felt lost ever since you left me but you or
some of your friends is the hole cause of it so fare you well until I hear from you.
Your husband H. H. Nelson Reply by the next stage to Harrisburg. Above all keep
this to your self I no you will if you are what I take you to be reply soon as I am
almost dead to hear from you.

O'BRYANT, JOSEPH—BOX 139, PACK 3934:
Est. admnr. Mar. 8, 1855 by Thos. Taylor, Jas. Dawson, W. W. Burris

bound to Wm. Hill Ord. Abbeville Dist. sum $1,200.00. He was the son. l. of Thos. Taylor. Jesse O'Bryant bought at sale. (Name also written O'Briant.)

OLIVER, JOHN—BOX 139, PACK 3935:
Will dated 1843 in Abbeville Dist. Filed June 9, 1854. Exrs: Jas. M. Latimer, Jas. Roberson. Wit: Wm. M. Bell, Peter Gibert, Jas. L. Beck. Chn: Elijah, Jas., Geo. W., Elizabeth, Susannah, Sarah Oliver. Covenant between parties made Dec. 12, 1855. Ment: Nathaniel Stinchcomb and wife Susan of La Fayette Co., Ga., Sarah Terrel of Elbert Co., Ga., Elizabeth Roberson of Abbeville Dist., Geo. W. Oliver of LaFayette Co., Miss.

POWER, JOHN, SR.—BOX 139, PACK 3936:
Will dated Feb. 14, 1855 in Abbeville Dist. Filed Apr. 2, 1855. Exr: Son, Henry F. Power. Wit: Hugh M. Prince, Sterling Bowen, J. H. Power. Wife ment. no name given. Chn: Henry F. Power, Mary Ann Magruder, Caroline A wife of G. W. Huckabee.

POWELL, WILLIAM R.—BOX 139, PACK 3937:
Est. admnr. June 10, 1854 by John T. Parks, Thos. B. Byrd, R. M. White bound to Wm. Hill Ord. Abbeville Dist. sum $10,000.00. John T. Parks states that Wm. R. Powell was a stranger in this community and had no blood relations living in this state, but a bro. and sis. of the whole blood living in the state of La. (Letter dated to J. T. Parks, Greenwood, S. C.)
Bosier Parish, La.
Mar. 16, 1854
Dear Sir
We received your letter bearing date of Feb. 22, we want you to administer on his est. there and pay all just demands that may be agains him according to law and the balance we want you to retain in your hand until we can get it and if it is in your power to bring it to us we would be glad and if you bring it you must write to us as soon as you get this letter and if you cannot bring it you must let us know as soon as possible and we will make other arrangement let us know soon and if you will bring it we will send you power of attorney we will bring to close by subscribing our names.
Gideon Powell
Sarah H. Powell

PRIOR, JOHN—BOX 139, PACK 3938:
Est. admnr. Jan. 2, 1855 by John H. Wilson, Lucien H. Lomax, H. A. Jones bound to Wm. Hill Ord. Abbeville Dist. sum $1,500.00.

PETTIGREW, ELIZABETH ANN—BOX 139, PACK 3939:
Est. admnr. Aug. 28, 1854 by Jas. A. Richey, Edmund Cobb, John G. Wilson bound to Wm. Hill Ord. Abbeville Dist. sum $10,000.00. Jas. A. Richey was a s. l. of said decd., and Thos. R. Pettigrew were the only distributees.

PETTIGREW, GEORGE G.—BOX 139, PACK 3940:
Est. admnr. Aug. 28, 1854 by Jas. A. Richey, Edmund Cobb, John G.

ABBEVILLE DISTRICT WILLS AND BONDS   545

Wilson bound to Wm. Hill Ord. Abbeville Dist. sum $2,000.00. Geo. Pettigrew was a bro. l. of Jas. A. Richey.

PRUITT, SAMUEL—BOX 139, PACK 3941:
Est. admnr. Oct. 3, 1854 by Saml. E. Pruitt, Jas. Martin, Thos. Hawthorn bound to Wm. Hill Ord. Abbeville Dist. sum $4,000.00. Saml. Pruitt was father of Saml. E. Pruitt. Sett. made Nov. 22, 1855. Present: Saml. E. Pruitt admnr., Jas. J. Pruitt in right of his wife Elizabeth, J. M. Pruitt son of Daniel Pruitt decd. 8 distributees viz: John Miller and wife Nancy, S. Bowen and wife Mary, Jas. Pruitt and wife Elizabeth, G. W. Bowen and wife Jane, Andrew Pruitt, Saml. E., Isaac Pruitt, chn. of Daniel Pruitt decd.

PETTIGREW, NANCY E.—BOX 139, PACK 3942:
Est. admnr. Aug. 28, 1854 by Jas. A. Richey, Edmund Cobb, John G. Wilson bound to Wm. Hill Ord. Abbeville Dist. sum $2,000.00. She was a minor. Jas. A. Richey, Thos. R. Pettigrew were the only distributees.

ROBINSON, SAMUEL—BOX 139, PACK 3943:
Will dated Dec. 19, 1854 in Abbeville Dist. Filed Mar. 19. 1855. Exrs: Chas. Evens, Wm. Gordon. Wit: Wm. G. Gordon, Saml. Reed, A. G. Hagan. Wife, Jane Robinson. Chn: Elizabeth Jane, John, Mary Robinson.

RUSH, JOHN, JR.—BOX 139, PACK 3944:
Will dated Dec. 18, 1854 in Abbeville Dist. Filed Jan. 1, 1855. Exr: Chas. Wm. Sproull. Wit: John Cothran, Hugh Moseley, Henry Rush. Wife, Mary Rush. Chn. ment. no names given.

RYKARD, THOMAS—BOX 139, PACK 3945:
Est. admnr. Sept. 18, 1854 by Levi H. Rykard, Henry Riley bound to Wm. Hill Ord. Abbeville Dist. sum $500.00. He died in May last. Was the father of Levi H. Rykard.

SALE, BENJAMIN W.—BOX 140, PACK 3947:
Will dated Dec. 8, 1854 in Abbeville Dist. Filed Jan. 3, 1855. Exrs: Johnson Sale, Jas. H. Wideman. Wit: Henry Jones, Joseph F. Trevet, H. F. Enlow. Wife ment. no name given. Chn: Jas. Leonard, Sara Jane, Martha Virginia Sale. Mrs. Martha Sale bought at the sale.

STRAWHORN, LEVI—BOX 140. PACK 3948:
Est. admnr. Dec. 1, 1854 by as. Strawhorn, John Barnett, H. G. Klugh bound to Wm. Hill Ord. Abbeville Dist. sum $2,000.00. He left no family. Jas. Strawhorn was a bro. Power of Atty. Know what I John R. Campbell of Cass. Co., Ga. have appointed Benjamin Pullman of said state and dist. my Atty. to receive his legacy and his wife Matilay Campbell of est. of Levi Strawhorn of Abbeville Dist., S. C. Sett. ment. 7 distributees: John Strawhorn, B. Pulliam in right of wife Frances, Thos. Strawhorn, Ezekiel Martin in right of wife, E. Rykard in right of wife.

SWAIN, ROBT.—BOX 140, PACK 3949:
Will dated Feb. 11, 1851 in Abbeville Dist. Filed Apr. 18, 1854. Exrs

Saml. Reid, Wm. Haggan. Wit: Wm. Gordon, Peter Henry, A. Stevenson. Wife, Nancy Swain. Chn: Jas. N., Jane Amanda, Elizabeth W. Swain. He died Apr. 4, 1854.

SWAIN, NANCY—BOX 140, PACK 3949½:
    Will dated Dec. 23, 1854 in Abbeville Dist. Filed June 19, 1855. Exr: Saml. Reid. Wit: Andrew, Jas. C. Stevenson, A. G. Hagen. Chn: Jane Amanda, Elizabeth Ward. Gr. son: Robt. Daniel Swain. Power of Atty. On Sept. 8, 1866 Robt. D. Swain of Lauderdale Co., Miss. appointed Elizabeth Swain his Atty. to receive his part of said est.

SMITH, JOEL—BOX 140, PACK 3950:
    Will dated May 20, 1853 in Abbeville Dist. Filed Feb. 26, 1855. Exrs: Son, Augustus Marshall Smith., S. l., Jas. M. Perrin. Wit: Thos. C. Perrin, John, W. H. White. Wife, Isabella Elizabeth Smith. "Give her land at Stoney Point." Chn: Augustus M. Smith, Mary Elizabeth wife of Jas. M. Perrin, Virginia Caroline, Wm. Joel, Lucy Jane, Emma Eliza, Geo. Miles, Isabella Smith. Partial sett. of est. made in Columbia, S. C. Dec. 17, 1862. Present: Col. D. Wyatt Aiken husband of Virginia C. Smith, Augustus M. Aiken husband of Emma E. Smith, Hon. D. L. Wardlaw one of the Exrs. of Col. A. M. Smith decd. Lucy Jane married a Bowie.

(BOX 140, PACK 3951—LOST)

THOMAS, THOS. WALTER—BOX 140, PACK 3952:
    Will date left out. Filed Feb. 1, 1855. Exrs: Son, Jas. Walter Thomas, Haskell, Jas. Taggart, Robt. M. Palmer. Lived in Abbeville Dist. Wife, Elizabeth Hamilton Thomas. Son, Robt. Walter Thos. Other chn. ment. but names not given. Sett. named J. W., D. W. Thomas, M. W. Parker, E. A. Thomas as heirs of est.

TRIBLE, DR. W. L.—BOX 140, PACK 3953:
    Est. admnr. May 7, 1855 by S. M. Trible, John R. Wilson, Robt. Ellis bound to Wm. Hill Ord. Abbeville Dist. sum $2,000.00. Dr. Trible was a bro. to S. M. Trible. His father was L. W. Trible.

TUSTEN, JAMES H.—BOX 140, PACK 3954:
    Est. admnr. Oct. 20, 1854 by Saml., Hiram T. Tusten, John G. Wilson, Augustus Lomax bound to Wm. Hill Ord. Abbeville Dist. sum $15,000.00. Jas. Tusten was father of said Saml. Tusten. Edny M. Tusten the wid. Sett. made July 8, 1856. Distributees: Saml. Tusten admnr., Hiram T. Tusten, Jas. A. Allen gdn. of John L. Tusten a minor, W. Fair represents Mrs. Sarah Allen wid. of John Allen decd.

TODD, ELIZABETH—BOX 140, PACK 3955:
    Will dated July 2, 1847 in Abbeville Dist. Filed Mar. 6, 1855. Exrs: Son, Jas. McCracken, S. l's: Benjamin F., Patrick H. Eddins. Wit: David Ourts, Squire J. Burnett, Willis Ross. Wid. Chn: Mary Ann, Elizabeth, Harriet Eddings, Rebecca, Jas. McCracken, Sarah Child decd. Gr. son: Wm. Child son of Sarah Child decd.

VANDIVER, LARKIN G.—BOX 140, PACK 3956:
Est. admnr. Dec. 15, 1854 by Wm. S. McBride, Wm. H. Simpson, Little-
ton Yarbrough bound to Wm. Hill Ord. Abbeville Dist. sum $2,000.00. Elizabeth
Vandiver bought at sale.

WATSON, JOHN—BOX 140, PACK 3957:
Est. admnr. Aug. 29, 1868 by Edmund W., Mary Watson, Jacob Miller
bound to Wm. Hill Ord. Abbeville Dist. sum $2,000.00. John Watson was s. l. of
Isaac Kennedy. Est. admnr. again Jan. 28, 1855 by Isaac Kennedy, Wiley Burnett,
Mary Watson, J. P. Kennedy bound to Wm. Hill Ord. Abbeville Dist. sum
$4,000.00. A. K. Watson recd. a share of est.

WALKER, DAVID—BOX 140, PACK 3958:
Will dated Sept. 12, 1854 in Abbeville Dist. Filed Oct. 24, 1854. Exr:
Irvin Hutchison. Wit: Edmond Walker, J. S. Chipley, M. Hutchison. Chn. ment.
only one given, John Fletcher Walker. Named also his Aunt Shelnut. Sett. made
Dec. 13, 1854. Present: Irvin Hutchison Exr., John C. Walker who married
Catharine Walker a dtr. of said decd.

WIDEMAN, JAMES A.—BOX 140, PACK 3959:
Est. admnr. Jan. 17, 1855 by Geo. R. Caldwell, Larkin Reynolds, M. W.
Coleman bound to Wm. Hill Ord. Abbeville Dist. sum $4,000.00. Abegall the
wid. Left 2 chn. After death of said decd. his wid. gave birth to one child who
lived about 6 wks. and died.

WATSON, WILLIAM—BOX 140, PACK 3960:
Est. admnr. Dec. 6, 1854 by Archibald Boggs, Kennedy, W. K. Bradley,
A. L. McCaslan bound to Wm. Hill Ord. Abbeville Dist. sum $6,000.00. Left a
wid. and 2 chn. Was a bro. l. to A. B. Kennedy. Wm. Watson at the time of his
death was gdn. of 5 minor chn. viz: John P., Isaac N., Sarah C., Rebecca A., Jas.
M. Kennedy.

WILSON, WILLIAM V.—BOX 140, PACK 3961:
Will dated Oct. 24, 1854 in Abbeville Dist. Filed Nov. 8, 1854. Exr: Bro.,
Saml. A. Wilson. Wit: Jas. M., John C. Chiles, Thos. Johnson. Mother, Lucinda
Wilson. Bro., Thos. Wilson. Sis., Elizabeth Tittle. Father, bros., and sis. ment. but
only these were given. Sett. men. 9 distributees including the parents. S. A., R. H.,
Thos. J., Jas. J., Nancy C. Wilson were legatees.

WALKER, MILES H.—BOX 140, PACK 3962:
Est. admnr. Feb. 1, 1855 by Jas. W. Child, M. O. McCaslan bound to
Wm. Hill Ord. Abbeville Dist. sum $150.00.

WIER, JOHN—BOX 140, PACK 3963:
Papers ment. John Wier as a lunatic. Nothing of interest in papers.

WATSON, JACOB M.—BOX 140, PACK 3964:
Est. admnr. Mar. 3, 1855 by Elihu Watson, Jas. Moore, Wright H. Blackmon bound to Wm. Hill Ord. Abbeville Dist. sum $1,500.00. Left no wife or chn.
but a father Elihu Watson and a mother, bros., and sisters.

ANDERSON, WILLIAM, SR.—BOX 141, PACK 3965:
Est. admnr. Oct. 2, 1855 by Wm. Anderson, Joel J. Cunningham, Jas. Creswell bound to Wm. Hill Ord. Abbeville Dist. sum $20,000.00. Sett. made Jan. 12, 1857. Present: Wm. Anderson Jr. admnr., Wm. Dickson who married Mary Ann a distributee, David Cleland who married Eliza P. a distributee, John Anderson a distributee, Wm. Anderson Jr. in Cartersville, Cass Co., Ga. in 1856.

ALLEN, EUGENE—BOX 141, PACK 3966:
On Aug. 16, 1855 Chas. H., Jas. A. Allen, John F. Livingston bound to Wm. Hill Ord. Abbeville Dist. sum $400.00. Chas. H. Allen made gdn. of Eugene Allen a minor. Chas. Allen father of said minor who is about 7 yrs. old. In the will of John E. Allen who died 1854 he left a legacy to said minor.

BUCHANAN, WILLIAM—BOX 141, PACK 3967:
Est. admnr. Jan. 19, 1856 by John A. Stuart, T. C. Griffin, Larkin Griffin bound to Wm. Hill Ord. Abbeville Dist. sum $12,000.00. Expend: 1852 Paid tutition for Miss Eliza Buchanan $4.00.

BUCHANAN, WILLIAM—BOX 141, PACK 3968:
Est. admnr. Feb. 15, 1856 by Francis Arnold, John, R. J. White bound to Wm. Hill Ord. Abbeville Dist. sum $1,500.00. Francis Arnold was a bro. l. to said decd. and states that Wm. Buchanan removed to La. where he died. Dudley Bryd was a distributee.

BOWEN, LACY B.—BOX 141, PACK 3969:
Est. admnr. Oct. 6, 1855 by Sterling Bowen, Thos. R. Cochran, Saml. A. Hodges bound to Wm. Hill Ord. Abbeville Dist. sum $200.00. Sterling Bowen father of said decd. states that his son died some few yrs. since.

BIGBY, THOMAS S.—BOX 141, PACK 3970:
Est. admnr. Nov. 15, 1855 by Geo. M., John W. Bigby, Jas. Robinson bound to Wm. Hill Ord. Abbeville Dist. sum $4,000.00. Geo. M. Bigby a bro. to said decd. and entitled to a share of est. of his father, Rev. Geo. Bigby decd. 9 distributees, mother and 8 bros. and sis.

BLACK, DR. WILLIAM P.—BOX 141, PACK 3971:
Est. admnr. Dec. 4, 1855 by Ellen Black, John Brownlee, Jonathan Johnson bound to Wm. Hill Ord. Abbeville Dist. sum $15,000.00. Ellen Black the wid. Left 2 infant chn. Jas. W. Black was a bro. to said decd.

BARNES, CHRISTIAN—BOX 141, PACK 3972:
Est. admnr. June 22, 1855 by Christian V. Barnes, Leroy J. Johnson, Jas. T., Z. W. Barnes bound to Wm. Hill Ord. Abbeville Dist. sum $20,000.00. Christian Barnes was father of said Christian V. Barnes admnr. Present at sett: C. V. Barnes admnr., John, Rosannah Barnes wid., Oscar, Franklin, Clarissa Barnes, Saml. Lockridge who represents Jas. F. Hodges and wife Amica, C. V. Barnes represents a sis. who was a wid. viz: P. Hodges, Michael Smith and wife Charlotte, Thos. Hellums and wife Alina were not present. Edward Barnes a son had been absent 14 yrs. had not been heard of, was never married and was reported

dead. Intestate died in May 1855. Had 9 chn. In July 1857 Oscar Barnes, Rosannah Barnes were in Haris Co., Ga.   (Letter)
Jefferson Co., Ark.
Oct. the third
Dear Brother
        I take the present opportunity to drop you a few lines the same leaves us all in tolerable good health we have had a good dead of sickness this season the health of the country has been generally bad for a long time you will please excuse me for not writing sooner I received a letter sometime ago the same accompanied by a check we have had several fine meetings since June there has been 50 or 60 professions in this neighborhood since the first of June I must cloze for the present from the fact the male will be on soon and I have just time to send this to the office.
        Mary Hodges to C. V. Barnes
        Received of C. V. Barnes a check for $500.00 the same being a part of Father's est. Mary Hodge.

BARMORE, FRANCES—BOX 141, PACK 3973:
        Est. admnr. Apr. 1, 1856 by David L. Donnald, Abner H. Magee, Jas. F. Donnald, G. B. Morrah bound to Wm. Hill Ord. Abbeville Dist. sum $5,000.00. Was a minor. Left 9 distributees: mother and 8 bros. and sis: E. E., Hugh R., Jas. L., Jane Barmore, D. L. Donnald, Mary E., Wm. C., Margaret W. Barmore recd. shares.

CALLAHAM, (MINORS)—BOX 141, PACK 3974:
        On Sept. 29, 1855 Robt. O. Tribble, John R. Wilson, Joseph Ellis bound to Wm. Hill Ord. Abbeville Dist. sum $5,000.00. Robt. O. Tribble made gdn. of Celestia C., Jas. R., Sarah E. Callaham minors of John L. Callaham decd. and Mary E. Callaham decd. who was a sis. to a Robt. O. Tribble. In 1875 J. R. Callahan and R. O. Tribble were of Oconee Co. In 1867 R. O. Tribble was of Townville, S. C. Richardson Tribble, Basil M. Callaham, Jas. M. Carwile, Bennet McAdams were relations of said minors. Sarah married a Harbin.

CHEVES, MARTHA—BOX 141, PACK 3975:
        Est. admnr. Sept. 18, 1855 by Joseph Ligon, A. Lewis Gillespie, John F. Livingston bound to Wm. Hill Ord. Abbeville Dist. sum $8,000.00. She died July 1855. Distributees: Joseph Ligon s. l. and his wife Eliza M. Ligon, Thos. A. Cheves, John Patterson and wife Martha A.

CALLAHAM, JOHN—BOX 141, PACK 3976:
        Will dated Nov. 30, 1853 in Abbeville Dist. Filed Oct. 2, 1855. Exrs: Sons, John L., Sherrod W. Callaham. Wit: G. M. Mattison, J. R., Benjamin M. Latimer. Wife, Nancy Callaham. Chn: John L., Sherrod W. Callaham, Elizabeth Carwile, the chn. of Sarah Carwile, David, Basdell Callaham, Lucy Caldwell, the chn. of Jane Rutherford, the chn. of Susan Bowen, Francis Callaham, Absalom Callaham, Mary Carwile, Dempsey Callaham, Clarissa Gray, Elenor Latimer. Martha Griffin, Cealia Wright, Gabrilla Pratt, Jas. S. Callaham, Wm. M. Callaham, Nancy Ann Pratt, Eliza Callaham. Power of Atty. Know that we, Addison

F., Madison M. Carwile, Sarah Rice formerly Sarah Carwile and Berry C. Rice
her husband all of Chattooga Co., Ga. do appoint Jas. M. Carwile of Abbeville
Dist., S. C. our Atty. to receive our shares of est. of John Callaham decd. Dated
this 13th May, 1857. Power of Atty. Chattooga Co., Ga. Know that we, Gabriella
Pratt wife of Chas. F. Pratt, Nancy A. Pratt wife of Joseph A. Pratt chn. of
John Callaham decd. of Abbeville Dist. do appoint Wm. Pratt Sr. of Abbeville
Dist. our Atty. Dated this 20 Jan., 1857. Expend: On Aug. 25, 1857 Wm. C.
Graham and Candis Graham recd. $61.66 as their share. On May 1, 1858 Mary
Pope dtr. of Sarah Carwile decd. $66.43 as her share. On Mar. 20, 1857 S. W.
Cochran and Frances Cochran recd. $301.65½ as their share. On Mar. 20, 1857
Jas., Eliza Williamson recd. $301.65 as their share. John Gray and Clarissa Gray
his wife on Feb. 14, 1857 were living in Chattooga Co., Ga. Andrew Caldwell
and his wife Lucy Callaham Caldwell were of *Meriwither* Co., Ga. in Dec. 1856.

COCHRAN, MAJOR JOHN—BOX 141, PACK 3977:
     Will dated Aug. 11, 1854 in Abbeville Dist. Filed Jan. 28, 1856. Exr:
Jas. N. Cochran. Wit: Chas. Smith, C. A. Cobb, B. Z. Herndon. Chn: Mary Ann
L. wife of Wm. McNary, Jas. N., John Wesley Cochran.

CALDWELL, EDNA—BOX 141, PACK 3978:
     Will dated Feb. 1, 1855 in Abbeville Dist. Filed May 16, 1855. Exrs:
Son, Geo. R. Caldwell, Stanmore Brooks. Wit: John Cothran, C. W. Sproull,
W. C. Hunter. Chn: Geo. R. Caldwell, Ann E. Webber, Margaret R. Caldwell.
Gr. dtr: Virginia Pickens Maynard. "Bequeath to Mt. Moriah Church."

CROSS, ELIZABETH—BOX 141, PACK 3979:
     Est. admnr. Aug. 22, 1855 by Jas. J. Devlin. Andrew Paul bound to Wm.
Hill Ord. Abbeville Dist. sum $1,600.00. Jas. Devlin sheweth that many yrs. ago
say in 1840 Elizabeth Cross died intestate, the wid. of Saml. Cross a Revolutionary
Soldier, and that arrears of pension may be obtained to the chn. of said Elizabeth
Cross from the U. S. Government. Left 2 chn., but one died leaving chn. David,
Mary Dansby recd. share of est. Martha Marsh recd. share also. On Jan. 31, 1860
Jas. O., Anna, Andrew B. McClane stated that they were entitled to a small est.
from that of our father, our gr. father John Webb and gr. mother Elizabeth Webb
and we are all minors of the age of choice and desire that Wm. Clinkscales be
appointed our gdn.

CALLAHAM, JOHN L.—BOX 141, PACK 3980:
     Est. admnr. Sept. 12, 1855 by Basil Callaham, Jas. M. Carwile, Jas.
Clinkscales bound to Wm. Hill Ord. Abbeville Dist. sum $3,000.00. Left a wid.
and 3 chn. Was a bro. to Basil Callaham. R. O. Tribble was gdn. of Celestia C.,
Jas. R., Sarah E. Callaham.

DONNALD, MAJOR JOHN—BOX 141, PACK 3981:
     Will dated June 23, 1855 in Abbeville Dist. Filed July 16, 1855. Exrs:
Sons, Jas. F., Saml. Donald. Wit: A. C. Hawthorne, R. R. Seawright, John B.
Gordon. Wife, Jane Donnald. Chn: Anny wife of Wm. Hill, Eliza wife of Larkin
Barmore, Sarah wife of Reuben Latimer, Lucinda wife of Robt. Brownlee, Mary

Jane wife of Saml. W. Agnew, Saml., Jas. F., Wm., John, David. L. Donnald. Grand dtr: Mary Jane Donnald. "Bequeath to the Greenville Church $200.00."

DONNELLY, REV. JAMES—BOX 141, PACK 3982:
Will dated Apr. 9, 1855 in Abbeville Dist. Prov. May 7, 1855. Exrs: John Brownlee, Jas. C. Harper. Wit: Jas. T. Baskin, Joel Lockhart. Wm. A. Giles. A Minister of the Gospel. Wife, Maria Donnelly. Chn: Francis Olin, Geo. Summerfield, Andrew Emory, John David Fletcher, Margaret Kizia Jane, Henrietta Donnelly.

DE BRUHL, STEPHEN C.—BOX 141, PACK 3983:
Est. admnr. Dec. 10, 1855 by J. Foster, Saml. S., J. W. W. Marshall bound to Wm. Hill Ord. Abbeville Dist. sum $30,000.00. Wid. Susan E. DeBruhl. 5 distributees viz: Susan C., Stephen C., M. T., M. P. DeBruhl, child of Mrs. Barkuloo.

DONNELLY, JAMES C.—BOX 141, PACK 3984:
Est. admnr. Dec. 10, 1855 by Jas. T., John G. Baskin, F. W. Davis bound to Wm. Hill Ord. Abbeville Dist. sum $200.00. He died Mar. 7, 1855 leaving a wid., no chn., but bro. and sis. Wid., Mary R. Donnelly.

DEVORE, JOHN S.—BOX 141, PACK 3985:
Est. admnr. Nov. 17, 1855 by Johnson, Sale, Wm. Andrews, Willis Ross bound to Wm. Hill Ord. Abbeville Dist. sum $1,500.00. Died Oct. 28. 1855. Wid., Mary Devore.

DIXON, JOHN J.—BOX 141, PACK 3986:
Est. admnr. Feb. 13, 1856 by Jas. Martin, L. J. Johnson, J. S. Reid bound to Wm. Hill Ord. Abbeville Dist. sum $400.00. He was a minor. 5 distributees viz: W. M. Martin and wife, R. S. Dixon, Martha M. Dixon, A. Stott and wife, Freeman B. Nixon minors.

DYSON, (MINORS)—BOX 141, PACK 3987:
On Feb. 5, 1856 John Sadler, Simeon Chaney, J. Wesley Fooshe bound to Wm. Hill Ord. Abbeville Dist. sum $1,811.92. John Sadler made gdn. of Wm. Thos., Mary Jane Dyson minors. Mary A. Thompson appointed her bro. John Sadler gdn. of her 2 minors.

FOSTER, JAMES H.—BOX 141, PACK 3988:
Est. admnr. Sept. 21, 1855 by Edmund G., John P. Kennedy, A. P. Conner bound to Wm. Hill Ord. Abbeville Dist. sum $3,000.00. Wid., Eliza Foster. Had 7 chn., no names given.

GRAY, JAMES—BOX 142, PACK 3989:
Est. admnr. Dec. 15, 1855 by Saml. Robinson, Jas. Carlisle, Jas. Irvin bound to Wm. Hill Ord. Abbeville Dist. sum $600.00. He died leaving no father, mother, bro., or sis. in this state. Was a cousin to Saml. Robinson.

GILES, JOSIAH P.—BOX 142, PACK 3990:
Est. admnr. Sept. 22, 1855 by Hamilton T. Miller, Sarah C. Giles, Allen

552 ABSTRACTS OF OLD NINETY-SIX AND

T. Miller, Jas. T. Liddell bound to Wm. Hill Ord. Abbeville Dist. sum $12,000.00. H. T. Miller was a bro. l. of said decd. Left a wife, Sarah C. Giles and 3 chn.

HOUSTON, ALEXANDER—BOX 142, PACK 3991:
Will dated Aug. 11, 1855 in Abbeville Dist. Filed Oct. 30, 1855. Exrs: Alexr. R. Houston, Wm. P. Noble. Wit: D. M. Rogers, T. T. Cunningham, W. W. Rogers. Chn: Robt. H., Jas. A. Houston, Matilda C. Noble, Elizabeth A. Cowen, John A., Joseph B. Houston, Susan A. Noble, Wm. J. Houston. Bequeath to my last set of chn. viz: Augusta G. Parks, Cornelius B., Armstrong P., Alice, Alexr. R. Houston, Jane C. Scott.

HIGGINS, HILYARD G.—BOX 142, PACK 3992:
Est. admnr. Oct. 22, 1855 by Frances Higgins, Daniel S. Beachum, J. K., John Vance bound to Wm. Hill Ord. Abbeville Dist. sum $6,000.00. Left wid., Mary Frances Higgins and 5 minor chn.

JAY, ABIGALE—BOX 142, PACK 3993:
Will dated July 27, 1849 in Abbeville Dist. Filed July 11, 1855. Exr: John Cothran. Wit: Robt. H. Wardlaw, Jas. M., Thos. C. Perrin. Chn: Henrietta Moriah Skinner, Joseph, Jesse, Tiry Jay.

JOHNSON, MARY—BOX 142, PACK 3994:
Est. admnr. Apr. 4, 1855 by Wm. A. Limbecker, John Bozeman. John T. Johnson bound to Wm. Hill Ord. Abbeville Dist. sum $5,000.00. Wm. A. Limbecker was an only son of said decd. Sett. made 1857 ment. that W. A. Limbecker had left the state.

LOMAX, SARAH JANE—BOX 142, PACK 3995:
On May 28, 1855 John W., Wm. A. Lomax, John J. Keller bound to Wm. Hill Ord. Abbeville Dist. sum $207.46. John W. Lomax made gdn. of Sarah Jane Lomax dtr. Is entitled to a legacy by the will of Mrs. Jane Houston.

LATIMER, CLEMENT T.—BOX 142, PACK 3996:
Will dated Nov. 10, 1854. Filed May 7, 1855. Exrs: Sons, Edmond F. Latimer, Jas. M., Benjamin M. Latimer. Wit: Noah R. Reev, Stephen Latimer. T. R. Latimer. Ment: Lived in Abbeville Dist. Wife, Isabella Latimer. Chn: Mary Trowbridge, Edmond F. Latimer, Harriet and Walter G. Johnson, Jas. M., Albert G., Stephen Latimer, chn. of Catharine Featherston, Micajah B., Benjamin M., Margaret Louisa Latimer, Sarah A. and husband Benjamin W. Mattison.

LOGAN, ANDREW—BOX 142, PACK 3997:
Will dated Jan. 11, 1851. Filed Apr. 21, 1856. Exrs: Sons, Isaac, Zachary Logan, Nephew, Dr. John Logan. Wit: Wm. A., Caleb A., A. M. Blake. Ment: Lived in Abbeville Dist. Chn: Zachary, Frances, Tyler, Leroy, Willis, Andrew J. Logan, Huldah Crawford, Frederick, Isaac, John Lewis Logan.

LINDSAY, L. T.—BOX 142, PACK 3998:
Est. admnr. Sept. 10, 1855 by A. P. Lindsay, D. O. Hawthorne, J. J. Bonner bound to Wm. Hill Ord. Abbeville Dist. sum $6,000.00. Was unmarried

and distributees are: mother, bros., and sis. A. P. Lindsay was a bro. 6 in all. W. Winn Lindsay, J. Oliver, A. P. Lindsay, J. J. Bonner recd. shares in est.

LATHERS, JOHN L.—BOX 142, PACK 3999:
Will dated Feb. 28, 1854. Filed Sept. 27, 1855. Exr: David Keller Esq. Wit: Jas. J. Gilmer, David Robison, Richard Thompson. Ment: Lived in Abbeville Dist. Wife, Nancy Lathers.
Will of Nancy Lathers in same package. Will dated Nov. 7, 1855. Exr: David Keller Esq. Wit: Jas. Irvin, Saml. Robinson, Thos. Gordon. Ment: Lived in Abbeville Dist. Bequeath to Ann Workman wife of John Workman, to Jas. Cunningham and his dtr. Mary Jane, to Robt. John Workman, Jas. Workman sons of John and Mary Workman decd., to Mary Phillips, Nancy Bedenbeau dtrs. of Ellender McGlothen, to Henry Anderson and family, to Elizabeth and Mary Jane Cunningham dtrs. of Jas. Cunningham.

McCOMB, BETSEY—BOX 142, PACK 4000:
Est. admnr. Sept. 1, 1855 by Eli Thornton, Saml. Link, John S. Dale bound to Wm. Hill Ord. Abbeville Dist. sum $800.00. She died in Oct. Robt. McComb was a bro. of said decd. Est. divided 4 shares viz: Est. of Robt. McComb, Eli Thornton and wife, Alex. Laugher, Wm. A. McCartney.

McCRACKEN, ANN—BOX 142, PACK 4001:
Will dated May 8, 1855. Filed Sept. 19, 1855. Exr: J. W. Hearst. Wit: John Robinson, Timothy Russell, Sarah Russell. Ment: Spinster. Lived in Abbeville Dist. Bequeath to Rebecca Robinson wid. of my half bro. Wm. Robinson Jr. decd., to Jenny McBryde wife of Thos. McBryde, to their dtrs. Margaret H. and Jenny Bell McBryde, to Mary Robinson, Jincy Robinson, Matty Davis wife of Wm. Davis, neighbors, Wm. White, Simpson Evans, Henderson Russell.

MORROW, (MINORS)—BOX 142, PACK 4002:
On May 8, 1855 Nancy Morrow, Jas. Dawson bound to Wm. Hill Ord. Abbeville Dist. sum $400.0. Nancy Morrow made gdn. of Permelia R. Morrow, Geo. A. Morrow minors. They were entitled to a pension allowed them by the U. S. Government on acct. of services performed by thier father who died in the Military Service of the U. S. in Mexico. Nancy Morrow was their gr. mother. Andrew Morrow decd. their gr. father.

MORTON, LUCINDA—BOX 142, PACK 4003:
Est. admnr. Aug. 18, 1855 by Augustus H. Morton, Silas Ray, John Burnett bound to Wm. Hill Ord. Abbeville Dist. sum $16,000.00. A. H. Morton admnr. was the only son and heir of his mother the said decd. She died July 15, 1855.

NEIL, MARTHA C.—BOX 142, PACK 4004:
Will dated Oct. 29, 1855. Filed Nov. 29, 1855. Exr: H. A. Jones Esq. Wit: B. P. Hughes, Wm. H. Parker, J. A. Allen. Ment: Lived in Abbeville Dist. Dtr. Mary Adalaide wife of Augustus Lomax. Husband, John P. Neil decd. of Newberry Dist.

OLIVER, ELIJAH—BOX 142, PACK 4005:
Will dated July 14, 1855. Filed Aug. 16, 1855. Exrs: Saml. L. Hill, Jas. T. Allen. Wit: Alexr. Oliver, J. Foster Hill, Jas. C. Harper. Ment: Lived in Abbeville Dist. Sis., Elizabeth Robinson, Susan Stinchcomb, Sarah A. Terel. Bros., Jas., Geo. W. Oliver.

PRUIT, ELEAZAR N.—BOX 142, PACK 4006:
Est. admnr. July 9, 1855 by Geo. B. Morrah, Alley Pruit, Saml. E. Pruit bound to Wm. Hill Ord. Abbeville Dist. sum $2,000.00. Was a minor son of Daniel Pruit decd. Left 8 distributees: mother and 7 bros., and sis. July 9, 1855 Recd. from Mrs. Alley Pruit the share of Eleazar in his father's est. $1,006.56.

PORTER, ELIZABETH D.—BOX 142, PACK 4007:
Will dated Mar. 28, 1854. Filed June 4, 1855. Wit: S. M. G. Gray, Mary A. Gray, A. N. Darracott. Lived in Abbeville Dist. Chn: Elizabeth wife of W. M. Griffin. (Letter)

Panola Co., Tex.
DeBerry P. O.
Nov. 12, 1874

Edward Noble,
Atty. at Law
Abbeville, S. C.
Dear Sir:
By the will of Elizabeth D. Porter decd. of your Co. and State, one hundred and sixty acres of land thereabouts situated about a mile from the Villiage of Cokesbury in your Co. now devised to the undersigned Elizabeth Griffin her dtr. and wife of W. M. Griffin for her life to her sole use and at her death to the heirs of her body of whom the undersigned John M. Mays, Anna L. Trosher and Mary E. Westmoreland are three and of age the other heirs of the body are Wm. Griffin a minor of 20 yrs. of age, Larkin P. Griffin 16 yrs., Lawton H. Griffin 14 yrs., Francis C. Griffin 10 yrs. All the parties interested reside in the State of Texas, Panola Co., etc.

PACE, SARAH—BOX 142, PACK 4008:
Est. admnr. Oct. 29, 1855 by John Davis, Jas. C. Ellis, Silas Ray bound to Wm. Hill Ord. Abbeville Dist. sum $12,000.00. Sarah Pace was the mother-in-law of John Davis. She died in Mar. 1855.

PURSLEY, NANCY E.—BOX 142, PACK 4009:
Est. admnr. July 7, 1855 by John C. Pursley, B. F. Hughes bound to Wm. Hill Ord. Abbeville Dist. sum $100.00. Wife of said John C. Pursley and had an interest in the est. of Henry Brooks decd. Sett. named 8 distributees as bros. and sis., no names given.

PARKER, MARGARET—BOX 142, PACK 4010:
Will dated Feb. 10, 1851 in Abbeville Dist. Filed Sept. 6, 1855. Exr: Bro. l., Zachariah Grayham. Wit: David W. McCants, John Moore, Williston W. Franklin. Bro., Jas. Parker. Sis., Elizabeth Grayham, Isabella Pool. Niece, Polly

Ann Grayham dtr. of my sis. Elizabeth Graham. Niece, Jane Pool dtr. of my sis. Isabella and Mathew Pool. Nephew, John W. son of Elizabeth and Zachariah Grayham. Nieces: Margaret E. Pool, Martha Jane Grayham. Nephews: Saml., Jas., Joel Addison Grayham. Sis., Sarah Parker now in the Lunatic Asylum in Columbia, S. C.

POOL, JANE—BOX 142, PACK 4011:
On Sept. 21, 1855 Benjamin S. Pulliam, Mathew Pool, Thos. B. Milford bound to Wm. Hill Ord. Abbeville Dist. sum $800.00. Benjamin S. Pulliam made gdn. of Jane Pool a minor about 19 yrs.

ATKINS, FRANCIS—BOX 143, PACK 4014:
Will dated Sept. 1, 1855 in Abbeville Dist. Filed Mar. 18, 1856. Exr: Son, Robt. Atkins. Wit: R. W. Lites, J. C. Lites, J. W. Lites. Chn: Robt. Atkins, Margarette Dale, Ravena, Jas. Atkins. Wife, Elizabeth Atkins. Sett. made Aug. 2, 1859. Dr. C. C. Porter was trustee for his wife Margaret Atkins a dtr. of said decd.

ANDREWS, JAMES A.—BOX 143, PACK 4015:
Est. admnr. May 9, 1856 by Mary A. Andrews, Jas. H. Cobb, Saml. Jordon bound to Wm. Hill Ord. Abbeville Dist. sum $15,000.00. Left a wid., Mary A. Andrew and 2 chn., Dr. Franklin Andrews, Catharine Zimmerman Andrews.

BOGGS, REBECCA—BOX 143, PACK 4016:
Est. admnr. Aug. 29, 1856 by John McCreery, Wm. Gibson, J. H. McCreery bound to Wm. Hill Ord. Abbeville Dist. sum $1,500.00. Sett. made Apr. 9, 1858. Present: John McCreery admnr., F. B. Robinson a nephew, Jane B. Lindsay niece wife of Josph Lindsay, Niece, Martha Davis wife of Wm. Davis, Margaret McCreery. Had a bro. and 2 sis. viz: Saml. Boggs left 1 child, Elizabeth A. Robinson left 9 chn., Mary McCreery left 3 chn. All 3 died before said decd. Elizabeth A. Robinson decd. sister of Whole blood left: Saml. B. dead, John dead, Mary living, Martha Davis and husband, Henry Robinson in Miss., Frederick Robinson in Abbeville, Jas. Robinson in Tex., W. H. Robinson dead in Abbeville, A. P. Robinson in Tex., Jane B. Lindsay wife of Joseph Lindsay in Abbeville, D. P. Robinson in Lancaster, S. C. Sis. Mary McCreery decd. left Margaret, John McCreery in Abbeville, Joseph McCreery, Jas. H. McCreery living in Abbeville. Martha Boggs died before Rebecca without heirs. Saml. Boggs decd. had 1 child, Mary.

BOWEN, JOHN—BOX 143, PACK 4017:
Est. admnr. Aug. 22, 1856 by Ezekiel Trible, R. F. Bell, David Cleland bound to Wm. Hill Ord. Abbeville Dist. sum $100.00. John Bowen died some yrs. past in the State of Miss. Son of Woody Bowen decd.

CALLAHAM, JOHN R.—BOX 143, PACK 4018:
Est. admnr. May 29, 1856 by Andrew H., Saml. J., David Callaham bound to Wm. Hill Ord. Abbeville Dist. sum $1,000.00. He died May 11, 1856. Was a bro. to Andrew H. Callaham.

CHEATHAM, MARTHA—BOX 143, PACK 4019:
Est. admnr. June 3, 1856 by Alfred Cheatham, J. Wesley Fooshe, John Sadler, J. W. Calhoun bound to Wm. Hill Ord. Abbeville Dist. sum $10,000.00. Was mother of said Alfred Cheatham. She died in May. Power of Atty. On Oct. 20, 1856 Washington Fooshe of Montgomery Co., Tex. appointed John Sadler of Abbeville Dist. his Atty. in right of his wife Lavinda Fooshe of est. of her late mother Martha Cheatham. Also entitled to a share from est. of her gr. father Col. Wm. Ware. Sett. made Apr. 9, 1858. Present: Alfred Cheatham son. Heirs: chn. of Robt. pre-deceased son viz. Amanda wife of Wm. Rotton and Wm. a minor. Chn. of John L. Cheatham decd. viz: Thos., John, Franklin Cheatham minors. Chn. of Milton Cheatham decd. viz: Martha Elizabeth, Mary Frances Cheatham minors. Hellena wife of Reuben G. Golding of Tex. Lavinda wife of G. W. Fooshe of Tex. Reuben G. Golding and wife Hellena were of Montgomery Co., Tex.

GAINES, CAPT. JOHN—BOX 143, PACK 4020:
Est. admnr. June 26, 1856 by Saml. Donnald, D. Donnald, Jas. F. Donnald bound to Wm. Hill Ord. Abbeville Dist. sum $200.0. On Dec. 4, 1857 Geo. Mattison and Ellis Sharp recd. their probate share of est.

GANTT, ELIZABETH Y. A.—BOX 143, PACK 4021:
On June 9, 1856 Elizabeth Y. Arnold, Alexr. Oliver, W. A. Pressly bound to Wm. Hill Ord. Abbeville Dist. sum $3,000.00. Elizabeth Y. Arnold made gdn. of Elizabeth Y. A. Gantt a minor. Elizabeth Arnold was her Aunt. Dr. A. B. Arnold decd. was her Uncle.

GIVENS, ELIZABETH—BOX 143, PACK 4022:
Will dated June 19, 1855. Filed May 8, 1856. Exrs: Son, Robt. Stuckey. Wit: E. Trible, Abram Haddon, Thos. Crawford. Ment: Lived in Abbeville Dist. Chn: Malinda wife of Geo. Williams, Margaret, Sarah, Jane, Elizam John Givens. Son, Robt. Stuckey. Expend: Oct. 14, 1856 Recd. from John L. Ellis share of said Elizabeth from est. of her decd. husband J. Givens $1,669.38.

HUEY, MARTHA P.—BOX 143, PACK 4023:
Est. admnr. Apr. 21, 1856 by Leroy J. Johnson, John Link. Jas. Taggart bound to Wm. Hill Ord. Abbeville Dist. sum $8,000.00.

HILL, MRS, MARY—BOX 143, PACK 4024:
Will dated Oct. 15, 1853. Filed Apr. 28, 1856. Exrs: Dr. Isaac Branch, Revd. Jas. Moore, David Keller Esq. Wit: R. Sondley, Edwin J. Taylor, Wm. C. Moore. Ment: Lived in Abbeville Dist. "My body should be buried at Upper Long Cane Graveyard." To bro. Hugh McCrone of Ireland $50.00. Sis., Ellen Bamfert of Ireland. Nephew, Hugh McCrone Jr. Niece, Mary McCrone. Will to the poor of *Bellyneere,* Ireland. Bequeath to the trustees of Episcopal Church at Abbeville, as it is the church of my choice.

HILL, J. FOSTER—BOX 143, PACK 4025:
Est. admnr. Feb. 10, 1856 by David F. Hill, Saml. L. Hill, Thos. O. Hill,

Richard S. Hill bound to Wm. Hill Ord. Abbeville Dist. sum $15,000.00. Jas. H. Whitner recd. a share of est. of Mrs. Eliza Hill decd. and J. Foster Hill. (Letter) Anderson
21st February, 1856
Wm. Hill Esq.
Sir
    Enclosed you will find a petition for Letters of Admnr. on the Est. of J. Foster Hill decd. late of your dist. the applicant is a bro. of his and J. F. Hill. Wife is also dead, she died on last monday the application is made in this way to save D. F. Hill the trouble and expense of coming to Abbeville as it a distance of 30 miles to ride, he wishes you to issue the citation for monday the 10th of Mar. next as he will be at Abbeville on that day of the weather will at all permit, and if not as soon there after as possible, he will of his bro. Richard Hill and Jas. A. Gray and probably Jas. Allen of your dist. as his securities. Hill and Gray are worth at least ten to fifteen thousand dollars as to Jas. Allen you know more of him than I do as to property they wish at this time simply to take out letters of administration and Warrant of appraisement and apply for a sale in the fall after the crop is made which has been begun and a contract for the year made by Hill in his lifetime by giving the notice upon the application you will confirm a favor on D. F. Hill and also on your humble servant.

A. Norris

McCREE, JAS.—BOX 143, PACK 4026:
    Est. admnr. June 13, 1856 by John A. Hunter, Edward Roche, Jas. H. Cobb bound to Wm. Hill Ord. Abbeville Dist. sum $400.00. Died May 25, 1856.

MURDOCK, (MINORS)—BOX 143, PACK 4027:
    On July 28, 1856 Stephen M. Fisher, Caleb Burton, Jacob Alewine bound to Wm. Hill Ord. Abbeville Dist. sum $200.00. Stephen M. Fisher made gdn. of Jesse, Stephen, Edna M., Jane, Joseph Murdock minors of Jas. Murdock decd. In 1866 Jane Murdock was wife of W. A. Ashley.

MARTIN, SARAH—BOX 143, PACK 4028:
    Est. admnr. Sept. 4, 1856 by Robt. Martin, Robt. McAdams, Jas. Elgin bound to Wm. Hill Ord. Abbeville Dist. sum $600.00. Sett. made Nov. 7, 1856. 7 distributees viz: Wm., Jas. about to remove from the state, Saml., Robt. Martin. Elizabeth Richey, Nancy Martin, minors of A. Webb. Nancy Richey was wife of Jas. W. Richey. John Webb was gdn. of John M. Webb a minor. Matthew. Manervey Williamson also recd. a share.

McWHORTER, LOUISA JANE—BOX 143, PACK 4029:
    On Apr. 8, 1856 Louisa Lesly, Wm., John W. Lesly bound to Wm. Hill Ord. Abbeville Dist. sum $5,000.00. Louisa Lesly made gdn. of Louisa Jane Mc-Whorter about 15 yrs. Under the will of D. Lesly decd. husband of Louisa Lesly, the said minor was entitled to a legacy. Louisa Lesly was an Aunt of said minor.

MANTZ, MARY—BOX 143, PACK 4030:
    Will dated Feb. 3, 1856. Filed Sept. 8. 1856. Exr: Nephew, David Glover.

Wit: John Cothran, Martha R. Zimmerman, J. A. Quarles. Ment: Lived in Abbeville Dist. Nephew, David Glover. Gr. niece, Harriet Glover. Gr. nephew, Vandal M. Glover chn. of said David Glover.

McCLINTON, JAS. R.—BOX 143, PACK 4031:
    Will dated May 10, 1856. Filed June 2, 1856. Exr: R. C. Sharp. Wit: Jas. Y. Sitton, Robt. Drennan, Robt. A. Archer. Ment: Lived in Abbeville Dist. Bro., Wm. McClinton. Sis., Jane, Caroline McClinton. Niece, Elizabeth Richey.

MADDOX, RICHARD—BOX 143, PACK 4033:
    Est. admnr. June 19, 1856 by Wm. Maddox, Jane Kirkpatrick, Jas. H. Shaw, A. M. Dodson, H. A. Jones bound to Wm. Hill Ord. Abbeville Dist. sum $20,000.00. Richard Maddox the father of Wm. Maddox and Jane Kirkpatrick died in 1855. Heirs were: Jane Kirkpatrick wid., Wm. Maddox, Jas. H. Shaw and Mary his wife.

POWER, HENRY F.—BOX 143, PACK 4034:
    Est. admnr. Apr. 7, 1856 by G. W. Huckabee, Jas. M. Latimer, John Brownlee bound to Wm. Hill Ord. Abbeville Dist. sum $40,000.00. Sett. made Jan. 19, 1858. Present: G. W. Huckabee admnr., John Williams Power an only son. Dr. John Logan gdn. of the minor chn. of Louisa R. wife of W. W. Logan decd. only heirs of intestate. Wm. R., Mary S. A. Logan were minors.

PORTERFIELD, (MINORS)—BOX 143, PACK 4035:
    On Jan. 24, 1856 Wm. W. Hunter, John Faulkner, J. F. McComb bound to Wm. Hill Ord. Abbeville Dist. sum $800.00. Wm. Hunter made gdn. of John H., Mary E., Margaret Porterfield minors.

ROSS, MOSES GLENN—BOX 143, PACK 4036:
    Will dated Mar. 19, 1855. Filed Aug. 13, 1855. Exr: Bro. l., Marcus A. Crews. Wit: C. H. Selleck, J. W. Appleton, Gilford Waller, Philip LeRoy. Sis., Isabella A. Crews wife of Marcus A. Crews.

RICHEY, WM.—BOX 143, PACK 4037:
    Est. admnr. Aug. 18, 1855 by Ezekiel Rasor, B. F. Moseley, G. M. Mattison, Saml. Agnew bound to Wm. Hill Ord. Abbeville Dist. sum $16,000.00. Left a wid. Virginia C. Richey and several chn. Sarah Jane, Letitia Richey, Sarah Jane Richey, Elmina and Fatina Ann Richey, by 2nd wife Antionette Richey.

RICHEY, WM. H.—BOX 143, PACK 4038:
    Est. admnr. Sept. 27, 1855 by Saml. T. Richey, Hezekiah Elgin, Saml. Martin bound to Wm. Hill Ord. Abbeville Dist. sum $500.00. Left a wid. and 2 chn. Saml. Richey was a bro.

ROBINSON, MARY AND JOHN—BOX 143, PACK 4039:
    Will of Mary Robinson dated Jan. 17, 1855. Exr: Dr. J. W. Hearst. Wit: John Bradley, D. L. Wilson, W. K. Bradley. Ment: Lived in Abbeville Dist. Bro., John Robinson. Will of John Robinson had same date, Exrs: Wit. Left est. to sis., Mary Robinson.

RUSSELL, JOHN—BOX 143, PACK 4040:
Est. admnr. May 21, 1856 by Sarah Russell, John A. Hunter, Edward Roche bound to Wm. Hill Ord. Abbeville Dist. sum $1,500.00. Died Apr. 23, 1855. Wid., Sarah Russell.

ROBERTSON, MARY KNIGHT—BOX 143, PACK 4041:
Will dated Oct. 23, 1854. Filed May 24, 1856. Exr: Bro. Wesley Robertson. Wit: J. Wardlaw Perrin, Langdon C. Haskell, Jas. S. Cothran. Ment: Lived in Abbeville Dist. Half bro., Wesley Robertson.

STEWART, JAS. D.—BOX 143, PACK 4042:
Est. admnr. Aug. 7, 1855 by G. M. D. Miller, Edward Noble, John A. Wier bound to Wm. Hill Ord. Abbeville Dist. sum $5,000.00. He died in the City of New Orleans, La.

SMITH, WM. H.—BOX 143, PACK 4043:
Will dated Dec. 1, 1855. Filed Dec. 31, 1855. Exr: Wm. Truwit. Wit: J. H. Jennings, A. B. Boyd, P. H. Bradley. Wife, Beda Smith.

TUSTAN, EDNA—BOX 143, PACK 4044:
Est. admnr. May 30, 1855 by Hiram T. Tusten, N. J. David, Hiram W. Lawson bound to Wm. Hill Ord. Abbeville Dist. sum $4,000.00. Edna M. Tusten was mother of Hiram T. Tusten. Saml. Tusten, Sarah A. Allen, John L. Tusten, J. A. Allen recd. shares.

WEBB, REVD. B. C.—BOX 143, PACK 4045:
Will dated May 30, 1855. Exr: Genl. S. McGowan. Wit: Thos. Williams, L. N. Durham, Thos Wilson. Ment: Lived in Abbeville Dist. Wife, Mary M. Webb. Son, Hylemon Alison. Aunt was, Mary L. Yon. Request my friends, Genl. S. McGowan, W. H. Parker of Abbeville, S. C. and my bro. Edward Webb and Rev. W. O. Prentiss of St. Bartholomews Parrish, S. C. to be advisers for my family. Chn. ment. but only one named. This will was written in Cleveland Co., N. C.

WATSON, MARGARET—BOX 143, PACK 4046:
Est. admnr. Apr. 3, 1856 by Geo. M. D. Watson, Robt. R. Tolbert, Stephen Elmore bound to Wm. Hill Ord. Abbeville Dist. sum $40,000.00. Margaret Watson died Mar. 11, 1856. Was mother of Geo. Watson, Thos. Anthony, Dorothy Jane, Jas. Franklin Watson. Wife of Jas. Watson decd. Geo. Watson was only one 21 yrs. of age.

WALKER, SOLOMON—BOX 143, PACK 4047:
Will dated Jan. 29, 1847. Filed June 19, 1855. Exr: Sanders Walker. Wit: Thos. Ferguson, Geo. W. Mitchell, L. Newby. Ment: Lived in Abbeville Dist. Wife, Nancy Walker. Chn: Elizabeth Dellishaw, Lucy Hardy, Saml. Walker, Sanders Walker, Margaret Martin, Barton Walker. Sett. made Feb. 12, 1858. Jas. F. Martin husband of Margaret Walker, Gallant Hardy husband of Lucinda Walker, Wm. Dellishaw gdn. for John Wesley Delashaw only child of Elizabeth Delashaw decd. Power of Atty. On Nov. 24, 1857 Saml. Walker of Coweta Co.,

Ga. appointed Barton Walker of Abbeville Dist. his Atty. to receive his part of est. of Solomon Walker decd.

WALKER, CROSKEY R.—BOX 143, PACK 4048:
Est. admnr. Feb. 26, 1856 by M. E. Walker, Jas. M. Perrin bound to Wm. Hil Ord. Abbeville Dist. sum $600.00. Left a mother and 4 bros., and sis. No names given.

WIDEMAN, CHAS.—BOX 143, PACK 4049:
On Dec. 6, 1858 C. Wm. Sproull, Jas. S. Cothran, Jas. Creswell bound to Wm. Hill Ord. Abbeville Dist. sum $1,527.96. C. W. Sproull made gdn. for Chas. Wideman a minor.

ZIMMERMAN, PETER—BOX 143, PACK 4050:
Nothing of importance in this package.

BYRD, THOS. B.—BOX 144, PACK 4051:
Will dated Jan. 7, 1856. Filed Feb. 13, 1857. Exrs: Albert Waller, Thos. C. Perrin, Francis Arnold, Allen Vance, Jas. M. Perrin. Wit: Emanuel Wiss, W. L. Templeton, H. W. Leland. Ment: Lived in Greenwood, Abbeville Dist. Wife, Elizabeth Byrd. Wm. Parks son of wife died recently in Tex. Leaves to chn. of my wife viz: Lewis, Jas., John T. Parks, Elizabeth wife of John Barrett, Jr. Bequeath to Catharine Ashe, Joseph Zebulen Hearst. Chn: John B. Byrs decd., Dudley Byrd, Frances wife of E. P. Vaughn. Dtr. in law, Frances E. S. Byrd wid. of my son John B. Byrd decd. (Letter to Joel Smith Esq., Stoney Point, S. C.)
Pickensville
Dec. 24, 1852
Friend J. Smith
Dear Sir
    I am in receipt of your esteemed favor enclosing the right end of ten hundred dollar bills and one twenty dollar bill as soon as you receive this enclose the left end of the above bills for your trouble in this matter I am under lasting obligations to you. In your next letter please give me all the news in your country if there has been any deaths among my old friends please inform me who they are write me how Aunt Betsey Adams' health is and how she is getting on vie me all the news that you think will be of interest to me as I am anxious to hear from all my old friends my own health is tolerable good and I am doing as well as could be expected I have broken up house keeping and am living with my chn. give my love to Mrs. Smith and all the chn. and enquiring friends. I remain your friend.

Frances Mitchell

    Power of Atty. On Apr. 6, 1853 Frances Mitchell of Pickens Co., Ala. appointed Joel Smith of Abbeville Dist. her Atty. Power of Atty. On Apr. 4, 1853 Burwell Ball of Siloam, Oktibbcha Co., Miss. appointed Joel Smith of Abbeville Dist. his Atty. to receive what was coming to him from est. of Rhoda Pulliam decd. wife of Jas. Pulliam decd. On Dec. 4, 1852 Lewis W. Ball, Parkes E. Ball of

Pickens Co., Ala. appointed Joel Smith of Abbeville Dist. their Atty. John Pulliam decd. of S. C. was a bro. to Rhoda Pulliam. He had lawful heirs 10 chn. in number 4 being dead and 6 living: John, Benjamin, David, Stephen dead; Wm., Richard, Joseph, Larkin Pulliam, Elizabeth wid. of Jas. Dobins, Sarah Christopher the wife of Wm. Christopher. Dated Mar. 30, 1833 in Pickens Co., Ala.

BURNETT, SARAH FRANCES—BOX 144, PACK 4052:
Est. admnr. Mar. 5, 1857 by W. B. Merriwether, Jas. W. Buchanan, John Foster bound to Wm. Hill Ord. Abbeville Dist. sum $4,000.00. Was a minor child of Sarah Burnett.

BOYD, JOHN L.—BOX 144, PACK 4052½:
Est. admnr. Oct. 9, 1856 by Wm. A. Boyd, Ruth R. Boyd, B. M. Cheatham, John H. Gray, Wm. H. Brooks, F. M. Brooks, Susana Brooks, Leroy J. Johnson, Jas. Giles bound to Wm. Hill Ord. Abbeville Dist. sum $100,000.00. Power of Atty. On Dec. 19, 1857 Wade Cowan of Tippah Co., Miss. gdn. of Rosaline S. Boyd, Alice J. Boyd minor heirs of John L. Boyd late of Abbeville Dist. appointed John T. Hughey their Atty. Sett. made Jan. 15, 1858. Wm. A. Boyd a distributee was gdn. of Sarah A., Joseph L. Boyd. Left a wid. and 5 chn.

BLACK, JOSEPH F.—BOX 144, PACK 4053:
Will dated Sept. 4, 1856. Filed Oct. 7, 1856. Exrs: Wife, Sarah M. Black, Bros., Jas., A., Wesley A. Black. Wit: Jas. Young, Richard Duncan, Almanza L. Black. Ment: Lived in Abbeville Dist. Wife, Sarah M. Black. Chn. ment. but no names given.

BEARD, STEPNEY—BOX 144, PACK 4054:
Man of color. Did not copy.

BURTON, POLLY ANN—BOX 144, PACK 4055:
In Jan. 7, 1857 John Smith, John T. Haddon, Aaron Ashley bound to Wm. Hill Ord. Abbeville Dist. sum $100.0. John Smith made gdn. of Polly Ann Burton a minor. Expend: Jan. 7, 1857 Recd. from est of David Russell decd. the amt. of ward's est. $27.00.

CAMPBELL, ANNA—BOX 144, PACK 4056:
On Feb. 2, 1857 Wm. L. Campbell, Joseph F. Bell, W. J. Campbell bound to Wm. Hill Ord. Abbeville Dist. sum $800.00. Wm. L. Campbell made gdn. of Anna Campbell a minor. Sett. made Jan. 28, 1860 ment. that she had married Jas. Cann.

CAMPBELL, JESSE—BOX 144, PACK 4057:
On Dec. 1, 1856 Sterling Bowen, Wm. B. Martin, Wm. M. Bowen bound to Wm. Hill Ord. Abbeville Dist. sum $658.00. Sterling Bowen made gdn. of Jesse Campbell a minor. On Jan. 24, 1856 he was about 15 yrs. of age. Was of age in 1862.

COOK, (MINORS)—BOX 144, PACK 4058:
On Oct. 20, 1856 L. Yarbrough, Mary C. Miller, W. Jas. Lomax bound to

Wm. Hill Ord. Abbeville Dist. sum $400.00. L. Yarbrough made gdn. of Margaret F., Mary B. Cook minors. John Baskin decd. was their gr. father.

CRAWFORD, NANCY—BOX 144, PACK 4059:
Will dated Aug. 3, 1854. Filed Oct. 7, 1856. Exr: Sis., Mary Crawford. Wit: D. O. Mecklin, Wm. B. Scott, Margaret N. Scott. Ment: Sis., Mary Crawford.

CARLILE, ISAAC N.—BOX 144, PACK 4060:
Est. admnr. Sept. 13, 1856 by Wm. H. B. Carlile, Frances Carlile, R. W. Shaw bound to Wm. Hill Ord. Abbeville Dist. sum $400.00. Lucinday was wife of said decd.

CASON, (MINORS)—BOX 144, PACK 4061:
On Aug. 4, 1856 Jas. Cason Sr., Wilson Watkins, Jas. Cason Jr. bound to Wm. Hill Ord. Abbeville Dist. sum $1,200.00. Jas. Cason Sr. made gdn. of Henry, Mary Jane, Cyntha Cason minors. Were the chn. of Benjamin A. Cason decd. who was a son of Jas. Cason. Amelia Cason was their mother.

DUNN, WM., SR.—BOX 144, PACK 4062:
Will dated Feb. 24, 1853. Filed Dec. 8, 1856. Exrs: Sons, Wm., Robt. Dunn. Wit: J. C. Williams, Joseph Dickson, Andrew Dunn. Ment: Lived in Abbeville Dist. Chn: Wm., Robt. Dunn, Nancy Norris, wife Nelson Norris, Margaret Dunn. Wife, Ally Dunn. Gr. chn: Ally Ann Dunn, Margaret Smith, Jane Dunn, Elizabeth Swancey. Sett. made June 17, 1859 named 4 distributees viz: Andrew, John Dunn, H. J. Richey and wife Polly, Chn. of Phoebe Hodges decd. viz: Jas., Robt., John C., Chas. R., S. Antoinette.

DOUGLASS, JAMES—BOX 144, PACK 4063:
Est. admnr. Nov. 5, 1856 by W. W. Perryman, Mathew McDonald, J. F. Livingston Jr. bound to Wm. Hill Ord. Abbeville Dist. sum $2,000.00. Mrs. M. Douglass bought at sale.

ELLISON, JOHN W.—BOX 144, PACK 4064:
On Nov. 24, 1855 Jas. M., John S. Carwile bound to Wm. Hill Ord. Abbeville Dist. sum $500.00. Jas. M. Carwile made gdn. of John W. Ellison a minor about 17 yrs.

FULTON, THOS.—BOX 144, PACK 4065:
Will dated July 10, 1848. Filed Dec. 19, 1856. Exrs: Robt. H. Wardlaw, Thos. B. Dendy. Wit: Thos. Thomson, Robt. A. Fair, Wm. Augustus Lee. Ment: Lived in Abbeville Dist. Wife, Sarah Ann Fulton. Chn: Richard B. Fulton, Amanda M. Ingram, Eliza A. Fulton, Jane Augustus Fulton, Frances C. Fulton, Lenore B., Anna Adolis, Jordan W. Fulton. Grand chn: Saml. J., John C. Fulton chn. of my decd. son Benjamin H. Fulton. Sett. Jesse A. Ingram and wife, Thos. Johnson and wife Jane recd. shares.

FOSTER, (MINORS)—BOX 144, PACK 4066:
On Jan. 29, 1857 Edmund G. Kennedy, John P. Kennedy, Isaac Kennedy

bound to Wm. Hill Ord. Abbeville Dist. sum $1,389.15. E. G. Kennedy made gdn. of John L., Sarah J., Wm. P., Emma, Mary, Josephine Foster minor chn. of J. H. Foster decd. and Eliza Foster. Power of Atty. Know that I Saml. P. McGaw of Henderson Co., Ill. gdn. of Sarah Jane, John L., Wm. P., Mary E., Nancy E., Frances L., Josephine Foster minors of Jas. H. Foster late of Abbeville Dist. have appointed John Kennedy our Atty. Dated this 11th Feb., 1858.

GOLMAN, CATO—BOX 144, PACK 4067:
    Was a man of color. Did not copy.

HOUSTON, GEO.—BOX 144, PACK 4068:
    Est. admnr. Oct. 29, 1856 by Jas. H. Baskin, John G. Baskin bound to Wm. Hill Ord. Abbeville Dist. sum $300.00. Geo. Houston died several yrs. ago. His est. is entitled to an interest in that of Martha Houston decd. Left a wid. and 2 chn.

HIGGINS, (MINORS)—BOX 144, PACK 4069:
    On Feb. 11, 1857 Mary F. Higgins, Daniel Beachum, J. Kincaid Vance, M. Strauss bound unto Wm. Hill Ord. Abbeville Dist. sum $7,000.00. Left a wid. Louisa C. Karr and 2 chn., Nancy Jane, Wm. Harvey Karr of Warrenton, Abbeville Dist. J. J. Gray was a bro. l. to Louisa Karr.

LOYD, REVD. JAMES—BOX 144, PACK 4071:
    Est. admnr. Sept. 27, 1856 by John B. Sample, W. S. Blake, John Sadler, Alfred Cheathan bound to Wm. Hill Ord. Abbeville Dist. sum $400.00.

MATHIS, LUKE—BOX 144, PACK 4072:
    Est. admnr. Jan. 29, 1857 by N. J. Davis, Wm. Adams, Thos. E. Owens, Hiram T. Tusten bound to Wm. Hill Ord. Abbeville Dist. sum $15,000.00. Left a wid. Mary Mathis and 3 chn. under 7 yrs. Was a bro. to W. T. Mathis.

McCOOL, JAMES—BOX 144, PACK 4073:
    Est. admnr. Dec. 9, 1856 by J. W. W. Marshall bound to Wm. Hill Ord. Abbeville Dist. sum $800.00. Mrs. Margaret McCool bought at the sale.

McKEWIN, JAMES—BOX 144, PACK 4074:
    Est. admnr. Jan. 26, 1857 by G. M. Mattison, Mathew McDonald, T. R. Cochran bound to Wm. Hill Ord. Abbeville Dist. sum $500.00.

McCOMB, ROBERT—BOX 144, PACK 4075:
    Est. admnr. Nov. 6, 1856 by Mary McComb, M. O. McCaslan, Jas. McCaslan, Jas. Taggart Ord. Abbeville Dist. sum $4,000.00. Left a wid. Mary McComb and 4 chn. Joseph McComb was a son.

MAGRUDER, (MINORS)—BOX 144, PACK 4076:
    On Oct. 4, 1856 G. W. Huckabee, Mary Ann Magruder, Joseph F. Bell bound to Wm. Hill Ord. Abbeville Dist. sum $300.00. Daniel Marbut was the gdn. of Ann W. P. Magruder, W. H. Bascom Magruder minors. Mary Magruder was the minor.

MARBUT, DANIEL—BOX 144, PACK 4077:
Est. admnr. Mar. 6, 1857 by John Marbut, Jas. W. Lipscomb, Wm. Carter bound to Wm. Hill Ord. Abbeville Dist. sum $300.00. Daniel Marbut was the father of John Marbut of Ninety Six, S. C. Left a wid. and 3 chn.

MALONE, HANIBAL—BOX 144, PACK 4078:
Est. admnr. Oct. 13, 1856 by Chas. R. Moseley, S. V. Cain, John McClellan bound to Wm. Hill Ord. Abbeville Dist. sum $400.0. Mrs. M. Malone bought at sale.

NICHOLS, MAJOR THOS.—BOX 144, PACK 4079:
Est. admnr. Nov. 17, 1856 by Henry Beard, Elizabeth B. Nichols, Thos. C. Lipscomb, Saml. Beard bound to Wm. Hill Ord. Abbeville Dist. sum $4,000.00. N. W. Stewart was gdn. of Thos. A., Elizabeth N., Wesly F., Susan Nichols.

RUSSELL, DAVID—BOX 144, PACK 4080:
Will dated Apr. 14, 1856. Filed Dec. 15, 1856. Exrs: Sons, Dr. John R., Jas. A., Robt. W. Russell, Nephew, Jas. A. Black. Wit: Wesley A. Black, Mary Young, Richard Duncan. Ment: Lived in Abbeville Dist. Wife, Elizabeth Russell. Chn: Dr. John R., Jas. A., Robt. W. Russell. Sett. Distributees: Wid. Russell, J. A. Russell, chn. of B. Hill 2, chn. of M. Martin 3, J. R. Russell, R. W. Russell.

SCOTT, JOHN O.—BOX 144, PACK 4081:
Will dated Oct. 6, 1856. Filed Oct. 15, 1856. Exrs: Bro., Thos. B. Scott, Bro. l., Saml. R. Morrah. Wit: M. O. Talman, J. Oliver Lindsay, P. LeRoy. Ment: Lived in Abbeville Dist. Wife and chn. ment. but no names given.

WIDEMAN, UEL—BOX 144, PACK 4082:
Will dated Jan. 31, 1857. Filed Feb. 3, 1857. Exrs: Wife, Emily Wideman, S. l., David J. Wardlaw. Wit: Chas. W. Cowan, Saml. H. Jones, Jas. C. Mathis. Ment: Lived in Abbeville Dist. Wife, Emily Wideman. Chn: Cornelius A. Wideman, Milley Elizabeth Wardlaw, Joshua Wideman, Agnes Emily Wideman.

WARE, COL. WM.—BOX 144, PACK 4083:
Will dated Feb. 24, 1852. Filed Nov. 5, 1856. Exrs: Son, Jas. A. Ware, Abner McGee, Capt. Saml. Agnew. Wit: Thos. C. Perrin, Jas. M. Perrin, S. McGowen. Ment: Lived in Abbeville Dist. Chn: Malinda E. Vandiver wife of Jas. M. Vandiver, Nicholas M. Ware decd., Patsey decd. wife of Chas. B. Fooshe, Jas. A. Ware. Gr. chn: Wm. J., Elizabeth S., Mary O., Cornelia Ware, Catharine Ware, Colistise Ware chn. of Nicholas M. Ware decd. Mary now the wife of Joel Fooshe, Jas. Fooshe, Washington Fooshe, Castledona wife of John Sadler chn. of Patsey Fooshe decd. Sett. made Oct. 29, 1859. Dr. Jas. A. Ware was of *Pontotoc*, Miss., Co. Ware died in Oct. 1855.

WILSON, LOUISA—BOX 144, PACK 4084:
Will dated Dec. 12, 1853. Filed Sept. 27, 1856. Exr: Bro., John B. Sample. Wit: Isaac Branch, Henry M. Branch, David R. Sondley. Ment: Lived in Abbeville Dist. Chn: Eliza Stewart Willson was only 1 mentioned. Sett. Dr. John Holland was her 2nd husband.

ALEXANDER, WM.—BOX 145, PACK 4085:
Est. admnr. Dec. 30, 1857 by David Knox, John Knox, Nathaniel Knox bound to Wm. Hill Ord. Abbeville Dist. sum $500.00.

ASHLEY, MOSES, SR.—BOX 145, PACK 4086:
Will dated Oct. 7, 1850. Filed Sept. 28, 1857. Exr: Son, Moses L. Ashley. Wit: Wm. Pratt, J. W. Brooks, J. M. Brooks. Ment: Lived in Abbeville Dist. Wife, Sarah Moseley. Chn: Moses, Margaret, Wm., Jas., Mary, Robison, Richard Ashley. Expend: On Mar. 25, 1858 Margaret Smith recd. her share of est.

BROOKS, SUSANNAH—BOX 145, PACK 4087:
Est. admnr. Oct. 16, 1857 by Wm. H., Jason T., Francis M. Brooks bound to Wm. Hill Ord. Abbeville Dist. sum $30,000.00. She died Sept. 25, 1857. Was mother of Wm. H. Brooks. Sett. made Feb. 17, 1859. Present: F. M., Jason T., Geo. W. Brooks in their own right, John J. Gray husband of Susan Ann Frances who is a dtr. of Amanda Cheatham decd. who was a dtr. of said decd., Tancey M. Seigler gdn. of Jas. B. Seigler who is the son of Permelia E. Seigler decd. a dtr. of Amanda Cheatham decd. and Wm. H. Brooks.

BUCHANAN, (MINORS)—BOX 145, PACK 4088:
On Feb. 1, 1858 Sarah Buchanan, John A. Stuart, W. M. Hughey bound to Wm. Hill Ord. Abbeville Dist. sum $629.74. Sarah Buchanan made gdn. of Ann E., Margaret E., Geo., Augusta, Sarah L. Buchanan minors.

BRANYON, REUBEN—BOX 145, PACK 4089:
Est. admnr. Dec. 24, 1857 by Joseph J., Polly Ann Branyon, Andrew H. Callaham, Jas. Shirley bound to Wm. Hill Ord. Abbeville Dist. sum $10,000.00. Polly Ann was his wife, Joseph J. was a bro. Had 1 child, Nancy A. Branyon.

BOTTS, THOS. C.—BOX 145, PACK 4090:
Est. admnr. Oct. 6, 1857 by Asa, Franklin Bowie, R. B. Eoyle bound to Wm. Hill Ord. Abbeville Dist. sum $3,000.00. He died about the 17th Aug., 1857. Sett. made Feb. 15, 1859. Present: Asa Bowie who represents his wife a distributee, Mrs. Emily A. McLelland, Thos. Botts, John G. Botts, Mrs. Nancy Botts wid., Henry Cannon, Jacob Clamp in right of their wives who are distributees. Dec. had 9 chn. Sarah Jane Botts recd. a share. Jacob Clamp and Mary E. Clamp recd. a share. Preston and Emily A. McLelland recd. a share.

BULL, MRS. SARAH—BOX 145, PACK 4091:
Will dated June 14, 1856. Filed Nov. 11, 1857. Exr: Son, Dr. Jas. Morrow. Wit: Jas. A. Richey, John T., Ft. Lyon. Ment: Lived in Abbeville Dist. Son, Dr. Jas. Morrow. Certificate of Citizenship. State of S. C. I Sarah Bull do solemnly swear that I was born near Belfast, in Down Co., Ireland in 1794 and resided there until Dec. 1818. When I arrived in the U. S. at Charleston in said state and after a night's stay in Charleston removed to Abbeville Dist., S. C. on or about the 20th Dec., 1818 since which last ment. time I have resided in this state and now reside near Willington in Abbeville Dist. Dated May 29, 1856.

BEVIL, MARY—BOX 145, PACK 4092:
Will dated Mar. 16, 1858. Prov. Apr. 5, 1858. Exr: Uncle, Nathaniel

Cunningham. Wit: Wm. C., W. W. D. Cozby, Eliel Stephens. Ment: Lived in Abbeville Dist. "Bequeath to Miss Sarah M. Fleming." Uncles, Nathaniel, Abraham Cunningham.

BLAIN, MARY—BOX 145, PACK 4093:
    Est. admnr. June 11, 1857 by Wm. P. Martin, Stephen Latimer, G. M. Mattison bound to Wm. Hill Ord. Abbeville Dist. sum $8,000.00. She died May 17, 1857. Sett. made May 3, 1859. Present: William P. Martin admnr., John Blain of Miss., Martha Norris wid., Mary Shirley wife of Richard Shirley. Was the wid of Wm. Blain decd. who made his will in 1829. Ment. their following chn: viz. Jas., John, Daniel, Wm. Y., Mary Shirley, Jane Smith, Martha Norris, Mahala, Wm. P. Martin in right of his wife and a decd. dtr. Elizabeth. Richard, Mary Shirley were of Green Co., Ala.

BOX 145, PACK 4094: MISSING

COFER, A. C.—BOX 145, PACK 4095:
    Est. admnr. Nov. 12, 1857 by W. C. Ware, Edward Noble, Isaac Branch bound to Wm. Hill Ord. Abbeville Dist. sum $200.00.

CRAWFORD, WADE—BOX 145, PACK 4096:
    Est. admnr. Oct. 21, 1857 by A. G. Harmon, Anthony Harmon, Stephen W. Willis bound to Wm. Hill Ord. Abbeville Dist. sum $10,000.00. He died in the spring. Left a wid. and 1 child. Cornlia Crawford recd. a share.

CLINKSCALES, JOHN B.—BOX 145, PACK 4097:
    Est. admnr. Sept. 18, 1857 by Wm. V., Albert J. Clinkscales, Larkin Barmore bound to Wm. Hill Ord. Abbeville Dist. sum $120.00. On Sept. 3, 1857 Wm. V. Clinkscales stated that his bro. John B. Clinkscales died Jan. 3 last in Smith Co., Tex.

DONNELLY, ANDREW EMORY—BOX 145, PACK 4098:
    Est. admnr. Mar. 10, 1858 by John Brownlee, John A. Wier, Henry S. Kerr bound to Wm. Hill Ord. Abbeville Dist. sum $2,000.00. 5 distributees viz: F. O., S., J. F., Margaret, Heneritta Donnelly.

DUNN, CAPT. WILLIAM—BOX 145, PACK 4099:
    Est. admnr. Nov. 2, 1857 by Andrew Dunn, J. F. Donnald, Robt. Dunn bound to Wm. Hill Ord. Abbeville Dist. sum $2,000.00.

DAVIS, EPHRAIM—BOX 145, PACK 4100:
    Will dated Sept. 8, 1857. Filed Nov. 2, 1857. Exrs: Wife, Mary Davis, Wm. C. Davis. Wit: Jacob Rykard, Robt. H. Rykard, R. S. Cobb, E. L. Davis. Ment: Lived in Abbeville Dist. Wife, Mary Davis. Chn: Wm. C., Benjamin F., John F., H. Davis. S. l., Henry Riley, Levi H. Rykard. Left 6 chn.

DAVIS, JOHN—BOX 145, PACK 4101:
    Will dated Sept. 6, 1853. Filed Sept. 11, 1857. Exrs: Sons, Edward, John Davis. Wit: Elias Earle, V. D. Fant, P. S. Vandiver. Ment: Lived in Abbeville Dist. Wife, Ursla Davis. Chn: Edward, John, Winston H. Davis, Lucy

Hadden wife of Wilson Hadden, Mandeline wife of Elias Kay was formerly the wife of one Theodore Baker by whom she had 2 chn., John T., Theodore Baker. Grand. dtr. Lucinda Tucker.

FRAZIER, CHARITY—BOX 145, PACK 4102:
Will dated May 16, 1846. Filed Aug. 25, 1857. Exrs: Thos. Thomson, C. H. Allen. Wit: Bartw. Jordon, Lewis Smith. S. S. Marshall. Ment: Lived in Abbeville Dist. Chn: Lucretia Devlin, Jas. W. Frazier. Gr. chn: Tallulah H., V. Antionette, Sarah C. Frazier. Nephew: John F. Livingston. Bequeeth to Charity Elizabeth and Mary Jane infant dtrs. of Martha B. Lites, Allen S. Walker. Dec. husband, Jas. Frazier. Lived at Cedar Springs. Legatees were: David T. Oliver, Sarah C., Oliver, Robt. and Lucretia Devlin.

GREER, CALEB W.—BOX 145, PACK 4103:
Est. admnr. Feb. 6, 1858 by J. J. McBath, J. L. Brock, B. G. Robinson bound to Wm. Hill Ord. Abbeville Dist. sum $500.00. Left a wid. Clarissa Greer and 1 child John J. Greer. On July 31, 1860 John J. Greer was a resident of Gwinnett Co., Ga. a minor under 14 yrs. Thos. J. Newborn was his gdn.

GABLE, ELIZABETH—BOX 145, PACK 4104:
On Feb. 1, 1858 Robt. R. Talbert, Esme Jones, J. R. Tolbert bound to Wm. Hill Ord. Abbeville Dist. sum $1,000.00. R. R. Tolbert made gdn. of Elizabeth Gable a minor. Expend: Mar. 1858 Recd. her share of her father's real est. in Anderson. $521.40.

HEARST, MARGARET—BOX 145, PACK 4105:
Est. admnr. May 5, 1857 by John W. Hearst, Jas. H. Wideman bound to Wm. Hill Ord. Abbeville Dist. sum $16,000.00. She died in the summer of last yr. Was wife of John Hearst. Joseph L. Hearst recd. share and was gdn. of J. T. J. Hearst a minor. H. L. Murphy and wife Martha recd a share.

HEMMINGER, NANCY ANN—BOX 145, PACK 4106:
Est. admnr. May 4, 1857 by Michael McGrath, Chas. Evans, Jas. M. Gillam bound to Wm. Hill Ord. Abbeville Dist. sum $500.00. Died Apr. 16, 1857. Michael McGrath was husband of her only child.

LIVINGSTON, HENRY AND MARY—BOX 145, PACK 4107:
Est. of Henry Livingston made Mar. 20, 1857 by Chas. H., Jas. A., Wm. A. Allen bound to Wm. Hill Ord. Abbeville Dist. sum $500.00. Est. of Mrs. Mary Livingston admnr. the same time by same admnrs. Petition of Chas. Allen sheweth that Henry Livingston died June 12, 1836 and that he was a Revolutionary Soldier. Mary Livingston died Dec. 2, 1856 leaving 2 surviving chn., Dr. John F. Livingston, Jane L. Allen.

LITTLE, PIERCE—BOX 145, PACK 4108:
Will dated Sept. 24, 1857. Filed Feb. 15, 1858. Exr: Wife, Tarasa Little, Simpson Waite. Wit: Jas. Owens, Daniel Rampey, Robt. Cheney. Ment: Lived in Abbeville Dist. Wife, Tarasa Little. Chn: Jas. R. Little, Sarah A. Little. Simpson Waite was a bro. to Tarasa Little.

LIGON, JOSEPH—BOX 145, PACK 4109:
Est. admnr. Jan. 26, 1858 by J. F. Livingston, Thos. Thomson, Chas. H.
Allen bound to Wm. Hil Ord. Abbeville Dist. sum $10,0000.00. Left a wid.
Eliza M. Ligon and 9 chn. viz: Richard C., Joseph A., Louisa M., Langdon C.,
Elizabeth E., M. A., Anna E. R., A. C. Ligon.

LOMAX, MARY A.—BOX 145, PACK 4110:
Est. admnr. Jan. 28, 1858 by Augustus Lomax, Jas. H. Cobb, John A.
Hunter bound to Wm. Hill Ord. Abbeville Dist. sum $50,000.00. Was the wife of
Augustus Lomax and dtr. of her mother M. C. Neil of this Dist. and Newberry
Dist.

LOMAX, MARY C.—BOX 145, PACK 4111:
Est. admnr. Jan. 28, 1858 by Augustus Lomax, Jas. H. Cobb, John A.
Hunter bound to Wm. Hill Ord. Abbeville Dist. sum $35,000.00. Was a minor
dtr. of Augustus Lomax.

MOSELEY, PHILIP H.—BOX 145, PACK 4112:
Will dated Mar. 9, 1847. Filed Mar. 30, 1858. Exr: Bro. John Moseley,
Wit: Wm. M., Martha A. Bell, Isaac H. McCalla. Ment: lived in Abbeville Dist.
Sis., Charlotte M. Moseley. Mother, Mary Moseley. Sis. l., Nancy Moseley. Bro.,
John M. Moseley. Nephew, Jas. H. B. Moseley.

MITCHELL, THOS. FINLEY—BOX 145, PACK 4113:
Est. admnr. Jan. 2, 1858 by J. Wardlaw, Jas. M. Perrin, Jas. S. Cothran
bound to Wm. Hill Ord. Abbeville Dist. sum $2,000.00. Thos. F. Mitchell of
Winston Co., Miss. died several yrs. ago. Entitled to est. from Jane Finley decd.
Mary A. Hughes wife of T. J. Hughes, Mathew C. Gage, Sarah J. Winston wife
of A. A. Winston, Nancy M. Hughes wife of D. L. Hughes, Jas. D. M. Gage,
W. A. Gage, uncles and aunts, heirs of Robt. A. Mitchell decd. son of said Thos.
F. Mitchell. All of Winston Co., Miss. Dated Sept. 4, 1859.

MURPHY, MARY—BOX 145, PACK 4114:
Will dated June5, 1857. Filed Dec. 23, 1857. Exr: Nephew, Revd. H. L.
Murphy. Wit: Robt. A. Archer, Robt. C. Grier, E. L. Patton. Ment: Lived in
Abbeville Dist. Sis., Esther Murphy.

MATHEWS, JOHN—BOX 145, PACK 4115:
Will dated Jan. 1, 1858. Filed Jan. 20, 1858. Exr: P. D. Klugh. Wit:
Andrew Cobb, Joseph Milford, Martin Delany. Ment: Lived in Abbeville Dist.
Wife, Nancy Mathis. Dtr. Mary A. Dabbs. Gr. son., John Mathis Dabbs.
(Name written Mathews and Mathis.)

MAJOR, JUDITH E. A.—BOX 145, PACK 4116:
On Sept. 14, 1857 John W. Major, Saml. B. Major, Jas. B. Black bound
to Wm. Hill Ord. Abbeville Dist. sum $280.22. John W. Major made gdn. of
Judith E. A. Major a minor of said John W. Major. Name was Judith Elizabeth
Ann Major.

MURDOCK, JAS.—BOX 145, PACK 4117:
Est. admnr. Aug. 29, 1857 by Wm. Pratt, Jas. M. Carwile, S. W. Callaham bound to Wm. Hill Ord. Abbeville Dist. sum $100.00. Died June 23, 1857. Was father in law of Wm. Pratt.

MOORE, FRANCES—BOX 145, PACK 4119:
Will dated July 1, 1856. Filed Sept. 7, 1857. Exrs: Joseph Kennedy, Jas. R. Cunningham. Wit: A. J. Clinkscales, A. Giles, Jas. M. Martin. Ment: Lived in Abbeville Dist. Bequeath to Joseph Kennedy and his wife Rebecca, to John W. Brooks. Gr. chn: Frances G., Wm. Y. Cunningham.

WALLER, ALBERT—BOX 145, PACK 4119½:
Est. admnr. Sept. 26, 1859 by P. A. Waller, C. D. Waller, Henry H. Creswell, Larkin Reynolds, Allen Vance, Francis Arnold bound to Wm. Hill Ord. Abbeville Dist. sum $40,000.00. Left a wid. J. E. Waller and 8 chn. viz: P. A., C. D., R. A. Waller were 3. Owned property in Ala. and Fla.

NORRIS, A. E.—BOX 145, PACK 4120:
Est. admnr. July 6, 1857 by Thos. Chatham, Wm. Smith, R. M. White bound to Wm. Hill Ord. Abbeville Dist. sum $1,500.00. J. J. Norris was gdn. of Fannie Norris.

PATTERSON, JOSIAH—BOX 146, PACK 4121:
Est. admnr. July 6, 1857 by Geo. S. Patterson, Jas. H. Wideman, R. W. Lites bound to Wm. Hill Ord. Abbeville Dist. sum $30,000.00.

PEARMAN. NATHANIEL—BOX 146, PACK 4122:
Est. admnr. Mar. 1, 1858 by Rachel Pearman, Wid., Welton Pearman. Jesse Robinson bound to Wm. Hill Ord. Abbeville Dist. sum $1,500.00.

PUCKETT, DR. C. C.—BOX 146, PACK 4123:
Est. admnr. Dec. 2, 1857 by David A. Jordon, John G. Wilson, John A. Wier bound to Wm. Hill Ord. Abbeville Dist. sum $800.00. He died Sept. 1857. M. F. Puckett the wid. requested that Admnr. be granted to her bro. l., Miles Puckett.

PURDY, WM. A.—BOX 146, PACK 4124:
Est. admnr. Dec. 16, 1857 by Jas. Irwin, Phillip, G. W. Cromer, Saml. Robinson bound to Wm. Hill Ord. Abbeville Dist. sum $3,000.00. Wm. Purdy was the nephew of Jas. Irwin. Was a minor.

PENNAL, WM.—BOX 146, PACK 4125:
Will dated Jan. 29, 1852. Filed Oct. 26, 1857. Exrs: Wife, Ellen D. Pennal, John Link. Wit: L. J. Johnson, J. W. Penny, J. H. Gray. Ment: Lived in Abbeville Dist. Wife, Ellen D. Pennal. Chn: Ment. but names not given.

RIDDLE, MARGARET—BOX 146, PACK 4126:
Will dated Oct. 25, 1856. Filed Aug. 26, 1857. Exr: John S. Reid. Wit: Wm. Pennal, Robt. S. Dixon, A. C. Ligon. Ment: Lived in Abbeville Dist. Neice, Rebecca Thornton.

REID, JANE—BOX 146, PACK 4127:
Will dated Apr. 29, 1857. Filed June 11, 1857. Exrs: Bro., Gabriel Cox, Octavius Porcher. Wit: W. Tennent, Paul Rogers, J. A. Gibert. Ment: Lived in Abbeville Dist. Wife of Wm. R. Reid. Bros: Gabriel, Christopher, Corneluis, Leroy, Bailey Cox. Sis: Bethana, Phereby Price.

REID, SAML.—BOX 146, PACK 4128:
Will dated left out. Filed Oct. 6, 1857. Exrs: Lemuel Reid, John R. Wilson. Wit: Jas. McCombs, Wm. Gordon, J. H. Wilson. Ment: Wife, Elizabeth Reid. Chn: Mary Wilson, Lemuel, Jas. C. Reid. Niece, Susan Wilson.

RICHEY, JAS. B.—BOX 146, PACK 4129:
Est. admnr. Aug. 20, 1857 by Geo. B. Richey, Jas. A. Lyon, Jas. P. Donald, Jas. Cowan, A. J. Lythgoe, H. T. Lyon bound to Wm. Hill Ord. Abbeville Dist. sum $50,000.00. Will dated Nov. 18, 1846. Exrs: Sons, Geo. B., Robt. Richey, Saml. Donald. Wit: John Donald Sr., John Seawright, Robt. Martin. Ment: Lived in Abbeville Dist. Wife, Martha Richey. Chn: Geo. B., Sarah Jane, Robt., Mary Ann Richey. Sarah Jane married Jas. A. Lyon; Mary Ann married Jas. F. Donald.

RYKARD, MARY—BOX 146, PACK 4130:
Est. admnr. Apr. 19, 1858 by Jacob Rykard, Jas. Edwards, Walter G. Keller bound to Wm. Hill Ord. Abbeville Dist. sum $10,000.00. Was mother of said Jacob Rykard. Sett. made Feb. 23, 1859. Distributees were: Peter Rykard, Wm. P. Leavell and wife Sarah C., Walter G. Keller and wife Mary M., S. P. Rykard a gr. son, and sis. of S. P. Rykard, Jacob Rykard, wife and chn. of Adam Rykard. Adam Rykard decd. left 8 chn.

ROBINSON, JOHN—BOX 146, PACK 4131:
Est. admnr. Jan. 4, 1858 by John W. Hearst, P. H. Bradley, J. H. Wideman bound to Wm. Hill Ord. Abbeville Dist. sum $40,000.00. Distributees were: dtr. Rachel Harvly decd. and her only son, Jno. Wm. Harvly, wife Elizabeth Robinson, sons Jabez P., Robt. J. Robinson. Benjamin B. Harvly was gdn. of John Wm. Harvly.

SPENCE, JOHN—BOX 146, PACK 4132:
Est. admnr. Dec. 17, 1857 by E. O. Reagin, John Patterson, Jas. C. Spence bound to Wm. Hill Ord. Abbeville Dist. sum $100.00.

SHILLITO, (MINORS)—BOX 146, PACK 4133:
On May 30, 1857 Hiram W. Lawson, H. H. Wilson, John White bound to Wm. Hill Ord. Abbeville Dist. sum $293.76. Hiram W. Lawson made gdn. of Mary A., Jas. A., Julia A., Harper H., Geo. A., John W. Shillito minors. Mrs. Jane Cameron decd. was their gr. aunt. Mary A. Shillito married T. Penney, Julia A. married J. W. Sign.

SHIRLEY, NANCY IRENE—BOX 146, PACK 4134:
Est. admnr. Sept. 10, 1857 by Benjamin Shirley, Jas. M. Latimer, Jr., Reuben Branyon bound to Wm. Hill Ord. Abbeville Dist. sum $1,500.00. She died May 1857. A sis. of Benjamin Shirley. Left 9 distributees viz: Benjamin R..

John, Jas., Geo., Amaziah Shirley. Chn. of Lavenia Branyon, Polly Ann Branyon, Leety Callaham.

STRAIN, A. THOMSON—BOX 146, PACK 4135:
Est. admnr. Oct. 30, 1856 by Nancy Jane Bowie, Robt. H. Wardlaw, John H. Wilson bound to Wm. Hill Ord. Abbeville Dist. sum $1,000.00. Was also admnr. of Louisa A. Bowie decd.

SHIRLEY, NANCY—BOX 146, PACK 4136:
Est. admnr. Sept. 7, 1857 by Jas. Shirley, Jas. H. Haddon, John R. Wilson bound to Wm. Hill Ord. Abbeville Dist. sum $18,000.00. Was mother of said Jas. Shirley. Sett. made 1859 ment: Jas., Richard, John, Amaziah, B., Geo., Shirley, Polly Ann Branyon, Letty M. Callaham, N. A. Branyon.

TILMAN, EDWARD—BOX 146, PACK 4137:
Will dated Sept. 25. 1855. Filed Sept. 3, 1857. Exrs: Wife Kitty Tilman, Son, Hiram Tilman, Dtr., Kity C. Tilman, S. l., W. A. Wardlaw. Wit: L. Yarbrough. W. Jas. Lomax, A. M. Smith. Ment: Lived in Abbeville Dist. Wife, Kitty Tilman. Chn: Kitty C. Tilman, Ivy wife of Wm. A. Wardlaw, Sarah C. Tilman, Hiram Tilman. "Give him land in Miss.", in Chickasaw Co.

WILLIAMS, STERLING Q.—BOX 146, PACK 4138:
Will dated Dec. 20, 1852. Filed Nov. 12, 1857. Exrs: Sons, Roger, Benjamin Williams, S. l., Wm. Spear. Wit. F. B. Clinkscales, A. Rice, W. C. Power. Ment: Lived in Abbeville Dist. Wife, Ann Williams. 5 chn. ment. but only 2 given viz: Roger, Benjamin Williams.

WILLIAMS, DAVID—BOX 146, PACK 4139:
On Aug. 3. 1857 H. A., D. F. Jones, B. V. Posey bound to Wm. Hill Ord. Abbeville Dist. sum S300.00. H. A. Jones made gdn. of David Williams a minor of Timothy D. Williams decd. and Esther Williams decd.

WEED, MARY—BOX 146, PACK 4140:
Est. admnr. Sept. 29, 1857 by John G. Gray, Mathew Goodwin. Michael McGrath bound to Wm. Hill Ord. Abbeville Dist. sum S150.00. Was gr. mother of John G. Gray.

WEBB, ELIZABETH—BOX 146, PACK 4141:
Est. admnr. Dec. 2, 1857 by Saml. Donnald, John A. Wier, Robt. H. Wardlaw bound to Wm. Hill Ord. Abbeville Dist. sum S1,000.00.

ZANER, HENRY—BOX 146, PACK 4142:
Est. admnr. Sept. 7, 1857 by Geo., Saml. C. Zaner, David McClain bound to Wm. Hill Ord. Abbeville Dist. sum S700.00. He died July 13, 1857. Geo. Zanor was a bro. Left a wid. Nancy and sis.

BANKS, (MINORS)—BOX 146, PACK 4143:
On Aug. 30, 1858 Jas. C. Jennings, Anthony Harmon, Jas. Newby bound to Wm. Hill Ord. Abbeville Dist. sum S400.00. Jas. C. Jennings made gdn. of Vincent and Saml. Banks minors.

BUCHANAN, JOHN—BOX 146, PACK 4144:
    Est. admnr. July 5, 1858 by Andrew J. Buchanan, Wm. McNary, Wm. M.
Hughey bound to Wm. Hill Ord. Abbeville Dist. sum $3,000.00. Was a bro. to
Andrew J. Buchanan. Sett. 7 distributees viz: Elizabeth Buchanan the mother,
Wm. M. Hughey and wife Elizabeth, Geo., Saml., Andrew J. Buchanan, Abner P.
Jones and wife Lavinda, chn. of Wm. Buchanan.

CARLILE, FRANCES—BOX 146, PACK 4145:
    Will dated Dec. 17, 1857. Filed June 7, 1858. Exrs: Sons, Wm., Daniel
E. Carlile. Wit: Jas. Grant, Mary L. Pressly, J. J. Grant. Ment: Lived in Abbeville
Dist. Chn: Daniel E., Robt. W. Carlile, Rebecca D. Causby, Ethel T. Carlile,
Jas. H., John J. P. Carlile, Elizabeth F. Lacky. Gr. son: Isaac N. Carlile.

COCHRAN, THOS. R.—BOX 146, PACK 4146:
    Will dated July 26, 1858. Filed Aug. 25, 1858. Exr: Wife, Mary L.
Cochran. Wit: Jas. H. Cobb, B. Johnson, T. F. Lanear. Ment: Lived in Abbeville
Dist. Nephew, Hamilton Stevenson. Wife, Mary I. Cochran. "Bequeath to Mrs.
Jane E. Stevenson."

CHANDLER, TIMOTHY B.—BOX 146, PACK 4147:
    Est. admnr. May 3, 1858 by D. O. Hawthorne, Thos. Hawthorne, J. R.
Hawthorne bound to Wm. Hill Ord. Abbeville Dist. sum $4,000.00.

CHILD, JAS. W.—BOX 146, PACK 4148:
    Will dated June 18, 1858. Filed Aug. 20, 1858. Exrs: Son in law, Thos.
C. Griffin, Z. W. Carlile. Wit: T. S. Blake, W. S. Blake, John Holland. Ment:
Lived in Abbeville Dist. Wife, Elizabeth Child. Chn: Louisa A. E., Arabella T.
Griffin, Mildred McCaslan, Jas. W. Child, Sarah R., Robt. R., Rugus A. Child.

CUNNINGHAM, THOS.—BOX 146, PACK 4149:
    Est. admnr. July 1, 1858 by Jas. R. Cunningham, Jas. Liddell, Joseph H.
Cunningham bound to Wm. Hill Ord. Abbeville Dist. sum $25,000.00. Left 6
chn. viz: J. H., Jas. R. Cunningham, Jas. T. Liddell in right of his wife. J. J.,
A. W. Cunningham, Wm. A. Giles in right of his wife J. Y. Giles. Mary Cunningham wife of said decd. Died Apr. 16,

FIFE, SAML.—BOX 146, PACK 4150:
    Est. admnr. May 31, 1858 by Thos. J. Roberts, Robt. Jones, Jas. M. Perrin
bound to Wm. Hill Ord. Abbeville Dist. sum $800.00. Mary Fife was the wid.

McCOMB, JOSEPH R.—BOX 146, PACK 4152:
    On Aug. 2, 1858 J. F. McComb, Jas. Taggart, M. C. Taggart bound to
Wm. Hill Ord. Abbeville Dist. sum $1,000.00. J. F. McComb made gdn. of
Joseph R. McComb minor.

McCOMB, (MINORS)—BOX 146, PACK 4153:
    On June 10, 1858 M. O. McCaslan, Jas., R. A. McCaslan bound to Wm.
Hill Ord. Abbeville Dist. sum $2,000.00. M. O. McCaslan made gdn. of Fannie
Isabella, Mary J., Rebecca R. McComb minors. Mary A. McComb was the mother.

SIMS, MARY R.—BOX 146, PACK 4154:
Est. admnr. Sept. 3, 1858 by John Mauldin, J. A. Lyon, John Dunn bound to Wm. Hill Ord. Abbeville Dist. sum of $800.00. Mary R. Sims was an old lady and had never married. Was an aunt to John Mauldin.

ROMAN, JOHN—BOX 146, PACK 4155:
Will dated Apr. 8, 1858. Filed July 16, 1858. Exr: Son l., Francis Aladen Buchanan. Wit: Robt. P. Buchanan, Martin Delany, Wm. P. Thompson. Ment: Lived in Abbeville Dist. Gr. Chn: John Robt., Mary Ann, Francis Pinkney Buch anan.

RUSSELL, WM.—BOX 146, PACK 4156:
Est. admnr. May 20, 1858 by Louis H. Russell, John A. Hunter, Robt. Jones bound to Wm. Hill Ord. Abbeville Dist. sum $12,000.00. Louis H. Russell was a gr. son of said decd.

WILLIAMS, WM. A.—BOX 146, PACK 4157:
Est. admnr. Mar. 22, 1858 by J. W. W. Marshall, Kitty F., Saml. S., J. Foster Marshall bound to Wm. Hill Ord. Abbeville Dist. sum $100,000.00. Died Feb. 11, 1858. Left a wid. Kitty F. Williams and 3 chn.

AGNEW, (MINORS)—BOX 147, PACK 4158:
On May 2, 1859 S. W., Wm. Agnew, S. R. Underwood bound to Wm. Hill Ord. Abbeville Dist. sum $580.50. S. W. Agnew made gdn. of M. E. Agnew, M. A., S. E., W. A. W., F. E. Agnew minor chn. of said S. W. Agnew. Entitled to a est. from John Donald decd. Margaret E. Agnew married W. T. McIlwain. Malinda Jane married S. R. Underwood. On May 25, 1861 Alonzo M. Folger recd. Mary Elizabeth's share.

ANDERSON, RICHARD L.—BOX 147, PACK 4159:
Will dated May 30, 1856. Filed Dec. 25, 1858. Exr: H. A. Jones Esq. Wit: Wm. C. Davis, L. H. Lomax, M. McDonald. Ment: Lived in Abbeville Dist. Wife, Sarah Elizabeth Anderson. Chn: Jas. Anderson, Sally Williams wife of Masten Williams, Peggy Agnew decd., Gilly Watson decd. Grand chn: Jas. Allen Watson of Ala., Nancy Watson, Sallie Williams, Emily Burnsides, Watty, John Anderson.

ADAMS, WM.—BOX 147, PACK 4160:
Est. admnr. Oct. 1858 by David M. Wardlaw, J. J. Devlin, A. L. Gray bound to Wm. Hill Ord. Abbeville Dist. sum $35,000.00. Died Sept. 19, 1858, leaving 3 chn: Saml., Mason, Ann Adams. John Adams decd. was their gr. father.

ADAMS, JOHN—BOX 147, PACK 4161:
Est. admnr. Aug. 21, 1858 by Wm. Adams, Jas. H. Cobb, Absolam L. Gray, John D. Adams, H. A. Jones, John G. Wilson bound to Wm. Hill Ord. Abbeville Dist. sum $60,000.00. Was father of said Wm. Adams. Sett. 9 dis triutees viz: Thos. Kirkpatrick and wife Elizabeth, Jas. Hughes and wife Susan, Edward, Wm., John J. Adams, John Hinton and wife Emily, Franklin, Saml. Adams, Sarah Tolbert decd. wife of Jas. F. Tolbert.

BOTTS, (MINORS)—BOX 147, PACK 4162:
On Apr. 9, 1859 Nancq Botts, Jacob Clamp, Henry Cannon bound to Wm. Hill Ord. Abbeville Dist. sum $450.00. Nancy Botts made gdn. of Chas. A., Joseph J. Botts minors of Thos. C. Botts decd. and said Nancy Botts. Chas. was of age. in 1862. Joseph of age in 1866.

CRAWFORD, JAS L—BOX 147, PACK 4163:
Est admnr. May 3, 1859 by A. G. Harmon, Wm. Harmon, Geo. Sibert bound to Wm. Hill Ord. Abbeville Dist. sum $2500.00. A. G. Harmon made gdn. of Jas. L. Crawford a minor about 4 or 5 yrs. old of Wade Crawford decd. and Cornelia Crawford.

CLARK, JAS.—BOX 147, PACK 4164:
On Oct. 4, 1858 J. B. Hammond, John Brownlee, Geo. W. Bowen bound to Wm. Hill Ord. Abbeville Dist. sum $200.00. J. B. Hammond made gdn. of Jas. Clark a minor about 13 yrs. old.

CALHOUN, (MINORS)—BOX 147, PACK 4165:
On Mar. 7, 1859 Nathan Calhoun, Saml. Agnew, Chas. R. Moseley bound to Wm. Hill Ord. Abbeville Dist. sum $2,298.80. Nathan Calhoun made gdn. of Jas. S., Malinda V., Robt. S., B. F. Calhoun minors. They recd. a share of est. of Geo. W. Calhoun.

CALHOUN, WM. L.—BOX 147, PACK 4166:
Will dated Sept. 19, 1858. Filed Oct. 9, 1858. Wit: L. Yarbrough, Saml. J. Hester, J. E. Lyon. Ment: Lived in Abbeville Dist. Wife, Kate Calhoun. Chn: John, Benjamin, Wm. Calhoun. Uncle, Jas. Edward Calhoun Sr. "My wish that my Uncle should consult with B. A. Putman of Fla. relating to my est."

CLINKSCALES, FRANCIS B.—BOX 147, PACK 4167:
Will dated Aug. 21, 1857. Filed Oct. 4, 1858. Exrs: Sons, Geo. B., Jas. W. Clinkscales. Wit: J. J. Cunningham, Jas., W., Jas. A. Black. Ment: Lived in Abbeville Dist. Wife, Barbary D. Clinkscales. Chn: Wm. V., Geo. B., Albert J., Mary C. Hamilton wife of John Hamilton, Jas. W. Clinkscales, Sarah Cowan decd. wife of John Cowan, Louisa Jane Merrimon. He died Sept. 1858. Sett: Sophronia C. Pratt, Jas. Pratt a legatee in right of her mother Sarah Cowan decd. John Cowan gdn. of their 3 minors, John Wesley, Wm. Tully, Sarah E. Cowan. Mrs. Mary L. Ellis, J. N. Seawright and Jane E. Seawright recd. share. Sarah Cowan left 7 chn. viz: J. M. Cowan, Mrs. Jane E. Seawright, Mrs. S. C. Pratt, Mrs. Mary L. Ellis, John W. Cowan, Wm. T., Sarah E. Cowan.

CAIN, DR. SAMPSON V.—BOX 147, PACK 4168:
Will dated June 26, 1858. Filed Oct. 5, 1858. Exrs: Nephew, W. C. Moragne, Allen Vance. Wit: Geo. M. Connor, Saml. R. Skillern, John T. Parks. Ment: Lived in Abbeville Dist. Wife, Caroline E. Caine my house and lot in Greenwood. Chn: John E. Caine, Martha P., Willie, Nonteith Cain, Mary Blanton.

CLAY, H. W.—BOX 147, PACK 4169:
Will dated Oct. 9, 1848. Filed Oct. 18, 1858. Wit: Wm. Q. Martin, Edwin Parker, L. Yarbrough. Ment: Lived in Abbeville Dist. "Bequeath to Mary Ann Clay wife of my bro., Elisha, W. A. Clay. Nieces: C. F. Wells, M. E. Wells. Mother, Elizabeth Clay. Josiah Wells was gdn. of Martha E., Catharine F. Wells.

COX, GABRIEL—BOX 147, PACK 4170:
Est. admnr. Apr. 15, 1859 by Agness Cox, Peter L. Guillebeau, E. Calhoun, Jas. H. Britt, Andrew Guillebeau, Wiley Newby bound to Wm. Hill sum $60,000.00.

DAVIS, JOSHUA—BOX 147, PACK 4171:
Est. admnr. May 10, 1859 by John David, Silas Ray, Jas. C. Ellis bound to Wm. Hill Ord. sum $25,000.00. Was the father of John Davis. Distributees were: Fanney Mathews, Polly Seals, Darkos Ellis, Nancy Robertson, Patsy Steward, Jane Turner, Wm. Davis, Drucilla Pace, John Davis, Polly Jones, Catharine Ray, Margaret Syfan, Frena Venell Elizabeth Benson, Susan Roberts, Milly Patterson, Catharine Roy, Rebecca Davis.

ELLIS, JOHN E.—BOX 147, PACK 4172:
Est. admnr. June 7, 1859 by Christopher, Ebenezer P. Ellis, Wm. Clinkscales, Basil Callaham bound to Wm. Hill Ord. Abbeville Dist. sum $20,000.00. Had 16 chn. viz: Elizabeth, Ellis, M. Davis, P. A. Hadden, L. Strawhorn, A. E. Ellis, Christopher, J. E., J. M., R. M., E. P., B., W. T., M. M., A. R., L. Y., P. S. Ellis.

FULTON, (MINORS)—BOX 147, PACK 4173:
On Oct. 8, 1858 Isaac John P. Kennedy, A. P. Conner bound to Wm. Hill Ord. Abbeville Dist. sum $2,050.00. Isaac Kennedy made gdn. of Saml. J. Fulton and John C. Fulton minors. Jane Burnett was their mother.

FRASER, MARY ANN—BOX 147, PACK 4174:
Will dated Jan. 13, 1859. Filed Jan. 26, 1859. Exr: Saml. Gilmer. Wit: Lemuel Reid, Leroy C. Wilson, Jas. W. Means. Ment: Lived in Abbeville Dist. "Bequeath to Archibald Fair, Thos. Livingston in trust for my dtr. Margaret Livingston of Madison Co., Fla. To my friend Saml. Gilmer a tract of land." Power of Atty. On Jan. 29, 1859. Taliaferro A. Livingston, Mary A. Wardlaw wife of Benjamin Wardlaw, David L. Kennedy and Charlotte M. Kennedy his wife, Geo. M. T. Benison or Brinson and Ann F. his wife and Wm. A. Livingston all of Madison Co., Fla., heirs of Mary Ann Freser do appoint Donald Livingston, Thos. J. Livingston, Benjamin F. Wardlaw our lawful Attys.

FOSTER, JOSEPH—BOX 147, PACK 4175:
Est. admnr. Oct. 20, 1858 by John Foster, Joseph S. Marshall, Bartw. Jordon bound to Wm. Hill Ord. Abbeville Dist. sum $40,000.00. John Foster was a son of said decd.

FOSTER, JOHN EDWARD—BOX 147, PACK 4176:
Will dated Jan. 6, 1859. Filed May 10, 1859. Exrs: Jas. McCaslan, Chas.

W. Cowan. Wit: W. P. Kennedy, A. J. Conner, J. L. Tittle. Ment: Lived in Abbeville Dist. Wife, Jane B. Foster. Chn: Robt. Jorden, Mary Caroline, John Edward, Jane Boman Foster. Bequeath to Chas. W. Cowan, Augustus P. Covan. Sett. made Apr. 15, 1863. Named wid. Jane B. Covin, Mary C., John E., Jane B. Foster.

GRAHAM, MARY—BOX 147, PACK 4177:
    Est. admnr. Oct. 6, 1858 by Wm. C. Graham, Wade H. Robinson, G. W. Roberson bound to Wm. Hill Ord. sum $300.00. Wm. C. Graham sheweth that his mother Mary Graham died some time 2 yrs. ago and was entitled to Bounty Land from her late husband. Left other chn.

GRAY, JOHN—BOX 147, PACK 4178:
    Est. admnr. Feb. 15, 1859 by Wm. J., Mary Ann, John O., Jas. A. Gray, Absolom Leonidas Gray, A. L. Gray bound to Wm. Hill Ord. sum $40,000.00. John Gray was the father of said Wm. Gray. Power of Atty. On Nov. 3, 1859 John O. Gray a resident of Austin Co., Tex. appointed his bro. Geo. C. Gray of same co. his Atty. to go to S. C. to collect his share of his father's est. John Gray of Abbeville. Dated at Bellville, Tex.

HARRIS, JAS. O.—BOX 147, PACK 4179:
    Est. admnr. Dec. 20, 1858 by John G. Baskin, Jas. H., W. S. Baskin bound to Wm. Hill Ord. Abbeville Dist. sum $1,200.00. The petition of Jas. M. Thomson and Julia E. Thomson his wife of Phillips Co., Ark. sheweth that Jas. O. Harris died intestate, entitled to certain funds now in the hands of the Commissioner in Equity of Abbeville Dist. and admnr. of est. of Jane Y. Caldwell the gr. mother of said decd.

HODGES, CATHARINE—BOX 147, PACK 4180:
    Est. admnr. June 17, 1859 by D. S. Benson, John A. Wier, J. H. Cobb bound to Wm. Hill Ord. Abbeville Dist. sum $150.00.

JOHNSON, JAS., SR.—BOX 147, PACK 4181:
    Will dated Jan. 18, 1856. Filed Sept. 3, 1858. Exrs: Son, Jas. Johnson, Abner H. Mafee Sr., Gabriel M. Mattison. Wit: Jas. R., Stephen, B. M. Latimer. Ment: Lived in Abbeville Dist. Wife, Julia Johnson. Chn: Jas. Johnson Jr., Sarah, Amanda A., Gabriel W. Johnson, Elizabeth Wilson, Henry A., Saml. V. Johnson. Grand. dtr. Martha A. Turner. Paper stated that he was about 60 or 70 yrs. old when he died. John Wilson was husband of Elizabeth. Power of Atty. On June 13, 1885 C. V. Johnson of Aiken Co., S. C. appointed J. C. Featherstone Esq. Atty. at law of Anderson Court his Atty. to collect what was coming to him from his gr. father's est. Jas. Johnson decd. On Nov. 14, 1877 W. T. Latimer recd. $134.00 the shares of Julia and Ida Latimer minors. Sarah Johnson married a Munroe. Amanda married a Latimer.

IRWIN, ELIZABETH—BOX 147, PACK 4182:
    Will dated Nov. 30, 1858. Filed Aug. 1, 1859. Exr: Dr. J. J. Wardlaw. Wit: Wm. Hill, Andrew McIlwaine, Wm. McIlwaine. Ment: Lived in Abbeville

Dist. Bequeath to Saml., Robt., Jas., John, Willie Irwin chn. of Jas. Irwin. Bequeath to Ellen Taylor wife of Wm. Taylor of Anderson Dist. Sis. in law, Jane the wid. of my decd. bro. John Donald. Niece, Anna H. Hill. Bequeath to my sis., Anna Taggart now living in Ohio and to her dtr.. Betsy wife of Jas. Irwin now living in Ill. and to her son Thos. Hawthorn now living in Ohio.

KAY, ALEXR. ELGIN—BOX 148, PACK 4183:
    Est. admnr. Jan. 24, 1859 by Geo. W. Bigby, John W. Bigby, Chas. David bound to Wm. Hill Ord. Abbeville Dist. sum $3,000.00. Left a wid. Melissa Kay and 9 chn. No names given.

KAY, REVD. JOHN—BOX 148, PACK 4184:
    Will dated May 19, 1859. Filed June 3, 1859. Exrs: Jas. B. Key, John Pratt, Joseph Ellis. Wit: John L. Ellis, John T. Miller, David Crawford. Ment: Lived in Abbeville Dist. Wife, Mary Key. Chn: Stephen, Mary, Jas. Berry, Francis Lemuel, Edny, Jane, Westly and Marshall Key. His wife was Mary Barmore before marriage. (Name written Kay and Key.)

LITES, ABRAHAM—BOX 148, PACK 4185:
    Est. admnr. Aug. 12, 1859 by Joel W. Lites, Jas. C. Lites, Bartw. Jordon, Augustus H. Morton, Robt. W. Lites bound to Wm. Hill Ord. Abbeville Dist. sum $80,000.00. Was the father of Joel W. Lites and Jas. C. Lites. A. P. Boozer married Eliza J. Lites.

LYON, BENJAMIN M.—BOX 148, PACK 4186:
    Est. admnr. July 28, 1858 by Wm. Lyon, Saml. Jordan, R. C. Mayson bound to Wm. Hill Ord. Abbeville Dist. sum $2,000.00. Wm. Lyon was the father of said decd. Distributees: Wm. Lyon the father, Dr. R. C. Mayson in right of his wife, R. N., J. F., Ann Lyon.

LYON, THOS. J.—BOX 148, PACK 4187:
    Est. admnr. Apr. 13, 1859 by Jas. H. Wideman, J. W. Hearst, W. H. Watson bound to Wm. Hill Ord. sum $30,000.00. Jas. H. Wideman was a bro. to Margaret C. Lyon. Left a wid. and 9 chn. J. S. Sybert was a s. l., Sallie P. Sibert. Thos., Martha, Jas., John, Wm., Leonard, Margaret were chn.

McCLAIN, JAS.—BOX 148, PACK 4188:
    Est. admnr. June 8, 1858 by John McClain, Jas. Shirley, John Webb bound to Wm. Hill Ord. sum $3,500.00. Mrs. E. B. McClain was the wid. Theodocia Elgin recd. a share. Left 9 chn. Jesse Robinson was a distributee in right of his wife Mary Ann.

MAJOR, SAM. B.—BOX 148, PACK 4189:
    Est. admnr. Jan. 28, 1859 by Matilda L. Major, John B. Johnson, Jas. F. Tolbert bound to Wm. Hill Ord. Abbeville Dist. sum $25,000.00. Distributees were: Mary, Joseph, Isabella M., Gamewell, Emma J., Anna R., Robt. W., Ella Major.

MABREY, LUCIAN L.—BOX 148, PACK 4190:
Est. admnr. June 23, 1858 by Thos. J. Mabry, John A. Wier, Robt. H.
Wardlaw bound to Wm. Hill Ord. sum $4,000.00. Was a bro. to Thos. J. Mabrey.

PERRIN, MARY E.—BOX 148, PACK 4191:
Est. admnr. Oct. 16, 1858 by Jas W. Perrin, John, Jas. S. Cothran bound
to Wm. Hill Ord. sum $75,000.00. Sett. made Feb. 12, 1859. Present: J. M.,
Joel Smith, Mary E., Jane E., Jas. M. Perrin. Joel Smith died in Feb. 1855 and
Mary E. wife of Jas. M. Perrin survived her father.

PEARMAN, (MINORS)—BOX 148, PACK 4192:
On Feb. 23, 1859 John T. Kerr, Wm. Duncan, Thos. M. Branuon bound
to Wm. Hill Ord. sum $2,000.00. John T. Kerr made gdn. of Sarah A., Weldon
C., John B. R., Isaac A., Leadie L. Pearman minors. Sett. of Nathaniel Pearman
decd. made Feb. 16, 1860.

PATTERSON, SAML.—BOX 148, PACK 4193:
Est. admnr. Feb. 4, 1859 by Jas. M. Perrin, Jas. Wardlaw Perrin, Jas. S.
Cothran bound to Wm. Hill Ord. Abbeville Dist. sum $300.00. He died in Ala.
Left wid. and 8 chn: Legatees: Wid., Wm., Catharine, Rebecca, B., John, New-
ton, Jas. Kennedy, Margaret Watson.

ROBERSON, HUGH—BOX 148, PACK 4194:
Will dated Nov. 14, 1857. Filed Dec. 10, 1858. Exr: Jas. W. Lipscomb.
Wit: Abraham P. Pool, Nathaniel McCants, John Sadler. Ment: Lived in Abbeville Dist. Wife, Louanna Roberson. Dtr., Jemima Eugenia Cook dtr. of my wife
by a former marriage. 1 paper stated that Wm. Roberson and Syth Roberson were
bros. of the whole blood and heirs of said decd. In 1859 Wm. Roberson was of
Tuscaloosa Co., Ala. Syth Roberson was of *Cherokee* Co., Tex. Was about 70
or 80 yrs. old when he died.

RUFF, JOHN—BOX 148, PACK 4195:
Will dated July 8, 1859. Filed July 27, 1859. Exrs: Sons, David F., Thos.
J. Ruff. Wit: Geo. W. Pressly, Wm. C. Smith, J. A. Myers. Ment: Lived in
Abbeville Dist. Wife ment. but no name given. Chn: Martha Adams, David F.
Ruff, Mary A. Hutchison, Joseph H., Thos. J., Geo. W. C., Henry B., Sarah V.,
Saml. A. C. Ruff.

RILEY, DR. DAN T.—BOX 148, PACK 4196:
Est. admnr. Apr. 21, 1859 by Jas. H. Riley, John G. Boozer, Birt Riley
bound to Wm. Hill Ord. sum $6,000.00. He died in Mar. leaving a wid. Was a
bro. to Jas. H. Riley.

RICHARDSON, JOHN—BOX 148, PACK 4197:
Est. admnr. Oct. 11, 1858 by Sarah Ann Richardson wid., David Keller,
Franklin Bowie, Wm. McIlwain bound to Wm. Hill Ord. sum $2,500.00. Left
7 chn. Jas. Richardson was a son.

ROBINSON, JESSE—BOX 148, PACK 4198:
    Est. admnr. Oct. 18, 1858 by Jas. Robinson, Geo., John W. Bigby bound
to Wm. Hill Ord. sum $8,000.00. Jas. Robinson was a bro.

SMITH, ROBT.—BOX 148, PACK 4199:
    Est. admnr. Mar. 5, 1859 by Williston W. Franklin, Christopher Smith,
Franklin Bowie bound to Wm. Hill Ord. sum $18,000.00. Decd. was unmarried.
Left 3 bros., 3 sis. living; 1 bro. dead who left one child. Distributees were: Jas.
Smith of Tex., Wm. S., Christopher Smith, Mrs. Malinda Bowie, Franklin Bowie,
Isaac Smith, Nathan Calhoun and wife. Jas. Smith was of Anderson Co., Tex.

SMITH, ISABELLA E.—BOX 148, PACK 4200:
    Will dated June 20, 1857. Filed June 2, 1859. Exr: Son, Wm. Joel Smith,
Jas. M. Perrin. Wit: Alexr. A. King, Thos. Stacey, 'John B. O'Neall. Ment: Lived
in Abbeville Dist. Chn: Geo. Miles Smith, Mary decd. Sett. Distributees: Augustus M. Smith, Virginia C. Aikens, W. Joel Smith, Lucy J. Bowie, Emma E. Aiken,
Geo. M., Belle Smith, Mary E. Perrin decd.

STOKES, ANNA R.—BOX 148, PACK 4201:
    Est. admnr. July 30, 1858 by W. Ludlow Hodges, G. W. Hodges, Lewis
Dantzler bound to Wm. Hill Ord. sum $10,000.00.

SMITH, (MINORS)—BOX 148, PACK 4202:
    On Mar. 9, 1859 Peter Smith, F. Ives, John Taggart bound to Wm. Hill
Ord. sum $107.60. Peter Smith made gdn. of Jewitt, Chas. A., Marietta Smith
minors.

TOGNO, DR. JOSEPH—BOX 148, PACK 4203:
    Est. admnr. Apr. 7, 1859 by John H., Leroy C. Wilson, Lucien H. Lomax
bound to Wm. Hill Ord. sum $3,000.00.

WATSON, RICHARD—BOX 148, PACK 4204:
    Est. admnr. Feb. 18, 1859 by W. W., Saml., R. M. Perryman, John G.
Barrett bound to Wm. Hill Ord. sum $25,000.00. Was an Uncle to W. W. Perry-
man. Left 3 chn: Lucy A., Richard, Saml. M. Watson. Lucy A. was the wife
of A. W. Ware.

WATSON, MARY PETTUS—BOX 148, PACK 4205:
    Will dated June 30, 1851. Filed Jan. 24, 1859. Exrs: John H. Mundy,
Wm. J. Arnold. Wit: Wm. McNairy, John Buchanan, O. J. Settle. Ment: Lived
in Abbeville Dist. Chn: Jubal Watson, Belinda Cunningham wife of Chas. N.
Cunningham, Matilda Strawhorn, Huldy Pulliam, Nancy Tharp wife of John J.
Tharp, John A. Watson. Gr. chn: Benjamin S. Pulliam, Mary Ann Tharp,
Moten Watson of Jubal Watson. Sett. made Mar. 23, 1861. Present: Exrs. John
Tharp and wife Nancy, Jubal Watson, Chas. Cunningham and his wife Belinda,
Benjamin Pulliam for his mother and self, Larkin Pulliam and wife Huldah.

WILSON, WALLACE—BOX 148, PACK 4206:
    Est. admnr. Oct. 16, 1858 by L. D. Merrimon, John G. Boozer, W. H.
Davis bound to Wm. Hill Ord. Abbeville Dist. sum $800.00.

WAITE, SARAH—BOX 148, PACK 4207:
Est. admnr. Mar. 7, 1859 by Simpson Waite, Wm. Hodge, John T. Johnson bound to Wm. Hill Ord. sum $1,500.00. Simpson Waite a son states that his mother died a wid. some 2 yrs. ago.

BARKSDALE, SHERARD—BOX 149, PACK 4208:
Est. admnr. Oct. 19, 1859 by Williams, Trewit, Sarah Barksdale, Jas. C. Willard, Joseph S. Britt bound to Wm. Hill Ord. sum $5,000.00. Left a wid., Sarah and 4 chn. Died in May. Mar. 23, 1869. Chn: Wm. W. Barksdale now 28 yrs. of Elyton, Ala., Jas. T. Barksdale 24 yrs., Geo. T. Barksdale of Edgefield Dist. 30 yrs. of age, John Lewis is dead.

BURNS, WM. C.—BOX 149, PACK 4209:
Est. admnr. June 21, 1859 by Stanley Crews, W. W. Perryman, W. W. Waller bound to Wm. Hill Ord. sum $1,000.00. Left neither wife nor child.

BARRATT, LAVINA—BOX 149, PACK 4210:
Will dated Oct. 22, 1859. Filed Nov. 3, 1859. Exrs: Son, John J. G. Barratt., S. l., Saml. S. Marshall. Wit: J. S. Chipley, Peter McKellar, Lemuel Bell, Jas. C. Ray. Ment: Lived in Abbeville Dist. Chn: John J. G. Barratt, Ann E. Marshall.

BARRATT, DR. JOHN P.—BOX 149, PACK 4211:
Will dated Nov. 10, 1856. Filed Otc. 14, 1859. Exr: Wife, Lavina Barratt. Wit: W. H. Bently, Henry Jones, A. A. Blyth. Ment: Lived in Abbeville Dist. Wife, Lavina Barratt. Chn: John J. G. Barratt, Ann Elizabeth Marshall.

BUCHANAN, J. WILLIS—BOX 149, PACK 4212:
Est. admnr. Oct. 15, 1859 by Robt. P. Buchanan, J. B. Sample, J. W. Buchanan, W. J. Arnold, Martin Delaney bound to Wm. Hill Ord. sum $20,000.00. Left a wid., Nancy J. Buchanan and 1 child. Was a bro. to Robt. P. Buchanan.

BUCHANAN, ELIZABETH—BOX 149, PACK 4213:
Est. admnr. July 6, 1860 by Nathaniel McCants, T. C. Lipscomb, W. L. Anderson bound to Wm. Hill Ord. sum $2,000.00. Left 2 chn.

BRAZEALLE, AIKEN—BOX 149, PACK 4214:
Est. admnr. Sept. 22, 1859 by Thos. Eakins, John Cowan, Joseph T. Moore bound to Wm. Hill Ord. sum $14,000.00. Left. a wid., several chn. by a former marriage who reside beyond the limits of this state. Distributees were: Abner, Jas. K. Breazeale, Elizabeth Lock, heirs of Newton Breazeale, heirs of Mrs. Margaret Woodruff, Heskey Dabney a dtr. Had wid. Louisa Brazeale and 6 chn.

BELCHER, WM. W.—BOX 149, PACK 4215:
Will dated Apr. 15, 1858. Exrs: A. P. Conner, Larkin Reynolds. Wit: Jas. Glasgow, Jas. M. Yarbrough, Wm. Burditt. Ment: Lived in Abbeville Dist. Nieces and nephews ment. but no names given. Warren P., Wm. W. Belcher were nephews. Sett. made Feb. 17, 1864. Present: J. C. Calhoun, Daniel Brown

who represents as gdn. for the minor chn. of Jas. Belcher, W. Belcher a distributee in right of his father Jas. Belcher decd., John White who represents Robt. White and wife. Jas. Belcher decd. had 6 chn., Edward Belcher had 8 chn.

BURTON, CALEB—BOX 149, PACK 4216:
Est. admnr. May 2, 1860 by Peter S., John A. Burton, Hugh Robinson, Michael Magee bound to Wm. Hill Ord. sum $35,000.00. Sett. made Dec. 13, 1861. Distributees: Robt. Burton, Robt. A. Tucker and wife Mary, Peter S. Jr., Wm. L. Burton, W. P. Magee and wife Dicey, Wm. Crowther and wife Amy, Jas. M. Hopkins and wife Elizabeth, J. F. Burton, W. F. Clinkscales and wife Lucinda, Bartley T. Gray and wife Sarah, Nancy L. Burton. Jas. M. Hopkins and wife were of Anderson Dist. Wm. P. Magee and wife Dicey of Tishomingo Co., Miss.

BRANSON, ELI—BOX 149, PACK 4217:
Will dated Nov. 14, 1859. Prov. Dec. 5, 1859. Exrs: Robt. A. Fair, Wm. Lyon, J. J. Devlin, J. L. Drennan, E. G. Kennedy, Isaac Kennedy. Wit: Jas. M. Purdy, Joel W., R. W. Lites. Ment: Lived in Abbeville Dist. Dtr. Mary Anna Dansby. "Bequeath ⅓ of est. to Associate Reformed Presbyterian Church Endowment and uses of her Theological Seminary in training young men for foreign missions."

COBB, EDMUND—BOX 149, PACK 4218:
Est. admnr. Oct. 26, 1859 by Jas. H., Elizabeth Cobb. Reid., Thos. Thomson, Nathaniel Cobb bound to Wm. Hill Ord. sum $30,000.00. Died Oct. 3, 1859.

WADKINS, REBECCA—BOX 149, PACK 4219:
Est. admnr. Oct. 7, 1867 by Jas. M., Joseph P. Young, Hiram T. Tustan bound to Wm. Hill Ord. sum $500.00. Rebecca Wadkins alias Caldwell left a husband, 3 sis., and nieces. Was a sis. to Wm. H. Caldwell decd. Est. of Saml. Y. Caldwell admnr. Oct. 7, 1867 by Jas. M., Joseph P. Young, Hiram T. Tustan bound to Wm. Hill Ord. sum $500.00. Was a citizen of Panola Co., Miss. Left a wife, bro., sis., and nieces. Joseph J. Caldwell est. admnr. same time was also of Panola Co., Miss.

CHEATHAM, BARTLET M.—BOX 149, PACK 4220:
Will dated Sept. 16, 1859. Exrs: John T. Cheatham, Wm. J. Cheatham. Wit: Edmund Cobb, A. J. Lythegoe, J. W. W. Marshall. Ment: Lived in Abbeville Dist. Chn: Permelia decd., Susan Ann Frances wife of John Jas. Gray, Mary wife of Jas. Thos. Wife ment. but no name given. Sett. Sarah E. Cheatham wid. Permelia Seigler a dtr. died about 1853. Wife of Tandy Seigler. Jas. Seigler was a son. B. M. Cheatham died about Sept. 18, 1859.

CROMER, PHILIP—BOX 149, PACK 4221:
Will dated Sept. 21, 1859. Filed Sept. 30, 1859. Exrs: Wife, Dorothy Ann Cromer, Son, A. F. Fletcher Cromer. Wit: Isaac Branch, Jas. Irwin, G. W. Cromer. Ment: Lived in Abbeville Dist. Wife, Dorothy Ann Cromer. Chn: Geo.

M., John P., A. F. Fletcher Cromer, Mary A. Elizabeth Tolbert, Sarah Virginia, Jane Amanda, Lucia Victoria Cromer. My little blind son Lindsay Harper. Sett. named 12 chn. viz: S. F., W. O., L. H., Thos. T. Cromer.

CUNNINGHAM, JOHN—BOX 149, PACK 4222:
Will dated Jan. 31, 1859. Prov. Feb. 21, 1859. Exr: Son, Joel Jasper Cunningham. Wit: John Brownlee, M. B. Latimer, Jas. W. Black. Ment: Lived in Abbeville Dist. Chn: Stephen W., Marthy V. Pool, Joel Jasper Cunningham. Gr. chn: John David, Josephine Antonia Cunningham.

CUNNINGHAM, (MINORS)—BOX 149, PACK 4223:
On June 12, 1860 T. T., J. H., Jas. R. Cunningham bound to Wm. Hill Ord. sum $6,000.00. T. T. Cunningham made gdn. of Francis C., Wm. T. Cunningham minor chn. of T. T. Cunningham.

DELLISHAW, JOHN WESLEY—BOX 149, PACK 4224:
Est. admnr. Mar. 5, 1860 by W. P. Dellishaw, J. F. Edmonds, Jas. A. Edmonds bound to Wm. Hill Ord. sum $3,000.00. Died June 21, 1858. Son of W. P. Dellishaw.

DAY, EDMUND—BOX 149, PACK 4225:
Est. admnr. Dec. 9, 1859 by J. W. Fooshe, Elizabeth Day wid., Wm. Carter, John Sadler bound to Wm. Hill Ord. sum $18,000.00. Distributees were: Frank, Nathaniel, John, Rebecca, Sumpter Day, Mrs. Jackson decd., who left a husband Caleb Jackson and 1 child.

DRAKE, JOHN—BOX 149, PACK 4226:
Est. admnr. Sept. 2, 1859 by Jas. A. Drake, R. R. Seawright, B. F Moseley, J. A. Lyon bound to Wm. Hill Ord. sum $1,000.00. Jas. Drake on Aug. 19, 1859 states that his bro. John Drake died about 12 months ago. Will dated Aug. 19, 1858. Ment. wife, Amanda Drake. Bro. l., Wm. W. Seawright. (Will not accepted.) Sett. Chn: Margaret wife of Wm. H. Austin, N. Jane wife of Alfred Sheriff who resided in Pickens Co., Jas., Andrew S. Drake, Elizabeth wife of N. P. Devore of Edgefield Co., Robt. W., Thos., John J. Drake, Amanda A. wife of Jas. W. Bell, Wm., B., Vashti Drake.

DENDY, CHAS.—BOX 149, PACK 4227:
Will dated Nov. 13, 1858. Filed Aug. 24, 1859. Exrs: Wife, Ellis Apsley Dendy, Son l., H. T. Lyon, Jas. A. Allen, Thos. Thomson. Wit: Geo. White, John G. Edwards, B. P. Hughes. Ment: Lived in Abbeville Dist. "Owned house and lot on the public square of Abbeville opposite John White's store extending down near to the Railroad." Wife Ellia Apsley Dendy. Chn: Thos. B. Dendy decd., Fannie E. Allen, Harriet B. Lyon, Sallie E. Dendy, Chas. N. Dendy. Gr. chn: Elizabeth Ellen, Jas. N., Thos. M. Dendy chn. of my decd. son Thos. B. Dendy.

THE END

A NEW INDEX
TO
"ABSTRACTS
OF
OLD NINETY-SIX
AND
ABBEVILLE DISTRICT
WILLS AND BONDS"

BY PAULINE YOUNG

Compiled By:

MARGUERITE CLARK
SHANNON, MISSISSIPPI

SOUTHERN HISTORICAL PRESS
%The Rev.S. Emmett Lucas,Jr.
P.O. Box 738
Easley, South Carolina 29640

ISBN 0-89308-059-4

Preface By Publisher

It is to be noted by the person using this Index to Pauline Young's "Abstracts of Old Ninety-Six and Abbeville District Wills and Bonds" that this is a brand new index, and is not the same as the one that appeared in the original edition or the reprint edition of this book.

The original index was not a complete index as many names were omitted from it that appeared in these records. This caused the person using this book to either think that his or her ancestor was not to be found in these records or else to examine each page line for line in hopes of finding the person they were looking for.

Much thanks must be given to Marguerite Clark of Shannon, Mississippi who began work on this new index some two years ago in hopes that it would be published and made available to the general public.

The Rev. Silas Emmett Lucas,Jr.+

1

4

5

7

9

Buchanan, Cont.
Robert 17, 31, 36, 54,
270, 286, 364, 419
Robert Bonds 17, 31, 36
Robert E. 17, 84, 98,
99, 364, 447
Robert P. 573, 580
Robertson 31
Samuel 19, 20, 87,
429, 572
Sarah 228, 305, 463,
565
Sarah L. 565
Thomas 20
William 17, 19, 36,
84, 168, 169, 228,
232, 304, 305, 325,
329, 345, 447, 465,
505, 548, 572
William, Sr. 20, 250,
262
William N. 23
Buck, John 198
Mary 43
Nancy 43
William 217
Buffington, Joseph 29
Moses 146
Bugg, Charlotte 378
Nicholas 378
Bull, Dicy42
John 42
John B. 283, 535
Martin 42
Mary 42
Sarah 535, 565
Thomas 42
William 309, 333, 414,
535
Bullion, Mary 30
Thomas 30
Bullock, Agnes 342, 356
B. S. 25
Bartlette 117
Daniel 357
Elihu 25, 138
Elizabeth 375
Hannah 357
James 25, 208
John W. 23
Luther M. 40
Martin L. 23, 288
Mary Ann 25
Nathaniel 443
Rebecca 375
William 23, 40, 333,
342, 356
William W. 40
Zachariah 69, 239, 427,
443
Bulow, Joachim 10, 298
Bumpass, Peggy F. 229
William 229
Bunting, Elsey 203
Helen 143
Isaac 56, 68, 88, 95,
115, 143, 162, 192,
315, 427
Mary Durret 88
Burkhalter, Christian 68
(Buckhatter), Michael
151
Burdette, Giles 31
(Burditt), William 580
Burdine, John 18, 435
Nathaniel 176
Reginald 18
Burley, William 296
Burnamof, Hickerson 467
Sarah 467
Burnett, Addline E. 451
Amanda 523
Andrew Jackson 539
Cradk. 382

Burnett, Cont.
(Barnett), Elizabeth
15, 560
(Barnett), Ester M. 20
(Barnett), J. H. 15
(Barnett), James 33,
280
Jane 462, 575
(Barnett), Jeremiah 360
(Barnett), John 43, 46,
103, 426, 446, 504,
523, 545, 553, 560
(Barnett), John J. 185,
195
(Barnett), Joseph 65,
161, 222
Littleberry 472, 513
(Barnett), Margaret 14,
451
(Barnett), Rosey Ann
280
Sarah Frances 513, 439,
561
Sumter D. 513
(Barnett), Susan C. 16
(Barnett), Thomas 318,
339, 360, 523
Wiley 462, 547
(Barnett), William, Sr.
33
(Barnett), William, Jr.
33
William N. 513
Burney, Andrew 36
Marthew 444
Burns, David 124
James 342
John A. 57
Luke 25, 329
Matty 25
Nancy B. 44
Rd. 44
Robert 67, 272, 307
William C. 25, 580
Burnsides, Emily 573
James 139
Burrelle, John 42, 455
Vashti (Bashti) 42, 455
Burris (Burrows), Samuel
13
(Burrows), W. W. 543
William 205, 222
Burson, Jonathan 124
Burt, Armistead 24, 43, 75,
81, 202, 234, 258,
346, 432, 472
Garland 345
Jared 290
(Bert), John 101, 346
Martha C. 75
Mathew 120, 346
Moody 63, 346
Thomas 468
Burton, Allen 24, 205
Beverly 24, 105, 342
Blackman 306
Caleb 21, 25, 40, 110,
184, 185, 275, 301,
557, 581
Caroline C. 21
Catherine 32
Charles 152
Delila 451
Douglass 32, 181
Ed. M. 260
Edy 32
Elizabeth 21, 32, 40
Frances 157
Henry S. 105
J. F. 581
James 21, 45, 166
John 21, 24, 32, 40,
85, 101, 177, 196,
219, 319, 337

Burton, Cont.
John, Jr. 40
John A. 21, 77, 166,
581
Joseph 32, 107, 194,
204, 216, 259, 337,
359, 451
Josiah 21, 25, 32, 45,
242, 259, 300, 451,
491
Mahatabel 32
Margaret 451
Mary (Polly) 21, 24, 25,
32, 45, 451
Nancy L. 581
Peter 21, 25, 169, 520
Peter S. 110, 136, 184,
185, 205, 275, 581
Peter S., Jr. 581
Phebe 389
Polly Ann 491, 561
Robert 21, 25, 581
Sarah 21, 32, 242
Sophia 491
Thomas 352
Timothy Marion 451
William 21, 32, 162,
275
William, Jr. 389
William L. 581
Busby, Benjamin 23, 44,
375, 380
(Buzbee), Elizabeth 23,
32, 106, 183, 375
(Buzbee), Jacob 380
Jane 23, 375, 380
(Buzbee), Jesse 380
John 23, 375, 380
(Buzbee), Lewis 42, 44,
245, 375
Mary 245, 380
Melinda 375
Micajah 19, 23, 44, 375
Moses 380
(Buzbee), Stephen 10,
23, 32, 34, 106,
213, 300, 364, 375,
380
Bussey, Charles 221
Butler, Ann 25
C. W. 133
Elizabeth 43
James 25, 32
John 62, 220
Larkin 43, 44, 353
Mary 32
Reuben 63
Sarah 121
Standmore 224
Thomas 35, 163, 220,
444
Washington 44
William 16, 35, 44, 88,
98, 136, 357, 543
Bynum, James 28
Cabell, Jane Charity 490
Cain, Abner 62
Barbary 62
Caleb 52
Caroline E. 574
Emily G. 263
Frances 72
Harold 62
James 9, 26, 35, 60,
66, 70, 72
James, Sr. 72
John 25, 62, 67, 102,
211, 215, 257, 330,
389
John E. 458, 574
John M. 257
John William 263
Jonathan 62, 67
Martha P. 574

10

Cain, Cont.
Mary (Polly) 60, 68, 69,
70, 88, 458
Michael 68, 145
Nancy S. 406
Nonteith 574
Patrick 62, 318
Peggy 72
Randal 72
Randolph 458
Richard 60
Dr. Sampson V. 263, 389,
457, 478, 523, 564,
574
Sara 60, 70
Thomas 77
William 18, 38, 69, 72,
207, 254, 458
Willie 574
Calbert, Permelia 290
Caldes (Codels), Richard
387
Robert 349
Caldwell, Abigail 50, 272
Agness J. 492
Alexander 53, 340
Andrew 62, 389, 550
Ann 48, 78, 256
Ann Elizabeth 74
Anthony 48, 141, 501
Charles 50, 59, 61, 64,
151, 165, 272, 346,
348, 374
Charlotte S. 74
Curtis 68
D. M. 451
David 62, 63, 428
David Robert 135, 335
E. W. 73
Edmund 25, 53, 106
Edna 48, 78, 256, 472,
492, 520, 521, 537,
550
Elizabeth (Betsey) 51,
53, 59, 62, 129, 308,
389, 402, 443, 456
Eliza Harris 63
Elizabeth Ann 335
Elizabeth Harris 63
Emily J. 456
Ezekiel 59
Frances 456
George 48, 72, 74
George F. 48, 270, 279,
288, 298, 315, 331
George R. 72, 492, 547,
550
Henry 59, 61, 64
Henry Nichols 386
James 20, 21, 48, 53,
61, 62, 63, 71, 74,
76, 77, 86, 90, 102,
105, 119, 141, 181,
195, 211, 222, 242,
272, 276, 302, 339,
347, 348, 359, 383,
386, 389, 443
James, Sr. 63, 151, 171
James, Jr. 171, 386
James B. 72, 492
James E. 456
James H. 81, 121, 384
Jane (Jean) (Jenny)
26, 59, 62, 152, 175,
377, 386
Jane Y. 492, 515, 576
Jesse 21, 22, 53
John 33, 50, 53, 61, 62,
63, 73, 86, 119, 121,
125, 126, 131, 141,
145, 151, 181, 295,
296, 300, 303, 304,
346, 375, 386, 389,
410, 436, 492

Caldwell, Cont.
John, Sr. 62
John, Jr. 62
John G. 21, 76, 77, 102,
119, 356, 394, 448,
456
John J. 77, 492, 515
John R. 384
John William 61
Joseph 59, 61, 64, 72,
308
Joseph J. 581
Jude 81
Letty 59
Lucy Callaham 549, 550
Margaret Rebecca 72,
550
Martha T. 518
Mary (Polly) 53, 129,
337
Mary J. 456
Mathew T. 53, 344
Nancy 61
P. C. 517
Peggy 53
Rebecca 48, 492, 581
Samuel 48, 75, 77, 87,
117, 140, 199, 259,
270, 288, 298, 308,
331, 344, 440
Samuel L. 515
Samuel Y. 492, 581
Sarah (Sally) C. 53, 59,
69, 73, 291, 305,
492
Sophia 384
Thomas 59, 63, 291, 308,
337, 358
Thomas F. 492
Thomas L. 73
Thompson 456
W. C. 73
William 53, 61, 62, 63,
75, 76, 96, 125,
259, 308, 386, 406
William D. 456
William Ezekiel 73, 159
William H. 26, 53, 73,
75, 77, 85, 86, 87,
88, 135, 149, 167,
174, 175, 195, 196,
216, 315, 319, 355,
392, 394, 406, 411,
456, 581
William H., Jr. 492
Calhoun, Agnes 52, 222,
492
Alexander 54
Alice (Alis) 52, 222,
492
Amelia 528
Andrew 81, 358, 436
Ann Eliza 56
Benjamin F. 537, 574
Caroline 79
Catherine 60
Dabney 367
Downs 20, 21, 22, 23,
39, 40, 42, 52, 74,
110, 112, 114, 156,
176, 194, 226, 228,
287, 304, 360, 383,
430, 431, 460, 469,
479, 492, 509
E. H. 68
Edwin Broyles 514, 515
Elizabeth M. 516
Ellen 515, 516
Dr. Ephraim R. 19, 22,
197, 201, 228, 267,
305, 310, 453, 465,
493, 506, 516

Calhoun, Cont.
Ezekiel 60, 61, 63, 85,
109, 148, 213, 321,
322, 329, 385, 400,
422, 435
Ezekiel, Sr. 175, 210,
334, 392, 444
Ezekiel, Jr. 60
Ezekiel Noble 54
Frances (Fanny) 61, 75,
136, 493
Frances A. 75, 263, 308
Frances J. 515
George W. 537, 574
Hugh 31, 99
Hugh, Sr. 60
Hugh, Jr. 60
James 22, 41, 49, 51,
54, 60, 62, 69, 73,
76, 77, 78, 79, 83,
171, 203, 205, 209,
226, 237, 287, 352,
387, 388, 405, 414
James, Sr. 78, 79
James, Jr. 18, 278, 319
James Edward 75, 574,
575
James Lawrence 75, 135
James Montgomery 51, 77
James Patrick 237
James S. 537, 574
Jane (Jennett) 49, 60,
78
John 34, 47, 52, 62,
66, 68, 69, 71, 78,
95, 120, 148, 161,
165, 193, 207, 211,
212, 215, 216, 339,
358, 365, 405, 515,
574
John, Jr. 68
John A. 77, 288, 373,
477
John C. 393, 580
John Ewing 48, 49, 52,
56, 60, 73, 307,
458
John L. 69, 79
John W. 537, 556
Joseph 51, 54, 56, 60,
67, 73, 75, 140,
145, 193, 203, 226,
237, 256, 285, 322,
380, 419, 427, 515
Kate 574
Kitty J. 78
Lavinda 383, 492
Leorana 300
LeRoy 51, 54, 383
Malinda Virginia 537,
574
Margaret (Peggy) 62,
71, 388
Maria L. 73, 78
Martha 49, 52, 56, 60,
73, 169, 458
Martha M. 383
Martha S. 73
Mary 383, 444
Mary Elizabeth 54
Mary Jane 56, 73, 310
Nancy 200
Nancy, Sr. 222
Nathaniel (Nathan) 52,
73, 95, 106, 156,
194, 209, 268, 347,
427, 469, 492, 528,
537, 574, 579
Patrick 19, 49, 51, 60,
62, 79, 80, 83, 105,
203, 222, 227, 237,
278, 302, 422

11

13

14

15

16

17

18

Davis, Cont.
Jefferson N. 81, 91,
  92, 261, 262
Jesse 84
John 9, 42, 88, 90, 103,
  127, 136, 241, 497,
  341, 346, 454, 481,
  494, 504, 554, 566,
  575
John B. 291, 340, 360
John F. 533, 566
John L. 340
John T. 346, 427
Joseph 51, 82, 85, 91,
  94, 106, 107, 157,
  236, 246, 255, 257,
  266, 289, 291, 305,
  306, 335, 433
Joshua 109, 163, 190,
  405, 575
Mrs. Laney 17
Lewis 94
Littleberry 84
Lucy W. 509
Malinda 88, 105
Margaret 87, 90
Marion J. 17, 258
Martha (Matty) 85, 87,
  90, 98, 282, 553,
  555
Martha Jane 110, 494
Mary A. F. 490
Mary (Polly) E. 63, 86,
  90, 253, 290, 458,
  566
Mary Isabella 533
Mildridge (Milley) 85,
  90, 575
Moses 31, 85, 86, 87,
  96, 181, 256, 392
Nancy H. 84, 85, 86, 90,
  331, 480, 494
Nathaniel J. 14, 91, 94,
  193, 239, 282, 467,
  473, 474, 482, 484,
  492, 504, 515, 518,
  563
Newton 169
P. H. 82
Patrick 82
Rachel W. 86
Rebecca 85, 90, 392,
  575
Richard D. 82, 113, 335
Robert 61, 85, 86, 87,
  90, 96, 125, 126,
  135, 300, 303, 362
Robert M. 258, 310, 454,
  480, 483, 525, 530
Samuel 84, 90, 128, 194,
  253, 267, 290, 291,
  340, 434
Sarah (Sally), A. 85,
  106, 113, 177, 197
Sarah M. 507
Susanna 84
Thomas 15, 216, 229,
  300, 362, 531
Thornton, 88
Timothy 90
Turner A. 82
Ursla 566
Waddey 362
William 28, 36, 38, 82,
  85, 86, 87, 88, 95,
  96, 145, 149, 216,
  282, 329, 335, 359,
  375, 392, 411, 500,
  553, 555, 575
William, Sr. 88
William, Jr. 41
William C. 516, 540,
  566, 573

Davis, Cont.
Winston H. 110, 535,
  542, 566, 579
Zachariah 86, 157, 217,
  362
Dawkins, Chole 82
Elijah 84
Elizabeth 84, 96
George 82
Hannah 82
Jean 406
John 84, 96
Joseph 82
Lewis 84
Margaret 84
Polly 82
Sally 84
Thomas 82, 84
Thomas, Sr. 96
Thomas, Jr. 96
William 64, 151, 406
William, Jr. 96
Dawson, Anne 79
Britton 36
James 543, 553
Jones 182
Joseph 121, 172
Day, Edmund 582
Elizabeth 460, 582
Frank 582
Hezekiah 41
James T. 44
John 95, 347, 460, 582
John R. 83, 85
Joseph 71
LeRoy 83, 85
Luke 72, 95
Mansfield 85, 427, 516
Nathaniel 582
Philip 95, 103, 347,
  516
Ransom 83
Rebecca 582
Sumpter 582
Dealwood, John 8
Dean, Edward 86
John B. 532
Julius 86
Sterline 478, 493
Susan 532
Thomas 29
William T. 532
Debruhl, M. P. 551
M. T. 551
Stephen C. 551
Susan C. 551
Susan E. 551
Delahowe, John 35, 352
Delaney (Deleney), John
  158
Martin 568, 573, 580
Delaughter, George 274
Delfudg, Robert 299
Dellechaux, Elizabeth 96,
  559
(Dellishaw), Jacob 94,
  96, 102, 394
(Dellishaw), James 17,
  32, 94, 96
(Delashaw), John Wesley
  559, 582
(Dellishaw), Nancy 94
(Dellishaw), Peter 94,
  96
Samuel 394
Sara 96
(Delishaw), Sarah
  Roberson 394
Susanna 96
(Dellishaw), W. P. 582
Deloach, Michael 31
Delph, Henry 83, 238
Mary (Polly) 87, 94
Muymons 83

Delph, Cont.
Robert 83
Robert P. 87, 338
Dendy, Charles 24, 75, 89,
  91, 131, 245, 325,
  335, 366, 411, 446,
  494, 496, 528, 582
Charles N. 582
Cornelius 296
Ellen 494
Ellia Apsley 582
James N. 494, 582
Mary Jane 494
Nancy 89
Sallie E. 582
Thomas B. 64, 89, 162,
  321, 477, 487, 494,
  498, 528, 562, 582
Thomas McClellan 494,
  582
Denham, Mary 90
Robert 90, 359
Dennard, John 176
Dennis, Joseph 368
Robert 90
Dennison, Patrick 129
Denton, John 328
Keziah B. 328
Margaret 328
Margaret C. 328
Rebecca H. 328
Derchaney, Peter 101
Desernett, Israel 409
Devall, Cecilia B. 338
Elizabeth (Eliza) 82, 89
Jacob 272
James 82, 246, 439
Joseph 82
Joseph A. W. 107, 336
Lucy 336
(DuVall), Macklin 89
Mary 272
(DeVauld), Matilday Ann
  82
(DuVall), Michael 66,
  89, 404
Otes 82
Samuel 82, 89
Sarah 82
Devaux, John 146
Devlin, Betsey 498
Charles 272
James 8, 13, 58, 62, 82,
  91, 112, 141, 158,
  184, 199, 236, 257,
  354, 359, 363, 368,
  403, 412, 458, 527
James, Jr. 54, 179, 238,
  346, 348, 351, 362
James H. 458
Devall, James J. 97, 257,
  261, 367, 474, 493,
  512, 519, 522, 535,
  550, 573, 581
Devlin, James M. 458
Jannet 82, 458
John 82, 85, 91, 169,
  179, 205, 215, 238,
  252, 256, 257, 261,
  268, 289, 295, 341,
  346, 348, 354, 357,
  382, 388, 391, 412,
  435, 437, 469, 474,
  493
John L. 458
Lucretia S. 112, 567
Margaret (Peggy) 179,
  362, 388
Martha 179, 357, 492
Martha M. 458
Mary 261, 382, 458,
  487, 493
Mary Ann 257
Oliver 567

20

Devlin, Cont.
    Peggy Ann 493
    Robert 16, 97, 107, 112,
        158, 194, 258, 264,
        367, 368, 382, 423,
        493, 522, 567
    Sarah C. 567
    William 175
Devore (DeFoor), Andrew 57,
    215
    (DeFoor), David D. 150
    David W. 493
    Elizabeth 582
    John S. 551
    Mary 551
    Mathew 32
    N. P. 582
Dewitt, John C. 105, 111
Deyampert, John 95
    L. Z. C. 205
Dial, Albert 303
    Elizabeth 302
    Hasting 302, 303
    James 302
    John 505
    Joseph Stalsworth 302
Dick, John 89
    Joseph 89, 217, 318
    Mary 89
    Thomas 89
    William 89
Dickert, Michael 298
Dickie (Dickey), Alexander
    72, 299
    Hector 124
    (Dickey), John 72
    Robert 124
    Susana 124
    Thomas 358
    (Dickey), William 275
Dickson (Dixan), Freeman
    Bates 313, 391, 494
    (Dixon), Hannah 85, 91
    Hugh 50, 73, 135, 180,
        268, 276, 293, 298,
        313, 335, 407, 524,
        536
    (Dixon), James 84, 85,
        313, 330, 345
    (Dixon), James N. 91,
        332, 418, 424, 459,
        494
    (Dixon), Jane Y. 494
    (Dickinson), Joel 395
    John 48, 49, 89, 144,
        494
    (Dixon), John Joseph
        494, 551
    John S. 494
    (Dickenson), Joseph B.
        73, 78, 86, 135,
        177, 202, 335, 367,
        451, 507, 530, 562
    Julia Ann 494
    (Dickinson), Marshall
        395
    (Dixon), Martha M. 494,
        551
    (Dixon), Mary 494
    (Dickinson), Mary Ann
        85, 91, 548
    (Dickinson), Mary A. E.
        W. 391, 494
    (Dixon), Nancy Y. 529
    Rachel Lucinda 177, 507
    Rebecca H. 149, 153
    (Dixon), Robert S. 494,
        551, 569
    Samuel H. 149, 153
    Samuel J. 494
    (Dixon), Starling 85,
        250
    Thomas 84, 212, 227,
        292, 307, 529

Dickson, Cont.
    Walter C. 366
    (Dixon), William 89,
        358, 548
Dilbone (Dilbon), George
    392
    Henry 86, 371
    John 86
Dilerd, James 11
Dinwoody, William 90
Doan, William H. 83
Dobbins (Dobins), Eliza A.
    248
    Elizabeth 561
    James 207, 561
    (Dobins), Samuel P. 248
    (Dobins), Sinthy 248
    (Dobins), Susannah M.
        248
Dobbs, E. H. 84
    Elipah 84
    Elizabeth 84, 98
    Fortune 303
    Jeremiah 257
    Jesse 82, 83, 84
    Mary 84
    Polly E. 84
    Susan 84
Dodds, Francis 321
    Jesse 90
    Sarah 90
    Thomas 90
Dodgen, James 212
    Olleyman 212
Dodson, A. M. 558
    Allen 455
    Charles 353
    Eli 346
    Elizabeth 76, 83, 95
    Enoch 83, 511
    James 83, 95
    Jane 194
    Mahaley 83
    Polly 83
    Thomas 223
    Wesley 95
    William 83
Doggens, James 292
Donahoe (Donohugh), Thomas
    95
Donald, Alexander 87, 393,
    494
    Amanda 205
    Andrew J. 133, 205,
        393, 403
    David L. 536, 549, 551,
        556
    Eugenia 536
    George 393
    Hezekia 393
    James 131, 250, 257,
        342
    James, Jr. 393
    James F. 461, 498, 549,
        550, 551, 556, 566,
        570
    James P. 570
    Jane 87, 516, 517, 550
    John 11, 87, 88, 94,
        95, 105, 120, 125,
        137, 168, 173, 175,
        191, 192, 200, 201,
        219, 234, 258, 259,
        263, 267, 268, 287,
        289, 304, 307, 319,
        325, 336, 338, 360,
        363, 372, 393, 433,
        483, 507, 529, 534,
        550, 551, 573, 577
    John, Sr. 459, 461,
        489, 570
    John, Jr. 459, 524

Donald, Cont.
    John A. 86, 87, 95, 97,
        133, 236, 240, 392,
        479
    Margaret 22, 451
    Martha 95, 494
    Mary 97, 507
    Mary (Polly) Ann 392,
        483, 524, 570
    Mary A. Lyon 498
    Mary Jane 551
    Robert 459
    Samuel 20, 46, 173, 192,
        234, 235, 336, 363,
        451, 459, 461, 475,
        529, 532, 534, 536,
        550, 551, 556, 570,
        571
    Susanna C. 150
    West 86, 125, 131, 250,
        306, 307, 393
    William 22, 431, 551
Donaldson, Jacob 237
    James 88
    Janet (Jenny) 88, 91,
        393
    Malinda 237
    Mary 88
    Matthew 91, 357, 393
    Reuben 88
    Thomas 88
    Thomas, Sr. 88
    William 88
Donnelly, Andrew Emory 551,
    566
    Francis Olin 551, 566
    George Summerfield 551
    Henrietta 551, 566
    James 551
    James C. 551
    John David Fletcher 551,
        566
    Maria 551
    Mary R. 551
    S. 566
Dooly, Hetha 517
Dornes, Elizabeth 8
    (Dorn), William 298
Dorrah, Margaret 150
Dorrio, Catherine 87
    John 87
    Margaret 87
    William 82, 87, 122,
        181, 316, 371, 397
Dorsett, Joseph 90
Doss, Joel 219
Dougharty, James 406
Douglass, Agness 84
    Archibald 35, 88, 100,
        149, 175, 375, 388,
        393, 400, 438, 460,
        486
    Catherine 84, 137, 511
    David 88
    Donald 14, 21, 52, 77,
        79, 94, 107, 180,
        184, 244, 270, 307,
        375, 391, 393, 403,
        417
    Eliza A. 137, 511
    Elizabeth 300, 393
    Elizabeth Cochran 79
    George A. 460
    Hugh 392
    James 98, 344, 516, 535,
        542, 562
    Jane 393
    John 33, 35, 79, 84, 85,
        88, 98, 114, 296,
        320, 350, 352, 375,
        403, 478, 493, 516
    Margaret 348
    Mathew 84, 562
    Matilda 460

21

22

23

24

25

Foster, Cont.
Mary (Polly) Ann 254,
396
Mary Caroline 109, 111,
576
Mary E. 563
Mary T. 323
Matthew 15
Moses 110, 122, 396
Nancy E. 563
Pamelia 333
Polly Perrin 106
Robert 30, 105, 106,
107, 108, 111, 144,
147, 166, 200, 228,
243, 253, 259, 272,
277, 302, 318, 353,
369, 382, 387, 388,
397, 408, 442
Robert, Sr. 106, 446
Robert Jordan 576
Samuel 62, 66, 106, 107,
108, 111, 169, 184,
210, 266, 299, 395,
397, 417
Samuel, Sr. 106, 107,
112, 120, 146, 171,
208, 210, 269, 272,
319, 392, 412, 413,
442
Samuel, Jr. 62, 106,
112, 147, 171, 212,
410
Samuel C. 108, 120
Sarah 106, 108, 122
Sarah Jane 563
Sarah M. 419
Savannah L. 506
Susanna 105
Thomas Jordan 19, 40,
108, 114, 359, 396
Virginia 251
William 56, 106, 111,
147, 413
William P. 563
Fowler, Catherine 111
Elizabeth 80
James C. 111, 113
John 80, 111, 221
Josephine 111
Nancy A. 111
Sarah 111
William 207, 249, 396
Fox, Catherine 397
Elizabeth 114, 397
John 397
Mary 276, 397
Mathew 38, 259, 397
Foy, Dinnes 61
Harmatal 113
John 367, 407
Peter 113, 407
Francis, Charlotte 15
Franklin, Asa 21, 105, 112
(Frankling), Benjamin
39, 11, 112
Benjamin, Jr. 495
(Frankling), Elisha 39
Ann 112
James 22, 82, 105, 112,
156, 170, 174, 186,
238, 253, 289, 347
Joseph 151, 255
Mahulda 528
Mary 106
Sarah 105
Sarah T. 106
Susan 112, 170, 495,
507
William 22, 112
William B. 105
Willison (William) W.
112, 233, 510, 528,
554, 579

Franks, John 427
Marshall 9, 372
Nehemiah 9
Frazier, Amanda 112
Ann 175
Benjamin 112
Charity 112, 567
(Fraser), Charlotte 15
(Fraser), Clara J. 113
(Fraser), David 105,
396
(Fraser), Donald 105,
175, 255, 292, 319,
394
Dorcas 210, 395
Edwin H. 112
(Fraser), Georgianna
113
(Fraser), Isabella 105
(Fraser), J. A. 507
James 90, 107, 112,
172, 567
James W. 112, 194, 258,
423, 567
John 65, 105, 106, 113,
252, 396, 418, 446
John B. 395
(Fraser), John G. 113
(Fraser), Margaret 105
Margery 184
(Fraser), Marshall 159,
498, 510
Martha B. 112
Mary 112
(Fraser), Mary Allen
22, 105
(Fraser), Mary Ann 575
Mary Elizabeth 498
Rebecca 112
Sarah A. 159
Sarah C. 567
Tallulah H. 112, 567
V. Antoinette 567
(Fraser), William 105,
106, 109, 346, 446
Frederick, James 182
John 182, 238, 294
Free, Jacob 32
John 484
Lewis 300
Martha Caroline 484
Nancy 484
Nancy Jane 484
Freeland, Daniel F. 515,
537
Freeman, Arthur 334
Caty Nolin 422
Centha 159
Charles 159, 160, 526
Elizabeth 334
George 105
Herod 38, 105, 359,
439, 511
Hugh 277
James 382
John 337, 423
Littleberry B. 160, 526,
527
Nancy 105
Polly 197, 378
Thomas 358
Washington 76
Wiley 340
French, George 452
Frith, Archibald (Archey)
109, 109, 146, 318,
369
Jacob 109
John 108, 109
Joseph 108, 109
Nancy 108
Susannah 109
Thomas 109

Fritz, (Frittes) Catreena
397
Peter 350
Frolick, Charles Edward 421
Frost, Edward 426
Jonathan 110
Mary 110
Fuller, Hannah 108
Henry 109
James 44
Jesse W. 108, 111
Silas 108
William A. 108
Fullerton, Agness 349
William 349
Fulmon, Levi 160
Fulton, Amanda 111
Anna Adolis 562
Benjamin H. 157, 462,
469, 562
Catherine F. 157
Charity 157
Elizabeth 107
Elizabeth A. 111, 562
Frances 111
Henry 103, 107, 172, 208
Horatio 107
Jane Augustus 111, 462,
562
John 103, 172
John C. 562, 575
Jordan W. 562
Leonore B. 562
Lucretia 107
Richard B. 111, 157,
347, 562
Samuel J. 562, 575
Sarah Ann 562
Thomas 111, 164, 172,
473, 562
Thomas J. 111
Furches, Elizabeth 396
John 396
Furr, Elizabeth 108, 113
Enoch 108
Henry 23, 108, 291, 435
Susannah Catherine 108,
113
Fuquay (Fuqua), Nancy 71,
300
William 71
Gabel (Gable), Elizabeth
566
Harmon (Herman) 122, 421
Henry 122, 374
Jacob 122
John 122
Margaret 122, 517
(Gable), Mary 374
(Gable), William 87, 517
Gabriel, C. B. 283
Gafford, John 118
Martha Ann Graham 118
Thomas 124, 162
William 223
Gage, James D. M. 568
Mathew C. 568
W. A. 568
Gailey, Alfred B. 27
Andrew 27
Elizabeth 27
Harriet Lomax 27
James 27, 126
(Galley), Margaret 126
Nancy 27
Polly 27
Gailliard, Archibald D. 158
Sarah S. 158
Gaines, Benjamin 290, 400
(Gains), David 58, 123
Edmund 106, 125, 422
Elizabeth 117, 296, 398,
399, 400, 539
Henry 106, 125, 238

26

27

28

29

Gunnin, Cont.
 Hannah Wardlaw 120, 399
 Isabella 120
 James 120
 Jane 116, 120, 399
 Margaret 116
 Mary 120
 Nathan 116, 399
Guthrie, John 67, 102,
 239, 430
Gutman, John 122
Guttrey, Aelnor 123
 Jean (Jennet) 123
 John 123
 Robert 368
 Thomas 123
Hackett, America E. 518
 Anna 141
 August G. 518
 Elijah C. 135, 141,
 341, 355, 518
 Elizabeth (Eliza) F.
 141, 142
 Joseph 444
 Lucy 444
 M. B. 523
 Martin 48, 79, 135,
 178, 308, 333, 334,
 539
 Michael 77
 Richard 274
 Robert 135, 207, 341,
 355, 427
 William 135, 141, 278,
 288, 333, 444
 William H. 141
Hackleman, Conrad 149
 George 149
 Jacob 149
 Michael 149
Hackney, John 123
 Joseph 345, 388
 Lydia 123
Haddon, Abraham 55, 86,
 143, 156, 187, 231,
 319, 381, 386, 451,
 556
 America Rowena Eliza
 232
 Andrew 134, 142, 143
 David 142
 Elizabeth 143
 Esther 153
 (Hatton), Francis 57
 Isaac 203
 (Hadden), James 416
 James H. 501, 571
 Jane (Jean) 49, 142,
 153, 156, 157
 (Hadden), John 86, 102,
 156, 296
 John, Sr. 156
 John T. 49, 451, 531,
 561
 Lewis 142
 Lilly 157
 Lucinda 143
 Mary 153
 Michael Lucy 567
 P. A. 575
 Robert, Sr. 153
 Robert, Jr. 153, 404
 Sally 156
 Thomas 106
 William 142, 143, 153,
 181, 203, 307, 351,
 419
 Zachariah 45, 156, 451,
 489
Hagan, Alexander G. 136,
 402, 485, 518, 531,
 545, 546
 Andrew B. 134, 136, 402

Hagan, Cont.
 Edward 136, 137, 230,
 313, 402, 489, 518,
 530, 536
 John 313, 489, 518
 Martha 518
 Mary 137, 518
 Nancy 530
 Rebecca Ann 485
 Robert 536
 Thomas 136, 402, 518
 W. A. 536
 William 136, 192, 205,
 402, 485, 546
Hagerty, Rebecca 169
Hagood, Eliza Ann 157, 406
 George 143
 James 256, 345
 John 28
 Partain (Partin) 353,
 439
 Randolph (Randel) 130,
 143
 Rebecca 143, 406
 Richard 143, 157
 William 124, 299
Haile, John 62, 271
Hairston, Ann 145, 149
 James 145, 149, 183
 James R. 157
 Jane 157, 158
 (Herston), John 34,
 149, 211, 214, 285,
 353, 374, 388
 Mandy 368
 (Herston), Peter 9,
 145, 149, 214, 252,
 368
 Robert 145, 358, 368
 Thomas 148, 149
 (Herston), William 9,
 70, 145, 148, 285,
 307
 William, Sr. 149
 William, Jr. 149
Hall, Caleb 138
 David 138
 Delila 330
 Elizabeth 138, 325
 Ezekiel 466
 Fenton 130, 138
 Fenton, Sr. 466
 Fenton B. 138
 Fleming 138
 G. W. 466
 J. D. 466
 James 148, 422
 Jesse M. 138
 John 34, 127, 138, 144,
 185, 253, 278, 315,
 325, 359
 Joseph B. 138
 Judith 315
 Laurel V. 138
 Margaret 138, 325
 Margaret Ann 519
 Mary D. 148, 325, 466
 Mary Elizabeth 541
 Rebecca 466
 Robert 407
 Samuel 321
 Sarah (Sally) 21, 138,
 144, 184, 185, 404
 Sarah Ann 138
 Ursula 138
 Vincent 404
 W. C. 541
 W. N. 466
 William 18, 108, 111,
 140, 141, 148, 346,
 466
 Zachariah 138, 306

Hallum, Basil 116, 149,
 165, 203, 204, 212,
 345, 352, 385
 Darkos 148
 James 148
 Jenny 148
 John 18, 148, 401
 John Y. 149
 Josiah 148
 Marsha 148
 Mary 149
 Rapley 149
 Robert Pickens 148
 Suckey 149
 Susannah 203
 Thomas 148
 William 148
Hambrick, George 342
 (Hamrick), John 231
Hames, Charles 66
Hamilton, A. T. 263
 Agness 147
 Alexander 7, 61, 134,
 144, 147, 154, 403
 Alexander C. 85, 134,
 139, 154, 230, 244,
 384, 418, 425, 433
 Andrew 54, 61, 121, 144,
 147, 205, 321, 389,
 392, 528, 529
 Andrew, Sr. 136, 147,
 445
 Anna A. 154
 Archibald 136, 144, 295,
 355
 Billy 144
 Caroline 336
 Christiana 518
 Elizabeth (Eliza) 155,
 486, 509
 Elizabeth Ann 145
 H. C. 322
 Harriett E. D. 134, 154
 Henry 65, 148, 177
 Isabella (Isbel) 144,
 145
 J. J. 486
 James 144, 155, 214,
 423, 509, 511
 James A. 134, 137, 261
 Jane (Jenny) 144, 294,
 307, 389
 John 31, 62, 134, 136,
 137, 145, 147, 151,
 180, 320, 404, 437,
 511, 528, 574
 John A. 121, 136, 137,
 482, 492, 511, 514,
 525
 Joseph 147, 165, 389
 Joseph A. 154, 157, 473
 Louisa A. 479
 Lucretia 157
 Luke 154, 155, 509
 Margaret 151
 Martha 159
 Mary 145
 Mary Anne 145
 Mary C. 574
 Moses 137
 Peter 66
 Richard A. 134, 154, 157
 Robert B. 134, 158
 Samuel 134
 Samuel S. 154
 Sarah (Sally) 155, 528
 Sarah A. 509
 Sophia C. 136
 Thomas 66, 151, 336
 Thomas Twining 52, 80,
 145, 340
 Walter 465

31

34

Irwin, Cont.
  John 9, 17, 20, 45, 68,
    123, 148, 161, 168,
    211, 218, 231, 352,
    408, 577
  John, Jr. 408
  Joseph 90, 210, 329,
    407, 489
  Joseph S. 506
  Martha 161
  Mary 408
  Nancy 168
  Parthenia 489, 506
  Rachel 161
  Robert 168, 519, 577
  Robert B. 161
  Samuel 117, 137, 173,
    205, 518, 519, 577
  William 168
  Willie 577
Issom, Abidien 162
  Edward 162
Ives, F. 579
Jabes, L. 164
Jack, John 34, 165
  John B. 165
  Mary 165
  Samuel A. 195, 363
  Thomas B. 165, 294, 335
Jackson, Mrs. 582
  Aaron 172
  Abel 67, 90, 165, 168,
    476
  Ann R. 264
  Caleb 582
  Daniel 254, 302, 320,
    422
  Elizabeth (Eliza) 63,
    161, 407
  G. M. 451
  G. T. 494
  Hezekiah 166, 168, 408
  Humphrey 451
  James 161
  John 375
  John M. 540
  Jordan 33
  Mark 29
  Martha Jane 494
  Mary 407
  Mathew 166, 168, 408
  Nancy 166
  Patsey 166, 168, 408
  Peggy 407
  Ralph 162
  Ralph, Sr. 162
  Robert 166, 168, 408
  Samuel 33, 66, 320, 422
  Thomas 7, 33, 127, 162,
    173, 283, 325, 334,
    367, 407, 422, 540
  William 63, 166, 211,
    284, 390, 407, 417
Jacobs, Daniel 330
  Moses 165, 314
  Moses, Jr. 472
  Synthia 162
  Thomas 162
Jame, T. J. 339
James, Charles 122, 161,
    408
  John Lashly 161, 408
Japp, John 162
Jarret, Peter 165
  Suckey 165
  Thomas 165
Jasper, Marion 87
Jastis, John 272
Jay, Abigail 166, 552
  Barzilla G. 164, 270,
    342, 511
  Clotilda 251
  David 371
  Elizabeth 106

Jay, Cont.
  Hiram 200, 482
  James 77
  James A. 251, 528
  Jane 201
  Jesse 166, 552
  John 29, 165, 166, 220
  Joseph 166, 176, 552
  Joseph, Sr. 166
  Lucinda 517
  Susannah F. 164
  Tyra (Tiry) 166, 208,
    276, 289, 298, 305,
    309, 310, 452, 482,
    517, 522, 552
  William 166, 320
Jefferies, Betsey 161
  John 299
  Mary 161
  Nathaniel 83, 161, 486
  Thomas 161, 346
Jenkins, Charles J. 255,
    256
  Francis 321
  John 321
  Mary 247
Jennings, Caleb 166, 213
  Caroline 469
  Coleman 469
  Ellenor 469
  J. H. 559
  James C. 571
  John 166
  Mary 166
  Robert 48, 340
  Robert T. 27, 166, 386,
    469
  Thomas 469
  William 468
Jernigan, Jesse 31, 278
Jester, Jenny 448
  Jesse 15
  Thomas 448
Johnson, Abbegil 166
  Adna 158
  Agness 243
  Albert 156, 450, 512
  Alse 163
  Amanda A. 169, 576
  Andrew R. 384, 512
  Anne 71, 162, 468
  Bartholomew 162, 299
  Benjamin 45, 68, 106,
    157, 163, 164, 346,
    369, 400, 418, 446,
    512, 572
  Benjamin F. 523
  Benjamin T. 163
  C. V. 576
  Caroline 169
  Catren 219
  Charles 36, 96, 149,
    163, 193, 196, 209,
    275, 314
  Cornelia Ann 469, 511
  Daniel 151, 162
  Elizabeth 161, 164, 408,
    468
  Elizabeth Catherine 163
  Elizabeth L. 164
  Frances Ann Elizabeth
    169
  Frances J. 468, 511
  Francis 162
  Gabriel W. 576
  George W. 162, 512
  Gideon 59
  Gideon H. 49, 164
  H. B. 517
  Harriet C. 540, 552
  Harry M. 484
  Henry 57, 158, 164, 207,
    277, 290, 291, 358,
    418, 432, 499, 511

Johnson, Cont.
  Henry A. 576
  Henry G. 163, 213, 400
  Henry O. 169
  Howell 238
  Hulda 511
  Isaac, Sr. 165
  Isiah 84, 117, 169,
    170, 183, 206, 319,
    329, 511
  Israel P. 169
  Jabez W. H. 47, 52, 73,
    114, 194, 245, 303,
    360, 365, 450, 469,
    484, 509, 511
  Jacob M. 165
  James 78, 115, 127,
    145, 162, 166, 168,
    169, 211, 228, 239,
    272, 288, 349, 364,
    372, 378, 389, 459
  James, Sr. 576
  James Wesley 164, 518
  Jane 47, 169, 518, 562
  Jane Augusta Fulton 111
  John 58, 71, 89, 161,
    165, 169, 195, 219,
    301, 336, 342, 356,
    408, 418, 468
  John B. 489, 577
  John H. 512
  John T. 469, 552, 580
  Jonathan 53, 114, 119,
    142, 154, 158, 186,
    201, 229, 267, 278,
    280, 291, 334, 365,
    432, 469, 485, 511,
    548
  Joseph 196, 314, 315
  Julia Ann 228, 576
  Lemuel 244, 342
  LeRoy J. 169, 459, 471,
    494, 538, 548, 551,
    556, 561, 569
  Levy 162
  Loocey 163
  Mahulda Ann 164
  Margaret 162, 511, 512
  Mark M. 442
  Martha 169, 209
  Mary (Molley)(Polly)
    57, 58, 163, 389,
    469, 552
  Mary Ann 511
  Matilda 244
  Nancy 58, 511
  Nathaniel 219
  Oliver 518
  Pamela 290
  Patrick 57, 166, 206,
    267, 373
  Patsey 336
  Rachel 166
  Reuben 18
  Robert 90, 404
  Robert D. 169, 306
  Samuel 168
  Samuel V. 576
  Samuel W. 169
  Sarah 162, 164, 165,
    511, 512, 576
  Sarah Agnes 163, 512
  Selina 469
  Sidney 512
  Sugar 280, 365
  T. L. 484
  Tacitus 49
  Thomas 111, 162, 164,
    165, 166, 167, 461,
    468, 473, 511, 518,
    547, 562
  Tidence 468, 518
  Tolivar 164, 166, 468,
    518

38

39

41

42

43

44

45

48

49

50

51

Means, Cont.
Sally 522
Sarah M. 335, 367
William 73, 189, 522
Meban, John 214
Margaret 214
Mecklin, Agness 211, 220
(Maclin), Ann 525
Charity 204
(Macklin), D. O. 77,
492, 562
(Macklin), David 204,
211, 220, 229, 242
Elizabeth 204, 492
George 203
(Macklin)(McLine), Hugh
211, 242, 247, 295,
306, 334, 350, 413
(Macklin), Hugh, Jr.
220
(Macklin), James 211,
220, 229
(Macklin), James S. 229
(Macklin), John A. 229,
448
Mary 204
(McLin), Oswell 454
(Macklin), Robert 211,
229
(Macklin), Unice 229
(Macklin), William A.
229
Medlin, Catherine 166
Michael 166
(Medling), Stephen 340
Medlock, Nancy 256
Meek, James M. 414
John 290, 414
Moses 67
Sarah 290
Tabitha F. A. 414
(Meaks), William 123,
341
William S. 414
Megin, Daniel 89
Mellown, A. L. 532
Elizabeth 532
Melville, Mary 222
Robert 222
Memminger, C. G. 117
Menary, Alexander 296
Meredith, Nancy 519
Meriwether, Ann 202
Barbara 393
Caroline 202, 227
Charles Waller 203
Evaline 203
Frances Ann 202
Francis 208, 223, 393
Frederick 202
John 16, 35, 74, 127,
202, 209, 220, 227,
345, 349, 355, 381,
392, 407, 419, 432,
446
John, Jr. 27
John H. 27, 202
John Lewis 202, 230
Joseph 27, 53, 127, 202,
203, 223, 227, 393'
Martha 202
Martha Elizabeth 202
Mary 419
Mary Lewis 419
Mary R. 202, 203, 209,
223
Nicholas 202, 203, 209,
393, 419
Robert 202, 227, 393
Robert H. 202
Sarah (Sally) 203
Thomas 202
Walter B. 484, 492, 561
William 202

Meriwether, Cont.
William Bickley 203
Zachary 25, 27, 28, 109,
139, 143, 194, 202,
209, 218, 220, 223,
227, 345, 354, 355,
385, 393, 405, 413,
419
Zachary, Jr. 393
Merriam, John 224
(Merryman)(Merrimon),
Lewis D. 234, 528,
579
Louisa Jane 224, 574
Messer, James 221
John 221
Robert 94, 101, 171,
318
Mewburn, Robson 122
Meyers, Catherina 421
David 421
(Myers), Elendor 475
Grace 421
(Myers), J. A. 235, 578
John 13, 30, 421
Jonathan 13, 30, 153,
221, 421
Leonard 278, 421
Michael 89, 128, 421
(Myers), Nelly 475
Sally 421
(Myers), Sarah J. 235
(Mayer), Ulrich (Ulrick)
421, 437
Michael, Bennet 181
Middleton, Answorth 374
Hezekiah 414
Hugh G. 112
James 374
John 239, 379
Mary E. 458
Milam, John 89, 162, 321
Miles, Lucy 222
Nicey 222
Peggy 299
Sarah 222
William 439
William, Jr. 222
Miller, Agness 224
Alexander H. 160, 191,
234, 467, 475
Allen 49, 134
Allen Thompson 43, 164,
202, 205, 224, 280,
297, 363, 506, 507,
552
Andrew 126, 134, 142,
201, 202, 210, 214,
368, 417
Andrew J. 417
Catherine (Kitty) 63,
419
Charles 145, 148, 216
Cornelia C. 497
David 214
Ebenezer 126, 142, 143,
203, 214, 244, 253,
280, 346
Elizabeth 214, 234, 420
Elizabeth Ann 475
Elizabeth C. 63
Elizabeth Stead 420
Esther 201, 210
George 57, 112, 201, 239
George A. 54, 135, 201,
394, 411, 464, 476
George McD. 530, 559
Hamilton T. 551, 552
Isabella 202, 205
Jacob 472, 517, 520, 547
James 21, 202, 221, 285,
291, 346
James S. 354

Miller, Cont.
Jane 148, 192, 214, 234,
473, 474
Jennet Lesley 359
Jesse William 474
John 38, 55, 97, 148,
162, 171, 172, 173,
182, 191, 192, 201,
206, 222, 224, 234,
239, 245, 259, 267,
295, 312, 320, 374,
396, 397, 419, 420,
475, 510, 534, 545
John, Sr. 29
John, Jr. 29, 210
John H. 17, 35, 54, 150,
295, 299, 337, 429,
464
John R. 234
John S. 214, 346
John T. 263, 515, 577
John W. 39
Joseph 72, 112, 181,
214, 273, 280
Lewis J. 473, 474
Lucinda 202
Margaret (Peggy) 70,
210, 214, 234, 280,
359
Margery 280
Martha 214, 285
Mary 202, 224, 417, 468
Mary C. 561
Mary E. 234
Mathew Thompson 117,
201, 304
Michael 34, 331
Nancy 331, 545
Nathaniel 162, 417
Nicholas 464
Nicholas H. 369, 476,
542
Rachel 201, 202, 346,
419
Robert 63, 214, 234,
419
Robert M. 224
Samuel 173, 192, 217,
234, 299, 349, 358,
511
Sarah 20, 68, 245
Sarah Ann 263
Susan 235
Thomas 58, 224
William 121, 161, 202,
224, 301
William C. 420
William McCrone 224, 234
Millford, Brittian 304
F. B. 158
(Milford), Henry 191
Jane Clelland 76
John 306, 518
Joseph 262, 568
Philip P. 306
Thomas B. 555
Thomas C. 76
William 191
William J. 518
Millhouse, Henry 109
Milligan, Andrew 17, 25,
100, 218, 248, 287,
291, 333, 347, 362,
408, 413, 419
Hugh 18, 100
(Mulligan), James 100,
152, 222, 419
Joseph 437
Mary 100
Rachel 100
Sarah 17, 413
Mills, Agness 251
Alexander 420
Alsey C. 305

52

53

55

60

67

69

70

Spieren, Cont.
  Thomas P. 26, 75, 174,
    280, 287, 288, 325,
    355, 379, 442, 502
Spikes, Amanda 517
  John 16
  William 345
Spiller, Amos 16
  (Spillars), Elenor Jane
    309
  (Spillars), Jane 309
  (Spillers), John 290
Splean, William 413
Spraggins, Martha 290
  Nathaniel 237, 301
  Thomas 194, 290, 301
  Thomas J. 54, 414
  William 82, 290, 301,
    332
Sprott, John 389
Sprouse, Alice 268
  (Spruce), John 34?
  (Spruce), John H. 25,
    125, 369
  Lew 268
Sprue, John 109
Spruill (Sproull), Charles
    159, 179, 233, 279,
    288, 338, 464, 471,
    545
  Charles W. 464, 550, 560
  (Sproull), E. H. 539
  Elijah 97
  (Sproull), Elizabeth
    288
  Gabriel 300
  George 88, 300
  (Sproull), Harriet 288
  (Sproul), James 105,
    288
  (Sproull), James C. 261,
    283
  Jepter 300
  John 217, 300
  John S. 46
  Luke 300
  Margaret (Peggy) 46,
    300
  Mary Ann 97, 288, 538
  Nancy 300
  Polly 300
  Ruth 300
  Sally 300
  Samuel 300
  Simeon 300
  Thomas 46, 300
  Thomas R. 464
  William 288, 300, 545,
    560
Stacy, Elizabeth Ann 174
  Thomas 174, 495, 507,
    579
Stallworth, Amon 193, 288,
    528
  Edmund 288
  (Stalsworth), Grace 302
  James 288
  John 288
  Joseph 137, 171, 289,
    302
  Margaret 288
  (Stasworth), Nicholas
    371
  Sarah 288, 289
  (Stalsworth), Thomas
    140, 193, 288, 302,
    345, 528
  Thomas, Sr. 342
  William 208, 288, 289,
    302, 319, 333, 345,
    418
Stainaker, Samuel 358
Standard, John 33
Standley, Lewis 344

Stanfield, Betsey 173
  John 299, 300, 331
  Richard 18, 300
  Robert 299
  Sarah 299
  Sarah, Sr. 300
  Sarah, Jr. 300
  William 66, 299
Stanton, Joseph H. 26
Stare (Starr), John 63,
    153, 436
  Mary 153
Starke, Catharine Jane 435
  Charles 80, 252, 286,
    295, 306, 312, 390
  Elizabeth G. 435
  James 286
  James H. 295, 306, 390
  Jeremiah 286
  Keziah 306
  Mary 286
  Newman 306
  Pinkney 435
  Reuben 228, 306, 435
  Robert 357, 443
  Samuel C. 306, 435
  Samuel J. H. 306, 312
  Sarah Ann 306
  Wyatt W. 202, 306, 435
Starkey, Caroline 484, 502
  Elizabeth 484, 502
  Isiah 484
  Lidia 484
  Polly 484
Starnes, Aaron 269
  Ebenezer 269, 358
Sted, Elizabeth 437
Stedman, James 298
  John 298
  (Steadman), S. 17
Steele, Aaron 60, 126,
    162, 300, 303
  Aaron, Jr. 300
  Abner 300, 303
  Archibald 344
  Charles 308
  Cynthia 295
  David 295, 297, 308
  Elizabeth 295, 300,
    303
  Henry 31
  James 61, 300, 303
  Jane (Jean) 295, 300,
    303
  Katharine 295
  Larkin 295
  Lucinda (Lucy) 295,
    308
  Mary 35, 295, 444
  Nancy 295
  Permelia 295
  Sarah 295, 308, 444
  William 28, 295, 300,
    308, 444
  William L. 308
Steen, James 296, 299
  Jean 296
  John 296
  John, Sr. 396
  John, Jr. 396
  Richard 296
  William 211, 296
Steger, Robert M. 83
Step, Jean 37
Stephens, Charlotte 57,
    290
  Edmond 372, 401, 444
  Edward 405
  Elizabeth 454
  Franklin 57
  (Stevens), James 290
  (Stevens), John 34,
    183, 220, 269, 310,
    353, 483

Stephens, Cont.
  Lyle 310
  Margaret 220
  (Stevens), Martha 290,
    454
  Mary 310, 454, 483
  (Stevens), Micajah 214,
    358, 439
  (Stevens), Pamela 290
  Sarah Jane 310, 454,
    483
  Thomas 310
  Thomas Lee 313
  Timothy 476
  (Stevens), William 302,
    400
Sterling, Ephraim 484
  James 484
  Robert 99
  Sarah 99
Stevenson, Alexander 172
  Andrew 286, 307, 320,
    346, 419, 489, 531,
    532, 546
  (Stephenson), Andrew T.
    286, 304
  Eliza T. 485
  (Stephenson), Elizabeth
    203, 230, 286
  Hamilton O. 531, 572
  Harmon 180, 468
  Isabella A. 485
  (Stinson), James 60,
    153, 172, 215, 286,
    295, 307, 320, 349,
    358, 404, 408
  James C. 531, 532, 546
  Jane E. 531, 532, 572
  (Stephenson), John 26,
    156, 172, 286, 304,
    307, 311, 312, 457,
    485, 503
  Jonathan 172, 382
  Joseph 172
  (Stinson), July A. 311
  Margaret 294
  Margaret Elizabeth 531
  Margaret S. 485
  Mary Jane 485
  Mary Louisa 531
  (Stinson), Nancy 18
  (Stinson), Pheoby 18
  (Stephenson), Rebecca
    286, 304
  Rebecca Ann 485
  Robert 294
  Samuel 172
  Sarah 286
  (Stephenson), Sarah M.
    304
  Susan Sanora 531
  Thomas 294
  William 531, 532
  William J. 312, 485
Steward, Caroline 47
  Mark A. 47
Stewart (Stuart), Adam
    100, 255
  (Stuart), Adam, Sr. 291
  Adam Levi 304
  Agnes 306
  (Stuart), Alexander
    23, 73, 145, 156,
    247, 248, 271, 290,
    293, 295, 304, 310,
    340, 431, 440, 443,
    459
  (Ewart), Andrew 58, 88,
    100, 289, 291
  Ann 100, 291, 306
  Archibald D. 306
  (Steward), Benton W.
    189, 311, 468, 484
  Caroline 479

71

73

77

78

79

RIVERS - CREEKS, Cont.

Mile Branch 421
Mill Creek 381, 445
Mountain Creek 85
Nine Creek 350
Ogechee River-Georgia 129
Ponch Creek 39
Pond Branch, Orangeburg
    Dist. 243
Reaburns Creek 10, 33
Reedy Branch (Creek),
    Edgefield Dist. 198,
    371
Reedy River 272
Richland Creek 103
Rocky River 205, 466
Saluda (Saludy) River 66,
    95, 153, 272
Sandy River 82
Santee River 318
Savannah River 61, 128,
    148, 215, 296, 422, 477
Seneca River 413
South Edisto River 161
Spanish Cut Off-Savannah
    River 128
Stephens (Stevens) Creek
    32, 412, 422
Thickety Creek 389
Tims Branch 129
Turkey Creek 422
Twenty Three Mile Creek
    202
Two Mile Creek 146, 222
Tyger (Tagger) River 34,
    121, 151, 165, 211,
    214, 242, 274, 316
Vans Creek-Ga. 223
Wateree 437
Williams Creek 153
Wilsons Creek 68, 512
Yarrow Branch, Orangesburg
    Dist. 243